Psychology

SECOND EDITION

Guy R. Lefrancois
University of Alberta

Wadsworth Publishing Company
Belmont, California
A Division of Wadsworth, Inc.

Psychology editor Kenneth King
Production editor Judith McKibben
Designer MaryEllen Podgorski
Copy editor Lorraine Anderson
Technical illustrators Stephanie McCann, Dorothy Cullinan, Lisa Palacio, John Dawson, Tim Keenan, Florence Fujimoto
Photo researcher Kay James
Page layout Wendy Calmenson
Cover painting Richard Diebenkorn: *Ocean Park #83*. In the collection of The Corcoran Gallery of Art, museum purchase with the aid of funds from the National Endowment for the Arts, the William A. Clark fund, and Margaret Hitchcock.

A study guide is available to help students master the concepts presented in this book. Order from your bookstore.

Printed in the United States of America

2 3 4 5 6 7 8 9 10—87 86 85 84 83

ISBN 0-534-01244-2

ISBN 0-534-02804-7 (International Edition)

Library of Congress Cataloging in Publication Data

Lefrancois, Guy R.
    Psychology.

    Bibliography: p.
    Includes indexes.
    1. Psychology.   I. Title
BF121.L4188   1982   150   82-10908
ISBN 0-534-01244-2

Preface

There is little doubt that my Uncle Raoul should have been a superb story teller. He had the rare ability to capture the essence of a person's character in one or two swift lines. "She had a face like a dried mushroom," he would say, "and her breath smelled of old bears in the spring." And he would launch into another fascinating anecdote. But by the time he was finished most of us would no longer be listening, no matter how exciting the tale or how brilliant my uncle's telling. His voice killed his audience; it was an absolutely deadly monotone.

In the end, my uncle told his stories mainly to my aunt. They were wonderfully amusing stories, and both would laugh hugely at his punch lines—always a twist, a hook, a clever surprise. And then my aunt would respond in kind, telling one of her stories, for she was also a magnificently gifted fabricator of dangerously tall tales with surprisingly moralistic and vastly important themes. Sadly, she too could scarcely hold our attention in spite of the fact that her voice was as lyrical and melodious as Uncle Raoul's was monotonous. It was simply that she had a peculiar speech defect that manifested itself in a drawn out, sibilant "s"—a piercing, screeching, whistling "s" that became more and more annoying the longer we listened to her. Most of us chose not to listen unless we had to.

Many years later when I became what my grandmother insisted on calling "le professeur," I was reminded repeatedly of my Uncle Raoul and Aunt Eugenie by many of the textbooks I chose for my sometimes unfortunate students. Although some of them told fascinating and important stories, a great many were written in the most deadly monotone imaginable; others grated rawly like my poor aunt's shrieking "s." It was as though in the author's mind the only important thing was the story and not the telling or the audience.

Characteristics of Psychology

So I wrote a textbook. In it, I tried to tell as fascinating a story as Uncle Raoul might, and one as important as Aunt Eugenie's, but without either monotone or speech defect. In short, I tried to write a textbook that would keep the reader's interest and attention but that would still tell the entire story in all of its magnificent and sometimes difficult detail. Thus *Psychology,* a comprehensive introduction to the field of psychology, is lively and compelling. It is marked by occasional flights of whimsy, vignettes, humor, and tongue in cheek. Equally important, it also has all the traditional content basic to the introductory psychology course.

Psychology has a number of outstanding characteristics intended to make it as useful a teaching-learning tool as possible. Among these are its graphic layout and format, designed with the student in mind. Pages are uncluttered, and text material flows with a minimum of interruption by extraneous material. Boxed inserts, used sparingly throughout, are always found at the bottoms of pages to allow students to move smoothly through the text. The graphics, which are of extremely high quality, are always found at the tops or bottoms of pages or in margins. Definitions of important terms are located in margins close to where they appear in the text and where they are most likely to be useful. In addition, all these definition are repeated alphabetically in the index/glossary at the end of the text. And the photographs not only make important points visually, but also serve to make the book a truly aesthetic piece.

What's New in the Second Edition of Psychology?

The second edition of *Psychology* retains all first-edition features to which students and instructors responded so favorably. In addition, there have been a number of important changes. There is a new chapter on emotion, a topic of considerable importance in our lives. The chapter on genetics has been deleted, but important material from that chapter has been placed in other chapters (heredity in the chapter that describes development from conception through childhood; nature-nurture in the section dealing with the development and measurement of intelligence; and sociobiology in a social psychology chapter).

Another important change in this edition involved removing all nonpsychological terms from the marginal glossary. Words that were difficult enough to warrant glossary definition even though they weren't specialized psychological terms were simply deleted from the text. The entire text was then extensively rewritten with painstaking attention to reading level, student interest, and the type of organization that would facilitate learning. Many chapters underwent significant reorganization (Chapter 2, for example), all were thoroughly updated, difficult sections and passages were simplified, and a number of topics were moved to chapters where their relevance would be more apparent (for example, creativity is now with problem solving in the chapter on thought and language; theories of motivation have been combined with a discussion of motives themselves). Comprehensive summaries in the form of main points have also been included at the end of each chapter. Among the many additions are an expanded treatment of adolescent sexuality, a critical look at the ape-language studies, discussions of eyewitness testimony, the Rescorla-Wagner model, situational or *milieu* therapy, and the Solomon-Corbitt pain theory as well as the role of endorphins.

Ancillary Materials for Psychology

User reactions to the first edition indicated that supplementary items to this text are particularly good. The main feature of the student study guide, prepared by George Semb, is its versatility. It is designed for use in a unit-mastery or PSI setting as well as in more traditional settings. The test item file, also prepared by George Semb (whose familiarity with the book is, by now, probably as great as mine), features some 2000 multiple choice items, more than a third of which are conceptual. These are available on printed cards as well as on computer tape. And the instructor's resource book, prepared by Jean and David Volckmann, may well be without parallel in the field. It includes information on teaching the course, a large number of lecture outlines, abstracts of current articles, and detailed instruction for classroom demonstrations.

My Thanks

to the hundreds of people who have contributed directly and indirectly to the success of this text, only a handful of whom can be named here. I am particularly grateful to Ken King, editor, who does more than most editors to put all this together; to Judith

McKibben, who not only served as a highly capable production editor, but also played a major role as prerevision reviewer; to Lorraine Anderson, whose contributions as copy editor were far greater than I had a right to expect; and to the many other members of an outstanding publishing team, including MaryEllen Podgorski, the designer; Wendy Calmenson, the art editor; Kay James, the photo researcher; and Marion Hansen, the permissions researcher. Many thanks, as well, to Judy Cameron and Sharon Seigel for their assistance with library research. And special thanks to George Semb, Jean Volckmann, and David Volckmann for preparing some truly outstanding ancillary material.

I also want to thank the many reviewers of the first edition, as well as those who reviewed parts or all of the second edition. This text owes a great deal to each of you, particularly: John B. Best, Eastern Illinois University; Robert Bundy, State University of New York, Buffalo; Garvin Chastain, Boise State University; Bernard Gorman, Nassau Community College; Nicholas J. Heidy, Fort Lewis College; Sally Hill, Bakersfield College; Gordon Hodge, University of Mexico; Daniel Kirschenbaum, University of Wisconsin, Madison; John M. Knight, Central State University; Herman H. Samson, University of Washington; and David R. Thomas, University of Colorado.

Finally, I want to thank the many hundreds of students and instructors who have written to me since the first edition appeared in 1980. Whether you scolded or praised, I was always glad that you responded, and only wish that I could have answered each of your letters personally. Please consider this edition part of that answer.

Brief Contents

Detailed Contents

Psychology

You and I are the subject matter of psychology. Given that there are very few subjects with which we are so intimately familiar, this should present some definite advantages. Sadly, however, it doesn't. We bring to our study of human behavior too many inaccurate notions, too many unquestioned beliefs. Our wishes, our cultural biases, our naive faith in the collective wisdom of our grandparents sometimes blind us to reality. This introductory chapter presents a short history of psychology and a description of the methods most commonly employed to discover truth, and to sort fact from fancy. In addition, it presents an overview of the subject matter of psychology—an overview that serves as a blueprint for this text.

INTRODUCTION

The Subject

Chapter 1
Psychology

Psychology

My grandmother, a well-respected source of wisdom and common sense, firmly believes that men can withstand more pain than women. This she has decided through some eighty years of personal pain and pleasure, and through the observation of pain among the men who have surrounded her for a good portion of those years. She, and other women she knows, would have gone to war had they been compelled to do so, but she believes they would have ill survived its physical hardships.

She also believes with equal if not greater conviction, and with at least as much supporting evidence, that boys who reach sexual maturity at an earlier than average age are often maladjusted later; that the proverbial hair's breadth allegedly separating genius from madness is more fanciful than factual; that dogs can't think; that those suffering from emotional disorders (the insane, as she so pointedly puts it) are dramatically different from herself and other sane people; and that psychologists have devious and uncanny ways of peering into one's very insides but that they can be fooled by anyone who is at least as devious. She is less convinced that if people were honest they could tell you their true motives, that babies can't really see anything until they are several weeks of age, and that rats can't be taught anything, although she is prepared to argue that these are facts.

Psychological research has not, in fact, supported these beliefs. That is not to say that all our folk wisdom is untrue or that psychology's **laws,* principles**, and **beliefs** are invariably correct (see Box 1.1). Indeed, psychologists frequently agree no better than two grandmothers who happen to be discussing the same matters.

Psychology's task, and our task in this book, is to separate fact from fiction; to weed out the trivial from the important; in short, to make the most logical affirmations

Laws Statements whose accuracy is beyond reasonable doubt. Laws should not be confused with truths, since laws can be refuted by sufficient contrary evidence. Physics has many laws (for example, $e = mc^2$); psychology, however, has very few.

Principles Statements usually relating to some uniformity or predictability. Principles do not have the same status as laws, since they are often open to doubt. Psychology is characterized more by principles than by laws, although the term *law* is frequently used where *principle* would be more accurate.

Beliefs Acceptance of something as accurate or truthful. Beliefs are more personal and less universal than principles, and ideally compose only a small portion of the body of knowledge characterizing a discipline.

---

*Terms defined in the marginal glossary are set in boldface type. These definitions are also listed in the index.

we can on the basis of the information at our disposal, and to admit freely and honestly when we don't know.

What Is Psychology?

Although it is sometimes useful to have clear and simple definitions of the subjects one is studying, these definitions are frequently misleading. Such is the case with psychology. The most widely accepted definition of psychology is simply that it is the science of behavior and experience. But this definition does not reflect accurately what psychology is, because psychology encompasses so many different interests and occupations that no single definition can include them all. Cates (1970) (see Box 1.2) surveyed members of the American Psychological Association and classified their areas of specialization as shown in Figure 1.1. Psychologists are not simply psychologists any more than engineers are simply engineers. In the same way that civil, mechanical, petroleum, or electrical engineers usually do different things, so developmental psychologists frequently concern themselves with different things from clinical psychologists. Although all psychologists are in some way concerned with behavior, some are more concerned with changes that occur as children develop (developmental psychology); some are concerned with behavioral and emotional problems (clinical or counseling psychology); some deal primarily with learning and instruction (educational psychology); and still others deal with other branches within psychology (see Table 1.1). Furthermore, regardless of their specialization, some psychologists teach, some do research, some attempt to apply their knowledge in real-life situations as consultants or practitioners, some write textbooks, some drive taxicabs or sell real estate, and some do nothing at all. In short, all that is human and all that affects human behavior, thought, and emotion, falls within the domain of psychology. This text, with its chapters and sections, represents the most common divisions, interests, topics, and issues in psychology. It is, in fact, a 275,000-word definition of psychology.

A Long Past

The beginnings of that definition are found in the history of psychology—a history that goes back at least as far as ancient Greece. It was in ancient Greek philosophical movements that psychology had some of its roots. In those days **philosophy** embraced

Philosophy The pursuit of wisdom; the study of realities, laws, and principles in an attempt to arrive at an accurate and unified conception of the universe and its nature. Since people are part of the universe, philosophy originally included attempts to understand humans. The study of human behavior eventually became the separate discipline of psychology.

BOX 1.1

True/False Folk Wisdom Psychology Test

Following are some common—but not universal—beliefs about matters related to psychology. Test your psychological wisdom by answering each item *true* or *false*.

1. Fat people are less "finicky" than those not so fat.

2. Dreams are often caused by indigestion.

3. People with photographic memories are usually exceptionally intelligent.

4. The grass is always greener. . . .

5. Trained psychologists can psychoanalyze people.

6. Absence makes the heart grow fonder.

7. A lot of people never dream.

8. Most mammals see the world in color; birds and insects usually see only in black and white.

9. If you concentrate on one thing only, you are likely to be totally unaware of other events around you.

10. The more you reward people for doing something, the more they will like what they are doing.

11. Some women are more likely than others to have sons rather than daughters.

12. Mental disorders are usually inherited.

Answers are provided in Box 1.5, p. 21.

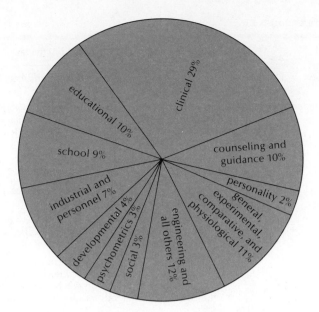

Figure 1.1 Areas of specialization among members of the American Psychological Association. (Based on data provided by Cates, 1970.)

most other disciplines, and it continued to include the **social sciences** for a long time. And it is in the Greek language that the term *psychology* originated. The Greek word *psyche* means soul; *logos* signifies a study or discussion.

More recently in psychology's history discoveries in medicine had a dramatic influence on our conception of the human being. When William Harvey discovered that the heart pumped blood into tubes throughout the body, a great many thinkers became convinced that people were nothing more than elaborate pumping machines. Many suspected as well that the ability to think originated in the blood. Much earlier, Aristotle didn't merely suspect this—he knew it. Certainly if a person's blood were entirely removed, it is unlikely that much evidence of thinking would remain.

Physics, too, in its earliest forms, was related to the development of psychological thought. The psychological importance of Sir Isaac Newton's observation that apples do fall when released, and that the direction of their fall is invariably earthward, may not be immediately apparent. But Newton's discovery illustrates a rather different way of looking at natural **phenomena.** The ancient Greek philosophers undoubtedly knew that apples and any number of other objects do in fact fall earthward. And had they wanted to know *why* apples fall, they would have spent some time thinking about the problem and holding learned discourses with colleagues. Their approach would

Social sciences Sciences concerned with the relationships of people to other people and to social institutions. The social sciences attempt to understand the organization of societies and the relationships between groups and individuals with respect to these societies.

Phenomena Observable events or happenings that can be experienced, reported on, and analyzed. What we observe are phenomena; hence phenomena are the data of psychology.

BOX 1.2

References

Throughout this and most other psychology texts, references are cited in the style approved by the American Psychological Association (APA). Thus, authors' names are followed by the year of the relevant publication (in parentheses). The bibliography at the end of the book lists all authors alphabetically, and includes all information necessary for locating sources referenced in the text. Each

direct quotation in the text includes not only the reference from which the quotation is drawn, but also the page on which the specific quotation may be found.

As an example, the reference "Cates (1970)" on p. 4 indicates the information was drawn from material published in 1970 by a person whose last name is Cates. The relevant bibliography entry (Cates, J. Psychology's manpower: Report on the 1968 National Register of Scientific and Technical Personnel. *American Psychologist,* 1970, *25,* 254–264) gives the author's name and initial, the title of the article, the journal in which the article was published (italicized), and, in order, the year of publication, the volume in which the article may be found (italicized), and the exact pages containing the article.

BIOGRAPHY
Wilhelm Wundt
1832–1920

Generally acknowledged as the founder of modern psychology, Wundt, the son of a Lutheran minister, obtained a medical degree at the age of twenty-four and subsequently became an instructor in physiology. His professional career was long: seventeen years at Heidelberg on the medical faculty, one year in Zurich as a professor of philosophy, and forty-two years at Leipzig. A quiet, unassuming man who seldom left his laboratory and his home, he wrote almost constantly. Boring (1950) estimated that Wundt wrote an average of one published word every two minutes, day and night, for sixty-eight years. His major textbook on psychology, unlike this one, appeared in three volumes in its first edition: 553, 680, and 796 pages of very complex German.

Science (a) A body of principles and procedures for dealing with observations; (b) an attitude toward the pursuit of knowledge emphasizing objectivity, replicability, and consistency.

American Psychological Association (APA) A large professional organization of psychologists. The APA exercises some control over its members through eligibility requirements for membership and guidelines and ethical standards for members' conduct. It disseminates psychological information through a large number of publications and through meetings and conventions, the largest of which is an annual conference usually held in late August, often attracting more than 20,000 psychologists. The APA is organized into a number of divisions that reflect its members' interests and activities.

Table 1.1 What Psychologists Do

Subfield	Major Concerns and Activities
Clinical	Diagnosis and treatment of illnesses and disturbances, frequently in a hospital or clinical setting
Counseling and guidance	Evaluation of and counseling assistance with behavioral, emotional, and other problems not serious enough to require hospital or clinical treatment; also assistance with important decisions (career, marriage, and so on)
Developmental	Study of changes that define growth and maturation from birth to death; application of findings in education programs
Educational	Research into ways psychology can be applied to teaching and learning; developing and applying learning programs
Industrial and personnel	Applying psychology in business and industry; developing and administering tests to evaluate aptitudes; conducting workshops and programs dealing with motivation, management, interpersonal relations, and related areas
Personality	Identifying and describing important, stable characteristics of individuals; developing classification schemes for personality characteristics as well as methods for identifying and assessing these characteristics
School	Identifying individual aptitudes and skills among learners in a school setting; developing and administering tests pertinent to school-related abilities
Experimental, comparative, and physiological	Conducting psychology as an experimental science; doing research on comparisons among species; investigating physiological functioning as it relates to psychological functioning
Psychometrics	Testing and measuring psychological characteristics and making sense of resulting measures; developing tests and measurement devices
Social	Doing research and consulting on the relationship between individuals and groups

*Needless to say, all psychologists do not fall neatly into any one of these categories. Many would identify themselves as belonging to several areas, both by the nature of their interests and by their activities. Others would hesitate to be classified in any of these subfields.

have made little use of the methods of **science** as we now know them. Newton, however, felt compelled to demonstrate and verify the phenomenon he had observed, and to investigate it by means of controlled experimentation. We are products of Newton's generation: psychology, anthropology, sociology, and other related fields are seldom referred to as the "social studies"; they are the social *sciences* (see Figure 1.2).

Recent Origins of Psychology

Scientific psychology is a product of the late nineteenth century and the twentieth century. In fact, my grandmother, had she been more gifted and differently inclined, could have been the founder of modern psychology. She wasn't. That honor is generally attributed to Wilhelm Wundt who, among other things, established the first psychological laboratory in Leipzig, Germany, around a hundred years ago. Many of Wundt's students later established laboratories of their own throughout Europe and North America. The first professorship in psychology was granted to James McKeen Cattell at the University of Pennsylvania in 1888; the first American journal of psychology was established in 1887 by G. Stanley Hall; and the **American Psychological Association** was founded in 1892. Hall, who was Wundt's first student, was also the first APA president, as well as its only two-time president.

Aristotle   Newton   Pavlov

Figure 1.2 Contemplation of their own experiences guided the ancient Greeks in learning about people. The result: the theory that the ability to think originates in the blood. Centuries later, Newton used *scientific observation and experimentation* to test theories about the physical world. By the twentieth century, psychologists were applying scientific methods to animals and people to learn about behavior. The result: psychology as it exists today.

Following these early beginnings, psychology departments were soon established at all major universities. Typically these began as branches of departments of philosophy, but in time the discipline became totally separate. Departments of psychology now claim far more students than do departments of philosophy.

Principles of Science

The scientific method is as much an attitude as a set of guidelines. It is an attitude that insists on objectivity, precision, and verifiability. Thus, science is based on **empirical** observations that are as precise and objective as possible, in sharp contrast to those ways of knowing that are based principally on subjective analysis. Subjective analysis refers to a process of thinking and reasoning that tends to be personal and unquantified; empirical observation is a more objective process of thought based on things outside the observer. The empirical world is the observable world—a world felt and experienced by most individuals in relatively similar ways. Science, as we now know it, is concerned principally with events that can be observed by a variety of individuals (that are objective rather than subjective), that can be measured or described in precise ways, and that can be observed again under similar circumstances (that are replicable) (see Figure 1.3 and Box 1.3). Attempts to explain and organize these observations take the form of **theories**. In other words, theories are collections of related statements

Empirical Relating to observable facts or experiences, sometimes contrasted with rational or deductive approaches which are based more on reasoning processes than on replicable observation. The sciences are typically empirical.

Theory In its simplest sense, an explanation of facts, where facts are observations. Theories emphasize which facts are important for understanding, and which relationships among facts are most important.

Figure 1.3 Science is principally concerned with events that can be observed, measured, and repeated under similar circumstances (**a**). The science of psychology is also concerned with subjective states that are not so easy to replicate (**b**).

a

b

BOX 1.3

Scientific Revolutions

In psychology, as in other sciences, we tend to view our present state of knowledge as the most advanced and accurate yet achieved. And we assume that this present state is a simple accumulation of all preceding discoveries. Explanation is added to explanation and will continue to be added to explanation so that in the end we might know much more, if not all.

Kuhn (1970) suggests that science does not progress cumulatively through the simple addition of more and more facts and explanations. Instead, it grows through *revolutions* that are brought about by new *paradigms* (models or theories). These new paradigms, if they are to lead to revolutions, have two things in common. First, they are sufficiently compelling, unprecedented, and promising (in terms of their usefulness for explaining things that seem important at the time) that they motivate a significant number of scientists to abandon older paradigms. Second, they are sufficiently open-ended that they leave many questions unanswered, thus providing obvious directions for new research.

Kuhn provides convincing evidence that progress in recent science has involved revolutions of this nature—the revolutions themselves having occurred principally as a result of competition among members of a scientific community. He notes, as well, that textbooks describing current knowledge in a science obscure the revolutions that led to the knowledge. That is, a textbook typically does not communicate a historical sense, except insofar as "important" people and ideas are referenced, and their relationship to present beliefs noted. Instead, textbooks present current conceptions and concerns and, at least by implication, dismiss as misguided, misleading, incomplete, uninformed, and certainly inaccurate theories that were once believed but are now "known" to be wrong.

It is not particularly reassuring to contemplate these thoughts, realizing that those things we now accept as truth may seem every bit as naive and foolish in 200 years as the belief that the earth is the flat center of the universe now seems to us. Note, however, that it was useful to consider the earth flat at a time when there was no reason to suspect otherwise; that doing so imposed no great intellectual strain, it being a simple and obvious belief; and that the earth's flatness and centrality were as "truthful" in former days as are our most precious current beliefs. In science, "truthfulness" is more easily measured in terms of the usefulness (fruitfulness), consistency, simplicity, and explanatory value of beliefs than by reference to irrefutable tests of objective and logical validity.

This does not mean that all of science is no more than *relativism*—that is, that scientific beliefs of dramatically opposing forms are each correct and valid in their *relative* circumstances. Scientists, Kuhn informs us, are puzzle solvers; and in the case of conflict among theories and explanations, those beliefs that promise to solve the greatest number of puzzles become dominant.

As you go through this text, you will become aware that there have been a great many "revolutions" in psychology; that there are currently more than a handful of competing explanations; that many beliefs once firmly held have been discarded (rather than added to). You will note, as well, that we are some distance from having solved all our important puzzles. But that we have solved a great many, and that a number of our approaches promise to solve many more, should also become evident. We have every reason to believe that our present state of knowledge *is* the most advanced and the most accurate yet achieved. But it is not yet in its final form.

intended to facilitate understanding of observations and to permit predictions, or **hypotheses**.

In spite of science's preoccupation with the objective, a great many things of interest to psychology are primarily subjective. Therefore, they cannot be observed and measured directly, but can only be inferred from behavior or from highly subjective self-reports. **Emotions**, for example, are subjective—as are thoughts. And even though an emotion might lead to behavior from which an observer could guess the underlying emotion, this is not always so. For example, I might be very angry or very sad, and you would not necessarily know it from my behavior. One of psychology's tasks has been to devise ways for determining the nature of these nonobjective events and states, and for studying them as objectively and scientifically as possible.

Sources of Psychological Information

The ways psychologists gather information vary greatly, depending both upon the psychologist and upon the topic being researched. What is invariably true, however, is that *observation* is the source of all psychological knowledge (just as it is the source of knowledge in other sciences). Psychological studies and experiments based on observation vary according to who is being observed, when, how, and under what conditions. We look at each of these variables in turn.

Observation

Observation in psychology takes a variety of forms. Observation can occur in natural settings (termed **naturalistic observation**) or in laboratories, hospitals, and other surroundings where the observer can exercise some control over the environment. Naturalistic observation is well illustrated by the research of Jane Goodall. Since 1960 she has lived among chimpanzees in the Gombe Stream Chimpanzee Reserve in Tanzania, simply observing these chimpanzees without disturbing them (see Figure 1.4). The assumption of naturalistic observation is that if the investigator does interfere, the behavior under examination may be affected. For example, chimpanzees that would be playful and bold in their natural state might become anxious and furtive when observed too closely. Naturalistic observation, then, takes place in surroundings that are not altered by the observer or by the requirements of the observation; nonnaturalistic observation occurs in more contrived surroundings such as laboratories. Both have their place in psychological investigation, as the following discussion of psychological studies and experiments shows.

Psychological Studies

Both naturalistic and nonnaturalistic approaches to gathering psychological information can be classified in terms of *who* is observed and *how* and *when* the observations are made. Thus, there are **case studies**, where single individuals (or single units such as a family) are observed, and **surveys**, where large groups of individuals (or larger groups of units such as a number of families) are studied. **Longitudinal** and **cross-sectional studies** differ in terms of when observations are made. Whereas longitudinal studies follow the same subjects over a period of time, cross-sectional studies look at different individuals of different ages at one time. Explanations and descriptions of each of these approaches follow.

Case Studies   A young Russian, known to us only as S, presented himself to a psychologist one day. S was confused and poorly adjusted. He hoped that the psychologist, the very well-known and highly respected Alexandr Romanovich Luria, would help him. His problem was that he had difficulty following ordinary conversations, that his mind was such a jumble of sights, sounds, tastes, and colors that he spent quite

Hypothesis   A prediction based on theory; an educated guess derived from the explanations and assumptions that make up theories.

Emotion   The feeling or affective aspects of human behavior. Emotions can often be evaluated as being positive or negative and include such reactions as fear, anger, pity, disgust, joy, sorrow, and grief.

Naturalistic observation   Observation that takes place in naturally occurring circumstances or environments rather than in contrived environments. Observation is said to be naturalistic when the phenomena being observed are not affected by the observer or by the requirements of the observation. Observations that occur in laboratory settings are not naturalistic.

Case study   A method of observation which involves the intensive examination of a single subject or unit.

Survey   A method of observation which involves large groups of individuals.

Longitudinal study   Psychological investigation where the same subjects are examined over time.

Cross-sectional study   Method of investigation that involves observing and comparing different subjects, usually at different age levels.

Figure 1.4 In *naturalistic observation,* the observer tries not to interfere with the behavior of the observed. Here, Jane Goodall observes chimpanzees.

```
6 6 8 0
5 4 3 2
1 6 8 4
7 9 3 5
4 2 3 7
3 8 9 1
1 0 0 2
3 4 5 1
2 7 6 8
1 9 2 6
2 9 6 7
5 5 2 0
x 0 1 x
```

Figure 1.5 Months after seeing it, Luria's patient could still remember every number in this table—grouped vertically, as here, or diagonally, horizontally, or all together—through the ability to see, hear, and even taste mental images. But the jumble of his mental sensations got in the way of ordinary conversation. (Table from *The Mind of a Mnemonist: A Little Book about a Vast Memory* by A. R. Luria, translated from the Russian by Lynn Solotaroff, p. 17. Copyright 1968 by Basic Books, Inc., Publishers, New York. Reprinted by permission of Basic Books, Inc. and Jonathan Cape Ltd.)

a lot of time absolutely overwhelmed and bewildered. From this initial meeting there developed a long relationship between the two, during which Luria conducted intensive and detailed investigations of his subject's memory. Luria discovered, among other things, that S could remember with incredible and uncanny accuracy. Nor did he remember as you or I might remember, painfully retrieving some isolated bit of information that we have succeeded in storing and protecting from the ravages of time. He could remember in infinite detail, retrieving from his memory not only the item requested of him, but a host of other associations that most people would never have even noticed initially, let alone remembered. As an example, one day Luria presented S with the table of single-digit numbers reproduced in Figure 1.5. S spent 3 minutes examining the table. He then reproduced the entire table in 40 seconds. He reproduced the numbers that form diagonals in 35 seconds, and within 50 seconds had read off each of the four-digit numbers that form the first twelve horizontal rows, plus the two-digit number in the thirteenth row. Finally, in 1 minute and 30 seconds, he converted the entire array into a single 50-digit number and read it off for Luria. Perhaps even more amazing, when S was requested to reproduce the same table after several months had elapsed (the table had not once been presented in the interim), he could do so unerringly and just as rapidly. The only difference was that the second time he required a brief period to "reimagine" the situation in which he had first memorized the table.

As a result of this intensive and prolonged case study, Luria discovered that S did not simply *hear* sounds but sensed them as colors, as tastes, or as other sensations; that he could remember the clothing he and Luria had been wearing on a given day years before; that he frequently remembered by "seeing" objects, events, or numbers in mental images of places where he had stored them. Sometimes he would imagine that he was walking along a very familiar street in his hometown, and he would mentally place different numbers on various fences, trees, and houses along this street.* Later, when called upon to remember these numbers, he would simply imagine the street and read off the numbers as he saw them. On one occasion when he couldn't recall a number he had memorized in this fashion, it eventually occurred to him that he had "placed" the number in question on a dark, heavily shaded piece of broken board and that he simply could not "see" it!

Luria's investigation of S's memory and his subsequent reports of the results of this investigation provide us with a striking example of a case study. Numerous other examples can be found in psychological literature, particularly in studies of abnormal behavior. Whenever a psychologist requires extensive and in-depth information concerning a single individual, a case-study approach is likely to be employed.

Surveys   Whereas a case study deals with a single case (an individual or single unit), surveys involve groups of individuals or groups of units. Case studies are clearly inappropriate when the intent is to discover something about a group of people. A psychologist who wanted to find out what the average person in the street thinks of a political event could not easily accomplish this by walking up to and questioning an "average" person. In the first place, there is no **average** individual: he or she is an invention. When a researcher refers to the average person, it is never a single person being referred to; it is, instead, the nonexistent, idealized product of a thousand surveys. A survey is a research technique that attempts to discover the qualities of the nonexistent average person by examining the qualities of a number of individuals. When Sorensen (1973) wanted to discover the sexual beliefs and behaviors of the average adolescent, he surveyed a large number of different individuals by means of interviews and questionnaires. He was then able to state that 49 percent of all adolescents between the ages of thirteen and nineteen have masturbated at least once. Had he conducted a case study instead, and generalized in the same manner, he would have had to state either that all adolescents between the ages of thirteen and nineteen have masturbated at least once, or that none of them have; and either conclusion would have been highly misleading.

Longitudinal Studies   When the goal of psychological investigation is to identify changes that occur within individuals or within a group of individuals over time, longitudinal studies may be employed. A longitudinal study examines the same individual(s) at different times, and makes direct comparisons between the individual at this point in time and the same individual at an earlier time. Consider, for example, the problem of determining whether **intelligence** changes with age. Direct comparisons of different individuals who belong to different age groups cannot answer this question. By definition, and because of the way intelligence tests are **standardized**, the average intelligence test scores of different age groups should be approximately the same (IQ = 100). Hence, comparisons of different age groups should reveal that intelligence test scores do not change as a function of age. Does this mean that your measured intelligence is the same now as it was when you were fifteen? ten? six? Or does it simply mean that your age group is still an average group with respect to measured intelligence? The problem can be resolved by a longitudinal approach that compares your IQ scores at the ages of six, ten, and fifteen to your present measured intelligence. Using this approach, investigators could determine whether an individual's intelligence test scores are fixed and stable or whether they vary with age. They could also determine the extent to which one can expect intelligence to vary. Terman's (Terman et al., 1959) studies of genius, in which he followed subjects from infancy to adulthood, provide one of the better known examples of longitudinal research in psychology. Terman found, among other things, that highly gifted children tend to

Average   A mathematical indication of central tendency. An average is obtained by summing the numbers that relate to a particular characteristic among a group of individuals and dividing the sum by the total number of observations involved. Although averages are often good descriptions of characteristics or qualities of groups, they do not describe individual members of groups.

Intelligence   An ill-defined characteristic of human functioning, measured by intelligence tests. It seems to refer primarily to the capacity of individuals to adjust to their environment.

Standardized   An adjective that, when employed in conjunction with tests, refers to the procedures by which the test makers arrive at scores that describe the expected performance of groups or individuals on the tests. Most contemporary intelligence tests are standardized so that the average performance of large groups is 100 and scores are distributed in predictable ways around this average.

---

*This memory device, termed the Loci Method, is described in more detail in Chapter 7.

become highly gifted adults, and that individuals highly gifted in one area are likely to be gifted in other areas as well.

In another longitudinal study, Hindley et al. (1966) attempted to determine at what ages children first learn to walk in various countries. They selected samples of newborns from five different cities: Stockholm, Paris, London, Brussels, and Zurich. Interviewers then visited mothers of these children when the children were 9 months of age, 12 months, 18 months, and 3 years. Mothers were asked at what age their child first started to walk alone. These investigators subsequently reported that children from Stockholm walked at the earliest age (12.44 months) and those from Paris at the latest (13.58 months). Although similar results might have been obtained simply by interviewing a **random** sample of mothers from each of these cities (without visiting them as the infants were growing), the results would have been highly dependent upon the honesty and memories of the mothers, and might also have been influenced by different national attitudes toward children. Some nations might place more emphasis on the early locomotor accomplishments of their children and parents might therefore attempt to accelerate these accomplishments or, having failed to do so, might tend toward slight and relatively harmless exaggeration. Frequent interviews with the mothers while the children were actually learning to walk would overcome some of these weaknesses, and would almost necessarily lead to much more reliable results.

Although results may be more reliable, considerably more time and effort are required in longitudinal research than in other types of research. Hence it can be much more expensive; and that can be a very important factor in determining what type of research will be undertaken.

Cross-Sectional Studies

Whereas longitudinal studies examine the same individuals over a span of years, cross-sectional studies examine two or more groups of subjects at approximately the same time. Cross-sectional studies are much less time-consuming and consequently much less costly; but they are not always appropriate.

Consider, for example, the problem of investigating language differences between two- and three-year-old children. A longitudinal study would examine a group of two-year-old children now and reexamine them a year later, and make relevant comparisons. The project would span at least one entire year. A cross-sectional study, by contrast, would identify and examine comparable groups of two- and three-year-olds— a simpler, less expensive, and quite adequate approach for this problem. If, however, the problem had been one of identifying the *sequence* of language development between ages two and three, a cross-sectional approach would have been inadequate.

For a comparison of surveys, longitudinal studies, and cross-sectional studies, see Figure 1.6.

Experiments

For some time it has generally been accepted that the **experiment** is a very powerful tool in science's quest for knowledge (see Box 1.4). One reason for this is that the experiment allows investigators to manipulate the environment, thereby enabling them to observe effects they might not normally observe. In brief, an experiment is a research procedure where experimenters control one or more of the **variables** of a situation and observe the effects of this control on other variables in the situation.

A variable may be a measurement, an outcome, or some other way of describing or classifying people or events. Intelligence test scores, environmental factors, physical characteristics, and so on, are all examples of variables. Those variables the experimenter controls and whose effects are being investigated are termed **independent variables**; variables that may be affected by changes in the independent variables are referred to as **dependent variables**. Independent variables are assumed to have an effect on dependent variables. Dependent variables are ordinarily what is measured at the end of an experimental procedure.

Random Due solely to chance. A sample is said to have been chosen randomly when every potential subject for the sample had an equal chance of being selected.

Experiment A definite, deliberately controlled arrangement of circumstances under which a phenomenon is observed.

Variable A characteristic or quantity that can be varied in an experiment.

Independent variable The conditions or circumstances in an experimental situation which are controlled by the investigator in order to determine whether they are causally related to the phenomenon under observation (dependent variable). The assumption underlying experimental procedures is that dependent variables are caused by independent variables.

Dependent variable The phenomenon (variable) that is being observed in an experimental situation where the object is to determine which of one or more specific factors (independent variables) is causally related to the phenomenon.

What is the average American IQ?

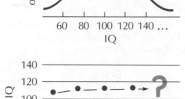

Surveys reveal information about groups of individuals at a specific time. But a single survey provides no information about change over time, and it gives only a composite picture of an idealized "average" individual.

How does IQ change over time?

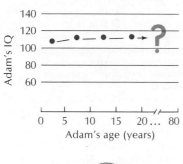

Longitudinal studies provide long-term information about one or more *real* people over a long term, often several years. But longitudinal studies are expensive and time-consuming. Many cannot be completed in the lifetime of a single researcher.

Does IQ vary according to age?

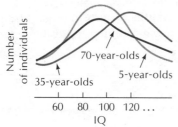

Cross-sectional studies can provide similar information about different groups at the same time. But, like surveys, they provide statistical averages and may not take all variables into account. For instance, did the 70-year-olds grow up with the same developmental stimulations as 35-year-olds, or 5-year-olds?

Figure 1.6 Surveys, longitudinal studies, and cross-sectional studies answer different questions.

As a simple illustration, consider the problem of determining which of two teaching methods is most effective. An experimental investigation of this problem requires that subjects be *assigned* to one or the other of these teaching methods, that the methods be put into practice, and that subsequent performance be measured and compared. In this case, teaching method is an independent variable; performance, a dependent variable. If teaching method does affect performance, it (the independent variable) may be employed to predict learning (a dependent variable).

For a comparison of research methods that differ in terms of who is observed, when, and how, see Table 1.2.

Ex Post Facto Studies   There is an important distinction between a true experiment and what is termed an **ex post facto study.** In a true experiment, the investigator assigns subjects to experimental conditions, controls these conditions, and controls as many other extraneous variables as is necessary and/or possible. In an ex post facto study, the experimenter simply *selects* subjects for study and does not exercise deliberate control over the conditions that lead to selection or rejection. To determine the relationship between social class and school achievement, for example, the investigator would simply *select* groups of subjects from different social classes and compare them on school achievement. This cross-sectional (subjects are selected from a cross-section of social classes and compared directly) ex post facto study is one of the most common approaches in psychological research.

There is one important caution in interpreting the results of ex post facto research. Such studies look for relationships between historical variables such as social class, parental rejection, or father absence, and current observations. And though such studies can establish the presence of relationships, they cannot provide sufficient evidence that one variable causes another. Although an ex post facto study might establish that

Ex post facto study   A study in which the experimenter does not assign subjects to experimental conditions or exercise control over these conditions; the experimenter simply selects subjects for study on the basis of differences that already exist among them.

Table 1.2 Common Types of Psychological Studies

	Case	Survey, Experiment (and Others)
Who	A single individual	More than one individual
	Longitudinal	Cross-sectional
When	The same individuals are observed at different times	Different groups of individuals are observed at the same time
	Experimental	Ex Post Facto
How	The experimenter controls relevant variables and *assigns* subjects to groups	The experimenter *selects* subjects, but neither assigns them to groups nor exercises control over independent variables

there is a relationship between father absence in early childhood and delinquent behavior in adolescence, it cannot prove that father absence *causes* delinquency, because any number of other uncontrolled variables (for example, poverty, mother absence, family size, and so on) might be causally related. Only a carefully controlled experiment can provide sufficient evidence of causation.

BOX 1.4

Animals in Psychology

Although psychology's ultimate concern is human behavior, a great deal of psychological research has involved nonhuman subjects. In this text, for example, you will find descriptions of research where:

Blowflies have had the nerve from their foreguts severed and have eaten until they burst (Chapter 9)

Rats have had parts of their brains tampered with and have subsequently become grossly obese (Chapter 9)

Infant monkeys have been separated from their mothers and reared in social isolation (Chapter 11)

Worms have been trained, minced, and fed to other worms (Chapter 7)

Dogs have been restrained and given mild electric shocks (Chapter 6)

These experiments were designed to provide information on the mechanisms that control eating and determine obesity; on the importance of mothers; on the nature of memory; and on the psychological effects of helplessness—all with respect to humans. The reason animals rather than human subjects were employed for these experiments is clear: none of these procedures can ethically be conducted with people. Furthermore, the results of research conducted on animals are very often generalizable to humans.

There are other reasons why animals are often employed instead of people, even when the experimenter's major interests relate to human behavior. Not only are animals frequently more docile and cooperative—and hence more manageable in certain circumstances—but they often present other specific advantages. The squid, for example, has immense nerve cells that function very much like human nerve cells. Their great advantage is their size, which permits observations that could not easily be made with human neurons.

Other advantages of animal subjects include the fact that experimenters can usually control an animal's experiences rather precisely, but can seldom do the same thing with humans. In studies of animal learning, for example, previous as well as present experiences are under experimental control. In addition, most animals reproduce far faster than do humans. Studies of heredity over eight generations of rats do not require eight generations of psychologists. One last reason for the study of animals is the interest science has in animals per se, as well as its interest in the relationship between humans and nonhuman animals.

But there are some disadvantages to the use of animals as experimental subjects when the primary goal is to understand people. A variety of human behaviors have no obvious parallels in nonhuman behavior. The courtship rituals of the North American male and female, although they might bear a vague resemblance to the strutting of peacocks, the head-butting of mountain sheep, and the dancing of the sage hen, have some distinctly "human" characteristics. Similarly, our use of language and its role in thought and behavior have not been greatly illuminated by animal research (although they might eventually be, as is shown in Chapter 8). In spite of this, however, the biological bases of these behaviors can, at least in part, be investigated through animal research. For example, the effects of hormones on sexual behavior have been extensively investigated among nonhuman primates (monkeys, apes, and lemurs), and some of these results generalize well to humans. Similarly, the role of the brain as well as of the vocal apparatus in the production of speech and in the comprehension of language has sometimes been clarified by looking at *differences* between us and other animals.

Besides, we too are animals.

Groups The experiment with which we are most familiar, as a result of the educational influence of television commercials, is that which makes use of an **experimental group** and one or more **control** (sometimes called comparison) **groups**. When the manufacturer of some exotic toothpaste with purple flecks assures us that use of this product leads to 40 percent fewer cavities, we assume, and indeed are sometimes told, that one group brushed regularly with the new product while a second group brushed with their regular toothpaste. Comparison of teeth between these two groups then enabled investigators to determine the extent to which the new product prevents cavities. Cavities are a dependent variable in this experiment; toothpaste employed is an independent variable. Similarly, the group to which something is done (in this case the group given the new toothpaste) is an experimental group; the group that is simply employed for comparison is a control group. Without the control group for comparison, we would never know whether simply brushing with *any* toothpaste decreases the incidence of cavities (see Figure 1.7). Any experimental design that does not employ comparison groups similar in as many relevant ways as possible to the experimental groups cannot be relied upon, since we have no way of determining whether outcomes might have been identical without any experimental treatment.

Experimental group The group of subjects which, in an experiment, is exposed to a treatment (independent variable) that is assumed to have an effect on the phenomenon under observation.

Control group A group of subjects as comparable to the experimental group as possible—ideally, identical to the experimental group in all respects save that they are not exposed to the treatment (independent variable) under investigation. Subsequent differences between experimental and control groups can then be assumed to be due to the only apparent differences between them—the independent variable.

Cautions in Interpreting Psychological Research

To what extent can we rely on an experiment such as the one just described, assuming, of course, that the results were reported accurately? Should we all run to our druggist and purchase armloads of the new toothpaste?

Would the results be affected, for example, if the control group had been selected from a small rural area where the drinking water is obtained from a questionably clean river, whereas the experimental group all reside in an urban area where fluoride is added to the water? Would the results be affected if the dentists who examined the subjects knew which ones were members of the experimental group and which were members of the control group? Is it important to know the number of cavities in the histories of members of each of these groups? These questions touch on various potential weaknesses of psychological research. We discuss each separately.

Experimenter Bias

An assortment of rats were divided among two groups of psychology students (Rosenthal & Fode, 1963). The students knew that psychologists had been successful in breeding strains of rats highly different with respect to their ability to learn how to run through mazes. These strains are appropriately and imaginatively labeled *maze-bright* and *maze-dull*. In this particular experiment, one group of students were told that they had been given rats of the maze-bright variety; the second group had to be content with allegedly maze-dull rats. In point of fact, however, both groups received randomly assigned rats of presumably equal intellect. Their task was simply to work with these rats over a period of time, and to train them in maze tasks. Significantly, those students who had been led to believe that they had bright rats reported considerably more success in training these docile creatures. In addition, they felt the rats to be more cooperative, more gentle, and generally more pleasant to work with than did those students whose rats were labeled dull (see Figure 1.8).

This experiment was among the first of many that have illustrated what is termed **experimenter bias**. It appears that the expectations of experimenters exert subtle and sometimes remarkable influences on their actual observations. A similar experiment conducted with elementary school children involved telling teachers that some of their students had been identified as potential "bloomers" (Rosenthal & Jacobsen, 1968). "Bloomers" were described as students of average or below-average achievement whose potential indicated they could easily achieve at a much higher level. The experimenters led the teachers to believe that they had developed a test that enabled them to identify those students who were most likely to show sudden acceleration of achievement during the coming academic year. Although these "bloomers" had been randomly selected, they did perform better than equally intelligent students who were not labeled the same. The results of this experiment have not always been supported in later research (see, for example, Barber & Silver, 1969–1970). Still, it seems that on occasion the expectations of teachers can dramatically affect not only the achievement of their students, but also their performance on objective measures of intelligence not ordinarily considered easily susceptible to teacher influence. Hence experimenter bias is now frequently referred to as the **Rosenthal effect**.

One of the most effective and most common means of guarding against the influence of experimenter expectations is simply to ensure that those responsible for gathering crucial experimental data do not know which subjects are members of experimental groups and which aren't. In the toothpaste experiment described earlier, if the dentists examining the children did not know which children had brushed with the new toothpaste and which were members of the control group, experimenter expectations would not likely affect the conclusions of the experiment. Experimental procedures where neither the examiners nor the subjects are aware of who is in the experimental group are termed **double-blind**. In a **single-blind procedure** either the subject or the examiner is unaware ("blind").

Subject Bias

Several decades ago in the Hawthorne plant of the Western Electric Company in Chicago, two psychologists (Roethlisberger & Dickson, 1939) experimented with different ways of increasing productivity among a group of women workers. In successive experiments the women were asked to work for longer periods of time, for shorter periods of time, for long periods with short rest breaks, for short periods with long rest breaks, with lights turned low, with lights turned almost off, with bonuses, without bonuses, and so on. The most striking finding from this series of experiments was that no matter what the experimental change, productivity increased. It appeared that as long as the workers thought they were members of an experimental group,

Experimenter bias The observation that experimenters' expectations may influence their observations. Experimenter bias is an unconscious process and is not to be equated with experimenter dishonesty. It is sometimes referred to as the *Rosenthal effect.*

Rosenthal effect The possibility that what researchers *expect* may influence what they observe. Also referred to as "experimenter bias."

Double-blind procedure An experimental procedure where neither the subjects nor the examiners know who is in the control group and who is in the experimental group.

Single-blind procedure An experimental procedure where either the investigators or the subjects are not aware of who are members of the experimental group and who are members of the control group.

scores reported by researchers who were told they had "maze-dull" rats

scores reported by researchers who were told they had "maze-bright" rats

Figure 1.8 How great a role does experimenter bias play in experimental results? The smaller rat represents lower scores reported by researchers who were told they had maze-dull rats; the larger rat represents higher scores reported by those told they had bright rats.

and as long as they assumed that the object of the experiment was to increase productivity and efficiency, they complied with these expectations. The observation that whenever subjects are aware that they are members of an experimental group, they tend to behave according to what they assume is expected or desired of them is now termed the **Hawthorne effect.** Ironically, however, subsequent examination of the original experiments suggests that they have been misinterpreted and exaggerated (Rice, 1982). In many of the experiments, productivity did *not* increase. In addition, experimental procedures were often unsupervised and poorly controlled. Nevertheless, the possibility that the outcome of an experiment may be affected by the fact that subjects know that they are subjects still exists and must be guarded against.

A single-blind procedure may also be employed to guard against subject bias. In this case, care is taken to ensure that subjects are not aware that they are members of an experimental group. Whenever possible, experimenters also try to prevent scorers or evaluators from knowing which subjects are members of experimental groups. A double-blind procedure is employed when neither the participants nor the examiners know who the subjects are. In the toothpaste experiment, a double-blind procedure would have required that all subjects be given similar, unmarked tubes of toothpaste. The control group would still have received an existing brand, and the experimental group, a new brand. In addition, the dentists examining the children's teeth would not have known which subjects had received the new toothpaste.

Sampling Bias

One of the most common weaknesses of many experiments has to do with inappropriate or biased sampling. There are two crucial **criteria** that should be met when selecting members of experimental and control groups. First, the subjects must represent the group to which the experimenters wish to **generalize**. Second, the experimental and control groups must be as similar as possible with respect to all relevant variables, and also with respect to the dependent variable(s) at the onset of the experiment.

Representativeness The importance of the first criterion (representativeness of subjects) relates to the usefulness of the experiment in providing information that is valid for groups other than those involved directly in the experiment. If the experimental group is significantly different from other groups, then the experiment will not provide information that can then be assumed to be more generally valid. Consider, for example, an experiment designed to compare the effectiveness of two teaching methods. If the experimenter intends to determine the relative effectiveness of these methods for all students in a given school system, it is important that the experimental and control groups be as similar as possible to all students in the system. Average intelligence, achievement, motivation, and other relevant variables of students

Hawthorne effect The observation that experimental subjects who are aware that they are members of experimental groups often perform better than subjects who are not aware they are. Sometimes subject bias can coexist with experimenter bias.

Criterion (plural, criteria) A standard, value, or goal by which something is judged; a necessary condition. If, for example, it is necessary to be able to type forty words per minute to pass ninth-grade typing, then the criterion for successful performance at the ninth-grade level is forty words per minute.

Generalization A process whereby conclusions derived in specific circumstances are extended to other similar circumstances. In experimental procedures the object is usually to generalize from a sample (subjects in the experiment) to a larger population (the group from which the sample is drawn). To increase the probability that generalizations will be valid, samples must be representative of the populations to which the generalizations presumably apply.

involved in the experiment should be as close as possible to those of all students in the system. If subjects are selected from a school where students have higher intelligence test scores, the results of the experiment might not be valid for other students.

Problems regarding the representativeness of samples are most evident in large-scale surveys where the intention is to generalize to a major segment of the population. Gallup polls and similar political forecasts would be highly unreliable if only one segment of the population were sampled. That is, it would be difficult to predict how a nation would vote if only academic populations or truck drivers were surveyed. To ensure that the results of such a survey apply to the entire population, experimenters must select their sample so that it matches the population in terms of as many relevant characteristics as possible. Thus, if 52 percent of the population is female, 52 percent of the sample should also be female; if 23 percent have college degrees, then 23 percent of the sample should also have college degrees. Similarly, in an ideal situation, the sample must match the general population in terms of age, religion, socioeconomic background, geographical location, and so on.

Comparability　The need for comparability of experimental and control groups is obvious in the toothpaste experiment. Suppose, for example, that the control group averaged 30 percent more cavities at the beginning of the experiment. Regardless of the effects of the new toothpaste, it would seem reasonable to expect that the rate at which the children developed cavities would be higher among those who initially had more cavities. Indeed, it would be relatively simple to select experimental groups and control groups who would serve as striking examples of the effectiveness of a new toothpaste even if both groups brushed equally religiously with the same toothpaste throughout the duration of the experiment.

Random Sampling　One way of attempting to ensure that experimental groups are representative of a larger population is to select group members *randomly*. Random selection requires that all members of the population have an equal chance of being selected. Given this condition, if enough representatives are drawn from the population, then there is a high probability that the experimental group's characteristics will be very similar to those of the entire population. In other words, if 23 percent of a population is male and 77 percent female, a large enough sample drawn randomly from this population should be close to 23 percent male and 77 percent female. By the same token, the sample should resemble the entire population closely in terms of average intelligence, racial background, and other variables that might be important. In most cases, a number of simple checks can be run to ensure this. The experimenter can determine the male-female ratio of a sample and compare this to that of the population. Similarly, average intelligence test scores, personality descriptions, and other important variables can sometimes be examined and comparisons made between samples and populations.

In the same way, *random* assignment of subjects to experimental and control groups is often employed to ensure that these groups will be comparable. Here again, simple checks can then be carried out to make sure this is so.

Other Problems of Psychological Research

Among numerous other problems that face researchers, as well as those of us who look for truth among their conclusions, are those of honesty, memory distortion, and inadvertent conceptual distortion. Surveys of sexual behavior, for example, must rely heavily on the honesty of participants. Many of these surveys (for example, Kinsey et al., 1948, 1953) have reported a significantly higher incidence of premarital and extramarital sexual activity among males than among females. However, given that our culture has for some time provided considerably more reinforcement for sexual behavior among men than among women, it is not unreasonable to suppose that some women would be more reluctant to disclose details of their sexual behavior. Similarly, studies of drug use and abuse have frequently provided inconclusive and contradictory results, probably largely because admitting to drug use is sometimes almost as bad as admitting to criminal behavior. In these and related studies, the honesty of subjects is a crucial factor that can do much to invalidate the results of research.

Related to the problem of subject honesty is that of having to rely on imperfect memories. Child development psychologists have had some difficulty establishing conclusively the average age at which children learn to walk, a problem related directly to the memories of their mothers. Unless the researcher is present whenever significant developmental events occur, reliance must be placed on the memories of the subject or of someone else who observed that subject. In either case, it is often wise to question the accuracy of results that are not obtained through direct observation.

Errors of conceptualization and interpretation that sometimes confuse scientific findings are related frequently to different meanings given to words and phrases. Most specialized disciplines have developed complex vocabularies that can be as confusing to the expert as they often are to the lay person. To say, for example, that children display a higher need for achievement if their parents are demanding and authoritarian is not particularly meaningful unless both the speaker and the listener (writer and reader) attach the same meanings to the terms *need for achievement, authoritarian,* and *demanding*. Unfortunately, both writers and speakers frequently blunder along as though everybody had highly similar vocabularies where each word and phrase has the same meaning.

A final pitfall in psychological research relates to the "correlational fallacy." The term **correlation** is frequently used and frequently misunderstood, both by academics and by others. Although a complete understanding of correlation requires more mathematical background and explanation than can comfortably and appropriately be included here, it is possible to explain it simply, so that you will be aware of the correlational fallacy.

In essence, a correlation is an expression of relationship between two variables. The toothpaste experiment could have been interpreted as meaning that there is a correlation between the decline of incidence of cavities and the use of different types of toothpaste. With the use of one toothpaste the number of cavities decreased (negative correlation). Conversely, with the use of the new toothpaste the order of dental health increased (positive correlation). In other words, a positive correlation exists between two variables when a change in one of these variables is reflected in a similar change in the other; a negative correlation is observed when a change in one variable is accompanied by an opposite change in the other. Numerically, correlation is expressed as -1.00 for a perfect negative correlation, $+1.00$ for a perfect positive correlation, and 0 for lack of correlation. Numerical expressions of positive and negative correlation, then, range from 0 to $+1.00$ and from 0 to -1.00, respectively (see Figure 1.9).

It would seem logical to assume that, if there is a high positive correlation between two variables, one must cause the other. Since there is apparently a high positive correlation between the use of a new toothpaste and the prevention of dental cavities, manufacturers of this toothpaste assume that the toothpaste prevents cavities. In point of fact, this may or may not be the case. *Correlation is not sufficient evidence of a causal relationship* (although it is *necessary* evidence); the assumption that it is sufficient is the correlational fallacy.

Consider, for example, the fact that there is a high positive correlation between the number of children in a family and the number of bedrooms in the home; between the number of churches and the number of liquor outlets in a community; between the number of prisons and the number of prisoners in a country. Do prisons cause prisoners? Do churches cause liquor outlets? Perhaps most striking, do bedrooms cause children?

Correlation A mathematical expression of relationship between two variables. Correlations may vary from highly positive relationships, where high or low values of one variable are always associated with corresponding high or low values in the second variable; highly negative, where high values in one variable are always associated with low values of the other and vice versa; or at or near zero, where values of one variable cannot be used to make systematic predictions about the second variable.

Who Can You Believe?

Have you by now developed an image of psychological researchers stumbling blindly among the numerous pitfalls of scientific research? This section is intended to persuade you that that image is considerably more appropriate for those whose knowl-

Figure 1.9 Plotting correlation on a graph.

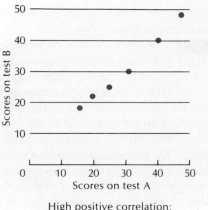

High positive correlation: individuals who did well on test A also did well on test B; those who did poorly on one also did poorly on the other.

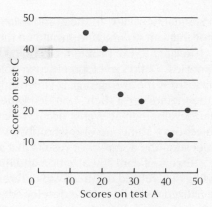

High negative correlation: individuals who did well on test A did poorly on test C; those who did poorly on test A did well on test C.

Low correlation: there is no apparent consistent relationship between scores on tests A and D.

Individual	Test score			
	A	B	C	D
1.	47	48	21	20
2.	32	30	23	12
3.	41	40	11	40
4.	20	22	40	10
5.	15	17	45	45
6.	25	23	25	50

edge of human behavior is primarily gathered haphazardly from daily experiences, newspapers, and television sets, and from the pronouncements of those who make pronouncements. Well-trained researchers generally are acutely aware of potential pitfalls and can thus more effectively guard against falling into traps that might deceive the less wary.

Philosophical Issues and Psychological Controversy

The search for explanations of human behavior is necessarily based on a number of **assumptions** that direct that search and that—in a very real sense—validate many of the beliefs resulting from the search. The most fundamental of these assumptions are philosophical in origin, have been subjects of controversy and debate that continue unresolved to this date, and cannot be tested or examined completely objectively. If they could, they would not be *assumptions* (which are, by definition, unproven) but would be laws or principles (beliefs more firmly grounded in objective observation).

Assumption A judgment or belief that is accepted as true even though it has not been proven and, in most instances, cannot be proven. Assumptions, many of which are not consciously recognized, are fundamental in most sciences, although they are often sources of error. Later investigations may prove assumptions false; or they may verify them, in which case they become principles or laws.

Most important among these assumptions are those which deal specifically with human nature: Is behavior a function of free will or is it determined by other forces? Are mind and body separate? Is behavior determined by underlying traits or characteristics in the person (termed *dispositions*), or is it determined by the immediate situation?

Although virtually all psychologists assume that behavior is orderly and consistent (otherwise there would be no point in searching for rules, laws, or principles to explain it), assumptions made with respect to many other questions often vary. Some psychologists premise their research and their beliefs on the notion that behavior is determined by immediate situations; others, on the notion that behavior results from underlying dispositions. Some attribute an important role to genetic factors; others to environmental forces. Some are primarily deterministic; others are more inclined to believe that we exercise deliberate control over our behavior. And the end result of these different assumptions is that psychology is characterized by a number of important and fundamentally different theories—a fact that has led Staats (1981) to describe psychology as being divided into "unrelated islands of information" (p. 239). But the different emphases and controversies that are represented by these "islands" are neither petty nor trivial. Their great value lies in the impetus they provide for a reexamination of assumptions and for gathering data that might be relevant for this reexamination. To a large extent, it is scientific controversy and the activity that results from the controversy that leads to scientific revolutions and that may eventually result in a unified psychological theory of the kind advocated by Staats (1981).

Many of these unresolved controversies are a fundamental part of the content of this book. Appreciating their origins and their potential contributions can lessen whatever frustration might come from trying to learn and understand a science that is sometimes gray rather than always black or white.

BOX 1.5

Answers for the True/False Folk Wisdom Psychology Test

None of the twelve items in the test is entirely true (although most can be true for some individuals under some circumstances). In general, then, all items are false.

1. Obese persons, very much like obese rats, tend to be more selective with respect to food than "normal" individuals. They will typically eat less of those substances that are not highly palatable (Chapter 9).

2. Dreams may on occasion be related to indigestion, although there is no evidence that this is *often* the case. In fact, no one knows for certain why we dream, but there are some interesting theories (Chapter 3).

3. Although there are some notable exceptions, those few individuals whose memories are photographic (termed *eidetic*) are quite normal in other respects (Chapter 7).

4. The grass is not invariably greener (on the other side of the fence or wherever). In fact, we tend to like our own choices better than other people's choices (Chapter 17).

5. Psychoanalysis is a psychiatric technique. Psychiatry is a branch of medicine; psychology is not. Psychologists are not usually psychoanalysts (Chapter 16).

6. Absence is likely to make the heart grow less fond; presence (nearness) often has the opposite effect. But in matters of love there are many exceptions (Chapter 18).

7. Virtually every normal person dreams, although not all remember their dreams (Chapter 3).

8. Many birds and insects see the world in color; by contrast, a great many mammals see only in black and white (and shades of gray) (Chapter 5).

9. Even when you concentrate intensely on a single thing (a conversation, for example), you are seldom totally unaware of other things happening around you, as is evident from the fact that you are likely to respond to your name even if it is spoken by someone to whom you are not listening (Chapter 4).

10. People whose activities are overly rewarded (termed *overjustified*) will often like those activities less, subsequently, than if they had been rewarded less (Chapter 17).

11. Fathers rather than mothers determine the sex of the offspring, because only the male produces the male sex chromosome (Chapter 11).

12. Although it is clear that heredity is involved in some types of mental disorders, it would be highly misleading to state that they are *usually* inherited (Chapter 15).

Psychology's Relevance

What do you want out of psychology? The question is not as simple as it might be in other fields. A bookkeeping course might teach you how to keep books; a course in dentistry, how to be a dentist; and a course in mathematics, how to do mathematics. But a course in psychology is not likely to teach you how to do psychology. Besides, what is involved in "doing" psychology is not at all clear. Clinical **psychologists** or **psychiatrists** "do" psychology in one sense; they attempt to apply some of what they have learned or discovered to the alleviation of the disturbances that are presented to them. Research psychologists also "do" psychology, but the thing they do is clearly different from the things done by psychiatrists. Your college professor "does" psychology; but that too is different. In any case, you will probably not do any of these things as a result of this single course. (See Figure 1.10.)

What then? Is psychology going to reveal the grand mysteries of the human psyche, expanding your understanding of yourself and of humanity? Will it enable you to function better as a human being, directing you along paths of growth and happiness? Or will it give you power—power to control the minds, the emotions, the wills, and, yes, the behavior of those less well informed than you; of those who have not been initiated in the secrets of our discipline?

Perhaps. Indeed, psychology's primary goal is to explain; and from explanation flow prediction and sometimes control. This does not mean that you will achieve all three; or even that psychology has achieved all three. There is much left to be explained, much that cannot be predicted accurately or reliably, and important practical limits on control, in addition to ethical objections (see Box 1.6).

It has become something of a cliché to point out that we have spent most of our recent history concentrating on attempts to understand the world in which we live— vegetable, animal, mineral—and that we have made absolutely remarkable progress in that direction. But we have spent almost none of our history in serious and systematic efforts to understand our own psychological functioning. We know our systems remarkably well in terms of their organic functioning. In cases of organic malfunction or breakdown, we frequently know exactly what should or can be done, although much still remains a mystery. But in cases of nonorganic breakdown we are more helpless—more, but not completely. And it is in this last qualifier that the excitement and the hope of psychology are to be found. What field could be more important than that which deals most specifically and most expressly with what is closest and dearest to us: ourselves? And what field could be more exciting and more challenging than that about which there remains so much that is unknown? That field is psychology. And this is your introduction.

This Book

The remaining chapters of this book provide, as was stated earlier, a definition of psychology. That definition takes the form of a division of psychological topics into those separate units that have made the field easiest to organize and understand. The units are further divided into chapters, each dealing with a different facet of human behavior, and each attempting to summarize and interpret what is known about that aspect of behavior.

Following this introduction, we move to a consideration of our biological aspects; brain and body. It is important to note that, even though it is possible to separate the human **organism** into parts and to deal with these individually (a nervous system here, a gland there), the functioning of these parts is linked in complex and often little-understood ways. Similarly, although we can divide our study of human behavior into units and chapters, we should not lose sight of the fact that it is the entire person with which we are concerned.

Psychologist A person who has studied psychology under professional guidance. In the strict sense, to be a psychologist requires certification or at least having met the criteria for certification by a psychological association. The APA certifies individuals as psychologists after two years of graduate training and one year of experience that relates directly to being a psychologist, or after three years of graduate training. Psychologists are not psychiatrists.

Psychiatrist An individual who, in addition to having medical degrees, has undergone intensive training and study in mental disorders.

Organism A living being composed of parts (organized), some of which may be specialized for different functions. Organisms include plants and animals, and are sometimes defined to include viruses and other single-celled beings. We are organisms; so are rats.

BOX 1.6

Explaining, Predicting, and Controlling

The goal of most sciences is to explain observed phenomena, predict their occurrence once explanation has been obtained, and eventually arrive at methods for achieving control. Meteorological forecasting, for example, is weather *prediction* based on our *explanations* of weather. And the ultimate application of explanation and prediction in this area lies in the possibility of *controlling* weather. Here, as elsewhere, there is potential for abuse.

Psychology is not different from other sciences in these respects. If we can explain human behavior, we can perhaps predict its manifestations. And ultimately we can exercise some degree of control.

There is a tendency to shudder when contemplating the possibility that human behavior might be controlled by something other than "free will" or the accidental arrangement of environments.

"Nothing and nobody will control me. I control my own life."

Not so. At least, not entirely so. Psychology reveals rather clearly that much of what you think and do is determined by environmental and innate forces over which you have relatively little control. This need not mean that you are a powerless prisoner of these forces. Nevertheless, they do limit and determine some of your options, and understanding these forces does enable psychologists and others to exercise some control.

Control is not intrinsically and by definition bad; nor is it usually direct and easy. Your attitudes cannot be casually manipulated, your behaviors precisely ordered, your emotions toyed with at will. Although each of these forms of control is possible to some extent, they are far from absolute. And they can often be applied extremely usefully. Psychology suggests methods (of varying effectiveness) for controlling classroom misbehavior, for promoting learning, for increasing memory skills, for dealing with maladjustment and emotional disturbance, for alleviating the distress of mental disorders, and for a great many other occasional and undesirable consequences of being human. There are enough of these consequences that there is little time or need to tamper with the joyful aspects of living except insofar as these too can be enhanced. Control of this nature is not to be feared, but to be welcomed.

The importance of biological factors in human thought and behavior can hardly be overestimated. Indeed, many of the important differences between human and nonhuman animals may be explained in terms of biology. It is not because an antelope is an antelope that it can run at 60 miles an hour, any more than it is because we are human that we can think about similarities among ourselves, antelope, and turkeys. One of these animals has a highly specialized arrangement of muscles and tendons, a big heart, and a timid nature; another has an unimpressive arrangement of leg muscles, a smaller heart, but an incredible brain. That incredible brain is the subject of a major portion of the second chapter. Suffice it to say that the third animal has feathers.

Of what are we aware, and how? Chapter 3 discusses various levels of consciousness, including sleeping, dreaming, being awake, and transformations of these states brought about through the use of drugs. The fourth and fifth chapters deal with the processes by which we become aware of our environments: our perceptual systems, which include the traditional five senses and a number of others less traditional but no less important.

Part II examines learning and thinking, and includes discussions of memory and language, tremendously important topics for understanding human behavior.

Part III looks at the why of behavior: human motivation. The area is fraught with frustration and promise. The chief source of frustration is the fact that our behavior is not nearly so predictable as science would like. Consequently, the generalizations that psychology is typically able to make often apply only to the nonexistent "average" person and are not particularly useful in dealing with any given individual. The promise lies in the fact that many of the generalizations do have "general" validity, and that psychology may one day understand the individual exception much more clearly.

Part III also deals with an area that has sometimes been neglected in the history of psychology, given our traditional preoccupation with topics that can be defined, observed, measured, and otherwise dealt with in objective ways. Affect, or emotions, are basically nonobjective reactions, not well understood by the individual experiencing them, and probably even less well understood by others. Yet emotion is fundamental to the quality of our lives; by the same token, it is fundamental to an understanding of psychology.

The fourth part looks at the span of human development from conception to death, and at the forces that shape the course of development.

Part V presents an examination of personality, normal and abnormal. One of psychology's important tasks has been to understand the human being as a whole functioning, feeling, and thinking organism. At the same time, one of its major contributions has been a greater understanding of the malfunctioning organism and the development of a variety of approaches to caring for and helping people who suffer from what are sometimes called mental disorders.

The concluding part (Part VI) looks at the individual in relation to society and attempts to assess the extent to which social forces influence individual behavior.

In brief, the breadth and substance of psychology are implicit in this arrangement of topics, and its definition, too, is implicit in them. Thus, it is not entirely facetious to say that the definition presented in this text requires several hundred thousand words. At the same time, however, the definition can be reduced to a single outline, as in Table 1.3, or can be reduced even further to a single statement: *Psychology is the study of behavior and thought.*

Main Points

1   All that affects human behavior, thought, and emotion falls within the domain of psychology.

2   Psychology had its origins in Greek philosophy (*psyche* is Greek for soul; *logos,* for study), was profoundly affected by medical discoveries which tended to reduce the mysteries of

Table 1.3 An Outline of This Text and a Definition of Psychology

Outline	Definition

1. Psychology
I. Physiology, Consciousness, and Perception
  2. The Nervous System and Its Brain
  3. States of Consciousness
  4. Perceptual Systems: Orienting, Hearing, Touching, and Savoring
  5. Perceptual Systems: Seeing
	Psychology is the study of behavior and thought. It looks at the physiological basis of behavior, at consciousness, and at the perceptual systems which are our contacts with external and internal events.

II. Learning, Memory, and Thinking
  6. Learning
  7. Memory
  8. Thought, Language, and Creativity
	It inquires about how we learn and remember, how we think, and how language relates to these intellectual activities.

III. Motives and Feelings
  9. Motivation
  10. Emotion
	It looks, too, at our reasons for behavior—at our motives and emotions.

IV. The Life Span
  11. From Conception through Childhood
  12. Adolescence, Aging, and Dying
	Psychology is concerned with developmental processes, and with the significant changes that transpire between birth and death.

V. Personality and Abnormality
  13. Descriptions of Personality
  14. Personality Assessment and Intelligence
  15. Psychopathology
  16. Therapy
	It examines human individuality and attempts to classify and sometimes to quantify in order better to understand. It studies abnormality and searches for ways to alleviate the distress that often accompanies mental disorders.

VI. Relationships and Others
  17. Social Influence
  18. Interpersonal Relationships
	And, finally, it looks at relationships between individuals and others.

the body to more mechanistic principles, and borrowed its scientific methodology from Newtonian physics.

3 Psychology as a contemporary science is approximately one hundred years old.

4 Science is an attitude that insists on precision and replicability. It is also a collection of methods based principally on empirical (observable or external) investigation, and geared toward gathering the best evidence possible for determining whether theories and predictions are valid.

5 Observation is the source of knowledge in all sciences. In psychology it can occur in natural surroundings (termed *naturalistic*) or in more contrived environments such as laboratories.

6 Case studies involve the observation of a single individual (or a single unit); surveys involve observation of larger groups of individuals. Observation may be direct or may employ a variety of tests, or instruments.

7 Longitudinal studies involve looking at the same individual(s) at different times; cross-sectional studies involve looking at different groups of individuals at the same point in time.

8 An experiment is a powerful research procedure where investigators control or manipulate important variables (dimensions that vary from one person to another or one situation to another) in order to determine what the effects of that variable (termed an *independent variable*) might be on one or more other variables (termed *dependent variables*).

9 An ex post facto study looks very much like a true experiment except that in the ex post facto study investigators do not have control over selecting subjects and deliberately manipulating independent variables. For example, investigators are not usually able to control a variable such as social class, but must instead select subjects on the basis of their membership in identifiable social groups. In a true experiment, the experimenter would assign (rather than select) subjects, and would manipulate social class, giving one group more and another less. In this case, a true experiment is clearly impossible.

10 In an experiment, a control (or comparison) group, as closely identical to the experimental group as possible, is often employed to ensure that any observed results are due to whatever

was done to or with the experimental group (but not to the control group), rather than to other factors not controlled by the investigator.

11 Single-blind procedures (where either the subjects or the investigator is not aware of who are members of the experimental group and who are members of the control group) and double-blind procedures (where neither the examiners nor the subjects know who is and who isn't in the experimental group) are employed to safeguard against experimenter and subject bias.

12 Experimenter bias is occasionally evident in the tendency of investigators to observe and/ or report evidence and conclusions that are compatible with their expectations. This appears to be a subtle unconscious process, and is sometimes termed the *Rosenthal effect*.

13 Subject bias is sometimes manifested in the greater tendency of individuals to perform well simply because they know they are members of an experiment (termed the *Hawthorne effect*).

14 In order to generalize experimental results to individuals and groups not included in the original experimental sample, the experimenter must study a sample representative of the population to which generalizations are to be made.

15 Other problems that face psychological researchers include those of subject honesty, distortions of memory, conceptual problems often arising from the use of identical words for different meanings, and the tendency to assume that if two events are correlated, one must have caused the other.

16 Psychological research is based on a number of assumptions; some of these are controversial (nature vs. nurture, determinism vs. free will), and can profoundly influence our conclusions. One fundamental assumption that is less controversial is that behavior is, at least to some extent, orderly and predictable. Otherwise, there would be little point in searching for rules and principles that describe it.

17 Psychology's primary goals are to explain human behavior, to make increasingly more accurate predictions, and to achieve a greater degree of control in alleviating human distress and in enhancing the joyful aspects of living.

18 An overview of this text may be summarized in terms of this definition of psychology:

Psychology is the study of behavior and thought (Chapter 1). It looks at the physiological basis of behavior (Chapter 2), at consciousness (Chapter 3) and at the perceptual systems, which are our contacts with external and internal events (Chapters 4 and 5). It inquires about how we learn (Chapter 6) and remember (Chapter 7), how we think, and how language relates to these intellectual activities (Chapter 8). It looks too, at our reasons for behaving—at our motives (Chapter 9) and our emotions (Chapter 10). Psychology is concerned with developmental processes (Chapter 11) and with the significant changes that transpire between birth and death (Chapter 12). It examines human individuality (Chapter 13) and attempts to classify and sometimes to quantify in order better to understand (Chapter 14). It studies abnormality (Chapter 15) and searches for ways to alleviate the distress that often accompanies mental disorders (Chapter 16). And finally, it looks at relationships between individuals (Chapters 17 and 18).

Further Readings

The history of psychology is traced in some detail in books such as the following:

Murphy, G., and Korach, J. *Historical introduction to modern psychology* (3rd ed.). New York: Harcourt Brace Jovanovich, 1972.

Fancher, R. E. *Pioneers of psychology.* New York: W. W. Norton, 1979.

For an entertaining and highly readable discussion of the role of research in the behavioral sciences, you are referred to:

McCain, G., and Segal, E. M. *The game of science* (4th ed.). Monterey, Calif.: Brooks/Cole, 1982.

For a provocative, highly readable, sometimes personal view of science's role, you might consult the following book, which presents a rather strong challenge to our traditional, well-reasoned views of the world.

Pearce, J. C. *The crack in the cosmic egg.* New York: Fawcett Books, 1971.

A physicist claims that a scientific revolution is under way, brought about by a new paradigm in physics, and with striking implications for medicine, psychology, and economics, in:

Capra, F. *The turning point: Science, society, and the rising culture.* New York: Simon & Schuster, 1982.

Interesting aspects of scientific methodology are highlighted in a critical look at various pseudoscientific theories:

Radner, D., and Radner, M. *Science and unreason.* Belmont, Calif.: Wadsworth, 1982.

Those interested in learning more about careers in psychology and relevant training programs might write to the American Psychological Association, 1200 Seventeenth St., N.W., Washington, D.C. 20036, for a copy of their free booklet: *A Career in Psychology.*

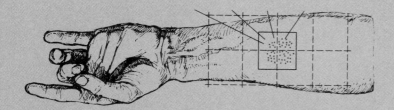

Among the most fascinating topics in psychology and philosophy are those concerned with the nature of reality and awareness. Unwilling to attribute our type of consciousness to any animal other than ourselves, we tend to believe that we are unique in our awareness of the world; that reality is that of which we are aware— no more and no less; and that our brains and nervous systems are the most remarkable of any species'.

In Chapter 2 we look at our nervous systems. Does the brain ever tell us all that there is to know about the brain? Or was Isaac Asimov correct when he suggested that those things that are understood must be simpler than those that understand, and that since the brain is equal to itself, it can never understand itself completely?

Chapter 3 looks at consciousness in its ordinary states: waking and sleeping. The emphasis here is on sleeping; most of the remainder of the text deals with being awake. The chapter also looks at less ordinary states of consciousness, including hypnosis, meditation, and drug-induced experience. Chapter 4 introduces the perceptual systems, the systems through which we are in contact with the environment and ourselves. These systems are organized around the traditional senses but include much more than simple sensation. Basic orientation, the haptic system (touching and feeling), the hearing system, and savoring (tasting and smelling) are treated in detail in Chapter 4. Chapter 5 examines the visual system, at once fascinating and incredibly complex.

PART ONE

Physiology, Consciousness, and Perception

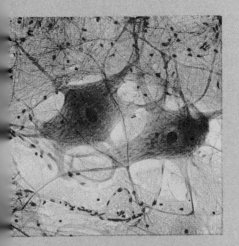

The Nervous System and Its Brain

We are animals; perhaps superior, but not in all ways. Take a bat, for instance. Bats, cunning beasts that they are, fly hectically about at what must be, for a bat, breakneck speed. Yet they don't break their necks on rafters and walls, or on brick buildings, in spite of the fact that they do most of this frantic flying when it is dark. And even if they flew during the daytime, they would still pay no attention to the ancient wisdom expressed so simply and so poetically in grandmother's admonition to look before you leap, and frequently not to leap at all, discretion being the better part of valor, in spite of the fact that faint heart ne'er won fair maid, and so on. The bat has little need of this wisdom, having long ago developed a magnificent imitation of our sonar. As they fly, bats emit a series of high-pitched squeals which bounce predictably off the various objects they encounter. Since sound travels at a relatively constant speed, it is a small trick for the bat to compute quite accurately—indeed, within a fraction of a centimeter—how far the sound has traveled from it to an object, and back again. You see, the bat responds to the echoes of its sounds. Of course, it has moved in the interim, but it has continued to emit squeaks, to listen, and to compute. Thus, it can not only avoid objects that might break its neck, but it can also detect smaller objects that might serve as food. A squeak bounces off a fly just as it bounces off a brick wall. And as the fly moves, the direction of the echo changes. Knowing this, the bat alters its movements and intercepts the fly in midair. Bats can hear sounds that we can't.

Penguins can smell smells that we can't (see Figure 2.1).

The golden eagle provides yet another example of how "lower" animals are not always lower in all respects. From precarious heights that eagle can, on a clear day, spot a green frog swimming innocently in green water, six inches below a slimy green surface, among lily pads which, as you guessed, are also green. True, the eagle must now suffer the risk of drowning miserably among those lily pads, or of being engulfed by a camouflaged crocodile, if it is to eat the frog. But the golden eagle, particularly since its cousin became a national bird, is no coward. Let us not, however, involve

Figure 2.1 While nonhuman animals may well be inferior to humans in some respects, many are superior to us in some areas of sensory development. For example, the penguins' sense of smell allows them to locate their own babies in large crowds.

ourselves in a discussion of the eagle's alleged bravery. Suffice it to say that its visual sense is superior to ours, as is that of the goat family. About pigs, I am less certain.

We could continue, but the point has almost been made. And what is the point, you ask? It is not specifically that the grizzly bear is physically stronger than we are, that the antelope is faster, that the kangaroo can jump farther, or that the seal swims with more grace. The point is that we, and all other animals, behave as we do largely because of our different physiologies, as well as because of our different nervous systems. And if we are to understand behavior, it is absolutely imperative that we understand something about our "wiring" and its functioning.

Evolution

We are *Homo sapiens,* the self-named wise one, ruler of the ash can, a comfortable position, due largely to our well-developed "new" brains, our opposable thumbs, the fact that we walk upright, and our ability to communicate through the use of arbitrary symbols.

But we don't have clever thumbs simply because we decided they would be a definite advantage; we did not invent our brains; we made no conscious decision to shift from a four-legged to a two-legged form of locomotion, thereby making our front legs obsolete and eventually changing their names to arms; nor did we, in council one day, decide that a language would be superior to the signs and signals we had previously been using. These great happenings were either the results of **evolution**, or they were the products of an inventive Supreme Being (**Divine Creation assumption**), or perhaps both. The issue cannot be resolved here and will not be discussed as an issue, although we will wander briefly back into the murky depths of evolutionary history.

Evolution, the adaptive progression of species from their origins, might at first glance seem an inappropriate topic for a study of human behavior. We are, after all, concerned with understanding your behavior, mine, and that of others. But perhaps something in evolution might help our understanding. Certainly, much in the biology

Evolution A scientific theory that holds that present life forms have developed from preexisting species through a series of modifications governed by laws of natural selection and diversification of species.

Divine Creation assumption The belief that present life forms were created by a Supreme Being.

PART ONE Physiology, Consciousness, and Perception

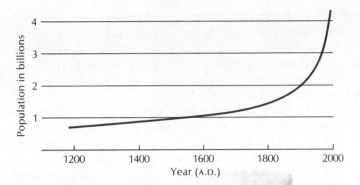

Figure 2.2 Population growth for *Homo sapiens* on earth. The part of the graph to the left that isn't shown would be about one kilometer long if it reached back to the time when humans first appeared.

of humans is related to behavior; and this biology is (perhaps)* the product of evolutionary processes.

Early Homo Sapiens

Much of the evidence upon which the details of evolutionary theory are based are drawn painfully from the few records nature has haphazardly provided: a fossil here, a bone there, a fragment of skull, a petrified dinosaur dropping. Those who can peer back into the dimness of geological time and read these records inform us that modern humans made their inconspicuous appearance on this planet approximately 1 million years ago (see Figure 2.2).† True, our immediate ancestors had diverged from their closest relatives, the great apes, perhaps 25 million years before that, but these ancestors were primitive in the extreme. Indeed, widely accepted speculation has it that the first tool makers did not appear until approximately 2 million years ago (Hawkes, 1963, 1976). There now remains only one species of humans in a world comprising approximately 1.5 million different species (Lerner, 1968). The human species belongs to the primate order, of which there are at least fifty-one living species (Campbell, 1966); its class is mammal; it belongs to the chordate phylum in the animal kingdom (see Table 2.1).

Table 2.1 Biological Classification of Humans

General Classification	Human Classification
Species	*Homo sapiens*
Genus	*Homo*
Family	Hominidae
Order	Primate
Class	Mammal
Phylum	Chordate
Kingdom	Animal

Why did this species of humans survive? Was it not physically inferior to the large carnivorous predators? Slower? Gifted with unexceptional vision and hearing? Relatively poorly developed in its sense of smell? Poorly protected against both heat and cold? Poorly made for climbing trees or digging holes? Unnatural in the water? Impossible in the air? Yes, it was all of these, and worse; it probably suffered incessantly from those odors that we now cleverly disguise with sprays, perfumes, repellants, powders, creams, and lotions. But it was more intelligent. If it could not outfight an enemy, it could still perhaps outwit the beast. It could also *stand upright,* a fact that would superficially seem to be of little advantage, since most four-legged animals except those with very short legs can run faster than a fully frightened human. But what those four-legged animals cannot ordinarily do is stand on their hind legs and use their front legs for purposes quite remote from those of locomotion. There, indeed, was the early human's great advantage. That animal could walk quite nicely

---

*The qualifier *perhaps* is included because evolutionary theory is, in fact, a theory. Even though the bulk of scientific evidence lends wide support to this theory, as is evident in that very few scientists dispute its general validity, there remain dissenters. Those who ask for proof may be supplied with considerable evidence, but not with proof. Theories, which are essentially attempts to organize and explain *facts,* can never be proven. Although they might be supported by all known facts, it is seldom possible to rule out undiscovered contradictory facts.

†Scientists don't always agree. Some estimates claim that modern humans are a mere 40,000 to 50,000 years old (see Thompson, 1975); others maintain that we are considerably more than a million years old (Leakey, 1971).

on just two of its legs, freeing the others for making tools, striking enemies while in full flight, gesticulating, and blowing the nose, an undertaking that was not at all hampered by the fine opposable thumb that we now take so much for granted. No other animal on this planet, save some higher monkeys, can move its thumb in apposition to its other fingers—and consequently no other animal can boast the manual dexterity that we have at our fingertips.

We now take for granted that the fittest survive, that this harsh law of evolution governed the development of our ancestors. Note, however, that the concept of *fitness* in an evolutionary context refers not so much to physical attributes like strength, agility, speed, cunning, and other talents and skills that would obviously be critical in societies of predators and prey. In effect, fitness refers primarily to the success with which species procreate. Clearly, only those species that are successful in procreating will survive. By the same token, however, the ability to survive physically from day to day is, for many creatures, necessary for their procreation and hence for species survival. This is particularly true of species that reproduce only after a long period of maturation. We are an excellent example of such a species.

Given our obvious physical disadvantages relative to certain other species, we must then conclude that our ability to walk upright, our superior **brain**, and our juxtaposed thumb were critical factors in our survival. Perhaps no less important, however, is a fourth factor, our development of language. And of these our brains (which, among other things, make language possible) are by far the most important of evolution's legacies.

Evolution and the Nervous System

The brain is part of our **nervous system**; our nervous system is the communication system within our bodies. It is because of our nervous system that our right hands know what our left hands are doing, that our legs alternate rather than compete when we walk, that we are sensitive to our environments. Indeed, the nervous system is implicated in all that we think, feel, and do; hence its tremendous importance in understanding human functioning.

In an evolutionary sense, our nervous systems are among the most complex and highly developed. They stand in sharp contrast to those of more primitive creatures—creatures to whom we are, nevertheless, related by evolution. At the lowest level, for example, there are single-celled organisms whose responsiveness and purposiveness are highly limited. There are also simple multicelled organisms such as sponges whose various "nervous systems" are not in communication with one another. Parts of the sponge contain specialized cells for reproduction or secretion, each of these functions being carried out independently of what might be happening elsewhere in the sponge.

The nervous systems of insects also provide an interesting evolutionary contrast to those of humans. In some insects, primitive clusterings of nerve cells coordinate simple functions. Here again, however, there is no single "command area"—no *brain* to oversee all functions. Cut off the head of a wasp and it will continue eating even though it has lost its abdomen. In much the same way, the male praying mantis will continue to copulate even as the female systematically devours him from the head down.

The more advanced nervous systems of fishes, reptiles, and eventually mammals, differ in a number of important ways from these more primitive nervous systems. Not only are they more complex in terms of function, but, in addition, their activity is coordinated by an increasingly large brain. Furthermore, brains in these more advanced animals have become increasingly specialized. Thus a large portion of the bat brain is devoted to hearing; the olfactory (smell) area of dog brains is far more developed than that of human brains; those parts of the brain that control rapid movement are more predominant in bird brains; and in humans, the area of the brain devoted to thinking, namely the cerebral cortex, is larger, proportional to the remainder of the brain, than in any other living creature (see Figure 2.3).

Brain A complex cluster of nerve cells centrally involved in coordinating activities and events in various parts of an organism. The human brain is reputedly the most complex structure in the universe.

Nervous system Parts of the body composed of nerve cells. Nervous systems are communication systems; they transmit messages. The major components of the human nervous system are the brain, the spinal cord, receptor systems associated with the major senses, and effector systems implicated in the functioning of muscles and glands.

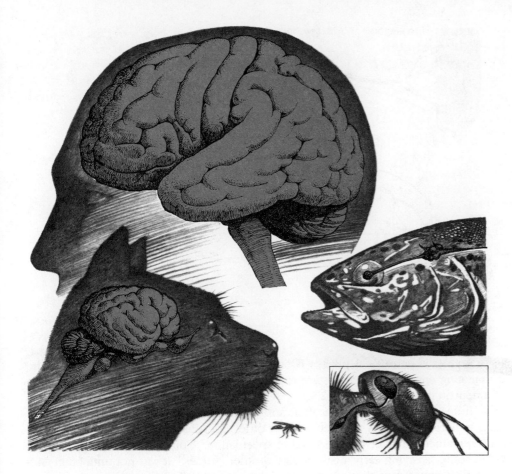

Figure 2.3 *Homo sapiens* may not see, hear, or smell as well as other species, but greater relative brain size and the greater relative size of the "thinking" part of the human brain, the cerebrum, have given us an evolutionary advantage.

It is this brain, the command center of our nervous system, that is largely responsible for what we are and for our behavior. Following sections of this chapter describe the structure and function of the nervous system and its brain, beginning with the smallest unit, the neuron.

The Neuron

The nervous system in humans, and indeed, in all other living organisms, can be described in terms of its smallest component, the **neuron**. Neurons, also called nerve cells, are those cells whose specialized function is to transmit impulses. There are some 12.5 billion such cells in the human body, the majority of them located in the brain (at least 10 billion). A mere 2.5 billion serve primarily as *receptors*; that is, they are concerned with the human sensory system and are concentrated in the skin, eyes, nose, tongue, ears, muscles, joints, and tendons. Many of these are highly specialized and respond only to very specific stimulation such as light or sound waves. Approximately 0.5 million nerve cells serve as *effectors,* instigating action, and are found in various muscular and glandular systems. The remainder are *connectors.* In essence, they serve as links between receptor (sensory) and effector (muscular or glandular) systems (see Figure 2.4). Most of the connectors (99 percent) are located in the brain.

Like all other living cells, neurons consist of a nucleus and surrounding matter. This matter is made up of the cell body, **axons**, and **dendrites**. The axon is the elongated part of a neuron; it may be microscopically short or as long as two or three feet, as is the case for some neurons located in the spinal cord. It may have an insulating sheath, termed a *myelin sheath.* Bundles of these elongated axons make up nerves. The dendrite is a hairlike extension of which there may be only a few or a great many, emanating from the cell body of the neuron. The space between the ends of one cell's

Neuron A single nerve cell, the smallest unit of the nervous system, and its basic structural unit. The function of the neuron is to transmit impulses.

Axon The elongated part of a neuron. Axons ordinarily transmit impulses from the cell body to adjoining dendrites.

Dendrite Hairlike extension emanating from the cell body of the neuron. Dendrites ordinarily receive impulses from adjoining axons.

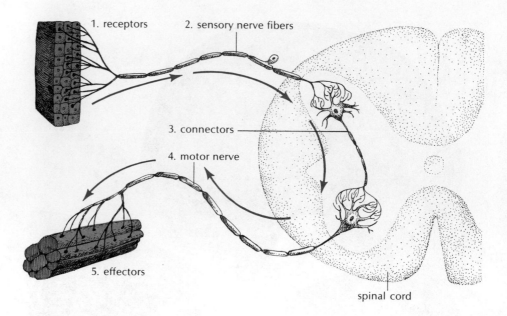

Figure 2.4 Schematic conception of the three components of the nervous system. *Receptors* (1) in eyes, tactile organs, nose, ears, taste buds, and kinesthetic senses send signals (2) to *connectors* (3) in the spinal cord, brain, and other neural pathways. Signals are then sent (4) to *effectors* (5) in muscles and glands. These neurons are microscopic, and are *not* drawn to scale with respect to the spinal cord.

1. receptors
2. sensory nerve fibers
3. connectors
4. motor nerve
5. effectors
spinal cord

axon and another cell's dendrites is termed a *synapse*. Enlargements found at the terminating ends of some axons are called *synaptic knobs*. The typical configuration of a neuron is shown in Figure 2.5.

Individual neurons have as their sole function the transmission of information via impulses over relays and networks of other neurons. How this is accomplished long remained a matter of considerable speculation. "Spirits" of various kinds provided some satisfying early answers, as did other "forces." It was not until Luigi Galvani's discoveries regarding electricity in the second half of the eighteenth century that explanations more acceptable to science were advanced (see Box 2.1).

Transmission between Neurons

With the discovery in the 1930s that the squid has a relatively huge neuron with an axon a full millimeter in diameter, it became possible to examine the nerve cell in detail and to describe its electrical and chemical functioning. More recently, new techniques involving quick-freezing and staining, together with the use of electron microscopes, have made this description easier.

The transmission of impulses from neuron to neuron involves both electrical and chemical activity (Figure 2.6). In effect, certain chemical changes make it possible for the action potential or impulse to bridge the synapse between adjacent neurons. Transmission proceeds from the cell body down the axon, across the synapse, to the dendrites and cell bodies of adjacent neurons. It also involves "microcircuits" within single neurons where transmission occurs among dendrites of one cell, or between dendrites and the cell body (Shepherd, 1978). Speed of transmission is considerably slower than the speed of an electric current. An electric current normally flows at the speed of light (186,300 miles per second). Neural transmission, depending on such factors as the diameter of axons and the presence or absence of a myelin sheath, travels at between 2 and 200 miles per hour. Part of the reason for this slower transmission is that at each synapse, a build-up in certain chemical transmitter substances is required.

A large number of chemical transmitter substances have been identified. Acetylcholine is one such substance. It is present, for example, at the ends of axons in muscle fibers and appears to be essential for movement of muscles. A number of poisons, including botulism toxin, apparently have their lethal effect by preventing the release of acetylcholine, thus causing paralysis of muscles involved in breathing.

Dopamine, norepinephrine (another name for noradrenalin), and serotonin are three other important transmitter substances. Neurons appear to be differentiated in

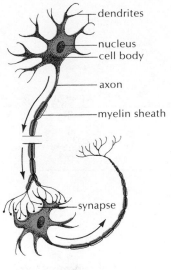

dendrites
nucleus
cell body
axon
myelin sheath
synapse

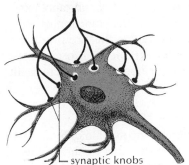

synaptic knobs

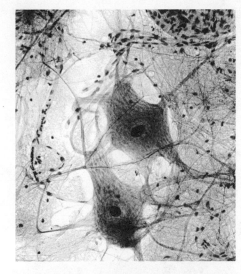

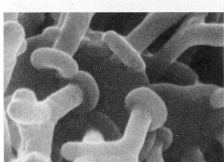

Figure 2.5 Electron micrograph photos of human neurons magnified many times. The accompanying illustrations present a stylized simplification of neurons and identify their principal parts.

terms of their chemical characteristics. Thus, *dopaminergic* neurons store dopamine and are thought to transmit impulses as a function of dopamine activity. Similarly, *noradrenergic* neurons store norepinephrine and *serotonergic* neurons store serotonin. For these types of neurons, norepinephrine and serotonin are the principal transmitter substances.

Numerous other neurotransmitter substances are still being discovered, some of which may, in fact, be far more important than acetylcholine, serotonin, dopamine, or noradrenalin (Carlson, 1980). Some of these chemicals belong to the chemical group known as peptides; in addition, certain amino acids are thought to be involved

---

Frog Legs

Luigi Galvani and his wife, Lucia, occasionally amused their dinner guests with dead frogs. On one propitious occasion, Luigi is reported to have laid the major portions of a dissected frog on the dinner table. To its head he attached a piece of wire, the other end of which was fastened to a metal rod perched either on the porch or on the roof (there are conflicting reports). This done, he then attached another wire to one of the frog's feet and ran the end of the wire into the well.

Either by design or by sheer good fortune, Luigi Galvani arranged to do all this just prior to a violent thunderstorm. When the storm came, with its thunder and lightning, the frog's leg jumped and twitched dramatically, much to the amazement and delight of the guests.

Following other related experiments with frogs, Galvani eventually concluded that nervous tissue contains electricity—a phenomenon that was not very well understood at the time. It turned out that he was sufficiently right to have made a striking contribution to the study of physiology. But was he entirely right?

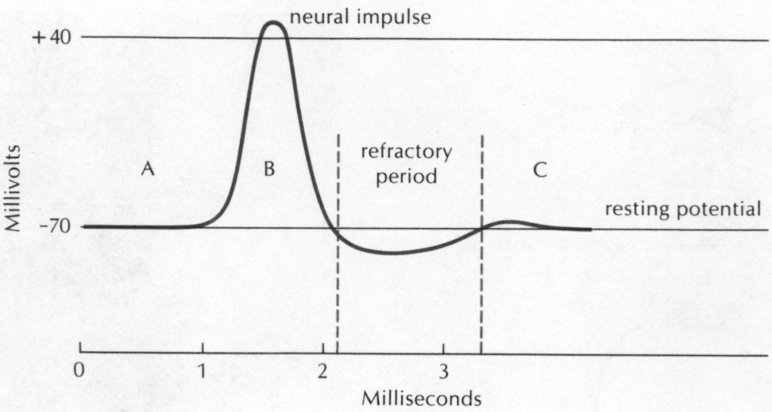

Figure 2.6 Representation of a neural impulse. At point A, there exists a state of readiness or "resting potential." At B, a stimulus leads to an electrical impulse. The impulse is followed immediately by a period termed *refractory*, during which the cell cannot fire or can fire only with intense stimulation. After the refractory period, the neuron is restored to the resting potential state, C. Certain chemical substances, including dopamine, norepinephrine, acetylcholine, and serotonin, play an important part in the temporary breakdown of neural membranes that allows the impulse to pass through the synapse.

Parkinsonism (also called Parkinson's disease, palsy, or paralysis agitans)   A central nervous system disease characterized by continuous coarse tremors, particularly of the hands, generalized weakness, slow movement, constipation, sleep disturbances, and sometimes depression. It is associated with low dopamine levels in the brain, and is frequently treated with the drug L-Dopa, a synthetic substance related to the production of dopamine.

Chorea   A neurological disorder characterized by spasmic, jerky, involuntary movements of large groups of muscles. These movements are particularly evident in the face, tongue, hands, and arms, and are often of short duration.

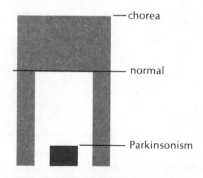

Figure 2.7 Certain chemical substances are known to be important in the transmission of electrical impulses across neural synapses. Dopamine is one chemical substance that is especially important in the brain's functioning. Studies show that the disease *Parkinsonism* is associated with low dopamine levels (autopsies show one-tenth the normal level). Another disease, *chorea,* is associated with abnormally high dopamine levels.

in neural transmission. And, to further complicate the matter, other substances known as neuromodulators appear to have an important effect on neural functioning. Among these, for example, are the endorphins, opium-like substances that are produced by the brain and whose effect is to lessen perception of pain (Bolles & Fanselow, 1982). Also included among neuromodulators are certain sex hormones that serve to facilitate or inhibit sexual behavior.

Chemical Transmitters and Behavior

It is now apparent that different transmitters may be involved in different behaviors, and that a number of neurological diseases and disorders may be due to chemical malfunctions. **Parkinsonism**, a disease characterized by shaking, generalized weakness, slow movements, constipation, sleep disturbances, and depression, is associated with low dopamine levels in areas of the brain where dopamine is usually most concentrated. Autopsies of patients who had Parkinson's disease found dopamine levels to be one-tenth of normal. This finding led directly to the use of L-Dopa, a synthetic precursor of dopamine, in the treatment of Parkinsonism. Pincus and Tucker (1974) report that approximately 80 percent of all patients so treated show a 60 to 70 percent improvement. Unfortunately, however, L-Dopa sometimes has undesirable side effects, principally related to emotional changes.

Another disorder associated with these chemical transmitter substances is **chorea**, characterized by involuntary muscle movements that are particularly evident in the face, tongue, hands, and arms. Chorea victims tend to jerk involuntarily. Chorea has been linked with high dopamine levels, as opposed to the low ones found in Parkinsonism (see Figure 2.7). And the drugs that can alleviate chorea are, not surprisingly, the same drugs (the major tranquilizers, among others) that can sometimes bring about the symptoms of Parkinsonism.

Related evidence suggests that high anxiety is sometimes related to high serotonin, mania to high receptivity to norepinephrine and dopamine, and depression to low norepinephrine and dopamine receptivity. These findings have had considerable impact on the treatment of neurological and emotional disorders.

Organization of the Nervous System

The brain and spinal cord together compose the **central nervous system**. Neural networks that fan out from the central nervous system into various parts of the body are labeled the **peripheral nervous system** (see Figure 2.8). This system includes all receptor and effector systems and is therefore linked to all sensory organs as well as the muscles and glands that are involved in behavior. In addition, the peripheral

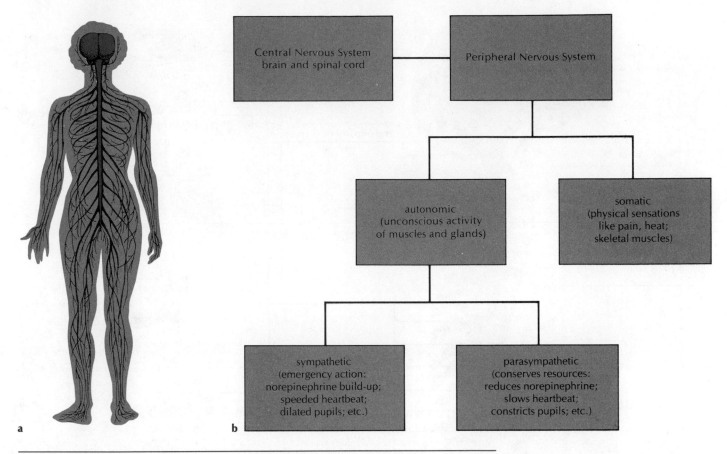

Figure 2.8 The human nervous system. Part **a** depicts the two major divisions of the nervous system: the central nervous system (red) and the peripheral nervous system. The organization and functions of each are described in **b**.

nervous system is involved in physiological activities such as respiration, heart action, sweating, and crying.

The peripheral nervous system has two parts. The **somatic system** transmits impulses relating to sensations of heat, cold, pain, and pressure to the central nervous system. It also transmits impulses in the opposite direction, from the central nervous system to muscles involved in behavior.

The **autonomic nervous system**, the other part of the peripheral nervous system, is directly involved in the action of those muscles and glands that are not ordinarily under conscious control (see Figure 2.9). The **sympathetic** division of the autonomic nervous system is, in a sense, responsible for the mobilization of the body's resources, particularly in emergency situations. It is your sympathetic nervous system that makes your heart beat fast, causes adrenaline to be pumped into your system, makes your pupils dilate, makes you tremble in anxiety or blush in shame, and causes the host of other physiological changes that transpire in moments of sudden fear and intense emotion. Clearly you have little immediate control over these reactions, a fact that led to the invention of the common lie-detector. In essence, a lie-detector is nothing more than an instrument that is capable of detecting physiological changes that result directly from activity of the autonomic nervous system. If you become anxious when you lie (as, apparently, most people do), your sympathetic nervous system reacts accordingly. As a result, your palms may perspire, your breathing change, your heart rate increase.

But your heart rate does not accelerate indefinitely, nor do you tremble more and more violently. The **parasympathetic nervous system** slows your heart rate,

Central nervous system The human nervous system that includes the brain and the spinal cord.

Peripheral nervous system The neural networks that fan out from the central nervous system to various parts of the body.

Somatic system Part of the peripheral nervous system concerned with bodily sensations (heat, cold, pain, and pressure) and with muscular movement.

Autonomic nervous system That part of the peripheral nervous system not ordinarily under conscious control. It regulates physiological functions such as respiration, heart rate, temperature, and digestion, and includes the sympathetic and parasympathetic systems.

Sympathetic nervous system Part of the autonomic nervous system which instigates the physiological responses that accompany emotion.

Parasympathetic nervous system Part of the autonomic nervous system that moderates physiological reactions that accompany emotion.

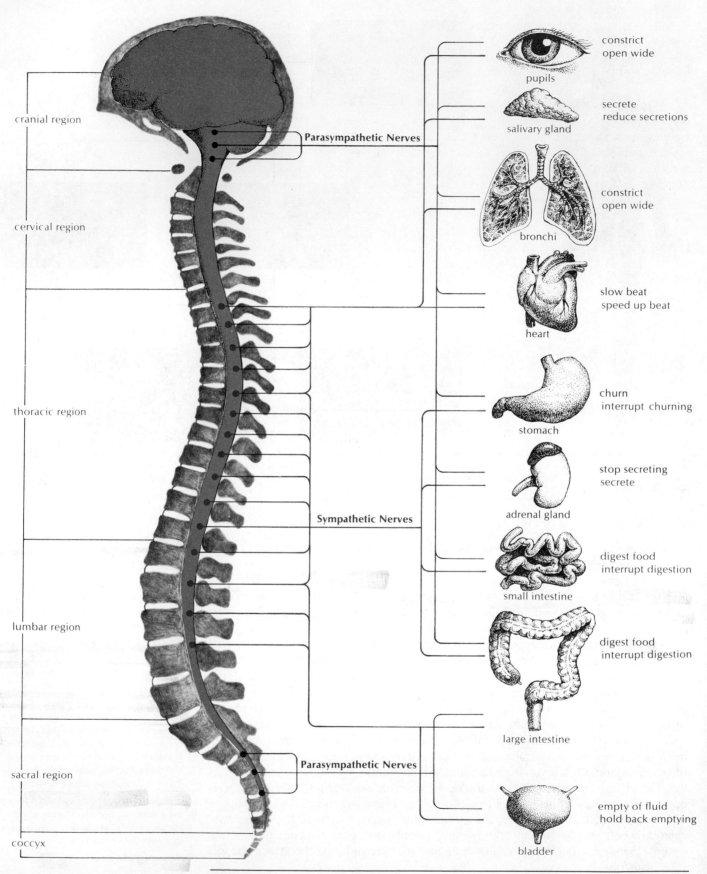

cranial region

cervical region

thoracic region

lumbar region

sacral region

coccyx

Parasympathetic Nerves

Sympathetic Nerves

Parasympathetic Nerves

constrict
open wide

pupils

secrete
reduce secretions

salivary gland

constrict
open wide

bronchi

slow beat
speed up beat

heart

churn
interrupt churning

stomach

stop secreting
secrete

adrenal gland

digest food
interrupt digestion

small intestine

digest food
interrupt digestion

large intestine

empty of fluid
hold back emptying

bladder

Figure 2.9 The autonomic nervous system.

steadies your trembling, increases your control over bowel and bladder functioning, and in other ways opposes some of the functions of the sympathetic nervous system. It is as though the parasympathetic nervous system conserves those bodily resources that are sometimes called upon too hastily and too greedily by the sympathetic nervous system.

Our awareness of the world as well as of ourselves is directly dependent upon the coordinated activity of our nervous systems. To summarize briefly what we have covered so far, a nervous system is, in effect, a complex but highly efficient and very rapid communication system. We have seen that communication between neurons is made possible by means of chemical and electrical activity. We have also described a number of divisions in the nervous system: central, including brain and spinal cord; peripheral, including somatic and autonomic, with the autonomic divided into sympathetic as well as parasympathetic. Although these can be differentiated in terms of location and function, it is important to bear in mind that they form a network of interrelated neurons and nerves. And, unlike the unlucky beheaded wasp, which continues to eat even though the food will never reach its abdomen, we have an organ that centralizes, coordinates, and integrates much of our nervous system activity: the brain. The remainder of this chapter focuses on the central nervous system, and especially on the brain; Chapter 4 deals with the somatic system.

The Brain

Would you believe that the brain is the single most complex structure in the entire universe? That it has more possible interconnections than the entire number of atomic particles in that same universe? That it consists of some 10 billion nerve cells (estimates vary slightly) and approximately ten times that number of **glial cells**—cells that are quite unlike nerve cells, and that are considered important as sources of nourishment and protection for neurons (as in myelin sheaths, for example)? Would you also believe that some animals have much larger brains than we have, and that others have higher brain-to-body-weight ratios than ours? All of these statements are believed to be true, although it is difficult to find out who counted the number of atomic particles in the universe.

Much of the information we have concerning the brain has been derived from the physical examination of brains removed from the dead (seldom the living); from observing the effects of injury to various parts of the brain; from surgical procedures sometimes required in cases of brain damage, epilepsy, tumors, or for other medical reasons; from the administration of drugs and the observation of their effects; and through the use of electrical recordings of brain activity (electroencephalography) and electrical stimulation of parts of the brain. Animals have been used extensively in this type of research.

Physical examination of the brain reveals a grayish mass inside most human heads (see Figure 12.10). Some of its various structures are identifiable through this type of examination. But determining the functions of these structures has presented a major problem: the structures themselves present few clues to their functions. Not only is the brain almost bloodless, particularly in death, but it has a lifeless appearance. In fact, the ancient Egyptians considered the brain so unimportant that they never bothered to preserve it in their mummies, removing it instead through the left nostril (Blakemore, 1977).

By the middle of the nineteenth century, the brain had been acknowledged as central in human behavior, but the functions of its various structures still remained very much a mystery. It wasn't until physicians began to note the effects of tumors and, later, of gunshot wounds that these functions became clearer. And, had it not been for Phineas Gage's unfortunate accident, we might have been some years longer before surmising that different parts of the brain might indeed have different functions.

Glial cells Cells found in the nervous system, but that are not nerve cells. Often described as *supportive* tissue because of their role in protecting and nourishing nerve cells.

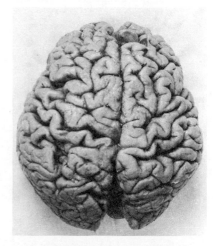

Figure 2.10 Top view of a human brain. The outer covering of the exposed brain is called the cerebral cortex.

Mapping Brain Functions

The 13th of September, 1848, although not a Friday, was an unlucky day for Phineas Gage, foreman of a construction gang then working on the Rutland and Burlington Railroad. Phineas and his co-workers were building a new line in Cavendish, Vermont. These were robust, hard-working men. Phineas, in particular, was reputed to be in excellent physical condition, strong and vigorous.

On the day in question, the gang had been using blasting powder to prepare the roadbed for new tracks. They would drill holes into the rock and gravel, pour in a measure of powder, tamp it down with a steel rod (a tamping iron), and retreat a safe distance as the blast was set off. Phineas's tamping iron was a smooth, cylindrical piece of iron, 3 feet 7 inches in length, an inch and a quarter in diameter, and a full 13 pounds 4 ounces in weight. Phineas Gage was still tamping the charge when it blasted prematurely. The forces of the explosion drove the iron from his hands, upward through the left side of his face, and out through the top of his head, slightly front of center.

Phineas was thrown to the ground by the blow. Far from being rendered unconscious, however, he spoke normally almost immediately after the accident. His men then carried him to a cart and drove him to his hotel, approximately 1 kilometer away. And although loss of blood had by then weakened him somewhat, he continued to speak rationally. Some time later, he went upstairs and to bed.

Phineas Gage's physical recovery was apparently complete, and his health and strength as good as ever. But his personality was never again the same. Although he had previously been a quiet, hard-working individual, as rational and cool in most situations as you or I, he now became moody, fitful, selfish, impulsive, and stubborn, and he persistently indulged in long bursts of highly profane language even in front of ladies. Indeed, so different was he that his employers and fellow workers remarked on more than one occasion that this man was not the Phineas Gage they had previously known.

Phineas Gage's accident provided some of the first crude evidence that the brain might be differentiated into separate functions. There was other historical evidence as well. Paul Broca, a neurologist, was sent a patient suffering from **aphasia**, a language disorder that we now know is linked to brain damage. The patient died within a few days, and Broca performed an autopsy, discovering lesions (structural abnormalities usually caused by injury, disease, or drugs) in the left temporal lobe. The area of the lobe that was affected by these lesions is now known as *Broca's region.* Subsequent research has established that aphasia may be linked to lesions that are almost always on the left side of the brain. Lesions in the right half of the brain rarely disturb language functions, particularly in right-handed individuals (Pincus & Tucker, 1974), leading researchers to believe that those functions reside primarily in the left half of the brain, in right-handed individuals and in most left-handed individuals (Milner, 1974). Most such investigations have relied heavily on evidence resulting from cases of injury or disease with resulting aphasia. The investigator notes the extent and nature of the aphasia; brain autopsies following the patient's death can then provide evidence of relationships between specific areas of the brain and given language functions.

This research is complicated by a number of factors, however. Unfortunately, tumors, injury, and disease, the most common sources of brain damage, are not often very specific in their effects. Tumors, for example, may distort relatively large areas of the brain, thus having an effect at some distance from their actual location. Accordingly, it is not particularly surprising that researchers have sometimes arrived at different and confusing conclusions with respect to the localization of language and other functions in the brain.

As Gardiner (1974) notes, the ideal experiment that might answer many of the unanswered questions about our brains would require a degree of control and precision that is not now possible, given that we are dealing with humans. Such an experiment would require that small parts of the brain be systematically removed and

Aphasia Any of a number of language disorders or impairments that result from brain damage. Difficulties with language which are not related to brain damage (for example, stuttering or stammering) are not examples of aphasia. Aphasia may take a variety of forms, including the inability to understand words (sensory aphasia, also called *word blindness* or *word deafness*), or the inability to speak or produce sounds that are intended. Other varieties include an inability to arrange words in proper sequence and unintended pauses or breaks in speech (groping speech). Aphasia is most often linked to injury or damage to the left side of the brain.

the resulting effects on behavior, personality, and other aspects of human functioning noted. The procedure has been employed with animals (particularly cats and monkeys) and has proven useful for identifying parts of the brain associated with motor functioning and with such easily observable reactions as rage in cats and overeating in rats. Some of these studies are described in later chapters. Unfortunately they tell us very little about language functions, that being a peculiarly human characteristic.

Other experimental procedures that have proven useful in identifying functions of the brain have involved placing electrodes in or on parts of the brain and stimulating those parts of the brain contacted. Using this procedure with patients undergoing surgery, Penfield and Roberts (1959; Penfield, 1969) were able to elicit specific reactions and memories in patients. Very small amounts of stimulation were sufficient to elicit what appeared to be memories of events years earlier that would not ordinarily have been available to the subjects. Few of these memories were very complex, however, and most of them could have been recalled under normal circumstances and without electrical stimulation of the brain. The majority of the reactions elicited by Penfield were simple sights and sounds.

Electrical stimulation of the brain could conceivably serve not only as a means for locating brain functions but also for discovering specific memory areas and perhaps for establishing whether or not material that we assume has been lost from memory is really lost. Unfortunately, experiments such as these cannot be carried out at will with normal subjects, but are typically the by-product of other neurosurgical procedures. Chapter 16, for example, describes several instances where electrical stimulation of the brain by means of microelectrodes is undertaken to determine the precise areas of the brain that might be involved in uncontrollable rage reactions. Similarly, stimulation of the brain is sometimes done during surgery undertaken to alleviate epileptic seizures or remove cysts and tumors. In all of these cases, the amount of time available for brain stimulation, and the area of the brain that is exposed, are highly limited. For these reasons the information we now have as a result of electrical stimulation of human brains is still rather small (LeVere, 1975).

From a combination of research methods, then, a picture of the brain's functioning has begun to emerge. It seems clear that some parts of the brain are more involved in certain functions than are others. These parts and their functions are described briefly in the following sections. It is important to bear in mind, however, that the brain is really not made up of a number of highly distinct and easily separated parts, but is an incredibly complex network of tissues which we have reason to believe is highly integrated in its functioning. Thus, although one area might be more closely associated with vision than any other, it is untrue that, if all other areas of the brain were removed, we would be left with an organism that could still see.

Cerebrum

The most recent brain structure in an evolutionary sense is the **cerebrum**, the outer covering of which is called the cerebral cortex. It is in the cerebrum that the major association areas of the brain are found. Association areas of the brain are distinct from other areas in that they do not appear to be concerned with specific aspects of human functioning such as vision or hearing, but are given over instead to higher mental processes such as thinking, feeling, remembering, creative problem-solving, and decision-making—in short, with *associations* among ideas, feelings, and so on. In addition, the cerebrum is centrally involved in sensation and perception. The cerebral cortex consists of two hemispheres (right and left), joined by a thick band of fibers labeled the *corpus callosum*. Through a variety of experiments involving the separation of these hemispheres by severing the corpus callosum, researchers have discovered a great deal about the dual functions of these hemispheres. These experiments and their findings are discussed later in this chapter.

The cerebrum is divided into major areas by deep fissures. These areas, termed *lobes,* have been differentiated in terms of function as well as location, and are depicted in Figure 2.11.

Cerebrum The most highly developed part of the human brain relative to the brains of lower animals. It is a wrinkled mass of brain tissue, the outer covering of which is labeled the *cerebral cortex.* The cerebrum contains the major association areas of the brain, and its principal functions appear to relate to higher mental processes. Its major divisions include the cerebral lobes.

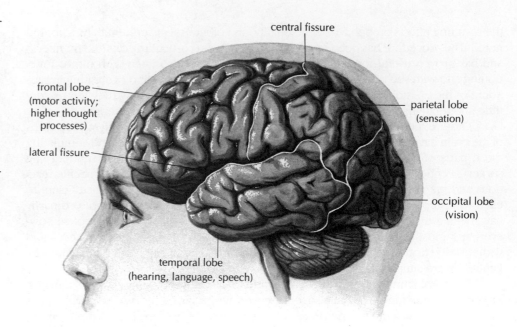

Figure 2.11 The cerebral lobes. Although functions are integrated, so that it is impossible to isolate one lobe from surrounding tissue in terms of function, each area is associated with certain specialized processes. The *temporal lobes* are associated with language, speech, and hearing; the *frontal lobes,* with control of voluntary muscles and higher thought processes; the *parietal lobe,* with body sensation; and the *occipital lobe,* with vision.

central fissure

frontal lobe
(motor activity;
higher thought
processes)

parietal lobe
(sensation)

lateral fissure

occipital lobe
(vision)

temporal lobe
(hearing, language, speech)

Hypothalamus A small structure at the base of the brain centrally involved in a variety of bodily functions, as well as in the functioning of most of the body's endocrine glands.

Endocrine system A system of glands whose functions are effected through the release of hormones directly into the bloodstream. Chief among these glands are the pituitary gland, the adrenal glands, and the gonads.

Hormone One of the variety of chemical substances produced by endocrine glands and secreted into the bloodstream. Hormones have important effects on growth, maturation, behavior, and emotions.

Thalamus A small structure at the base of the brain which serves as a major relay center between incoming sensory stimulation and other parts of the brain. Almost all sensory information is channeled through the thalamus.

Other Brain Structures

Other identifiable structures, most of which would not be evident from an external examination of the brain, become apparent when the brain is sliced in different ways. Figure 2.12 shows the major structures revealed in sagittal transection. Many of these structures are related to physiological functioning, to the action of the endocrine glands, and to motor coordination. Not surprisingly, these are the parts of the brain that are most highly developed in lower animal forms. In fact, as one progresses up the evolutionary scale the relative proportion of the brain given over to biological and sensory functioning declines, and the areas of the cortex increase.

The **hypothalamus** is centrally involved in the activity of endocrine glands which are themselves central to the regulation of growth and maturation, sexual behavior, and kidney functioning. In addition, the hypothalamus is directly involved in other functions such as eating, drinking, and sleeping, and in autonomic nervous system activity. The **endocrine system** includes those glands that secrete **hormones** directly into the bloodstream and are therefore known as the ductless glands. The endocrine glands include the pituitary (involved in regulating growth and in regulating other glands); the thyroid (involved in metabolic rate and physical growth); the pancreas (involved in sugar metabolism); the adrenal glands (involved in emotional reactions and adaptation to stress); the ovaries (which secrete hormones related to the development of secondary sexual characteristics and sexual arousal and behavior in females); and the testes (which have a similar function in the male). The relationship of the hypothalamus to the endocrine glands is by way of the pituitary, a small gland located at the base of the hypothalamus. The pituitary is frequently termed the *master gland* because of its role in regulating the activity of the other glands. Indeed, its relationship to the endocrine system is very much like the relationship of the brain to the remainder of the nervous system. It is the pituitary that regulates the secretion of hormones. It, in turn, responds directly to secretions from the hypothalamus.

The **thalamus** serves as the brain's major relay station, its principal function being to relay input to appropriate parts of the brain which lie above it. Almost all sensory information the brain receives—sight, hearing, taste, and body sensations—is channeled through the thalamus. To say that the thalamus is nothing more than a relay station, however, is to oversimplify, since it also appears to regulate the signals it transmits to the cortex. In other words, sensory messages don't simply get routed through the thalamus on their way to appropriate areas of the brain like telephone

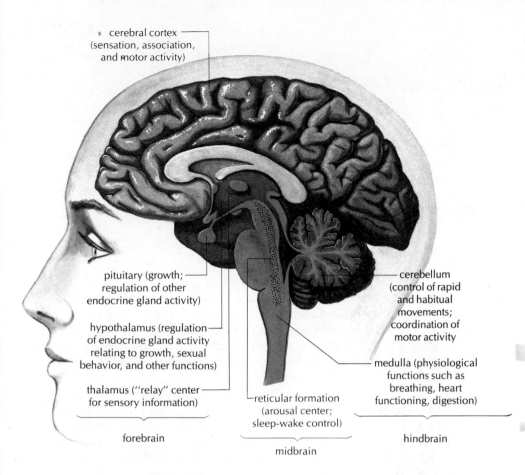

Figure 2.12 A sagittal (bisected front to back) view of the human brain showing major structures and some of their principal functions.

cerebral cortex (sensation, association, and motor activity)

pituitary (growth; regulation of other endocrine gland activity)

hypothalamus (regulation of endocrine gland activity relating to growth, sexual behavior, and other functions)

thalamus ("relay" center for sensory information)

reticular formation (arousal center; sleep-wake control)

cerebellum (control of rapid and habitual movements; coordination of motor activity

medulla (physiological functions such as breathing, heart functioning, digestion)

forebrain

midbrain

hindbrain

calls might be routed through a switchboard to appropriate outgoing lines. Unlike the switchboard, the thalamus may hold some calls and modify others.

The **cerebellum's** primary functions appear to relate to the coordination of motor activity and the maintenance of balance. Removal of or injury to the cerebellum typically results in jerky, uncontrollable motor movements. The **medulla** is a small formation in part of what is referred to as the *brain stem:* it is concerned with physiological activities such as breathing, digestive processes, and regulation of heart functioning.

Another structure located in the brain stem is the **reticular formation** (also called the *reticular activating system*). There is considerable evidence that one of its most important functions is to control the arousal level of the organism (J. D. French, 1957; Hebron, 1966). Physiological **arousal** refers to changes in heart rate, respiration, electrical activity in the cortex, and the skin's electrical conductivity. Under conditions of low arousal, the individual may be resting, asleep, or in a coma. With increasing arousal, individuals become more vigilant, more alert, and better able to react to the environment. However, very high levels of arousal (panic) can detract considerably from the effectiveness of the individual's response to the environment. A second major function of the reticular formation appears to involve the control of sleeping and waking cycles. A third function of the reticular formation relates to motivation, and is discussed in detail in Chapter 9.

Spinal Cord

Although the **spinal cord** is not part of the brain, its intimate relationship with that organ is of central importance to an understanding of human behavior. It is via the spinal cord that most of the major neural pathways conduct impulses between brain centers and various glandular, muscular, and sensory systems. In short, the spinal cord is the major neural conductor in the human body. In addition, it appears to be

Cerebellum One of the major portions of the brain, attached to the rear of the brain stem. Its principal functions appear to be coordinating motor activity and maintaining balance.

Medulla The lowest part of the brain, found at the very top of the spinal cord and containing nerve centers involved in regulating physiological activity such as breathing, digestion, and heart functioning.

Reticular formation (Reticular activating system) The portion of the brain stem assumed to be responsible for the physiological arousal of the cortex. The reticular formation is also involved in the control of sleeping and waking, and may be important in human motivation.

Arousal Both a physiological and a psychological concept. As a physiological concept, it refers to changes in heart rate, respiration, electrical activity in the cortex, and the skin's electrical conductivity. Psychologically, the term relates to degree of alertness, awareness, vigilance, or wakefulness.

Spinal cord The major link between the brain and the sensory and motor areas of the body. It is involved in reflexes—automatic reactions to physical stimulation such as the knee-jerk reflex. It is therefore a direct link between receptors and effectors, although its primary function is to link receptors and effectors with the brain. Anatomically, it is the major neural tract that runs from the base of the brain to the tip of the spinal column; it is encased throughout its length by bony structures called spinal vertebrae. Spinal injury often results in death or paralysis.

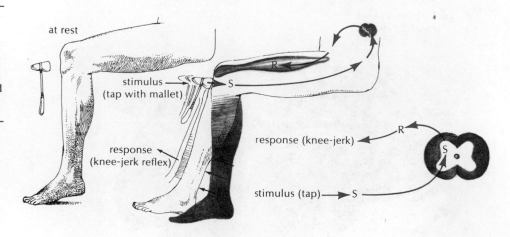

Figure 2.13 The knee-jerk reflex, illustrating what is termed a *spinal arc.* The brain is not involved in this type of reflex. The mallet striking the tendon activates receptors (S), initiating a neural impulse that proceeds to the spinal cord, synapses to an outgoing motor nerve, and terminates at the effector neurons (R), which initiate the knee-jerk response.

at rest

stimulus
(tap with mallet)

response
(knee-jerk reflex)

response (knee-jerk)

stimulus (tap)

Reflex An unlearned connection between a stimulus and a response such that the presentation of the stimulus leads automatically to a simple, predictable, and uncontrollable response. Blinking in response to a puff of air blown in the eyes is an example of a reflex; an infant's sucking in response to stimulation of the mouth is another.

importantly involved in some primitive **reflex** behaviors. A reflex is an unlearned, automatic response to a specific stimulus. A stimulus is a condition, external or internal, that affects the organism and can lead to behavior. Light waves are stimuli; hunger produces stimuli; a word is a stimulus; a punch in the nose is also a stimulus. In other words, stimuli include, but are not necessarily limited to, all aspects of our internal and external environments to which we are sensitive.

Among the better-known reflexes in the human repertoire are the knee-jerk reflex, the sneezing reflex, and the eye-blink reflex. When a doctor strikes your patellar tendon (knee joint) with a rubber mallet, it is not the force of the blow that causes your leg to jerk, but the neural links between your patella and those muscle systems responsible for the knee jerk, via the spinal cord (Figure 2.13). If your spinal cord were completely detached from your brain, your knee might still jerk when your patella was appropriately stimulated, even though you would neither feel the tap of the mallet nor be able to move your knee consciously. Consciousness seems to require the brain—or at least half of it.

The Split Brain

Epilepsy Includes a number of neurological disorders characterized principally by convulsions which may vary considerably in frequency and severity. "Petit mal" convulsions may be almost unobservable, and patients typically do not lose consciousness and may in fact be unaware of suffering from epilepsy. In "grand mal" seizures, convulsions are more violent, frequently involving loss of awareness. Certain rarer forms of epilepsy may be characterized by excessive and brutal violence which patients will typically not remember.

Hemisphere Literally, half of a sphere. The cerebral hemispheres are the two halves of the cerebrum. The major neurological and physical link between them is a thick tract of nerve tissue, the corpus callosum.

Corpus callosum The major neural link between the two cerebral hemispheres. In "split-brain" research on animals, the corpus callosum is frequently cut surgically. Severing of the human corpus callosum is sometimes used to eliminate or alleviate epileptic seizures.

Much of the information we have concerning the functions of various parts of the cerebral cortex is derived from studies of individuals whose brains have had to be "split." For obvious ethical reasons, this was not originally an experimental procedure, but was instead an operation found helpful in cases of severe **epileptic** seizures. A major epileptic seizure may be described in oversimplified fashion as the result of massive and random discharge of neural activity in the brain. Typically, a seizure begins with electrical activity in one **hemisphere**; with a sufficiently severe seizure, the activity progresses to the adjacent hemisphere, thus involving a large portion of the brain. The major link between these hemispheres is the **corpus callosum**, a broad band of fibers that may be severed with no apparent ill effects on the patient. One cranial hemisphere thus becomes neurologically isolated from the other; what transpires in one hemisphere does not have any direct effect on what happens in the other, since the major neurological connections have been physically cut.

Dual Functions

In a series of intriguing studies, Sperry (1964) and his associates have investigated the roles of the two hemispheres in the behavior of humans and other animals. These studies have involved subjects whose corpus callosum had been surgically severed, usually to control epileptic seizure. After surgery, patients typically do not manifest any signs of brain damage; indeed, they function normally, particularly when the

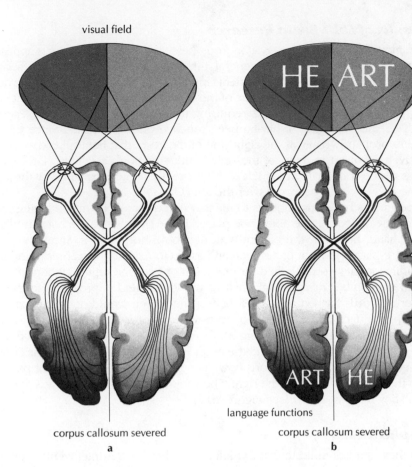

visual field

corpus callosum severed

a

language functions

corpus callosum severed

b

Figure 2.14 (**a**) In a typical split-brain subject, the corpus callosum has been severed as shown to prevent generalization of epileptic seizures. Note that the right half of each eye projects from the *left* visual field to the right hemisphere (as it would with a normal subject); the left half projects from the *right* and to the left hemisphere. Unlike the normal brain, the split brain cannot transmit impulses from one hemisphere to the other. (**b**) When the word *heart* was flashed before the split-brain subject's eyes, the subject was only aware of seeing *art*—the portion of the word that registered in the language-dominant left hemisphere. If asked to point at what she had seen with her left hand, though, the subject would point to the word *he*—not to *art*.

operation has succeeded in eliminating or alleviating the epilepsy. But in some ways they are quite different from you or me. And it is in these differences that researchers have been able to discover a great deal about the roles of the cerebral hemispheres.

Our motor functions are typically controlled by the opposite cerebral hemisphere: Movements of the left side of the body are under control of the right hemisphere; movements of the right side of the body are controlled by the left hemisphere. Since both hemispheres are generally in close contact via the corpus callosum, it is ordinarily impossible to demonstrate this except in cases of brain damage to one or the other hemisphere. With the corpus callosum severed, however, it is relatively simple to provide a message to one or the other hemisphere in order to determine the extent to which the patient understands the message and is able to respond to it. This is simple only because of the way the eyes work; the ears and the other senses do not appear to work the same way.

The left and right eye in a normal human being transmit impulses to both the right and the left hemispheres (see Figure 2.14). The right half of each eye transmits to the right hemisphere; the left half, to the left hemisphere. Interestingly, however, the left half of each retina (the light-sensitive portion of the eye) projects from the right side of the visual field; the right half of the retina projects from the left side of the field. The result is that the right hemisphere receives impulses relating to the left half of the visual field whereas the left hemisphere receives impulses relating to the right half of the visual field.

The first split-brain studies with human patients date back to 1961, when a forty-eight-year-old war veteran underwent surgery that involved cutting through his corpus callosum. Within the next five years, a total of ten patients underwent the same operation; four of these have been studied extensively by Gazzaniga (1967, 1970, 1972) and by Sperry (1964, 1968).

Results of Split-Brain Research

The most striking initial observation from these studies was that patients appeared to be unaffected in temperament, general intelligence, and personality. A second important observation was that most patients initially favored the right side of the body and, indeed, appeared to have lost some of the finer muscle control over the left side. This was particularly evident in tasks requiring the manipulation of objects. Patients frequently seemed unaware of having been touched on the left side. Since the left hemisphere ordinarily controls the right side of the body, that hemisphere would be more actively involved in many of the right-handed person's activities. If conscious awareness resides primarily in the left hemisphere, this might explain why the right side of the body would be favored over the left (Ornstein, 1973).

Experiments requiring subjects to identify objects solely by manipulating them presented little difficulty if the object was placed in the right hand. When it was placed in the left hand, however, the patient typically could not name it. Similarly, when subjects were placed in front of a screen and asked to fixate on its center point, they could readily identify words flashed for one-tenth of a second on the right portion of the screen (remember that the right half of the visual field is projected to the left hemisphere). Words flashed on the left half of the screen would not be recognized by the subject. In fact, in the majority of cases where words were flashed on the left, subjects would claim they saw nothing. If, for example, a single word were flashed with half of the word on one side and the other half on the opposite side, the subject would "see" only one half. The word *heart* was presented to a number of patients, the *he* on the left half, the *art* on the right. The subjects' typical response was that they had been shown the word *art* (see Figure 2.14).

Implications

Do these studies indicate that the left hemisphere is the intelligent, conscious hemisphere and that the right hemisphere is vastly inferior? Not exactly. What they do demonstrate is that the left half of the brain ordinarily controls language and speech functions. This does not mean that the right hemisphere is unaware of visual stimulation, but simply that it is less able to communicate that awareness in language. Amazingly, when subjects in the "heart" experiment were asked to point, *with their left hand,* to what they had seen, they would invariably point to the word *he*. This portion of the experiment, replicated many times, demonstrated clearly that both halves of the hemisphere were aware of what had been presented to them, and that manifestation of this awareness depends on the opportunity presented to subjects to express themselves. Since the left hemisphere is **dominant** for language, subjects who are asked to point to a correct object with either hand will most likely point to whatever object is presented in the right half of the visual field; similarly, if asked to express verbally what they have seen, that expression will relate to the right half of the visual field. If, for example, a word has been presented only on the left half of the visual field (right hemisphere), subjects will deny having seen anything. But that they *have* seen something becomes apparent under different instructions—and sometimes in the absence of any instruction. In one variation of this study, a female patient was presented with a drawing of a female nude. The information was presented only to the right hemisphere (left visual field). As expected, the woman denied that she had seen anything—but she laughed nervously although she couldn't explain why.

Further evidence that the right hemisphere is aware of what is occurring even if it can't always communicate that awareness is provided by studies where either a red or a green light is presented to subjects who must then make a correct verbal response (Gazzaniga, 1967). When the light is presented in the right visual field, subjects experience no difficulty in responding verbally; when the light is presented in the left visual field, there is similarly no difficulty in pointing to the correct solution. When, however, the light is flashed only in the left visual field, and subjects are required to make a verbal response, the accuracy of those responses is only at a chance level.

Dominance With respect to the brain, describes (but does not explain) the fact that certain portions may take precedence over others in controlling certain motor or sensory activities.

example   left hand   right hand

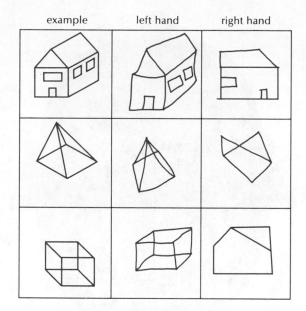

Figure 2.15 Although language abilities are normally centered in the left hemisphere, the right hemisphere is superior in spatial tasks. Right-handed split-brain subjects could copy the example with neat, clean lines with the right hand, but the left hand (right hemisphere) was able to indicate depth far more clearly. (From *The Bisected Brain* by M. S. Gazzaniga. New York: Appleton-Century-Crofts, 1970. Reprinted by permission of Plenum Publishing Corporation.)

What is striking about this experiment, however, is that when subjects are given a second chance without being told by the experimenter whether they are right or wrong, they improve their scores remarkably. If they were correct the first time, they do not change their minds; if they were not correct, chances of their altering their responses increase dramatically. It appears that, in these cases, the right hemisphere is providing clues to the left hemisphere. In one patient, these clues were obvious. When the patient answered incorrectly, his right hemisphere would make him frown and shake his head, whereupon he would change his response. If the response were initially correct, no negative information would be provided.

Continued investigation of separate brain halves in human subjects has now made it clear that in most individuals the right hemisphere is not highly verbal, that language and speech processes reside largely in the left hemisphere. Although these conclusions are clearly true for right-handed individuals, they are not necessarily true for those who are left-handed. Nevertheless, the majority of left-handed individuals also have left-hemisphere speech and language dominance. Evidence suggests that this dominance is not present at birth and develops before the age of ten (Basser, 1962). Prior to this time, language functions appear to be represented in both hemispheres.

Other related research has demonstrated that the right hemisphere is superior to the left hemisphere in spatial tasks although both can perceive spatial configurations. One simple illustration of this involved having subjects who had undergone split-brain surgery attempt to copy a three-dimensional design with their right and left hands. Results of this experiment are depicted in Figure 2.15. Note that the left hand succeeded much better than the right hand in reproducing the three-dimensional aspects of the figures in spite of the fact that the patient was right-handed. Drawings by the right hand (controlled by the left hemisphere), although less shaky than those executed by the left hand, are clearly inferior in showing depth.

Additional evidence also suggests that the right hemisphere may be more centrally involved in musical abilities than the left hemisphere (Milner, 1974); that symbolic functions, including language and mathematical skills, reside primarily in the left hemisphere. A relatively crude representation of the cortex's allocation of functions is depicted in Figure 2.16. It should be noted that much of the information implicit in that figure is somewhat speculative and, further, that there is considerable overlap in functions among adjacent areas of the brain as well as across from one hemisphere to the other.

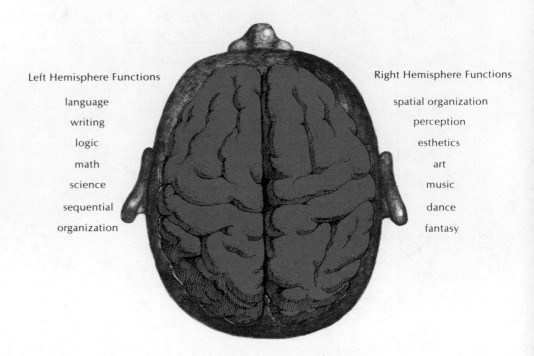

Figure 2.16 Dominant abilities of the right and left hemispheres. How accurate is this "division of labor"? Kinsbourne and Cook (1971) describe a simple experiment to illustrate right and left hemisphere functions. They have a person balance a wooden dowel on the index finger of first the right hand and then the left. For right-handed individuals, balancing is easier on the right hand. But when the person is asked to speak while balancing the dowel (speech is a left hemisphere function), balancing time decreases for the right hand but increases for the left.

Left Hemisphere Functions

language
writing
logic
math
science
sequential
organization

Right Hemisphere Functions

spatial organization
perception
esthetics
art
music
dance
fantasy

Biology and Behavior

The purpose of this chapter is not to make you an expert in human biology, but instead to show you that there is scarcely a subject of interest to the student of human behavior that does not implicate the nervous system and body. Just how much of our behavior is a product of our biological makeup? To start with, having developed throughout evolution a magnificent brain in an insignificant body has made certain things difficult for us and other things far more possible. Thus, we can design a computer but can scarcely climb a tree. Our biology may also account for some far less obvious characteristics. As a case in point, recent speculation suggests that altruistic (self-sacrificing) behavior may be genetically linked (Wilson, 1975), and that many other social behaviors may also be the product of evolutionary forces. Sociobiology, discussed in Chapter 17, is a new discipline that attempts to relate social behavior to biology and evolution.

Other links between biology and behavior, some discovered only recently, span a wide range of topics in psychology: learning, development, motivation, and personality, to name a few (see Lumsden & Wilson, 1981; Fantino & Logan, 1979). As one example, certain animals appear to be biologically prepared to learn specific behaviors. Quail who are poisoned (but not killed) by blue-colored water learn immediately to avoid all blue-colored liquids. Rats, on the other hand, experience considerably more difficulty in learning to avoid blue-colored liquids, but can easily, after a single learning episode, learn to avoid foods with a particular smell. The quail has excellent color vision, and relies extensively on visual cues to identify edible fruit, berries, and seeds. In contrast, the rat sees only in black and white, but relies heavily on smell cues to identify edible substances. It makes sense, then, that the rat should be prepared to learn smells, and the quail, sights. In much the same way, we appear to be prepared to learn language.

Still, biology does not explain everything about us (see Box 2.2). There is little doubt that you would be quite different today had you been born and raised in the place and under the circumstances that I was. And I too would be different had I been in your place. So we are products of our biological makeup (nature) in interaction with our environments (nurture). One of the longstanding and absolutely fundamental controversies in psychology concerns precisely this question: To what extent do nature and nurture share in determining human behavior and personality? We examine this question a number of times in this text, not with a view to answering it (it has no answer at this time), but to clarify how biology and the environment interact and to discover how we are limited by each—and also how each might make possible that of which we have yet scarcely dreamed.

Main Points

1 The special navigational skills of the bat, the eyesight of the eagle, the strength of the bear, and our own intellectual skills are made possible by our biology; hence the importance of the nervous system and its brain.

2 The theory of evolution describes the progressive adaptation of species through natural selection and the survival of the fittest. We are one of the products of evolution, characterized by our ability to walk upright, our juxtaposed thumbs, and our large brains.

3 Our nervous system appears to be the most complex of all animals', and may be described as an elaborate communication system consisting of receivers (sensory systems), connectors (the brain and spinal cord), and transmitters (also termed *effectors,* and found in the muscles and glands).

4 Advanced brains tend to be more specialized than those more primitive (insect or reptile brains, for example). Thus bat brains are specialized for hearing; dog brains, for smelling: bird brains, for rapid movement; and human brains, for thinking.

5 The neuron is the smallest unit of the nervous system, and consists of a cell body, an elongated part termed an *axon,* and hairlike extensions called dendrites. Transmission of impulses ordinarily proceeds from the cell body down the axon to the dendrites of an adjoining cell.

BOX 2.2

Mind and Body

Although many of the relationships between the brain and behavior might seem obvious, a fundamental philosophical question concerning that relationship remains unanswered. We have begun to map correspondences between specific brain structures (and functions) and behavior, but we have not discovered the *mind.* We don't even know very clearly what it is. What we do know is that we can feel and think; we suspect, as well, that we are characterized by volition (will). And, for the sake of argument, we can say that feeling, thinking, and volition are properties of the mind. Are they also properties of the brain (body)? Is it because of a history of specific chemical and electrical events in my brain and body that I have a sense of being *me*—a self consciousness that, at this moment, seems completely divorced from my immediate physical environment?

There have been three historical resolutions for this problem. One maintains that there is no such thing as mind; that all attributes we might ordinarily associate with the mind are a direct product of the body (in this sense, body includes all of the nervous system). A second maintains that the body is a product of the mind, and that the sensible aspects of the physical world also exist only in the mind. These two positions are termed *monistic,* since they accept the existence either of the mind or of the body, but not of both. The first, that mind is a product of the body, is labeled *physical monism* or *materialism.* The second, that matter is a product of the mind, is termed *mental monism* or *idealism.*

The third philosophical resolution of the mind-body problem is *dualism,* which maintains that the mind and body exist separately. Dualism is often associated with Descartes and is therefore referred to as a Cartesian position. Descartes believed that there were two basic substances in the world: the mind or soul, which is a thinking substance; and a second substance which is material and exists in space. The mind, even though it is immaterial, was believed to exercise its effects on the body through the pineal gland.

Recent pronouncements on the mind-body problem are generally restatements or modifications of these three classical resolutions. In fact, however, none of these positions is really a resolution; they are simply beliefs that might seem more or less reasonable depending on the information we have at our disposal. Although we might strongly suspect that if we knew more about the brain's functioning, we would eventually discover that mind is a structure of neural processes (physical monism) (see Pribram, 1971), we can at this stage do no more than suspect. We might equally strongly suspect that, since we know the material world only in our minds, the mind is separate from the physical world. And we might assert, with Rosenblueth (1970) that there is no physical interaction between mental processes and neurological events (dualism). But here, again, we are forced to admit that we really don't know. Will science ever solve this essentially philosophical problem?

6 Transmission between neurons involves electrical and chemical activity. Chemical changes involving one of a number of neural transmitters (acetylcholine, serotonin, dopamine, and noradrenaline are the best known) make it possible for an electric charge to cross the gap (termed a *synapse*) between the terminating ends of an axon and adjoining dendrites or cell bodies.

7 Imbalances in chemical transmitter substances have been associated with a number of mental and physical disorders, the best known of which is Parkinsonism associated with low dopamine levels and characterized by coarse tremors, fatigue, depression, and other symptoms.

8 The brain and spinal cord together comprise the central nervous system. Other parts of the nervous system are more peripheral (away from the center) and are labeled the *peripheral nervous system.*

9 The peripheral nervous system consists of two parts: the somatic system, concerned with the body (sensations of heat, cold, pain, and pressure); and the autonomic system, concerned with functioning of smooth muscles and glands not under conscious control (heart rate, respiration rate, digestion, and so on).

10 The autonomic nervous system consists of two systems with different functions: the sympathetic nervous system is responsible for mobilizing resources of the body in times of crisis (increases heart rate, infuses adrenalin in blood stream, and so on); the parasympathetic nervous system works to temper the results of sympathetic nervous system activity (reduces heart rate, slows respiration, and so on).

11 The brain coordinates all of these diverse activities; it consists of more than 10 billion of the total 12.5 billion or so neurons that compose the nervous system.

12 Much of the information we have concerning the brain comes from physical examination of brains following death: from observation of results of injury to various parts of the brain; from administration of drugs and observation of their effects; through the use of electrodes to stimulate various parts of the brain; and as a result of removing parts of brains and observing the results. This research is conducted with animals except in cases where surgery, drugs, or electrodes might be used to remedy human conditions resulting from brain damage, epilepsy, tumors, or disease.

13 The cerebrum, the outer covering of which is termed the *cerebral cortex,* is the most highly developed brain structure in humans and is intimately involved in higher thought processes—hence its common label, *association area.*

14 Other brain structures include the hypothalamus, which regulates eating and drinking, sexual behavior, and the endocrine system; the thalamus, which serves as a major relay station transmitting information particularly from the senses to appropriate parts of the brain, and regulating the signals that are transmitted; and the reticular formation, which is involved in arousal, in control of sleeping and waking, and in motivation.

15 The spinal cord, part of the central nervous system, is the major nerve pathway in the body. In addition, it is the seat of certain reflexive behaviors that do not involve the brain.

16 Split-brain research indicates that the two halves of the cerebral cortex might have different functions. Specifically, the left half of the brain (which controls motor activity in the right side of the body) is implicated in language and verbal behavior including logic, mathematics, and science, while the right half is involved primarily in spatial organization, perception, music, and art.

17 Biology not only makes some behaviors possible and others very difficult (we find speaking easy but climbing trees more difficult), but also makes some behaviors probable and others improbable. However, the environment too contributes to what is possible and probable.

Further Readings

The following two books are standard, comprehensive textbooks in physiological psychology. They provide considerably more detail than it is possible to include in a single chapter:

Carlson, N. R. *Physiology of behavior* (2nd ed.). Boston: Allyn and Bacon, 1980.

Kalat, J. W. *Biological psychology.* Belmont, Calif.: Wadsworth, 1981.

A highly readable, extraordinarily well-written, and somewhat speculative account of the great events that might have transpired in the course of evolutionary history is:

Eiseley, L. *The immense journey.* New York: Random House, 1957.

More recent developments in evolutionary theory, and a thoughtful account of links between evolution and behavior, is provided in:

Dawkins, R. *The selfish gene.* London: Oxford University Press, 1976.

Current accounts of split-brain research and of what is known of hemisphere functioning are presented in:

Springer, S. P., and Deutsch, G. *Left brain, right brain.* San Francisco: W. H. Freeman, 1981.

Gazzaniga, M. S., and LeDoux, J. E. *The integrated mind.* New York: Plenum, 1978.

States of Consciousness

On a bitterly cold night last January, I spoke to my grandfathers. More than that, I implored them to help me: I wailed and screeched, spluttered and babbled, moaned and whispered. Perhaps I even chanted a little: "Ayai-yai-yai-yai."

I had come to a Cree Indian sweat lodge—my first such experience and, thus far, my last (see Figure 3.1). The sweat lodge is among the most fascinating of the spiritual and cultural rituals of the North American Plains Indians; when asked whether I would like to participate in a "sweat" I scarcely hesitated. The plain truth is that I knew too little about the experience to hesitate. More honestly, I knew virtually nothing.

We arrive in silence, my host for the evening having decided that I should experience the sweat without any preconceived notions. Previously we had purchased tobacco and cloth. Now we sit in a loosely defined circle on the floor of the medicine man's home, wrapping the tobacco in bright squares of cloth so that we might make an offering to the grandfathers. At the appointed time we shed our clothing and file out of the house, barefoot and naked, carrying our tobacco offerings through the snow to the lodge, about thirty yards away. The sweat lodge is a circular, dome-shaped affair, perhaps ten feet in diameter and no more than four feet high at its apex. It is constructed entirely of animal hides stretched tightly over a wooden frame. There is but a single small doorway covered with four or five layers of animal skins. To enter, we must get down on our hands and knees and crawl in. But first, all participants must walk three times clockwise around the fire before the hut. By now the fire is a bed of smoldering embers. It has burned all day, heating the stones that have just recently been removed and placed in the pit in the very center of the sweat lodge.

Thrice around the fire and past the buffalo skulls, naked and shivering; kneeling and crawling inside; handing the offering to the medicine man, who hangs it with the others amid the poplar rafters. The heat is startling, intense. We sit cross-legged around

Figure 3.1 Throughout history, different cultures have had ways of altering states of consciousness. Some methods have been more pleasant than others. For instance, Indian sweat ceremonies may involve several hours in a sweat lodge, where temperatures typically rise to painful levels.

the fire pit, backs to the wall. There are no windows, no cracks in the lodge. Light filters dimly through the partially open doorway. My legs are cramped, awkward. The heat is intense but still welcome.

There are ceremonies before the sweat, and for these the main door flap remains open. Inside, the medicine man lights a bunch of sweetgrass, an herb that grows wild on the plains of the northern United States and southern Canada. It smolders, filling the lodge with its pungent incense. The sweetgrass passes from hand to hand around the circle, each of us wafting it deliberately to and fro several times before passing it on, clockwise. The medicine man finally receives it again and discards it. He lights the peace pipe and draws deeply of its smoke before passing it on. It too must go around the circle; and we each taste the sweet smoke before the pipe is laid beside the sweetgrass. A wooden gourd is now dipped into a water container. The medicine man sips sparingly and pours a few cold drops on his head and back; we all sip and sprinkle in turn, and our skins shiver slightly at the rude, cold touch.

"Let the sweat begin!" The medicine man's sudden shout startles me. The outside flaps are dropped into place and the lodge is pitched into sudden and almost absolute blackness—almost but not quite, for the feverishly heated rocks in the center pit glow eerily. And although we can see them, they do not provide enough light to enable us to see anything else.

The temperature begins to rise at once, and the medicine man speaks. Softly at first, he asks the grandfathers for guidance and prays that each of us might have a good sweat, that we might be rid of bad thoughts and bad feelings, and that our spirits might be lightened and gladdened. And as he speaks, he splashes water upon the rocks, the steam instantly scalding. By now I am drenched in perspiration and I breathe the burning air with difficulty. The medicine man begins to chant: "Ayai-yai-yai-yai-yai; ayai-yai-yai-yai." And others, not novices, join in. I too chant, the sound and the effort distracting me from my discomfort.

We pray then, each person individually but aloud, imploring the grandfathers to help us. "Help me, grandfathers . . . ayai-yai-yai-yai." The heat continues to rise, and soon people moan and groan, some swaying from side to side, others bent over, trying to suck cooler air from the earthen floor. With the rising heat, the volume of discordant voices also rises—the chants and implorations, the words *grandfather . . . grandfathers,* the moaning and the scarcely disguised screams—until, when I am certain that I can stand it no longer, the medicine man shouts, "Open the door."

The cold air sifts in slowly, and we bend low to the ground so that we might breathe it. "It is done," I think to myself. "I have done it."

But it is not done. After only a few minutes, the medicine man asks that the door be shut, and the sweat begins again. This time it is longer and more painful, the supplications are less restrained, and I begin to panic toward the end, realizing that there is no easy and fast way out of the lodge except over the glowing hot stones. Finally the medicine man again provides short-lived relief, before we begin the third sweat. And there is a fourth as well. One of the younger Indian lads, recently recovering from some sickness, is forced to leave before the fourth sweat. The medicine man tells us that there is no shame, no dishonor, in having to leave the sweat. Sometimes when you are not right in your body or your spirit, the ordeal is too great and the grandfathers cannot help you enough that you might stay and benefit from the whole sweat. Sometimes it is better to leave. I agree silently, but remain seated on the sweat-soaked earth. Perhaps I am beginning to hallucinate. During the fourth sweat, when the medicine man speaks of the eagle feathers, I distinctly sense a swift light stroke across my left foot. Frantically I search the darkness with my hands to discover what has touched me. Somebody's hair, perhaps. But there is nothing. In agony now, I half lie on the earth, my head turned away from the rock pit, my mouth at the far lower reaches of the lodge, trying desperately to fill my lungs with fresh air. There is none. I hold my breath but find that I have done that too many times already. My body screams for oxygen, my skin hurts from the heat, and every pore is clogged with perspiration, but the heavy air will evaporate no more. When I scream to the grandfathers, the scream is not a ritual—an empty sound sanctified by tradition. It is real; I scream for help.

"Open the doors!" It is done and we file once more around the fire and through the frigid, 30-below January night, scarcely feeling any cold. The sweat is done.

Later I speak with the medicine man, trying to discover why people willingly suffer the sweats. It does different things for different people, I am told, and these things cannot always be put into words. There is much in life that can only be sensed; much that is as conscious and as real as anything that you or I might touch or say, but that can neither be touched nor put into words. There is much that is beyond our ordinary and our scientific comprehension; and perhaps there are things that are neither conscious nor unconscious. Words, logic, and science might not always be enough.

Consciousness

But words, logic, and science are the stuff of which textbooks are made. And they are the means by which we examine the subject of this chapter: consciousness.

Consciousness is a term from which many meanings can be squeezed. Unfortunately, it is seldom defined precisely or employed consistently. The term that is most often employed synonymously with consciousness is *awareness*. Although to be *conscious* is to know, consciousness is usually defined as involving more than simple knowledge. At one level, consciousness appears to result from personal introspection by which we are aware of events within ourselves. The processes or events that seem to characterize consciousness are unique for each person, so they do not lend themselves to definition in terms of objective "things" with universal meaning. Psychologists' insistence on scientific rigor, precision, and objectivity did much to discredit the study of consciousness at the turn of this century, although there is evidence that it is once again emerging as a legitimate subject.

Some psychologists inform us that there are three states of consciousness, having relatively recently discovered that there are more than two. The original two, still valid, were considered to be the awake state and the asleep state. Now, however, distinctions are made between two states of sleep: REM (rapid eye movement) sleep and NREM (no rapid eye movement) sleep.* Levels and characteristics of consciousness also vary in the awake state, sometimes due to physiological factors (fatigue, for example), and sometimes due to the influence of drugs, meditative techniques, or hypnosis. Each of these states of awareness is discussed in some detail in this chapter.

So consciousness, although easily sensed, is not easily defined. Nor is *sense* exactly the right word, since sensation implies the apprehension of the physical qualities of the environment. It is true that to be conscious (or *aware;* the terms are used synonymously here) is to be sensitive to the environment, but consciousness is more than simple sensation.

Have you ever noticed how you talk to yourself? It's a very private thing; at the same time, it is a phenomenon that you take so much for granted that you may never have thought about it very much, or even talked about it with anyone else. I suspect that you, like me, continually give yourself little verbal directions—not out loud, of course; if you did, people might think you were deranged. You tell yourself what you are doing or what you are going to do, or how you are going to do it. Stop right now. That is, stop reading these words for thirty seconds and pay attention to what is going on in your head.

You're back. Were you talking to yourself about what you were reading? Perhaps. But more likely you were talking to yourself about what you were doing, which was not reading, but listening to yourself talk to yourself about listening to yourself talking to yourself. All of which is a truly marvelous illustration of the **stream of consciousness**, a phenomenon noted, named, and described by William James (1890). That there is a stream of consciousness—an unending string of thoughts chasing each other through your mind—is one of the characteristics of consciousness. It is your own personal proof that you are aware (see Figure 3.2).

But you are not aware of everything around you. Certainly you are not at this time, or weren't until I mentioned it, aware of the feeling of the clothing you have on your body. If you were constantly aware of all the sensations that surround you, you would probably become unbearably mad in very short order. Awareness is therefore limited by attention, attention being simply the responsiveness of the individual to the environment.

Awareness, or consciousness, also includes notions of **self**—notions, which although real and meaningful for each of us, remain nebulous and ill-defined. Few topics lend themselves less well to scientific research or logical analysis. A self cannot be observed objectively; it can only be felt subjectively. It cannot be set apart and measured; it cannot be divorced from sensation or perception; it cannot easily be separated from ongoing thought processes; it is imbued with feelings and emotions; it is private. Self is at once part of my immediate functioning and separate from it. In other words, although I feel that my self is directly involved in whatever I am now doing, I cannot rid myself of the notion that there is some undefinable, elusive part of me that can somehow stand apart from what is happening—that can evaluate, make

Stream of consciousness A descriptive phrase employed by William James to emphasize that consciousness is continuous rather than a series of discrete states or events. The expression is now used more often in literature than in psychology, and often refers to a process similar to free association wherein individuals express in uninterrupted fashion whatever is occurring in their consciousness at the time.

Self Another ill-defined term. Its many meanings may be reduced to two components: (a) the concept you have of your *person* (your self-notions, often derived from the reactions of others to yourself); (b) the self as an individual. Thus the self may be seen as a complex arrangement of all of the characteristics that make up an individual, or as the notions that an individual has about his or her own personal characteristics. Since neither definition is objective, they lack precision. Nor is it clear that we have single selves.

---

*Distinctions can also be made among *four* stages of sleep defined largely in terms of changes in brain-wave activity (see Figure 3.5).

Figure 3.2 What William James called *stream of consciousness*—an unending string of loosely connected thoughts that are a constant part of being alive, awake, and conscious.

BIOGRAPHY
William James
1842–1910

comments, amuse me with self-talk, react emotionally. Do I control my self or does it control me? Is the self that I was when I was 6 the same self that I sense myself to be now that I am 106, more or less? Do I have only one self? Eve White (the subject of *The Three Faces of Eve*) had three (Thigpen & Cleckley, 1954). William James believed that we all have more than one. Co-consciousnesses, he called them. These are dissociated selves, distinct selves that are frequently unaware of other selves. Some of these selves allegedly manifest themselves in dreams (many of which we don't recall); others become apparent under the influence of hypnosis. Unlike those of Eve White, however, our dissociated selves do not constitute separate identities. We can live with all of them and still think we are one. Studies of split-brain patients described in the preceding chapter provide evidence that each half of the brain may be conscious of totally different things (see also Jaynes, 1977). In fact, however, since our brains are ordinarily in close and immediate neural contact, there is no reason to suppose that the hemispheres represent separate selves.

Let us not, however, lose our*selves* in circular and time-consuming contemplations of our selves. We will return to them later.

Waking

The type of consciousness, or self-awareness, we have been discussing (in a one-sided manner, to be sure) is evident primarily in our waking state but is not limited to it. As will become clear in subsequent sections of this chapter, sleep states are by no means unconscious states.

It may seem pointless to attempt a discussion of the waking state, since that is the state with which we are all so intimately familiar. Indeed, discussions of almost any psychological topic—hence the major portion of this book—are inevitably concerned with various characteristics of the waking state in the human animal. We spend perhaps two-thirds of our lives more or less awake. We are rather completely aware of that state. Consider, however, that we spend the remaining third of our lives in sleep states—states about which we subjectively know incredibly little, except for those portions revealed to us through our remembrance of dreams. It is not an exaggeration to say that you have been a stranger to yourself for a third of every day of your life.

William James was born into a wealthy Irish-American family, fourteen months before the birth of his equally famous brother, Henry. Their father, a highly educated man, was also a writer, although he achieved very little fame. The brothers, William and Henry, were educated in various schools in Europe, in the United States, and by private tutors. William, undecided about a future career, went to the Amazon in 1865 thinking he might be a biologist; but he hated collecting and soon returned to Harvard, where he obtained an M.D. in 1869. Shortly thereafter, he was invited to teach physiology at Harvard. Among his first lectures was one which dealt with the relationship between physiology and psychology. James was later to remark that the first lecture he ever heard on psychology was the first lecture given by himself. James established a psychological laboratory at Harvard in 1875. Shortly thereafter, he signed a contract with Holt for a psychology textbook, apologizing that it would take him a full two years to complete it; it took him twelve. But the resulting text, *Principles of Psychology,* laid the groundwork for the birth of a new science.

Figure 3.3 The innocent are reputed to sleep like babies and angels—although angels sleep less publicly.

Sleep

Sleep An altered state of consciousness characterized by loss of muscle tone, loss of immediate awareness of surroundings, and changes in such physiological functions as heart rate, blood pressure, respiration rate, body temperature, and electrical activity of the brain. Sleep appears to be universal among animals and occurs in regular cyclical fashion.

What is **sleep**? It is the state that ensues when you close your eyes and eventually lose immediate contact with your environment. It ends when you regain awareness of external events. Does that mean we are unaware of our physical environments as we sleep? Not exactly. The sound of a crying baby awakens its parents. Clearly the parents hear the sound and are able to respond to it. If I place an object delicately on your chest as you sleep, you may incorporate the feeling of an object on your chest into your dreams. Part of you is therefore aware of tactile stimulation. And as you lie precariously on your narrow bed, a dangerous height above your stone floor, you have little fear of falling and bruising that part of you in which you keep your brain and other things. You casually assume that your body has some control over its movements during sleep, and that it is responsive to signals that might indicate it has moved you dangerously close to the edge of your sleeping platform. All of this provides strong evidence that you are not totally unconscious while you are asleep, that part of you or of your brain remains alert (see Weitzman, 1974, 1975).

That you can be awakened while you sleep is added evidence that you are not totally unconscious. And the fact that you, or at least someone you know or have heard about, can walk and talk while apparently asleep provides still more evidence. Furthermore, you can think while you are asleep (to the extent that dreams are thoughts), and you can remember some of this thinking (to the extent that dreams can be remembered). (See Figure 3.3.)

Sleep, then, is not unconsciousness, but clearly involves altered consciousness. Physiologically it does involve, as was mentioned earlier, closing of the eyes, reduction of muscle tension, reduction of heart rate, lowering of blood pressure, slowing of respiration rate, and a marked decrease in body temperature. In addition, **electroencephalographs** (**EEGs**) indicate that brain activity is altered during sleep, ranging from typical alpha waves (8 to 12 waves per second, relatively high amplitude) to delta waves in deeper sleep states (large, slow waves: frequency 0.5 to 4 per second) (see Figures 3.4 and 3.5).

Electroencephalograph (EEG) A graphlike representation of changes in electrical potential that occur in the brain. These changes are detected by means of sensitive electrodes ordinarily placed on the surface of the skull but sometimes in or on the exposed brains of animals.

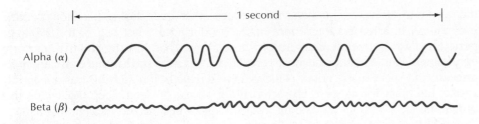

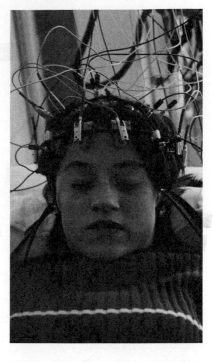

Figure 3.4 Graphic portrayals of electrical activity in the brain are most frequently obtained by placing ultrasensitive electrodes on (not in) various parts of the skull, amplifying signals picked up by these electrodes, and recording these changes on paper. The most common brain waves are labeled *alpha* and *beta*. Alpha waves are of relatively high amplitude with a frequency of 8 to 12 per second. Beta waves are of considerably lower amplitude but have a much higher frequency: 18 to 30 per second. Alpha waves correspond to relaxed but wakeful states; beta waves typically occur most frequently when the subject is more alert.

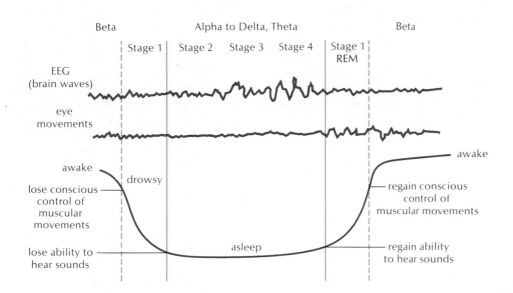

Figure 3.5 Physiological changes during stages of sleep.

Laird and Muller (1930) long ago noted regular patterns in going to sleep and waking up. In particular they established that an individual first loses the ability to control muscular movement consciously; the ability to hear noises is last to be lost and is never, of course, lost entirely. Just as parents remain very sensitive to their baby's cry even though they might sleep peacefully through the sounds of a nearby freight train, so if your name is mentioned while you are asleep, there is a high probability that you will awaken. The sequence during waking up is exactly the opposite, with the ability to respond to noises regained first and the ability to exercise conscious control over muscular movements regained last.

Why We Sleep

We still do not know why we sleep although, as Carlson (1980) notes, the insistent nature of sleepiness leads us to believe that sleep is absolutely essential. In addition, the fact that all mammals and even reptiles, amphibians, and fish have periods of sleep (or at least sleeplike periods), would also lead us to believe that sleep is essential. Is it essential, and what does it do for us?

One way of approaching this question is by looking at what happens when people are deprived of sleep. In one marathon, single-case experiment, a New York disc jockey undertook to remain awake for 200 hours (Luce & Segal, 1966). During this period he continued to do a daily 3-hour radio show, a feat he accomplished competently to

Hallucinations False perceptions that appear so compellingly real that those experiencing them believe firmly in their reality. Hallucinations are primarily auditory or visual, and may take the form of voices or sounds in the absence of any object or person producing those sounds, or of vivid visual images that do not relate to the immediate visual environment. Although hallucinations are often associated with abnormality or with drugs, they are also sometimes experienced by normal people without the mediation of drugs.

Paranoia (adjective, paranoiac) A condition where subjects feel persecuted, chased, hunted, or followed. Paranoia is characteristic of a number of mental disorders of varying severity, and, in its milder forms, is also frequently characteristic of otherwise normal individuals. In its more extreme forms, paranoia is often accompanied by delusions of grandeur (the conviction, for example, that one is an important historical figure), which often provide some rational justification for the feelings of persecution. Those who think they are Christ or Hitler might not have much difficulty in deciding they have enemies.

Figure 3.6 Peter Tripp, New York disc jockey, after being awake for 200 consecutive hours. His behavior became increasingly irrational during this marathon.

the very end. However, his behavior at times other than during his show became increasingly bizarre, irrational, and ineffective during the last half of the 200-hour period. He was frequently unaware of where he was, had lost the ability to perform exceedingly simple mathematical or verbal tasks, began to **hallucinate**, became **paranoiac**, and spent many hours panicked and terrified. Although he was apparently awake, his brain waves were characteristic of a state of deep sleep. Following this ordeal, he slept without awakening for 13 hours. When he did awaken, his hallucinations, his paranoia, and his inability to solve simple problems had all disappeared (Figure 3.6).

The Luce and Segal study has been widely interpreted as meaning that without sleep our behavior would probably become very bizarre, that we might suffer from hallucinations, and that our ability to respond to the environment would be significantly impaired. Other research has not always borne out these conclusions, however. When Randy Gardner stayed awake for 264 consecutive hours in order to get into the *Guinness Book of World Records,* he suffered from no hallucinations or paranoia, his concentration appeared to be unimpaired, and his motor coordination remained sufficiently good that he was able to beat psychologist William Dement one hundred times in a row at a penny arcade baseball game (Gulevich, Dement, & Johnson, 1966). An earlier study by Kleitman (1963) found much the same thing. Subjects who were deprived of sleep for two or three days still performed normally on a variety of tasks provided the tasks were short. Longer and more boring tasks were more difficult.

The most logical conclusion to be derived from these apparently contradictory studies is that sleep deprivation does not necessarily lead to hallucinations, paranoia, and other disturbances. Indeed, it is quite possible that the disturbances apparent in the disc jockey after 200 sleepless hours were due as much or more to the stress associated with having to continue doing the radio show as to any physiological effects caused by sleep deprivation.

Sleep deprivation research with animals has shed little light on this question. Although prolonged sleep deprivation in animals sometimes results in their death, researchers can seldom be certain that the effect is due to sleep deprivation itself rather than to the usually stressful methods that must be employed to keep animals awake. Whereas human subjects can be persuaded to stay awake, and will then actively cooperate in order not to go to sleep, animals must sometimes be prodded into sleeplessness by electric shock or by using water. In one ingenious experimental method, mice or rats are placed on a tiny surface completely surrounded by water. As they fall asleep their muscles relax and they droop slowly toward the water until, touching it, they rudely awaken. This technique is termed the *flower pot technique* since the surface on which the animal is placed is often an inverted flower pot (Fishbein & Gutwein, 1977).

Although we do not know for certain what would happen if we did not sleep, we can theorize about what the effects of sleep are. Coyne (1968) summarizes five theoretical explanations for sleep. The circulatory theory maintains that sleep occurs as a result of the brain's being deprived of a normal amount of oxygen. Related to this is the chemical theory, which also holds that oxygen deprivation leads to unconsciousness (sleep). A neurological theory is that cell changes that transpire during waking hours must be repaired during sleep. A fourth theory speculates that a specific sleep center in the brain simply shuts off activity in other parts of the brain, thereby causing sleep. Finally, a biological theory makes reference to the rhythms and cycles that are apparently characteristic of all life; sleep is simply one of the cycles to which we are heir (see Box 3.1). It is possible that sleep is an evolved mechanism whose survival function lies in the fact that sleeping animals (which are typically concealed) are less likely to be preyed upon, particularly if their sleep cycles correspond with predation cycles. It also appears reasonable to suppose that sleep might have evolved as a system for conserving energy (Zepelin & Rechtschaffen, 1974). Furthermore, none of these explanations is necessarily exclusive; that is, sleep might result from a combination of factors.

BOX 3.1

Biorhythm Theory

Many of us intuitively feel that we have good days and bad. And perhaps we wish occasionally that we knew beforehand which days would be which so that we might plan our behavior accordingly. Biorhythm theory presumes to tell us about good days and bad. It informs us, first, that there are three broad, recurring (hence rhythmic) cycles that govern our lives (Thommen, 1973): A twenty-three-day cycle relates to our physical selves—our strength, endurance, and energy. A twenty-eight-day cycle governs our emotional lives and is reflected in our moods, our happiness, and our creativity. A thirty-three-day cycle is reflected in our intellectual lives and manifests itself in our reasoning power, our memories, and our intelligence. The theory states, further, that each of these three cycles originates at birth and continues uninterrupted throughout life; hence it is necessary to know only your date of birth to determine at which phase of each of these cycles you now find yourself. Each of the cycles can be described in terms of two half-cycles, one positive and one negative. In addition, for each cycle there are several "critical" periods, each extending for perhaps twenty-four hours on either side of a critical day. These occur at each of the shifts from positive to negative or from negative to positive. Also, there are peak negative periods when individual cycles are at their maximum negative phase, or when more than one cycle is negative. When all three cycles are maximally negative, it might be a very bad day indeed. In fact, the theory predicts that during these times the probability of accidents, depression, suicide, and other unfortunate events should be considerably higher than when cycles are positive. It is not a difficult theory to test, given that it makes rather specific predictions.

Biorhythm theory has been investigated in a variety of ways, and by a variety of individuals. A great many of these investigations have shown substantial relationships between accidents and critical days or negative periods. Unfortunately, however, the experimental procedures employed have not always been impeccable (Wolcott et al., 1975). In spite of this, biorhythm theory has been employed fairly widely in business and industry.

A carefully controlled investigation of 4,008 civil aviation accidents in the United States in 1972 looked at the relationship between biorhythms and accidents (Wolcott et al., 1977). Of these accidents, 3,253 were attributed to the pilot and only 755 to other causes. Since accidents due to pilot error would more likely be under the influence of prevailing biorhythms, analyses were conducted separately for those two groups of accidents. Biorhythm theory would predict a greater-than-chance number of accidents on those days when multiple cycles are negative, as well as on other critical days. The findings contradict this prediction emphatically. In fact, there was no correlation between critical days, negative cycles, or multiple negative cycles and number of accidents.

Other research has not been any kinder to biorhythm theory. Wood, Krider, and Fezer (1980) looked at hospital emergency room records of 700 injuries and found that 27.4 percent of these accidents occurred on critical days, compared with the 26.6 percent that would have been expected by chance. Haywood (1979) found that archers performed every bit as well on critical days as on noncritical days. Prytula et al. (1980) conducted experiments that indicate that randomly generated biorhythms are as accurate and as believable for the subjects involved as are biorhythm charts based on birth dates. Demuth (1979) studied 250 individuals who had identified their own critical days: 200 of them had dropped in to a counseling center, unable or unwilling to wait for an appointment; 50 of them had committed suicide. When these critical days were compared with what should have been critical days based on biorhythm theory, absolutely no relationship between the two was found.

In summary, the theory is not valid. As Louis (1978) put it: ". . . biorhythm theory [is] absurd" (p. 95). Yet it sometimes works. At least on occasion, predictions based on the theory are correct far more often than would be expected by chance. And when factory workers are given biorhythm information and are told that they should be more careful on specific critical days, accident rates often decrease dramatically. Why?

Wolcott et al. (1977) suggest that the explanation might be quite simple. If workers are told to be careful during their critical periods, they are, in effect, being told to be more careful approximately 50 percent of the time (since critical periods extend twenty-four hours on either side of a critical day, and since there are a number of critical periods for each of the three cycles). It is hardly surprising that biorhythm theory should appear to work in these circumstances.

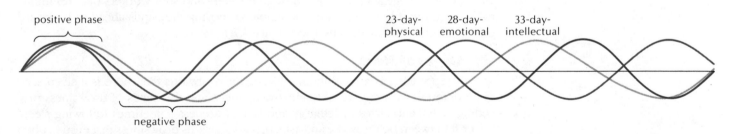

A biorhythm chart, indicating physical, emotional, and intellectual cycles. Can you spot the "bad days"? (Critical days occur at each crossover.)

In effect, none of these explanations have been clearly substantiated (Thompson, 1975). Animals who have had their brains removed continue to sleep; there is no physiological evidence that sleep involves unconsciousness due to oxygen deprivation; the theory of cell damage remains unsupported; and no toxins or other harmful substances have been discovered to accumulate in the body's cells that must be destroyed through sleep. Nor is there any significant change in the body's overall consumption of energy during sleep, so that the commonly held belief that the body needs to sleep in order to conserve and restore its energy levels does not appear to be substantiated either. Despite marked declines in physiological functioning during sleep, the level of energy consumption increases dramatically during the first hour of sleep, although it falls off rapidly after that. Why do we sleep? The question remains unanswered.

Biological Clocks

Circadian rhythm *Circadian* means "around one day"; circadian rhythms are the twenty-four-hour cycles that appear to exercise some influence on the lives of lower animals as well as humans. Also termed *biological clocks,* they are most evident in sleep-waking cycles and in temperature cycles.

One of the theoretical explanations for sleep made reference to certain cycles and rhythms to which we are heir. These rhythms, called **circadian rhythms** or biological clocks, appear to be common to a great many lower animals as well as to our species. Rats who are kept in unchanging light conditions for prolonged periods of time continue to eat and sleep following regular twenty-four-hour patterns. So it appears to be with people. Every twenty-four-hour period is more or less regularly divided into periods of waking and sleeping, accompanied by appropriate changes in physiological functioning. Thus, it is true to say that we tend to sleep when our temperatures are lowest. Is it also true to say that our temperatures tend to be lowest when we sleep? Perhaps. In point of fact, however, when the sleep-wake cycle is disrupted abruptly, the temperature cycle may continue to adhere to old rhythms for a while, and psychological functioning and general well-being may be adversely affected.

Jet lag, a frequently noted phenomenon resulting from air travel through several time zones, is most often explained in terms of disruption of circadian rhythms. K. E. Klein et al. (1972) flew eight students from the United States to Germany, where they remained for eighteen days before returning home. Psychological tests were conducted beginning three days prior to departure, continuing up to thirteen days after arrival in Germany, and for thirteen days after their return home. Peak performance on a number of tasks did not reappear for as long as twelve days after the flight; even some easier tasks required six days before students could perform at top capacity. Interestingly, body temperature did not readjust to the new cycle for approximately two weeks following the initial flight. Other studies, many involving a restructuring of the sleep-wake cycle rather than actual flight, have demonstrated that the effects of jet lag are not due to lack of sleep, but to the disruption of circadian rhythms (see Kripke, 1975). Our biological clocks can be reset; travelers and shift workers bear testimony to that fact. But the process is not as simple as moving the hands ahead or backward on our mechanical timepieces. (See Figure 3.7.)

Stages of Sleep

Hypnagogic An adjective that relates to drowsiness, or more specifically to the state that precedes sleep. It has not been extensively investigated, but it is generally recognized that hallucinations are not uncommon during this state.

Sleep-waking is a continuum. Although it is obvious that there is a sleep state quite different from a state of being awake, there are also states of drowsiness preceding sleep, and states of lethargy and semiawareness sometimes following sleep. That rift between being awake and asleep, that luxurious drowsiness that ensues when you realize that sleep is inevitable unless you consciously chase it away, that indescribably and overwhelmingly good feeling that can be cultivated by being deliberately aware of it, is termed **hypnagogic**. Although it has been reported and described by a number of writers, very little scientific research has been conducted on it. Pearce (1971) speculates about the possibilities of the hypnagogic state. He notes Selye's (1964) assertion that every important scientific idea that he knew of had occurred in "the twilight state between waking and sleeping." "The hypnagogic's strawberry vision is free of half-ripe, bird-pecked, imperfect berries; free of gnats, dirt, sore knees, or aching back," Pearce tells us. But that is the judgment of a poet, not of a scientist.

The scientist tells us that there are two types of sleep, distinguishable largely by the presence or absence of rapid eye movements which can be detected as shown in Figure 3.8 and represented graphically (Dement, 1974). **REM sleep** (rapid eye movement), first discovered by Aserinsky and Kleitman (1953), comprises between 20 and 25 percent of our normal sleep. **NREM sleep** (no rapid eye movement) makes up the remaining 75 to 80 percent. Some of the marked differences between these two sleep states, apart from their typical duration and the presence or absence of rapid eye movements, include differences in brain-wave activity, in heart rate, and in breathing. During REM sleep these physiological functions are very similar to those expected in a normal, awake person. Heart rate ranges between forty-five and one hundred beats per minute, breathing is irregular, and EEG patterns are similar to those evident in wakeful and alert states (alpha). Because of the surprising presence of the kinds of waves expected from a subject who is awake, REM sleep is often called *paradoxical* sleep. In contrast, delta waves appear during NREM sleep, breathing becomes regular and substantially slower, and heart rate is slow and steady. One of the more surprising findings of sleep research is that, in spite of the apparently deeper sleep of the NREM state, it is often considerably easier to awaken subjects from this state than from REM sleep.

Three other characteristics of REM sleep are noteworthy. First, during this state males almost invariably manifest partial or complete penile erection, whether they be infants or elderly men. It has been substantiated that this phenomenon is unrelated to the sexual content of any dreams that might have been occurring at the time. Second, during REM sleep most of our dreams take place, an observation that has led to common use of the expression D sleep (D for dream) for REM sleep, and of S sleep (S for sleep) for NREM sleep. C. Hall (1951) reports that subjects awakened from REM sleep claim 80 percent of the time that they have been dreaming; only 20 percent of awakenings from NREM sleep result in reportings of dreams. Third, even though REM sleep is characterized by high cortical activity, there is a dramatic loss of muscle tone during this stage. In effect, the muscles become completely relaxed—essentially paralyzed.

REM sleep occurs fairly regularly at approximately ninety-minute intervals, and lasts for twenty-five minutes or more. It does not begin for thirty or more minutes

REM sleep A stage of sleep characterized by rapid eye movements (REM). Also called paradoxical sleep because of the presence of EEG patterns similar to those characteristic of the waking state.
NREM sleep Stage of sleep that is not characterized by rapid eye movements (hence NREM).

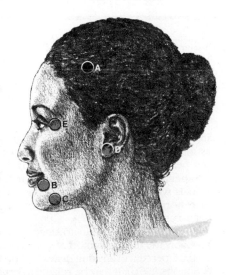

Figure 3.8 The electrodes this subject is wearing are placed in specific locations on the head for specific reasons. Electrode A is to map brain waves; B and C are to record muscle tone (a sudden droop of the chin frequently marks the onset of REM sleep); D is a neutral indicator; and E records REMs.

Figure 3.9 Cycle of REM-NREM sleep. During a normal sleep cycle, REM sleep occurs fairly regularly at about ninety-minute intervals and lasts for twenty-five minutes or more. If we are awakened from NREM sleep, REM sleep will not begin for thirty minutes or more after the onset of sleep. If we are awakened during REM sleep (as in a dream-recording experiment), the result is shorter NREM periods between REM states during the subsequent night.

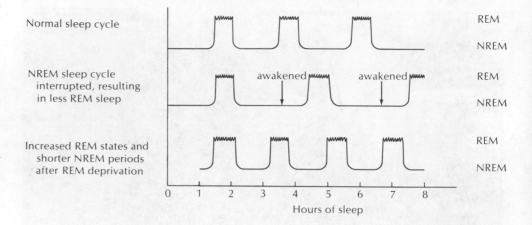

following onset of sleep. If a subject is awakened from NREM sleep and kept awake for a few minutes, REM sleep will not begin for at least thirty minutes, even if the subject had been in NREM sleep for the last hour or more (see Figure 3.9). Thus it is possible to deprive subjects of REM sleep simply by waking them whenever there is evidence of the beginning of rapid eye movements. One of the results of this procedure is that subjects who are deprived of one type of sleep tend to make up for it during subsequent nights. A subject deprived of REM sleep one night will simply experience much shorter NREM periods between REM states the next night. (See Box 3.2.)

Other effects of REM deprivation are much less clear. While some early studies reported increased irritability, mild anxiety, and a lessening of the ability to concentrate (for example, Dement, 1960), subsequent research in which subjects were deprived of REM sleep for as long as 16 days found no appreciable impairment of psychological functioning or well-being (Dement, 1974). Nor have studies of NREM sleep deprivation been any more revealing (see Carlson, 1980). In summary, research on the effects of

---

Sleep Disturbances

In the absence of violent physical or emotional disturbances (such as might result from having a bucket of cold water deposited on our persons), most of us sleep during a good deal of the time that we spend in bed for that purpose. But there are a number of individuals who sleep less well than normal, who sleep much more than normal, or who sleep abnormally. Their complaint: a sleep disturbance.

Insomnia, the inability to sleep for a normal period of time, is probably the most common of sleep disturbances, affecting an estimated 6 percent of all adult males and 14 percent of females (Kripke & Simons, 1976). It may be related to drugs that facilitate sleep but, when withdrawn, often lead to severe insomnia; or perhaps to psychological factors, the most likely being stress or tension. *Apnea,* the temporary paralysis of breathing mechanisms (or their total relaxation), sometimes accompanied by a collapse of throat muscles, accounts for as much as 5 percent of all insomnia complaints (Mitler et al., 1975). What apparently happens in apnea is that the transition between drowsiness and sleep is accompanied by a ces-

sation of breathing which, in turn, reawakens the individual. Occasional, fleeting moments of apnea are quite common, particularly among heavy snorers. Severe apnea, which is fortunately quite rare, can endanger life. Relief in such cases has been provided through a tracheotomy (a small slit in the throat and into the windpipe into which a plastic tube is inserted, thus enabling the subject to breathe even though throat muscles might be completely collapsed).

Hypersomnia, a tendency to sleep too much or too often, frequently takes the form of unpredictable "sleep attacks," which are labeled *narcolepsy.* Subjects suffering from narcolepsy may "fall" asleep so suddenly and unexpectedly that they literally fall from their chairs in midsentence. Other sleep disturbances include enuresis (bed-wetting), sleepwalking, and nightmares. These disturbances are not well understood, but they tend to be rare among adults (C. Fisher et al., 1973). Sleepwalking in particular usually disappears by the age of twelve or thirteen. And, contrary to popular belief, sleepwalkers do on occasion injure themselves (Mitler et al., 1975). Although there are no reliable methods for preventing these sleep disorders, it may sometimes be wise to arrange the environment so as to minimize the risk that a sleepwalker will suffer injury. Locking or barricading the bedroom door or setting up an alarm system that will awaken another person might be effective. In the case of enuresis, changing bed clothing is recommended. In serious cases, certain conditioning techniques, under the direction of a psychologist, might be recommended.

sleep deprivation in general or of deprivation of only one kind of sleep has not yet provided us an explanation either of why it is that we sleep, or of what specific physiological or psychological functions sleep might serve. But sleep does make dreams possible.

Dreams

And what are these **dreams** made of? C. Hall (1951) classified the content of 1,000 dreams. The predominant activity in these dreams involved some form of movement; the second most common activity was talking; playing, thinking, socializing, and so on were all less frequent (see Figure 3.10). Your typical, average, American dream involves only two or three people and perhaps the same number of mundane objects.

Twenty percent occur in a living room (your own), more often than in any other room; some 43 percent of the people in the dream, other than the dreamer, appear to be strangers, with 1 percent being drawn from among the famous; men dream about other men twice as often as they dream about women; women dream about men and women equally often; some 30 percent of all reported dreams have some color in them, and the remainder are colorless. Sex-related dreams are not uncommon (Husband, 1936; Kinsey et al., 1953), although the literature is vague as to their actual frequency. These quite often lead to orgasm in both men and women, but more often in men. Relatively few dreams are nightmares. Interestingly, those that are tend not to occur during an REM state, but rather toward the end of an NREM period (Broughton, 1968; Webb & Cartwright, 1978) (see Figure 3.11). Nightmares are slightly more common among emotionally disturbed adults and among younger children (DeMartino, 1955).

Contrary to some of our more naive beliefs, everybody dreams (Faraday, 1972). We simply do not all remember our dreams with equal clarity. In fact, research demonstrates that most people remember only a small portion of what they dream. Nor, as is popularly believed, is a dream a condensed version of real-time events. Indications are that the amount of time that might have elapsed had dream events been real is very similar to the amount of time during which the dream occurred. Evidence that

Dream A noun with connotations of unreality. Dreams may take one of two forms: daydreams (which typically involve sequences of fantasy); and night dreams (relatively coherent sequences of imagery, primarily visual). Although the reasons for and functions of dreaming remain unclear, we know that it is almost universal.

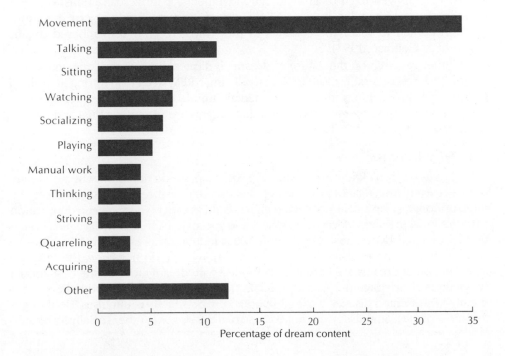

Figure 3.10 What are dreams made of? In Hall's analysis of the content of 1,000 dreams, the activities shown here were most regularly reported. Most dreams involved only two or three people, close to half of them (43 percent) total strangers. (Based on data from Hall, 1951.)

Figure 3.11 Relatively few dreams are nightmares, and they tend to occur toward the end of NREM sleep—not during REM sleep, as do the majority of other dreams.

this is so is derived from tracings of eye movements, from verbalizations, or from movements corresponding to an event in a dream. Subsequently, subjects are awakened and asked to relate the contents of their most recently remembered dream (Dement & Kleitman, 1957).

Other research on the nature of dreams indicates that sleepwalking and sleeptalking occur considerably more frequently during NREM sleep than during REM sleep (Jacobson & Kales, 1967); that environmental stimulation is quite frequently incorporated into dreams (Berger, 1963); and that dreams are primarily visual and passive rather than active (C. Hall, 1951).

Why Dream?

Just as we don't know for certain why we sleep, we do not know why we dream. We can't even investigate the effects of not dreaming, since doing so requires the interruption of sleep and any observed effect could as well be due to sleep deprivation as to dream deprivation. Social researchers and speculators, however, have never been unduly daunted by the absence of verifiable scientific observation in their quest to advance theory and explanation. Therefore, although we do not *know* the purpose and function of dreams, we have been provided with dream theories, the best-known of which is clearly Sigmund Freud's (DeMartino, 1959). In brief, Freud believed that dreams represented disguised manifestations of **unconscious** impulses. He thought that most of these impulses were linked to sexual desires or to other socially forbidden

Unconscious The term *unconscious* has numerous confounded and confounding meanings, many of which are contradictory. In the Freudian sense, the unconscious is the part of the person that includes activities, events, impulses, and so on that are not accessible to conscious examination (in other words, that are beyond ordinary awareness), but have a powerful effect on conscious processes and events.

inclinations. Hence they were disguised, even in dreams, as a form of self-protection or, more precisely, as a form of sleep protection. Were they not disguised, we would continually awaken horrified at our vile and base cravings. If the father we want to murder appears in a dream as a spider, we can step on that creature and feel no guilt. Only Freud and a number of other gifted psychoanalysts would be expected to recognize the spider. And we don't really have to believe them in any case, if we find it overly disturbing.

According to Freud, then, dreams have a hidden meaning—what he termed a *latent* meaning. Their apparent meaning is largely irrelevant, relating primarily to events, objects, or people that populate our immediate days. The dream serves the purpose of relieving tensions resulting from impulses that have not or cannot be attended to; the symbolic, unrecognizable nature of the dream serves to ensure that we obtain our sleep relatively undisturbed.

Theories such as Freud's, although intriguing, are high speculative. They do not lend themselves easily to scientific verification. A more recent theory of dreams is no less speculative. Hobson and McCarley (1977) agree with Freud that dreams are often related to the dreamer's personality and experiences, but they disagree with the notion that dreams serve as expressions of unconscious and disguised wishes. Their argument is that the content of dreams may be related more to physiology than to personality.

Hobson and McCarley conducted experiments with 120 cats. Although it cannot be established conclusively that cats dream, most cats being noticeably reluctant to discuss such things, their patterns of REM and NREM sleep are remarkably similar to ours. By monitoring electrical activity in various parts of cat brains before, during, and at the onset of REM sleep, these investigators arrived at the notion that signals for the onset of a dream originate in the reticular activating system (RAS). Recall that most neural impulses go through the RAS, that it functions as an arousal center, and appears to control waking and sleeping. Hobson and McCarley argue that the rapid eye movements of REM sleep provide, via the RAS, a sequence of impulses to the cortex. To make sense of these incoming impulses, the cortex generates a dream, incorporating into the dream other external impulses that are immediately present. Thus, an individual who is physically cold may well incorporate feelings of being cold into an ongoing dream.

Seligmann and Begley (1978) note that Freud believed psychologists would one day be able to provide a biological explanation for dreaming. These recent notions may constitute the beginning of that explanation.

The Usefulness of Dreams

Although psychologists have not yet provided a definite answer for the question of why we dream, research does suggest a number of ways in which dreams may be useful. To begin with, there is the possibility that, as Freud believed, dreams serve as a release for impulses that cannot easily be acted upon in reality. This possibility has not been investigated experimentally since it is, in effect, impossible to deprive an individual completely of dreams. Partial and temporary dream deprivation, however, accomplished by waking individuals at the onset of REM periods, suggests that dreaming may have a beneficial effect on psychological functioning (R. D. Cartwright, 1977). Cartwright argues that one of the functions of dreams is to permit the individual to attend to fantasy and to examine impulses. In the absence of dreams, the individual finds it difficult to attend to reality upon awakening but tends instead to pay attention to "imaginative thoughts and inner feelings."

A second function of dreams is to regulate inner feelings, thus helping the individual adapt to the stresses of life. R. D. Cartwright (1977) notes that the various dreams collected from a single individual on the same night typically present such a coherent pattern that it is impossible to believe that dreams represent random happenings. She argues that dreams may be purposive, since they often appear to be directed toward the resolution of conflict-laden situations. It may be important to note, in this connection, that schizophrenics tend to have very bland and sterile dreams—dreams less "crazy" than yours or mine (Dement, 1955; R. D. Cartwright, 1972).

The contribution of dreams to intellectual functioning is not at all clear. Although a number of attempts have been made to show that dreams can sometimes contribute to the solution of problems or to the production of creative works, most of the evidence is contradictory and unsatisfactory. It may be that, as R. D. Cartwright (1974) argues, a dream does not contribute to psychological functioning until the content of the dream is consciously analyzed and worked with. In other words, the contribution of dreams to cognition may be indirect rather than direct.

Hypnosis

Hypnosis A state characterized by heightened suggestibility (willingness of the subject to perform whatever acts are required by the hypnotist; readiness to believe whatever is suggested). *Hypnotism* is the process by which this state may be induced.

Hypnosis is a big word out of which many meanings can be squeezed. Like many other concepts in psychology, it should not be defined in one sentence, but should instead be described. How do you do it, and what does it look like once you have done it?

A rather surprising recent discovery is that, in terms of physiological functioning, a hypnotic state is much more similar to a waking state than to a sleep state. EEG waves are typically alpha; respiration and heart rate may be those of deep relaxation, but may also be those of strenuous physical activity. The single most striking feature of a hypnotic state is the willingness of subjects to do what is asked, and the indifference and matter-of-factness that accompany even the most bizarre behaviors requested of them (see Figure 3.12). This, however, does not mean that hypnotized subjects will do anything that is asked of them. That people under hypnosis will do nothing they would not do while fully conscious, that no behaviors that go against fundamental

---

BOX 3.3

Hypnopaedia

Considerable research has been conducted in Russia and more recently in other countries, including the United States, concerning the possibility of learning while sleeping. Since brain activity does not cease during sleep, and since a sleeping individual does not become totally insensitive to the environment, it would appear reasonable to suppose that certain forms of learning would be possible while one is sleeping. In fact, an impressive assortment of learn-while-you-sleep tapes have been put on the market, the majority of them promising that you can learn a foreign language effortlessly while in the arms of Morpheus or in whoever else's arms you choose to do your learning.

S. Rubin (1968) reports a large number of studies that have attempted to validate claims made on behalf of hypnopaedia (sleep learning in its impressive Latin-derived disguise). Most of these studies are of extremely poor quality, offering very little substantive evidence that sleep learning is effective or even possible. Balkhasov (1968) taped thirty Italian lessons and listened to each of these seven or eight times between six and seven in the morning, presumably while asleep although there is no way of verifying this. He reports that some six months later he could competently translate articles published in Italian medical journals. The experiment is described as "a personal experiment"; no impartial investigator was involved. A number of other similar studies are reported where the

experimenter is at once the subject, the evaluator, and the person who prepares the tapes. It is clear that no conclusions can be based on the type of evidence that might result from these studies. Other investigations, such as the German Experiment described by Rubin (1968, p. 237), provide no controls for whether the subjects were in fact asleep. Only two subjects were employed in the German Experiment. One of them recalled having heard parts of the tape while presumably asleep; the other did not fall asleep until the tape had been played through in its entirety.

Studies that have taken steps to ensure that subjects were asleep have found no evidence of learning. In one study, the material was no more complex than ten taped words repeated eighty-two times. Upon awakening, subjects were asked to select these ten words from a list of fifty, but could not do so (Emmons & Simon, 1956). Subsequently, the New York attorney general banned the advertising of a "sleep-learning" language-teaching machine. He argued that there was no evidence to substantiate the contention that a language could be learned while the learner was asleep (*Consumer Reports*, 1970).

A number of studies with apparently better controls, however, do seem to indicate that some learning is possible through hypnopaedia (Curtis, 1960). Typically, although subjects are apparently incapable of remembering whatever it is they were taught while asleep, they then learn the material slightly more rapidly than if it hasn't been presented hypnopaedically. Perhaps the most valid, though tentative, conclusion to be drawn from sleep-learning studies is that although there is no evidence that immediately demonstrable learning occurs during sleep, learning may subsequently be facilitated.

a

b

Figure 3.12 Many misconceptions surround hypnosis, partly owing to years of demonstrations of bizarre activity on stage (**a**). The practice originated in the late eighteenth century with a Viennese physician, Anton Mesmer, from whom the original name *Mesmerism* was derived. Only within the past few decades has it become a serious focus of psychological research (**b**).

moral or religious beliefs can be elicited from these subjects has been firmly and frequently contended. Still, no research can easily be directed toward proving this. For obvious ethical reasons, it would not be advisable to conduct research where individuals are compelled, through hypnosis, to perform acts that they would otherwise find highly immoral. Certainly the extent to which a hypnotized individual will engage in such extreme behaviors as rape or murder cannot easily be investigated directly.

Nevertheless, a number of investigations have looked at the extent to which hypnotized subjects will engage in less extreme forms of antisocial behavior. In some earlier studies, Rowland (1939) and Young (1952) found that their hypnotized subjects would throw what they believed to be nitric acid into the face of a research assistant and pick up a poisonous snake barehanded. (What they threw was water, and they were stopped before they actually touched the snake.) Orne and Evans (1965) replicated these studies and found very similar results. Their hypnotized subjects would indeed throw "nitric acid" into an assistant's face and would approach a poisonous snake with no apparent fear. Interestingly, however, a second group of six subjects who had not been hypnotized but who had been asked to behave as though they were hypnotized (described as *simulators*) willingly engaged in the same acts. Since subjects who are *not* hypnotized will perform antisocial acts, demonstrating that those who are hypnotized will engage in the same behaviors does not provide evidence that hypnosis gives the hypnotist a degree or kind of control that stems from hypnosis alone. Nevertheless, it is clear that people under hypnosis can often be made to perform dangerous acts. The fact that the same thing can happen under other circumstances may be irrelevant.

A second characteristic of the hypnotic state is that the experiences of that state are direct products of the individual's mind. In other words, the hypnotist cannot elicit feelings that might correspond to experiences totally new to the subject. Pearce (1971) writes of the Russian, Vasiliev, and his experiments with hypnotized peasants who were administered fake mustard plasters. Those peasants who had never been subjected to mustard plasters and who knew nothing about them didn't react. Those who had received real plasters earlier in their lives developed rashes, blisters, and itches, and sweated copiously. Once the first group of subjects had been awakened and mustard plasters had been explained to them, they could then be rehypnotized and would produce the characteristic rashes and perspiration.

By the same token, hypnosis cannot give an individual superhuman powers. Although it is true that stage hypnotists have frequently moved subjects to exhibit tremendous feats of strength, these are not feats that could not be performed under normal circumstances given proper motivation. Hypnosis does provide great motivation—an overwhelming desire to do whatever is required. What is involved, essentially, is heightened suggestibility. Suggestibility is a characteristic of a hypnotic state wherein subjects become exceedingly ready to believe whatever is *suggested* by the hypnotist, and willing to perform whatever activities are asked of them. If I told you now that your left leg had fallen off, you probably wouldn't believe me. In fact, you might not even check to make sure that I was incorrect. If, however, you allowed me to hypnotize you before I made that suggestion, you would in all probability believe me. You would also believe me if I told you that you had three legs. You, my friend, would simply be incredibly suggestible. It's not something to be ashamed of; we are all quite suggestible, although we vary in that respect. Certain tests of suggestibility commonly employed prior to hypnosis are described later.

Most people can be hypnotized. Estimates are that only 5 percent of the population cannot be (Petrel-Petrelevicius, 1975), this 5 percent consisting of the mentally defective, infants, and those who refuse. As is well understood now, you cannot be hypnotized against your will, although if certain drugs are employed first, your will may not be so opposed. In addition, ease of conditionability and depth of hypnosis vary widely for different individuals, as well as for the same individual at different times.

Behavior under Hypnosis

As was mentioned earlier, a hypnotic state closely resembles a waking state except for the extreme suggestibility of the subject and a strong desire to comply with the wishes of the hypnotist. Under these conditions, an interesting range of behavior, including catalepsis, anesthesia, hallucinations, amnesia, age regression, and posthypnotic action, can be induced in the subject by appropriate instructions (Kihlstrom, 1979). These phenomena are what has made hypnotism so attractive as stage entertainment. Catalepsis (or **catalepsy**) implies rigidity or inability to exercise conscious control over motor movements. It is strikingly illustrated when a subject is made to lie rigid, suspended foot and neck on the backs of two chairs. Although this act appears difficult, it can be performed by most individuals in a waking state (Meeker & Barber, 1971).

Anesthesia is lack of sensation and is possible even in a relatively light **trance** (see Table 3.1). It has been most dramatically illustrated in instances where the hypnotist suggests to the subject that one hand can feel no pain—that it is as though there were an iron glove over that hand. The hypnotist then nonchalantly sticks a pin deep

Catalepsy A state in which the body adopts a rigid, immobile position in which it may remain for a considerable period. It is occasionally a symptom of some mental disorders and is also possible in some of the deeper states of hypnosis.

Anesthesia Loss of sensitivity to stimulation. Anesthesia is often induced through drugs for surgical reasons and may also be a characteristic of a hypnotic state.

Trance A state that is sleeplike in that it involves altered consciousness. Characteristics of the trance might include loss of contact with the immediate environment and a reduction or loss of the ability to act voluntarily. The term is frequently employed as a synonym for hypnotic states as well as for the results of profound religious or mystical experiences.

Table 3.1 Stages and Symptoms of Hypnosis

Depth	Degree	Obtainable Symptoms (with appropriate suggestions)
Not hypnotized	0	
	1	
	2	Relaxation
	3	Fluttering of eyelids
	4	Closing of eyes
	5	Complete physical relaxation
Light trance	6	Inability to open eyes
	7	Inability to move limbs
	10	Total body catalepsy (body rigidity)
	11	Gloved anesthesia (insensitivity to pain in hand)
Medium trance	13	Partial amnesia
	15	Posthypnotic amnesia
	17	Assumption of different personality
	18	Simple posthypnotic suggestions
	20	Total amnesia
Deep trance	21	Ability to open eyes without breaking trance
	23	Posthypnotic illusions
	25	Ability to walk without breaking trance
	26	Pleasant posthypnotic hallucinations (visual)
	27	Pleasant posthypnotic hallucinations (auditory)
	30	Unpleasant (negative) visual or auditory hallucinations

into the hand; the subject neither winces nor faints, but, in fact, denies all pain. Physiological measures taken during controlled demonstrations of anesthesia indicate, however, that muscular tension and brain-wave activity do correspond to pain. In other words, although the subject may not consciously be aware of pain, some part of the brain appears to recognize it (Hilgard, 1973, 1975). This particular feature of hypnosis has long been employed in medical and dental practice, although its use has never been extensive. Chambard (cited in Lassner, 1960), as far back as 1881, employed hypnosis in childbirth.

Age regression also presents an interesting phenomenon that has quite frequently been employed in psychotherapy. Subjects in a deep trance are asked to return to a time when they were much younger and to act as they did then, or to describe what transpired on given days in their past. Many of these subjects can describe in impressively overwhelming detail events that would ordinarily be presumed to have been forgotten, a fact that has led many psychologists to believe that we never forget anything, but simply can't ordinarily remember a lot of things. Hypnosis might provide a key to the memories of our stored experiences; then again it might not. Orne (1951) conducted a series of experiments with a number of college students who were hypnotized and asked to describe their sixth birthdays. Although students responded in great and intricate detail, when compared with actual records, some of which were obtained directly from parents, their responses were found to be as much fiction as fact. One subject who had spoken only German at the time of his sixth birthday forgot this fact and reported the birthday as though it had taken place in English. When Orne reminded him that he could speak only German, he reverted to a childlike imitation of German and spoke no more English until the session was complete. Following these and similar studies, Orne has concluded that much of what is observed during hypnosis is the result of clever role-playing. Be that as it may, it remains true that hypnotized subjects willingly undergo experiences to which they would not subject themselves without some powerful incentive.

Posthypnotic suggestions are commands given to the subject while in a trance, but whose effects do not become apparent until some time after the trance is over.

Age regression A process where subjects are asked in a hypnotic state to return to an earlier period and to relive or describe events and experiences that occurred during that period.

Posthypnotic suggestion A command given to the subject, not after the hypnotic trance is over, but during the trance. The suggestion is *post*hypnotic in that it relates to activities the subject is being asked to engage in after the trance. When subjects are given a definite time span after which they must perform the commanded activity, the posthypnotic act typically takes place at almost exactly the appointed time, in spite of the fact that subjects do not appear to be conscious beforehand that they will feel impelled to perform the activity.

For example, a hypnotist may suggest to a subject that ten minutes after he is awakened, he will become unbearably warm and begin to remove his outer clothing. The subject will of course comply—at least up to a point. It is up to the hypnotist to provide additional posthypnotic suggestions relating to when the warmth will cease and the clothes can be put back on.

Subjects who are told, while under the influence of hypnosis, that they will remember nothing of what has transpired during the session, do in fact appear to remember nothing, a state of selective **amnesia**. The testimony of a large number of apparently reputable people who have been hypnotized makes it unlikely that this form of amnesia is the result of role-playing. Nor is the type of control over physiological functioning that is required for the production of heat rashes and perspiration likely to result from the simple decision on the part of subjects that they are going to "play the role."

Amnesia Sudden and temporary loss of memory for no apparent organic reason. Amnesia may take a variety of forms and is sometimes associated with mental disorders. In hypnosis, amnesia can be induced in subjects if they are told they will remember nothing of what transpired while in a hypnotic state.

Hallucinations are also readily obtained in hypnotic trances, and are used extensively for the amusement of those who pay to observe the antics of others in the hands of a stage hypnotist.

Suggestibility

We do not know why, but we are not all equally susceptible to hypnosis. As was mentioned earlier, some 5 percent of the population cannot be hypnotized, the majority of this group being made up of the mentally retarded, infants, and those who are unwilling. Suggestibility, a crude measure of the likelihood that you can be hypnotized and of the ease with which this can be accomplished, appears to be linked with age, though not with sex. That is, men and women appear to be approximately equally suggestible. Very young infants are not demonstrably suggestible prior to their acquisition of language. Suggestibility apparently increases rather dramatically beginning around the age of six, reaches its peak between eight and ten, declines between ten and fourteen, and remains relatively stable at least until the early twenties (Barber, 1969).

Suggestibility, defined as an unconscious willingness to please or to follow instructions (Petrel-Petrelevicius, 1975), can be assessed in a number of ways. The better-known susceptibility scales are the Stanford Hypnotic Susceptibility Scales and the Stanford Profile Scales developed by Weitzenhoffer and Hilgard (1959, 1962, 1967). These incorporate a number of the suggestibility tests commonly employed by stage hypnotists. The most familiar of these include the body-sway test and the hand-clasp test. In the first test, the hypnotist has the subject stand before him, back turned, with eyes either closed or fixed on some point on the ceiling. The hypnotist then places his hands on the subject's shoulders and informs him that these appendages are, in effect, powerful magnets that will draw him backward when they are removed. These instructions are repeated a number of times, the subject is assured that he will be caught as he begins to fall, and the hands are removed. A good subject (that is, a highly suggestible subject) will in fact lose his balance and fall backward at this point.

The hand-clasp test requires that subjects clasp their hands tightly together. It is particularly useful in stage presentations of hypnosis since it can be employed to eliminate a large number of less suggestible subjects at one time. The hypnotist informs these subjects that as he counts (or sings, or plays, or talks), their hands will become welded together more and more tightly, and that when a certain number has been reached, they will not be able to tear their hands apart no matter how hard they try. Again, highly suggestible subjects now find it impossible to separate their hands, whereas those less suggestible are returned to their seats to serve as amusees rather than amusers.

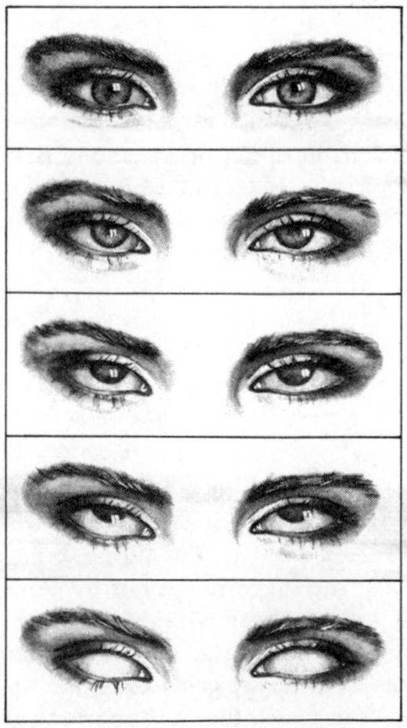

Figure 3.13 Eye-rolling ability has been found to relate to suggestibility. (From Spiegel, H. The Hypnotic Induction Profile (HIP): A review of its development. *Annals of the New York Academy of Sciences,* 1979, *296,* p. 130.)

Another test for assessing suggestibility, labeled the *Hypnotic Induction Profile* (HIP) and developed by Spiegel (1974, 1979), is based largely on the subject's ability to roll the eyes upward (see Figure 3.13). Why eye-rolling ability should be related to hypnotizability is not at all clear, although research suggests that the test is useful (Eliseo, 1974). And why anyone would have thought of using eye-rolling ability as a measure of suggestibility in the first place might seem strange as well. Clinical psychologists who had been employing hypnosis in therapy frequently came across patients who were difficult or impossible to hypnotize; they also noticed that patients with eye-rolling ability were easier to hypnotize, and so began investigating the connection (Spiegel, 1972).

Although tests of suggestibility might be useful, particularly in therapeutic situations, suggestibility is not a fixed personality characteristic, measurable and unchanging in each individual. In fact it varies a great deal, depending on the subject, the hypnotist, the relationship between the two, and the immediate environment (Bowers, 1976) (see Box 3.4). It can also be affected by drugs. Chemically induced or facilitated hypnotic trances can be brought about with various anesthetics (for example, chloroform or sodium pentathol) administered in small doses, and even through the use of barbiturates. Their effectiveness is probably due largely to the relaxation they bring about.

Hypnosis: Real or Faked?

Attempts to establish that hypnosis represents a "real" state of consciousness have often taken the form of demonstrations that subjects behave differently under hypnosis than they would in a normal waking state. In fact, however, most of the

---

BOX 3.4

Hypnotic Techniques

There are a number of widely accepted and practiced methods of inducing hypnotic trances. I will describe one in some detail, and several only in passing. I should caution you that these are not recipes for party games; they can be the toys of charlatans and quacks. Hypnosis can be, and has been, abused by the unscrupulous and by the semi-ignorant. A little ignorance may be considerably more dangerous than a lot.

Hypnotism by fascination is rather fascinating. You've seen it in your childhood comic strips and cartoon shows. The hypnotist stares into the subject's eyes, perhaps raising two fingers in the manner of a fallen peace sign, pointing these digits flamboyantly and devastatingly at the eyes of the subject. Zap! Perhaps, but not usually, unless the subject is very highly susceptible or the procedure is employed as the result of a posthypnotic suggestion.

The swinging-pendulum technique, employed extensively in nineteenth-century France and Germany, and often depicted in graphic portrayals of psychoanalysts plying their trades, involves the fixation of attention by means of a moving object. It is not the pendulum, the gold watch on its heavy chain, that induces the trance, but the words that accompany the swinging.

In what Chertok (1961) labels the *fixed-object technique,* the subject is asked to stare at a fixed point, perhaps a thumbtack on a wall, while the hypnotist repeatedly suggests progressive relaxation, fatigue, sleepiness, warmth, drowsiness, and eventual sleep. The word *sleep* is used in most hypnotic sessions simply as a metaphor for a state that appears to be some distance removed from real sleep. There is no way of describing it more accurately to the peasants who flock upon the hypnotist's stage. Besides, sleep is close enough.

The technique that I first learned is, according to Chertok, over ninety years old. It is perhaps the most common and the easiest, and has sometimes been referred to as the method of "fractional relaxation." The subject is asked to close her eyes. The hypnotist might then proceed in a manner similar to this: "I want you to relax. Just listen to my voice and relax. You are growing very tired. Very sleepy. So tired. Imagine your feet. You can feel them growing limp and warm and heavy. Your feet are limp and warm and heavy. You are completely relaxed, and warm and sleepy. Relax. Your feet are limp and warm. Sleepy. You can feel the drowsiness moving up your legs. Your whole body feels warm and sleepy. You are very drowsy. You want to go to sleep. Let yourself go to sleep. Sleep. Warm and loose and heavy. You are tired and drowsy. Your feet and legs are warm and limp and completely relaxed and your thighs and hips are warm and limp. You can feel the drowsiness moving up your body. You want to go into a deep, deep sleep. Deep, deep sleep."

Et cetera, et cetera. The hypnotist continues in this vein, progressively relaxing the subject's body, moving upward beyond her chest, down each of the arms, relaxing hands and fingers, and finally paying considerable attention to the neck and face. Depth of the trance can be ascertained at any time by reference to the symptoms described in Table 3.1. Gloved anesthesia, body catalepsy, and so on can be suggested (usually repeated a number of times) to the subject and appropriate tests carried out to check for the extent to which the subject is able to respond to these suggestions.

Awakening the subject is as simple as telling her that she will awaken upon a given signal (a dramatic and impressive snap of the fingers, a mundane count to three, or whatever). Before being awakened, the subject will ordinarily be given posthypnotic suggestions relating to how well she will feel, or to the fact that she will no longer wish to smoke, eat excessively, or engage in other habits she might wish to be rid of. Other posthypnotic suggestions might relate to whether or not the events of the session will be remembered, or to future hypnotic sessions. It is possible, for example, to establish a posthypnotic suggestion whereby the subject, if willing, will immediately fall into a deep hypnotic trance whenever the hypnotist says a specific word or phrase. Similarly, it is possible to transfer the subject from one hypnotist to another simply by means of suggestion.

behavior evident during hypnosis can be shown by an intelligent individual who is determined to deceive the hypnotist or to cooperate in deceiving an audience. And the argument, made earlier in this chapter, that subjects under the influence of hypnosis will often engage in behaviors and suffer indignities and pain that they would not normally allow themselves to experience, really offers little proof in that direction.

A number of recent studies offer much more convincing evidence that a hypnotic state is both genuine and different from a normal waking state. In most of these studies, investigators make use of simulators—individuals who have been instructed in some of the characteristics of hypnosis, and who are asked to pretend that they are hypnotized. Simulators are often told that the hypnotist will not be aware of which subjects are really hypnotized and which are merely faking. Thus, simulators serve as experimental controls. Evidence of the genuineness of the hypnotic trance has been found primarily in differences between simulators and real subjects.

An experiment that is particularly relevant in this connection was conducted by F. J. Evans and Orne (1971). In a previous investigation, they had found that if the proceedings are interrupted indefinitely while the subject is being hypnotized, or after the subject has already been hypnotized, the hypnotic state will continue for some time, but will eventually disappear completely. In that experiment (Orne & Evans, 1966), subjects were hypnotized by means of instructions recorded on tape. Arrangements were made for a power failure to occur just before the termination of the session. Thus, after subjects were hypnotized, the tape recorder suddenly stopped playing, the lights went off, and the experimenter went quickly from the room muttering "the damn fuse." Subjects were then observed through a one-way mirror for the next thirty minutes. After approximately twenty minutes, all hypnotized subjects were fully awake and remained alert and inquisitive when the experimenter returned. In contrast, simulators remained in their trancelike state for the full thirty minutes.

The findings might have been puzzling, given the expectation that once the simulators were no longer being observed, they would return to a more normal state. In this case, however, the one-way mirror might well have indicated to simulators that they were being observed, that the power failure was an experimental ruse, and that they should continue to behave as though they were still in a hypnotic state. A second study examined this interpretation. In this study (Evans & Orne, 1971) the two-way mirror was covered and observation was accomplished by means of an unobtrusive aperture in a silk-screen print on one wall. Real subjects continued to behave much as they had originally, coming out of the state in fifteen or twenty minutes, and being awake and alert when the experimenter returned. Simulators behaved very differently. They ceased to pretend almost as soon as the experimenter left the room. But when they heard him returning after thirty minutes, they at once returned to their simulated hypnotic states.

Additional evidence that a hypnotic trance represents a truly altered state of consciousness may be found in studies of pain. Hypnotized individuals who are told that they will feel no pain, even when subjected to what might otherwise be painful (a pinprick, for example), will report no pain (see Figure 3.14). As indicated earlier, measures of physiological change indicate clearly that the pain is being felt at some level.

In an ingenious set of experiments, investigators have succeeded in obtaining actual reports of pain from hypnotized subjects who had been told they would feel no pain (Hilgard, 1973; Knox et al., 1974). Subjects were told that a part of them (dubbed the "hidden observer") was aware of everything that went on in their bodies, and that the hypnotist would have access to the hidden observer whenever he touched the subject on the shoulder. During the experiment, subjects were exposed to severe pain (for example, placing the hand in ice water, or stopping blood flow to the hand by means of a tourniquet, and then requiring the subject to exercise the hand). Their verbal reports of pain indicated that they felt very little discomfort; but when touched on the shoulders they suddenly reported very high levels of pain. Subjects later reported

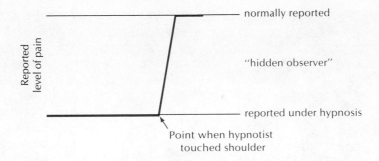

Reported level of pain

normally reported

"hidden observer"

reported under hypnosis

↑ Point when hypnotist touched shoulder

Figure 3.14 Under conditions that most people would consider extremely painful (holding the hand in ice water or applying a tourniquet to cut off blood circulation to the hand, then releasing the tourniquet and exercising the hand), subjects under hypnosis reported little or no discomfort—until the hypnotist touched their shoulders in a prearranged signal to their "hidden observer." Still under hypnosis, at this point they were able to report very high levels of pain.

that they sensed two parts of themselves: a hypnotized part that was quite unaware of pain, and another part that was equally aware of pain. Evidence is convincing that hypnotized subjects do not consciously experience pain under conditions of anesthesia, but that some aspect of their selves (termed a *dissociated self* by Hilgard, 1977) is aware of the pain.

Hypnosis and Learning

Can hypnosis make learning easier? Research results remain unclear. A number of studies have apparently demonstrated that learning, motivation, and retention can be improved as a result of posthypnotic suggestion. Henderson (1968), for example, reports a study conducted by Parrish involving two classes in a child development course. One class was hypnotized and told that they would have little difficulty in understanding and remembering a lecture; the other was not hypnotized and knew nothing of the competitive nature of the experiment. Both classes were then presented with identical lectures and tested on their understanding and retention of lecture material. The hypnotized class performed **significantly** better. Similarly, W. L. Fowler (1961) reports an experiment involving educational psychology classes where experimental subjects not only performed better, apparently as a function of hypnotic suggestion, but continued to report, some eighteen months later, greater ability to concentrate, increased understanding, faster reading, and better memories.

A number of studies, however, have failed to find any differences between experimental groups and control groups, particularly when control groups are highly motivated. It seems that hypnosis can be very effective in increasing motivation, but that it does not, per se, increase intelligence and its manifestations. There is virtually no evidence that it has any harmful effects.

Significant Better than would be expected by chance. The term *significant* in research refers to findings that cannot be accounted for solely by chance factors. Such findings are usually interpreted to mean that the independent variables have a real effect on the dependent variables.

Meditation

Sleeping, waking, and hypnosis are all referred to as natural states. That is, there is nothing mysterious or magical in them, nor do they result from chemical changes brought about through the use of drugs. Are the **meditative** states also natural? Are they supernatural rather than unnatural? Are they real? What is real? Is that which is in your mind real? Does a transcendental state, one which by definition transcends the bounds of ordinary sensory or perceptual experience, exist only in the mind? Would that make it unreal? (See Figure 3.15.)

Qualities of a Mystical Experience

Accept, first, that the chief goal of all meditative techniques, quite apart from any other tangible or intangible benefits they might have, is the attainment of a mystical experience. Words are miserable beggars in their attempts to describe these experiences. That, of course, is as it should be, for if an experience truly transcended the boundaries of your small sphere of reality—actually cracked your "cosmic egg"—you

Meditation A process or state involving serious contemplation or thought, typically with the object of achieving a mystical experience. A wide variety of processes is involved, many of them with little in common. Zen and yoga are traditional meditative techniques.

would have no words to describe it. You could only sputter gibberish. Yes, the most meaningful thing you could say is, "You will have to experience it yourself." But we Westerners want to know what it is that we have to experience. We want you to describe it to us, masters of Zen, of Zazen, of yoga. (See Figure 3.16.)

Deikman (1966a) tried. He described five features of the mystical experience, the first of which is *realness*. Although those who experience states that transcend our ordinary realities cannot easily describe them, cannot show them to us, cannot point to them and say, "See, there is an example of what I mean," they are overwhelmingly convinced of the reality of their experience: "It is more real than thinking or talking."

Mystical experiences, says Deikman, also usually involve *unusual perceptions*. These are perhaps best described by one of Deikman's (1966b) subjects who was involved in an investigation of the effects of meditation:

> *Shortly I began to sense motion and shifting of light and dark as this became stronger and stronger. Now when this happens it's happening not only in my vision but it's happening or it feels like a physical kind of thing. It's connected with feelings of attraction, expansion, absorption and suddenly my vision pinpointed on a particular place and . . . I was in the grip of a very powerful sensation and this became the center. (p. 109)*

Subjects in this experiment were asked to concentrate on a blue vase for increasing periods of time (a maximum of fifteen minutes) during twelve sessions spread over three weeks. Instructions were to simply try and see the vase as it existed while excluding all other thoughts and feelings from the mind. Almost all subjects eventually reported altered perceptions of the vase as well as changes in their own personal feelings (Deikman, 1963).

Another characteristic of the mystical experience Deikman described is *unity*. The widely accepted hallmark of the true mystical experience is a realization of a sense of oneness—with the universe, with the self, with whatever it is with which we are one. I can't describe the feeling.

Ineffability, or more simply the inability to describe what has been perceived or felt, is yet another striking characteristic of a mystical experience. This should be obvious from the preceding passages.

Figure 3.16 Instead of the more rigid and demanding techniques of yoga and Zen (or Zazen), millions of people have learned Transcendental Meditation techniques in attempts to achieve altered states of consciousness.

The final characteristic described by Deikman relates to the last two: a mystical experience involves *transsensate phenomena*. This simply means that mystical experiences go beyond ordinary sensation; they transcend. In short, they are transcendental.

The Promise Examined

Some Oriental religions promise their more devout and dedicated practitioners health and peace, creative energy and purpose, tranquility and joy, serenity and long life, wisdom and selflessness. Whether their followers attain these qualities cannot easily be measured. But the physiological changes that occur in meditative states can be measured, and do serve as an index of their effectiveness.

Wallace and Benson (1972) conducted a controlled investigation designed partly to assess the truthfulness of the many previously reported studies of physiological functioning among Zen and yoga masters. The most frequently replicated finding from these studies is that brain-wave activity and respiration rate sometimes change dramatically, particularly among those most skilled in attaining the meditative trance (for example, Kasamatsu & Hirai, 1966). For their study, Wallace and Benson selected thirty-six subjects who had been trained in Transcendental Meditation and who had been

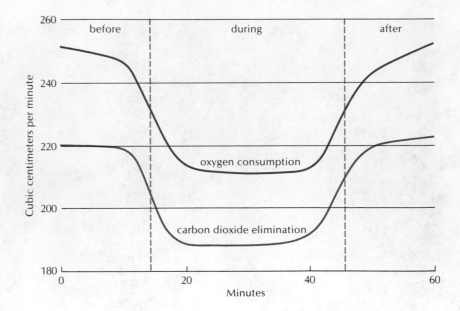

practicing their training for an average of two to three years. Physiological measures were obtained before meditation sessions, during the sessions, and after the sessions. Figure 3.17 presents some of their findings. Most striking were the following: Oxygen consumption decreased dramatically during meditation, as did the elimination of carbon dioxide; respiration rate was significantly reduced; alpha rhythms predominated (corresponding to a highly relaxed state or to sleep); there was an increase in the skin's resistance to electricity (technically, a decrease in galvanic skin response—GSR—thought to indicate anxiety or arousal when resistance is low); and there was a marked reduction in blood lactate (also probably indicating anxiety and tension when high).

In short, the physiological evidence points toward the *possibility* that meditative techniques can sometimes provide a form of control over physiological functions that have until now been considered under the direction solely of the autonomic nervous system and various glands. (See Box 3.5).

Biofeedback

The meditative techniques are not the only methods that offer some promise of giving the individual control over autonomic functioning; **biofeedback** is another. The term *biofeedback* refers specifically to information (feedback) the individual receives about specific aspects of biological functioning like heart rate, blood vessel constriction or dilation, conductivity of the skin to electricity (GSR or electrodermal response), or electrical activity of the brain. Measuring electrical activity of the brain by means of "alpha recorders" has been the most popular biofeedback technique. Recall that alpha waves are a type of brain wave thought to be associated with relaxation, in contrast to beta waves, which are associated with more highly aroused states. The term **alpha state,** widely used in connection with various meditative techniques, exotic religions, drug-induced spaces, or mystical trances, refers specifically to the type of brain activity expected to result from methods designed to bring about relaxation.

Numerous early biofeedback experiments, some with animals and others with humans, apparently demonstrated that a subject can exercise some control over brain-wave activity without any specific training (Hart, 1968; Kamiya, 1968). A typical exper-

Biofeedback   The information we obtain about our biological functioning. In a more specialized sense, it refers to procedures whereby subjects are given information about physiological functioning that they would not ordinarily have with the object of achieving control over specific aspects of physiological functioning.

Alpha state   Literally a state of consciousness where brain waves are predominantly of the alpha variety, ordinarily associated with restful but waking states of consciousness. Therefore the expression *alpha state* is typically used to imply states of relaxation.

iment involves placing electrodes on appropriate parts of the subject's head in order to monitor brain waves and transforming the signals obtained into a tone corresponding to either the presence or absence of alpha waves, or simply to an increase in alpha relative to beta. The subject is then asked to experiment with the apparatus in an attempt to produce the tone as much as possible (if it represents alpha) or to keep it off (if it represents absence of alpha).

In one experiment, Knowlis and Kamiya (1970) paid twenty-six college students two dollars each to participate in an experiment on learning how to control brain waves. The experimental procedure was much as just described. Electrodes were attached to the subjects so that they would receive immediate auditory feedback for the presence of alpha waves. They were then instructed to keep the tone on as much as they could. In a later stage of the experiment, they were asked to keep the tone off. Many subjects were successful. A similar experiment conducted by B. B. Brown (1970) employed a light bulb that was turned on and glowed more brightly as brain-wave activity decelerated; here, too, results were highly positive (see Figure 3.18).

More recent studies with biofeedback have not always replicated earlier findings (see N. E. Miller, 1978). Perhaps more important, it has been found that eye movements can produce changes in the electrical field that block input to an ordinary alpha recorder (Hardt & Kamiya, 1976). In other words, apparent control of alpha waves in a biofeedback experiment may result from changes in eye movement rather than from actual changes in brain activity. In much the same way, control of heart rate has sometimes been found to be an artifact of other behaviors. Anand and Chhina (1961) examined yogis who claimed to be able to stop their hearts. Indeed, an ordinary

BOX 3.5

Meditative Techniques

In a highly popular book entitled *The Relaxation Response,* Benson argues that all successful forms of meditation have very similar results—specifically, a *relaxation response.* To the extent that this observation is valid, it follows that meditation should have many of the beneficial effects that relaxation has, and that it might, for example, lead to a reduction in blood pressure and to a lessening of anxiety. There is, in fact, some evidence that this is the case (Benson, 1975; Hassett, 1978).

Many of us incorrectly assume that the benefits of meditation are available only to those who have devoted a large part of their lives to mastering the sometimes difficult and demanding meditative techniques of mysterious Oriental religions. Not so. Transcendental Meditation, for example, although it is based on ancient yogic techniques, requires little training and little personal sacrifice. Essentially, it is a Westernized form of yoga developed and popularized by the Maharishi Mahesh Yogi and thousands of his followers. Like yoga, it makes use of a word or sound called a mantra, one of the more popular examples of which is the sound *Ohmmm.* The mantra used in Transcendental Meditation is given privately to the meditator at the time of training, and remains secret. Essentially, it is a meaningless, nondistracting sound that the meditator repeats mentally during a fifteen- or twenty-minute period each morning and evening. During this period of meditation, the individual is asked to sit quietly and comfortably where distractions

are unlikely, and to make no effort to *concentrate* on the mantra or on any other thought. As thoughts appear unbidden, the meditator simply ignores them, returning quietly to the mantra.

In contrast to Transcendental Meditation, Zen meditation advocates *focused* concentration on a specific question, called a koan and exemplified in questions such as "What is life?" A single koan can sometimes serve as a focus of meditation for years. Other forms of meditation require the meditator to focus attention on some external stimulus such as a candle's flame or, in some Oriental religions, an abstract symbol called a mandala.

For those unwilling or unable to devote the time and energy required to learn Zen, yoga, or even Transcendental Meditation, there are simple forms of meditation that might have very similar benefits. For example, Benson (1977) provides instructions for a form of meditation highly similar to Transcendental Meditation. These instructions can be summarized as follows.

Once or twice a day (but always more than two hours *after* the last meal), sit comfortably in a chair, feet on the floor, eyes closed, and hands loosely on your lap. Begin by attempting to relax your muscles, starting with your feet and progressing deliberately upward to your face. Breathe deeply, slowly, and consciously, repeating the number *one* mentally every time you exhale. Continue this process, uninterrupted, for a twenty-minute period, opening your eyes only to check the time. Don't be alarmed if distracting thoughts enter your mind during meditation. Simply ignore them and continue to repeat the number *one.* After the twenty-minute period, relax for a few minutes before continuing with your other activities.

If you try these simple instructions, do not expect dramatic insights, radical alterations of consciousness, or spiritual ecstasy. But you might be justified in expecting that some of the benefits of relaxation will occur in time.

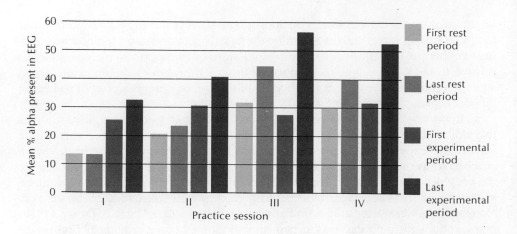

Figure 3.18 How easily can normal people learn to exercise control over their own brain waves? In experiments like Brown's a light bulb glowed more brightly whenever the subject's brain waves decelerated. As the diagram shows, the feedback worked, and the subjects' brain waves did slow down to the alpha state. Even in controlled experiments like this, though, the results may not be as clear-cut as they seem. It was recently shown that changes in eye movements can affect alpha-wave recordings. Did the feedback from the light bulb mechanism affect the subjects' state of consciousness or merely the recording device? (Based on data from B. B. Brown, 1970.)

stethoscope failed to find any evidence of heartbeat in these subjects. An electrocardiogram recording, however, revealed that the heart was beating even faster than normal. What had happened, in effect, was that the yogis had learned to control pressure in the thoracic cavity and were able to shut off the return of blood to the heart, thereby eliminating the characteristic noise of the heartbeat.

Other related research has found that blood pressure and heart rate can be controlled through subtle muscular movements, or sometimes through changes in breathing (Levenson, 1976). Accordingly, studies that have demonstrated the *learning* of blood-pressure or heart-rate control might, in fact, be demonstrating control over muscular responses which then affect autonomic functioning.

In our earlier discussion of alpha waves and meditation, we assumed that alpha corresponds to relaxed states. Although this assumption is probably valid for most individuals, it cannot be generalized as an absolute principle of human functioning. N. E. Miller (1978) cites research that indicates that, for some individuals, alpha states are perceived as unpleasant. In addition, the finding that eye movements can block the functioning of an alpha recorder, making it *seem* as though the individual had achieved control over brain-wave activity, raises serious questions about the sorts of changes that might be occurring in various meditative states.

The application of biofeedback procedures in medicine (for alleviating tension, migraine headaches, insomnia, high blood pressure, heart irregularities, and so on) has tremendous, but largely unproven, potential. N. E. Miller (1978) suggests that research in this field should proceed as it does in drug research, through three phases: (1) pilot studies, which determine whether there are any effects worth investigating, and which attempt to identify practical problems and undesirable effects; (2) controlled comparisons, where new treatments are compared with other treatments or with placebos (procedures where patients are duped into believing that they are receiving an effective treatment when in fact they are receiving nothing but the conviction that they are being treated); and (3) clinical trials with large samples, long-term follow-up studies, and ordinary practitioners (in contrast to enthusiastic researchers). Miller contends that most biofeedback research has been at the first phase (pilot studies that have shown some promise), and that it is now time to move to the second phase before reaching unwarranted generalizations or attempting indiscriminate, wide-scale applications of techniques that are still highly experimental, and whose effects are still a subject for debate. Can those people who suffer from anxiety neuroses learn to relax by means of biofeedback? Can high blood pressure be reduced? Can nonrhythmic heart action be made rhythmic again? We may know tomorrow.

Drugs

Sleeping and waking are natural states of consciousness, which we each regularly and predictably experience. Hypnosis and the various meditative techniques represent attempts to alter these states, the alteration seldom being very violent. There is yet another means of altering consciousness, a means that is sometimes highly dramatic: **drugs.**

History

Did you know that Chief Sitting Bull mixed marijuana with tobacco in his peace pipe (Leander, 1967)? Perhaps he knew that marijuana would pacify his enemies. Did you know that the English word *assassin* may have originated from an Arabian group of murderers who called themselves *hashashi* and used marijuana prior to committing murder? And that the term *hashish* is also derived from this group of murderers (Thompson, 1975)?

Drugs are clearly not new. Alcohol was common in biblical times. Opium was supposedly known to the Sumerians in 5000 B.C. (Jalkanen, 1973). Marijuana is said to have been included in the legendary Emperor Shen Nung's pharmacopoeia in 2737 B.C. (Blum and associates, 1970). Several thousand years ago *soma,* a drug from an unidentified plant, was in use in India (Osmond, 1964). When the Spaniards invaded Mexico, they found three varieties of psychedelic drugs in common use: ololiuqui, teonanacatl, and peyote. Peyote was also used by the North American Plains Indians (Osmond). In short, most of the naturally occurring drugs in use today have been known for centuries. Such is not the case for the synthetic drugs (uppers, downers, LSD, and so on), all of which were discovered recently.

Incidence

Drug abuse in the United States (excepting abuse of alcohol) was originally a lower-class phenomenon, largely relegated to the ghettoes of major cities and restricted primarily to Oriental and Caucasian groups. In time, an increasing number of blacks and Puerto Ricans came to be included in the expanding circle of **drug dependence** (Jalkanen, 1973). With the popularization of marijuana in the 1930s, the discovery of the hallucinogenic properties of LSD in 1943, and the rise of a number of self-appointed missionaries of the drug cult, the affluent middle class entered the drug scene. One conservative estimate is that well over 26 million Americans misuse drugs at the present time (Jalkanen). Countless surveys, some highly reliable and others highly suspect, have been undertaken in response to widespread alarm caused directly by this mushrooming drug scene.

Nicotine and alcohol continue to be among the most widely used drugs in spite of widespread and concerted efforts by health and government agencies to curb their use. Johnston (1973), in a survey of several thousand eighteen-year-olds, found that 30 percent of the males and 25 percent of the females smoked (nicotine). Percentages for young adults (ages eighteen to twenty-four) are much higher. The *National Survey on Drug Abuse* (1977) found that 47.3 percent of respondents had used nicotine in the preceding month; 70 percent had used alcohol. Cahalan, Cisin, and Crossley (1969) reported that in a study of adults (twenty-one and older) a striking 12 percent could be classified as heavy drinkers. Only 22 percent had never used alcohol. Here there were marked sex differences, with 21 percent of the men being heavy drinkers and only 5 percent of the women. In Cahalan's study, use of alcohol appeared to be closely related to cigarette-smoking. Among males, 38 percent of the abstainers smoked; 60 percent of the heavy drinkers smoked. The relationship for females was even more striking: 19 percent of the abstainers smoked; an overwhelming 81 percent of the heavy drinkers also smoked.

Drug   A chemical or organic substance that has one or more of a wide range of effects on the human body and nervous system. Drugs that are of principal interest in psychology are those that affect the nervous system.

Drug abuse   Refers primarily to the "recreational" use of drugs as opposed to the use of drugs for medical or psychiatric purposes. Drug abuse is classified as a disorder by the American Psychiatric Association because behaviors apparently resulting from drug use impair social or occupational functioning. Defined in this way, drug abuse stops short of drug dependence.

Drug dependence   Also a disorder as defined by the American Psychiatric Association. It results from repeated use of a drug in sufficient dosages that a strong desire to continue taking the drug develops.

Physiological dependence, frequently referred to as *addiction,* is a type of dependence in which the desire to continue taking a drug is partly or entirely organically based—that is, the body eventually becomes dependent upon the drug. Physiological dependence is characteristic of the "hard drugs"—for example, heroin, morphine, and codeine. After the individual has become physiologically dependent, cessation of drug use typically results in "withdrawal" symptoms.

Psychological dependence, sometimes referred to as *habituation,* is a strong, sometimes overwhelming, desire to continue using a drug, usually attributed to its psychological rather than its physiological effects. Drugs that relieve anxiety or that lead to euphoric (intensely happy) states may lead to psychological dependence even in the absence of physiological dependence.

Surveys of marijuana use have resulted in widely varying estimates of typical usage, probably because most of these studies necessarily involved either interviews or questionnaires. Since these are totally dependent on the honesty of respondents, and since admitting to drug use frequently amounts to admitting to a crime, there is some reason to doubt that all respondents would be equally honest. For example, Weil, Zinberg, and Nelson (1968) reported that they had extreme difficulty in finding "marijuana naive" subjects for an experiment in Boston, while Wozny (1971), in a large-scale investigation, found that only 21 percent of a university freshman class had tried marijuana at least once. Another 18 percent claimed that they would try it under the right circumstances; 61 percent claimed that they would not try it under any circumstances.

Berg and Broeker (1972) reviewed a large number of surveys of the extent of drug use. One of their striking findings related to the increase in marijuana usage between 1969 and 1972. Whereas only 22 percent of a college sample had tried marijuana in 1969, 42 percent had tried it one year later, and 51 percent another year after that. Similarly, use of hallucinogens had increased from 4 percent to 18 percent during the same period. One-time use of cocaine was 7 percent in this study; only 2 percent of the sample had tried heroin at least once. The authors point out, however, that there are indications that the extent of drug use peaked in the early seventies, and is now remaining stable or declining slightly. In contrast, surveys reviewed by McClothlin (1975) and by Hollander and McCurdy (1978) show no decline between 1968 and 1978, and present indications are that cocaine use, particularly among the affluent middle class, has recently increased.

Drugs Most Often Abused

Drugs most frequently abused in the Western world include alcohol, tobacco, marijuana, LSD, stimulants, barbiturates, opiates, and inhalants. Various classifications of these drugs have been offered, based on effects rather than on composition. There are the narcotics, addictive drugs that produce sensations of well-being; sedatives, such as tranquilizers and barbiturates; stimulants, such as the amphetamines; and the hallucinogenic drugs (also called psychedelic, psychomimetic, or psychoactive), such as LSD, mescaline, and PCP. Marijuana is also ordinarily classified as a hallucinogenic drug, although its effects are seldom as dramatic as those of LSD or mescaline (see Table 3.2).

Another frequently used classification is based on the distinction between "hard" and "soft" drugs. Included among hard drugs are those that lead to physiological dependence (in other words, are addictive). This simply means that the body adjusts to the drug and has to go through a more or less severe period of readjustment upon its withdrawal. Heroin is perhaps the best-known of the hard drugs. Soft drugs, by definition, are those that are not physiologically addictive; they may, however, lead to psychological dependence.

Marijuana A mildly hallucinogenic drug derived from the hemp plant *Cannabis sativa* and containing the active ingredient tetrahydrocannabinol (THC). Hash or hashish is derived from the same plant and contains the same active ingredient, but in a higher concentration.

Marijuana The drug **marijuana** is derived from the annual hemp plant *Cannabis sativa*. This plant grows in both male and female varieties. Popular opinion has held for some time that only the female plant produces the active ingredient in marijuana, tetrahydrocannabinol (THC). Research undertaken by the Ledain (1972) Commission indicates that this belief is incorrect. Both male and female forms of the plant contain THC, although there is frequently a higher concentration in the female. (See Figure 3.19.)

The physiological effects of marijuana include increased heart rate and blood pressure, a lowering of body temperature, and a subsequent tendency to sleep or rest. Subjective, psychological effects are more difficult to identify and describe. They appear to vary with a number of factors, the most important of which are the user's personality, past experience with marijuana and other drugs, present attitudes, and other immediate situational variables. Goode (1969) reports that the primary effect is a pleasant

Table 3.2 Classification of the Most Frequently Abused Drugs

Class	Examples
Narcotics	Opium Morphine Heroin Codeine Methadone
Sedatives (downers)	Barbiturates (Phenobarbitol, Seconal, Nembutal) Tranquilizers (Valium, Librium, Vivol) Alcohol
Stimulants (uppers)	Cocaine Amphetamines (Benzedrine, Dexedrine, Methedrine)
Hallucinogens (psychoactive, psychotropic, psychedelic, psychomimetic)	LSD Mescaline Psilocybin Marijuana PCP STP
Inhalants	Glue Paint thinner Aerosol sprays Solvents
Unclassified (or sometimes classified as stimulant)	Nicotine

emotional state related more to the "experience enhancement" effects of the drug than to the drug itself. In other words, marijuana is reported to enhance other activities such as eating, talking, listening to music, and making love. A number of controlled studies have not found any significant differences between users and nonusers with respect to their reported enjoyment of these same activities. Sorensen's (1973) investigation of the sexual behavior of adolescents revealed that the majority of the adolescents in that study did not think marijuana enhanced their sexual pleasure. Evidence suggests, in fact, that lower testosterone (a male sex hormone strongly implicated in sexual maturation and arousal) levels may be associated with heavy marijuana use (Kolodny et al., 1974).

The Ledain (1972) Commission's extensive review of literature related to the effects of Cannabis (marijuana and hashish) presents evidence of possible adverse reactions, cognitive changes, "peak" or transcendental experiences, and a wide variety of other subjective reactions. Among the positive reactions are

> *happiness, increased conviviality, a feeling of enhanced interpersonal rapport and communication, heightened sensitivity to humour, free play of the imagination, unusual cognitive and ideational associations, a sense of extraordinary reality, a tendency to notice aspects of the environment of which one is normally unaware, enhanced visual imagery, altered sense of time in which minutes may seem like hours, changes in visually perceived spatial relations, enrichment of sensory experiences (subjective aspects of sound and taste perception are often particularly enhanced), increased personal understanding and religious insight, mild excitement and energy (or just the opposite), increased or decreased behavioral activity, increased or decreased verbal fluency and talkativeness, lessening of inhibitions and emotional control, and at higher doses, a tendency to lose or digress from a train of thought. Feelings of enhanced spontaneity and creativity are often described although an alteration in creative performance is difficult to establish scientifically. (pp. 49–50)*

Figure 3.19 The behavioral effects of marijuana vary.

Less positive reactions to marijuana have also been reported, including panic, severe depression, perceptual distortion, suicidal tendencies, disorientation, nausea, headaches, and confusion (C. J. Schwartz, 1969). There is some evidence that, in sufficiently high doses and in sufficiently pure forms, marijuana may have hallucinogenic effects similar to those sometimes characteristic of LSD or mescaline (Gershon & Angrist, 1967; Krikstone & Levitt, 1975). There is evidence, as well, of apathy and loss of motivation following prolonged abuse (see Coleman, Butcher, and Carson, 1980).

LSD-25 (D-lysergic acid diethylamide tartrate) A particularly powerful hallucinogenic drug that is a relatively inexpensive, easily made, synthetic chemical.

LSD The most powerful semisynthetic hallucinogenic drug known is D-lysergic acid diethylamide tartrate (**LSD-25**, commonly known as LSD or acid). It was discovered by Albert Hoffman in 1938, but its hallucinogenic properties remained unknown until he accidentally ingested a small amount in 1943. Subsequently Timothy Leary and Richard Alpert (now Baba Ram Dass) were instrumental in popularizing its use among college students.

LSD is derived from ergot, a fungus that grows on rye and various other grains. It is a white, tasteless, odorless powder, effective in doses as small as 50 to 150 micrograms. More massive doses sometimes employed therapeutically may be as high as 300 to 450 micrograms. LSD is easily concealed on a cube of sugar, a stick of chewing gum, or other food substance. It is also relatively easy to manufacture in the laboratory. The effects of one dose may last for the better part of an entire day.

Drug tolerance A physiological reaction to prolonged drug use in which the body requires a progressively higher dosage of the drug in order to experience the same effects. Tolerance commonly develops with continued use of drugs such as heroin.

Like marijuana, LSD is not physiologically addictive, although marked **tolerance** for it may develop after frequent use. Interestingly, this tolerance extends to such other hallucinogens as mescaline and psilocybin, and vice versa, even if the individual has taken only one of these drugs.

The predominant characteristic of an LSD "trip" appears to be a heightened sensory experience with frequent perceptual distortion (Ebin, 1961). On occasion, this experience may be extremely satisfying and rewarding; at other times it may be nightmarish. The specific reasons for the unpredictability of an LSD experience remain unknown. While under the influence of "bad trips," individuals have been known to inflict serious harm on themselves or others—even to commit suicide. Others have subsequently found themselves in various treatment centers for emotional and mental disturbances.

There is evidence, some of it highly subjective, that an LSD experience may lead to profound insights, to mystical or transcendental experiences (Lilly, 1972; B. E. Smith

& Sternfield, 1970). Accordingly, LSD is being employed as means of studying mental imagery and consciousness through the analysis of hallucinations (Van Der Horst, 1980). In addition, there is evidence that LSD may be effective as a therapeutic agent in the treatment of some emotional disturbances. Recently it has also been employed therapeutically in treating heroin addicts (Savage & McCabe, 1971) with apparent success. An experimental group subjected to a single "peak" experience by means of a 300 to 450 microgram dose of LSD as part of their therapeutic program fared better in terms of being cured of their heroin addiction than a comparable group that was simply given conventional therapy without LSD. Twelve months after treatment, 41 percent of the experimental group continued to refrain from using heroin, compared with 6 percent of the control group. One of the explanations for the apparent effectiveness of LSD in this situation is that it forces subjects to face themselves; that it places them in direct confrontation with whatever it is that is troubling them. In contrast, heroin had previously provided them with an escape from themselves.

Other Hallucinogens The drug **mescaline** was originally derived from the peyote cactus. It has now been synthesized in the laboratory and is produced as a white powder. This powder can be dissolved and injected directly into the bloodstream (mainlined), or it can be mixed with fruit juice or taken in capsule form. Its effects are very similar to those of LSD, although they are not considered to be as dramatic or as unpredictable. Other hallucinogens include STP, MDA, and PCP, with PCP probably being the most common of these. It was first used as a tranquilizer for horses. It is sometimes mixed with marijuana (called angel's dust), and can lead to powerful hallucinations. It has also been associated with psychotic episodes, severe depression, and death.

Mescaline A drug originally derived from the peyote cactus that has now been synthesized and can be made in the laboratory as a white powder.

Opium and Derivatives Heroin, morphine, codeine, and **opium** are all derived from juices of the opium poppy. Morphine, codeine, and opium each have a history of medical use, primarily in the alleviation of pain. Codeine has also proven very effective as a cough suppressant; it has been a frequent component in various cough syrups and tablets, and has therefore been relatively easy to obtain.

Opium A highly addictive narcotic drug derived from the opium poppy. Opium and related drugs have a long history of medical use, primarily to alleviate pain. Heroin, morphine, and codeine are all derived from the same plant. Of these, heroin appears to be the most highly addictive.

The primary effect of each of these highly addictive narcotics is a feeling of euphoria that ensues almost immediately upon use, particularly when the drug is injected directly. Although they do not have the hallucinogenic effects of LSD or mescaline, they are considered more dangerous, largely because they are so addictive. Heroin, probably the most prevalent and most feared of these drugs, may result in addiction after only a few injections. In addition, the body quickly develops marked tolerance to the drug, requiring increasing doses in order to achieve the same reaction. Once the body is addicted, abstinence results in severe pains, chills, fevers, trembling, and other symptoms of extreme ill-being.

Cocaine The drug **cocaine**, like the amphetamines, is a stimulant. In its pure form, it is a white powder that typically is sniffed. In its original form it is simply chewed as a leaf from the coca plant (the source of pure cocaine), a practice that remains common among certain South American natives. Cocaine may also be dissolved and injected into the bloodstream, or it may be mixed with heroin for the same purpose (called a speedball). Although cocaine is not universally considered to be addictive, there is some speculation that when it is mainlined, addiction may result. And although withdrawal of use is not characterized by the sometimes violent symptoms of alcohol or heroin withdrawal, some individuals appear to develop an intense craving for cocaine and a need to increase dosage (Krikstone & Levitt, 1975).

Cocaine A stimulant drug which, in its pure form, is a white powder that typically is sniffed.

The primary effects of cocaine are reportedly a euphoric high and occasional hallucinations. Since it is very expensive it is not in widespread use except among the affluent. Indications are that its use has increased dramatically in recent years, however (S. Cohen, 1976).

Inhalants Glue and other similar toxic substances (aerosol sprays, paint, various cleaning fluids, and so on) that result in a short-lived euphoria similar to the occasional effects of alcohol consumption are readily available and not uncommon in the lower and middle school grades. Substances are typically poured or sprayed into a plastic bag, onto a cloth, or onto a cloth inside a plastic bag, and the fumes are inhaled directly. Intoxication initially results after two or three deep breaths, but with prolonged use, tolerance increases and more of the substance is required. Some of the less desirable eventual effects of inhalant use include speech and motor impairment, double vision, and sometimes hallucinations. There is also tentative evidence that prolonged use of these substances may lead to permanent brain damage or to other physical and psychological disturbances. There is little doubt that they are considerably more dangerous than marijuana.

Barbiturates and Other Sedatives

Barbiturates Any of a large number of drugs that have a powerful sedating influence on the body, and that are also addictive. Barbiturates are often prescription drugs.

The American public (and private) is estimated to consume some 1.5 tons of **barbiturates** every day (and 40 tons of aspirins)(S. Cohen, 1971). There are over 2,500 different varieties of barbiturates, and a large number of the milder depressants commonly called tranquilizers. These are in extremely widespread medical use, and are virtually indispensable for many of the purposes for which they are employed. Unfortunately, however, they are extensively overused. Their primary effect is relaxation and drowsiness (hence they are called "downers," as opposed to the stimulants, which are called "uppers"). Extensive overuse results in physiological addiction. The consequences of withdrawal are often more severe than those of withdrawal from the narcotic drugs such as heroin, and may result in death. Overdosing, which may be unintentional, can also be fatal, as can the use of barbiturates with alcohol.

Amphetamines

Amphetamines A class of drugs known as stimulants (uppers). Methedrine (commonly known as speed), Dexedrine, and Benzedrine are trade names of common amphetamines.

The better-known stimulants (uppers) include the **amphetamines** (see Figure 3.20). Some of their common trade names are Benzedrine, Dexedrine, and Methedrine. They are used extensively in medicine to counteract narcolepsy (involuntary attacks of sleep), sometimes to overcome drowsiness that might be due to sedatives, and most frequently in weight-reducing programs. The effects of amphetamines include increases in energy, dissipation of fatigue, and loss of appetite, although their effectiveness in reducing appetite disappears with prolonged use. They are typically taken as tablets but may also be dissolved and injected directly into the bloodstream, a practice that is common with Methedrine (speed). The effect of mainlining speed (and of injecting heroin) has frequently been compared to an orgasm. It is not at all uncommon for a chronic user of speed to go without eating or sleeping for a number of days. Eventually succumbing to fatigue, the user may then sleep for several days prior to awakening, ravenous.

Although amphetamines are not considered to be physiologically addictive, psychological addiction and increased tolerance are frequently such that users, particularly those who mainline speed, will begin shooting up almost immediately after their prolonged sleep. The user may inject eight or more times per day to maintain the high.

Alcohol

Alcohol A legal drug whose principal effect is depression of central nervous system activity.

One of two legal drugs considered in this section, **alcohol** remains the drug of choice in our society. The frequency of its use has been well documented. There is no evidence that with the increasing popularity of other drugs during the last several decades, use of alcohol has declined; in fact, it may have increased (Alden, 1980).

Alcohol is a central nervous system depressant. Its principal psychological effect is a reduction of inhibition, which frequently leads drinkers to act as though they had taken a stimulant. With the intake of greater amounts, the sedating effects become more apparent. Some of the effects of excessive consumption are obvious and well known: impaired judgment, reduced self-control, deterioration of muscular control, loss of balance, nausea, blackouts, amnesia, and, if taken in sufficient doses, paralysis of the heart and lung muscles, sometimes leading to death (Harger, 1964). Among its long-term physiological effects are its known contribution to cirrhosis of the liver, one of the ten leading causes of death in the United States. It is also implicated in 50 to 70 percent of all traffic fatalities.

Nicotine The effects of **nicotine** are not nearly so clear as those of most other drugs. It does not produce a high; it does not sedate; there is some evidence that it might stimulate, but there is also the speculation that it relieves tension and leads to relaxation. Nor is it clear that nicotine is addictive. If it is, the addiction is not comparable to alcohol or heroin addiction. What is clear is that it is strongly habituating (leads to psychological dependence): individuals experience considerable difficulty in getting rid of the habit once it has been acquired.

The dangers of smoking nicotine have been highly publicized. Tobacco-linked deaths now exceed traffic deaths, with most of these due to lung cancer and coronary heart disease. Cigarette-smoking has also been linked with chronic bronchitis, emphysema, cirrhosis of the liver, pneumonia, and cancer of such tissues as the tongue, lips, esophagus, and mouth.

The symptoms of drug use and abuse are summarized in Table 3.3.

Drugs and Consciousness

The preceding discussions of the nature and effects of various drugs may, on the surface, appear to be only tangentially related to the central topic in this chapter: consciousness. Bear in mind, however, that consciousness refers to our personal conceptions of the realities that surround us, *and of what we are*. For many, these realities

Nicotine The principal active ingredient in tobacco. Although its psychological effects remain unclear, it is highly habituating. Its physiological effects are more clearly established.

Table 3.3 Symptoms of Drug Use and Abuse

Drug	Signs and Early Symptoms	Long-Term Symptoms
Narcotics	Medicinal breath Traces of white powder around nostrils (heroin is sometimes inhaled) Red or raw nostrils Needle marks or scars on arms Long sleeves (or other clothing) at inappropriate times Physical evidence may include cough syrup bottles, syringes, cotton swabs, and spoon or cap for heating heroin	Loss of appetite Constipation
Sedatives	Symptoms of alcohol consumption with or without odor: poor coordination and speech, drowsiness, loss of interest in activity	Withdrawal symptoms when discontinued Possible convulsions
Stimulants	Excessive activity Irascibility Argumentativeness Nervousness Pupil dilation Dry mouth and nose with bad breath Chapped, dry lips Scratching or rubbing of nose Long periods without sleep Loss of appetite	Loss of appetite Possible hallucinations and psychotic reactions
Hallucinogens Marijuana	Odor on breath and clothing Animated behavior or its opposite	None definite
LSD	Bizarre behavior Panic Disorientation	Possible contribution to psychoses Recurrence of experiences after immediate effects of drug
Inhalants	Odor of glue, solvent, or related substance Redness and watering of eyes Appearance of alcoholic intoxication Physical evidence of plastic bags, rags, aerosol glue or solvent containers	Disorientation Brain damage

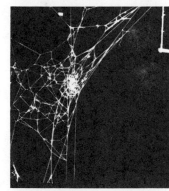

Figure 3.20 Effect of an amphetamine on a spider's ability to construct a web. (**a**) Normal web; (**b**) web constructed about twelve hours after a small dose of dextroamphetamine was given to the same adult female spider. (**c**) After twenty-four hours of recovery, a third web is still not normal.

are extremely painful. Drugs provide a simple, passive means of altering reality, sometimes dramatically—indeed, sometimes much too dramatically. There is little doubt that it is often easier to change yourself chemically than to change what surrounds you, or to change what you feel inside. And it is precisely this observation that provides one of the explanations for drug use and abuse. There are obviously others. Much drug use, particularly in schools, results from peer pressure; some is due to a desire to experiment; the possibility of transcendental experiences lures a number; the promise of escape from boredom or from personal problems is yet another attraction. Whatever the initial reason for drug use, continued use of drugs may be motivated by entirely different factors. The adolescent who begins using drugs simply for the experience involved may become psychologically or even physiologically addicted. The lure is no longer a vision of new experiences; the trap has been sprung. But there are ways of escaping. Some succeed, unharmed; others may succeed, considerably harmed; an unfortunate group may never escape.

Main Points

1 Ordinary states of consciousness include being awake and being asleep. There are two sleep states: REM (rapid eye movement) and NREM (no rapid eye movement).

2 Consciousness appears to result from a personal, introspective process culminating in *awareness*. Psychological investigations of consciousness generally study ordinary consciousness and less ordinary states such as those brought about through hypnosis, the effects of drugs, and meditative techniques.

3 Sleep is not an unconscious state, but represents a state of altered (with respect to the awake state) consciousness. It is characterized by loss of muscular control, relative loss of ability to hear noises, and altered patterns of electrical activity in the brain.

4 We do not know why we sleep. Sleep deprivation does not appear to lead to bizarre behavior, hallucinations, or paranoia except where sleepless individuals are placed under high stress.

5 Theoretical explanations of why we sleep include circulatory theories (sleep occurs when the brain is deprived of a normal amount of oxygen); chemical theories (also an oxygen-deprivation theory); neurological theories (cell damage that occurs during awake periods must be repaired); sleep center theories (part of the brain simply shuts off); and biological theories (we inherit sleep-wake cycles, perhaps as a protective mechanism). None of these theories has been clearly substantiated; perhaps a combination of them explains sleep.

6 Circadian rhythms are daily sleep-wake, temperature, and general arousal cycles spanning twenty-four-hour periods. Many animals seem to be heir to these cycles.

7 The two recognized types of sleep are the REM and NREM states. We spend between 75 and 80 percent of our normal sleeping time in NREM states. It is during the remaining 20 to 25 percent of sleep time (REM sleep) that most of our dreams occur. REM states do not ordinarily begin for thirty to forty-five minutes following the onset of sleep, and last for between twenty and thirty minutes. NREM states last for perhaps ninety minutes at a time. The states alternate.

8 Everybody dreams, although not all remember doing so. Most of our dreams involve familiar individuals in familiar locations; roughly one-third of them are in color; and relatively few of them are nightmares, these tending to occur toward the end of an NREM period rather than during an REM period.

9 Freud believed that dreams had an apparent and a latent (hidden or symbolic) meaning, and that they functioned as an outlet for forbidden impulses. Some research indicates that dreams may serve a useful psychological function, allowing us to attend to our fantasies during the night, and freeing us to attend to reality during the day.

10 Hypnosis is a nonordinary state of consciousness induced through suggestion, and characterized by an increased willingness to accede to the wishes of the hypnotist.

11 Some of the behavior possible during hypnosis includes catalepsy (rigidity—loss of muscular control); anesthesia (loss of sensation, insensitivity to pain); age regression (recollection of events that have transpired in the far past); obedience to posthypnotic suggestions

(carrying out the hypnotist's commands after the hypnotic session has been terminated); and amnesia (loss of memory for events that have occurred during hypnosis).

12 Individuals vary in terms of the degree to which they are suggestible—that is, in terms of the ease with which they can be hypnotized. Several tests are available to measure suggestibility.

13 Evidence that hypnosis represents a genuine and different state of consciousness has been obtained in studies employing simulators (individuals who pretend they are hypnotized), where differences have been found between the behaviors of those who are simply pretending and those who apparently aren't. Studies of pain tolerance employing "the hidden observer" suggest that some dissociated part of an individual may continue to remain *aware* during hypnosis although the individual is not conscious of this.

14 There is little good evidence of significant improvements in learning and memory using hypnosis.

15 Meditation is a process involving contemplation or thought, and intended to lead to relaxation, peace, happiness, and, ultimately, to a mystical experience (a state that is said to appear *real,* to lead to a feeling of unity or oneness, to be ineffable or difficult to describe, and to go beyond ordinary sensation).

16 Biofeedback is a technique whereby individuals are provided with information that they would not ordinarily have concerning their physiological functioning (for example, information concerning brain wave activity). Biofeedback techniques typically try to help subjects gain control over brain wave functioning.

17 Drugs, chemical substances that have any of a range of effects on the human body and nervous system, have been used for many years. Alcohol and nicotine are the most widely used and abused drugs in contemporary Western societies. Also widely used are mild hallucinogens such as marijuana, stronger hallucinogens such as LSD and PCP, sedatives such as tranquilizers and barbiturates, and a variety of inhalants. Most of these have been associated with a variety of physical and mental disorders, although they don't affect all individuals in the same way.

Further Readings

A relatively simple and interesting account of research on sleeping and dreaming is the following:

Cartwright, R. D. *Night life: Explorations in dreaming.* Englewood Cliffs, N.J.: Prentice-Hall, 1977.

Bowers presents a straightforward description of hypnosis and hypnotic techniques in:

Bowers, K. S. *Hypnosis for the seriously curious.* Monterey, Calif.: Brooks/Cole, 1976.

The following collections of readings represent current and provocative examinations of speculation and knowledge in the area of human consciousness:

Ornstein, R. E. (Ed.). *The nature of human consciousness: A book of readings.* New York: Viking Press, 1973.

Goleman, D., and Davidson, R. J. (Eds.). *Consciousness: Brain, states of awareness, and mysticism.* New York: Harper & Row, 1979.

An intellectually oriented, thought-provoking, and somewhat controversial book which attempts to trace the evolution of consciousness in humans is:

Jaynes, J. *The origin of consciousness in the breakdown of the bicameral mind.* Boston: Houghton Mifflin, 1977.

Carlos Castaneda, apprentice to Don Juan, a Yaqui sorcerer, recounts his troubling experiences with other realities and his explorations of altered consciousness in:

Castaneda. C. *The teachings of Don Juan: A Yaqui way of knowledge* (1968); *A separate reality* (1971); *Journey to Ixtlan: The lessons of Don Juan* (1972); *Tales of power* (1974); *The second ring of power* (1978); and *The eagle's gift* (1981); all published by Simon & Schuster, New York.

The Castaneda books, fascinating as they are, may well be more fiction than fact. See:

de Mille, R. *Castaneda's journey.* Santa Barbara: Capra Press, 1976.

Perceptual Systems: Orienting, Hearing, Touching, and Savoring

4

Some years ago I found myself on a warm Atlantic beach off Virginia's east coast. I remember rather clearly staring in awe at that mighty ocean and wading headlong into the first big breaker, imagining that it would simply toss me carelessly over its shoulder and bounce me up and down on its crest. Instead it swept me into its bowels, turned me in a dozen different directions, pointing various parts of my anatomy up, down, and sideways in rapid succession, and left me submerged, suffocating and absolutely disoriented. I would not have panicked, I assure you, had I known immediately which way was up and which direction was shoreward. But I had absolutely no idea, and might, in my understandable terror, have plunged my head quite madly into the sand had another wave, or perhaps the same one, not picked me up and tossed me unceremoniously onto shore.

I was reminded of this event earlier this evening when my ski instructor spoke of avalanches, and what one should do if buried by one. Someone in the class advanced the opinion that it might be appropriate to pray. I suggested that in such a situation I would not, of course, deliberately choose to quarrel with the Almighty, but that a more direct course of action might seem equally appropriate. "One should endeavor to dig one's way out," I offered in academic tones.

"And which way is out?" asked the instructor.

"Up," I ventured somewhat more timidly, sensing a trap. One cannot long be a professor without becoming highly sensitive to such things. I was right.

"Would your finger not point up if you told it to?" I asked her, smiling disarmingly (another academic trait, that. We can all smile so disarmingly.). She remained armed.

"It might not. It might point straight down, or sideways." I recalled Virginia then. My well-practiced index might not have pointed up. It probably wouldn't have pointed anywhere, even if it had had time. It wouldn't have known where to point. And that, apparently, is what might well happen if you were to be buried (alive of course) in an avalanche. Your finger would be useless. Your perception of up and down might be totally confused.

The solution that promises some possibility of escape from an avalanche might be considered indelicate in present circumstances. Textbooks are supposed to be ceremoniously and seriously tasteful and delicate. I see no harm, however, in telling you that what you must do is gather whatever saliva you can in your mouth and spit as vigorously as circumstances allow. Even when buried by an avalanche, spittle has the good sense to fall downward.

Our Contacts with Reality

It is clear that existence as a human being is bound up with our ability to **apprehend** the qualities of the objective world. Not to be able to apprehend those qualities would amount to being blind and deaf, devoid of taste and smell, and unable to sense physical contact. Perhaps even worse, we would not know up from down or sideways. In addition, we would be totally oblivious to our bodily positions, to our movements, to feelings of hunger, to pain, to heat and cold. In fact, in the absence of these abilities, we might not even be aware of being. Our brains, hidden as they are, surrounded by flesh and bone, need our **senses**. Our senses are our contacts with reality.

Aristotle spoke of five senses: vision, hearing, touch, taste, and smell. J. J. Gibson (1966), too, speaks of these same senses, although he combines taste and smell into a single system: the savor system. In addition, he considers the basic orienting system as a separate system. It is our basic orienting system that tells us which way is up and which is down (when it has not been buried by an avalanche or tossed about by an Atlantic wave). Table 4.1 outlines these five perceptual systems, four of which are dealt with in this chapter.

The five perceptual systems are related to the functioning of specialized organs (eyes, ears, and so on) and are responsive to external stimulation. It is by means of these systems that we become aware of what is "out there." It should be kept in mind that although each of the perceptual systems is treated separately, they often function in combination and in cooperation, sometimes telling us very much the same thing in different ways. My ears might inform me that a turkey is very close if I hear it; my eyes might tell me the same thing if I see it, revealing as well that it is colored; my hands might confirm the nearness of the bird and suggest too that it is both soft and warm; and my nose might tell me things I would prefer not to know about a turkey at this moment, although both my nose and my mouth might later tell me things I quite enjoy knowing. In short, the perceptual systems sometimes give us information that is redundant, and redundance might be an important factor in the perceptual process; in addition, they work together to make us more fully aware of our environments.

Sensation and Perception

How the senses make us aware of our environments is a different matter. Some psychologists maintain that the senses merely translate various forms of energy (an electromagnetic wave for vision or hearing, for example; a molecule for taste or smell; a movement, a pressure, a form of radiant energy) into neural impulses. They term this process *sensation* and say that it is complemented by a second process, *perception*. Perception subjectively interprets those neural impulses, which in and of themselves have no meaning. Sensation most often involves one or more of the specialized organs with which we are endowed: eyes, ears, nose, tongue, and a variety of other sensors

Apprehend Literally, to take hold of or seize, as in "to apprehend a criminal." As a psychological term, it refers to the simple awareness of an object, or the process of becoming aware. Apprehension goes somewhat beyond perception, but implies something less than comprehension.

Senses Any of a number of responses to stimulation involving the activity of specialized organs such as eyes, ears, taste cells, and olfactory cells (smell). The responses of these organs are translated into neural impulses, which can then be interpreted by the brain or otherwise reacted to by the body. This process defines sensation.

Table 4.1 The Perceptual Systems

Name	Mode of Attention	Receptive Units and Anatomy	Activity of the Organ	Stimuli Available	External Information Obtained
Basic orienting system	General orientation	Mechanoreceptors: vestibular organs in the inner ear	Body equilibrium	Forces of gravity and acceleration	Direction of gravity, being pushed
Auditory system	Listening	Mechanoreceptors: cochlear organs with middle ear and auricle	Orienting to sounds	Vibration in the air	Nature and location of vibratory events
Haptic system	Touching	Mechanoreceptors and possibly thermoreceptors: skin (including attachments and openings), joints (including ligaments), muscles (including tendons)	Exploration of many kinds	Deformations of tissues Configuration of joints Stretching of muscle fibers	Contact with the earth Mechanical encounters Object shapes Material states (solidity or viscosity)
Savor system	Smelling	Chemoreceptors: nasal cavity (nose)	Sniffing	Composition of the medium	Nature of volatile sources
	Tasting	Chemoreceptors and mechanoreceptors: oral cavity (mouth)	Savoring	Composition of ingested objects	Nutritive and biochemical values
Visual system	Looking	Photoreceptors: ocular mechanism (eyes, with intrinsic and extrinsic eye muscles, as related to the vestibular organs, the head and the whole body)	Accommodation Pupillary adjustment Fixation Convergence Exploration	Variables of structure in ambient light	Everything that can be specified by the variables of optical structure (information about objects, animals, motions, events, and places)

Note: From *The Senses Considered as Perceptual Systems* by James J. Gibson. Copyright © 1966 by James J. Gibson. Reprinted by permission of Houghton Mifflin Company.

found over most of the surface of the body as well as inside it. Perception depends upon these sensors, but also upon the activity of the brain (see Figure 4.1). Blue, for example, does not exist out there. It may, but whether it does or not is irrelevant. Certainly, there is a wavelength that corresponds to your perception of the color blue. But who can demonstrate that a wavelength *has* or *is* color? What we can demonstrate is that most of us will select the same color plate if asked to point to the blue one among a number of others. Similarly, hardness or softness of objects, although *real* attributes of objects dependent upon their molecular structures, are not *real* properties of the light waves that are reflected from them to our retinas. Nor are they real properties of the cellular displacements they might bring about in our hands when we feel them. Yet hardness and softness are perceived by our brains through our eyes and hands, and perhaps through other parts of our bodies as well.

An increasing number of psychologists have ceased to treat the senses as no more than receptors sensitive to various types of stimulation and designed to translate that stimulation into neural impulses to be perceived by the brain. They maintain that although it is true that the sense organs do translate physical energy into neural impulses, they do much more. Experiments have demonstrated that the senses can become more sensitive, more selective, more discriminating—in short, that a type of learning occurs that would not occur were the senses simply organs that translate physical energies into neural impulses. J. J. Gibson (1966) was among the first to treat the senses as *perceptual systems* rather than as simple translators. His argument, elaborated as well by Neisser (1976), is that we perceive with our eyes as well as with our brains. As will become clear in Chapter 5, our eyes don't simply register all that they are exposed to, leaving it up to the brain to sort out those things of which we are then aware. Nor do our ears translate all sounds that they are capable of translating into neural impulses. Our senses are directed and limited by something called attention.

Figure 4.1 Perceptual systems translate energy from the environment into neural impulses, and we can usually depend on these signals to help us keep in touch with reality. Sometimes, however, human senses become confused and perception becomes distorted—and the effects may last longer than the stimulus. Have you ever tried to walk a straight line after emerging from one of these?

Attention A state of the reacting organism which, as it increases, narrows the focus of perception. Attention denotes a state of readiness to perceive and/or respond. In addition, it implies selection and emphasis. It is both a state (wherein an individual is more likely to respond to certain events than to others) and a process (whereby an individual increases the probability of responding to one event and not another).

Attention and Perception

If you take a moment from your important studies with the deliberate intention of becoming aware of everything you possibly can be aware of at this very moment, you may not return for some time. Not only is there an impressively large array of visual stimuli available, even if you do not turn your head, but there are sounds, tastes, smells, and tactile sensations of which you were not aware a minute ago if you were paying attention to what I am now writing. Visually, you can study minute details, light and shadow, patterns, colors, movements. But you cannot study these effectively while listening carefully for the various sounds that might be around you. This does not mean, of course, that only one sense is active at one time. All may be active, but your **attention** is likely to be focused primarily on one. Similarly, you can sense the feeling of your clothing on your body; you can taste the inside of your mouth; you might even be able to detect some odor. Spend a few minutes sensing and perceiving right now.

If you were, at this moment, completely aware of the thousands of stimuli impinging upon you, you would probably go mad. If you were constantly aware of the feeling of your clothing, you would probably become a nudist in an attempt to escape madness. Fortunately for us, we are aware of only a few sensations at any given time. Which ones, and why?

The Cocktail Party Problem

Cherry (1953; Cherry & Taylor, 1954) investigated the problem of how an individual at a social gathering such as a cocktail party can listen to a single conversation despite the fact that there may be several going on within easy hearing distance. These other conversations appear to have no effect on individuals not involved in them, although if their names are mentioned even casually and in a conversational tone, they may well become immediately aware of it and begin paying attention to a second conversation. Similarly, if another conversation runs haphazardly into a subject that is of interest to someone busily engaged in a separate piece of social repartee, that individual may also turn immediately to the conversation that is of interest.

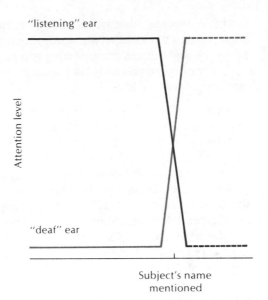

"listening" ear

Attention level

"deaf" ear

Subject's name
mentioned

Figure 4.2 How much do we hear of things we aren't listening to? In the cocktail party experiment, subjects heard two simultaneous messages, but they were instructed to attend to only one. (To ensure this, they repeated—or shadowed—everything as they heard it on the tape for the "listening ear.") Even when a word was repeated thirty-five times on the tape for the "deaf ear," subjects denied having heard that word. But when the subject's name was mentioned on the tape for the "deaf ear," attention quickly shifted from the tape the subject had been listening to.

Cherry and his associates investigated this problem by feeding two different messages simultaneously to an individual by means of stereophonic headphones. Subjects were instructed to pay attention to a single message (left or right ear). In order to ensure that this was being done, they were also instructed to repeat everything they heard in that ear, as they heard it. The process is called *shadowing;* it is based on the apparently valid assumption that directing energy in one direction (that is, attending to one source) leads to a reduction of energy directed elsewhere (see Figure 4.2). •

Among a number of interesting findings from these and related experiments is that subjects almost invariably remember absolutely nothing of the message that has been fed to the ear not being attended to. The message in that ear can, for example, switch from one language to another without the subject's being aware of it (Treisman, 1964); the same word can be repeated as many as thirty-five times and the subject will later deny having heard it (Moray, 1959). Yet a single presentation of the subject's name is usually sufficient to alter attention (Schneider & Shiffrin, 1977). It appears clear that subjects do "hear" those messages to which they are not attending, but that the messages are not retained in ordinary memory. These observations also suggest that there is a type of ongoing filtering or analysis of all messages received (Broadbent, 1952, 1958). If this were not the case, subjects would not respond when they hear their names or, in the cocktail party situation, when the subject of another conversation is of greater interest to them than the one in which they are presently engaged. It is no secret that we continue to be aware of a wide variety of sensory stimulation even when we are attending to a single source of input, but that much of this awareness is marginal. Subjects in the cocktail party situation are probably aware of a great number of conversations, as is evident in their ability to shift attention upon hearing their names.

Determinants of Attention

Attention precedes perception. It is, in effect, a state of readiness—a heightened responsiveness. William James (1890) defined attention as holding in the mind one of a number of competing thoughts. Since, however, perception is not solely a mental phenomenon, it is perhaps better defined as the state of the organism that leads to a narrower focusing of perception. If you are at this moment attentive to what you are reading, you are more likely to perceive it, to understand it, and perhaps even to remember it. However, if you are attending primarily to your ongoing daydream, you might be reading these words almost unconsciously. It is possible to read an entire page—that is, to look at all the words sequentially—while being so engrossed in some private thought that nothing of what you have read will remain with you.

Experimentation and observation reveal that the following are among the important determiners of attention:

Change Stimulation that presents a sudden change is relatively likely to alter attention, even among such lowly animals as rats. If a rat is placed in a Y-maze (see Figure 4.3) with glass barriers at the juncture of the Y so that it can visually explore the arms of the maze, but is prevented from entering them, some interesting things can be discovered about rat behavior when the glass barriers are eventually removed. In a series of experiments (Dember, 1956; H. Fowler, 1958), rats were exposed to arms of the same color, arms of different color, simple arms, complex arms, and so on. Consider three different situations. In the first, the rat is allowed to explore the maze visually when the two arms are of different colors—one is black, the other is white. After visual exploration, the white arm is exchanged for a black arm so that both arms are now of the same color, the glass barriers are removed, and the rat is allowed to go into either or both of the arms. Interestingly, the rat now spends more time in the arm that was originally white but has now been changed to black. The inference is simply that the rat is responding to change. There is considerable anecdotal evidence that we are no different.

Novelty In a second situation, the arms of the Y-maze are of identical colors for the initial visual exploration with the glass barriers in place. One arm is then exchanged for a different-colored arm. Now the rat spends more time in the arm that has a new color. It appears that rats respond to novelty as well as to change, a phenomenon that can easily be demonstrated with human infants as well as with adults. It is, however, more challenging to demonstrate the same property with rats.

Complexity In the third situation, the rat is placed in the Y-maze with no glass barriers. One arm of the maze is plain (white or black); the other has a relatively complex black and white pattern. The rat, hero of twentieth-century psychology, can be relied on to spend more time in the more complex arm. Complexity of stimulation also appears to have attention-focusing properties.

Repetition Within limits, repetition can also increase attention, particularly when some variation is involved (in which case novelty may be the determining factor). Jingles used in television advertising serve as good illustrations of this fact. A parent's repeating a child's name eight times may also illustrate the attention-related effect of repetition.

Intensity The more intense a stimulus, the more likely it is to attract and hold attention, a fact that has not been overlooked by the advertising media. Thus printed advertising frequently struts boldly across pages carrying heavy letters, flaming colors, compelling borders, and arresting designs.

Change, novelty, complexity, repetition, and intensity are all properties of stimuli that can affect attention. In addition, a number of very important subjective conditions are directly related to attention as well as to the nature of perception. In brief, what is perceived must first be attended to, but what is perceived is not always accurate. We are subject to a number of perceptual distortions and inaccuracies, some of which are dealt with in the section on visual illusions in Chapter 5. We are also prone to completely erroneous perception, sometimes as a function of our interests and our expectations.

Interest Attention is often directed by our learned interests and preoccupations. Thus, on a nature walk a geologist may perceive rocks; a botanist, flowers; a zoologist, animal life; an artist, colors and forms; and a lover, . . .

Attention is also directed by our immediate interests, these being in turn highly influenced by our prevailing needs and moods, which impose certain search require-

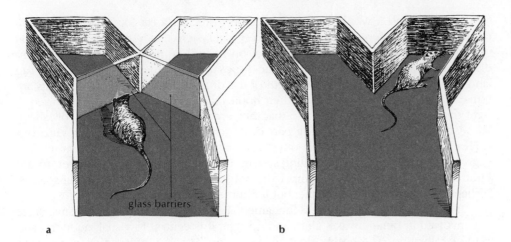

glass barriers

a   b

ments on our sensory/perceptual systems. Thus, when you are walking along a downtown street, hunger will make you notice (attend to and perceive) restaurants and bakeries, a desire to buy music will lead you to notice record shops, an upcoming fishing excursion may bring sporting-goods stores to your attention, or your avid interest in psychology may lead you to notice the expressions on people's faces. Psychology can sometimes be depressing.

Expectations   Science records numerous instances of erroneous perceptions predicated on false expectations. For example, when Leeuwenhoek invented the first crude microscope, initial inspection of sperm cells revealed what had been well known for some time: inside each sperm cell there is a miniature replica of the animal from whom the cell was taken. Inside a human sperm cell, there is a tiny human; inside a rooster's sperm, there is a little rooster, and inside the sperm of an ass, there is a little creature with long asslike ears. For an embarrassingly long time, researchers continued to perceive this miniature animal inside sperm cells—and sometimes inside egg cells too. This led to a heated controversy between the *animalculists* and the *ovists,* the former being convinced that the miniature animal was inside the sperm cell, and the latter being equally convinced that the egg cell (ovum) contained the complete tiny organism (Hunt, 1961). The controversy continued until the development of more refined microscopes permitted what we now consider to be an accurate perception, unaffected by erroneous expectations. The little animal is inside the sperm cells, and the debate goes to the animalculists.*

Every fall countless horses, cows, sheep, and a few hunters fall prey to misperceptions occasioned by intense interests, highly directed search requirements, and well-honed expectations. To some extent, what we perceive is what we expect, what we want, and what we are looking for. Most of us do not allow the world to present us with too many surprises.

The Basic Orienting System

We have, in effect, five principal modes of attending to our environment: orienting, looking, listening, touching, and savoring. These modes operate within specific perceptual systems, not as passive receptors, but as active, exploratory, and highly cooperative and sometimes interdependent systems. We discuss each of these systems in turn, beginning with the **basic orienting system.**

Basic orienting system   The perceptual system whose principal function is to provide the organism with information relating to positions of the body, body movements, and relationship to the gravitational plane. It allows us to remain upright, informs us which way is up and which way is down, and allows us to determine whether we are moving and in what direction. The organ that appears to be most central to the basic orienting system is the vestibular organ.

---

*Do you expect to be able to believe everything you read? This statement is false.

I don't think it would be unkind of you to recruit a cat for a well-known but rather remarkable demonstration of a perceptual system that appears to be common to all animals. You can hold a purring cat on its back a mere foot above the floor, distract it by whatever means are at your disposal, and suddenly drop it. That it can land on its feet despite the short length of the drop illustrates not only that cats are remarkably gifted to be able to put their bodies through the contortions required to right themselves in midair, but also that they are instantly aware not only of falling, but also of falling with the wrong part of the anatomy pointing up. This **righting reflex**, present in many animals other than cats but often to a much less marked degree, illustrates the basic orienting system. It would be less kind, however, to use a human baby (or adult) in an attempt to demonstrate the righting reflex in our species. Perhaps we did have it at one time, but it now seems to have disappeared.

The basic orienting system is fundamental to all other perceptual systems. Since it is involved in being awake, alert, and upright, it is central to visual, auditory, and tactile exploration. The basic orienting system provides us information concerning our body position, movement, and our relationship to the gravitational plane. As pointed out earlier, it tells us which way is up and which down, but more than that, it tells us whether we are moving upward, downward, sideways, straight ahead, or in a circle. Its close relationship with the visual and auditory systems is obvious. If I see an interesting object, I may turn toward it. My eyes will now tell me that I am, in fact, facing the object. That, of course, is oversimplified and somewhat inaccurate. Information derived from the light waves entering my eyes may lead my brain to make the instantaneous and perhaps conscious decision that I am facing the object. At the same time, my basic orienting system indicates that my head has turned, and will also be sensitive to my bodily movements should I decide to approach the object. Some of the information obtained through the visual system and the basic orienting system will be redundant, as will information that might be derived from the **haptic** system should I reach the object and touch it, and from the savor system should the object have a detectable odor.

Functions

The basic orienting system has three distinct functions, all of which have been mentioned. First, it maintains orientation to the earth by its sensitivity to the gravitational plane. It tells us what is up. Second, it permits orientation of other perceptual systems to aspects of the environment to which they are attending. This is accomplished through movements of the head, the eyes, and sometimes the whole body. Third, it is centrally involved in purposeful locomotion: approaching, departing, or, on a much grander scale, finding the way to distant places. Geographical orientation is not simply a matter of following learned directions, of reading maps, or of boarding the right bus, train, ship, or airplane. It involves a sense of direction, conventionally labeled north, south, east, west, and points in between, sensitivity to changes in direction, and some apprehension of distance. Clearly, the visual system is also involved in locomotion.

The Vestibular Organ

Part of our inner ear comprising an elaborate arrangement of canals and sacs is not involved in hearing; it is involved in basic orientation. This **vestibular organ*** consists of the semicircular canals, the utricle, and the saccule (see Figure 4.4). These are fluid-filled enclosures which also contain a large number of hairlike sensory receptors. A crude notion of how this system works may be obtained by swirling a glass partly filled with water, moving it backward, forward, up, down, or sideways. In each case, movement of the water is highly predictable. Laying the glass on its side also has

---

*There are, in fact, two vestibular organs, most people having two ears. Presumably the information obtained by one is simply complemented by information obtained by the other.

Righting reflex A reflexive response, easily observable in cats, which involves going through the contortions necessary to ensure that the organism lands upright after falling or being dropped.

Haptic Pertaining to the sense of touch: the perceptual system concerned with sensing pressure as well as heat, cold, and pain, both internally and externally.

Vestibular organ A part of the inner ear consisting of the semicircular canals, the utricle, and the saccule. It is centrally involved in detecting movement and in maintaining balance, and is the principal organ of the basic orienting system.

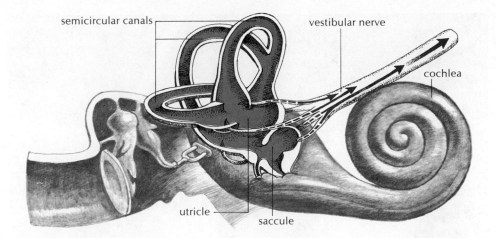

semicircular canals — vestibular nerve

cochlea

utricle

saccule

Figure 4.4 The vestibular orienting system. Motion of fluid and of a heavy gelatinous substance inside the three semicircular canals, the utricle, and the saccule is caused by any movement of the head. Hair cells within the canals act as receptors: when the fluid moves, they sway, and this motion triggers an impulse which is sent through the vestibular nerve to the brain.

very predictable results. In much the same way, the fluid in the vestibular organ responds to changes in movement or position. These changes are sensed by the hairlike receptors within the organ and are translated into neural impulses that mean you are upright, sideways, or upside-down; you are moving; you are accelerating; you are stopping; you have stopped; or you are turning. The vestibular organ is particularly sensitive to movements of the head because of its location, a fact of considerable importance in its cooperative role with the visual, auditory, and taste-smell systems.

Deceiving the Basic Orienting System

Like all our perceptual systems, the basic orienting system, remarkable though it may be, is some distance from being perfect. It responds impressively in determining self-initiated direction and movement. In conjunction with our motor systems, it even permits such activities as riding bicycles and walking tightropes, the latter probably not much more difficult than the first. A bicycle presents some incredibly complex problems of equilibrium (D. E. H. Jones, 1970) which are handled with ridiculous ease by a well-practiced vestibular organ. But the basic orienting system does not always respond well to movement that does not involve direct activity of our own bodies. It did not evolve inside cars, airplanes, or spaceships. And when it is constantly jostled inside one of these, it sometimes responds by making us feel nauseated and sick. Nor did it evolve on a cliffside, and in a large number of us it responds with muscular tension and dizziness in high places. Our vestibular organs together with our visual systems do not judge vertical distance in the same manner as they judge horizontal distance. Looking across a football field seldom produces the sensations that frequently accompany looking down from a twentieth-story balcony.

Our basic orientation systems are accustomed to horizontal and vertical rooms and can easily be deceived in rooms that do not conform to these expectations. The famous Witkin (1959) tilting chair and room apparatus has frequently demonstrated this phenomenon (Figure 4.5). The apparatus consists of a chair inside a room. Both the chair and the room are arranged so that they can be tilted on the same axis—that is, from one side to another, although not forward or backward. A subject sitting in this chair when both the room and the chair are in the upright position has no difficulty judging that both are upright. If the chair is tilted to one side but the room remains stationary, most subjects again experience no difficulty in determining the extent to which they are tilted. If, however, the room is tilted, or both the room and the chair are tilted, the subject may become quite confused. A tilted room, provided the tilt is not too severe, is likely to produce the feeling that it is the chair that is tilted and not the room. Visual information now competes with information from the basic orienting system as well as with information from the haptic system.

Figure 4.5 The basic orienting system can be deceived. In this photograph of the Witkin tilting-room tilting-chair apparatus, both the chair and the room are tilted. Accurate judgments of the subject's position are difficult under these circumstances and, unless the room is drastically tilted, are likely to be based on the subject's belief that the chair is tilted. In this situation, subjects will often perceive themselves as *more* tilted than they are, and the room as *not* being tilted.

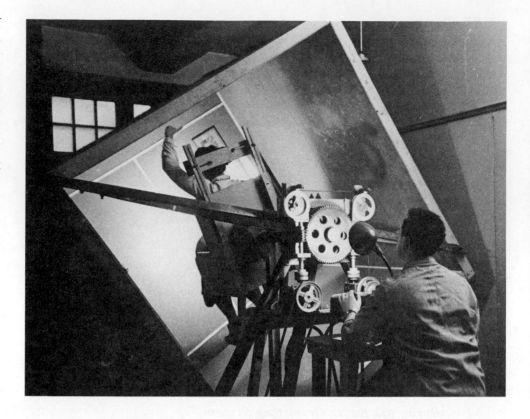

Another situation in which there is frequently confusion between information from the visual system and the basic orienting system is flying. It is not uncommon for pilots to sense that the earth is tilting when the plane is in a banked attitude; to feel that the plane is banked in the opposite direction when it skids in a flat turn; to experience a strong sensation that a level plane is tilted following recovery from a roll; or to feel that the plane is flying level when it is climbing or dropping slowly (Bartley, 1972, from Vinacke, 1947). In short, our basic orienting systems are inadequate inside airplanes that move easily in three dimensions, going incredibly faster than the human body would dream of going, and producing gravitational forces that exceed those to which we are accustomed. The plane's own orientation systems are considerably more reliable.

The Auditory System

What is there to say about the ear, that insignificant-looking, immobile, partially recessed piece of skin and cartilage spiraling loosely from each side of the head? Scientists have gone beyond this external ear, which they name the **pinna**, to the middle and the inner ear. And, in their terse, analytical manner, they have said the following.

Function

The function of the ear is not simply to permit us to hear—to sense vibrations and to make sense of (perceive) them. It has three other important functions. First, it allows us to detect the direction of a sound source, its distance (within limits), and (also within limits) the nature of its movements. It is largely because we have two ears rather than just one that we are able to use our **auditory systems** as direction finders. Sound waves, the physical energy to which our ears are sensitive, strike our ears at

Pinna The Latin term for the outer ear; the skin and cartilage that we identify as ears.

Auditory system A perceptual system whose principal sensory organs are the ears and whose function is to permit detection of sounds, of their direction and distance, and of other characteristics of vibrations that are important in our understanding of the environment.

PART ONE Physiology, Consciousness, and Perception

slightly different times unless we are facing directly toward or away from the sound source. It is then a simple matter to orient the head so that the source of sound is faced directly, which puts our noses in the general direction of that source. Laboratory research has found that two sounds separated by as little as 0.0001 second, and fed to the ears by means of stereophonic headphones, will be perceived as coming from the left or right depending on which sound is fed first (Békésy, 1971; Griffin, 1959). Certain characteristics of sound waves also allow us to deduce distance. Movement is reflected in changes in the direction from which the sound is emanating. Interestingly, however, we are able to orient toward sound primarily in one plane, that, of course, being horizontal. Sounds that emanate from above or below cannot be located nearly as rapidly or as easily, as anyone who has attempted to find a high-flying plane or to locate a whistling flock of goldeneye ducks can testify. The owl, in contrast, has its auditory canals at different angles, enabling it to locate sound sources in more than one plane. This is fortunate, since it does much of its hunting in full flight, and in the dark.

A second function of the auditory system is to permit identification. We have no difficulty differentiating between thousands of different sounds: bird calls and all manner of wildlife; the countless mechanical sounds of our cities with their automobiles, trucks, buses, bells, chimes, rings, growls, grunts, whooshes, and wheezes. We can identify falling rain, flowing water, showers, drips, lakes, and oceans. My Remington typewriter pulses arrhythmically when it doesn't click or clack. And I would know it anywhere. But perhaps more important than all this, it is my marvelous auditory system that enables me to recognize a hundred voices on my telephone. And it is largely because of that system as well that you and I could communicate outside my Remington if you were here, or I there. In a real sense, then, communication is the last function of the auditory system.

The auditory system has sometimes received less attention than it might, partly because of the greater importance accorded the visual system. But hearing does have some advantages over sight, not the least of which is that it can take place in total darkness. Sound waves are dependent upon a molecular medium, air being the medium of choice, although water and other solids also conduct sound waves. Vision, however, is dependent upon light; it cannot occur in the dark.

Sound Waves

The phrase **sound waves** is something of a misnomer. A wave is not a sound any more than a wavelength is a color. The sound is the subjective effect of what J. J. Gibson (1966) terms a *vibratory event*. Vibrations, described as back-and-forth movements, are caused by mechanical disturbances or dislocations: the movements of vocal cords, the rupturing or breaking of solids; the movements of liquids; movements of the mechanisms inside my Remington typewriter. The vibrations themselves move through a medium such as air in the form of waves resulting from the alternate compression and rarefaction of air molecules (as illustrated in Figure 4.6). The waves move spherically outward from the center of the disturbance, much as waves created by dropping a pebble on calm water travel over its surface. Since sound waves travel at relatively constant speeds, the wave front relates directly to the distance between the perceiver and the source. As mentioned earlier, direction of the source is then determined in terms of the time that lapses between reception by one ear and by the other.

Waves can be described in terms of the number of waves that are set up in a given unit of time, the amplitude of these waves, and their complexity (see Figure 4.7). The number of waves per second corresponds to the speed of the vibration. Obviously, a rapidly vibrating tuning fork will create more waves per second than one that is vibrating more slowly. Number of waves per second is called **frequency** and is measured in Hertz units (Hz), named after a nineteenth-century German physicist,

Sound waves Displacements of air molecules caused by vibratory events, whose subjective effect is the perception of sound. Waves are physical events definable in terms of molecular changes; sound is a subjective interpretation of the effects of these waves.

Frequency One of three characteristics of waves that give rise to perceptions of sound. Frequency is defined by number of waves per second, measured in Hertz units. Frequency of sound waves is related to perception of pitch.

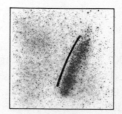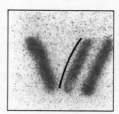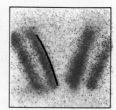

Figure 4.6 A vibrating rod in slow motion. Successive illustrations demonstrate that the rod creates sound waves by alternately compressing (darker red) and rarefying the surrounding molecules. The graph at the bottom illustrates the wave created by the vibrating rod.

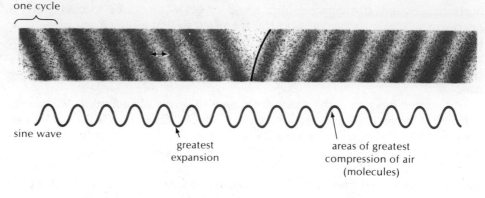

one cycle

sine wave

greatest expansion

areas of greatest compression of air (molecules)

Figure 4.7 Why do sound waves differ from one another? Sound waves can vary according to three dimensions. They can vary in pitch, which is a function of the number of waves per unit of time (frequency) (**a**); they can vary in loudness, which is a function of the height of the wave (amplitude) (**b**); and they can vary in timbre, which is a function of the individual frequencies of waves combined to yield a different subjective experience of sound (complexity)—for instance, when a cello and a flute play a duet (**c**).

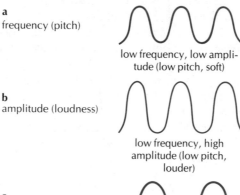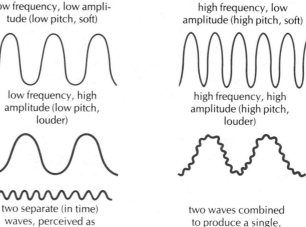

a
frequency (pitch)

low frequency, low amplitude (low pitch, soft)

high frequency, low amplitude (high pitch, soft)

b
amplitude (loudness)

low frequency, high amplitude (low pitch, louder)

high frequency, high amplitude (high pitch, louder)

c
complexity (timbre)

two separate (in time) waves, perceived as separate sounds

two waves combined to produce a single, more complex sound

Amplitude One of three characteristics of waves that produce sounds, defined physically as the height of wave peaks. Amplitude corresponds to the violence of the vibratory event that gave rise to the wave, and is related to perception of loudness.

Complexity One of three characteristics of sound waves, physically defined in terms of the mixture of waves that emanate from a vibration source. Complexity of sound waves corresponds to subjective impressions of timbre.

Heinrich Hertz. One Hertz unit corresponds to one vibration per second. The **amplitude** of a wave, defined physically as the vertical distance between wave peaks, corresponds to the violence of the vibratory event and is not constant throughout the wave field. That is, maximum amplitude occurs next to the sound source and decreases in an outward direction. Amplitude is measured in decibels. **Complexity** refers to the mixture of waves that emanate from the vibration source, most waves being composed of a number of waves of different frequencies and amplitudes. (See Box 4.1.)

Our Perception of Sound Waves

We perceive auditory wave characteristics as pitch, loudness, and timbre. Wave frequency determines the pitch we hear; amplitude determines loudness; and complexity determines timbre (see Figure 4.7).

Pitch   High or low tones (pitch) are a function of frequency. Some sounds are too high for the human ear; their frequencies are too great. Some are too low (their frequencies are too low), which is quite different from not being sufficiently loud. A normal human ear is sensitive to frequencies ranging from 16 Hz (16 waves per second) to 20,000 Hz (children hear higher frequencies than adults; and women hear higher frequencies than men). Waves below and above this range respectively are referred to as subsonic and supersonic. A number of animals, the most notable probably being the dog, the bat, and the porpoise, are sensitive to sounds considerably

---

BOX 4.1

Echolocation

Many porpoises and whales find their prey in murky oceans through the use of a natural sonar system similar to that employed by bats. The process, termed *echolocation*, involves responding to the echo that results when sounds emitted by these creatures bounce off objects. Blindness poses no real problems for these animals, but it does for humans. Nevertheless, some blind people often display an almost uncanny ability to avoid all obstacles, often claiming they can sense them through their hands or faces. Is that, in fact, the case? Science looked at the problem many times between 1890 and 1940, turning away inconclusively each time. Finally Dallenbach of Cornell, with two graduate students (Michael Supa, who was blind, and Milton Cotzin, who wasn't), tackled the problem (reported by Griffin, 1959). They arranged a series of screens as obstacles along a corridor. A number of subjects were recruited, some of them blind and others not. Those who weren't spent several days wearing blindfolds in an attempt to learn how to avoid obstacles. In the experiment, subjects were asked to indicate when they first sensed that they were approaching an obstacle, and then to approach it as closely as possible without touching it. Obstacles were moved periodically so that subjects never knew where to expect them, or indeed, whether to expect them at all. A number of subjects, both sighted and blind, could detect obstacles and avoid them reliably. In fact, they could detect them from an average of 6.9 feet away.

In order to determine how these obstacles were being detected, investigators attempted to eliminate information that might be derived from other senses (vision having already been ruled out), one at a time. Subjects had their faces and hands completely covered with heavy felt. If sensations do come through the hands or face, this might prevent their being perceived. It didn't. Subjects could still detect obstacles from an average of 5.25 feet away.

Subjects were then deafened as much as possible. They wore wax earplugs, cotton earplugs, ear muffs, and padding over the sides of their heads. Thus bedecked, they walked unsuspectingly into every obstacle placed in their paths. They had lost all ability to detect obstacles. Does this demonstrate conclusively that hearing is involved in detection of obstacles among the blind? Science, my friends, is a thorough person. Perhaps, the investigators reasoned, blind people detect obstacles by means of some other sense that is somehow muffled when mufflers are put over the ears. The sense might not be hearing at all. How does science examine a question of this complexity?

The investigators had an answer. Subjects were placed in one room and handed a telephone receiver. This receiver was connected to a transmitter that was then carried by a subject walking the obstacle course. Now, only the sounds that the subjects would hear if they were walking the course would be transmitted to them. The results were highly reassuring. Subjects predicting obstacles simply as a function of the sounds they could hear on their telephones performed almost as well as they would have in the course proper. They could now detect obstacles at an average of 6.4 feet. Would this experiment satisfy science? No. What if there is some subtle change in the breathing or in the footsteps of the person carrying the transmitter? Or unconscious telepathic communication?

In the next phase of the experiment, the microphone was placed on an animated cart. Its breath would not change, and it would alter its course only as subjects guided it, for the controls would be in their hands although they would be in another room! Acting now on the hunch that footsteps created echoes that might provide the clues to obstacle location (having already found that subjects in bare feet on carpet performed much more poorly than well-shod subjects on harder floors), the cart was also equipped with a loudspeaker.

Subjects could still detect the obstacles, though perhaps not quite as effectively. There appears to be little doubt that humans, too, can and do make use of echolocation.

Certain animals such as the whale use *echolocation* (a word that means exactly what it says—judging location by the length of time sound waves take to echo). Studies show that many people, both blind people and sighted people who wear blindfolds over a period of time, not only can avoid walking into obstacles, but can detect an obstruction from as far as 7 feet away.

Table 4.2 Decibel Values of Some Ordinary Sounds

Source of Sound	Decibel Value	Consequences
Electric guitars in rock concerts	125	
Loudest woman in 1973 British shouting contest		
Hammering on steel plate two feet away	115	Pain threshold for humans
Loudest man in 1973 British shouting contest		
	105	
Riveter 35 feet away		
Subway train		
Pneumatic drill at ten feet	95	Possible hearing damage with prolonged exposure
	85	
	75	
Noisiest spot at Niagara Falls		
Ordinary conversation at three feet	65	
Department store shopping		
Quiet automobile ten or more feet away	55	
	45	
Night noises in a city	35	
	25	
Quiet garden in London		
Average whisper at four feet	15	
Rustle of leaves in gentle breeze		
Quiet whisper five feet away	5	
	0	Hearing threshold: arbitrary value for point below which an acoustic wave at 1,000 Hz will not be heard
A butterfly at 6 feet		
Butter slowly melting		

beyond those we perceive. The silent dog whistle is silent only because it creates vibrations in excess of 20,000 Hz. Porpoises and bats emit sounds in the range of 100,000 Hz which they use for echolocation.

Decibel A measure of perceived loudness of sounds. Zero decibels is the threshold for human hearing.

Loudness   Loudness corresponds to the amplitude (intensity) of waves and is measured in **decibels** (dB units). Zero dB has been arbitrarily set as the threshold (lower limit) for normal hearing given a tone of 1,000 Hz, loudness being *in part* a function of frequency (for example, tones below 100 Hz or above 15,000 Hz reach threshold at 40 dB or more). A sound ten times louder is 10 dB; one 10,000 times louder is 40 decibels (10^4). In other words, perceived loudness increases logarithmically with increasing decibels. Table 4.2 presents some ordinary sounds and their approximate decibel values. Exposure to sounds that are too loud can result in permanently impaired hearing. Kryter's (1970) extensive review of the effects of noise on humans, however, does not support the popular view that it might induce other severe stress-related psychological and physiological ill effects. Indeed, the literature points strongly to the fact that we adapt rather well to working and even to sleeping in what might be described as noisy environments. *Noise* in this context does not refer simply to the loudness of a sound, but to the ongoing patterns of background auditory stimulation as well. Although excessive noise probably does not typically have serious consequences (other than impairing hearing, which is itself serious), it does have other less

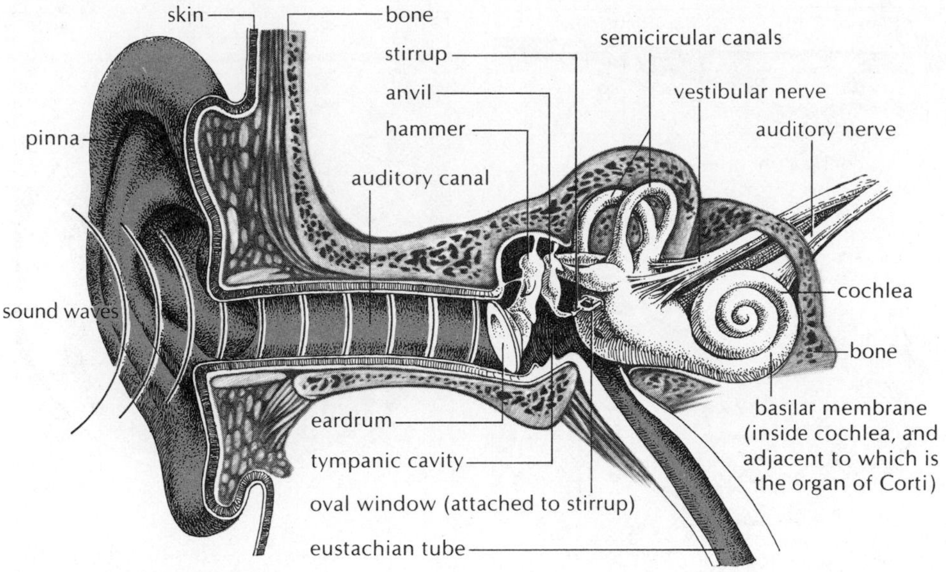

Figure 4.8 The human ear is a complex arrangement of tubes, canals, containers, fluids, membranes, and nerves.

Diagram labels: skin, bone, stirrup, anvil, hammer, auditory canal, pinna, sound waves, semicircular canals, vestibular nerve, auditory nerve, cochlea, bone, basilar membrane (inside cochlea, and adjacent to which is the organ of Corti), eardrum, tympanic cavity, oval window (attached to stirrup), eustachian tube

severe effects. Kryter includes among these the masking of speech sounds and other sounds that we might be attempting to hear; auditory fatigue, defined as a temporary loss of hearing acuity; excessive loudness of speech, probably as compensation for interacting in continual noise; a vague and general bothersomeness of noise; and the startle reaction, particularly in response to such extreme noises as sonic booms.

Timbre   Sounds are almost never pure. That is, they do not consist of waves with identical frequencies, but are instead a mixture of frequencies. Even a single note played on a piano has overtones—slightly different auditory waves. Subjective interpretation of these mixtures gives rise to what is termed *timbre,* and accounts in large part for the richness of auditory perceptions. The same notes played on different musical instruments can usually be differentiated easily, particularly by musicians and others who are familiar with the instruments. Similarly, human voices present great varieties of timbres, and great variation within these varieties. The physics of loudness and pitch are simpler than those of timbre. Consequently, the perhaps more important, though more elusive, perceptions made possible by our responses to the complexity of sound waves have tended to be overlooked. We take too much for granted our ability to discriminate between a whisper and the rustling of silk sheets; our mother's voice and those of other mothers.

The Auditory Apparatus

In your ear there is a complex arrangement of tubes, canals, containers, fluids, membranes, and nerves, arranged as depicted in Figure 4.8. For convenience, logical simplicity, and because nature might have intended it to be that way, scientists group these various components into three general areas: external ear, middle ear, and inner ear—unimaginative but relatively accurate labels.

The external ear includes the pinna, the oval, wrinkled, spiraling extremity mentioned earlier. Although three muscles attach each of these visible ears to the head, the ears remain virtually immobile, unlike those of most nonhuman animals. This external ear spirals into a circular tube approximately one-quarter inch wide and one inch long, the auditory canal. At the end of this wax-filled canal is the tympanic membrane, commonly called the eardrum.

The middle ear consists of a small air-filled space called the tympanic cavity. Inside this cavity are the three minute bones (ossicles) popularly named after the objects they closely resemble: the hammer, the anvil, and the stirrup. This last ossicle fits over a small membrane (oval window) which leads into the inner ear.

Figure 4.9 The inner ear (cochlea) viewed from the interior as it would appear if uncurled and cut in half longitudinally (**a**); and as it would appear if uncurled and cut cross-sectionally (**b**). The last of the middle ear ossicles, the stirrup, vibrates against the oval window, setting up waves in the fluid of the cochlea. These waves are transmitted to the basilar membrane, stimulating hair cells on the organ of Corti, and thus initiating neural impulses in the auditory nerve.

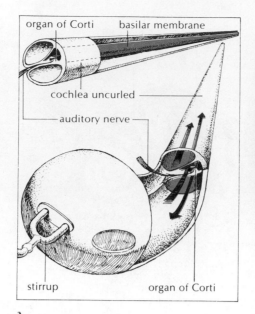

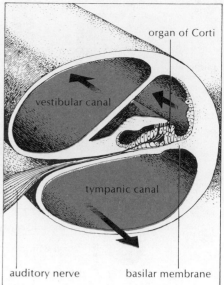

a

b

The inner ear is filled with a thin fluid contained in a spiral structure (the cochlea). This structure contains a membrane (basilar membrane) adjacent to which are the nerve cells that act as sound receptors and translators. That is, it is in the cochlea that waves are translated into neural impulses. These nerve cells are arranged in a line and are collectively labeled the organ of Corti. Interestingly, and fortunately, the organ of Corti is isolated from the blood supply. If this were not the case, we would all be deafened by the roaring of our bloodstreams and the pounding of our pulses. As it is, there are apparently some individuals who are so sensitive to sounds that they can hear, when placed in an absolutely quiet room, the random movements of molecules.

How the Ear Works

Auditory waves are gathered by the pinna. From there, these waves are funneled into the auditory canal toward the eardrum, which they set to vibrating much as an ordinary drum might vibrate, although the vibration is very minimal. The vibration corresponds physically to the characteristics of the sound waves (which, in turn, are specific to the event that precipitated them). The vibrations of the eardrum are transmitted to the three ossicles of the middle ear, which amplify them. The direct physical connection of the last of these ossicles, the stirrup, to the inner ear through the oval window sets up wavelike motions in the fluid contained in the cochlea. Hair cells on the organ of Corti respond to these waves as they strike the basilar membrane, initiating neural transmission via the auditory nerve to the auditory centers in the brain (see Figure 4.9). Each ear feeds signals to both the right and left temporal lobes, much as each eye relays impulses to the visual cortex in both the right and left hemispheres.

From a physical point of view, functioning of the auditory system involves the conversion of acoustic energy (sound waves) into mechanical energy at the tympanic membrane and through the ossicles, into hydraulic energy in the fluid of the inner ear, and finally into electrical energy at the organ of Corti (Figure 4.10).

One of the truly amazing features of this intricate conduction of vibrations is its fidelity. Wever and Bray (1930) demonstrated this phenomenon by inserting an electrode in the cochlea of an anesthetized cat, amplifying the signals picked up by this

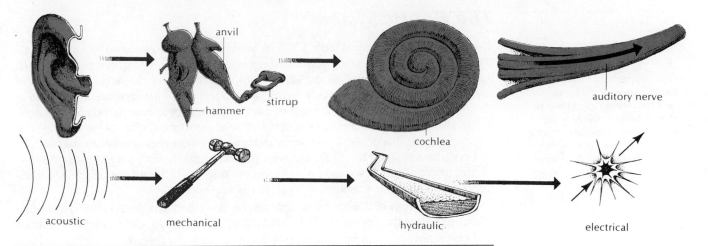

anvil

hammer stirrup

cochlea

auditory nerve

acoustic mechanical hydraulic electrical

Figure 4.10 Sensation involves the conversion of energy. This is most clearly demonstrated in the auditory system, but it occurs in other perceptual systems as well. The acoustic energy of sound waves is translated into mechanical energy as the tympanic membrane and the ossicles (hammer, anvil, and stirrup) vibrate. In the fluid of the inner ear, the mechanically transmitted energy is converted to hydraulic energy, which triggers an electrical impulse in the organ of Corti.

electrode, and transmitting them through a loudspeaker. Music that is fed into the cat's ear can be transmitted in this manner with virtually no distortion. So finely tuned is this system, and so independent from other systems, that it is possible to do the same thing with a dead cat. There are easier ways of listening to music, however.

Precise details of how the inner ear (cochlea) translates fluid motion into electrical impulses that we can then interpret as sound remain unknown (Dallos, 1981). There are, however, a number of theoretical explanations for this phenomenon. The **place theory**, attributed to Helmholtz and Békésy, maintains essentially that waves of different frequency give rise to different neural impulses by causing displacement of different parts of the basilar membrane (the organ of Corti and the basilar membrane are adjacent). Békésy (1956) showed that high-frequency tones cause displacement at one end of the basilar membrane, and that tones of intermediate frequency cause displacement further up the membrane. The next observation, however, weakened the theory considerably: lower-frequency tones cause displacements along the entire area of the basilar membrane.

A second theory, the **frequency theory**, holds that perception of pitch is a function of the frequency with which impulses are transmitted, and that this frequency corresponds in one-to-one fashion with the actual frequency of the auditory waves. Thus, a wave of 500 Hz would give rise to 500 neural impulses per second. Since, however, a neuron cannot ordinarily fire more than 1,000 times per second, frequencies in a higher Hz range could not be accounted for by the repeated firing of a single neuron. Wever and Bray (1930) therefore proposed the **volley theory**, which speculates that for frequencies greater than 1,000, single neurons alternate, firing every second, third, fourth cycle, and so on, and that other neurons would then fire on cycles that had been missed by the first neuron. Thus, neurons would be firing in rhythmic volleys.

Bartley (1969) advances the supposition, as do a number of other researchers, that a correct explanation may well involve a combination of these theories. For example, place and volley mechanisms might account for the perception of higher frequencies, whereas frequency of transmission might explain perception of lower frequencies.

Place theory A theory of hearing that suggests that different waves give rise to different neural impulses because they cause displacement of different parts of the basilar membrane.

Frequency theory The frequency theory of hearing suggests that neural impulses correspond in frequency to the frequency of sound waves. This means that a wave with a frequency of 400 units per second would give rise to 400 neural impulses per second. Since a neuron cannot ordinarily fire more than 1,000 times per second, this theory cannot explain perception of sounds corresponding to higher frequencies.

Volley theory A theory of hearing that hypothesizes that for sounds that are of such high frequency that neural impulses cannot correspond to them in one-to-one fashion, single neurons fire rhythmically in alternating fashion.

The Haptic System

The term *haptic* is derived from a Greek word meaning "to be able to lay hold of." When it was more popular to separate the senses into as many as might possibly exist, the haptic system included all the skin senses, of which there might be four, plus the kinesthetic sense. **Kinesthesis**, a word for which there is no accurate equivalent in ordinary speech, refers to awareness of our bodies and awareness of our movements. It has also been called the *muscle, tendon, and joint sense*. The physiology of the sensory systems that underlie the haptic perceptual system remains somewhat obscure and controversial (see Box 4.2). As a wise person probably once said, the clarification of obscurity and the resolution of controversy must await new facts or greater intelligence. Failing these, it is always possible to oversimplify.

The function of the haptic system can be described simply. It is the system that allows us to feel the presence of objects next to our bodies, to detect certain qualities and characteristics of these objects, to sense our bodies relative to these objects, and to sense our bodies themselves. Sensors pertinent to the haptic system are found throughout the body, with the exception of in brain matter. They tend to be concentrated near the surface of the body and in the muscles, joints, and tendons. These sensors have been described as mechanoreceptors because they are sensitive to mechanical energy. Thermal receptors are also involved, these being sensitive to temperature. For discussion here, we divide sensors into skin systems and kinesthetic systems.

The Skin Senses

We are responsive to heat and cold, to pain, and to pressure. The stimulation that gives rise to each of these sensations cannot be quantified physically as can sound waves or light waves. Nor has it been possible to identify specific types of sensors that respond to each of these different sensations. A number of very different nerve endings in the skin have been identified, and human bodies have been mapped with respect to areas that appear to be sensitive only to pressure, only to temperature, and only to pain. Woodworth and Schlosberg (1954) report an often replicated procedure for mapping these points. A grid is drawn on a subject's arm, the subject is blindfolded, and a hair, a cold rod, a hot rod, and a needle are systematically applied to the arm within this grid. The subject indicates the nature of the sensation, if any. Figure 4.11 depicts this procedure and indicates the relative density of heat, cold, pain, and pressure spots on the human body. Results of this procedure led quickly to the belief that there are different receptors for each of these sensations. Microscopic examination of successive layers of skin tissue eventually revealed that this belief was erroneous. Several unexpected findings also helped dispel the belief. One, referred to as *paradoxical cold,* occurs when a point on the skin is touched with a hot rod (around 110° Fahrenheit). Subjects occasionally report a distinct sensation of *cold.* The other involves the subjective response to grasping two intertwined metal pipes, one of which contains warm water, and the other cold (Figure 4.12). The perception in this case is frequently of heat. Although the first experiment (paradoxical cold) might be explained in terms of the types of receptors activated, the second presents a different problem. Since our hands can sense both heat and cold, it does not appear reasonable to suppose that subjects sense heat because no cold receptors are activated. A final explanation is yet to come.

Several other characteristics of skin sensation are worth noting. One is that those parts of the body that are most sensitive to pressure include the parts covered with hair or nails, the tongue and lips, and the hands (Darian-Smith, 1982). At the base of each hair is a concentration of neural receptors, as at the base of each fingernail. Very slight pressure on a nail or the very gentle bending of a whisker can easily be felt. Whiskers are relatively stiff, and their movement displaces and activates nerve cells at

Kinesthesis A part of the haptic perceptual system, relating specifically to knowledge of the movements of the body or of its limbs. Sometimes considered to include three separate sensory systems: the muscle sense; the tendon sense; and the joint sense.

BOX 4.2

Pain

It has proven difficult to isolate specific areas of the brain, precise receptors, or identifiable neural pathways that are involved in pain. This is partly because pain may result from a variety of stimuli that affect different parts of the body, or may occur in the apparent absence of any stimulation. Intense noise, blinding lights, cold, heat, pressure, or actual tissue damage are often painful. On occasion, patients report intense pain in a limb that they have lost (termed *phantom limb* pain). Similarly, psychiatric patients frequently report very severe pain for which there is no organic basis (Veilleux & Melzack, 1976).

Traditional physiological explanations for pain are based on the notion that there are pain receptors in the body, many of which also provide simple sensations of heat, cold, or pressure, and that stimulation of these receptors beyond a certain *threshold* (the pain threshold) results in pain sensation. Hebb (1949) advanced a *pattern* theory of pain, which held that intensity or amount of stimulation is related to sensations of pain, and that no specific pain receptors are therefore necessary. This theory might explain why intense noise or blinding lights are sometimes perceived as painful.

A more recent pain theory has been advanced by Melzack (Melzack & Wall, 1965; Melzack & Perry, 1975). It provides explanations both for pain sensation and for the inhibition of pain. Known as the *gate-control theory,* it may be described briefly as follows. Pain is initiated by the activation of nerve fibers, labeled *C-fibers,* which in turn activate specific neural cells known as *dorsal horn cells.* These connect to sensory areas of the brain involved in pain sensation. The C-fibers may be activated by intense stimulation, injury, and other events that we interpret as painful or, on occasion, by the absence of stimulation (as in the case of certain psychiatric patients or of individuals with phantom limb pain). Put another way, the activation of C-fibers open a *gate,* so that impulses may then proceed to the brain's pain centers. A second, critical aspect of the theory proposes that another type of nerve fiber, labeled *A-fibers,* has an effect directly opposite to that of the C-fiber; in other words, activation of these fibers may close the gate entirely or in part. A-fibers conduct impulses more rapidly than C-fibers.

This theory explains a number of situations that cannot easily be explained by other pain theories. Consider, for example, that music has been shown to reduce the felt intensity of pain associated with a dentist's drill. Pattern theory cannot explain this phenomenon in view of the fact that music does not decrease the amount or intensity of painful stimulation; in fact, it represents an increase in stimulation. Gate-control theory, however, simply suggests that whereas the dentist's drill activates C-fibers, music activates A-fibers. Thus, music partially closes the gate, thereby reducing the intensity of pain. In the same way, phantom limb pain might be explained on the grounds that, in the absence of the limb, A-fibers remain inactive and the gate remains open. Melzack (1970) reports that applying gentle pressure to the stump (in the case of a phantom leg) relieves pain. His explanation is that this pressure activates A-fibers. In the same way, he suggests that the effectiveness of acupuncture in relieving pain is related directly to the fact that the needles employed are inserted in such a way that they activate major A-fibers, thus blocking all pain sensations.

One of the major potential contributions of Melzack's gate-control theory of pain lies in the possibility of controlling pain (perhaps through drugs or surgically). Evidence suggests that the "gate" may be located in a specific part of the spinal cord known as the *substantia gelatinosa,* where the C-fibers synapse prior to activating the dorsal horn cells. The inhibitory effect of the A-fibers may simply prevent the transmission of pain information to the C-fiber synapses. If the theory is correct, additional information about the substantia gelatinosa may lead to major medical breakthroughs.

Although the Melzack pain theory provides a useful explanation for some of the characteristics of pain and its alleviation, we still do not know a great deal about this subject (Weisenberg, 1977). For example, as we mentioned in Chapter 2, scientists have only recently discovered the presence of naturally occurring opiates (endorphins and enkephalins) in the brain, and are just beginning to explore their role in the alleviation of pain (Bolles & Fanselow, 1982). It now seems clear that these substances do reduce pain. That they do so by closing gates is not as certain. It appears, as well, that the effectiveness of other opiates such as morphine may well be due to the fact that these substances are very similar to naturally occurring opiates such as the endorphins or enkephalins (Coren, Porac, & Ward, 1979).

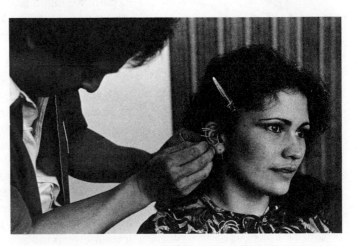

What causes pain? According to Melzack's gate-control theory, intense stimulation activates certain nerve fibers known as C-fibers, which open a "gate" to let pain impulses proceed to areas of the brain involved in pain sensation. Another type of nerve fiber, known as A-fibers, may close the "gate," inhibiting pain impulses from reaching the brain. Melzack's theory might help to explain acupuncture and the soothing effect of music, both of which may activate A-fibers.

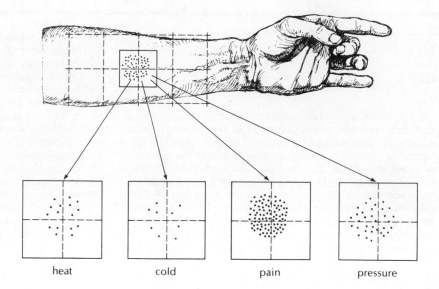

Figure 4.11 A procedure for mapping receptors on the skin. While the subject is blindfolded, a hair, a warm rod, a cold rod, and sharp needle are systematically applied to the arm, upon which a grid has been drawn. Although this procedure is useful for disclosing the relative sensitivity of different parts of the body to heat, cold, pain, and pressure, it has not led to the positive identification of different sorts of receptors.

heat   cold   pain   pressure

Habituation   Progressive reduction in sensitivity or reactivity to stimulation.

warm

cold

Figure 4.12 Tricking the skin senses. When two metal pipes are intertwined, one containing cold water and the other containing warm water, the person who grasps the coils will feel the sensation of heat—not of warmth, coldness, or tepidness, as one would expect.

their base. This principle is evident in certain rodents and in members of the cat family, whose long, stiff whiskers serve effectively as exploratory sense organs, enabling them to move quickly in near-darkness and through small spaces with little fear of colliding with walls.

A second characteristic of touch sensitivity concerns the wide disparity among pressure receptors on the body. This can easily be demonstrated. If you touch people at two places on the back, they may detect only a single point of pressure even if the touches are separated by as much as three inches. Two touches on the tongue, however, will be sensed as being distinct even if they are only a fraction of an inch apart.

One final important feature of these receptors is that some are highly subject to **habituation** and others are not. Receptors habituate very quickly, for example, to sensations of touch. If this were not the case, we would constantly be aware of the sensations caused by the clothing we wear, our hair, and other sources of tactile stimulation. Pain, however, is less easily habituated to. Much that hurts continues to hurt until the cause of the pain is removed. Although we do habituate to pain to some degree, not habituating obviously has very high survival value. If we habituated easily to pain, we might find ourselves dying frequently of minor causes, and Hemingway's epic statement might become more appropriate than ever: "People are dying who have never died before."

Kinesthesis

That we sense bodily position and movement is taken almost entirely for granted. With your eyes closed, you have little difficulty in describing where each of your limbs is, or in moving them in various well-controlled ways. The information that allows you to do this emanates from sensors located in three places: the muscles, the joints, and the tendons. These sensors appear to respond principally to muscular contraction and relaxation, and to movement of the joints.

There are, in addition, other sensors in various parts of the body besides the skin, many of these serving to make us aware of pain. Interestingly, they appear to function differently depending on where they are. Pain sensors next to the outer skin layer respond to cuts, blows, squeezes, burns, itches, and so on. Pain sensors in the intestine respond acutely to intestinal gases, which might be interpreted as intense pressure. They do not, however, respond to cuts: the human intestine can be sliced absolutely painlessly. Similarly, the brain can be surgically manipulated with no pain, although the skin and skull must be anesthetized. The explanation for this is, as was mentioned earlier, that there are no pain receptors in the brain.

The Savor System

Psychologists have for some time considered the **savor system** the "lower" senses, relegating vision and hearing to the "higher" position, but it has never been entirely clear why. Certainly vision and hearing are no more essential for survival than are tasting and smelling. Indeed, tasting and smelling are, in a sense, defensive systems designed at least in part to prevent us from poisoning ourselves. Consider, for example, that our tongues are most sensitive to bitter tastes and least sensitive to sweet tastes. Many substances that are bitter contain alkaloids, which are poisonous. The ability to detect even minute quantities of these, combined with our natural avoidance of bitter foods, must surely have had some survival value in those days when our foods were not entirely preselected, preprocessed, and prepackaged.

The savor system is variously known as two separate senses, taste and smell; as a chemical sense (or as two chemical senses), since it is responsive to chemical properties of certain substances and gases; as the gustatory sense; or as the taste-smell system. Its functions appear to include detection, discrimination, and appreciation, primarily with respect to materials that reach the mouth, but also with respect to substances that evoke perceptions of odor. That is, within limits, this system allows us to detect the nature of materials, to discriminate among different materials, and to respond emotionally—in short, to appreciate or not to appreciate. Interestingly, although subjective emotional reaction is intimately linked with savoring, relatively little has been written about the aesthetics of taste. One achieves little fame by having a better-developed, more exacting savor system. We do not often assume that gourmets taste with more skill than we do, but are more likely to think that they are simply more given to self-indulgence. The professional wine tasters, cheese samplers, and "smellers" are rare exceptions. We do not try to emulate them.

The savor system does not depend solely on those specialized organs responsive to tastes and smells, but includes as well reactions to pain, temperature, and touch (see Figure 4.13). The taste of food, as is well known, is highly dependent upon its odor. It is not as well known, but just as intuitively true, that the texture, consistency, granularity, and other physical properties of food affect our subjective reactions to its taste. Furthermore, temperature plays an important role with respect to tasting many foods and beverages. Cold coffee does not taste the same as hot coffee, and cold mashed potatoes are most unappetizing. That pain is sometimes involved in the subjective experience of savoring food is illustrated by the delight with which some individuals eat banana pepper sandwiches with hot mustard. As J. J. Gibson (1966) suggests, the mouth is a highly sensitive haptic organ—an exploratory organ—as well as a taste organ. Despite the fact that smell, taste, and various other haptic and visual systems are all involved in savoring, the traditional sense of smell (olfaction) and taste are treated separately here for the sake of simplicity.

Olfaction

It is widely believed, and probably accurately so, that olfaction is not nearly as well developed in humans as it is in most nonhuman species. Indeed, the part of the human brain that is given over to olfaction is minimal; in dogs, approximately one-third of the cortex is devoted to olfaction; and in many fish, the entire cortex is olfactory. The dog's olfactory sense is estimated to be 1 million times more sensitive than man's (Droscher, 1969). Bedichek (1960), in his intriguing account of notable and less notable noses, reports the case of Geisha, a spaniel trained to detect coffee smugglers in West Germany. She hardly ever failed. Dogs are now in wide use in the postal service, in law enforcement agencies, and in security agencies because of their olfactory sensitivity. They can be trained to find heroin or marijuana, to detect gas leaks, to track fugitives, to find missing persons, and to locate all manner of game for the hunter.

Savor system The perceptual system concerned with tasting and smelling.

Figure 4.13 The savor system depends on other sensory input besides that received from the olfactory epithelium and taste buds.

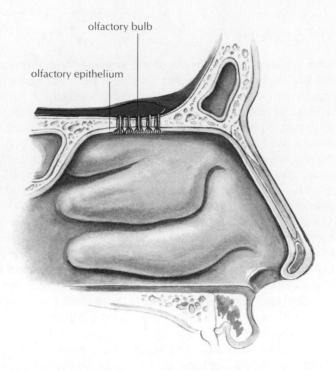

olfactory bulb

olfactory epithelium

We cannot do these things. It has sometimes been suspected that we can detect four separate odors and combinations thereof; it has also been thought that we can detect six distinct odors and their combinations; others have believed that we can discriminate reliably among seven. It was also believed that the shapes of different molecules could perhaps account for the different subjective olfactory impressions to which they give rise. There is virtually no evidence to corroborate these beliefs. One of the difficulties in this type of research is that perception of odor is subjective; odor is not a physical property of an object or of the gaseous molecules that emanate from it. Another difficulty is simply that we do not have an olfactory vocabulary. We are absolutely lost when we try to describe smells and must almost always do so by reference to other smells, or to objects that give rise to fairly typical smells. Consider, for example, Amoore et al.'s (1964) list of the seven odors to which we are sensitive. *Musky.* Now there is one of the few words that refers more often to smell than to anything else. Can you describe a musky smell? *Flowery.* Does a begonia smell like a rose? And does a wild rose smell like a florist's rose? *Camphorlike.* Camphor is a substance. Granted, it does have an odor. *Etherlike.* What, other than ether, smells etherlike? *Pepperminty.* There is a sweet smell. But sweet is a taste. Or is it? *Putrid.* Burning rubber is putrid. So is an unwashed hogsty in the middle of a muggy day. But they are quite different. *Pungent.* Yes, perhaps they are pungent as well.

Judging on the basis of our language, it would appear that we smell very imprecisely. But that may not be entirely true. Perhaps we have simply not found it necessary or useful to speak of odors with our enemies or friends ("even your best friend won't tell you!"). But we do know intuitively what is pleasant and what isn't. And the number of associations evoked by odors for which we have no names attests to the potential of our noses.

The nose is not really our olfactory organ, impressive though it might sometimes appear, and useful though it is as a breathing passage. In effect, in the course of breathing, it allows potentially odorous molecules to reach the true olfactory organ, the **olfactory epithelium**. This organ, directly connected to the olfactory regions of

Olfactory epithelium (plural, epithelia) The true olfactory organ, the olfactory epithelium is a thin mucous membrane located in each nostril. Odor-sensitive cells are located on the olfactory epithelium.

the brain (olfactory bulbs) by means of very short neural pathways, is found some distance up the nose, in each nostril. It is a thin mucous membrane approximately the size of a dime (see Figure 4.14). Its odor-sensitive cells are capable of regeneration in most vertebrates (Graziadei & Dehon, 1973).

Incidentally, have you ever noticed that noses invariably point downward? This presents two distinct advantages. One is that odors frequently originate from warmer sources and therefore tend to move upward; the other is that a nose that points downward is less likely to become filled with rain and other objects falling from the sky (see Box 4.3).

Taste

Taste, as indicated previously, is our subjective reaction to the chemical effects of certain substances in materials we put into our mouths, together with effects related to odor, touch, temperature, and pain. The principal organ of taste has long been considered to be the tongue. In fact, however, individuals who cannot detect odors are often unable to differentiate between foods that to others seem to taste quite different.

The cells sensitive to taste are located in taste buds on the tongue. It is believed that these cells regenerate frequently (as often as every seven days), but that with advancing age they do so less frequently or cease regenerating altogether. This explains the fact that very old people frequently lose all ability to taste food. Middle-aged people sometimes find themselves using considerably more salt and spices, presumably because greater stimulation is required to evoke the same subjective response.

Psychologists generally agree that we can detect four distinct tastes and their combinations: salty, sweet, sour, and bitter. Various parts of the tongue are more or less sensitive to these tastes, although there is somewhat more overlap than might be suggested by Figure 4.15. Again, the precise physiology of taste is unknown. It appears unlikely that specific cells respond only to one of these four tastes. It is probable that here, as in the other senses, patterns of neural activity are linked to subjective taste. There is no explanation, for example, for phenomena such as that described by Bartoshuk et al. (1972): if you eat a piece of artichoke heart and then drink a glass of water, the water will taste approximately as sweet as if it contained two teaspoons of sugar. This effect lasts for a few minutes following eating the artichoke.

Figure 4.15 The human tongue, showing taste buds and areas of greatest sensitivity to four distinct tastes.

BOX 4.3

Notable Noses

Anosmatic noses cannot detect smells. For an exceptionally gifted nose, we have another label, *macrosmatic*; and for noses not so notable, though not quite anosmatic, yet another: *microsmatic*.

There is some evidence that women may be more macrosmatic than men, at least with respect to certain odors that may be related to sexual attraction and behavior. It is no scientific secret that sexual behavior among numerous nonhuman species is highly dependent upon smell. Frequently the female in heat exudes odors that are highly attractive to the male, as any owner of a bitch will attest. Male moths can detect female moths at a distance of several miles and can then locate them. Owners of female moths might attest to

this as well. Science, for its part, would like to attest to the fact that the olfactory acuity of women is greater than that of men for certain ketosteroid compounds in urine. In fact, they can identify as many as seventeen of these compounds, with their acuity being directly related to the estral cycle (Money, 1965). Perhaps more striking, Bartley (1972) reports that *between menstrual periods,* women can easily detect a synthetic odor analogous to a sexual attractant among mammals. Men, and girls prior to puberty, can smell this odor only faintly or not at all.

What science has not yet established is the nature of women's reaction to this synthetic sexual attractant. Nor is it possible, at this time, to assert that primitive woman's sensitivity (and man's too, for that matter) might have been even greater. It is entirely possible that a small amount of this synthetic (or of the real stuff, perhaps) would have been considerably more effective than traditional courtship. But, as Hassett (1978) notes, "No scientist working in this field believes that a clear link has been established between a specific smell and human sexual behavior" (p. 45).

Main Points

1 Our senses are our contacts with reality.
2 Sensation is the translation of various forms of energy into neural impulses; interpretation of these impulses (as a sound or color, for example) is perception. In practice, it is difficult to separate sensation and perception; we perceive with our eyes, our hands, our noses, and so on as well as with our brains. It is for this reason that we speak of the senses as perceptual systems.
3 Attention is a state of readiness that serves to focus perception. Not attending is, in effect, not perceiving.
4 We ordinarily attend primarily to one source of stimulation at a time. This does not mean that we are totally unaware of other stimulation (as the cocktail party phenomenon shows).
5 Attention is generally drawn in the direction of change, novelty, complexity, repetition, and intensity, and is affected as well by our interests and expectations—with a number of exceptions.
6 The basic orienting system provides us information concerning the position of our body and its parts, movement, and our relation to gravity. Among other things, it permits us to remain upright.
7 The organ associated with the basic orienting system is the vestibular organ in the inner ear. It consists of the semicircular canals, the utricle, and the saccule, structures that contain the liquids whose movements tell us about our body's movements and positions.
8 The auditory system not only permits us to hear, but enables us to locate the source of a sound, to estimate its distance, and to detect its movements (within limits). This information is important in identifying aspects of the environment as well.
9 Sound waves are molecular disturbances brought about by the rapid movement (vibration) of a sound source. Sound waves can be described in terms of number of waves per second (frequency), size of the waves (amplitude), and their complexity.
10 The subjective effect of a sound wave is a sound that varies in loudness or intensity (corresponding to the amplitude of a wave); in pitch (corresponding to frequency, with higher frequencies being associated with higher pitches), and timbre (corresponding to complexity).
11 Translation of a sound wave (acoustic energy) into neural impulses involves changing that wave into an actual vibration (mechanical energy) at the tympanic membrane and through the ossicles; transforming the mechanical energy into wave motions (hydraulic energy) in the fluid of the inner ear; and finally translating this fluid energy into electrical energy at the organ of Corti.
12 The haptic system, our "feeling" system, includes the kinesthesic sense (awareness of our bodies and of movements, also called the muscle, tendon, and joint sense), and what are termed the skin senses (our ability to sense heat, cold, pain, and pressure). The physiology of the haptic system is not clearly understood.
13 The savor system includes the gustatory sense (taste) and the olfactory sense (smell). It also includes reactions to pain, temperature, and touch.
14 The true olfactory organ is not the nose, but the olfactory epithelium. Olfaction is not as highly developed in humans as in such animals as dogs.
15 Taste buds on various parts of the tongue detect four distinct tastes: salty, sweet, sour, and bitter.

Further Readings

The perceptual systems are described in more detail in the following two books:

Goldstein, E. B. *Sensation and perception.* Belmont, Calif.: Wadsworth, 1980.

Coren, S., Porac, C., and Ward, I. M. *Sensation and perception.* New York: Academic Press, 1979.

Gibson presents his views of perception in a readable and important book:

Gibson, J. J. *The senses considered as perceptual systems.* Boston: Houghton Mifflin, 1966.

Neisser discusses the role of learning, experience, and intellectual activity in perception. See especially the second chapter of:

Neisser, U. *Cognition and reality: Principles and implications of cognitive psychology.* San Francisco: W. H. Freeman, 1976.

Perceptual Systems: Seeing

All living things, from the smallest amoeba to the largest mammal, are sensitive to light. Even the sunflower turns its face to the sun almost as though the flower were an eye.

There are a number of interesting nonhuman eyes. The cat, for example, is reputed to have excellent night vision, a fact that is due not solely to its ability to open the pupil very wide, allowing a great deal of light to enter the eye, but also to a kind of mirror behind its retina (the light-sensitive portion of the eye, analogous to the film in a camera). This mirror, termed a *tapetum,* reflects light back onto the retina. It accounts for the fact that cats' eyes appear to glow when your automobile headlights surprise one at night. Headlights do not reflect off human eyes in the same way.

A number of insects also have very interesting eyes, many of them being of the compound variety. Dragonflies, for example, have several thousand separate eyes, each with its own pupil and its own light sensor. We have only two. It was long believed that each of these dragonfly eyes provides a separate image—a thousand pictures. If one picture is worth a thousand words, how many words can a dragonfly eye be worth?

In fact, compound eyes do not appear to provide separate images. Each "eye" has a single receptor; each, therefore, registers only a small portion of the total visual field, while other "eyes" register different portions of the same field. The result is a composite picture of a much wider visual field than the one we ordinarily perceive without moving our eyes. That is, each "eye" points in a slightly different direction so that, taken all together, the eyes of a dragonfly cover a greater area than human eyes. The dragonfly eye is very sensitive to movement but lacks the acuity of the human eye. It is also much better adapted for vision in conditions of low light—that, too, at a cost in visual acuity (see Figure 5.1).

Figure 5.1 A comparison of the images detected by the compound eye of a dragonfly and a human eye. Each "eye" in a compound eye is connected to only a single receptor and so registers only a small portion of the visual field. The result is not the millions of tiny pictures that we once thought insects saw, but a single, somewhat fuzzy picture from both eyes, with an extremely wide visual range (a result of the great surface exposure). Human eyes have a far more complex receptor system for picking up images (see Figures 5.3 and 5.4). The result is greater visual acuity, although range is diminished.

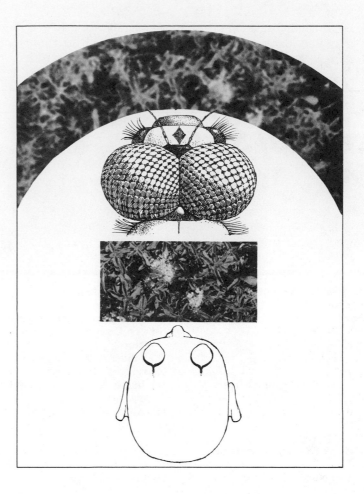

Other remarkable nonhuman eyes are those of the goat family (including the antelope) and those of some of the great birds of prey, which see clearly at distances far beyond those we can see without special aids such as binoculars or telescopes.

We might never have noticed that we only have two eyes had we not also noticed that many insects have a great many more than two. It might also have taken us some time to notice that our eyes point in the same direction, and to discover the advantages and disadvantages of that situation, had we not noticed that the eyes of many animals point in different directions. In general, the eyes of most predators point in the same direction. The advantage of binocular vision (both eyes looking at the same field) is that it permits a much more accurate judgment of distance, speed, and size, thereby making it considerably easier for the predator to intercept the prey. The eyes of many animals that are preyed upon point in different directions. The advantage of this for preyed-upon animals is that it provides them with a much greater field of vision, and consequently reduces the likelihood that they will be surprised and eaten. Thus, the eyes of the cat family, of dogs and wolves, and of hawks and eagles all point toward the front. Humans, too, have the eyes of predators. Most birds, most rodents, members of the deer family, rabbits, and a host of other animals have eyes that point to either side. The eyes of a chicken point in two different directions. If the chicken sees two visual images at once, how does it decide which one to look at? And what about a cross-eyed chicken?

Comparative studies of animal eyes also provide clues for the explanation of color vision. Most birds, many insects, and humans (as you are no doubt well aware) see a world of color. It is strongly believed that dogs and most other nonhuman mammals except cats do not, that theirs is a world of black and white. From the point of view of survival, it is doubtful that color vision presents any real advantages. There is very little important information in a color photograph, for example, that is not also in a black and white photograph—save hue (color). Comparisons among eyes of animals that are sensitive to color and those that aren't have enabled scientists to discover differences that might account for color vision.

Functions of Visual Perception

The eye, we have been told repeatedly, is like a camera. This is a good analogy for the *structure* of the eye, but, like most analogies, it is misleading. In its functioning, the eye is not like a camera. It is like itself and nothing else, as is made clear in these pages.

The eyes, like all other sensory organs, may be considered to have evolved to make it possible for us to perceive. They are part of a perceptual system, even as the hands, the nose, the tongue, the ears, and most portions of our bodies are parts of perceptual systems. But the information they provide and the perceptions that result are rather different from those resulting from other systems.

The primary function of visual perception is obvious: it permits us to detect our surroundings, and to detect changes in those surroundings. It also provides a means of detecting movement and of controlling it. Although it is true that some of the other perceptual systems provide us with information about our environments, about changes, and about movement, the information provided by the visual system is of a different nature, not dependent upon the same circumstances. Auditory perception, for example, enables us to detect certain aspects of our environment (I can hear my Remington complaining), to detect changes (I can hear it as the words *to detect changes* miraculously appear), and to perceive movement (with my eyes closed I can identify the sounds that correspond to its carriage shifting). Certain qualities of my immediate environment are discernible through odor, as well. This dusty Remington does smell rather bad. I can also touch it, and learn about its contours, its resistance, its texture. But only by looking at it do I perceive clearly its shape, its position relative to other objects in its surroundings, and its color. I can stand apart from it, it can be absolutely silent, and its distinctive odor can be cleverly camouflaged with an aerosol spray reminiscent of the piny woods. Provided there is some light, I will *see* it.

Structure of the Eye

The marvelous organ that is sensitive to light waves and thus permits visual perception is the eye (Figure 5.2). It is somewhat spherical, covered by a transparent coating called the **cornea**, and relatively isolated from the bloodstream. The cornea itself has no blood supply and can therefore be transplanted with little risk of rejection. The **lens**, too, has no blood supply. Nutriments for the cornea and lens are obtained from the aqueous humor, the fluid in the eyeball, which is changed continually. A complete change of aqueous humor is thought to occur approximately once every four hours.

Each eyeball is controlled by an intricate arrangement of muscles that rotate it in different directions in all planes. The eyeballs are in continual motion, the motions being relatively smooth when a moving object is being followed, and jerky when a stationary object is being looked at. In the absence of any movement, visual acuity quickly fades. More precisely, if eye tremors did not move an image on the retina, the image would eventually disappear completely.

Another muscle that is of considerable importance to the eye is the **iris** which, in humans, creates a round opening (the pupil) that allows light to enter the eye. Interestingly, humans are among the few animals that have circular pupils, most other animals having almond-shaped, slit, or oval eyes. Note that the pupil is not a structure, but is simply an opening created by the iris muscle. It is also in the iris that eye color is found.

Cornea The transparent coating that covers the eyeball in humans. The visible white of the eye seen through the cornea is the sclera.

Lens In the human eye, a transparent structure capable of changing its shape, thereby focusing light waves emanating from closer or farther objects directly on the retina.

Iris A muscle in the eye that creates the pupil. The iris is the colored portion of the eye.

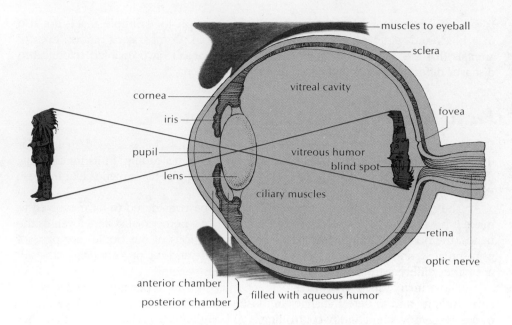

Figure 5.2 Parts of the human eye, the marvelous organ that is sensitive to light waves and permits visual perception.

muscles to eyeball

sclera

cornea

iris

pupil

lens

vitreal cavity

fovea

vitreous humor

blind spot

ciliary muscles

retina

optic nerve

anterior chamber

posterior chamber

filled with aqueous humor

Retina The interior lining of the back of the eyeball including several layers, one of which consists of more than 100 million light-sensitive cells.

Rods Light-sensitive cells on the retina; rods respond primarily to brightness and are centrally involved in night vision.

Cones Light-sensitive cells on the retina; cones respond primarily to color and are extensively involved in daylight vision.

Immediately behind the iris is the lens, which focuses incoming light waves on the retina. Here, again, an analogy to a camera would be inexact. A camera focuses incoming light waves by increasing or decreasing the distance between the lens and the film. The human lens focuses by elongating, thus becoming thinner, or by contracting, thus becoming thicker. With advancing age, accommodation of the lens becomes more difficult, and people typically become more farsighted, a condition that can be corrected with the use of artificial lenses (eyeglasses). (See Colorplate 1.)

The light-sensitive portion of the eye is the **retina**. It is lined with more than 120 million nerve cells capable of translating light waves into neural impulses. Figure 5.3 illustrates the structure of the retina. Note that the receptor cells are *behind* a layer of nerve cells, much as though the film in the human eye had been put in backward with its light-sensitive portions facing away from the source of light.

Those neural cells sensitive to light are labeled **rods** and **cones** after their physical appearance. Rods outnumber cones by about 20 to 1. The cones are found throughout the retina but are concentrated in its center (termed the *fovea*), which is some distance from where the optic nerve branches out to the visual portions of the brain. There is a blind spot where the optic nerve exits, there being neither rods nor cones there. Figure 5.4 illustrates how you can verify that you too have a blind spot.

Rods and cones have different functions in visual perception, some of which are treated in more detail in the sections on color vision and night vision. Rods respond primarily to brightness, are involved in night vision, and are more sensitive in responding to light. Cones are employed primarily in daylight, are involved in color vision, and provide the clearest detail, although they are considerably less sensitive. Since light coming into the eye from directly in front tends to strike the retina in the area of the fovea (where cones are most concentrated), greater detail and sharper colors may be perceived in daylight by looking directly at an object. At night, however, it is often possible to see an object more clearly by looking slightly away from it so that the majority of the light waves strike the retina in an area away from the fovea, thereby coming into contact with a greater number of rods.

In brief, then, the eye functions in some ways like a color television camera. Light waves are reflected on the retina from some object, focused thereon by means of the lens, inverted, miniaturized, and constantly changed by virtue of both eye movements and changes in the environment.

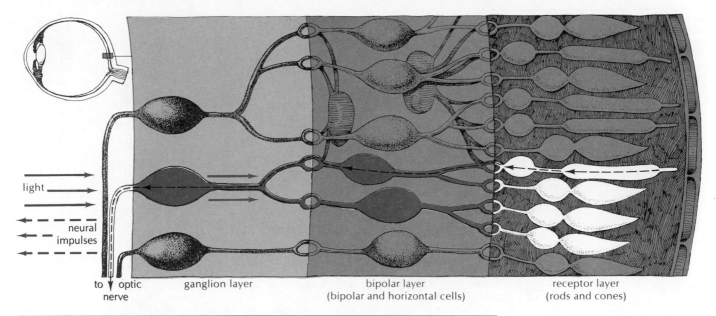

light

neural
impulses

to ↓ optic
nerve

ganglion layer

bipolar layer
(bipolar and horizontal cells)

receptor layer
(rods and cones)

Figure 5.3 The retina is composed of three layers of cells. Farthest from the light source are the rods and cones. The function of rods is to respond to brightness; the cones are involved in color vision and visual acuity. Rods and cones change light energy to neural impulses. The second layer of cells consists of bipolar and horizontal nerve cells that receive neural impulses from the rods and cones. From the bipolar layer, impulses are transmitted to the ganglion cells, and the axons of this last set of cells eventually lead to the optic nerve.

Figure 5.4 The blind spot is "blind," because there are no rods or cones in the area where the optic nerve leaves the eye: no image can be transmitted from the impulses that reach that small section. To find your blind spot, stare at the triangle with your right eye closed and move the book back and forth between eight and twenty inches away. At the appropriate distance, the circle will disappear. To find the blind spot in your right eye, close the left, stare at the circle, and move the book until the triangle disappears.

Eye and Brain

Although the eye permits visual perception, it does not see. It merely reacts to stimulation by light waves, translating these waves by way of the rods and cones into neural impulses. Perception of color, form, texture, and so on occurs in the brain. To trace the connection between eye and brain, let's follow a neural impulse as it leaves the eye via the optic nerve.

As noted in Chapter 2, information from the right half of each eye (left visual field) goes to the right brain hemisphere; information from the left half of each eye (right visual field) goes to the left brain hemisphere. The crossover occurs at the optic chiasma (see Figure 5.5). From there our neural impulse traveling along the optic nerve goes to the thalamus, the brain's major relay station, with some branching to the reticular formation. The majority of impulses then go from the thalamus to the visual areas of the cortex (in the occipital lobe at the back of the brain); others go to a part of the midbrain where they make synaptic connection with nerves that control eye movements. What we perceive, in the end, is an image—not a retinal image, inverted, miniaturized, flat, and in two dimensions like a photograph, not even an image in the brain. What we perceive through vision is an image of what is out there. That is the way we perceive it! Who would be so presumptuous as to quarrel with the conviction that seeing is believing?

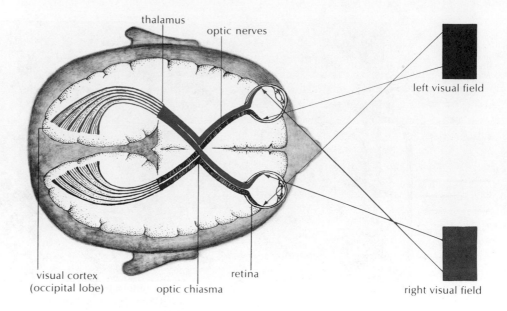

Figure 5.5 Images from the left visual field are transmitted to the right side of each retina, then on to the right hemisphere. Images from the right visual field are transmitted to the left half of each retina, then on to the left hemisphere. The optic nerve is the passageway that carries impulses from the retina through the optic chiasma (where half of the ganglion cells cross over from one side to the other) and on through the thalamus (then, usually, on to visual centers of the occipital cortex).

Light Waves and Vision

All eyes, no matter to whom they belong, are responsive to certain characteristics of light. Light can be described in terms of waves, much as sound waves were described. Recall that the three characteristics of sound waves to which we are sensitive are wave frequency (cycles per second measured in Hertz units and giving rise to perceptions of pitch); amplitude (corresponding to loudness, measured in decibels); and complexity (describable in terms of wave mixture, giving rise to subjective sensations of timbre). In light waves, frequency corresponds to hue, amplitude to intensity or brightness, and complexity to saturation or purity.

Wavelength and Color

Light waves, at 186,000 miles per second, are considerably faster than sound waves. Their frequencies, given their constant speed, are a function of **wavelength**. Perceived color relates to wavelength. Blue light, for example, has a wavelength of approximately 1/70,000 inch; red light, of 1/40,000 inch (Gregory, 1973). Some idea of the incredible speed and frequency of these light waves is given by the notion that some 70,000 waves could occupy a mere linear inch of space, and that these waves could reach the moon and back in just 3 seconds. Some idea of the vastness of space is given by the notion that a light year is the distance light will travel in one calendar year. The farthest astral grouping visible to the naked eye on a clear night is the Andromeda nebula. Consider, when next you look at it, that you are seeing it as it was some million years before primitive man first gazed upon the stars. Would we know if it were no longer there?

Wavelength is seldom measured in terms of frequency per inch, given the very high numbers that result, but is measured instead in terms of nanometers, each nanometer being one-billionth of a meter. In these terms, visible light ranges from just below 400 nanometers (violet) to below 800 nanometers (red). Electromagnetic waves, of which visible light is but an infinitesimally small part, range from gamma rays and X rays to the various radio bands. The gamma rays have considerably higher frequencies; radio waves have much lower frequencies and consequently much greater wavelengths (see Colorplate 2). These waves remained unknown until scientists developed instruments sensitive to them or capable of creating them. Wavelength, within the narrow band of electromagnetic activity to which our eyes are sensitive, corresponds to hue (color) in much the same way as acoustic wavelength corresponds to pitch.

Wavelength In vision, a property of light waves measured in nanometers (a nanometer is one-billionth of a meter) and related to the perception of color. The shortest wavelengths visible to the human eye are approximately 400 nanometers and are perceived as violet or dark colors; the longest perceptible wavelengths are between 700 and 800 nanometers and are perceived as red. Between are all the colors of the rainbow.

Amplitude and Brightness

Amplitude, with respect to light waves, gives rise to the subjective experience of brightness or intensity. When middle C is played softly on a piano, sound waves are created at the rate of 256 per second. Each of these 256 waves will have relatively low amplitude, this amplitude decreasing as a function of distance from the piano (the sound becomes less loud with increasing distance). Obviously, if you are too far away, you won't hear the note. When the key is struck more firmly, the waves are still created at the same frequency, but now the amplitude is much greater. The subjective effect is that the note is heard as being louder, and will continue to be heard at a greater distance. The effects of light waves are similar. A given hue has a specific wavelength (or more precisely, a wavelength mixture). Increasing the amplitude of light waves does not result in a change in perceived hue any more than striking a piano key more or less firmly results in a different note. But in the same way as the note will appear louder or softer depending on its amplitude, so a hue will appear brighter or less bright as a function of wave amplitude (see Figure 5.6).

Complexity and Color Purity

Mixtures of acoustic waves give rise to the experience of timbre. As was noted in Chapter 4, very few sounds are "pure." That is, most of them consist of various mixtures of different acoustic waves. Similarly, there are virtually no "pure" wavelengths with respect to perceived light, unless they have been created artificially. What we perceive is a function of mixtures of different wavelengths. The subjective experience of these mixtures is saturation or purity. More simply, a pure wavelength gives

Michael Maslin

Figure 5.6 Like sound waves, light waves can vary in amplitude without causing a change in hue (for sound, the analogy is a change in pitch). Instead, greater amplitude simply causes us to experience greater intensity or brightness; less amplitude means a decrease in brightness, with hue remaining constant.

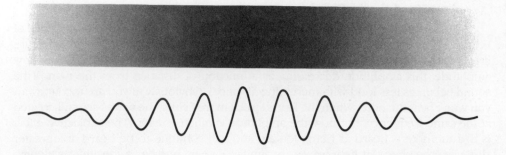

Table 5.1 Wave Characteristics and Subjective Experience: Light and Sound

Wave Characteristics	Color Experience	Sound Experience
Frequency	*Hue*	*Pitch*
High ∿∿∿∿	Purple/blue	High
Low ∿∿	Red	Low
Amplitude	*Brightness*	*Loudness*
High ∿∿	Bright	Loud
Low ∿∿	Dull	Soft
Complexity	*Saturation*	*Timbre*
Pure ∿∿	Saturated	Simple, pure sound
Complex (mixed) ∿∿	Grayer or murkier	Harmony, disharmony, or cacophany

rise to a sensation of pure color (pure red, for example); various mixtures may give rise to reds that are less saturated—that tend progressively toward gray with increasing complexity. Although this observation is essentially correct, it is oversimplified. In a later section on color vision, it will become apparent that mixtures of different wavelengths can give rise to entirely different colors—that we do not, in fact, respond to pure wavelengths when we perceive color, but that we respond to various mixtures of wavelengths (see Colorplate 3).

In summary, color, brightness, and purity are the subjective effects of our sensitivity to light waves. Color is a subjective experience dependent upon wavelengths and wavelength mixtures; purity of a color depends upon complexity of wavelength mixtures, and brightness upon wave amplitude (see Table 5.1).

Color Blindness and Color Vision

Normal perceptual systems all appear to function in similar ways. And when they do not, in most cases we remain unaware of any differences between the way we perceive and ways in which other people perceive. Subjects who wear goggles that drastically distort the visual world adapt quickly and easily to these distortions, provided they are systematic. There is little reason to suppose that children will be aware of their own abnormal vision. Indeed, many people who are color blind do not discover their failing until late in life, if ever. Science did not discover the existence of colorblindness until the nineteenth century. Yet color blindness is perhaps the most obvious of genetically based perceptual defects. It affects approximately 10 percent of all men but only 1 percent of women (Gregory, 1973). It can easily be detected by means of a color test (see Colorplate 4), and can be described as being one of three varieties: red-green, blue-yellow, or all colors.

Red-green color blindness is by far the most common. It involves a confusion between red and green, but in many cases this confusion is not absolute, so that colors of higher intensities can still be differentiated. Blue-yellow color confusion is very rare, as is total inability to detect colors.

Whereas 10 percent of us suffer from varying forms and degrees of color blindness, the remaining 90 percent of us can identify as many as 319 different hues (Bartley, 1969). How we do so is still not completely clear, although two distinct theories provide some plausible explanations.

Trichromatic Theory

One theory suggests that in order to see these 319 hues we do not need 319 different types of cones; we need only three. This theory is based on the observation that mixing only three colors can produce all other colors. The theory was proposed by Young and Helmholtz, and is now known as the *Young-Helmholtz trichromatic theory.* It suggests that there are three types of cones in the retina, each sensitive to a single color: red, green, or blue. Furthermore, each of these cones is linked to different color-producing areas of the brain. Mixtures of different wavelengths, which account for all other colors, give rise to differential activity in two or more of the three cone systems, and this combined activity then leads to the subjective experience of a color other than red, blue, or green. Yellow, for example, results from the stimulation of red and green color systems.

Opponent Process Theory

Later experiments with afterimages suggested that cone systems might function as dual color systems, reacting to complementary colors rather than to just one of the three primary colors. Colorplate 5 illustrates how our eyes project an afterimage. In most cases, the hue of the afterimage is an exact complement (opposite) to the hue of the image we observed beforehand. Red and green are complementary, as are blue and yellow. We cannot see reddish greens or bluish yellows. This observation led to *Hering's opponent process theory* of color vision, which speculates that there is a red-green system and a blue-yellow system. Opponent process theory also proposes that there is a third system, a light-dark system, which responds to black and white and accounts for the perception of brightness.

The fact that color blindness is most often of the red-green variety and sometimes of the blue-yellow variety lends support to this theory. The theory also suggests that the cones themselves are responsive to different wavelengths. Cells activated by shorter wavelengths are inhibited by longer wavelengths. Mixtures of wavelengths activate different cells, giving rise to different perceptual experiences of color. The red-green system is an opponent system: When the red member of the pair is active, the green member is inactive. Interaction among red-green and blue-yellow systems, together with the light-dark (black-white) system, produces all other colors.

Why Two Theories?

There is convincing evidence that the Young-Helmholtz trichromatic theory is correct. In fact, there appear to be three distinct types of cones differentiated not in terms of their shapes, but in terms of their chemical compositions (Mollon, 1982). At the same time, Hering's opponent process theory, initially based largely on speculation, is also supported by considerable evidence, and provides a useful explanation of color blindness (Coren, Porac, and Ward, 1979). Can both theories be correct?

Goldstein (1980) says yes. He argues that trichromatic theory is a good explanation of how retinal receptors (cones) work, but that opponent process theory is a better explanation of functioning beyond the receptors (specifically at the level of bipolar cells).

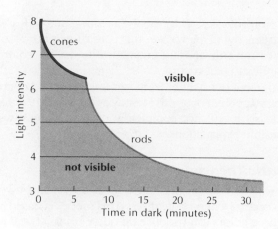

Figure 5.7 Rods and cones adapt differently to increasing darkness. Rods continue to become more sensitive (adapt) for as long as 30 minutes following a reduction in light intensity (light red line); cones adapt more quickly, but do not become as sensitive (dark red line).

Adaptation In this context, adaptation refers to an *increase* in sensitivity to light following a sudden decrease in the amount of available light (for example, going from daylight to a dark room).

Vision in Low Light

Like our other senses, our eyes do more than simply translate physical energy into neural impulses, as might an unsophisticated camera. They also make possible a kind of learning that is evident in the fact that they can become more or less sensitive under different circumstances. For example, when we go from a brightly lit yard to a dimly lit outhouse, we initially see only very faintly. But as time passes, our eyes become accustomed to the gloom, become increasingly sensitive, and eventually allow us to read headlines, if not finer print. This phenomenon is labeled **adaptation.**

The eyes' adaptation (increased sensitivity) to darkness or dim light has been extensively studied under laboratory conditions. It has been found that cones are considerably less sensitive to conditions of low light than are rods. Cones adapt about as much as they will within seven or eight minutes; rods continue adapting for as long as half an hour or more (see Figure 5.7). Since cones are responsible for color vision and rods for brightness (light-dark), vision is less colorful in dim light. Under conditions of very low light, vision is in black, white, and gray (Land, 1977). This also explains why objects can sometimes be seen better in the dark when the subject looks slightly away from them so that light strikes away from the fovea, which contains a concentration of cones but not rods.

Experiments with frogs' and cats' eyes suggest that adaptation to darkness is in part due to regeneration of visual pigment (bleached during exposure to white light) in the retina. The pigment appears to be bleached only minimally with exposure to red light; hence the use of red light bulbs in photo-developing labs and in other situations where workers alternate between darkness and light. Once the eyes are dark-adapted, they will continue to be so following exposure to red light.

As has been noted, sensitivity to detail and to color is dramatically reduced in conditions of near darkness. It is perhaps not as obvious, but no less true, that the amount of time required for the brain to perceive a visual scene under conditions of low illumination is significantly greater. The *Pulfrich Pendulum effect* illustrates this dramatically. A weight is suspended on a length of string and made to swing in a straight arc in front of a subject who has one eye responding to low light and the other to ordinary light. (This is accomplished by placing a dark sunglass lens or dark photograph negative over one eye.) Since messages from the covered eye reach the brain slightly later than those from the uncovered eye, the pendulum is seen as describing an ellipse although its path is straight.

The implications of perceptual delay in dim light are obvious. In dim light reaction times are slower, and driving an automobile or piloting an airplane is more dangerous. It is also more difficult to catch a baseball, to avoid being hit by a tennis ball, or to net a butterfly.

Characteristics of Visual Perception

Visual perception is not solely, perhaps not even primarily, a function of the light-sensitive characteristics of the eye. It is easy to overlook the role of the brain and of learning in visual perception. And even when we do not overlook their role, it is difficult to make precise statements about the relationship of brain and eye. The most important point that needs to be made here, and that is illustrated in the sections that follow, is that the brain continually makes adjustments based on our experiences and expectations, and that as a result we do not always *see* things in ways that correspond exactly to relevant light waves. The **constancies** are a case in point.

The Constancies

We know that most windows are square or rectangular, most oranges are orange, and most elephants are large. We almost always perceive them in these ways; these are constant characteristics of these objects. Our perceptions illustrate color constancy, size constancy, and shape constancy.

Color Constancy   We take for granted that colors do not change with changing light conditions or with changing backgrounds. We continue to see our orange as being orange even when there is so little light that we could not possibly identify the color orange *unless we had learned it beforehand.* In much the same way, we perceive the orange of our orange in a constant way in spite of highly contrasting or highly orange backgrounds. In brief, since we generally know the colors of familiar objects, we tend to perceive them that way, somehow compensating for brighter or darker conditions, or for the effects of contrast or the lack thereof.

Size Constancy   How large is the face that looks at you from your mirror? About the same size as your own face? In fact, it is smaller, since it is halfway between you and yourself. That is, light waves reflected from you back to you must travel the distance between you and the mirror twice. If you fog up your bathroom mirror, an amusing pastime on a dull Sunday afternoon, and circle your reflection with a finger, you may be amazed at how small the circle you have made actually is. Yet you perceive your reflection as being of the same size as you imagine yourself to be.

Size constancy is illustrated throughout your everyday activities. The size of the retinal image is a function of the distance between you and what you see. The farther you are from an object, the smaller will be the image projected on your retina, in the same way as photographs of an object taken at different distances will depict objects of measurably different sizes. At great distances, even a large elephant casts only a small retinal image. Subjectively, however, the perceived size of the elephant does not change with distance. In the same way, you do not assume that as an automobile approaches it is getting bigger, even though the size of the retinal image increases. Quite the opposite: as the retinal image increases in size, you know the car is approaching. Our knowledge that the sizes of things in the physical world stay constant shapes our visual perceptions in the same way as knowledge about the colors of familiar objects serves to color them. Figure 5.8 illustrates how distance can serve as a clue to size. The retinal images cast by the three candles held at different distances are quite different, but the candles are perceived as being the same size.

In the absence of clues concerning distance, however, and when dealing with unfamiliar objects, perceptual judgment can be erroneous. Turnbull (1961) took a Bambuti pygmy with him up a mountain. The pygmy had spent all his life in the forest, and had consequently never seen a mountain, let alone climbed one. In addition, the visual spaces to which he had been accustomed were limited by the density of his forest home. From the top of this mountain, Turnbull and the pygmy looked down upon a herd of buffalo. These fascinated the pgymy, who had also never seen any buffalo except for the small woods buffalo that he might occasionally have encountered in the forest. "What type of insects are those?" he asked in a foreign tongue. He had

Constancies Properties of visual perception that enable us to perceive color, size, and shape of objects as being constant under a great variety of conditions even though the light waves reflected from these objects would be different under these different conditions. Although these constancies govern much of our visual perception, there are numerous circumstances under which perception of size, shape, and color are inaccurate.

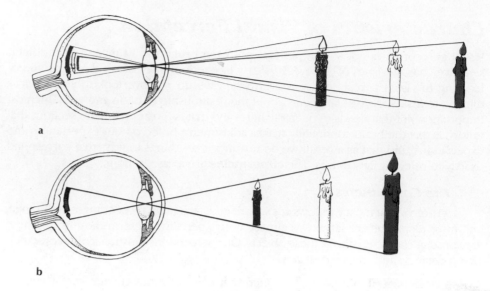

Figure 5.8 Size constancy. In **a**, candles of identical lengths project progressively smaller retinal images at greater distances, yet they are perceived as being equal in height. In **b**, candles of different lengths project the same retinal image, since they are at different distances, yet they are perceived as being different in height.

apparently misjudged their distance and interpreted their size accordingly (in relation to the size of their projected retinal images). As Turnbull and the pgymy drove down the mountain toward the buffalo, the pygmy watched in disbelief. The buffalo grew larger and larger. Magic! Witchcraft! Never having had to look beyond a few yards, the pygmy's mind had not learned to make perceptual corrections for great distances.

The Ames room (Figure 5.9) provides a well-known example of how perception of size depends on environmental cues. When observed from a single peephole, the room appears square, although it is actually trapezoidal with a sloped ceiling. When two people are placed in the room, the observer uses the distance between their heads and the ceiling as a cue for judging their sizes. People of the same height thus appear to differ dramatically in height.

Figure 5.9 The Ames room creates an illusion by its distortion of context. The photograph (**a**) shows a short girl at left and a much taller girl to the right. The diagram (**b**) reveals that the room is trapezoidal rather than square. In addition, the ceiling is sloped upward from right to left. In fact, the girl at left is as tall as the one at right.

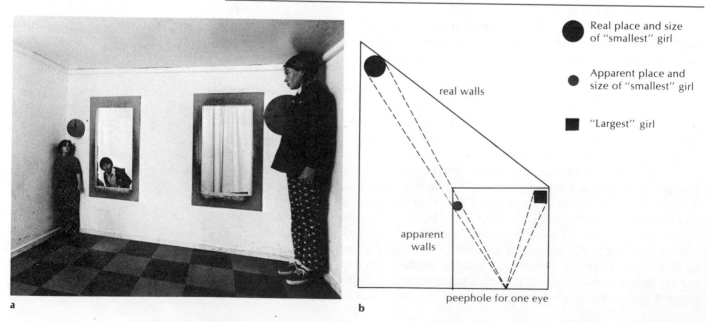

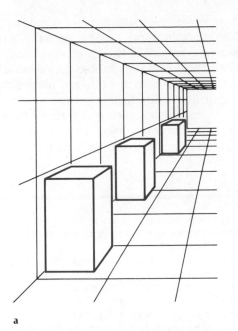
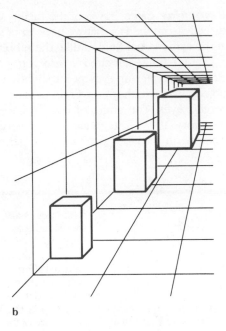

a

b

Figure 5.10 Perspective as a cue to size. In **a** the boxes are perceived to be the same size, although the nearest is actually larger. In **b** the farthest box appears larger, although all three are actually the same size. In both pictures, the lines across the side wall provide false cues about the relative size of the boxes.

Since perception of size seems less related to size of retinal images than to other environmental cues, including distance, it would appear reasonable that at very great distances our judgments of size would be considerably less accurate. Research has not shown this to be true. J. J. Gibson (1950) set up a series of upright stakes in a flat field over a rather long distance. These stakes ranged from 15 to 99 inches in height. Closer to the subject was a second row of stakes for comparison. Subjects had to indicate which stake in the comparison group was most nearly identical in height to a test stake. Gibson found that subjects were remarkably accurate and consistent in their judgments of height at distances of up to half a mile. At that distance, a 71-inch stake, almost invisible to the eye, was judged to be an average of 74.9 inches high. It appears that estimation of size is excellent for virtually as far as we can see an object, provided we are not misled in our perceptions of distance. Figure 5.10, for example, illustrates how perceptions of size can be distorted through perspective. Given identical retinal images, objects that are perceived as being farther away will be judged as being larger. This is, in effect, one explanation for the moon illusion (see Box 5.1).

Shape Constancy Under most circumstances, our use of environmental cues, together with previous knowledge of the sizes, shapes, and colors of objects, leads to relatively accurate perception. This is no less true with respect to shape than with respect to size and color. If you hold a cup at an angle in front of you, the retinal image of the cup's mouth is oval rather than circular. Yet you would not judge it to be oval (see Figure 5.11). Similarly, most doors and windows are rectangular. In fact, however, the retinal image of a door is rectangular only when we face the door directly. As it opens, it projects retinal images that change considerably in shape. We do not ordinarily perceive these changes, however, but continue to see the door as rectangular. So shape, like color and size, remains constant under a variety of circumstances.

Perception of Depth and Distance

A retinal image is a relatively flat pattern of neural stimulation, but its interpretation is not flat. The world, as we perceive it, has depth (sometimes referred to as three-dimensionality), and we perceive objects as having distance from us and distance relative to each other. What causes us to perceive depth and distance? A number of cues, some of which depend upon our ability to see with two eyes, some of which don't.

Figure 5.11 Shape constancy. The mouth of the cup is perceived as being round no matter what its position is relative to the viewer.

Binocular Cues Two of the means whereby we judge distance and depth result directly from the fact that we have *binocular* vision; that is, we have two eyes that look at the same visual field, unlike the rabbit whose eyes look at two different worlds.

One binocular cue is *convergence*. When we look at a single object at a relatively close distance, our eyes point slightly inward so that both are directed toward the object. In short, they converge. Cross-eyed individuals simply have permanently converged eyes. The angle of convergence in normal vision serves as a range finder (Gregory, 1973). The greater the convergence, the closer the object. That we do judge distance in terms of optical convergence can be demonstrated through the use of

---

BOX 5.1

The Moon Illusion

An example of size distortion is the well-known moon illusion: the moon looks considerably larger when it is near the horizon than when it is higher in the sky. Numerous early explanations were advanced for this phenomenon, some relating to the different tilt of the eyeballs and the head when the moon is viewed at the zenith (straight up) and at the horizon; others to apparent differences in the moon's color and brightness when it is at different positions relative to the horizon; and some relating to the use of surface land cues in estimating the distance and consequent size of the moon on the horizon, and the absence of these cues when looking straight up. It was later discovered, perhaps by some pioneer grandmother washing her hair outdoors early on a moonlit evening, that the moon illusion persists even when it is viewed upside down from between the legs, so position of the eyeballs does not appear to account for it. Later studies illustrated that the nature of surface land cues is also irrelevant (Kaufman & Rock, 1962a, 1962b). In these studies, artificial moons were pasted or projected onto artificial skies. The illusion persisted.

The moon illusion can also be illustrated and studied in terms of visual afterimages (King & Gruber, 1962). Subjects are presented with a bright flash (as from a camera flash apparatus) in a darkened room and then asked to look at screens at different distances, whereupon the afterimage appears on the screen. Although the retinal size of the image does not change, the perceived size changes drastically as a function of the distance of the screen. When the afterimage is viewed on a distant screen, it appears to be larger than when it is viewed on a nearer screen. When subjects project this afterimage onto an artificial sky at the horizon and at the zenith, they perceive a difference in the size of the afterimage similar to the moon illusion.

The most remarkable explanation for the moon illusion derived from these various studies relates to our typical conceptions of the sky. Most of us think of the sky as a flattened dome. We then see the moon as being on the underside of this dome. Since our distance from the edges of the dome (the horizon) is greater than from the zenith, we perceive the moon as being larger at the horizon.

Why does the moon look larger at the horizon and smaller as it rises?

prisms, which converge the eyes in predetermined ways when they are looking at objects that remain stationary. When subjects' eyes are made to converge dramatically they judge objects as being close. Conversely, they judge objects to be farther when the eyes are less converged.

Stereoscopic vision is another binocular cue to depth and distance. Since the eyes are set approximately 2.25 inches apart, the images presented to each retina are slightly different. In other words, each eye sees the same field from a slightly different angle. The combination of these two different pictures yields an impression of depth (De Valois and De Valois, 1980).

Monocular Cues   Other cues to depth and distance do not depend on our having two eyes: hence the term *monocular* (see Figure 5.12). *Size* is one such cue. When a tree is seen as being very small, we know that it is probably very far away. If we didn't know how large an ordinary tree is, our judgments of distance might be inaccurate, as was the case for Turnbull's pygmy. Experiments with oversized objects in surroundings that provide no contextual cues as to their actual sizes typically lead the perceiver to assume that the object is closer than it actually is.

Interposition provides a second monocular index of distance. Objects are typically seen as being in front of or behind other objects, with the partly hidden objects always being perceived as being farther than the objects that are not hidden. *Perspective,* our position in relation to what we are perceiving, is a third index of distance. Lines appear to converge with increasing distance. This phenomenon is referred to as *linear perspective* (see Figure 5.13). A second type of perspective is labeled *aerial.* It refers to the fact that objects seen at greater distances appear hazy and less brilliant than those seen close up. Similarly, details of texture (clarity) tend to disappear with increasing distance, shadows provide clues to depth and distance, and colors become less bright and bluer when seen from afar (Colorplate 6).

Perception of Movement

Not only do we perceive objects in depth, complete with judgments of size, shape, distance, and color, but we perceive movement as well. One of the simpler explanations for this fact is that as an object moves it creates a succession of different images on the retina. But perception of movement is not as simple as that. If you turn your head slowly around with your eyes open, you will create a succession of different retinal images, but you will not perceive any motion of those images. What you will perceive is that you have yourself moved, and your brain has somehow coordinated the changing visual scene with your own movement. Further, when an unchanging object moves across the visual field and is followed by the eyes, the retinal image does not change, but we perceive motion.

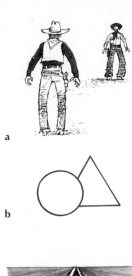

a

b

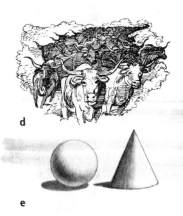

c

d

e

Figure 5.12 Besides the binocular cues provided by convergence and stereoscopic vision, there are also monocular cues to depth and distance to which we would respond even with one eye: (**a**) size, (**b**) interposition, (**c**) perspective, (**d**) clarity, (**e**) shadows.

Figure 5.13 Linear perspective. Lines appear to converge with increasing distance, providing an impression of depth and distance.

Similarly, it might seem clear that changes in an object's position relative to its background account for our perception of movement. In fact, however, we still perceive motion when there is no background whatsoever. As Gregory (1973) points out, this can be illustrated simply by having someone move a lighted cigarette in a dark room. It will be perceived as moving even though there are no background cues. The explanation for this appears to be that the brain is capable of interpreting eye movements as indicative of movement of an object out there, despite the fact that the world does not move when you simply move your eyes.

So it seems, then, that movement is detected through the interplay of what Gregory (1973) describes as two systems: the image-retina system, and the eye-head system. The image-retina system responds to changes in the visual field that result in alterations in the retinal image; the eye-head system responds to movements of the head and eyes.

Misperception

Visual perception, as must be clear by now, is subject to various forms of misperceptions and illusions. It is important to note, however, that these misperceptions are due less to weakness of the sensory aspects of the system than to inappropriate judgments. Frequently these judgments are based on rules that are clearly appropriate most of the time and are therefore relied on even when they are no longer appropriate. Misperception of the Ames room (Figure 5.9) is a case in point.

Illusory Movement Illusions of movement can be created in a number of ways. Perhaps the most familiar is the motion picture that is, in reality, simply a succession of static pictures. These pictures are presented sufficiently rapidly that they are perceived as smooth, continuous movement. Ordinarily they are presented at a rate of twenty-four frames per second, a speed that would result in perception of jerky movement, since each image would be seen separately. But each motion picture frame is presented three times by means of a flutter shutter, so the viewer actually sees seventy-two frames per second. The type of illusory movement created by a motion picture is termed the **phi phenomenon**.

> **Phi phenomenon** The illusion of motion created by presenting a succession of static pictures.

> **Autokinetic effect** A phenomenon whereby stationary objects are perceived as though they were in motion.

A second movement illusion is termed the **autokinetic effect**. When a single, stationary dim light is observed in a darkened room, it will not appear to remain stationary, but will appear to move, often in random and erratic ways. A large number of explanations have been advanced for this phenomenon. Perhaps the most reasonable is Gregory's (1973) hypothesis that fatigue from looking at a single point results in impulses to move the eyes. If they are deliberately held stationary, the brain tends to interpret the resulting muscular tension as indicative of movement. Evidence that this explanation may be correct is derived from a simple experiment employing a lighted cigarette in a dark room. If the eyes are held hard to the left for a period of time, and then moved swiftly to look at the lighted cigarette, the glow will appear to move swiftly to the left or right. Thus tension of the eye muscles appears to have effects similar to those of actually moving the eye to follow a moving object.

> **Waterfall effect** A visual illusion involving perception of movement in a direction opposite to that previously perceived.

The **waterfall effect** is illusory movement that occurs in a direction opposite to previously perceived movement. Its name derives from the fact that if you stare at moving water for a period of time and suddenly shift your view to a stationary object, the object will appear to be moving in the opposite direction. If you stare at a record while it is rotating, then shut off the turntable suddenly, it will appear to begin rotating in the opposite direction.

> **Induced movement** A sensation of movement that is induced by the observation of movement in other objects.

A final example of illusory movement is generally labeled **induced movement**. This illusion is sometimes illustrated in a stationary automobile parked next to a moving vehicle, when the occupants of the stationary vehicle perceive themselves as moving backward. It is also common in passenger trains. Passengers in two trains on adjoining tracks may have the illusion of moving forward, of moving backward, or of being stationary when none of these is happening. An often replicated laboratory demonstration of induced movement is Duncker's (1939) spotlight experiment. In the

Figure 5.14 Mirages do not deceive the eye, but they often do deceive the brain. The lake in this photograph, complete with its reflection, is a mirage.

experiment, a single tiny beam of light is projected onto a screen. The screen is then moved a short distance sideways. Subjects almost invariably perceive the spot as having moved. It seems that the brain can more easily believe that a small object has moved than a large one.

Mirages   Seeing is believing. Not only do we believe what we see, but we tend to believe that we see all that there is to see. In fact, however, sometimes we see much less, and sometimes much more. Consider mirages, for example, those ghostly apparitions that popular literature has relegated to the parched deserts of the world, adorned with their mesas, piñon trees, and vibrant colors. Some friends and I recently saw a mirage on a frozen northern lake. The central body of this lake has no islands. In the winter it is a circular expanse of barren snow-covered ice perhaps seven or eight miles across. That morning, however, it had long peninsulas covered with spruce and aspen reaching from either side of the lake on the far side, and several smaller islands scattered haphazardly near the horizon. Beyond these islands and peninsulas, the lake continued to its farthest shore. The mirage was "real"; that is, we all could see it. What we might not have noticed, had we not known that the lake has no islands and no peninsulas, was that the perspective was wrong. When you stand on a small lake in front of an island, you cannot see the lake on the other side of that island. But we could. It was as though the entire lake was tilted upward from the illusory peninsula to the far shore. It was simply nature playing tricks with light. Since our eyes respond to light first, and to objects only incidentally and only to the extent that they reflect light, our eyes were not at all deceived. We each saw exactly the same mirage; we could even photograph it. It is only our minds that were deceived. (See Figure 5.14.)

Other Visual Illusions   A number of visual illusions have been mentioned in previous pages, sometimes as explanations of perceptual phenomena, and sometimes simply as illustrations. There are a large number of very simple geometric illusions, most of which appear to be due in part to certain expectations that we have governing relationships among perspective, distance, shape, and size. The Ames room effect is a case in point. Another simple illusion that is so common that we tend not to consider it an illusion involves the uncanny way in which the subjects of photographs look directly into your eyes no matter where you stand. You cannot hide. You can sneak up very quietly in the dark, suddenly turn on the light, and they will be staring directly at you. Figure 5.15 illustrates this illusion. Where the subject has looked directly into

Figure 5.15 A common visual illusion that we still can't totally explain. Why is it impossible to escape Uncle Sam's gaze? The illusion works with photographs and paintings, but not with three-dimensional art such as sculpture.

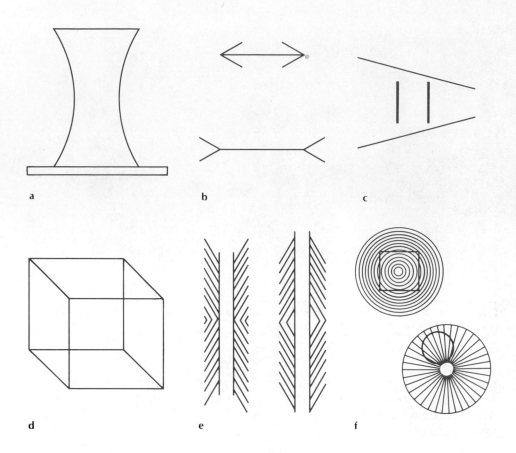

Figure 5.16 Visual illusions. The top hat illusion (**a**) looks as though the hat is taller than the brim is wide, but both dimensions are equal. The Müller-Lyer illusion (**b**) contains parallel lines of equal length. In the Ponzo illusion (**c**), the heavy lines are of equal length. If you stare at the Necker cube (**d**) it eventually reverses itself. (**e**) The vertical lines are parallel. (**f**) The two figures in the circles are actually square or circular.

the camera, or directly at the painter, the illusion persists; if the subject's vision was directed to the side, there is no comparable illusion. Luckiesch (1965) suggests that since the same illusion cannot be created with a sculpture, the fact that photographs and paintings are in two rather than three dimensions may be related to an explanation for the illusion.

The top hat, Müller-Lyer, and Ponzo illusions (Figure 5.16) can perhaps all be explained quite simply in terms of our tendency to perceive in depth and in more than two dimensions. Thus, the top part of the hat (Figure 5.16a) looks longer than its width because it suggests perspective—distance. Similarly, the arrows in the Müller-Lyer illusion (Figure 5.16b) suggest expansion or compression—distance or its opposite. The Ponzo illusion (Figure 5.16c) is clearly affected by perspective and may be interpreted in terms of our tendency not to perceive the background as being flat. The reversing figures in Figure 5.17 are simple ambiguous figures that do not really qualify as illusions. The fact that there are two competing perceptions possible for each is due to the absence of cues pertaining to depth. Quite simply, we have no way of determining which is the front and which the back.

Gestalt Principles of Perception

At the beginning of the fourth chapter, we noted that perception is to a large extent a selective process. That is, we not only select the significance we will assign to sensory stimulation, but we also select those aspects of the environment of which we are aware from moment to moment. Recall that *attention* is the general term that describes this selectivity. Attention is affected by a range of factors, including expectations, needs, interests, and so on.

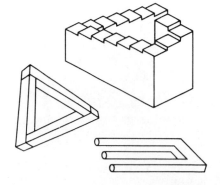

Figure 5.17 The impossible figures seem possible at a quick glance.

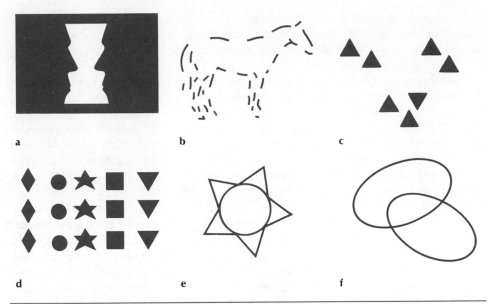

a   b   c

d   e   f

Figure 5.18 Gestalt principles of perception. (**a**) Figure-ground: what is perceived is a function of what is considered background and what is considered figure. This object is either a vase or two faces. Although we can alternate from one to the other, we cannot perceive both at once. (**b**) Closure: incomplete patterns are perceived as complete. (**c**) Proximity: objects that are close together tend to be perceived as being related. The eye sees the triangles as three distinct groupings. (**d**) Similarity: similar objects tend to be perceived as related. This array is perceived as vertical columns rather than as horizontal rows. (**e**) Continuity: perceptual phenomena tend to be perceived as continuous. This figure is perceived as a circle within a five-pointed star, not as five quasi-triangular figures. (**f**) Praegnanz: perception tends to result in "good forms." This law governs all other laws of perception, since complete, proximal, similar, and continuous objects are better forms than those that are incomplete, nonproximal, dissimilar, or incomplete. This figure is perceived as two overlapping circles, not as three irregular-shaped objects.

A number of other factors affect what is perceived. These include what are called principles of perceptual organization. These principles were introduced by a number of German psychologists, chief among whom were W. Köhler (1927, 1959), Werthei-mer (1959), and Koffka (1925, 1935). These psychologists have come to be known as the **Gestalt** psychologists, *gestalt* being a German word meaning "configuration" or "whole." They were so called because of their interest in the principles that govern the perception of "wholes." Perception, argued the Gestalt psychologists, tends toward the recognition of forms or shapes. We tend not to see just parts of objects or figures, even when the visual stimulation we have is only partial. The mind fills in the missing parts.* The most important Gestalt principles of perceptual organization, illustrated in Figure 5.18, are *figure-ground, closure, proximity, similarity, continuity,* and *praegnanz.* These are best described and illustrated with respect to visual perception, although they apply to other forms of perception as well.

Whatever is perceived is generally part of a larger background of other percep-tual information. The object perceived is referred to as the figure; the background, as the ground. What is actually perceived is frequently a function of what is considered to be figure and what is ground. For example, Figure 5.19 depicts either a young woman or an older, somewhat less attractive woman variously described as a hag, a witch, an old crone, or sometimes in even less kind terms, the likes of which you would be hard-pressed to find in this respectable text. Similarly, Figure 5.18a can be seen as a vase or as two faces eye-to-eye, depending again on what is figure and what is ground. One of the interesting features of these ambiguous figures is that the two

Gestalt A German term meaning "con-figuration" or "whole." *Gestalt* was the label originally applied to the school of German psychologists whose principal preoccupation was with perception, and whose most widely recognized beliefs were summarized in the expression that the whole is greater than the sum of its parts.

---

*Gestalt psychology has had a much more profound influence on psychology than these few lines would indicate, as is shown elsewhere in this text. Its influence, for example, is evident in the cognitive theories of personality, learning, motivation, and interpersonal behavior, as well as in various therapies.

Figure 5.19 What do you perceive in this picture? People bring their own frame of reference to bear in interpreting ambiguous images. If you have just been reading about elegant fashions at the turn of the century, you will probably see a young lady dressed in furs; if witches have been on your mind, you will see a very inelegant old woman.

alternatives that present themselves cannot be perceived at the same time. It is very much as though the human brain, having determined what is figure and what is ground, can only perceive the figure in its entirety, and experiences some difficulty in reversing the figure-ground relationship.

An example of the human tendency to fill in missing parts is provided by the illustration of *closure* in Figure 5.18b. Unless viewers are aware of the nature of the experiment, and unless they are provided with a great deal of time to study the pattern, they will, in fact, perceive a horse rather than a number of isolated lines. An even more striking example of closure is provided by a simple demonstration of the blind spot. Recall that in Figure 5.4 you were invited to locate the distance at which a spot disappeared completely from your vision. Light waves reflected from the circle at that distance and location are concentrated at the point where the optic nerve leaves the eye (presumably loaded with colorful messages for the brain). At a distance of approximately three feet, the blind spot covers a roughly circular area perhaps two inches across. Now let us suppose that you are looking with one eye at a much larger circle that is either patterned or of a single color. Since there is a blind spot that covers some three square inches of the larger pattern, there should be a blank space in your visual perception. But there isn't. The solid color or the pattern continues uninterrupted throughout the circle. Obviously, the brain does not see the blind spot even if it knows there is one!

The remaining Gestalt principles of perceptual organization are also easy to illustrate. Figures that are in close *proximity* (Figure 5.18c) tend to be perceived as belonging together. The same principle is evident in listening to music, where notes and melody lines are organized according to temporal proximity. Indeed, temporal proximity is largely what determines rhythm patterns of drums. It is also this principle that explains how a melody or a conversation can be detected and, indeed, listened to in spite of other contrasting melodies or other background noise. *Similarity* (Figure 5.18d) is also involved in auditory perception. We experience no great difficulty in following a conversation amid other conversations. There is a *continuity* (another Gestalt principle, Figure 5.18e) provided not only by the proximity of words, but also by the fact that there are recognizable similarities among the sounds of the words, since they are ordinarily delivered by the same person. The situation would not be nearly so simple if every word in the conversation were taped by a different individual. Similarly, you would experience some difficulty in reading these words if th eywe re n ot spa ced prop e rly O Rif they were printed in different colors without regard for the rules of proximity. The final Gestalt principle of perception, *praegnanz* (Figure 5.18f), maintains that the subjective result of perception tends toward the best, most pleasing, most perceptually acceptable form in accordance with the other principles of perception.

Inborn Capacities and Learning in Vision

If, in the interests of science, your eyes had been blindfolded at birth and the blindfold not removed until much later in your childhood, do you suppose that you would immediately *see* whatever there is out there? That you would see it in the same way as you might see it had your eyes never been blindfolded? Or is learning involved even at this level of visual perception? We look at these questions next.

The Influence of Experience

Clearly, many of our perceptions are influenced by learning. That this is the case is perhaps most evident in studies of perceptual behavior among different cultures. Unfortunately, many of these studies are not studies in the true sense, but are simply anecdotal evidence gathered by anthropologists and other world travelers who have been impressed with apparent differences between their views of the world and those of the more primitive peoples with whom they have worked. Perhaps best known and most misleading among these gems of anecdotal evidence are those that relate to the influence of vocabulary on the perception of color.

Rivers (1901) studied the color vocabularies of New Guinea tribes, Eskimos, Australians, and a variety of other people. In several instances he found tribes who had no distinct terms for blues, greens, and violets. In subsequent tests they confused these colors hopelessly. His interpretation, like that of a number of other researchers, was that innate perceptual differences made it impossible for these people to perceive the differences that we note among colors, and that terms had therefore not been invented for them. That this is true is very difficult to prove. As Rivers himself suggested, it is quite possible that people who have no words for certain colors are simply not interested in them. They might *perceive* differences among them, even as we do, but simply lump them all together. And certain language problems that frequently exist between the investigator and the investigated might also partially explain the apparent confusion among different colors.

A second explanation was later advanced by Whorf (1940) and by Sapir (1928), who maintained that inability to perceive does not account for lack of terms, but that lack of specific terminology accounts for the inability to perceive. The question is in some ways reminiscent of the chicken and the egg. As Segall et al. (1966) note, evidence linking culture and language with different perceptions is highly equivocal. There has now been more than one hundred years of research in this area. Perhaps the next hundred years will result in one or two well-accepted facts.

Cross-cultural research on visual perception that has been more experimental and less concerned with the possible role of language has yielded some clearer results. Bagby (1957) presented pairs of photographs to Mexican and American subjects by means of a stereoscope whereby each eye was presented with a different picture. The two retinal images that result simultaneously lead to what is called binocular rivalry. Under these circumstances, only one image will actually be seen. In this demonstration, one picture of each pair depicted U.S. scenes, the other, Mexican scenes. Mexican subjects saw Mexican scenes at least half the time; American subjects always saw U.S. scenes. The evidence points clearly to the influence of culture, or, alternatively, of familiarity, in determining perceptual dominance in cases of binocular rivalry.

There is evidence to suggest, as well, that exposure to educational influences and, perhaps most importantly, to pictures and photographs, is related to the development of an ability to perceive depth in photographs and paintings. W. Hudson (1960) tested groups of South Africans, some illiterate, others attending school, and still others who were teachers. He found that, in general, cues involving overlap and size were employed most frequently in judging depth, and that perspective was used least often. Perhaps most important, there was a marked relationship between educational level and the ability to perceive depth in a photograph.

Following an extensive review of studies that have attempted to identify and explain cultural differences in perception, Segall et al. (1966) concluded that many of these studies are ambiguous, inconclusive, and subject to a variety of interpretations. Nevertheless, it appears clear that perceptual processes are frequently influenced by "culturally mediated experiences" (p. 67).

Another series of studies that bears on the role of experience in visual perception makes use of a variety of distorting goggles (I. Kohler, 1962). Some of the goggles invert the world, some discolor it, some color it, and others distort it in other ways. One of the revealing findings is that, given sufficient time, subjects are able to adapt to a world that is upside-down, systematically curved, half-blue and half-yellow, or consistently rubbery. There is frequently a difficult period of orientation, after which the brain appears to compensate for distorted images. Subjects wearing prisms with the bases both pointing either left or right, for example, are exposed to expanding or contracting images, depending on whether they are looking right or left. After two or three weeks of continually wearing the prisms, the eye (or the brain) learns to compensate for the distortion even though it occurs in two directions. The only goggle effect to which adaptation has been impossible involves the use of prisms whose bases are in different directions; that is, one points left and the other right. The subjective effect of wearing these glasses is described as an intense color distortion where various colors appear closer or farther than they actually are, so that a woman wearing a red blouse is seen as disembodied, with her arms swinging unattached beside where her torso should be, and her blouse moving nonchalantly some distance behind her (Kohler, 1962). A tentative explanation for the effect of these inverted prisms (termed the *color-stereo effect*) is simply that the information presented to the eye consists of random and virtually unpredictable distortions and displacements of color. It is perhaps because these distortions are unpredictable that the individual is unable to adapt to them.

It seems clear, then, that experience can have dramatic effects on visual perception. But experience alone cannot account for all the characteristics of perception.

Inborn Capacities

The influence of innate factors on visual perception has been investigated in a number of studies of perception in infants. Presumably, to the extent that visual perception is dependent on genetic factors, vision would be highly similar among infants and adults. Differences between infant and adult perceptions might provide clues to the role of learning. Unfortunately, however, the results of these studies are not sufficiently clear to provide easy generalizations. Human infants, like the young of nonhuman species, are nonverbal; they cannot communicate the effects of a perceptual experience. Science does have some ways around these problems, however.

Among the first important studies of visual perception with the young were studies conducted by Fantz on baby chicks. Unlike human infants, who are essentially helpless at birth, chicks and the young of many other wild animals exhibit purposeful behavior almost immediately upon hatching or being born. In the Fantz (1961) experiments, chicks that were hatched in the dark, and therefore had no previous exposure to light, were presented with a number of plastic-coated shapes—plastic-coated so that touch or smell would presumably have no effect on the chicks' behaviors. Some of these objects were flat, either triangular, square, or circular; others were square, rectangular, or prismatic in three dimensions. As chicks will, these experimental subjects immediately began pecking the imitation plastic seeds. Significantly, however, they did not peck at random, but preferred the seed-shaped objects, pecking the flat circle ten times more often than the pyramid. Here is striking evidence of form recognition among chickens, independent of experience.

A technique developed to examine form perception among human infants was later employed by Fantz (1961). Reflections from an infant's eyeballs can be monitored so as to indicate precisely where the child is looking. Subjects, aged between one and fifteen weeks, were systematically exposed to a series of pairs of test patterns, some complex (bull's-eyes, checkerboards, and stripes) and others plain. On the average, the more complex patterns elicited significantly more looking behavior measured in terms of total fixation time.

In a later study, Fantz (1963) exposed infants as young as ten hours (some were as old as five days) to six circular patterns, one bearing an illustration of a human face, one with concentric circles, one covered with newsprint, and the remaining three plain white, yellow, and red. Again, infants spent considerably more time looking at the complex patterns than at the plain circles. The most preferred stimulus object, if fixation time is an index of preference, was clearly the human face (see Figure 5.20).

These studies indicate not only that human infants are capable of discriminating among different perceptual forms and patterns at a very early age, but also that they exhibit a marked preference for certain patterns over others. The evidence is clear that some aspects of perceptual behavior are not entirely dependent upon learning.

Evidence of early depth perception in infants is provided by the E. J. Gibson and Walk (1960) studies of the "visual cliff." The visual cliff apparatus consists of a large, heavy sheet of glass raised a foot or more above the floor. A sheet of patterned material is placed underneath the glass, flush with it on one half; the other half of the glass is

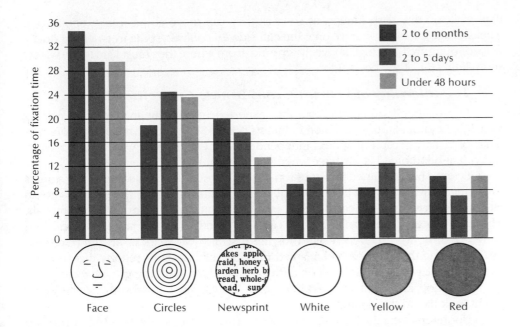

Figure 5.20 Are human infants, like chicks or other young animals, predisposed toward visual stimuli that will help them survive? The six patterns here were shown to human infants, and their preference was measured by monitoring the time they spent looking at each pattern. The clear winner was the pattern most closely resembling the human face. (From "Pattern Vision in Newborn Infants" by R. L. Fantz, *Science*, Vol. 140, pp. 296–297, April 1963. Copyright 1963 by the American Association for the Advancement of Science. Reprinted by permission.)

left bare, suspended above the floor, but the same patterned material is placed on the floor below it. Thus, although the entire surface of the apparatus is solid, the appearance of solidity ends at the halfway point, where vision would clearly tell adult subjects that they are on the edge of a cliff (see Figure 5.21). Infants who have been tested on the visual cliff have been six months of age or older, since it is important that they be able to crawl if they are to indicate their recognition of depth or the absence thereof. Of twenty-seven infants placed on the apparatus, only three ventured over the edge of the cliff; the others refused, even when called by their mothers from the other side. Not surprisingly, a few of them cried when their mothers called them, apparently trying to entice them to fall down.

Use of the same visual cliff with animals indicates that perception of depth is developed very early in life. Goats at only one day of age leap over the chasm rather

Figure 5.21 Use of the glass-floored visual cliff indicates that depth perception is developed at a very young age in human and other animal babies. In **a**, an infant refuses to cross over the cliff to his mother even when she calls him. In **b**, a baby goat won't step over the cliff—although, unlike the human, it can jump to the other side. Goats show this response at the tender age of one day; humans can't accurately be tested until they are much older and able to move by themselves.

than walk on the glass; kittens, as soon as they can move about freely (about four weeks of age), seldom venture onto the cliff side. In contrast, some tree-nesting ducks whose young are born high above the ground, from where they must leap to the water, show little fear of the deep side!

The Interplay of Learning and Innate Capacities

Cross-cultural studies indicate that experience can play an important role in visual perception. Studies of vision in infants provide evidence that certain characteristics of visual perception appear independently of experience. What, then, does an individual blindfolded at birth *see* when the blindfold is finally removed?

Science has examined this question directly through a series of intriguing studies involving individuals who have been blind through most of their lives, but who, in later years, have been subjected to successful cornea transplants or cataract removals. There have been more than sixty such cases reported in the literature. A typical case is that of S. B., who had been blind for the first fifty-two years of his life (Gregory, 1973). During that time he had adapted impressively. Gregory reports that he rode about on a bicycle with his hand on a friend's shoulder, built things with tools in his own workshop, and spent a good portion of his time trying to discover what the world might look like to the sighted.

Upon removing the bandages after the cornea transplant, he faced a blurred and indistinct world. He quickly learned to recognize those objects with which he was already very familiar, but had little sense of perspective, of depth, or of speed. He imagined, for example, that he could lower himself easily to the ground from the window ledge of his hospital room, although it was more than thirty feet up. He also became terrified of crossing streets, although he had done so confidently all his life when blind. S. B., like most other individuals in similar circumstances, suffered increasingly from depression after his operation, eventually choosing to spend long periods of time sitting at home in the dark. Some three years later, after having essentially given up active living, he died.

A number of studies have been conducted on cats, chimpanzees, and monkeys who are reared in darkness, with bandages on their eyes, or with translucent goggles that allow light to enter the eye but do not permit actual pattern vision. Studies with chimpanzees (Riesen, 1960) indicate that after a prolonged period of sightlessness, many hundreds of hours are required before the animal can recognize objects, follow movements, and guide its own movements and manipulations. In a large number of cases, experimental subjects never do achieve normal visual behavior.

Early studies of kittens (Held & Hein, 1963) also indicated that normal visual perception is affected by early learning. In one experiment, for example, two kittens were exposed to the same visual stimulation. One cat, however, was kept immobile, while the other was responsible for all locomotion. After ten days, when both kittens were permitted to live in more normal environments, the cat who had done the walking appeared to have developed normal perceptions. The other kitten would not blink at the sudden approach of an object, or put up its paws in self-protection.

Following these early investigations, a large number of studies of visual deprivation have been conducted with animals, mostly cats. One of the major emphases of these studies has been to identify changes that occur in the brain as a result of early deprivation and, by the same token, to describe the course of normal development. Hubel and Wiesel (1968, 1970, 1974), two of the principal researchers in this area, shared a Nobel prize in medicine in 1981 for their discoveries relating to the role of the striate cortex (part of the occipital lobe at the back of the brain) in vision.

The most general finding from visual deprivation research is that visual stimulation during infancy (during the first four months for cats) is crucial for the development of neural synapses in the striate cortex, as well as for the specialization of neurons. Specifically, certain neurons in the visual cortex seem to be involved in monocular vision; others make use of binocular cues. There is evidence, as well, that some cells are sensitive to vertical stimulation and others to horizontal. Research involving sewing shut one or both of an animal subject's eyes indicates that in the absence of appropriate stimulation, many of these specialized neurons simply become nonfunctional, and there are fewer neural synapses in the visual cortex relative to subjects reared with visual stimulation. When the animal is deprived of stimulation through only one eye, when the stitches are removed neurons in the striate cortex continue to respond only to stimulation coming from the eye that was not deprived. What this evidence strongly suggests is that cells in the striate cortex are predisposed to respond to certain kinds of stimulation, and in the absence of this stimulation during critical developmental periods, the cells do not become functional. In other words, visual development is not simply a matter of learning as a function of visual experience, but is very much dependent on neural development. In turn, early visual experience is essential for neural development in the striate cortex. Perhaps the same might be true for other forms of perception. Are musically talented individuals those whose genes were appropriate *and* who were exposed to experiences related to relevant neural development?

Extrasensory Perception

We can see. We have been able to see as far back as we can remember. And way back then we assumed quite confidently that we could see all there was to see. We know now that we see only certain wavelengths not much beyond 400 and 700 nanometers. We know too that we cannot hear all there is to hear: Dogs and porpoises detect sounds we can only imagine. Science has also told us that we respond to certain odorous molecules and not to others; that some materials lead us to perceive taste, and others not. What else might there be beyond the range of our accepted perceptual systems? In short, what might there be in extrasensory perception?

Extrasensory perception is variously referred to as ESP, Psi (from the Greek letter, which, incidentally, symbolizes psychology), paranormal phenomena, or psychic phenomena. Its study is called parapsychology. It has, for years, been something of a taboo topic in psychology partly because, as Thouless (1972) puts it, Mrs. Grundy, guardian of our decency, finds that a number of subjects offend either her social scruples or her scientific priggishness. Presumably Psi offends scientific priggishness. One extreme scientific position maintains, in fact, that since parapsychological phenomena cannot be accounted for by either physics or physiology, they cannot exist. The other extreme simply insists that in spite of whatever violation may be done to existing notions of physics and physiology, Psi phenomena are demonstrably real. The issue has not been resolved, and cannot be resolved here, but both sides are presented briefly.

Several phenomena are included in studies of Psi. These include telepathy, the communication of thought from one person to another without the use of language, writing, or other known forms of communication; precognition, the perception of an event that has not yet occurred; clairvoyance, the perception of immediate objects and events that are not now in any direct contact with any of the senses; and psychokinesis (PK), the manipulation of physical bodies or systems indirectly, presumably through some action of the mind (see Box 5.2).

Research in extrasensory phenomena has a long history, the principal well-known investigators being Rhine, Sidgwick, and Schmeidler. There are a number of standard experimental procedures. Perhaps the best known involves the use of a deck of cards developed by Rhine in 1927. It consists of twenty-five cards, each having one of five designs on it (see Figure 5.22). In an experiment on telepathy, the "sender" looks at a card hidden from the subject's view and attempts to influence the subject's decision as to what the card is. In an experiment on clairvoyance, subjects attempt to guess what the next card will be without having anyone look at it. Automatic shufflers are sometimes used to eliminate the possibility that the shuffler might influence the subject. In an experiment on precognition, the same procedure might be employed;

Extrasensory perception Perception of phenomena without use of the ordinary senses. Instances of ESP are sometimes described as *paranormal* (beyond the normal). The scientific study of ESP is called *parapsychology*.

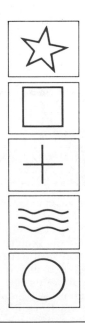

Figure 5.22 Cards like these, developed by J. B. Rhine, are used in studies of extrasensory perception. They were first developed to test telepathy. The sender used a deck of twenty-five cards of these patterns, randomly shuffled. The sender would look at a card hidden from the subject's view, and the subject would attempt to guess the card.

in an experiment on psychokinesis, subjects might attempt to influence the card shuffler. Other experiments have employed dice, cards with clock faces on them where the hands point to one of twelve different hours, or the reproduction of drawings (Thouless, 1972).

For

The results of numerous experiments and a vast burden of anecdotal evidence can be cited in support of paranormal phenomena. Only two are mentioned here: one an anecdote, the other an experiment.

Schmeidler (1972) uses numerous anecdotes to illustrate paranormal phenomena in real life. Among them is the following:

> I was blackleading my grate when I suddenly said to my sister who was visiting me, "Mr. G. has just dropped dead." The gentleman in question was an old rector of our parish church who had left the district some years previously. My sister said, "Whatever made you say that?" But I couldn't give her any explanation. I just saw in a flash, like a photograph, the old gentleman dropping down on to the pavement. Later that same evening, my sister called again to show me a local evening paper. It gave the news that the Rev. D. B. G. had died suddenly in the street that morning. (pp. 215–216)

An experiment conducted by H. Schmidt (1969) also presents supporting evidence. The study made use of an electronic device programmed to light one of four different colored lamps. The subject's task was to depress a lever indicating which of the four lights would come on. Subject responses did not affect the order in which the lights went on, that order being determined electronically, and being unknown to the experimenter as well. Tabulation of hits (correct guesses) and misses was automatic.

In the experiment, subjects were employed who had previously shown evidence of possessing psychic powers. These subjects were apparently successful more often than would be expected by chance (see Figure 5.23).

BOX 5.2

The $10,000 Challenge

A famous Israeli entertainer, Uri Geller, is self-described as remarkably gifted in extrasensory powers of clairvoyance, psychokinesis, and ESP. He has demonstrated these powers widely, and many have believed in their genuineness. Two physicists obtained Geller's cooperation in what were intended to be scientifically controlled demonstrations of these powers. Geller convinced the physicists, and the results of this investigation were subsequently published (Targ & Puthoff, 1974). Among other things, Geller succeeded in calling out which side of a die had come up on eight out of ten tosses, with the die inside a steel box; he refused to "guess" on the other two tosses. The probability of being correct solely by chance is less than 1 in 1 million. Impressive.

In 1973, Geller appeared as a guest on a British television show, along with Professor John Taylor, who was asked to judge the authenticity of the performance. During this show, Geller bent spoons and forks, ostensibly psychokinetically (through the power of the mind). Taylor was convinced. Following additional demonstrations after the program, he was even more convinced (J. Taylor, 1975, 1976).

The majority of the scientific community remained highly skeptical, however. Hanlon (1974) suggests that Targ and Putoff did not take sufficient precautions to prevent Geller from cheating. In fact it is simple for a magician (which many claim Geller to be) to switch a transmitter-equipped die for the original. Such a die transmits a signal indicating which side is up. Similarly, Randi (1975) points out that, prior to the BBC television program, the tray of forks and spoons that Geller was to bend was in his dressing room; the attendant who was to guard them was sent on an errand by Geller.

Randi (1976) has challenged Geller to perform a single psychic feat that he ("The Amazing Randi") cannot explain or duplicate—a feat for which he will pay Geller $10,000. Geller has not accepted.

It is perhaps significant that Geller refuses to perform if he knows there is a professional magician in his audience. The evidence strongly supports natural (magic) explanations for the Geller feats. But that Geller is "a fake" (Randi, 1980) does not *prove* that ESP does not exist as a real phenomenon. As Randi notes, however, the burden of proof still lies with those who believe in paranormal phenomena. And Randi's check for $10,000 is there for *anyone* with that proof. Details may be obtained by writing to: Randi Challenge, 51 Lennox Avenue, Rumson, NJ 07760.

Colorplate 1 The figures of El Greco (1541–1614) are typically elongated, as shown in his painting "Saint Martin and the Beggar." It has been suggested that he suffered from astigmatism, a structural defect in the cornea that causes images to be drawn out in a line. But if that actually were the case, he would still have painted in proportion. A proportional painting might have appeared elongated to him, but then elongation would have seemed normal. It is probably more accurate to attribute his style to his eccentricity and his training.

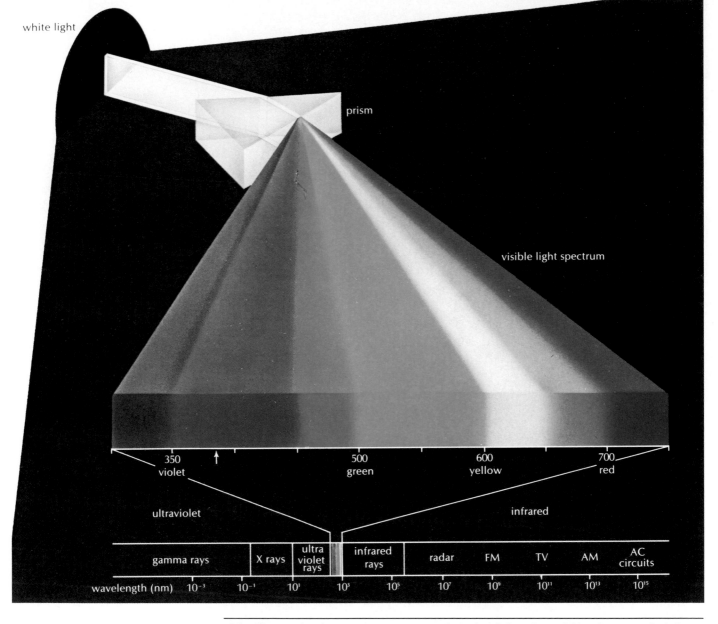

white light

prism

visible light spectrum

| 350 | | 500 | 600 | 700 |
| violet | | green | yellow | red |

ultraviolet

infrared

gamma rays		X rays	ultra violet rays	infrared rays	radar	FM	TV	AM	AC circuits

wavelength (nm) 10^{-3} 10^{-1} 10^1 10^3 10^5 10^7 10^9 10^{11} 10^{13} 10^{15}

Colorplate 2 The electromagnetic spectrum. When white light is directed through a prism, the light is broken down into its component colors: violet, blue, green, yellow, orange, and red. The human eye can perceive only this narrow band of colors. The rest of the spectrum—from gamma rays to long-wave radio waves and beyond—cannot be seen directly.

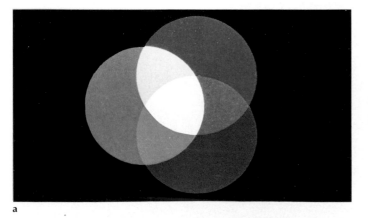

a

b

Colorplate 3 Mixing lights (**a**) and mixing pigments (**b**) produces different colors. Thus, mixing the three lights yields white; mixing the three color pigments yields black. The result of mixing color pigments is not as predictable as that of mixing lights.

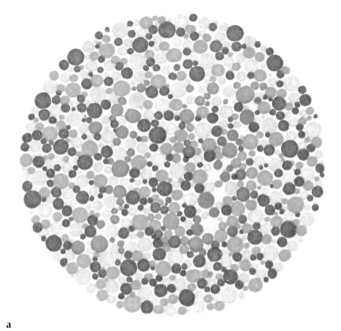

a

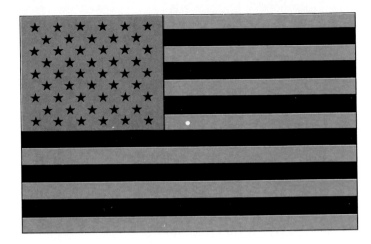

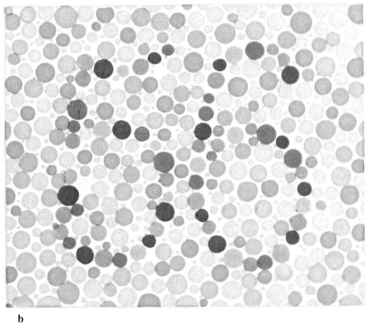

b

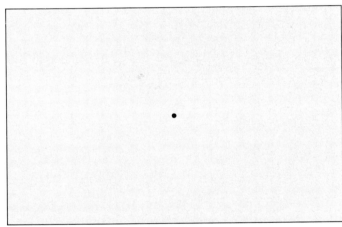

Colorplate 5 Afterimage. Stare at the center of the flag for 15 to 30 seconds. Then shift your gaze to the gray rectangle at the bottom. What you see is an afterimage. Its colors are opposite (complementary to) those of the original image—hence it is called a negative afterimage.

Colorplate 4 Two common tests for color blindness, a phenomenon that is not always all-or-none, but that is often partial. If you are not color-blind, you should have little difficulty seeing the number 15 in **a** and 56 in **b**.

a

b

Colorplate 6 The same photograph in color (**a**) and black and white (**b**) shows how color adds to depth clues. In both photographs distant objects appear lighter in tone and less distinct than nearby objects. However, in **a** the hues of distant objects shift toward blue (as they do in reality). Also, the depth clues provided by overlapping objects are enhanced by color differences. Warm colors appear closer, cool colors farther.

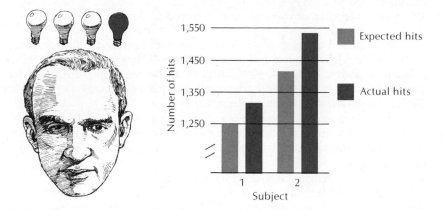

Subject	Number of trials	Hits expected by chance	Hits above chance	% above chance
1	5,000	1,250	66	1.3
2	5,672	1,418	123	2.2
Totals	10,672	2,668	189	

Figure 5.23 Two subjects (the first a professional medium and the second an amateur psychic) attempted to predict which of four bulbs would light next. In other words, they were given an opportunity to demonstrate the psychic phenomenon of *precognition*. Since the bulbs lit in random order, subjects would be expected to predict correctly 25 percent of the time by chance. If precognition is a valid phenomenon (for these subjects at this time and in this situation), the number of correct responses would exceed the chance level. The chart indicates that this was the case. In 10,672 trials, subjects were correct 189 more times than would be expected by chance: they were correct 2,857 times rather than 2,668 times. Critics have been quick to point out that, although these results may be statistically significant, they are not very impressive. (Based on data from H. Schmidt, 1969.)

Against

And what is the case against Psi other than science's priggishness—its refusal to accept as valid anything that so flagrantly violates all that is known of physics and physiology? The arguments are many. First, anecdotal evidence must always be regarded as suspect. Whatever occurs in day-to-day life is generally replicable in the laboratory, or at least under more controlled conditions. This has not always been the case with Psi phenomena.

Second, laboratory experiments that ostensibly demonstrate the existence of ESP should be easily replicable. In point of fact, they have not been. Even the most devoted researchers and passionate believers in these phenomena have frequently lamented the fact that highly convincing results obtained by one investigator have not always been obtained by other investigators employing identical methods and equipment.

Third, scientists have argued that the extraordinarily large numbers of trials that have been employed in psychical research have frequently been necessitated by the desire to achieve statistical significance (see Statistical Appendix). The results have seldom been dramatically convincing even when they do reach statistical significance. Consider, for example, that in one experiment (Pratt & Blom, 1964) a subject faced with a two-choice decision was correct 917 out of 1,600 times. By chance, the subject should have been correct an average of 800 times if the experiment were repeated a large number of times. Does 117 correct guesses more than chance expectation convince the skeptic?

A Resolution?

Proponents of ESP typically respond by claiming that these powers are not like memory or intelligence, available at any time and ready for testing whenever the psychologist wishes to test them. Mood, atmosphere, relationship between the investigator and the subject—all of these and perhaps other unknown factors are of importance. They might well explain why it is that some experiments have been supportive and some less so.

The question remains unresolved. Some Psi researchers are convinced that there is no longer any need for experiments to demonstrate the existence of psychic phenomena, that experiments should now be directed toward understanding them. Others believe that there is a just marginally adequate basis for belief in their existence. And a number, by far the majority, remain unwilling to accept the legitimacy of the evidence, although most are now willing to accept the legitimacy of the inquiry.

Main Points

1 The eyes of predators generally point to the front, thus making binocular vision possible, and making it easier to estimate distance. The eyes of the preyed-upon point in different directions, thus giving the animal a wider field of vision, but reducing accuracy of depth perception. We have the eyes of a predator.

2 The principal function of visual perception is to detect changes in our surroundings, as well as to detect the surroundings themselves at a distance.

3 The eye focuses incoming light (by means of a lens that accommodates by becoming thicker or thinner) onto light-sensitive cells that form part of the retina. Rods in the retina respond primarily to brightness; cones, of which there are far fewer (perhaps one-twentieth as many) respond primarily to color. These cells translate light energy into neural impulses that are transmitted to the brain via the optic nerve.

4 The part of the brain that is involved in vision is in the occipital lobe at the back of the cortex. Information from the right half of each eye (left visual field) goes to the right half of the brain; information from the left half of each eye (right visual field) goes to the left half of the brain.

5 The eyes respond to light waves, describable in terms of frequency (number of waves per unit of time), amplitude (height of wave) and complexity (mixture or purity).

6 Wavelength is a function of frequency and gives rise to subjective experiences of color. We perceive waves varying in length from approximately 400 nanometers (1 nanometer is 1 billionth of a meter) which are perceived as violet or dark, to between 700 and 800 nanometers, where light waves are perceived as red. In between are other colors of the rainbow. Beyond the reds (750 or so nanometers) are infrareds; and beyond the violets (below 400 nanometers) are ultraviolets.

7 Amplitude of a light wave gives rise to a sensation of brightness or dullness, with higher amplitude corresponding to brighter colors (in the same way as sound waves of higher amplitude correspond to louder sounds).

8 Complexity of light waves gives rise to the subjective experience of color saturation or purity, with simpler waves being associated with more saturated colors, and more complex waves being associated with "grayer" colors.

9 Color blindness is often genetically based, and is far more common among males than females. The most common form is red-green blindness, a defect that in many cases is not absolute. That is, many red-green color blind persons can nevertheless distinguish among various hues of red and green.

10 The Young-Helmholtz trichromatic theory suggests that we have cones differentially responsive to three colors: red, green, and blue. According to this theory, colors other than these three give rise to precise mixtures of activity among them which we then interpret in terms of an appropriate color.

11 Hering's opponent process theory proposes that we have three dual color systems: a red-green system, a blue-yellow system, and a light-dark system. There is evidence to support the existence of these systems.

12 Adaptation (increased sensitivity) to low light is far greater for rods than for cones, a fact that explains why we don't see color well at night.

13 Among the stable characteristics of visual perception is a tendency to perceive color, size, and shape as being constant for objects even when the stimulation we receive varies considerably. Without the constancies, we might be more confused by our environments.

14 We judge depth and distance by means of binocular cues such as convergence (our eyes point more toward the center when the object we look at is closer) and stereoscopic vision (the retinal images in each of our eyes are slightly different). We also make use of what are termed monocular cues—monocular because we don't need two eyes to see them. These include interposition (objects between us and something else must be closer than the something else); perspective (parallel lines tend to converge with increasing distance); and size (distant objects appear smaller).

15 We perceive movement as a function of changes in retinal images and of movements of our own heads and eyes.

16 Common illusions of movement include the phi phenomenon (apparent movement of motion pictures, for example); autokinetic movement (where a single, stationary light in a dark room appears to move); and the waterfall effect (where movement in one direction ceases and is then perceived as movement in the opposite direction).

17 Visual illusions frequently occur as a function of our tendency to perceive in depth and in two dimensions, and in terms of perspective and expectations.

18 Gestalt principles of perception include praegnanz (a tendency toward "good form"); proximity (figures close together tend to be perceived as though they go together); similarity (objects that are similar tend to be perceived as though they belong together); and continuity. These principles explain why we can listen to a conversation when others are going on around us. That is, words and gestures in a single conversation form a logical continuity, display similarity in terms of voice, tone, source, and so on, and tend to occur in some sort of proximity.

19 Cultural experience probably influences how we perceive things, as well as what we are likely to perceive. Experiments with distorting goggles indicate that we adapt very well to a variety of perceptual distortions, providing that these exhibit some order and predictability. These findings seem to indicate that experience plays an important role in visual perception.

20 Infants appear to be sensitive to visual stimulation at birth, indicating that some aspects of visual perception are not dependent upon learning.

21 Visual perception seems to depend upon an interplay of learning and innate capacities. Research with animals suggests that without appropriate stimulation during early development, certain neurons in the visual cortex either atrophy or fail to establish synapses with other neurons, essentially becoming nonfunctional.

22 Extrasensory perception (ESP, Psi or paranormal phenomena) is the perception of phenomena without use of the ordinary senses—hence the label *extra*sensory. ESP phenomena include telepathy (communication without voice, language, or other ordinary means); precognition (knowing events in advance of their occurrence); clairvoyance (perception of objects and events not now in immediate sensory contact); and psychokinesis (movement of objects through nonphysical means).

23 Some claim that the existence of ESP has been established: the majority claim not. In fact, there is as yet no reputable scientific evidence to substantiate claims made by proponents of paranormal phenomena.

Further Readings

Visual perception is described in more detail in the following three books. Gregory's two books provide fascinating accounts of some of the characteristics of visual perception in humans and other animals. The first also contains interesting accounts of visual illusions. Hochberg's book provides a more advanced look at perception theories.

Gregory, R. L. *Eye and brain: The psychology of seeing* (2nd ed.). New York: McGraw-Hill, 1973.

Gregory, R. L. *The intelligent eye.* New York: McGraw-Hill, 1970.

Hochberg, J. *Perception* (2nd ed.). Englewood Cliffs, N.J.: Prentice-Hall, 1978.

Extrasensory phenomena and relevant research are described and evaluated in the following four books. Holroyd asserts that a new scientific paradigm is emerging that must and will include parasensory phenomena. Mishlove's is a complete account of research on the nonmaterial dimensions of being, from pre-recorded history to contemporary laboratory experiments. Mitchell is a noted astronaut; his monumental work covers every area of psychic research. And Targ and Puthoff are the physicists who studied Uri Geller.

Holroyd, S. *Psi and the consciousness explosion.* New York: Taplinger, 1976.

Mishlove, J. *The roots of consciousness.* New York: Random House, 1975.

Mitchell, E. D. *Psychic exploration: A challenge for science.* New York: G. P. Putnam's Sons, 1974.

Targ, R., & Puthoff, H. *Mind reach: Scientists look at psychic ability.* New York: Delacorte, 1977.

For a devastating antidote to pro-ESP literature, this book, written by a master magician, is a must:

Randi, J. *Flim-flam: The truth about unicorns, parapsychology, and other delusions.* New York: Lippincott and Crowell, 1980.

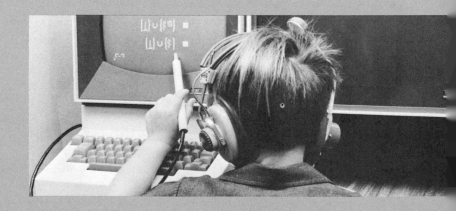

The processes involved in learning, remembering, and thinking have long presented intriguing problems for psychologists. A number of sometimes contradictory and sometimes complementary explanations have been advanced for these phenomena. Chapter 6 looks at some of the most important and influential explanations of learning; Chapter 7 describes memory processes and suggests some interesting possibilities for improving memory; Chapter 8 discusses thinking, language, and creativity. It is interesting that these predominantly human topics have been extensively investigated among nonhuman animals. Not only is some of this research fascinating in itself, but also much of it has contributed significantly to our understanding of our own behavior; there are sometimes remarkable similarities between us and other animals.

PART TWO

Learning, Memory, and Thinking

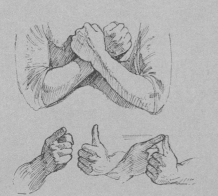

Chapter 6
Learning
Chapter 7
Memory
Chapter 8
Thought, Language, and Creativity

Learning

There is an oft-told tale that demonstrates the power of precise and rigorous scientific investigation in psychology. It concerns a psychologist, a well-known expert on learning processes and an avid investigator of conditioned responses in fleas. Unvarnished rumor, as reliable as any rumor, has it that this psychologist was remarkably successful in conditioning fleas to jump in response to the verbal command: "Jump!"

In one noteworthy variation of his basic experimental procedure, the professor investigated the effects of removing a conditioned flea's legs, one pair at a time. A flea having six legs, the procedure was carried out in three stages. At each stage, the psychologist made careful and detailed entries in his notebook, specifying, among other things, the exact procedure and the precise observation. Thus, after removing the first pair of legs, he noted:

> *Time: 1:38. Frontal left and right legs removed. Subject placed on jumping table. Command given as per approved procedure (1904). Observation. Flea jumps; mean height, 7.23 cm.*

When the next pair of legs was removed, the flea still jumped on command, although the mean height had been reduced to 5.21 cm. But when the last pair of legs was removed, the flea lay quivering on the table, unresponsive to repeated exhortations to "Jump!" The final entry in the lab book: "When a flea has all six legs removed, it becomes deaf."

Does this experiment prove that deafness is learned? Or does it prove that fleas hear with their hind legs?

What Is Learning?

Psychology deals with all the things we do and feel; with our perceptions and our awareness; with our personalities and our motives; with our interactions in groups and with our development as individuals. It deals too with the biological facts of existence and with the relationships between biology and behavior. These are the subjects of this book.

Psychology deals as well with changes that occur in behavior. Some of these changes are temporary; they might result from fatigue or from the use of drugs. Other changes appear to be primarily biologically determined; they accompany the natural, normal processes of maturation (the physical growth of the organism including, for example, changes that usually occur with sexual maturation); or they might result from injury or disease, particularly of the brain or other parts of the nervous system. There is yet another class of changes in behavior; it includes all changes that result from experience, and is illustrated by most of the behaviors we engage in daily. These changes in behavior that result from experience, but that are not due to fatigue, maturation, drugs, injury, or disease, define learning.

It should be noted that although we look to behavior for evidence that learning has occurred, changes in behavior do not always happen following experiences that we might have expected to lead to learning. In many cases there is no evidence of learning until an opportunity to display a behavioral change is presented; and in some cases, that opportunity never occurs. As a case in point, consider a classic learning experiment conducted by Buxton (1940). In this experiment, a number of rats were left in large mazes during the course of several nights. These mazes had "start" and "goal" boxes. In the morning, the rats were removed and placed back in their cages. There was, of course, no evidence that any of these rats had learned anything. Their behavior in their cages, or in the mazes, did not change in any apparent way. But when Buxton later gave the rats a very small taste of food in the goal boxes, and immediately placed them in the start boxes, more than half the rats ran directly to the goal boxes without making a single error. It is clear that they had learned a great deal about the mazes during the nights they had spent in them, but that this learning had simply been latent until they were presented with an opportunity to use the learning. Thus **learning** is more properly defined as an actual or latent change in behavior due to experience.

Learning An actual or latent change in behavior due to experience.

Approaches to Learning

Learning is not easily separated from the other major topics in psychology. Changes in behavior are centrally involved in motivation, personality, perception, development—indeed, in all of our behaviors. We are not simple, highly predictable organisms with unchanging patterns of behavior. Only fools do not profit from experience, and we are not fools; we are *Homo sapiens,* the self-named wise one.

Given that learning is so centrally involved in behavior, it is not surprising that the history of psychology can be traced through a study of the development of theories of learning. Most of the important early psychologists devoted considerable effort to discovering the laws and principles of learning. These early efforts, particularly in the United States, were governed by the prevailing spirit of those times in psychology. It was a spirit that had rejected the more philosophical and intuitive approach of an earlier age, a spirit of scientific empiricism. Empiricism involves itself with the objective and observable facts of nature. It accepts as true only those phenomena that can be objectively demonstrated. Accordingly, the earliest learning theorists looked at objective aspects of human functioning, and sought rules that might govern relationships between **stimuli**—observable conditions that can give rise to behavior—and **responses**—objective manifestations of behavior. Their theories have come to be known as *S-R theories* (stimulus-response theories), as *associationistic theories* (since

Stimulus (plural, stimuli) A highly general, widely employed psychological term. It may be defined as something, either internal or external to the organism, which has an effect on an organism. Stimuli are ordinarily associated with sensory processes (that is, they are usually visual, auditory, tactile, and so on).

Response The effect of stimulation. A response may be a muscular or glandular reaction or may take the form of a mental process where there is no detectable glandular or muscular change. Psychological orientations such as the behavioristic have emphasized stimuli and responses that are objective and observable; other emphases in psychology have been more concerned with stimuli and responses that are *inferred* rather than always observable.

they deal primarily with associations that might form between stimuli and responses), or as *behavioristic theories* (since they deal with the observable aspects of behavior). And although these theories have sometimes been accused of leading to a mechanistic and inexact description of human learning, they have contributed a great deal that continues to be both valid and valuable.

There have been numerous approaches to the study of human behavior in addition to the purely **behavioristic** approach and its many variations, but a relatively limited number of other approaches have withstood the assaults of time. **Humanism** (also referred to as *third-force psychology*) is sometimes considered one of these approaches. In essence, it advocates a more individual and more affective (emotional) approach to psychology, where the uniqueness of every individual is considered more important than the more general and mechanistic principles attributed to behaviorism. Accordingly, topics such as the development of self and of self-awareness are central in humanistic psychology. In fact, however, although humanism presents a contrast to behaviorism, it does not present specific explanations for learning and is therefore not considered in the present chapter. (It is considered in more detail in Chapter 13, however.)

Cognitive approaches present yet another way of looking at learning. These approaches are not so much alternatives as attempts to explain facets of human behavior that cannot easily be explained with traditional behaviorist theories. Cognitive theories are distinct from behaviorist theories primarily with respect to their topics and methods. Whereas behaviorist theories concern themselves with such observables as stimuli and responses, cognitive theories attempt to explain mental processes involved in thinking, problem-solving, decision-making, perceiving, and attributing meaning, motives, causes, and so on.

This chapter deals primarily with behaviorism. Chapters 7, 8, 11, and 13 look at research dealing with cognitive topics.

Behaviorism An approach to psychology that considers only objective evidence of behavior and does not consider consciousness and mind.

Humanism A philosophical and psychological orientation that is primarily concerned with *humanity*—the worth of humans as individuals and those processes that augment their human qualities. The humanistic movement in psychology is also referred to as *third-force psychology*, the other two forces being behaviorism and psychoanalytic theory. The principal concerns of humanistic psychology are the self and emotions.

Cognitive Pertaining to intellectual processes. Since *cognize* is to *know*, cognitive theories are principally concerned with the processes whereby organisms obtain knowledge.

Pavlov's Dogs: Classical Conditioning

The process whereby an association is formed between a stimulus and a response is termed **conditioning.** Conditioning is, in some respects, a simple phenomenon, easily explained and understood, and of tremendous value in understanding some aspects of human functioning.

Ivan Pavlov, a distinguished Russian physiologist, is closely associated with the simplest form of conditioning, now referred to as **classical conditioning**. Pavlov made extensive use of dogs in a variety of experiments on digestive processes (for which he was awarded one of the first Nobel prizes in medicine). In the course of these experiments, he noticed that some of his more experienced dogs began to salivate at the mere sight of their handlers. The less experienced dogs also salivated, but they did so only when presented with food. Pavlov rightly guessed that his older dogs had learned something that the more naive dogs had yet to learn. More precisely, they had learned to associate the sight of a handler or of a food dish (stimulus) with salivation (response) (Figure 6.1). Alternatively, it could be said that they had learned an association between a handler and food, both of which are stimuli, but only one of which would initially lead to a predictable response (salivation). In other words, they had learned to substitute one stimulus (handler) for another (food). Accordingly, classical conditioning is sometimes referred to as stimulus substitution. That a previously neutral stimulus (sight of handler) eventually leads to a response ordinarily associated with some other stimulus is evidence that learning has taken place. In short, there has been a change in behavior (specifically, in the response to the handler) as a result of experience (repeated pairing of the handler and food).

Subsequent Pavlovian experiments did much to clarify the laws of classical conditioning. In the classic experiment, a dog is placed in a harnesslike contraption similar to the one depicted in Figure 6.2. The apparatus is so arranged that food powder can

Conditioning A process whereby a response becomes dependent upon specific circumstances (stimuli). Conditioning theory is therefore a learning theory—that is, a theory which seeks to explain processes involved in learning. It gives two specific explanations for learning: classical conditioning and operant conditioning.

Classical conditioning A process whereby the repeated pairing of two stimuli, one of which is associated with a specific response and one of which is not, eventually leads to the association of the response with the stimulus not ordinarily associated with that response. Classical conditioning is also sometimes referred to as stimulus substitution, since once learning has occurred it is possible to substitute one stimulus for another in order to evoke highly similar responses.

Figure 6.1 What Pavlov first noticed was that the sight of the handler alone was enough to cause many of his experimental dogs to salivate. Through further experiments, he reconstructed and validated the process that must have produced the effect.

Figure 6.2 Pavlov's dogs were placed in a harness like this one. Food powder can be placed either in the dog's mouth or in the dish. Saliva is measured as it drops into a tube in the dog's mouth. The resulting movement of a tiny balancing mechanism in the tube is transmitted to a pen, whose movement in turn is recorded on a revolving drum. In the experiment illustrated here, the unconditioned stimulus (food) is paired with a conditioned stimulus (light shining in the window).

Unconditioned response A response that is unlearned. Withdrawing the hand upon touching a hot object is an example of an unconditioned response.

Unconditioned stimulus A stimulus that elicits an unlearned response. All stimuli capable of eliciting reflexive behaviors are examples of unconditioned stimuli (for example, food is an unconditioned stimulus for the response of salivation).

Conditioned stimulus A stimulus that does not elicit any response initially but, as a result of being paired with an unconditioned stimulus and its response, acquires the capability of eliciting that same response. For example, a stimulus that is always present at the time of a fear reaction may become a conditioned stimulus for fear.

Conditioned response A response that is elicited by a conditioned stimulus. In some obvious ways, a conditioned response resembles its corresponding unconditioned response. The two are not identical, however.

either be inserted directly into the dog's mouth or, alternatively, can be dropped into a dish in front of the dog. Salivation occurs when food powder is placed in the dog's mouth. This is an unlearned response: all normal dogs salivate under these conditions. This behavior is therefore labeled an **unconditioned response** (UCR). The stimulus that gives rise to the UCR is termed an **unconditioned stimulus** (UCS). Most animals, including humans, are born with a number of these prewired stimulus-response associations (UCS-UCR bonds). Since they are simple and unlearned, they are called *reflexes*. More complex behaviors that are also unlearned are termed *instincts* (see Chapter 9). Human reflexes include the tendency to blink when material approaches the eye, to salivate in response to food, to withdraw from painful stimulation, and to jerk the knee in response to a sharp blow below the kneecap.

Every time Pavlov's dog has food powder inserted in its mouth, a buzzer sounds. The procedure is repeated a number of times. Then the experimeter simply sounds the buzzer without providing any food powder. The dog still salivates. The animal has been *conditioned* to respond to a buzzer by salivating (see Figure 6.3). The buzzer is termed a **conditioned stimulus** (CS); the response of salivating upon hearing the buzzer is a **conditioned response** (CR).

Acquisition

A number of factors have been found to be directly related to the ease with which a classically conditioned response can be acquired. One is the distinctiveness

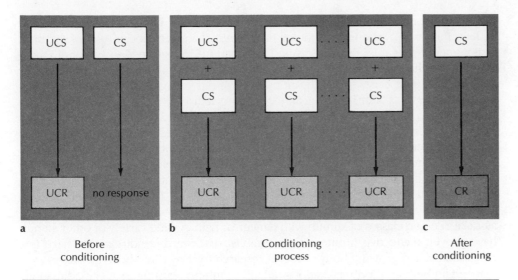

BIOGRAPHY
Ivan Petrovich Pavlov
1849–1936

Figure 6.3 Classical conditioning. Initially the conditioned stimulus does not lead to a response (**a**). After repeated pairings with an unconditioned stimulus (**b**), the conditioned stimulus eventually does lead to a response (**c**).

Pavlov, the son of a village priest in Russia, received his early education in a local seminary. From there he went to the University of St. Petersburg, specializing in animal physiology and in medicine. After he obtained his medical degree, he went to Germany, where he studied physiology and medicine for another two years. He then returned to St. Petersburg and worked as an assistant in a physiology laboratory until he was appointed professor of pharmacology and head of a physiology department at the age of forty-one. His work, for which he received a Nobel prize in 1904, continued to deal almost exclusively with physiological topics, specifically with digestive processes. It wasn't until the age of fifty that he began to study classical conditioning, these studies lasting another thirty years. To the end, however, he insisted that he was a physiologist and not a psychologist. In fact, he viewed psychology with considerable disdain, and fined any of his laboratory assistants who used psychological rather than physiological terms (R. I. Watson, 1971).

of the CS. Not surprisingly, a stimulus that is easily discriminated from other stimulation will more easily become associated with a response.

A second factor of critical importance is the timing of the conditioned stimulus and the unconditioned stimulus. The ideal situation, delayed or forward-order conditioning, presents the conditioned stimulus prior to the unconditioned stimulus, with the CS continuing during the presentation of the UCS (Schwitzgebel & Kolb, 1974). In the classical Pavlovian experiment, for example, fastest learning is obtained by sounding the buzzer just before the presentation of food powder, and continuing the sound of the buzzer while the food powder is being injected into the dog's mouth. Other alternatives are to have the CS begin and end before the UCS, termed *trace conditioning;* to have the UCS and the CS *simultaneous,* neither beginning nor ending before the other; or to present the UCS prior to the CS (termed *backward conditioning*). Figure 6.4 summarizes these pairing sequences.

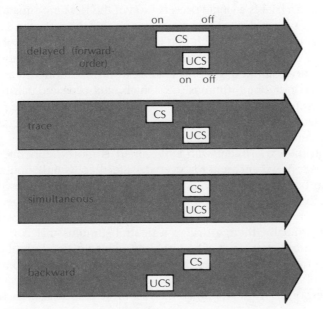

Figure 6.4 The pairing sequences are shown here in the order of effectiveness. Acquisition of conditioning takes place most quickly in the delayed sequence, when the conditioned stimulus (for instance, the buzzer) is presented shortly before the unconditioned stimulus (food powder) and continues throughout the time the UCS is presented.

BIOGRAPHY
John Broadus Watson
1878–1958

The founder of U.S. behaviorism, John Watson was born in Greenville, South Carolina, in 1878. By his own admission, he was not a particularly good student (Murchison, 1936), although on one occasion he was the only person who passed a final Greek exam, an accomplishment that he attributed to having spent the previous afternoon drinking an entire quart of Coca-Cola syrup and cramming. He took his graduate training at the University of Chicago, working his way through school as a rat caretaker. After obtaining his degree he lectured at the University of Chicago. Several years later he was offered a full professorship at Johns Hopkins, where he remained until his wife apparently discovered his infidelities (with his assistant, Rosalie Rayner) and sued him for divorce. The ensuing front-page scandal led to his being fired from Johns Hopkins. From there he went to New York, married Miss Rayner, had two more children (he had already fathered two), and went to work for the J. Walter Thompson advertising agency. His first job with them required that he go up and down the Mississippi River asking people what brand of rubber boots they wore, and he moved from there to virtually every department in the company until he became its vice-president. During this time he wrote popularized psychology articles for such magazines as *Harper's*, *McCall's*, *Liberty*, *Collier's*, and *Cosmopolitan*. These activities, for which he was well paid, did little to endear him to his former colleagues, who spent some time and effort criticizing the articles. He never returned to academic life.

Generalization The transference of a response from one stimulus to a separate stimulus. A child who responds with fear in a new situation that resembles an old fear-producing situation is showing evidence of stimulus generalization.

The least effective sequence, backward conditioning, has generally not resulted in learning, except when the stimulus has certain characteristics. In one of the most striking studies of this, Keith-Lucas and Guttman (1975) succeeded in conditioning avoidance behavior in rats by shocking them electrically and then presenting a plastic hedgehog in their cages. A significant number of rats exposed to the hedgehog one, five, or ten seconds after receiving an electric shock displayed avoidance behavior the following day. Backward conditioning had been established after a single trial. Other rats who experienced a forty-second delay between the presentation of the shock and the appearance of the hedgehog showed little evidence of being conditioned.

The significance of these results is that the long-held belief that *any* neutral stimulus can be conditioned through appropriate presentation no longer appears to be true. In the case of the rat, Keith-Lucas and Guttman (1975) speculate that the effectiveness of the plastic hedgehog relates to an evolutionary tendency in the rat to associate certain classes of stimuli with danger or pain. A wide variety of other stimuli have proven ineffective in attempts to establish backward conditioning. There is a considerable and growing body of recent research relating directly to the observation that certain biological predispositions can aid or inhibit learning in specific situations and with specific organisms. The importance of this research is considerable. It is therefore treated in more detail in a later section following a discussion of other forms and principles of conditioning.

Generalization and Discrimination

A dog trained to salivate in response to a buzzer may also salivate in response to a bell, a gong, or a human imitation of a buzzer; then again, it may not. The probability that the response will generalize from one situation to another seems to depend on the similarity between the two situations. For example, if the human imitation of the buzzer is a good imitation, **generalization** is likely to take place.

An early investigation of conditioning among humans involved the legendary case of Little Albert (J. B. Watson & Rayner, 1920). J. B. Watson, one of the principal proponents of classical conditioning, had earlier observed that children react with fear whenever they hear loud noises. He reasoned that this fear reaction was, in fact, an unconditioned (unlearned) response, and that it could be conditioned to any other distinctive stimulus. Accordingly, he and Rayner arranged for Little Albert to be placed in proximity to a white laboratory rat. Initially, Little Albert showed no fear whatsoever of the rat, but cooed and gurgled as an eight-month-old infant will. On successive occasions, Watson and Rayner made loud noises whenever the rat was brought before Little Albert. As expected, he reacted fearfully to the noise. After a relatively small number of trials (a trial is a single presentation of the learning situation), Little Albert responded with a great deal of fear whenever he saw the rat, even in the absence of any noise. This is a clear, although perhaps unethical, illustration of *affective* (emotional) learning brought about through classical conditioning. In this case the loud noise was an unconditioned stimulus leading to unconditioned fear responses. The white rat was a conditioned stimulus (CS) which, after repeated pairings with the UCS (loud noise), eventually led to a conditioned fear response (CR) (see Figure 6.5). Little Albert continued to respond with fear to a variety of other furry objects, some of them inanimate, evidence of generalization.

Although the experiment with Little Albert is more deliberate and systematic than most situations we encounter in everyday life, there is little doubt that emotional responses can be classically conditioned, and that these responses generalize from one situation to another. Witness, for example, the fear that many people experience upon hearing sounds similar to those of a dentist's drill. The sound of the drill is really quite painless. Initially, then, a drill is a neutral stimulus that comes to serve as a conditioned stimulus as a result of being paired with pain. Similarly, the white clothing typically worn by dentists and their assistants, the odors peculiar to a dentist's office, and a variety of other neutral stimuli may come to be associated with pain and give rise to fear responses. Note, too, that many of these responses may be unconscious.

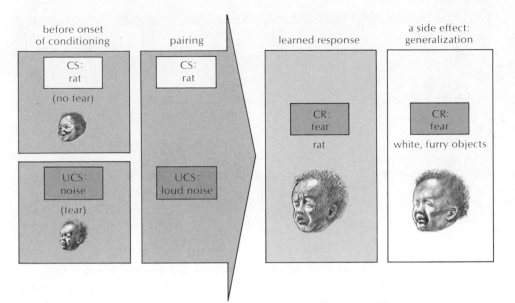

before onset of conditioning	pairing	learned response	a side effect: generalization
CS: rat (no fear)	CS: rat	CR: fear rat	CR: fear white, furry objects
UCS: noise (fear)	UCS: loud noise		

Figure 6.5 Watson and Rayner's 1920 experiment in classical conditioning to bring about a response of fear for a white rat. After pairing the white rat—a stimulus to which Little Albert clearly had no aversion before the experiment—with an unpleasant UCS (a loud noise), Albert became conditioned to react as if the white rat alone was as frightening as the noise had initially been. A common side effect of conditioning also took place in the experiment on Little Albert. The child *generalized* his response to stimuli that were similar to the conditioned stimulus. White, furry objects that weren't rats also became sources of fear.

They may take the form of such physiological changes as increases in respiration rate, heart rate, blood pressure, and muscular tension (termed *conditioned emotional reactions,* or CERs). Interestingly, all of these behaviors over which we ordinarily have no conscious control may be conditioned to a variety of stimuli, a fact of which Pavlov was well aware.

Not all classically acquired responses generalize to all other similar situations. Indeed, in many cases, the most important aspects of learning involve **discrimination** between situations where a response is appropriate and another where the response might be inappropriate. Thus, although an individual may be classically conditioned to fear certain stimuli associated with a dentist's office, that same individual may respond in quite the opposite manner to the sound of an electric motor in a toothbrush.

A curious and rather bizarre illustration of discrimination is provided by one of Pavlov's (1927) early experiments. A dog was trained to discriminate between a circle and an ellipse (a squashed circle). The procedure was simply to pair food with the circle but never with the ellipse. In time, the dog learned to salivate reliably in response to the circle, and not to salivate in response to the ellipse. Having demonstrated discrimination learning, Pavlov then changed the experimental conditions, altering the shape of the ellipse so that it became rounder with every succeeding trial, and flattening the circle slightly, so that it was slowly becoming elliptical. For a period of time, the dog continued to discriminate between circle and ellipse. Finally, however, a point was reached where the dog could no longer tell the difference between the two. At this point it showed symptoms of highly deranged behavior, attempting desperately to extricate itself from its harness, whining, growling, barking frantically, and urinating and defecating rather impolitely. Similar procedures have since been employed to induce experimental neuroses in monkeys and other animals.

Extinction

Just as numerous responses can be classically conditioned very easily, they can also be unlearned very quickly. To bring about the **extinction** (cessation) of a classically conditioned response, it is necessary to present the conditioned stimulus a number of times without the unconditioned stimulus. Extinction is said to have occurred when (and *if;* it needn't always occur) the conditioned stimulus no longer elicits the conditioned response. Thus, once Pavlov's dog had learned to salivate in response to the tone, continued presentation of the tone without pairing it with food would lead

Discrimination A process of detecting differences; essentially opposite to that involved in generalization. Whereas to generalize is to respond to similarities in different situations, discrimination involves responding to differences. In discrimination, an organism reacts differently to similar but not identical situations (that is, it discriminates between situations where the response is appropriate and similar situations where the response is not appropriate).

Extinction A conditioning procedure whereby a learned response is eliminated. Extinction may involve the repeated presentation of a conditioned stimulus without the accompanying unconditioned stimulus, or may involve the withdrawal of reinforcement. Extinction is said to have occurred when a previously conditioned stimulus no longer elicits a conditioned response, or when a previously reinforced behavior is no longer reinforced and ceases to occur.

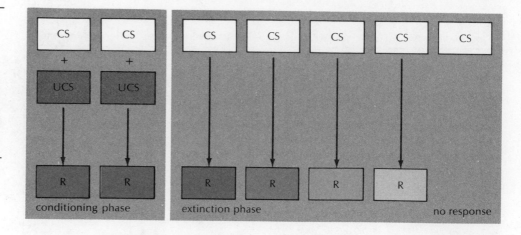

to a rapid decline in salivation in response to the tone, and eventually to its extinction. The same observation generally holds true for the variety of emotional responses that have been conditioned to neutral stimuli. Even Little Albert might have been cured of his fear of rats (and of his generalized fear of other furry white objects) if these were presented to him often enough in the absence of other fear-inducing stimulation (see Figure 6.6). Unfortunately, Little Albert was removed from the hospital where Watson had been working with him the day before Watson was to begin "deconditioning" procedures.

Once a classically conditioned response has been extinguished, it can be reacquired much more easily than initially. A dog who has initially learned to salivate in response to a tone, and whose response to the tone has then been extinguished, will learn to salivate again following only one or two trials pairing the tone with food powder. In fact, an extinguished response sometimes recurs in the absence of any training. This phenomenon, termed *spontaneous recovery,* illustrates that behaviors that are apparently extinguished are not necessarily completely forgotten.

Relevance to Daily Life

It appears that classical conditioning in everyday life is largely an unconscious process, dependent more on the whims and vagaries of life's events than on any intentions we might have. The inexplicable fears we sometimes sense, and the more positive emotions too, may often be the results of associations whose origins we do not know. Hence descriptions of the role of classical conditioning in everyday life are difficult and speculative. In the scientific laboratory, conditions leading to observed behaviors are often very clear; in our daily laboratories, conditions are more complex. Nevertheless, we can speculate that at least some of the meanings that events and situations have for us derive from classically conditioned associations. We know that we feel good in certain places; we react positively to certain odors; we become tense in other situations (see Box 6.1). We can logically assume that these feelings were present at other times under similar circumstances, and that they have become learned responses as a result. Thus classical conditioning may be centrally involved in our emotional lives as well as in the host of unconscious habits and responses that are part of our daily repertoire.

Why Does Classical Conditioning Work?

When I was five years old, my grandfather's dog attacked me. I remember a huge hound, teeth like razored spikes, growl as ugly as any that might populate the most horrible of nightmares. In fact, it was probably only a small dog, since I was only a small child. And perhaps it didn't attack me as savagely as I remember. My skin was broken in only two places.

I have not been bitten by a dog since, and I have raised a number of dogs and cats, not to mention a few children. And I have loved them all.

But last week when my truck broke down on the way to the lake and I had to walk into a farmyard for assistance, the farm dog came bounding across the snowy field, barking, and I tasted fear. As I have on many other occasions since I was five. I am conditioned to fear strange dogs. I have no control over my physiological reactions when I meet one.

Why does an emotional (or other) response become conditioned to a particular stimulus (or class of stimuli)? There are two distinct explanations for classical conditioning. The first, and oldest, is the one that Pavlov and Watson believed to be correct. It maintains that the simultaneous or near-simultaneous presentation of a stimulus and a response leads to the formation of a physiological or neural link between the two. In this view, what is most important in the conditioning situation is the closeness in time (termed **contiguity**) of the stimulus and response. A contiguity explanation of classical conditioning maintains that all of the stimuli associated with "dog" (appearance, smell, sound, and movement of the beast) were also associated with my initial fear response (not to mention a little pain); thus the sight, sound, or smell of a dog continues to plague me in my otherwise peaceful adult life.

Although contiguity might appear to be an adequate explanation for what happened to Pavlov's dogs, and perhaps even for what happened to me, there are a number of relatively simple experimental situations which it does not explain. One of them,

Contiguity Closeness in time. Two events are said to be contiguous (or in contiguity) when they are simultaneous or nearly simultaneous. Contiguity provides one important explanation for the effects of classical conditioning procedures.

BOX 6.1

A *Classical Conditioning Lie-Detector*

Polygraphs, instruments capable of sensing and recording changes in such physiological responses as blood pressure, respiration rate, heart rate, and electrodermal response (galvanic skin response, or GSR), have been employed by law-enforcement and judicial groups since as far back as 1895 (Reid & Inbau, 1977). The technique is based on the simple observation that deception is often accompanied by physiological changes indicative of increasing emotion or tension (increased physiological arousal). With the continued refinement of instruments and polygraph methodology, experienced examiners are sometimes remarkably successful in separating those who are lying from those who aren't, with accuracy of judgment occasionally running over 90 percent (Horvath & Reid, 1977). The method is by no means foolproof. Nor is the voice stress analyzer or psychological stress evaluator, an instrument that detects voice tremors presumably due to stress and *sometimes* associated with deception, and that can be employed via telephone, radio, television, or in person without the consent of the subject (see Rice, 1978).

Another lie-detection technique serves as a startling demonstration of the influence of classical conditioning. Using this technique, subjects (more accurately, suspects) are conditioned to signal their lies. The procedure, pioneered by Jafee, Millman, & Gorman (1966), has been further developed by Golden (1967). In the Golden procedure, subjects are questioned in two stages, the first stage being a conditioning process and the second, a test process. In the conditioning process, subjects are instructed to *lie* every time they are asked their name and to signal the lie by depressing a key. If, for

example, the subject's name is John, he will be asked, "Is your name John?" He is to respond by saying "no" and depressing the key. He is also instructed to answer other questions correctly and *not* to press the key. If, for example, he is asked, "Is your name Tom?" he is to answer "no" and *not* depress the key.

Following the conditioning period, after which the subject reliably and virtually automatically answers "no" and depresses the key every time he is asked whether his name is John, he is asked a series of questions (test phase). Some of these questions are irrelevant, some refer to his name, and others are relevant to the crime of which he is suspected. The hope is that he will have been sufficiently conditioned so that he will press the key each time he lies. One example of a series of questions presented to a subject whose name was John and who was suspected of having stolen one hundred dollars from a Mr. Smith is provided by Golden (1967, p. 387):

Is your name John?	(conditioning question)
Were you born in Illinois?	(irrelevant question)
Is your name John?	(conditioning question)
Do you live in Chicago?	(irrelevant question)
Is your name John?	(conditioning question)
Do you know who stole Mr. Smith's $100?	(relevant question)
Is your name John?	(conditioning question)
Did you steal Mr. Smith's $100?	(relevant question)

In a large-scale investigation of this procedure, 795 *actual* suspects who had been diagnosed as being untruthful by other methods were questioned, not in a laboratory, but as part of ordinary police procedure. Of these, an impressive 33 percent actually signaled that they were lying in response to relevant questions—and 72 percent of them later confessed!

This method too is not foolproof.

investigated by Kamin (1969) involves what is termed *blocking*, a phenomenon where conditioning to one stimulus is made difficult or impossible as a result of conditioning to another stimulus. Blocking experiments typically involve conditioning one group of animals to respond to a specific stimulus; a second group is not initially conditioned to this same stimulus. In the second phase of the procedure, both groups are given a number of learning trials where the initial stimulus is present but is now paired with a second, distinctive stimulus (for example, a light might be paired with a tone, and both might be associated with an electric shock). Subsequent trials where only the second stimulus is presented to members of both groups now reveal that subjects who had initially been conditioned with the first stimulus alone have learned virtually nothing from the second phase of the procedure. In contrast, animals who have been conditioned only in the presence of both stimuli exhibit learning when presented with either stimulus.

Contiguity does not explain blocking. Clearly, if conditioning depends only on the simultaneous presentation of a stimulus and response, there is no reason why both groups of animals should not have learned the same things.

Contingency provides a second explanation—one with far reaching implications. In this context, contingency refers to the interdependence of two or more events—to a sort of cause-and-effect relationship. If obtaining a scholarship depends on your getting good grades, then the scholarship is contingent upon your grades. And if not getting shocked in a cage depends upon the rat's depressing a lever at a crucial time, shock avoidance is contingent upon bar pressing. A contingency explanation of classical conditioning says, in effect, that what is learned is not a simple pairing of stimulus and response as a function of contiguity but the establishment of relationships between stimuli. This explanation, elaborated and investigated by Rescorla and Wagner (see Rescorla & Holland, 1976, 1982; Rescorla & Wagner, 1972; Wagner & Rescorla, 1972), is commonly termed the *Rescorla-Wagner model*. What this model says, in effect, is that the animal learns what goes with what. In a conditioning situation, what is important is the information a stimulus provides with respect to the probability of other events. When a dog salivates in response to a tone, it is because the tone now predicts the presentation of food. Put another way, the dog has learned a contingency between tone and food—a dependency relationship between two stimuli. And in the blocking experiments, animals who have learned that stimulus A means shock find it difficult to learn that B also means shock when A and B are subsequently paired because, in the context of the Rescorla-Wagner model, there is no new information provided by stimulus B in the learning situation. As Rescorla and Holland (1976) put it: "Pavlovian conditioning should be viewed as the learning about relations among events" (p. 184). And, as they make clear, this learning is not limited to discovering temporal relationships (shock always follows stimulus A), but includes as well what they term *informational* relationships. It appears that even rats in simple conditioning experiments acquire information about possible contingency relationships between stimuli. And I too, not to be outdone by a mere rat, have learned a contingency relationship from my grandfather's dog.

There are also important contingency relationships between behavior and its consequences, a topic that is central to the second form of conditioning that learning theorists have investigated: operant conditioning.

Skinner Boxes: Operant Conditioning

Another form of conditioning may account for much learning that is beyond the explanatory scope of classical conditioning. It was systematically investigated by Thorndike (1911, 1913) and elaborated by B. F. Skinner (1953, 1957, 1961, 1977), one of the most influential psychologists of this age.

Skinner begins with the observation that although classical conditioning is adequate to explain some simple forms of learning where responses are elicited by specific

Contingency A dependency relationship. An event is said to be contingent upon another when its occurrence is dependent upon the occurrence of the other. The Rescorla-Wagner conditioning model maintains that learning involves the discovery of contingencies.

Figure 6.7 B. F. Skinner distinguishes between two different types of behavior that may involve different learning processes. *Operants* (**a**) are deliberate behaviors that are seldom associated with a specific stimulus. In contrast, *respondents* (**b**) are reactions, often unconscious or uncontrollable, to obvious stimuli.

stimuli (termed **respondent** behavior), most of our daily behaviors are not of that variety. And the Pavlovian argument that all learning stems initially from associations that originate with unlearned stimulus-response bonds, and that are then elaborated by being associated with other stimuli (*second-order* or *higher-order conditioning*), presents a cumbersome and unconvincing explanation for such complex behaviors as walking, talking, reading, or even scratching one's nose when it isn't itchy. In effect, Skinner's system is admirably suited to explaining why some people scratch non-itchy noses, as well as a variety of other behaviors that are not elicited by obvious stimuli. Skinner describes these behaviors as **operant**, partly because they are, in one sense, operations that are performed on the environment (rather than in response to it), and partly to distinguish them from behaviors that are more clearly respondent (Figure 6.7). Thus Skinner speaks of respondent conditioning (essentially the same as classical conditioning) and of **operant conditioning**, also called *instrumental* conditioning. Most of his research has been directed toward discovering the principles underlying the learning of operant behaviors, and elaborating procedures for bringing about this type of learning. His most important findings are detailed in the following sections of this chapter.

An Illustration

Imagine, if you will, a small, squarish, cagelike structure with a metal grid for a floor. At one end of this structure is a lever; above it, a light; below it, a small tray. Outside the structure are various mechanical and/or electronic devices, so adjusted that if the lever inside the cage is pushed down, the light will go on, a click will be heard (if someone is listening), and a food pellet will drop into the tray.

Imagine, now, that an ordinary, reasonably intelligent, brown rat is placed inside this cage. This naive rat, Eric, knows nothing of Skinner, operant conditioning, or

Respondent A response that is elicited by a known, specific stimulus. Unconditioned responses of the type referred to in classical conditioning are examples of respondents.

Operant A response not elicited by any known or obvious stimulus. Most significant human behaviors appear to be of the operant variety. Such behaviors as writing a letter and going for a walk are operant, since they are not ordinarily associated with any known stimuli.

Operant conditioning A type of learning that involves an increase in the probability of a response occurring as a function of reinforcement. Most of the experimental work of B. F. Skinner investigated the principles of operant conditioning.

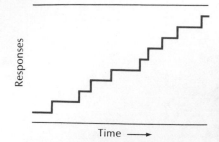

Responses

Time →

Figure 6.8 The photo shows a rat in a small Skinner box. When the bar is pressed, a food pellet appears. The graph shows a typical learning curve recorded on a revolving drum. The scroll-type drum revolves at a fixed pace, so that horizontal distance on the paper provides an easy measurement of time elapsed. Each time the rat emits the desired behavior (in this case, pressing the bar), a pen fixed to the scroll moves up a notch. The more frequent the bar-pressing, the sharper the ascent of the curve. This type of recording device provides a cumulative curve of the response rate over a known time period.

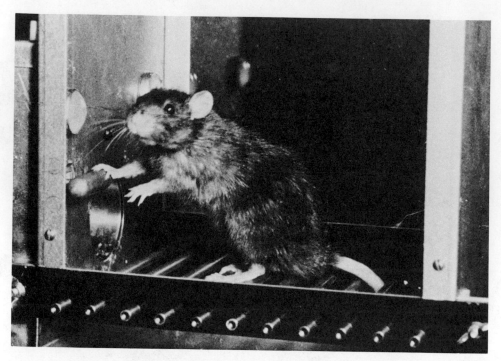

Reinforcer A stimulus that increases the probability that a response will reoccur.

Reinforcement The effect of a reinforcer; specifically, an increase in the probability of a response reoccurring.

Skinner boxes, that being the affectionate name for the cagelike structure (Figure 6.8). The rat now explores its environment, as rats are wont to do, and in the course of its wanderings, it accidentally depresses the lever, hears a click, finds a food pellet, and eats it.

Has Eric learned to depress the lever? No. He is simply not that intelligent. A child in the same situation might have made the connection immediately and would, if placed in the box again, go directly to the lever and press it. (Presumably, the food dispenser would release some aromatic health food rather than a rat pellet.) But Eric does not run directly to the lever and press it again. He does so eventually, but again accidentally. His bar-pressing behavior is simply an operant, an emitted behavior. Again, however, the light, the click, and the food.

Shortly, Eric's rate of bar-pressing behavior increases dramatically. Press, light, click, food, eat, press. . . . Now a switch is flicked on the apparatus. Eric presses; no click, no light, no food. He presses again, and again, and again. Suddenly, light, click, food. Eat, press, press, press, food! Slowly, Eric's bar-pressing behavior is being modified. Not only has he learned to press the lever to obtain food, but his rate of bar-pressing is being *controlled* by the administration of food. When he is given food once every ten bar presses, but the food is released randomly, he presses constantly at a high rate. When food is presented only after every thirty-five seconds following bar-pressing, he ceases to press the bar until the thirty-five-second interval is almost over. Then he presses rapidly until he again receives food (Figure 6.9).

So? What does bar-pressing in a rat have to do with scratching a nose that doesn't itch? Patience, while we become more technical, and introduce terms that have more general value than bar-pressing, food pellet, click, light, and rat. We will look at the nose later.

The Basic Model

First, let us call the rat an *organism*. We, too, are organisms. The bar-pressing is an *operant*—an emitted behavior. The rat does not depress a lever as an unlearned response to the cage or to anything specific in the cage. The food is termed a **reinforcer**; **reinforcement** is its effect. Any stimulus (condition or consequence) that

162

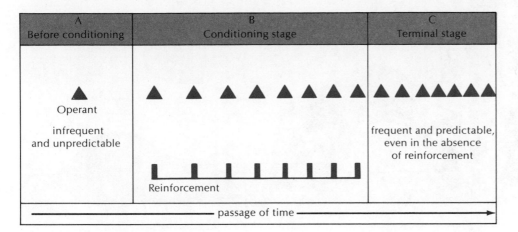

A Before conditioning	B Conditioning stage	C Terminal stage

Figure 6.9 Schematic model of operant conditioning. In A, the operant behavior alone is not rewarded. In B, conditioning begins. The operant behavior takes place by chance; it is immediately reinforced. It occurs again, by chance or deliberately, and the reinforcement is repeated. As the time-line chart shows, repetition becomes more and more frequent as the learner catches on. Eventually, the operant behavior continues even without reinforcement at the terminal stage (C).

increases the probability of a response occurring is said to be reinforcing. Thus, in the preceding example, the light too is a reinforcer. The click of the food-releasing mechanism serves as a signal that food has been released. It is termed a *discriminative stimulus,* and may be defined as any distinct feature of the situation which may, in the course of learning, become associated with a reinforced behavior. When conditioning bar-pressing and related behaviors in rats, for example, it is common to train the rat beforehand so that it recognizes an association between the click (or a light) and the presentation of food. In this type of training, termed *magazine training,* the click or light may be described as a discriminative stimulus which leads to whatever operant behaviors are required to reach the food tray and obtain reinforcement.

What happened to Eric in the cage may be described simply as follows: A naive rat (untrained organism) is placed in a situation. The organism emits a specific operant (bar-pressing); the operant is reinforced; eventually the probability of the operant occurring again increases dramatically. At this point the organism may be said to have *learned* the operant. When placed in the same situation on another occasion, the organism may begin to emit the operant immediately. At this stage it is accurate to say that an association has been formed, not only between the operant and reinforcement, but also between the operant and specific aspects of the situation. In other words, the organism discriminates between this situation and others where the operant is impossible or will not be reinforced. The operant may then be said to be affected by discriminative stimuli as well as to be under the control of its consequences (at least to some extent) (Figure 6.10).

In brief, Skinner's explanation of learning is based not on associations that might be formed between stimuli and responses (classical conditioning), but on associations that are established between a behavior and its consequences. Any other distinctive stimulus that happens to be present at the time of those consequences may also come to be associated with them and with the operant. And in the same way as responses that have been established through classical conditioning can sometimes be generalized to other stimuli, so operant behaviors learned in one situation will often be repeated in different circumstances (generalized to other discriminative stimuli).

Shaping

In a whimsical moment, I imagined I saw the king's men trying to train a rat to kneel in front of royal personages. They sat around various rat cages, waiting for the appropriate operant to appear. Each person's thumb was poised above the food-dispensing trigger, ready to dispense reinforcement immediately upon the appearance of the first acceptable genuflection. In time the rats grew gray and wizened with age, developed inoperable cancers, suffered fatal coronaries, and otherwise ceased to exist. Some of the king's best and brightest went in the same direction; others were simply

BIOGRAPHY
Burrhus Frederic Skinner
1904–

B. F. Skinner, like many of psychology's pioneers, did not enter graduate school with the intention of becoming a psychologist. Instead, he studied biology, but in the course of his studies he was exposed to the writings of Watson and Pavlov, and these profoundly influenced his career. In 1931 he obtained his Ph.D. in psychology from Harvard and spent the next five years doing research before beginning a career as lecturer, researcher, and writer. Chief among his early works was his 1938 book *The Behavior of Organisms,* which laid the groundwork for operant conditioning principles. A novel, *Walden II* (1948b), did much to popularize his conception of an ideal society based on scientific principles of human behavior, and engineered in such a way that positive rather than aversive techniques of control would predominate. He was soon recognized as the leading proponent of the behavioristic position—a position which has not had universal acceptance, and which he has had to defend on numerous occasions. His book *Beyond Freedom and Dignity* (1971) presents a highly readable exposition and defense of Skinner's beliefs.

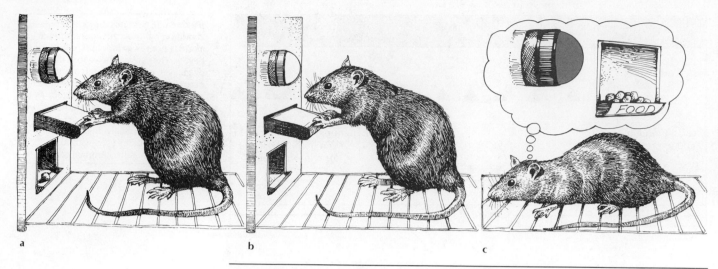

Figure 6.10 Learning discrimination in operant conditioning. In **a**, the pellet of food appears when the light is already on and the bar is pressed. In **b**, the rat presses the bar when the light is off. No reinforcement follows. After several repetitions of situations **a** and **b**, the rat learns to discriminate the second factor in the reinforcement process. At this stage, it is more likely that the rat will emit the operant behavior under the conditions where the discriminative stimulus is present.

Shaping A technique whereby animals and people are taught to perform complex behaviors not previously in their repertoire. The technique reinforces responses that come increasingly closer to the desired behavior. Shaping is also called the *method of successive approximations,* or the *method of differential reinforcement of successive approximations.*

beheaded, both as punishment for failing to comply with the king's wishes and as a means of easing the taxpayer's burden.

Skinner and I would have fared better. One does not teach a rat a complex behavioral sequence by waiting for it to appear, fully formed, and reinforcing it. Instead, one shapes the animal's behavior through the differential reinforcement of successive approximations, a process that sounds more complex than it actually is. **Shaping** is an operant conditioning technique where the experimenter reinforces small steps in the sequence of behavior that will (it is hoped) ultimately lead to the desired final behavior (often referred to as the *terminal* behavior). Thus the animal (or person) does not learn a complete final response at once, but is reinforced instead for behaviors that come progressively closer to that response—hence the phrase "differential reinforcement of successive approximations." Using shaping procedures with a rat requires that the first behavior in the sequence be reinforced. When the rat reliably emits that first behavior, it is not reinforced again until it executes a second behavior that more nearly approximates the desired terminal behavior.

Using shaping techniques, pigeons have been taught to bowl, chickens to play baseball, mules to dive into shallow waters from precarious heights, and pigs to point to pheasants.

Schedules of Reinforcement

Skinner's primary interest has been with discovering the relationships between behavior and its consequences, and in determining the extent to which behavior is controlled by its consequences. Many of his early investigations made extensive use of rats and pigeons. These provide the clearest illustrations of the variables involved in operant conditioning, and of their relationships to behavior.

Chief among these variables are the frequency and manner in which behavior is reinforced (termed the *schedule of reinforcement*). Clearly, there are a number of alternatives. Every correct behavior (called a "trial") might be reinforced (*continuous* reinforcement), or only some responses might be (*partial* or *intermittent* reinforcement). The second alternative leads to a number of other systematic alternatives. Intermittent reinforcement can be based on a proportion of trials (*ratio* reinforcement) or on the passage of time (*interval* reinforcement). These last two alternatives present two additional alternatives each (life is never simple): reinforcement can be

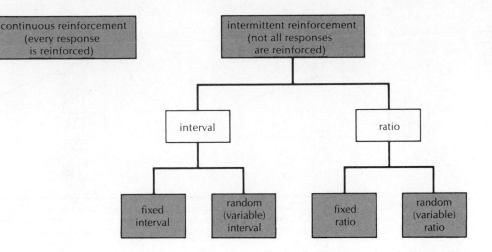

Figure 6.11 The five basic schedules of reinforcement: continuous, fixed interval, random interval, fixed ratio, and random ratio. These may be combined in a variety of ways.

regular (*fixed*), or irregular (*random* or *variable*). Figure 6.11 clarifies this, and reference to Eric can clarify it further.

Continuous: Eric is reinforced very time he presses the bar.

Fixed ratio: Every tenth (or twelfth, or fifth, and so on) response is reinforced.

Variable ratio: One out of ten (twelve, twenty, and so on) responses is reinforced, but in random fashion (the first, the twelfth, the fourteenth, the thirty-ninth, and so on).

Fixed interval: Reinforcement occurs after the first correct response that follows a specific time period (twenty seconds, thirty seconds, and so on).

Variable interval: Reinforcement occurs an average of once every twenty (thirty, forty, and so on) seconds, but at unpredictable times (fifth second, thirty-seventh second, sixtieth second). It always follows a correct response (but not *every* correct response).

Effects of Schedules   There are three ways in which operant learning may be measured. First, the experimenter might be concerned with the speed of learning (acquisition rate); second, concern might be for the strength of the learned response as reflected in the length of time during which it will persist following the cessation of reinforcement (extinction rate); finally, the experimenter's interest might be in the rate at which a particular response is emitted (response rate). Studies with rats and pigeons illustrate clearly that different schedules of reinforcement have different effects on each of these variables (see Figure 6.12).

Rate of acquisition is almost always best with continuous schedules of reinforcement. In his experiments, Skinner would typically reduce the animal's food intake for a period of time, thus increasing the effectiveness of the reinforcer. In the initial training stages, all correct responses are reinforced. Indeed, behaviors that are not quite correct, but that are close, are often reinforced as well. Learning has been found to be slow, haphazard, or nonexistent with intermittent schedules of reinforcement.

In contrast, extinction rate is considerably more rapid following continuous reinforcement than it is if intermittent schedules have been employed. Under a continuous schedule of reinforcement, two things may happen: frequently the animal becomes satiated and ceases responding for a period of time; even when the animal has not been satiated, if reinforcement is discontinued, the animal will generally cease responding after a very short time. Generally, extinction rate will be slowest for animals who have been reinforced under a variable ratio schedule. Hence the best combination of training schedules is usually a continuous schedule in the early stages, followed later by a variable ratio schedule.

Response rate is very much a function of schedule. Indeed, animals who have been conditioned by operant means frequently behave as though they had developed

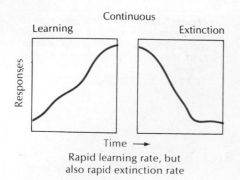

Continuous

Learning / Extinction

Responses

Time →

Rapid learning rate, but
also rapid extinction rate

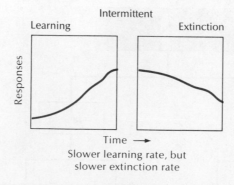

Intermittent

Learning / Extinction

Responses

Time →

Slower learning rate, but
slower extinction rate

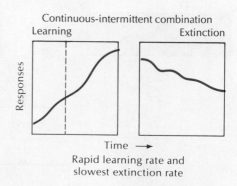

Continuous-intermittent combination

Learning / Extinction

Responses

Time →

Rapid learning rate and
slowest extinction rate

Figure 6.12 Effectiveness of learning using various training schedules. The best combination of training schedules is to begin with continuous reinforcement, then phase into variable ratio reinforcement. This combination produces the most rapid acquisition of new behavior, and also the slowest rate of extinction.

expectations with respect to reinforcement. Thus, an animal who is reinforced for every correct response after an interval of thirty-five seconds will often cease responding, or respond at a very low rate, until just prior to the end of the thirty-five-second period. Another who is reinforced on a variable ratio basis will continue to respond at a relatively high rate for long periods of time. Skinner reports the case of one pigeon who, after complete withdrawal of reinforcement, emitted more than 10,000 pecks before extinction was complete.

Schedules of reinforcement are also at play in our lives, although their effects might not always be as dramatic or as obvious as they can be in the laboratory. Witness, for example, the persistence with which people play slot machines on a variable ratio reinforcement schedule. In contrast, consider the hypothetical case of an individual who has always caught fish in a particular stream. Once the fish in that stream stop biting (cessation of continuous reinforcement), it is likely that the person will abandon the stream much more quickly (after fewer trials) than someone else who only occasionally catches fish in a stream (intermittent reinforcement).

Superstitious Behavior Recall that a fixed interval schedule of reinforcement provides reinforcement for the first correct response following a specified period of time. A small variation of this schedule provides reinforcement following a specific time interval regardless of what the animal is doing at the time. This schedule is referred to as a *superstitious schedule.* Its effects are intriguing. Skinner (1948a) once left eight pigeons on such a schedule overnight. The following morning six of the eight birds had learned something. One had learned to turn clockwise; another to toss its head toward a corner; and several to sway in a manner quite unnatural to an ordinary pigeon. It appeared that each had learned whatever it happened to be doing at the time of reinforcement, and now acted as though it had come to believe that its behavior was somehow responsible for the reinforcement. In other words, each had learned a superstition. We too are apparently subject to the same kind of learning, a fact that might explain why someone would scratch a nose that is not itchy.

Stimulus Control The effects of operant learning are manifested among people in a variety of ways, not all of which are immediately apparent. It follows from operant conditioning principles that whatever we happen to be doing at the time of reinforcement may, with sufficient reinforcement, tend to recur under similar circumstances. In this sense the circumstances, describable in terms of the discriminative stimuli, are said to have acquired *stimulus control* over our behaviors. The phenomenon of stimulus control is a widespread consequence of operant learning. If my students smile at me when I grin at them in the middle of a lecture, they can perhaps reinforce my behavior sufficiently that I will subsequently grin my way through as many lectures as

Figure 6.13 Two kinds of extrinsic reinforcement. Food is a primary reinforcer; we don't have to learn that it is rewarding. Money is a secondary reinforcer; its value is learned.

I can. Students in lecture halls would, at that point, have acquired stimulus control; that is, the lecture situation would, through operant conditioning, have acquired some degree of control over my grinning behavior.

Types of Reinforcers

The fact that a pigeon would wear its beak to a frazzle, were it more fragile, before ceasing an apparently unreinforced behavior may be evidence that reinforcement is not nearly as simple or as obvious as these few pages might suggest. We have some basis for concluding, in fact, that pecking itself is for the pigeon a pleasurable activity that requires no *extrinsic reinforcement* to be maintained. Extrinsic reinforcement includes the variety of external stimuli that might increase the probability of a behavior. *Intrinsic reinforcement,* a variable not intensively investigated in studies of animal learning, may be loosely defined as satisfaction, pleasure, or reward that is inherent in a behavior, and that is therefore independent of external rewards. The satisfaction that people sometimes derive from their work is a form of intrinsic reinforcement; the money and the praise that might also result are forms of extrinsic reinforcement.

Skinner distinguishes between two broad classes of extrinsic reinforcers (Figure 6.13). **Primary reinforcers** are stimuli that are rewarding for most people, most of the time, without anybody having had to learn that they are rewarding. Those objects or events that satisfy such basic needs as eating, drinking, sleeping, and being comfortable are examples of primary reinforcers.

Secondary reinforcers include the wide range of stimuli that may not be reinforcing initially, but that eventually becoming reinforcing as a function of having been associated with other reinforcers. In other words, secondary reinforcers are learned (they are also called *conditioned* reinforcers for that reason); primary reinforcers are not. Social prestige, praise, money, and applause are all very powerful secondary reinforcers. The light in Eric's cage also served as a secondary reinforcer. In fact, had the experimenter discontinued providing him with food for correct responses, but had the light continued to go on instead, it is probable that he would have continued to depress the lever. The light would, in this case, have served as reinforcement for bar-pressing behavior.

Primary reinforcers Stimuli that are reinforcing in the absence of any learning. Such stimuli as food and drink are primary reinforcers since, presumably, an organism does not have to learn that they are pleasant.

Secondary reinforcers Stimuli that are not initially reinforcing, but that are present so often at the time of reinforcement that they eventually come to be reinforcing for a wide range of activities. Stimuli such as social prestige, praise, and money are secondary reinforcers for human behavior.

Negative reinforcers Stimuli that have the effect of increasing the probability of occurrence of the desired response when they are removed from the situation.

Escape learning A type of conditioning in which the organism learns responses that reduce or terminate unpleasant stimuli.

Avoidance learning A type of conditioning in which the organism learns responses that prevent the occurrence of unpleasant stimuli.

Punishment The presentation of an unpleasant stimulus or the withdrawal of a pleasant stimulus as a consequence of behavior. Punishment should not be confused with negative reinforcement.

Since a reinforcer is *any* stimulus (situation) that increases the probability of a response occurring, this stimulus does not have to be pleasant or rewarding. Consider, for example, what might have happened if the grid floor on which Eric was standing had a very mild electric current running through it. Would he have learned to jump? Probably, if that's what the experimenters had in mind, and if they reinforced jumping behavior by turning off the current whenever Eric jumped. This illustration presents an example of negative reinforcement. In short, a **negative reinforcer** is a stimulus that increases the probability of a response through its removal when the desired response is made. In contrast, a positive reinforcer is effective through being added to the experimental situation following the emission of the desired response. Negative reinforcement has sometimes been employed in animal experimentation to bring about avoidance learning or escape learning. If Eric learned to turn off an electric current by jumping, his jumping would be a form of **escape learning** (escaping from actual painful stimulation). If he learned to jump in order to prevent the electric current from being turned on, his behavior would illustrate **avoidance learning** (behavior designed to prevent the occurrence of painful stimulation).

There is frequently confusion between negative reinforcement and **punishment**. The two are in fact quite different. Recall that negative reinforcement has the effect of *increasing* the probability of a response. The intended effect of punishment is precisely the opposite.

In essence, the consequences of behavior can involve the removal or presentation of stimuli that are pleasant or unpleasant. In addition, behavior can have no noticeable or important consequences. The addition or removal of pleasant or unpleasant stimuli as a consequence of behavior presents the four distinct possibilities that are relevant to operant learning: positive reinforcement, negative reinforcement, and two types of punishment. Distinctions among these four possibilities can perhaps be made clearer by reference to Woods' (1974) labels: presenting a pleasant stimulus (positive reinforcement) is termed *reward;* presenting an unpleasant stimulus is *punishment;* removing a pleasant stimulus (punishment) is labeled *penalty;* and removing an unpleasant stimulus (negative reinforcement) is termed *relief.* (Table 6.1 diagrams these possibilities.) Each can be illustrated by reference to ordinary human behavior. A person is complimented on a new hairstyle: the addition of a pleasant stimulus (positive reinforcement; reward). A tablet relieves a headache: removal of an unpleasant stimulus (negative reinforcement; relief). A child is given two lashes for wearing long fingernails: addition of an unpleasant stimulus (punishment). Another child has his jelly beans confiscated for throwing one at a crippled cat: removal of a pleasant stimulus (second type of punishment; penalty).

Objections to Punishment

There has been considerable controversy concerning the ethical aspects of punishment and its effectiveness. Psychology offers some tentative advice. First, punishment is very often not particularly effective in eliminating undesirable behavior. Certainly, it is not nearly as effective as reinforcement is in bringing about more desirable behavior. In many cases, punishment may lead to the suppression of the punished behavior, but not to its extinction—nor to its being forgotten (Clarizio & Yelon, 1974).

A second objection to the use of punishment is that it frequently leads to undesirable emotional side effects which, interestingly, can sometimes as easily become associated with the punisher as with the punished behavior. It is conceivable, for example, that punishment might lead a child to dislike and fear the punisher, and might result in efforts to avoid punishment rather than efforts to avoid the transgressions for which the punishment was administered (see Box 6.2).

A third objection is that punishment does not present a guide for desirable behavior, but emphasizes instead behavior that is considered undesirable. Its contribution to learning is therefore limited. Finally, there is a very practical objection to its use, in addition to the many theoretical and ethical objections that might also be raised. Research has demonstrated that punishment sometimes has effects opposite to those

Table 6.1 Punishment and Reinforcement. Woods' labels are given in parentheses

	Nature of Stimulus	
	Pleasant	Unpleasant
Added to the situation	Positive reinforcement (reward)	Punishment (punishment)
Removed from the situation	Punishment (penalty)	Negative reinforcement (relief)

intended. Sears et al. (1957) report studies that indicate that children whose parents punish them when attempting to toilet train them are more likely to wet their beds. Similarly, Bandura and Walters (1959) report that children whose parents punish them severely for being aggressive are more likely to be aggressive.

It should be noted that most of these objections to the use of punishment apply primarily to one type of punishment: that involving the presentation of unpleasant stimuli. More specifically, the objections are most pertinent in the case of physical punishment. And although it is true that the bulk of psychological opinion has been opposed to physical punishment, this is not the case with respect to other forms of punishment. Verbal reprimands, loss of privileges, and so on have long been considered legitimate and sometimes effective means of controlling behavior. There are instances when punishment appears to be effective in suppressing destructive, aggressive, and dangerous behavior in children (and sometimes in adults as well; Parke, 1970). Like reinforcement, it appears to be most effective when it follows behavior immediately, and least effective when it is delayed. Also, punishment by a parent who

BOX 6.2

Learned Helplessness

Anecdotal evidence has long supported the belief that death can result directly from the efforts of a vengeful medicine man, from curses, from destroying sacred relics, and from a variety of other spiritual and mystical causes. Burrell (1963), for example, witnessed six Bantu men being cursed and told to their faces that they would die at sunset. They did, and subsequent autopsies could not establish the cause of death.

Death by voodoo, magic, or curse is characterized by a feeling of absolute and utter helplessness on the part of those who know they are about to die. Recently Seligman (1975) and others have investigated the dimensions of helplessness and its effects on humans. One of the original series of studies, performed with dogs, is discussed briefly here, since it bears directly on the possible effects of using an aversive stimulus to control behavior. These studies and many variations thereon have been conducted by S. F. Maier (1970), Seligman (1974), and S. F. Maier et al. (1973), among others.

In a typical experiment, dogs in the experimental group are placed in a sling of the type used by Pavlov and administered moderately painful electric shocks *from which they cannot escape*. That is, there is nothing the dog can learn or do that will prevent the shock. The dog is later released from the sling and is placed in a box that is divided into two compartments by a barrier shoulder-high to the dog. Thus, in order to go from one side of the box to the other, the dog need only jump over the barrier—an extremely simple task for most dogs. If a naive dog (not experimentally trained or previously shocked) is placed in one of the compartments, and an electric current is turned on so that it is receiving a mild shock, it will run around somewhat frantically, but will soon jump over the barrier, thus escaping from the shock, which is administered only on one side. After several trials, naive dogs will learn to jump the barrier at the first indication of shock. Indeed, if the shock is preceded by a signal such as a light or tone, the dog will jump calmly from one side of the box to the other, never once getting shocked.

The experimental dog, who has previously been shocked a number of times under conditions over which it has absolutely no control, reacts in a strikingly different fashion. Such dogs may become frantic at the onset of the first shock in the shuttle box, and may pace back and forth inside the box. A number do jump the barrier, and some of these eventually learn to associate a signal with the electrical shock, thereby learning how to avoid being shocked. The great majority, however—some two-thirds of all subjects—simply give up (Seligman, 1975). They lie down and whine quietly.

Seligman's argument is that helplessness is learned, often as a function of punishment in circumstances over which we have no control. And learned helplessness might serve as a partial explanation for such dramatic deaths as those that result from curses, as well as for many other physical and psychological complaints (see Huesmann, 1978). Put simply, individuals who feel helpless may give up. Perhaps there is an additional argument here against the use of punishment, particularly of a physical nature.

Figure 6.14 Punishment (**a**) and reward (**b**). Both can have profound effects on behavior.

is ordinarily warm and loving is more effective than punishment by a parent who is cold and distant (Aronfreed, 1968). And there is no evidence that punishment administered by a loving parent disrupts affectional bonds between parent and child (or between teacher and child, for that matter) (Walters & Grusec, 1977). (See Figure 6.14.)

Traditional Behaviorism: A Brief Summary

Traditional behavioristic theory has recognized two general classes of behaviors, respondent and operant (elicited or emitted), and two general sets of rules and principles to account for these (Herrnstein, 1977a). Classical conditioning theory, attributed largely to Pavlov, has been found most useful for explaining learning involving automatic and reflexive reactions over which we ordinarily have no conscious control. Thus, eye-blinking in response to a puff of air and salivation in response to food have been identified as responses easily amenable to classical conditioning. But certain other behaviors in the same general class cannot be so easily conditioned. The knee-jerk reflex in humans is highly resistant to conditioning, as is pupil dilation. Why?

Operant conditioning has generally been thought to apply to all behaviors that were not respondent—that is, to all behaviors that were not elicited by specific, identifiable stimuli, but that simply occurred and could then presumably be brought under control of reinforcement. A number of standard, although initially arbitrary, responses in certain animal species were found to lend themselves admirably to operant conditioning procedures, and were employed widely in laboratories in efforts to discover the laws that might govern relationships between behavior and reinforcement. Chief among these were bar-pressing in rats and disk- or key-pecking in pigeons.

Whereas classical conditioning appealed to principles of contiguity (near simultaneity of events that were to be associated), operant conditioning invoked a law that behaviors followed by reinforcement tend to be repeated (hence learned); those that are not (or that are followed by punishment) tend not to be repeated.

Early behaviorists had hoped that the laws of learning that might be derived from the experimental study of animal and human learning would prove sufficiently general to explain most human behaviors. As Seligman and Hager (1972) note, the use of arbitrary responses in investigations of behavior was premised on the assumption that if *any* response could be shown to conform to the principles of operant or classical conditioning, the generality of these principles could more easily be established.

Challenges to Traditional Behaviorism

Unfortunately, behavior does not prove to be as simple as behavioristic theory might indicate. A number of animal behaviors are not explained by traditional conceptions of behaviorism, and have led to a reexamination of some of its broader generalizations (see Herrnstein, 1977b).

Instinctive Drift

The Brelands (1951, 1961) undertook to train a number of animals and put them on display at fairs, conventions, exhibitions, and other public gatherings. Students of Skinner's, they applied the well-known methods of shaping and differential reinforcement, and taught pigs to carry large wooden nickels to a piggy bank and deposit them therein; they taught raccoons a similar trick with coins, where reinforcement for the raccoon was contingent upon the raccoon picking up a coin and depositing it in a metal tray; they taught chickens to pull a rubber loop, thereby releasing a plastic capsule down a slide from where the capsule could be pecked out of the cage with one or two swift blows of the beak, following which the chicken would be reinforced. The tricks were amusing and apparently simple. But in many cases, they did not work.

Although the animals showed themselves to be capable of performing the tasks set for them, many eventually began to behave in strange ways. In Breland and Breland's (1961) terms, they "misbehaved." Pigs took longer and longer to carry the wooden coins back and deposit them in the bank. As the weeks went by, they became progressively worse, sometimes tossing the coin in the air, dropping it to the ground, pushing it with their noses ("rooting" it), picking it up again, rooting it again, and so on. In the end, some of the pigs became so slow that the number of reinforcements they earned in a day was insufficient for their needs.

Raccoons behaved no better. Although they could be easily and quickly trained to pick up a coin (their hands are very much like ours in terms of manipulative skills) and deposit it in a tray, they seemed progressively more reluctant to let go of the coin as time went by. They walked slowly with it, rubbing it back and forth in their hands, very much like misers. And indeed, the commercial act that resulted featured a raccoon as a miser. The raccoon would pick up the coin, rub it as it walked back to the tray, dip it into the tray, but retrieve it again immediately and rub it again, very much as though it were washing its food, a trait that is common to wild raccoons.

There are numerous other instances of animals who condition with difficulty, who stop working remarkably soon after initial learning, or whose behaviors drift toward what appear to be genetically related behaviors. It is surely no accident that raccoons "wash" their coins, that pigs root, or that chickens peck, for these are the things that pigs, raccoons, and chickens ordinarily do with respect to eating behavior. This **instinctive drift**, also known as the *Breland effect,* presents a problem for traditional operant theory. It has now become apparent that not all behaviors can be conditioned and maintained by schedules of reinforcement (Hulse et al., 1975); that, in other words, there is some degree of competition between instinctual (unlearned and genetically based) tendencies and the conditioning of related behaviors. This

Instinctive drift Refers to the tendency for organisms to revert to instinct.

competition is expressed in the principle of instinctive drift: Whenever strong instinctual tendencies are related to a conditioned response, repeated exposures to the relevant situations will eventually lead to a "drifting" toward the instinctual behavior, even at the expense of the conditioned response and its contingent reinforcement.

Autoshaping

Autoshaping Refers to responses that are learned in experimental situations in spite of the fact that they are not related to reinforcement. In some cases, autoshaped behaviors may be learned even though they actually prevent reinforcement.

Instinctive drift is one example of an animal behavior that cannot easily be explained by reference to the established principles of operant conditioning; **autoshaping** is another. An autoshaped behavior is a response (or combination of responses) that is learned in the absence of direct reinforcement. This may be simplified by illustration. If a pigeon is reinforced at certain intervals, regardless of what it is then doing or has been doing (response-independent reinforcement), and if a light is brightened or darkened prior to the presentation of food, the pigeon may learn to peck at the light (P. L. Brown & Jenkins, 1968). In this situation, there is no causal relationship between pecking the light and the appearance of food: reinforcement will appear regardless of what the pigeon does. It is as though the pigeon shapes its own pecking behavior—hence the term *autoshaped*.

Early explanations for autoshaping relied on the principles of classical conditioning. The light is, in a sense, a signal that reinforcement is about to occur, and becomes associated with it (Hearse & Jenkins, 1975). This, of course, does not really explain why the pigeon would peck at the light, unless it can be assumed that the initial pecking behavior, an operant behavior, has been reinforced by the appearance of food, and has consequently become learned much as a superstitious response might be learned.

A related experiment reported by D. R. Williams and H. Williams (1969) presents a more serious problem for traditional behavioristic explanations. In this experiment a similar procedure was employed to condition pigeons to peck at a light (autoshaping), but the conditions were so set up that the pecking behavior *prevented* reinforcement from occurring. Nevertheless, pigeons continued to peck at the light despite the fact that doing so meant they would go without food.

Biological Constraints

Biological constraints A highly general term referring to the observation that certain behaviors are more easily learned by some organisms than by others and, conversely, that other specific behaviors are not learned at all easily. Biological constraints are essentially genetic predispositions that either *prepare* or *contraprepare* organisms for specific learning.

That there are limits to the types of behaviors a given species can learn is an interpretation of studies on instinctive drift and autoshaping advanced by Seligman (1975), Seligman and Hager (1972), Hinde and Stevenson-Hinde (1973), and a growing number of other theorists. Moreover, these **biological constraints** make the learning of other behaviors highly probable and relatively easy. The overriding general principle is that behaviors with genetic survival value (and, therefore, an evolutionary history) are more probable in a given species than are other behaviors. In Seligman's terms, we and other species are *prepared* for certain types of learning; by the same token, we are *contraprepared* for others. Thus, it is almost impossible to teach a rat to depress a lever to escape an electric shock (Bolles, 1970). A rat's natural response to danger is to fight, flee, freeze, or become frantic; it is not to approach a lever and depress it. Therefore, a rat can be trained to *jump* to escape shock. The ease with which this is accomplished demonstrates *preparedness*. That the rat cannot be trained to depress a lever illustrates *contrapreparedness*.

Taste Aversion

Taste aversion An inclination to avoid certain tastes (an *aversion* is a strong dislike). Organisms appear to be biologically predisposed to acquire marked aversions for substances that make them ill. These predispositions illustrate biological constraints.

Biological constraints are evident in other forms of learning as well, and have been dramatically illustrated in a series of studies of **taste aversion** (Garcia et al., 1966; Rozin & Kalat, 1971). It is highly significant biologically that if we eat a substance that poisons but does not kill us, we frequently experience a marked distaste for that substance later. For example, on one particularly memorable occasion my grandmother sautéed a small rabbit I had snared, fricasseed the beast, roasted it for a short period, boiled it, and finally stewed it with small onions, potatoes, mushrooms, and carrots. Some hours later she delivered it to the table, where we promptly devoured it.

The occasion, memorable enough in itself, would not have been nearly so memorable had we not both become violently ill later that evening. My grandmother, resourceful person that she was, let the illness run its nauseous course. In time we both recovered, the only major change in our lives being that a number of rabbits that might otherwise have found their way to our table continued to gambol in the bushes and do whatever else it is that rabbits do in bushes on a winter evening.

Learned taste aversions are common in both humans and nonhuman animals. Rats who drink a lithium chloride solution become ill and subsequently show a marked aversion to any substance that tastes of lithium chloride. Perhaps more striking, rats who are exposed to low dosages of radiation after eating or drinking (the radiation makes them ill) display a strong aversion to the food or drink as long as thirty-two days later—and this after a single pairing of food or drink and illness that is not caused by the food or drink. Classical conditioning theory, dependent as it is on temporal relationships between conditioned and unconditioned stimuli, does not provide an explanation for single-trial *delayed* conditioned reactions of this nature.

Evidence of biological constraints in taste-aversion studies can be derived from cross-species studies, as well as from a number of single-species studies. It has repeatedly been shown, for example, that although rats can readily be conditioned to avoid a food substance if they are rendered ill following feeding, their avoidance behavior does not generalize to the sights and sounds that might be present at the time of the initial learning (Garcia et al., 1966). Thus, flashing lights, beepers, buzzers, or metronomes paired with the food, contrary to what classical conditioning theory would surely predict, do not later elicit avoidance reactions. But if a distinctive perfume is sprayed in the chamber where the conditioning occurs, the rat will later eat or drink less in the presence of the same perfume than in its absence (Garcia et al., 1966; Garcia & Koelling, 1966). It is highly relevant that olfactory cues are closely linked with eating, whereas audiovisual stimuli are not: it makes biological sense that a perfume present at the time of poisoning would be associated with taste aversion, and that sights and sounds would not.

A single cross-species study makes the same point in a dramatic way. Wilcoxon et al. (1971) induced taste aversion in rats and in quail by giving them flavored water and, half an hour later, injecting them with an illness-inducing drug. In some of the experimental conditions, the flavored water was also colored blue. Subsequent taste-aversion tests demonstrated clearly that both the rats and the quail had learned an aversion for the flavored water. More important, however, the quail had also learned to avoid blue water, but the rats had not. The most plausible explanation would appear to be that quail have excellent color vision (rats don't) and that visual cues are closely related to their feeding behaviors. It would therefore be biologically important for them to learn to recognize edible and inedible substances on the basis of their appearance rather than their taste. Rats, however, are more likely to make use of smell-taste cues, and not to respond as well to visual cues. Thus, what is learned is subject to biological constraints.

Insight

Bertrand Russell made the interesting observation that U.S. and German rats must be quite different. He is quoted as saying:

> *Animals studied by Americans rush about frantically, with an incredible display of hustle and pep, and at last achieve the desired result by chance. Animals observed by Germans sit still and think, and at last evolve the solution out of their inner consciousness. (In Commons & Fagin, 1954, p. 28.)*

He was referring to the fact that U.S. psychology was then largely dominated by the behavioristic notion that responses are learned as a result of the reinforcement of a

Insight The sudden recognition of a correct solution for a problem, often described in contrast to trial and error. The original definition of this term implied that the solution occurred suddenly and completely or not at all. Synonymous terms are illumination and inspiration. There is now a general recognition that insight may be a gradual process rather than a sudden inspiration.

"correct" response that occurs by chance (or as a result of trial and error, as Thorndike (1911) maintained). At the same time, German psychologists had been heavily influenced by Wolfgang Köhler's work with apes, and had begun to consider the role of **insight** in problem-solving, even among lower animals.

There are two classic types of studies attributed to Köhler, a German psychologist who spent four years in the Canary Islands during World War I studying apes. One is referred to as the "stick problem," the other as the "box problem." Both problems are essentially the same; only the solutions differ. In both, an ape finds itself unable to reach a tantalizing piece of fruit, either because it is too high or because it is outside the cage, some distance beyond its reach. In the stick problem, the solution involves inserting a small stick inside a larger stick in order to reach the fruit (Figure 6.15). In the box problem, the solution is to place several boxes one on top of the other, again in order to reach the fruit.

The solution, asserts Köhler (1927), does not involve trial and error, although some of that type of behavior may be displayed in the early stages. When the ape realizes that none of its customary behaviors is likely to obtain the bananas, it may sit at some length, apparently pondering the problem. And when the solution is eventually executed, it appears to have occurred in a flash, with a sudden burst of insight. The ape leaps up, quickly joins the sticks or piles the boxes, and reaches unhesitatingly for the prize.

Insight, according to the Gestalt psychologists, involves the sudden perception of relationships among elements of a problem. It is a complex, largely unconscious process, not easily amenable to scientific examination. Nevertheless, they assumed that the laws that govern ordinary perceptual phenomena would also apply to more cognitive problems. Recall (from Chapter 5) that these included the laws of closure, of praegnanz or good form, of continuity, and of similarity. The tendency, in thinking as in perceiving, is to achieve closure (recognition of a complete pattern or form). Insight is nothing more than sudden closure.

Cognitive Maps

The behaviorists were, in fact, hard-pressed to explain the behavior of Köhler's ape without resorting to nonbehavioristic concepts like *insight*. Nevertheless, they did come up with a behavioristic explanation: that the ape tried a number of apelike behaviors, eventually resorting to combinations of these behaviors when none of the simple behaviors was rewarded. Through a process of trial and error, the solution was eventually achieved; the ape's recognition of that solution did not occur until the bananas had been obtained.

Quite a number of psychologists, however, were reluctant to accept any behavioristic explanations for the phenomenon of insight, a phenomenon which is common enough among our species that its existence is difficult to deny. In time, the lowly rat was allowed to contribute in a small way to the study of insight. Tolman and Honzik (1930) pioneered the *blocked-path study,* which involves allowing a rat to become totally familiar with a maze in which there are several alternative routes to the goal. Once the rat has learned the maze completely, barriers are introduced into the maze so that the rat has to choose one of the alternatives. Typically, a rat will always select the shortest route, rats being considerably more intelligent than most people give them credit for. Behaviorists are not terribly upset at this evidence of intelligence in the rat. Their successive choice of alternatives that are always "next best" simply serves as evidence that they have developed a preference for the shortest routes, perhaps as a result of receiving reinforcement more quickly following these routes than they do when they meander nonchalantly through various lengthy detours.

Figure 6.16 presents Tolman and Honzik's arrangement of barriers. The maze offers three alternatives. Route 1 is the most direct and is almost invariably chosen when there are no barriers. When there is a barrier at A, the rat would be expected to choose route 2. This is, in fact, the case some 93 percent of the time. When the barrier is at B, rats might again be expected to select route 2, since its opening is not

Figure 6.15 In the stick problem (Köhler, 1927), the chimp inserts a small stick into a larger one to make a long enough implement to reach the fruit.

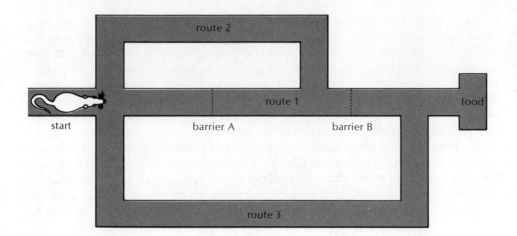

Figure 6.16 Do rats develop cognitive maps? Tolman and Honzik's 1930 experiment suggests they do. When barriers are erected at either A or B after the rat has become familiar with the maze, it will consistently choose the shortest route to the goal box. Interestingly, naive rats seem to develop a cognitive map even when no tangible reinforcers are present at the end of the maze.

blocked. They don't. These clever rats now run all the way around route 3, despite the fact that they should still have a higher preference for route 2. The cognitive explanation is simply that they have developed a **cognitive map** of the entire maze, and that they understand that a barrier at B also blocks route 2.

Subsequent experiments with rats have demonstrated that a rat will develop knowledge of a maze in the absence of any tangible reinforcement. Rats who are allowed to explore a maze without food learn the maze considerably more quickly than naive rats when food is introduced. Such observations indicate that rats, too, have some understanding of their environments that goes beyond the formation of simple associations among stimuli, responses, and rewards.

Indeed, there is evidence that the rat is more intelligent with respect to learning about space than we might have suspected. Olton and Samuelson (1976) released hungry rats in the middle of a "sunburst" arrangement of 8 maze arms. At the end of each of these arms was a small morsel of food. None of these rats had previously been in this type of maze arrangement, and would therefore not be expected to have any previously learned "maps" of this particular space. Yet, without knowing anything about the rules of this game, on their first 8 forays into arms of the maze, rats went into an average of 5.6 *different* arms. And after only 5 separate experiences in this maze, a great many of the rats went into 8 different arms in 8 trips (average, 7.6). Variations of the procedure indicated that these rats were not making use of olfactory cues; nor did they have some systematic strategy, such as we might employ (always going to the next left alley, for example). In fact, it seems, as Bolles (1979) put it, that "the rat finds it trivially easy to make eight different trips to eight different places without repeating itself very much" (p. 217).

Current Directions in Behaviorism

The explanatory powers of traditional behavioral theory do not easily encompass these diverse findings. Instinctual drift, autoshaping, delayed taste aversion, the fact that some autonomic responses cannot be conditioned (pupil dilation, for example) by classical methods and that others can be conditioned through operant means (see N. E. Miller, 1969), insight, and cognitive maps all present serious problems for traditional behavioristic theories. Do the findings invalidate the theories? And should they lead us to discard the theories completely and to search for new explanations?

The answer is no. What these findings point to is a need for models that have greater generality, like the Rescorla-Wagner model. Recall that this model provides a powerful explanation for many of the phenomena of classical conditioning, saying, in effect, that conditioning is primarily a matter of learning about things that are likely

Cognitive map A mental representation of physical space. That we know how to get from home to school is evidence of the existence of a relevant cognitive map.

to occur in the environment—of, as Bindra (1978) put it, learning *expectancies*. A conditioned stimulus in a classical conditioning situation comes to elicit a response because it *predicts* the occurrence of an unconditioned stimulus. The Rescorla-Wagner model can be generalized to apply to operant conditioning also: Discriminative stimuli lead to a response because they predict some consequence (reward or punishment). And building on this model, we can say that biological constraints simply make it more or less likely that certain types of associations will be formed. Rats happen to be very good at developing expectancies that have to do with space; and all organisms, including humans, are very good at developing expectancies that have to do with the possibility of reward or punishment. Indeed, it is likely that biological constraints favor the development of these expectancies since they relate directly to our survival, and since the fundamental biological principle that underlies all behavior is that of survival. So the generality of the Rescorla-Wagner model allows it to encompass findings not explained by earlier, more specific theories.

Current directions in the study and explanation of learning appear, therefore, to have the following in common (with some exceptions): an increasing recognition of the importance of biological factors in human learning; the recognition that classical and operant conditioning are far more similar than was once thought, and that both can be explained by reference to similar models; and the realization that the more cognitive processes that might be involved in learning about space, in achieving insight, in inferring cause-and-effect relationships, and in learning what predicts what in the environment are all available to lower organisms as well as to humans. In short,

John Caldwell

learning theories of the last small piece of this century, and perhaps into the next, might be biologically based, behavioral-cognitive models. These models emphasize the processes by which we relate things to one another so as to make predictable sense of what we hope to be a relatively orderly world.

Practical Applications of Behavioral Principles

There are countless everyday applications of reinforcement theory. People are controlled and manipulated by organizations and by other people, sometimes quite unconsciously—although often consciously as well. Performers' behaviors are shaped by the responses of their audiences; the behavior of teachers is shaped by the responses of their students; consumers' behaviors are shaped by advertising media. Examples are everywhere. Indeed, one of the more potent explanations for the acquisition of social behavior is premised on a model of operant conditioning (Bandura & Walters, 1963), and is referred to as "observational learning," or learning through imitation (see Chapter 13).

Programmed Instruction

Although the originator of **programmed instruction** is generally considered to be Sidney Pressey (1932), Skinner is most responsible for the flurry of excitement that surrounded the use of programs in the 1950s and 1960s. These programs represent one of the best-known attempts to apply theoretical knowledge to the practical aspects of education (see Figure 6.17).

Programmed instruction An instructional procedure that systematically presents information in small steps (frames), usually in a textbook or some other device. Programs typically require learners to make responses and provide them with immediate knowledge of results. Knowledge of being right is assumed to act as a reinforcer.

Figure 6.17 Programmed instruction represents one of the best known attempts to apply theoretical knowledge to the practical aspects of education. In this illustration, the boy is learning simple arithmetic.

Table 6.2 A Comparison of Linear and Branching Programs

	Linear	Branching
Theorist	Skinner	Crowder
Frame length	Short	Long
Answer format	Emitted	Selected
Prompts	Many	Fewer
Remedial frames	None	Many
Difficulty level	Low	Higher
Reinforcement	Knowledge of correctness	Knowledge of correctness
Diagrammatic representation	$1 \rightarrow 2 \rightarrow \ldots n$	(branching diagram: from 1 to nodes 3, 5, 8; to 2; from 2 to nodes 4, 6, 9; to 7)

Essentially, programmed instruction involves the systematic presentation of information in such a way that the learner does not require the intervention of a teacher. Traditionally, there are two ways of organizing such material, one developed by Skinner (1954), and another by Crowder (1961). Both can be understood in terms of an operant conditioning model. Programs present questions, problems, or situations that encourage the learner to emit a response. Following that response, learners are immediately told whether they are correct or incorrect. Knowledge of a correct response may be assumed to be reinforcing.

Linear programs, associated with Skinner, present small bits of information, require frequent learner responses (encourage the emission of operants), and provide immediate knowledge of whether the response is correct or incorrect (provide immediate reinforcement).

Branching programs, associated with Crowder, present larger frames (chunks of information and explanation) and provide alternative routes through the program dependent on the accuracy of the learner's responses. Table 6.2 compares the two types of learning programs.

Educational researchers have spent considerable time evaluating the relative effectiveness of programmed instruction and teachers, and in comparing branching and linear programs. Schramm (1964) reviews 165 of these studies, and concludes that programs do teach; they sometimes appear to teach as well as teachers; sometimes they do not teach as well as teachers. Neither linear programs nor branching programs are generally superior to the other.

Perhaps because of these somewhat equivocal findings, and due as well to the great deal of time and expense required to produce good programs, programmed instruction is not in nearly as widespread use as had once been predicted. Many programs are currently being used in various forms of computer-assisted instruction (CAI), but the classroom teacher has not been replaced and does not appear to be in any immediate danger.

Behavior Modification

Behavior modification Changes in the behavior of an individual. Also refers to psychological theory and research concerned with applying psychological principles in attempts to change behavior. Since many of these attempts relate directly to behavior problems or mental disorders, the expression *behavior therapy* is often used as a synonym.

A second application of operant conditioning principles is in widespread use in schools and institutions for children with behavioral and emotional problems, as well as in psychotherapeutic practice (the treatment of mental and emotional disorders). Essentially, **behavior modification** involves the deliberate and systematic use of reinforcement (and sometimes punishment) in attempts to modify behavior. It makes extensive use of reinforcement administered under various schedules, and of the withdrawal of reinforcement in order to eliminate undesirable behavior. Behavior modification is discussed and illustrated in Chapter 16.

Beyond Freedom

The immediate practical applications of operant conditioning techniques and principles present a very useful and sometimes dramatic approach to therapy, as well as to teaching and to the resolution of behavioral and emotional problems. In addition, their deliberate or unconscious use in the ordinary affairs of daily life, in advertising and merchandising, in political persuasion, and in a variety of other areas has a tremendous influence on our beliefs and behaviors. But the implications of operant conditioning and of the view of humans that is implicit in this position go considerably beyond its immediate practical applications. They speak, as well, to some very basic philosophical notions concerning the nature of being human.

If Skinner's system presents a valid description of the human condition, it follows that we are not free—that we are, in fact, controlled by the reinforcement contingencies of our behaviors and, indirectly, by our environments. The freedom of which we are so proud is nothing but an illusion. Indeed, Skinner (1971) asserts that the autonomous man (and presumably woman too) is a myth. "Autonomous man," he explains, "is a device used to explain what we cannot explain in any other way. He has been constructed from our ignorance, and as our understanding increases, the very stuff of which he is composed vanishes" (p. 200). Skinner's science of human behavior is premised on the notion that the control of behavior rests not in mind or will, but in the environment. True, it is an environment we ourselves have created, at least in part. In that sense, humanity is in control of itself. But the control is indirect and is in the hands of society, not of the individual.

This estimate of the human condition has come under severe critical attack, as Skinner had predicted it would (Rogers & Skinner, 1956). Behaviorism presents a more mechanistic view of people than most of us intuitively have. We are uncomfortable with the notion that our actions might not result from choice; that we might be controlled by an impersonal and imperfect environment for which we, individually, accept little responsibility. Such notions bring into question our personal worth and dignity, undermine our faith in traditional beliefs concerning the ability of every individual to shape destiny, to overcome the limitations of restrictive environments. We want to believe that we are captains of our ships and rulers of our souls; that where there is a will, there is a way.

Skinner is not a pessimist. He believes strongly that a science of human behavior can be employed in the interest of humanity; that an environment can be created which will optimize the development of individuals and of societies. One immediate step in that direction would be to remove the countless techniques of aversive control currently in use. These include the punitive aspects of such social institutions as legal systems, schools, and churches, where the emphasis is sometimes as much (or more) on the punishment of undesirable behavior as on the reinforcement of desirable behavior. Techniques of aversive control, argues Skinner, must be replaced by the conscious and open application of positive control.

Main Points

1 Learning is defined as changes in behavior that result from experience and are not due to fatigue, maturation, drugs, injury, or disease. Learning may not always be manifested in *performance* (actual behavior), but is sometimes *latent*.

2 Behavioristic approaches to the study of learning emphasize stimuli and responses and the relationships that exist between them. Humanistic approaches are more concerned with human individuality and emotional growth. Cognitive approaches deal with cognition (knowing) or awareness, and are more concerned with the intellectual processes that underlie knowing, remembering, problem solving, decision making, and so on.

3　Conditioning is a process by which an association is formed between stimulus and response, or between a response and its consequences.

4　Pavlov, the Russian physiologist, is closely associated with classical conditioning because of his experiments with dogs.

5　In a classical conditioning procedure, an initially neutral stimulus (conditioned stimulus or CS) is presented at the same time as another stimulus (unconditioned stimulus or UCS) that reliably gives rise to a response (unconditioned response or UCR). Following a number of pairings, the previously neutral stimulus (CS) will give rise to a response (conditioned response or CR) very similar to that originally associated with the unconditioned stimulus.

6　The most effective sequence for UCS and CS in classical conditioning is usually (from most to least effective): delayed or forward order (CS before UCS but overlapping in time); trace (CS before UCS and not overlapping in time); simultaneous; and backward (CS after UCS and not overlapping in time).

7　Generalization occurs when a subject responds to situations (stimuli) in terms of their similarities—thus making the same response for two different stimuli. A child who responds to a stranger by smiling may have generalized the smiling response from familiar people to the stranger.

8　Discrimination, essentially the opposite of generalization, involves responding to differences. Essentially, to discriminate is to make two different responses to similar, but not identical, situations.

9　Extinction is a conditioning procedure whereby a learned response is eliminated. In classical conditioning, it involves the repeated presentation of the conditioned stimulus without pairing it with the unconditioned stimulus.

10　Classical conditioning models are particularly useful for explaining emotional learning (conditioned emotional reactions or CERs).

11　Conditioning models typically are explained by one of two theories: contiguity, which maintains that the simultaneous or near-simultaneous occurrence of two events is sufficient to account for the formation of an association between them; and contingency, which maintains that what is learned is an interdependency between two or more events—a sort of cause-and-effect relationship. Rescorla and Wagner argue that contingency explanations are valid even for simple illustrations of classical conditioning. In effect, Pavlov's dog learned an association between buzzer and food—not between buzzer and salivation!

12　Operant conditioning is a procedure whereby an association is formed between an emitted behavior (an operant) and its consequences. Essentially, operant conditioning increases the probability that a response will occur by reinforcement—or reduces its probability by lack of reinforcement.

13　A reinforcer is a stimulus that has the effect of increasing the probability that a response will occur. Reinforcement is the effect of a reinforcer.

14　Shaping (the differential reinforcement of successive approximations) is a procedure whereby animals and humans may be taught complex behaviors by being reinforced for simple behaviors leading toward the terminal behavior.

15　Continuous schedules of reinforcement (where every correct response is reinforced) seem to be more effective in early stages of training. Subsequently, intermittent schedules of reinforcement, which can be either fixed or random and which can be based on the passage of time (interval) or on the number of responses emitted (ratio), are more effective in maintaining a high rate of responding, and in leading to slower extinction.

16　Primary reinforcers are stimuli that are innately reinforcing; they include food, drink, and sex. Secondary (or generalized) reinforcers are learned reinforcers. They include money, power, prestige, and so on.

17　Positive reinforcement increases the probability of a response by being contingent on that response; negative reinforcement also increases the probability of a response occurring, but as a result of being removed contingent upon a response. Punishment, unlike negative reinforcement, does not increase the probability of a response, but rather decreases the probability of a response.

18　Operant and classical conditioning theories do not explain all behavior. Certain simple responses cannot be conditioned (knee-jerk reflex in humans); other behaviors can be easily conditioned, but are eventually abandoned in favor of some more primitive response, even if this results in a loss of reinforcement (instinctive drift); and some behaviors appear to be learned even when they compete with behaviors that might lead to reinforcement (autoshaping).

19 It appears that there are *biological constraints* on learning—inherited predispositions that make learning certain things easy and highly probable (preparedness), and other things very unlikely and sometimes impossible (contrapreparedness). Rats are apparently prepared to learn to avoid smells associated with being sick; we are prepared to learn language.

20 Insight is the sudden recognition of a correct solution for a problem, and is not easily explained by traditional behavioral theories.

21 Even rats seem to be able to develop sophisticated spatial knowledge (cognitive maps) in the absence of tangible reinforcement; this too cannot easily be explained by behavioral theory.

22 Some current directions in the study of learning include a greater reliance on the role of expectations and the learning of contingencies (cause-effect relationships); an increasing recognition of the importance of biological factors in learning and behavior; and a greater emphasis on the essentially cognitive processes by which we relate things to one another so as to make sense of our world.

23 Practical applications of behavioral principles include programmed instruction and behavior modification.

Further Readings

Systematic and easily read accounts of major learning theories, including those discussed in this chapter, are presented in:

Lefrancois, G. R. *Psychological theories and human learning* (2nd ed.). Monterey, Calif.: Brooks/Cole, 1982.

Chance, P. *Learning and behavior.* Belmont, Calif.: Wadsworth, 1979.

A much more detailed and more biologically oriented discussion of conditioning is presented by:

Fantino, E., and Logan, C. A. *The experimental analysis of behavior: a biological perspective.* San Francisco: W. H. Freeman, 1979.

The following two paperbacks present very brief and simple introductions to operant conditioning principles:

Keller, F. S. *Learning: Reinforcement theory* (2nd ed.). New York: Random House, 1969.

Reynolds, G. S. *A primer of operant conditioning* (rev. ed.). Chicago: Scott, Foresman, 1975.

The most definitive statement of Pavlovian classical conditioning is Pavlov's own series of lectures, translated in 1927:

Pavlov, I. P. *Conditioned reflexes* (G. V. Anrep, Trans.). London: Oxford University Press, 1927.

A provocative presentation of Skinner's position and its implications for society and for our view of such concepts as freedom and dignity is:

Skinner, B. F. *Beyond freedom and dignity.* New York: Alfred A. Knopf, 1971.

Memory

7

Much to the amusement of his numerous grandchildren, and to the occasional embarrassment of our grandmother, our grandfather became increasingly forgetful with the passing years. Most days he would lose at least one important thing. Sometimes his glasses; at other times, his newspaper, his slippers, his favorite red cushion with the yellow tassels on each corner. Whenever he lost one of these, he would shuffle miserably about the house, assuring our grandmother and whoever else happened to be present that he knew for certain, without any doubt whatsoever, that he had left his glasses right here by the piano, or his cushion right over there on the green rocking chair. Sometimes he would find the missing item himself; more often our grandmother would interrupt her work and retrieve the glasses or the slippers.

Some days, our grandfather lost much grander things, and on a far larger scale. His many dogs were easily lost, and he would sometimes spend hours walking around the garden or the barn, or through the small woods behind the house looking for Pouf who, old as he was, seldom strayed very far from the shady nook underneath the back porch. Other people's houses were easily lost as well. More than once, the old man set out to visit someone down the road, only to return some hours later grumbling that they had moved again without telling him. One day, it was his own house that he lost. And had my grandmother not eventually gone out and shown him where it was, it is possible that he would never have found it again.

"His memory isn't always as good as it used to be," my grandmother explained, seemingly proudly. And we too were proud of this old man, about to begin the tenth decade of his life.

And then there came the day of his most ambitious forgetting. It was one of those soft days of early spring when we had all gathered at our grandmother's to watch her bake and to help her make holes in her doughnuts and in her pies and cookies. Our grandfather had retired into his bedroom to change into his early spring gardening clothes. Perhaps an hour or so later when he had still not returned, our grandmother noticed that he was gone, and went to look for him.

And found him, dressed like the proverbial jaybird, parading majestically in front of the boarding school next door, picking early spring crocuses and singing an aria from some obscure opera, much to the delight of the school's giggling occupants.

When she asked him later how he, Frank Francoeur of all people, could behave so unthinkably, he confessed at once that, only for a short moment, he had forgotten who he was.

The Role of Memory

You know who you are (or at least you think you know) during every waking moment of your life, provided it is not too terribly clouded by alcohol, drugs, fatigue, or illness. You take this knowledge almost entirely for granted. There is no need for you to look into your wallet when you first awaken in the morning to discover your identity in cold print corroborated by a photograph. The information is already in your memory.

You understand the meaning of this sentence. You take that understanding for granted as well, never realizing that all sentences would be absolutely meaningless if you did not remember their beginnings once you have reached their ends.

July 4, July 1, June 22, 1492, 1984, Churchill, and a variety of other dates and names may have meaning for you. Their meanings are not implicit in the names or dates themselves; these are only reflections of light waves or disturbances in the air. The meanings are in your memory.

Various bits of poetry, passages from plays, memorable lines, and assorted pearls of wisdom occasionally suggest themselves to you. These too are in your memory.

Memory is centrally implicated in all aspects of human functioning. For example, the learning processes discussed in the previous chapter would be meaningless without the intervention of memory. In a very real sense, to learn requires memorization. It is clear that there must be some lasting change as a function of experience if learning is to take place; and that lasting change describes one type of memory. In fact, the principal difference between learning and memory, from a psychologist's point of view, has to do primarily with procedure. A measure of learning is provided by looking at performance immediately; a measure of memory involves looking at performance after a time lapse (Hall, 1976).

We often speak as though a memory were a *thing* that people have—a thing that varies from one individual to another in terms of how well it functions. In fact, however, we have no single standard by which to judge this "thing." If I say that I have a good memory, as anybody might from time to time, I might mean any number of things. Perhaps I have just remembered a date or a name. Alternatively, I might have obtained a high score on some measure of achievement. My good memory might also refer to the fact that I have been successful in recalling a poem that I intended to memorize. Then again, it might refer to the fact that I can read a chapter and recall its meaning, or that I can recall some of its sentences and perhaps some of the pages on which specific information can be found. I might even remember the general location of an item on a page. That I have a good memory might also refer to the fact that I have just discovered myself capable of something I haven't done for many years.

In contrast to a good memory, a bad memory may be seen as one that is sometimes incapable of some of the activities just described. Good and bad memories, however, are not the simple manifestation of some inherited ability. Remembering may be related to learning, to the organization of material, and to a variety of other factors.

Memory: A Cognitive Topic

Behaviorism, as we have seen, is a psychology of stimuli and responses; it deals with the objective, observable aspects of human behavior. And historically, its search has been for the laws and principles that might govern the formation of associations between stimuli and responses (as well as among various stimuli and various responses). Behavioristic concerns are well illustrated in the work of such behaviorists as Watson and Skinner, among others.

Cognitive psychology, in contrast, is a psychology of mental processes and structures far removed from such objective and observable components of behavior as stimuli and responses. Its subject matter is knowing, decision making, thinking, organizing, and remembering. It doesn't deal with associations among stimulus and response events so much as with events that might be considered to occur primarily in the brain. And it doesn't search for laws and principles so much as for *metaphors*.

In a very real sense, cognitive psychology is a psychology of metaphor. It seeks the most useful and fruitful metaphors for intellectual processes. It attempts to understand mental processes and to explain them in terms of these metaphors. Thus, cognitive theories in psychology are generally based on hypothetical structures and processes. A cognitive theory says, in effect, that we behave *as if;* it compares through metaphor.

Remembering, an absolutely fundamental aspect of knowing, is primarily a cognitive topic in contemporary psychology. This does not mean that memory cannot be studied in terms of stimuli and responses. It can, and continues to be. What this statement means is that most of our current explanations for memory processes, and most of our approaches to research in this area are now based on cognitive models. They are the subject of this chapter.

The Filing-Cabinet Metaphor

The first, and probably the oldest, of metaphors for memory says that memory is a filing cabinet. It is apparently a huge, limitless, grayish cabinet into which we can toss a great variety of material which is thus kept out of the way until we have some use for it. It has large and small drawers into which we file things.

Several related processes are involved in the filing operation. Much as a clerk must first record material if it is to be filed, so it is necessary for us to learn before we can remember. If the material is not very important and is not likely to be necessary very often if ever again, there is little point in cluttering the files with it. Better to leave it on the desk for a short while, use it, and throw it in the wastebasket. We have a system very much like that, which is extremely useful in ensuring that we do not clutter our cabinets. We look for telephone numbers or get them from the operator, record them, use them, and promptly forget them.

If, however, the material is important, it is filed in such a way that it can later be retrieved. The clerk may use an alphabetical system. Such a system makes it extremely easy to enter the file, find the pertinent information, and retrieve it—provided the clerk knows how the material was filed. Does Mr. Jones, who has just had an accident and who has not paid his premiums, belong under *J* for Jones, *A* for Accidents, *U* for Unpaid, or *D* for Do Not Renew? Cross-referencing the file may solve the problem.

We cross-reference our memories as well, although not always as systematically as a file clerk.

The three Rs of filing—recording, retaining, and retrieving—are analogous to the three processes involved in remembering: coding, storing, and retrieving. Is everything that is learned, stored? Can everything that is stored be retrieved?

A Three-Stage Model of Memory

Research has shown that the filing-cabinet metaphor recognizes only one of three different and distinct kinds of memory. This is not to say that we have three separate areas in our brains, each of which corresponds to a different type of memory. In fact, distinctions among types of memory are based primarily on the techniques that psychologists have devised to investigate remembering. Thus we study retrieval that occurs some time after learning and we refer to **long-term** or *secondary memory;* we examine the retrieval of information just presented and speak of **short-term** or *primary memory;* and we note that some information never appears to be learned in a traditional sense, but is available for recall only within a second of presentation, in which case we refer to **sensory** (or *iconic* or *echoic*) **memory**. The principal differences among these three types of memory relate not to the nature of the material so much as to the type of processing that takes place.

Sensory Memory

Consider the case of a typist. He sits hunched over a typewriter, words moving from a handwritten letter through his head, down certain neural pathways, out his fingers, through the keyboard, and eventually onto a white sheet of paper. His typing is usually several words behind his reading. Now the phone rings. He answers it. I am on the other end. After a polite introduction, I ask, "What is the next word you were going to type?" The typist doesn't remember. The word was in his mind when he answered the phone, but has now been forgotten. In fact, the word was never learned. It was simply in what is called *sensory memory.* It appears that whenever we sense something in the environment, the sensation continues to be available for a fraction of a second after the stimulus has ceased. If there is no need to remember it, it is forgotten immediately.

The nature of sensory memory has been investigated through a series of ingenious experiments. Sperling (1963) projected an array of 12 letters in rows of 4 letters each for a very brief time, using a tachistoscope (an instrument that flashes visual stimuli for seconds or fractions thereof). Only a few milliseconds after presentation, subjects heard 1 of 3 tones, indicating which of the 3 rows of 4 letters they were to try and remember. As will be shown later, only very rare individuals are capable of remembering 12 discrete items, 7 or fewer being a much more common memory span (Miller, 1956). It would be expected, then, that subjects would have occasionally remembered the correct row, and occasionally not. In fact, however, when asked to report only 1 row of letters, accuracy of recall was over 90 percent, provided that recall occurred immediately after presentation. When subjects were asked to recall after half a second had elapsed, they did very poorly. Similarly, when they were asked to recall all 12 letters rather than just 1 row of 4, they remembered an average of only 4.5 letters (Figure 7.1).

This type of experiment illustrates that sensory memory is extremely brief. It is as though there is a visual image of material that continues to be available for only a fraction of a second following presentation. If the subject is asked to concentrate on a small portion of this array, it is then possible to recall it. If the question comes later, the material is no longer available for recall. Witness the typist who has no difficulty remembering the next word when in the process of typing, but who can no longer

Long-term memory A type of memory whereby with continued rehearsal and recoding of sensory input, material may become available for recall for an indefinite period of time.

Short-term memory A type of memory in which some material, although it is not learned in the sense that it will be available for recall at a later time, will nevertheless be held in memory for short periods.

Sensory memory The simple sensory recognition of stimuli.

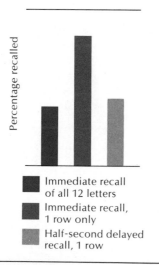

Percentage recalled

■ Immediate recall of all 12 letters

■ Immediate recall, 1 row only

■ Half-second delayed recall, 1 row

Figure 7.1 Sensory memory. Sperling (1963) projected twelve letters in rows of four on a screen for a very brief period and then asked subjects to recall the letters immediately or shortly after exposure. Almost no subjects could remember the whole chart, but recall for a single row was 90 percent accurate immediately afterward (at the signal of a tone right after the row was projected). Retention was short-lived, however. Even half a second after seeing the letters, subjects had markedly poorer recall, even for a single row.

recall the word once interrupted for a brief period. Recent findings (Sakitt, 1976) indicate that this kind of visual sensory storage occurs in the rods of the retina.

In summary, sensory memory, as described by Sperling (1960, 1963) involves very short-term availability of stimulus effects for processing. For vision, this memory is in the form of an icon—an image of the visual display at the retinal level. For auditory stimuli, Neisser (1967) suggests the effect is very similar, taking a form like an echo— hence his label, *echoic memory.*

Eidetic Imagery   A peculiar and rare form of memory involving longer-term sensory storage is **eidetic imagery**, popularly referred to as "photographic memory." Psychologists have sometimes distinguished among three types of imagery: afterimages, mental images, and eidetic images. An afterimage, described in Chapter 5, appears to be the result of a simple perceptual process. It may be elicited by looking intently at a brightly lit source such as a television screen and then looking away. A mental image refers to what results from conscious attempts to recall visual material; it is subject to the changes that often accompany memory.

An eidetic image shares some of the characteristics of both mental images and afterimages. It too is a visual representation. Unlike an afterimage, however, it is subject to a degree of conscious control; that is, the subject can to some extent choose to "see" or not to see an eidetic image. Such is not the case for an afterimage, which persists in spite of any intentions we might have. And, unlike a mental image, an eidetic image is not highly subject to distortions and changes; in a sense, it is an accurate, photographlike recollection of a visual stimulus.

Ahsen (1977a, 1977b) describes one of the most common procedures employed in investigations of eidetic imagery. First, subjects are usually known to be gifted in this respect. Many of these subjects are very young, because eidetic imagery is more common among young children and becomes less common after adolescence. Subjects are generally seated in front of a blank screen, often gray, and told to fix their attention on the screen. Various squares of different colors may then be placed on the screen for a short time and removed. Subjects are then asked what they can "see." After this, designs or photographs of varying complexity and detail may be shown, removed, and subjects required to describe them or to answer specific questions concerning the visual stimulus.

Research of this nature reveals that an eidetic image is "real" in the sense that the subject actually "sees" the image and can attend to its details in much the same way as we might attend to the details of an actual photograph or painting if we were asked questions about it. If, for example, subjects are asked how many flowers there are in a bouquet, after the picture of the bouquet has been removed, they do not immediately answer correctly, but must first take whatever time is actually required to count the flowers (Figure 7.2). Haber and Haber (1964) report that a subject's eyes move during this process, in much the same way as they might move if the subject were looking at an actual image.

The amount of time a subject needs to look at an image before forming an eidetic image varies from one individual to another. In some cases, only a few seconds of exposure is sufficient to elicit an eidetic image; in other cases, more time is required. The duration of the eidetic image varies as well, ranging from a few minutes to as long as several hours (G. W. Allport, 1924).

There are certain rare cases of eidetic imagery being available for recall years later. Luria's (1968) subject, S, described in Chapter 1, is a case in point. He made extremely effective use of visual imagery, even when recalling verbal material years after he had first learned it. Luria describes his behavior as follows:

> *In fact, some of these experiments designed to test his retention were performed (without his being given any warning) fifteen or sixteen years after the session in which he had originally recalled the words. Yet invariably they were successful. During these test sessions S would sit with his eyes closed, pause,*

Eidetic imagery   A particularly vivid type of visual image in memory. In many ways it is almost as though the individual were actually able to *look at* what is being remembered.

Figure 7.2 Eidetic memory is often tested by showing a subject a picture, like this one, for a brief period. The subject is then asked specific questions about details in the picture: How many oranges are in the tree? What animals are in the picture? How many stripes are in the skirt of the flute player? People with eidetic memory can reconstruct these details through a process very much like that involved in looking at the picture for the first time: their eyes move as if they were actually counting the oranges in the tree.

then comment, "Yes, yes . . . This was the series you gave me once when we were in your apartment . . . You were sitting at the table and I in the rocking chair . . . You were wearing a grey suit and you looked at me like this." (p. 12)

A second illustration of remarkable eidetic imagery is provided by Stromeyer's (1970) description of a woman who could look at a page of poetry *in a foreign language* and reproduce it exactly years later. She, like S, is clearly an exception. Among children who possess some degree of eidetic imagery, there is typically no transfer to long-term memory and consequently no obvious advantage in terms of their ability to learn and remember material. In addition, their recollections are frequently imperfect. Like our more adult memories, they too are subject to moods, wishes, and various other fanciful distortions.

Short-Term Memory (STM)

Consider now our same typist, who has returned to the typewriter, only slightly annoyed at my interruption. Psychologists telephone frequently, anxious to demonstrate for their students the vagaries of human memories. Our typist is tolerant though not glad, only half-believing his grandmother's admonition to suffer fools gladly. Sitting there tolerantly typing, he finds a word he suspects is misspelled. He leaves the desk, moves to a large dictionary, finds the word, returns to his typewriter, and finishes the letter.

Later that evening, I call him again. "Did you look up any words in your Funk and Wagnall today?" I inquire politely. He thinks so. "What words?" I inquire, again very politely. He doesn't remember. I should have called earlier.

There is clearly a difference between the type of memory involved in recognizing a word, typing it, and forgetting it immediately, and the memory involved in looking up a word's spelling in a dictionary and correcting it in typing. In the second case, the word has to be kept in memory for a period of time, but is later forgotten. The label for this type of memory is *short-term*. It has been intensely investigated by psychologists, beginning with Ebbinghaus's (1885) pioneering use of nonsense syllables. One of the problems implicit in investigating memory is that it is difficult to control for previous learning. Nonsense syllables, meaningless arrangements of letters, provide

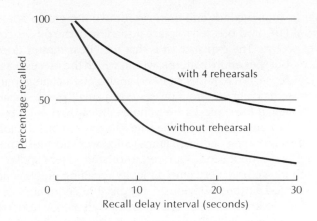

Figure 7.3 The black line shows a typical short-term memory curve. Forgetting of three-consonant units begins within seconds and is virtually complete after twenty seconds. If subjects are allowed to rehearse material, however, retention is considerably improved (as shown by the red line), sometimes becoming coded in the long-term memory system. (Based on data from Hellyer, 1962.)

some control for this. Syllables such as *gur, kar, lev, zib, tel,* and *cez* may be assumed to have less meaning for most subjects than ordinary words.

Literally thousands of experiments have been conducted with nonsense syllables (see Wickelgren, 1981). Some require simply that the subject remember as many words as possible after learning (free recall); others present nonsense syllables paired with meaningful words and later require subjects to recall the syllable when given the meaningful word (cued recall). Still others present series of nonsense syllables and require subjects to recall words in their correct order (serial recall). A wide variety of other experiments have looked at the effect of previous and subsequent learning on retention of a list of words, or at the effects of activities that intervene between learning and recall. The most reliable (most often replicated) and most important findings from these studies are summarized here.

Characteristics of STM   Immediate recall of short lists of syllables (seven or fewer) presented at a rate of one per second is usually close to 100 percent (Peterson & Peterson, 1959). Errors in this kind of experiment are typically due to faulty perception rather than faulty recollection. A subject may say *gar* instead of *gur,* for example, simply because *gar* is the syllable that was perceived. This observation has led to the widely held belief that memory span for short periods of time is limited to seven discrete items (G. A. Miller, 1956). Subsequent research indicates that it is frequently even lower than this (Broadbent, 1975), although some individuals can recall more than seven items. If the list is longer than seven items, some of these have a greater probability of being recalled than others. Among these are the last items presented (*recency effect*) and the first (*primacy effect*) (Jahnke, 1963).

Another significant finding is that short-term memory declines extremely rapidly (see Figure 7.3). Without rehearsal of learned materials, forgetting begins within a few seconds and is usually complete before twenty seconds have elapsed. In one variation of their study, for example, Peterson and Peterson (1959) prevented subjects from rehearsing by having them count backward in time to a metronome, beginning immediately after presentation of the last syllable. Under these circumstances, subjects recalled less than 10 percent of the material correctly after only eighteen seconds had elapsed. Even when subjects are asked to repeat the list immediately after learning, if they are forced to speak very slowly, thus increasing the passage of time, they typically make significantly more errors (Conrad & Hille, 1958). If they are allowed to rehearse the material, however, it is typically retained for considerably longer (Hellyer, 1962), sometimes eventually becoming part of the store in long-term memory.

Chunking   It should be noted here that the apparent limits of short-term memory can be partially overcome through processes of *grouping* information. Chase and Simon (1973) report the well-known ability of chess masters to glance at a chessboard

```
D   E   S   7

    S   A   N   O

1   U   W   D

6   F   N   N
```

Figure 7.4 Chunking and memory. (**a**) Look briefly at this figure and then test your short-term memory by trying to duplicate the letters and numbers. Did you make some mistakes? Look at the same grouping as it is arranged on page 192.

for a mere three or four seconds and then reproduce the entire board faultlessly. A novice player would be hard-pressed to place just a few of the pieces correctly following so brief an exposure. The explanation is that the chess master does not "see" all the separate pieces, but sees entire patterns, within which the pieces have well-ordered positions. (See Figure 7.4.) G. A. Miller's (1956) analogy to a change purse is apt here. If short-term memory is compared to a purse, it is a small purse, capable of holding seven pieces of money. If these pieces are pennies, its capacity is no more than seven cents; if, however, they are nickels or dimes, its capacity is considerably greater. Evidence that *chunking* (grouping of related items) improves short-term memory is easily obtained. Although we cannot recall fourteen unrelated letters spoken at the rate of one letter per second, we have very little difficulty recalling entire sentences spoken within the same period of time. Obviously, predictable sequences of words within sentences based on our knowledge of grammar, as well as our understanding of the meanings of sentences, greatly facilitate recall. But also, the mere grouping of letters into words improves our recall: Three or four unrelated words can also be recalled immediately after presentation in spite of the fact that they do not convey a unified meaning.

Sequential or Parallel Processes?   As we have seen, short-term memory is an active, extremely short-lived process whereby a highly limited amount of information is momentarily accessible, but will be lost if it is not rehearsed, coded, and transferred to longer-term storage. But between being lost forever or going into long-term storage, this small number of items (seven, plus or minus two) remains accessible. How do we access this information?

There are, in effect, two possibilities. The first is that we have immediate access to all STM material, simultaneously (termed *parallel processing*); the other is that we access each STM item in sequence (termed *serial* or *sequential processing*). Consider, for example, the following STM problem. A subject is presented with a set of four separate digits (say, numbers, 8, 1, 2, and 5). These are presented very briefly so that they will be available only in STM and not in long-term memory (LTM). And immediately after their presentation, the subject is presented with a fifth number (say 3), and is asked whether this fifth number was present in the first group of four digits. If retrieval from STM involves parallel processing, the subject simply compares the fifth digit with each of the first four *simultaneously;* but if processing is sequential, the subject must now compare the fifth digit with each of the first four *in turn*. How are we to find out which occurs?

Sternberg (1966, 1967, 1969) solved the problem using the following rather clever logic. The comparison of the fifth digit with the remaining four will take longer if it is sequential than if it is simultaneous. Furthermore, if processing is parallel, the amount of time required to answer correctly in this situation should be independent of the number of digits presented to the subject, If, on the other hand, processing is sequential, the more digits there are in STM, the longer it will take the subject to process the information required for a correct response.

Results of a large number of studies conducted by Sternberg and others (see Solso, 1979) are generally in agreement: retrieval from short-term memory involves sequential rather than parallel processing. The more items there are in short-term memory, the longer it takes for processing. (See Figure 7.5.) In fact, it takes approximately 250 milliseconds to process a single item in STM. But since STM is limited to seven items (more or less), total processing time remains very short.

Long-term memory, by contrast, contains all of our stable information. Sequential processing at that level would be so time-consuming as to be impossible. At the same time, parallel processing would require immediate access to so much information that it too is unlikely. As we see later, a different type of processing is probably employed at that level.

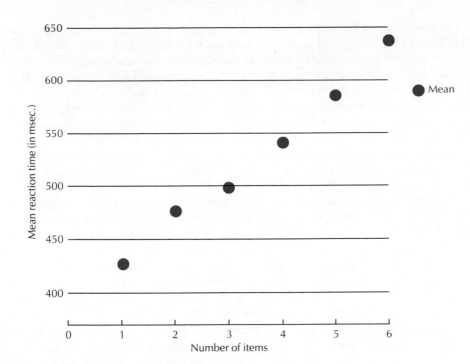

Figure 7.5 The time it takes subjects to process items in short-term memory grows longer as the number of items increases, indicating processing is sequential. (Adapted from *"Memory Scanning: Mental Processes Revealed by Reaction Time Experiments"* by S. Sternberg, *American Scientist,* 1969. Used by permission.)

Long-Term Memory (LTM)

Material that is remembered over long periods of time is said to be stored in long-term memory. Such material obviously includes most of what we retain from our educational experiences, a wide variety of daily happenings, and all our stable information about the world.

Most of the early research in memory dealt primarily with short-term memory. There were a number of reasons for this, not the least important of which is the fact that it is far easier to control the subject's relevant experiences in studies of STM. In studies of long-term memory, the experimenter frequently has little control over experiences that might intervene between initial learning and the recall of material some time later.

With the recent development of cognitive models and a renewed interest in information processing, there has been a dramatic shift in memory research. Nonsense syllables have given way to a study of meaningful material; studies of interference and memory span are being replaced with studies of cognitive organization and retrieval strategies. As a result, we know more about characteristics of LTM, and processes involved.

Characteristics of LTM Material stored in long-term memory is, by definition, relatively stable; that is, it tends to be recalled indefinitely. Interestingly, however, what is recalled is not necessarily what was perceived or learned in the first place. Numerous studies have established that memory is in part a constructive process. Among the first of these was Bartlett's (1932) investigation of memory for printed material. He had his subjects read an unusual story adapted from Native American folklore. The tale concerned two young men who were approached by strangers one foggy night and were invited to come along and fight with them. One of the two went along; the other did not. They fought, and many were killed. But before the fight was done, one of the strangers said that they must leave because the young man who had come with them had been hit. The young man, feeling no pain and no illness, concluded that these strangers must be ghosts. He returned home to tell his story. Having told the story, he fell quiet. The sun rose. He died.

b

Figure 7.4 (**b**) Chunking, or grouping figures according to some system, improves recall. The more obvious the logic of the system, the easier it will be to remember (as a general rule).

Zeigarnik effect The tendency of individuals to remember those problems or tasks that they have not yet finished rather than those they have finished.

In paraphrasing this story for you, I have changed much of the style and some of the content of the original story, just as Bartlett's subjects did. Our cultures, our experiences, and our customary ways of depicting and expressing, all affect our memories. We tend to remember certain aspects of visual scenes, for example, and fill in the rest, sometimes quite convinced that we are remembering accurately. Again, the extent to which this inexact recall is a function of an imperfect memory and the extent to which it is dependent upon faulty perception or simply to inattention cannot easily be determined. Figure 7.6 presents a series of reproductions of a relatively ambiguous and imperfect stimulus. Successive drawings over a period of two months probably come closer to the subject's idealized notion of what the original stimulus was in the first place.

In my introductory classes, I have frequently invited a stranger into class on some more or less flimsy pretext, and later had students attempt to describe the stranger. Invariably, a class of several hundred students will cover the entire range of physical characteristics by which individuals can be identified. Some are convinced that the stranger was blue-eyed, well-dressed, clean-shaven, and wore glasses; others are equally convinced that the dark-eyed, casually dressed, mustached gentleman wore no glasses. Perhaps the only attribute that has never been mistaken by these students was the visitor's sex. Faulty memory, or faulty perception? (See Box 7.1.)

Meaningful material is more easily learned and remembered for longer periods of time (Ausubel & Robinson, 1969). Similarly, events that are particularly striking may be recalled indefinitely, regardless of their importance or their duration. An accident, a painting, a scene, a feeling, or a person may be recalled for a long time (Bower, 1981; Leight & Ellis, 1981). Less striking but frequently rehearsed items like your driver's license number, your Social Security number, or your current telephone number may also be recalled for a long time. Interestingly, however, even when these are rehearsed countless times, they are soon forgotten when they are no longer required. If your telephone number has changed recently, you might well be unable to recall your previous number.

One additional characteristic of long-term memory is termed the **Zeigarnik effect**. Zeigarnik presented a series of relatively simple problems to her subjects. Most of these could have been solved had enough time been provided, but students were interrupted prior to their completion. Subjects were later asked to recall as many of these problems as they could. One obvious expectation would be that those problems that had been completed would be remembered more often than the incomplete problems, since subjects had spent more time on them. The opposite was found to be true: subjects tended to remember incomplete problems. Quite simply, the Zeigarnik effect is the apparent tendency that we have to recall interrupted activities. This phenomenon is probably best explained by reference to the Gestalt notion that we tend toward closure (completion) both in perception and in thought (see Chapter 5). An unsolved problem is one for which we have not achieved closure; hence the tendency to remember an unsolved problem rather than another problem with which we are finished.

Words versus Pictures A picture is worth a thousand words, they tell us, and *they* may be right, for a change. Subjects have been shown as many as ten thousand pictures, and later shown some of these same pictures paired with other pictures that they had not seen. Under these conditions, they were able to recognize more than 90 percent of the pictures they had already seen (Standing, 1973). A related study (Babrick et al., 1975) presented subjects with photographs of former classmates taken from yearbooks. Recognition was 90 percent accurate after two months, and almost as accurate some fifteen years later. It appears that capacity for long-term memory of pictures may be almost unlimited.

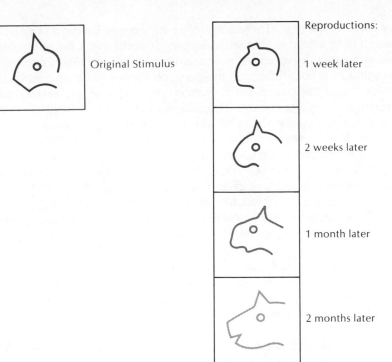

Original Stimulus

Reproductions:

1 week later

2 weeks later

1 month later

2 months later

Figure 7.6 Although long-term memory is relatively stable, the way we remember material tends to change over time. Within a week, the subject's memory of the original stimulus had changed considerably. After two months, the reproduction still resembled the original, but it had taken on more character of its own. In this sense, long-term memory is *generative*.

Much of what is stored in LTM appears to be either verbal or pictorial, although there isn't a great deal of agreement with respect to which is most prevalent. Paivio (1971), for example, describes memory as a dual coding system where information is coded either as an image or verbally or both. He assumes that concrete information is more often coded in images, and more abstract information, verbally. Certain processes also permit the individual to associate pictorial and verbal information, to give images verbal labels, or to visualize abstract information. Other theorists (Bugelski, 1970, for example) believe that mental pictures rather than verbal material are stored in memory, that we recall images and then elaborate them verbally. Still other theorists maintain that memory is primarily verbal except for material that is itself pictorial (Bower, 1972).

Although this apparent controversy cannot be resolved here, it is worth noting that memory for pictorial and verbal material appears to be quite different, no matter how this material might be stored. The two studies mentioned earlier, for example, illustrate that recognition of individuals in photographs is highly impressive. For our purposes, it is irrelevant whether the form of storage is itself pictorial, verbal, or both. Time of recall has also been shown to be different for pictorial and verbal material, with verbal material being recalled faster than pictorial material. It is possible to rehearse mentally the entire alphabet *verbally* in approximately four seconds; rehearsing images of alphabet letters requires minutes rather than seconds.

There is little doubt that images are more memorable than words. This is demonstrated not only by research such as that cited earlier, but also by the simple observation that when we are desperately attempting to remember something but cannot do so, we often explain our failure in terms of our inability to "picture it." Any memory that has a strong visual component is typically more easily available for recall than are purely verbal memories. Herein lies the importance of graphic representations in textbooks. It is also this principle that underlies most of the more powerful memory aids that are described later in this chapter.

Consolidation In this context, a theory that suggests that the physiological activities that accompany learning and that therefore underlie memory continue for a period of time following the actual activities associated with learning.

Retrograde amnesia A type of amnesia that usually results from a blow to the head or from electrical shock. Loss of memory is limited to events immediately *preceding* the blow or shock, thus it is termed *retrograde*.

Consolidation Theory There is evidence that a **consolidation** period is required for material to be stored in long-term memory. Material that is being learned remains unstable and easily disrupted for at least thirty minutes after its presentation. Given sufficient time, it is consolidated in memory and cannot easily be removed.

Evidence for this consolidation theory comes from cases of **retrograde amnesia**, a type of memory loss that usually results from a blow to the head or from electrical shock. It is not uncommon for those who have suffered head injuries in automobile accidents to be unable to remember any of the events that immediately preceded the accident. Similarly, patients who are administered electrical shock therapy (termed *electroconvulsive therapy* or ECT) do not remember events that preceded the therapy. Typically, a period of approximately thirty minutes preceding ECT or head injury cannot be remembered. This would tend to substantiate the theory that it takes about that long for learning to be consolidated before it is stored in long-term memory.

Additional supportive evidence for this consolidation theory has come from a large number of studies where animals are trained to perform various tasks and are then administered electric shocks. Hudspeth et al. (1964) administered shocks to rats immediately after training, twenty seconds later, thirty minutes later, and one hour later. Rats shocked immediately showed no retention; those shocked later had partial retention. If the shock was administered one hour after training, rats typically exhibited complete retention.

There is another experimental situation that parallels retrograde amnesia to a limited extent and bears out consolidation theory. Tulving (1969) presented subjects with lists of fifteen words at one-second intervals. Subjects were asked immediately to recall as many words as possible, within thirty seconds. As would be predicted from the *recency principle,* words presented last in the lists tended to be recalled most often. Then certain high-priority words were inserted in some of the lists. High-priority words were easily identified, since they were the names of well-known individuals (Columbus, Freud, Aristotle); other words were names of ordinary objects. Subjects were now instructed to make certain that they remembered high-priority words whenever these occurred, as well as to try to remember as many other words as possible.

BOX 7.1

Eyewitness!

We seldom quarrel with the conviction that "seeing is believing." Indeed, when we are most skeptical, we are most likely to say "show me." But if we can't be shown, we rely on others who *have* been shown—who have *seen.* And if we have faith in the honesty of those who have seen, of our *eyewitnesses,* we then have almost boundless faith in their descriptions of what it is that they have seen. Understandably we have far less faith in those who have not themselves seen, but who have been told. We dismiss them easily: "That's just hearsay. You weren't actually *there.*" Accordingly, our systems of justice are firmly anchored on our belief in the validity of eyewitness testimony—and on the unreliability of hearsay evidence. Should we be so trusting of eyewitnesses?

Extensive research on the reliability of eyewitness testimony leaves little doubt that eyewitnesses are very often in error (Loftus, 1979a, 1979b; Yarmey, 1979; Wells, Lindsay & Ferguson, 1979). Many of these studies involve situations where subjects view a staged crime and are later asked to identify the criminal; or situations where subjects view films and are then questioned about what they saw. In one typical staged-crime study, subjects were shown six photographs and asked to identify the criminal. Only 31 percent made accurate identifications. Thirty-four percent of the subjects could make no identification on the basis of these photographs (one of which was a clear photograph of the "criminal"), and an astounding 35 percent made false identifications (Leippe, Wells, & Ostrom, 1978).

Other studies have shown that witnesses can be made to "remember" things that didn't happen. Loftus (1979) had subjects view a film in which a sports car was involved in an accident, and then questioned them about what they had seen. Among the questions asked was one of the following: "How fast was the sports car going when it passed the barn while travelling along the country road?" or "How fast was the sports car going while travelling along the country road?" Later, subjects were asked whether they had seen a barn in the film. Seventeen percent of those who had been asked the question that contained the only mention of a barn in the entire series *remembered* seeing a barn. Fewer than 3 percent of the others thought they had seen a barn.

As a result of these and related studies, Loftus argues that much of what we remember can be modified by subsequent events. Not only does the passage of time dull our recollections, but our memories of events that we have clearly witnessed can be manipulated. Perhaps fewer than half of us will later be able to identify the thief; even fewer will remember the color of his eyes, his hair, or his umbrella; and some of us will remember things we could not possibly have witnessed.

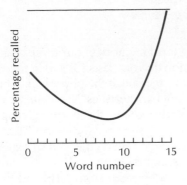

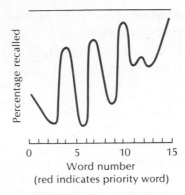

a Recency principle

b Memory span in high-priority/low-priority text

Figure 7.7 Tulving (1969) had subjects listen to a list of fifteen words read aloud at one-second intervals. Immediate recall of the list typically followed the *recency principle,* with words heard most recently remembered best (**a**). When subjects were told ahead of time to look out especially for high-priority words (such as names of famous people), those words were best remembered, and the words immediately preceding each high-priority word were rarely recalled (**b**). Tulving's explanation was that the *consolidation period* had been disturbed.

The findings from this study that are of relevance here are that the probability of remembering the word just preceding the high-priority item was significantly reduced, whereas the probability of remembering the high-priority item was very high (close to 100 percent if it occurred near the end of the list) (Figure 7.7). Tulving suggests that this is additional evidence that a consolidation period is required for remembering, even with respect to short-term memory. His hypothesis is that the consolidation process for any one word overlaps into the presentation of the next word, and that the presentation of a high-priority word disrupts this process, thereby inhibiting recall of the preceding item. Significantly, when the rate of presentation is decreased to one word every *two* seconds, evidence of memory loss preceding high-priority words disappears. Equally important, memory for terms that follow the high-priority word is not affected.

Two Kinds of LTM?   Tulving (1972) makes a distinction between two different kinds of long-term memory. On the one hand, there is all of our stable information about the world, our abstract knowledge, our knowledge of language and grammar, of facts and principles, of theories and strategies. This type of memory is labeled **semantic** (or sometimes generic). On the other hand, there is our personal memory of all events that have happened to *us*. These, argues Tulving, are not abstract memories like your memory of the date the Pilgrims landed at Plymouth Rock. They are highly personal memories tied to a time and place. They are our autobiographical memories; they always involve us in particular episodes, and are therefore labeled **episodic**. My recollection of the methods by which I can find the length of the diagonal in a rectangle is an example of semantic memory. My recollection of the specific event during which I was taught this tidbit of information is an episodic memory.

Semantic memory   Abstract memory of facts like historical dates, grammar, principles, theories.

Why make this distinction? Tulving suggests that it might be a very useful distinction to the extent that there are important differences between the two types of memory. For example, episodic memory appears to be far more susceptible to distortion and forgetting than does semantic memory. I now have considerable difficulty remembering when and where I first learned that chickens lay eggs (an episodic memory, absent in this case), but am not likely to forget that they do, indeed, lay eggs (semantic memory).

Episodic memory   Highly personal memories of experiences, tied to a particular time and place.

A number of researchers do not agree that a distinction between generic and episodic memory is valid or useful. Wickelgren (1981) points out that it is almost impossible to recall an *episode* without having abstracted it to some extent, and related it to other items of information. Others suggest that even if generic and episodic memory can be separated, the advantages of considering them separately might not be very great (Mcloskey & Santee, 1981; Baddeley, 1976).

Summary: Short-Term and Long-Term Memory Compared

The distinction between short- and long-term memory in our three-stage model clearly involves more than the banal observation that one lasts for a long time and the other for only a short time. There is evidence to suggest that the physiological processes involved may be quite different. Certainly, the characteristics of long-term memory would imply that some relatively permanent changes in the brain accompany the memory; such changes would not be required for short-term memory. The precise nature of these changes remains unknown, although several theoretical explanations have been advanced. These are examined later in this chapter.

In addition to the obvious time differences between short-term and long-term memory, there are three other clear distinctions. First, short-term memory involves an active, ongoing rehearsal process that is very easily disrupted. Almost any delay between the presentation of material and its recall decreases the accuracy and completeness of recall. In contrast, long-term memory, although it initially requires active involvement, eventually becomes a more passive process, subject to the distortions of time, but not easily disrupted by any of a variety of specific interruptions. If you know the seven spectral colors of white light today, you will in all likelihood know them tomorrow in spite of whatever else you might learn between today and tomorrow.

Second, as was mentioned earlier, short-term memory is of very limited capacity. If you were to hear twelve unrelated letters during a space of twelve seconds, it is highly unlikely that you would remember them all. You would most likely recall some of the first letters presented, and a slightly larger number of the last ones (the recency and primacy effects described earlier). In this sense, short-term memory is very much like *attention span*. The terms have occasionally been used interchangeably, since evidence that a subject can attend to something is implicit in the ability to recall details of the presentation. In the same way as we can recall seven digits or seven numbers immediately following their presentation, so we can identify groups of six or seven objects without having to count them. Larger groups, unless they are organized in recognizable patterns, need to be counted individually. In contrast to the limited storage capacity of short-term memory, the capacity of long-term memory appears to be relatively unlimited. Psychology has not yet provided any evidence that after a lifetime of storing material in long-term memory, our memories become overcrowded and incapable of learning new material until some old material has been forgotten (see Figure 7.8).

A third important distinction between short-term and long-term memory has to do with the ease with which material may be retrieved from each. Recall in the case of short-term memory is easy and automatic. The individual either remembers immediately or does not remember, in which case recall is unlikely to occur later. With respect to long-term memory, recall may be slower and more difficult, sometimes requiring some form of "search" and the occasional elimination of incorrect responses. Such retrieval is not always immediate (the tip-of-the-tongue phenomenon discussed in Box 7.2 is a case in point) but may occur some time after the individual intends to remember. Frequently, however, information that has been well learned can be recalled immediately and easily. The point is that material in short-term memory is *always* available immediately (if it *is* available); material in long-term memory may not be.

The major differences between short- and long-term memory are summarized in Figure 7.9, and the relationships among the components of memory in our three-stage model are represented in Figure 7.10.

A Levels of Processing Model of Memory

Older, more traditional models of memory have typically portrayed the mind as some sort of catalog or camera that saves a complete, sequential record of our experiences. Time and other factors subsequently erase some of this record; what is left is our

memory. The most notable feature of this particular model, first described by Koffka (1935), is that it is *not* associationistic. That is, the model does not concern itself with the possibility that items of information might be related one to another in our memories.

Almost without exception, current models of memory are **associationistic**. They are based on the fundamental assumption that all items of information in our memories are associated in various ways (Baddeley, 1976; Estes, 1980; Wickelgren, 1981). That this is the case with respect to long-term memory would seem obvious. While short-term memory rarely contains more than seven items of information, long-term memory contains an uncounted number of items. We are clearly incapable of processing all of this information *simultaneously* when trying to retrieve something from memory. And at a mere 250 milliseconds per item, a *sequential* search might require most of a lifetime to recall something as trivial as our birthdates; hence the need for search strategies based on *associations* among items.

Associationistic models   Models of memory that concern themselves with the way items of information in our memories are associated with each other. The levels of processing model is associationistic.

BOX 7.2

Tip-of-the-Tongue Phenomenon

"What's his name. . . . It starts with an *S*. It's a Scottish name. Shoot! I'm blocking on his name again." So spoke my grandfather with a name on the tip of his tongue. It is not an uncommon phenomenon. It applies not only to people's names, but to all manner of information that cannot quite be recalled immediately. It is information that you are fully aware of knowing, and that you are convinced you will eventually recall. What do psychologists know about the tip of the tongue that goes beyond its taste buds and coloration?

R. Brown and McNeill (1966) read definitions of rare English words to a group of subjects and asked them whether they could think of the word being defined. In this way, they produced a variety of tip-of-the-tongue phenomena. Numerous subjects were convinced they knew the word even though they could not remember it immediately. Subjects were then asked to select from a list of forty-nine words, words that might be similar or different. Many were able to select words that were highly similar, particularly in sound. Frequently, the first letter of the word could be recalled as well. On other occasions, providing the first letter is sometimes a sufficient cue for retrieval of the correct word.

Studies of the tip-of-the-tongue phenomenon illustrate again that memories are frequently available but not accessible. They illustrate as well that memory is not necessarily an all-or-nothing phenomenon. That is, memory does not always result in the complete, correct response or in no response at all, but frequently results in a partially correct response. Memory is perhaps more like an artist reproducing a painting than like a camera duplicating a scene. We seldom have access to the photograph, but must instead generate our own paintings.

Short-term

Active rehearsal process, easily disrupted
Limited capacity: 7 ± 2
Immediate, automatic recall

Long-term

Relatively unaffected by activities interpolated
between initial learning and recall
Unlimited capacity
Recall sometimes more difficult and slower

Figure 7.9 Major differences between short-term and long-term memory.

One of the principal tasks of researchers in recent years has been to attempt to understand and describe how we form associations. The *levels of processing* model described by Craik and Lockhart (1972; Cermak and Craik, 1979) is the result of one such attempt. In essence, this model says that memory results from the *processing* of information—specifically, from the *level* of processing that occurs. Information that is not processed leaves only a momentary sensory impression; other information may be processed to different degrees and in different ways, depending in part on its importance (to the processor), the time available, and the amount of energy and effort invested in processing. For example, subjects who are asked to learn and remember

Figure 7.10 The three-stage model of memory. Sensory information first enters sensory memory (iconic or echoic memory); from there it may go into short-term memory (also called primary memory), where it is available as a name or word, for example, as long as it is rehearsed. Some of the material in short-term memory may then be coded for long-term storage, where it might take the form of meanings and concepts. It is important to note that these three components of memory do *not* refer to three different locations in the brain or other parts of the nervous system, but refer to a model of how we remember—or, more precisely, how we study memory.

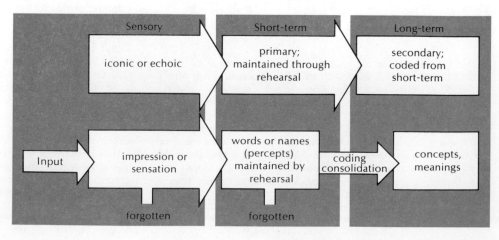

a series of words can process these words at one of three levels. At the shallowest level, the subject might attend only to the word's physical appearance (structure); at a slightly deeper level, processing might take into consideration the word's pronunciation; and at the deepest level, processing would involve consideration of the word's meaning (semantic processing).

Studies that have looked at the levels of processing model have typically found that semantic processing does result in greater retention. These studies have also found that simple rehearsal (without elaborating or forming new associations) does not increase retention. In one ingenious experiment, Craik and Watkins (1973) presented subjects with a series of words, asking them to remember the last word in the list that began with a specific letter. For example, subjects might be asked to remember the last word beginning with the letter *M* in the series: woman, image, man, money, table, flower, book, message. . . . Later, subjects were asked to recall as many of the *M* words as they could. Clearly, words beginning with the letter *M* should have been held in STM (rehearsed) for only a short period of time if they were immediately followed by another *M* word, but would have been rehearsed for much longer if the next word beginning with *M* didn't occur for a long time. It follows that if simple rehearsal is important for recall, *M* words followed by a long sequence of non-*M* words would have been remembered more easily. However, that was not found to be the case, and the researchers concluded that rehearsal does not automatically lead to retention.

A number of other studies have attempted to demonstrate the importance of level of processing for retention. Among the first of these was one reported by Hyde and Jenkins (1969) where subjects were presented with a series of words and asked to make different judgments about these words. The different judgments required were designed to bring about different depths of processing. For example, subjects might be asked to note whether or not there were any *e*'s in the words (low level of processing) or to rate the pleasantness of the words (deeper level of processing). Subjects were not told beforehand that this was a memory task. Significantly, those asked to rate the pleasantness of words recalled almost twice as many words as those asked simply to note the presence of a specific letter.

Although research has often been kind to the levels of processing model, the model has not escaped criticism entirely. Chief among these criticisms is the observation that the model's main belief is the not particularly earth-shattering notion that meaningful material seems to be more easily remembered than material that is less meaningful. A second criticism is that the model has led to a circular form of reasoning—specifically, if something is well-remembered, we conclude that it has been deeply processed; evidence of depth of processing is then obtained from measures of memory. In other words, since we have no measures of depth of processing that are independent from measures of memory, it is difficult to validate the principal beliefs of the theory.

Which Model?

Thus far we have looked at three metaphors or models of memory: the filing cabinet analogy; the three-stage (sensory memory, STM, and LTM) model, and the levels of processing model. In addition, there are a number of other models that make use of such abstract concepts as *node,* and that are described as node models or sometimes as semantic memory node models (see, for example, Bower, 1977; Wickelgren, 1981). In these models, a node is simply a metaphor for whatever it is that can be represented in memory. The single most important characteristic of a node is that it *represents;* and representation involves associations. It is important to keep in mind that the associations of which the cognitive theorists now speak are not the stimulus-response associations of the behaviorists. Quite the contrary, they are associations based on meaning or significance.

Although most memory researchers generally agree on the associationistic nature of memory, they do not yet agree on which of the various proposed models will prove to be the most useful. Further research may lead us closer to the ultimate metaphor. (See Box 7.3.)

Ways of Measuring Memory

It might seem obvious that if we want to know whether an individual has an item in memory, we simply need to ask for its retrieval. In fact, that is only one of several ways of measuring memory. Recognition and relearning provide two additional measures. Interestingly, each of these has a higher degree of sensitivity than pure **recall**.

Recall

Recall The retrieval of material from memory.

When subjects are asked to recall items in a memory experiment, they are simply being asked to produce a correct response from memory. Different types of experiments sometimes require different types of recall. *Free recall* is involved when subjects are simply asked to remember as much as they can; *cued recall* makes use of various cues (aids, hints) and is therefore more sensitive to what might be in the subject's memory than is free recall. For example, if I ask you to tell me what you remember of your eighth birthday, your response would initially be based on free recall. If, however, I have been able to obtain information concerning where you were living at that time, and who was present at your birthday party (assuming you had one), you might be able to recall considerably more. The fact that you can now remember what your presents were indicates that this information was in your memory—that it was, as the psychologists would put it, available but not immediately accessible.

Recognition

Recognition Literally, to cognize (understand, know) over again. Recognition is the awareness that objects or items have been experienced previously.

If I were now to ask you to name as many of the people who were in fourth grade with you as you can, your list might be very short. Now if I present you with a long list of names among which are the names of your fourth-grade classmates, you might easily recognize most of them. **Recognition** simply involves remembering after restimulation. It is considerably easier than recall, and provides a more sensitive measure of what might be in your memory.

BOX 7.3

Generative Theory

One of the results of increasing interest in information-processing aspects of memory is *generative theory*. Generative theory maintains that memory is more than a simple question of retrieval, that it involves the actual construction or *generation* of material. Bransford and his colleagues (Bransford & Franks, 1971; M. K. Johnson et al., 1973) have elaborated this theory through a series of ingenious experiments. In a typical experiment, subjects are presented, not with nonsense syllables, isolated words, or lists of terms, but with meaningful sentences. Subjects are later tested to see what they are able to recall.

In one experiment (Johnson et al., 1973), subjects were presented with a number of sentences, among which were the following:

John was trying to fix the birdhouse. He was pounding the nail when his father came out to watch him and to help him do the work.

Among the sentences later presented to the same subjects as memory tests was this one:

John was using the hammer to fix the birdhouse when his father came out to watch and to help him do the work.

Even though subjects had a choice of both sentences in the memory test, they overwhelmingly agreed that they had seen the second sentence but not the first. A plausible explanation, based on generative theory, is that what we remember frequently takes the form of meanings and concepts. In other words, we store abstract ideas (for example, the idea that a hammer was being used to fix the birdhouse, even though only a nail was mentioned but not a hammer), and later recall the abstraction and then *generate* a version of the original.

Consider how often you meet people, *recognize* them, but are then unable to remember their names. The first is a recognition task; the second requires recall. Students typically prefer multiple-choice examinations over the more subjective essay examination. In fact, multiple-choice items are usually easier than essay items when both cover the same material. The first presents a recognition task; the second, a recall task.

Relearning

A final measure of memory has not been employed as extensively, although it provides an even more sensitive measure than recognition or recall. Quite often, even when subjects find themselves unable to recall or recognize anything associated with a previous learning experience, attempts to relearn the same material prove considerably easier than they would otherwise have been. Burtt (1941) read passages of Greek to his son when the boy was between fifteen months and three years of age. As might be expected, these passages were, indeed, all Greek to him. At the age of eight, the boy showed no evidence of remembering any of these Greek passages. Burtt then had him learn various passages, some of which had been included in the original readings, and some of which were totally new. The familiar passages required 27 percent fewer trials prior to learning.

Burtt's investigation provides a classic example of how memory can be measured through **relearning**. This method, also called the *method of savings,* demonstrates that even when an individual appears to retain little, if anything, from previous experience, some influence of that experience might remain. Ebbinghaus (1885), a pioneering investigator of memory, was among the first to note and study this phenomenon. Using himself as his own subject, he attempted to memorize long lists of nonsense syllables (for example, *gar, lev, kur*). Among his many findings was that even though he might not remember a single item on a list learned in the past, he could now learn that list much more rapidly than if he had been seeing it for the first time.

Relearning A highly sensitive measure of memory in which subjects are asked to relearn material they have previously learned or been exposed to but have since forgotten. Evidence of memory is implicit in the observation that material being relearned is typically learned more easily than original material.

Why We Forget

One of the most general conclusions to be derived from studies of learning and remembering is that most of what we forget is lost very rapidly after learning, and that materials retained over a period of time are less likely to be forgotten (see Figure 7.3). In spite of this observation, however, it is also clear that we eventually forget a great deal of material that was originally retained for some time. Our old phone numbers and addresses are a case in point. So is a great deal of the information we learn in schools.

Psychologists have advanced several distinct explanations for forgetting (Figure 7.11). Each appears to have some validity.

Fading Theory

Some forgetting appears to result quite simply from the gradual deterioration of any traces that learning might have left somewhere in the brain. These are termed *memory traces;* their nature is unknown. (More about them shortly.) It is as though there is a passive type of memory decay that occurs as a function of disuse—hence the term *fading theory.* Although we do appear to forget a great deal with the passage of time, particularly if the information is not periodically recalled to mind, there is evidence that memory traces may not completely disappear. Studies of subjects under hypnotic trance suggest, but cannot prove, that there might be a great deal more in memory than we can ordinarily recall. Similarly, studies of memory that have employed recognition or relearning, rather than simple recall techniques, illustrate convincingly that availability and accessibility are not necessarily synonymous. Perhaps we never do forget, to the extent that forgetting involves a complete loss of a memory trace.

Table 7.1 compares the ways of measuring memory.

Table 7.1 Ways of Assessing Memory (Methods B, C, and D are more likely to provide evidence of memory than is Method A)

A. Free recall
What is the Greek letter that symbolizes psychology?

B. Cued recall
What is the capital of Turkey? It starts with an I.

C. Recognition
Which of the following symbolizes psychology?

D. Relearning
Go back to Chapter 2 of this book and review the discussion of impulse transmission among neurons. (Easier the second time around?)

Figure 7.11 Why we forget. This figure illustrates three types of *trace-dependent* forgetting. In each instance, forgetting is related to changes that occur in the memory trace itself.

Distortion Theory

A second explanation for forgetting can be derived from Ausubel's (1963) description of learning as involving the incorporation of new material into existing conceptual frameworks. With the passage of time, this new material changes (is *distorted*) and becomes more like things we have previously learned, eventually becoming part of existing cognitive material (hence the term *distortion theory*). When the new material can no longer be separated from previously learned material, it can be said to have been forgotten. This explains why we sometimes have difficulty recalling a specific face following the passage of time. Like many other faces that we might also have forgotten, it has become incorporated into our general notion of what faces look like, and can no longer be separated from our more general concept of faces.

Repression Theory

A very popular theory of forgetting is based on Freud's observation that individuals sometimes *repress* highly unpleasant, anxiety-provoking (traumatic) experiences. Repressed material is not lost from memory (as can sometimes be demonstrated by recalling it through hypnosis), although it is not accessible to ordinary waking memory.

Evidence of repression has not been derived in controlled experimentation but has been gathered solely from clinical observation. Since it applies only to emotion-laden material or to highly unpleasant or otherwise disturbing experiences, it is of limited value as a general explanation of forgetting.

Interference Theory

Some forgetting appears to result from the interference of previous or subsequent learning. It is relatively simple to demonstrate, for example, that if subjects are required to learn two lists of nonsense syllables in succession, recall of either list will not be as perfect as if only one list were learned. The prevalent explanations for this observation are twofold: if recall for the first list is found to be impaired, investigators assume that learning the second list has interfered with recall of the first. This is termed *retroactive interference* (or retroactive inhibition): *interference* because recall has been lessened; *retroactive* because new learning has interfered with the recall of old learning. If recall for the second list is tested and found to be less correct and complete than might be expected, learning the first list is now assumed to have interfered with recall of the second. This is termed *proactive interference* (or inhibition): *proactive* because old learning has interfered with the recall of new learning. In other words, proactive interference involves an effect that moves forward in time; retroactive interference involves interference with recall of previous learning. Experimental models for the illustration of these interference effects are presented in Tables 7.2 and 7.3. Numerous studies have been based on these models or on variations of them, and have consistently shown that proactive and retroactive interference do occur. What these experiments cannot show, however, is precisely how interference works. Does learning a great deal of similar material impose too great a task on storage capacity? Does it lead to confusion among retrieval cues? Or does it hasten a decaying process? As R. C. Atkinson and Shiffrin (1968) note, the concept of interference may well be more descriptive than explanatory. The same comment can be made with respect to other theories of forgetting.

Here is one example of interference in everyday life. Frequently, beginning teachers have little difficulty in learning and remembering the names of all their students. In succeeding years, the task becomes progressively more difficult, probably because of the interfering effect of previous learning (proactive inhibition). In addition, they now find it difficult to remember the names of students in their first classes (retroactive inhibition).

As a summary of these theories of forgetting, consider again the analogy of the filing cabinet. This particular cabinet belongs to a large, long-established firm (an old person's memory). Assuming, now, that all pertinent material has been recorded (learned)

Table 7.2 Testing Retroactive Interference

	Experimental Group (A)	Control Group (B)
	1. Learn X	Learn X
Time sequence	2. Learn Y	
	3. Recall X	Recall X

Note. Lower scores of group A relative to group B indicate the extent to which learning Y has interfered with recall of X.

Table 7.3 Testing Proactive Interference

	Experimental Group (A)	Control Group (B)
	1. Learn X	
Time sequence	2. Learn Y	Learn Y
	3. Recall Y	Recall Y

Note. Lower scores of group A compared with group B indicate the extent to which learning X has interfered with recall of Y.

and filed (stored in memory), the clerk (old person) may experience various difficulties in retrieving appropriate files when they are required (forgetting). Some of the files have been in the cabinet for so long that they have simply deteriorated, paper and ink not being completely impervious to the passage of time (fading theory). In this case, it would do absolutely no good to recover the appropriate file, since it is now illegible. A number of the files might have become confused with one another, so that information that originally belonged to one file is now to be found in other general files. The clerk can no longer separate pertinent items of information, although the general files still remain intact (distortion theory).

In addition to these deteriorated and misplaced files, there are a number of entries dealing with sensitive issues. Some years ago, because of the possibility of some scandalous revelations, the clerk locked all sensitive files in a small strongbox in one of the dark corners of the bottom drawer. Not only can the clerk no longer remember what is contained in these files, but the key to the box has been lost (repression theory).

Finally, this filing cabinet contains so much material from so many different years that pertinent files are sometimes almost impossible to find. Old and new files are hopelessly confused. As a result, the unhappy clerk finds yesterday's files when searching for files several years old (retroactive interference), and sometimes finds old files when looking for new ones (proactive interference).

Forgetting, or Retrieval Failure?

There may be two different kinds of forgetting, one involving the memory trace itself, and the other dependent upon loss of cues. Forgetting involving memory traces is sometimes termed **trace-dependent**; that which relates to loss of cues, **cue-dependent** (Tulving, 1974; Tulving & Madigan, 1970). The four theoretical explanations described earlier all relate to trace-dependent forgetting. They are premised on the belief that memory traces can fade, change, be repressed, or be interfered with. However, the observation that items that are not immediately recallable are not necessarily gone may serve as evidence that remembering depends as much on appropriate cues for retrieval as it does on storage.

Improving Learning and Memory

Studies of learning and of memory have a number of very direct and useful applications. For convenience and simplicity, these applications are sometimes divided into means of learning (acquiring information, studying) and means of improving memory. In practice, it is extremely difficult to make any distinctions between learning and memory, since evidence of learning must always be based on measures identical to those employed in studies of memory.

A classic study in this area presented experimental subjects with seven strategies for improving learning (Woodrow, 1927). Subjects were taught these strategies and then given three hours to practice them. A control group was taught no rules, but was allowed to practice memorizing, also for three hours. After the three-hour period, both groups were given various memory tests. Final results showed that learning by the experimental group had improved 36 percent; learning by the control group had improved only 4.5 percent. The seven strategies, listed briefly, include some of the suggestions described in the following sections.

1. Learn by wholes.
2. Use active self-testing.
3. Use rhythm and grouping.
4. Pay attention to meaning and take advantage of picturing.
5. Be mentally alert and concentrate.
6. Use secondary association.
7. Have confidence in your ability to memorize.

Trace-dependent Explanations of forgetting that describe changes in memory traces (physical changes assumed to result from learning) as a result of the passage of time (fading theory, distortion theory), because of the nature of the traces (repression theory), or because of interference from other traces (proactive and retroactive interference).

Cue-dependent Explanation of forgetting that suggests that much that we cannot remember is not necessarily gone from memory but simply cannot be retrieved because of organization or the individual's inability to make use of cues.

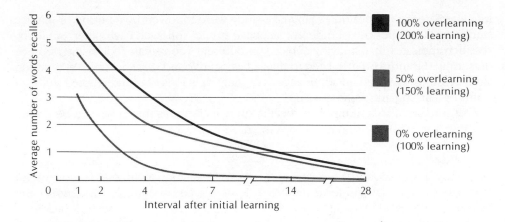

Figure 7.12 Improved retention through overlearning. Subjects were given twelve single-syllable words to learn, one word presented every two seconds. The point at which a subject can recall all the words correctly is defined as 100 percent learning, or 0 percent overlearning. Overlearning occurs when the subject is given additional learning trials after first recalling the words correctly. That is, if the list was learned in ten trials, an additional five learning trials is 50 percent overlearning; an additional ten trials is 100 percent overlearning. The subjects were asked to recall the words one, two, four, seven, fourteen, and twenty-eight days after the learning trials. As the graph shows, overlearning greatly improves long-term retention. (Based on data from Krueger, 1929.)

Reducing Interference

One of the principal causes of forgetting may well be interference. Several strategies have proven useful in reducing proactive and retroactive interference. Most of these have been highly researched. Among them is **overlearning**, the process of repeating and reciting material after it has been learned, of continuing to "learn" it. Whether this results in a different type of memory trace (more deeply engrained, perhaps) or provides a larger number of associations that might be useful for retrieval is unclear. What is intuitively and experimentally clear, however, is that material that is overlearned tends to be recalled more easily and for a longer time (see Figure 7.12).

Interference can also be reduced by making the material more meaningful. Studies employing nonsense syllables have repeatedly demonstrated that this type of material is considerably more difficult to learn in the first place than is more meaningful material, and that it is not retained for very long. In fact, nonsense syllables are typically employed in studies of short-term rather than long-term memory. A student studying for an examination should be considerably more concerned with long-term than with short-term memory.

Since interference may be induced in experimental situations by placing experiences between initial learning and recall, it follows that a reduction of interference can be brought about by paying particular attention to the activities that intervene between learning and recall. In fact, it has been found that subjects who are allowed to sleep after learning typically perform better on a test the next day than students who are asked to go about their routine activities in the interim (Figure 7.13) (Jenkins & Dallenbach, 1924).

Interference also appears to be related to similarities among learning situations as well as among the materials learned. Thus, a student would probably experience

Overlearning A learning procedure where performance or practice of what is being learned continues beyond the point where the learning can be said to have become correct or adequate. It appears to be related to the ease and correctness with which material can later be remembered.

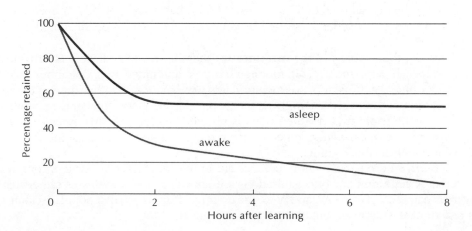

Figure 7.13 One way of reducing retroactive interference after learning is by sleep. Jenkins and Dallenbach had subjects learn a series of ten nonsense syllables immediately before going to sleep. They were awakened and tested for recall at intervals of one, two, four, or eight hours. In a second test, the same subjects learned another list of syllables, went about their routine activities, and were also tested at one of the four intervals. The subjects who slept during the interval between learning and testing had significantly better retention than those who remained awake. (Adapted from "Oblivescence during Sleep and Waking" by J. G. Jenkins and K. M. Dallenbach, *American Journal of Psychology*, 1924, *35*, 605–612. Reprinted by permission of the University of Illinois Press.)

less interference if a period of language study were followed by a period of science study than if two periods of different language studies followed each other. Similarly, research indicates that studying subjects in different rooms can reduce interference drastically (Strand, 1970). Related to this, it has been found that short breaks between study sessions have certain advantages over longer periods of uninterrupted study, in terms of learning and remembering.

There are also a number of specific study techniques that appear to be useful. Of these, the SQ3R method is perhaps the most popular.

SQ3R

Survey, question, read, recite, and review. This study technique is most useful for textbook material and lecture notes. It is simple and systematic. First, *survey* the material to be read. This involves paying particular attention to section headings, outlines, and summaries in order to obtain a general idea of what the *entire* text, chapter, or section is about. It also involves skimming sections. Intelligent and effective skimming is not a random process, but is determined by section titles and is geared toward the recognition of material related to that title. The second step involves the formulation of *questions.* Most section headings and titles can be rephrased as questions. For example, this section, "SQ3R," simply becomes "What is SQ3R?" It is useful at this point to write down the various questions. They, in turn, guide the third step, that of *reading.* Reading, although it should be thorough and complete, is undertaken specifically to answer the questions that you have formulated. Thus, instead of reading this section to find out what might be of interest in it, you read it specifically to find out what the SQ3R method is.

The fourth step is obvious. Once you have read the material, you *recite* answers for the questions formulated earlier. If you can satisfactorily answer each of these, chances are the material has become both meaningful and highly familiar, and that it will be recalled later. Questions for which your answers are uncertain indicate which sections of the material need to be reread. Finally, having recited a number of appropriate answers, you then *review* the material again, perhaps by rereading the summary, by reskimming the material, by looking at notes you might have made, or by reciting answers for your questions once more.

Simple Mnemonic Devices

There are a number of relatively simple devices, sometimes referred to as tricks or memory crutches, that can be useful aids to recalling. Most of these are, in effect, systematic retrieval cues, many of which are probably very familiar to you. Others are more elaborate coding systems that require more effort, but that can lead you to prodigious feats of memory, and perhaps eventually to a stage career as a mnemonist (professional memorizer). Do you think you could stand before a thousand people, have them name or show you twenty-five unrelated objects while your assistant writes their names in appropriate numbered spaces on a chalkboard out of your line of vision, and then recall each of these items in order, backwards, by odd or even numbers, or in any other order requested by your audience? You probably could—with some effort.

Mnemonic Pertaining to memory.

Among the simplest of the **mnemonic** (memory-related) devices are rhymes. Thirty days hath September. . . . In fourteen hundred and ninety two, Columbus sailed the ocean blue. Patterns, too, are memory aids. Five million, five hundred and fifty-one thousand, two hundred and twelve is a more difficult telephone number to remember than 555-1212; triple five, double twelve is probably easier yet. This mnemonic aid involves the use of *chunking,* a method for reducing large quantities of information into a number of smaller units.

Acronyms are simply letter cues that aid in the recall of more or less complex material. A large number of organizations are known by their acronyms rather than by their names: NATO, NOW, and WAC, for example. Roy G. Biv, that popular scientist, is red, orange, yellow, green, blue, indigo, and violet.

Acrostics are generally expressions or sentences whose first letters serve as cues for recalling specific material. "Every good boy does fine" allows simple folk to recall the notes on the lines of the treble clef; "Men very easily make jugs serve useful nocturnal purposes" recalls the planets in order from the sun.

Use of mnemonic devices such as these has sometimes been criticized on grounds that they facilitate rote learning but do very little to improve meaningful learning. Although this may well be true, there is no obvious meaning in the order of planets, in the number of days in each month, or in the colors of prismatic light. Some material would probably never be learned if its learning depended upon the discovery of its inherent meaning. Besides, if invisible crutches allowed you or me to run a mile in less than four minutes, would we be so foolish as not to use them when we wanted to run?

More Complex Mnemonics

There are some even better "crutches": the *loci system,* the *link system,* the *peg system,* and the *phonetic system* (described by Higbee, 1977). The first three are not particularly difficult; the last requires more work.

Each of these systems makes direct use of our apparently unlimited facility for recalling images (for example, recall some of the experiments mentioned earlier where individuals are shown as many as 10,000 different pictures and correctly recognize over 90 percent of them later). Essentially, these memory aids require that some form of pictorial association be made between whatever you wish to remember and some more familiar object, or simply between the items in question.

The Link System Suppose you have a shopping list consisting of the following items: butter, bread, flour, sugar, thumbtacks, and dog food. True, you could write the list down and take it to the store with you. Alternatively, you might try to memorize the list much as you might memorize several lines of poetry, reading, reciting, and testing yourself. Or you could use the *link system,* which involves the formation of mental images linking each of these items. It is surprisingly simple and effective. Picture a glob of butter smeared on a subdued slice of bread. Try to see the image as vividly as you can. It can be bizarre or very ordinary, the important point being simply that you should try to concentrate on the first image that suggests itself, since that is the one you are most likely to recall first. Now associate bread and flour. That same slice of buttered bread might be wrapped around a bag of flour; the flour might be in the sugar bowl which, fakir fashion, is resting on a bed of thumbtacks. And now you see the thumbtacks protruding from a can of dog food (Figure 7.14b).

The link system, like the other systems described shortly, does not require that you actively try to *memorize* and rehearse images. It asks only that you visualize each image as clearly as you can, even if only for a few seconds. When you are in the process of forming associations for items further along in the list, you should not attempt to recall early associations. Once the list is complete, you may well be amazed at the ease with which you can recall it in its entirety and in the correct order. The link system is therefore particularly useful for learning serial material.

One additional point should be made. It is sometimes difficult to remember the first item on the list unless an association has been made between it and some other image that is likely to serve as a cue. The grocery list, for example, might be associated with the store to which you are going. You might visualize a pound of butter lying in a grocery cart. Despite its effectiveness and usefulness, the link method does have one major weakness: if you forget one item on the list, you may not be able to recall any of the subsequent items.

The Loci System This second system overcomes the principal limitation of the link system. It does not involve forming associations between individual items on a single list, but associations between these items and specific locations (*locus* is Latin for place or location; *loci* is its plural). Imagine, for example, that you are taking a walk through

a

b

Figure 7.14 Two methods of using mental images to remember things. How could you remember a shopping list of butter, bread, flour, sugar, thumbtacks, and dog food? (**a**) The *loci method* involves putting each object in an imaginary location in a familiar environment—like your house—and then taking a mental room-by-room tour. (**b**) The *link system* involves constructing a visual image that connects all the objects to be remembered.

your house. Visualize a number of specific locations in the house; these are your loci. Now place each of the items you wish to remember in one of these locations (or perhaps two or three items in the same location, if you have a lot of material to remember). Form a strong visual association between the item and its location; then move to the next item, very much as you did for the link system. Later you can retrieve your items at will, in the order in which you learned them, if your mental walk through your house follows the same paths. And if you forget one of the items, you can still move to the next location and retrieve other items (Figure 7.14a).

Experimental evidence of the effectiveness of this technique is provided by a study conducted by Bower (1973). Subjects were instructed in the use of the loci system and were then presented verbally with five lists, each containing twenty unrelated words. One word was presented every five seconds. Subjects who had learned the method correctly recalled 72 percent of the words; others who had not been taught any method recalled an average of 28 percent of the words.

The Peg System Several mnemonic techniques allow individuals to recall items in order, although not necessarily sequentially. Employing a loci or link method, for example, a subject would have to pause for some time before being able to determine what the twentieth or twelfth item is; and a subject who responded incorrectly would almost surely be unable to identify the twenty-first or thirteenth item. The *peg system* overcomes this limitation by forming associations between numbers or letters and the

Table 7.4 The Phonetic System

Digit	Consonant Sound	Memory Aid
1	t, d, th	T and d each have one downstroke
2	n	Two downstrokes
3	m	Three downstrokes
4	r	Last sound for the word "four" in several languages
5	l	Roman numeral for 50 is L
6	j, sh, ch, soft g	Reversed script j resembles 6 ( )
7	k, q, hard c, hard g, ng	7 resembles a skeleton key ( ); k made of two 7's ( )
8	f, v, ph	Script f resembles 8 ( )
9	b, p	Both resemble 9 when inverted
0	z, s, soft c	z = zero, c = cipher

Note. From *Your Memory: How It Works and How to Improve It,* by Kenneth L. Higbee, pp. 137–138. Copyright © 1977. Reprinted by permission of Prentice-Hall, Inc., Englewood Cliffs, New Jersey.

items to be recalled. It is slightly more complicated in that it requires that subjects first learn visual images for numbers or letters. A number of relatively simple lists of appropriate images have been suggested, many of them based on rhymes. For example, 1 is a bun, 2 is a shoe, 3 is a tree, 4 is a door, and so on. Alternatively, A is hay, B is a bee, C is a sea, D is a deed. . . . Once you have learned these associations, it is relatively simple to form visual associations between items to be remembered and each of the images conjured up by the number or letter. The principal weakness of these systems is that they become very cumbersome for long lists of material, since a different association must be formed for every number or letter. In addition, use of letters does not allow the subject to recall the twenty-third or twelfth item unless the numerical positions of the letters have also been learned.

The Phonetic System Even these limitations are overcome by the *phonetic system.* The phonetic system has you associate numbers with consonants, form words from those consonants, associate the words with the numbers, and associate items to be remembered with the words which are in turn associated with the numbers. It requires more work to learn than any of the other systems, but it is without doubt the most powerful. I suggested that you could become a mnemonist. You can.

The number 1 suggests a *t* or perhaps the letter *d,* each of these having a single downstroke. The letter *n* has two downstrokes; *m* has three; they suggest the numbers 2 and 3, respectively. Indeed, all digits can be represented by one or more consonants (see Table 7.4).

Assuming, now, that vowels don't count, it is possible to write a variety of words that represent numbers. For example, TOE is number 1; it is easily visualized and can serve as a useful image with which to pair another item that you are trying to learn. Double consonants that make only one sound are a single number. Thus PUT is 91, as is PUTT. Similarly, NOT is 21, TON is 12, and so on. Having learned the number-consonant correspondences in Table 7.4, you can develop your own words to represent any number you wish. Try, initially, to establish strong visual images of words that correspond to the numbers 1 through 25. Now, with a little more practice perhaps, you are ready to face your audience of thousands. As they present items, you associate them consecutively with the images you have for numbers 1 through 25, and when they ask you to recall the items by twos, backwards, it is a simple matter to recall your visual associations for NAIL (25), NAME (23), NUT (21), TUB (19), right on down to 1. A professional mnemonist's course might not teach you much more.

Remembering Names

There are a number of courses and textbooks designed to help you improve your memory. Most of them spend some time dealing with people's names. Despite the fact that people's names are very precious and very important to them, most of us frequently fail to remember names, sometimes under the most acutely embarrassing circumstances. In most cases, it is not a failure of memory so much as a failure of learning. We do not remember a name because we never learned it.

How do you learn a name? Pay attention to it, making certain that you hear it correctly; repeat it, politely to be sure; focus on some distinctive and lasting feature of the person's face or body (facial hair, glasses, and blond wigs have a habit of disappearing or of reappearing in altered form; you can't even be too certain about eye color); create some sort of visual image associated with the name, and, in turn, associate this image with the distinctive feature you have noticed; finally, review the association and repeat the name. By the time you have finished, the person may have walked away in utter boredom. Try to be more subtle.

The Physiology of Memory

Engram The neurological something that is sometimes called a memory trace. If learning causes permanent changes in nervous tissue, the results of these changes are engrams. Engrams are hypothetical; their existence and nature have not yet been established.

Researchers have not yet been able to determine the precise physiology of *what* is stored in memory, *how* it is stored, or *what happens* to it after it is stored. However, they have agreed on a label for the effects of a memorable experience: **engram**. The engram has been looked for and speculated about for centuries, but it has not yet been found. Nevertheless, science offers us some theories about it.

Electrical?

One hypothesis is that since mental activity involves electrical activity, engrams might be things that facilitate electrical activity. If two events occur in our lives in close association, electrical activity in our brains corresponding to these events might also occur at the same time. Engrams might then facilitate activity between the two neural events so that the activation of one might lead to the activation of the other (Hebb, 1966). Not only would this explain the engram, but it would explain conditioning as well. The hypothesis is highly speculative, however, and has not been supported by research. Studies with animals that hibernate, and whose brain temperatures can be lowered to the point where all electrical activity ceases, later awaken with apparently intact memories. Similarly, individuals who undergo electroconvulsive therapy also experience a brief cessation of electrical activity in the brain, but this does not disrupt memories that were established an hour or more prior to therapy.

Chemical?

A second hypothesis is that since brain activity also involves chemical changes, the engram might be found in these chemical changes. The evidence for this hypothesis is again very tentative, and it fails to describe the nature of the engram. Studies with rats exposed to enriched environments (Krech et al., 1966), who would presumably have more memories than deprived rats, have found that these rats' brains are richer in acids and enzymes involved in neural transmission. But the differences are general rather than specific, and cannot be related directly to memory.

A third hypothesis, also chemical, has been extensively researched by means of the controversial "cannibal" experiments. This hypothesis maintains that RNA molecules may be the engram units. Like DNA, RNA is a fundamental component of all life forms and is present in all neurons. Interestingly, it increases and decreases in amount as intellectual ability increases or decreases with age. In the initial "cannibal" experiments, McConnell (1962) trained flatworms (planaria) to curl in response to light. This was accomplished through classical conditioning by pairing the presentation of light with a mild electric shock. Planaria are not easy to condition, but after many trials they do appear to curl in response to light.

After training, these unfortunate creatures were ground up and fed to untrained planaria. Amazingly, there appeared to be a transfer effect. The newly fed but naive planaria now learned to curl in response to light much more rapidly than would otherwise have been expected. In subsequent experiments, RNA molecules were extracted directly from the sacrificial planaria and injected into their untrained friends, with the same results (McConnell, 1976; Zelman et al., 1963).

Additional support of the RNA hypothesis has been derived from studies where animals are given injections of drugs that block the formation of RNA. After these injections, the animals appear to be incapable of remembering simple tasks that they earlier performed with ease (Flexner, 1967).

Unfortunately, replications of these and related experiments have not always been successful. Many that were successful were only moderately so. Those that weren't point to the many difficulties involved in this type of research. First, it is difficult to condition planaria to curl in response to light; having done so, it is hard to be sure that the curling response is occurring specifically for the light. Planaria frequently curl for a variety of other reasons. Second, the process of mincing planaria and feeding them to other planaria is extremely crude and is vaguely reminiscent of the ancient belief that eating the brains of the wise would make the eater wise as well. Third, it is difficult to extract pure RNA from an organism as small as a planarian. Nor is it simple to inject it into another, sometimes reluctant, planarian.

A final chemical hypothesis currently being investigated has obtained considerable empirical support (Dunn, 1980). Since the discovery that certain protein substances, many of these specific to the brain, undergo changes as a function of learning, investigators have hypothesized that proteins may be centrally involved in learning and remembering. After numerous investigations with animals who are trained and whose brains are then examined under electron microscopes and subjected to detailed chemical analyses, Hyden (1973; Hyden & Lange, 1972) concludes that *both* RNA and specific proteins undergo changes as a function of learning. In addition, if a serum blocking changes in identified brain proteins is injected into the brains of experimental animals, it inhibits further learning. Glassman et al. (1973) report similar findings with different proteins, as do a number of other researchers (Dunn, 1980).

Although the evidence still remains tentative, it is highly suggestive. It appears very likely that protein substances, RNA, and perhaps other chemicals as well are implicated in learning and memory. The precise nature of the changes they undergo and of the mechanisms by which they interact with learning and behavior remains unknown.

Main Points

1 Learning and memory are difficult to separate, since both involve the effects of experience, and both are usually measured by looking at performance. In one sense, measuring memory involves looking at performance after a time lapse; measuring learning involves looking at the effects of experience immediately.

2 Contemporary models of memory are primarily cognitive; they deal with hypothetical structures and metaphors rather than with observable stimuli and responses.

3 One early metaphor compared memory to a filing cabinet, where items are coded, stored, and retrieved. This metaphor has proven inadequate since it recognizes only long-term memory.

4 The three-stage model of memory speculates that we remember as if some material is not processed but is available only for a split second as a sensory impression (sensory memory); as if other material is available for a few seconds and then forgotten (short-term memory); and as if some material is rehearsed, coded, and stored for longer periods of time (long-term memory).

5 A special form of sensory memory, eidetic imagery, is a phenomenon where photograph-like recollections of visual images appear to be available to the subject for a period of time. It is more common among young children than among older children or adults.

6   Short-term memory is very similar to attention span, and seems to be limited to seven, plus or minus two, items.

7   It appears that processing at the level of short-term memory is sequential rather than parallel. That is, we have access to the seven or so items in short-term memory one after the other rather than simultaneously.

8   Material in long-term memory is relatively stable and available for a longer period of time. It is subject to considerable distortion with the passage of time, however.

9   Images appear to be far more memorable than verbal material.

10 Consolidation theory suggests that a period of time is required for material that has just been learned to become firmly established in memory, and is supported by the observation that certain traumatic events (a blow on the head, for example) frequently lead to loss of memory (retrograde amnesia) for events that have transpired just prior to the trauma.

11 Tulving distinguishes between two kinds of long-term memory: episodic, which includes all our autobiographical memories (where I was when I learned this or that); and semantic or generic, which includes all our abstract memories—our total store of stable information about the world including facts, theories, principles, languages, and so on.

12 The most important differences between short-term and long-term memory are that short-term memory is an active, ongoing process whereas long-term memory is more passive; short-term memory is highly limited in capacity whereas long-term memory appears to be virtually unlimited; and retrieval from short-term memory is generally immediate and automatic (or simply does not occur), whereas retrieval from long-term memory is frequently a longer, more deliberate process.

13 Contemporary models of memory are associationistic in that they maintain that we store information in terms of more or less complex, hierarchical arrangements of *related* information. The levels of processing model suggests that we remember material we have processed at a meaningful level longer than material we have processed at a shallow level.

14 Memory may be measured in terms of recall (bringing back from memory); recognition (identifying things that have been experienced previously); and relearning.

15 Among important theories of forgetting are fading theory (memory traces dissipate with the passage of time); distortion theory (what we learn *changes* so that we cannot separate it from other things we might have learned); repression theory (emotion-laden experiences are put out of conscious memory as a sort of self-protective measure); and interference theory (new learning interferes with the recall of previous learning in retroactive interference, or old learning interferes with the recall of new learning in proactive interference).

16 There is some evidence that much of what we apparently forget is not forgotten in the sense of being completely gone, but that we simply cannot *retrieve* it. In other words, much forgetting is cue-dependent (due to retrieval failure) rather than trace-dependent (due to the loss of memory traces).

17 Memory improvement can result from attempts to reduce interference, through the use of specific study techniques such as SQ3R (survey, question, read, review, recite), and through the use of mnemonics.

18 Some simple mnemonics include the use of rhymes, patterns, acrostics (for example, a sentence where every first letter stands for something else), and acronyms (such as NATO).

19 More complex mnemonics typically make use of powerful visual images, sometimes linked together sequentially (link system); sometimes associated with familiar locations (loci system); or sometimes associated with images that have been paired with specific numbers or words (peg and phonetic systems).

20 We have reason to believe that memory mechanisms are both chemical and electrical, although the precise physiology of memory remains unknown.

Further Readings

The following two books present more detailed information on memory-related research and models.

Seamon, J. G. *Memory and cognition: An introduction.* New York: Oxford, 1980.

Klatzky, R. L. *Human memory: Structures and processes* (2nd ed.). San Francisco: W. H. Freeman, 1980.

Research relating to the levels-of-processing model has been gathered in:

Cermak, L. S., and Craik, F. I. (Eds.). *Levels of processing in human memory.* Hillsdale, N.J.: Erlbaum, 1979.

Those interested in the reliability of eyewitness testimony are referred to either of the following excellent acounts of relevant research:

Loftus, E. F. *Eyewitness testimony.* Cambridge, Mass.: Harvard University Press, 1979.

Yarmey, A. D. *The psychology of eyewitness testimony.* New York: Free Press, 1979.

There are numerous popular books on how to improve memory skills. The following are simple and practical:

Higbee, K. L. *Your memory: How it works and how to improve it.* Englewood Cliffs, N.J.: Prentice-Hall, 1977.

Lorayne, H., and Lucas, J. *The memory book.* New York: Ballantine Books, 1974.

Thought, Language, and Creativity

"Thinking about thinking is like dreaming about dreaming," Sam said, perhaps a little truculently, when I asked him for his thoughts. "When you dream that you are dreaming, you're not really dreaming, are you?" he asked, though the question was more statement than query.

"Not so," I interjected, sensing a rare gap in his thoughts and seeking at once to fill it with some brilliance. "Not so. You cannot think about thinking without thinking."

"Thinking what?" he asked, disarmingly it seemed, and I was instantly on guard.

"What? . . . Thinking what, what? I mean . . . what *do* you mean?"

"What is it that you are thinking when you think about thinking?" he asked, continuing before I could answer, "because whatever you think about thinking while you are thinking should be a thought relevant to the process of thinking. Don't you see?"

"I think . . ."

"Therefore you are!" He finished my thought before I could think it. Thinking myself rather confused, I asked to be excused, not thoughtlessly but politely, as is my custom.

"Excuse me, please, I think I must go now."

"Think what you will. They're your thoughts," he replied quickly, "but let me leave you with one thought. De Bono (1976) informs us that God does not need to think. Thinking is for those who do not have adequate information."

Presumably she has information that is at least adequate.

The Stuff of Thinking

Is thinking limited to the acquisition of information for those of us, less than gods, whose information is inadequate? Or does it, as Greene (1975) suggests, include daydreams, fantasies, the elaboration of new and of old wishes, organizing, speculating, imagining, problem solving, planning, decision making, and self-talk? And if it does, what do these activities have in common that might suggest a definition of thinking? Obviously, they are all symbolic rather than actual activities; they are most often conscious though not always deliberate, and their principal medium is usually, though not necessarily, language. Thought, then, is symbolic mental activity that is usually both verbal and conscious, although it can be nonverbal and unconscious. It permeates every aspect of our waking existence, is absolutely central to our notions of who we are and what the world is; it is, in effect, one of the principal hallmarks of being human. Not that nonhuman animals cannot think; but there is no evidence that they can do so with nearly the elaboration, the precision, the richness, and the productivity that is ours. Can they use language in thought? We examine this question later in this chapter.

Psychology has traditionally paid lip service to the richness of thought and to its incalculably important contribution to human life. But the richness of thought and its role in life are subjects more fit for gods and poets than for scientists. Thinking is, as a whole, too complex, too convoluted and involved, too inaccessible, and too private, to expose itself quietly to science's microscopes and gauges. Accordingly, only a few aspects of thought processes have been examined in detail, and psychological discussions of thinking are inevitably limited largely to just these aspects. Chief among them are discussions of theoretical explanations of thinking, problem solving, and concept formation. Each of these is discussed in following sections of this chapter. It should be kept in mind, however, that these topics do not fully represent what thinking is. It is also worth noting that the raw material of thought processes is derived from past experiences, and that thinking and memory cannot, therefore, be neatly separated—except in textbooks of psychology. Similarly, we can discuss language and thought in entirely different sections even though these are intimately related in our day-to-day affairs (see Figure 8.1).

Thinking: A Cognitive Topic

Thinking has not always been a fashionable term in Western psychologies. Indeed, it was largely avoided by the behaviorists, whose theoretical preoccupations were with the objective and observable aspects of human behavior. Thinking is not directly observable, although much of our behavior is necessarily a manifestation of thought processes. Behavior alone is observable. Behaviorists fervently hoped, and sometimes firmly believed, that a complete explanation of human behavior could be arrived at simply by looking at behavior and its relationships to external events; that whatever transpires in the nervous system would not be directly relevant to that explanation. However, as Chapter 6 indicated, the simple behavioristic explanations of learning have proven inadequate for the conceptual processes involved in human behavior.

Consider, for example, a simple arithmetic problem: $2 + 5 = 7$. It is possible, as some behaviorists would insist, that the correct response has been paired so frequently with the given stimulus that it has been learned through some form of conditioning by association or, alternatively, that the correct response has been reinforced

Figure 8.1 Thinking cannot easily be separated from language and memory.

sufficiently frequently that it has been learned. Perhaps the same could be said of a problem such as 49 ÷ 7. But the conditioning explanations begin to fall apart when more complex problems are considered, even though their answers might all be identical: 1,533 ÷ 219; −1,477 + 1,484; 2,978 −2,971; 2,177 ÷ 311. It is inconceivable that each of these problems will have been presented sufficiently frequently with the correct response for the solution to have been learned through association or reinforcement. What has been learned, in effect, is not a single solution to a variety of problems, but an integrated set of logical and mathematical rules that govern thinking.

Mathematics presents one clear example of the inadequacy of simplistic explanations of thought processes; verbal behavior presents yet another. There is no adequate behavioristic explanation for the learning of grammar or for the ability each of us has to generate sentences and paragraphs that have never been generated before. What we have learned clearly goes far beyond the simple words and sentences that a child might be expected to learn through reinforcement; we have learned rules for decoding meanings and for generating novel combinations of words that also have intended meanings.

Cognitive theories are explicitly concerned with thought processes. Piaget's theories, described in Chapter 11, attempt to describe the evolution of thought processes in the child's development; Bruner's theory, described later in this chapter in connection with the attainment of concepts, attempts to describe strategies that we sometimes use in classifying events; and **artificial intelligence** models present a novel attempt to duplicate human thought processes in machines.

Artificial Intelligence

Artificial intelligence is, in the words of Bertram Raphael (1976), that branch of computer science that attempts to make computers smarter. There are a number of reasons why we might want to make a computer smarter, quite apart from the fact that we might feel particularly intelligent if we were successful in making a truly smart computer. To begin with, at a very practical level, a smart computer ought to be able to do a whole variety of things for us, freeing us to do all manner of other things for ourselves. The second reason why we might want to make a smarter computer is far more relevant for our purposes: not only might making such a computer clarify many of the questions we now have about our own intellectual processes, but also the computer itself, once it had been made, might tell us new things about ourselves. This second possibility motivates many of those who work in artificial intelligence.

As the term implies, *artificial* intelligence deals with an intelligence that we are not quite ready to admit might be real. And sometimes we continue to labor under a number of myths concerning computers. The first of these maintains that computers are nothing more than computational machines. In reality, the functioning of a sophisticated modern computer involves countless operations that are not strictly computational: storing in memory, organizing and sorting, retrieving, sensing and responding to the environment, and so on (see, for example, Boden, 1977).

The second myth is that a computer is no more than a docile slave, subservient to its operator, or at least to its programmer. While it is true that computers do what they are programmed to do, it is not true that they are always programmed so that their activities will be completely predictable. There are now chess computers that can in fact sometimes beat their programmers, a feat that would have been virtually impossible a mere decade ago. In 1968 David Levy, an international chess master, wagered £1250 (approximately $2500 at the time), that a computer could not be programmed to beat him at chess within the next ten years (interview with David Levy, *Omni,* 1979). Ten years later, David Levy played a computer in Toronto. "The eyes of the world will be on the match as a sort of struggle between man and machine," he

Artificial intelligence A branch of computer science concerned with the use of machine or computer models either to simulate human behavior or as metaphors for some aspects of human cognitive processes.

said before the match. "This will inevitably make me a little shaky, but of course it will not affect my opponent." Perhaps Levy was a little shaky. He drew one game, and actually lost one. True, he won the other three, thus emerging the victor and retaining his money. But he emerged far less confident than he had been prior to the contest. Indeed, he is convinced that within the next few years, the world chess champion may well be a computer. And Levy, together with *Omni* magazine, is offering a prize of $5000 to the programmers of the first computer to win a match against him.

Clearly, the day of the clever computer is here; now researchers can face the fundamental challenge of using *artificial* intelligence to achieve insight into *natural* intelligence. As we noted, there are two broad approaches to this challenge. One is to program the computer to generate models or metaphors of human functioning; the second is to look at how the computer imitates the functioning of the mind. Hence the relevance of our next question: Can machines think?

Can Machines Think?

The question is not entirely frivolous. If a thinking machine could be designed, it might reveal a great deal about thinking. Indeed, the very construction of such a machine would presuppose considerable knowledge about thinking (Figure 8.2).

The classic answer for this question was provided by the late A. M. Turing (1950), who rephrased the question as "Can machines imitate?" Presumably, if a machine can imitate a process that would require humans to think, it too can think. In an amusing discussion of the "imitation game," Turing describes a situation where a man (*A*) and a woman (*B*) are placed alone in a room. An interrogator (*C*) in another room must discover whether *A* is a man (*X*) or a woman (*Y*). That is, the interrogator must be able to say "*A* is *X* and *B* is *Y*" or, alternatively, "*A* is *Y* and *B* is *X*." To discover who *A* and *B* are, the interrogator is allowed to ask questions, to which *A* and *B* type their responses. The object of the game for *A* is to impede the interrogator; *B*, on the other hand, attempts to be helpful. But *C* does not know this. *A* might, for example, answer as though he were a woman, in which case *B* might point out that *A* is lying. Obviously, *A* can now lie too, and claim that *B* is lying.

Turing's next question is the crucial one: "What will happen when a machine takes the place of *A* in this game?" His answer is that it will soon be possible to construct a machine that will outwit the interrogator at least 70 percent of the time. Clearly, the machine can imitate the human; ipso facto, it can think!

Or can it? Gunderson (1964) presents a sequel to the imitation game, the "toe-stepping game." In this situation *A* and *B* are again placed in a room. At the bottom of one wall in this room is an aperture large enough for *C*, in an adjoining room, to insert one foot. Again, *C* is required to determine which of *A* and *B* is a woman, and which a man. This *C* must determine by placing a foot in the aperture and allowing *A* and *B* to step on it, each in turn. *A*'s task is again to try and stump *C*; *B*'s is to help *C*. "Now what would happen," asks Gunderson, "if a machine were to take *A*'s place?" This machine would simply need to be a box filled with rocks of various sizes and shapes—a "rock box" to be precise. These would be released on *C*'s foot one after the other. Gunderson has little doubt that it will soon be possible to construct such a machine, and that it will confuse the interrogator at least 70 percent of the time.

The point of Gunderson's parody is simply that to demonstrate that a machine can imitate is not to demonstrate that it can think—unless, of course, a box filled with rocks is capable of rational thought. But the rock box does not need to think in order to accomplish its purpose. He concludes: "In the end the steam drill outlasted John Henry as a digger of railway tunnels, but that didn't prove the machine had muscles; it proved that muscles were not needed for digging railway tunnels" (p. 71).

So. What have Gunderson and Turing established? Both have shown that a machine might be as effective as a human in a rather silly attempt at deception, a fact which

Figure 8.2 Can machines think?

does not demonstrate that a machine can (or cannot) think, but which does show that thinking is not necessary for such trivial exercises. And herein lies the usefulness of the Gunderson and Turing games. They emphasize that it might be possible to imitate something rather impressively, but to employ functions and processes that are totally unlike those employed by whatever is being imitated. Thus, a computer that is programmed to play chess as well as a chess master does not *need* to employ the same cognitive processes in its decision-making sequences. Nor is it likely to feel elation when it wins or dejection when it loses.

We might learn a great deal from the computer, but we have to be careful that what we learn is not simply what we assumed to be true beforehand, and what we therefore made inevitable through our programming. And we also have to be careful to distinguish between using computers to imitate human functioning, and using computers (or, more often, computer programs) simply as analogies for human functioning. Computers do not have to be able to "think" for us to fruitfully compare our functioning to theirs. We will look at some of these useful analogies next.

Some Computer and Machine Analogies

Computers and humans are analogous in many respects. The electronic circuitry of advanced computers has sometimes been compared to the neurological make-up and functioning of humans (G. A. Miller et al., 1960); computer programs to human capacities for information processing (Hovland, 1960; Hovland & Hunt, 1960). In addition, a number of attempts have been made to design computer programs that would function in ways analogous to the ways in which we imagine ourselves to function.

Problem-Solving Analogies

For instance, how we solve problems can be illuminated by writing computer programs that solve problems like we do. Best-known among attempts to do this are the efforts of Newell, Shaw, and Simon (1957, 1958; Newell & Simon, 1956, 1972). It is important to note that in the theories of Newell et al., computers are not analogous to human functioning; the *programs* are analogous. One program developed by Newell et al. used axioms and mathematical processes to discover proofs for theorems. When it was presented with fifty-two theorems, it was able to discover proofs for thirty-eight, many in less than one minute. Longer proofs took more time. Advanced theorems, presented in isolation so that the computer could not make use of earlier proofs, were often impossible for the program to prove. A later program incorporates problem-solving strategies that might be employed in a variety of fields, including mathematics and chess.

What do computer programs like these tell us about human problem solving? Basically, they provide evidence that our problem-solving strategies may be hierarchically arranged, so that the use of successive strategies is more or less predictable; that human problem-solving behavior relies heavily on previous experience and knowledge; and that in the course of solving some problems, we acquire information that may be essential for the solution of other problems. The analogy is also useful for other reasons. It has highlighted a number of factors in problem solving that we have sometimes casually dismissed. Perhaps the most central of these factors is whether we use **deterministic** or **stochastic models**. A deterministic model for problem solving is one in which the outcome of the operation, which is selected from among a number of alternatives, can be predicted accurately, given complete knowledge of the problem. A stochastic model, however, allows for the effect of random variables so that the outcome of an operation can only be predicted within some error range. Would an accurate model of human behavior be deterministic if we had sufficient information about humans and how they function, and complete information about a specific individual? Or must it necessarily be stochastic, with sometimes frustratingly large probabilities of error in prediction?

A second factor in problem solving is whether we use **algorithms** or **heuristics**. A problem is solved algorithmically when all possible alternatives are considered; it is solved heuristically when certain strategies are employed to maximize the probability of being correct, and to minimize the time and effort involved in the solution. It is theoretically possible, for example, to program a computer to play chess so that it will never lose. Such a program would have to be algorithmic; that is, it would have to consider all possible moves, all of their possible implications, all possible countermoves given all possible opponent moves, and so on, a task which is practically impossible given the astronomical number of possibilities presented by the game (approximately 10^{120}). The numerous chess programs that have been developed are heuristic; they respond not in terms of algorithms but in terms of strategies for the attainment of subgoals (such as protect the king, control the center). Today, they are still no match for the great chess masters.

Feedback Analogies

Another aspect of our functioning that can be likened to a computer's is that we regulate our thought processes based on **feedback** we receive from the environment. Feedback in a machine generally refers to information concerning whether the machine is performing or not performing a specific operation. Ordinary human functioning is governed by feedback from the perceptual systems, which provide messages concerning movement, position, pain, and other sensations. The principles involved in the control of functioning by feedback are of central importance in analogies drawn between the operation of machines and human functioning. The application of feedback theory to the study of thinking is termed **cybernetics** (Weiner, 1948).

Deterministic models Problem-solving models that assume that, given complete, accurate, and adequate information concerning all variables involved in an operation, it is possible to predict the outcome of the operation precisely.

Stochastic models Probabilistic models, where the outcome cannot be determined precisely beforehand but can be predicted with increasing accuracy as the number of operations increases. The outcome of flipping coins is stochastic.

Algorithms A problem-solving procedure where all possible alternatives are systematically considered.

Heuristics A problem-solving procedure where strategies are employed to maximize the probability of being correct as well as to minimize the time and effort involved in the solution.

Feedback Information that an organism or a machine receives about its functioning.

Cybernetics Theoretical approach that sees thinking as self-regulating, based on feedback.

Cybernetic theories consider three components of human behavior: input, processing, and output. They are essentially *machine* models of human behavior, and perhaps best understood by reference to a common analogy between an ordinary household heater that is thermostatically controlled and the cybernetic components of human functioning. The heater itself is a processor; it changes cool air into warmer air. Its thermostat is both a sensor and a regulator. It is sensitive to the heater's functioning to the extent that it can detect changes in surrounding air temperature. The warmer air is the heater's output. Its input is the information it derives from the thermostat. Put another way, the heater receives feedback about its functioning via the thermostat. All feedback systems are capable of two types of information: negative or positive. *Negative feedback* is exemplified when the surrounding temperature has reached the level at which the thermostat has been set. The feedback the heater now receives indicates that functioning should cease. *Positive feedback,* by contrast, indicates that functioning should continue. As long as the heater is functioning, it is receiving positive feedback. Once the feedback becomes negative, functioning ceases. A system like this involves continuous testing of the environment, and continuous regulation of functioning as a result of feedback obtained from this testing. We are similar to self-regulated machines like this heater in the sense that our thought processes are governed by information we obtain about them (see Figure 8.3).

Let me elaborate on how human functioning based on feedback resembles the functioning of self-regulating machines. Elsewhere I (Lefrancois, 1982) describe a certain obese, bearded, and fastidious individual who, having dined regally on a turkey, found with the tip of his tongue a small piece of meat lodged next to his left eyetooth. He extracted a well-used gold toothpick from a small gold toothpick case, guided the toothpick to the offending meat, and flicked at it decisively. This done, he again passed his tongue gently over his teeth, discovering that the morsel remained firmly entrenched. Again he reached toward it with his toothpick, attempting to weaken its hold; and again he checked the results with his tongue, finding once more than the remnant remained. And again he activated the toothpick; once more the tongue. A sigh of contentment. *Fait accompli.* "Now that," I concluded, "is a marvelous example of a TOTE sequence" (p. 221).

It may not be marvelous, but it does illustrate a TOTE unit. The letters are an acronym for the words *test, operate, test, exit.* Essentially, these represent the functioning of self-regulated machines. In this case, they also represent a model for human functioning described by G. A. Miller, Galanter, and Pribram (1960). Basically the model is simple. Behavior is initiated by a *test* designed to determine whether environmental conditions match some standard. In the preceding illustration, passing the tongue over the teeth was the test; it served to determine whether these were clean. The *operation* is a behavior initiated as a result of positive feedback and designed to bring about a match between observed and desired conditions. After this operation (tooth-picking), a second *test* is employed. In the illustration, feedback was again positive, so that the operation had to be repeated. Finally, after a test resulting in negative feedback, operation ceases (*exit*). The toothpick is returned to its case. A TOTE sequence is represented in Figure 8.4.

In a further attempt to clarify the nature of human thinking and behavior, Miller et al. (1960) postulate that operations (behavior or thought) are governed by what they term *plans,* a plan being "any hierarchical process in the organism that can control the order in which a sequence of operations is to be performed" (p. 16). At the highest level, our plans are *molar;* these are the plans that govern large segments of behavior. At a lower level, plans become more *molecular.* It is in this sense that plans can be considered hierarchical. A molar plan can also be considered as a strategy for some major segment of behavior; a molecular plan is more similar to a simple tactic. For example, my decision to write you this increasingly long letter comprises the activation of a molar plan; the molar plan, in turn, gave rise to a large number of more molecular plans governing specific activities in which I must engage if I am ever to present you with my final signature.

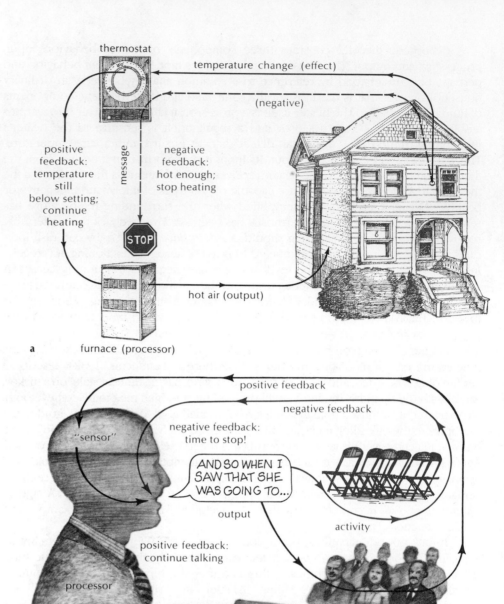

Figure 8.3 Do humans think like machines? (**a**) A classic depiction of feedback: how a thermostat regulates temperature. (**b**) An example of human self-regulation based on feedback.

A second concept that plays a fundamental role in this model of human behavior and thought is that of *images*. These are defined by Miller et al. as "all the accumulated organized knowledge that the organism has about itself and its world" (p. 17). Images are our world views; they are all that we know and think, including our plans for behavior (Figure 8.5). It is important to note that plans are not limited to overt behavior: we also have plans for acquiring information, for storing it, for processing it, and so on.

You might, by now, have noticed that this presentation of an abstract cybernetic model does not provide an explanation of human behavior and thought. It is, in effect, simply a model—a model premised on the notion that we behave and think *as though* we are responsive to feedback, and *as though* we had hierarchical arrangements of alternative means of behaving and thinking.

Robots

A robot is simply a machine that performs some function or a series of functions that might otherwise be performed by a human. There are thousands of robots in

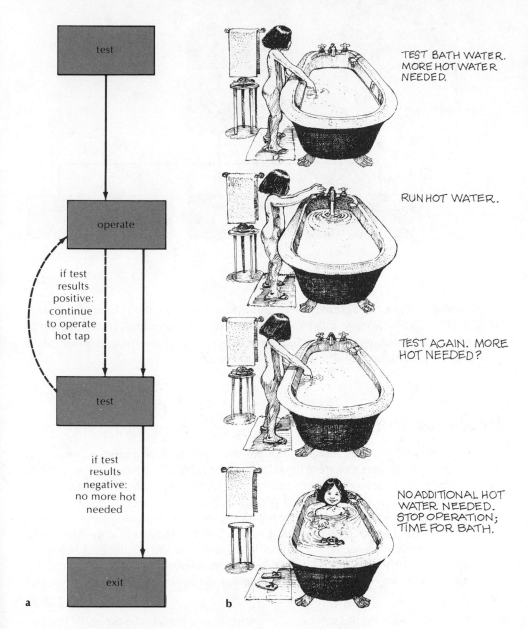

Figure 8.4 A simple depiction of stages in the TOTE sequence, a cybernetic model of human functioning. Notice the broken-line feedback loop. If test results are positive at this stage, the operate-test stage can be repeated indefinitely (or at least until the bath overflows) until feedback is negative. (Based on G. A. Miller, Galanter, and Pribram, 1960.)

countless factories throughout the world. They screw nuts, weld, sew, paint, solder, and mold. One suffered a breakdown in a Japanese automobile factory and stabbed a human worker, killing him. It was a mechanical and not a nervous breakdown. While these robots might be of great practical value, they are of limited interest to students of artificial intelligence.

Of more interest are the few robots that have been deliberately designed to appear less mechanical—more intelligent. How do we make a robot *seem* more intelligent? Usually by giving it some *purpose*. Among the first of the "purposive" robots was a small creature developed at Johns Hopkins University in the early 1960s. This little robot, affectionately named the Hopkins Beast, consisted of a peculiar arrangement of sonar, electrical circuits, photocells, wheels, and lenses. It moved up and down the hallways in its building at Johns Hopkins, keeping itself equidistant from either wall, never hitting them and hurting itself. And always, it looked for electrical outlets. That was its *purpose*. And when it found one, it would hungrily reach out its little "hand," plug it in, and feed. Full, it would move on again, looking, always looking.

The Johns Hopkins Beast was not, of course, the ultimate robot. The ultimate

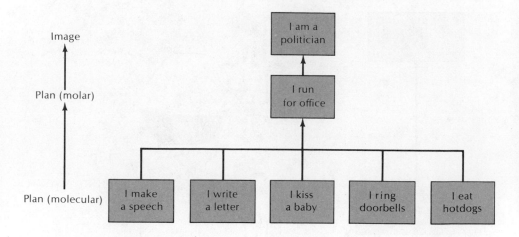

Figure 8.5 Images, plans, and behavior. In G. A. Miller, Galanter, and Pribram's (1960) conception, operations or behaviors are organized hierarchically. At the lowest (*molecular*) level, a would-be politician makes a speech (or a would-be psychology student reads Chapter 8 of this text) because of a higher-level, or *molar,* plan: the politician wants to win an election (or the student wants to pass a test). The hierarchy doesn't stop there. Our plans and behaviors, both large and small, are governed by *images* we have of ourselves and the world. Computers can be programmed to operate according to a hierarchy of plans, but it is questionable how far the cybernetic analogy can be stretched to include self-imagery.

robot would be capable of far more humanlike functions. Like the robots of *Star Wars* or of *2001: A Space Odyssey,* this robot would have a "personality." It would have its own whims, its moments of unpredictable behavior. But, in the main, it would solve problems in predictable fashion. And always correctly.

Problem Solving

Problem An incomplete situation; a situation where certain elements are known but others must be found, discovered, provided, implemented, begged, borrowed, or stolen. A puzzle differs from a problem in that puzzles initially provide few of the elements that are required for a solution, although they might provide some indication of the methods that might be employed.

One of the clearest manifestations of thought processes is in **problem** solving. This does not mean, of course, that thinking is limited to problem solving; as it was defined earlier, it includes a variety of other functions. Problem solving, however, is easier to investigate than are most other mental processes, principally because problems can be defined in terms of objectives (their solution), and can frequently be analyzed in terms of the mental operations required to attain these objectives (Figure 8.6). There are, however, many different types of problems, and a variety of different behaviors involved in solving them. Greene (1975) provides one useful classification of problems based on the amount of old and new thinking that is required of the problem solver (p. 18):

Level 1: Solver already knows solution (for example, that Paris is the capital of France)

Level 2: Solver already knows the rules for obtaining solution (for example, formula for doing long division)

Level 3: Solver learns correct responses during task (for example, finding the way through a maze)

Level 4: Solver has to select and evaluate operations for obtaining a solution (for example, doing a crossword puzzle)

Level 5: Solver has to reformulate problem or produce some unusual method of solution (for example, inventing a new kind of windshield wiper)

Level 6: Solver has to realize that a problem exists at all (for example, Newton realizing that the falling apple needed explanation)

Clearly, any given problem may be at a number of levels, depending on whether the learner knows its solution, the means of obtaining that solution, and so on. Consider, for example, the problem of determining the area of the geometric shape presented in Figure 8.7. One learner may recall from past experience that the correct answer is 2 (level 1); a second might know the rule expressed by the formula, area

Figure 8.6 Problem solving is among the most highly researched of thinking processes. This is because problems can often be analyzed in terms of the sequential processes involved in their solution.

= length × width (level 2); yet a third might revisualize the form and eventually arrive at a correct solution (level 5).

It might also be noted that a majority of the exercises, activities, and examinations presented to children by formal education require lower-level problem-solving skills. These frequently do not require the learner to go beyond simple recall; or, at best, they require the learner to apply previously learned rules in well-defined situations. These are the types of skills that are involved in what Guilford (1967) terms **convergent thinking**: the type of thinking that leads to a single correct solution. It is this type of thinking that is most crucial in school achievement as well as on measures of intelligence (see Chapter 14). Higher-level problems, however, frequently require **divergent thinking**: a type of thinking that does not immediately and necessarily lead to a single correct solution. Divergent thinking and creativity are frequently equated in psychological literature for precisely this reason. To the extent that creative thinking requires the generation of a variety of possible solutions, it involves divergent thinking. More about creativity shortly. First, we focus on various experiments that have examined problem solving.

Convergent thinking To *converge* is to come together. Hence, convergent thinking is a type of thinking that leads to a single solution or thought. Problems that have a single correct solution generally require convergent thinking.

Divergent thinking To diverge is to go in different directions, to come apart. Hence, divergent thinking involves the production of a variety of thoughts or solutions.

Strategies and Hypotheses

The first two levels of problems are ordinarily not considered in the literature on problem solving, since they involve no more than the recall of previous solutions or the application of previous learned rules. For this reason, they are perhaps more closely related to memory than to thinking.

Level 3 problems, requiring the learning of correct responses during the task, have also been extensively investigated in studies of memory. Typical experiments at this level require subjects to learn series of words or digits (serial learning), or associations between words, some of them frequently nonsense syllables (paired associate learning). Other experiments have been employed to demonstrate that, even at this

Problem: What is the area of the shape?

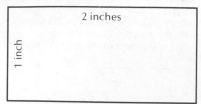

Level 1: Subject recalls that a rectangle of these dimensions is 2 square inches in area.

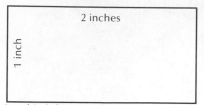

Level 2: Subject applies known formula: area = length × width. Answer is 2 square inches.

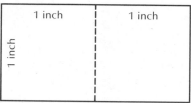

Level 3: A new approach: Learner may not remember either the rectangle's area or the formula, but may recall the area of a 1-inch square. Learner obtains the answer by dividing the rectangle into 2 equal halves, then adding their known areas.

Figure 8.7 Three levels of problem solving.

Strategy   A plan of attack; an orderly, sequential, and purposeful approach to the solution of problems or to the execution of behavior. Strategies typically have heuristic value in that they facilitate the solution of problems while at the same time reducing the amount of energy and effort required for solution.

Rote   A form of memorization requiring neither understanding nor comprehension, but the simple reproduction of the material to be learned. Rote learning is generally accomplished through repetition.

Concept   A meaning, an idea, a categorization, or a property that relates two or more objects or events.

level, more than simple memory may be involved. Numerous studies of memory (see Chapter 7) have shown, for example, that a subject who is able to develop and employ a **strategy** for grouping items, for relating them, or for developing associated visual imagery is better able to recall items correctly.

One of the classic problems that illustrates the usefulness of strategy is Katona's (1940). He presented subjects with the following number: 581215192226. Some subjects learned simply by **rote**; others were told to look for patterns in the sequence of digits. If sufficient time was allowed, all subjects generally succeeded in learning the entire digit. However, those who had discovered a simple rule could recall the entire digit and could, in fact, continue to generate it indefinitely, much longer than the rote memorizers. They only needed to remember that the first digit was 5, and that the entire number resulted from alternately adding 3 and 4 to preceding numbers.

Rats, too, are capable of developing strategies. In an intriguing investigation of problem solving in rats, Krech (1932) found that rats behave as though they are capable of generating rules and hypotheses. The maze arrangement employed in these studies is shown in Figure 8.8. Note that the barriers can be swung over so as to open either alternative at each of the choice points. In a maze of this sort, it is relatively simple for a rat to learn a simple alternating route (for example, left, right, left, right), its reverse, or more complicated routes (left, left, right, right, and all other possible combinations). Alternatively, instead of learning a route based on the direction of each turn, the rat might learn a route based on whether the passage is lighted or dark. Thus, it might learn to enter only passages where the light is on or off, or to enter light and dark passages in turn. In short, the rat does not merely learn a route, but appears to learn certain rules for finding that route. Impressive as this might be, even more impressive is the finding that, if the experimenter alters the light-dark and right-left variables on every trial so that the rat cannot readily discover a correct rule, it behaves as though it were testing hypotheses and systematically eliminating them. It might begin, for example, by trying all left passages first, moving then to all right passages, then perhaps to all those that are lighted, all that are dark, and so on.

The relevance of this type of research for the understanding of human behavior is twofold. First, it highlights the importance of formulating and testing hypotheses; second, it suggests that if animals such as rats are capable of cognitive approaches to problems, the intellectual gap between us and animals may be somewhat narrower than we have assumed.

Concept Attainment

Level 4 problems offer some intriguing possibilities for experimentation. These are problems where the solver has to select and evaluate alternative ways of reaching a solution. Bruner et al. (1956) have suggested that we solve this type of problem through concept attainment. A **concept** is simply a representation of related things or events. As Bruner puts it, it is a means of **categorizing** the world and of relating to it. All our nouns, for example, represent concepts. *Book* is a concept that includes a large number of items related by virtue of the fact that they are printed, bound, and expensive; *Caligula* is a concept that includes large, turkey-colored, turkey-sounding, highly edible, ignoble birds. It is the Latin word for turkey.

According to this cognitive position, all of learning may be viewed as involving the acquisition of concepts. Not only are these used to organize information, but they also allow us to make predictions about likely events, and to respond to the world. We identify objects and events only when we can place them in categories (concepts) of other related objects or events; our categories include our knowledge of how we should respond to these objects. For example, I recognize an ordinary piece of white chalk because I have a category (concept) that says, among other things: "Short, stick-like, whitish, chalky objects found on chalkboard ledges are chalks." This category also says, at least implicitly, that chalk is useful for making marks on chalkboards, but that it is less useful for eating. Indeed, my category *chalk* is related to a wide number of other categories, as is depicted in Figure 8.9. All knowledge is thus organized in

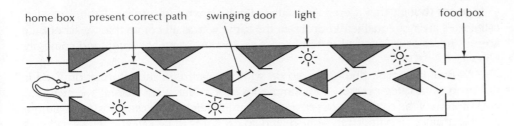

home box   present correct path   swinging door   light   food box

hierarchical **coding systems**. These are hierarchical in the sense that lower-level categories are highly specific (chalk, for example), whereas successively higher-level categories become progressively more generic (general, inclusive). Thus, they include an ever-widening array of specifics (things with which to write, for example). And it is precisely because my *chalk* category is not included in my coding system of *things to eat* that I know it might be inappropriate to eat a piece even though I might be hungry.

Bruner draws a distinction between the formation of concepts and their attainment. Individuals may be said to *form* concepts when they arrive at the notion that some things belong together and others do not. I have formed a concept, for example, when I realize that certain fungus growths are edible and others are not. *Attaining* a concept is slightly more difficult; it involves learning the characteristics (called *attributes* by Bruner) of those objects that belong to the concept. Thus, I will not have attained a concept of edible mushrooms until I have learned the important characteristics of those mushrooms that are edible and of those that are not.

Early research on concepts looked for strategies subjects might use in attaining concepts. Unfortunately, the various strategies identified in this type of research have not always related directly to ordinary human behavior (see Box 8.1). Accordingly, recent research in this area has focused less on identifying strategies problem solvers use, and more on analyzing categories in terms of their characteristics, their relationships one to the other, and some features of how they are developed by problem solvers (Mervis and Rosch, 1981).

Contrary to what might have been expected, research suggests that children do not typically begin by learning the most specific concepts, and progress from there to the most generic; nor do they begin with the most generic. Instead, they begin by learning concepts of intermediate generality. Thus, a child learns the general concept "cat" before learning related specific concepts such as "Angora," "Siamese," or "alley." The more generic concepts, cat family or mammal, are learned much later, if ever.

A second finding from recent research on categorization is that items problem solvers include in the same category are not always equal, even though we may react

Figure 8.8 Level 3 learning. Krech (1932) tested rats' abilities to learn while solving a problem, using a maze in which swinging doors and lights could be arranged in varying patterns, precluding the possibility that the rat would memorize the solution. Rats reacted by attacking the problem systematically, as if testing hypotheses. For instance, a rat would go to all the right-hand doors first, then all the left-hand ones; or to all the dark doors before all the lighted ones. (From "The Genesis of Hypotheses in Rats" by D. Krech, *Publications in Psychology,* 1932, 6, 45–64. Reprinted by permission of the University of California Press.)

Coding system A hierarchical arrangement of related categories. Since categories are concepts, coding systems are arrangements of concepts in terms of their generality. In a coding system, the most inclusive concept is at the apex of the system, with progressively more specific concepts falling lower in the hierarchy.

Categorizing A process described by Bruner which involves placing objects or events into groups (categories) on the basis of their common characteristics. To categorize is to form concepts.

Objects to Write With

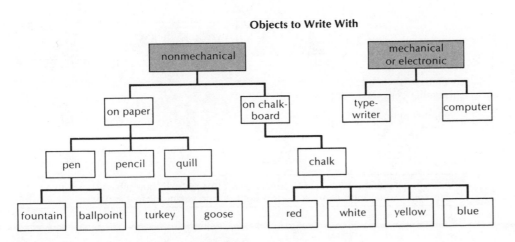

Figure 8.9 A tree diagram illustrating a partial coding system. Lower-level categories are highly specific; higher-level categories become progressively more generic.

to them as though they were. Thus, all individuals who fit into our "thin" or "fat" categories are not equally thin or fat, in the same way as all colors that we label blue are not necessarily identical in terms of wave length. Some are fatter, and some are bluer.

A final important finding has to do with the nature of the information used in the process of categorization. At a simple level, it might seem that all we need is a clear notion of the characteristics required for membership in a category (for example, an object must be cylindrical, whitish, and so on if it is to be categorized as a chalk). After this, a simple sensory process would allow us to match an object with a category.

BOX 8.1

Concept Attainment Strategies

If concept attainment is important in solving Level 4 problems, how exactly do we attain concepts? Systematic investigations of strategies used in concept attainment have been conducted by Bruner and his associates, and replicated by a number of other investigators (for example, Cole et al., 1971). Material for the experiments consists of eighty-one separate cards representing all possible variations of four attributes: number of figures, shape of figures, color of figures, and number of borders. There are three different values possible for each of these attributes. In a typical experiment, subjects are presented with a single card and told that it is an example of a concept. They are then allowed to select other cards, and are told whether these new cards are also examples of the same concept. The object is simply to discover what the concept is. The experimenter's task is to discover whether subjects employ identifiable strategies in the attainment of these concepts, and then to attempt to determine whether strategies that are employed in the laboratory might have some relevance for the attainment of concepts in everyday life.

Following these experiments Bruner et al. (1956) have identified four decision sequences that subjects might employ in concept attainment.

Simultaneous Scanning The first strategy, *simultaneous scanning*, involves generating all possible correct combinations, and testing each of these in turn. This approach requires tremendous intellectual prowess, and is seldom used in practice.

Successive Scanning A second strategy, *successive scanning*, imposes very little cognitive strain on subjects. It involves simply making a guess about the correct concept immediately, and testing it directly with the choice of the next card. If the guess was correct, the solution has been achieved in the fastest possible time; if it was incorrect, only one of six possible hypotheses has been eliminated.

Conservative Focusing Perhaps the best of all strategies is *conservative focusing*. Employing this strategy, subjects begin by accepting the first card as a hypothesis and then choose cards that change only one attribute value at a time. Say the first card has two borders and three red circles. This is then the hypothesis. Let's assume that the correct concept is simply *red circles*. Say the next card the subject chooses has a single border and three red circles, and the experimenter says that this is also an example of the concept. The subject now knows that number of borders is irrelevant. The next card chosen has two borders and three black circles, and the experimenter says it is not an example of the concept. The changed attribute value, color, was relevant. Therefore the subject now knows that red is part of the concept. The next choice, altering the shape or the number of figures, will lead the subject directly to the concept.

Focus Gambling In a slight variation of conservative focusing, the subject chooses cards that change more than one attribute value at a time. If the card continues to illustrate the concept, the subject will have reduced the number of trials required to attain the concept; if it does not, the subject will have learned little, since either or both of the changed values could be relevant. In essence, the subject is "gambling" on being right; hence the label, *focus gambling*.

Unfortunately, life is seldom as systematic and deliberate as the psychological laboratory. Although there is reason to believe that we make use of various strategies, frequently unconsciously, in our attempt to make sense of the world, we cannot yet identify and describe them simply.

Attributes	Values		
number of figures	2	3	1
number of borders	2	1	3
shape	triangle	circle	square
color	black	red	gray

Examples of stimulus cards used by Bruner et al. (1956) to study how subjects formed concepts. A wide range of variation was possible for presenting the four attributes.

In fact, however, the process appears to be far more complex than this. In most cases, the criteria used for category membership are *abstract:* they cannot be sensed directly. Fatness and thinness are a case in point. We don't sense them directly, but infer them on the basis of abstract intellectual processes. That is, fatness depends on an abstract personal judgment based on a complex relationship between height, age, weight, and expectations. Indeed, it appears that abstraction is involved in virtually all acts of categorization (Mervis and Rosch, 1981).

Insight and the Effects of Set

Solution of level 5 and 6 problems requires reformulation or production of unusual solution methods, and thus involves insight. Solution of insight problems by both animals and humans has been intensively investigated. Recall, for example, from Chapter 6, Köhler's (1927) "stick" and "box" problems with bananas and apes. When the ape finally "saw" the solution to the problem, *insight,* defined as the sudden restructuring of the elements of a problem, had been achieved. These topics are examined in more detail in the section on creativity which follows shortly.

Wason and Johnson-Laird (1972) presented subjects with an extraordinarily simple problem: discover the rule that governs the production of a list of numbers such as 2, 4, 6, 8, 10. . . . Subjects were allowed to generate new lists and were told whether these lists also represented the same rule. They were asked to state the rule only when they were certain of it, but to keep a record of all their hypotheses. In this case, the rule was not, as most subjects immediately expected, all even numbers in ascending order. It was simply any number in increasing order. There was no way to prove that this was the rule, except by eliminating all other possible alternatives. Many subjects, however, simply generated sequences of even numbers consecutively, thus confirming their initial hypothesis, but not rejecting any others. Even after stating their hypothesis and being told that it was wrong, some subjects continued to generate sequences that still confirmed their original hypothesis. This type of experiment simply illustrates how **set**, a predisposition to respond in a given way, can sometimes impede the solution of relatively simple problems.

Numerous other examples of problems whose solutions require insight, but where set interferes with the solution, are presented in Duncker's (1945) classic work. Among these is the now famous "nine-dot" problem shown in Figure 8.10a. Subjects are required to connect all dots with no more than four consecutive straight lines. Those who are not familiar with the problem are impeded by their preconceived notion (set) that these four lines should all be within the boundaries of the nine dots. The solution (Figure 8.10b) therefore requires overcoming the effects of set, and may be said to involve insight.

Functional Fixedness Another manifestation of the negative effects of set has been labeled *functional fixedness* by Duncker. It involves using objects and ideas in terms of preconceived notions that we have of their functions, and sometimes failing to think of new functions as a result. Sometimes these new functions can be instrumental in solving problems that cannot easily be solved otherwise. Perhaps the most famous of Duncker's (1945) illustrations of functional fixedness is the one in which a subject is presented with candles, string, thumbtacks, a box of matches, and sometimes other irrelevant material. The subject's task is to place the candle on a wall or screen in such a way that it can be used to provide light. A correct solution simply involves emptying the matchbox, tacking it onto the screen, and placing the candle inside it. If the box were initially empty, the solution would be obvious to most subjects. Since it isn't, however, many subjects eliminate it as a potential part of the solution since its function appears to be simply to hold matches. The string, however, has no obvious function among the collection of materials, and is more likely to be employed in attempted solutions.

A similar situation is presented by N. F. Maier's (1931) string problem (Figure 8.11a). Two strings are suspended from a ceiling far enough apart that a subject cannot

Set   A predisposition to perceive specific stimuli rather than others, to respond in predetermined ways rather than in others. In other words, set predisposes or facilitates certain perceptions or responses. Set is a description (but not really an explanation) of how we sometimes find things we are looking for more easily than things we are not looking for.

Figure 8.10 (a) The nine-dot problem: join all the dots with no more than four continuous straight lines (that is, without lifting your pencil). The solution is on p. 230.

Figure 8.11 (a) The Maier string problem. The person cannot reach both dangling strings at the same time. The task: to tie the two strings together while standing on the floor, using no materials other than those you can see. To find the solution, turn to p. 230.

Figure 8.12 Water jar problems of the Luchins type. The first eight problems can be solved by the formula $B - A - 2C$; the last is much simpler ($A - C$) but presents greater difficulty if it is not presented first. Set is clearly detrimental in solving problem 9, but it is helpful in solving problems 2 through 8.

	Use jars with these capacities:			Measure this amount:
	A	B	C	
1.	9	20	3	5
2.	4	12	1	6
3.	20	59	4	31
4.	10	41	5	21
5.	21	74	3	47
6.	34	94	6	48
7.	12	38	3	20
8.	13	47	11	12
9.	19	71	3	16

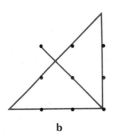

b

Figure 8.10 (**b**) The solution to the nine-dot problem. Did set interfere with your approach?

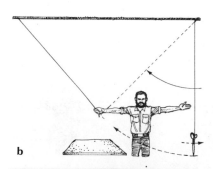

b

Figure 8.11 (**b**) The reason most people don't immediately solve the Maier string problem is because of *functional fixedness,* a type of set, concerning the use of scissors. They are more likely to solve it if it is called the Maier pendulum problem.

reach both of them at the same time. The room may be barren except for a pair of scissors tossed apparently carelessly on a table. The subject is asked to tie the two strings together while standing on the floor. The solution, which simply requires overcoming any set the subject might have with respect to the function of scissors, is illustrated in Figure 8.11b. And if it was not immediately obvious to you, it probably would have been had the problem been described, as it often is, as the Maier pendulum problem. That description would have given you a different set.

Usefulness of Set   Set is not always a detriment to problem solving. Indeed, predispositions to approach problems in set ways probably arise as a result of the effectiveness of these methods in solving most problems. Life demonstrates the usefulness and time-saving qualities of set much more frequently than it demonstrates its negative effects. Consider, for example, the Luchins and Luchins (1950) water jar problems illustrated in Figure 8.12. After solving a long list of problems that could always be solved by the formula $B - A - 2C$, subjects experience considerable difficulty with a simpler problem ($A - C$, for example). Most subjects continue to employ the original formula. Although this illustrates the negative effect of set for a specific problem, it also illustrates that human problem solvers develop strategies and rules (which are themselves sets) that do work and are helpful for precisely that reason. On the other hand, our strategies and rules don't always work; sometimes we need to be creative.

Creativity

George Bernard Shaw, allegedly a very **creative** person, was once asked by his biographer, Stephen Winsten (1949), to comment on the proverbial hair's breadth that separates genius from madness. "The matter-of-fact man prefers to think of the creative man as defective, or at least akin to madness," Winsten said. And Shaw characteristically replied, "Most of them are, most of them are. I am probably the only sane exception" (p. 103). And it is true that there have been notable instances of madness among some of the world's best-known creative people. It is also true, however, that there have been many instances of madness among more matter-of-fact people, but these, for obvious reasons, have been much less notable.

The literature presents a bewildering array of definitions for creativity. Some suggest that it is simply the ability to make remote associations and to produce "new

Figure 8.13 Creativity is not a simple concept. Does it describe the outcome of a special process (the painting), the process itself (the act of painting), or a personality characteristic (something in the artist that we might label "creativity")?

combinations with either meet specified requirements or are in some way useful" (Mednick, 1962, p. 221); others define it in terms of such factors as originality, fluency, and flexibility (Guilford, 1959); still others insist that creativity involves the production of "a novel work that is accepted as tenable or useful or satisfying by a significant group of others at some point in time" (Stein, in Parnes & Harding, 1962, p. 86). Applying these abstract definitions to specific people and products is difficult: creative products, creative persons, and the creative process may be quite different (Figure 8.13). That is, a creative product can result accidentally (science employs the term **serendipity** for such accidents) from the activities of an otherwise very ordinary person. Another person, highly gifted, clever, and original, might approach problems in a variety of unusual ways but produce nothing that others consider creative.

For our purposes, then, creativity may best be defined as a quality of a person that is, at least on occasion, manifested in behaviors that might be judged creative (either because of their results or because of what they tell us about the individual). Psychology is less interested in judging the relative creative qualities of works of art, for example, than it is in identifying and studying the personality characteristics of those who produce the works.

Measuring Creativity

To measure creativity, several batteries of tests have been designed, most of them allowing for the production of a variety of responses none of which is necessarily correct. Best-known among these tests are the Minnesota Tests of Creative Thinking (Yamamoto, 1964). They present items similar to the following: How many uses can you think of for a silk stocking? a brick? an old tire? How many ways can you think of to improve a bicycle? How many titles can you think of for this picture? These tests may then be scored in terms of fluency (number of responses), flexibility (number of times the respondent shifts from one class of responses to another), and originality (number of unusual responses). Table 8.1 presents an example of one item from a creativity test and how it might be scored.

There is as yet little evidence that measured creativity is highly related to creative productivity as it might be judged by teachers or by the public. In other words, the

Creative An adjective that may be used to describe people, products, or a process. The term *creativity* generally refers to the capacity of individuals to produce novel or original answers or products.

Serendipity The act or the process of finding something while looking for something else. A serendipitous finding is accidental, although it might be unwise to assume that serendipity is as likely to occur to the stupid and the unprepared as it is to those more wise and better prepared. And if it does happen as frequently to the less wise, the resulting serendipitous findings may not be particularly momentous.

Table 8.1 Sample Answers and Scoring Procedure for One Item from a Test of Creativity

---

Item: How many uses can you think of for a nylon stocking?

Answers:

*	wear on feet
@#*	wear over face
*	wear on hands
#*	make rugs
*	make clothes
@#*	make upholstery
#*	hang flower pots
*	hang mobiles
@#*	make Christmas presents
#*	use as a sling
#*	tie up robbers
@#*	cover broken wine bottles
@#*	use as ballast in a dirigible
#*	make a fishing net

Scoring:
* Fluency: 14 (total number of different responses)
# Flexibility: 10 (number of shifts from one class of responses to another)
@ Originality: 5 (number of unusual responses: those that occurred less than 5 percent of the time in the entire sample)

---

validity of these tests has not been firmly established. In addition, there is some evidence that individuals can successfully rate themselves for creativity (Taylor & Holland, 1964). Conversely, there is evidence that teachers are not particularly good at rating students: they fail to recognize approximately 20 percent of the most gifted students (Gallagher, 1960). There is intriguing evidence as well that simply instructing students to behave as though they are creative or noncreative can make them appear to be so. L. Hudson (1968) asked groups of sixth-grade children to answer items as though they were "inhibited scientists" or "bohemian artists" and was thus able to obtain extremely creative responses from apparent noncreative students, and very ordinary responses from those who had previously been judged as being highly creative. Recent evidence suggests, in fact, that creativity is probably not very separate from other intellectual abilities, that what separates the highly creative person from one who appears less creative is probably a host of personality variables and motivational factors (Vernon, 1970).

Promoting Creativity

Even though creativity cannot easily be measured or defined, there is little argument with the belief that it is one of the more valuable and precious of human qualities. The intellectual processes involved in being creative may not be fundamentally different from those involved in being intelligent (Cropley, 1965; Pribram, 1963), but the attitudes with which creative people approach life and its problems may be quite different. There is good reason to believe that some of these attitudes can be learned,

"I like the metaphorical symbolism and the chromatic nuances, but I don't like the fish in the corner."

George Dole

and that people can be made more creative or, at the very least, can be made to behave in ways that result in the production of creative ideas.

Among the many programs that have gained popularity as methods of fostering creativity are Osborn's (1957) brainstorming and de Bono's (1970) lateral thinking. What these have in common is that they encourage the deferment of evaluation and the production of novel and sometimes bizarre ideas. That is, they take pains to ensure that participants do not evaluate ideas as they are being produced, and that problems are looked at in novel ways so as to stimulate unusual ideas. Each is described briefly here.

Brainstorming One of the better known techniques for creative problem solving, brainstorming involves a group of five to twelve people who are brought together specifically to produce creative ideas. Often, these people are from a variety of backgrounds. The brainstorming session typically begins with the leader explaining the rules of brainstorming. The first, and by far the most important of these rules, is that of **deferred evaluation**. By this is meant that members of the group are not allowed to evaluate any of the ideas that might be presented during the session. Laughter, ridicule, head nodding, and other subtle signs of approval or disapproval are also discouraged, since these too are forms of evaluation. Three other rules are also important: (1) modification or combination with other ideas is encouraged; (2) quantity of ideas is sought; and (3) unusual, remote, or wild ideas are sought (Haefele, 1962, p. 142).

Deferred evaluation Deliberately refraining from evaluating an idea. This is considered an important aid to creativity.

Typically, a brainstorming session is a free-wheeling, wide-ranging affair with ideas coming very rapidly in the beginning and somewhat more slowly at the end. A great many of the good ideas produced during brainstorming sessions come when familiar ideas have been completely exhausted. Specific techniques sometimes used to foster ideas during brainstorming include the use of checklists that suggest different ways of looking at problems. One such checklist is presented in Table 8.2.

Anecdotal evidence suggests that brainstorming sessions can be very valuable when they are used for specific purposes. They do result in the production of many ideas, some of which may, upon later evaluation, prove to be entirely appropriate. In addition, several studies suggest that simply being involved in a brainstorming session may increase scores on tests designed to measure creativity (H. H. Anderson, 1959; Haefele, 1962).

Lateral Thinking De Bono (1970) suggests that if one is to dig a hole deeper, then one must dig vertically; if the hole is to be made in a different place, then one must dig laterally. Similarly, if the object is to discover more about something, or to arrive at a conventional, accepted, convergent solution for a problem, vertical thinking is acceptable; if unusual, divergent, creative solutions are required, lateral thinking is indicated. Accordingly, he has devised programs to teach thinking (de Bono, 1976) and a program designed to foster lateral thinking (1970, 1976). Unlike brainstorming and its variations, de Bono's approach does not ask participants to solve specific problems, but encourages them instead to develop new ways of approaching all problems—more precisely, lateral rather than vertical approaches.

Subjects are presented, for example, with various geometric designs and asked what each might be (Figure 8.14). They are then encouraged to produce as many variations of initial descriptions as possible. Other exercises are designed to make people ask why, to suspend judgment, to challenge assumptions, to isolate crucial factors in problem situations, to break distracting sets, to brainstorm, and to produce analogies. An example of a specific technique is that of the "block problems." Subjects are asked to arrange four blocks so that they touch each other in specific ways. Blocks are considered to be touching if any part of two flat surfaces are in proximity; edges and corners do not count. Try the following arrangements before looking at Figure 8.15. Take four oblong blocks or boxes and attempt to arrange them so that (a) each

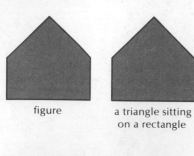

figure | a triangle sitting on a rectangle

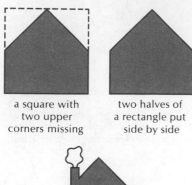

a square with two upper corners missing | two halves of a rectangle put side by side

end view of a house

Figure 8.14 One of the lateral thinking exercises described by de Bono. Descriptions of the figure illustrate unusual perceptions. (From *Lateral Thinking: A Textbook of Creativity* by E. de Bono, 1970, Ward Lock Educational Company Limited. Reprinted by permission.)

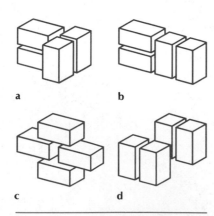

a   b

c   d

Figure 8.15 Solutions to the block problems.

Table 8.2 Checklist for Eliciting More Ideas from Brainstorming Groups. (This checklist was created in an attempt to solve a problem with classroom discipline.)

Technique	Examples
1. Put to other uses	The class might be used as something other than a learning situation. For example, it might be given the responsibility of entertaining the school at a social evening.
2. Adapt	Adaptation involves using ideas from other sources. Perhaps a school could be run like a factory, like a prison, or like a playground.
3. Modify	This suggests changing the composition of the class, changing teaching methods, or changing the approach to discipline problems. This entire checklist could be applied to any of these changes; it would suggest possible forms for them to take.
4. Magnify	Class size could be increased, as could number of teachers, number of assignments, or magnitude of punishment or reinforcement.
5. Minify	Class size could be decreased, as could number of assignments, number of reprimands, or number of school days.
6. Substitute	A new teacher might be substituted, the entire class might be exchanged, or a few members of the class might be replaced by students from other classes.
7. Rearrange	The seating plan could be rearranged so as to separate troublemakers, as could the physical arrangement of the room. Perhaps the desks shoud all face toward the rear.
8. Reverse	The last idea came one point too early. However, the teacher might face the front as a sort of reversal. Another reversal would be to have the students take turns teaching.
9. Combine	This suggests, first, that a combination of the previous suggestions might provide a solution; and second, that the teaching-learning function might possibly be combined with other functions such as entertainment, problem solving, or the discussion of noncurricular topics of interest.

Note. Based on Osborn (1957), modified by Parnes (1967), and reprinted from Lefrancois (1982, p. 277).

block is touching every other; (b) one block is touching one other, one is touching two others, and one is touching three; (c) each block is touching two others; (d) each block is touching one other.

Techniques for lateral thinking encourage creating the new and challenging the old. To this end, de Bono (1970) suggests the use of a new word, *Po,* a word that will be to lateral thinking what the word *no* is to logical thinking. He argues that logical thinking is based on rejection and selection, and that the major role is played by rejection. Hence negation is the most important function in logical thinking. Its opposite, *yes,* would not be suitable either for lateral thinking, which is concerned with challenging established thought and ideas, not to create chaos and confusion, but to bring about order and clarity. Hence the word *Po,* a word that means nothing and everything; that permits us to do or say whatever we want to do or say; that does not judge but requires no justification; that, in de Bono's words, is the laxative of language and thinking. And if I say to you, "Po psychology is a strange beast," you are not to say, "Yes it is," or "No it isn't." Instead, you are to examine it, challenge it, make variations on it, brainstorm it, analogize for it. In short, you are to think laterally about psychology. *Po* is not a condemnation, a rejection, or a criticism, real or implied. It is simply an invitation to think laterally.

Po!

Po?

Once more if you have time. Po.

Figure 8.16 Language is more than a means of transmitting information; it is our principal means of storing knowledge and is crucially involved in transforming and discovering information.

Language

In the first part of this chapter we have dealt at length with some of the questions that are of interest to those who study thinking, but have yet to touch on one of the most fundamental but most difficult of these questions. We know that thinking is more than the solution of problems; that it goes beyond the formation and attainment of concepts; that insight and set describe only a few of its possibilities and limitations. We suspect that it sometimes involves conceptual gyrations and contortions that we haven't begun to isolate and understand; and we suspect, as well, that among the most important factors in our thought processes is our ability to use **language**. And the question, still largely unanswered, that is most fundamental here concerns the relationship between language and thought.

Language is more than a tool for thinking—or its servant; the point has yet to be resolved. It is probably the single greatest cultural force among human societies, serving not only to bind people together, but also to store and transmit knowledge and wisdom indefinitely. Today's spoken or written word can be preserved in various forms, to be looked at or heard exactly as it is now, at virtually any time in the future. Even at the dawn of civilization, prior to the invention of writing, the word could be stored in various memories and passed on from generation to generation (Figure 8.16).

Wouldn't one language have sufficed? Probably, but given geographical, religious, ethnic, and national isolation, thousands developed. More than 5,000 languages are used at present. In addition, a large number of languages are now extinct, some of which are still studied as "dead" languages. More than 800 attempts have been made to develop a single universal language, the best-known of which is Esperanto. All have failed.

Elements and Characteristics of Language

Our language, as I write and you read, is English. It consists of some forty-five different sounds, called **phonemes**, sounds that are the basic units of language, but

Language Language is not necessary for communication, but it is nevertheless a form of communication. Animals communicate but, as far as we know, do not employ language.

Phoneme The simplest unit of language, consisting of a single sound.

Morpheme Combinations of phonemes that make up the meaningful units of a language.

that do not necessarily have meaning. They are represented by our different pronunciations of vowels and consonants. These phonemes achieve meaning as **morphemes**, the simplest meaningful units in the language. Permissible and current morphemes in the English language number over 100,000. The sounds associated with the letter *e* are phonemes; such sound units as are represented by the letter combinations *he, the, let, were, ere,* and *zeal* are morphemes.

There is more to language, however, than morphemes and phonemes, the sounds that define these, and the meanings associated with them. Nor is meaning simply a matter of an unvarying correspondence between a sound or written word and a specific event or object. Consider the following groups of words, for example:

I bear no grudge.

Bear left by the barn.

I can't bear it any more.

I can bear him on my back.

Don't shoot the bear.

Bare? Again?

I won by a bare margin.

Prosody Modes of expression, intonations, accents, and pauses peculiar to a particular language.

It appears that meaning can be a function of context. It can also be a function of intonation and inflection, termed **prosody**. *Stop,* depending on how, when, where, and why it is said, might mean "Don't move, there's a small rattlesnake near your left foot"; "You don't mean I should stop?"; "Do stop by and visit the turkeys"; "I've had all that I can take!"; "I move that we discontinue feeding the birds"; "Stop this vehicle"; or a number of other things.

Thus, the things a word refers to, its context, and the manner in which it is said all contribute to its meaning. But language is even more complicated than this, as you well know—and also, in one sense, more simple. **Syntax** (grammar), the implicit and explicit rules that govern the use of words, has much to do with meaning. Certainly, it is because of well-understood syntactical rules that "You don't know," "Don't you know?", "No you don't," and "No? Don't you?" have such different meanings. Grammar simplifies language in that, having learned the rules, we do not have to learn all the possible associations of words that we might need to express the meanings we intend. Because of these rules we can create entirely new combinations that contain our intended meanings (Figure 8.17). It might amaze you to consider, for example, that of the numerous statements you might make this very day, there are a number that have probably never been said in exactly the same way by anybody else. Language makes you creative.

Syntax The grammar of a language, consisting of the set of implicit or explicit rules that govern the combinations of words comprising a language.

In summary, the basic elements of any language are its units, phonemes and morphemes; certain characteristics of intonation and inflection, termed *prosody;* and the rules that govern word combinations, termed *syntax.* Its defining characteristics, according to R. Brown (1973) are *displacement, meaningfulness,* and *productiveness.* Language involves displacement in that it permits the representation of objects and events that are not immediate. That is, it employs symbols as arbitrary representations of objects and events that are, were, or might be real, or that are abstract and hypothetical. To think about turkeys does not require the manipulation of real turkeys, live or dead, or even of miniature replicas of turkeys. The word *turkey* is a symbol that denotes the actual object. And because a word has similar meaning for each of us, we can speak, you and I, of turkeys and be reasonably sure that we are speaking of the same thing. Finally, a language is characterized by productiveness. Beyond the simple words and phrases that we might learn mechanically, we can produce an incredible variety of expressions and sentences by applying the rules of syntax. With a mere hundred words, some people can talk forever.

Building Blocks		Rules
phonemes	morphemes	prosody (inflection)
(simple sounds)	(simplest sound units with meaning)	Help!
		Give him some help.
		You need help?
f in *fire*	morph	
s in *sit*	eme	syntax (grammar)
e in *eat*	let	man-eating shark
e in *help*	him	shark, eating man
m in *my*	est	shark-eating man
		context
		sharpshooter
		sharp knife
		sharp dresser
		sharp mind

Figure 8.17 Language is a combination of building blocks and rules. They can be put together in countless ways to produce innumerable variations.

Language and Nonhumans

Language has frequently been defined as the means by which we communicate. In fact, however, it does not appear that language, as we know it, is essential for communication. A wide variety of "lower" animals communicate in limited but highly effective ways. The simple, reflexive communication of impending danger is probably most obvious: whitetail deer flag their long tails; pronghorn antelope bristle their rump patches; beavers slap the water resoundingly with their tails; ground squirrels utter piercing whistles; crows crow; and turkeys gobble. Barnett (1967) reports a slightly more advanced phenomenon among certain baboons whose vision is not nearly so acute as that of the gazelles with whom they sometimes feed. The signs of danger that the gazelles emit are picked up and heeded by the baboons.

At a slightly higher level, some animals communicate meanings that go beyond simple danger. Lorenz (1952) interprets the various calls of the jackdaw as meaning "food," "danger," or "let's go." Dolphins, too, have been extensively studied because of widespread speculation that the relatively complicated sounds they emit might constitute a language. Wardaugh (1976) reports that, in fact, they have a very limited range of calls, and that there is no evidence these are used for conversation. The sounds of the Atlantic bottlenose dolphin, for example, appear to be used primarily to locate objects, including other dolphins, and perhaps as unlearned expressions of a small number of emotions.

The amazing communication system of bees has been widely discussed in psychological literature as well, following Frisch's (1953) description of the bee dance. Bees returning to a hive after foraging in the open perform a complicated dance which indicates to other bees both the direction and the distance of whatever food source the dancing bee might have discovered (Figure 8.18).

Wardaugh (1976) points out that although the dancing language of bees is universal, there are slight differences among bees—differences that might be analogous to differences in dialect that sometimes develop among groups of people who speak the same basic language, but who live apart. Austrian and Italian bees apparently have some difficulty communicating with each other, and consistently misinterpret each other's dances. Italian bees never go far enough when responding to an Austrian bee's dance; by the same token, Austrian bees go farther than they have to.

Animal forms of communication, like our languages, are symbolic, involving both displacement and meaningfulness. Unlike human languages, however, they are non-

"round" dance   "wagging" dance

Figure 8.18 In 1973 Karl von Frisch shared the Nobel prize in medicine and physiology with two other ethologists, Konrad Lorenz and Nikolaas Tinbergen. Von Frisch is perhaps best known for his research into the "language" of bees, certain aspects of which are depicted above. A foraging bee finds a food source, returns to the hive, and performs a "dance," the symbolic meaning of which appears to be clear to other bees in the hive. A "round" dance indicates that the food is within a hundred yards; a "wagging" dance means that food is further. In addition, the duration and vigorousness of the dance relate to the amount of food discovered, and the axis of the dance relative to the position of the sun precisely indicates its direction. Interestingly, bees of different subspecies do not understand each other's dances at all well, and sometimes become hopelessly confused in their attempts to locate the food source. This is why von Frisch believes the communication systems of bees to be inherited rather than learned.

productive. That is, as far as we know, animal communication symbols—whether sounds, gestures, or movements—are not governed by rules analogous to syntax and cannot be combined in novel ways to express different meanings. Thus, although many animals can communicate at a limited level, none has achieved language in the wild.

Can Animals Learn Language?

My friend's grandmother has a parrot. "Does your parrot talk?" I once asked the old lady, after she had introduced me to her parrot, Pipi. "Sure he can," the gentle woman replied, proceeding to exhort Pipi to make some verbal expression. "Parle, Pipi, hein. Parle, Pipi," said the old lady. Pipi responded with a hoarse, raspy, croakish, throat-clearing sequence of meaningless sounds followed by the single phrase: "Pipi, maudit cracker!"

Pipi can imitate some human sounds, many of which are best left untranslated, but he cannot communicate with these sounds. He remains absolutely incapable of generating new sequences of words with the clear intention of conveying different meanings. He can imitate, but he has not acquired language.

Gua   If any animal could learn language, our closest living relatives would seem the most likely to do so. It was with this in mind that the Kelloggs (Kellogg, 1968; Kellogg & Kellogg, 1933) adopted a seven-month-old female chimpanzee, Gua, and attempted to rear her with their ten-month-old son. Gua was given toys, dressed, talked to, cuddled, played with, given her own bed and high chair, and otherwise treated like a typical middle-class baby. A careful record was kept of her development as well as of Donald's, the Kelloggs' son. Initially, Gua was more active than Donald, but less imitative. In fact, the experiment was later abandoned because the Kelloggs feared that Gua's presence was retarding Donald's development.

Nine months after Gua had been adopted, she understood 95 words; Donald fewer than 107. But whereas Donald could also say a number of these words, Gua had not learned to speak a single one. The Kelloggs tried desperately to teach her to say "Papa," and failed dismally.

Viki Some twenty years later, the Hayeses (C. Hayes, 1951; K. J. Hayes & Hayes, 1951) adopted a little girl chimpanzee when she was only a few days old. They had no children of their own. Their intention was to teach Viki to speak. Following months of their laborious and painstaking efforts, she finally said "Mama." But the response was not a result of simple imitation. Indeed, teaching a parrot to say "Mama" would have been considerably easier. Her teachers had to sit repeatedly with Viki, holding her lips, and physically shaping her mouth, all the while saying "Mama," while she grunted, squealed, and made other typical chimpanzee sounds. In the end, she learned three other words—*Papa, cup,* and *up*—but she never did learn the ordinary meanings of these words. Her pronunciation was atrocious, so that what she was saying was frequently very unclear. She sometimes used the word *cup* to indicate that she wanted a drink of water, but used the other words apparently only to obtain attention. She, like Gua, had failed to learn language.

Washoe In 1966, the Gardners (1969) adopted Washoe, a ten-month-old female chimpanzee. Realizing by now that it might never be possible to teach a chimpanzee to speak, they attempted to teach Washoe American Sign Language (ASL), the contemporary sign language of the deaf. There are two forms of this language, one of which spells out the letters of the words. This form would clearly be very difficult and probably impossible to teach to an illiterate chimpanzee. The second form makes use of symbols for concepts and objects, several of which are depicted in Figure 8.19. Washoe, who was kept in a trailer in the Gardners' back yard, was exposed to a rich, naturalistic environment in which people spoke to her only in sign language, although they were permitted to make certain expressive sounds. Through a combination of operant conditioning, frequently employing tickling as reinforcement (Washoe was a tickling addict), physical assistance in shaping her hands, repeated prompting, and imitation, Washoe learned 38 different signs in her first two years. These signs were rapidly generalized to a variety of related objects, so that the sign for dog, for example, came to mean not only the animal dog, but a picture of a dog, a simple drawing of a dog, or the sound of a bark. One year later, the number of signs in Washoe's repertoire had increased to 85; by the age of five, she had mastered more than 160 signs.

Early in her acquisition of signs, Washoe apparently began to put them together in novel ways: *hurry open; listen dog; you drink; you me tickle; Roger Washoe tickle* (Roger Fouts was her trainer). There is little doubt that Washoe has learned to use ASL to communicate. What is less clear is the extent to which her use of signs is governed by syntactical rules. A large number of different signs in any order appear to have highly similar meanings for her. Thus, when faced with a locked door, she has on different occasions made all of the following signs: *more key, gimme key, open key, gimme more key, gimme key more, open gimme key, in open help, help key in, key help hurry,* and a number of others (Gardner & Gardner, 1969). In addition, Washoe apparently remains incapable of using signs to refer to past or future events, but uses them only for the present.

There is, of course, the possibility that Washoe is an extremely rare chimpanzee that found her way into the laboratory, to the great good fortune of the Gardners. Fouts (1973) provides evidence that this is not at all probable. He and some student volunteers undertook to teach four chimpanzees, two male and two female, ten signs from American Sign Language. The technique they employed was one of "molding" rather than imitation, this having been found to be the simplest and most effective way of teaching signs to chimpanzees. For example, the trainer would show the chimpanzee an object, "mold" the chimpanzee's hands in the presence of the object, and reward it (usually with a raisin).

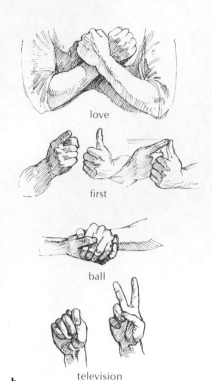

love

first

ball

television

b

a

Figure 8.19 (**a**) Starting at the age of ten months, Washoe mastered more than 160 signs by the age of five. What is she saying? (**b**) Some common signs in American Sign Language (ASL).

Several findings from this project are important. First, all four chimpanzees learned all ten signs, the fastest requiring an average of 54 minutes per sign, and the slowest requiring 159.1 minutes. Second, although there were marked individual differences in the rate at which individual chimpanzees learned signs, some signs were consistently more difficult to learn than others. By the same token, a number of signs were relatively easy for all chimpanzees. Particularly easy was the sign for *listen* (hand to ear); more difficult was the sign for *look* (finger near the eye). Given the natural inclination primates have for protecting their eyes, they may have an instinctual tendency not to place a finger near the eye, and this tendency may account for slower learning of this sign.

Other Apes; Other "Languages"   Other "languages" are also being taught to chimpanzees. Premack (Premack & Premack, 1972) has developed a series of plastic shapes that stand for various objects, and has successfully taught the meanings of these shapes to a six-year-old chimpanzee, Sarah. Not only can she respond correctly when presented with specific objects such as a cup, but she has also learned such abstract symbols as *same as* or *different*. Thus, she can respond with the symbol for *same as* when presented with the symbols for "apple is red" and "red color apple." There is evidence, as well, that she is not learning simple associations between symbols and objects, but that she is responding to their meanings. For example, she was told that "brown is the color of chocolate." She could later use the symbol for brown appropriately, indicating that her concept of color is such that her memory of chocolate leads her to the correct association.

Sarah's training was rather different from Washoe's. She was kept in an ordinary laboratory environment and given systematic training sessions one hour every working day. These training sessions provided reinforcement under regular schedules. Sarah was not allowed to play with her symbols as Washoe played with ASL, and has not made the same use of her knowledge for communicating wishes to her trainers. Her tasks have been deliberate attempts to demonstrate that she can "name" objects, make

Figure 8.20 To what extent can Koko reason?

yes, no, same as, and related decisions, and describe certain physical activities appropriately through the use of symbols (for example, putting an object in a dish). She has learned over a hundred different symbols, and can write sentences with these, vertically, top to bottom, in response to specific situations and questions. There does remain some controversy over whether she has succeeded in learning a productive language, or whether she has simply learned some problem-solving skills employing symbols rather than concrete objects.

A group of Georgia psychologists report another "language" training program with a two-year-old chimpanzee, Lana (Rumbaugh, 1977; Rumbaugh et al., 1973). Lana has been taught a number of arbitrary, nondescriptive word characters that are represented on a computer keyboard. By depressing appropriate keys in the right order, she can activate machinery that will open windows, show movies, and provide food or drink and various other things that she might want. She is also able to "read" sequences of these characters as they appear on a screen, and to erase those that are incorrect. In effect, Lana has learned to associate various symbols and symbol orders with specific reinforcers, and to "converse" by means of these symbols (see Box 8.2).

Washoe, Sarah, and Lana have come a long distance from Gua and Viki. Will the United States ever have a chimpanzee president? Or a gorilla?

Koko Washoe, Sarah, Lana, Booee, Bruno, Cindy, Thelma, and other primates who have amazed psychologists and linguists by learning to understand and use various languages have all been chimpanzees. They are small and reasonably intelligent. A gorilla, by comparison, is large, and biologists have generally believed, not sufficiently intelligent for such a heady accomplishment as learning a language.

Not true. Francine Patterson of Stanford borrowed a young female gorilla from the San Francisco Zoo in 1972 (H. T. P. Hayes, 1977). Like Roger Fouts and the Gardners, she attempted to teach ASL to this gorilla, Koko, using a "molding" approach—that is, by shaping the gorilla's hands to conform to the appropriate sign. A number of deaf assistants worked with her as well. Within a mere twenty-nine months, Koko had mastered over 200 different signs, had learned to put them together in various meaningful combinations, invented new combinations for unfamiliar objects ("eye hat" for mask; "white tiger" for zebra), and "talked" to herself constantly while she played (Figure 8.20). And on nonverbal tests of intelligence, she performed within the normal range for four- or five-year-old humans (Linden, 1980).

Have They Really Learned Language? One of the principal characteristics of any language is that it is generative. Having learned both the vocabulary of the language and its syntax, we can combine words in novel ways to convey intended meanings. In the absence of this ability to *generate* meaning, we have probably not learned anything that resembles what we call language. As noted earlier, it is possible to communicate without language. A cat presumably does so when it rubs against your leg, if it wants you to do something as a result. If it is merely itchy, then perhaps it is just scratching, and not talking.

Conversations with Lana

Lana, a female chimpanzee, has learned to communicate by depressing keys that correspond to word characters, and to operate a machine which, if she depresses appropriate keys, dispenses food and drink, plays music, opens windows, and otherwise makes her life agreeable. Below are several of her conversations.

1. Tim enters the room and substitutes chow for water in the machine.
Lana: ?You move water out-of machine.
Tim: Yes.
Lana: You put chow in machine.
Tim: Yes.
    Conversation ends. Lana had not previously used the expression *out-of* except in connection with her own person being removed from the cage. She subsequently used it on numerous occasions (Gill, 1977, p. 239).

2. Lana has previously named an "orange box" on several hundred occasions. The box is therefore highly familiar. Was she deliberately "lying" in the following conversation (Rumbaugh & Gill, 1977, p. 185)?
Tim: ?What name-of this which-is orange.
Lana: Can.
Tim: ?What name-of this which-is orange.
Lana: Color.
Tim: ?What name-of this which-is orange.
Lana: Cup.
Tim: No. (At this point Tim was exasperated and took a break. He returned five minutes later with the same question.)
Tim: ?What name-of this which-is orange.
Lana: No name-of this bowl.
    No name-of this which-is orange.
Tim: No. Box name-of this which-is orange.

3. Lana eventually generalized the use of many terms and expressions. The following conversation illustrates her use of the concept *more* (Rumbaugh & Gill, 1977, p. 187):
Lana: Please you give cup of juice.
Tim: Yes (and gave her a cup of juice, which she emptied).
Lana: ?You put Coke in cup. (No Coke was present).
Tim: No Coke.
Lana: ?You put more juice in cup.
Tim: Yes.
Lana: ?You put juice of.
    ?You put.
    ?You give juice to Lana.

(Excerpts from *Language Learning by a Chimpanzee: The Lana Project*, D. M. Rumbaugh (ed.), Academic Press, 1977. Reprinted by permission.)

Tim: Yes. (Thereupon he gave her the juice to drink, though he kept possession of the cup.)
Lana: ?You give cup.
    ?You give cup of juice.
Tim: Yes. (And he gave her the cup of juice to drink.)
Lana: ?You put more of.
    ?You put more juice in cup.
Tim: Yes. (The cup being empty, Tim put more juice into it as specifically requested by Lana.)

Lana the chimp pushing keys at her computer keyboard.

Language goes beyond mere communication, however: It also involves the use of symbols. But even pigeons can communicate with symbols. Epstein, Lanza, and Skinner (1980) taught one pigeon to ask another what color was lit on a panel that was not visible to the first pigeon. The second pigeon had been taught to respond by pressing one of three keys, appropriately labeled *R, G,* or *Y* (for red, green, or yellow). The first pigeon would then thank the second one (by depressing a key that said "thank you" and caused the second pigeon to receive a reinforcer), select the appropriate color on his panel, and peck it to receive his own reinforcement.

Had these two pigeons learned language? No. They had simply learned that reinforcement was contingent upon pecking appropriate keys in response to specific stimulation. That the keys were labeled *R, G, Y,* and *Thank You* is completely irrelevant. Is it possible that Washoe and Koko, like our two pigeons, have merely learned relatively complex gestures that are directly associated with approval, food, and other forms of reinforcement—that they have grasped neither the symbolic nor the syntactical nature of language?

Patterson (1978) and others have sometimes made extravagant claims for the abilities of the apes in their charge. Washoe, for example, is supposed to have "invented" combinations such as "water bird" for swan. And Koko, far more impressive than any chimpanzee to date, is credited with such gems as "white tiger" for zebra, "elephant baby" for a Pinocchio doll, and "eye hat" for a mask. Perhaps even more impressive, Koko has been reported to joke and to tease. When she is asked to sign for a drink, she touches her ear: A joke. She is asked to smile, but frowns: She is teasing.

It's possible that Koko might not have been teasing or joking; she might simply have made a mistake. And perhaps Washoe did not invent the "water bird" but merely

"He's learned a lot. The other day he corrected Edwin Newman."

Gerald Emerson

made the signs for both water and bird, not being certain which of the two Roger Fouts was pointing at.

Terrace (1979a; 1980) spent five years teaching a young chimpanzee, Nim Chimpsky (named after the famous linguist, Noam Chomsky who, incidentally, does not believe apes capable of language). Nim learned as had Washoe and Koko, and initially impressed Terrace very much. But in the end, Terrace was no longer at all impressed (Terrace, 1979b). It seemed that almost 90 percent of Nim's utterances were direct imitations; that is, he required immediate prompting. Careful examinations of videotapes of "conversations" with other chimpanzees revealed the same thing. What looked like sequences of words with sentence-like structure were simply sequences of subtle imitations. As Terrace put it, "I could find no evidence confirming an ape's grammatical competence, either in my own data or those of others" (1979a, p. 67).

Indeed, careful analysis of videotaped "conversational" sequences revealed: that chimpanzees typically imitate signs that their teachers have just begun, presumably because they have learned an association between reinforcement and imitation; that they often imitate a sequence of signs repeatedly and in a number of different orders, thereby appearing to "generate" sentence-like sequences; that most two- or three-sign combinations are completely random, although researchers tend to remember those that appear to be meaningful and creative, such as "water bird"; that numerous mistakes involve confusing signs; and that extended sentences are typically nonsensical and repetitive. Terrace's conclusion: Apes have not learned language. Their "signing" appears to have as its sole function, not the communication of meaning, but the obtaining of a reward that cannot be obtained in a more direct way (such as by grabbing, for example).

Terrace is not alone in his severe criticism of ape-language claims. Sebeok and Umiker-Sebeok (1979; 1980) present what Gardner (1980) describes as "the most powerful indictment in print of the early work on talking apes" (p. 4). Suffice it to say that they too point to how the alleged "cleverness" of the "talking" chimpanzees, their lying, joking, and teasing, can more easily be explained in terms of mistakes than in terms of a genuine understanding of language; that researchers have often unwittingly sifted from an ape's many movements those few that make sense to the researcher, though not necessarily to the ape.

We do not yet know, in fact, whether language makes sense to an ape, or whether they simply learn to imitate, and to order certain gestures (or depress certain keys) in ways that are most likely to be rewarded. We do know that until their language is proved to be meaningful and productive, it cannot truly be considered language.

Language Acquisition

How do we humans learn language? The sequence of language acquisition in children has been extensively researched, beginning with early studies of vocabulary size at different ages (M. E. Smith, 1926) (Table 8.3), and progressing to more complex recent analyses of the structure of children's language. The sequence of learning has been found to be remarkably consistent among children, although the ages at which children reach different levels can vary a great deal. Gurney (1973) describes three stages, recognized by most psychologists, although sometimes with different labels: sounds, words, and grammar.

The earliest of the child's sounds is the birth cry, an undifferentiated cry whose meaning is obscure at best. It is probably no more than a sound, reflexive and unintentional—biologically significant, perhaps, but devoid of any **semanticity** (meaning). Very shortly after birth, however, the infant's cries become associated with contentment, pain, hunger, and perhaps a few other simple infant states, and can sometimes be differentiated on this basis if they are heard in context.

Semantics The study of meanings of words and of other symbols or the collection of rules that describe the ways in which words and other symbols relate to objects and events.

Within six or seven weeks of birth, children begin to engage in a second activity that has in it the roots of speech: *babbling*. The sounds of every language in the world may be found in the babbling of young infants, no matter which language surrounds them. In fact, all these sounds are also found in the babbling of deaf children (Lenneberg, 1969).

Babbling is erratic and unsystematic prior to the age of six months (Irwin, 1949). After the age of six months, however, it becomes more systematic, frequently displaying what has been termed *lalling*—the deliberate repetition of a single sound. "Dadadadada," and "bahbahbahbah" are common examples. Lalling is followed by echolalling. *Echolalia* is a tendency to echo what others say. Echolalic babbling involves the infant's repeating sounds that others have produced. Thus, "bye-bye" becomes "byebyebyebyebyebyebyebyebyebyebyebye." Echolalic behavior, which begins around nine or ten months of age, is also accompanied by a rapid decline in the production of sounds that are not in the child's environment. Many of these sounds, so easy at this stage, and so useful for learning Swahili and Chipewyan, become exceedingly difficult later in life.

What has sometimes been termed the *prespeech* stage of development culminates with the systematic babbling of the child toward the end of the first year, and terminates with the appearance of the first meaningful word. This first meaningful word may be seen as the initial step toward an acquisition of syntax. The space between this word and an adultlike production of complex grammatical structures may be seen as involving six major stages (Wood, 1976). They are presented in Table 8.4 and described in the following sections.

Table 8.3 The Early Growth of Vocabulary in Children

Age (years-months)	Average Number of Words
0–8	0
0–10	1
1–0	3
1–3	19
1–6	22
1–9	118
2–0	272
2–6	446
3–0	896
3–6	1,222
4–0	1,540
4–6	1,870
5–0	2,072
5–6	2,289
6–0	2,562

Note: From "An Investigation of the Development of the Sentence and the Extent of Vocabulary in Young Children" by M. E. Smith, *University of Iowa Studies in Child Welfare*, 1926, 3, No. 5.

Table 8.4 Six Stages in Children's Syntactic Development

Stage of Development	Nature of Development	Sample Utterances
1. Sentencelike word (*holophrase*)	The word is combined with nonverbal cues (gestures and inflections) to produce several meanings.	"Mommy." (I see Mommy) "Mommy!" (Pick me up!) "Mommy?" (Where is Mommy?)
2. Modification	Modifiers are joined to topic words to form declarative, question, negative, and imperative structures.	"Pretty baby." (declarative) "Where Daddy?" (question) "No play." (negative) "More milk!" (imperative)
3. Structure	Both subject and predicate are included in the sentence types.	"She's a pretty baby." (declarative) "Where Daddy is?" (question) "I no can play." (negative) "I want more milk!" (imperative)
4. Operational changes	Elements are added, embedded, and permuted within sentences.	"Read it, my book." (conjunction) "Where is Daddy?" (embedding) "I can't play." (permutation)
5. Categorization	Word classes (nouns, verbs, and prepositions) are subdivided and used consistently for recognized grammatical functions.	"I would like *some* milk." (use of "some" with mass noun) "Take me *to* the store." (use of preposition of place)
6. Complex structures	Complex structural distinctions are made, as with "ask-tell" and "promise."	"Ask what time it is." "Tell me what time it is." "He promised to help her."

Note: Based on *Children and Communication: Verbal and Non-Verbal Language Development* by Barbara S. Wood, p. 148. Copyright © 1976. Reprinted by permission of Prentice-Hall, Inc., Englewood Cliffs, New Jersey.

The Sentencelike Word

At around one, children utter their first meaningful words. Actually, it is hard to determine exactly when this occurs, since the transition between the babble and the word is not particularly dramatic. A frequently babbled word, tired and meaningless, suddenly finds itself dressed in new meaning—not one meaning, but perhaps a great many. *Bah* might mean food. Does it mean *banana?* Yes. But is also means *food, give me, I'm hungry,* and a variety of other states, activities, and objects that have been associated with food. This single word with uncounted meanings is termed a **holophrase**. It is much more than a word, although it is often only a single morpheme; there is evidence that it is, in fact, a sentencelike structure. That is, sometimes the child uses holophrases like nouns, sometimes like verbs, and frequently like entire phrases.

McNeill (1970) argues that children develop notions of grammatical structure before they arrive at notions concerning how to express them. In effect, the majority of holophrases are used as nouns. This is probably no accident, since a noun can be used in a variety of grammatical senses without endangering its meaning. Thus, *banana* might mean "Give me the banana," "I'm hungry," "I sat on a banana," and so on. The verb *give,* however, would be subject to a wider array of possible interpretations and misinterpretations. Gurney (1973) notes, in this connection, that holophrases are not used simply for naming. The young child often has less interest in saying "This is a banana and that is an apple" than in saying, "I am hungry" (see Table 8.5).

Modification

By the time the child reaches eighteen months, the single-word utterances of holophrastic speech begin to merge into two-word utterances. This phase of language development has sometimes been described as being *telegraphic,* since it omits a large number of words (principally determiners, such as *the, a, an,* and modifiers) in expressing relatively complete, sentencelike thoughts. It has also been analyzed in terms of the functions of the members of pairs of words (Braine, 1963). Thus, there are *pivot words* and *open words.* The pivot words are those most frequently used. They can be combined with virtually any available open word, but will seldom be used alone or with another pivot word. Open words, however, may be employed alone or with other open words. *All gone* is a common pivot word (even though it is really two words, it is used as a single pivot term and not as a phrase consisting of two separate words), frequently paired with such open words as *Mama, Daddy, banana,* and so on.

Simple syntactical or grammatical rules now become more evident in the child's production of two-word expressions. These rules may be expressed in the form of three alternatives. A sentence may be (1) simply an open word; (2) a pivot word and an open word (in either order); and (3) two open words (again in either order). Table 8.6 presents a number of common open and pivot words and illustrations of how they might be used in sentences following each of these three alternative rules. Essentially the rules describe how words can be combined by twos to modify each other, or how they can be used alone, all in the interest of producing meaningful statements.

Initial development of two-word structures is slow, as is the development of vocabulary in its early stages, but is accelerated rapidly. Braine (1963) cites as one example the case of a boy who produced 14 two-word combinations in his nineteenth month, 24 the next month, and then, in succeeding months, 54; 89; 1,400; and more than 2,500.

Structure

By the age of two to two-and-a-half, children gradually move from two-word combinations to multiple-word sentences. "Pretty baby" becomes "That's a pretty baby," following an intermediate stage where the expression might be "That pretty baby" or "That a pretty baby." Although it has sometimes been argued that the child's short-term memory is initially incapable of coping with multiple-word productions, the real significance of the transition from two-word to multiple-word expressions lies in the

---

Holophrase A single word or sound which, early in the development of language, may take on a great variety of meanings. If a child uses the word *cat* to mean cats, horses, light bulbs, mothers, and other "things," then *cat* is a holophrase for that child. For you and me, *cat* is simply a noun.

Table 8.5 Single-Word Utterances (Holophrases) and Their Many Meanings

Holophrase	Possible Meanings
Noun	
Milk	I'm thirsty.
	There is the milk.
	Here comes the milkman.
	Daddy is nice.
Verb	
Go	Let's go.
	Are you going?
	Please go.
	Daddy is nice.
Preposition	
On	Turn the light on.
	The car is running.
	The light is on.
	Daddy is nice.
Adjective	
Pretty	You're pretty.
	I'm smart.
	I like my cookie.
	The cat is nice.

Table 8.6 Pivot Words and Open Words: Modification Stage of Syntactic Development

---

Pivot: gone pretty see   *Open:* milk baby dog

Syntactical rules in "18-month-old language"
1. *Pivot words* are seldom used alone.
   ("See Mama," but rarely just "see")

2. An *open word* expresses a complete meaning by itself, so it frequently appears alone.
   ("milk" = "give me milk," or "That is milk," or "I'm thirsty")
   ("dog" = "I see a dog," and so on)

3. Two *open words* form a meaningful expression by themselves.
   ("Dog milk" = "Give the dog some milk" or "The dog is drinking milk")

4. Pivot and open word combinations also form meaningful statements.
   ("Baby gone," "Pretty dog," and so on)

---

grammatical structure employed. For the first time, children begin to use complete subjects and predicates. In addition, they now make use of pronouns in sentences and of inflected endings such as *ing*. Thus, a two-word expression such as "Daddy go" now becomes "You going?" and eventually "Are you going?" Nouns are being replaced with noun phrases and with pronouns; verbs with verb phrases.

Operational Changes

Between the ages of two-and-a-half and three or four, children acquire some of the more complex aspects of syntax that permit them to make changes in the simple structures of their earlier sentences. These changes, termed *transformations* and discussed in more detail in a later section, are of three kinds: *conjunction, embedding,* and *permutation* (Wood, 1976). Simple conjunction is illustrated by the joining of two simple sentence structures to form a third, more complex. "We go" becomes "Where we go?" following the conjunction of *we go* and *where*. Similarly, "Me eat nice banana" may be seen as a conjunction of *me eat* and *nice banana*. Embedding involves the introduction of words within a simple sentence. Thus, *no* embedded in *me eat* transforms the sentence into "Me no eat." Permutation is the reordering of words within a sentence and is required to transform a declaration into a question. Initially, children's questions make use of inflection rather than permutation. "I can eat," a simple declaration, becomes a question, without permutation, when *eat* is inflected as in "I can *eat*?" The permutation rule for transforming "I can eat" into a question changes the word order: "Can I eat?" There is sometimes a relatively long period during which children make use of a question such as "why" or "where" without transforming the declaration: "Why I can't go?"

Categorization

Implicit in the preschool child's use of language is a recognition of the grammatical functions of various words and phrases. Nouns and noun phrases, verbs, adjectives, and adverbs are all used as though they have been categorized as such. That is, nouns are treated as nouns, and not as predicates; adjectives are no longer treated as verbs. Increasing mastery of syntax, however, requires further categorization. Not all nouns are the same, for example: some are plural, others singular. The child's manifestation of an understanding of this type of categorization is reflected in the choice of verbs and determiners (for example, *the, that, these*). Thus, "box empty" eventually becomes "*That* box *is* empty" or "*Those* boxes *are* empty," as the case may be. Before mastering these categorizations, children make such characteristic errors as "This boxes is empty."

Complex Structures

The final stage of syntactical development involves learning the subtleties implicit in the complex grammatical structures of adult language usage. Much of this learning occurs in the first three or four grades of elementary school and involves, among other things, learning distinctions between commands, requests, and promises; asking and telling; and so on (Wood, 1976). These are distinctions that we as adults know so well and so intuitively that we take them almost entirely for granted; such is not the case for young children. "I asked him to go," "I told him to go," and "I ordered him to go" are quite different, but in ways sometimes too subtle for the five-year-old to understand.

Theories of Language Acquisition

Learning syntax is a complicated and intriguing affair long neglected by psychology. What psychology has known for some time, however, is that none of our traditional explanations of learning could adequately account for language learning. Skinner's (1957) insistence that a theory of verbal behavior should be completely divorced from such mentalistic notions as ideas, meanings, and grammatical rules, and that it should instead be tied directly to the laws of operant conditioning, has fallen short of being a complete explanation. It was Skinner's contention that children learn labels (*tacts*) and demands (*mands*) as a function of being reinforced for using the right labels or for requesting the right things. As Chomsky (1965) notes, the countless expressions employed by adults and young children alike that they have never used before, and that have therefore not received any direct reinforcement in the past, can hardly be explained through operant conditioning.

Similarly, explanations based on theories of imitation have not proven adequate. There is little doubt that imitation is central to language acquisition. If this were not the case, we could not predict as reliably as we now can that those children who are reared by French parents will learn to speak French rather than Stony. But the appearance of expressions that are not present in the language that surrounds children indicates that there is more to learning a language than simple imitation. Most striking among these expressions, and perhaps most damaging for imitation theories, are those that involve **overregularization**. Children invent certain grammatical rules, but do not immediately learn all the exceptions that accompany them. Accordingly, they apply their rules everywhere. There is a rule that says that adding the sound *s* to a verb makes it appropriate for a third-person-singular subject. It is a good rule: I eat, he eats; I talk, she talks; I buy, he buys; I groan, it groans. Sometimes it is less good, as in "he doos." It is as a result of overregularization that children say, "It goed," "I sayed," "I runned," "I writed," and so on.

One of the most amazing and puzzling features of language development is that the intuitive ability to employ grammatical rules develops in the absence of any formal training. Because this is so, because it occurs in no other animal, and because it occurs at about the same age in all normal children—sometimes very much in spite of their environment—Lenneberg (1967) argues that the ability to learn language is species-specific and largely innate. To further support this contention, he has documented a remarkable correspondence between the acquisition of motor skills and the development of language, in both normal and retarded children. Lenneberg et al. (1964), for example, studied language and motor development of sixty-one people, aged two to twenty-two years, with Down's syndrome (mongolism). Perhaps the most striking observation was that, *regardless of age,* when children were at a babbling stage of language development, they were crawling; and when they had begun to walk, they were capable of simple one-word utterances (see Table 8.7).

Chomsky (1957, 1972), too, has advanced a biological theory of language development. He proposes that all humans have a built-in predisposition to learn grammar, a proposition with which many now agree (Lenneberg, 1967, for example). It is as though there are innate neurological mechanisms that somehow correspond to grammar, thereby facilitating the child's acquisition of syntax. This prewired neurological something has been labeled a **language acquisition device** (LAD) or an *acquisition model* (AM). Its existence would explain some of the facts that cannot easily be explained otherwise, but it does remain highly speculative.

Overregularization A process in the acquisition of language where children apply rules in all possible relevant instances without regard for exceptions. Because our language is not entirely regular (not entirely predictable), overregularization leads to errors.

Language acquisition device (LAD) A label employed by Chomsky to describe the neurological *something* that corresponds to grammar and that is assumed to be innate.

Table 8.7 Correspondence between Motor and Language Development

At the Completion of:	Motor Development	Vocalization and Language
12 weeks	Supports head when in prone position; weight is on elbows; hands mostly open; no grasp reflex.	Markedly less crying than at 8 weeks; when talked to and nodded at, smiles, followed by squealing gurgling sounds usually called *cooing*, which is vowel-like in character and pitch-modulated; sustains cooing for 15–20 seconds.
16 weeks	Plays with a rattle placed in hands (by shaking it and staring at it), head self-supported; tonic neck reflex subsiding.	Responds to human sounds more definitely; turns head; eyes seem to search for speaker; occasionally some chuckling sounds.
20 weeks	Sits with props.	The vowel-like cooing sounds begin to be interspersed with more consonantal sounds; labial fricatives, spirants and nasals are common; acoustically, all vocalizations are very different from the sounds of the mature language of the environment.
6 months	Sitting: bends forward and uses hands for support; can bear weight when put into standing position, but cannot yet stand with holding on; reaching: unilateral; grasp: no thumb apposition yet; releases cube when given another.	Cooing changing into babbling resembling one syllable utterances; neither vowels nor consonants have very fixed recurrences; most common utterances sound somewhat like *ma, mu, da,* or *di.*
8 months	Stands holding on; grasps with thumb apposition; picks up pellet with thumb and finger tips.	Reduplication (or more continuous repetitions) becomes frequent; intonation patterns become distinct; utterances can signal emphasis and emotions.
10 months	Creeps efficiently; takes side-steps, holding on; pulls to standing position.	Vocalizations are mixed with sound play such as gurgling or bubble blowing; appears to wish to imitate sounds, but the imitations are never quite successful; beginning to differentiate between words heard by making differential adjustment.
12 months	Walks when held by one hand; walks on feet and hands—knees in air; mounting of objects almost stopped; seats self on floor.	Identical sound sequences are replicated with higher relative frequency of occurrence and words (*mamma* or *dadda*) are emerging; definite signs of understanding some words and simple commands.
18 months	Grasp, prehension and release fully developed; gait stiff, propulsive and precipitated; sits on child's chair with only fair aim; creeps downstairs backward; has difficulty building tower of three cubes.	Has a definite repertoire of words—more than three, but less than fifty; still much babbling but now of several syllables with intricate intonation pattern; no attempt at communicating information and no frustration for not being understood; words may include items such as *thank you* or *come here,* but there is little ability to join any of the lexical items into spontaneous two-item phrases; understanding is progressing rapidly.
24 months	Runs, but falls in sudden turns; can quickly alternate between sitting and stance; walks stairs up or down, one foot forward only.	Vocabulary of more than fifty items (some children seem to be able to name everything in environment); begins spontaneously to join vocabulary items into two-word phrases; all phrases appear to be own creations; definite increase in communicative behavior and interest in language.
30 months	Jumps up into air with both feet; stands on one foot for about two seconds; takes few steps on tiptoe; jumps from chair; good hand and finger coordination; can move digits independently; manipulation of objects much improved; builds tower of six cubes.	Fastest increase in vocabulary with many new additions every day; no babbling at all; utterances have communicative intent; frustrated if not understood by adults; utterances consist of at least two words, many have three or even five words; sentences and phrases have characteristic child grammar; they are rarely verbatim repetitions of an adult utterance; intelligibility is not very good yet, though there is great variation among children; seem to understand everything that is said to them.
3 years	Tiptoes three yards; runs smoothly with acceleration and deceleration; negotiates sharp and fast curves without difficulty; walks stairs by alternating feet; jumps twelve inches; can operate tricycle.	Vocabulary of some one thousand words; about 80 percent of utterances are intelligible even to strangers; grammatical complexity of utterances is roughly that of colloquial adult language, although mistakes still occur.
4 years	Jumps over rope; hops on right foot; catches ball in arms; walks line.	Language is well established; deviations from the adult norm tend to be more in style than in grammar.

Note: From *Biological Foundation of Language* by Eric H. Lenneberg. Copyright 1967 by John Wiley & Sons Inc., New York. Used by permission of John Wiley & Sons, Inc.

Psycholinguistics

Much of what has thus far been said about language concerns its structure, a topic that falls in the realm of linguistics; much of what has been said also concerns its function and acquisition and falls within the realm of psychology. These two areas have recently been bridged by a mushrooming new discipline: psycholinguistics. It is no longer necessary to draw artificial separations between the acquisition of language, its role in communication and thought, and its more fundamental structure. Current psycholinguistics bridges all these interests, with emphasis on the relationship between grammar and meaning.

Transformational Grammar

A major contribution to psycholinguistics has been Chomsky's (1972) discovery and elaboration of *phrase-structure rules* and *transformational rules* that we employ in the production and understanding of language. Phrase structure refers to the types and functions of word units that make up phrases. *The turkey,* for example, is a noun phrase. Its structure consists of two words: an article and a noun. According to phrase-structure rules, a noun phrase can consist of a noun (*turkeys*); an article and a noun (*the turkeys*); an article, an adjective, and a noun (*the ugly turkeys*); and so on. Transformational rules are the rules that allow us to transform the structure of phrases, to combine phrases—in short, to make meaningful sentences. By the same token, these rules allow us to understand meaningful units of speech. A transformational rule might state, for example, that a sentence can be composed of a noun phrase and a verb phrase (*A turkey ate the eagle*). **Transformational grammar**, encompassing phrase-structure rules and transformational rules, is a set of highly precise rules for generating acceptable sentences (see Figure 8.21).

Where did these highly precise rules come from? Chomsky says that, in effect, children discover (or invent) these rules to permit them to generate sentences and eventually to recognize and avoid nonsentences. This conceptualization of language-learning has some clear advantages over most traditional explanations. Consider, for example, that when a child has learned a simple phrase-structure rule for generating a noun phrase such as *the dog,* it becomes unnecessary for that child to learn the phrase *the girl* or any equivalent phrase, since thousands of them can be generated simply by substituting equivalents: *the horse, a girl, the boy,* and so on. What has been learned, in effect, are large classes of equivalent words and certain rules for treating them appropriately.

Deep and Surface Structure

There are two fundamental tasks involved in speaking and understanding. One is to produce a sequence of sounds that corresponds to some intended meaning (more about meaning shortly). The production of meaningful speech sounds is termed *encoding.* The other task is to extract meaning from sequences of sounds. This is termed *decoding.* Chomsky describes the sounds of a verbal expression as its **surface structure**; its meaning, as **deep structure**. The two are not identical. The problem involved in understanding language is essentially one of deriving deep structure from surface structure. We do this through an implicit knowledge of phrase-structure and transformational rules.

There are three obvious situations where surface structure might be misleading were it not for our knowledge of phrase-structure and transformational rules (Chomsky, 1965). Sometimes different orders of words (different surface structures) have identical meanings (identical deep structure). For example, "Luba ate the turkey" is semantically equivalent to "The turkey was eaten by Luba," in spite of the very different surface structures of these two sentences.

Second, there are situations where sentences with identical surface structures (in terms of order) have *different* meanings. These differences immediately become apparent when the sentences are analyzed in terms of phrase structure. "Bob is afraid

Transformational grammar A set of highly precise rules, which we discover or invent as children, for generating acceptable sentences and distinguishing nonsentences. Transformational grammar encompasses phrase-structure rules and transformational rules.

Surface structure The sounds of a verbal expression. Surface structure is not to be confused with meaning, since it does not go beyond the outward appearance or sound of a language expression.

Deep structure The meaning of a language expression. Meaningfulness is derived from the surface structure of a sentence or of a verbal expression, but often requires as well that the interpreter take context and other cues into consideration.

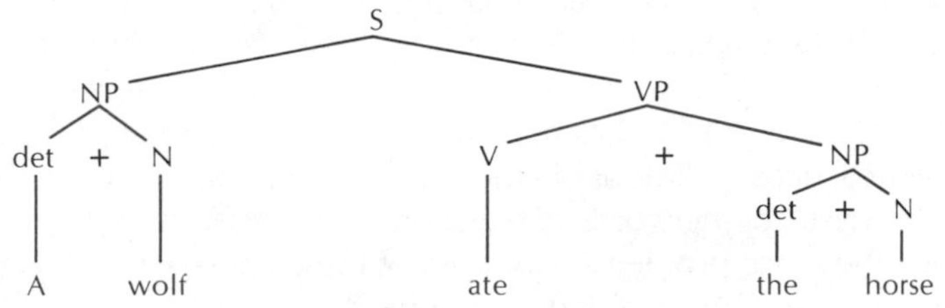

Figure 8.21 Some simple rules of transformational grammar and their application in a tree diagram. (Based on Chomsky, 1972.)

1. S (sentence) = NP (noun phrase) + VP (verb phrase)

2. NP may consist of:

N (noun)	(wolves)
determiner + N	(some wolves)
adjective + N	(gray wolves)
pronoun	(they)
pronoun + adjective + N	(his gray wolves)
determiner + adjective + N	(some gray wolves)

3. VP may consist of:

V (verb)	(ate)
auxiliary + V	(can eat)
V + NP	(ate the horse)
V + adverb	(ate quietly)

Given these rules, a sentence may be constructed as follows:

```
                           S
              NP                        VP
       det  +   N        V    +              NP
                                       det  +   N

        A     wolf       ate            the   horse
```

to lose" has the same surface structure as "Bob is easy to lose." The difference between these two sentences lies not so much in the fact that *afraid* and *easy* have different meanings, as in the fact that they are embedded in different phrase structures. In the first case, *Bob* is the subject; in the second, *Bob* is the object.

A third example of potentially misleading surface structure can be found in expressions where a single sentence can have two or more meanings. Consider, for example: "They are racing horses" or "Helping mothers can be fun." The first sentence might mean that a group of horses are racing horses, not plow horses, *or* that a group of people are racing horses, not cars. The underlying phrase structure determines their meaning. It, in turn, can often be determined only from context.

Meaning

Although Chomsky's transformational grammar and phrase structure analysis has stimulated a great deal of research and contributed considerably to our appreciation of the complexities of language (and of the magnitude of the tasks that face children in their attempts to master language), much of the recent emphasis in psycholinguistics has been directed toward understanding *meaning*.

One of the primary functions of language is the communication of meaning—of what is termed *semanticity*. Meaning, however, is by no means a simple concept; accordingly, there is not yet any obvious consensus with respect to the meaning of meaning, or concerning the most fruitful approaches to understanding understanding. The following summary presents only a small hint of the complexities involved, by describing very briefly several theoretical approaches to meaning and by raising questions that each approach cannot adequately answer (based in part on H. H. Clark & Clark, 1977).

Referential Theory The meaning of a word is what the word refers to. Thus *dog* means "dog" because it refers to an animal to which we both know I intend it to refer. What does *and* refer to? Or *although, if, is, whether*?

Image Theory   Words mean whatever image they evoke. Thus, *horse* means "horse" because it evokes an image of an animal that we both recognize as being a horse. Unfortunately, images are idiosyncratic. My image for *horse* at this moment is of Ruling Tinda, wearing the number 3, sporting the colors of the Winfield stable (purple and white), and hitting the wire an easy four lengths up front. My image might be quite different tomorrow; yours might be quite different right now. Has the meaning of *horse* changed?

Componential Approach   The meaning of a word is determined by those properties an object must have in order to be what it is. In other words, the meaning of *turkey* may be expressed in terms of the criterial attributes of turkeys (bird, gobbles, noble). Ryle (1951) notes that a number of words cannot be defined in terms of any attributes that they *must* have (for example, *work, playing, fighting*): In other words, it is possible for activities that we would recognize as being one of these to have nothing in common.

Quantificational Approach   Meaning may be represented in terms of the combined evaluational judgments of a number of people. For example, the meaning of *mother* is "good" or "soft" if people react to the word in those terms. This approach, exemplified by Osgood (1957), has been useful for studying attitudes and emotional reactions to words, but says little about their specific referents, or about the properties typically characteristic of the words in question.

Although there are problems with each of these approaches, this by no means suggests that they are all invalid and should be discarded. They should, instead, be thought about. The problems involved here are essentially conceptual. Unlike many of the problems that concern psychologists, the meaning of meaning is perhaps much more likely to be revealed in intelligent and concentrated *thinking* than in the results of experimental research.

Language and Thought

The relationship between language and thinking has been a matter of some speculation and controversy. One position holds that language is necessary for thought; another that thought is necessary for language; a third, that the two are independent. There are virtually no contemporary psychologists who adhere strictly to any one of these alternatives, although some lean more in one direction than the other.

Whorf's Hypothesis

Whorf was one psychologist who didn't mind taking sides. His (1941, 1956) hypothesis, in its most extreme form, maintains that language is necessary for thought. It is based on the notion that all thinking is verbal, and that the forms thoughts take must therefore be limited to the possibilities inherent in language. The evidence most often cited in support of this position is based on studies of perceptual and cognitive differences between people who speak different languages. That the Eskimos have twelve or more different words for snow has sometimes been interpreted as evidence that they can perceive and think about snow in ways quite foreign to most of us. Similarly, numerous studies of color perception among primitive tribes has uncovered a number of groups with limited color vocabularies. Some evidence has suggested that people who do not have different terms for colors such as blue and green are, in fact, unable to perceive the differences between these hues, and therefore do not think about them as we do (Rivers, 1901). Subsequent research has revealed, however, that where language indicates perceptual differences, it is nevertheless possible to teach people terms that were not initially in their vocabularies, and to have them use these terms appropriately. It might be, however, that accurate perception occurs only *after* the appropriate terms have been learned.

Bernstein's Language Codes

Bernstein also presents evidence that language is central to thought. He speculates that the inferior school achievement of children from disadvantaged backgrounds may be linked directly to inadequacies in their language. He describes the language of disadvantaged parents (and children) as a **restricted language code**; in contrast, more advanced language usage is termed an **elaborated language code**. Hypothetical examples of each are given below (Lefrancois, 1983):

Restricted:

Mother: Clean your feet.

Child: Why?

Mother: Because.

Child: Because why?

Mother: I said clean your feet, that's why.

Child: But why clean my feet?

Elaborated:

Mother: Clean your feet, Henry. They are about to dirty the carpet.

Child: Why you don't want it to dirty the carpet, Mom? Why, Mom? Why you don't want?

Mother: Because it's messy, Henry, and we must keep the carpet clean for when Daddy comes home, because Dad doesn't like to have mud all over the carpet.

Restricted language has the following characteristics (Bernstein, 1958): It is employed to express emotion or to control, rather than to express information or to rationalize; it is less personal, less precise, and more global; sentences are short, grammatically simple, and often incorrect; gestures and other expressions are frequently used in place of language; and it is liberally sprinkled with idiom and colloquialism. To the extent that these observations are true, it is not particularly surprising that children with restricted language backgrounds should initially do less well in school. It should be pointed out, however, that their sometimes inferior achievement may not be indicative of inferior language development so much as of *different* language development. Baratz (1969) found, for example, that black and white children who performed differently on measures of standard English performed equally well when presented with language codes outside their primary code. It appeared not so much that the blacks were at an inferior level of language development as that they had developed different language codes—language codes which, since they were not standard English, did not serve them as well in school.

Piaget's and Vygotsky's Theories

Not all theoretical positions maintain that language is necessary for thought. Piaget (1923) points out, for example, that the development of certain logical concepts frequently precedes the understanding of words corresponding to those concepts. Words such as *bigger, smaller, longer, farther,* and so on are not understood until the logical properties themselves are understood. H. H. Clark (1973) advances much the same argument (Figure 8.22).

Vygotsky's (1962) position is only slightly different. He contends that language and thinking have separate roots—that, in short, the two initially develop independently. Certainly, there is unquestionable evidence of thought among nonverbal animals, and in the preverbal child. There is anecdotal evidence, as well, that many people can "think" music or imagine physical activity without any accompanying verbalization. Vygotsky suggests that it is not until around the age of two that thought becomes verbal and, at the same time, speech rational—although adult thought need not always be verbal, or speech always rational.

Restricted language code A term employed by Bernstein to describe the language typical of children from disadvantaged backgrounds. Restricted language codes are characterized by short and simple sentences, general and relatively imprecise terms, idiom and colloquialism, and incorrect grammar.

Elaborated language code A phrase employed by Bernstein to describe the language of children from "advantaged" backgrounds (usually "middle" or "upper" class). Elaborated language codes are grammatically correct, complex, and precise.

Figure 8.22 The development of certain logical concepts frequently precedes the understanding of words for those concepts.

In Conclusion

Investigations of the contribution of language to thinking and problem solving present some difficulties of interpretation. Since we cannot ordinarily communicate thought except in language, it is extremely difficult to separate the two. Even nonverbal (performance) tasks like those sometimes employed in intelligence tests ordinarily require the understanding of verbal directions. In addition, the execution of these tasks may be accompanied by verbalization, sometimes expressed and sometimes covert.

The most reasonable conclusion regarding the relationship of thought and language appears to be that the two are intimately related despite the fact that they can occur independently. As Sokolov (1959) contends, it is through language that most thoughts are formulated, and it is language that makes it possible to analyze, synthesize, abstract, and generalize. More than this, it is primarily through language that we become aware of the thoughts of others—and they of ours. Language is without doubt the single greatest binding force of all cultures.

Main Points

1 Thought is symbolic mental activity, usually conscious and usually verbal. It is manifested in daydreams, fantasies, organizing, speculating, problem solving, remembering, imagining, self-talk, and so on.

2 Thinking is essentially a cognitive activity. Behavioristic explanations are inadequate for processes like solving abstract mathematical problems or using language.

3 Artificial intelligence is a branch of computer science that uses computers to simulate human cognitive processes or as analogies for these processes. It tries to make computers smarter primarily to learn about humans.

4 Machines can imitate a variety of human processes, sometimes involving relatively silly games such as "toe-stepping," and sometimes involving more complex activities such as chess-playing. That a machine can imitate a behavior that requires us to think does not mean that the machine itself can think.

5 Computer and machine analogies for human thought processes take a couple of forms: problem-solving analogies, where a computer program solves problems in ways similar to those we might employ; and feedback analogies, where the computer's self-regulation in response to feedback serves as an analogy. In this analogy our behavior can be described with terms and concepts, like the TOTE sequence, borrowed from computing sciences.

6 The theory of Miller et al. describes behavior and thought in terms of arrangements of plans, TOTE (test, operate, test, exit) sequences, and images that serve as the source of plans and of tests for plans.

7 A robot is a machine that performs a function or a series of functions that might otherwise be performed by humans. Although there are numerous robots in factories, they are of limited interest to artificial intelligence. The ultimate robot will be of greater interest.

8 Problems, situations that are in need of solutions, may be described in terms of the amount of new thinking required for their solution. Convergent thought processes result in a single, correct solution; divergent (creative) thought processes result in a variety of solutions, none of which is necessarily *the* correct solution.

9 A strategy is an orderly, purposeful approach to the solution of problems. Bruner describes a number of strategies that might be employed to attain concepts. Most of these are designed not only to ensure that the concept will be attained, but also to minimize the amount of cognitive strain (demand on memory and thought processes).

10 Research suggests that children acquire concepts of intermediate generality prior to more specific concepts, and the most generic concepts are often acquired last (cat before Siamese before cat family).

11 Bruner describes concept formation as a process of learning what goes with what—of forming categories and learning rules that can then be used to classify different things in the same categories. Most of the criteria that are employed to determine whether or not something belongs to a specific category are abstract.

12 Set is a tendency to perceive specific stimuli and to respond in one way rather than in another. Set may be a hindrance to the solution of a problem when it prevents us from seeing new relationships or new functions (functional fixedness); it can also be highly helpful when it suggests effective and time-saving ways of solving problems.

13 *Creative* is an adjective that can describe a person, a process, or a product. It generally refers to that which is novel or original.

14 Although there are a number of tests designed to measure creativity, there is little evidence that what they measure is highly related to creative behavior or to the production of objects, ideas, or works that might be judged as creative by others. Self-ratings are sometimes as valid as these tests.

15 Brainstorming, one of the group techniques that has been developed to promote creativity, is based on the principle of deferred evaluation, and encourages people to produce a variety of wild and unusual ideas.

16 De Bono describes lateral thinking in much the same way as others have described divergent thinking; it is geared toward the production of a variety of responses, and encourages new ways of approaching problems.

17 Language is a verbal form of communication that makes use of sounds in particular combinations to communicate meaning; it is not necessary for communication, however.

18 Language consists of simple sounds (phonemes) arranged so as to have meanings (morphemes are the simplest meaningful units). In addition, prosody (intonation and inflection)

and syntax (grammar—rules that define permissible combinations and sequences) give language its meaning.

19 Three important characteristics of language are meaningfulness (also called semanticity); displacement (that which is represented by language can be physically remote); and productiveness (language allows each of us to create or generate meaning).

20 Attempts to teach chimpanzees and gorillas human language have failed. Attempts to teach them American Sign Language have been considerably more impressive, and have given rise to a rather significant current controversy. Have these primates actually learned language, as most of their trainers claim? Or have they simply learned to imitate certain gestures that reliably lead to reinforcement, as a number of critics claim? We honestly don't yet know whether language makes sense to an ape as it does to a child.

21 Language acquisition in the child progresses from meaningless sounds to meaningless babbles (repetitive sounds); from babbles to sentencelike words; to combinations of words with increasingly complex structure; finally to a stage where transformational changes are possible, and where an impressive knowledge of grammar is implicit in the child's use of language.

22 Behavioristic and imitation theories of language acquisition cannot easily explain the ease and rapidity with which children acquire language; nor can they explain the large number of nonimitative errors that children make when they overregularize their newly-learned rules (as in "I goed"; "I dood"; "I sayed").

23 Knowledge of phrase-structure and transformational rules is implicit in the child's use of correct phrases and sentences.

24 That language and thought are intimately related is clear. The Whorfian position is that language is necessary for thought; Piaget and Vygotsky suggest that language is not always necessary for thought and that, on occasion, thought precedes language. Evidence of thought in nonhuman animals and in pre-verbal children support this latter hypothesis.

Further Readings

Computer simulation of human thought processes and computer analogies for these processes are described in:

Newell, A., and Simon, H. A. *Human problem solving*. Englewood Cliffs, N.J.: Prentice-Hall, 1972.

A collection of some of Bruner's most important and highly readable articles is contained in:

Bruner, J. (Ed.). *Beyond the information given: Studies in the psychology of knowing*. New York: W. W. Norton, 1973.

For an analysis of the relationships between thought and language, and for a useful description of problem solving, see:

Greene, J. *Thinking and language*. London: Methuen, 1975.

Brown describes the development of language in young children in:

Brown, R. *A first language: The early stages*. Cambridge, Mass.: Harvard University Press, 1973.

An excellent account of research on problem solving and thinking, together with a fascinating collection of problems that have been used in this research, is presented in:

Mayer, R. E. *Thinking and problem solving: An introduction to human cognition and learning*. Glenview, Ill.: Scott, Foresman, 1977.

Osborn's book, translated into dozens of languages, has been widely employed by groups and individuals interested in promoting creativity:

Osborn, A. *Applied imagination*. New York: Charles Scribner's, 1957.

Provocative and highly readable books by de Bono address themselves to the problems of teaching for thinking and for creativity, and contain a large number of useful exercises:

de Bono, E. *Lateral thinking: A textbook of creativity*. London: Ward Lock Educational Limited, 1970.

de Bono, E. *Teaching thinking*. London: Temple Smith, 1976.

There is considerable current controversy concerning whether or not apes can learn language. The following three references present an introduction to this controversy. Premack's book says yes; the first part of Terrace's book shows why many researchers have said yes, although the second part shows why at least some should have said "no"; and the Sebeok and Umiker-Sebeok collection presents a strong critique of many of the conclusions reached by ape-language research.

Premack, D. *Why chimps can read.* New York: Harper, 1976.

Terrace, H. S. *Nim: A chimpanzee who learned sign language.* New York: Knopf, 1980.

Sebeok, T. A., and Umiker-Sebeok, D. J. (Eds.). *Speaking of apes: A critical anthology of two-way communication with man.* New York: Plenum, 1980.

Much of the psychological endeavor can be described as a search for the average person. Although we should always be aware that the average person does not exist—that there are *individual differences* among people—it is virtually impossible to arrive at an understanding of perceptual processes, developmental progressions, learning, thinking, and remembering without first reducing these processes and phenomena to that which is common to the greatest number of people. With respect to such topics as perception, for example, the reduction is not particularly difficult. We tend to see things in pretty much the same way.

Motivation and emotion present more difficult problems, because our motives are more individualistic, and our emotions more private. These are the psychological dimensions that most clearly differentiate us one from another. Not only has it been very difficult to determine how the average person feels and expresses emotion in different situations, but it has been even more difficult to generalize this knowledge to a specific individual in a given situation.

In spite of these difficulties, motives and emotions are absolutely central in any consideration of the human condition. Accordingly, Chapter 9 looks at a number of specific motives, ranging from basic physiological motives such as hunger and thirst to more humanistic motives such as those expressed in our attempts to know and understand, and to relate to other people. Chapter 10 examines human emotions.

PART THREE

Motives and Feelings

Chapter 9
Motivation
Chapter 10
Emotion

Motivation

Inspired by the conviction that education might eventually make something not entirely shameful of me, my parents sent me away when I reached ninth grade. Isolated as we were in the woods of northern Saskatchewan, higher education was considered a rare commodity, well worth pursuing no matter how lonely the places where it could be found.

It was a lonely place. Although the little hamlet that boasted the high school had more people than I'd ever seen before, most were strangers. The woods were strangers too, friendlier than the people, but not mine, as *my woods* were a scant five miles away.

One of the good sisters pioneered a taxidermy course that year, thinking perhaps that taxidermy might motivate her students more than Latin and algebra. "Bring in any dead animals or birds you find," she insisted, "and we will stuff them." I had not known that this was the stuff of which high schools were made.

Dead cats and dogs were numerous; crows and magpies, too. Beavers and muskrats. Gophers and weasels; owls and hawks; frogs and mice. All were skinned and dried, tanned and stretched, stuffed and shaped, till the walls of the classroom resembled nothing more than a grotesque caricature of a haphazard museum, for most of us had neither the skill nor the talent for our duties. Birds looked like rats, rats like frogs. Our beavers were lumpy and deformed, their noses skewed, their eyes crossed, and sometimes of different colors. The good sister smiled through it all, speaking algebra and Latin, extolling history and science, whispering French verbs as we skinned and cut, stuffed and sewed, painted and combed.

And then the skunk was brought in. "Lovely specimen," proclaimed the good sister. "Who wants to skin it? In the barn."

"I will," I volunteered graciously, "but I don't have to do it in the barn. It's too cold there. Besides, I've skinned many skunks." All of which was true.

Sitting quietly in the skinning corner, I attacked the skunk, quickly and expertly exposing the scent glands, peeling the skin back, and moving on to the safer parts of its anatomy.

Had I not glanced out the window then, pausing to rest, I probably would not have been quite so overcome by the crisp October morning, by memories of my woods in the fall, by a yearning to walk into the hills and follow the river back to its source. Had it been a blustery, rainy October morning, I might not have drawn the knife gently across the glands, already holding my breath. That I reached the door even before the carcass hit the floor is as much a tribute to my foresight and agility as it is to the nefariousness of my character.

The school sat silent and pungent for almost a week. And I, the cause of its silence, found myself in some slight difficulty. Three of the good sisters were driven by horse carriage to our home. After a painfully long, closeted conversation with my parents, they called me in for judgment. I faced a single question: "Why did you do it?" Clearly a motivational question.

Guilty without trial, I grinned sheepishly at my feet: "The devil made me do it."

Motivation

In the wisdom of later years, I will now concede that the devil might have been blameless. But sitting here today thinking of the unborn pages of this chapter, I wish that I could honestly say, "Folks, all that you do not understand about human behavior, I will now explain. We have found all those hidden motives which you expect psychology to discover for you. The ultimate motive is, as I knew so long ago, the devil. That is now the end of this chapter. Nothing more need be said, and we move to Chapter 10." Sadly, though, science will accept neither devils nor gods in its search for truth.

Motivation, science tells us, is what instigates behavior, directs it, and accounts for its cessation. Thus, motivation relates to all aspects of human functioning (learning, development, perception, and so on). But its emphasis is on explanation; it addresses the question "why?" (Figure 9.1). And, to a large extent, it provides an explanation for the distinction often drawn between learning and performance. Recall that *learning* is a change in behavior. *Performance* refers to actual, manifested behavior. In many situations, however, learning does not lead directly to performance. For example, a trained gymnast does not incessantly repeat whatever she has learned; her performance does not continually reflect her learning (or her personality, abilities, skills, and so on). Performance clearly depends on more than learning; it depends on appropriate *motivation*. Put yet another way, motivation describes the factors that account for actual behavior, its direction, and its termination. A trained animal may perform, for example, if it is hungry and has learned that food will be the reward for its performance. The motivation that accounts for its actual behavior (its performance) might, in this case, be limited to hunger. Thus, the *onset* of the behavior may be attributed to hunger. Similarly, the *direction* the behavior takes may also be related to hunger in the sense that the behavior will presumably be of the sort that has some probability of resulting in food; and its *termination* will, in all likelihood, relate to the alleviation of hunger. Hunger motivates; it urges and drives. And so we speak of a *hunger drive,* and of other drives and motives as well. We speak, too, of other primitive urges—what we term instincts.

Instincts

A Canada goose was banded in northern Alberta and ended up on a picnic table in California. A monarch butterfly was labeled in Ontario, Canada, and was later seen on a picnic table in Mexico. Salmon struggle desperately to return to the places that

Figure 9.1 Motivation. Usually the reasons people behave as they do are more complex than "because it's there."

spawned them. One could be found on my picnic table last June. These complex behaviors are common to all members of a species, are apparently unlearned, and are little affected by learning. They are labeled **instincts**.

We assume that instincts motivate behavior, at least in animals. Why do ducks migrate? Because they have an instinct to do so. Actually, this is hard to prove (How do we know they have an instinct to do so? Because they do so. Why do they do so? Because . . .) but instinct labels for certain behaviors seem useful and have not been entirely discarded. The existence of an instinct is assumed to be demonstrated if all individuals of a species behave in highly similar ways without apparently having to learn these behaviors. That a lone salmon should return to its native waters to spawn cannot easily be explained by reference to traditional accounts of learning; the behavior required is simply too complex. Hence we assume there must be genetic influences that account for the behavior, and we label these influences *instinct* (Figure 9.2).

Instincts Biologically determined tendencies or predispositions to react in specific and predictable ways. Instinctive behaviors are generally related to species or individual survival, and are therefore highly adaptive. Although generally considered to be unlearned, their manifestation is subject to environmental influences. Hibernation and migration are clear examples of instincts among nonhuman animals; there are no clear illustrations of instincts among humans.

Figure 9.2 The instinct model.

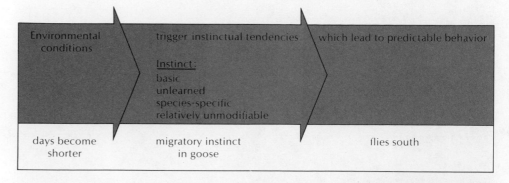

Environmental conditions	trigger instinctual tendencies	which lead to predictable behavior
	Instinct: basic unlearned species-specific relatively unmodifiable	
days become shorter	migratory instinct in goose	flies south

Research with animals has found that instincts can be modified through experience. Rats who are not allowed access to natural environments where they can carry objects around in their mouths do not engage in nest-building behavior when about to give birth (H. G. Birch, 1956). Apparently, lack of appropriate stimulation and experience has disrupted their nesting instincts. However, given relevant early experiences—which do not include lessons in nest construction or prenatal classes and obstetrical advice relating to probable time of delivery—virtually all pregnant female rats build adequate nests at appropriate times. Even domestic cats and dogs are no different.

Given the presence of important instincts among nonhuman animals, it is not surprising that early motivation theorists looked for instincts among humans. It seemed logical that any behavior common to all or most members of the human species might be attributable to an instinct. If this were the case, the search for explanations might be almost over. Mothers care for their young; hence, human females have a maternal instinct. Adults mate; hence, they have a mating instinct. We fight; therefore we have aggressive instincts. We establish homes; therefore we have territorial instincts. Based on their observations of behavior, some early theorists listed hundreds of supposed human instincts (McDougall, 1908, for example). The lists multiplied dramatically, the most brilliant and imaginative observers discovering more new instincts every month. Bernard (1924) counted some 6,000 of these, ranging from such common instincts as gregariousness, maternal urges, and sexual urges, to such exotic and rare instincts as the tendency "to avoid eating apples that grow in one's own garden" (p. 212). The irony of the situation soon become obvious. Nothing was being explained. Behaviors were simply being observed and labeled as instincts. To attribute fighting to an aggressive instinct is, in the final analysis, no more revealing than to say that people fight because they fight.

Imprinting

Though the search for human instincts has largely been abandoned, the search for parallels between imprinted social behaviors in animals and imprintinglike behaviors in humans continues. Imprinted behaviors are complex, instinctlike behaviors manifested by certain animals. Unlike instincts, however, imprinted behaviors are not entirely innate but are acquired, in the sense that they do not appear unless the animal is exposed to appropriate stimulation (termed a **releaser**) at the appropriate time (termed the **critical period**) (see Figure 9.3).

The clearest and most extensively researched example of **imprinting** involves the "following" behavior of newly hatched birds and mammals of certain species. In general, newly hatched ducks, geese, and chickens, and a variety of infant mammals including zebras, moose, goats, and deer, will follow and apparently become attached to the first moving object or the first large object they see *during a critical period* (Sluckin, 1965). Lorenz (1952) gained considerable notoriety from a film that depicts him with three happy goslings behind him (Figure 9.4). To demonstrate some of the characteristics of imprinting, he had simply arranged to be the first moving object seen by these goslings after they hatched. Had he waited three or four days after hatching, the goslings would have been difficult and perhaps impossible to imprint. Similarly, lambs that are removed from their mothers at birth and not brought to them for a week or more do not ordinarily develop any attachment to them (Thorpe, 1963). Perhaps equally striking, mothers of these lambs completely reject them, sometimes butting the hapless youngsters out of the way if they come too close.

The search for imprinted behaviors among humans has not been highly rewarding. A number of researchers have argued that behaviors such as smiling are imprinted behaviors, subject to critical periods, and difficult to establish if not imprinted during those periods. Others suggest that the mother-infant bond is highly dependent upon early contact between mother and infant (Kennell, Trause, & Klaus, 1975; Klaus &

Releaser The stimulus or situation to which an organism must be exposed during the critical period in order for imprinted behaviors to become manifest.

Critical period The period during which exposure to appropriate experiences or stimuli will bring about specific learning much more easily than is the case at other times.

Imprinting A process whereby an animal exposed to appropriate stimulation at the appropriate time acquires a certain behavior. Unlike instincts, imprinted behaviors are acquired, not innate.

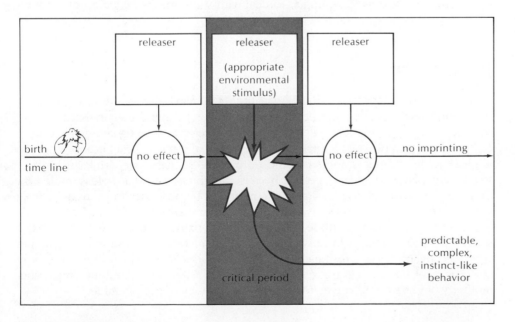

Figure 9.3 A model of imprinting. Under appropriate environmental conditions, exposure to a releaser during the critical period leads to imprinting, which is manifested in predictable behaviors in response to specific environmental conditions. Imprinting does not occur in the absence of a releaser, or if the releaser is presented too early or too late.

Figure 9.4 Imprinting. By arranging events so that he would be the first moving object seen by these geese after they hatched, Lorenz became a "surrogate mother" to this brood. Had he waited a few days longer, it would have been too late for imprinting to take place.

Kennell, 1976). In support of this position, Gray (1958) reports a number of studies that have examined the development of children deprived of social contact during infancy. Some of these studies have reported social maladjustment, apathy, listlessness, general unresponsiveness, and sometimes death, allegedly as a result of such deprivation (Spitz, 1945, 1954). However, these results have not always been replicated in other studies.

Nevertheless, the possibility remains that human social adjustment or, in its absence, hostility, anxiety, and maladjustment are related to imprintinglike behaviors brought about by early social contact. These maladaptive social behaviors are, interestingly enough, highly reminiscent of behaviors often observed in young chickens who are kept in isolation sufficiently long that they do not imprint on any object, animal, or person. Science can ill afford to overlook the possibility that Olive Schreiner (1883; quoted in Sluckin, 1965) was correct: "The souls of little children are marvellously delicate and tender things and keep forever the shadow that first falls on them." Although psychology is ill equipped to deal with souls, the investigation of shadows may not be beyond its capabilities and interests.

Hedonism

Another historical approach to the explanation of human behavior has taken the form of an intuitively appealing and obviously true cliché: people usually behave so as to achieve pleasure and to avoid pain. This position is referred to as *psychological hedonism,* or as the pain-pleasure principle. It says, essentially, that we eat because doing so is pleasurable and not doing so would be painful. Similarly, we drink, make love, work, fight, play, and, in sum, behave because the things we do are pleasurable now or are expected to lead to pleasure in the future, or because they move us away from pain or are expected to move us away from pain in the future. It is, in fact, virtually impossible to quarrel with these statements, since pain and pleasure are subjective states. Bizarre and unattractive behaviors that we sometimes observe in others do not contradict the principle. Presumably eating razor blades is more pleasurable for those who eat razor blades than not eating razor blades. "Chacun à son goût," my grandmother would have said, never realizing the profundity of her platitude.

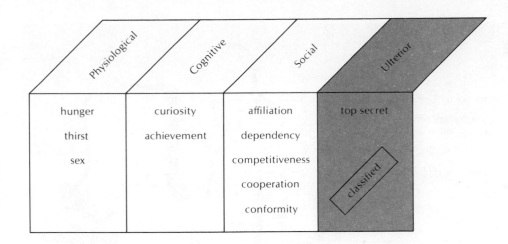

Figure 9.5 The three major categories of motives, plus a fourth. Physiological and cognitive motives are discussed in this chapter; social motives, in Chapter 17. Ulterior motives have not yet been the topic of major psychological research.

In fact, psychological hedonism provides a useless account of human motivation. Unless general principles can define the nature of pain and pleasure, knowing that people are more likely to seek one rather than the other tells us no more than we have always known.

Four Classes of Motives

As we have seen, a distinction is sometimes made between basic, unlearned tendencies to behave in given ways, and behaviors that appear to be learned rather than innately determined. Another way of making this distinction is to refer to the physiological systems that all organisms have, and to the behaviors that are related to those systems. Thus, it is clear that we need to eat and drink and that these **needs** relate directly to the physiological systems we have. The tendencies to act which arise from these needs when they are unsatisfied are termed **drives**. Sex, too, is often considered an unlearned need which gives rise to a basic drive. Thus, we can speak of hunger drives, a thirst drive, and a sex drive.

But eating, drinking, and copulating are not everything, however important they might be. There are a large number of specific human behaviors whose most apparent motives are generally ascribed to other causes—other urges. We explore, we fight, we achieve, we conform, we make friends and enemies. In short, we sometimes behave as though we had altruistic motives, dependency needs, achievement needs, curiosity urges, and so on.

This chapter examines two major classes of human motives: the *physiological motives,* which are related directly to individual or species survival, and the *cognitive motives,* which are more related to our intellectual functioning as well as to other activities that do not appear to be closely involved in physiological survival. A third major class is labeled *social motives;* these give rise primarily to our interaction with others, and are therefore dealt with in Chapter 17 rather than here. A fourth, more mysterious type, the ulterior motive, is not discussed in this chapter. (See Figure 9.5.)

Some Physiological Motives

Hunger, thirst, and the sex drive are the most obvious of the traditional physiological motives. They are considered physiological because they relate directly to physiological systems involved in individual and species survival. Drinking and eating are clearly necessary for individual biological survival. Sex is not needed for individual survival;

Needs and drives Terms such as *need, drive,* and *motive* are often used synonymously, although each can be distinguished. *Motive* is the most general term, refers to all forces, internal or external, involved in accounting for the instigation, direction, and termination of behavior. *Needs* are specific deficits or lacks in an organism, the satisfaction of which will increase the organism's welfare. *Drives* are the effects of the deficits or lacks that define needs. More specifically, drives are tendencies or urges to act in specific ways, determined by the nature of the need that gives rise to the drive. For example, an unsatisfied need for food gives rise to a hunger drive. The hunger drive may then be seen as a motive for behaviors relating to eating.

Figure 9.6 Cannon and Washburn's 1912 experiment to test whether hunger pangs result directly from stomach contractions. The subject (Washburn) swallowed a balloon, which was then lightly inflated inside his stomach. Pressure on the balloon (A) resulting from stomach contractions was recorded on a moving graph (pen B). At the same time, pen C recorded time elapsed, and pen D recorded the subject's feelings of hunger, which he indicated by depressing a key. Pen E recorded respiration movements of a belt around the abdominal area. The subject could not see the recording device during the experiment. Although Cannon and Washburn found a strong correlation between stomach contractions and hunger pangs, later findings indicate that the balloon itself may actually cause contractions (R. C. Davis et al., 1959) and that the duodenum is probably more involved in hunger feelings than is the stomach. (From *Psychology: A Scientific Study of Man* (3rd ed.) by F. H. Sanford and L. S. Wrightsman, Jr. Copyright © 1970 by Wadsworth, Inc. Reprinted by permission of the publisher, Brooks/Cole Publishing Co., Monterey, Calif.)

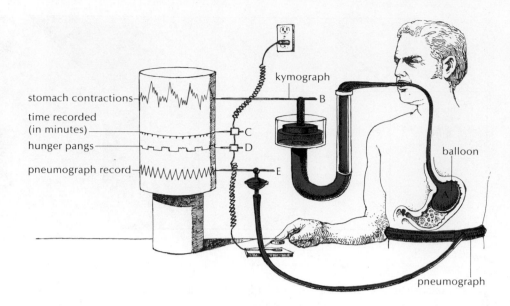

stomach contractions

time recorded (in minutes)

hunger pangs

pneumograph record

kymograph

B

C

D

E

balloon

pneumograph

yet, in some ways, it is as important as either drinking or eating. From an evolutionary point of view, the individual is of considerably less importance than the species. And if individuals do not have a powerful drive urging sexual behavior, the species is doomed to extinction.

Hunger

Subjectively, hunger may be described as the bodily sensations that result from not eating for a period of time. Such sensations range from mild discomfort (the gentle growlings of a hollow belly) to severe pain (the tortured pangs of intense hunger). Normally, death by starvation is preceded by cessation of hunger pains.

Stomach Contractions   Given these subjective observations, it seems reasonable to assume that feelings of hunger are caused by the emptiness of the stomach and its resulting contractions. Early theorists speculated that, as the stomach becomes empty, its walls rub on each other, giving rise to sensations of hunger. Cannon and Washburn (1912) developed an ingenious test designed to discover whether subjective feelings of hunger were in any way related to stomach contractions. Washburn swallowed a balloon which was then inflated inside his stomach. This balloon was connected to a recorder in such a way that when the stomach contracted, a running graph would indicate the contraction. Whenever he felt a hunger pang, Washburn was to depress a key which would indicate the pang on the same graph (see Figure 9.6). Their observation? Washburn's stomach eventually contracted (sometimes he had to wait a long time before this happened); he felt hunger. The correspondence between the two was sufficiently impressive that for many years thereafter most psychologists and physiologists believed that hunger results directly from the actions of an empty or nearly empty stomach.

But truth in the early decades of this century was no less elusive than it is today. It was found later that people with no stomachs also get hungry; that hunger persists even when neural pathways from the stomach to the brain are severed; and that even a full stomach can feel hungry when passage to the small intestine is blocked (Cofer & Appley, 1964). R. C. Davis et al. (1959) later replicated the Cannon and Washburn experiment, using electrodes to monitor stomach contractions. They apparently found that there were no contractions unless a balloon was first inserted in the stomach! Subsequently, however, there have been numerous experiments employing "gastric" balloons (Schachter, 1971). Contractions may sometimes be involved in sensations of hunger, although it is likely that the duodenum (upper part of the small intestine) is even more involved.

Figure 9.7 Hunger is a function of certain physiological mechanisms relating to survival; it is also a function of taste, smell, appearance, and learning, and does not always relate to nutrition.

Taste-Smell Factors But that, not surprisingly, is far from the whole story. The black blowfly *(Phormia regina meigen)*, proboscis extended, tells a small part of the same story. The blowfly normally has a retracted proboscis (an oral appendage similar to that by which a mosquito obtains its nourishment). When its feet come into contact with a sweet substance, and if its gut is empty or nearly empty, its proboscis will extend and it will begin to feed. As the stomach fills, feeding slows down and the proboscis slowly retracts. Typically it will not retract fully at once, but will extend again for short periods of feeding until the fly is finally full. In a fascinating series of experiments, Dethier (1966, 1967) examined factors related to the blowfly's feeding behavior. One of the experiments involved cutting the nerve from the foregut. Under such bizarre experimental conditions, the poor fly does not seem to realize when it is full and continues to feed quite happily until it literally bursts. A second experimental variation presents the fly with a sugar substitute—very sweet but without nutritive value. Again, the fly feeds quite happily, insisting on eating the sweeter substance when given a choice between that and something more nutritious but less sweet. And it eventually starves to death.

Several observations are noteworthy. First, feeding in the blowfly does not depend solely on the condition of the gut (full or empty stomach). It depends also on the presence of sweet substances on the chemical receptors in the feet. This might have implications for understanding human eating behaviors—specifically, for understanding why individuals who should be satiated can nevertheless ingest a wee dessert. Second, feeding in the blowfly relates less to the physiological condition of the fly than to the "taste" of its food. Thus, it can starve to death when presented with non-nutritive but highly appealing foods.

Hunger in humans is also a function of taste-smell factors. Personal evidence suggests strongly that we, like the blowfly, often prefer tasty over less tasty food, regardless of nutritional value (see Figure 9.7; Box 9.1). Even the rat likes to taste its

BOX 9.1

Junk-Food Addicts

White bread, sugar-glazed cereals, soft drinks. Candies and cake. Would we, like the unfortunate blowfly, starve to death, particularly as children, if allowed to eat whatever and whenever we want? Would we forgo nutritive substances in favor of tasty junk food?

D. M. Davis (1928), in a widely cited experiment, allowed infants to select from a variety of available foods. Contrary to popular expectation, their long-term diets were well balanced, and they developed in a normal, healthy fashion. The study was subsequently criticized, however, on the grounds that the choice of available foods made it highly unlikely that any of the infants would have selected a nonnutritive diet.

Nevertheless, subsequent research with rats provides some corroboration for Davis's findings (Richter, 1942–1943). Various dietary deficiencies have been produced artificially in these rats by removing specific glands. The animal typically compensates for the deficiency by eating increased amounts of appropriate foods: rats with adrenal glands removed increase their salt intake; those whose parathyroid glands have been removed increase their calcium intake; and those whose pancreases have been removed dramatically decrease their sugar intake. Even in the body of the lowly white Norway rat there is a little wisdom. It is unlikely that the human body, which survived for perhaps a million years before the appearance of the first registered nutrition expert, has lost all its wisdom. However, we have only recently had to contend with overprocessed, mass-manufactured, "empty" foods. Coping with modern nutrition may well require more wisdom than our bodies naturally have. A case in point is a recently labeled medical condition; the "overconsumption–undernutrition" syndrome (Bland, 1982). The disorder, characterized by fits of aggressive behavior and assorted physical complaints, is attributed to high sugar–low vitamin diets (candy, soft drinks, chocolate milk, cookies), and to a resulting vitamin deficiency (particularly the B vitamins).

In a recent study, LeMagnen (1974) found that rats would eat significantly more if presented with four differently flavored foods than if given only one food. He argues that satiety is closely related to taste-smell factors and that, given sufficient variety, the organism will reach satiety later than if a bland or uniform diet is presented. Sclafani and Springer (1976) report very similar results in a study where they were successful in inducing obesity in a number of rats simply by presenting them with a "supermarket" diet rather than their ordinary diet of lab chow. These rats were allowed to select from at least seven different foods at any time, including chocolate-chip cookies, salami, cheese, bananas, marshmallows, chocolate milk, Crisco fat and Purina powder, and peanut butter. It is worth noting, however, that not all experimental animals became obese when placed on this diet. Like some adult humans, a number remained relatively trim.

Food intake and taste. In Scalfani and Springer's experiment, groups of rats were offered two different diets, both in unlimited amounts. The control group received regular lab chow; the second group a "supermarket" diet. The results: many of the "lucky" rats turned out to be not so lucky. A high proportion became obese. (Adapted from "Dietary Obesity in Adult Rats: Similarities to Hypothalamic and Human Obesity Syndromes" by A. Scalfani and D. Springer, *Physiology and Behavior,* 1976, *17,* 461–471. Copyright 1976 by Pergamon Press, Ltd. Reprinted by permission.)

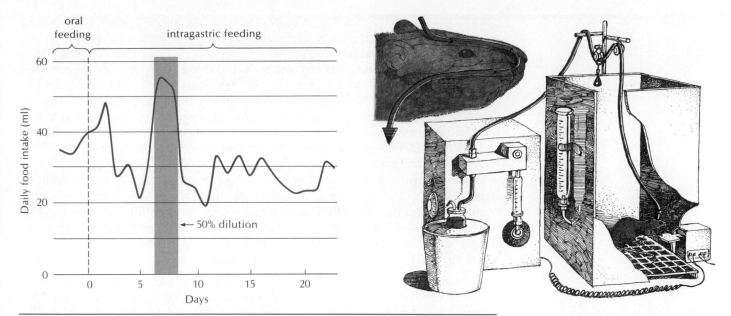

Figure 9.8 Epstein and Teitelbaum studied the role of taste and smell in regulating food intake with the apparatus seen here. Rats were trained to depress a lever to obtain liquid food that went directly into the stomach, so the rats could neither smell nor taste it. Significantly, rats continued to regulate their food intake so as to maintain body weight. As the graph shows, food intake increased markedly when the food was diluted during a two-day period. (From "Regulation of Food Intake in the Absence of Taste, Smell, and Other Oro-pharyngeal Sensations" by A. N. Epstein and P. Teitelbaum, *Journal of Comparative and Physiological Psychology,* 1962, *55,* 753–759. Copyright 1962 by the American Psychological Association. Reprinted by permission.)

food, and eats less when it is prevented from doing so. In an ingenious experiment, Epstein and Teitelbaum (1962) inserted a tube (a nasopharyngeal tube to be precise) into a rat in such a way that it could be fed without having the food come into direct contact with its mouth and nasal regions (see Figure 9.8). Rats were then trained to feed themselves by depressing a lever, giving them control over the amount of food they would ingest. Under these conditions, rats ate approximately 25 percent less than they would when feeding normally. It is significant, however, that they continued to eat enough to maintain their normal weights.

Metabolic Factors   Motivation seeks to explain what instigates behavior, what directs it, and what terminates it. Thus, in order to understand such behaviors as eating, it is necessary to answer questions relating to its onset, its maintenance, and its termination. The preceding discussion provides partial answers for some of these questions. There are other partial answers, some of which relate to body **metabolism**, and others, to brain structure.

It is now suspected that blood sugar levels may be correlated with hunger. As levels of glucose (a form of sugar) in the blood drop, hunger increases; as blood glucose levels rise, there is a decline in hunger (Stunkard et al., 1955). This has been dramatically illustrated by injecting glucagon, which causes a rapid increase in glucose level, into hungry subjects. Stomach contractions and hunger cease very quickly. It would be tempting at this point to conclude that hunger and its cessation are caused by blood sugar levels. In fact, however, this appears to be only half true. Hunger is *initiated* by lower blood glucose levels (more precisely, by lower utilization of blood sugar), but it does not appear to be *terminated* by a corresponding increase in blood sugar level. In fact, since eating ordinarily stops when digestion has scarcely begun, the termination of hunger is probably not ordinarily associated with an increase in blood glucose (save when it is injected directly into the bloodstream). This does not contradict Stunkard et al.'s (1955) finding that hunger drops with increasing blood

Metabolism   The biological processes concerned with building up or breaking down living cellular material and tissue. Basic metabolic processes include those involved in digestion, elimination, and the oxygenation of red blood cells.

glucose levels. The point is that an individual with high blood glucose levels would not ordinarily be hungry; but hunger would cease (presumably after eating) before blood sugar levels could have increased.

More recently, Friedman and Stricker (1976) have proposed that the stimulus for hunger is supplied to the brain, not by the stomach or the bloodstream, but primarily by the liver. Their argument is that the liver is the most important organ in the metabolic processes involved in converting food into usable fuels, and that it is therefore the organ most likely to be sensitive to changes in the supply of metabolic fuels. Since under normal circumstances fuel utilization does not vary dramatically in body tissues (and even less in the brain), it is unlikely that alterations at those levels would trigger hunger or indicate satiety. Hunger ensues before our cells begin to starve; and, as noted, eating generally terminates long before blood sugar levels have risen, but not before metabolism has changed in the liver (as well as in the intestines). In other words, although it is true that changes in blood sugar levels are related to hunger, as are stomach contractions, these events may not be causally linked with hunger or satiety; that is, they often accompany hunger but do not necessarily cause it.

The Brain   Certain parts of the hypothalamus are involved in eating behavior, it was concluded following the discovery of tumors on that portion of the brain among a number of patients suffering from **hyperphagia** (overeating) and consequent obesity (Grossman, 1967). Subsequently, research with rats has done much to clarify the role of brain structures in both eating and drinking.

Among the most salient findings from research on eating in rats is that **lesions** in the *ventromedial* (central lower) part of the hypothalamus (termed *VMH*) cause hyperphagia (Hetherington & Ranson, 1942), and that lesions in the *lateral* (side) part of the hypothalamus (termed *LH*) cause its opposite, **aphagia** (insufficient eating). Subsequent research employing more refined and more precise surgical techniques indicates that the hypothalamus itself is probably not directly involved in the control of eating behavior, but that it acts as a neural transmitting station to other parts of the brain. Thus, it is the severing of the neural pathways rather than the destruction of a brain structure that causes aphagia or hyperphagia (Gold, 1973).

There is also some intriguing evidence that a number of neurotransmitters are centrally involved in the control of appetite. Woods et al. (1981) found, for example, that appetite in obese rats was significantly reduced when they were injected with one of a number of hormones belonging to the chemical group labeled *peptides*. In contrast, injections of beta-endorphins serve to increase appetite (Margules et al., 1978). Recall that the endorphins are opiate-like chemicals produced by the brain, and known to be involved in lessening the perception of pain. Precisely how these chemicals interact with each other, with other hunger-control mechanisms, and with the brain is still a matter of ongoing research.

Hunger Control: A Summary   Hunger is a motive of considerable importance to our physical survival. It is not particularly surprising, therefore, that the relevant underlying physiological systems involve a variety of different mechanisms for the control of food intake. We have seen, for example, that stomach contractions (particularly duodenal contractions) and blood sugar utilization serve as signals for eating or for stopping eating, as do the presence or absence of certain peptides. Each of these mechanisms relates specifically to the immediate and short-term control of eating behavior, and may often have its effects through mediation of specific parts of the hypothalamus. More precisely, research suggests that the LH is involved in the initiation of eating (when it is destroyed or damaged, organisms tend not to eat); in contrast, the VMH is involved in the termination of eating (when damaged, organisms tend to overeat). We have seen, as well, that there is reason to believe that the hypothalamus regulates body weight. It has been hypothesized that our upper and lower body-weight limits are "set" in the VMH and LH respectively, and that these "set points" serve as long-term regulators of our eating behaviors. Both humans and nonhuman animals

Hyperphagia   Derived from Latin terms meaning excessive *(hyper)* and eating *(phagia)*.

Lesions   Structural changes in tissue. Lesions may be caused by injury or disease, or surgically—as is often the case in research. A surgically produced lesion might be a small cut or might involve the removal of part or all of a structure.

Aphagia   The Latin prefix *a* signifies "against" or "opposed to." Aphagia therefore indicates insufficient eating.

appear to eat so as to maintain body weight within these limits. And, in addition to these short-term and long-term hunger-control mechanisms, there is also the savor system: the taste and smell of food are clearly implicated in hunger motivation.

Obesity Unfortunately, our hunger control systems do not always work perfectly, a fact of which I was again reminded this morning when my radio spoke to me of fat people, almost as if it knew that my cognitive processes were somewhere among them. Authoritative as always, it informed me that Americans will spend over 10 billion dollars this year in efforts to lose weight, mostly on drugs, physicians, weight-reducing programs, patent weight-reducing medications, and weight-reducing literature. An impressive 30 percent of all those who seriously attempt to lose weight will be substantially successful. Ironically, only 6 percent of these—hence less than 2 percent of all who try to lose weight—will maintain their reduced weights for any length of time.

What motivates a person to become obese? A number of early studies of fat people suggested that they respond to their internal states differently from normal individuals. For example, although a high correspondence has typically been found between stomach contractions (particularly duodenal contractions) and feelings of hunger, obese people do not always exhibit the same correspondence. They report hunger at times when they would not be expected to do so, based on their physiological conditions. Schachter (1971) hypothesized that obese people might be less tuned in to their internal states, and more to environmental stimulation. He speculated that many obese people may be unable to recognize hunger states and so may eat whenever it seems appropriate to do so or whenever something particularly appetizing is easily available. He and his associates (Schachter et al., 1968) found some corroboration for this prediction in a study of airline pilots. Obese pilots were compared with normal pilots on international flights. Obese pilots tended to eat whenever mealtime arrived, no matter what country they were in or how recently they had eaten. In contrast, normal pilots were much more likely to eat according to their ordinary biological functioning, apparently being motivated to eat by sensations of hunger rather than by knowledge of time. In another study, L. B. Ross (1969) found differences in amounts of nuts consumed by fat and normal people under conditions of high and dim light. In well-lit surroundings, where the external stimulus would be highly prominent, fat people consumed more nuts. In dimmer light, where the stimulus would be more subdued, normal individuals ate more. (See Figure 9.9.)

Although this evidence suggests that obesity is associated with a greater responsiveness to external cues and a lesser responsiveness to internal cues, the validity of this hypothesis is far from being firmly established. Rodin (1981) notes that a number of experiments have not borne out the hypothesis, and suggests this is partly because not *all* obese persons are more responsive to external stimulation than internal stimulation; nor are all thinner people better able to interpret internal evidence of hunger or nonhunger. In addition, differences between obese and nonobese subjects are probably not as extreme as a simplistic interpretation of the external-internal hypothesis might suggest.

Recent research has also looked at genetic and metabolic factors that might contribute to obesity. Evidence of genetic influences is found in the observation that infants born to obese parents are far more responsive to external food-related cues than other infants, initially of the same weight, but born to thinner parents (Milstein, 1980). Metabolic factors are indicated in a study that found that among pairs of individuals of identical weights and of similar exercise patterns, there were a number of pairs where one member ingested twice as many calories as the other (Rose & Williams, 1961). In summary, although it is likely that many obese people differ from those less obese in terms of their responsiveness to external and internal cues, the difference is not as general or as extreme as was once thought. It now seems clear that in addition to psychological and environmental factors, there are some important genetic and metabolic influences that contribute to obesity.

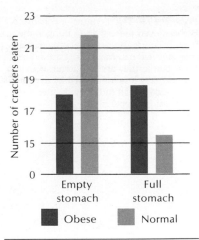

Figure 9.9 Some obese people respond more to taste and other external cues such as appearance than to internal states (that is, hunger). Subjects in this experiment were given substantial quantities of solid food such as roast beef sandwiches, then allowed to "sample" crackers. Note that the condition of the obese person's stomach appears to have no effect on the number of crackers eaten. (From "Some Extraordinary Facts about Obese Humans and Rats" by S. Schachter, *American Psychologist,* 1971, *26,* 129–144. Copyright 1971 by the American Psychological Association. Reprinted by permission.)

Figure 9.10 Thirst-control mechanisms. Perhaps even more than in hunger, the hypothalamus appears to play a central role in thirst: external factors are not as important as they are in hunger. People are normally less influenced by the smell of a good glass of milk than by the smell of a meal in preparation.

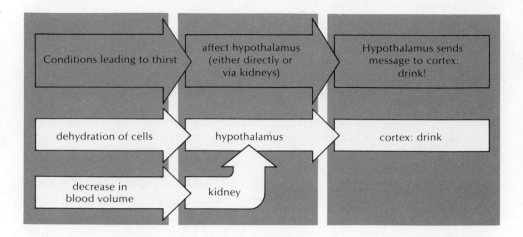

Thirst

Appetite comes with eating, we are told, and that is not far from the truth if the food tastes good. Thirst, however, does not come with drinking; it goes. And if we drink often enough, it never comes.

The human body is approximately 75 percent fluid that is saturated relatively evenly with about 0.9 percent salt. Fluid balance and salt level are critical to survival and are maintained largely through metabolic functioning, provided that sufficient fluids are taken in. We, like other animals, seem to have a strong liking for salt, and typically consume more of it than we need, a fact that has been linked to high blood pressure (Contreras, 1978). Excess fluids are simply excreted, primarily in the form of urine, but also through perspiration, feces, and breath. When we are deprived of water for a time, urination is less frequent, reduced in amount, and contains a higher concentration of other waste products. Although we can survive for a long time without food, two or three days of fluid deprivation are sufficient to lead to death.

How do we know when to drink, and how much? Initial speculation and experimentation implicated the mouth and salivary glands in these processes, claiming that as the inside of the mouth becomes dry, thirst develops. Conversely, drinking reactivates the salivary glands and moistens oral linings (Cannon, 1918). Evidence now suggests that, although these factors are probably involved in thirst, they are by no means central. People who have emerged parched from the deserts of the world continue to drink long after their mouths are moistened; one form of diabetes leads to almost insatiable thirst even if drugs are administered to stimulate salivary flow or to inhibit it.

In fact, the center for the thirst drive appears to be the hypothalamus. It responds to two sorts of stimulation. One is a drop in body fluids, which causes body cells to become dehydrated, or dried out. The hypothalamus responds to this dehydration and translates its responses into a "thirst" message. A second source of stimulation is the decrease in blood volume and pressure which results from a drop in fluid level. The kidney responds to this decrease in blood pressure by stimulating the blood to produce an enzyme. The enzyme is monitored by the hypothalamus, which again responds with a message to drink. Figure 9.10 summarizes this process in simplified form.

Sexual Motivation

And where does the message to have sex come from? From the genitals (sex organs)? No. External genitalia may be removed (in the wider interests of science) or denervated (neural pathways severed) without affecting sexual urges. The thought is not particularly comforting.

Hormonal Factors A variety of evidence suggests that sexual urges are linked to hormonal factors. Among most mammals, sexual behavior is cyclical (Jolly, 1972). Such behavior does not occur unless the female is receptive; receptivity is a function of the ovulatory cycle, which is itself a function of hormonal changes. Thus, it is typically the female's receptivity that determines whether sexual behavior will occur. Not surprisingly, the female is most receptive during those times when the probability of conception is highest (Beach, 1975).

The situation with nonhuman males is quite different. Their sexual behavior is less an immediate function of sex hormones than of the availability of a receptive female. Rhesus monkeys, for example, have relatively precise breeding seasons. During those periods when no females are receptive, males remain sexually inactive, but when brought into contact with a female who has been made receptive through the injection of **estrogen**, they immediately become sexually active (Vandenbergh, 1969). This phenomenon has been replicated in the laboratory as well. Thus males, whose hormonal balances do not fluctuate appreciably, are not in a constant state of sexual arousal, but become aroused in the presence of appropriate stimuli. The parallel with human behavior is obvious.

Estrogen One of the principal hormones produced by the ovaries. Often referred to as a "female" hormone, estrogen is centrally involved in sexual maturation and sexual arousal of females. It is also found in males, although in lesser quantities.

The role of hormones in sexual behavior has been investigated in several ways. One method is to remove the gonads (sex glands: testes in the male and ovaries in the female) and to observe subsequent sexual behavior. Among lower animals, the result is typically cessation of sexual activity. Such is not the case among humans, however. In those few documented cases where males have been castrated, the timing of the operation appears to be the single most important factor in determining sexual interest and behavior. Boys who have been castrated prior to puberty frequently develop no sexual interest or behavior. If castration occurs after puberty, however, sexual behavior may continue much as before. Similarly, females whose ovaries have been removed for medical reasons do not ordinarily report any noticeable reduction in sexual interest and behavior. Nor does sexual interest disappear when females cease to ovulate (at menopause).

A second method of studying the influence of hormones has been to inject them directly into subjects. In both males and females, hormones are produced by the gonads as a function of stimulation from the pituitary gland. Among other things, these hormones are centrally involved in the development of secondary sexual characteristics such as breasts, pubic hair, and voice changes. The two principal **androgens** (male sex hormones) are testosterone and androsterone, the more important of which is testosterone. The principal female sex hormone is estrogen. It is important to note that the gonads produce male and female hormones both in males and females.

Androgens Male sex hormones. The principal androgens are testosterone and androsterone.

A number of findings from hormone-injection studies are particularly important. Thompson (1975, p. 358) summarizes them as follows:

1 Hormone injections in immature animals can elicit sexual behavior typical of mature animals.

2 Hormones injected in animals that have been castrated or whose ovaries have been removed can produce a return to presurgical levels of sexual behavior. In this connection, hormone injections are sometimes used therapeutically with individuals born with specific **chromosomal aberrations** and who would not, therefore, mature sexually. By means of such injections, children whose secondary sexual characteristics would not ordinarily develop can be stimulated to develop normally.

3 Sexual behavior can be elicited in cyclical animals by injecting them with appropriate hormones at times when they would not ordinarily breed.

4 Injection of male hormones in very young or unborn female animals may produce sexual behavior typical of males. Striking evidence of this has been provided in studies of monkeys where pregnant females received testosterone injections. In one study (W. C. Young et al., 1964), a female whose fetus was genetically female

Chromosomal aberrations Abnormalities, inconsistencies, deformities, or other abnormal characteristics of chromosomes. Those that involve the sex chromosomes are sometimes manifested in inappropriate or arrested development of secondary sexual characteristics.

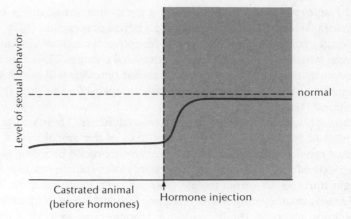

Figure 9.11 Effects of hormone injections on behavior and physical characteristics. The graph shows typical low levels of sexual behavior in a castrated animal (from which hormone-producing gonads have been removed). Injections of sex hormones (testosterone, for example) restore levels to normal for a male, as shown in the colored portion of the figure.

Level of sexual behavior

normal

Castrated animal
(before hormones)

Hormone injection

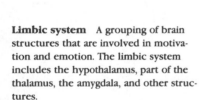

Limbic system A grouping of brain structures that are involved in motivation and emotion. The limbic system includes the hypothalamus, part of the thalamus, the amygdala, and other structures.

was given daily injections of testosterone from her 42nd to her 122nd day of pregnancy. Subsequently, she gave birth to a hermaphrodite (possessing both male and female sexual characteristics). Although the infant was genetically female, she had a well-formed penis. On later measures of aggression and dominance, her behavior was clearly that of a male (see Figure 9.11).

The Brain The hypothalamus becomes progressively more important as we discover more about it. Recall that it is implicated in eating and drinking; not surprisingly, it is implicated in sexual behavior as well. Several lines of evidence support this conclusion. Studies with animals indicate that sexual behavior, in both males and females, can be completely inhibited by surgical manipulation of the hypothalamus. Conversely, electrical stimulation of appropriate areas of the hypothalamus can elicit very intense sexual behavior. One study (Vaughan & Fisher, 1962) reports twenty ejaculations in a single hour for a male whose hypothalamus was being stimulated.

Considerable medical literature implicates other parts of the brain as well in human sexual behavior. Impotence and reductions of sexual drive have frequently been associated with tumors or lesions in the **limbic system**, which includes part of the hypothalamus (Blumer & Walker, 1967). Other evidence suggests that stimulation of that area may lead to sexual arousal. Heath (1964) reports four cases of electrical stimulation of the limbic system, three of which involved men who experienced penile erection during stimulation, and one of which involved a woman who experienced orgasm.

In humans, unlike other animals, the cortex plays an important role in sexual arousal and behavior. The human male does not respond to a woman in estrus (ovulating) with overwhelming sexual urges; indeed, he ordinarily cannot consciously recognize this state. He responds, instead, to a variety of stimuli which presumably derive their sexual significance, at least in part, through activity of the association areas of the cortex.

Other neural structures that are centrally involved in the human male's sexual responses are at the level of the spinal cord. Penile erection, pelvic movements, and even ejaculation occur as spinal reflexes. Thus, those whose brains have been separated from their spinal cords (paraplegics) are still capable of these sexual behaviors.

External Factors Although hormones are directly implicated in sexual behavior through the mediation of certain brain structures, they are not the only important factors. As was shown, even in nonhuman primates, sexual behavior among males appears to depend on external stimulation as well as on hormonal factors. Males become sexually active in the presence of a receptive female. The sexual behavior of nonhuman females appears to be more directly related to hormonal than to external factors.

Unlike most animals, the human female is not cyclically receptive, although there is evidence of greater sexual activity at times of peak estrogen production (Udry &

Morris, 1968; see Figure 9.12). And, unlike most animals, the human male is not dependent upon the presence of a receptive female for sexual arousal. It is clear that nonhormonal factors are much more important in human sexual behavior than they are in the sexual behavior of other animals. This text will not be so pedantic as to attempt to enumerate these factors, obvious as they are to each of you. Descriptions of sights, sounds, touches, smells, and tastes that might serve as erotic stimuli would be wasted in this context, editorial wisdom being what it is. Suffice it to say that an incredibly large array of external stimuli are related to sexual motivation.

Previous learning, too, is related to sexual behavior, as primate research clearly shows. Harlow (1971) raised a number of monkeys in isolation, devoid of all social contact—no mothers, no fathers, no brothers and sisters, no monkey friends. When these monkeys were later put into cages with other monkeys, they didn't know how to behave. Male monkeys, when confronted with receptive females, became agitated but failed to behave as normal monkeys undoubtedly would. Studies of monkeys in their natural state reveal that, although the males of many monkey species do not achieve sexual maturity for nine or more years, they engage in a great deal of imitative, precopulatory behavior, including mounting (almost all monkey species mount from the rear). It is likely that these early experiences play an important role in adult sexual behavior.

Female monkeys reared in isolation fare somewhat better. Many of them do achieve copulation when sexually receptive and when paired with an experienced male. When their infants are born, however, they fail to display typical maternal behavior, completely rejecting their offspring. And it is perhaps significant that far fewer of these females become pregnant than would be expected if they were raised normally.

The role of experience in human sexual behavior cannot be investigated in the same manner, for obvious ethical reasons. Consequently, it remains unclear. Given that adult sexual behavior is typically secretive, it is unlikely that children learn these behaviors through imitation. However, unlike monkeys, we can speak with each other of such matters, we can read about them, or we can view them on celluloid (see Box 9.2). How do you suppose an adult male and female would react to each other had they been reared in complete and absolute isolation until maturity?

Sex Differences in Sexual Motivation and Arousal

That there are biological sex differences between males and females is obvious. To some extent, these define male and female, although other factors are clearly implicated as well (Money & Erhardt, 1972). That there are basic differences in sexual behavior was once considered to be an established fact, but is no longer.

Among the first detailed investigations of human sexual behavior were the studies of Kinsey and his associates (1948, 1953). Among other things, these studies revealed that males experience sexual arousal in response to a wider range of stimuli than women; that they probably desire orgasm more urgently; that virtually all males experience orgasm prior to marriage, but that only some 30 percent of females have that pleasure; that females first engaged in intercourse at a later age than males despite the fact that they matured at a younger age; and that more men than women engaged in extramarital sex.

Science has experienced some difficulty in separating fact from fancy in attempting to interpret these and related studies. There is not, in fact, any physiological evidence that males desire orgasm more urgently than women, or that it is a more intense and more satisfying experience for them. There is evidence, however, that a great many more women now experience orgasm than reported doing so to Kinsey, and that they engage in sexual behavior more freely than was once thought to be the case. Packard (1968) reported that in the mid-1960s approximately 60 percent of men and 40 percent of women had engaged in premarital sexual intercourse. Athanasiou (1973) reports later data indicating that 78 percent of females and 80 percent of males had engaged in premarital sex. M. Hunt (1974) reports similar figures. Thus, although incidence has gone up for both sexes, it has increased more for females (Figure 9.13).

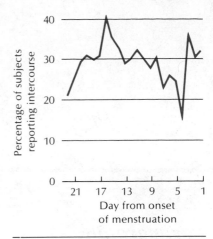

Figure 9.12 Although human females are not cyclically receptive to sexual activity, variations in the estrogen level during the menstrual cycle do appear to be linked to the frequency of intercourse. Estrogen levels are highest at about the fifteenth day and lowest at about the fourth day of the menstrual cycle. (From "Distribution of Coitus in the Menstrual Cycle" by J. R. Udry and N. M. Morris, *Nature*, 1968, *220*, 593–596. Reprinted by permission.)

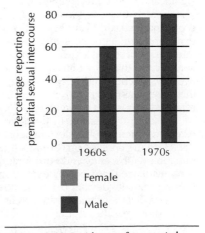

Figure 9.13 Incidence of premarital sexual intercourse has increased for both sexes, but more for females. (Based on data from Packard, 1968; Athanasiou, 1973; and M. Hunt, 1974.)

A number of recent studies indicate strongly that male-female differences in sexual beliefs and behavior are rapidly converging. This does not mean, of course, that they have completely converged. Indications are that there is still some distance to go, however small. Science remains uncertain about the precise distance.

There is something disquieting about clinical discussions of sexual behavior. We know at once that there is much more to sexual behavior than hormones and glands, brain structures and arousal, copulation and ejaculation. What these discussions fail to take into consideration are the affective aspects of sex: liking and loving. We look at these in Chapter 18.

Pornography

Are sexual violence and other forms of sexually deviant behavior caused or affected by sexually explicit books, movies, and other forms of erotica, often collectively labeled *pornography*? Research presents some answers. And some questions. Many of these questions and answers may be gleaned from the massive report of the Commission on Obscenity and Pornography (1970) and its ten volumes of supporting research. In addition, recent literature abounds with isolated studies that have looked at the specific effects of pornography under a variety of conditions.

The research generally agrees that pornography is associated with sexual arousal in a large majority of viewers of either sex (Mosher, 1970). And, contrary to what has sometimes been popular belief, women report sexual arousal approximately as often as men. Nor are women more responsive to "love" than to "lust" themes— another popular belief. W. A. Fisher and Byrne (1978) showed subjects an erotic film, describing it to some subjects as depicting a recently married man and woman (love) and to others as depicting a man who has purchased the services of a prostitute (lust). In a second experiment, a third condition was added: the material was described as representing a man and a woman who have just met at a dance, are attracted, and have returned to her apartment (casual sex). Not only were male and female subjects equally aroused by the films, but it made no difference to either sex whether the theme established was one of love or lust. However, both sexes became significantly more aroused when the theme was casual sex.

Research that has looked at the extent to which exposure to erotic material stimulates sexual behavior has also shown that such exposure *can* increase sexual behavior (both masturbation and interpersonal sexual activity), but that these effects are by no means general and that they tend to disappear completely within one or two days (Liebert and Schwartzberg, 1977). It is important to note that the effects of exposure to erotic material tend to diminish with repeated exposure (Mann et al., 1974).

The central question in pornographic research concerns the extent to which sexually deviant behavior is affected by erotic material. Here the conclusions are much less clear. Although the Commission on Obscenity and Pornography (1970) reported that there is no evidence that sexually explicit materials play a major role in causing sexually deviant behavior, a large number of studies have indicated that there may be an increase of aggressiveness following such exposure; other studies have not found any increase in aggressiveness. Some even report that aggression may be decreased following exposure (Frodi, 1977). It is worth noting that most of the studies that have shown increases in aggressiveness have typically looked at male aggression toward other males. In one study where

the object of aggression was either male or female, the results showed no greater aggressiveness toward females than toward males (Donnerstein & Barrett, 1978).

The results of these studies should probably not be interpreted as convincing evidence that sex crimes and other forms of sexually deviant behavior are not affected by pornographic materials. One of their most obvious limitations is that the measures of aggressiveness typically used (willingness to administer mild electric shocks, willingness to become verbally abusive) might bear relatively little relationship to sexual aggressiveness in real life. Hence some of the most socially important questions in this area remain unanswered.

The relationship between pornography and sex-related crimes is still not clear.

Drive Reduction and Incentives

Hunger, thirst, and the sex drive, the three principal physiological motives central to our lives, are each fundamental biological needs linked with survival and the propagation of our species. Each of these needs gives rise to predictable behaviors. As we said earlier, there is a drive or an urge associated with an unsatisfied need. Thus, the need for food gives rise to a hunger drive; drink, to a thirst drive; and for sex, to a sex drive. According to Hull (1943, 1952), the individual who is motivated by a drive is moved to engage in behavior that results in a reduction of the drive. Thus a hungry person eats, eating decreases the need for food, and the hunger drive is consequently reduced (Figure 9.14). Hull's **drive-reduction model** of human motivation went one step further; it maintained that the reduction of a drive is *pleasant,* and therefore reinforcing. Hence drive reduction was not only a basic motivational principle, but was also used to account for learning.

Many theorists believe that we not only have physiological needs such as those relating to eating, drinking, maintaining body temperature, procreating, and resting, but that we also have psychological needs. Psychological needs include the needs for love, affection, belonging, achieving, and so on; they pertain to the cognitive or affective aspects of human behavior. Early theorists attempted to explain them in the same way as they explained physiological needs—by reference to drive reduction.

Subsequent investigations of a number of behaviors that do not appear to have any obvious rewards, but that are undertaken for their own sake (exploration, for example), presented serious difficulties for need-drive theorists. In addition, although physiological drives can be assumed to be common to most individuals, this is not the case with respect to psychological needs. For example, some individuals appear to manifest a high need to achieve; others do not. This calls into question the appropriateness of employing the label *needs.* Indeed, it may be more suitable and more profitable simply to consider psychological needs as learned, without discounting the possibility that they may also be influenced to an as yet unknown degree by genetic factors.

Dissatisfaction with drive-reduction models eventually led to new theoretical positions. One of the major weaknesses of the "reducing" models was that they attributed behavior to *inner* states and urges—to tensions that accompany these states and are subsequently reduced as a result of appropriate behaviors. Given the obvious importance of external stimulation, however, even with respect to physiological needs, it became apparent that a more complex explanation of motivation would also take into account the **incentive** function of external stimulation. Put simply, stimulation has incentive value when it actually leads to behavior.

The importance of incentives is evident even in rat studies. Food was long considered to be a reward, important in a learning situation simply because it served as reinforcement by reducing the animal's state of drive. It had been established to psychology's satisfaction, for example, that hungrier rats performed better than less hungry rats. Presumably, they were in conditions of higher drive, and food was a more powerful reinforcer than if they had not been so hungry. Subsequently, a number of studies showed that if a rat was starved too long, it did not perform as well. Other studies showed that monkeys who were not starved performed as well or better than monkeys who were quite hungry (Harlow, 1953). It appeared that drive-state, defined in physiological terms, might not be as important as had once been thought. One simple study confirmed this. Zeaman (1949) gave a number of rats a small taste of food before they entered a maze, at the end of which was more of the same food. These rats had previously learned the maze and knew of the waiting food reward. Other rats were given no appetizer, but were simply released in the maze. Drive-reduction theory would predict unblushingly that the hungrier rats should run faster. They didn't. Reward prior to goal-directed behavior appears to serve as an incentive (Figure 9.15).

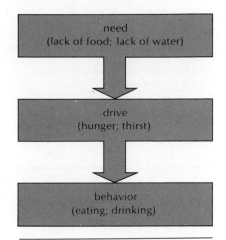

Figure 9.14 The need-drive model. A lack or need leads to an urge or drive, which in turn leads to a behavior that satisfies the need and reduces the drive. Although the need-drive model explains many physiologically based behaviors, it does not explain most others. Why is it that some people like to read mystery books and others. . . .

Drive-reduction model A motivational theory based on the notion that a need gives rise to tensions which are reduced when the need is satisfied.

Incentive A motivational concept that relates to the attractiveness, or subjective value attached to a behavior or goal, and thus to its effectiveness as a motive for behaving. It is appropriate to speak of goals or objectives as having low or high incentive value, incentive value being reflected by the amount of effort the organism will willingly expend in order to obtain the goal.

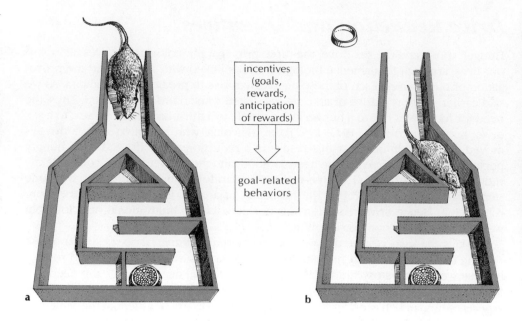

Figure 9.15 Incentives. Drives alone can't explain behavior. In Zeaman's 1949 experiment, rats who had already been given some food (**b**) performed better on a maze that they knew led to food than did hungry rats (**a**).

incentives (goals, rewards, anticipation of rewards)

goal-related behaviors

BIOGRAPHY
Clark Leonard Hull
1884–1952

Hull was not a healthy child. In addition to his illnesses, he suffered from very poor eyesight. But he was a brilliant mathematician and logician and could easily have had a distinguished career in these fields. Instead, he turned to mining engineering at the University of Wisconsin, but never finished his program. Psychology seduced him and he emerged, in 1918, with a Ph.D. in psychology. Among his early research interests was hypnosis, to which he devoted a full ten years. In 1928 he was first exposed to Pavlov's work, and in 1929 he became a research professor at Yale. From then until his death in 1952, he devised and elaborated one of the most complex and influential learning theories yet advanced: a mathematico-deductive system which was meant to include all behavior, and which has probably generated more empirical research than any other single system in psychology. The final formulation of his system appeared in his 1952 text, *A Behavior System*. He died before he could read the typesetter's proofs.

Current cognitive theories of motivation, although they do not all use the same language, generally recognize the importance of incentives for human behavior. We do not have to know beforehand, gifted as we are with imaginations; we can anticipate the consequences of our behavior. And there is little doubt that our anticipations, whether of pain or pleasure, are powerful influences in directing our activities.

Cognitive Theories

A useful, although oversimplified, comparison of the more behavioristic theories like need-drive theory and cognitive theories can be based on their different views of human nature. Early behavioristic (and instinct) positions were characterized by a mechanistic and, perhaps more important, a passive view. Motives for behaving were seen as internal or external prods of which we were the helpless victims. This attitude is not particularly surprising in view of the large number of animal studies employed to demonstrate the effects of drive, rewards, and incentives on behaviors. It is highly surprising, however, in view of what we intuitively suspect about our own behavior. Cognitive theories, at least in this one sense, contradict our intuition less than did earlier beliefs. In effect, they present an active, rather than a passive, view of the human animal. They take into account the wealth of human emotions and intellectual processes involved in behavior, dealing with these not as forces over which we have no control, but as something we actively and sometimes very consciously manipulate. The cognitive theorist does not look for motives so much as for some general understanding of the sequence of ongoing human behavior in natural situations. As Bolles (1974) maintains, motivation is not some special force. There are no unmotivated behaviors. For the cognitive theorist, the search focuses on the nature of the cognitive processes that determine the direction of behavior and changes that occur in sequences of behavior.

This cognitive view of behavior emphasizes two things: The first is the role of intention. As Deci (1975) notes, it is not goals that motivate our behavior, but rather our intentions of reaching them. The second emphasis of cognitive theories of motivation is on our ability to discover causes and effects. If not for the fact that we can attribute certain effects to our behaviors and to that of others, we would be hard-pressed to make much sense out of our existence. That is, we need to know what the likely effects of our behaviors are; we need to know whether our successes and failures should be attributed to this or that behavior, to luck or skill, or to the malice of others or their friendship.

Attribution theory is a loose collection of cognitive theories based on the role of cause and effect inferences in human behavior (Kelley & Michela, 1980). One specific attribution theory deals with achievement motivation and is described in this chapter. Others deal with interpersonal relationships and are described in Chapter 18.

Attribution theory Attribution theories in personality, social psychology, motivation, and other topics in psychology look at external circumstances and personality characteristics that influence processes of assessing and assigning responsibility or cause.

Some Cognitive Motives

Among our less physiological motives are a number of powerful urges, evident in lower animals as well, to explore, to manipulate, and to understand our environment. Psychology's acceptance of the existence of these urges as separate and important motives has not been immediate and unanimous. Only after considerable evidence had accumulated of behaviors that could not be explained in any traditional way did theorists begin to consider the possibility that we do some things for no apparent reason other than to do them. In the end, however, the result is more than simply having done something; cognitive changes also result.

Curiosity

Behaviors that have obvious goals have traditionally been favored as subjects of psychological investigation. This is not surprising, since goals can be defined and manipulated, and behaviors can be described in terms of their relationships to these goals. Eating, drinking, and sexual activity are among the extensively researched goal-directed behaviors. **Curiosity**, however, need have no goal other than the activities that relate to it (H. Fowler, 1965). In other words, curiosity-motivated behavior is simply behavior designed to do, to see, to feel, to hear, and so on. Defined yet another way, curiosity manifests itself in behaviors that seek stimulation, in contrast with behaviors such as drinking and eating that can be interpreted as reducing stimulation.

Curiosity A tendency to act that does not have specific, identifiable goals other than whatever might be gained from investigating, obtaining information, experiencing, or doing. Defined another way, *curiosity* describes behaviors whose primary motive appears to reside in the activities themselves rather than in identifiable objectives.

Exploratory and manipulatory behaviors unrelated to hunger, thirst, or sex are extremely common among humans. Even those who study rats and monkeys are demonstrating curiosity! And they have frequently observed related behaviors in these nonhuman animals—animals that we assume would be more moved by basic drives than we are. For example, recall some of the experiments mentioned earlier in connection with studies of attention and perception. Dember (1956), H. Fowler (1958), and a number of other researchers demonstrated, by means of T or Y mazes, that rats "preferred" novelty, change, and complexity. Animals who are allowed to become thoroughly familiar with a maze will, when aspects of that maze are changed, spend more time exploring the altered maze. There need be no obvious reward attached to such behavior; exploration appears to be a sufficient motive.

In a series of intriguing studies, Harlow and his associates (Harlow, 1953; Harlow et al., 1956) presented monkeys with mechanical puzzles. They were neither told nor asked to play with these puzzles or to attempt to solve them; nor were they rewarded for doing so. Yet they spent hours trying to undo them. And most of them were successful. When compared with naive animals some two weeks later, Harlow's experienced monkeys put them to shame. Harlow (1953) also reports the case of an orangutan who was given two blocks of wood, one with a square hole and one with a round hole, and two plungers, one round and one square. "Intellectual curiosity" drove the animal to work on the puzzles for long periods. The orangutan eventually learned to place the square peg in the square hole, and the round peg in either hole; but, like some of our most astute philosophers, he never succeeded in inserting the square peg in the round hole. Harlow concludes, "in defense of this orangutan, let it be stated that it died working on more complex problems than are investigated by most present-day learning theorists" (p. 30). Cause of death: perforated ulcers; time of death: within one month of initial presentation of round hole and square peg!

Figure 9.16 Stimulus material employed by Berlyne in investigations of the properties of stimuli that command attention. Which figure in each pair do you look at longer? The inclination to look more closely at the right half of each grouping illustrates what Berlyne calls *epistemic* curiosity—curiosity directed toward acquiring knowledge. (From "The Influence of Complexity and Novelty in Visual Figures on Orienting Responses" by D. E. Berlyne, *Journal of Experimental Psychology*, 1958, 55, 289–296. Copyright 1958 by the American Psychological Association. Reprinted by permission.)

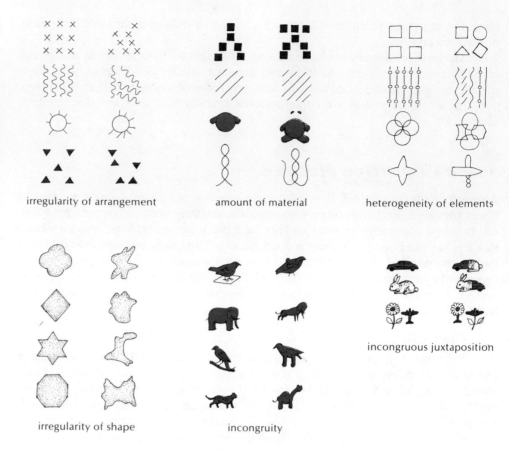

irregularity of arrangement   amount of material   heterogeneity of elements

irregularity of shape   incongruity   incongruous juxtaposition

Berlyne (1960), whose motivational theories are based heavily on considerations of curiosity, investigated some of the variables that are most likely to lead to exploratory behavior in humans. He, like most theorists, assumes that exploration results largely from external stimulation, and that it does not, like hunger and thirst, derive from internal conditions. (Recall, however, that hunger, thirst, and sex drive are not solely dependent on internal factors, either. A succulent turkey leg may give rise to hunger in the absence of any real *need* to eat.)

In Berlyne's (1958) classic experiment, undergraduate college students were presented with pairs of stimulus figures projected onto a screen for ten seconds. One member of each pair was more complex than the other (see Figure 9.16). A record was kept of the amount of time each subject spent fixated on one or the other member of the pair. The hypothesis was simply that the more complex figures would be explored at greater length than the simpler figures. That this was, in fact, the case has two important implications. First, it confirms the existence of this nebulous motive that relates curiosity, exploration, and manipulation, sometimes discussed as a *perceptual curiosity motive*. Since time spent examining either member of stimulus pairs was, as far as subjects knew, irrelevant to the outcome of the experiment, there is no reason to suppose that anticipation of some type of reward would motivate them to spend more time examining the more complex figures. That they did so is evidence of some systematic motive, common to all subjects and, presumably, to most humans. A second implication of the study is that certain variables appear to most directly stimulate exploratory behavior. Among these are incongruity (disharmony), irregularity, heterogeneity (variety), and a host of other factors that, together, define complexity.

In later discussions of curiosity, Berlyne (1960) identifies a number of stimulus variables involved in curiosity-motivated behavior. Among these are novelty, complexity, intensity, and change. Quite simply, we are moved to explore the aspects of the environment that are most salient, most complex, and most novel. In addition,

Berlyne has elaborated a theory of epistemic curiosity—curiosity that is directed toward the acquisition of knowledge. Thus, curiosity is not manifested simply in perceptual exploration, but in cognitive exploration as well.

Curiosity is not a completely frivolous motive. That is, although exploratory behaviors might seem to have no specific function, they can be considered to be extremely useful biologically. At a simple level, for example, it is largely through curiosity-based behaviors that many nonhuman animals are able to discover food sources, not to mention hiding places, sunny places, and other creatures with whom to mate. As many researchers of animal behavior insist, it makes biological sense for an organism to engage in a great deal of exploratory and manipulatory behavior that does not appear to be directly related to the immediate probability of reward. Although rumor has it that many cats have died at the hands of the assassin curiosity, rumor is probably incorrect. Our most reliable scientific evidence suggests quite the contrary: it is likely that many cats have been saved as a result of curiosity.

Achievement Motivation

The word *motive,* like so many of our elegant words, is derived from Latin: its source is *motere,* "to move." We have many of these "movers," some complex and not easily discerned; others apparently simpler. The urges that propel us toward achievement are among the complex movers, not easily defined or measured, although their influence is real enough.

McClelland and his associates began investigating **achievement motivation** (alternatively called *need for achievement,* and abbreviated *nAch*) several decades ago. Clearly, nAch should be evident in a person's actual achievement. That is, those with a higher need for achievement should achieve more than others with a lower need, all other things being equal. In fact, however, nature does not ordinarily make all other things equal. Those more intelligent, more talented, more persistent, and perhaps luckier might be the high achievers.

Faced with these problems, McClelland et al. (1953) resorted to a fantasy measure. They presented subjects with a series of images taken from a personality test, the Thematic Apperception Test (TAT), and had them fantasize about events that might be transpiring in the picture (Figure 9.17). Typically, the pictures depicted people involved in some form of achievement-related behavior (a boy playing a violin; two men at a machine). Subjects were asked to write stories about what was happening in the picture, who the people were, what they were thinking, and what would happen in the future. Subsequently, scorers read the stories and enumerated the number of achievement-related themes that appeared in them.

The reliability of this measure of need achievement has sometimes been questioned. Although trained scorers agree remarkably well with one another in respect to incidence of achievement imagery, subjects do not perform at consistent levels from one testing situation to another. Thus, it appears that the tests may not measure nAch entirely accurately—or that achievement motivation is not a particularly stable characteristic.

In spite of these problems, a number of relationships have been found between scores on measures of nAch and other behaviors. The existence of these relationships provides some evidence of the validity of the measures. In a large number of studies, children who do well on measures of school achievement also attain high nAch scores. Other behaviors can also be predicted on the basis of nAch scores. For example, children with high scores tend to be moderate risk takers; those with lower scores tend to be either very low risk takers or very high risk takers. McClelland (1958) involved a group of young children in a ring-toss game where subjects would win prizes for accurate tosses and could stand as close to the target as they wanted. Those with high nAch tended to stand neither too far nor too close. Those with low nAch either ensured success by standing very close to the target or ensured failure by standing very far away; when there is very little probability of success, failure carries little stigma.

Figure 9.17 When assessing need for achievement (nAch), McClelland and his associates (1953) presented subjects with photographs from the Thematic Apperception Test (TAT) similar to this one. The photographs typically depict two or more people engaged in some activity. Subjects are asked to write a short paragraph keeping in mind four sets of questions: (1) What is happening? Who are the people? (2) What has led up to this situation? (3) What is being thought? What is wanted? By whom? (4) What will happen? Analysis of the stories begins with a search for *achievement imagery* (AI). In the absence of AI, analysis is terminated. If the paragraph does contain AI, the examiner searches for more specific evidence of achievement orientation (expression of specific needs, description of activities directed toward goals, and so on).

Achievement motivation or need for achievement (nAch) The need to meet some inner standard of excellence. Achievement motivation is a personality variable which appears to differ from one individual to another. In other words, some individuals are highly achievement-oriented, others are not.

Fear of failure A motive or personality characteristic that acts in opposition to forces that direct the individual toward achievement.

After a number of studies indicating that predictions based on knowledge of nAch scores were not always simple and straightforward, J. W. Atkinson (1964) proposed that there were two competing forces involved in achievement behavior: One is the desire to achieve success, or to attain some standard of excellence; this, in fact, is McClelland's original definition of nAch. A second force acts in direct opposition to the first, however; concomitant with a desire to achieve is a **fear of failure**. Thus, achievement-oriented behavior may be seen as a combined function of approach tendencies (resulting from a desire to achieve) and avoidance tendencies (resulting from fear of failure). Atkinson then proposed that a more accurate measure of achievement orientation might be obtained by measuring both the traditional nAch and fear of failure, and subtracting the second from the first. In some cases, the result might be negative in spite of the fact that an individual had a relatively high nAch score. Subsequent research has found a fairly strong relationship between Atkinson's more complex measure of achievement motivation and actual achievement-oriented behavior.

Sex Differences in Achievement Motivation Most of the early research on achievement motivation was conducted with boys, partly because results were clearer with them, and perhaps because achievement had traditionally been a masculine endeavor in male-dominated societies. The few early studies that did employ girls as subjects often found marked differences between the sexes in favor of boys. And in certain experiments involving competitive behavior, girls did achieve at lower levels than boys. That, however, is not true in school situations, where girls perform at least as well as boys (Maccoby & Jacklin, 1974). Because of these studies, a number of researchers assumed that nAch illustrated a clear difference between the sexes, and that it might easily explain why so few women find themselves in positions comparable to those of high-achieving males. Subsequent research has shown, however, that these assumptions are not entirely warranted. TAT pictures employed to test nAch in earlier research consisted entirely of pictures of males. The assumption that boys project their own achievement aspirations, hopes, and fears when responding to these pictures might be justifiable; the assumption that girls would be projecting their personal achievement aspirations into descriptions of males doing "masculine" things is more tenuous, to say the least.

Horner (1969) had male and female college students write essays beginning with the open-ended statement: "After first-term finals, John/Anne finds himself/herself at the top of his/her medical school class." The names and pronouns corresponded to the sex of the respondent. Here, too, Horner found striking evidence of male-female differences, with males consistently scoring higher on counts of achievement imagery. The most important difference, however, was in what Horner labels "motivation to avoid success." Women typically expressed such feelings as guilt, anxiety, and fear of social rejection. According to Horner, it is as though women actively seek to avoid too much success. In fact, 65 percent of female respondents described undesirable personal attributes and unpleasant consequences when speaking of highly successful women; only 10 percent of the men did likewise when speaking of the men.

Does this warrant the conclusion that there are basic differences between men and women with respect to need for achievement? In fact, it doesn't. Monahan et al. (1974) conducted a very similar study with adolescent boys and girls, also employing success stories of males and females. The results were identical, to the extent that the studies are comparable. Boys described more positive, achievement-oriented themes; girls gave more negative, failure- and rejection-oriented themes. However, when boys were asked to describe female stories and girls, male stories, the results were entirely reversed. Boys now showed more evidence of "fear of failure" themes when describing girls; conversely, girls described males in achievement-oriented ways.

These studies indicate that there are, in fact, some very basic *cultural* differences in the way men and women view achievement and failure. But they do not indicate that there are intrinsic differences between the sexes in achievement orientation.

a b

Figure 9.18 Test your own feelings about achievement by men and women. Are your feelings about the person in **a** different from your feelings about the person in **b**?

Given cultural standards that would accept and encourage achievement among women as much as our standards now encourage achievement among men, there is every reason to believe that these differences would disappear. Figure 9.18 will help you check your own reactions.

It should be noted, as well, that the measures of nAch described in these studies typically involve a competitive element. As is shown in Chapter 17, there are some marked differences between males and females with respect to competitiveness. Interestingly, those few studies that have attempted to examine nAch under noncompetitive situations have found that girls scored as high as boys (Maccoby & Jacklin, 1974).

An Attribution Theory of Achievement Motivation As mentioned earlier, attribution theories are based on the role of cause and effect inferences in human behavior. Weiner (1972, 1974a, 1974b) has developed a specific attribution theory to explain achievement motivation. Weiner begins with the assumption that individuals attribute the causes of their successes and failures to internal or external sources. If I am **internally oriented** (possess a high degree of "felt powerfulness"), I will tend to take responsibility for my own actions and their consequences. Thus, I will attribute these consequences either to my ability or to my effort, both of which are under personal control. If, however, I am **externally oriented** (possess a high degree of "felt powerlessness"), I will ascribe success or failure to the difficulty of the tasks I face or to luck (or both). These factors are not under personal control, so that, in effect, the externally oriented individual does not accept responsibility for either success or failure.

Weiner (1974a) further differentiates between causes that are stable and those that are unstable. Ability and task difficulty are stable factors; that is, they do not vary for a given task and a given individual. Effort, however, can be high or low; and luck can be present or absent. Thus, these are unstable variables. A complete tabulation of these factors is presented in Figure 9.19. There are a number of other causal factors to which we also attribute our successes and failures. Mood, fatigue, and illness are perhaps the most obvious. Although these can be extremely important in our behavior,

Internal orientation or internality A personality characteristic describable in terms of the extent to which individuals will accept credit or blame for the outcomes of their behaviors.

External orientation or externality A personality characteristic identifiable in terms of the extent to which individuals will attribute the causes of their successes and failures to external factors (for example, luck or task difficulty).

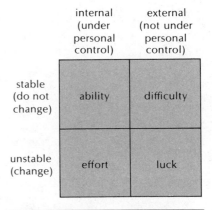

	internal (under personal control)	external (not under personal control)
stable (do not change)	ability	difficulty
unstable (change)	effort	luck

Figure 9.19 Attribution theory: explanations of success or failure. (After Weiner, 1974a.)

they are highly personal, highly variable, and not easily amenable to scientific investigation or analysis. Effort, luck, ability, and task difficulty have been investigated more systematically.

One of the striking and consistent findings that has emerged from studies of causal attribution is that people who are high in need for achievement are much more likely to attribute causes to internal factors. In other words, those who have a high need to strive and to be successful are likely to think that ability and effort are responsible for their successes. Individuals low in measured need for achievement may attribute success to any of the four causal factors. When those with high nAch are not successful, they continue to invoke internal causes, frequently blaming their failure on lack of effort. When those with low nAch are not successful, they are more likely to attribute the outcome to lack of ability (Weiner et al., 1971).

As Bolles (1974) suggests, attribution theory presents an active view of people. We do not simply behave; we actively evaluate our behaviors and try to make sense of them. Thus, we do not simply accept success or failure as the consequence of behavior, but instead we attempt to find deeper reasons for successes and failures. Depending on our predispositions, our personality characteristics, and our previous histories, we ascribe causes to specific factors. The attribution process is clearly not random. As we have seen, much of it can be predicted from knowledge of the individual's orientation toward achievement. The reverse is also true. Causal attribution can, to some extent, be predicted after individuals have succeeded or failed, given knowledge of their general power orientations (internal or external) and their needs for achievement.

Arousal

We have looked at instincts and imprinting, at hedonism and physiological needs, and finally at cognitive theories and motives. We look now at a physiological-cognitive-emotional theory—a theory that provides explanations for behaviors not easily explained in other ways, and that also provides a basis for other explanations. **Arousal theory** relates to physiological drives, to cognitive activity, and to emotions.

The term *arousal* has both physiological and psychological connotations. As a physiological term, it refers primarily to activity of the sympathetic nervous system manifested in bodily functions such as heart rate, respiration rate, perspiration, and brain-wave activity, and mediated through functioning of the reticular formation in the brain stem. As indicated in Chapter 2, these activities are related to and accompany emotional reaction. Generally, with more intense emotional reaction, there is also more intense physiological reaction. Physiological arousal ranges from states of very low activity in sleep or deep comas (alpha, theta, or delta waves; low galvanic skin response; low respiration and heart rate) to very high activity, such as in extreme anger, fear, or panic.

As a psychological term, *arousal* refers to the alertness or vigilance of the organism. Thus, a highly aroused individual is one who is very alert and attentive. One at a low level of arousal might be asleep.

Level of Arousal

Arousal theory is premised on two simple assumptions (Hebb, 1966). The first is that there is an optimal (best) level of arousal for different behaviors, and that this level varies both for different individuals and for different behaviors. The second is that individuals behave so as to maintain an optimal level of arousal.

The first assumption is, up to a point, obvious. At very low levels of arousal, behavior will be ineffective. A sleeping person is unlikely, for example, to respond correctly when asked a question. A drowsy person may have to become considerably more alert (more aroused) before solving a mathematical problem. As arousal level increases, behavior becomes more effective. Put in other terms, increases in physiological arousal relate to effectiveness of behavior as well. However, if arousal increases

Arousal theory Arousal refers to activity of the sympathetic nervous system, and therefore relates to emotion; it also relates to degree of alertness. Arousal theory maintains that we behave so as to maintain arousal at an optimal level, sometimes seeking stimulation and sometimes trying to reduce it.

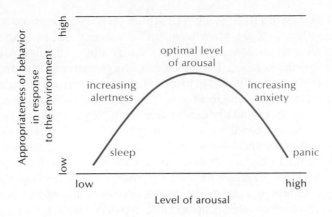

Figure 9.20 The relationship of level of arousal to effective behavior. As arousal increases, behavior becomes more appropriate until an optimal level is reached. If arousal increases beyond the optimal level, effectiveness again decreases.

beyond the optimal level, effectiveness of behavior again declines. At extreme levels of arousal, totally inappropriate, highly rigid behavior patterns may appear. This provides one explanation for panic behavior (Box 9.3). The relationship of arousal level to effectiveness of behavior is depicted in Figure 9.20. Note that this is a hypothetical relationship, although its general characteristics are well substantiated by research.

The second assumption predicts that individuals will behave in such a way as to maintain an optimal level of arousal. The validity of this assumption is obvious with respect to highly arousing situations which tend to be perceived as unpleasant. Thus, although it might be said that a person flees from a burning building in order to escape the painful consequences of being burned, it can also be said that one of the effects of running from fire is a reduction of arousal.

The assumption is double-edged, however. It predicts not only that people behave so as to reduce arousal when it is too high, but also that they will attempt to increase arousal when it is inappropriately low. Experimental evidence supports this prediction as well.

In a classic experiment, Hebb and his colleagues (Heron, 1957) paid a number of college students to do absolutely nothing. In fact, they were prevented from doing anything. For as long as they cared to, they lay on a cot, twenty-four hours a day, getting up only to go to the bathroom and to sit on the edge of their cots at mealtime. Their ears were covered with U-shaped foam pillows, their eyes with translucent visors, their hands with cardboard cuffs. Overhead, a fan hummed ceaselessly. Although they could hear, see, and feel, their stimulus world was unchanging.

BOX 9.3

Panic

Schultz (1964), in a fascinating account of panic behavior, describes several horrendous fires—horrendous not because they were mighty conflagrations, but because great numbers of people died in them. In the Coconut Grove nightclub fire in 1942, some 500 of the 800 people involved died, the majority because they panicked. *Newsweek* (December 7, 1942, pp. 43–44) described the fire as follows:

Every available table was taken ... a girl, her hair ablaze, hurtled across the floor screaming "Fire!"

That shriek heralded catastrophe. Some 800 guests, insane with panic, lunged in a wild scramble to get out the only way they knew—the revolving-door exit. Flames flashed with incredible swiftness.... Smoke swirled in choking masses through hallways. The revolving doors jammed as the terror-stricken mob pushed them in both directions at the same time. Blazing draperies fell, setting women's evening gowns and hair on fire. Patrons were hurled under tables and trampled to death. Others tripped and choked the 6-foot-wide stairway up from the Melody Lounge. Those behind swarmed over them and piled up in layers—layers of corpses.

The fire was quickly brought under control, but the fatal damage was done.

Numerous other instances of inappropriate behavior accompanying panic can be gleaned from the anecdotes of old people. In these anecdotes, there is a clue for the development of a comprehensive motivational theory based on the concept of *arousal*.

This was the first of a large number of studies on sensory deprivation and sensory restriction (see Zubek, 1969). Many have had consistent and striking results. First, subjects typically cannot endure the isolation for very long. In the original experiment, two days was the usual duration. In conditions of more extreme deprivation—where, for example, subjects are immersed in brine solutions in silence and darkness, floating unfeeling and unattended—length of stay is considerably shorter. More important, perhaps, most subjects eventually experience some impairment of perceptual and intellectual functioning. Tasks that are very simple before isolation become extremely difficult and sometimes impossible after prolonged sensory deprivation. In addition, subjects display emotional changes and rapidly fluctuating moods ranging from nervousness and irritability to anger or fear. The most striking finding, although it has not always been replicated, involves the appearance of hallucinations among some of the subjects. These uncontrolled "apparitions," typically visual, are mildly amusing at first and can be gotten rid of if the subject wishes. Later, however, they become more pronounced, less amusing, and quite persistent.

The implications of sensory deprivation research are manifold. It appears that humans have a need for variety in sensory stimulation. If this is so, perhaps some of our otherwise unexplainable behaviors might be accounted for. Such behaviors as exploration, for example, might be related to cognitive needs—that is, to a need to know. It might be equally plausible, however, to attribute them to a need for stimulation (Reykowski, 1982). In fact, the behavior of subjects in sensory isolation cannot easily be explained in any other way. During Hebb's experiment, subjects whistled, sang, talked to themselves, attempted desperately to engage the experimenter in conversation whenever food was brought in, and otherwise behaved so as to increase the amount of stimulation they were receiving. One of the effects of sensory stimulation is to increase arousal. Later, when these activities became boring, some of the subjects began to hallucinate. One possible explanation for these hallucinations is that, following prolonged lack of sensory stimulation, the cortex takes control from individuals, exposing them to hallucinations.

Sources of Arousal

Knowing that people behave so as to maintain an optimal level of arousal would not be particularly useful if we did not also know what some of the principal causes of arousal are. The physiological changes that accompany arousal changes provide a clue. Since these changes are under autonomic nervous system control, they are not ordinarily under the individual's conscious control. That is, most individuals cannot "will" their skins to become more conducive to electricity, their hearts to beat faster, and their brain-wave activity to change. However, these changes are under control to the extent that they can be brought about through appropriate activities. Simply imagining highly arousing scenes, or seeing them depicted in pictures, films, or words, can in fact increase physiological arousal. Research reviewed in Chapter 3 indicates that it is sometimes possible to lower physiological arousal through the use of biofeedback. Although biofeedback instrumentation is typically not used to increase arousal, it might be effective in doing so.

It appears then that one source of arousal is internal stimulation; a second obvious source is external stimulation. At one extreme, emotion-laden experiences can increase arousal dramatically, as is evident in panic situations. More generally, however, all external stimulation is a source of arousal (Zuckerman, 1979). Recall from your reading of Chapter 2 that physiological arousal is mediated through the activity of the reticular formation, a small portion of the brain stem. Major nerve trunks going to the cortex also branch out into the reticular formation, whose function seems to be that of bombarding the cortex in random fashion. Thus, it alerts the brain to incoming stimulation (arousal). It is as though all meaningful stimuli have two functions. Hebb (1966) describes these as the *cue* function and the *arousal* function. The term *cue* refers to the specific message associated with the stimulus. It is the cue function of a stimulus

Figure 9.21 Cognitive arousal theory. In Berlyne's (1960) epistemic theory, novel or problematic situations increase arousal. The learning process involved in becoming familiar with new situations reduces the initial gap between problem and solution (need to understand and actual level of understanding); at the same time, it reduces arousal level.

that allows individuals to determine what they are perceiving and, consequently, what behaviors might be appropriate in response, if any. The arousal function is a general, alerting function (J. D. French, 1957).

The types of stimulation that appear to have the greatest arousal functions are those associated with emotion. In addition, the *amount* of sensory stimulation appears to be important, although it is not nearly so important as variety. In the isolation experiments, for example, there is, in fact, considerable sensory stimulation. Individuals can hear a fan, can feel cardboard cuffs, can see light, can probably taste the insides of their mouths, can feel their clothing. This stimulation is constant, however, and arousal level consequently drops dramatically. Brainwave recordings of subjects during isolation indicates that their brain-wave functioning is more like that of the deeper stages of sleep than like that of subjects who are awake.

A Cognitive Arousal Theory

On the basis of these observations, Berlyne (1960) has proposed an arousal-based cognitive theory to explain epistemic behavior and exploration. Recall that epistemic behaviors are designed to obtain information and solve problems. Berlyne proposes that problem situations have arousal properties, and that their solution results in a reduction of arousal. More precisely, he argues that certain stimuli increase arousal by bringing about conflict, and that reduction of this conflict is attempted in order to bring about a decrement in arousal.

Berlyne's research indicates that it is not the amount of stimulation that affects arousal so much as specific properties of stimuli such as surprisingness, novelty, meaningfulness, ambiguity, and complexity. The conflict to which these properties give rise results from the discrepancy between expectations and observation. Obviously, a stimulus cannot be novel unless it is unexpected; nor can it be ambiguous, surprising, or complex unless it is different, in some respect, from other stimuli. These, then, are not intrinsic properties of stimuli, but subjective interpretations of them based on comparisons between them and other possible stimulation. In one sense, it is this violation of expectation, this subtle conflict between cognitions, that increases arousal. Becoming familiar with a novel stimulus removes its novelty, and decreases arousal. Thus learning may be seen as an arousal-related behavior (Figure 9.21).

Arousal theory predicts that, following periods of monotony, of unchanging arousal level, organisms will seek an increase in arousal. Put another way, it predicts that organisms will seek stimulation, since this is the principal means of controlling arousal level. Harlow's monkeys who manipulated and *learned* mechanical puzzles in the absence of any reinforcement for doing so, Hebb's isolation subjects who whistled, sang, and talked to themselves, animals and people who explore, who manifest curiosity—all of these illustrate behaviors that result in increases in arousal.

Arousal theory, then, provides a simple integration of a number of motivational theories and observations. The prediction of specific individual behaviors on the basis of arousal level and the measurement of arousal do present some real problems, however. At present, arousal theory is more useful as a general, underlying framework for other theoretical explanations than as a specific motivational theory.

Social Motives

The Canada lynx is a solitary creature, fierce and cunning. It prowls its secluded haunts in dark hours, avoiding all contact with human or beast except those it must eat. And only when driven by powerful sexual urges does it seek out its own kind.

We, a different animal, are gregarious in the extreme. We actively seek the company of others, their friendship, love, and assistance; and we give of ourselves, to greater or lesser degrees. In short, many of our behaviors relate neither to physiological drives nor to cognitive motives. They relate, instead, to social aspects of our nature and may be classified as social motives. There are at least two broad categories of social motives: those involved in competitive, aggressive interaction; and those involved in cooperative, affiliative, helping interaction. Although these motives are not always separate in practice, theory can do things of which practice would never dream. So can books and authors.

Chapter 17, which deals with the social aspects of human behavior, discusses these and other social motives.

Ulterior Motives

The old lady looked me right in the eye, pursed her lips, and coined an expression that I would blush to repeat. Shocked, I lifted my water-wrinkled feet from our communal tub and prepared to leave. I assure you I wasn't frightened, although I might have been a little pale. Shocked, obviously.

"The spare bedroom!" she exclaimed. "For research!"

"For research, yes. My office is too crowded," I explained again.

Undaunted, my grandmother leveled her finger in the direction of my nose.

"I know you better than that," she claimed, asserting once more the superiority of her folk psychologies. "You have ulterior motives!"

She totally misinterpreted my excitement. You see, I had decided to terminate this chapter when it started to rain last night. A discussion of ulterior motives had not occurred to me, but now that she had mentioned them, I realized what a serious omission I might otherwise have committed.

I have now spent many long minutes poring through learned journals and some of the heavier books that surround me. Would you believe that no motivation theorist has yet dedicated any concerted effort to the investigation of the ulterior motive? True!

An ulterior motive is, by definition, hidden; it does not show! If you see someone taking a drink and you *know* that there is an ulterior motive involved, then you also know, immediately, intuitively, and brilliantly, that *thirst* is not the motive. If someone agrees with you repeatedly, smiling in friendly fashion all the while, and stroking your cheek, beware! If an ulterior motive is involved, it is neither altruism nor sex! It is hidden.

Consider the challenge: a search for the hidden motive. Naturally, nothing can be said about the ulterior motive at this time, since it does not flaunt itself flagrantly like the more shameless motives: hunger, sex, thirst, need for achievement. But there is no doubt that an entire book could be devoted to The Ulterior Motive.

A Humanistic Closing

Maslow (1970) suggests that human actions may be accounted for in terms of two systems of needs: the basic needs, and the **metaneeds**. The basic needs consist of physiological needs (food, drink) and psychological needs (security, love, and self-esteem). Metaneeds are higher-level needs and include cognitive needs, aesthetic needs, and the need for self-fulfillment. Alternative labels for these two broad categories of needs are *deficiency needs* and *growth needs*. Basic physiological and psychological needs are called deficiency needs because when they are unsatisfied, indi-

Metaneeds   A term coined by Maslow to describe a group of human needs that are superior to the basic physiological needs. Metaneeds include aesthetic needs and the need for self-actualization.

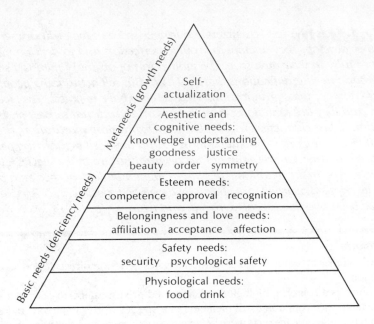

Figure 9.22 Maslow's hierarchy of needs. The lower-level needs must be satisfied before higher-level needs are attended to. The growth needs are fundamental to mental health and happiness.

viduals engage in behaviors designed to satisfy them. The metaneeds are called growth needs because activities relating to them do not result from deficiencies, but from the organism's tendency toward growth.

The basic needs are, according to Maslow, hierarchically arranged as depicted in Figure 9.22. What this means, in effect, is that lower-level needs (physiological, for example) are initially more important than higher-level needs in the sense that they must be satisfied before other needs are attended to. For example, a person who is starving is not likely to pay much attention to self-esteem. Indeed, starving people may well engage in behaviors that would ordinarily be highly damaging to their self-esteem, stooping to steal from their grandmothers.

The metaneeds are not hierarchically organized. All supersede the deficiency needs and attain importance as lower-level needs are satisfied. In other words, we pay attention to beauty, justice, order; we explore and search for truth; we try to become whatever it is that we are capable of becoming when our basic needs are more or less satisfied.

Maslow's concern was less with the development of a scientific theory of motivation than with the organization of existing principles and knowledge within a framework what would encompass the more "human"—though highly elusive—qualities of behavior that are involved in what he terms our "higher nature." The theory views behavior tendencies toward growth as instinctual (*instinctoid* is Maslow's term). These tendencies define our very essence and are absolutely fundamental to mental health and happiness. Chief among these higher-level growth needs is the need to self-actualize. Unlike the more basic needs, whose satisfaction can be ensured through appropriate activities (eating, for example), **self-actualization**, as a need, is never satisfied. The process of becoming is less a movement toward a state of being than a movement toward a process. Although to self-actualize is to develop one's potential—to become whatever it is that one is capable of becoming, should become, indeed, needs to become—a final, fully actualized state is an ill-defined state of happiness that does not lead to cessation of behavior.

Maslow (1970) studied about two dozen individuals whom he identified as self-actualizing. Among them were Albert Einstein, William James, Eleanor Roosevelt, and Albert Schweitzer. He interviewed nine of these directly, and examined case histories and historical references for the others. As a result, he arrived at a description of self-actualization. In his words:

Self-actualization The process or act of becoming oneself, of developing one's potential, of achieving an awareness of one's identity, of fulfilling oneself. The term *actualization* is central in humanistic psychology.

Our subjects [the self-actualizers] *no longer strive in the ordinary sense, but rather develop. They attempt to grow to perfection and to develop more and more fully in their own style. The motivation of ordinary men is a striving for the basic need gratifications that they lack. But self-actualizing people in fact lack none of these gratifications; and yet they have impulses. They work, they try, and they are ambitious, even though in an unusual sense. For them motivation is just character growth, character expression, maturation, and development; in a word self-actualization. Could these self-actualizing people be more human, more revealing of the original nature of the species, closer to the species type in the taxonomical sense? Ought a biological species to be judged by its crippled, warped, only partially developed specimens, or by examples that have been overdomesticated, caged, and trained? (p. 159)*

Main Points

1   Motivation may be defined as that which instigates behavior, directs it, and accounts for its cessation.

2   An instinct is a complex, biologically determined predisposition to react in a specific and predictable way, common to all members of a species (for example, migration in birds). Although at one time instincts were believed to motivate human behavior, that explanation is no longer accepted.

3   Imprinting is a phenomenon where certain behaviors are typically learned by all members of a species as a function of exposure to appropriate stimulation (a *releaser*) during a specific developmental period (termed a *critical period*). Researchers have speculated that some human behaviors depend on imprinting, but conclusive proof has not been found.

4   Hedonism is the belief that people behave so as to obtain pleasure and avoid pain. Motivation was once explained in these terms but since this explanation tells us no more than we already know, it is not really useful.

5   Physiological needs are lacks, the satisfaction of which will contribute to the animal's welfare. Thus we have needs for food, drink, sex, maintaining body temperature, and so on. Drives are urges associated with needs. Thus hunger is a drive associated with the need for food; thirst is a drive associated with the need for drink.

6   Taste and smell as well as metabolic factors (blood sugar levels; stomach contractions; activity of the hypothalamus, and the presence or absence of certain neurotransmitters such as the endorphins) all appear to be involved in hunger.

7   Some evidence suggests that obese people are more responsive to external food-related cues, and less responsive to internal, hunger-related cues, than thinner people. Metabolic factors and genetic factors are also involved in obesity.

8   Thirst appears to be regulated by cell dehydration and by increases and decreases in blood volume, monitored by the hypothalamus.

9   Sexual motivation is closely related to sex hormones: in males, androgens (especially testosterone); in females, estrogens. In addition, a large number of external factors are associated with sexual arousal. There is evidence that sexual beliefs and behavior are more similar among males and females now than in the past.

10   The drive-reduction model of motivation maintains that drives give rise to certain urges or tensions, which in turn cause behavior, which if appropriate reduces the tension—an outcome which is pleasant and which therefore reinforces the behavior in question. This model does not explain psychological motives such as needs for love and affection; nor does it explain curiosity-based behavior or stimulation-seeking behavior.

11   Current cognitive theories of motivation generally recognize the importance of incentives for human behavior.

12   Behavioristic theories of motivation tend to describe a relatively passive organism, highly responsive to external stimulation and to internal drives. Cognitive positions describe a more active organism, less responsive to the demands of basic needs, but curious, exploring, *actively* trying to make sense of the environment.

13   Curiosity is a cognitive motive that moves us to explore and to manipulate, apparently for no other reason than to seek stimulation. Epistemic curiosity is directed toward the acquisition of knowledge.

14   Achievement motivation may be described as a need to meet or surpass some inner standard of excellence—in other words, as a need to achieve. People who have a high need

to achieve tend to do better in school, and are moderate (as opposed to extreme) risk-takers. Fear of failure may sometimes reduce need for achievement.

15 Some evidence suggests that males are higher in need for achievement than are females, particularly in competitive situations, a difference that is probably culturally engendered.

16 Attribution theories of human motivation are based primarily on the notion that we try to make sense out of our behaviors and that of others by looking for causes and effects. Thus we *attribute* our behaviors to internal factors or to external factors, depending on our personalities and on the immediate situation. People who are high in need for achievement tend to attribute the outcomes of their behaviors to internal rather than to external factors.

17 Arousal has both a physiological and a psychological component. There is an optimal level of arousal for different behaviors, and individuals behave so as to maintain arousal level at or near an optimal level. Arousal increases with amount and variety of stimulation. Boredom, associated with low arousal levels, is related to unchanging, monotonous stimulation.

18 Arousal theory proposes that knowledge-seeking behavior is motivated by a need to either increase or decrease arousal. Problems or lack of information may be seen as arousing; solving them reduces arousal and is reinforcing.

19 Social motives relate to our gregarious (sociable) nature, and are evident in our needs to establish and maintain relationships with others. They include competition, cooperation, altruism, and aggression.

20 An ulterior motive is, by definition, hidden.

21 Maslow suggests that humans are motivated by both basic needs and metaneeds. Basic needs, or deficiency needs, are for food, drink, safety, belongingness, and self-esteem. When these have been filled, metaneeds, or growth needs, become important. The highest metaneed is for self-actualization, which is the process of fulfilling one's potential.

Further Readings

The biological bases of motivation are typically covered in detail in physiological psychology textbooks. For example:

Carlson, N. R. *Physiology of behavior* (2nd. ed.). Boston: Allyn & Bacon, 1980 (especially Chapters 11, 12, and 13).

A readable summary and discussion of research on obesity, together with suggestions for controlling weight, is given in:

Stuart, R. B., and Davis, B. *Slim chance in a fat world: Behavioral control of obesity.* Champaign, Ill.: Research Press, 1972.

For recent research on obesity, see:

Stunkard, A. J. *Obesity.* Philadelphia: W. B. Saunders, 1980.

Among the many recent books that look at sex differences in motivation and behavior, as well as cultural stereotypes with respect to the sexes, are the following. The first two are paperbacks. The third is a popular text that deals with sexual anatomy as well as behavior.

Deaux, K. *The behavior of women and men.* Monterey, Calif.: Brooks/Cole, 1976.

Grams, J. D., and Waetjen, W. B. *Sex: Does it make a difference?* North Scituate, Mass.: Duxbury Press, 1975.

McCary, J. L. *Human sexuality.* New York: D. Van Nostrand, 1978.

Among the best descriptions of curiosity as a motive is:

Fowler, H. *Curiosity and exploratory behavior.* New York: Macmillan, 1965.

A more detailed overview of different approaches to motivation is presented in:

Petrie, H. L. *Motivation: Theory and research.* Belmont, Calif.: Wadsworth, 1981.

A short paperback by Cofer provides an excellent overview of different motivational theories:

Cofer, C. N. *Motivation and emotion.* Chicago: Scott, Foresman, 1972.

The following collection contains excellent and important articles relating primarily to cognitive views of motivation:

Weiner, B. (Ed.). *Cognitive views of human motivation.* New York: Academic Press, 1974.

Maslow's motivational theory is described in:

Maslow, A. H. *Motivation and personality* (2nd ed.). New York: Harper & Row, 1970.

Emotion

10

My cousin, Luke, stole a truck when he was twelve. It wasn't much of a truck. Just an old Ford pickup that had spent all of its life hauling manure and firewood on the farm, or chugging along the country road between the farm and the store. It belonged to my uncle—Luke's father. We knew that he had once loved it dearly, although it now seemed that with its dented and rusted fenders, its cracked windshield and weathered tires, he must find it much less lovable.

The truck was still full of manure the day we stole it. I mean, the day Luke stole it. Martin and I just happened to be there. Luke's father didn't happen to be there.

The excitement! The heady, nerve-tingling, whoopee! sheer, tremulous excitement of it all, tearing down that brown dust road, swooping over hills and around corners. Just a tiny prickle of fear sharpened our exhilaration. We would only go for a small ride; we did not dare risk more this first time.

And then Luke, not yet a practiced driver, veered too far into a corner, and the old truck plunged madly into the ditch at full throttle. Perhaps twenty miles an hour: just fast enough to roll over, gently like an arthritic old dog, great clouds of fluffy manure floating softly through the open windows.

The fear! The raw, heart-thumping, dry-mouthed, wide-eyed panic of it all, choking in the putrid dust, scrambling to get out.

Then the relief of being alive and unhurt, brushing manure from our clothes, spitting and coughing.

Luke crying, not terrified anymore, but afraid that his father might still love the old truck.

Martin crying. Embarrassed that his trousers needed to be washed—that it was not just cow manure.

And I, feeling a confused mixture of emotions; crying too, knowing they would think it had been my idea. Young chicken thieves often have bad reputations.

Now, many years later, even Luke's father laughs when we remember. . . .

Figure 10.1 Even when the context seems clear and the emotion powerful, its nature is not always obvious. Is this girl terrified, ecstatic, or in pain? Or has her younger brother just fired his water pistol at her?

What Is an Emotion?

Emotions have caused a great deal of difficulty for psychologists. They cannot easily be defined or described; they are almost impossible to measure; their physiological bases do not clearly differentiate among them; and yet they are a fundamental part of the experience of being human. In fact, it is almost impossible to imagine any human experience that does not involve emotion.

What is this thing called emotion or affect? In general, it appears to have two broad dimensions, the first being intensity. Intensity of an emotional reaction can range from very high to very low. For example, the emotion of anger might range from petty annoyance to rage; disgust, from mild distaste to sickening revulsion; joy, from contentment to absolute ecstasy.

Not only can emotions be described in terms of intensity, but also in terms of whether they are pleasant or unpleasant. Joy, love, and happiness are generally pleasant emotional states; anger, rage, and disgust are clearly more negative. Knowing that emotional (or affective) reactions vary both in terms of pleasantness and in terms of intensity, we are now in a position to offer a tentative definition of emotion.

In general, emotion may be described as the "feeling" or "affective" component of human behavior, where "feeling" describes an internal or subjective state. This state varies in intensity as well as in terms of whether it is perceived as pleasant or unpleasant. In addition to being an internal state, emotion is accompanied by certain physiological changes and, quite often, by behaviors that may be directly related to the emotion. Thus, the emotion of anger is an internal feeling, usually perceived as negative and as more intense than displeasure but less intense than rage. It is generally accompanied by increased heart and respiration rate as well as by other physiological changes, none of which are necessarily detected (or detectable) by the person experiencing the anger. Finally, this emotion may also be accompanied by certain behaviors

including facial expressions, clenching of fists, and raising of the voice. (See Figure 10.2.)

Davitz (1969) amused himself by counting words that refer to emotions in *Roget's Thesaurus,* a book of synonyms. He found over 400 of them. A brief examination reveals that they may be classified in a number of ways, but that no one is likely to agree on the precise number of *different* emotions of which we are capable. Not all emotions fall neatly within our classification of emotions as either pleasant or unpleasant. Is surprise pleasant or unpleasant, for example? Perhaps it isn't even an emotion, but a general reaction to the unexpected. The reaction then takes on emotional connotations dependent on the nature of the stimulation. In fact, however, emotion is not a property of stimulation, but a property of subjective responses to stimulation (both internal and external). Yet "surprise" has often been listed as an emotion in spite of the fact that we cannot readily agree about what it is. And even if we could agree on which emotions are pleasant and which unpleasant, we would still be left with the problem of ranking our emotional reactions in terms of their intensity. Sadness, sorrow, hurt, depression, despair, and grief are related unpleasant emotions. However, our language of emotions is so imprecise that the behavioral scientist is hard-pressed to talk rationally about them.

Emotional Expression

To define an emotion is to speak about what we presume to be the subjective experience of being in that emotional state. Emotion, however, has other dimensions. Among the most important of these for human interaction is its expression. Emotions can be expressed in behavior, as, for example, when you run from an irate turkey or run after a less irate chicken. Thus, emotions may be seen as having approach or avoidance tendencies, not all of which will always be expressed overtly.

Emotions may also be expressed verbally. Much of the richness of human conversation derives from the expression and interpretation of emotion. So, too, our books, movies, and art forms play on and with our emotions. In fact, there is probably nothing we do that does not have emotional overtones, although we do not always pay attention to them. Emotions and their expression are an absolutely central concern for each of us.

Emotions are expressed nonverbally as well. Facial expressions and gestures have been extensively studied as manifestations of emotion. Many emotional expressions are learned and culture-specific. Applause in North America indicates approval but means the opposite in certain European countries; so, too, with whistling which, in European countries, means what booing means in North America. Klineberg (1938) examined some Chinese novels to discover how their authors describe emotional expression. It might seem strange to us that sticking out the tongue means surprise; clapping the hands indicates **anxiety** or disappointment; and scratching the ears shows happiness. The Chinese might be equally surprised to find us frowning when we are puzzled, chewing our lips in concentration, pounding fist in palm to signal determination or anger, and wetting our lips in anticipation. In Europe and North America, spitting is a sign of contempt, the violence of the act corresponding well with the intensity of the emotion; in Arab countries, spitting is a courtesy—more, it is a blessing.

Not all expressions of emotion are learned and therefore culture-specific, however. It seems that there are a number of emotional expressions that are innate and common to all members of our species. Raising the eyebrows is a quasi-universal expression of greeting or acknowledgment; smiling, a universal gesture of approval and friendliness (Eibl-Eibesfeldt, 1974; Morris, 1977). Darwin (1872) was among the first to note the similarity of these expressions across very different cultures. Accordingly, he sent a list of questions concerning facial expressions to a number of researchers in different countries in an attempt to discover precisely which gestures are universal and might, therefore, be genetic. After gathering this data, the bulk of which was purely anecdotal, he concluded that typical facial expressions accompanying joy, sorrow, anger, surprise, and so on are largely genetic. This view was uncritically accepted for a considerable period of time (see Ekman, 1973).

Subsequently, however, a number of noted anthropologists gathered volumes of cross-cultural evidence which they interpreted to mean that expressions of emotion were culture-specific (for example, Klineberg, 1938; Birdwhistell, 1963). These researchers based their conclusions on evidence which was often no more convincing than Darwin's collections of anecdotes. For example, if a researcher in some preliterate jungle village notes that people smile at a funeral, should we conclude that expressions of grief are not universal—that they are specific to our cultures? Ekman (1973) says no. He makes the important point that we are probably not justified in assuming that identical situations in two different cultures give rise to the same emotions. Another culture might teach its people that dying is a happy thing. If its people then insist on smiling at funerals, it is not because they have chosen to express grief by smiling, but it is precisely because they feel no grief.

Should we now agree with Darwin who believed that at least some expressions of important emotions are universal—that, indeed, they are present in nonhuman primates as well as in all humans? Or should we accept the view of at least some anthropologists that culture determines how we manifest our emotions?

A number of experimental studies have attempted to answer this question. Ekman and his associates (Ekman, 1972; Ekman, Sorenson, & Friesen, 1969; Ekman, 1973), for example, examined a group of some 3000 photographs to identify those highly representative of facial expressions we ordinarily associate with one of six emotions: happiness, sadness, anger, fear, surprise, and disgust. They selected 30 of these photographs and showed them to a total of 455 subjects in five different cultures (U.S., Brazil, Chile, Argentina, and Japan). Subjects were asked to match each of the pictures

Anxiety An unpleasant emotional reaction whose most identifiable characteristic is fear. Anxiety can vary from mild trepidation, frequently not associated with any specific situation or stimulus, to severe panic. One of the most common characteristics of a great number of mental disorders is anxiety; in fact, psychoanalytic theory suggests that anxiety is at the root of virtually all mental disorders.

Percentage Agreement in How Photograph Was Judged across Cultures				
United States (N = 99)	Brazil (N = 40)	Chile (N = 119)	Argentina (N = 168)	Japan (N = 29)
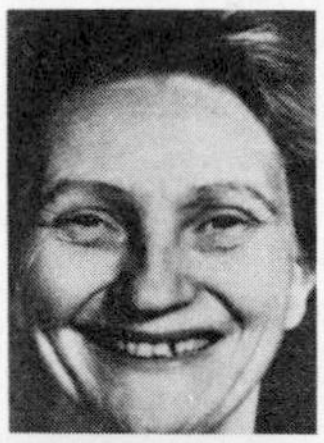 97% Happiness	95% Happiness	95% Happiness	98% Happiness	100% Happiness
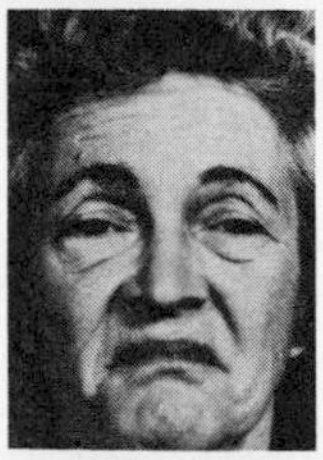 92% Disgust	97% Disgust	92% Disgust	92% Disgust	90% Disgust
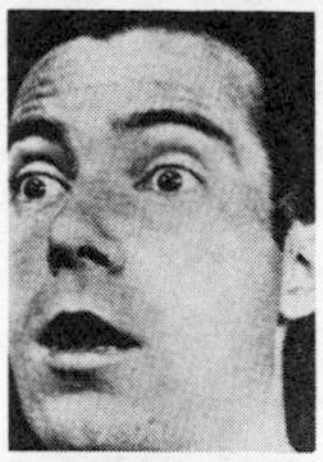 95% Surprise	87% Surprise	93% Surprise	95% Surprise	100% Surprise
 84% Sadness	59% Sadness	88% Sadness	78% Sadness	62% Sadness
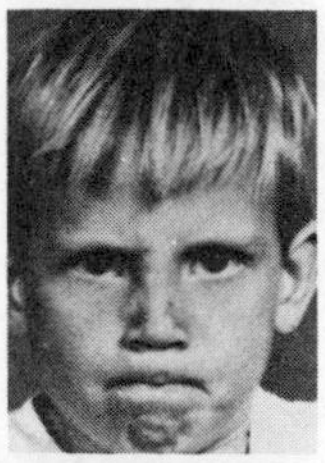 67% Anger	90% Anger	94% Anger	90% Anger	90% Anger
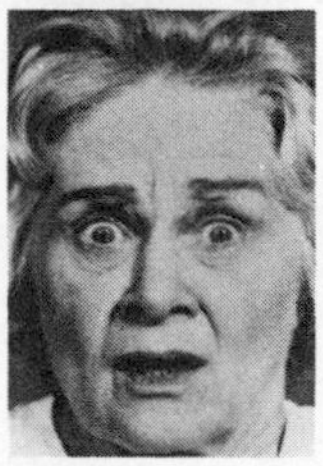 85% Fear	67% Fear	68% Fear	54% Fear	66% Fear

Figure 10.3 Results of an experimental study by Ekman et al. People from different cultures interpret emotional expression in very similar ways. From "Cross Cultural Studies of Facial Expression" in P. Ekman (ed.), *Darwin and Facial Expression: A Century of Research in Review,* Academic Press, 1973. Reprinted by permission.

to one of the six emotions. Results for 6 of the photographs are shown in Figure 10.3, and are representative of results obtained for the entire sample of 30 photographs. The results provide strong evidence that people from different cultures interpret emotional expression in very similar ways. In a later study, researchers had members of a preliterate New Guinea tribe try to show (through facial expression) what emotion the person in a story would feel (Ekman, 1972). Stories were short, simple tales meant to connote fear, happiness, or anger. Videotapes of these subjects were later shown to American college students who experienced no difficulty in identifying the emotion being portrayed.

That many emotional expressions (crying, laughing, smiling, fearing) will be understood by most people from many countries has by now been well documented. But that many subtler emotions will be misunderstood has also been demonstrated. For example, Klineberg (1951) had Chinese and American subjects identify emotional expressions in photographs of Americans and Chinese. Although all subjects recognized a great many emotions, Americans had considerably less difficulty with American photos and Chinese, with photographs of Chinese people.

The Physiology of Emotion

In addition to its experiential and expressive features, emotion is also related to activity of the autonomic nervous system. Popular literature abounds with descriptions of physiological activity that are so meaningful, given their contexts, that the reader need not be told anything more about the nature or intensity of the emotion. "My heart beat fast/stood still/quaked/shivered/jumped/was in my throat/stopped." "My breath caught in my throat/halted/came fast and hoarse/was silent." "My hair stood on end." "Shivers ran up my spine." "My hands were cold/clammy/perspired/trembled/shook."

The Autonomic Nervous System

We ordinarily have no control over these physiological reactions. We do not begin to tremble in front of an audience because we want to; we don't consciously accelerate our heart rates; we have no control over the dryness in our mouths. All of these reactions are under control of our autonomic nervous systems. (See Figure 10.4.)

What, precisely, does your autonomic nervous system cause to happen in your body in moments of great fear? A number of things. A message goes to your adrenal glands, which rapidly secrete adrenalin in your bloodstream. Your heart reacts at once: its rate increases dramatically, sometimes doubling. At the same time, your respiration rate increases, providing an increased supply of oxygen to the blood which is, in fact, coursing more rapidly through your body, and supplying more oxygen to your muscles. Your skeletal muscles, in turn, contract slightly. In an animal, the result is that the hair stands on end, a phenomenon that is sometimes highly apparent on the neck of an angry dog; in humans, the result is a slightly less threatening display of goose bumps. At the same time as these changes are occurring, blood vessels to the stomach and intestines constrict and the process of digestion is interrupted. Also, action of the salivary glands is impeded and your mouth consequently becomes dry. Bowel and/or bladder control may also be lost temporarily.

The biological significance of these changes is clear. They prepare the organism to fight or, alternately, to flee. They serve, in a very real sense, to mobilize the resources of the body. And in the event that these resources are not immediately required, the parasympathetic division of the autonomic nervous system begins to counteract the effects of sympathetic nervous system activity almost at once. As noted in Chapter 2, your heart rate does not increase indefinitely.

The Brain

Our knowledge of the physiology of emotion is not limited to what we know about autonomic nervous system functioning. The brain too is centrally implicated. Specific structures that are known to be involved in emotional behavior include the hypothalamus and parts of the limbic system. Research conducted primarily with animals, but sometimes with humans who have suffered brain damage through injury or disease, has led to a number of observations. We know, for example, that the amygdala (one of the structures in the limbic system) is strongly implicated in anger and rage.

Damage to certain parts of the amygdala can turn a wild animal into a docile creature (G. V. Goddard, 1964); damage to other parts of the amygdala can turn a docile creature into a raging beast (Bard & Mountcastle, 1948). Charles Whitman, the man who shot thirty-eight people from a tower at the University of Texas, killing fourteen of them, had a malignant tumor on the amygdala (Sweet, Ervin, & Mark, 1969).

Stimulation of portions of the hypothalamus can turn a cat into a quiet killer—a killer that does not hiss or slash violently at its victims but stalks quietly and kills unemotionally and with professional dispatch (Levison & Flynn, 1965). Stimulation of other parts of the hypothalamus can turn a cat into an enraged killer—a killer that does not hunt methodically but attacks violently and senselessly, a killer who strikes out at anything that comes close (Flynn, 1967). Stimulation of parts of the amygdala can elicit mild or intense fear, sometimes causing animals to flee in panic (G. V. Goddard, 1964). Lesions in the septal area can bring about rage reactions similar to those associated with hypothalamic stimulation or lesions in the amygdala (Brady & Nauta, 1955).

These and a variety of other observations that bear directly on the relationship between the brain and emotions have done relatively little to simplify our understanding of the physiological basis of emotion. Although it seems clear that the limbic system is involved in emotional reaction, the relationship of these structures to specific emotions is complex and not entirely certain. In addition, evidence suggests strongly that hormones and other chemical substances (for example, acetylcholine, serotonin, and other neurotransmitters) are also involved in emotional reactions, as are some of the higher brain centers (see Box 10.1).

BOX 10.1

Pleasure Centers

The brain may have an area, or several, devoted to pleasure. Olds (1956) implanted electrodes in the brain of a rat and discovered, quite accidentally, that stimulation of specific areas of the hypothalamus was highly rewarding. When the electrodes were connected in such a way that rats could stimulate their own brains by depressing a lever, they appeared to find electrical stimulation more pleasurable than food or sex. Hungry rats would ignore a tempting food dish in order to stand before the lever, playing with their brains. One rat stimulated himself more than 2,000 times per hour for twenty-four consecutive hours (Olds, 1956). If the electrodes were implanted somewhat lower in the hypothalamus, however, rats experienced not pleasure but pain, and went to great lengths to avoid being stimulated.

It is possible that stimulation of appropriate portions of the hypothalamus has the same emotional effect as a good meal, a fine drink, or a moving sexual experience. There are some important differences, however, between the effects of brain stimulation and those of such primary reinforcers as food or drink. Whereas animals eventually become satiated following repeated reinforcement with food or water, this is not the case with brain stimulation. One rat stimulated himself nearly 7,000 times in a single hour (Olds & Milner, 1954). In addition, brain stimulation appears to take precedence over other types of reward. Rats will go without food or drink in order to stimulate their brains; they will even cross an electric grid to gain access to a lever associated with self-stimulation; and female rats will abandon their squealing newborn pups in favor of self-stimulation (Sonderegger, 1970).

However, when self-stimulation is discontinued, extinction is remarkably more rapid than it would be if food or water had been employed as a reward. And perhaps most puzzling, it is ordinarily impossible to train maze-running in rats, or to employ schedules of reinforcement in other learning situations, when brain stimulation is the reinforcer. Although stimulation of the appropriate parts of a rat's brain appears to be highly rewarding, its effect is quite different from that of the common primary reinforcers.

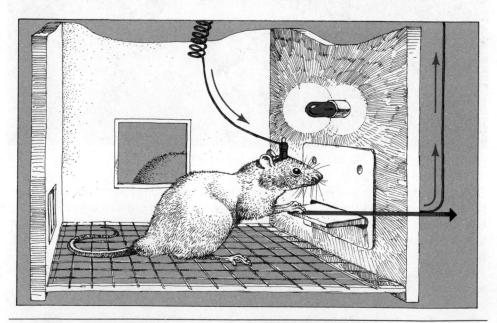

Do "pleasure centers" exist in the brain? Olds (1956) implanted electrodes in rats' hypothalami. The rats could trigger an electrical stimulus by depressing a lever. Clearly, the region where the electrode was implanted was involved in pleasure sensation: rats stimulated themselves as many as 7,000 times in one hour, passing up opportunities for food, drink, and anything else in favor of the "pleasure machine." (From "Pleasure Centers in the Brain" by James Olds. Copyright © 1956 by Scientific American, Inc. All rights reserved.)

Pert (interview, 1982) goes so far as to suggest that there might be specific neurotransmitters associated with very specific emotions, and that the receptors for these transmitters are located in very specific areas of the brain. In the same way as we have "opiate" receptors that respond to endorphins, so too do we appear to have "valium" receptors. One line of speculation is that the brain manufactures endorphins and other neurotransmitters as a sort of reward for itself—a self-reward system. Research continues.

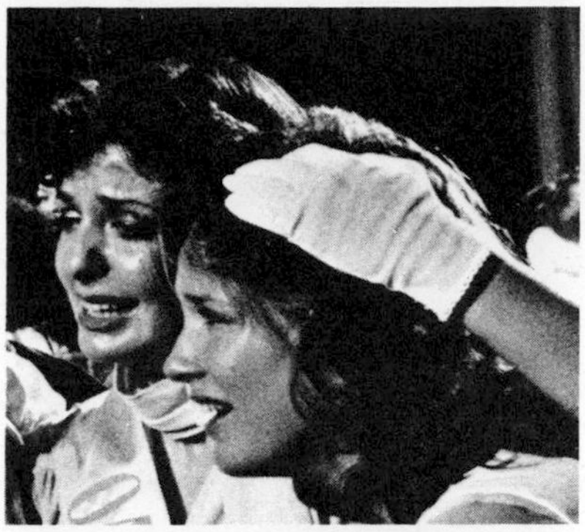

The Search for Specifics

Language is not always adequate to describe emotions precisely. When asked to describe the difference between great joy and great sorrow, for example, we are most likely to resort to describing differences in the situations that give rise to each. Alternately we might try to differentiate between them by reference to synonyms for each. Another approach to this problem would be to describe differences in the physiological reactions that might accompany one or the other. Thus for great joy, we might laugh; and for great sorrow, we would most likely weep. But sometimes we weep with joy (see Figure 10.5). Would it be better, then, to measure more subtle physiological changes such as heart rate, blood pressure, conductivity of the skin to electricity? Unfortunately, a variety of emotions give rise to very similar physiological changes (Grossman, 1967).

In summary, gross physiological changes related to emotional arousal (and to autonomic nervous system activity) do not appear to be very specific to different emotions. There is a possibility, however, that chemical changes in the brain and specific patterns of neural activity might be associated with identifiable emotions, although those precise relationships have yet to be identified.

Figure 10.5 What emotions do you think these two young women are expressing? Once you've decided, turn to Figure 10.6.

Theories of Emotion

We have attempted to define and describe emotion; we have looked at its physiological bases. We turn now to a handful of theories that have helped clarify our understanding of our emotional lives.

Physiological Theories

Early theorists made much of the physiological changes that accompany emotions. William James (1884) went so far as to say that emotion results from them, and based an entire theory on this notion. These same ideas were also being developed simultaneously by a Danish psychologist, Lange, so that the theory came to be known as the *James-Lange theory*. In essence, it maintains that an emotion-related stimulus gives rise to certain physiological changes; the individual perceives these physiological changes (for example, becomes aware of increased heart rate, of perspiration, perhaps of imminent tears), and subsequently attributes an emotional feeling to the situation or event that gave rise to the physiological changes (see Figure 10.7a). In other words, awareness of bodily changes leads to an emotional state.

Serious objection to the James-Lange theory was presented by two individuals, Cannon (1929, 1939) and Bard: hence the *Cannon-Bard theory*. Cannon demonstrated that if he cut nerves linking the brain to those parts of the body most obviously involved in emotional reactions, animals still behaved as though they felt emotion. He proposed, then, that it was awareness of the emotional significance of an object or event that led to emotional reactions. Bard later performed a series of experiments implicating the thalamus in emotional reaction (subsequently it was discovered that the hypothalamus should have been the organ of choice). Accordingly, their theory states that when an individual perceives an emotion-related situation or object, the hypothalamus sends messages both to the cortex, where the emotion is felt, and to the body, where physiological reactions take place. Thus, awareness of emotion and awareness of physio-

logical changes are independent, although they result from the same source of stimulation. The Cannon-Bard theory is depicted in Figure 10.7b.

Cognitive Labeling Theory

Maranon (1924) injected epinephrine into human subjects. This compound is very similar to the adrenalin released by the adrenal glands when responding to **stress**. Like adrenalin, epinephrine produces a variety of physiological reactions similar to those that accompany intense emotion. Maranon's prediction was that his subjects should experience emotion if they were subjected to physiological reactions that ordinarily accompany emotion. But this was not the case. In a few instances, subjects reported that they felt "as if" they should be afraid, or "as if" with respect to some other emotion, but they insisted that they actually felt no emotion.

Subsequently Schachter replicated the Maranon studies in hope of clarifying the relationship between physiological changes and cognitions in the production of emotional states (Schachter & Singer, 1962). All subjects in the experiment were told they would receive injections of a new drug, "Suproxin," which would improve their performance on a test of visual perception. Some subjects actually received injections of epinephrine; the others received a **placebo**. After the injections, they were given one of three sets of instructions concerning the effects of the drugs. The *informed* group were told what the actual effects of the drug might be, and how long these effects normally lasted; the *ignorant* group were told that the drug would have absolutely no side effects; and the *misinformed* group were told that they might experience a slight numbness and itchiness.

Stress A physiological and essentially adaptive response to disturbances which may result from emotional experiences, physical injury or disease, or other factors. Since anxiety is one of the principal results of stress, the two terms are often used interchangeably.

Placebo A "sham" drug; often a harmless and ineffective saline (salt) injection or a "sugar" pill. Placebos typically have little direct physiological effect, although research indicates that they can often have powerful psychological effects.

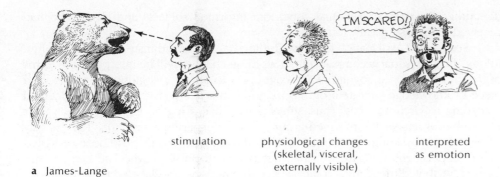

stimulation   physiological changes   interpreted
(skeletal, visceral,   as emotion
externally visible)

a James-Lange

Figure 10.7 Two historical explanations of emotion. In the James-Lange model (**a**), the physiological change leads to and is interpreted as emotion; in the Cannon-Bard model (**b**), physiological change and emotional interpretation are simultaneous but independent.

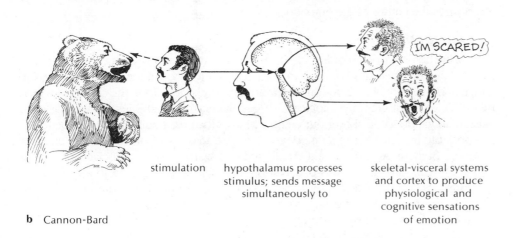

stimulation   hypothalamus processes   skeletal-visceral systems
stimulus; sends message   and cortex to produce
simultaneously to   physiological and
cognitive sensations
of emotion

b Cannon-Bard

Subjects were assigned to one of two experimental conditions, or to a control group. The control group waited quietly for a period of time, and were then interviewed with respect to their emotional reactions. Not surprisingly, they reported no particular emotion, as had been the case in the earlier Maranon studies.

In one of the experimental groups, named the *euphoria* group, subjects were left to wait in a room with another individual who was introduced to them as a fellow subject. In fact, however, the person was a confederate of the experimenters and had been instructed to perform a standardized "euphoric-manic" routine. This stooge danced, played basketball with crumpled pieces of paper, made little projectiles and launched them with rubber bands, played with a hula hoop, and otherwise tried to convey the impression that this was a hilarious episode in the life of a college student.

In the second experimental group, termed the *anger* group, subjects were again left with a confederate, but were asked to fill out a questionnaire while waiting. The questionnare was long (it required a full hour to complete), highly detailed, and sometimes embarrassingly personal. It asked about the personal hygiene of every member of the subject's family, how often they took a bath, brushed their teeth, and who had the most disagreeable body odor. The questionnaire did not permit the subject to answer "No" or "None" to the more embarrassing questions. One question read: "With how many men (other than your father) has your mother had extramarital relationships? 4 and under—: 5-9—: 10 and over—." The stooge, acting according to precise directions, became progressively angrier while completing the questionnaire, finally crumpling it up and leaving the room.

Following this, all subjects were interviewed individually in order to uncover their emotional reactions. Results were as follows: subjects who were uninformed or misinformed and who had received epinephrine exhibited and felt anger or euphoria, depending on the experimental condition; informed subjects and those who had received placebos typically did not.

Schachter's explanation for these findings is simple and instructive. Given physiological changes that accompany emotion, these changes will be interpreted in terms of the most plausible cognitions (to cognize is to know; a cognition is therefore a piece of knowledge—an item of information). In other words, they will be labeled according to circumstances. Thus, subjects who had a logical explanation for their physiological states (the informed group) did not experience emotion. They simply labeled their physiological states in terms of the explanations that had been provided by the experimenter. Those who had not been informed or who had been misinformed attributed their physiological states to emotions, and labeled these emotions according to the confederate's behavior. In short, although physiological changes are clearly involved in emotional reaction, the individual's cognitive label for the change determines the nature of the emotion.

Attribution Theory

Schachter's work provides the basis for an attribution theory of emotion not unlike that described in Chapter 9 in connection with motivation. Quite simply, the nature and intensity of an emotion appear to depend largely upon the causes to which the individual attributes physiological changes. Such a theory implies that we may have considerably more control over our emotional lives than has traditionally been believed. It is possible that, at least to some degree, we are masters of our emotions, and not prisoners of them. An experiment conducted by Lazarus and his associates (Koriat et al., 1972) bears directly on this observation. Subjects were exposed to a number of presentations of a film depicting accidents in a woodshop. For example, one man lacerates the tips of his fingers, another cuts off a finger, and a third is skewered through the midsection by a plank propelled from a circular saw. He dies.

In some experimental conditions, subjects were asked to detach themselves from events in the film; in others they were told to involve themselves in the film. In neither case were they told how to do this. Records were kept of heart rate changes for every individual during presentation of the film; in addition, reports were obtained of subjective emotional states. Significantly, subjects who were asked to detach themselves from the film showed evidence of greatly reduced emotional reaction in terms of both their heart rates and self-reports. Those who were told to involve themselves were highly successful in bringing about profound emotional reactions. The procedures employed by members of the two groups were simple and effective. A majority of the *involvement* group imagined that they were the person to whom the accidents were happening, or attempted to relate the accidents to other accidents they might have witnessed or in which friends or relatives had been involved. Members of the *detachment* group pretended that the events had been "staged" for the filming, or paid particular attention to the technical details of the film. (See Figure 10.8.)

The most important point of this study is not that we are able to exercise some control over emotional reactions. Rather, it is that we *do,* in fact, deliberately exercise control through various strategies that we ourselves develop. As is shown in Chapter 15, these strategies are not always healthy, effective though they may be. Lazarus (1974) discusses the coping functions of the cognitive control of emotions, citing numerous studies which indicate not only that it is possible to exercise considerable control over emotional reaction, but also that doing so can be of considerable benefit. A study of patients before and after surgery revealed that those who adopted detachment strategies, not wanting to know details of their surgery or symptoms of recovery or complications, experienced more rapid and smoother recoveries than patients who were more involved. Lazarus speculates that paying undue attention to possible signs of complications, or even to signs of recovery, is probably associated with more anxiety (stress) and is negatively associated with recovery.

In Lazarus's view, a position closely related to Schachter's as well as to Weiner's attribution theory of need for achievement, cognitive activity does a great deal to

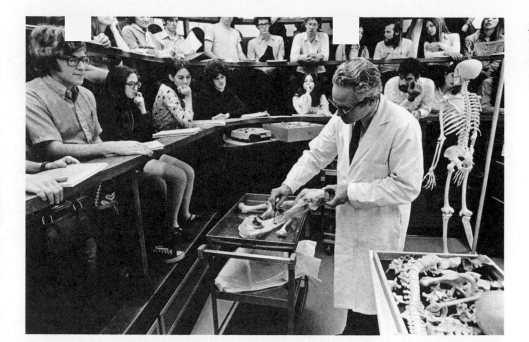

control emotional states. He argues that emotion is seldom a single, identifiable response to a given situation, but is more often a complex of responses. Moreover, this complex shifts continually. Anger turns into despair; grief into elation; rage into apathy; joy into sorrow; anxiety into relief. Emotions ebb and flow as we appraise our situations, our relationships with people and things, our probabilities of attaining or not attaining goals. The fundamental point is that *we* are the ones doing the appraising; the emotion resides not in the situation but in our appraisal of it. Furthermore, we exercise control over our appraisals, sometimes deliberately reducing emotional reaction, as may be the case with anger or fear; sometimes deliberately enhancing it, as with love or joy.

Opponent Process Theory

Unfortunately, we cannot always deliberately control our emotional reactions; in some circumstances, we appear to be enslaved by them. Love is sometimes a case in point; other addictions are too. Indeed, any really extreme emotion can exercise a powerful motivational force on an individual. It appears, however, that we are not designed to withstand the continual tension of a prolonged extreme emotion. At a physiological level, for example, the changes instigated by activity of the sympathetic nervous system are eventually compensated for by opposing reactions brought about by activity of the parasympathetic nervous system. This tendency to maintain a physiological *balance* is termed **homeostasis**. Homeostasis is evident not only in the opposing reactions of the sympathetic and parasympathetic divisions of the autonomic nervous system, but also in certain basic physiological functions involved in survival. Thus there are homeostatic mechanisms involved in the regulation of eating and drinking. These ensure that the amounts and varieties of substance ingested are sufficient for our needs—in other words, they ensure a balance between what we take in and what we need.

Homeostatic mechanisms also seem to be operative at the psychological level. With respect to arousal, for example, we noted that there is an optimal level associated with various behaviors, and that individuals tend to behave so as to maintain arousal at or near this level. The same appears to hold true with respect to specific emotions (all of which are, incidentally, accompanied by arousal as well). Solomon and Corbit (1974; Solomon, 1977) have advanced a simple model of emotion and motivation

Homeostasis Tendency to maintain balance, evident at both a physiological and a psychological level. Homeostasis is the basis of the opponent process theory of emotion.

based specifically on this assumption. The model is labeled the opponent process model. It says, in essence, that all emotional reactions are accompanied by an opposite reaction. If a specific situation gives rise to feelings of great joy, then there will also be feelings of sadness; fear will be tempered with relief; excitement with boredom; love with hate. It is important to note, however, that the opposing emotion is always aroused *after* the initial emotion, and is initially so weak that it cannot easily be detected. With repeated exposure to the same specific emotion-related situation, however, the dominant emotion becomes progressively weaker whereas the opposing reaction becomes stronger. That, in brief, is the Solomon-Corbit opponent process model of emotion and motivation.

As an illustration of this model, Solomon and Corbit refer to a study of emotional reactions among sky divers (Epstein, 1967): The initial dominant emotion in this situation is one of fear—perhaps even of terror. The opponent emotion, relief, is extremely weak. When the sky diver lands following a first jump, there is still little immediate relief. The general reaction is akin to being "stunned" or "overwhelmed." With repeated jumps, however, the dominant emotion lessens: Terror gives way to fear, eventually to anxiety, finally perhaps to momentary concern and vigilance. At the same time, the opponent process strengthens with every repetition. Relief becomes more apparent, giving way eventually to joy; then perhaps to elation. In the end, according to the Solomon-Corbit model, people engage in risk-taking behaviors because of the dominance of the opponent emotion. The lure of a terrifying rollercoaster ride is not so much terror, as it is the relief (and perhaps later the sheer exhilaration) that follows the terror. In the same way, the appeal of masochism (a masochist is one who apparently enjoys pain, particularly in a sexual context) is not the pain that might be suffered, but the opposing pleasure that follows the pain (Solomon, 1980).

In the same way as intense negative emotions might eventually give way to intense pleasant emotions, so too might emotions that are initially pleasant come to be replaced by more negative reactions. This phenomenon, according to Solomon and Corbit (1974), is a useful explanation for drug tolerance and addiction. When a drug user first experiences a drug such as heroin, the accompanying emotional reaction is intensely pleasurable. Opponent process theory suggests, however, that this intensely pleasurable emotion will also be accompanied by an opponent reaction. And if the person continues to take the drug over a period of time, the negative opposite reaction will become progressively stronger, and the initially dominant pleasurable reaction will become correspondingly weaker. Put another way, it will take higher doses of the same drug to achieve an intensely pleasurable state; hence the development of tolerance. Accordingly, the user will be tempted to take the drug more frequently, perhaps not so much to maintain the pleasant state as to avoid the unpleasant opposing emotion. Thus, in the same way as a high-risk-taker might be moved to leap from a plane because of the pleasant opposing emotion, so too might a drug addict be moved to quickly smoke another cigarette or inject once more to avoid the unpleasant opposing reaction.

Manipulation of Emotions

To some unknown degree, our emotions control us. They make us do things. When we speak of experiences that have moved us, we speak of things that have evoked profound emotion. We can as easily speak of the emotions themselves as being moving, for novelists have not yet counted all the things we do in the name of passion. Love is a motive as surely as hunger is. So too, hate, fear, and the vast array of more subtle, less passionate emotions.

But we are not necessarily prisoners of our emotions, although in certain pathological cases the person does appear to be the victim and emotion, the controller. Normally, however, we exercise considerable control over emotional states. Much of this control may be cognitive, as has been shown. Perhaps even more of it takes the form of seeking out situations likely to lead to pleasant emotions, and avoiding those with unpleasant possibilities.

There are other forms of control as well. The sometimes dramatic mood-altering effects of drugs, discussed in Chapter 3, provide an increasingly common method of controlling emotions. There are, in addition, a number of more extreme methods for controlling emotions, many of which have been employed therapeutically with patients suffering from mental disturbances, epilepsy, Parkinsonism, and **cerebral palsy**. Early studies indicated that rage, sometimes real and sometimes only partial (termed "sham" rage), could be evoked in cats, dogs, primates, and other animals by stimulating appropriate areas of their brains (Flynn, 1967; Hess & Akert, 1955). These studies, as mentioned earlier, also showed that violent emotional reactions could be completely inhibited in these animals. Demonstrating his confidence in such procedures, Delgado (1969) entered a bull ring armed only with a radio transmitter. The bull facing him, menacingly angry, had radio-activated electrodes implanted in his brain. With a flourish and a flick of the switch, Delgado stopped him in his tracks, turning him into an apparently docile, quite friendly beast. Numerous studies with monkeys and other primates have since confirmed that electrical stimulation of the brain, or the introduction of certain chemicals via chemotrodes (small inserts, similar to electrodes, that deliver precise dosages of a drug to a small and specific portion of the brain), can control a variety of emotions. What is being controlled, however, is not always clear. Whether Delgado's bull had actually become docile, whether it was simply confused, or whether its motor system was paralyzed remains unclear.

Research with humans has been no less promising, although much work remains to be done in mapping the cortex to locate areas where electrodes may be implanted or drugs introduced. The treatment of severely violent patients by chemical or electrical means, and of mental disorders that are accompanied by severe, debilitating emotion, has successfully been undertaken in a number of cases. Sem-Jacobsen and Styri (1975) report successful mood changes in sixty-six patients, twenty-six of whom were diagnosed as schizophrenic. Nine suffered from other mental disturbances, twenty-six from Parkinson's disease, two from epilepsy, two from cerebral palsy, and one from phantom limb pain.

Brain surgery provides another extreme form of emotion control. It too has been employed with mentally disturbed people for whom all other forms of therapy have proven unsuccessful. The practice of removing parts of the cortex (for example, **prefrontal lobectomy**), once relatively common, has largely been abandoned since the discovery that very small lesions have many of the same positive effects without the same side effects.

Cerebral palsy A syndrome (collection of symptoms) which results from brain injury. The motor areas of the brain are most often affected, which accounts for the motor problems and occasional paralysis that sometimes accompany cerebral palsy. The condition is usually due to brain damage which occurs during birth. A minority of affected individuals are also mentally deficient.

Prefrontal lobectomy Surgical removal of the prefrontal areas of the frontal lobes. Not to be confused with the lobotomy, a surgical procedure whereby nerve fibers that connect the frontal lobes with the thalamus are cut.

Specific Emotions

Some of the more obvious emotions have been subjected to considerable research and speculation. In particular, such "negative" emotions as anxiety, fear, stress, rage, and anger have been researched. Aggression is sometimes included in this list, although there is some doubt as to whether the term *aggression* denotes an emotion or a pattern of behaviors sometimes associated with rage and anger. Aggression is discussed in more detail in Chapter 17. In the remainder of this chapter, two specific groups of emotions are looked at. The first, stress-related emotions, are pervasive and often negative; the second, love and happiness, are more positive.

Stress

Stress is a term for the body's reactions to environmental conditions with which we cannot easily cope. Thus, we can speak of stress as a bodily response, and of *stressors* as those situations in the environment that present challenges or that are disturbing and unsettling, and that lead to stress. The emotion that accompanies stress is labeled anxiety. For this reason, the terms stress and anxiety are often used interchangeably.

Situations that are stressful are, in effect, those that require the body to make adaptive changes. In other words, they require the mobilization of certain resources. These adaptive changes can usually be observed in measures of autonomic functioning. For example, individuals subjected to stressors may experience increased blood pressure and higher electrodermal responses (GSR). Kasl and Cobb (1970) recorded blood pressures for a group of men who subsequently lost their jobs. A comparable group of men who were similarly employed but who did not lose their jobs served as a comparison group. Presumably, knowledge that one is about to lose employment as well as the actual loss would prove stressful. As was expected, there was no change in blood pressure readings for those men who retained their jobs; in contrast, those who were laid off manifested increases in blood pressure in anticipation of losing their jobs and continued to have higher than normal blood pressure readings after being terminated. This and a number of related studies have established that stress may be an important factor in hypertension (high blood pressure) and related circulatory and cardiac problems (Haynes, Feinleib, & Kannel, 1980).

Some celebrated studies with animals have also linked stress to the formation of **peptic ulcers**. Brady (1958) placed pairs of monkeys in restraining devices where each of them would receive a mild electric shock every twenty seconds (a source of stress) unless one of them, the "executive" monkey, depressed a lever to prevent the shock. The executive monkey developed ulcers; the control monkey did not—presumably because, having no responsibility for preventing the shock, he was not exposed to the same degree of stress as his counterpart. In an earlier study, Sawrey and Weisz (1956) housed rats in an environment where they would have to submit to an electric shock whenever they approached food or water. After only two weeks in this environment, many of the rats had developed ulcers and some had even died of hemorrhages.

The executive monkey studies have not always been replicated, however. J. M. Weiss (1968, 1971) found, for example, that rats in the passive rather than executive position developed more ulcers (they also ate less, drank less, lost weight, and in general began a rapid downhill slide). In the original studies, monkeys had not been randomly assigned to the executive (or passive) role, but had been selected on the basis of the speed with which they learned to avoid shock. It may well be that the executive monkeys were initially more anxious or less resistant to pain, and that their ulcers resulted not from the executive position so much as from their predispositions combined with the stress of being shocked. In fact, both the Brady and the Weiss studies illustrate the possible effects of stress on the development of ulcers (Figure 10.9).

Later studies have shown that the tendency to develop ulcers in stressful situations is also a function of certain biological predispositions. Some individuals produce more pepsinogen (a substance which, together with hydrochloric acid, is involved in digestion) than others. It has been found that individuals exposed to stressors who are high pepsinogen producers are more likely to develop ulcers than individuals exposed to the same stressors who are low pepsinogen producers. In short, although stress is an important contributing factor, biological predispositions are probably of considerable importance as well.

Identifying Stress We are constantly exposed to stress. Change implies stress; decisions are stressful; all of life, no matter how simple, is stressful. But part of learning and adapting involves learning how to deal with stress. In fact, our life experiences prepare us to cope with an amazing amount of change, and most of us suffer no ill effects from the continual stresses to which we are exposed. Consider, however, that our day-to-day lives are filled with the expected, or with the pleasant unexpected. With

Peptic ulcers Painful lesions in the wall of the stomach resulting from the stomach lining being "eaten away" by excess hydrochloric acid.

Figure 10.9 "Executive" ulcers? In a famous study by Brady (1958), pairs of monkeys were administered electric shocks; one monkey could press a lever to turn off the electricity for both of them. The "executive" monkey developed ulcers; the passive monkey did not. Weiss set up a similar study for rats, but obtained the opposite results (1968, 1971). The rat in the pair who could stop the administration of shocks to its tail by turning a wheel developed fewer ulcers than the passive rat. The tendency to develop ulcers seems to be more complex than a simple executive-nonexecutive situation can explain; biological predispositions are also involved.

these we can cope. It is when life is filled with the unexpected and the unpleasant that our capacities to adapt to stress are genuinely taxed. (See Figure 10.10.)

Holmes and Rahe (1967) attempted to identify the most stressful changes that might occur in a person's life. They listed forty-three events, termed *life-change events,* ranging from the death of a spouse to changes in eating habits, vacations, and so on (see Table 10.1). They then had 400 subjects, representing a wide variety of ages and backgrounds, rank each of the changes in terms of the adjustment it required, taking into account the significance of the change and its duration. Subsequent research with this scale (Rahe, 1972) found it was possible to predict with significant accuracy who would stay healthy and who would become ill during the following year. Those who were to stay healthy had reported an average of 150 life-change units (LCUs); those who developed illnesses reported up to 300 LCUs. Other studies have confirmed the general finding that those who experience many significant changes are more susceptible to physical illnesses as well as to mental disorders (Eron & Peterson, 1982).

A Theory of Stress Hans Selye (1956, 1974) has proposed one of the more widely accepted theories of stress. He claims that there is a general pattern of reaction to stress, termed the *general adaptation syndrome.* This adaptation syndrome involves three stages of responding (Figure 10.11). The initial response to stress is one of alarm and is manifested in the many physiological changes that occur with emotional reactions. If stress continues, the individual goes into a second stage—a stage of resistance. During this period, physiological manifestations of emotion decrease markedly and

Figure 10.10 When we are faced with a life-changing event, such as a funeral, our ability to handle stress is shaken.

the individual appears to be coping successfully with the stress. In other words, outward behavior appears normal. With prolonged stress, however, the body's resources are being depleted; and if stress continues, or if additional stress is confronted during this stage, the individual may reach a point of exhaustion. With respect to physiological stress (injury, disease, exposure), exhaustion may result in death. According to Selye, psychological stress rarely leads to exhaustion. Evidence suggests, however, that it may well lead to a variety of mental disorders, many of them with physiological manifestations.

Love and Happiness

The more positive emotions that have received the greatest amount of attention include love and happiness, both of which are extremely difficult to define and study. (See Figure 10.12.) Not surprisingly, the major early studies of love were undertaken with monkeys, with love being defined in terms of attachment and measured objectively in terms of amount of time spent with the "love-object." In the most famous of these studies, Harlow (1959) investigated some of the variables that might be related to the development of attachment between an infant monkey and its mother. Tradi-

Figure 10.11 Selye's stress model—the general adaptation syndrome. The model depicts the three stages of reaction to continued stress.

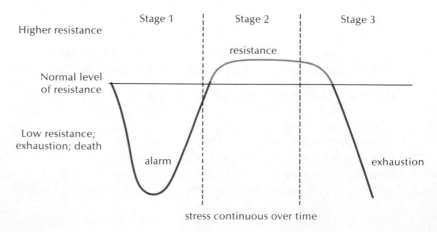

Table 10.1 Social Readjustment Rating Scale

Rank	Life Event	Mean Value (Life-change units)
1	Death of spouse	100
2	Divorce	73
3	Marital separation	65
4	Jail term	63
5	Death of close family member	63
6	Personal injury or illness	53
7	Marriage	50
8	Fired at work	47
9	Marital reconciliation	45
10	Retirement	45
11	Change in health of family member	44
12	Pregnancy	40
13	Sex difficulties	39
14	Gain of new family member	39
15	Business readjustment	39
16	Change in financial state	38
17	Death of close friend	37
18	Change to different line of work	36
19	Change in number of arguments with spouse	35
20	Mortgage over $10,000	31
21	Foreclosure of mortgage or loan	30
22	Change in responsibilities at work	29
23	Son or daughter leaving home	29
24	Trouble with in-laws	29
25	Outstanding personal achievement	28
26	Wife begins or stops work	26
27	Begin or end school	26
28	Change in living conditions	25
29	Revision of personal habits	24
30	Trouble with boss	23
31	Change in work hours or conditions	20
32	Change in residence	20
33	Change in schools	20
34	Change in recreation	19
35	Change in church activities	19
36	Change in social activities	18
37	Mortgage or loan less than $10,000	17
38	Change in sleeping habits	16
39	Change in number of family get-togethers	15
40	Change in eating habits	15
41	Vacation	13
42	Christmas	12
43	Minor violations of the law	11

Note: From "The Social Readjustment Rating Scale," by T. H. Holmes and R. H. Rahe, *Journal of Psychosomatic Research*, 1967, *11*, 213–218. Reprinted by permission of Pergamon Press, Ltd.

tional theories have long maintained that infant-mother attachment must result from the fact that the mother is the principal caretaker—that she is always there when the child is being reinforced. Most important, according to this point of view, is the mother's role as provider of nourishment.

In the Harlow studies, infant monkeys were separated from their mothers at birth, and reared with surrogate mothers. The surrogates were wire monkey-mother models with wooden blocks for heads and heating elements for warmth. In the most important variation of the studies, one mother was covered with soft terry cloth; the other was left bare. Infants were reared by both mothers—that is, both models were present in the cage. In one situation, a milk bottle was inserted in the wire model's breastwork at approximately the place that a breast might have been had this been a real mother; in other cages, the terry cloth mother was equipped with the bottle and the wire model was left milkless. There were four infant monkeys in each of these situations.

Figure 10.12 Love is not easily measured or defined among humans, a fact that makes it no less real. Is it more easily defined and measured among nonhumans? And does it exist in the same way among monkeys, for example, as among men and women?

The experimental situation provided for two measures of attachment. One was simply the amount of time spent by the infant on each of the models; the other was the infant's reaction when a fear-inducing stimulus was presented.

The results were clear, and devastating for traditional theory. No matter which of the models fed the infants, they became overwhelmingly attached to the soft, terry cloth mother (see Figure 10.13). In addition, they invariably ran to the cloth model and clung to it desperately when frightened. Even more convincing, if the two models were placed close to each other, infants would typically feed from the wire mother while holding on to the cloth mother.

In view of the fact that satisfaction of basic needs does not seem to be of great importance in the development of maternal attachment, what is? No one knows precisely. Harlow suggests that the "contact comfort" derived from the cloth model is *one* of the variables. How important is it, and what are the others? And do these findings apply to human infants as well? (See Box 10.2.)

If this were all, it would indeed be a miserly description of love. An emotion so precious, so pervasive, so powerful, surely deserves better. We speak again of love in Chapter 18.

Happiness. That too is precious, perhaps above all else, for that is what the gods promise, along with peace. Everlasting.

Yensen (1975) tells us that there are no physiological ways of measuring happiness or, indeed, any other objective means. Relevant research has focused on attempting to identify factors associated with self-reports of happiness (Bradburn & Caplovitz, 1965). The reliability and validity of these reports is open to question. Although a number of "happiness" tests have been constructed, none can be said to be adequate. All are necessarily based on what the investigators consider to be the areas in life most likely to contribute to happiness. Most have used arbitrary weightings for different

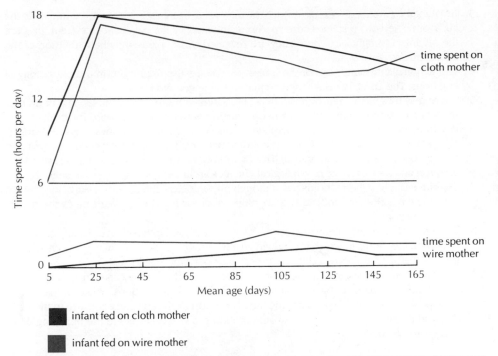

Figure 10.13 Amount of time spent by infant monkeys on cloth and wire surrogate mothers. The results show a strong preference for the cloth mother regardless of whether the infant was fed on the wire model (red line) or on the cloth model (black line). (From "Love in Infant Monkeys" by Harry F. Harlow. Copyright © 1959 by Scientific American, Inc. All rights reserved.)

areas, assuming that some were more important than others, but never knowing for certain which ones, and how much more important. And all have assumed that the same factors contribute to happiness in the same way for all individuals. Most of these assumptions are patently untenable. Here, more than anywhere else, what is sauce for the different stroke is a different folk gander, chacun à son goût, and so forth.* As George Bernard Shaw observed in *Major Barbara:* "A lifetime of happiness! No man alive could bear it: it would be hell on earth." Not to fear, George. Jane Austen assures us in *Emma* that it is most uncommon: "Perfect happiness, even in memory, is not common." In any case, perhaps we should not know too much about happiness or how to obtain it. We should not prepare for it, Austen tells us: "Why not seize the pleasure at once? How often is happiness destroyed by preparation, foolish preparation!"

Main Points

1 Emotion is the "feeling" component of human behavior. It varies in intensity as well as in terms of whether it is perceived to be pleasant or unpleasant, and is accompanied by certain physiological changes and behaviors.

2 Emotion may be expressed in behavior, in gestures (particularly facial), and verbally. Many emotional expressions are learned and culture/language-specific; a number appear to be universal (smiling and frowning, for example).

---

*All of which means, as my grandmother so aptly put it, "different streaks for different freaks."

3 Involuntary emotional reactions such as increased heart rate are under control of the autonomic nervous system. These reactions, initiated by the sympathetic system, prepare the organism to fight or to flee. They are reversed by the parasympathetic division of the autonomic nervous system.

4 The hypothalamus and parts of the limbic system are also implicated in the physiology of emotions. The amygdala is strongly implicated in anger and rage.

5 There may be specific neurotransmitters associated with specific emotions. The brain may manufacture endorphins and other neurotransmitters as a sort of reward for itself.

6 Physiological theories attempt to explain emotion by relating it to physiological changes. The James-Lange theory holds that the individual feels the physiological change first and then associates an emotion with it. The Cannon-Bard theory proposes that awareness of emotion and awareness of physiological changes are independent but simultaneous.

7 Cognitive labeling theory holds that although physiological changes are clearly involved in emotional reaction, the individual's cognitive label for the change determines the nature of the emotion.

8 The attribution theory of emotion states that the nature and intensity of an emotion depend largely on the causes to which the individual attributes physiological changes. Such a theory implies that we have a great deal of control over our emotional lives.

9 The opponent process explanation for emotion is based on homeostasis, the tendency of an organism to maintain balance. It says that all emotional reactions are accompanied by an opposite reaction, aroused after the initial emotion. With repeated exposure to the same emotion-related situation, the dominant emotion grows weaker while the opposing emotion grows stronger.

Security Blankets

Infant monkeys reared without real monkey mothers apparently develop strong attachments to inanimate objects and show a marked preference for those that are soft—that provide "contact comfort." Experiments of the kind conducted by Harlow with infant monkeys cannot easily be duplicated with little humans. There are, however, some naturally occurring situations that are somewhat related. My eighteen-month-old son is a case in point. He has an eighteen-month-old green and white blanket which he appears to love at least as dearly as his father, although perhaps somewhat less than his mother. It accompanies him everywhere. And in this respect he is like no less than half of all middle-class North American children (Weisberg & Russell, 1971).

In an intriguing series of studies, Passman and his associates (Passman, 1974; Passman & Weisberg, 1975) have investigated the role of the blanket (and sometimes the teddy bear and other similar objects) in the life of the child. Among other things, they have found that children who are attached to an inanimate object display no more anxiety in strange situations (provided their "attachment" object is present) than do children who show no similar attachments but whose mothers are present. In fact, they play and explore *more* than similar children who have neither blanket, nor toy, nor mother present. "Security" blankets are as effective as mothers in most learning situations, unless the situations are highly stressful. With increased stress, mothers are more effective in reducing anxiety.

Since it is sometimes awkward to bring a mother along on a date, it is reassuring to discover that a blanket or what-have-you might well be just as effective.

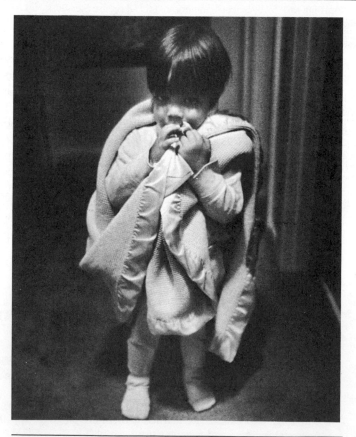

It is not only adults who need the comfort and reassurance of security blankets.

10 Emotions can be manipulated cognitively, through drugs, and through brain surgery or the use of electrodes or chemotrodes in the brain.

11 Stress is a global term for the body's reaction to change. Stressful changes are those that require the greatest physiological and psychological adaptation. High stress is associated with cardiovascular problems, peptic ulcers, and a variety of other physical and mental complaints.

12 Holmes and Rahe identify a number of *life-change* events that are importantly related to stress. Individuals who experience a great number of such events in a short period of time are at greater physical and psychological risk, although there are marked differences in our abilities to tolerate stress.

13 Selye hypothesizes that there is a general pattern of reaction to stress, consisting of three stages: alarm, resistance, and exhaustion. He calls this pattern of reaction the general adaptation syndrome.

14 Studies of attachment in infant monkeys suggest that the satisfaction of hunger and thirst drives may not be nearly as important as simple contact in the formation of early mother-infant bonds.

15 Happiness does not lie still for the scientist.

Further Readings

The following book presents a comprehensive look at research dealing with emotions as well as a detailed discussion of specific emotions including joy, surprise, distress, anger, disgust, fear, shame, shyness, and guilt:

Izard, C. E. *Human emotions.* New York: Plenum Press, 1977.

An absolutely fascinating, profusely illustrated book that looks at the expression of emotions among humans as well as at the variety of other nonverbal signals by which we communicate is the following:

Morris, D. *Manwatching: A field guide to human behavior.* London: Jonathan Cape, 1977.

The following presents a collection of current research on stress and related topics:

Selye, H. (Ed.). *Selye's guide to stress research,* Vol. 1. New York: D. Van Nostrand, 1980.

Studies of happiness, its measurement, and its distribution by income, social class, sex, age, and so on, are presented in:

Bradburn, N. M., and Caplovitz, D. *Reports on happiness: A pilot study of behavior related to mental health.* Chicago: Aldine, 1965.

Research and discussion relating to love and its various manifestations are presented in the following text (see also Chapter 18 of this text):

Walster, E., and Walster, G. W. *A new look at love.* Reading, Mass.: Addison-Wesley, 1978.

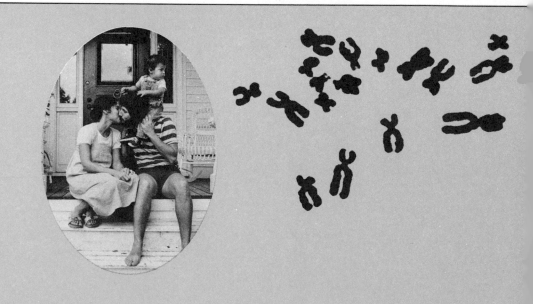

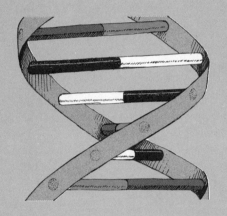

In this section we turn to a description of the course of human development. In textbooks of this nature, there is a danger that the reader will lose sight of the principal subject under examination. It is important to keep in mind that division of our subject into six parts and eighteen chapters, although conceptually useful and logically necessary, does not reflect the actual state of affairs. We are much more than brains, perceptual systems, genetic predispositions, and developmental tendencies. We are persons: complex, perplexing, and not easily reduced to a four-handed fistful of chapters.

PART FOUR

The Life Span

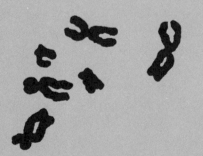

Chapter 11
From Conception through Childhood
Chapter 12
Adolescence, Aging, and Dying

From Conception through Childhood

In an unexplained and unusual moment of weakness, I agreed to go shopping, leaving this communication behind and unattended. How much wiser it might have been to have left our youngest son behind. A shopping trip at the best of times is only slightly more attractive than a forced march without rations through any of this world's great deserts. And this was not the best of times.

The trip began uneventfully enough. That we ran out of gasoline only a short distance from the shopping center was not really a stroke of bad fortune. Nor was it deliberate, as my wife immediately suspected. And I did agree to meet her in front of Frebelle's Funtastic Fashions as soon as I had taken care of my immediate automotive difficulties. My slight discomfiture, standing in front of my incapacitated vehicle, waving like a silly new father at my eighteen-month-old son as he and his mother marched resolutely toward that suburban mecca, the shopping center, was only a small taste of things to come.

Courageous to the end, I eventually found my way to Frebelle's Funtastic Fashions, silently hoping that Frebelle's stock still remained largely intact. A mannequin in the window lay on her side, like a dummy, my pride and joy perched delicately on her plastic bosom, his small finger in her plastic eye, pale pink lingerie, a Frebelle Funtastic Original, crumpled inelegantly around her plastic thighs. And behind, his mother looking at me and explaining to Frebelle herself that here was the boy's father, a psychologist.

"But he doesn't know yet that his father's a psychologist," she explained, rescuing our unlikely progeny, smiling disarmingly all the while.

"I am a psychologist," I explained to the boy as we hurried toward the supermarket. "A psychologist's son does not sit on a plastic dummy."

"Dummy!" he exclaimed loudly, and I quickly flashed what I assumed to be a conspiratorial smile at all who seemed to be looking and who might have heard.

321

We wasted little time in the supermarket—just the basic necessities for a poor man with a large family. Two carts, well loaded, and a generous armful of toilet tissue.

"Hold daddy's pants because daddy can't carry you right now and you can't ride in the cart because it's full," I advised the young one. Reassuringly obedient, he wrapped his small fist around my pant leg.

An individual on whom the gods smile more generously would have been sufficiently disgraced and humiliated for a single short afternoon. Not I. As we walked past the eggs, my charming little responsibility said loudly, proud of his budding linguistic skills, "Egg!", released my pants, and quickly procured a dozen of these objects.

I must confess that if I had not dropped my load of toilet paper on him, he might not have dropped the eggs. Under the circumstances, I considered it fair that I should pay for these unripe chickens, and made no objection when the supermarket manager suggested I do just that. But I did consider it unfair of my wife to explain to him, "He doesn't yet know that his father's a psychologist." And I must confess that I was pleased when he didn't believe her.

"That's an old story," he said, pausing to coin a phrase, "a story as old as the hills."

History of Attitudes toward Children

The study of children is neither as old as the hills, nor as old as the art (or science) of producing them. Development historians argue that for many centuries children were not considered particularly worthwhile as subjects of study; that, instead, they were treated as nothing more than miniature adults. Not only were they considered miniature adults physically, but also emotionally and psychologically. Thus, they could reason, but less completely; they felt the same emotions, but less keenly; they had the same abilities, but less well developed.

The sciences of a more child-centered age have devoted considerable research and speculation to identifying possible differences between children and adults, and to discovering the forces that shape children into adults. The search has been for qualitative rather than quantitative differences. A quantitative difference would be manifest, for example, in the child's increments in physical size. If the child were nothing more than a miniature adult, all differences between adults and children would be quantitative. Qualitative differences would be evident in those characteristics (qualities) of children that are different from the characteristics of adults.

The history of child rearing is replete with instances of abuse, neglect, and exploitation of children. DeMause (1975) traces six evolutionary trends in their treatment. Antiquity is reported to have dealt with millions of children through infanticide. The Middle Ages saw a dramatic reduction in infanticide. Instead of being killed, unwanted children were simply abandoned. And there were, in those years, millions of unwanted children, for children were an economic burden, likely to die of starvation, injury, or infection in any case. Parents could ill afford to become attached to a child who was likely to die. The Renaissance is reputed to have been characterized by an ambivalent attitude toward children. The humanistic movements of more enlightened regions of that age would hardly have been compatible with the brutal and inhuman practices of an earlier age. But economic and social conditions were still a far cry from today's. The eighteenth century resolved the preceding century's ambivalence largely through its industrial revolutions. No longer would children be an economic burden; they had now become an economic necessity (Figure 11.1). Young children, sometimes no older than five or six, could be made to work long hours deep in the bowels of some badly ventilated, cramped coal mine, crawling knee-deep in rank water, suffocating in oxygen-poor darkness, scratching black riches from the guts of the earth with their bare hands (Kessen, 1965). That many became ill and died is hardly surprising.

Figure 11.1 Dramatic changes have taken place in the way Western society views children. Only in the past few decades, however, has early development become a focus of serious study.

The nineteenth century saw many improvements in the plight of children. Child-labor laws plucked them from the cellars and factories, fields and fisheries, shops and mines. And it dumped great numbers of them into schools. Education suddenly became a massive enterprise; it is even more massive today.

Finally, the twentieth century stumbled in, a century as child-centered as any has ever been, particularly in the affluent countries. Children's rights have become a battle cry of the socially conscious. We are, according to DeMause (1975), at the threshold of a deep-seated helping attitude toward children.

The Average Child

It is, in one sense, misleading to begin a chapter on human development with a description of the average child. The average child, like the average person, does not exist. Psychologists and others have invented the average child to make it simpler to talk about children. We would be lost without this average child. I could not tell you that children learn to talk at the age of one, but would, instead, have to tell you that some children begin to speak at the age of three months and that others have still not learned by the time they are ninety-four years of age. Some cautions are in order, however. Not only does this child not exist except as an abstraction, but the average child may not even be *normal* in the ordinary sense of that word. Thus, if our hypothetical average child learns to walk by the age of twelve months, another child who does not learn before fifteen months cannot be said to be exactly average; and children who have learned by the age of nine months cannot be said to be average either. Is either of them abnormal? (See Figure 11.2.)

The notion of the average child is misleading in yet another way. Treating children as average or nonaverage tends to rob them of their individuality; it renders static a dynamic process; it separates into various age, stage, or topic layers what is, in effect, a single, dynamic, conscious individual. But, as noted elsewhere (Lefrancois, 1983), children do not fit neatly between the covers of a book.

Figure 11.2 Although there is an average age for various early accomplishments (such as learning to walk), children vary a great deal in their personal ages of accomplishment. The nonaverage child is not, by virtue of that fact alone, abnormal.

In order to make sense of human development, it is necessary to dissect, to analyze, to treat various parts of the child as though they were separate and separable when they really are not. There is a danger of losing the child in the process. Beware.

Forces That Shape Development

It is customary among those who give any thought to the problem to consider the forces that determine the course of human development as falling neatly within one of two camps. There are, on the one hand, those forces that are hereditary, the genetic blueprint. On the other hand, there are those forces that exert their influences externally, the environmental forces. Had we three hands, we might have found a third set of forces to explain all the things we don't understand. Having neither three hands nor a third grouping of shapers of development, we have no choice but to ignore what we cannot yet explain, or simply to admit that there are a few things psychologists do not yet understand completely.

Genetic Forces

Why does an acorn become an oak tree (if it does become a tree, and if it is an acorn from an oak tree)? Why does a yellow-bellied sapsucker egg become a yellow-bellied sapsucker? And why does the sperm of an ass together with an ass egg become a long-eared ass even though neither the sperm nor the egg has long ears? Why indeed? **Genetics** is the name given to the science that answers these questions (see Figure 11.3). We look briefly at that science here.

The following discussion of genetics is based on what is termed *Mendelian genetics*, named after Gregor Mendel, who in 1866 published his first studies of the inherited characteristics of garden peas. He interbred parents with identifiably different traits and examined the resulting *hybrids* (offspring resulting from interbreeding of different strains) for the presence or absence of these traits. In this way, Mendel was able to make inferences about relative dominance and recessiveness of genes, but not about structure of the genes themselves. *Molecular genetics,* a recent and highly

Genetics The scientific study of heredity and variation of organisms. Genetics is important to psychology to the extent that heredity predisposes individuals to behave in certain ways.

Figure 11.3 Genetics helps to explain many things about why individuals are the way they are.

promising approach to the study of inheritance, attempts to understand genetic transmission through an examination of the structure of genes. It is based largely on J. D. Watson and Crick's (1953) discovery of the molecular structure of deoxyribonucleic acid (DNA). A segment of DNA corresponds to a Mendelian gene. The chemistry is complex, and though molecular genetics may clarify heredity considerably, it is not likely to simplify it. Thus, for the sake of simplicity we stick to Mendel here.

Sperm and Egg   Every mature human female releases a single, mature egg approximately once every twenty-eight days, usually somewhere around the eleventh or twelfth day of her menstrual cycle. Some women produce more than one egg at a time, thus giving rise to the possibility of multiple births. At other times, a single egg can separate after fertilization, also leading to a multiple birth. A mature human male normally produces several billion sperm cells every month.

The egg and sperm cell are the immediate origins of life. After activities beyond the scope of this textbook, there occurs a union of sperm and egg in a **Fallopian tube**, division of the resulting zygote, its movement down the Fallopian tube into the uterus, or womb, and its attachment to the uterine wall. All of this takes place within seven days. During the next short while, the placenta and umbilical cord form, the **placenta** being a flat membrane that links mother and embryo. The **umbilical cord** is a tubular affair perhaps eighteen inches in length, containing two veins and an artery, linked to the placenta at one end and to what will eventually be the child's navel at the other. There are no nerves in the umbilical cord, and the child's developing nervous system is never linked with the mother's.

A number of other changes that are not of immediate concern then occur. Some 266 days after conception, barring accident or design to the contrary, a child will be born. Why will it be this child, and not another?

Chromosomes and Genes   The answer lies in large part in the **chromosomes** contained in the sperm and egg cells, and more specifically, in the particular complement and arrangement of **genes** within these chromosomes. Every cell in the human body contains twenty-three pairs of chromosomes, one member of each of these pairs having been inherited from the mother, and the other member from the father. These

Fallopian tubes   Tubes that link the ovaries and the uterus; where fertilization (conception) ordinarily occurs.

Placenta   A flat, thick membrane attached to the inside of the uterus during pregnancy and to the developing fetus by means of the umbilical cord.

Umbilical cord   A long, thick cord attached to what will be the child's naval at one end and to the placenta at the other. It transmits nourishment and oxygen to the growing fetus from the mother.

Chromosomes   Microscopic bodies in the nucleus of all animal and plant cells containing the genes—the carriers of heredity. Each mature human sex cell (sperm or ovum) contains twenty-three chromosomes.

Genes   The carriers of heredity. Each of the twenty-three chromosomes contributed by the sperm cell and the ovum at conception is believed to contain between 40,000 and 60,000 genes.

Figure 11.4 A photograph of the twenty-three pairs of chromosomes in a human cell. The actual hereditary information (the genes) carried in the chromosomes is contained in DNA molecules.

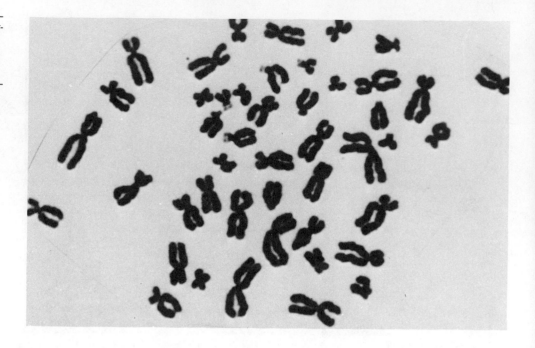

chromosomes are the carriers of hereditary information (Figure 11.4). They are what determine whether a child will have dark or light hair, blue or brown eyes, whether it will be male or female, and so on. These are among the obvious influences of heredity. Even more obvious, so obvious that it usually escapes our attention completely, these chromosomes carry information relating to the fact that we have two legs, two eyes, one head, and all the other physical trappings that have become characteristic of *Homo sapiens*. In one sense, the similarities among humans are vastly more important than the differences, although we often pay considerably more attention to differences than to similarities.

The actual units of heredity are the genes, there being perhaps 1,000 genes on each chromosome, perhaps 40,000, perhaps 150,000. Science cannot yet agree. Their number may be less important at this stage of genetic knowledge than their functioning. That story can be told in a relatively straightforward manner.

As we've said, chromosomes are ordinarily arranged in pairs, termed *homologous pairs*. Genes can be viewed as segments of chromosomes, arranged in rows (somewhat like beads on a string). They are also arranged in pairs in terms of their relative position on the chromosomes. Corresponding genes on corresponding (homologous) chromosomes are termed *alleles*.

Mitosis The division of a single cell into two identical cells. Mitosis occurs in body cells rather than in sex cells.

Meiosis The division of a single cell into two separate cells, each consisting of 23 chromosomes rather than 23 pairs of chromosomes.

Cells reproduce by two means: **mitosis** and **meiosis**. Mitosis involves the splitting of a cell, together with its twenty-three pairs of chromosomes, into two identical cells, each bearing twenty-three identical pairs of chromosomes. Body cells reproduce in this fashion, accounting for the fact that every cell in your body is identical in terms of genetic structure. Meiosis, however, involves the splitting of a cell into cells that are not identical (see Figure 11.5). Sex cells reproduce in this fashion, giving rise to cells that do not contain twenty-three *pairs* of chromosomes, but contain twenty-three *single* chromosomes. Thus, a mature ovum and a mature sperm cell each contain twenty-three single chromosomes. After the union of sperm and egg, however, the zygote will again contain its full complement of twenty-three pairs of chromosomes, half from the father, and half from the mother.

It is thus true that half of our heredity comes from our father and half from our mother. It is also true that half of our father's heredity came from his father, and half

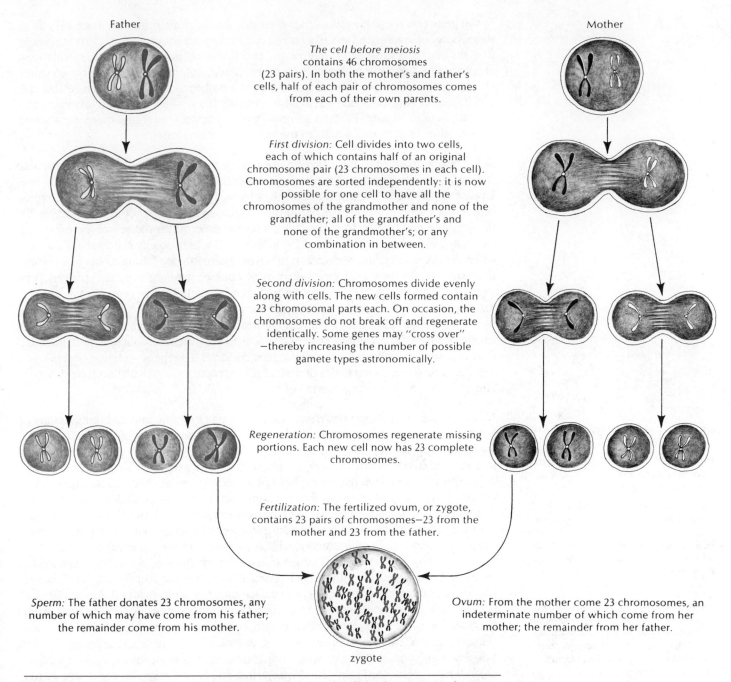

Father

Mother

The cell before meiosis contains 46 chromosomes (23 pairs). In both the mother's and father's cells, half of each pair of chromosomes comes from each of their own parents.

First division: Cell divides into two cells, each of which contains half of an original chromosome pair (23 chromosomes in each cell). Chromosomes are sorted independently: it is now possible for one cell to have all the chromosomes of the grandmother and none of the grandfather; all of the grandfather's and none of the grandmother's; or any combination in between.

Second division: Chromosomes divide evenly along with cells. The new cells formed contain 23 chromosomal parts each. On occasion, the chromosomes do not break off and regenerate identically. Some genes may "cross over" —thereby increasing the number of possible gamete types astronomically.

Regeneration: Chromosomes regenerate missing portions. Each new cell now has 23 complete chromosomes.

Fertilization: The fertilized ovum, or zygote, contains 23 pairs of chromosomes—23 from the mother and 23 from the father.

Sperm: The father donates 23 chromosomes, any number of which may have come from his father; the remainder come from his mother.

Ovum: From the mother come 23 chromosomes, an indeterminate number of which come from her mother; the remainder from her father.

zygote

Figure 11.5 Meiosis is cell division in which the new cells have only half the chromosomes of parent cells. For simplicity, only one of the twenty-three pairs of chromosomes is depicted here. The new cell— the fertilized egg, or zygote—contains the full complement of twenty-three *pairs* of chromosomes.

from his mother. But it is *not* true that one-quarter of our heredity comes from each of our four grandparents via our parents. This is due to one of the most important features of meiotic cell division. When a sex cell is reducing from twenty-three pairs of chromosomes to twenty-three single chromosomes, the chromosomes are sorted independently. What this means is that any gamete (sperm or egg) might have twenty chromosomes from one grandparent and three from the other, all chromosomes from one grandparent, or any combination from either. In addition, the structure and order of the genes on these chromosomes does not always remain intact. Figure 11.5 illustrates how separate members of a pair of chromosomes (homologous chromosomes) may on occasion cross over, intertwine, and break off, forming two essentially new chromosomes, each of which will be in a separate cell along with twenty-two other chromosomes. The number of possible new combinations is so immense that the production of two identical individuals is virtually impossible. Each of us is genetically unique, save those who have an identical twin. That's no big thing: there are some 4 billion other unique individuals in the human species alone!

Sex Chromosomes   One pair of these twenty-three chromosomes is of particular interest, since it determines the sex of the offspring. The female produces only one type of *sex chromosome,* appropriately labeled X. Males, however, produce two types, one X, the other, Y. An XX pairing in the fertilized egg will result in a female; an XY pairing, in a male. Therefore, the father's sperm determines the sex of the offspring. As I noted elsewhere (Lefrancois, 1983) Henry VIII was probably not aware of this fact when he disposed of his succession of wives ostensibly for failing to bear him sons. If science could have told him just that, of course, it might not have proven very helpful. What it could also have told him, had it been slightly more mature, is that the male sperm cell is somewhat more agile than the female egg, but also somewhat less hardy. A current, although not entirely validated, theory speculates that when ovulation can be predicted relatively accurately, it is possible to time intercourse so as to increase the probability of conceiving male or female children. The theory is based on evidence that the chemical characteristics of discharges that accompany ovulation have different effects on X- and Y-bearing sperm cells.

Dominance and Recessiveness   Genes, in pairs or in complex combinations of pairs, are directly responsible for the hereditary characteristics of offspring. There are, for example, pairs of genes corresponding to eye color, pairs of genes corresponding to a specific characteristic of hair (straight or curly, for example), and groups of genes corresponding to virtually every other identifiable physical characteristic of an individual. There are genes corresponding to intellectual and psychological characteristics as well, but—as will become clear—it has been extremely difficult to assess the precise nature and extent of their influence. Our inherited chromosomal makeup is our **genotype**; the observable characteristics that it produces is our **phenotype**.

The simplest explanation of gene functioning involves dominance and recessiveness. From research with animals, particularly with the fruitfly, and from observations of human reproduction, scientists have determined that certain members of pairs of genes are dominant over their corresponding member. It is known, for example, that the gene for normal colored skin is dominant over the gene for albinism (lack of pigment). What this means is that if an individual inherits a gene for pigmented skin from one parent and a gene for unpigmented skin from the other, that individual will have pigmented skin. It also means that all albinos have two **recessive genes** for skin pigmentation. Individuals with pigmented skin, however, might have two **dominant genes** (both for pigmented skin) or one dominant gene (for pigmented skin) and one recessive gene (for unpigmented skin). Figure 11.6 presents another example.

If each human characteristic were determined as a function of the dominance or recessiveness of genes in a single pair (**major gene determination**), matters of genetics would be considerably simpler. They aren't. Many traits are a function of an indefinite number of gene pairs. They result from **polygenetic determination**. Also, genes are not dominant or recessive in any absolute sense, but only in relation to other genes. Thus, a gene that may be dominant over another may be recessive for a third. In addition, genes sometimes undergo *mutations,* changes due to environmental forces such as irradiation, mustard gas, cosmic rays, drugs such as thalidomide, or other unknown causes.

Genotype   Our inherited chromosomal, or genetic, makeup.

Phenotype   The observable characteristics in an individual that are assumed to be genetically determined.

Recessive gene   A gene whose characteristics are not manifest in the offspring unless it is paired with another recessive gene. When a recessive gene is paired with a dominant gene, the characteristics controlled by the dominant gene will be manifest.

Dominant gene   The gene that takes precedence over other related genes in genetically determined traits. Because genes occur in pairs (alleles) on corresponding chromosomes (one from the male and one from the female), the presence of a dominant gene as one member of the pair means that the hereditary characteristics it controls will be present in the individual.

Major gene determination   The determination of a characteristic as a result of the presence or absence of dominant and recessive genes in a single pair.

Polygenetic determination   Determination of a characteristic as a result of the interaction of more than a single pair of genes. Most human characteristics are determined polygenetically.

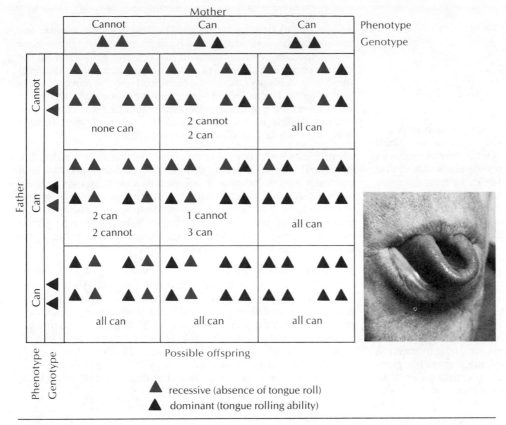

recessive (absence of tongue roll)

dominant (tongue rolling ability)

Figure 11.6 Can you roll your tongue as shown? An illustration of dominance and recessiveness, given various combinations of maternal and paternal traits. If you can roll your tongue, would you be prepared to wager that either your mother or your father can also?

Genetic Defects Genetic defects are either sex-linked or non-sex-linked. Hemophilia (bleeder's disease), baldness, night blindness, and color blindness are four common **sex-linked defects**. The genes that give rise to these defects are found on the X chromosome. Recall that a male possesses a single X chromosome and a Y chromosome; a female possesses two X chromosomes. Since the Y chromosome does not have genetic material corresponding to these defects, it cannot counteract them with a normal, dominant gene. Thus, if a male inherits a single recessive gene for baldness, for example, that male will eventually be bald (should he live so long). Since the Y chromosome can only have been inherited from the father (recall that only males produce Y chromosomes), baldness is inherited from the mother, just as hemophilia, night blindness, and color blindness may be. Why are there so few bald, hemophiliac, color-blind women? Because they possess two X chromosomes, and there is a very high probability that one of these will contain the dominant gene that will counteract any recessive genes relating to these defects.

Sex-linked defects provide clear illustration of how a genotype is not always reflected in the observed phenotype. Mothers who themselves appear to be free of defects (their phenotypes are defect-free) are carriers for defects that are phenotypical (manifested) in their sons but seldom in their daughters. The probabilities are high, however, that sons born to their daughters will also manifest the same defects.

Non-sex-linked defects are discussed in Box 11.1.

Chromosomal Aberrations In addition to the various defects and diseases that are genetically transmitted, a number of abnormalities are linked to defects in chromosomes rather than to the effects of specific genes. Some of these are characterized

Sex-linked defects Defects due to the action of genes located on the sex chromosome. Such defects are typically due to the action of recessive genes on the X chromosome and are much more likely to be manifested in males than in females.

Non-Sex-Linked Defects

Genetic abnormalities that are *not* related to genes on the sex chromosomes are said to be non-sex-linked. These abnormalities are seldom related to dominant genes; and if they are, they do not result in early death, impotence, or very severe illness. Otherwise they would soon be completely eradicated from the human genetic pool. This, of course, is not the case for abnormalities that are linked to recessive genes, since these genes will be carried by many individuals who do not manifest the abnormality. Some of the more common genetic abnormalities are the following:

Sickle-cell anemia This genetically based disease is linked to a recessive gene and is characterized by red blood cells that are abnormal in composition and in shape (sickle-shaped, in fact). These cells carry less oxygen than normal cells. Thus, individuals suffering from this disease become ill at high altitudes; indeed, they are frequently ill throughout much of their lives. Many die in childhood. One of the initially puzzling features of this disease is that it is highly prevalent among blacks living in coastal Africa (40 percent of the population carry the recessive gene); in contrast, it is gradually being eliminated among the U.S. black population (less than 9 percent; Thompson, 1975) with a similar genetic ancestry. The reason for this striking discrepancy became apparent when it was discovered that individuals who possess only one recessive gene with respect to sickle-cell anemia are resistant to malaria. In the malaria-prone coastal areas of Africa, natural selection would favor these individuals over those who possessed only the corresponding normal gene. In the United States, however, where malaria is virtually nonexistent, normal individuals would be favored. The consequent decline in the incidence of the sickle-cell anemia gene presents a dramatic example of current evolution.

Huntington's chorea A severe disorder that does not manifest itself until later in life (between the ages of thirty and fifty) is of particular interest because it is linked to a dominant gene. *Huntington's chorea* is characterized by progressive mental deterioration, involuntary movements, and death. In spite of the fact that it is dominant and fatal, the gene continues to be transmitted. This is because its effects appear late enough in life that parents can reproduce before they die of the disease.

Phenylketonuria (PKU) *Phenylketonuria*, or *PKU*, is characterized by progressive mental retardation that begins shortly after birth and becomes severe and irreversible by the age of four to six months (Thompson, 1975). Fortunately, it is an easily detectable defect caused by the presence of two recessive genes that are somehow related to the body's inability to oxidize the amino acid phenylalanine. Routine tests ordinarily given within two days of birth typically lead to the early identification of PKU. Simple dietary treatment (a diet low in phenylalanine) has proven highly effective in preventing symptoms of the disease.

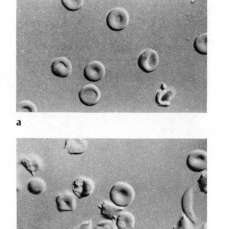

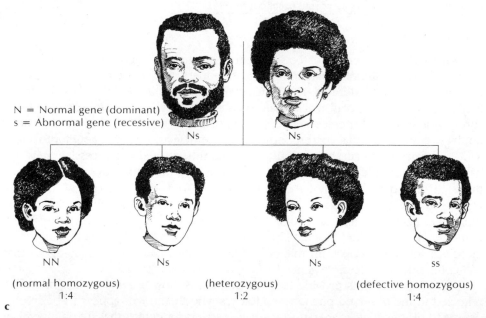

N = Normal gene (dominant)
s = Abnormal gene (recessive)

Ns   Ns

NN   Ns   Ns   ss
(normal homozygous)   (heterozygous)   (defective homozygous)
1:4   1:2   1:4

Sickle-cell anemia. The photographs show normal oxygenated red blood cells (**a**) and sickle cells (**b**). Sickle cells are a recessive trait: an individual who is genetically homozygous for sickle cells (who has two recessive genes) will inherit sickle-cell anemia, but a heterozygous individual (who has one recessive and one dominant gene) will not. The diagram shows that, although heterozygous parents will not have sickle-cell anemia themselves, their child will have one chance in four of inheriting it. (**c**).

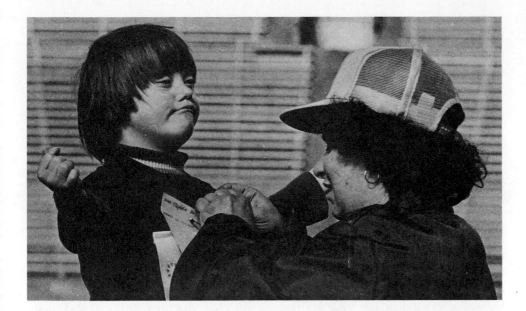

Figure 11.7 The most obvious characteristics of Down's syndrome, some of which can be seen in this child, are not always present at birth. The syndrome (also called trisomy 21 or, infrequently now, mongolism) can be detected by means of a chromosomal examination.

by abnormal chromosomes; others by the presence of extra chromosomes or by the absence of one or more.

A relatively common chromosomal aberration results from the presence of an extra chromosome attached to the twenty-first pair of chromosomes (geneticists have labeled chromosomes by numbering them). Its medical name is accordingly *trisomy 21;* more popularly, *Down's syndrome* has been called *mongolism.* Children suffering from this defect tend to be short and stocky, and have small, squarish heads, defective hearts, and characteristic folds of skin over the corners of the eyes (see Figure 11.7). Mental retardation is also fairly common among these children. Some 10 percent of all people in institutions for the mentally retarded in the United States suffer from Down's syndrome (Thompson, 1975). Not all children afflicted by Down's syndrome will manifest all these characteristics. The presence of the condition is frequently difficult to ascertain by looking at the child immediately after birth. A chromosomal examination, however, provides a sure test.

The cause of trisomy 21 remain obscure, although it is clear that they are linked to the age of the mother. The probability of bearing a child with Down's syndrome is less than 1 in 1,500 for mothers between fifteen and twenty-four years of age; it is a frightening 1 in 38 for mothers over forty-five (Hamerton et al., 1961).

A small number of female children (1 out of 5,000; Thompson, 1975) suffer from *Turner's syndrome,* lacking one member of the pair of X sex chromosomes characteristic of normal females. These are designated as 45, X (having 45 chromosomes, the missing one being an X sex chromosome), or as XO (indicating the absence of a second X chromosome). Many of these are aborted spontaneously. Those who do survive may be atypically short, sometimes physically unattractive, devoid of secondary sexual characteristics, and infertile (Money, 1975). Initial manifestations of the disorder sometimes include swelling of the extremities which eventually disappears, leaving loose folds of skin, particularly in the neck region and on the fingers. Injections of the sex hormone estrogen prior to puberty are often helpful in bringing about a greater degree of sexual maturation among these girls (Timiras, 1972).

Another chromosomal aberration linked to the sex chromosomes involves the presence of an extra X chromosome in a male child; hence the designation 47, XXY, since there are 47 chromosomes, the extra one being an X. *Klinefelter's syndrome* is found in 1 out of every 400 males (Thompson, 1975). Affected males frequently have both male and female secondary sexual characteristics, often with underdeveloped testicles and overdeveloped breasts. Their voices tend to be higher-pitched as well, and facial hair is minimal or absent. Treatment with the male sex hormone testosterone can enhance the development of male sexual characteristics and increase sex drive (H. R. Johnson et al., 1970). It is interesting that the reason for the sex test given female athletes at Olympic meets relates to the finding that some highly successful "female" athletes in relatively recent Olympics were in fact males with Klinefelter's syndrome.

Males with an extra Y chromosome are characteristically tall and muscular. There is some evidence, as well, of lower intelligence. Interestingly, the *supermale syndrome* was first discovered among prisoners where the incidence ranges between 2 and 12 percent; only 0.1 percent of the general population have the syndrome (Telfer et al., 1968; Jarvik et al., 1973). This observation led quickly to the somewhat premature conclusion that criminality and the XYY syndrome are closely associated. Falek (1975) indicates that the public immediately accepted as fact the supposition that extreme aggressiveness and the XYY syndrome go hand-in-hand. Immediate speculation was that the extra Y chromosome, being the male chromosome, simply increased the XYY male's aggressiveness. However, subsequent investigations revealed that the crimes for which XYY individuals were imprisoned were not typically violent crimes (Witkin et al., 1976). It may well be that the greater than chance number of XYY males among prison populations is due not to their greater aggressiveness but simply to their lower intelligence (Kalat, 1981).

Heredity Isn't Everything   In summary, the particular chromosomes that you have inherited, together with their arrangement of genes, are responsible for a great many of the qualities and characteristics you now manifest. This is most obvious with respect to your physical appearance, less so with respect to your psychological characteristics. There is some evidence that predispositions toward certain personality traits, abnormal or otherwise, may be inherited. There is also considerable evidence that these same personality traits are affected by environmental forces. The complex interaction between heredity and environment is not at all well understood with respect to psychological characteristics. It is important to keep in mind, nevertheless, that the influence of heredity, either directly or in the form of certain predispositions and tendencies, cannot be discounted when considering any aspect of human behavior. It is also important to keep in mind that, although heredity may make certain outcomes more probable than others, environmental forces play their own games of probability. No matter what your genetic endowment, your chances of becoming whatever you are now (or are in the process of becoming) would have been considerably reduced had you been born and brought up among the Mundugumor on the banks of the Sepik River.

Environmental Forces

Environmental forces that shape development are so general and all-inclusive that they cannot easily be listed, let alone described, in an ordinary book-length manuscript. I shall describe only a few of the more obvious ones—and briefly at that—in a series of small sections in an ordinary, chapter-length chapter.

Nutrition   A sound mind in a sound body. An apple a day keeps what's his name away. Thus spake my grandmother, displaying wisdom far beyond her own comprehension. Science has not yet told us whether we should take the apple seriously, although at least some religions assure us that we should. But science has begun to tell us that the sound body and the sound mind may be more closely related than we had reason to suspect in our duller years. Adelle Davis, in a number of best-selling books (for example, *Let's Have Healthy Children,* 1972), did much to popularize science's recent claims that psychological as well as physical health are highly dependent upon nutrition. She also did much to make us more aware of the fact that, although we have great respect for science and its research, we are slow to put its findings into effect if doing so requires any major change. Although we now know more than we ever did about producing healthy bodies, they are not as healthy as they could be. Perhaps the same is true of our minds. That more of us reach old age than used to in our forebears' day is perhaps due less to our individual attention to things that might prolong life than to the medical sciences.

Intelligence, too, is suspected to be affected directly by nutrition. Lewin's (1975) findings suggest that the brain undergoes a developmental spurt toward the final stages of fetal development. Malnutrition during this period (particularly protein deficiency) appears to have measurable effects on later intellectual functioning. He cites other research which suggests that malnutrition in the early years of life can harm intellectual development (Figure 11.8).

Family   Other environmental forces that are of great importance to the developing child include its entire social-cultural milieu. The most important component of this milieu ordinarily is the immediate family. The influence of the family on the child's development is, again, so general and so pervasive that it does not lend itself easily to description in these academic spaces. Much of the literature in this area deals with the vast number of studies that have attempted to find relationships between parental characteristics and characteristics later found in their children. Many of the results are inconclusive and contradictory. Parental and child characteristics are difficult to identify and to measure, and they interact in complex ways. There is no reason to believe that all parents affect all children in the same way. People being what they are, it is simply not possible to control for all relevant factors in this type of research (Figure 11.9).

One family variable about which science feels more secure concerns the effects of birth order on children. Galton (1869), who noticed that most of Britain's eminent people came from very few families, also noticed that there was a preponderance of first-born children among these leaders. Subsequent research has confirmed the accuracy of this observation. It appears that first-born children have an advantage in several areas of development. They speak more articulately than those born later; they appear to be more responsible and to be better planners; and they score higher on a variety of measures of intellectual achievement (Koch, 1955). Other research indicates that they are more achievement-oriented (Sampson, 1962); they perform better academically (Altus, 1965); they are more competitive (Koch, 1955); and they are more likely to attend college (Bayer, 1966). *Newsweek* (1969) reported that, of the seven original astronauts, two were only children (hence first-born), and the remaining five were the oldest in their families. Even more convincing, of the first twenty-three men to travel in space, twenty-one were either first-born or only children; one had an older brother who had died as an infant; and the other was a full thirteen years younger than his older brother.

The most reasonable explanation for the frequently replicated finding that first-born or only children have an advantage (on the average) in a large number of areas is based on the speculation that the type of interaction these children have with their parents differs from that of later-born children. The language models that surround them are most likely adult; they receive more attention, on the average, from these adults than do children who come later.

Television   Violence, we are told by today's finger waggers, has become a contemporary way of life; and it is a way of life that owes much to that great electronic medium, the household television set. Yesterday's finger waggers said much the same thing as they decried the breakdown of the family, the loss of the good old values, the rejection of worthwhile literature, and the undermining of religion. They didn't have television to blame, but they had comic books and fairy tales. "Violence in content, ugliness in form, and deception in presentation," said Wertham (1954) of comic books, claiming

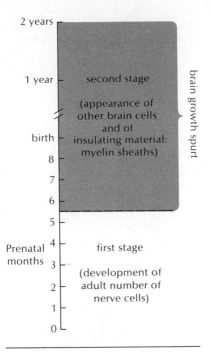

Figure 11.8 Nutrition is vital for the development of the brain, not just during early childhood, but before birth, too. Studies suggest that the brain undergoes a developmental spurt during the last months of pregnancy. Malnutrition during this period, particularly protein deficiency, can impair later intellectual functioning.

Figure 11.9 The influences of the family on children are highly variable and difficult to isolate and measure.

Aggressive An adjective descriptive of individuals who engage in, or have a strong urge to engage in, actions that are hostile, that cause fear, or that result in injury or damage to people or property. The term *aggression* is also commonly employed to signify less violent behaviors. For example, dominant, intrusive behaviors such as might be characteristic of successful business people are frequently described as being aggressive. Thus, aggressive behavior may be seen as a continuum ranging from mildly attack-oriented behavior to such crimes as physical assault and murder.

that they qualified neither as literature nor as art, were antieducational, and demonstrated that the greatest evil is certainly not crime but stupidity, for only the stupid get caught. Fairy tales were attacked less passionately, but were frequently placed out of the reach of small children. Recently Bruno Bettelheim (1976) has returned fairy tales to the child. In his moving book, *The Uses of Enchantment,* he speaks of the symbolism in fairy tales, and of the potential benefits of these symbols. "If our fear of being devoured takes the tangible form of a witch, it can be gotten rid of by burning her in the oven." The fairy tale, says Bettelheim, allows children to examine their monsters; it gives substance and form to their greatest anxieties, and allows them to be dealt with. And fairy tales all have happy endings. Ever after!

There is widespread fear in the hearts of grandmothers and others that television may now be having many of the effects that were once ascribed to the comic book and perhaps to fairy tales. Early studies demonstrated a relationship between children's **aggressive** behavior and the viewing of violent programs, whether cartoon animation or live actors (Bandura et al., 1963). The typical study had subjects view a film where one of the characters behaved violently and aggressively with an inflated plastic Bobo Clown. Subsequently, children were left alone with a Bobo Clown and their behaviors observed. Almost invariably, children who had been exposed to violent programs behaved in a highly imitative, violent manner.

It is probably unrealistic to generalize from studies such as these to real-life situations. Television violence is not often directed against inanimate objects, but rather against people. And when it is directed against objects, it is generally directed against real property rather than against objects similar to the Bobo Clown. Not only do children learn early in life that aggression upon people and upon people's property is likely to be punished, but they also learn that it is permissible to aggress upon certain inanimate objects usually presented in the form of toys. In some ways, it would appear both reasonable and intelligent for a child to assume that a Bobo Clown that was soundly beaten up by a film character was, in fact, designed for that purpose by its makers (Figure 11.10).

In 1969, the United States government allocated 1 million dollars for research on the impact of television. The results are contained in a five-volume report published in 1972 (for example, Murray et al., 1972). They can be summarized briefly.

First, the studies looked at the nature of television programming. To no one's surprise, they found that violence is the predominant television theme, and that it is six times more prevalent in children's programming than in adult programming. One study reports that over 98 percent of all children's cartoons contain violent episodes (Gerbner, 1972).

Second, the studies looked at who watched television. Most people do. N. Johnson (1969) had earlier reported that by the time an average American male reaches the age of sixty-five, he will have spent nine full years of his life watching television. Three age groups spend the greatest amount of time watching television: young children, young adults, and the elderly. Of these, young children spend the greatest amount of time so engaged.

Third, the studies focused on the influence of television. Here the results are much less conclusive. Some of the studies suggested that television does have real effects on the behavior of children. Stein and Friedrich (1972) exposed various groups to violent episodes, prosocial (as opposed to antisocial) programs, and neutral programs. After four weeks of viewing programs according to the groups in which they had been placed, children were observed to determine whether their behaviors had changed (they had been observed prior to the experiment). Results indicated that children who were initially more aggressive had become even more aggressive after exposure to violent programs. Perhaps more significant, those who had viewed prosocial programs demonstrated an increase in cooperative, sharing behavior. Other studies placed children in situations where they could ostensibly inflict harm on other children (Liebert & Baron, 1972) after exposure to violent programs. Here again, experimental-group subjects showed a greater willingness to be aggressive.

Critics of these studies point out that the situations in which behavior is observed are typically unnatural, and that very few studies have been designed to look at behavior in natural situations.

One study (Feshbach & Singer, 1971) that has employed less contrived observation was a long-term study which controlled television viewing patterns of boys nine to fifteen years old living in private homes for the underprivileged or in residential boarding schools. One group of boys was allowed to watch violent programs; the other watched situation comedies, variety shows, and other nonviolent programs. Among the striking findings was that boys who watched nonviolent programs engaged in more than twice as many fist fights as those who watched violent programs; they also engaged in more angry arguments. Of those who watched violent programs, those whose subsequent behavior showed the greatest decline in aggressiveness were boys whose previous aggression had been highest in terms of various behavioral measures.

The apparent contradiction between the Feshbach and Singer (1971) study and a variety of others that have shown increases in aggressive behavior following exposure to television violence may be due to the "real-life" aspects of the Feshbach and Singer research. In their study, subjects in both groups were allowed to talk to one another, and would have been aware that each group was being exposed to different television fare. It is possible that members of the "nonaggressive" television group felt frustrated and rebellious and that these feelings accounted for their greater displays of aggressiveness when they were observed later. Leyens et al. (1975) conducted a field study very similar to that of Feshbach and Singer, but in a situation where they could observe and monitor subjects carefully. In contrast to the earlier study, Leyens et al. report significantly more aggressive behavior among subjects exposed to violent movies nightly for one week.

In the rush to establish whether television violence is truly harmful, its potentially beneficial effects have been left in the shadows. Speculation is that language development may be helped by television, particularly among some of the lower socioeconomic groups. In addition, there is evidence that intergroup attitudes among children may be beneficially influenced through exposure to programs featuring minority-group participants (Gorn et al., 1976). It is possible, too, that television-reared children will manifest a wider range of interests and will display considerably more general information. It is also possible that they will be more passive and more easily bored. Having been exposed to all the marvelous sounds, sights, and colors that television can bring them, adolescence may find them jaded and drowning in boredom.

Sex Roles A sex role is a learned pattern for behavior based upon obvious sexual characteristics. Social development of children is intimately linked with the development of sex roles and the adoption of behaviors appropriate to these roles (*sex typing*). Sex roles in Western cultures have traditionally been very clear. They are reflected in dress, behavior, and occupations; they permeate children's toy markets; they are identifiable in our literature and in our television shows. These roles have said, in effect, that boys will be masculine and girls feminine. To be masculine is to be "tough," aggressive, and unemotional, to be interested in contact sports and in the outdoors. To be feminine is to be tender, compliant, and emotional, to be interested in art and literature. There has traditionally been little confusion between boys and girls. If their different interests and activities were not always obvious, their clothing and hair styles were.

Recent decades have seen a dramatic alteration of these sexual stereotypes. They are slowly being changed by the forces of feminism—a movement that might have been primarily female-inspired in its beginning, but that finds its support in male circles as well. Unfortunately, however, traditions change slowly. Boys and girls still have little difficulty identifying **masculine** and **feminine** traits. Not only do they agree as to what boys should be like and what girls should be like, but they also agree that the masculine characteristics are more desirable (Spence & Helmreich, 1978). Parents, too, agree about how boys and girls should behave. Lambert et al. (1971) found high agreement among them that boys should be more aggressive, more boisterous, more adventurous; girls should be more passive, more emotional, more tender (Figure 11.11).

Considerable literature has been devoted to the basic inequities of culturally ascribed sex roles. There is little doubt that this has been a male-dominated society (Bardwick, 1972; Roszak & Roszak, 1969). There does remain some confusion, however, concerning the reality of sex differences, and the extent to which these are inevitable given different genetic background.

Maccoby and Jacklin (1974), in a large-scale review of relevant literature, have identified four areas in which there has been some agreement concerning sex differences: females have greater verbal ability than males, most evident in the early school years; males excel in **spatial-visual ability**; males excel in mathematical ability; and males are more aggressive. Indications are that measured achievement orientation may also be greater for males than for females (L. W. Hoffman, 1972; Horner, 1969; see Chapter 9).

The possibility that some or all of these differences might be genetically based (at least in part) has led to a great many studies both with animals and with humans. The case for the genetic basis of differences in aggressiveness appears to be the clearest. Lynn (1974) presents the following argument. If a difference is genetically linked, (1) it would be manifest at a very young age, before environmental forces could account for it; (2) it would not be restricted to a few cultures, but would probably be universal; (3) it would probably be evident among subhuman primates; and (4) sex hormones would have an effect on it. All of these conditions appear to have been met with respect to aggression. Males are more aggressive than females at an early age (Bandura & Walters, 1959); this finding is true of other cultures and of nonhuman primates as well (Mitchell et al., 1967); and the administration of male hormones to pregnant mothers has been shown to increase the aggressiveness of female children later born to them (Money & Erhardt, 1968).

The case with respect to sex differences in language, mathematics, and spatial-visual ability is not at all clear. Some authors, citing evidence of greater spatial ability in male than in female rats, argue that observed spatial-visual differences between

Masculine and feminine Adjectives descriptive of those traits and characteristics ordinarily associated with the male and female, respectively. Their use should not be taken to imply that the traits they subsume are limited to people of one sex and therefore are undesirable in people of the other.

Spatial-visual ability Ability to see relationships among objects in space, to identify objects, and, in short, to deal with the world of physical space as it is perceived through vision. The ability to maintain orientation in a strange place is sometimes a manifestation of spatial-visual ability.

Figure 11.11 To what degree are sex roles culturally imposed? Should girls be more feminine, boys more masculine?

males and females must be genetically based (Buffery and Gray, 1972). In contrast, McDaniel et al. (1978) examined space-related experiences of boys and girls and concluded that observed differences in spatial ability are related more closely to experience than to gender. And the same argument can be advanced with respect to apparent differences in verbal and mathematical ability. As Tobias (1982) notes, "Until and unless girls can experience the world as boys do, we cannot assume that sex differences in math are genetic" (p. 14). The same holds true for language differences.

In spite of the apparent genetic basis of greater aggressiveness in males, and in spite of the possibility that genetic influences might be involved in visual-spatial and linguistic sex differences, environmental factors are clearly important. Research leaves little doubt that parents treat manifestations of aggression differently in boys and girls, encouraging it in the one and punishing it in the other (Lewis, 1972). In addition, occupations that require aggression have traditionally been male-dominated; males have been provided with more opportunities, and at earlier ages, to develop independence and aggression, and females have been guided toward the more passive, nurturant roles (see Holland, Magoon, & Spokane, 1981).

In summary, Lynn (1974) attributes the development of sex roles to the interaction of three separate forces: biological, family-based, and cultural. Biological forces are evident in basic predispositions for the sexes to think, feel, and act differently; family influences are most evident in the sexual characteristics and behaviors of parents and siblings; cultural forces are manifest in the models provided by television, schools, churches, and other trappings of culture. To the extent that cultural and family influences change, so too will sex roles.

Nature-Nurture Interaction

Thus far in this chapter, we have looked at the two great forces that determine the eventual outcome of the developmental process. On the one hand there is nature, a complex of genetic forces that, in a sense, both limits and directs development. On the other, there is nurture, the host of environmental forces that make certain developmental outcomes more probable than others. Psychologists are fond of saying that heredity and environment interact in determining whatever it is that you and I have become and are becoming. Most of us assume immediately that we know exactly what is meant by the interaction of these two great forces; and most of us are at least partly wrong. We incorrectly assume that if we understand the separate effects of nature and of nurture, we might then understand their combined effects. That is, we assume that heredity accounts for this or that trait, that environment accounts for other characteristics, and that the sum total of their effects is you and I. It bears repeating that we are wrong.

A couple of simple examples of interaction might illustrate why this assumption is wrong. Consider, first, a simple substance like water or salt. One results from the interaction of hydrogen and oxygen; the other from the interaction of sodium and chloride. But neither the wetness and taste of water, nor the granularity and taste of salt can be understood just by knowing the separate elements of hydrogen, oxygen, sodium, and chloride.

As a second illustration of interaction, Schaefer (1976) refers to what was once a controversial question in studies of human learning: Is it better to distribute learning over a longer period of time with rest periods between study periods, or is it better to attempt to do all the learning at once (distributed vs. mass practice)? Studies sometimes provided evidence in favor of one method; sometimes in favor of the other; and on occasion, in favor of neither. Eventually it was discovered that one of the crucial variables in studies of massed vs. distributed practice was the meaningfulness of the material to be learned. Highly meaningful material can often be learned better with massed practice; but as the material becomes less meaningful, massed practice becomes less effective and distributed practice, more effective. This situation is a clear illustration of interaction (between learning method and type of material to be learned), and suggests a useful definition: "Interaction means that the relation between one variable and behavior actually changes as levels of one or more other dimensions vary" (Schaefer, 1976, p. 104).

The meaning of interaction with respect to heredity and environment is no different. In brief, the effects of heredity on specific behaviors or characteristics vary depending on any of a variety of environmental influences. And it is precisely for this reason that we should be wary of estimates of the extent to which variability in certain characteristics is due to heredity. Under some circumstances, heredity might well account for 80 percent of the variability in our manifested intelligence (Jensen, 1974); under different environmental circumstances, however, it might account for only 20 percent. Although we don't yet know the precise dimensions of nature-nurture interaction, we do know that the relationship is far from a simple additive one.

So with the knowledge that both nature and nurture are interacting in complex ways as a child develops, we turn next to an important developmental theory before taking a closer look at some of the developmental characteristics of infants and children.

Developmental Theory

A theory may be described as a set of concepts that attempts to organize related observations. Thus, theories have descriptive and explanatory functions; they may also have predictive value. The Darwinian theory of evolution, for example, seeks to describe and explain historical biological changes. It can also predict change in the future. Less obvious, but no less true, it can predict in retrospect. That is, it can be employed to predict certain events that have already occurred but that have not yet been confirmed through observation—indeed, that may never be confirmed through observation. The "missing link" in the chain of human evolution is a product of retrospective prediction: that life forms served as evolutionary links between the most advanced subhuman primate and the most primitive human can only be inferred on the basis of theory.

Theories in the social sciences are not fundamentally different from those in the natural sciences. True, the observations with which they deal are sometimes less reliable and less easily measured. But the organizational, explanatory, and predictive functions of the theories are the same.

In yet another sense, a theory may be seen as encompassing a specific point of view or combination of viewpoints. All theories bring with them certain biases implicit in the assumptions they must make about the nature of the subject matter with which they are concerned. Three main theories of developmental psychology have thus far survived the harsh tests of time. Each has its biases; probably none is entirely accurate; all are very useful, although sometimes for very different purposes. These are the theories of Sigmund Freud, Jean Piaget, and Erik Erikson. Piaget's theory is discussed in this chapter, Erikson's in the next, and Freud's in Chapter 13.

Piaget's Theory

Piaget's background in the biological sciences is fundamental to his description of development. As a biologist, he sought to clarify the evolution of intelligence and the child's adaptation to the environment. He asked two biology-related questions of human development: What are the mechanisms that allow the child to interact with the environment and to adapt to it? How can the course of human development be classified (as zoological or botanical species are classified)? Answers to the first question compose his general theory of human functioning; answers to the second classify development into a series of stages. Both are discussed here.

Mechanisms of Adaptation

Development is a process of adaptation. Children are not born knowing how to cope with external reality. Indeed, they are born with only a limited number of simple reflexes in their behavioral repertoire. Some of these reflexes are crucial to biological survival (sucking, sneezing, and swallowing, for example); others are of very limited value (the knee-jerk reflex, for example). Even those reflexes that are important for survival are sometimes poorly suited to the demands of the environment. From the very beginning of life, changes are required in the infant's behaviors. These changes define **accommodation**. A complementary process, **assimilation**, is manifested when the child makes use of previously acquired or innate activities without having to modify these activities.

Assimilation and accommodation are the two ways we have of interacting with the environment. We make use of aspects of our environment for certain activities that we already know (assimilation); and we modify our activities in order to be able to make use of certain aspects of the environment (accommodation). Piaget illustrates these complementary processes by reference to the infant's sucking behavior. When first born, children are capable of sucking, this behavior being reflexive (unlearned). They can therefore assimilate nipples in the activity of sucking. Not all objects can be sucked in exactly the same manner, however. It is therefore necessary to learn to change the shape of the mouth, the placement of the gums, the amount of suction employed, the rhythm of the activity, and so on. All these changes define accommodation. All behavior involves both accommodation and assimilation. And it is through the interplay of these twin processes that the child progressively adapts to the world, for as accommodation is required, changes occur in the child's behavior and in the capability for behavior.

Several related concepts are central to Piaget's account of development. Children are born with a limited repertoire of unlearned behaviors. They can suck, grasp, blink, and execute a variety of other behaviors. These behaviors are labeled **schemas** (also called *schemata* or *schemes,* translations from French to English not always being exact). As a function of interaction with the environment through assimilation and

Accommodation Involves the modification of an activity or an ability that the child already has in order to conform to environmental demands.

Assimilation The act of incorporating objects or aspects of objects in previously learned activities.

Schemas (also schemes or schemata) A label employed by Piaget to describe units in cognitive structure. A schema is, in one sense, an activity together with its structural connotations. In another sense, a schema may be thought of as an idea or as a concept. It usually labels a specific activity: the looking schema, the grasping schema, the sucking schema. A great deal of Piaget's theorizing and research deals with the processes by which the schemas with which a child is born become elaborated, progressively more complex, and progressively more "adultlike" as a function of interaction with the environment.

Piaget is widely recognized as the leading development psychologist of this century. He was born in Neuchâtel, Switzerland, received his early training in biology, and was awarded a Ph.D. in zoology at the age of twenty-two. His dissertation was not on children; it was on mollusks. In fact, by the age of twenty-four, he had published some two dozen papers on zoological topics.

After he obtained his Ph.D., Piaget spent several years working in various clinical centers in Europe, eventually coming under the direction of Simon, one of the two originators of an intelligence test that, after a number of revisions, is still one of the most widely used and respected measures of intelligence (the Stanford-Binet, originally the Simon-Binet).

His first articles on child development appeared in 1921 and 1922, followed shortly by his first book (Piaget, 1923). After that, often in collaboration with Barbel Inhelder, he published hundreds of articles in addition to dozens of books, many of which have not yet been translated into English. His productivity continued, unabated, until his death at the age of eighty-four.

Table 11.1 Piaget's Stages of Cognitive Development

Stage	Approximate Age (years)	Some Major Characteristics
Sensorimotor thought	0–2	Motoric intelligence World of the here and now Language, thought, and notions of objective reality are not present initially, but develop gradually

Preoperational thought
  Preconceptual
	2–7
	2–4
		Egocentric thought
		  Recognition of classes of objects, but logical weaknesses in classifying objects

Intuitive	4–7	Logic and imagination dominated by perception
Concrete operations	7–11 or 12	Ability to conserve Logic of classes and relations Understanding of numbers Thinking bound to concrete Development of reversibility in thought
Formal operations	11 or 12–14 or 15	Complete generality of thought Propositional thinking Ability to deal with the hypothetical Development of strong idealism

accommodation, schemas change. They develop as the child acquires control over motor activities and acquires the capacity to use schemas in a wider variety of situations. Thus, through assimilation and accommodation (functioning), mental growth begins to take place. And mental growth is the principal concern of Piaget's *cognitive* theory.

Stages of Cognitive Development

As children develop, their primitive schemas give way to more advanced representations of the world, and to new ways of dealing with the world on a mental level. Piaget's description of development is, in a sense, a description of the development of the child's mind. This description is classified into four major stages and a variety of substages, the stages providing useful guides for the analysis of development. These stages are depicted in Table 11.1 and are described in the following sections.

Sensorimotor Thought During much of the first two years of life, the world of the child is a world of the here and now. Children understand their environment principally in terms of the activities they can perform on it and the sensations they derive from it; hence the label *sensorimotor* (Figure 11.12). It is a world of sensation and movement, a world that is not represented in imagination and that therefore ceases to exist when it is not being immediately perceived. Indeed, only toward the end of the first year do children begin to realize that objects have a permanence and an identity all their own, completely independent of their perceptions. With this realization of *object permanence* or *object concept* comes symbolization, for in order to realize that an object exists when it is not being seen, it is necessary to remember that object. And in order to remember an object, it is necessary to have some sort of internal representation of it. This representation makes it possible for the child to imagine, to begin to think, to imitate objects and people who are not immediately present, and eventually to develop language.

In summary, the intellectual achievements of the first two years of life are singularly impressive. Initially, the young of the human species seem inferior to the young of most other animals. Their helplessness is considerably greater at birth and does not show signs of lessening during the first few months of life. Indeed, in most cases a full year will elapse before the child can move in an upright position, and even then, the movements are awkward, uncertain, and slow. Consider, however, that by the time children can walk, they have begun to understand the language that surrounds them, they have made remarkable progress in their understanding of the physical aspects of their environment, and they have begun to manifest the type of intelligence that is involved in understanding causality.

Figure 11.12 The sensorimotor world of the infant—a palpable, smellable, chewable world of the here and now.

Preoperational Thought   The preoperational period, spanning the approximate ages of two to seven, is frequently divided into two subperiods: preconceptual (two to four) and intuitive (four to seven).

Preconceptual thought is the child's increasing ability to deal with concepts, global representations of related objects or events. It is now possible for children to identify dogs, birds, people, and houses. Presumably they have a concept for each of these—a concept of birdness, of peopleness. But the generality of these concepts is limited: hence, *pre*conceptual. Although children at this stage can distinguish among individuals of different classes, they cannot easily discriminate between two individuals of the same class where these individuals are highly similar. This is why the preschooler has no difficulty believing that there is a Santa Claus even after seeing ten of them in different places on the same day.

The child's reasoning during this period manifests several logical weaknesses. It is said to be *syncretic* and *transductive*. Syncretic reasoning is illustrated in the idiosyncratic and changing criteria children employ when asked to sort objects into groups according to common characteristics. For example, a two-year-old who is placed in front of a table containing a variety of objects and is asked to put "those that go together in one pile" may proceed something like this: "The truck goes here because it's a truck, and this truck goes with it because it's a truck too, and this ball goes with it because it's blue, and the orange ball goes with the orange pencil and the pen goes with the pencil too."

Transductive reasoning involves making logical inferences on the basis of particular characteristics, proceeding from particular to particular rather than from particular to general or general to particular:

A has fur.
B has fur.
Therefore *B* is an *A*.

If *A* and *B* are both dogs, transductive reasoning leads to a correct conclusion. If, however, *A* is a dog but *B* is a cat, the same reasoning process leads to an incorrect conclusion.

The period of *intuitive thought* is characterized by **egocentric**, perception-dominated thought. The child's egocentricity is evident in an inability to adopt an objective point of view. Children find it very difficult at this stage to describe what the other side of a mountain is like, or what it would look like from the top or the bottom. The entire world tends to be perceived from the child's private viewpoint.

The role of perception in the preschooler's thought processes is illustrated by problems in conservation (*conservation* is defined as the realization that characteristics such as weight, volume, and mass do not change in spite of misleading perceptual changes). In a conservation of mass problem, for example, a four-year-old child might be presented with two identical balls of modeling clay. After the child admits that both balls contain the same amount of clay, one of the balls is rolled into a long, thin, sausagelike shape; the other is left untouched. Most preoperational children will now maintain that the changed object has more clay because it is longer, or that it has less because it is thinner. They are misled by the perceptual features of the problem and

Egocentric   An adjective derived from the Latin words for *self* (ego) and *center*. Literally, it describes a self-centered behavior, attitude, or personality characteristic. Although egocentrism often has negative connotations of selfishness, as applied to the child's perception of the world it is simply a descriptive label. Egocentric perception is characterized by an inability to assume an objective point of view.

Figure 11.13 Characteristics of preoperational thought. During the preconceptual period, thought is preconceptual, transductive, and syncretic. During the intuitive period, thought is intuitive, perception-dominated, egocentric, and prone to errors of classification.

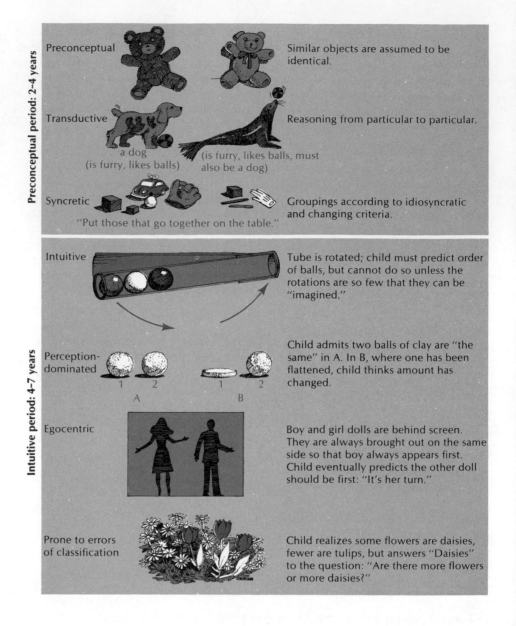

Preconceptual period: 2–4 years

Preconceptual — Similar objects are assumed to be identical.

Transductive — Reasoning from particular to particular.
a dog (is furry, likes balls) — (is furry, likes balls, must also be a dog)

Syncretic — Groupings according to idiosyncratic and changing criteria.
"Put those that go together on the table."

Intuitive period: 4–7 years

Intuitive — Tube is rotated; child must predict order of balls, but cannot do so unless the rotations are so few that they can be "imagined."

Perception-dominated — Child admits two balls of clay are "the same" in A. In B, where one has been flattened, child thinks amount has changed.

Egocentric — Boy and girl dolls are behind screen. They are always brought out on the same side so that boy always appears first. Child eventually predicts the other doll should be first: "It's her turn."

Prone to errors of classification — Child realizes some flowers are daisies, fewer are tulips, but answers "Daisies" to the question: "Are there more flowers or more daisies?"

have not yet developed the logical abilities that will permit them to arrive at a correct conclusion.

In addition, the child is prone to errors of classification during this period. Classification errors can easily be illustrated by reference to Piaget's class-inclusion problems. Suppose, for example, that a child is presented with a handful of candies, 90 percent of which are jellybeans, and 10 percent of which are chocolate drops. In response to the question, "Are there more jellybeans or more candies?" the typical answer is "more jellybeans." Dividing the class *candy* into its subclasses has the practical effect of destroying the parent class.

Figure 11.13 presents some of the major characteristics of preoperational thought and illustrations of these characteristics. It is important to keep in mind throughout this discussion of Piaget that the ages given are approximations. Numerous studies have found considerable variation in the ages at which each of these stages is reached; but few have found any variation in the sequence of attainment. It is therefore the sequence rather than the ages that is important.

Concrete Operations   Transition from preoperational thought to the period of *concrete operations* is marked by the acquisition of concepts of conservation, as illustrated in the modeling-clay problem. A child in the concrete-operations stage can reason that amount has not changed in spite of changes in appearance. There are three alternative explanations the child can employ to support this conviction. Each illustrates a different rule of logic, none of which was present in earlier developmental periods. These rules of logic are of tremendous importance to children's intellectual development and specifically to their ability to deal with problems of ever increasing complexity. The child can reason (1) that the clay ball could be reshaped into whatever it was before and that it would then have the same amount; it must therefore have the same amount now; (2) nothing has been added or taken away, so an identical amount remains; or (3) the deformed object seems to have more in one dimension, but less in another; these changes compensate for each other so the amount has not really changed. These rationalizations illustrate *reversibility, identity,* and *combinativity,* respectively. Although they are most clearly illustrated in the various problems of conservation (Figure 11.14), they are nevertheless general. In other words, they permeate the child's thinking and make many of the errors prevalent in preoperational thought literally unthinkable during the concrete-operations stage.

It is also during the concrete period that children manifest new abilities with respect to classification, seriation, and numbers. The problem of the jellybeans and chocolate drops is so simple for eight-year-olds that they would be embarrassed at having to answer it. Similarly, a seriation problem of the type illustrated in Figure 11.15 would present insurmountable problems for a three-year-old, but would be ridiculously simple for an eight-year-old. Given the ability to classify and to seriate, understanding our number system becomes relatively simple. In order to understand the meanings of real numbers (as opposed to imaginary numbers) it is necessary to understand that a number represents a grouping of objects or events (it has class properties). It is also necessary to understand that numbers are ordered in terms of the magnitude of groupings they represent, three being greater than two, but less than four (its serial properties).

In summary, the eleven-year-old child has acquired the ability to deal with a wide range of problems systematically and logically, and is very much at home in the world of symbols. But there do remain a number of limitations to thought during this period, the most obvious of which is the child's continued inability to deal with the hypothetical; hence the label *concrete.* The logic of concrete operations is tied to the real. Children do not yet have the freedom made possible by the more advanced logic of formal operations.

Formal Operations   The single most important achievement of the period of *formal operations* is the transition from logic bound to the real and concrete, to a more advanced logic that deals with hypothetical states and events. This transition is at once the culmination of all the developmental stages that have gone before, and the beginning of the final stage of intellectual development: the stage of formal operations. It should be noted, however, that the ability to deal logically with the hypothetical is not a characteristic that governs all adolescent and adult thinking. Rather, it is a form of thinking that is now *possible,* whereas it had previously been beyond the child's abilities. Although formal thought may be clearly evident in individual instances, it is by no means evident in all cases. Chapter 12, which deals with adolescent development, treats formal operations in greater detail.

Each of Piaget's developmental stages can be interpreted as the culmination of those stages that preceded it and as a preparation for the next. Within this framework, development is a continuous process made possible by the child's interaction with the environment. Piaget's primary concern was with the development of cognitive

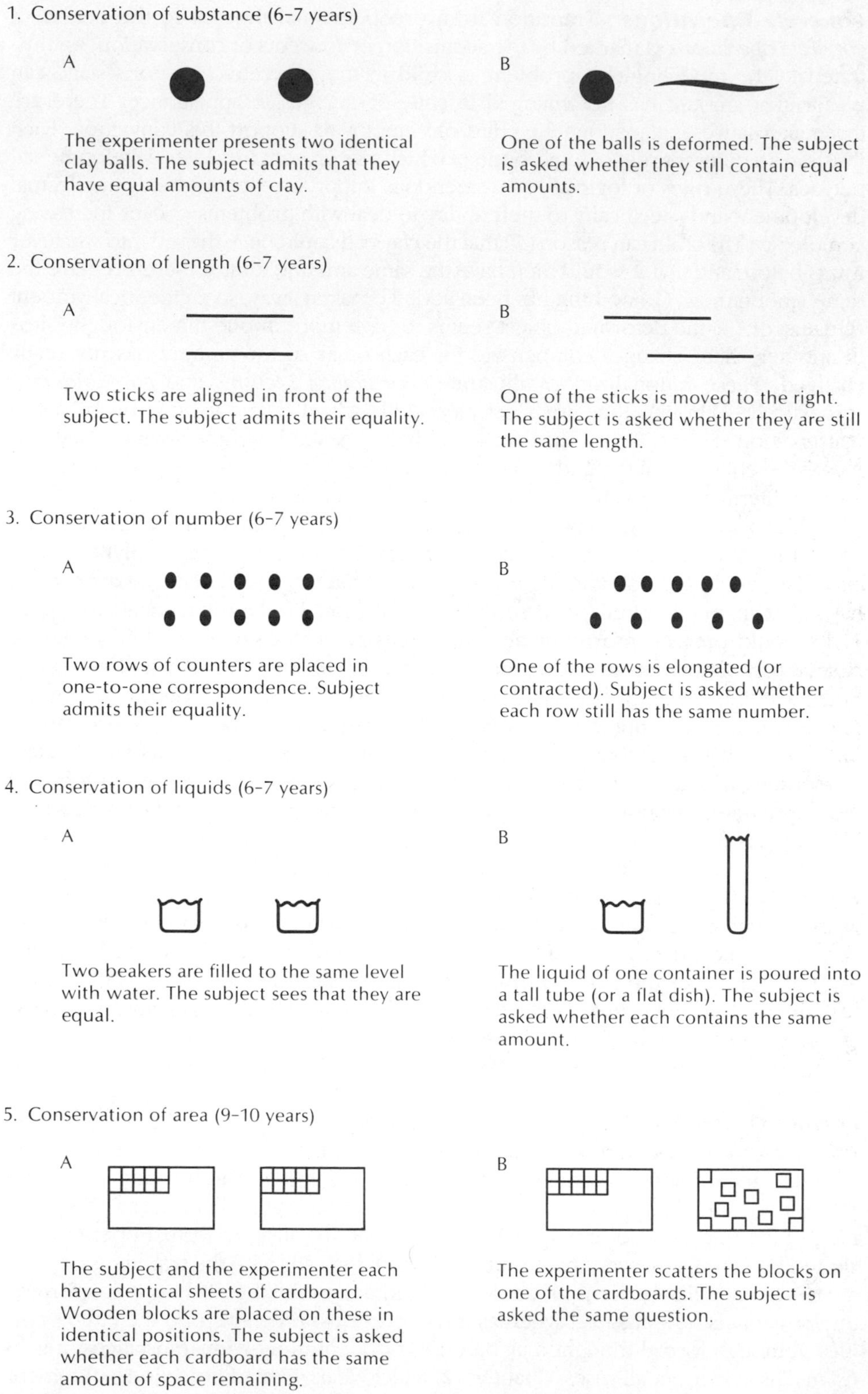

Figure 11.14 The stage of concrete operations is characterized by the acquisition of concepts of *conservation,* the realization that attributes of objects do not change despite changes in appearance. Some examples of conservation problems are given here, accompanied by the approximate ages at which children are likely to be able to answer them correctly. Children between the ages of six and seven years can accurately answer questions on the conservation of substance, length, number, and liquids. Children between nine and ten years can accurately answer questions on the conservation of area.

1. Conservation of substance (6–7 years)

A

The experimenter presents two identical clay balls. The subject admits that they have equal amounts of clay.

B

One of the balls is deformed. The subject is asked whether they still contain equal amounts.

2. Conservation of length (6–7 years)

A

Two sticks are aligned in front of the subject. The subject admits their equality.

B

One of the sticks is moved to the right. The subject is asked whether they are still the same length.

3. Conservation of number (6–7 years)

A

Two rows of counters are placed in one-to-one correspondence. Subject admits their equality.

B

One of the rows is elongated (or contracted). Subject is asked whether each row still has the same number.

4. Conservation of liquids (6–7 years)

A

Two beakers are filled to the same level with water. The subject sees that they are equal.

B

The liquid of one container is poured into a tall tube (or a flat dish). The subject is asked whether each contains the same amount.

5. Conservation of area (9–10 years)

A

The subject and the experimenter each have identical sheets of cardboard. Wooden blocks are placed on these in identical positions. The subject is asked whether each cardboard has the same amount of space remaining.

B

The experimenter scatters the blocks on one of the cardboards. The subject is asked the same question.

skills involved in imagining, remembering, reasoning, and problem solving. He described himself as a "genetic epistemologist." *Epistemology* refers to knowledge, *genesis* to development. In short, Piaget's theory seeks to account for the development of ways of knowing.

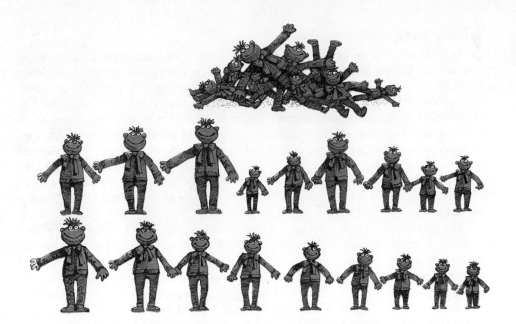

Cognitive, Social, and Emotional Development

There is more to the development of children, of course, than is presented in the preceding account of the forces that shape development and of Piaget's theory. To try and stuff all that is left into one small part of a chapter would engorge it. Accordingly, the following sections present only the most salient, interesting, and important information concerning cognitive, social, and emotional development in infancy and childhood. We begin, first, with a look at the capabilities of the newborn. Adolescence and adulthood are described in the next chapter.

Perception in the Newborn

It was long believed that the newborn's world was all "blooming, buzzing, confusion"; that, in particular, vision and hearing were so poorly developed as to be virtually useless. Recent evidence has dispelled many of these early beliefs. We now know that infants are sensitive to light almost immediately after birth, that they arc capable of visually following moving objects within a few days, that they are sensitive to patterns and contours as early as two days after birth (Fantz, 1964, 1965; Haith, 1966), and that they are born with the ability to see color (Bornstein & Marks, 1982). With respect to hearing, evidence suggests that, unlike the young of many species (dogs and cats, for example), which are deaf at birth, the human neonate is sensitive to a wide range of sounds and can also locate the direction of these sounds (Eisenberg et al., 1963).

The smell system, too, is functional in newborns. When presented with unpleasant odors, newborns attempt to avert their faces (Lipsitt et al., 1963). In contrast, the taste system appears to be less well developed (Pratt, 1954). Substances such as salt, sugar, citric acid, or water typically do not elicit different responses in the infant until around the age of two weeks. Fortunately, sensitivity to pain is not very pronounced in the newborn (McGraw, 1943), since the process of birth might otherwise be rather painful.

Learning in the Newborn

In addition to being remarkably perceptive very shortly after birth, human newborns are capable of learning. Indeed, some evidence suggests that they can learn even before being born. Spelt (1948) conditioned fetuses to react to vibrations using a classical conditioning procedure. He used a loud noise as an unconditioned stimulus, and obtained increases in fetal activity (detected by means of a stethoscope) as an unconditioned response. He then paired the loud noise with the vibratory sensations that resulted from placing a door chime, soldered closed, on the mother's abdomen (conditioning stimulus). Because the door chime was soldered shut, it did not ring but simply vibrated. After fifteen or twenty pairings of noise with the door chime's vibrations, Spelt obtained increases in fetal activity in response to the chime's vibrations alone.

The validity of these results has sometimes been questioned, because they have not always been replicated, and the possibility of conditioning the fetus in utero still remains uncertain. That the infant can be conditioned shortly after birth, however, has been demonstrated in a number of ways. As an example, Lipsitt (1971) conditioned a *rooting* response in infants by employing an operant conditioning procedure. Rooting is the infant reflex of turning the head when the cheek or corner of the mouth is stroked (the head turns in the direction of the stroking; thus the reflex is of value in locating nipples). Two-day-old infants lying on their backs had their cheeks stroked as a tone was sounded. If they turned in the appropriate direction, they were reinforced by being allowed to suck briefly on a nipple, thereby obtaining "formula." Within a half-hour of training, newborns, who had initially turned in response to the tone an average of 25 percent of the time, now turned 75 percent of the time. They had clearly been conditioned. Perhaps even more striking, when a different tone was introduced and the newborns were *not* reinforced for turning in response to the second tone (when their cheeks were stroked), but were still reinforced for the first tone, they continued to respond to the second tone only 25 percent of the time. Thus, not only is it possible for newborns to be conditioned, but it is possible as well for them to discriminate between different sounds.

Infant States

It has been found to no one's overwhelming surprise that not all infants are identical in terms of their typical behaviors and reactions; that there are, in fact, identifiable differences among infants; and that these differences, present very early in life, might have implications for understanding differences that exist among adults. The differences are described in terms of *infant states,* most frequently classified as regular sleep, disturbed sleep, drowsiness, alert activity, or focused activity (Prechtl & Beintema, 1964; Wolff, 1959, 1966). The terms are self-explanatory, with the possible exception of *alert* and *focused activity.* Alert activity is active response to the environment; focused activity is directed and unchanging. Crying is one focused activity; playing with objects is an alert activity (Figure 11.16).

Research on infant states reveals one predominantly important finding: individual infants vary greatly in the amount of time they spend in each of these states. Thus, in a study of six infants, J. L. Brown (1964) found that although the babies spent approximately one-third of their time sleeping, one infant slept 56 percent of the time and another 22 percent of the time (Figure 11.17). One infant cried 35 percent of the time; another, 17 percent of the time. One was alert 40 percent of the time; another, 10 percent of the time.

Present speculation is that infant states are to some degree genetically determined. At the same time, it is clear that they are highly influenced by environmental factors. Rocking or singing to a baby may bring about a change from an alert to a drowsy or sleeping state; if the cat now jumps on the sleeping infant, another change in state might be brought about.

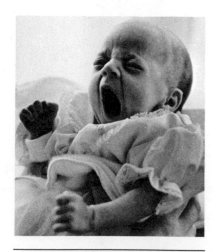

Figure 11.16 Infant states are highly individualistic. This infant is in a state of drowsiness.

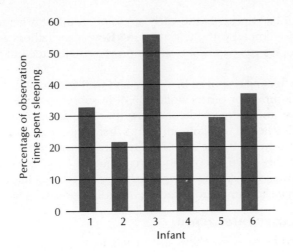

Figure 11.17 In observations of six infants for the first five to seven days after birth, the time each infant spent in various states was recorded. The observation time was approximately one hour each day and occurred about one hour after feeding. One infant slept only 22 percent of the observation time, whereas another slept 56 percent, illustrating the wide range of individual differences in infant states. (Based on data from J. L. Brown, 1964.)

Infant Emotional Reactions

Investigating emotional reactions in infants presents several obvious difficulties. Given that infants are preverbal and have little understanding of such abstract notions as love and fear (as we define them), these emotional reactions can only be inferred from their behavior. The danger here is that the investigator will invest the infant with emotions that adults might experience in similar circumstances. In fact, we have no way of ascertaining that a crying infant is afraid or hungry, angry or insulted, humiliated or simply bored.

In spite of these problems, psychologists have generally accepted that infants are capable of reacting with such basic emotions as fear, rage, and love (J. B. Watson & Rayner, 1920), and that a limited number of stimuli will initially evoke these responses. Fear, for example, is assumed to result from hearing a loud noise or from sudden loss of support. Subsequently, some infants come to fear an increasing range of stimuli; others remain unperturbed in the face of their environment. Fear of heights appears to be almost universal among infants by the age of thirteen to eighteen months, and is present in approximately 20 percent of all children by the age of seven months (Scarr & Salapatek, 1970). *Stranger anxiety* does not ordinarily manifest itself until around the age of six months, and becomes most common by the age of two years.

Lack of stranger anxiety in the first few months of life is assumed to be related to infants' inability to discriminate between familiar people and strangers, and to the absence of any strong attachments to their caretakers (Ainsworth, 1967). That fear does eventually develop has been explained on the basis of an *incongruity hypothesis* (Hebb, 1946; J. M. Hunt, 1964). In essence, this hypothesis maintains that as children become familiar with their environment and begin to recognize some of its features, of which the parent is probably among the most important, they develop certain expectations relative to the environment. The appearance of the unexpected is incongruous with their expectations and results in anxiety (Figure 11.18). Indirect confirmation of this hypothesis is provided by Schaffer's (1966) finding that only two variables correlate highly with the incidence of fear of strangers: number of siblings in the home, and exposure to strangers. Children who had the greatest number of brothers and sisters, and who were exposed to the greatest variety of strangers early in infancy, manifested the least amount of stranger anxiety.

Research indicates that fears in later life are closely related to parental fears, to intelligence, and to socioeconomic level. Economically disadvantaged children appear to be most afraid of scolding, starvation, punishment, and divorce; economically well-off children are most afraid of being left alone, of physical punishment, and of the dark (Angelino et al., 1956).

Figure 11.18 Fear of strangers (stranger anxiety) is not uncommon after the age of six months. Mothers provide considerable security—as do other "attachment" objects such as teddy bears and blankets.

And what of happiness? Is the early smile of an infant a genuine smile? How many mothers have argued with their mothers? How many fathers with their fathers? He can smile? No, it's gas pains. She smiles now! No, she's teething. Let psychology settle the dispute.

Smiling is a fleeting response in a warm and well-fed infant. It can occur as early as two to twelve hours after birth (Wolff, 1963)! In subsequent weeks and months, it occurs in response to an ever widening array of stimulation. The true social smile, said to arise as a function of recognition, occurs first in response to a voice, sometimes as early as the third week. By the age of 3.5 months, infants smile in recognition of a human face, sometimes more readily and more frequently if the face is familiar (Gewirtz, 1965). The selective social smile follows shortly, and becomes increasingly selective. It occurs in response to stimulation that the infant recognizes as familiar.

Infant-Mother Interaction

Relationships between mothers and infants have been studied in a number of ways. Indirect studies have dealt in detail with the effects of separating infant monkeys from their mothers, of rearing them in isolation, or of rearing them with substitute mothers (see, for example, Harlow, 1958, 1959). These studies, reviewed in Chapter 10, point strongly to the importance of the mother for the child's emotional, social, and sexual well-being.

Studies of this nature are clearly not possible with human infants. There are, however, a number of naturally occurring situations that are not dramatically different. These have involved children raised in institutions and therefore deprived of mothers—and sometimes of mother figures as well in the larger, more impersonal institutions (Bowlby, 1953; Casler, 1961). They include, as well, situations where infants have been moved from foster homes which, to all intents and purposes, would provide emotional bonds similar to those that might otherwise have been provided by their biological parents, and placed in adoptive homes (Yarrow & Goodwin, 1973). Results of these studies indicate that separation from the mother after the age of six months is especially traumatic, and is evident in decreased social responsiveness, increased stranger anxiety, and such specific disturbances as crying, colic, other feeding difficulties, and sometimes rejection of the new caretaker (Yarrow & Goodwin, 1973; see Figure 11.19). More complete maternal deprivation, sometimes evident in institutional settings, apparently has more extreme effects. Spitz (1945, 1954) reports that institutionalized children in South Africa had significantly higher mortality rates, were retarded in physical development, and were emotionally immature and incompetent to the extent that many of them withdrew, became seriously depressed, and sometimes died.

The father's role in the emotional, physical, and social well-being of the infant has not been extensively investigated. This is not particularly surprising, since fathers have typically spent relatively little time with very young infants in this society.

Play

In the very beginning, which you probably don't remember too clearly, your parents were all-important. Not only were they essential for your physical comfort, even for your survival, but they provided for all your psychological needs. They were the source of love.

As children grow older, peers become progressively more important. That does not mean, however, that parents immediately become less important. Indeed, it is debatable that they become less important before adolescence—and even then peers and other individuals outside the family ordinarily do not completely replace parents either as a source of love or as a source of profound influence on interests, values, and decisions.

The progressive socialization of the child does, therefore, begin in the family, since it is there that children first become aware of the many implicit and explicit rules that govern behavior in their culture. *Socialization* may be viewed simply as the

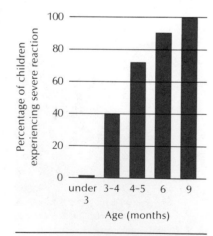

Figure 11.19 Studies of children moved from foster homes into adoptive homes show how maternal separation becomes increasingly traumatic as the infant matures. (Based on data from Yarrow and Goodwin, 1973.)

process of developing an individual who is aware of the mores, the values, the traditions, and the accepted ways of behaving in society, and who is capable of functioning in society. Much of the child's early socialization occurs through play.

And what is **play**? Sadly, many adults have forgotten the joys of true play. We abandon ourselves reluctantly and guardedly to the joys of madness and the ecstasies of whimsy. We know too carefully what reality is and we fear too passionately the possibility of confusing the imaginary with the real—or we fear that others might think we have confused the two. There is no such fear in the hearts of children. The games they play, unlike the games we play, are played solely for their enjoyment. They are designed neither to impress nor to deceive; neither to persuade nor to annoy. We work at our play; we take it seriously. We imbue it with an element of desperation, scarcely bothering to pay lip service to the hoary maxim, "It's not whether you win or lose; it's how you play the game." But children are uncorrupted. Their games have players, but neither winners nor losers. What are these games?

Children's games may be classified into three broad categories. There is sensorimotor play, social play, and imaginative play (Figure 11.20). Many games obviously share characteristics of all three. And some of the games we play as adults, in spite of what was just said, are highly similar to the games children play. But most of us don't indulge ourselves in many of these games.

Sensorimotor play involves manipulating objects or performing activities simply for the sensations involved. Thus, rope-skipping, creeping, crawling, hopping, waving, pushing a toy car, or blowing bubbles in a bathtub are all forms of sensorimotor play. This type of play is evident in the countless solitary games young children play. Note, too, that children play solitary games before they engage in more social games, and that even when two children are playing side by side, they are frequently playing separately. Piaget (1932) drew attention to this progression in children's games, pointing out that, prior to truly social play, there is parallel play where children play together (in the sense of being in physical proximity) but neither share the activities employed in the game, nor follow mutually accepted rules.

Social play involves interaction between two or more children and the use of rules, and is characterized by cooperation. Hence the tremendous importance of games in the socialization of the child. Piaget (1932) investigated the progression of children's understanding of rules. Before the age of three, children do not play according to rules and do not understand them. This stage is followed by an intermediate period during which children imitate rules, but do not really understand them, and therefore change them constantly as they are playing. Interestingly, during this period they believe that rules come from God or some similar source, and that they are therefore fixed and unchangeable. In the third stage (by the age of seven or eight) children have begun to play in a truly social manner, with rules that are accepted by all players and rigidly adhered to. Again, their verbalized notions of the nature of rules during this period dramatically violate their adherence to these rules. They now believe that rules are made by people, and that they can therefore be changed by mutual consent. Yet they seldom change them. "That's the rule!" It is not until the age of eleven or twelve that the nature of rules is completely understood; now they can be adhered to or changed by agreement as the situation warrants (see Table 11.2).

Imaginative play is perhaps the most interesting of the three types. It begins very early, continues throughout life, and takes a variety of forms. Most obvious are the host of make-believe games and activities prevalent in the preschool years—games where children pretend that their activities are something they are not: that they themselves are something else; that objects with which they are playing are something else. Thus, the child who walks about on all fours, sniffing crumbs on the carpet, licking people's hands, and barking *is* a dog; the pencil in his mouth *is* a bone; and the chair leg *may well be* a fire hydrant.

Another type of imaginative play becomes increasingly common in the later preschool years and continues well into adulthood, although we spend little time

Play Activities with no goal other than the enjoyment derived from them.

Sensorimotor play Play activity involving the manipulation of objects or the execution of activities simply for the sensations that are produced.

Social play Play activity that involves interaction between two or more children and frequently takes the form of games with more or less precisely defined rules.

Imaginative play Play activities that include make-believe games.

Figure 11.20 The three categories of children's play: (**a**) social, (**b**) imaginative, and (**c**) sensorimotor.

talking about it. Daydreaming is a form of play. Most of us are too ambitious, too achievement-oriented, and too guarded to admit that we daydream; indeed, some of us are simply too occupied to allow ourselves the luxury of undirected thinking. Not so the child. Theoretical speculation has it that daydreaming may be very important in the resolution of fears, anxieties, and a wealth of related problems. It is not at all unlikely that it is also centrally involved in the development of interpersonal skills, providing as it does an opportunity for the imaginary exercising of these skills. There is, too, the imaginary playmate with whom as many as one-third of all preschool children play constantly (Singer, 1973). These imaginary friends are loved, spoken to,

Table 11.2 Piaget's Description of Rules as They Are Understood and Practiced by Children

Approximate Age	Degree of Understanding	Adherence to Rules
Before 3	No understanding of rules	Do not play according to rules
To 7 or 8	Believe rules come from God (or some other high authority) and cannot be changed	Break and change rules constantly
To 11 or 12	Understand social nature of rules, and that they can be changed	Do not change rules; adhere to them rigidly
After 11 or 12	Complete understanding	Change rules by mutual consent

taken on trips, dressed, and played with. Psychology has not yet interviewed any of them in depth. Most of them go away in the earlier school years and never reappear. Schaefer (1969) found that college students who recalled having had an imaginary playmate tended to be more creative than those who didn't. This does not necessarily mean that they had an imaginary playmate because they were more creative; it might simply mean that those who were more creative were more concerned with their fantasies and were therefore better able to recall imaginary playmates than those less creative.

Morality

Part of socialization involves learning what is right and wrong. Perhaps more important, the socialization process contributes very directly to the tendency of individuals to act rightly or wrongly. Research has shown that the two are not necessarily the same; that the probability of transgressing moral principles sometimes depends as much on the likelihood of being caught as on any moral convictions an individual might have (Havighurst & Taba, 1949; Hendry, 1960). Following a recent upsurge in research on **morality**, there is a current controversy regarding this very issue. One of the principal figures in morality research, Kohlberg (1964, 1973), has demonstrated a close correspondence between beliefs and behavior, as have a number of researchers employing his theoretical framework. Haan et al. (1968) found that subjects who functioned at the highest level of moral orientation on the Kohlberg scales (described shortly) tended to be more active politically and socially. And Fodor (1972) found that those who were delinquent typically exhibited lower levels of moral orientation.

In contrast, studies of cheating behavior have found that an amazing number of individuals will cheat if the likelihood of getting caught appears remote. In one study (Feldman & Feldman, 1967), students were given the opportunity to mark their own examination papers from a key that had been placed on a chalkboard. Subjects were unaware that the examinations had previously been marked by the investigator. Shortly after subjects began marking their papers, the instructor was called from the room. Incidence of cheating was then determined by comparing the students' marks with those previously computed by the investigator. Figure 11.21 presents some of the results of this study. While sex differences in cheating in seventh grade were not significant, more boys than girls cheated in twelfth grade, a finding that has frequently been corroborated in other research (for example, Hartshorne & May, 1928).

Stages of Moral Development

Kohlberg's description of moral development is the result of an attempt to find universal stages in moral orientation. It appears that these stages do exist, that they are sequential, but that they are not discrete. In other words, children will not typically exhibit a level II or III moral orientation before having exhibited a level I orientation, and they will continue to exhibit lower levels of moral orientation even after they have demonstrated that they can operate at higher levels.

Morality The ethical aspects of human behavior. Morality is intimately bound to the development of an awareness of accepted and unacceptable behaviors and is therefore linked to what is often called *conscience*.

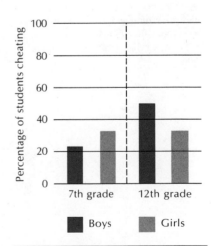

Figure 11.21 Cheating as a function of grade and sex when children were permitted to mark their own exam papers. (Based on data from Feldman and Feldman, 1967.)

Table 11.3 Kohlberg's Levels of Morality

A dying woman needs a drug that was discovered by a local pharmacist who charges such an exorbitant price that the husband can't pay. Should he steal the drug?

Level I Premoral	Stage 1: Punishment and obedience orientation	"If he steals the drug, he might go to jail." (Punishment.)
	Stage 2: Naive instrumental hedonism	"He can steal the drug and save his wife, and he'll be with her when he gets out of jail." (Act motivated by its hedonistic consequences for the actor.)
Level II Conventional Role Conformity	Stage 3: "Good boy" morality of maintaining good relations, approval of others	"People will understand if you steal the drug to save your wife, but they'll think you're cruel and a coward if you don't." (Reactions of others and the effects of the act on social relationships become important.)
	Stage 4: Authority maintains morality	"It is the husband's duty to save his wife even if he feels guilty afterwards for stealing the drug." (Institutions, law, duty, honor, and guilt motivate behavior.)
Level III Morality of Self-Accepted Principles	Stage 5: Morality of contract, of individual rights, and of democratically accepted law	"The husband has a right to the drug even if he can't pay now. If the druggist won't charge it, the government should look after it." (Democratic laws guarantee individual rights; contracts are mutually beneficial.)
	Stage 6: Morality of individual principles of conscience	"Although it is legally wrong to steal, the husband would be morally wrong not to steal to save his wife. A life is more precious than financial gain." (Conscience is individual. Laws are socially useful but not sacrosanct.)

Note. After Kohlberg, 1969 and 1971.

Conscience An internalized set of rules governing an individual's behavior. Conscience may or may not reflect the teaching of religious principles in childhood.

Initially, children respond primarily to punishment or to fear of punishment. This lowest level of moral orientation is termed *premoral*. The intermediate level is characterized by a rigid, rule-bound, highly conforming type of morality, where the child's primary considerations relate to maintaining good relations with authority. Finally, the highest level of moral orientation involves the acceptance of self-determined moral principles. It will not be manifest until the individual has examined rules of **conscience** and behavior, and has made personal decisions about the rightness and wrongness of these rules. These three levels of moral orientation, and the types of moral judgments characteristic of each, are presented in Table 11.3. It should be noted that most children and a great many adults never operate beyond the second level. That is, we are typically rule-bound, authority-submissive, and good-relations-oriented. Only 10 percent of Kohlberg's sample of twenty-four-year-olds operated at level III. The great majority operated in terms of the impact of immediate authority or in terms of the pain-pleasure consequences of their behavior.

Prosocial Behavior

Investigations of altruism among children have begun to clarify the processes by which altruism and other forms of prosocial behavior are acquired (for example, Peters, 1977). Paulson (1974) reports, for example, that children who were exposed to the *Sesame Street* series designed to foster cooperative behavior displayed significantly more cooperative behavior than children who had not watched the series, provided that the testing situations were highly similar to those in the series. Cooperative behavior did not appear to transfer readily to other situations. Other investigations (for example, Elliot & Vesta, 1970; M. C. Hoffman, 1976) reveal, as no great surprise, that cooperation and sharing can be increased through modeling and reinforcement. Some studies have found sex differences in prosocial behavior, with girls frequently being more cooperative and less competitive than boys (McKee & Leader, 1955). Others have failed to find any sex differences (Kagan & Madsen, 1972). There is more general agreement concerning the finding that competitiveness increases with age. There is also general agreement that cultural influences are important in determining prosocial behavior or its absence. Studies with Israeli children (typically kibbutz children) have almost invariably found greater cooperation than comparable studies with American children (Shapira & Madsen, 1974).

A Look Back

There is an incredibly impressive distance between the eleven- or twelve-year-old child, standing on the edge of sexual maturity, and the neonate lying just barely on this side of the womb. Between these two there are dramatic physical, social, and cognitive changes. A relatively helpless little human, capable of experiencing and reacting only in limited ways, becomes a person. But the process of development is far from complete at the termination of childhood. The story has only begun. We continue in the next chapter.

Main Points

1. The history of attitudes toward children is characterized by instances of abuse, neglect, and exploitation, in dramatic contrast with the child-centeredness of the present century.

2. Genetic and environmental forces shape the child's development.

3. Mendelian genetics sees hereditary characteristics in terms of recessiveness and dominance of genes; molecular genetics examines the structure of genes and the chemistry of the DNA molecule.

4. The egg and sperm cell are the immediate origins of life. They reproduce by meiosis, splitting into cells that contain twenty-three single chromosomes. After their union, the zygote again contains its full complement of twenty-three pairs of chromosomes, half from the mother and half from the father.

5. Of our twenty-three pairs of chromosomes, a single pair determines whether we will be male or female. Females produce only one type of sex chromosome (X); males produce two types (X and Y). An XX pairing of sex chromosomes results in a female; males result from an XY pairing.

6. Sometimes a single pair of genes can determine a characteristic, in which case one member of the pair, corresponding to one value of the characteristic, may be dominant over the other (major gene determination). In most cases, however, human characteristics are determined by a combination of genes (polygenetic determination).

7. Our inherited chromosomal makeup is our genotype; the observable characteristics that it produces is our phenotype.

8. Sex-linked defects, associated with genes on the sex chromosome and far more common among males than females, include hemophilia, baldness, night blindness, and color blindness.

9. Nutrition, family, television, and culturally approved sex roles are a few of the environmental factors that shape a child's development.

10. First-born and only children appear to have an advantage in several areas including academic achievement, measured intelligence, probability of attending college, and verbal development.

11. There is tentative evidence that viewing violence on television may be associated with greater aggressiveness among children. At the same time, there is evidence that viewing television may be associated with increased prosocial behavior, as well as with enhanced language development, particularly among less advantaged socio-economic groups.

12. Sex-role stereotypes influence children's social development as they adopt behaviors appropriate to these roles. Some sex-role differences may be genetically based; others are enforced in the family and by culture. The feminist movement of recent decades has raised awareness of sex-role stereotypes and their harmful effects.

13 The interaction between heredity and environment is not simple and additive, and cannot easily be understood simply by understanding each separately, any more than the wetness of water can be understood through an intimate knowledge of hydrogen and oxygen.

14 Developmental theories attempt to describe, explain, and predict child development. Piaget's is one of three major developmental theories; it deals mainly with the cognitive development of the child.

15 Piaget, a biologist by training, attempted to discover what it is that enables children to adapt to an increasingly complex environment. He described two processes by which we interact with the world: assimilation involves exercising already learned behaviors; accommodation involves modifying behaviors in the face of environmental demands.

16 According to Piaget, a child's schema, units of cognitive structure, develop through four major stages: sensorimotor thought, preoperational thought (divided into preconceptual and intuitive stages), concrete operations, and formal operations.

17 The sensorimotor period (from birth to approximately two years) is a world of the here and now, characterized initially by the absence of language and an inability to represent objects that are not immediate.

18 Preoperational thought (two to seven, approximately) is egocentric (based on the child's personal point of view), and characterized by weakness in classifying objects and a strong reliance on perception.

19 Concrete operations (seven to eleven or twelve) is marked by the advent of the various conservations, by the child's increasing ability to classify and to seriate, and by an eventually complete understanding of numbers. Thinking is still bound to the concrete, however; that is, it is limited to the real or to the potentially real.

20 Formal operations (eleven or twelve onward) is a completely logical form of thinking, not bound to the concrete but capable of dealing with the abstract and hypothetical. In many cases, formal thinking is not characteristic of most adolescents or even adults.

21 Infants are able to see color, to detect sounds at birth, and to sense various tastes and smells very shortly after birth. In addition, they are capable of learning as soon as they have been born, and may also be capable of simple conditioning prior to birth.

22 Infants vary greatly according to the amount of time they spend in different identifiable states: regular sleep, disturbed sleep, drowsiness, alert activity, and focused activity.

23 Infants are capable of reacting with such basic emotions as fear, rage, and love; a limited number of stimuli will initially evoke these responses. The social smile usually arises as a function of recognition.

24 Maternal deprivation appears to have harmful effects on the infant's social, emotional, and physical development, particularly if it occurs after the infant has already formed a strong attachment to a mother (or other caretaker).

25 Much of the child's early socialization occurs through play, activities with no other goal than enjoyment. In sensorimotor play children manipulate objects for the sensations involved. In social play, children interact and use rules. Imaginative play includes make-believe games and daydreaming, and has been linked to creativity.

26 Children develop morality during the process of socialization. Kohlberg says there is a close correspondence between beliefs and behavior but this conclusion is controversial. He has identified three levels of morality: premoral, conventional role conformity, and morality of self-accepted principles. Each level has two stages. We are typically rule-bound and authority-submissive and thus seldom operate beyond the second level.

27 Prosocial behaviors such as cooperation and sharing can be increased through modeling and reinforcement and are prone to cultural influences.

Further Readings

The following presents a readable and comprehensive account of the relationship between genetics and behavior:

McClearn, G. E., and DeFries, J. C. *Introduction to behavioral genetics.* San Francisco: W. H. Freeman, 1973.

Kessen gives a fascinating account of how children were sometimes treated in the past:

Kessen, W. *The child.* New York: John Wiley, 1965.

Numerous short books provide simple explanations of Piaget's most important beliefs and discoveries. Among them:

Ginsberg, H., and Opper, S. *Piaget's theory of intellectual development* (2nd ed.). Englewood Cliffs, N.J.: Prentice-Hall, 1979.

A provocative and informative discussion of sex-roles, their origins, and their effects, is contained in each of the following:

Frieze, I. H., Parsons, J. E., Johnson, P. B., Ruble, D. N., and Zellman, G. L. *Women and sex roles: A social psychological perspective.* New York: W. W. Norton, 1978.

Spence, J. T., and Helmreich, R. L. *Masculinity and femininity: Their psychological dimensions, correlates and antecedents.* Austin: University of Texas Press, 1978.

A book that looks at the role of the father in the upbringing of children and reviews some of the research in this area is:

Lynn, D. B. *The father: His role in child development.* Monterey, Calif.: Brooks/Cole, 1974.

A more detailed presentation of most of the topics discussed in this chapter may be found in:

Lefrancois, G. R. *Of children: An introduction to child development* (4th ed.). Belmont, Calif.: Wadsworth, 1983.

Adolescence, Aging, and Dying

Toward the middle of a highly vigorous life, my aunt attempted to relieve her boredom by obtaining employment in a home for retired men and women. Residents of the home ranged from sixty-five to somewhat riper ages, but all were active and in good health. Those less active and healthy were unceremoniously removed to a nursing home or to the local hospital. When, for example, Mr. Broacus, a retired shopkeeper, found himself disinclined to come to the cafeteria for his dinner, my aunt was sternly forbidden to bring him food: "If he can't come to eat, he shouldn't be here." Since Mr. Broacus was well enough to come for dinner the next night, he was not sent away. And that he had missed three meals apparently bothered no one except, perhaps, Mr. Broacus, although my aunt too claimed some slight reaction.

She reacted somewhat more violently some time later when one of the old gentlemen, having had too much good wine and merriment in a local tavern, found himself unable to climb the short steps into the hallway leading to his room. Having tried several times to negotiate this obstacle, and realizing now that the feat was quite beyond his present capabilities, the old gentleman stretched himself regally across one of the tables in the parlor and promptly fell asleep. Some time later, he fell upon the floor. The noise awakened my aunt from one of several short rests that character-istically punctuate her duties and brought her timidly into the parlor; the same noise, though at a much closer distance, had failed to awaken the sleeping gentleman, who now lay in a silent and sodden heap upon the floor. Alarmed, my aunt ran to fetch her supervisor so that they might assess the old man's condition and perhaps help him to his bed.

"Let him be," said the supervisor.

"But he might be hurt," rejoined my aunt. "He might even be dead."

To which the supervisor replied, "Well, never mind. If he's dead he won't show up for breakfast."

Sadly convinced that nobody cares very much about old people, my aunt now relieves her boredom in other ways. Mostly she looks after my uncle.

Figure 12.1 Is the best yet to be?

Does nobody care? Not true. Some do. But how many and how much is a different question. About youth, however, there is little question: we have made a cult of youth. When we are no longer young, we exhort ourselves to think and act as though we still were. And none of our lotions, creams, potions, toupees, dyes, tonics, salves, pigments, tinctures, unguents, and countless other cosmetic aids (chemical, natural, and surgical) are designed to make us look elderly. Only the adolescent and perhaps the young adult can be excused for really believing "Come along and grow old with me; the best is yet to be." Yet, perhaps it is! (See Figure 12.1.)

Adolescence

Adolescence The period from the onset of puberty to adulthood, typically including the teen years (thirteen to nineteen).

Continuous culture A culture that does not clearly demarcate passage from one period of life to another.

In Western cultures, transition between childhood and adulthood is accomplished by means of passage through the prolonged and sometimes turbulent period of **adolescence**. Ours is a **continuous culture**, one with no clear demarcations between different life stages. Other cultures, sometimes considered more primitive when viewed through our cultural blinders, do not all require their young to spend a period between childhood and adulthood. Instead, they demarcate the passage clearly and celebrate it with pomp and ritual—and sometimes with circumcision, scarring, and other forms of physical mutilation. This cross-cultural comparison is intended to make only one point: adolescence is not necessarily a universal phenomenon, at least in terms of its psychological implications. It is, nevertheless, universal in terms of the biological changes that accompany it, and that sometimes define it.

Physical Changes

Pubescence Changes that occur in late childhood or early adolescence and that result in sexual maturity.

Puberty Sexual maturity following pubescence.

For convenience, adolescence is most often defined in terms of an age span—twelve to eighteen or nineteen, for example—or in terms of the teen years. Biologically, however, it can be considered to begin either with **pubescence** (changes that precede sexual maturity) or with **puberty** (the onset of sexual maturity), and to terminate with adulthood. Since the beginning of adulthood is arbitrary, and since the timing of puberty and pubescence vary greatly in different individuals as well as between the sexes, the biological definition cannot be very precise.

The most important physical changes of adolescence are those that lead to sexual maturity. These are the changes of pubescence (Figure 12.2). Their external manifestations are well known. Among the first signs in both boys and girls is the appearance of pigmented pubic hair. Pubic hair that might exist before this period is not pigmented and is soft rather than coarse and kinky. At about the same time, boys' testes begin to enlarge, as do girls' breasts. Among girls, there is then a period of rapid physical growth, the occurrence of the first menstrual period (termed *menarche*), the growth of armpit hair, and a slight lowering of the voice. Among boys, there is also a growth spurt, a dramatic change in voice, the growth of armpit hair, the development of facial and chest hair (not universal), and the ability to ejaculate semen. It is worth noting that these changes occur approximately two years earlier for girls than for boys, temporarily placing them ahead of boys in height, weight, and sexual maturity. Table 12.1 presents height and weight data for the period of adolescence. It is also worth noting that boys are sexually mature as soon as they can ejaculate semen, but girls usually remain infertile for a year or more after their first menstrual period.

Early and Late Maturation   The average adolescent matures at twelve or fourteen, depending on sex. Many mature earlier; many, later. Given that maturity tends to be judged in terms of physical appearance, the age at which the most obvious changes of pubescence occur can be of tremendous psychological importance to the child. The psychological implications of early and late maturation have been extensively investigated in several series of longitudinal studies (Ames, 1957; M. C. Jones, 1957, 1965; M. C. Jones & Mussen, 1958). The findings are remarkably consistent for boys, but less so for girls. In general, early-maturing boys tend to have a definite advantage over their slower-maturing peers in several areas, probably because they frequently excel in activities that are prized by the adolescent male culture. Since they are larger and stronger at a younger age, they are often better athletes; since they are more socially mature, they tend to be leaders; since they are sexually mature, they are more likely to engage in highly reinforced heterosexual activities. Research suggests that they tend to be better adjusted, more popular, more confident, and to have more positive self-concepts. In contrast, late-maturing boys are frequently more restless, more attention-seeking, less confident, and have less positive self-concepts.

However, the initial advantages of early maturation, particularly in areas of social behavior, and the concomitant disadvantages of late maturation, are not always evident in later life. Peskin (1967, 1973) reports findings which suggest that early maturers frequently become dependent, less intellectually curious, less active, and more prone to temper tantrums. In contrast, late maturing boys are often more active, more intellectually curious, more independent, and more adaptive in later life. Thus, early maturers may have an advantage in terms of social development whereas late maturers may have a slight advantage in terms of intellectual functions (Clausen, 1975).

The picture with respect to girls is not quite so clear. Jones and Mussen (1958) found that early-maturing girls were at a disadvantage, particularly with respect to social adjustment and acceptance by their peers. In contrast, Douglas and Ross (1964) found that they might have some slight advantages over girls who matured later. Subsequent findings indicate that early maturation is initially a disadvantage for girls whose age-grade mates have not yet begun to mature, but that it later becomes an advantage when other girls begin to mature and the **precocious** girl's greater maturity becomes something to be admired (Peskin, 1973).

The effects of early and late maturation are by no means universal. The advantages and disadvantages are evident when groups are compared in terms of their average performance, adjustment, and so on. There are numerous individuals for whom the effects might be quite the opposite, or might be nonexistent. It is always dangerous to generalize from research such as this to any specific individual.

Figure 12.2 The most important changes of adolescence are those that lead to sexual maturity—the changes that define pubescence.

Table 12.1 Height and Weight at the Fiftieth Percentile for American Children

	Height (in.)		Weight (lb.)	
Age	Girl	Boy	Girl	Boy
12	59¾	59	87½	84½
12½	60¾	60	93¼	88¾
13	61¾	61	99	93
13½	62½	62½	103¾	100¼
14	62¾	64	108½	107½
14½	63	65	111	114
15	63½	66	113½	120
15½	63¾	66¾	115¼	125
16	64	67¾	117	129¾
16½	64	68	118	133
17	64	68½	119	136¼
17½	64	68½	119½	137½
18	64	68½	120	139

Note: Adapted by the Health Department, Milwaukee, Wisconsin; based on data by H. C. Stuart and H. V. Meredith, prepared for use in Children's Medical Centre, Boston. Used by permission of the Milwaukee Health Department.

Precocious   Advanced; more developed than would ordinarily be expected. Early-maturing adolescents may be said to be sexually precocious. Children who are highly advanced in motor or intellectual skills are sometimes described as being precocious in a more general sense.

Social and Emotional Development

Much has been written concerning the supposed turmoil and turbulence of adolescence, a period frequently characterized (and anglicized) as one of "storm and stress" following G. Stanley Hall's (1905) more Germanic assertion that it is a time of *"sturm und drang."* The popular press, too, has done much to paint a stereotype of discontent and alienation; of rebelliousness or apathy; of communication breakdown and silence in the gap between generations. Events of the 1960s did much to confirm this stereotype and led many social prophets to predict violent youth-based strife and upheaval for the 1970s. But the 1970s did not fulfill these predictions, and we are now left with little excuse for propagating myths, or sometimes half-truths, concerning typical adolescent rebelliousness, delinquency, apathy, and abject and total degeneracy. True, there are rebellious adolescents, and delinquent and degenerate ones, too. But these are clearly as much the exception as the hard-core criminal is an exception in adult society. And although it is important to study instances of adolescent delinquency and rebellion, viewing adolescents only from that point of view is misleading at best, and entirely erroneous at worst. Nevertheless, some profound changes do occur in the social and emotional development of the child during adolescence; and, too, profound frustrations sometimes result from being an adolescent too long. Not all adolescents adjust well to these changes. Some rebel; others simply drop out in one of a variety of ways. The vast majority, however, go happily through adolescence.

Socialization   One of the profound changes that is required of adolescents concerns their changing relationships with peers and parents. Numerous studies have attempted to examine these relationships. Bowerman and Kinch (1959) interviewed a sample of 686 students from grades four to ten, asking them such questions as who understood them best; whom they most liked to do things with; whose ideas were most like theirs with respect to right and wrong. Predictably, they found a gradual shift from family to peer orientation between grades four and ten. Originally, 87.1 percent of the children had been more family-oriented; by tenth grade, only 31.6 percent were more family-oriented (Figure 12.3). The most revealing finding, however, was that this change involved "association" rather than "identification." In other words, children in later grades tend to associate more with their peers, preferring to do things with them, but they continue to identify strongly with their parents. They still consider themselves to be more like their parents than their peers in terms of values, and still prefer to be the types of adults their parents are, or the types of adults they think their parents want them to be, than the types of adults they think their friends will be. Other research has also found very high correspondence between adolescent values and parental values (for example, Reiss, 1966).

The process of socialization in late childhood and adulthood was the subject of an interesting study by Dunphy (1963). Dunphy spent slightly more than three years as a "participant observer" among youth groups in Sydney, Australia. During these years, he hung around on corners, in "milk-bars," on beaches, and at parties, and he observed the social organization of 303 adolescents. He initially identified two separate types of groups: cliques and crowds. A *clique* is a small, highly cohesive group of friends, with three to nine members. Cliques, with related interests and usually of similar ages, interact in various ways to form larger groups called *crowds*. Among the sample of 303 adolescents, there were forty-nine identifiable cliques that, in turn, formed twelve distinct crowds. Crowds, on the average, consisted of three cliques, and could easily be distinguished in terms of age: older cliques tended to form crowds separate from those of younger cliques. Furthermore, older cliques tended to include both boys and girls, whereas younger cliques were exclusively of one sex. Membership in a clique appeared to be determined primarily by similarity of interests, values, sex, and age. In other words, individuals who were most alike in obvious ways were most likely to become intense, close friends. Those few individuals who were too dramatically different from any of the cliques were simply not accepted by them. They remained

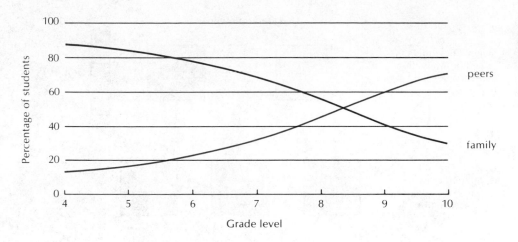

Figure 12.3 Students were asked questions like "Who understands you best?" and "Whom would you rather spend time with?" to measure family versus peer orientation in fourth- through tenth-graders. The red line indicates "peer" answers; the black line, "family" answers. (Based on data from Bowerman and Kinch, 1959.)

socially isolated. Ostracism from a group most often occurred as a result of failure to conform to group authority, or as a result of failure to achieve at the same level as other group members with respect to heterosexual activity.

The chronological progression of peer-group relationships during adolescence is of particular interest. Figure 12.4 diagrams this progression. Note that early adolescence is marked by the absence of crowds or heterosexual cliques. Boys and girls interact in small exclusive groups of "buddies" or "best pals." Later a number of these cliques may be brought together by virtue of similar interests, often related to athletic or social activity. Dunphy notes that crowds serve different purposes than cliques. Whereas the primary activity in clique gatherings is conversation, crowds exist to permit more organized social activity such as playing or dancing. Eventually some of the upper-status members of these crowds (made up of single-sex cliques, but containing both sexes) begin to interact with one another, forming new, heterosexual cliques. Thus, the initially single-sex clique has given way to heterosexual cliques through the formation of crowds. In turn, these heterosexual cliques now interact in crowds which will eventually disintegrate as heterosexual couples pair off.

Identity and Self-Esteem In part through interaction with peers, and in part through interaction with parents, teachers, and others, adolescents develop notions of self—notions of *me*. There is nothing more personal or more absorbing in our lives than our personal *me*'s. As James (1890) noted: "No mind can take the same interest in his neighbor's *me* as in his own" (p. 289).

The self is, in effect, an abstraction. It is, according to G. H. Mead (1934), the conglomerate of notions that arise from our observations of how other people react to us. That is, we decide whether our selves are good or bad, strong or weak, serious or whimsical largely as a function of how we perceive others perceiving us. Given the tremendous biological and social changes that accompany adolescence, it is inevitable that the child will be faced anew with the task of establishing an identity (Erikson, 1968).

The importance of the self-concept is difficult to measure, but it can hardly be overestimated (Rosenberg, 1979). One aspect of self-concept that is particularly crucial is the value we place on ourselves—our **self-esteem**. In a classic study, Coopersmith (1967) examined self-esteem among eighty-five boys. In Coopersmith's words, self-esteem indicates the "extent to which the individual believes himself to be capable, significant, successful, and worthy. In short, self-esteem is a *personal* judgment of worthiness that is expressed in the attitudes the individual holds toward himself" (p. 5).

Self-esteem Our personal estimate of our own worth. Self-esteem seems to be a crucial factor in adjustment.

Coopersmith's most important findings were that individuals with higher self-esteem found it easier to make friends, were more likely to assume an active rather than a passive role in group discussions, were less likely to be highly conformist,

Figure 12.4 Dunphy's diagram of stages in peer-group development during adolescence. Cliques are small, cohesive groups of three to nine friends; crowds are much larger, consisting usually of three cliques. (From "The Social Structure of Urban Adolescent Peer Groups" by D. C. Dunphy, *Sociometry*, 1963, *26*, 230–240. Copyright 1963 by the American Sociological Association. Reprinted by permission.)

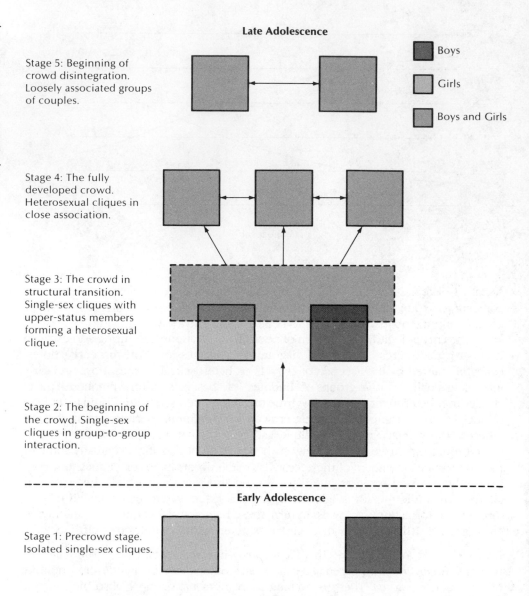

Late Adolescence

Stage 5: Beginning of crowd disintegration. Loosely associated groups of couples.

▪ Boys
▫ Girls
▪ Boys and Girls

Stage 4: The fully developed crowd. Heterosexual cliques in close association.

Stage 3: The crowd in structural transition. Single-sex cliques with upper-status members forming a heterosexual clique.

Stage 2: The beginning of the crowd. Single-sex cliques in group-to-group interaction.

Early Adolescence

Stage 1: Precrowd stage. Isolated single-sex cliques.

scored higher on measures of creativity, were less self-conscious, were less sensitive to criticism, tended to be more intelligent, appeared to be happier, and achieved better in school. It is potentially significant that parents of boys with high self-esteem tended themselves to have favorable self-concepts, and were more emotionally stable.

Given the correlation between self-esteem and adjustment, it would seem important to determine whether there is a *causal* relationship between the two. Does high self-esteem lead to success and happiness? Or do success and happiness lead to high self-esteem?

Delinquency   Self-esteem also appears to be related to delinquency. Ahlstrom and Havighurst (1971) found that delinquents typically think less well of themselves than do nondelinquents.

Delinquency is a legal rather than a scientific category. A delinquent is a juvenile who has been apprehended and convicted of some criminal offense. Obviously, the precise meaning of this definition varies from one jurisdiction to another and is related to legal rather than moral prescripts. Defined in this manner, however, surveys of its incidence, based on police and other legal records, are quite accurate. One such survey (Ball et al., 1964), involving 25,000 boys and girls in Kentucky, found the incidence of delinquency to be 2 percent for boys and 0.5 percent for girls. Other surveys, based on interviews designed to discover whether subjects had broken laws rather than whether they had been arrested and convicted, have typically found a much higher incidence of delinquency. This is partly because many crimes are never reported (Vaz & Lodhi, 1979). Short and Nye (1957–1958), by using interview techniques, found that more than 80 percent of all individuals in their sample had broken some law at least once.

A number of factors appear to be related to delinquency. Sex is clearly implicated, with far more boys than girls being classified delinquent. Traditionally, delinquent boys have been involved in the more aggressive transgressions and girls in the more passive, a large number in prostitution or sex-related offenses and in *statute* offenses (defined by age). Recent years have seen two major changes: drug-related offenses have increased astronomically, and girls have been more involved in such aggressive activities as breaking and entering and car theft (Vaz & Lodhi, 1979).

Social class is related to delinquency, with the lower classes significantly over-represented. This consistent finding is confounded, however, by the probability that law-enforcement agencies deal differently with lower-class and minority-group offenders than they do with the more affluent, dominant, White Anglo-Saxon Protestant majority (Chambliss, 1974).

The influence of peer groups is also significant in delinquent behavior and has been extensively studied, particularly as it is reflected in the behavior of gang members. There is little doubt not only that gang leaders serve as models of delinquent behavior, but that gang members do much to reinforce this behavior among their members (Bloch & Neiderhoffer, 1958; D. S. Cartwright et al., 1975). Delinquent peer groups are perhaps most evident in juvenile correctional institutions and detention centers. Not surprisingly, some 60 percent of all admissions to these institutions are readmissions.

Fathers, too, play a role with respect to delinquency. Research suggests that fathers of delinquent boys tend to be more **authoritarian**, more punitive, more prone to alcoholism, more rejecting, and more likely to have engaged in delinquent behavior. Boys and girls from fatherless homes are more likely to be delinquent (A. S. Friedman, 1969; Herzog & Sudia, 1970).

None of the factors that are related to delinquency should be interpreted as being its *causes*. The nature of the research does not warrant causal inferences. There is, for example, a definite and obvious correlation between age and delinquency. Clearly, it would be unreasonable to suggest that age causes delinquency. In the same way, it cannot be argued that social-class variables cause delinquency any more than do sex, father characteristics, peer groups, or wayward grandmothers. Although the data may be suggestive, they are by no means conclusive (Figure 12.5).

Authoritarian An adjective descriptive of people who consistently exhibit the need to dominate. Such individuals are frequently aggressive, imperious, intolerant, and demanding.

Adolescent Sexuality

Our sexual drives are related to hormonal changes that occur at the onset of adolescence. Among other things, these hormonal changes manifest themselves in more or less urgent desires to achieve sexual release. Not surprisingly, therefore, sexual behavior and relationships are a matter of concern for many adolescents. It would be misleading, however, to suggest that sexual matters are of primary concern for all, or perhaps even for most, adolescents. When Kermis, Monge, and Dusek (1975) asked 532 adolescents to rank topics in terms of which they would like to obtain more information about, sexual matters typically ranked below arts, sports, crafts, future work opportunities, and understanding other people. This, of course, might not mean that they were less interested in sex than in these other matters; it might simply mean that most of them felt they had sufficient information.

Sexual Behavior and Beliefs Researchers have experienced some difficulty in investigating the sexual beliefs and behaviors of adolescents (and adults as well). For many years, these topics were not considered suitable for scientific research. And even when they became more acceptable, prevailing attitudes toward the privacy of sexual

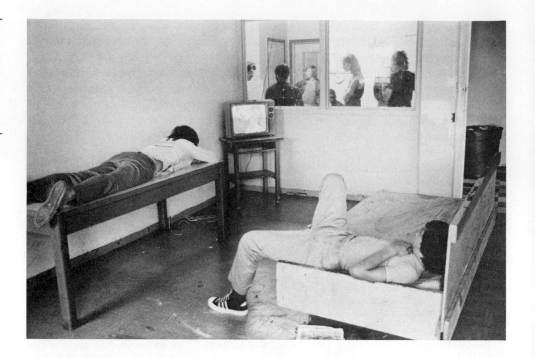

Figure 12.5 A detention center. Although a number of factors are significant correlates of delinquency—for instance, sex (male), lower socioeconomic class, and authoritarian or absentee fathers—data are neither consistent nor conclusive enough to determine any cause-and-effect relationships.

matters did much to hamper our quest for knowledge. Even in this age of greater sexual freedom, the honesty and cooperation of subjects can seldom be assured. In spite of this, several surveys of the sexual behaviors and beliefs of adolescents have resulted in the following collection of tentative "facts."

Whereas female virginity prior to marriage was common before the 1960s (approximately 75 percent of all new brides; Bell, 1966), it was much less common among males (Luckey & Nass, 1969). More recently, both male and female virginity are reportedly much rarer (perhaps 20 percent at marriage) with very little difference between the sexes (*Involvement in Developmental Psychology Today,* 1971). These findings are not meant to suggest that indiscriminate, matter-of-fact sexual relations have become commonplace. Indications are that, although there has been a distinct decline in adherence to the double standard (sex is acceptable for males but not for females), love and affection are still important in premarital sexual intercourse. J. K. Collins (1974) reports that sexual intimacy is not the typical outcome of a casual date or of a chance meeting, but is increasingly likely to occur after couples have become involved to the point of "going steady" or becoming engaged. (See Figure 12.6.) And here there appears to be a distinct difference between the beliefs of adolescents and of their parents. Contemporary adolescents are far more likely than their parents to view premarital sexual relations as being acceptable for *both* men and women providing there is affection between them. The trend appears to be away from the double standard to a single standard accepting sexual behavior provided there is affection (Dreyer, 1975).

Sexual Outlets The occasional urges for sexual release that begin to occur following the onset of adolescence vary in frequency and intensity for different individuals. These appear to be tied closely to hormonal changes, but are affected as well by a wide range of environmental stimuli. It was long thought that males were far more responsive than females to environmental stimuli and that they therefore desired orgasm more urgently and more frequently. As noted in Chapter 9, however, our best evidence suggests that there is little difference between males and females with respect to their responsiveness to erotic stimuli (Mosher, 1970; Fisher & Byrne, 1978), or with respect to the nature and intensity of their orgasms. But that there is still a difference between them in terms of actual sexual behavior is evident as well, with females typically engaging in premarital sex less frequently and with fewer partners.

Indications are that masturbation is the most frequent form of sexual outlet among adolescents, the practice being more common among males than females (Sorensen, 1973). Virtually all males have reached orgasm prior to marriage; the percentage for females is lower. Kinsey (1953) found that only 30 percent of the females in his sample had actually reached orgasm through masturbation. A later study reported a much higher percentage: 66 percent (Gagnon & Simon, 1969). And indications are that half of all adolescents who masturbate experience some guilt. Thirty-two percent feel guilty frequently; 17 percent only occasionally.

Petting to orgasm and actual intercourse provide the second most frequent form of sexual outlet among adolescents. As noted earlier, the sexual revolution of recent decades is reflected, in part, in increased sexual intimacy for both males and females. There is little evidence, however, that this intimacy is casual and primarily physical. Sexual intimacy is most likely to occur only when there is affection and some degree of commitment between partners.

There is no evidence of any notable increase in incidence of homosexual behavior among adolescents, although the phenomenon has become considerably more visible. Both Sorensen (1973) and Hunt (1974), following extensive surveys of sexual beliefs and behaviors, report that more than 80 percent of all male adolescents have not had any homosexual experience whatsoever; the corresponding figure for females is well over 90 percent. These figures are in very close agreement with the Kinsey figures obtained more than two decades earlier. In the Sorensen study, only 9 percent of all adolescents reported one or more homosexual experiences. Sorensen reports that the prevailing attitude among adolescents seems to be highly tolerant of homosexuality in spite of the fact that it is not a major concern for most of them.

Implications of Sexual Behavior   In spite of the greater permissiveness of recent decades, prevailing sexual mores and social customs still make it difficult for the adolescent to attend to what can be very powerful, biologically based sexual urges. The consequences of sexual unemployment, or of occasional and often surreptitious sexual employment, can take a variety of forms. These might include guilt, fear of peer disapproval, or fear of parental disapproval. They might also include venereal disease, some forms of which have almost reached epidemic proportions (Schroeder, 1977). This is most notably true of gonorrhea, some strains of which are highly resistant to penicillin, and of herpes (also called herpes simplex or *herpesvirus hominis*).

Another possible consequence of adolescent sexual activity is pregnancy, a condition that appears to be almost as common after the advent of the Pill and other forms of birth control as it was some decades ago. Indications are that many adolescents are misinformed or ignorant with respect to many of the facts of birth control (Apkom et al., 1979). And even of those who are well informed, a significant number continue to use no form of protection, believing that pregnancy is not something that is likely to happen to them (Herold & Goodwin, 1979). It is hardly surprising that approximately half of all high school marriages result from pregnancy or from fear of pregnancy. Howard (1971) reports that between 50 and 85 percent of all new teenage brides are pregnant when they marry. One of the unfortunate aspects of teenage pregnancy-forced marriages is that the divorce rate for these marriages is three to four times greater than it is for the general population (Landis & Landis, 1963).

Before concluding this section, it is worth noting that the majority of adolescent girls do not become pregnant; that only a small percentage marry before leaving high school; and that sexual matters are frequently far more joyful than problematic. Furthermore, sexuality is not the constant, overriding concern of most adolescents; it is only one aspect, albeit a very important one, of their development. We turn now to another important aspect of adolescent development.

Cognitive Development

Consider the following problem. A subject is presented with five test tubes, each filled with a different, unidentified substance. Certain combinations of four of these test tubes with a fifth, which is identified as potassium iodide, will yield a yellow precipitate. The problem is to discover which combination or combinations will yield the yellow precipitate. A child presented with this problem might approach it in one of two ways. The first is to predict which of the combinations might be the desired one and test this combination empirically. If it is incorrect, other combinations might be tried, each serving as a direct test of a single hypothesis. Employing this method, the subject may succeed in discovering one of the correct solutions, or perhaps even both, but will not likely be able to determine whether there are any other solutions.

A second approach is to combine the four test tubes in all possible ways, and to add the fifth to each of these combinations. Such a procedure is an exhaustive test of all possible hypotheses and yields all correct solutions, as well as all incorrect solutions (see Figure 12.7).

Some of the principal differences between thought processes at Piaget's formal level of operations and at the concrete level are implicit in children's approaches to this problem. Typically, a child at the stage of concrete operations will attack the problem in the manner first described. Every combination serves as a direct test of a single prediction. The child does not conceive of all possibilities and systematically eliminate each. In contrast, adolescents at the formal level are frequently able to consider all possible combinations and to solve the problem systematically. The first approach illustrates the concrete nature of preadolescent thought; the second reflects the hypothetical and deductive capacities of adolescent thinking. The child has moved from a limited, *concrete* logic to the more advanced and more powerful logic of propositions. A *proposition* is simply a statement that may be true or false. Each of the possibilities in the test-tube problem may be seen as a proposition (for example, "*A* plus *B* yields a yellow precipitate" may be either true or false). The proposition is hypothetical, despite the fact that it can be tested empirically. There is a fundamental difference between considering the problem in this manner and simply testing a single prediction concretely and directly.

Propositional thought is further reflected in the adolescent's ability to contemplate *ideal* states; to delve into the realm of the possible rather than simply the actual. Indeed, one of the fundamental differences between formal operations and the preceding stage, concrete operations, is that the adolescent is no longer bound to the concrete. Reasoning about hypothetical states of affairs—about ideas and concepts that do not need direct links to the concrete—is now possible. Recall that the sensorimotor

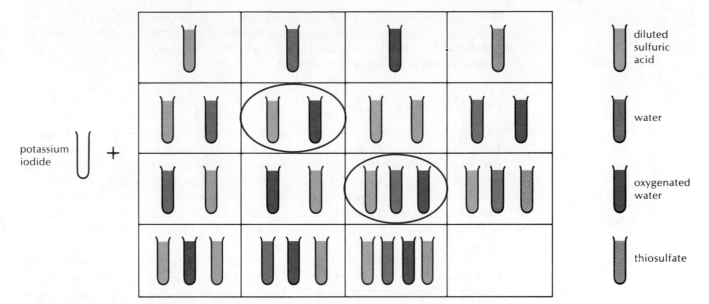

potassium
iodide

Figure 12.7 A systematic plan to test all possible combinations of the four test tubes to which the fifth can be added to discover the combination(s) yielding a yellow precipitate. (The correct solutions are circled.) At the concrete-operations level, a child will typically attack the problem haphazardly, making single hypotheses and testing them, without a master plan. Not until the level of formal operations (twelve to fifteen) can the child devise a logical, step-by-step hypothesis like this one. Piaget's theory of cognitive development has been criticized on the ground that not all adults manifest this logical level— and certainly most of us don't manifest it consistently.

child's world was a world of the here and now—a world that existed only when it was being reacted to. All stages of intellectual development prior to formal operations are concerned with developing the logic and the knowledge that permit interaction with the real world.

One of the consequences of these new mental abilities may be an intense new idealism, based in large part on the adolescent's sudden and very personal realization that things are not necessarily as they should be, that they are certainly not as they could be. Frequently, this idealism translates itself into a profound dissatisfaction with the world as it is and with those who have let it get this way. This is, in fact, one of the occasional sources of conflict between the new generation and the one that is already here—the Establishment.

Formal Operations Reexamined Recent investigations of formal thought, particularly with adults, have thrown considerable doubt on the generality of this Piagetian stage (for example, Papalia, 1972; K. H. Rubin et al., 1973). In particular, these investigations reveal that many individuals do not manifest formal thought between the ages of twelve and fifteen, as Piaget claimed, but that the transition occurs considerably later and sometimes not at all. In addition to these individual differences in age of attainment, the characteristics of formal thought are sometimes manifested in one area (on one type of problem) but not in others, so the usefulness of this concept as a general description of thinking might be considerably more limited than was anticipated. Piaget (1972) reexamined his theorizing in the light of these and related findings and conceded that we have not yet demonstrated the existence of cognitive structures (at the adult level) common to all individuals. He noted, too, that social influences, as manifested in different cultures, and individual aptitudes and interests are probably much more importantly involved in intellectual development, and specifically in the transition from childhood to adulthood, than his original theorizing foresaw.

These findings do not mean that Piagetian theorizing is irrelevant to an understanding of adolescence or adulthood, but they do indicate that we should be cautious about generalizing across cultures, as well as within cultures. As Riegel (1973) and Schaie and Gribbin (1975) suggest, other models of cognitive development, or modifications of existing models, might eventually prove more accurate and more useful in psychological studies of the life span.

Adulthood

Developmental theory and research have traditionally focused on infancy and childhood. One of the principal reasons for this lies in our sometimes explicit assumption that most significant developmental events occur prior to adulthood; that, in fact, adulthood signifies the end of positive development and the beginning of a more or less gradual decline culminating, inevitably, in death. A wealth of recent data challenges this assumption and serves, in part, to legitimize the study of adulthood and aging and to highlight its importance for understanding human behavior (see Baltes, Reese, & Lipsitt, 1980).

There are relatively few comprehensive theoretical descriptions of development beyond adolescence, although there are a number of general sequential descriptions. Among the more recent theoretical descriptions is Levinson's (1978) description of the "seasons" of a man's life (his research sample included no women). Levinson describes four broad developmental stages: childhood and adolescence (birth to age twenty-two); early adulthood (seventeen to forty-five); middle adulthood (forty to sixty-five); and late adulthood (sixty to death). Between each of these stages (the ages vary) are important periods of transition.

A second, better-known theory is Erikson's (1950, 1968). The bulk of Erikson's theorizing concerns pre-adult development; only the last three of his stages deal specifically with adulthood. Nevertheless, the entire theory is described briefly here, since parts of it that are less relevant to this chapter are nevertheless relevant to the preceding chapter.

Erikson's Developmental Theory

Whereas Piaget's major concern was with intellectual development, Erikson has dealt primarily with social development. Erikson describes the course of human development in terms of eight developmental stages, each marked by the presence of a conflict stemming from the person's need to adapt to the social environment. Resolution of each conflict results in the development of a new competency. These stages are described briefly here, and are summarized in Table 12.2.

Trust versus Mistrust   The conflict characteristic of the first year of life centers around children's basic mistrust of a world about which they know nothing, and the need to arrive at feelings of security and trust with respect to this world. Resolution of this conflict is not complete during the first stage; indeed, resolution of all conflicts described in Erikson's developmental stages continues throughout life.

The basic mistrust characteristic of infancy centers primarily around bodily functions such as eating. It is as though infants are impelled to place objects in their mouths yet, at the same time, must overcome the mistrust and fear associated with putting something new in the mouth. According to Erikson, a safe, predictable environment, engineered largely by the parents, will do much to help the child overcome this basic mistrust and eventually develop into something other than a suspicious old person.

Autonomy versus Shame and Doubt   During the second stage, children begin to realize that they are authors of their own actions and, consequently, that they are responsible for them. They actively seek to develop the autonomy that this realization implies, but are beset at the same time with doubts concerning their own behaviors, and feelings of shame at withdrawing some of the trust they had previously learned to place in their environment and in their parents. The ultimate resolution of the conflict is, as the label implies, the development of a sense of autonomy.

Table 12.2 Erikson's Developmental Phases

Psychosocial Crises	Radius of Significant Relations	Psychosocial Modalities	Psychosexual Stages	Approximate Ages
1 Trust versus mistrust	Maternal person	To get; to give in return	Oral-respiratory, sensory-kinesthetic (incorporative modes)	0–8 months
2 Autonomy versus shame and doubt	Parental persons	To hold (on); to let (go)	Anal-urethral, muscular (retentive-eliminative)	8–18 months
3 Initiative versus guilt	Basic family	To make (= going after); to "make like" (= playing)	Infantile-genital, locomotor (intrusive, inclusive)	18 mos.–6 yrs.
4 Industry versus inferiority	Neighborhood, school	To make things (= completing); to make things together	Latency	6–9 years
5 Identity and repudiation versus identity diffusion	Peer groups and outgroups; models of leadership	To be oneself (or not to be); to share being oneself	Puberty	9–11 years
6 Intimacy and solidarity versus isolation	Partners in friendship, sex, competition, cooperation	To lose and find oneself in another	Genitality	11 years—adulthood
7 Generativity versus self-absorption	Divided labor and shared household	To make be; to take care of		Adulthood
8 Integrity versus despair	"Mankind" "My Kind"	To be, through having been; to face not being		Toward the upper ages

Note: Adapted from "Identity and the Life Cycle" by Erik H. Erikson. From *Psychological Issues*, Vol. 1, No. 1. By permission of W. W. Norton & Company, Inc. Copyright © 1980 by W. W. Norton & Company, Inc. Copyright © 1959 by International Universities Press, Inc.

Initiative versus Guilt Having discovered that they are responsible for their own actions, children now face the problem of discovering who they are—in Erikson's words, of developing an identity. The development of notions of self constitute, within Erikson's theory, the single most important developmental task that life provides. The conflict of this period stems from the guilt children may feel as a result of occasional inclinations to abdicate the responsibility and initiative that are now required by their social environment, and to revert to the comfort and security of earlier modes of interacting. Resolution of this conflict, according to Erikson, is as much a function of interacting with peers and of such solitary activities as daydreaming as of identification with the parent of the same sex.

Industry versus Inferiority This phase is characterized by the child's discovery that the self is not only distinct but worthwhile, that it can do things. Children now avail themselves of all opportunities to learn. They become passionately interested in the world and in the competencies that they seek to develop. They all want to be "great" ball players, nurses, doctors, writers. They want to be good. In short, they want to be able to *do* things. At the same time, they continue to experience feelings of inferiority, never being quite certain that they are people of importance. Through continued industry, however, these feelings gradually diminish. The end result: resolution of the conflict.

BIOGRAPHY
Erik Homburger Erikson
1902–

Erik Erikson was born near Frankfurt shortly before the separation of his parents. His mother soon remarried a physician, Dr. Homburger. Young Erik attended local schools but could not decide what he would be when he grew up. Accordingly, he spent a year wandering through Europe, finally deciding that he would be an artist. After several years of art school, he obtained a job teaching art in Vienna. As fate would have it, one of the founders of the school was Freud's daughter, Anna. Like her father, Anna was a psychoanalyst. Erikson began analysis with Anna shortly after starting his teaching career, became friends with the Freud family, and, with the encouragement of Sigmund himself, entered the Vienna Psychoanalytic Society school, graduating as a psychoanalyst in 1933. Almost immediately he left for the United States, where he has remained. His academic posts have included positions at Harvard, Yale, and Berkeley. He retired from Harvard in 1970.

Identity and Repudiation versus Identity Diffusion   Erikson (1968) notes that the term *identity* has seldom been clearly defined in psychological writing. Essentially, it appears to involve notions of self. To have an identity is simply to be somebody, to have clear and stable notions of who one is. According to Erikson, the development of identity, the principal quest of the adolescent during this period, involves not so much discovering who one *is* as discovering who one *can be*. In other words, there is not a single self that the adolescent must discover; instead, the self is something one becomes. Obviously, there are a number of alternatives available to most individuals, many of these determined by the social and cultural environment. The conflict that arises during the sometimes turbulent years of adolescence stems in large part from the uncertainty adolescents experience in their quest to determine who they are (or are likely to become). The term for this uncertainty is *identity diffusion*. It is as though much of the adolescent's time is spent in trying out different identities, some of which are described by Erikson as being *negative*. These are identities that run counter to established social norms. They are illustrated in the identity of the delinquent, the rebel, or the social nonconformist. Toward the end of this period, a stable, positive identity will ordinarily become dominant, thus ending the adolescent conflict.

Intimacy and Solidarity versus Isolation   Development does not end with the onset of adulthood. The identity the adolescent has developed is, according to Erikson, insufficient for continued happy adjustment. Accordingly, young adults seek out other young adults of the opposite sex in efforts to develop a sense of shared identity. It is in the intimacy of a marriage relationship that this sense of identity is most often achieved; and it is in the isolation outside marriage that the young adult finds frustration and conflict. The competency toward which the individual now strives is adulthood; and the demonstration of that competency is effected through love and through work.

Generativity versus Self-Absorption   *Generativity* does not mean procreation so much as the establishment of the sorts of caring relationships that benefit the community and the world. The developing adult now begins to acquire a sense of responsibility in relation to family and offspring, as well as in relation to work, education, community—in short, to the entire social-cultural environment. The competing tendency is one that would move the individual toward selfish absorption in personal goals and a consequent rejection of larger responsibilities.

Integrity versus Despair   Integrity, or wholeness, is the culmination of the developmental life cycle. Like a great wheel, life has brought the person from an initial sense of trust, through six distinct phases, and finally back to the highest possible form of trust: trust in the integrity of oneself and of others. With the development of this feeling of integrity, there is no fear of death, just as with the initial development of trust, children have no fear of life. They are then on their way to developing the trust that leads them from the first developmental phase to the next, and eventually on through the cycle. A circle has neither beginning nor end.

Erikson's Theory Reexamined

Erikson's theory provides a very general framework for interpreting some of the major changes that occur during the life span; its usefulness is limited by its generality. Peck (1968) argues that the three developmental stages that span the last forty to fifty years of life are insufficiently detailed to account for other issues that become particularly important in middle age. In addition, the developmental task posed by the last of Erikson's stages is frequently taken care of very early in adulthood.

Accordingly, Peck suggests that additional developmental tasks center around the physical and intellectual changes of aging, and are determined as well by social-environmental variables. With declining physical powers, stamina, and health, individuals are faced with the task of valuing wisdom above physical powers (Figure 12.8). In Eriksonian terms, the conflict for this stage is *valuing wisdom versus valuing physical powers*.

Figure 12.8 With age, wisdom and knowledge become more important—physical accomplishments, less.

A second developmental task concerns a reassessment of sexuality: *socializing versus sexuality*. This task also relates to physical changes to the extent that sexual inclinations and sometimes ability might be affected by age. Perhaps more important, it is determined to a large extent by changes in social roles that require a redefinition of relationships between men and women. In many cases, companionship and the purely social aspects of human relationships become more valued as sexual and competitive aspects decline in importance.

A third developmental task concerns the need to develop and manifest emotional flexibility (termed *cathectic flexibility*): *cathectic flexibility versus cathectic impoverishment*. Changes in human relationships, brought about by death, separation or divorce, and changes in occupational status, frequently require that the individual realign emotional commitments. This might require considerable emotional flexibility, and adjustment might therefore be hampered by rigidity (cathectic impoverishment).

The final developmental task described by Peck is highly similar to the third, but concerns mental rather than emotional flexibility: *mental flexibility versus mental rigidity*. Unlike cathectic flexibility, which is concerned primarily with emotional reactions to human relationships, *mental flexibility* refers to the individual's ability to continue to profit from experience rather than relying solely on past experience, past judgments, and past beliefs. Mentally flexible individuals are those who continue to find themselves capable of changing their beliefs, attitudes, and opinions during middle age.

These four developmental stages are thought to be most descriptive of middle age. Peck suggests that a number of additional conflicts present themselves in old age, many of these having to do with changing work roles (retirement), problems of health, and impending death. Accordingly, it becomes necessary for individuals to redefine their worth in terms of themselves rather than in terms of their occupations and professions (*ego differentiation versus work-role preoccupation*), and to accept without fear the idea of death (*ego transcendence versus ego preoccupation*) (see Figure 12.9).

Aging Processes

The significance of theories such as Erikson's and Peck's becomes more apparent when we contemplate what is involved in the process of aging. This chapter does not pretend to cover all aspects of that process in detail but selects, instead, some of its most salient and psychologically relevant aspects.

Figure 12.9 Erikson's theory has been revised to bring problems and stages of adult development more clearly into focus. In this figure, Peck (1968) defines several additional adult development tasks during the last two stages of Erikson's scheme.

1. Trust vs. mistrust

2. Autonomy vs. shame and doubt

3. Initiative vs. guilt

4. Industry vs. inferiority

5. Identity and repudiation vs. identity diffusion

6. Intimacy and solidarity vs. isolation

7. Generativity vs. self-absorption

8. Integrity vs. despair

7. Valuing wisdom vs. valuing physical powers

8. Socializing vs. sexuality

9. Cathectic (emotional) flexibility vs. cathectic impoverishment

10. Mental flexibility vs. mental rigidity

11. Ego differentiation vs. work-role preoccupation

12. Ego transcendence vs. ego preoccupation

Physical Changes

Height is relatively invariant after the age of twenty or earlier. Weight, however, is not. As Bischof (1969) notes, after adolescence we stop growing at both ends and begin to grow in the middle. Whereas 10 percent of an adolescent's weight is fat, this figure rises to 20 percent of a middle-aged person's weight. The implications of this change for those whose self-images and self-confidence are closely related to their appearance and physical prowess might be considerable.

Other important physical changes concern health and strength, both of which tend to decline after the age of twenty-five or thirty. This, of course, is not true in all cases. Athletes, for example, sometimes evidence no marked decrements in strength (or related skills) until well after thirty. Nor are all changes in health necessarily negative. Adult susceptibility to infections such as colds and flu is generally less than that of children, although recovery time is often longer. In addition, many adults "outgrow" allergies that plague children, and also suffer fewer accidents. Heart and respiratory functions in particular tend to decline after adolescence, although the rate of decline is not the same for all organs (or functions) (Leaf, 1973).

Other physical changes of aging are manifested in loss of skin elasticity, hair-thinning and receding hairlines, changes in voice quality, relaxation of posture, slowing down of movements, and changes in motor coordination and elasticity.

Although none of these changes is, at present, preventable or reversible (Hayflick, 1975), there is considerable evidence that they can be retarded somewhat through diet and exercise.

Perceptual Changes

Sensory apparatus too undergoes gradual, although not always significant, deterioration with aging. The lens in the eye begins to age at birth, for example, making accommodation progressively more difficult, so that by the age of fifty most individuals require at least one pair of glasses (Schaie & Gribbin, 1975). Similarly, there is a gradual loss of hearing among many individuals, particularly among men. Since sensitivity to high tones seems to be most affected, hearing loss does not always present a very serious problem in day-to-day activities (Timiras, 1972). As noted in Chapter 4, smell and taste are affected, too, so that foods often taste more bland and require more spices and more salt.

Sexual Changes

The Kinsey et al. (1948, 1953) data indicated that a rather drastic reduction in sexual interest and activity begins in the thirties (for both men and women). The reliability of these data has been questioned, given the general reluctance of the aged to participate in sexual surveys. In addition, its applicability to the aged of today cannot be clearly established (Figure 12.10). Pfeiffer et al. (1972), for example, found that sex continues to play an important role at least until the age of seventy-five. For some it is important considerably longer. In general, however, there is a reduction in sexual behavior, although it is probably not as dramatic as earlier studies indicated. Health and other physical changes, coupled with the emergence of other preoccupations and interests, may account for many of these changes.

Cognitive Changes

Schaie and Gribbin (1975) review a number of studies that have looked at differences in learning ability between older and younger subjects. Although some differences have been found in favor of younger subjects when timed tasks are employed, these results have not always been replicated. There is evidence to warrant a tentative conclusion that ability to learn declines slightly, as does ability to remember (the two are, in effect, very difficult to separate). With increasing age, decrements often become more obvious, but they cannot always be attributed to a "normal" process of aging since disease is often implicated. In addition, Botwinick (1969, 1973) has found that older people are often more cautious than younger people, and that differences in performance, particularly on timed tasks, may often be attributed to this greater caution.

Creativity and productivity appear to reach their peak during adulthood. In a massive, classic study in this area, Lehman (1953) looked at the average age of maximum productivity in the sciences, the arts, athletics, and philosophy (Figure 12.11). Selected results of this study are shown in Table 12.3. Although athletic ability tends to peak by the age of thirty (with a few exceptions, like golf and bowling), general trends in our society show that at thirty the "best is yet to come" in terms of leadership, income, and creativity (or at least in the recognition these command).

Whether intelligence itself declines with age, and at what point it begins to decline, are still highly controversial questions. Cross-sectional studies have been extensively employed to investigate intellectual decline; longitudinal studies have also been used, although less often. Recall that a cross-sectional study compares individuals of different ages at one point in time, whereas a longitudinal study looks at the same individuals at different points in time. Both approaches have serious drawbacks. In particular, cross-sectional studies that have compared one age group with a different one are, in fact, comparing different age cohorts. Identical age cohorts are people who are born at approximately the same time, and who therefore have similar histories. Different age cohorts are born at different times and can have quite different histories. For example, a comparison of seventy- and thirty-year-olds in 1980 is, in effect, a comparison of people born in 1910 and 1950, respectively. Any differences observed between the two groups can as easily be a function of their different histories as of changes that *necessarily* accompany age.

Another problem that hampers research in this area concerns the instruments that are employed. As Krauss (1976) argues, it may well be that many of the tests that have been used to assess adult intelligence are totally inappropriate. Most of them were developed for use with children and adolescents, and most are designed to predict school and college success. Furthermore, many older adults have had little or no experience with some of the test forms that are frequently employed, and consequently are quite overwhelmed at the complexities of electronically scored answer sheets.

In spite of these difficulties, a number of researchers have concluded that intellectual performance declines with increasing age (Horn, 1975, 1976). In particular, intellectual abilities that are labeled *fluid* (Cattell, 1971) rather than *crystallized* have

Figure 12.10 Sexual behavior does not disappear with age, although the relative importance of companionship and socializing may increase.

Figure 12.11 Not all abilities inevitably decline with age. Some individuals, such as the artist Matisse shown here, are highly productive in their later years.

Table 12.3 Age Ranges: Peak Creativity, Leadership, and Achievement

Discipline or Area	Age Range
Physical Sciences, Mathematics, and Inventions	
Chemistry	26–30
Mathematics	30–34
Physics	30–34
Electronics	30–34
Practical inventions	30–34
Astronomy	35–39
Biological Sciences	
Psychology	30–39
Medical discoveries	35–39
Music	
Instrumental selections	25–29
Vocal solos	30–34
Symphonies	30–34
Grand opera	35–39
Writing	
Poetry	25–29
Short stories	30–34
Novels	40–44
"Best books"	40–44
Best sellers	40–44
Art	
Oil paintings	32–36
American sculpture	35–39
Modern architecture	40–44
Income	
Movie actors who are "best money-makers"	30–34
Movie actresses who are "best money-makers"	23–27
Outstanding commercial and industrial leaders	65–69
Athletics	
Professional football players	22–26
Professional prizefighters	25–26
Professional ice hockey players	26
Professional tennis players	25–29
Leading contestants at chess	29–33
Professional golfers	31–36
Breakers of world billiards records	31–36

Note: From *Age and Achievement* by Harvey C. Lehman. Copyright 1953 by the American Philosophical Society; published by Princeton University Press. Brief excerpts from pp. 324, 325, 327 reprinted by permission of Princeton University Press.

been most subject to decline. *Fluid abilities* are described as being basic to general intellectual functioning. They are relatively independent of experience or education and contribute highly to intellectual performance in many areas. Fluid abilities are most evident in inductive-deductive abilities, general reasoning, attention span, and related abilities. In contrast, *crystallized abilities* are highly influenced by experience, and increase with experience and education (mathematical or verbal skills, for example). These have traditionally shown little decline with increasing age (Horn, 1976).

It should also be pointed out that the conclusion that intelligence declines with age has sometimes been based on longitudinal studies which do not present the problem of different age cohorts. These studies are often limited, however, by unanticipated and uncontrollable subject mortality, particularly when they span a long period of time. In the study of aging, for example, many studies must be planned to go beyond the research lifetime of a single investigator or group of investigators. And many of the original subjects, for one reason or another—not the least of which is death—will have been eliminated from the final accounting. If there are any specific and systematic factors that account for subject dropout, the results of the study might be considerably less reliable than anticipated.

In view of these shortcomings, Baltes and Schaie (1974, 1976; Schaie, 1974; Schaie & Gribbin, 1975) argue that the widespread belief in intellectual decline as a function of age is largely a myth, unsubstantiated by research. Although they do not deny that decline is often observed, they claim that what the research shows most clearly is that there are large individual differences in patterns of intellectual growth and decline, that intelligence is a multidimensional grouping of abilities, and that often there are significant cohort differences in intellectual performance. Accordingly, they argue that the most fruitful lines of research in this area would not be directed toward finding invariant and genetically ordained developmental functions in adulthood, but rather toward identifying conditions that are most likely to affect intellectual growth.

The controversy cannot be resolved on the basis of existing data, particularly in view of the fact that these often have serious limitations. Although most researchers agree that some intellectual functions do decline with age, many do not accept the notion that general decline is an inevitable part of aging (Schaie & Gribbin, 1975). Furthermore, decline of abilities related to verbal meaning, reasoning, and numbers does not occur until the late sixties, and appears to be occurring later for succeeding generations (Schaie & Labouvie-Vief, 1974). As Schaie and Gribbin (1975) suggest, it may well be that, given appropriate environments (or environmental intervention), intellectual abilities can actually *increase* into old age (p. 72).

Life Span and Life Expectancy

Wines and brandies mature; apples and oranges ripen. But do they not also rot? We are perhaps more like apples than like wines, for there is one affliction from which none of us is likely to escape: death. And if it does not come earlier from other causes, it will come later from aging (see Box 12.1).

It is perhaps revealing that although two-thirds or more of us will reach the age of seventy, and that we will therefore age at least to that extent, we know very little more about aging now than was known many centuries ago (Hayflick, 1975). In fact, science has not been systematically interested in aging or dying until very recently. Like sex—perhaps even more than sex—aging and dying are shrouded in mystery. They are our great social taboos. But denying aging and death has become increasingly difficult as life expectancy has increased. The number of people over the age of sixty-five in the United States has increased from 4.1 percent of the total population in 1900 to 10.5 percent in 1975 (3 million to 22.4 million), and is continuing to increase (Figure 12.12). **Life expectancy** has almost doubled in that period (from forty-eight to seventy; yet **life span** has remained virtually unchanged throughout history (Hayflick, 1975). That is, although medicine and improved nutrition have given us an additional twenty-two years of life (on the average), there are still very few people who live to be one hundred. If we reach the age of seventy, our life expectancy is another twelve years, which is not very different from what it was a century ago. If we become terminally ill during this period, medical science can substitute for most of our functions. We can be fed intravenously, machines can breathe for us and eliminate our wastes, our hearts can be stimulated electrically or chemically. In short, we can be kept alive long past what might otherwise have been our appointed time. But in the end we succumb, having lived no longer than those who lived a long time and a long time ago. The only difference is that more of us now make it to old age.

The point of these observations is simply that life span (in contrast to life expectancy) will not be increased until the biological causes of aging are slowed or stopped (Hayflick, 1975). That they *should* be slowed or stopped (if that were possible) is highly debatable as well.

Current research and speculation on aging generally agree that biological limits to life are inherent in cellular material (Leaf, 1973; Hayflick, 1975). Tissue cultures raised *in vitro* (in the laboratory rather than in the living organism) do not multiply indefinitely, but eventually atrophy and die. Human tissue regenerates perhaps fifty times; tissue from longer-lived animals produces more generations, and that from shorter-lived animals, fewer (Hayflick, 1975). In contrast, certain defective cells, usually cancerous, appear to regenerate almost indefinitely (Leaf, 1973).

Biology has also discovered that molecules themselves are subject to an aging process. It may be that DNA molecules, the basis of all life, are also subject to aging, and that the eventual inability of cells to regenerate is a function of aged DNA material (Leaf, 1973). A related hypothesis speculates that the immune system of the body deteriorates with age, so that our ability to recognize and destroy foreign and potentially harmful cells is impaired, and that this impairment is manifested in aging (Rockstein and Sussman, 1979).

In summary, we do not yet know why we do not age as gracefully and purposefully as a fine brandy. But that we are more like beer, which does not age at all well, makes biological sense. Most animals do not live many years after they become sexually productive and have ensured the continuity of their genetic material. Given that our offspring are helpless for so long, it is reasonable that we should live long enough to

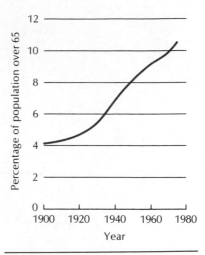

Figure 12.12 A changing society. In 1900, only 4.1 percent of the population were over sixty-five; by 1975, 10.5 percent were—and thanks to modern medicine and the declining birth rate, the percentage is still climbing. No wonder society and psychologists are becoming more conscious of the aging process. (Based on U.S. Bureau of the Census data cited in *Information Please Almanac Atlas and Yearbook,* 31st ed., Simon and Schuster, 1977.)

Life expectancy The expected duration of human life.

Life span The total length of an individual life, as opposed to statistical predictions of its average length.

ensure that most of them have a reasonable chance of continuing our genetic material. But that we should live much longer than that would make considerably less sense (biologically speaking, of course).

Death

As we have seen—and as we presumably knew all along, although most of us spend relatively little time in its contemplation—death must eventually come. How will we react? And what do we know of death?

We have long assumed that children know nothing of death—that they do not understand its finality (Kastenbaum & Costa, 1977)—but that we adults do know and understand. There is considerable indirect evidence, however, that we often prefer not to think of death, either in scientific or in personal terms. The "death-awareness" movement is a recent newcomer to psychological concerns, judging from the scarcity of writing and research on that topic until just recently.

Kübler-Ross (1969, 1974) stands out as one of the most recognized writers in this field. Her major concerns have been the needs of those who are dying and those

---

Ripening without Rotting

In most parts of the world only 2 or 3 people out of every 100,000 live to be 100; 1 in 1 million reach 105; and only 1 in 40 million live to be 110 (Hayflick, 1975). Occasionally, however, the popular press tantalizes us with visions of healthy old people, sometimes 120 or more years of age, living happily clustered in some remote, exotic, dreamlike, and certainly very faraway place. Three such groups of people have received the greatest amount of attention: the Vilcabambans in Ecuador, the Hunzukuts in the Karakoram Range of Kashmir, and the Russians in parts of the Caucasus of the Georgian Republic, U.S.S.R. Scientists have visited each of these parts of the world, interviewed the inhabitants, and attempted to determine what they might have in common (Leaf, 1973).

The Vilcabambans live in primitive circumstances far removed from the sanitary conditions of our own lives. Their average caloric intake per day is 1,200 for each adult, with very little animal fat or protein. Pigs and chickens share their modest mud huts, situated along the banks of a river in which they only rarely bathe (some hadn't had a bath for ten years). Infant mortality is high, but so is longevity. Indeed, had there been 100,000 villagers, 1,100 of them would have been over 100 (compared with 2 or 3 in the United States).

Among their more interesting and potentially significant habits are those of smoking between forty and sixty cigarettes per day, and imbibing an unspecified amount of a potent local rum. Is that why they live so long? Why else might they live so long?

More pertinent, do they live so long? Leaf (1973) reports that ages were verified by reference to birth certificates. Hayflick (1975) reports that birth certificates were not always in existence, and those that were found proved highly unreliable. In addition, a gerontologist (aging specialist) who revisited the Vilcabambans five years later interviewed a number of villagers who now claimed to be seven to ten years older than they had been when interviewed five years previously.

The Hunzukuts and the Georgians provide data that are no less unreliable. Identity cards came into use in Russia in 1932 and were,

at that time, based solely on verbal reports, totally unsubstantiated by any documentation. The Hunzukuts are illiterate and have no written language. As Hayflick (1975) says, "they cannot even point to falsified birth records" (p. 37).

Rum and cigarettes may not be the answer after all.

The gentleman shown in this photograph is an octogenarian. It is his wedding.

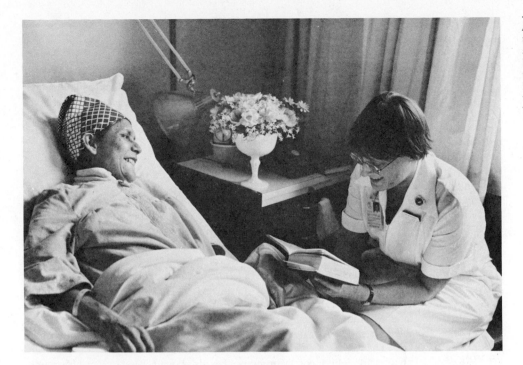

Figure 12.13 Kübler-Ross believes that terminally ill patients pass through five stages of awareness of death. She has been criticized, though, on the ground that different individuals may react to knowledge of their impending death in very different ways.

they leave behind. She describes five stages through which a terminally ill patient progresses after having been informed of the illness (Figure 12.13). First there is often a *denial* of the immediate reality: the patient does not believe that the end might be near. This is followed by *anger*—"Why me?"—and then by a *bargaining* stage, where patients may look after unfinished business with God or affairs of life, promising to do these well and religiously in exchange for life or less suffering. The fourth stage is that of *depression,* where the patient would prefer not to see anyone—to be left alone to grieve. Finally, if the patient lives that long, there may be an *acceptance* of death. Kübler-Ross cautions that it is important that the patient be allowed to grieve if there is to be acceptance, and that the acceptance that is part of dying with dignity is less likely if life is prolonged artificially for too long.

Studies of death awareness in childhood reveal that children are far from being as naive as was once thought (Tallmer et al., 1974). Literature, and particularly television, have done much to demystify the finality of life. Other findings are that many adolescents and young adults *expect* to die within a few years, most from violent causes (Teahan & Kastenbaum, 1970).

In summary, we still know relatively little of the psychological impact of impending death or of the death of those close to us, except insofar as these effects are manifested in mental disorders (see Chapter 15). Although Kübler-Ross (1974) has done much to make people aware of some of the needs of the dying (she provides questions and answers such as "Should you tell a person that he or she is dying?"; "Who should tell?"; and so on), her description of stages of death has been criticized (see Kastenbaum & Costa, 1977). These criticisms deal primarily with their highly subjective nature, lack of empirical evidence of their existence, and lack of evidence that people generally progress through these stages in the order described. The stages leave little room for individual differences and lead to the disturbing possibility that friends and family might react in what would otherwise be regarded as a callous and indifferent manner, rationalizing their behavior by claiming that the patient is simply going through the "anger" or the "grief" stage. Not all go through these stages, and in this order; dying is a highly individualistic process. It is clear that considerable research needs to be done on death and the implications of dying if psychology is to contribute significantly to making our departure more pleasant (or at the very least, less unpleasant) (see Box 12.2).

Main Points

1 A continuous culture (such as ours) does not clearly demarcate the passage from one life stage to the next. Pubescence, the physical changes that signal impending sexual maturity (*puberty*), provides a vague beginning for adolescence—vague because age of pubescence varies a great deal from one individual to another.

2 Among the important physical changes of pubescence are external manifestations of sexual maturity (breasts and the first menstrual period in girls; facial hair and the capacity to ejaculate semen in boys; armpit and pubic hair in both sexes).

3 Boys who mature early appear to be at an advantage particularly with respect to athletic and social leadership; this advantage often disappears in adulthood. Early-maturing girls appear to be at less of an advantage than early-maturing boys, but may be at more of an advantage later.

4 The stereotype of the adolescent as a social misfit, and as rebellious, nonconformist, irresponsible, and worse, does not fit the majority of adolescents. Nevertheless, adolescence is for most a time of stress and strain due to the profound changes undergone.

5 One of the major changes of adolescence involves the increasing importance of peer group and a gradual movement from same-sexed peer groups to heterosexual groups and finally to boy-girl pairs associated in loosely knit larger groups.

6 Self-esteem, a personal judgment of worthiness, has been found to correlate with success in both achievement and social roles. Delinquents typically have lower self-esteem than nondelinquents.

7 More boys than girls are delinquent. Delinquency has also been related to social class, peer group, and authoritarian fathers.

8 The trend in premarital sexual intercourse seems to be away from the double standard to a single standard accepting sexual behavior provided there is affection.

BOX 12.2

Life after Life

Does the life span end with death? Or is there more? Elizabeth Kübler-Ross, Raymond Moody, and Michael Sabom insist that there is. "I know beyond a shadow of a doubt that there is life after death," states Kübler-Ross (*McCall's,* 1976). Raymond Moody, a psychiatrist, says much the same thing in his book *Life after Life* (1976), as does Michael Sabom (1982a, 1982b). And the stories that these *independent* researchers tell are remarkably similar. They are based on reports of individuals who have come very close to dying without actually doing so, or who, in some cases, have been pronounced clinically dead but have then been resuscitated. In addition, they are corroborated by hundreds of anecdotal reports. Moody was initially struck by the fact that individuals who have been very near death all report highly similar experiences; and the stories told to Kübler-Ross and Sabom are no different. What is life after life?

In fact, we know little of it, since those who tell the stories are not dead. But the generalized story of "almost" dying may be abbreviated as follows:

There is initially a buzzing, ringing, or roaring noise—not out there, but inside the head. At times, the noise may be more musical. Shortly, the individuals feel themselves being transported rapidly through a long dark tunnel. At this point, they sense a separation from their physical bodies, but later lack the words to describe exactly what body they are in. (Moody speaks here of a "spiritual body.") As they progress through the tunnel, individuals are aware of dying and may see themselves looking down at their bodies. They may also sense the anguish of those they are leaving, and may

witness attempts to revive them. They find themselves in a state of intense emotional upheaval, resisting death. As they come through the long tunnel, they glimpse the "spirits" of friends and relatives who have previously died—and sometimes of strangers as well. A light then appears, dimly at first, but rapidly getting brighter, until they realize that this light is a real person—a "loving spirit" toward which they are irresistibly drawn. In response to an unspoken question, the dying evaluate their lives, particularly in terms of how well they have loved and learned. At this point, they find themselves approaching a dark barrier—a barrier that perhaps represents the boundary between life and death—the point of no return.

Kübler-Ross, Moody, and Sabom have spoken only with those who have stopped on this side of the boundary—who have returned from near death. These individuals typically bring back with them a sense of the importance of love and of knowledge, an absence of the fear of dying, and a conviction that there is life after life. And well there might be. But, as Siegel (1980) cautions, the evidence presented by Moody, Kübler-Ross, and Sabom can just as easily be explained in terms of hallucinatory activity of the brain.

Indeed, as far back as 1892, a man by the name of Heim (translated 1972) described "near-death" experiences highly similar to those reported in current life-after-life literature. He called this phenomenon depersonalization, and described it as a type of disorder whose symptoms included peculiar hallucinations at the time of death. The purpose of these hallucinations seemed to be one of reassuring the victim, and making dying acceptable. Noyes and Kletti's (1976) investigation of a number of near-death experiences has led them to corroborate Heim's initial descriptions, and to agree with him that a number of individuals, faced with death and unable to do anything about it, can "depersonalize" (or, in Siegel's term, "hallucinate")—that is, they can remove themselves from the experience and "face life's end with serenity, even acceptance" (p. 27).

9 Masturbation is probably the most common sexual outlet for adolescents. Those who engage in intercourse risk guilt, parental or peer disapproval, venereal disease, and pregnancy. About half of all high school marriages result from pregnancy or fear of pregnancy.

10 Cognitive development during adolescence is characterized by the transition from concrete operations to formal operations. There is often an accompanying idealism that translates itself into a dissatisfaction with the world as it is, one of the sources of the generation gap.

11 Erikson's comprehensive theory of development identifies eight phases in the life cycle of the individual. During each phase a conflict must be resolved in order for the individual to go on to the next phase. Only the last three stages in Erikson's scheme deal specifically with adulthood: intimacy versus isolation, generativity versus self-absorption, and integrity versus despair.

12 Peck suggests that a number of important developmental tasks center around the intellectual and physical changes of aging. These include the task of valuing wisdom above physical powers, as physical strength declines; a reassessment of sexuality where social aspects of relationships become more important than sexual and competitive aspects; increasing demands on emotional flexibility as death, separation, divorce, and other changes force emotional realignments; and a need to be mentally flexible and open in the face of changing social conditions, rather than relying exclusively on past experience.

13 Aging manifests itself in physical changes such as decreased health and strength, in perceptual changes such as hearing loss, in sexual changes such as reduction in activity and interest, and in cognitive changes. Nonetheless, creativity and productivity appear to reach their peak during adulthood, and intelligence has not been proven to decline with age.

14 Life span is the total length of an individual's life; life expectancy is how long an individual is expected to live given knowledge of how long other individuals of the same sex typically live. Life expectancy has increased considerably over the last several centuries; life span of the human species does not appear to have changed, perhaps because aging is largely a biological process that we have not yet been able to arrest.

15 Studies of death and dying have led some researchers to suggest that individuals who are dying may progress through a number of stages. Kübler-Ross describes five such stages: denial, anger, bargaining, depression, and finally acceptance. Not all individuals—perhaps not even most—go through all of these stages, nor in the prescribed order.

Further Readings

Adolescent development is covered in more detail in a number of adolescent psychology textbooks, among which is the following:

Lefrancois, G. R. *Adolescents* (2nd ed.). Belmont, Calif.: Wadsworth, 1981.

A book on adolescent sexuality that is geared toward answering important questions regarding adolescent sexual behavior, contraception, abortion, venereal disease, and so on, is:

Gordon, S., Scales, P., and Everly, K. *The sexual adolescent: Communicating with teenagers about sex* (2nd ed.). North Scituate, Mass.: Duxbury Press, 1979.

In her highly readable and high provocative book, Margaret Mead examines the generation gap:

Mead, M. *Culture and commitment: The new relationships between the generations in the 1970s* (rev. ed.). New York: Columbia University Press, 1978.

The following two references are valuable sources of information on adulthood. Levinson presents an insightful discussion of stages in the life of the North American male. Kalish presents a clear analysis of aging and of the problems of research on aging.

Levinson, D. J. *The seasons of a man's life.* New York: Alfred A. Knopf, 1978.

Kalish, R. A. *Late adulthood: Perspectives on human development.* Monterey, Calif.: Brooks/ Cole, 1975.

The classic work on dying is:

Kübler-Ross, E. *On death and dying.* New York: Macmillan, 1969.

Those interested in life after life, see:

Moody, R. A. *Life after life.* Covington, Ga.: Mockingbird Books, 1976.

Sabom, M. B. *Recollections of death.* New York: Harper & Row, 1982.

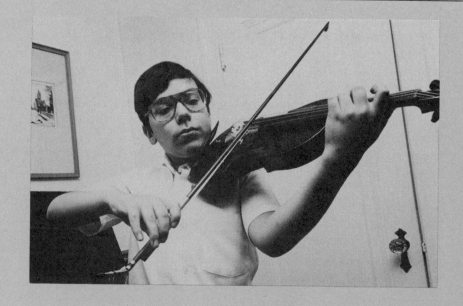

The first four parts of this book present descriptions of "average" human functioning, paying some attention to individual variations; Part Five makes a transition from "average" to "individual." It looks specifically at the characteristics that make each of us different from every other: our personalities. Tea leaves, stars, our palms, bumps on our heads, and our handwriting might provide clues for the wise and the gullible; psychology looks not in leaves or wrinkles, at skulls or stars. It looks instead to its theories, tests, ratings, and instruments. And it provides a magnificent, although still incomplete, painting. Parts of this painting are drawn in Chapters 13 and 14 in the form of discussions of normal personality and personality assessment. Chapter 15 then looks at abnormality; Chapter 16 discusses several of the hundreds of different ways of treating or preventing mental disorders.

PART FIVE

Personality and Abnormality

Descriptions of Personality

13

Ken, who should probably remain nameless, and I, who shall remain nameless, were sitting peacefully in the local tavern. We scarcely knew it was Halloween.

The tavern is in a small town populated with hard-working, sober individuals. Although they laugh as loudly as the next person when they hear a joke, and although they have a vague appreciation for some of the things that are not entirely common in their town, they are not overly given to madness or whimsy. Theirs is a hard lot, comforted periodically by the simple joys of good food, cheap whisky, and married love. Television too provides some comfort.

The tavern was perhaps a trifle more crowded than usual, but there was nothing particularly different when we first arrived. Sitting there, we could overhear snatches of farm conversation. Pigs, cows, the odd chicken, and the stupidity of land speculators—these were the topics of conversation, as they almost always are.

Until the new people arrived. They came in droves from scattered parties. Men dressed as women, hairy legs bared to the October winds, their wives' borrowed brassieres overfull with balloons and rags; rouge and lipstick heavy; wigs too tight; mincing and prancing in primitive caricature of seductive females. With them, their wives, only one dressed as a man, grotesque in overalls too large, boots too big, whiskers too polished. The others, a Mata Hari; a Jill, her Jack in tow; a rabbit, long ears flopping; an Indian; assorted queens and princesses.

They descended on the sober tavern like celebrants plucked by whimsy from history's great Saturnalias, Bacchanalias, Mardi Gras, and Bingo Bouts. They whooped and shrieked, hollered and laughed. One of the men, dressed as a rather unattractive middle-aged woman, danced madly with a barmaid, spilling her tray of drinks amid loud applause from his group.

Then Jill spotted Ken. And despite the fact that Jack was always at her elbow, smiling to be sure, she streaked to our quiet table.

Figure 13.1 What is personality? The term, rooted in the Latin word *personae* (the role masks worn by Roman actors), refers to the way people see us—which in turn has a great deal to do with the way we see ourselves.

"I like your hair," she announced brightly, displaying a certain dullness of observation or perhaps simply a slight lack of taste. "Come to a party with us."

"I'm with my friend," he excused himself, pointing vaguely in my direction, but eyeing Jack all the time.

"Bring him," Jack condescended, convincing Ken immediately.

It was not your ordinary small-town middle-class party. The house, owned by a sheik, was bathed in black light. All the furniture had been removed, although no one seemed quite sure where to or why; there were bottles, cups, and glasses everywhere; and people. Strange people doing very strange things. Things so strange that they cannot be described in a respectable book of this nature.

"You look shocked," Jill said. "We're just ordinary people. Tomorrow we'll be just like we were yesterday. But tonight. . . ."

I was less shocked than bewildered. I knew they were ordinary people, having met many of them before. What I hadn't known was that they were also extraordinary people—that given the right circumstances, their entire manifested personalities changed. These ordinary people do not make the study of human personality any simpler.

Personality

The language of smells is incomplete and imprecise, as you may recall from Chapter 4; the language of emotions is vast, but also touched by imprecision; the language that describes human personality is even more abundant, and no less confusing for all that. People can be shrewd or simple, courageous or cowardly, assertive or accepting; they can be forthright, bright, quick, stable, emotional, creative, or any of their opposites; they can behave with fortitude, speak with candor, play with abandon, or approach with caution. These nouns and adjectives are just a few of more than 17,000 words that may be used to describe personality (G. W. Allport & Odbert, 1936); can we also define it?

A Definition

More than forty-five years ago, G. W. Allport (1937) was able to find no fewer than fifty distinct definitions for *personality*. The oldest is perhaps the most interesting. It goes back to the very roots of the term, a Latin word, *personae,* which referred to the masks worn by Roman actors. Using these masks, a single actor with good voice control could play many different roles in a single play. A persona was, in a very literal sense, a means of changing one's personality, a way of becoming somebody else (Figure 13.1). And in one sense we all make use of **personae** (masks or roles). That is, we appear to be different people in different situations (Figure 13.2). But are we really different? Does our *self* change? And is *self* synonymous with *personality?* These terms have been a source of some confusion in the literature, although they need not be. The self is essentially the person viewed from inside. My self is me as I see myself. Personality is the self, too, but from a different view; it is the self as viewed from the outside. In other words, it includes those aspects of my self that I present to the world. The correspondence between the two may be very high (as in an "open" person) or quite low. Presumably, the more closely our personae resemble our true selves, the more similar will be our selves and our personalities.

Tournier (1957) makes a useful distinction among the person, the personality, and the personage. He uses the term *personage* as others have used the term *persona* (Goffman, 1959, for example), to signify the roles we might adopt in different situations. The *person* is the organism complete with all that the term denotes: will, reason, emotion, physiology, and so on. *Personality,* according to Tournier, is something of a compromise between what the person actually is and the personage. This position assumes that each of us is a unique individual—that the structure of our personality is very much our own—but that each of us behaves in different ways, these different

Personae (singular persona) The masks we choose to show the world; the different roles we adopt in different situations.

Figure 13.2 Manifestations of personality are highly influenced by context. That is, we behave differently in different situations. Does that mean that our personalities are different?

behaviors not always reflecting what we are. The psychologist who evaluates personality strives to acquire a clear notion of what the person is, but is blocked by masks. Put another way, the view the psychologist obtains of the person through the personage is what we have chosen to call personality.

The confusion between the "real" self and its outward appearance is compounded by the fact that we cannot easily separate ourselves from our actions. Thus, although we assume that we (our selves) are the authors of our actions, we must nevertheless admit that our behaviors are subject to a variety of influences over which we have no control. Actually, research has shown that, although we sometimes behave very differently in different circumstances (Mischel, 1968), there is some consistency to normal behavior (Block, 1971). Only in the case of severe mental disturbance, frequently referred to as personality disorders, does behavior become random and unpredictable.

The task of the psychologist, then, is to identify and measure the factors that determine consistency in behavior. For example, having observed that an individual is *typically* assertive, outgoing, and aggressive in a variety of situations, it becomes reasonable to infer that this person is *basically* assertive, outgoing, and aggressive— that these are reliable and stable personality traits (characteristics) for that individual. In a more practical sense, then, **personality** can be defined as the stable characteristics of a person, including abilities, talents, habits, preferences, weaknesses, moral attributes, and a number of other important qualities that vary from one person to another. Most measures of personality are concerned with specific manifestations of qualities that are important in social interaction.

Personality The set of characteristics that we typically manifest in our interactions with others. Psychologists usually distinguish between the self, the persona, and the personality. The personality is the glimpse others get of the self through the persona.

Types and Traits

The thousands of adjectives, nouns, and phrases that can be employed to describe people are all examples of *trait* names. More simply, a *trait* is any distinct, consistent quality in which one person can be different from another. There are physical traits (blond, big, black), behavioral traits (quick, quiet, quarrelsome), moral traits (bad,

Table 13.1 Cattell's Personality Traits

Casual	Controlled
Conservative	Experimenting
Emotional	Stable
Expedient	Conscientious
Forthright	Shrewd
Group-tied	Self-sufficient
Humble	Assertive
Less intelligent	More intelligent
Placid	Apprehensive
Practical	Imaginative
Relaxed	Tense
Reserved	Outgoing
Shy	Venturesome
Sober	Happy-go-lucky
Tough-minded	Tender-minded
Trusting	Suspicious

base, benign)—more than 17,000 possible traits. One approach to the study of personality has been to attempt to reduce the total number of possible traits to a few highly representative, useful adjectives. The most useful would be those most often displayed in human behavior, most variable from one person to another, and most distinct. Typically, all synonyms or near-synonyms are excluded from such lists, and an effort is made to pair the words as opposites. Thus, a person can be emotional or stable, humble or assertive, outgoing or withdrawn. Another way of looking at a trait is to say that it implies a prediction about behavior (Levy, 1970). In other words, to say that an individual is bold is, in fact, to predict that that person is more likely to act boldly than timidly in a given set of circumstances.

Type is a more inclusive term than trait. Whereas a trait is inferred from a tendency to behave in a given way in certain situations, a type may be seen as a grouping of related traits. It is important to note that traits and types are not the causes of behavior, but indicate, instead, certain identifiable consistencies in behavior. Thus, people do not fight *because* they are hostile; but because they fight, we describe them as hostile. And if causes can be identified, they may be as much in the situations as in the person (Mischel, 1973, 1977).

Trait Approaches   Among the best known of the trait approaches to the study of personality is that advanced by Cattell (1946), who reduced Allport and Odbert's list of 17,000 + adjectives by eliminating all synonyms, obscure and infrequent words, and apparently irrelevant terms. After extensive analysis of individuals who had been rated by close friends employing Cattell's adjectives, he further reduced the list to sixteen pairs of traits, presented in Table 13.1. Cattell identified these traits using popular adjectives that could be used to describe people in meaningful ways. Note that these traits are arranged in pairs of opposites. Using a similar approach, Gough (1954) isolated ten personality traits that he felt were the most important and the most consistent; Edwards (1954) identified fifteen. There is, in fact, relatively little overlap among these three lists. Assessment methods and instruments have been developed relating to each of these lists of traits, and to many others as well. Some of these are discussed in the next chapter.

Type Approaches   Recall that a *type* is a clustering of traits. One of the oldest type approaches to the study of personality was that of the Greek philosophers, most notably Galen, who spoke of four distinct *types* of individuals. There were those who were *sanguine* (optimistic and happy); the *melancholic* (unhappy, depressed); the *choleric* (of violent temper); and the *phlegmatic* (apathetic, not easily moved to excesses of emotion) (see Figure 13.3). They accounted for each of these personalities in terms of what were then called "humors"—fluids in the body. Thus the sanguine individual had a preponderance of blood; the melancholic, of black bile; the choleric, of ordinary bile; and the phlegmatic, of phlegm. Unfortunately, science has revealed us not to be so simple.

A more generally accepted typology is the one originated by Carl Jung (1923), who proposed that great clusters of traits might be accounted for by two adjectives: **extroverted** and **introverted**. These are the two possible attitudes with which all people approach life. On the one hand, people sometimes run toward it, adventurous, bold, eager to live and to experience, concerning themselves with others, with sports, with all the external world. This is an extroverted attitude, shown by those who are fun-loving, outgoing, friendly, active. On the other hand, people sometimes turn away from the world, inward, and concern themselves more with subjective than with objective realities. This is an introverted attitude, shown by those who are timid and quiet, who avoid social interaction, who dislike adventure and physical risk. There is no evidence that introversion and extroversion are *general* personality types descriptive of individuals in all situations. That is, many people will manifest both introverted and extroverted behaviors in different situations. Jung's theory, a fascinating and complex description of human personality, is discussed under the heading of "Psychodynamic Approaches" later in this chapter.

Extroverted   An adjective which describes behaviors (or individuals) that are predominantly oriented toward the outside rather than the inside. Principal characteristics include concern with and involvement in social activity and a relative disinterest in subjective states.

Introverted   An adjective descriptive of behaviors (or persons) that turn inward. The most obvious introverted behaviors involve a disinterest in social contact, and a preoccupation with internal states.

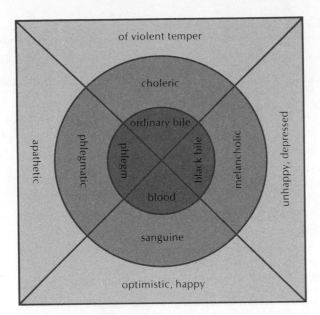

Approaches to Personality

Psychology offers a variety of theories of personality. Jung's theory and the other type and trait approaches discussed above are just a few of the approaches that seek to describe and explain personality. It is not particularly fruitful to view these as alternative explanations, among which a choice must be made. None is exclusively correct; and none is absolutely wrong. In effect, they simply represent different orientations and emphases. The various approaches are usually not completely exclusive, and the theoretical positions of each sometimes have a great deal in common.

The theories vary according to what the theorists assume to be the underlying bases of personality; the specific personality variables emphasized; the attitudes about people they reflect; and the importance they assign to the different forces that affect behavior. This chapter describes five principal approaches to personality theory: the biological (premised on the notion that personality variables are determined or highly influenced by genetic factors); the psychodynamic (which describes personality in terms of the interplay of powerful psychic forces, many of which are unconscious and based in instinct); the social (which views personality as a conglomeration of learned habits, attitudes, and predispositions); the cognitive (which looks at the contribution of intellectual processes to behavior and emotion); and the humanistic (which is concerned with the worth, dignity, and individuality of self). Before moving to each of these five principal approaches, we look briefly at the common-sense approach. These six approaches are compared in Table 13.2.

The Common-Sense Approach

It is important for each of us to have some understanding of others, of their likely and unlikely behaviors, of their probable reactions to our behaviors. Effective interaction in the social environment requires this intuitive understanding. Those unlucky individuals who are less able than others in this respect are frequently labeled "inept," "tactless," or "socially stupid." However, even those who pride themselves on their "social intelligence" tend to operate with highly general notions of what other people are like, and of what they are like themselves. Stagner (1958) provides a striking demonstration of this. An unethical salesman (experimenter) approached a number of personnel managers with a new personality test. In fact, the test was absolutely

Table 13.2 Approaches to Understanding Personality

Approach	Major Concerns	Representative Theorists
Common-sense	Why did she do that? Does he like me? What is she *really* like?	You My grandmother
Biological	Genetically determined or influenced traits and types	Sheldon Eysenck
Psychodynamic	The interplay of psychic forces Conflicts between instincts and reality Unconscious forces	Freud Jung
Social	Personality as learned habits, attitudes, predispositions	Bandura
Cognitive	Rational contributions to behavior and emotion, decision-making, attribution, cognitive control, cognitive styles	Rotter Harvey
Humanistic	The self: worth, dignity, individuality	Maslow Rogers

worthless, but managers were told that it was an excellent personality test and were invited to take it themselves, and to buy it only if they were impressed with the personality reports that would be given to them once the test was scored. After taking the test, each of sixty-eight personnel managers was presented with "personality reports" containing statements such as the following:

> *You prefer a certain amount of change and variety and become dissatisfied when hemmed in by restrictions and limitations.*

> *While you have some personality weaknesses, you are generally able to compensate for them.*

> *You have a tendency to be critical of yourself. (p. 348)*

In this study, 91 percent of the managers thought the first statement about them was "rather good" or "amazingly accurate"; 89 and 92 percent thought the same thing of the second and third statements, respectively. It is little wonder that charlatans posing as graphologists (handwriting analysts), phrenologists (those who interpret personality on the basis of head contours, bumps, and so on), astrologers (it's in the stars, the planets, and the moons), and palmists (palm readers) have sometimes not required a great deal of training in their respective endeavors.

The point of the Stagner experiment, for our purposes, is not simply that personnel managers may be gullible, but that there are certain things that most people believe about themselves. A common-sense approach to personality would accept these beliefs as descriptive of all people. In fact, however, none of the three statements given as examples is particularly revealing. They say nothing about what makes people different from one another, or even very much about how people might be alike.

Biological Approaches

Approaches to the study of human personality concerned primarily with the importance of genetic forces are referred to as biological approaches. Two such approaches are described here. The first, Sheldon's, looks at possible relationships between the body and personality; the second, Eysenck's, attributes differences in personality to inherited differences in the nervous system which manifest themselves in general personality characteristics.

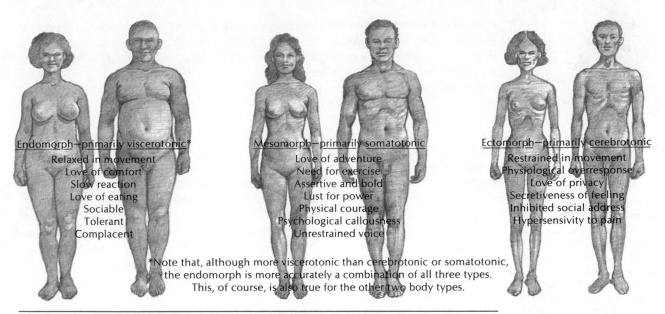

Endomorph—primarily viscerotonic*
Relaxed in movement
Love of comfort
Slow reaction
Love of eating
Sociable
Tolerant
Complacent

Mesomorph—primarily somatotonic
Love of adventure
Need for exercise
Assertive and bold
Lust for power
Physical courage
Psychological callousness
Unrestrained voice

Ectomorph—primarily cerebrotonic
Restrained in movement
Physiological overresponse
Love of privacy
Secretiveness of feeling
Inhibited social address
Hypersensivity to pain

*Note that, although more viscerotonic than cerebrotonic or somatotonic, the endomorph is more accurately a combination of all three types. This, of course, is also true for the other two body types.

Figure 13.4 Sheldon's (1936) classification of body types and personality traits, an interesting but controversial approach to personality theory that has received both support and criticism in recent years. Do your own acquaintances fit neatly into these categories?

Sheldon's Body Types

Among the first well-known systematic investigations of the relationship between biologically determined characteristics and personality traits was the monumental study of body types (somatotypes) presented by Sheldon (1936, 1954). He investigated some of the common stereotypes people have about physical appearance and personality. Is the fat person really happy and outgoing? Is the well-built person athletic and adventurous? And is the frail person intellectual and artistic?

Sheldon's approach to this problem was initially to take 2,000 photographs of people and to sort them in various ways. In the end, he arrived at a classification of three general body types: endomorph, mesomorph, and ectomorph (Figure 13.4). **Endomorphs** are the larger individuals. They are, according to Sheldon, characterized by massive viscera (internal organs), are more obese than other individuals, and are said to have *viscerotonic* temperaments. **Mesomorphs** are muscular and strong, of medium weight, and with higher specific gravities. If they fall in water, they do not float as easily as endomorphs. Their temperaments are described as *somatotonic* (concerned with the body). **Ectomorphs** are frail and slender, and are described as *cerebrotonic* (concerned with mind).

After classifying body types into categories, Sheldon and his co-workers interviewed large groups of individuals to determine the relationship between body type and personality. They found an extremely high correspondence between the two, with the principal characteristics of each being as described in Figure 13.4. Thus, Sheldon apparently confirmed that endomorphs are complacent, tolerant, concerned with eating, and highly sociable; that ectomorphs are withdrawn, secretive, and concerned with intellectual matters; and that mesomorphs are adventurous, bold, and loud. Sheldon cautioned, however, that very few individuals fall solely into one category. Although individuals tend to be more mesomorphic than ectomorphic, or more ectomorphic than mesomorphic, most are actually a combination of all three body types. Thus, it is possible to identify the predominant temperament of an individual by analyzing body type, but personality characteristics pertaining to other body types may also be present.

Sheldon's measures of body type do not involve a simple placement of subjects into one of three categories according to their appearance. The procedure requires

Endomorph One of Sheldon's somatotyping classifications; endomorphs are believed to love comfort, be relaxed and sociable, and love eating.

Mesomorph One of Sheldon's somatotyping classifications; mesomorphs are believed to love adventure, exercise, and activities that demand boldness and courage.

Ectomorph One of Sheldon's somatotyping classifications; ectomorphs are described as withdrawn and concerned with intellectual matters.

BIOGRAPHY

Hans J. Eysenck
1916–

Like Freud, Eysenck had to leave Germany with the rise of Nazism; and like him, he went from Germany to London. But whereas Freud's career was ending when he left Germany, Eysenck's was just beginning.

Eysenck enrolled at the University of London with the intention of becoming a physicist. Among his teachers was Burt, probably the most mathematically inclined psychologist of that time, and a man who profoundly influenced Eysenck's later work, with its insistence on rigor and precise quantitative techniques.

Much of Eysenck's early work dealt with topics such as hypnosis, humor, and aesthetics. He later turned to clinical psychology, not because of any profound interest, but because "one has to live and I made a living by going into psychiatry" (D. Cohen, 1977, p. 111).

After World War II, Eysenck joined the faculty of the University of London, where he has enjoyed a highly prolific career of research and writing which includes a number of popular books. He has also become identified with the IQ controversy, where his largely genetic position has earned him considerable criticism. Another controversy concerning the effectiveness of psychotherapy stems largely from some of his early research, which indicated that there was little evidence for its effectiveness.

Eysenck's research and theorizing continue (D. Cohen, 1977; R. I. Evans, 1976).

that photographs be taken from three angles: front, side, and rear. A total of seventeen measurements of diameter are then made on the photographs, principally to arrive at indexes of width relative to height. These measures are combined to yield three scores, ranging from 1 to 7, one for each body type. Scores are presented in the following order: endomorphy, mesomorphy, and ectomorphy. Thus a score of 7-1-1 indicates extreme endomorphy; 4-4-4 would be in the middle of all three.

Related Studies Later studies found a number of computational errors in Sheldon's original data (Lubin, 1950). In addition, it was revealed that the same raters had been employed to assess both body types and personality characteristics. Given what is now known about the relationship between experimenter expectations and experimental outcomes (see Chapter 1), the majority of theorists subsequently concluded that Sheldon's theory of body types was not valid. More careful replications (for example, Hood, 1963) found very low relationships between body type and personality characteristics, thus confirming the wisdom of those who had already decided the theory was invalid. For years, psychology courses presented students with Sheldon somatotyping and then informed them that what they had learned had no scientific basis. There is evidence, however, that Sheldon might not have been entirely wrong. Cortes and Gatti (1965), employing actual body measurements rather than measurements based on photographs, and using self-report methods for assessing temperament, found very substantial relationships between body type and personality.

These authors also report a number of studies that have looked at the relationship between motivation and physique. Interestingly, need for achievement is positively related with mesomorphy: mesomorphs tend to have higher measured achievement needs than do ectomorphs or endomorphs.

Why Body Build? Why should body build be related to personality characteristics such as aggressiveness, intelligence, and achievement orientation? Sheldon's argument was that temperament is constitutional (hereditary) in the same way as is body build, and that environmental influences are of minimal importance. More popular explanations have generally argued that the types of activities and interactions facilitated by body build are more directly responsible for any relationship that might be found between personality and physical characteristics. The mesomorph, whose body is better suited to robust physical activity, is naturally more likely to be athletic, and to become aggressive and assertive. The frail ectomorph, by contrast, may experience difficulty with physical activity. One of the consequences of this may be subsequent difficulty with social interaction, since much of the early learning that is important for effective socialization occurs in the physical activities of childhood. Consequently, the ectomorph turns inward, becomes withdrawn, and is more likely to develop solitary interests such as are exemplified by the arts. The endomorph may be seen as compensating for a tendency toward obesity by becoming gregarious and outgoing, by adopting a loving, good-willed, pleasure-oriented approach to life.

There is yet a third possible explanation, based on the effects of social expectations. This argument maintains that the frail person is expected to be interested in intellectual matters; the person who looks like an athlete is expected to be aggressive and active; and the larger person is expected to be friendly and relaxed. According to this explanation, the pressures of social expectations determine personality development. We tend to become what we appear to be.

An Evaluation Several important points should be made here. First, the relationship between somatotype and personality, although it has been shown to exist in a number of careful studies, is not very high. Correlations (statistical measures of relationship) are typically considerably lower than those first presented by Sheldon. What this means, in effect, is that although body build may account for some personality variables, a great deal of the variability among people must be accounted for in other ways.

A second important point, and one that is pertinent for most psychological research, is that conclusions from studies such as these apply to the average. Although there is a tendency for individuals of a given body build to have *relatively* similar personality characteristics, any given individual within a group of endomorphs might be much more like an ectomorph than many ectomorphs. Thus, generalizations derived from even a detailed knowledge of somatotyping cannot be applied to a specific individual. Generalizations derived from a superficial knowledge of somatotyping should probably not be applied even to fictitious individuals.

A final word of evaluation. In the last section, we spoke of three explanations for possible relationships between body type and personality. It is highly likely that all three of these explanations are valid in some cases. Certainly, research does not allow us to say that only one is right, or that one is wrong. In short, body type and temperament are to some extent related; this is due in part to innate genetic factors, to environmental factors relating to activities that are made most likely by the individual's physical attributes, and to the effects of social stereotypes concerning the most likely behaviors and qualities of individuals with different body constitutions.

Eysenck's Biological Theory

A second biologically based personality theory is one developed by Hans Eysenck (1947, 1967). Only a few of his most important ideas are reviewed here.

One of Eysenck's basic premises is that we are born with tendencies to behave in certain ways. In large part these tendencies determine whether we will be intelligent or stupid, introverted or extroverted, and neurotic or stable (see Figure 13.5). Eysenck has been most concerned with extroversion and **neuroticism.** He employs the terms *extroversion* and *introversion* in much the same way as did Jung. Neuroticism, discussed more fully in Chapter 15, refers to mild personality disorders most often characterized by anxiety. Analysis of numerous personality inventories (tests) has led Eysenck to the conclusion that neuroticism and extroversion are essentially independent. That is, an individual can be high on one without being high on the other, or can be high or low on both. Although the tendency to be neurotic or extroverted (or their opposites) is thought to be highly influenced by genetic factors, Eysenck does not rule out the influence of environment. What he says, essentially, is that individuals who score high on the neurotic factor have less stable types of nervous systems, and are more likely to acquire conditioned anxieties to neutral situations. This is principally because they react too strongly to situations that would evoke less intense emotional responses from individuals lower on a neuroticism scale.

Research Evidence   Much of Eysenck's experimental work has been geared toward establishing the validity of these personality dimensions and their biological basis. A fundamental assumption underlying the theory is that the nervous systems of extroverts and introverts differ, as do those of neurotics and normal people. Accordingly, he predicted that extroverts should have lower levels of cortical excitation (low arousal levels; see Chapter 9) than introverts. Pavlov had already demonstrated that conditioning is closely related to level of cortical activity, with animals whose brains were most active conditioning more rapidly than others whose brains were typically at lower levels of arousal. If, in fact, extroverts have more inhibited cortexes (lower arousal levels at resting states), they should condition more slowly than introverts. This prediction has been borne out in research (Eysenck, 1967; Hebron, 1966).

Other indirect tests of Eysenck's theorizing may be derived from studies of personality disorders. Individuals high on the neuroticism scale who are also high on introversion (hence high on conditionability) are more likely to develop personality disorders characterized by withdrawn behavior, and private fears and anxieties. Individuals high in extroversion and neuroticism would be expected to manifest disturbances that are termed **hysterical** (for example, psychological paralysis of an arm). In one of his earliest studies, Eysenck (1947) found this to be largely the case among a group of 700 patients who had been independently rated by various psychiatrists.

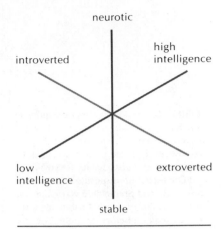

Figure 13.5 Eysenck's three main dimensions of personality: neuroticism-stability; introversion-extroversion; and high intelligence-low intelligence. Each dimension is independent of the others.

Neuroticism or **neurosis** A classification of mild mental disorder. In its most common sense, neuroticism refers to disorders characterized primarily by anxiety that can manifest itself in a variety of physiological and psychological symptoms. Although neuroticism may be associated with considerable personal distress (unhappiness), it does not involve bizarre behaviors, loss of contact with reality, or other symptoms of the more serious disorders.

Hysterical disorders A classification of mental disorders, not usually employed by contemporary psychiatrists, whose primary symptoms include loss of perceptual functioning in one sensory mode. There is no apparent physiological or neurological basis for the disorder. Thus there is hysterical blindness (individuals cannot *see* although the eyes and all related neurological systems are intact); hysterical mutism (individuals cannot speak); hysterical anesthesia (they cannot sense pain); hysterical deafness (they cannot hear); and hysterical paralysis (they cannot use one or more limbs). Waves of hysteria swept through Europe in the eighteenth century, but the disorder has virtually disappeared.

The Structure of Personality Eysenck's view of the structure of personality may be summarized as follows. Our nervous systems differ in important ways from those of people who have fundamentally different personality characteristics. Basically, we inherit greater or lesser tendencies toward introversion-extroversion, or toward neuroticism-stability, these tendencies being evident in the functioning of our nervous systems. In turn, these tendencies give rise to behavioral predispositions, labeled *traits*. The traits themselves are translated into patterns of responding that we label **habits**. Specific habits manifest themselves in our actual responses. Thus, personality is hierarchically structured.

As an illustration, consider the case of Ebenezer Goring, who customarily tells jokes to a group of strangers on a commuter train out of New York. There is a high probability that he would score near the top on an extroversion scale; hence his type is extrovert. The dimension is in fact a continuum. That is, few individuals are entirely extroverted or introverted; most fall somewhere between the two extremes, sharing characteristics of each. Ebenezer may be typed as high extrovert-low introvert; the trait he is manifesting might be labeled *sociability;* the relevant habit is entertaining strangers; and the specific behavior is simply telling this story, at this time, in this situation (Figure 13.6). Had we known beforehand the extent of Ebenezer's extroversion, we might have predicted a behavior not unlike that observed. Theorists who have been more concerned with the identification and measurement of specific traits, however, would point out that, had we been aware of the extent of his trait of sociability, the same prediction could have been made. And if we had known of his habit of telling jokes to strangers, our prediction would have been even more accurate. Consider, however, how much simpler and more economical it is to be able to classify traits or types than to classify habits. In addition, habits change; traits and types are more enduring (Block, 1971).

Psychodynamic Approaches

The psychodynamic approaches to personality have attempted to identify deep psychological forces, sometimes instinctive, sometimes unconscious, that interact with the environment to produce manifested personality (Solomon, 1974). They are referred to as *dynamic* approaches, since they emphasize the active, though mentalistic, aspects of personality. Chief among them is Sigmund Freud's psychoanalytic theory.

Freud's Psychoanalytic Theory

Among the most basic of Freudian notions is the belief that powerful *instinctual* tendencies account for human behavior and development (J. A. C. Brown, 1961; Freud, 1914; Roazen, 1975). Most important among these are the urge to survive and the urge to procreate (labeled **eros** after the Greek term meaning love). Since the urge to survive is not ordinarily thwarted by reality, it is of secondary importance. The urge to procreate, however, does meet with considerable social resistance. Hence the overriding importance of sexuality in Freud's writings (sexual urges are so important, in fact, that they warrant a separate label: **libido**).

A second important instinctual urge in the Freudian system is often described as the *death wish* (labeled **thanatos** after the Greek word meaning death), which is thought to be manifested in high-risk behaviors (such as car-racing, skydiving, and related sports) and, more importantly, in aggressive behaviors. Sexuality and aggression are thus accorded a central position in Freud's theory, since they are assumed to be the prime motivators of our behaviors. It is important to note, however, that their influence is largely unconscious (Solomon, 1974). That is, Freud believed we are not ordinarily aware that many of our behaviors have sexual or aggressive significance.

The Structure of Personality Freud's theory describes three levels of human personality. Popular literature and the mutterings of amateur psychology have made

---

Habits Learned behaviors or sequences of behaviors, usually simple, that have been repeated so frequently that they have become virtually automatic (habitual). In other words, habits are strong and consistent predispositions to behave in specific and predictable ways in given situations. For example, I habitually put my left sock on before my right. The usefulness of habits is implicit in the simple fact that I do not have to choose between my feet every morning and can get on with the more important business of buttoning my shirt.

Eros A term employed by Freud to describe the life instinct, the urge for survival and procreation.

Libido A Freudian term denoting sexual urges.

Thanatos A Freudian term denoting the death wish or death instinct.

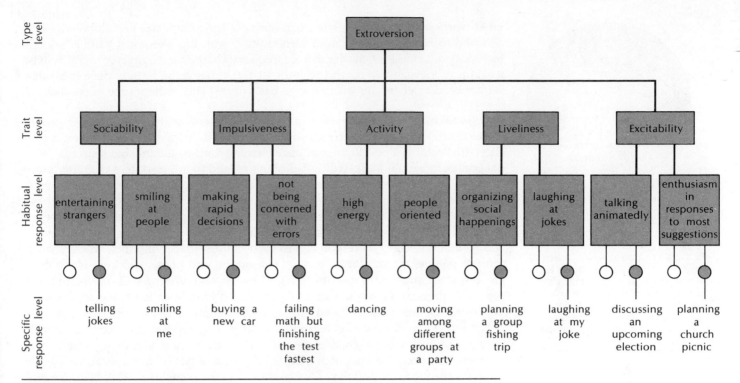

Figure 13.6 Ebenezer Goring's gregariousness is predictable to all who know him. Eysenck's hierarchical model of personality helps to explain why Ebenezer can be expected to collect a group of strangers on the 5:45 express. At the *type* level, Ebenezer is a clear extrovert. As such, he mainfests many *traits,* including sociability. Several *habitual responses* accompany the trait of sociability, one of which is entertaining strangers. Therefore, *specific responses* like telling jokes on a commuter train are predictable. (Adapted from *The Biological Basis of Personality* by H. J. Eysenck, 1967. Courtesy of Charles C Thomas, Publisher, Springfield, Illinois. Used by permission.)

you aware of them: id, ego, and superego. In a simplified sense, your **id** includes your more primitive and more basic desires; your **ego** represents your awareness of reality and of the extent to which you can satisfy the desires of your id; and your **superego** is your conscience. Thus, your id and your superego are in constant conflict, each wanting different things; your ego mediates between these warring factions (Figure 13.7). Again in a simplified sense, personality disturbances are reflections of unresolved conflicts between superego and id. Less disturbed personalities have been able to resolve conflicts through the mediation of the ego.

The human child is not born with these three levels of personality. In the beginning, the infant is all id: basic, instinctual, primitive urges; a seething bundle of reflexes, demanding satisfaction. The infant has no conscience, no notion of what is right or wrong, possible or impossible.

As a function of repeated and abrupt collisions between instinctual desires and reality, children begin to develop notions of what is possible and impossible. In short, they develop notions of reality. Hunger cannot always be satisfied immediately; gratification is more and more frequently delayed. Out of these realizations grows the ego. Now this second level of personality begins to work with the first, the id, toward the satisfaction of the child's desires. Instead of simply demanding immediate and complete satisfaction, the ego includes the realization that it is sometimes necessary and even important to delay. The ego is rational; it looks for other ways of reaching the same goals.

The third level of personality, the superego, arises out of contact with social rather than physical reality. Unlike the ego, it sets itself up in opposition to the id. Basically, it includes the ethical aspects of personality, notions of right and wrong. In

Id In Freudian theory, all the instinctual urges that humans are heir to; the level of personality that contains human motives; in short, eros and thanatos.

Ego According to Freud, the rational, reality-oriented level of human personality, which develops as the child becomes aware of what the environment makes possible and impossible.

Superego According to Freud, the level of personality that defines the moral or ethical aspects of personality.

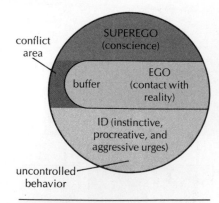

conflict area

uncontrolled behavior

Figure 13.7 The Freudian conception of the three levels of personality: id, ego, and superego. The id, consisting of instinctive urges, develops first. The ego and superego (conscience) develop later. In normal personality development, the ego acts as a buffer between the id and superego, which are in conflict with each other. Personality disorders may arise from unrestricted conflict when the ego fails to mediate successfully.

Oedipus complex A Freudian concept denoting the developmental stage (around four years) when a boy's increasing awareness of the sexual meaning of his genitals leads him to desire his mother and envy his father.

Electra complex A Freudian stage (around four years) when a girl's awareness of her genital area leads her to desire her father and to become jealous of her mother.

Identification The process of assuming the goals, ambitions, mannerisms, and other personality characteristics of another person—of *identifying* with that person.

other words, superego is conscience. It does not arise until later in childhood, and is believed to result primarily from identification with the like-sexed parent. Since it includes prescripts for behavior that are frequently based on religious or moral beliefs, it is almost inevitably in conflict with the id, the id being the level of personality that is interested solely in the satisfaction of basic urges. This is the source of conflict.

Psychosexual Stages Parallel to the development of the three levels of personality is the child's progression through what Freud labels the *psychosexual* stages. A psychosexual stage is a developmental stage characterized by identifiable sources of sexual gratification and, therefore, by behaviors related to these sources of gratification. Through the course of development, these sources of gratification change; with each major change, a new developmental phase appears. To make matters simple, these stages are labeled according to the area or activity that provides the greatest source of sexual gratification. In chronological order, they are *oral, anal, phallic, latency,* and *genital.* The ages corresponding to each of these stages and their major characteristics are summarized in Table 13.3. During the oral phase, children derive their greatest satisfaction from sucking, biting, chewing, and otherwise exercising the oral region. In the next phase, the source of gratification gradually shifts to the anal regions. This does not mean that children no longer derive any pleasure from oral areas, but rather that a new source of gratification has begun to supplant the previous source. During the phallic stage, children become more concerned with their genitals, and masturbation becomes common. It is also during this period that children allegedly progress through the troubling **Oedipus** or **Electra** complexes. The existence and importance of these complexes has sometimes been questioned. For the male child, the Oedipus complex results from his increasing, although subconscious, awareness of the significance of his genitals, and a concomitant desire to seduce his mother. The father thus becomes the child's rival, in a subconscious and perhaps symbolic sense. The child is then like King Oedipus of the Greek legend, who killed his father and married his mother. The Freudian child does not resolve his Oedipal conflict through murder, but through strong **identification** with his father and a concomitant repression of any sexual desires that might remain for his mother. As a function of this identification, he begins to develop the superego described earlier. Identification, in a Freudian sense, involves a subconscious desire to *be* somebody else. Consequently, it involves the adoption of values and beliefs, as well as of habits and mannerisms.

For the female child, the Electra complex involves desiring the father and being torn between love and hatred for the mother—love because the mother has always been loved, and hatred because she is a rival. Freud has written considerably less about the Electra complex than about the Oedipus complex. Its resolution involves identification with the mother and rejection of all carnal desires for the father.

The latency period is so called because Freud believed that there was a long period in early childhood during which the child was not very interested in any form of sexual gratification, particularly of a heterosexual nature. He felt that, during this time, children continued to identify with same-sexed parents and to associate with same-sexed peers, thereby developing and solidifying the superego. After this long period of sexual neutrality, the child enters the final psychosexual stage, becoming increasingly concerned with adult modes of sexual gratification.

Partial Summary In brief, Freud's theory attempts to account for human behavior and development by reference to basic sexual urges he assumes are implicit in our genes. Much of development can be viewed, within this framework, as a struggle to satisfy these basic urges (id) in the face of a reality (ego) that does not always make their satisfaction possible, and in the face of social and moral prescripts (superego) that do not always make their satisfaction desirable. The psychosexual stages which describe the course of human development are simply age classifications premised on the assumption, and sometimes on the observation, that modes of sexual gratification change with time.

Table 13.3 Freud's Stages of Psychosexual Development

Stage	Approximate Age	Characteristics
Oral	0–8 months	Sources of pleasure include sucking, biting, swallowing, playing with lips.
		Preoccupation with immediate gratification of impulses.
		Id is dominant.
Anal	8–18 months	Sources of sexual gratification include expelling feces and urination, as well as retaining feces.
		Id and ego.
Phallic	18 months–6 years	Child becomes concerned with genitals. Source of sexual pleasure involves manipulating genitals. Period of Oedipus or Electra complex.
		Id, ego, and superego.
Latency	6–11 years	Loss of interest in sexual gratification. Identification with like-sexed parent.
		Id, ego, superego.
Genital	11–	Concern with adult modes of sexual pleasure, barring fixations or regressions.

Normal and Abnormal Personality Freud proposed that, in a simplified sense, there are three routes the individual may take in the course of development. One is implicit in the progression of stages described in Table 13.3 and would ostensibly result in a normal personality. A second possibility is *fixation,* the cessation of development at a certain stage, sometimes because of trauma (severe emotional shock) and sometimes because of excessive sexual gratification at that stage. The third possibility is *regression,* which involves reverting to a previous development stage, again sometimes because of trauma, or perhaps because of insufficient sexual gratification at that stage. The behavior of adults who are fixated at a certain stage, or who have regressed to that stage, is related to the forms of sexual gratification characteristic of that stage. Thus **oral characters** (fixated or regressed at the oral stage) are those who chew their nails, bite their lips, smoke, chew gum, and otherwise exercise their mouths. **Anal characters** are compulsive, orderly, stingy, and perhaps aggressive—these characteristics presumably being related to the pleasure (sexual gratification) associated with the retention and expulsion of feces during the anal stage. **Phallic characters** are principally concerned with the immediate satisfaction of their sexual urges without regard for the object of their satisfaction: they are sadists and rapists (according to Freudian theory).

Defense Mechanisms Freud's theory has frequently been described as considerably more useful for understanding abnormal rather than normal personality. That this should be so is not surprising, since the theory was developed primarily as a result of Freud's attempts to help his disturbed patients. In this regard, it is worth noting that the highly restrictive cultural mores of that period, particularly on the issue of sexual freedom, probably contributed a great deal to Freud's theorizing. According to him, the root cause of much abnormal behavior lay in conflicts between the id and the superego. He believed that id impulses, primarily sexual and aggressive, do not abate with the passage of time if they are not satisfied. Thus, if the individual cannot find satisfactory ways of dealing with these basic tendencies, there is a continual build-up of tension. The ego, realizing that this tension is unhealthy, may instigate a defense reaction, which may take one of a variety of forms termed **defense mechanisms.** Defense mechanisms are unconscious distortions of reality to reduce anxiety. Chief among the defense mechanisms are repression, rationalization (also called intellectualization), displacement, reaction formation, and projection. These are described briefly here, and summarized in Table 13.4.

Oral characters Individuals who have fixated or regressed at the oral stage of development. Although the oral character may be identified by such obviously oral activities as smoking or chewing gum, Freud describes some more subtle personality characteristics. You may be optimistic, for example, because you had particularly pleasurable suckling experiences as an infant.

Anal characters Individuals with a pattern of personality traits associated with fixation at the anal stage of development or regression to that stage. Freud believed that two kinds of sexually related pleasures were associated with the anal period: those related to the expulsion of feces, and those related to their retention. He suggested that pleasures associated with anal expulsion would be associated with ambition, generosity, conceit, and suspicion; those associated with anal retention would lead to compulsiveness, orderliness, and stubbornness. Since an anal character might have resulted from both types of pleasures, all of these characteristics or any combination of them might be descriptive of that person.

Phallic characters Among many ancient peoples, the phallus, representing the penis and testes, has been an object of religious worship, often as a symbol of fertility and power. For these people, phallic worship was normal; in a Freudian sense, arrestation of development at the phallic stage or regression to that stage, manifested in the phallic character, is abnormal. According to Freud, largely because of excessive pleasures associated with masturbation during the period of phallic development, phallic characters later manifest an overwhelming preoccupation with immediate and selfish sexual satisfaction without regard for the objects of their satisfaction.

Defense mechanisms Relatively irrational, unconscious, and sometimes unhealthy methods people use to compensate for their inability to satisfy their basic drives and to overcome the anxiety accompanying this inability.

Table 13.4 Some Freudian Defense Mechanisms

Mechanism	One Possible Manifestation
Repression Unpleasant experiences are stored deep in the subconscious mind and become inaccessible to waking memory.	A soldier comes very close to death, but remembers no details of the event.
Rationalization Behavior is stripped of its emotional concomitants, and is justified on "logical" grounds.	A grown man who loves his mother too dearly treats her with extreme consideration, kindness, and devotion but convinces himself that he is motivated by duty and not by love.
Displacement A suppressed behavior is directed toward a substitute object.	A potential murderer hunts nonhuman primates.
Reaction formation Behavior is the opposite of how the individual would like to behave.	A woman loves an unobtainable man and behaves as though she dislikes him.
Projection Persons come to believe that their own undesirable feelings or inclinations are more descriptive of others than of themselves.	A claustrophobic individual who unconsciously avoids closed spaces is amazed at the number of persons who suffer from claustrophobia.

Repression A defense mechanism whereby anxiety-provoking thoughts and experiences become inaccessible to the waking mind.

Rationalization A defense mechanism whereby anxiety-provoking behavior is justified (excused) on "rational" grounds, and thus rendered less anxiety-provoking.

Displacement A Freudian defense mechanism referring to the appearance of previously suppressed behavior in a somewhat more acceptable form.

We often flatter ourselves on our ability to repress unpleasant events and feelings, claiming loudly that we "have repressed it for years." What we mean is that we have been successful in not thinking consciously about something as a result of a deliberate attempt to put it "out of our minds." Freud's use of the term is quite different. It refers to an *unconscious* process whereby events or feelings are effectively eliminated from our conscious memories in spite of ourselves. Freud believed that **repression** is an extremely powerful mechanism—so powerful, in fact, that the repression of anxiety-provoking sexual desires might, for example, occasionally lead to impotence. And repression, like other defense mechanisms, is virtually impossible to identify in our own behaviors. For that reason as well, it cannot easily be eliminated once it has been employed.

Like so many other Freudian terms, **rationalization** has become part of ordinary speech. When we speak of individuals who rationalize, we speak of those who find excuses and reasons that *justify* their feelings and behaviors. Freud employed the term in much the same way. By it, he meant the mechanism that attempts to make our behavior seem rational and nonthreatening. Common expressions of rationalization often follow simple failures that we find threatening. Thus, the individual who fails to pass an examination may rationalize the failure by believing that the questions were unfair, the markers were in error, or a splitting headache interfered with normal functioning. Note that rationalization, like other defense mechanisms, is unconscious. We do not deliberately attempt to convince ourselves that we had a splitting headache, knowing that we did not have one or that it was irrelevant. But in the end, we actually believe that a headache accounts for our failure.

Given social and cultural realities, various impulses can give rise to considerable anxiety, particularly if they are acted upon. Thus, individuals who find themselves the victim of almost overwhelming sexual urges may find an acceptable outlet for these urges, or may use **displacement** to direct the urges in directions that are more socially acceptable. Thus, powerful feelings of hostility may be expressed against other people (or things) when the object of the hostility cannot safely be aggressed upon. How many dogs (and wives? and husbands? and children?) have displaced their owners' employers and received the displaced kick?

Do people who hate children organize and operate adoption agencies? Do those whose private impulses and fantasies envision unlimited sexual freedom replete with tantalizing perversions violently crusade against pornography? Perhaps. This is not to say that all who crusade against pornography are voyeurs, masochists, rapists, and related types, or that all who operate adoption agencies have an intense dislike for children. But, according to Freudian theory, these conditions may be true for some who have successfully defended against the anxiety associated with these behaviors and feelings through the defense mechanism of **reaction formation**. In essence, this defense mechanism involves behaviors directly opposed to those that would be in accordance with the basic impulse. Since the reaction is unconscious, and the defense mechanisms assume an absolutely convincing air of reality, the individuals concerned are totally unaware of any contrary inclinations.

Reaction formation A Freudian defense mechanism whereby individuals behave in a manner opposite from their inclinations.

When feelings that give rise to anxiety are ascribed to others, the individual may be said to be using **projection**. It is not uncommon, for example, to assume that many other people feel the same way we do, so that our feelings need not cause us alarm. Claustrophobic individuals are sometimes amazed at how many people are afraid of small spaces; their feelings have been projected in an unconscious attempt to reduce anxiety. Similarly, the conviction that it is not we, but somebody else, who expressed hostility in a social encounter, illustrates projection.

Projection A Freudian defense mechanism whereby individuals attribute anxieties that are really their own to someone else.

An Evaluation Freud paints a dark and cynical picture of human nature: seething, primordial forces drive us relentlessly into conflict with social reality. From the moment of birth, our most basic "selves," our ids, react with anxiety and fear—fear that id impulses will not be satisfied, and anxiety that accompanies the fear. It is this *birth trauma* which, according to Freud, serves as the prototype of all adult anxieties: many of our patterns of responding in the face of anxiety are established at birth or soon thereafter. Indeed, our adjustment and our ability to cope realistically with anxiety are largely determined by the time we are five years old.

Many of Freud's students and followers have not accepted his position entirely. Although there is little doubt that he is among the most influential of all social thinkers and theorists, the theory itself has not been spared criticism. Chief among these criticisms are the following:

1 The theory is clearly weak from a scientific and methodological standpoint (Rothstein, 1980). Freud's data derive from a limited number of cases (and thus may not be very general), were obtained in uncontrolled and unsystematic fashion, were seldom quantified, and are subject to biased interpretation. It should be pointed out, however, that although the theory is not a *scientific* collection of rules

"David, you're denying your feelings again, aren't you?"

Drawing by Koren; © 1981 The New Yorker Magazine, Inc.

BIOGRAPHY
Sigmund Freud
1856–1939

There are volumes of information about the early life of Sigmund Freud, first of eight children born to a wool merchant and his wife in Moravia (now part of Czechoslovakia). That his body was covered with black hair at birth and that he still wet his bed at the age of two are perhaps less important than that he was the only one of eight children who was allowed to have an oil lamp in his room rather than a candle; his precocity had been noticed very early and was strongly encouraged by his family.

Freud started school a year earlier than normal. A brilliant student, he graduated with distinction and went on to study medicine at the University of Vienna. Because of his interest in a variety of fields, he took eight years to complete his medical degree.

Freud had intended to be a scientist and a researcher, but financial pressures forced him into private practice as a clinical neurologist. A year later he began a stormy courtship, which lasted four years prior to his marriage and the beginning of a family of six children.

Freud's professional career is generally divided into two periods: the first, where he founded and elaborated the principles of psychoanalytic psychology; the second, where he extended these principles to a consideration of wider social problems. By the early 1900s he had been granted international recognition and had attracted a growing number of followers.

In 1923 Freud, who habitually smoked twenty or more cigars a day, discovered he had cancer of the mouth. Over the next sixteen years he underwent thirty-three separate operations; finally his speech was almost unintelligible. But he continued to work to the end. The Nazi invasion of Austria in 1938 finally forced him to leave for England. Although his books had been confiscated and burned in Austria, he was not allowed to leave until remaining copies in Switzerland had been returned and destroyed; the Nazi regime did not favor psychoanalysis.

Freud died of cancer a year later (D. P. Schultz, 1969; Clark, 1980).

and principles, it does present a largely intuitive and in many ways brilliant description of the human condition. It is probably unfair to judge the accuracy or usefulness of that description by applying conventional scientific criteria.

2   Considerable confusion has arisen in the interpretation of Freudian theory, often as a result of his ambiguous use of terms and concepts. Solomon (1974), for example, presents a detailed analysis of the central Freudian concept of "unconscious motivation" and notes that Freud moved freely among the very different concepts of "The Unconscious," "unconscious processes," "processes which are unconscious," and "processes of which (the subject) is not conscious" (p. 193). In other words, it is never clear whether Freud intended *the unconscious* to be a particular "level" in memory, inaccessible to conscious thought; whether it included processes of a specific and identifiably different type; or whether it is defined simply in terms of whether or not the subject is aware (conscious) of the processes. Given this ambiguity, it is not surprising that not all interpretations of Freudian theory are exactly alike.

3   Many major predictions based on the theory cannot be empirically confirmed. This is not only because of problems of definition and interpretation, but primarily because the same underlying concepts can lead to opposite predictions. Consider, for example, the case of people whose aggressive impulses are directed toward their children. One Freudian prediction might be that these individuals would display some aggression when interacting with the children; another equally Freudian prediction might be that they would treat them with exaggerated kindness (reaction formation); a third plausible prediction could be that they would be aggressive toward other children or toward their cats (displacement). Since any of these behaviors could be explained by reference to the same underlying psychodynamics (unconscious motivation), the existence of the underlying construct cannot easily be established, and its usefulness is somewhat limited.

Several detailed reviews of research dealing specifically with Freudian theory have sometimes reported some scientific evidence for a limited number of predictions based on the theory. For example, Fisher and Greenberg (1977) report that Freud's description of some of the characteristics of oral and anal personality types appear valid in the sense that they form related clusters of traits (though not necessarily in terms of the origins Freud assigned to these types). Kline (1972), too, reviews a number of studies ostensibly supporting aspects of Freudian theory. In general however, a great many predictions based on Freudian theory have not stood up to scientific investigation, including his notion of dreams as a mechanism that protects sleep and reveals hidden motives; his beliefs concerning the effectiveness of insight in therapy; and his description of the importance of the Oedipal conflict and of its resolution (Fisher & Greenberg, 1977, pp. 394–395).

4   Freud's excessive emphasis on sexual and aggressive impulses as the principal determining forces in the shaping of personality has often been criticized. In this connection, a large number of his students departed significantly from his basic teachings in that they placed considerably more emphasis on social and cultural forces in personality development (for example, Erikson, discussed in Chapter 12). As noted earlier, Freud's theorizing occurred during a period of limited sexual freedom (the Victorian age)—a time when guilt and anxiety associated with sexual impulses would presumably be common. It is likely that such feelings are not nearly so prevalent today, and that sexuality is therefore not nearly so important as a possible source of mental disturbance.

In spite of these criticisms, Freud's theorizing still stands as one of the great contributions to social thought. He drew dramatic attention to the possibility that maladjustment might be the manifestation of "unconscious" forces and desires, that early childhood experiences are crucial in later development, and that sexuality might be centrally implicated in psychological functioning. In large part, he paved the way for research on human sexuality, a topic that had long been taboo. And perhaps more important than all this, he presented psychiatry with a method for treating mental disorders: **psychoanalysis**. Psychoanalytic therapy, almost inextricably linked with Freud, is treated in more detail in Chapter 16.

Freud attracted a number of students, many of whom became fervent disciples of the new psychoanalysis. These included a number of brilliant individuals who later developed their own systems, basing much of their thinking on Freudian interpretations, but departing from him in significant respects as well. Two of these psychodynamic systems are examined very briefly here: those of Alfred Adler and Carl Jung.

Adler's Individual Psychology

Adlerian psychology is considerably simpler than Freud's. Not only does it deal with a number of simpler concepts, but Adler's writings are much easier to read and understand (see Ansbacher & Ansbacher, 1973; Sperber, 1974).

The major break between Adler and Freud concerned the importance of biological drives. Whereas Freud believed that biologically based sexual and aggressive strivings were the basis of all behavior, Adler believed humans to be primarily social rather than biological. Accordingly, he placed great emphasis on the child's social environment in an effort to understand the behavior of the adult. Sexuality plays a small role in this system, and the unconscious, an even smaller one. According to Adler, we are conscious of our motives even if we might not understand their sources, and we actively direct our own lives.

Inferiority and Superiority   In Adler's theory, the force that most directly influences our behavior is a constant striving, basic to each of us, for *superiority,* by which is meant competence (*perfection* is Adler's synonym). We all have, at the very core of our existence, some powerful feelings of inferiority. And the progress we make in our lives is a function of the extent to which we strive to overcome our feelings of inferiority—in other words, to achieve superiority.

The inferiority of which Adler speaks refers to the feelings of helplessness and dependence that are a necessary part of childhood. To the extent that the child can progressively overcome helplessness and dependence, feelings of competence and superiority will result. But if the child is unsuccessful in overcoming the inferiority, an **inferiority complex** may result. This "complex" is later manifested in the individual's inability to overcome problems—in other words, in maladjustment.

Adler identified three principal causes of inferiority complexes that serve as his primary explanations for adult maladjustment: *organic inferiority, spoiling,* and *neglect.* Organic inferiority is, as the term implies, an actual physical or intellectual inferiority in the individual. Obvious examples include smallness, weakness, or lack of intelligence. Adler believed that such individuals frequently work much harder than others in efforts to compensate for their organic inferiority, and are often successful in doing so. But if the weak boy tries very hard to become a football player *and fails,* the result will likely be an inferiority complex.

Spoiling leads to an inferiority complex when it is carried to such an extreme that the child finds it unnecessary (and sometimes impossible) to develop any competence. Once removed from the protective environment of the family, such a child is overwhelmed by feelings of inferiority.

Neglect, according to Adler, communicates feelings of being unloved and unwanted and leads naturally to a sense of worthlessness—of inferiority. Neglect, like spoiling or organic inferiority, does not *necessarily* lead to an inferiority complex. The child may compensate and develop adequate feelings of superiority.

It is possible, as well, to overcompensate, to develop a *superiority complex.* Whereas the individual with an inferiority complex feels incapable and worthless and cannot deal with the problems of life, the one with a superiority complex is arrogant and conceited and carries an exaggerated opinion of personal capabilities.

The possible courses of individual development proposed by Adler's theory are illustrated in Figure 13.8.

Psychoanalysis The elaborate psychotherapeutic system developed by Freud and based on his theories of personality. Its principal techniques involve free association, analysis of dreams, and interpretation of manifestations of unconscious impulses as might be revealed, for example, in "Freudian slips." The object of psychoanalysis is to provide patients with insight into the source of their difficulties. The assumption is that insight may cure or at least alleviate the disorder.

Inferiority complex An Adlerian concept referring to a repressed (therefore unconscious) though powerful conviction of being inferior. Adler thought that the bases for inferiority complexes were laid very early in life, largely as a result of the child's inability to overcome the feelings of inferiority common to all children, and that these feelings, once repressed (once they have become complexes), become powerful dynamic forces in determining adjustment problems and mental disorder.

Figure 13.8 In contrast to Freud, Adler sees social influence rather than biological needs or drives as of prime importance in determining adult personality. The first five years are the most crucial in determining an individual's life-style. Pitfalls like spoiling, neglect, and inherent weaknesses can be overcome, but only with great effort (and the danger of *over*-overcoming them is developing a superiority complex). Notice how, in contrast to Erikson's and Peck's theories of development, the individual has "arrived" when she or he becomes a competent adult.

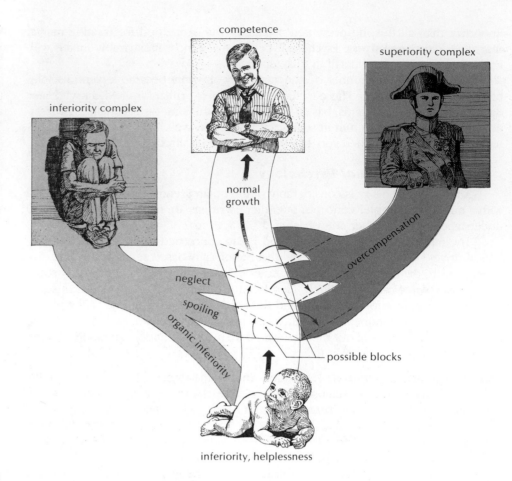

BIOGRAPHY
Alfred Adler
1870–1937

Adler was born in Vienna, the city that was home to Freud for most of his long career. His parents were wealthy. One of two boys in his family, Alfred describes his childhood as unhappy. He was sick much of the time, did not walk until the age of four, and thought himself too small and quite ugly. In addition, he despaired of ever being as good in any way as his older brother.

Alfred Adler attended the University of Vienna, becoming a physician with a specialty in ophthalmology. He set up private practice and began attending Freud's weekly sessions, where he soon became a great favorite of Sigmund's. In 1910 he was named president of the Vienna Psychoanalytic Society, but by 1911 he had become openly critical of Freud. After a presentation to the society in which he criticized Freud's emphasis on sexual motivation, he was denounced and forced to resign as president. Shortly thereafter he severed all ties with the society, formed his own group, and began to attract an increasing number of followers. He gave several lecture tours in the United States and moved there in 1935, becoming professor of medical psychology at Long Island College of Medicine. He died two years later while on a lecture tour in Aberdeen, Scotland (Nordby & Hall, 1974; D. P. Schultz, 1969).

Life-Style   A concept central to Adler's interpretation of human personality is that of **life-style**. A life-style is a characteristic way of reacting to life; it is established very early in life and determines much of our future behavior. Adler's emphasis here, unlike Freud's, was on the uniqueness of every individual. This emphasis gives Adler's system its common label, *individual psychology*.

Although each of us is beset by feelings of inferiority, and is moved by a need to overcome inferiority and achieve superiority, we all have different styles for doing so. These styles reflect our unique personalities, our habits and weaknesses, our strengths and predispositions. We begin to develop our unique styles upon our first encounters with inferiority, and by the age of five they are relatively firmly established. This does not mean that our future behavior and adjustment are irretrievably determined by the age of five, but that our major personality characteristics have already been formed.

In connection with the development of life-style, Adler paid particular attention to social-cultural variables, for it is in interaction with others that our personalities develop. Among other things, he noted that order of birth is crucial in determining personality characteristics. A first-born child sufers a major, disruptive shock when the second child is born, and this shock may be manifested later in a general cynicism, preoccupation with order, and insecurity. In contrast, last-born children frequently do not have to compete with other siblings for the attention and affection of the parents. Such children frequently develop very rapidly in an attempt to become as competent as older brothers and sisters.

Adler was careful to point out that the effects of birth order might be very different on different children. The most important point does not concern what the specific effects of being born first or last might be, but rests instead on the great importance that Adler attributed to the process of socialization. In this respect, his position is fundamentally different from Freud's.

An Evaluation   Adler's theorizing is subject to many of the same criticisms as Freud's. Many of his concepts are ambiguous and not easily amenable to scientific investigation. He has also been accused of having presented a theory that is too simple to account for the details of personality development, and of having relied too exclusively on the imprecise observations of common sense. Among his major contributions in the development of personality theories are his emphasis on the importance of social variables and his insistence on the self-determination of the individual. Adler believed strongly in the creative power that each of us has—a power that frees us from the shackles of biological forces and gives us some control over our destinies.

Jung's Analytical Theory

Carl Jung's theorizing, termed **analytical** rather than *psychoanalytical* (Jacobi, 1968; Jung, 1923) is based on a wealth of quasi-mystical and entirely fascinating speculation, only a small portion of which can be described here. His major break with Freud concerns what Jung felt to be Freud's overemphasis on sexual instincts. Unlike other neo-Freudians, who became more involved with the effects of the socialization process, Jung was principally concerned with discovering the "instinctual tendencies" that Freud had overlooked (Lundin, 1974).

The Collective Unconscious   According to Jung, personality is divided into two levels, in contrast with Freud's three levels of id, ego, and superego. The *conscious* level includes the ego, the self, and our persona—our mask. It is through our persona that others come to know our personality. The *unconscious* level of personality is composed of successive layers, the most accessible of which include our personal memories of events that have occurred in our own lives, together with some notions of self. This is termed the *personal unconscious*. Far less accessible are deeper unconscious levels, within which powerful instinctual tendencies are found. These instinctual tendencies exist in the **racial** or **collective unconscious**. They consist of memories that are species-specific, built into the brain, and that manifest themselves in **archetypes**: universal concepts that we do not recognize consciously, but that possess a magnitude of energy not unlike that ascribed to sexual urges by Freud.

Among the most common of archetypes are the *anima* and *animus,* the man/woman dichotomy that is present in each of us and that manifests itself both in our symbols and in our behaviors. The animus is male: aggressive, confident, assertive. Yet men are sometimes afraid and submissive; that is their anima. And there is a tendency in each of us, says Jung, to recognize and accept the archetype. Thus, there is an unconscious, sometimes acknowledged, but often repressed, tendency toward masculinity and femininity in all human males and females. Similarly, there is an archetype corresponding to *self.* Like so many other archetypes in the great collective unconscious, it has manifested itself in the artistic symbols of many races and generations. The *mandala,* a representation of a figure within a circle, is found in the art of so many different cultures that Jung assumed it must represent the *self* archetype (Figure 13.9). Similarly birth, rebirth, death, God, and the hero are all archetypes. Evidence of their existence in the collective unconscious is to be derived from the observation that many individuals appear to have an unconscious desire to experience and to meet with the actual representation of these concepts. Power, too, is an archetype—a concept of tremendous motivational strength. It is recognizable in many symbols as well as in behavior.

For Jung, an archetype is more than an inherited memory; it is really a powerful motive. At one level, he believed it explained why people found it easy to believe in God. God is an archetype. We have a universal, collective memory of God. At another level, the concept of archetype explains why we find it so easy to be afraid of snakes. Snakes have been a source of danger and of fear throughout much of our history; thus we have a universal, collective memory of the snake.

Personality Functioning   Jung described two fundamentally different orientations toward life. One is directed inward and is labeled *introverted;* the other is

---

Life-style   As an Adlerian term, *life-style* refers not only to individuals' characteristic ways of reacting to life, but more specifically to the methods by which people overcome feelings of inferiority. Adler employed the terms *life-style, personality,* and *character* almost synonymously.

Analytical   Pertaining to *analysis,* a logical thought process that involves separating a problem into its elements and examining its parts. To analyze is, in essence, to break down. In a highly specialized sense, analytical refers to the psychological system advanced by Jung.

Collective unconscious   (also called racial unconscious)   A Jungian term for the inherited aspects of our unconscious minds. Jung believed that the elements of the collective unconscious arose from primitive models (archetypes) reflected in concepts that appear to be nearly universal. These concepts appear among peoples who have never been in contact, and have done so throughout history. They are particularly evident in religious worship and ritual which revolves around such central themes as birth, rebirth, death, God, hero, man, and woman. All of these are, in fact, Jungian archetypes.

Archetype   The first, or original, model. For Jung, a sort of universal thought—a thought present in all our minds, throughout human history, but essentially unconscious.

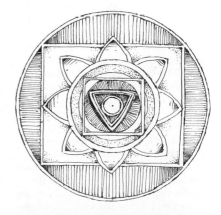

Figure 13.9   A mandala is an abstract symbol employed extensively in the meditative practices of Hinduism and Buddhism. It usually consists of intricate patterns of squares within circles, and is designed to draw the eyes toward its center, freeing the mind of other thoughts and thus facilitating meditation. The mandala is prevalent in the art of numerous widely separated cultures—an observation that led Jung to the belief that it is a universal symbol of the self.

Jung was born in a Swiss village, first of two children of a Swiss reform pastor. His mother suffered from a hysterical disorder and was away much of the time. Since his sister was eight years younger than he, he was very much alone in a profoundly religious atmosphere—eight of his uncles were also pastors. During his adolescence he is reported to have suffered severe religious turmoil, eventually deciding to become a psychiatrist after some occult experiences (sometimes reported as nothing more than a dream). He received his M.D. from the University of Basel in 1900 and went to work as a psychiatrist at the University of Zurich. Several years later he resigned to devote his time to private practice, research, and writing.

Soon thereafter he read Freud's book on dreams, began corresponding with him, and eventually established a very close friendship which was to last only six years. Largely because of Freud's efforts, Jung became the first president of the International Psychoanalytic Society. Freud apparently feared that the society would do better if it were not headed by a Jew, because of strong anti-Semitic sentiments in Vienna. Jung and Freud had traveled to the United States together to lecture the previous year, but now their friendship began to deteriorate. A year after his appointment as president of the society, Jung published a major book which advanced some significant departures from Freud's emphasis on sex. A year later, they terminated their correspondence. Jung resigned from the society and founded his own Analytical Society, and the two men never saw each other again. Jung went on to establish his system and to attract followers. By the time of his death, his collected works filled nineteen volumes and covered topics ranging from religion and social problems to ESP, astrology, art, fortune-telling, alchemy, and flying saucers (Nordby & Hall, 1974; D. P. Schultz, 1969; Brome, 1978).

directed outward and is labeled *extroverted*. As we have seen, these are the basic dimensions that Eysenck investigated and incorporated into his theory of personality.

In addition, Jung believed people can be differentiated in terms of their dominant modes of intellectual functioning. There are four of these, two rational, and two nonrational (which is quite different from irrational). *Thinking* and *feeling* are rational functions; *sensing* and *intuiting* are nonrational. Thinking is a reality-oriented process, highly rewarded and dominant in many Western societies. Feeling refers to affective responding such as liking and disliking, loving and hating. Sensing describes the perceptual processes; intuiting is an unconscious form of perception where only the final idea becomes conscious. All four of these functions are present in every individual, though not to identical degrees. Jung felt strongly that Western societies overemphasize thinking to the detriment of other functions, particularly intuiting and feeling. He maintained that individuals grow as they learn to use all functions.

A Brief Summary

Psychodynamic theories, of which there are a great variety, emphasize the interplay of conscious and unconscious forces in the shaping of personality. Most are biologically based in that they assume that the most primitive and most powerful human tendencies are inherited. Both Jung and Freud describe the translation of inherited tendencies into powerful, although often unconscious, desires that are manifested in behavior or that remain unexpressed but potent. Competing tendencies, instinctual or learned, conscious or unconscious, give rise to behaviors designed to reduce anxiety. Adler placed considerably more emphasis on the social environment than did Freud or Jung.

Social Approaches

Biological approaches to understanding personality focus on the relationship between inherited predispositions and personality; psychodynamic approaches are concerned with interactions among competing or cooperating psychic (mental) impulses; social approaches are more concerned with the role of social interaction. It should be noted, however, that although these divisions are theoretically clear and conceptually useful, most theoretical positions have elements of all approaches. This is no less true of the social approaches.

Social approaches to the study of personality are concerned more with manifestations of personality than with its causes. Where the biologically or psychoanalytically oriented theorist would search for the sources of behavior, the social theorist typically limits observation and explanation to manifested behavior. For this reason, the social approaches are frequently described as learning-theory explanations.

Among the most useful of the social approaches are those that have attempted to apply principles of learning theory to an understanding of behavior. To the extent that societies define acceptable ways of behaving, and to the extent that the behavior of individuals is somehow responsive to social pressure, it is appropriate to argue that behavior is as much a function of social context as of biological or psychodynamic forces (Mischel, 1979).

Bandura and Walters's Observational Learning

Following ideas earlier advanced by N. E. Miller and Dollard (1941), Bandura and Walters (Bandura, 1971; Bandura & Walters, 1963) have proposed a comprehensive theory of social learning based on the effects of **imitation**, or *observational learning*. Their argument is simply that a great deal of complex social learning cannot be accounted for by traditional learning theories. Learning to drive a car, for example, is not a question of classical conditioning, of trial and error, or of shaping. Psychologists would be hard-pressed to develop an effective driver-training course if they were

Figure 13.10 Imitation isn't always this obvious.

limited to only one of these approaches. A more fruitful approach is simply to *instruct* the learner in certain fundamentals, to *show* the learner the positions and purposes of various controls, to *demonstrate* their operation, and allow the learner to attempt the task with verbal and sometimes physical guidance. In effect, what has happened is that a number of **models** have been presented and imitated.

A model is not simply a person doing something which can then be imitated by a learner; it includes all the patterns for behavior that complex societies present their members. Books, verbal directions, film and cartoon characters, and a variety of other real or symbolic objects, people, or situations can serve as models. Their prevalence, in both primitive and more complex societies, is highly evident, as is their effectiveness (Figure 13.10). Western societies present a preponderance of achievement-oriented, aggressive, assertive, outgoing models for men. Not surprisingly, a great many males in these societies are aggressive, achievement-oriented, assertive, and outgoing. In contrast, the Zuni culture presents models of cooperation and selflessness, and these are the primary characteristics of its members.

It would be possible to list thousands of such examples from anthropological and cross-cultural studies, examples which indicate strongly that manifested personality characteristics are highly influenced by social context. This does not mean that theories based on the notion that there are inherited dispositions toward specific personality traits are incorrect. What it does indicate is that biological predispositions will not necessarily be dominant over social influences. A complete understanding of human personality will require that both sources of influence be taken into account.

Relevance

The importance of social-learning theories of personality is not that they contribute to the identification of personality traits or to their measurement; nor are they particularly useful for understanding the structure of personality or the biological and dynamic forces at play. But they do facilitate an understanding of the manifestation of personality. A great majority of the personality characteristics that have been identified as being most basic and most important are meaningful only in social interaction. Honesty, aggression, extroversion, sociability, dependency, and so on are all qualities of human interaction. That is, they describe typical ways of relating to social realities. Furthermore, they are not characteristics that individuals manifest regardless of their

Imitation A process whereby individuals learn new behaviors, change the direction of their behaviors, or inhibit certain behaviors as a function of the observation of models; also termed *observational learning.*

Models Patterns for behavior that can be copied by someone else, or people who provide the patterns that will be imitated. The term is not restricted to human models, but includes symbolic models such as movies, television programs, verbal and written instructions, and religious, literary, musical, or folk heroes.

immediate social context. For example, highly aggressive individuals might well display their aggressive tendencies in athletics and other physical activities where aggression is socially approved; few are likely to display aggression in the church choir or university classroom.

In summary, social approaches to personality highlight the tremendous influence of social customs, traditions, expectations, and situations on the manifestation of personality characteristics. They argue that acceptable and unacceptable social behaviors are learned. Specifically, Bandura and Walters contend that much of this learning is due to the effects of observing various kinds of models—models that are represented by rules and laws, taught in schools and churches, displayed in movies and on television, described in books and magazines, and exemplified in "significant others"—those people whose opinions and behaviors matter to us in a personal way (parents, teachers, ministers). Understanding human personality requires some understanding of the effects of social influences. More about these in Chapter 17.

Cognitive Approaches

If you are now overwhelmed by the seemingly impossible complexities of this vast and important topic, personality, take whatever comfort you can from the realization that this is an almost shameful abbreviation of relevant theories; many dozens more could have been included, many of which history may, in its strange and whimsical fashion, find more important than some that have been included.

Consider yet another approach to the understanding of our persons. Cognitive personality theorists look neither at biological determinants nor at warring psychic factions. Nor are they engrossed by the pressures of social realities. On several occasions throughout this text, we have noted that cognitive psychologists take the view that humans are active, exploring beings, trying to make sense of the world. The cognitive psychologist, as the label implies, deals with cognitions; and cognitions are items of knowledge—they are the things we know. Accordingly, cognitive psychologists concerned with learning processes have emphasized how we process information, how we abstract information from sensory data, and how we make decisions. Cognitive motivational theorists have been most concerned with how we direct our behavior so as to explore the environment, and how we discover cause-and-effect relationships. True to this tradition, cognitive personality theory looks for individual consistencies or regularities in cognitive behavior. Accordingly, many of the cognitive theories mentioned in relation to motivation, emotion, and learning are directly pertinent to an understanding of cognitive approaches to personality.

One of the questions of central concern to cognitive personality theory deals with personality characteristics that might underlie our attributions (Kelley and Michela, 1980). Recall that an attribution is a personal judgment of cause. If I attribute my behavior to stupidity, then I am simply saying that the cause of my behavior is stupidity. The important question is, are there underlying personality characteristics that consistently affect an individual's attributions?

Rotter's (1966, 1975) research, along with that of a large number of other investigators (see Jackson & Paunonen, 1980), suggests that there *are* certain personality characteristics that affect attribution. Rotter identified two principal tendencies with regard to locus of control—that is, with regard to where we place the responsibility for our actions. These tendencies are labeled *externality-internality,* and they appear to have a profound influence on how we perceive our own behavior and its effects.

Externally oriented individuals are those who believe that their rewards and punishments are beyond their control—in short, that luck, fate, or other uncontrollable circumstances determine the outcomes of behavior. In contrast, internally oriented individuals are those who accept personal responsibility for the outcomes of their behavior (see Figure 13.11). Recall that Weiner's theory of motivation (described in Chapter 9) is based precisely on this same distinction. We noted there that individuals

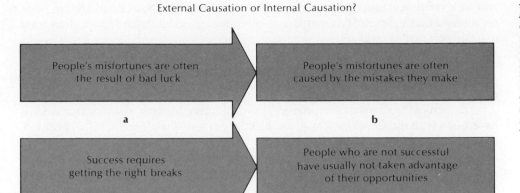

People's misfortunes are often the result of bad luck

People's misfortunes are often caused by the mistakes they make

a

b

Success requires getting the right breaks

People who are not successful have usually not taken advantage of their opportunities

Figure 13.11 Items similar to those employed by Rotter (1966) to assess an individual's externality or internality. People whose orientation is internal perceive themselves as being responsible for their behavior and its consequences. In the two sample items, externally oriented people would be most likely to select the first statement (**a**) of each pair as being more true.

who are internally oriented also tend to be higher in achievement motivation. Conversely, individuals low in achievement motivation are more likely to be externally oriented.

The importance of Rotter's concept of locus of control as a personality variable relates to his notion of **expectancy**. In effect, an expectancy is a belief about likely sources of reinforcement. If I am externally oriented, then I expect rewards and punishments from sources over which I have no control (chance, personal favoritism, prejudice, and so on). And I will govern my behavior accordingly. Research suggests, for example, that internally oriented individuals will react with considerably more frustration than externally oriented individuals when prevented from choosing between two tasks (Moyer, 1978). Similarly, internally oriented children experience less frustration with delayed reward when they are themselves responsible for the delay; in contrast, externally oriented children become frustrated with self-imposed delays, but are far less frustrated when the delay is imposed by someone else (Miller, 1978). These observations appear reasonable in view of the fact that internally oriented individuals are predisposed to accepting personal responsibility for rewards and punishments.

Locus of control is an area of considerable ongoing research activity. One of the important preliminary findings from this research is that externality-internality is an extremely complex dimension that interacts with other personality variables as well as with individual situations in ways that are not yet clearly understood.

In summary, cognitive theorists look for regularity in individual judgment, interpretation, and belief, and search for ways in which people can be identified on the basis of differences in their dominant modes of cognitive functioning. The field is young, and cognitive functioning is extremely complex. But there is every indication that personality differences exist in this area that are perhaps every bit as important as those that have enjoyed a longer history in the annals of psychology.

Expectancy A belief about likely sources of reinforcement. Cognitive theorists regard this as an important determinant of some aspects of personality.

Humanistic Approaches

The opening pages of this chapter, now a long distance before these words, spoke of personality and self in humanistic terms. I suggested there that the self (Tournier's person) is an integral part of personality, but that it cannot easily be differentiated from behavior. Mention was also made of the fact that one of the great difficulties in personality research and theorizing is that the psychologist does not see the person, but only the persona. The next chapter describes some of the methods that have been invented in an effort to remove the mask and look at the quivering self.

Humanistic psychologists speak of the self. They speak, too, of the uniqueness of the person, and of the futility of trying to understand that uniqueness from an objective, scientific point of view. This is not to say that all humanists are antiscience and antiexperimentation. What it does indicate is that their primary emphasis has been on subjects that are even less amenable to objective examination and experimentation than are personality traits and types, cognitive processes, social influences, and perhaps even psychodynamic forces.

Maslow's Concept of Self-Actualization

Like most humanistically oriented psychologists, Maslow's principal concerns have been with the development of the healthy person. Fundamental to his position, as you will recall from Chapter 9, is the notion that we are moved by a hierarchy of needs, the lowest of which relate to physiological survival and the highest, to the fullest and most desirable blossoming of the person (see Figure 9.22). The process of growth is one of self-actualization—of *becoming* in the most abstract sense of the term. This involves a recognition of what one is, of what one can and should be, and a striving for fulfillment.

Maslow (1970) admits that the concept of self-actualization is extremely difficult to define. It is characterized first by the absence of "neurosis, psychopathic personality, psychosis, or strong tendencies in these directions" (p. 150). In addition, self-actualized people "may be loosely described as [making] full use and exploitation of talents, capacities, potentialities, etc." (p. 150). Using these rather loose criteria, Maslow's search for self-actualized people among a group of 3,000 college students yielded only one actualized person and one or two dozen "potentials." Maslow concluded that a fully actualized person is much more likely to be found among older people. He then selected a small number of cases (twenty-three) from among his contemporaries and historical figures. He interviewed them (extremely informally—socially even) where possible, or read accounts of their lives. Maslow subsequently described some of the principal characteristics of these self-actualizers (Figure 13.12).

Given its highly subjective nature, Maslow's account is no more than suggestive. Science might shudder to consider that individuals were defined as being self-actualized by Maslow and were then interviewed or studied (also by Maslow) in order to determine what self-actualized people were really like. The process is only slightly different from deciding that authoritarian people are psychopaths, selecting a group of psychopathic-authoritarian people, and interviewing them in order to determine whether authoritarian people are really psychopathic. The only surprises possible are those that might arise from errors in selection or in interviewer judgment. Nevertheless, Maslow made a noteworthy contribution by establishing the importance of studying the best we might expect of ourselves in a field that had long been fixated on the abnormal and the *worst* we might expect of ourselves.

Rogers's Person-Centered Psychology

Humanistic positions concern themselves primarily with the individual at the center of realities that are, in essence, self-created. This makes humanism **phenomenological**, concerned with the world as it appears rather than as it actually might be. The argument is that no two people see the world in exactly the same way, and that understanding people requires understanding their notions of the world.

Carl Rogers's theory of personality may be described most simply in terms of a set of statements. These are based principally on his own summary of his theoretical beliefs (Rogers, 1951, Chap. 11).

1   Every individual exists in a continually changing world of which that person alone is the center. The person's world is thus private, unknown and unknowable by anyone else. As the existential philosophers have pointed out, existence is lonely; it is necessarily always alone.

2   My perception of the world is real. So is yours. We have our separate realities. If we are to understand each other, you must try to understand my world, and I yours.

BIOGRAPHY
Abraham Maslow
1908–1970

Maslow was born in Brooklyn, N.Y. He reportedly felt isolated and developed as a shy adolescent, resisting his father's insistence that he become a lawyer. This profound disagreement with his father worsened when Maslow fell in love at the age of sixteen, while still in high school. In an attempt to avoid the strained relationship with his father, Maslow left New York City, went to Cornell, and embarked on law studies. Two years later he transferred to Wisconsin, began to study psychology, and, at the age of twenty, married the girl he had fallen in love with at sixteen. And although marriage appeared to do much to increase his confidence and determination, he was still so shy that when he had a paper accepted for presentation ("Psychoanalysis and Mental Hygiene as Status Quo Social Philosophy") he did not show up for the meeting.

Early in his career, Maslow was very interested in behaviorism, which he soon rejected in favor of the humanistic approach. Until his death in 1970, he had a varied and highly productive academic career which included posts at the University of Wisconsin, Columbia, Brooklyn College, and Brandeis (Frick, 1971; Maddi & Costa, 1972).

Phenomenology   A phenomenon is an event, or occurrence. Thus phenomenology is concerned with the world of appearance; that is, with the world as it appears to the individual.

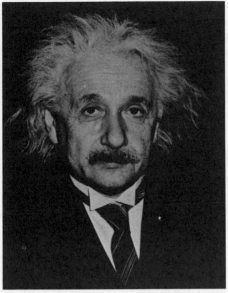

Figure 13.12 Maslow identified these three historic figures (Beethoven, Einstein, and Eleanor Roosevelt) as being highly actualized. He described the actualized personality as being free from defects such as neuroses, and as having made full use of all capabilities and talents. Using these criteria, actualization may be obvious in figures such as these, but less easy to detect among plumbers and taxi drivers.

3 We have one basic tendency—actualization. In short, we have an inner, directing need to develop ourselves in Maslow's sense of the word.

4 Behavior is essentially a goal-directed attempt to satisfy needs, some of which are clearly physiological. The most important concern is growth or self-actualization.

5 The best vantage point for understanding behavior is from the internal frame of reference of the individual. Open communication is therefore the great facilitator of mutual understanding.

6 The structure of self—notions of I or me—develops as a result of interaction with the environment and, particularly, interaction with others.

7 Values attached to notions of self are obtained either as a result of direct experience, or indirectly through what is termed *introjection*. In other words, I can learn that I am good as a result of engaging in good behavior; or I can introject the value of "goodness" into my concept of self as a result of hearing my grandmother telling me I am good.

8 Most of our ways of behaving are consistent with our notions of self. That is, we tend to engage in behaviors that do not violate our internalized conceptions of what we are like—our values and ideals, for example. One source of conflict that sometimes leads to personality disturbance involves behaviors that are not consistent with notions of self.

An Evaluation

Humanistic approaches to personality are difficult to evaluate by the standards that might be applied to other approaches. The most common criteria of science—demonstrability, verifiability, replicability, and so on—are inapplicable. Humanistic positions do not present theories; most other approaches attempt to do so. Instead, they present a new emphasis, a new way of looking at people. Based as they are on the literary and philosophical humanism of an earlier age, they have sought more to glorify the importance of the individual, the nature of being, and the sanctity of personal experience than to analyze and dissect in the sometimes impersonal laboratories of science. Their impact on mental health and counseling has been considerable.

BIOGRAPHY
Carl Ransom Rogers
1902–

Carl Rogers was born into a fundamentally religious family in Oak Park, Illinois, the fourth of six children (five boys). Family life was strict, although not unpleasant. Drinking, smoking, playing cards, and sexual interest were explicitly forbidden. As a result, Rogers recalls considerable guilt when he had his first bottle of lemonade—and reports as well an early preoccupation with obtaining information about sexual matters (Marquet, 1971).

When Carl was twelve, his father purchased a farm thirty miles from Chicago and moved his whole family there, partly to apply scientific principles to farming, and partly to insulate his growing family from the evils of association with a society that tolerated the many activities expressly forbidden in this religious family. Carl apparently loved farming and worked very hard as an adolescent, getting up at five in the morning to do farm chores, attending school, and working again on the farm after school. When he entered the University of Wisconsin he enrolled in agriculture. Shortly thereafter, however, he switched to religious studies and was accepted as a member of a Christian delegation going to China for a conference. Carl stayed a full six months before returning to a theological seminary. In his third year, he transferred to clinical and educational psychology programs. He later went to the University of Ohio as a faculty member, then to the University of Chicago, and finally to the University of Wisconsin. During this time he developed his humanistic and person-centered approaches to personality and counseling, wrote, and lectured widely, activities which he continues at the Center for Studies of the Person (R. I. Evans, 1976; Marquet, 1971; Nordby & Hall, 1974).

Situation-trait controversy A controversy that revolves around the issue of whether behavior is predictably consistent with underlying personality characteristics or whether it can only be predicted on the basis of knowledge of the immediate context.

Traits and Situations

A sometimes explicit, more often implicit, goal of personality research has been to arrive at a description of individuals that would make it possible to predict their behavior (for example, Cattell, 1974). This has been most evident in the trait theories, since a trait is, in effect, simply a label for a regularity in behavior. Thus, individuals who regularly behave aggressively are said to be aggressive. Conversely, to say that someone is aggressive is to predict that that person will behave aggressively more often than will someone who is recognized as being nonaggressive.

One of the fundamental questions of personality theory is whether there are sufficient regularities in behavior to make it possible to identify and label these regularities in useful ways. In other words, can it be shown that behavior is at least moderately consistent with an assumed personality structure? In this context, the phrase *personality structure* simply means the pattern of traits (characteristics) that are unique to a given individual.

Trait theorists have generally assumed, often without question, that behavior is indeed highly consistent. Accordingly, their endeavors have been directed toward identifying consistencies from which they can infer traits or motives which might be useful in predicting subsequent behavior. Recently, however, this assumption has been seriously challenged by a number of theorists who share the belief that behavior is so often specific to a given situation that a search for underlying traits is often fruitless (see, for example, Mischel, 1968, 1977). These theorists are often described as *situation theorists* because of their emphasis on present situations, and the resulting controversy is sometimes called the **situation-trait controversy**. (See Figure 13.13.)

Social-learning theory presents one clear example of a situation theory. Its major concern is not with underlying traits so much as with the immediate context in which the behavior occurs. In other words, it looks at the ways in which social variables affect behavior.

Evidence that traits have not proven particularly useful for predicting specific behaviors is not difficult to obtain (Rotter, 1954). More than five decades ago Hartshorne and May (1928) investigated the relationship between moral behavior and beliefs and reported that the probability of doing right and wrong was much less a function of moral beliefs than of the likelihood of getting caught. In other words, even those individuals for whom the trait label *honest* would be highly appropriate do not consistently behave honestly. Moreover, predicting an individual's behavior in this specific situation might be more accurate if the situation (likelihood of apprehension) were considered apart from any knowledge the predictor might have about the individual's honesty.

Situation theorists (also self-named "contextualists" because of their emphasis on context) also argue that a trait is not in the behaving subject, but in the observer (Mischel, 1968). In other words, traits are often inferred from our preconceived notions about how people should behave, rather than from their actual behavior. Cantor and Mischel (1977) presented subjects with lists of descriptive adjectives pertaining to one of a number of fictitious characters, some of whom had been identified as introverted, and others as extroverted. Memory tests for these lists of adjectives indicated that subjects were biased in the direction of being able to recognize more adjectives related to the generic labels (extrovert or introvert) than unrelated adjectives. The global impression provided by the labels prejudices memory in the same way it might prejudice observation (Schneider, 1973).

Still, trait theories have not necessarily been irreparably damaged. Block (1971) cites impressive evidence of consistency in a longitudinal study where subjects were administered the same personality scales ten years apart.

What do these observations mean? Knowledge of *specific* traits does not appear to be particularly useful in predicting *specific* behaviors in *specific* situations. Yet there is considerable evidence that *major* identifiable traits are relatively stable within a given individual over time. There is considerable evidence as well that behavior is

Figure 13.13 The situation-trait controversy in personality theory centers on the question of whether behavior is a function of the situation in which the individual behaves or whether it is more a function of personality traits within the individual. Put another way, are we likely to be able to predict (or explain) the behavior of these seven boys in terms of their apparent environments, or would it be more profitable to look at their individual personality characteristics? Or both?

often highly responsive to a specific situation, although Bem and Allen (1974) have shown that this observation is more true for some individuals than for others. Indeed, it is possible that consistency is itself a personality trait. Some individuals vary their behavior a great deal in different situations; others do so much less.

The implications of these findings, and of the trait-situation controversy, point toward a merging of the two approaches. It is clear that behavior is not sufficiently consistent to be predictable solely on the basis of inferred personality characteristics; hence the importance of considering situational variables. Conversely, general descriptions of traits (and types) might prove highly useful when situational variables are also taken into account. In this context, it is reassuring to note that one of the theorists closely identified with the beginning of the situation-trait controversy, Mischel, has now adopted precisely this point of view. In his words, "... undoing the role of dispositions" was not his intention; his aim "was to call attention to the specific reciprocal interactions between person and context and hence to the need to examine those interactions in fine-grained detail" (1979, p. 740). This approach will not make the study of human personality any simpler, but it might make it considerably more meaningful.

A Last Word

What should we now believe about human personality? Should we look for it in inherited predispositions? Is it to be found in the fitful struggles of dynamic, internal forces? Does it reveal itself in social interaction, prisoner to cultural context and social expectations, shaped by external influences? Is it developed and manifested through the application of conceptual and perceptual processes? Is it so unique and so private that it cannot be analyzed, measured, and dealt with, but must simply be recognized and allowed to develop in the best way possible?

All of these. These are not different descriptions of different things. We are what we are no matter what we or others say we are. The oft-quoted Sufi tale of the elephant is appropriate. Five blind men each feeling a different portion of the same great elephant may develop very different notions of what the elephant is, but the elephant is an elephant for all that. Five "blind" scientists each looking at a different manifestation of personality might develop very different notions of what personality is. But it is what it is for all that.

Main Points

1 Psychologists have distinguished between the self, the persona, and the personality. The self is who we experience ourselves as being, from the inside; the persona is the role or mask we adopt in a certain situation; and the personality is the set of characteristics that we typically manifest in our interactions with others.

2 A trait is a distinct, consistent quality in which one person can be different from another; a type is a grouping of related traits. Some psychologists have attempted to study personality by listing basic traits; some by classifying personality according to types. Jung's typology of the introvert (turning inward; preoccupied with self) and the extrovert (turning outward; preoccupied with others) is one accepted type approach.

3 The common-sense approach to personality makes assumptions of wide generality and is not particularly useful in explaining or describing personality.

4 Biological approaches to the study of personality are concerned primarily with the importance of genetic forces.

5 Sheldon's description of body types and corresponding personality characteristics is a biological approach to personality. Endomorphs (large) are described as relaxed, comfort-seeking, sociable, and highly tolerant; mesomorphs (intermediate) are assertive, bold, and courageous, love adventure, and tend to be loud and boisterous; ectomorphs (slight) are timid, private, restrained, secretive, highly sensitive to pain, and more concerned with intellectual matters.

6 Although the correlation between body type and personality is not very high, it has been demonstrated in a significant number of cases. This relationship has sometimes been explained in terms of genetics, in terms of the activities that are made possible and probable by different physiques, and in terms of social expectations associated with different body types.

7 Eysenck's biological approach proposes that we are born with tendencies to behave in certain ways, along three major dimensions: high intelligence-low intelligence, introversion-extroversion, and neuroticism-stability. In Eysenck's hierarchy of personality, types lead to traits, which lead to habits, which lead to specific responses.

8 Psychodynamic approaches to personality are concerned with the interplay of powerful psychic forces in the mind. Many of these forces are assumed to be innate or instinctual.

9 Freud's psychodynamic personality theory is based on the notion that we are born with powerful instinctual urges associated with procreation and survival (eros) and therefore with sexuality (libido). These urges compose the most basic level of personality, the id. With exposure to the world, the individual develops a notion of reality (of what is possible and what isn't), these notions becoming the second level of personality (the ego). The third level of personality, the superego, represents conscience and arises as a result of experience with parental, religious, and other constraints and restraints.

10 Freud identified a series of psychosexual stages in child development, related to the level at which sexual gratification is obtained: oral, anal, phallic, latency, and genital. He said that during the phallic stage, children progress through Oedipus or Electra complexes. Normal personality development can be impeded by either fixation or regression.

11 Freud also identified a series of defense mechanisms individuals use unconsciously, distorting reality to reduce anxiety. Chief among these mechanisms are repression, rationalization, displacement, reaction formation, and projection.

12 Freud's theory has been criticized on scientific and methodological grounds, because of its ambiguous use of terms and concepts, and because many of its predictions cannot easily be tested. Still, it was the first to acknowledge the importance of unconscious forces and sexuality in psychological functioning.

13 Albert Adler, Freud's student, believed social forces to be more important than biological in determining personality. He proposed that we all strive for competence and that if we are thwarted by organic inferiority, spoiling, or neglect, we may develop an inferiority complex, or we may overcompensate and develop a superiority complex.

14 Jung's analytical psychology describes human personality in terms of a conscious level (including the ego, or self, and personality) and an unconscious level containing memories of events that have occurred in our own lives as well as dim species- or race-specific recollections (the collective unconscious). These collective memories manifest themselves as powerful urges and motives, and are evident in certain universal themes (such as self, God, hero, man, and woman) labeled *archetypes*.

15 Jung believed people can be differentiated according to their basic orientation toward the world: either introverted or extroverted; and according to their dominant modes of intellectual functioning: either thinking, feeling, sensing, or intuiting. He believed that Western societies overemphasize thinking and that individuals grow as they learn to use all functions.

16 Social approaches to the study of personality are concerned with manifested behavior. Bandura and Walters argue that we learn much of the behavior we manifest by observing various models (observational learning).

17 Cognitive approaches to personality look for ways in which personality characteristics can be identified on the basis of differences in individual modes of cognitive functioning. One cognitive dimension along which people differ is internality-externality of locus of control. People develop expectancies about likely sources of reinforcement, either internal or external, and behave accordingly.

18 Humanistic approaches to personality study do not attempt to measure or quantify but instead appreciate the uniqueness of the person and the importance of the self.

19 Maslow established the importance of studying the most psychologically healthy individuals in society. He saw the process of growth as one of self-actualization—of recognizing what one is, what one can and should be, and striving for fulfillment.

20 Rogers's theory of personality is person-centered; that is, he sees the person as the center of self-created reality. He proposes that the one basic tendency is toward actualization, that behavior is a goal-directed attempt to satisfy needs, that we develop notions of self as a result of interaction with others, and that we behave in accordance with our notions of self.

21 Trait theorists believe that behavior is consistent with identifiable traits; situation theorists believe that behavior is more situation-specific and that predictions based on inferred traits are not very useful. The two approaches seem to be merging into a more meaningful description of personality.

22 In the final analysis, none of these approaches to personality is mutually exclusive, and personality remains personality no matter how it is explained and described.

Further Readings

Among the best general sources of information on personality theories is the widely used text:

Hall, C. S., and Lindzey, G. *Theories of personality* (3rd ed.). New York: John Wiley, 1978.

The following text also presents a clear introduction to personality:

Liebert, R. M., and Spiegler, M. E. *Personality: Strategies for the study of man.* Homewood, Ill.: Dorsey Press, 1975.

Freud's life and ideas are clearly presented in:

Wollheim, R. *Sigmund Freud.* New York: Viking Press, 1971.

Clark, R. W. *Freud: The man and the cause.* New York: Random House, 1980.

For an impartial examination of evidence relating to the scientific value of Freudian theory, see:

Fisher, S., and Greenberg, R. P. *The scientific credibility of Freud's theories and therapy.* New York: Basic Books, 1977.

The advanced student of Freudian theory is referred to the following more difficult, theoretically oriented, book:

Feffer, M. *The structure of Freudian thought.* New York: International Universities Press, 1982.

The following book presents a humanistic approach to personality:

Maddi, S., and Costa, P. T. *Humanism in personality.* Chicago: Aldine-Atherton, 1972.

Personality Assessment and Intelligence

My Uncle Robert, far from the stupidest of my many uncles, once found himself in the embarrassing position of "failing" an eye test. The school nurse, having little else to do at the time, had asked each of the seventh-grade boys to read an eye chart—from the prescribed distance, one eye at a time. Uncle Robert saw the big *E,* but only a blurred image of the smaller letters. As a result, he was sent to the closest city so that a qualified person might determine precisely what glasses he would require.

Sitting in the doctor's office, he spotted the eye chart on a far wall. Never a fool, my uncle approached it at once and quickly copied the entire chart on the palm of his right hand. When the doctor finally arrived and checked his vision, he was understandably amazed that a school nurse should have referred a boy with such excellent vision, although he did express some concern at the fact that my uncle's left arm was sufficiently sore that he had to use his right hand to cover both his right and his left eye.

Some time later my nearsighted uncle took a brief personality test designed to screen applicants for a far northern appointment. He was selected for the position and later confessed that he had found out beforehand that the company was interested in adventurous, courageous, and well-adjusted people. Upon further inquiry, he had also been told that well-adjusted people didn't have personality problems, liked other people and especially their mothers, and that they were highly adaptable. He claims to have pretended that he was adventurous, courageous, and well-adjusted, and to have fooled the testers in much the same way as he had fooled the eye doctor some years earlier.

As luck would have it, once he went north he behaved as though he were courageous, adventurous, and well-adjusted. The company then offered to send him back south for advanced training so that he might be promoted to a more senior and better-paying position. Never one to turn up his nose at the smell of money, my uncle accepted readily. But one final test awaited him: an intelligence test.

Uncle Robert made a number of discreet inquiries and discovered that an intelligence test requires people to behave intelligently. This information provided little room for cheating. And since his teachers had never made a big issue of his intelligence save to note unkindly on several occasions that he would have to work hard to succeed, he decided to pretend that he was intelligent just as he had pretended that he was courageous and well-adjusted.

The pretense failed, a fact that did not upset him in the least.

"I'm not stupid," he claimed loudly. "I'm just different."

Psychological Assessment

That we are different from one another is obvious. Personality, learning, and developmental theorists have all had to recognize at least some of these differences. We do not all learn as rapidly or as well; developmental rates vary from one individual to another; and each individual can be described in terms of a unique arrangement of characteristics.

One of the more practical problems that has faced psychologists is that of identifying and measuring individual differences. The task has not always proven simple, but its usefulness has seldom been questioned (Figure 14.1).

The practical significance of being able to measure individual differences goes considerably beyond whatever contribution it might make to a theoretical understanding of human behavior. At a more concrete level, it is important for teachers to know the capabilities of their students, their likelihood of future success, and their past achievements. Similarly, it can be of practical significance for a clinical psychologist to be able to arrive at a relatively clear description of a person in need of help.

This chapter looks first at the general principles underlying psychological assessment. It then looks at personality assessment, with special attention to the measuring instruments that are employed to provide a description of common personality variables. Finally it looks specifically at the definition, development, and measurement of intelligence.

Characteristics of Good Measuring Instruments

Validity The extent to which a psychological test measures what it purports to measure, and not some other variable(s).

Reliability The extent to which a psychological test measures consistently what it is supposed to measure. A good instrument has both validity and reliability.

Psychological tests can be said to be good instruments to the extent that they measure what they purport to measure, and to the extent that they do so consistently. These two characteristics are called **validity** and **reliability**. Thus, a thermometer is a valid measure of temperature if it is affected in some predictable way by temperature changes and not affected by irrelevant changes such as time of day, season of the year, or phases of the moon. A thermometer is reliable to the extent that specific conditions of heat or cold result in consistent readings on the thermometer. In other words, the thermometer is reliable if it says 20 every time the temperature is 20; it is also reliable if it says 30 every time the temperature is 20, although in this case it is not entirely valid (see Box 14.1).

Psychological variables cannot be described or defined as objectively as height, length, weight, or temperature. Thus we cannot always be absolutely certain that the tests we employ measure what they are intended to measure and nothing else. Nor can we always be certain that they measure accurately whatever it is that they do measure. There is little doubt, for example, that measures of intelligence can be influenced by fatigue, illness, mood, and other variables. Although we would justifiably expect our rulers to yield the same measures for the same objects on different occa-

sions, we cannot reasonably expect the same thing of our intelligence and personality measures. But what we can expect is that they will be as valid and as reliable as possible under the circumstances.

Estimating Reliability

The most obvious proof of reliability with respect to a ruler is that it yields the same measurements repeatedly. So too with psychological assessment. If we can assume that the characteristic being measured is relatively stable (does not fluctuate erratically over a short period of time), reliability of an instrument will be evident in a high similarity of test scores obtained on different occasions. This index of *test-retest reliability* may be obtained by presenting the test to the same individuals on different occasions and looking at the *correlation* between their test scores. Those who score high on the first testing would be expected to score high on the second; those who score low on the first testing would be expected to score low on the second. To the extent that this is true, the resulting correlation would be high and positive. If there is little relationship between the two test scores, the correlation (hence, the index of reliability) will be low. A high negative correlation would indicate that those who scored high on the first administration of the test were now scoring low on the second, and vice versa—an extremely unlikely situation.

A test-retest estimate of reliability can sometimes be artificially inflated if subjects remember their previous responses and therefore answer the same way when given the test again. There are two ways of estimating reliability that take this possibility into account. One is to administer a second, parallel, form of the test instead of using the same test twice. Such testing demonstrates *parallel-form reliability*. A second method is to divide the original test into halves and look at the relationships between scores on each half. If the two halves of the test are composed of items whose levels of difficulty are comparable, each individual should have similar scores on the two halves, provided the test is reliable. If the test is not reliable, then scores on each half might be quite different. Again, a numerical estimate of reliability can be obtained by looking at the correlation between these "split halves" of the test—hence, the label *split-half reliability* for this index.

If a test is not reliable, it cannot be valid. However, a test can be quite reliable without being at all valid. Confusing? If weight does not change in a given individual, but scale readings fluctuate, the scale is obviously not measuring what it purports to measure, and nothing else. Thus, to be valid, the scale must be reliable. However, if I use a tape measure to arrive at a weight index, I will obtain the same measurement day after day. Perfectly reliable, but desperately invalid.

Estimating Validity

We know that a ruler is valid as a measure of length because we can define length in an objective way and design our measuring instrument according to our definition. That is sometimes possible in psychological measurement, but to a much more limited extent. Certainly there has been too little agreement with respect to the definition of such characteristics as intelligence, creativity, and other personality variables such as aggressiveness, authoritarianism, and so on to permit the construction of a single instrument that all researchers would judge to be highly valid. There are, however, other ways of estimating validity.

If I have a box into which I can place objects that are no more than 6 inches long, I can use a ruler to determine which objects will fit into my box. Thus my pen, at 5 7/16 inches, will go in; my letter opener, at 9 inches, will not; and my left shoe, at 12 1/4 inches, will not. These statements are, in effect, predictions that I can then verify

---

The Validity and Reliability of My Ruler

Why is a ruler a good measuring instrument for determining the length of my red pen? When I lay the pen along the edge of the ruler, it reaches from its beginning to a point exactly 5 7/16 inches down the ruler. I can repeat the measurement over and over again, today or tomorrow, and my pen's measured length is always 5 7/16 inches.

That is one reason why the ruler is a good measuring instrument for length. It provides the same index repeatedly. In measuring terms, it is highly *reliable*, reliability being a measure of the consistency of the instrument.

There is a second reason why the ruler is a good instrument for measuring length. It measures length and nothing else. We know that this is so because length can be objectively defined in a way that permits us to measure it in spite of any other irrelevant characteristics of the object being measured. The length of my red pen is always 5 7/16 inches in spite of the fact that it is red and not blue, that it is round, and that it weighs less than an ounce. My ruler is unaffected by weight, circularity, or color of the object it is measuring. It measures length and nothing else. In measurement terms, it provides a *valid* measure, validity being defined as the extent to which a test measures what it purports to measure.

by actually putting these objects in the box, or by at least attempting to do so. If my predictions are accurate, I might then assume that my measuring instrument had high *predictive validity*.

Many personality tests can be evaluated by looking at their predictive validity. For example, I can define intelligence as a quality that is important for success in school. If this definition is of any value, a valid measure of intelligence should allow me to predict school success and failure. Thus, I could estimate the predictive validity of my intelligence test by looking at the relationship between scores on my test and actual school performance. If the relationship were high and positive (those who scored high on the test also achieved well in school, and vice versa), the predictive validity of the test would be high.

Other evidence of validity may be obtained by looking at the content of the measuring device. In many instances, a valid measuring instrument *appears* to be measuring what it is measuring. Thus, a mathematics test generally has mathematics items in it; a test of intelligence would contain items that seem to be related to the processes we associate with intelligent behavior. In short, to the extent that test items test a representative sample of the behaviors the examiner wishes to assess, a test may be said to have *content validity*. In some instances, however, the appearance of an instrument is a poor clue to the characteristics it intends to measure. This is most notably true of some of the personality tests described later, where the individual taking the test often remains unaware of the characteristics being measured.

Evidence of validity may also be obtained by looking at the relationship between related instruments. For example, a new intelligence test may be compared to one or more established tests in order to estimate its validity. If a new test measures intelligence and other established tests do likewise, the scores it yields should be highly comparable to scores obtained on other tests. This is termed *concurrent validity*.

A fourth measure of test validity is somewhat more complex than the preceding three. It is labeled *construct validity*. A *construct* is an abstract network of relationships between behaviors and characteristics. As an example, *anxiety* is a construct. There are a variety of behaviors that might be related to anxiety; hence it is defined in terms of its relationship to other characteristics (such as extroversion-introversion), in terms of its relationship to mental disorders or physical disturbances, and so on. An instrument designed to measure anxiety can then be validated by looking at the extent to which individuals identified as high or low in anxiety manifest other characteristics or behaviors that are part of the construct, anxiety. Thus, as Lanyon and Goodstein (1971) note, establishing construct validity requires the accumulation of a variety of evidence that demonstrates a logical network of relationships between the measure and other relevant concepts.

When interpreting the results of psychological testing, it is always extremely important to keep in mind that the instruments employed, unlike weight scales, rulers, and thermometers, have less than perfect reliability and validity. Tests measure things they are not intended to measure, and they do not measure entirely accurately (see Figure 14.2).

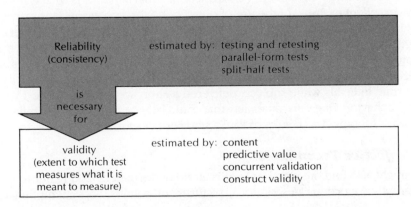

Figure 14.2 The two necessary qualities of a good psychological measuring instrument: reliability and validity.

Measuring Personality Variables

The preceding chapter described a recent controversy in personality theory: the trait-situation controversy. Are traits stable, and can behavior be predicted from a knowledge of underlying personality traits, or does it depend on the situation? To the extent that behavior is *not* consistent in different situations, personality tests may have low validity. Similarly, to the extent that behavior is a function of immediate circumstances, psychologists may be able to learn more about personality by looking at "naturally occurring behaviors . . . in real-life settings" (Mischel, 1977, p. 248). One of the important functions of personality measurements is to provide evidence that might be useful in resolving this conflict, and that might give us more accurate and more fruitful descriptions of personality. In addition, personality tests are sometimes very useful in clinical situations where they can provide psychologists with important insights, and in schools and colleges where they might be employed to guide career decisions.

How can we find something out about someone's personality traits? There are numerous ways, some highly subjective and difficult to validate, others highly objective. Here we discuss four important methods: self-reports and ratings, behavioral observation, projective techniques, and scales and inventories.

Self-Reports and Ratings

Among the more subjective approaches to personality assessment are *self-reports* and *ratings*. I can find out whether Joan is afraid of the dark by asking her (self-report). I can do this directly in an interview, or I can mail her a questionnaire. The question might be very direct ("Are you afraid of the dark?") or more indirect ("Do you sleep with your lights on?").

Alternatively, I might ask someone else whether Joan is afraid of the dark. A panel of experts who have observed her behavior in different circumstances might be asked to provide a rating of Joan's reaction to darkness.

Behavioral Observation

Still another alternative would be to observe Joan's behavior in specific situations. This might take place in natural situations (in her boarding house, for example) or in more contrived situations (in a laboratory where the lights are suddenly turned off). In either case, assessments of Joan's fear would be based on direct observations of fear reactions.

Behavioral observation has become an increasingly common way of assessing personality characteristics, particularly in situations where relevant characteristics are manifested in specific observable behaviors. Clinical psychologists interested in treating maladaptive behaviors, for example, often find it useful to assess the nature and extent of the behaviors through direct observation prior to treatment. Following treatment, identical observation techniques can be employed to determine the effectiveness of the treatment. Using this procedure, it is not necessary to make any inferences about the personality characteristic (or construct); actual behavior is what is important.

An excellent example of the use of direct behavioral observation is provided by Paul's (1966) investigation of the relative effectiveness of three types of therapy for alleviating public-speaking anxiety. In this study, anxiety was determined not through questionnaires or tests, but through direct observation. Trained observers simply recorded the frequency of specific anxiety-related behaviors (such as licking the lips) at fixed time intervals while subjects delivered a short speech (see Table 14.1). This yielded a behavioral measure of anxiety that could later be compared to similar observations after therapy. The results of Paul's study are described in Chapter 16.

Projective Techniques

I might also find out whether Joan is afraid of the dark by asking her to respond to apparently innocuous descriptions, pictures, or sounds, and attempting to find

Table 14.1 Checklist Used in Behavioral Observation of Public Speaking Anxiety

Behavior Observed	Time Period								
	1	2	3	4	5	6	7	8	9
1. Paces									
2. Sways									
3. Shuffles feet									
4. Knees tremble									
5. Extraneous arm and hand movement (swings, scratches, toys, etc.)									
6. Arms rigid									
7. Hands restrained (in pockets, behind back, clasped)									
8. Hand tremors									
9. No eye contact									
10. Face muscles tense (drawn, tics, grimaces)									
11. Face "deadpan"									
12. Face pale									
13. Face flushed (blushes)									
14. Moistens lips									
15. Swallows									
16. Clears throat									
17. Breathes heavily									
18. Perspires (face, hands, armpits)									
19. Voice quivers									
20. Speech blocks or stammers									

Note: Reprinted from Paul, G. L. *Insight vs. desensitization in psychotherapy* with permission of the publishers, Stanford University Press. © 1966 by the Board of Trustees of the Leland Stanford Junior University.

evidence of fear or confidence *projected* into her descriptions. This approach, although not particularly suitable and highly uneconomical for purposes such as this one, has been used extensively in personality assessment. The assumption underlying the use of projective tests is simply that unconscious fears, desires, and other personality traits may be *projected* in descriptions of stimuli apparently unrelated to the underlying personality characteristics. Since these traits are *unconscious,* the argument goes, they would not ordinarily be revealed in conventional measures of personality.

Rorschach Inkblots   Among the best-known of the projective devices is the *Rorschach inkblot test,* so called because it presents the subject with stimulus cards printed with figures sometimes vaguely reminiscent of an elaborate and careful inkblot (Figure 14.3). The test consists of ten such cards. Most of the "blots" are black, although two have some red and three others are in pastel shades. Administration requires considerable expertise, and interpretation of responses is even more complicated. The scoring procedure is elaborate, detailed, and not well validated. In addition, the interpretations of different experts vary a great deal. Furthermore, the relationships of scorer interpretations to the actual behavior of testees has been very difficult to establish (Suinn & Oskamp, 1969).

Literally thousands of separate studies have looked at the validity and reliability of the Rorschach. Although these studies seldom arrive at precisely the same estimates, in total they provide very little evidence of either validity or reliability (Jensen, 1970). In spite of these well-known and widely accepted observations, more than five decades after its introduction the Rorschach continues to be the most widely used of all clinical

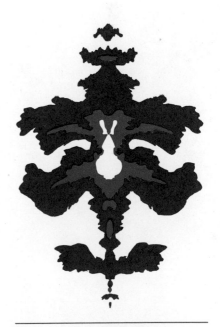

Figure 14.3 An inkblot similar to some used in the Rorschach inkblot test, a projective measure of personality.

measures in the United States. And this, even though it is also among the most expensive and time-consuming tests to employ, and it generally requires a year or more of concentrated training and considerable clinical experience before "expertise" is reached.

In all fairness, however, it should be noted that projective measures such as the Rorschach lend themselves particularly well to the exploration of fantasy. In addition, such measures, in contrast to many other personality measures, are not highly subject to deliberate faking. That is, although an intelligent subject might find it easy to "pretend" on a straightforward paper and pencil test (or to deceive in an interview situation), organizing responses to an inkblot with the intention of producing a definite clinical impression is considerably more difficult.

The TAT H. A. Murray's (1938, 1943) *thematic apperception test* is a second well-known projective technique. It consists of thirty black and white pictures showing people in various situations. Recall that a number of picture cards from the TAT have been widely used in investigations of need for achievement (Chapter 9). There, too, it is used as a projective device, with scorers looking for achievement-related themes in subjects' descriptions of the pictures.

Use of the TAT as a more general personality test also requires that subjects tell a story that is suggested to them by each of the pictures. They are told that this is a test of imagination, and are then presented with a sequence of cards selected on the basis of the age and sex of the subject. Respondents are urged to tell as dramatic a story as they can, describing what is happening in the picture, what has led up to the present situation, what each of the characters is thinking and feeling, and what the outcome will be.

"It looks as if someone spilled ink on a piece of paper and then folded it in half."

Thomas Cheney

Evaluation of TAT responses is based on two important assumptions. The first is that respondents project their own inclinations, wishes, fears, and so on in their description of the "hero" in the story; the second is that the environment described in the story includes significant features of the respondent's personal environment. To the extent that these assumptions are valid, the examiner hopes to obtain information relating to the mental or psychic state of the individual (unconscious wishes, fears, and so on), as well as some insight into features of the environment that might be a source of pressure or conflict. The following response to the TAT card shown in Figure 14.4 might be interpreted as revealing considerable inner turmoil:

> *The old lady has a plan. She wants the younger woman to seduce the landlord. She's supposed to do it before they tell the landlord they can't pay the rent. The young woman doesn't really want to because she wants to get married. But she already lost her job because she wouldn't give in to her boss in the factory, and now they might lose their room if she doesn't go ahead with the old lady's plan. The old lady isn't too sorry about the situation, because she thinks she would go ahead and do it if she were younger. The young lady is scared and confused, but in the end she'll go through with it.*

Unfortunately there are no widely accepted procedures for interpreting TAT responses (except with respect to need for achievement and related research where it is not employed as a *general* personality test); and reliability and validity have not been experimentally established. Its principal purpose has been clinical; that is, clinicians (therapists and counselors) frequently employ the TAT as a means of obtaining greater insight into the subject's fantasies. Although the test does not *measure* specific personality characteristics, it may be highly suggestive of preoccupations, fears, unconscious needs and desires, personal relationships, and related themes.

Figure 14.4 One of the picture cards used in the TAT. Subjects are asked to tell a story concerning what is happening in the picture, what has led to the situation, what the characters think and feel, and what the outcome will be. (Copyright 1943 by the President and fellows of Harvard College; © 1971 by Henry A. Murray. Reprinted by permission.)

Scales and Inventories

There are hundreds of paper-and-pencil personality tests, usually referred to as **scales** or **inventories**. Scales measure specific dimensions of personality (sociability, neuroticism, and so on); inventories are more general. Typically, inventories consist of a number of different scales and yield a profile of personality characteristics. One of the best known and most rigorously developed personality inventories is the *Minnesota Multiphasic Personality Inventory (MMPI)*.

The MMPI There are various forms of this test, the best-known consisting of 550 items (plus 16 repeated items that are sometimes employed if the test is to be scored by machine). Ordinarily, it is scored for fourteen scales. That is, it yields measures on fourteen different dimensions. Some of these are termed *rational scales* and provide indications of the extent to which an individual's responses may be considered reliable and valid; others are diagnostic scales (also called *empirical scales*) and provide a basis for clinical judgment with respect to several dimensions of personality.

The development of the diagnostic scales is of particular interest. A number of criterion groups were identified in terms of other ratings and measures. These groups consisted of individuals who had been clearly diagnosed as hypochondriacs (individuals who manifest undue concern over health), depressives, psychopaths, and so on. Scores obtained by these individuals were then compared to scores obtained by a "normal" control group, and items were selected on the basis of how well they discriminated between specific criterion groups and the control group. If, for example, hypochondriacs always responded in one way to ten items, and controls always responded differently, these ten items would then make up the hypochondriasis scale (Hs scale). Theoretically, it would then be possible to identify people who respond like hypochondriacs by looking at their scores on that scale. Ten clinical scales were developed in this fashion:

Scale 1 (Hs) hypochondriasis: profound and debilitating concern over physical health

Scale 2 (D) depression: overwhelming feelings of hopelessness, despair

Scales In psychology, test items, questions, or problems which, alone or in combination, have been assigned numbers that are assumed to represent the qualities the scale is intended to measure.

Inventories An inventory is a list. Personality inventories are, accordingly, lists that may be employed to assess personality. Such lists typically take the form of sentences that describe personality, or simply of questions that are typically answered yes or no. Although inventories are usually not characterized by specific rules governing the assignment of numbers to different responses, they often provide *norms*, based on the typical responses of large numbers of individuals, to facilitate interpretation of results.

Scale 3 (Hy) hysteria: manifestations of physical symptoms for which there is no organic cause; frequently involves paralysis following trauma or extreme stress; not uncommon among soldiers in wartime

Scale 4 (Pd) psychopathic deviate: sometimes termed *character disorders;* characterized by apparently conscienceless behavior—lying, stealing, and so on—usually without any indication of remorse

Scale 5 (Mf) masculinity-femininity: used to differentiate between males and females primarily in terms of culturally ascribed interests and behaviors

Scale 6 (Pa) paranoia: strong, irrational fears and suspicions in relation to other people

Scale 7 (Pt) psychasthenia: obsessive fears, anxieties, guilts

Scale 8 (Sc) schizophrenia: marked distortions of reality; bizarre forms of behavior and dress

Scale 9 (Ma) hypomania: overactivity, excitability, irritability; fluctuating, high-energy moods

Scale 10 (Si) social introversion: a measure of introversion similar to that described by Jung and Eysenck

In responding to the MMPI, subjects are required to answer true or false to each of the 550 or 566 items. Since many of these items relate to bizarre and pathological feelings and behaviors, subjects are sometimes offended. Many become defensive; some attempt to fake their responses; and others either refuse to answer specific items or indicate that they don't know. Accordingly, a number of scales have been devised to look at specific "rational" characteristics of the respondents.

The ? scale consists of all items that subjects have answered with a question mark (or "I don't know"). A high score on this scale would indicate that the subject is defensive, evasive, or indecisive. Interpretation of other scales would then have to be modified accordingly. The scales are not groupings of separate items, but patterns of items. Thus, any one item may be scored for a number of different scales. If many items are marked ?, then all scores might be lower.

The L scale is a lie-detection scale. It consists of all items to which most people would always answer "true" or "false." For example, "I do not like everyone I know" is answered "true" by most people who are answering honestly. Deviation from keyed responses on L scale items indicates that the respondent has probably been less than completely honest. Typically, subjects score very low on the L scale, meaning they are answering honestly.

The F scale consists of all items for which less than 10 percent of the members of the original control group gave the keyed response. That is, 64 items are keyed for highly unusual and improbable responses. The average score on the F scale is around 6.4. Individuals who score considerably higher than this have either answered without reading items carefully or are trying to call attention to themselves.

The K scale presents a slightly more difficult concept. A number of individuals in some of the diagnostic groups (hypochondriacs, for example) scored relatively low on the clinical scale (Hs in this case). The assumption is that these individuals have been unduly defensive in answering items pertaining to their disorder, but have scored higher on certain other items. These other items compose the K scale. Scores on the K scale may then be used to correct for the effects of defensiveness and the consequently lower scores on specific diagnostic scales.

In many ways, the MMPI is a masterpiece of empirical test construction. Evidence suggests that it is useful in making discriminations between groups of people and in preliminary **diagnosis** of abnormal behavior. It has had its critics, too, who have claimed that the criterion groups were too small and that they were selected on the basis of psychiatric assessments that vary considerably, depending on the individual doing the assessment. Be that as it may, there is little doubt that few instruments have been used more widely in personality diagnosis and research, and few have stimulated more research.

Diagnosis Classification on the basis of symptoms. Essentially, diagnosis involves identifying a condition (for example, a disease or abnormality) on the basis of its observable manifestations and origin.

Although the MMPI is simple to administer and to take, it is not simple to score by hand. There are no great difficulties involved, but it can be extremely time-consuming to score 550 items and to sort them into their various scales to obtain a profile of the subject. Fortunately, the scoring can be done by machine, and computer printouts can provide scores on each of the scales, profiles for each subject, and a clinical evaluation (one of these is presented in Figure 14.5). The evaluation is based more on the individual's profile (pattern of scores) than on single scores in separate scales.

The CPI   The California Personality Inventory (CPI), modeled after the MMPI, uses 200 original MMPI items and 280 new items. All MMPI items that were thought to be offensive and to bring about defensive reactions were eliminated. In addition, the CPI was designed primarily to arrive at a measure of personality characteristics not associated with abnormality. Thus, it presents eighteen scales for the measurement of characteristics such as dominance, tolerance, self-control, achievement via independence, achievement via conformity, flexibility, and so on. Criterion groups were not obtained through psychiatric reports, but were obtained through peer ratings. That is, members of criterion groups were selected on the basis of their being described by others as being leaders, achievers, and so on.

Other Inventories   A number of other personality inventories are in relatively wide use. The Kuder Occupational Interest Survey and the Strong Vocational Interest Blank are used extensively in career guidance. The Maudsley Personality Inventory (MPI) was developed to assess Eysenck's dimensions of neuroticism and introversion-extroversion. The 16 Personality Factor Questionnaire (16PF) measures sixteen traits, including tough-minded versus tender-minded, forthright versus shrewd, placid versus apprehensive, and so on. The Jackson Personality Research Form (JPRF) contains a wide variety of well developed scales including scales for autonomy, adaptivity to change, cognitive structure, and understanding. Perhaps the most comprehensive of all scales is the Edwards Personality Inventory (EPI), which provides measures for fifty-three personality traits. It consists of five separate booklets, each containing 300 items. Unlike most other personality inventories, it asks subjects to answer questions as they think somebody who knows them well might answer. Thus an attempt is made to obtain a greater degree of objectivity.

I have just returned from counting personality tests in print. According to Buros, editor of a comprehensive catalog and description of available psychological tests, there were 350 nonprojective and 84 projective tests when the 1975 edition went to press; by 1978, 72 *new* personality tests had been introduced (Buros, 1975, 1978). We could continue this section almost forever, but we'll end it right here.

Use of Tests

T. C. Wade and Baker (1977) surveyed 500 clinical psychologists in an attempt to discover their opinions of psychological tests and to determine the extent to which these tests are actually used. Results indicate that psychologists are well aware of the predictive limitations of tests and of their often very low reliability and validity coefficients, but that a substantial proportion of psychologists use tests extensively in any case. Indeed, 71.8 percent of all respondents indicated that they ordinarily would employ at least one test at some stage in the treatment process, and that they spent over one-third of their clinical time in the administration, scoring, and interpretation of tests. These tests are employed primarily in diagnosis and assessment (47.4 percent) and to a lesser degree for assigning clients to treatments (16.2 percent). Less than 1 percent of all respondents employed standardized tests to determine the effectiveness of their treatments (Figure 14.6).

Respondents were also asked to list which tests they considered most important for future clinical psychologists to be exposed to in their training. The Rorschach inkblot test was named most often, followed by the TAT, the Wechsler Adult Intelligence Scale (described later in this chapter), and the MMPI. It is revealing to note that the two tests mentioned most often are projective tests which lend themselves much

Figure 14.5 Profile of personality characteristics as measured by Minnesota Multiphasic Personality Inventory (MMPI). Sample computer printout showing (**a**) one individual's scores on a number of different scales. The first set of scores (?, L, F, K) is designed to detect inconsistent or irrational answers. This subject's answers score high on the F scale, indicating a high percentage of unusual answers. (**b**) The computer also prints out a clinical evaluation in the form of a narrative report. (From "Computer Interpretation of the MMPI" by R. D. Fowler and M. L. Miller, *Archives of General Psychiatry*, 1969, *21*, 502–508. Copyright 1969, American Medical Association. Reprinted by permission.)

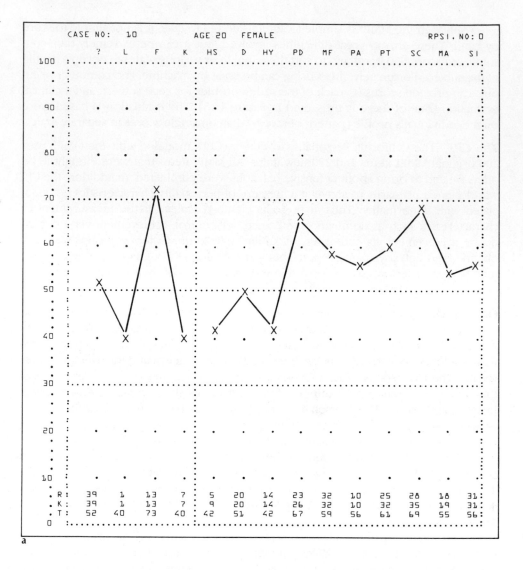

a

CASE NO: 10   AGE 20 FEMALE   RPSI. NO: 0

	?	L	F	K	HS	D	HY	PD	MF	PA	PT	SC	MA	SI
R:	39	1	13	7	5	20	14	23	32	10	25	28	18	31
K:	39	1	13	7	9	20	14	26	32	10	32	35	19	31
T:	52	40	73	40	42	51	42	67	59	56	61	69	55	56

CRITICAL ITEMS

THESE TEST ITEMS, WHICH WERE ANSWERED IN THE DIRECTION INDICATED, MAY REQUIRE FURTHER INVESTIGATION BY THE CLINICIAN. THE CLINICIAN IS CAUTIONED, HOWEVER, AGAINST OVERINTERPRETATION OF ISOLATED RESPONSES.

27   EVIL SPIRITS POSSESS ME AT TIMES. (TRUE)
48   WHEN I AM WITH PEOPLE I AM BOTHERED BY HEARING VERY QUEER THINGS. (TRUE)
170   I AM WORRIED ABOUT SEX MATTERS. (TRUE)
200   I BELIEVE MY SINS ARE UNPARDONABLE. (TRUE)
44   MUCH OF THE TIME MY HEAD SEEMS TO HURT ALL OVER. (TRUE)
337   I FEEL ANXIETY ABOUT SOMETHING OR SOMEONE ALMOST ALL THE TIME. (TRUE)
354   I AM AFRAID OF USING A KNIFE OR ANYTHING VERY SHARP OR POINTED. (TRUE)

b CASE NO. 10   AGE 20   FEMALE   RPSI NO. 0
                                       JANUARY 14, 1969

THE PATIENT'S RESPONSES TO THE TEST SUGGEST THAT SHE UNDERSTOOD THE ITEMS AND FOLLOWED THE INSTRUCTIONS ADEQUATELY. IT APPEARS, HOWEVER, THAT SHE MAY HAVE BEEN OVERLY SELF CRITICAL. THE VALIDITY OF THE TEST MAY HAVE BEEN AFFECTED BY HER TENDENCY TO ADMIT TO SYMPTOMS EVEN WHEN THEY ARE MINIMAL. THIS MAY REPRESENT AN EFFORT TO CALL ATTENTION TO HER DIFFICULTIES TO ASSURE OBTAINING HELP. THIS SUGGESTS THAT SHE FEELS VULNERABLE AND DEFENSELESS, WHICH MAY REFLECT A READINESS TO ACCEPT PROFESSIONAL ASSISTANCE.

THIS PATIENT HAS A TEST PATTERN WHICH IS OFTEN ASSOCIATED WITH SERIOUS PERSONALITY DISORDERS. PSYCHIATRIC PATIENTS WITH THIS PATTERN FREQUENTLY SHOW OBVIOUSLY DEVIANT BEHAVIOR. THEY ARE USUALLY DIAGNOSED AS HAVING A PERSONALITY DISORDER OR PSYCHOTIC REACTION. USUAL MANIFESTATIONS ARE

POOR SOCIAL ADJUSTMENT, AND UNUSUAL OR BIZARRE THINKING AND BEHAVIOR, FREQUENTLY IN THE SEXUAL AREA. MEDICAL PATIENTS WITH THIS PATTERN ARE CHARACTERIZED BY VAGUE PHYSICAL COMPLAINTS AND CONSIDERABLE ANXIETY. MANY APPEAR TO BE EARLY PSYCHOTIC REACTIONS, ALTHOUGH THEY RARELY SHOW FRANKLY BIZARRE BEHAVIOR.

IN GENERAL, PEOPLE WITH THIS TEST PATTERN ARE SEEN AS ODD OR PECULIAR. IT SHOULD BE EMPHASIZED THAT THE PRESENCE OF THIS PATTERN IS NOT CONCLUSIVE EVIDENCE OF A PERSONALITY DISORDER. HOWEVER, THE HIGH INCIDENCE OF UNUSUAL BEHAVIOR AMONG PATIENTS WITH THIS PATTERN SUGGESTS THAT THE PATIENT SHOULD BE CAREFULLY EVALUATED.

SHE IS A RIGID PERSON WHO MAY EXPRESS HER ANXIETY IN FEARS, COMPULSIVE BEHAVIOR AND RUMINATION. SHE MAY BE CHRONICALLY WORRIED AND TENSE, WITH MARKED RESISTANCE TO TREATMENT DESPITE OBVIOUS DISTRESS.

THIS PERSON FEELS UNABLE TO DEAL WITH THE ENVIRONMENTAL PRESSURES FACING HER, OR TO UTILIZE HER SKILLS OR ABILITIES TO FULL ADVANTAGE. AT PRESENT SHE FEELS UNABLE TO COPE WITH LIFE AS SHE SEES IT. SHE MAY RESPOND TO HER FEELINGS OF INADEQUACY WITH INCREASINGLY RIGID BEHAVIOR OR WITHDRAWAL DEPENDING UPON INDIVIDUAL FACTORS.

THE TEST RESULTS ON THIS PATIENT ARE STRONGLY SUGGESTIVE OF A MAJOR EMOTIONAL DISORDER. APPROPRIATE PROFESSIONAL EVALUATION AND CONTINUED OBSERVATION ARE SUGGESTED. PSYCHIATRIC CARE MAY BE REQUIRED.

NOTE: ALTHOUGH NOT A SUBSTITUTE FOR THE CLINICIAN'S PROFESSIONAL JUDGMENT AND SKILL, THE MMPI CAN BE A USEFUL ADJUNCT IN THE EVALUATION AND MANAGEMENT OF EMOTIONAL DISORDERS. THE REPORT IS FOR PROFESSIONAL USE ONLY AND SHOULD NOT BE SHOWN OR RELEASED TO THE PATIENT.

more readily to a global and intuitive assessment than to a standardized scoring procedure. In this connection, respondents emphasized the importance of insightful, subjective evaluations. A large number felt that tests were much more valuable than estimates of reliability and validity would indicate.

Do clinical psychologists employ tests because there are no easy alternatives? T. C. Wade and Baker's (1977) research suggests that this is probably not the case. Psychologists were asked to list alternatives to testing. Most often cited as alternatives were behavioral observation and interviewing, with interviewing being employed as an assessment technique by a majority of those who claimed they rarely (if ever) used tests. It seems clear that the majority of respondents felt that tests contributed something to their practice (only 73 out of 500 said they seldom employed tests).

Why do psychologists employ one test rather than another? Are their decisions based on validity and reliability data? Are they determined by the specific purposes for which the tests were constructed? On many occasions, both of these factors are clearly important, but the single most important factor was previous experience with the test. In other words, most psychologists tended to employ a relatively limited number of tests selected from among those with which they had had the greatest amount of experience. Presumably, repeated experience with the same instrument would contribute to the subjective insights that might be derived from the test.

Some Cautions

Although personality inventories and other assessment devices have proven useful in a number of situations, both practical and theoretical, it cannot yet be argued that any specific personality trait can be measured with unquestioned validity and reliability (Weiss & Davison, 1981). Results obtained from different inventories for the same individual are sometimes different, and not all predictions made on the basis of diagnostic instruments have been entirely reliable (Bersoff, 1973). For these reasons, interpretation of test scores requires both restraint and wisdom. There are ethical considerations here as well. Tests such as these can be dangerous in the hands of those who are not fully aware of their weaknesses. Users must constantly bear in mind that the stability of personality characteristics is still a matter of theoretical debate. Thus, a test that reveals an individual to be tense does not establish that anxiety is a pervasive and predominant personality characteristic in that person. Personality tests measure mood, fatigue, feelings of happiness or dejection, and a variety of other affective states. And we know from our private experience that none of these is necessarily permanent.

Figure 14.6 How useful are psychological tests? Although well aware of the tests' limitations, close to 72 percent of responding clinical psychologists in one survey used at least one test on clients, usually in making a diagnosis. Subjective projective tests, like the Rorschach inkblot shown here, are most frequently employed (T. C. Wade & Baker, 1977).

Intelligence

Personality was defined earlier as the stable characteristics of a person, including abilities, talents, habits, preferences, weaknesses, moral attributes, and a number of other important qualities that vary from one person to another. Perhaps the most important and most controversial of all personality characteristics is intelligence. Intelligence has been defined in many ways, beginning with Boring's assertion that "intelligence is what the tests test" (1923, p. 35), and culminating in a variety of more or less complex descriptions of intellectual functioning.

General Factor or Special Abilities?

A number of definitions of intelligence are based on the belief that it consists of separate, identifiable abilities. One example of this **special abilities** approach is provided by Thurstone (1938) who identified seven "primary mental abilities" on the basis of test results:

S (space) visualization of geometric figures

N (number) speed of computational skills

Special abilities theory A theory of intelligence that does not recognize the existence of a single underlying factor but instead proposes that intelligence consists of separate, identifiable abilities.

P (perceptual speed) speed of perceiving details

V (verbal meanings) grasp of meanings of words

W (word fluency) speed of manipulating single words

M (rote memory) facility in memorizing simple material

I (induction) logical reasoning ability

Other definitions are based on the assumption that intelligence is a single underlying ability, although it might manifest itself in a number of more specific abilities. This assumption is commonly known as a **general factor theory** of intelligence, and is exemplified by Wechsler's (1958) definition of intelligence as "the global and aggregate capacity of an individual to think rationally, to act purposefully, and to deal effectively with his environment" (p. 7).

A complex "special abilities" model of human intelligence has been organized around three main aspects of human functioning: operations, products, and content (Guilford, 1959, 1967). An *operation* is a major intellectual process involving such things as cognition, memory, divergent thinking, convergent thinking, and evaluation. Each of these operations may be applied to different kinds of information, labeled *content*. Thus, there is figural content (numbers, for example), symbolic content (abstract representations), semantic content (words), or behavioral content (motor or emotional responses). The result of applying an operation to content is a *product*. It can take one of six different forms: single items of information (units), sets of related items (classes), relationships among items or groups (relations), more complex organizations of information (systems), changes of information (transformations), or generalizations and predictions from information (implications). Given that each operation can be applied to every type of content separately, and that the result can be any or all possible products, a total of 120 separate "abilities" are represented by this model (Figure 14.7). Not every one of these has been isolated in practice, however. The two dimensions that have stimulated the greatest interest and research are those of convergent and divergent thinking, which are thought to be centrally involved in creativity and intelligence. Creative abilities involve a preponderance of divergent operations (the production of a variety of solutions); other operations are involved as well, however. Clearly, memory and evaluation play an important role in creative behavior. Convergent thinking, the production of single "correct" responses, is related to measured intelligence.

There is no definite agreement concerning whether intelligence is better considered as a single quality or as a combination of separate factors, but most currently used measures of intelligence are premised on the assumption that, although intelligence might be manifested in a number of different ways, there is a general, underlying ability that contributes to performance in all areas. This does not mean that a given individual will perform at the same relative level on all tasks that require intelligence. It simply means that there is a tendency for performance in different areas to be related.

Measuring and Describing Intelligence

I amused myself earlier by counting the number of personality tests currently available, but I would not be so foolish as to try to count the number of intelligence and aptitude tests available. There are many.

The principal use of intelligence tests is for prediction. An intelligence test score is, in fact, a prediction that an individual will do well or less well on tasks presumably requiring intelligence. Even when tests are being employed to sort people into categories, there is implicit in the sorting process a prediction that some categories can function better than others. Indeed, a widely accepted definition of *intelligence* is "the ability to do well in school." Given this definition, the most valid intelligence tests would be those that predict school achievement most accurately.

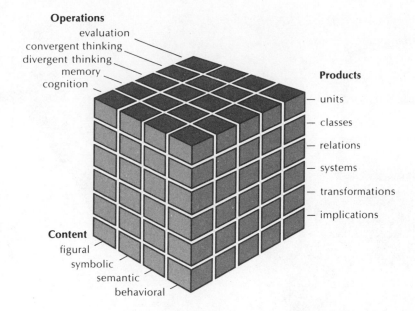

Operations
- evaluation
- convergent thinking
- divergent thinking
- memory
- cognition

Products
- units
- classes
- relations
- systems
- transformations
- implications

Content
- figural
- symbolic
- semantic
- behavioral

Figure 14.7 Guilford's "special abilities" model of intelligence, based on three aspects of human functioning. Five types of operations may be applied to any of four types of information or content to result in any or all of six types of products. In all, 120 separate abilities can be distinguished. (From "Three Faces of Intellect" by J. P. Guilford, *American Psychologist*, 1959, *14*, 469–479. Copyright 1959 by the American Psychological Association. Reprinted by permission.)

Given the global and imprecise nature of the term *intelligence*, a large number of tests that might otherwise be termed intelligence tests, and that do, in fact, attempt to measure many of the same things that traditional intelligence tests attempt to measure, are called *aptitude tests*. Since an **aptitude** is generally defined as a specific ability or capacity to learn, it does not have the same connotations that IQ scores do. Being told that you have a low aptitude for scholastic work does not cause the same feelings of personal inferiority that being told you have low intelligence might.

Many traditional intelligence tests describe what they measure by assigning it a number: an **intelligence quotient** (IQ). IQ was originally derived in a simple, easy to understand manner. Suppose that the majority of five-year-old children are capable of solving problems of difficulty X; most four-year-olds are capable of problems with difficulty levels of $X - 1$; most six-year-olds, of problems with difficulty levels of $X + 1$. Average five-year-old children may be said to have mental ages of five, mental age simply referring to the average mental functioning of a five-year-old. Clearly, however, not all five-year-old children have a mental age of five; only the average do. Some are more intelligent and consequently solve problems that older children solve; their mental ages are six or seven or higher. Others have lower mental ages. A simple way of describing intelligence is in terms of a relationship between chronological (real) age and mental age. Thus, an average five-year-old has identical chronological and mental ages. The intelligence quotient for this average child is the ratio of mental to chronological age, multiplied by 100 to simplify matters. Hence, $5 \div 5 \times 100$ yields an IQ of 100. Average IQ is thus 100 for any large, representative, "average" group of people. Those whose mental ages are greater than their chronological ages have higher IQs (for example: MA = 6; CA = 5; IQ = 120) (Figure 14.8).

The earliest recognized measure of intelligence was based on this reasoning. Binet and Simon, in 1905, devised sets of questions, arranged them in increasing order of difficulty, and allocated them to age levels. All items that 65 to 75 percent of the five-year-olds passed were placed in the five-year level, and so on. Mental age was computed by presenting children with these questions until they reached levels that were too difficult for them.

Later revisions of the Binet tests, the most popular of which is the Stanford-Binet (revised by Terman at Stanford) made use of large, representative standardization samples. This revision also used the "deviation IQ," a concept introduced earlier by Wechsler and now employed in virtually all contemporary measures of intelligence.

Aptitude A specific ability or capacity to learn. Aptitude tests measure the extent to which individuals are likely to profit from future experiences. When psychologists speak of *special aptitudes* they mean specific aptitudes (for example, music aptitude), rather than aptitudes that are most outstanding. They speak as well of *general aptitudes:* a capacity for acquiring knowledge or proficiency in a number of areas. *Scholastic aptitude* tests measure the capacity to profit from educational experience and are very similar to intelligence tests.

Intelligence quotient (IQ) A simple way of describing intelligence by assigning it a number: the ratio of mental to chronological age, multiplied by 100. Average IQ is thus 100, and is based on a comparison between an individual and comparable others.

Figure 14.8 Although intelligence manifests itself in a large variety of specific abilities and behaviors (such as playing the violin), there is no accepted method of measuring it in an absolute sense (as we measure distance or weight, for example). Thus measures of intelligence always involve comparisons between an individual and the average performance of other comparable individuals.

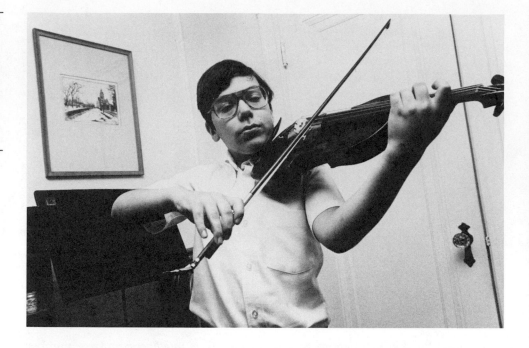

Normal distribution A mathematical function which can be represented in the form of an inverted U-shaped curve (or a bell-shaped curve right side up). A large number of naturally occurring events, or events determined by chance, are normally distributed. What this means, essentially, is that the vast majority of scores cluster around the middle of the distribution (around the average or median), with progressively fewer scores being further and further away from the average.

A deviation IQ is not computed as a function of chronological and mental age, but is read directly from tables that accompany each test. Tests are standardized so that the average scores for any age group are at or very close to 100, and scores vary from this average in predictable ways. Intelligence, like many other events and personality characteristics, illustrates **normal distribution**. That is, if you took all the scores obtained by a large group of people on a large number of individual measures, and plotted them in terms of frequency, the distribution would look like the shaded area in Figure 14.9. Most people tend to cluster around the mean (average), with progressively fewer people scoring further and further from it in each direction. The normal curve can be expressed as a mathematical equation with definite properties, the most important of which concerns the number of cases that will be found in different areas of the curve (see Box 14.2 and Appendix). Note, for example, that approximately two-thirds of all individuals score between 85 and 115; 95 percent score between 70 and 130.

Representative Tests

In general, there are two types of intelligence tests: individual and group. *Individual tests* can be given to only one person at a time and typically require a trained tester. These tests are expensive and time-consuming, but usually more reliable than *group tests*. The great advantage of group tests is that a single examiner can present the test to large groups of subjects at one time. Unlike individual tests, they are primarily of the paper and pencil variety.

Stanford-Binet The *Stanford-Binet* is one of the most widely used individual intelligence tests, particularly for young children (as young as age three). It is a highly verbal test that tends to correlate highly with success in school. The test requires approximately an hour (sometimes more) and considerable training and practice to administer. It yields a single score that can be converted to an intelligence score basically identical to an IQ.

The Wechsler Scales The *Wechsler tests* yield a number of different scores relating to specific abilities. In addition, different scores are grouped together as verbal scales and performance scales. Thus, the test yields scores for each separate ability, a performance score, a verbal score, and a composite score. Scale scores are sometimes

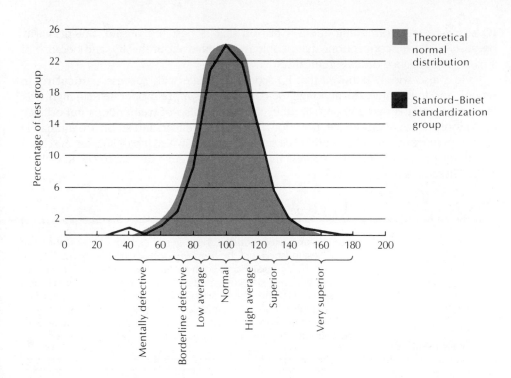

useful in establishing a profile (pictorial representation) of the subject's specific strengths and weaknesses. Verbal and performance scores can each be converted to intelligence scores (deviation IQs), and the composite score yields a single measure of intelligence highly comparable to that obtained with the Stanford-Binet (Figure 14.10).

There are various forms of the Wechsler tests: The WAISr (Wechsler Adult Intelligence Scale, revised, ages sixteen to seventy-five); the WISCr (Wechsler Intelligence Scale for Children, revised, ages five to fifteen); and the WPPSI (Wechsler Preschool and Primary Scale of Intelligence, ages four to six-and-a-half). The various subtests of the WISCr are described in Table 14.2. Those for the WAISr are highly similar.

Draw-a-Man Test   This intriguing group test was devised by Goodenough (1926) and later revised by D. Harris (1963). It is based on the assumption that children's drawings reflect their conceptual sophistication. The child is simply asked to draw the best man (or woman in the Draw-a-Woman Test) possible and is given no time limit. Drawings are scored primarily for detail and completeness according to a well-established set of criteria. Raw scores are then converted to an IQ equivalent (Figure 14.11). The test is appropriate for children aged three to fifteen years.

Otis-Lennon Mental Ability Test   Of the hundreds of aptitude or intelligence tests, the Otis-Lennon (1967) is one of the most widely used. It is suitable for a wide age range from kindergarten to adult, and is intended to provide a measure of what the authors term "general mental ability" or "scholastic aptitude." A more recent form of the Otis-Lennon, the Otis-Lennon School Ability Test (1979) is described not as an intelligence test but simply as a test of scholastic aptitude. It is designed to measure abstract thinking and reasoning, and to predict success in school.

Myths about IQ

A number of common misconceptions surround the use of the IQ. It is frequently assumed, for example, that all individuals have an IQ, as though it were a fixed something that a person has or doesn't have. In fact, IQ is simply a mathematical expression based on ability to perform a number of tasks in prescribed situations. IQ is not some mystical hidden quality known only to clever psychologists. And the secrecy that has long surrounded the use of IQ scores has been justified, not on the grounds that an

IQ score reveals something about a person that is best left unsaid, but primarily because of the misconceptions that people might have about the IQ, and because of a naive overreliance on its significance.

It is also widely believed that IQ scores correlate with success, particularly in school. And in fact, they do, although the correlation is more moderate than high. The important point is that a variety of other factors are also of tremendous importance for school success. Persistence, need for achievement, effort, and so on are intimately related to performance. And numerous studies have shown that past success in school is a better predictor of future success than is an intelligence test score (D. K. Cohen, 1972; Thorndike & Hagen, 1977).

Family Size and the IQ Slump

Between 1962 and 1974, average scores of high-school seniors on the Scholastic Aptitude Test (SAT), in effect a measure of intelligence, dropped from 490 to less than 460. The evidence suggests strongly that seniors in the early 1970s were *less intelligent* than were seniors in the early 1960s (Tavris, 1976). Why?

People blame IQ tests, television, a deteriorating educational system, or an era of permissiveness which has infected young people with apathy and loss of ambition and industriousness.

Zajonc (1975) has another explanation. He and Markus have investigated the relationship between birth order and intelligence and have arrived at a simple model of intellectual development. The Zajonc-Markus model describes intelligence as being in large part (although not entirely) a function of the intellectual climate of the home; and they have derived simple formulas for computing an index of intellectual climate. In essence, this index is an average of the intellectual levels of all family members. Parents are arbitrarily assigned a value of 30; a newborn has a value of 0; and the intellectual index increases between birth and adulthood. Thus, a first-born child is brought into a home with an intellectual climate of $(30 + 30 + 0) \div 3 = 20$. Children born later, particularly if there is little space between succeeding children, have a lower intellectual environment (for example, $30 + 30 + 6 + 4 + 2 + 0 \div 6 = 12$).

The Zajonc-Markus model suggests a close correspondence between intellectual climate in the home and performance on measures of intelligence. A direct test of the model is provided by data on birth-order advantage (see Chapter 11). In addition, a number of large-scale studies provide strong evidence that children born later in large families score lower on measures of intelligence than children born earlier, or than children born into smaller families (Zajonc, 1975; Grotevant et al., 1977; Page & Grandon, 1979). There appears to be little doubt that, *on the average,* birth order and size of family are closely related to intellectual development, with children born later or born into larger families having a disadvantage (Melican & Feldt, 1980).

How does this explain the decline in SAT scores? Children taking the test in the late 1960s and early 1970s were the products of the postwar baby boom. They came from larger families, and their average birth order was later than had been the case for those taking the SAT in the early 1960s (see the graph).

These observations, however valid they may be, apply only to average scores and average birth order. Numerous individuals pro-

vide striking exceptions to these generalizations. It has not been clearly established that the *most important* variables in intellectual climate are family size and birth order. Page and Grandon's investigation of family size and intelligence led them to the conclusion that social class and ethnic variables might be even more important. Larger families tend to be more common among lower social classes and in certain ethnic minorities. Intellectual climate is not likely to be a simple concept, tied only to family size and birth order.

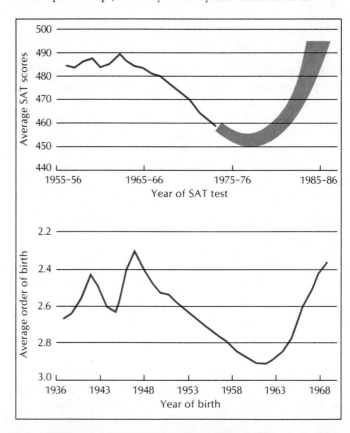

An explanation of the "IQ slump." The lower graph shows the average birth order of U.S. children born between 1936 and 1963; the upper graph shows how those children scored seventeen years later on the SAT. The postwar baby boom's big families began a twelve-year slide of test scores. If this theory is correct, then the lower birth rates and smaller families of recent years should reverse the trend; the shaded range in the top graph indicates predicted higher scores. (From "The End of the IQ Slump" by C. Tavris, *Psychology Today,* April 1976, 69–73. Copyright © 1976 Ziff-Davis Publishing Company. Reprinted by permission.)

Figure 14.10 This child is taking the Stanford-Binet intelligence test.

A third misconception is that IQ tests measure all that is important. In fact, however, IQ tests, like all other personality tests, may not measure all the important things. Sadly, we cannot be absolutely certain of everything they do measure, but to the extent that they are unreliable and invalid (and all of them are, more or less), we can be certain that they do measure other things and that they do not measure perfectly accurately whatever it is they are measuring.

A final misconception with respect to measured intelligence concerns its origins, and can take one of two forms: a naive belief that intelligence is fixed because it is

Table 14.2 Tests Included in the Wechsler Intelligence Scale for Children (WISCr)

Verbal Scale	Performance Scale
1. *General information.* Questions relating to information most children have the opportunity to acquire.	1. *Picture completion.* Child indicates what is missing in pictures.
2. *General comprehension.* Questions designed to assess child's understanding of why certain things are done as they are.	2. *Picture arrangement.* Series of pictures must be arranged to tell a story.
3. *Arithmetic.* Oral arithmetic problems.	3. *Block design.* Child is required to copy exactly a design with colored blocks.
4. *Similarities.* Child indicates how certain things are alike.	4. *Object assembly.* Puzzles to be assembled by subject.
5. *Vocabulary.* Child gives meanings of words of increasing difficulty.	5. *Coding.* Child pairs symbols with digits following a key.
6. *Digit span.* Child repeats orally presented sequence of numbers, in order and reversed.	6. *Mazes.* Child traces way out of mazes with pencil.

Figure 14.11 Two examples of the Goodenough-Harris Draw-a-Man Test. Both subjects were boys aged 10¾ years. The raw scores and IQ equivalents, respectively, for the drawings are (**a**) 41 and 110; (**b**) 4 and 54. The child who drew **b** also had a low Stanford-Binet IQ score. (From *Children's Drawings as Measures of Intellectual Maturity* by Dale B. Harris. © 1963 by Harcourt Brace Jovanovich, Inc. Reproduced by permission of the publisher.)

genetically ordained; an equally naive belief that intelligence is totally plastic because it is determined by the environment. This, the classical nature-nurture controversy with regard to intelligence, is the subject of the next major section of this chapter.

Heredity, Environment, and Intelligence

Is intelligence inherited? This is a central question in one of the longest and most bitter debates in psychology. Variously referred to as the nature-nurture controversy or the heredity-environment question, this debate has raged virtually unabated for more than a century. Extremists have typically adopted one point of view or the other. John Locke proposed that the mind is a blank slate at birth; experience writes its messages. Presumably, good experiences write clearly and intelligently; less good experiences scribble and doodle. John Watson (1930) took Locke's wisdom seriously. He asserted that, given a dozen healthy infants of any background whatsoever, and given complete freedom to do with them as he wished, he could probably make anything conceivable of them. Galton (1869) would have disagreed; he believed that intelligence and a variety of other psychological characteristics are hereditary.

Over the years, less extreme psychologists have frequently attempted to assess the extent to which heredity and the environment are responsible for such traits as intelligence. Virtually nobody now believes exclusively in the power of genetics or the power of environment. It is clear that both are involved in determining the outcome of human development. We have touched on this topic in earlier chapters, particularly in Chapter 11. We take it up again here as we explore the origins of individual intelligence.

Nature and Nurture in Animal Intelligence

Much of our evidence about the origins of intelligence comes from a large number of controlled studies conducted on a variety of animals. Two of the classic and highly illustrative series of studies conducted with rats are discussed here.

In the first series of studies, Tryon (1940) began with a parent generation of 142 rats. Each of these rats was run through a seventeen-unit maze—an intricate arrangement of barriers and pathways where rats had to learn seventeen correct choices before they could run most directly through the maze. He counted the total number of errors made by each rat in learning the maze. The "brightest" rat made only 14 errors; the "dullest" made 174. Next, Tryon selected the brightest rats and mated them; similarly, dull rats were mated with other dull rats. The progeny from these arranged pairings were then run through the same maze and their errors again tabulated. The brightest of the bright group were mated together when they reached maturity; the dullest of the dull group were paired. The procedure continued unchanged through a total of eighteen rat generations, the brightest of the bright rats always being paired together, and the dullest of the dull. Dull rats in the bright group were systematically eliminated, as were bright rats in the dull group. After a mere eighteen generations, there was no longer any overlap between the groups. That is, the dullest rat in the bright group was brighter, on this specific maze, than the brightest rat in the dull group (see Figure 14.12). It appears clear that genetic factors are involved in the maze-learning ability of the white rat.

Hebb (1947) investigated the effects of environmental stimulation on four groups of rats. Two of these groups were blindfolded—one at birth, and the other at maturity. A third group was raised as ordinary laboratory rats in cages. The fourth group was reared as people's pets, in their homes. In subsequent tests of maze-learning ability, rats blindfolded at birth performed least well. No one was surprised. What may have been more surprising was that rats reared as pets did significantly better than those

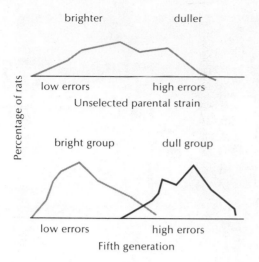

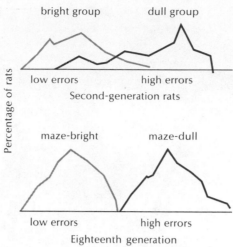

Figure 14.12 An approximate representation of Tryon's successful attempt to produce maze-bright and maze-dull rats through selective breeding. (From "Genetic Differences in Maze Learning in Rats" by R. C. Tryon, *39th Yearbook of the National Society for the Study of Education,* 1940, 111–119. Reprinted by permission.)

reared as laboratory animals. It seems clear that environmental factors are closely involved in the maze-learning ability of the white rat.

In summary, these and a variety of studies cannot easily establish that heredity is more important than environment, or vice versa. What they demonstrate is that *both* can be important. The optimal situation would clearly be one where both genetic factors and environmental forces favor the development of characteristics considered desirable.

Comparisons of Intelligence in Twins

Ethical and social considerations prevent the experimental use of human subjects in breeding experiments. It would therefore have remained very difficult to assess the relative influences of heredity and environment on the development of certain human attributes had it not been for the natural provision of one of the best-controlled experimental situations possible. Approximately one out of every eighty-six live births is that of twins, most of whom are fraternal, resulting from the nearly simultaneous fertilization of two different ova by two different sperm cells. The result is two individuals who are no more alike genetically than any other pair of siblings (siblings are brothers and sisters), but whose environments, given that they share the same uterus at the same time, and that they are always of the same age throughout their development, are considerably more similar than are those of most other siblings. A small number of twins, however, are identical (Figure 14.3). They result from the division of a single fertilized egg, and are therefore completely alike genetically. It follows, then, that any greater similarity between identical twins relative to fraternal twins would reflect a genetic effect. By the same token, any greater similarity between fraternal twins relative to other siblings should reflect environmental effects.

A strikingly large number of studies have reported a variety of correlations for identical twins, fraternal twins, siblings, parents, and children. A number of studies have even looked at twins who were reared apart. Erlenmeyer-Kimling and Jarvik (1963) summarized the results of studies that looked at intelligence test scores for ninety-nine different groups of such individuals. This summary is presented in Figure 14.14. What does it reveal?

First, it is clear that intelligence test scores are increasingly similar with increasing genetic similarity. Consider, for example, that the median (midpoint) correlation for unrelated people reared apart is around 0, indicating complete lack of relationship, but that for identical twins reared together it approaches 0.90 (very high positive relationship). What this correlation means, in effect, is that if one member of a pair of twins has a very high intelligence test score, the other twin will probably also have a

Figure 14.13 Identical twins. Clearly, genetics plays a part, but environment also plays an important role.

very high score. Similarly, if one member has a low score, the probability that the other will also have a low score is very high.

Second, the summary in Figure 14.14 also indicates that similarity of intelligence test scores increases with increasing environmental similarity. Thus, identical twins reared apart are more different in terms of measured intelligence than those reared together. Similarly, unrelated people reared together resemble each other more closely than unrelated people reared apart.

A more recent review of 111 studies that have looked at IQ correlations among relatives was undertaken by Bouchard and McGue (1981). Like most other researchers in this field, they too conclude that "the higher the proportion of genes two family members have in common, the higher the average correlation between their IQ's" (p. 1055). It must be noted again, however, that all of these studies also report higher correlations between individuals who are reared together or in similar environments than between those reared apart or in very different environments. In this connection, a number of recent studies of IQ correlations between parents and their adopted children, as well as between adopted children in the same family have also revealed higher than chance correlations even though none of these individuals is closely related genetically (Scarr & Weinberg, 1978; Horn, Loehlin & Willerman, 1979; Bouchard & McGue, 1981).

The best conclusion to be derived from this great variety of studies is quite simply that there is a strong genetic basis to measured intelligence, but that environmental forces are nevertheless very important. There does remain some controversy, however, concerning the extent to which each is important.

The Jensen Hypothesis

The highly publicized Jensen research (1968, 1969) has added fuel to the fire. The argument he advances is relatively simple. If measured intelligence were simply a function of genetic factors, the correlation coefficients for identical twins would be perfect (1.00). However, obtained correlations for identical twins are not perfect. The difference between a perfect correlation and that actually obtained must then be due to the environment. Since the obtained correlation for identical twins *reared apart* is around 0.75, it might be accurate to say that 25 percent of the variation in measured intelligence is due to the environment and 75 percent to heredity. A second method for arriving at an estimate of the heritability of intelligence would be to look at the

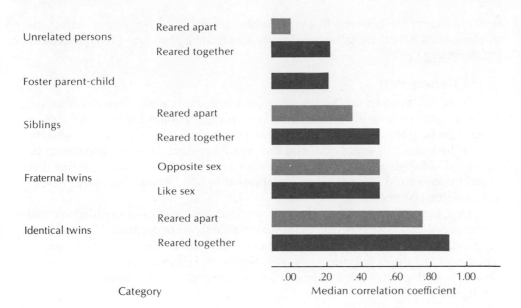

Unrelated persons
- Reared apart
- Reared together

Foster parent-child

Siblings
- Reared apart
- Reared together

Fraternal twins
- Opposite sex
- Like sex

Identical twins
- Reared apart
- Reared together

Category

Median correlation coefficient

.00   .20   .40   .60   .80   1.00

Figure 14.14 Median correlation coefficients for intelligence test scores from studies totaling ninety-nine different groups. The high correlation for identical twins shows the strong genetic basis of measured intelligence. The greater correlation for siblings or twins reared together compared with those reared apart supports the view that environmental forces are also important in determining similarity of intelligence test scores. (Based on data from "Genetics and Intelligence: A Review" by L. Erlenmeyer-Kimling and L. F. Jarvik, *Science*, 1963, *142*, 1477–1479. Copyright 1963 by the American Association for the Advancement of Science. Used by permission.)

correlation for unrelated people who are reared together. Jensen reports that these correlations average around 0.24. Thus the **heritability coefficient** for intelligence derived in this fashion is still around 75 percent. Various mathematical corrections for the inaccuracy of the tests employed yield overall heritability coefficients of around 0.81. It is important to note that these measures of heritability are indicators of the extent to which *variations* in intelligence test scores for groups reflect genetic differences among these groups. They do not refer to the proportion of intelligence that is genetic for an *individual*, but only to variation among groups. In summary, then, the Jensen hypothesis is simply that approximately 80 percent of the variation (among groups) in intelligence test scores is due to genetic factors, with 20 percent being accounted for by the environment.

Although there is some agreement with Jensen's general notion that genetic factors are more important in determining intelligence than are environmental factors (Vernon, 1979), a second aspect of his work has met with severe criticism. Following the often replicated finding that American blacks typically score below "comparable" whites on measures of intellectual performance, and given the assumption that black and white groups represent different gene pools, it apparently follows that observed racial differences in intelligence test scores may have a genetic basis. Jensen has advanced this notion, proposing that these racial differences cannot be accounted for solely by environmental factors.

The criticisms? J. S. Kagan (1969) and a number of geneticists point out that the races do not comprise separate gene pools. There is so much overlap among races that no single gene exists in one group alone, in spite of the fact that certain genes are more frequent in some groups than in others. Furthermore, and perhaps more important, variations within any single group are typically five to ten times greater than variations among different groups. If heredity is such a potent force, why is there so much variation within groups?

Other critics of Jensen's hypothesis point to the difficulties inherent in attempting to substantiate heritability coefficients (J. M. Hunt, 1969); to the very small samples he employed in some of his studies (Crow, 1969); to his failure to take into account such powerful environmental forces as nutrition (Brazziel, 1969); and to the biases inherent in most measures of intelligence—biases that typically favor white, middle-class children. As Crow points out, even if only 20 percent of the variation in measured intelligence can be accounted for by the environment, there is really no guarantee that the

Heritability coefficient An index which generally indicates the extent to which variation in characteristics is related to genetic factors. A heritability coefficient of 70 does not indicate that 70 percent of a characteristic (for example, intelligence) is determined by heredity; it indicates that 70 percent of the *variation* in intelligence scores appears to be accounted for by genetic factors. In other words, a heritability coefficient is an index of variation rather than of absolute amount.

observed difference between black and white groups does not simply reflect the environment's 20 percent influence, a point also made by Hawkins (1977) and Scarr and Weinberg (1978).

A Conclusion

It should be noted that Jensen advances a hypothesis rather than a conclusion; it cannot easily be proven or disproven. Vernon (1979), following a careful look at Jensen's data and at that of other major researchers in the field (see Box 14.3), suggests that the hypothesis of greater genetic than environmental influence appears to be supported, although a number of estimates are somewhat lower than those first presented by Jensen (60 percent genetic as opposed to 80). Vernon also makes several very important points.

First, heritability describes a genetic tendency that applies to populations with similar genes, and not to specific individuals within those populations. Thus, for any given individual, the influence of environment or genetics can be substantially greater than they are for the population as a whole. Stern (1956) summarizes this point in the form of an analogy between intellectual functioning and the length of a rubber band (see Figure 14.15):

> The genetic endowment in respect to any one trait has been compared to a rubber band and the trait itself to the length which the rubber band assumes when it is stretched by outside forces. Different people initially may have been given different lengths of unstretched endowment, but the natural forces of the environment may have stretched their expression to equal length, or led to differences in attained length sometimes corresponding to their innate differences and at other times in reverse of the relation (p. 53).

Second, it is imperative to keep in mind that genes do not *cause* intelligence; they interact with the environment, the end result being a certain level of manifested intelligence. And the nature of that interaction, as we noted in Chapter 11, is often

---

BOX 14.3

IQ, Heredity, and Fraud?

Sir Cyril Burt (1883–1971) conducted and reported one of the most influential studies of heredity and intelligence using pairs of twins, some reared together, and others reared apart (Burt, 1966). His finding, that intelligence is largely hereditary, has been used extensively by others who also argue for the heritability of intelligence (for example, Herrnstein, 1973; Jensen, 1974).

It now appears that Burt's data may be useless, for a number of reasons (see, for example, N. Wade, 1976a), not the least of which include serious and sometimes quite implausible errors in his data and in his analysis of those data (Kamin, 1974). He reports, for example, that the correlations between IQ scores of identical twins reared apart is exactly 0.771 in three separate studies and, similarly, that the correlation for identical twins reared together is 0.944, also in three separate studies. That these figures should be the same in each of these studies is extremely unlikely. Furthermore, he often fails to provide critical information about his subjects (their ages, sex, the types of tests employed, actual test scores, number of subjects, and so on).

After these exposures, many researchers who had relied heavily on Burt's data recognized that they were now useless. Among them, Jensen (1974) published the first account of Burt's errors, acknowledging in this account that Kamin was the first to recognize publicly in lectures the weakness in Burt's data. Others had suspected the data, but no one had systematically reexamined them and reported their suspicions.

Whether Burt's "errors" are the result of deliberate fraud, honest error, or both has not been determined (although there are strong opinions on every side). In any case, the reasons behind the deception are probably irrelevant for science. The crucial point is that much of the data can no longer be used (Vernon, 1979).

How devastating is the loss of these data to the hereditarians' argument? Jensen (1974) claims that the important results have now been replicated, and that no conclusions need be dramatically altered. Similarly, Scarr and Weinberg (1977) believe that the loss of Burt's data simply means that estimates of heritability have to be scaled downward, although not dramatically. Vernon (1979) agrees.

Recent research in this area, reviewed extensively by DeFries and Plomin (1978), Bouchard and McGue (1981), and Vernon (1979), indicates that almost all studies of heritability (twin studies, adoptive studies, and other family studies) support a belief in the partial heritability of cognitive abilities (see, for example, Scarr & Weinberg, 1977). But few of these studies provide heritability estimates as high as those based on Burt's data.

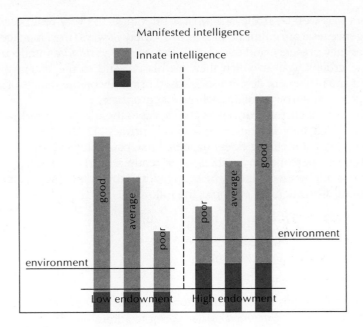

Manifested intelligence

Innate intelligence

Figure 14.15 The "rubber-band hypothesis." Individuals with high or low intellectual potential (genetic endowment) can manifest varying degrees of intelligence depending on the "stretching" effects of environmental forces.

extremely complex. It is quite possible, for example, that certain parents react one way to children with particular genes for intelligence, but react quite differently to other children whose endowments are different. We are not likely to be able to sort these influences easily.

Finally, it bears repeating that our measures of intelligence are not yet perfect; and one of their imperfections is that the most commonly employed tests tend to favor children from some environments (notably white, middle class, dominant majorities) and to penalize others (social-ethnic minorities). As we note in the next section, intelligence tests can be abused in a number of ways.

Misuses and Abuses of Tests

Given that intelligence tests and personality tests are less than perfectly valid and reliable, it is not surprising that they are sometimes misused. This section discusses briefly a number of ways in which tests and test results can be used or interpreted inappropriately.

First, it is extremely important to bear in mind with regard to intelligence tests that an IQ is simply a numerical expression that in some ways relates to performance in various areas, the most obvious of which is school achievement. It is not a completely stable, unchanging quality of an individual; nor is it always a highly significant predictor of achievement. In spite of this, a great many crucial decisions, particularly in schools and colleges, are premised almost entirely on the results of intelligence tests. It should be clear that this procedure can be highly unfair to specific individuals whose scores might be adversely affected by any number of factors, including illness, fatigue, language deficits, lack of motivation, and so on.

Related to this is the widely accepted observation that most intelligence tests in current use have been developed with white middle-class individuals in mind, and have been standardized on samples of such individuals. Numerous studies have shown repeatedly that various groups (most notably the poor, a group which frequently includes ethnic minority groups such as blacks or Hispanic Americans) perform less well on these tests than the white middle-class majority (for example, Loehlin et al., 1975) (see Box 14.4). Whether these differences are due largely to environmental factors or not may well be irrelevant; what is relevant is the very real possibility that most intelligence tests are culturally biased in a variety of ways (the language they use, the examples they present), and that they therefore *underestimate* intellectual potential for those groups against which they are biased. And to the extent that school advancement and placement decisions are based primarily on the results of such tests, their use with certain groups might well be inappropriate.

Another area of current concern with respect to the use of psychological tests is the extent to which they invade an individual's privacy. There are several ways in which this can (and sometimes does) happen. First, psychological tests—particularly those dealing with personality variables—frequently require individuals to disclose information that might not ordinarily be revealed, and that sometimes is embarrassing or incriminating. Consider, for example, the following:

Has anyone in your family been in a mental institution?

Does anyone in your family have a criminal record?

Have you been in a mental institution?

How frequently do you masturbate?

Requiring such relevations is not always appropriate, particularly when examiners do not obtain the individual's *informed consent* prior to administering the test. Informed consent requires that the individual be aware of the nature of the test, its purposes, and its usefulness, and that there not be any coercion involved in obtaining consent. The conditions required for obtaining informed consent do not always exist. In some

---

BOX 14.4

The Chitling Test

In a semiserious reaction to traditional intelligence tests, designed for and standardized with white middle-class populations and consequently often biased against individuals whose cultural backgrounds are significantly different, black sociologist Adrian Dove designed the Dove Counterbalance General Intelligence Test (the "Chitling Test"). It draws freely on black language and culture, and a low score on this test might be indicative of cultural deprivation—at least with respect to the black culture.

1. A "handkerchief head" is: (a) a cool cat, (b) a porter, (c) an Uncle Tom, (d) a hoddi, (e) a preacher.

2. Which word is most out of place here? (a) splib, (b) blood, (c) gray, (d) spook, (e) black.

3. A "gas head" is a person who has a: (a) fast-moving car, (b) stable of "lace," (c) "process," (d) habit of stealing cars, (e) long jail record for arson.

4. "Down-home" (the South) today, for the average "soul brother" who is picking cotton from sunup until sundown, what is the average earning (take home) for one full day? (a) $.75, (b) $1.65, (c) $3.50, (d) $5, (e) $12.

5. "Bo Diddley" is a: (a) game for children, (b) down-home cheap wine, (c) down-home singer, (d) new dance, (e) Moejoe call.

6. If a pimp is uptight with a woman who gets state aid, what does he mean when he talks about "Mother's Day"? (a) second Sunday

in May, (b) third Sunday in June, (c) first of every month, (d) none of these, (e) first and fifteenth of every month.

7. "Hully Gully" came from: (a) East Oakland, (b) Fillmore, (c) Watts, (d) Harlem, (e) Motor City.

8. If a man is called a "blood," then he is a (a) fighter, (b) Mexican-American, (c) Negro, (d) hungry hemophile, (e) Redman or Indian.

9. Cheap chitlings (not the kind you purchase at a frozen-food counter) will taste rubbery unless they are cooked long enough. How soon can you quit cooking them to eat and enjoy them? (a) 45 minutes, (b) two hours, (c) 24 hours, (d) one week (on a low flame), (e) one hour.

10. What are the "Dixie Hummingbirds"? (a) part of the KKK, (b) a swamp disease, (c) a modern gospel group, (d) a Mississippi Negro paramilitary group, (e) Deacons.

11. If you throw the dice and seven is showing on the top, what is facing down? (a) seven, (b) snake eyes, (c) boxcars, (d) little Joes, (e) 11.

12. "Jet" is: (a) an East Oakland motorcycle club, (b) one of the gangs in "West Side Story," (c) a news and gossip magazine, (d) a way of life for the very rich.

13. T-Bone Walker got famous for playing what? (a) trombone, (b) piano, (c) "T-flute," (d) guitar, (e) "Hambone."*

Note: From "Dove Counterbalance General Intelligence Test" by Adrian Dove. Copyright 1968 by Newsweek, Inc. All rights reserved. Reprinted by permission.

*Those who are not "culturally deprived" will recognize the correct answers are 1. (c), 2. (c), 3. (c), 4. (d), 5. (c), 6. (e), 7. (c), 8. (c), 9. (c), 10. (c), 11. (a), 12. (c), 13. (d).

cases it is not possible to tell testees the purpose of the test without completely invalidating it. This would be the case, for example, if the test were designed to discover whether people cheat or lie. And in other cases, even when individuals can be completely informed, there remains an element of coercion. If the test is being used as a screening device for a job or for school admissions, for example, it is highly impractical—and probably impossible—to refuse consent.

Violations of personal rights might also be involved in the secrecy which has traditionally surrounded psychological testing. IQ scores, for example, have often been closeted in school files, accessible to school personnel and law-enforcement agencies, but seldom to parents or children. Increasing concern with individual rights, however, has recently been reflected in a federal law in the United States affecting all publicly funded educational institutions (Public Law 93-380). In effect, this law grants parents of children under eighteen access to education records; the right to challenge the accuracy and appropriateness of these records; the right to limit access to these records; and the right to be made aware of individuals and agencies who are permitted access to the records. All of these rights become the child's after the age of eighteen.

In summary, psychological tests can be patently unjust when used inappropriately or with groups for whom they were not intended; they can violate individual rights; and they can be highly threatening. In short, they can be misused in ways that are unethical and sometimes illegal. And it would be misleading to suggest that the misuse of psychological tests is rare; unfortunately it isn't.

In spite of these observations, intelligence tests provide a highly useful basis for such important decisions as school placement, college admission, job placement, scholastic awards, and so on. In the same way, personality tests can provide important information for career decisions, in clinical practice, and in other areas. In one sense, they are impeccably *objective* and *impartial*. The test does not know whether the testee is rich, poor, brown, or purple. And if used appropriately, tests can be far more just than might be the subjective opinions of teachers, personnel officers, and academic administrators. The single most important proviso is that those who make use of tests must not only respect the rights of testees, but must be fully aware of the very real limitations of psychological tests in their present stage of development.

Main Points

1 Psychological tests are good instruments to the extent that they are reliable and valid. They are valid to the extent that they measure what they purport to measure, and they are reliable to the extent that they do so with consistency.

2 Reliability of a psychological test may be determined by looking at the relationship between *parallel forms* of the test; by looking at the relationship between two halves of the test (*split-half*); or by giving the test twice (*test-retest*).

3 Validity of a psychological test may be determined by the accuracy with which it predicts (*predictive validity*); by looking at the content of the test to determine whether it represents a valid sample of the behaviors the examiner wishes to test (*content validity*); by comparing the test with other similar tests (*concurrent validity*); or by analyzing the test in terms of its relationship with underlying theoretical concepts and in terms of its logical consistency (*construct validity*).

4 Self-reports and ratings by independent observers are two simple ways of measuring personality characteristics. A third alternative, labeled *behavioral observation,* involves direct observation of samples of a subject's behavior.

5 Projective approaches to personality assessment involve asking the individual to respond to abstract stimuli. The basic assumption is that people unconsciously *project* many of their fears, wishes, fantasies, anxieties, and so on, when responding.

6 Rorschach inkblots and the thematic apperception test (TAT) are two well-known projective tests. Although the validity and reliability of these tests has not been established, they are particularly useful for exploring fantasy, and in the hands of a skilled analyst can lead to important insights.

7   There are hundreds of paper and pencil personality tests, referred to as scales and inventories. Scales measure specific dimensions of personality, while inventories are more general.

8   The Minnesota Multiphasic Personality Inventory (MMPI) is one of the best-known and more rigorously developed personality inventories. It yields measures on fourteen different dimensions, some of them rational scales and some of them diagnostic scales.

9   Personality assessment devices often have very low reliability and validity coefficients; thus, interpretation of test scores requires restraint and wisdom. A substantial proportion of clinical psychologists use tests extensively, most often for diagnosis and assessment.

10   Of the many definitions of intelligence, some are based on the notion that intelligence is a general ability that underlies a great many behaviors; others are based on the notion that separate abilities are essentially unrelated.

11   A special abilities model of intelligence is Guilford's description of five mental *operations* (evaluation, convergent thinking, divergent thinking, memory, and cognition) that can be applied to four types of mental *content* (figural, symbolic, semantic, or behavioral) to yield one of six different types of products (units, classes, relations, systems, transformations, and implications). The result is 120 separate abilities, not all of which have actually been identified and measured.

12   Intelligence tests are used mainly for prediction of how well an individual will do on tasks presumably requiring intelligence. Many traditional intelligence tests describe what they measure by assigning it a number: an intelligence quotient (IQ).

13   The IQ was initially derived by comparing an individual's *mental age* with *chronological age* to arrive at some notion of whether the individual was functioning at an "average" level or not. Current measures of intelligence typically provide IQ scores without reference to mental age, but still on the basis of average performance of large groups of individuals of similar chronological ages. Average IQ for large, unselected populations is typically around 100, and is normally distributed (approximately two-thirds of all individuals score between 85 and 115; only 5 percent score below 70 or above 130).

14   Individual intelligence tests are administered to one subject at a time and typically require a trained examiner. The Stanford-Binet and the Wechsler Scales are among the best-known of individual intelligence tests.

15   Group intelligence tests can be administered to many subjects at one time, are typically paper-and-pencil tests, can often be machine scored, and do not ordinarily require a trained examiner. The Otis-Lennon Mental Ability Test, and the Draw-a-Man test are two examples of group intelligence tests.

16   Misconceptions concerning the IQ include the notion that IQ is a fixed, mysterious something, highly correlated with success, and stable throughout life.

17   The nature-nurture (genetics-environment) controversy with respect to intelligence is one of the oldest controversies in psychology. Animal studies (of enriched rats and selectively bred rats) as well as studies of twins (reared together and apart, by their biological parents and by adoptive parents) all indicate that with increasing genetic similarity, IQ scores typically correlate more highly (a nature argument), but that with increasing environmental similarity, the same is also true (a nurture argument).

18   The Jensen hypothesis is that a greater proportion (perhaps as high as 75 or 80 percent) of the variation in intelligence test scores is due to genetics than to environment. The hypothesis appears to be generally supported, although more recent estimates are somewhat lower than Jensen's. These heritability figures apply to populations; for any given individual, the influence of heredity might be considerably lower. It is also worth noting that genes do not *cause* intelligence, but that they interact with the environment, the end result being the manifestation of intelligence in behavior.

19   In addition to their less than perfect validity and reliability, many tests of intelligence and personality currently in use are biased against certain ethnic and social minorities; none take into account important personal factors such as motivation, fatigue, and illness; and their use sometimes constitutes an invasion of privacy. Tests can be misused if these limitations are not acknowledged and taken into consideration.

Further Readings

A basic but comprehensive introduction to personality testing and measurement in psychology and education is provided by:

Thorndike, R. L., and Hagen, E. *Measurement and evaluation in psychology and education* (4th ed.). New York: John Wiley, 1977.

An excellent review of research relating to heredity, environment, and intelligence is presented in:

Vernon, P. E. *Intelligence, heredity and environment.* San Francisco: W. H. Freeman, 1979.

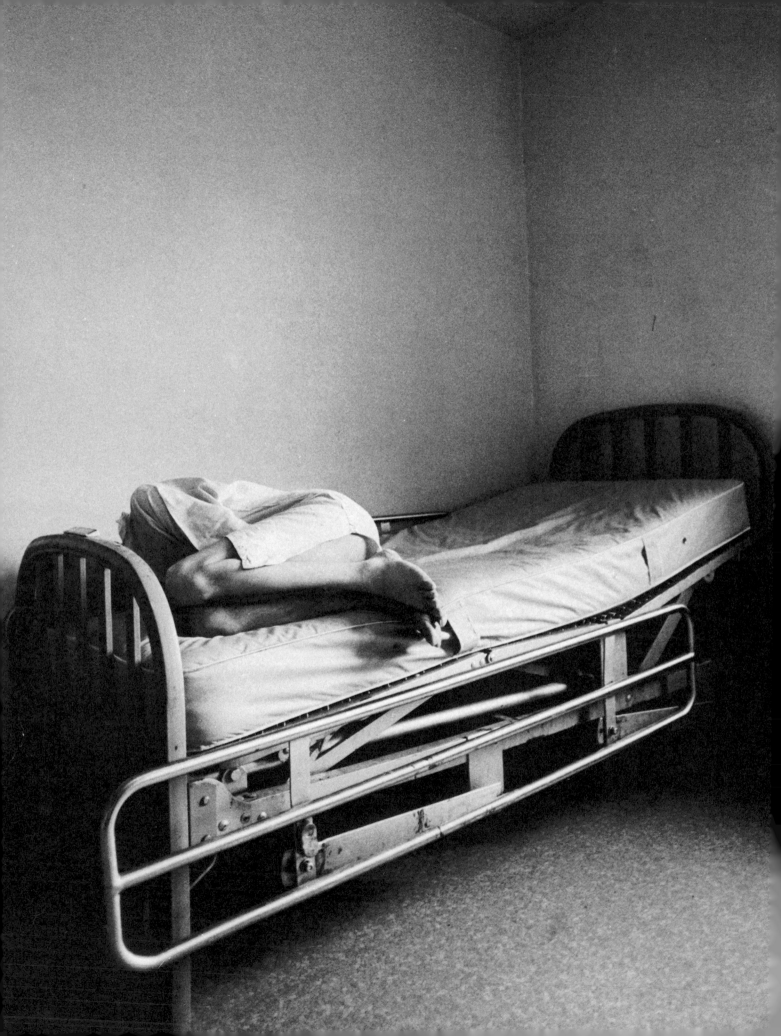

Psychopathology

15

Yukon Joe died last week. He was a friend. A horse kicked him in the head somewhere in Oregon and he died.

His girlfriend, Diana, phoned me from Oregon. She had found my phone number in his wallet. She knew none of his friends, none of his family. All she had were small scraps of paper with phone numbers. Local authorities could not release his body until they had notified next of kin. Diana was not next of kin; she was just a girlfriend.

Did I know where his family was? No. I met Yukon in California in the fall of 1975. I met him in a small town that he had temporarily taken over. "I'm fifty-two, you know," he boasted, and most were amazed because Yukon looked ten years younger. He was in marvelous physical condition. And he was a storyteller without equal. He told tales of personal adventures in the high Arctic that left his listeners breathless; and tales of years in the African jungles, fighting as a mercenary, that also left us speechless.

Throughout that winter, he enchanted that little town, entertaining in its bars, buying drink and dinners for his friends. As he told everyone, he had recently found wealth in Alaska.

And in the spring, when I was no longer there to be enchanted by his tales, he began investing in various enterprises—some local, and some very far away. People flocked to him with money and favors; he impressed them and they loved him.

Later that summer, Yukon came to visit me, and we wandered among the hills, fishing our way through August and into the fall. When the ducks left, he left too. Later in the winter, I returned to California, to the same little town. Yukon was no longer there. All his business ventures had failed; all his love affairs had failed. And he had left owing much money, and perhaps much love too.

Yukon never returned to the little California town. He came back to my home to fish one time, from some vague place in Idaho; and then he disappeared again.

Then a horse kicked him in the head and the authorities had to find his family.

They did. He had been in the Navy once, thus leaving a tiny record in his wake. It was one of the few.

Yesterday I spoke with Yukon's son; he is now eighteen.

Yukon had never been to the Yukon; nor had he ever been to Africa. And he was not fifty-seven years old when he died; he was only forty-seven. For eighteen years, he had been married to the same woman; he had lived in the same town; he had had the same bricklaying job. He was a stable, dependable father and husband, moderate in all his habits, honest and hardworking. He loved his wife and his two sons.

But at 4:30 on the morning of March 15, 1975, in the middle of a raging blizzard, Yukon Joe got into his truck and drove out of his life. He said nothing to anyone. He simply drove away. And his family did not hear another thing about or from him until the phone call that informed them that he was dead.

Was he mad? Insane? Crazy? Deranged? Disturbed? Touched? Strange? Queer? Eccentric? Odd? Abnormal? Lunatic? Neurotic? Schizophrenic? Psychopathic? Distracted? Disordered? Or was he simply your average person trying hard to deviate?

Will you be his judge? Will I?

No. Let history be his judge.

A Brief History of Madness

History is a sometimes harsh, but always fickle, judge. The Bible, as proud a historical document as there is, judged as follows: "[He scratched] on the doors of the gate, and let his spittle fall down upon his beard. Then said Achish unto his servants, Lo, ye see the man is mad: wherefore then have ye brought him to me?" (1 Sam. 21:13–14).

Petronius, who died in A.D. 66, attributed madness to learning, in his *Satyricon:* "We know that you are mad with much learning." John Dryden agreed: "Great wits are sure to madness near allied" *(Absalom and Achitophel)*. Michael Drayton, also in close agreement, spoke of a "fine madness" essential for the poet: "For that fine madness still he did retain/Which rightly should possess a poet's brain" *(Of Poets and Poesie).*

Lord Byron sensed the contagious nature of madness: "the madmen who have made men mad by their contagion" *(Childe Harold).* And David Lawrence, in the wisdom of a more enlightened age, blamed neither learning nor contagion: "Money is our madness, our vast collective madness" *(Money Madness).*

But madness has not historically been the domain solely of the Bible and the poets. Simpler people, baffled and awed by its manifestations, invented their own explanations and cures. Skulls from the Stone Age are sometimes found with holes in them—holes that appear to have been made deliberately with sharp instruments. Archaeologists inform us, speculatively to be sure, that these holes were a primitive attempt to release the evil spirits that might have been assumed to possess those afflicted with madness. **Trephining** is the medical label for this "cure" (which might occasionally have been effective when it succeeded in relieving pressure).

Demons, Witches, and Masturbation

Many ancient human cultures attributed madness to evil spirits—to demons. Demonology, the belief that behavior is in part a function of good or evil spirits that enter a person and assume control, was particularly widespread in the Middle Ages (Zilboorg & Henry, 1941). The cure for "possession" may take a number of forms, depending on what you believe about demons. If you believe that they are amenable to reason and supplication, you might talk to them directly, gently, but firmly: "Get thee hence, Satan, Beelzebub, or whoever you are." If you need assistance, you might

Trephining A technique employed in brain surgery, involving the removal of a small, usually circular, portion of the skull.

call upon a greater power: "God we pray thee to remove these demons from this poor woman that she might be employed once more in your service" (a little bribery doesn't necessarily hurt).

If neither the Lord's intercession nor your gentle persuasions are effective you might resort to more violent language, more passionate supplications, and perhaps the use of some foul language as well, attempting to get down to the demon's level, as it were. Holy water, properly administered, various cleansing and exorcising rites, religious ceremony, and displays of the organized power of different religions might also be involved. All these failing, there are more extreme measures. Flogging, starvation, and physical torture might drive the demons out. And if the demons still persist, then execution might be the only alternative.

Demonology and witchcraft were closely allied for long periods of our relatively recent history. Traditionally, there have been two kinds of witches: good and evil. There have also been two kinds of demonological possession: involuntary, where the devil assumes control over a body as a form of punishment for sins, and voluntary, in which a person makes a pact with the devil in order to attain supernatural powers over natural events. Essentially, a witch is one who has made such a pact. In fact, however, neither kind of possession was treated very kindly; nor were "good" witches treated better than the evil ones. **Insanity**, in any of its manifestations, was typically treated as evidence of possession. Similarly, the ability to effect "miraculous" cures, or the supposed ability to bring about floods, pestilence, or any natural catastrophe, was also considered evidence of possession.

In 1484, Pope Innocent VIII issued a papal bull (edict) exhorting all clergy to search constantly for witches. Two well-intentioned monks subsequently compiled a manual documenting the existence of witches and explaining how they might be hunted. Various signs that could be employed to prove that a suspect was a witch were described. Most important among these were the red marks sometimes left by the devil's claw on the witch's skin, and the fact that witches do not sink when bound and tossed into water. In addition, this "divinely inspired" manual described the many methods of torture that might be employed to convince the devil that a confession would be in order. Individuals found guilty of being witches were generally executed publicly. Witch-hunting proved a popular diversion and accounted for the deaths of many thousands of individuals. Massachusetts, in the seventeenth century, was the scene of massive witch hunts which led to the arrest of 250 suspects within a few months, and in 1692 to the Salem witch trials, resulting in the execution of 19 "confirmed" witches. France executed its last witch in 1745, and Poland in 1793 (Szasz, 1970).

History does not consider demons to be the only cause of insanity. Masturbation must be given its due. Szasz (1970) traces the history of belief in "masturbatory insanity," beginning with such books as Tissot's *Onania or a Treatise upon the Disorders Produced by Masturbation,* published in 1758. Tissot alleged that among the many disorders known to be caused directly by masturbation was insanity. From then until the twentieth century, physicians preached the harmful effects of "self-abuse," ascribing to it all manner of ills including blindness, deafness, impotence, epilepsy, depression, homosexuality, insanity, and sometimes death. The "habit" was acknowledged to be extremely insidious and frequently impossible to cure by ordinary means. Surgical procedures were sometimes employed, including castration or the denervation of the genitalia (cutting nerves leading from the genital areas or cauterizing appropriate portions of the spine).

History makes a habit of acknowledging the error of its old beliefs and the rightness of those more current. In time, it relegated witchcraft and masturbation to other areas of concern, separating them from insanity. Poverty, skin color, ethnic origin, or the vengeance of a wrathful God, sometimes believed to be the causes of various forms of madness, have also been discarded as explanations of insanity (discarded by science, at any rate). Our more current beliefs are discussed later.

Insanity A legal term for mental disorder based on an individual's recognition of right and wrong and control of personal actions. Individuals are no longer described as being insane, no matter what the nature of their mental disorders, unless they have been pronounced insane by a court of law.

Treatment Yesterday

Not surprisingly, treatments of mental disorder are directly related to beliefs about its causes. Thus, demons are released through holes in the head, exhorted to leave through verbal supplication, frightened away with such substances as holy water, forced to flee through torture, or exorcised by killing their host. If insanity is caused by masturbation, it is prevented by preaching against the vices of the habit, or through surgical means. Generally, madness has historically been viewed as mysterious and frightening. And those suffering have sometimes been avoided, locked up, or exiled. At other times, they have been subjected to bizarre cures or even executed (Figure 15.1).

Early facilities for the disordered were, by our standards, primitive and cruel. Believing the insane to be insensitive to temperature and taste, authorities frequently housed them in unheated **asylums** and fed them unpalatable gruels (Deutsch, 1937). Many were confined in chains, particularly if they were suspected of being dangerous. In most respects, early asylums were very much like jails. Indeed, even after the establishment of medically oriented treatment centers, the more dangerous of the insane were typically jailed as any criminal might be.

In the late eighteenth and early nineteenth centuries, governments began to assume more responsibility for the mentally disturbed. Consequently, an increasing number of "mental hospitals" were built. Before this time, many of those judged "deranged" or "distracted" had remained the responsibility of their relatives or of their towns. Parallel with the growth in numbers of facilities dedicated to the care of the mentally ill, there occurred a radical change in the medical profession's view of insanity. This change was largely a result of the discovery that a common cause of insanity was terminal **syphilis**. Syphilis was curable, as might be other mental disorders. Theories of mental disturbances and accompanying therapies multiplied rapidly. Mental illness had finally become a medical rather than a religious or social problem.

Definitions and Models of Mental Disorder

Insanity is a legal term, defined by law and through court precedents in terms of an individual's knowledge of right and wrong, and control of personal actions. This definition recognizes the possibility of temporary insanity and is premised, as well, on the assumption that cures are possible. Thus, individuals found not guilty by reason of insanity are frequently provided with treatment rather than punishment. In fact, however, legal definitions of insanity are not at all clear, but must rely on the individual judgments of people trained in diagnosing mental disturbances. Such definitions are applicable only when an individual has committed a crime or is suspected of having done so. And, in the end, the definition will still be legal rather than medical.

It should be noted that the term *insanity* is no longer widely employed in medicine and psychology, although it has been retained by the courts. The terms *abnormality, mental illness, personality disorders, emotional disorders,* or other more specific descriptions are employed instead. These too, however, present some horrendous problems of definition. What, precisely, is a mental disorder?

A Statistical Model

One way of defining abnormality is by reference to the prevalence of specific behaviors among groups of individuals. According to this approach, those whose behaviors or personality traits are demonstrably different from the majority are abnormal in a statistical sense (Figure 15.2). Thus, those whose weights are considerably above the average are abnormally obese; those whose weights are considerably below the average are abnormally thin. But although individuals in both of these groups may

Asylum A once common term for institutions in which individuals suffering from mental disorders were held. The term is now actively avoided, as is the equivalent expression *mental hospital.* Instead, such euphemisms as *state hospital, sanitarium, "home,"* or *treatment facility* are employed.

Syphilis The most dangerous, although not the most common, of the venereal diseases. It is ordinarily transmitted through sexual intercourse, but in later stages it may be communicated through other bodily contact. Its initial symptoms are neither obvious nor painful in the male or the female and may go undetected. Its long-term neurological effects, if left unchecked, include progressive deterioration of both physical and mental abilities characterized by delusions, mental disorder, and eventual paralysis. The technical term for the resulting "disease" is *general paresis.* Prior to the advent of the germ theory of disease, the discovery of the relationship between syphilis and paresis, and the discovery of antibiotics, many notable and less notable individuals contracted syphilis and eventually died from its effects. Routine tests such as the Wassermann, compulsory for obtaining a marriage license in most jurisdictions, together with the effectiveness of penicillin in curing the disease, have made it unlikely that anyone will suffer from syphilis-induced paresis.

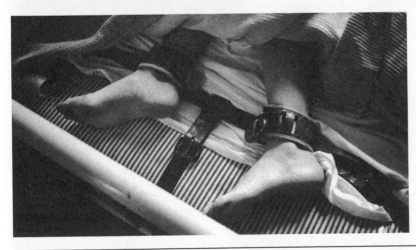

Figure 15.1 This pictorial history of the treatment of insanity shows only a few of the restraining and treatment devices that have been employed in institutions for the mentally disturbed.

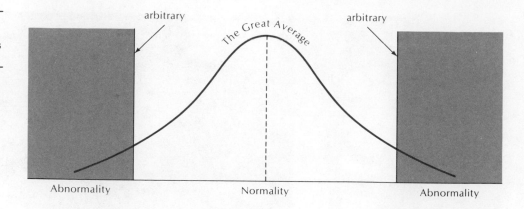

Figure 15.2 A statistical model of abnormality. According to this model, being different from most other people is abnormal.

arbitrary

The Great Average

arbitrary

Abnormality   Normality   Abnormality

be said to be abnormal, the nature of their abnormality is probably not pertinent to a definition of mental health. Abnormality with respect to emotional functioning, social behavior, perception, and so on may, however, be directly related to what is generally perceived as mental health. Deviance is manifested in behaviors and characteristics that have low frequency. Thus, to be afraid of dirt is deviant, since most people are not afraid of dirt. To be afraid of a poisonous snake or of a psychopath with a gun is not at all deviant; indeed, not to be afraid in these situations is improbable and may be considered deviant.

The statistical model is useful in that it provides a relatively objective method for identifying abnormal behavior. It says, quite simply, that to the extent that being like most other people is normal, being different from most other people is abnormal. Its major weaknesses are that it cannot specify which behaviors are most crucial for normality, and it cannot provide any "absolute" definitions, given the unstable nature of social norms. For example, various forms of sexual behavior that were once considered highly abnormal may now be accepted as being normal insofar as they are characteristic of a large segment of the population. Other models must also be employed to provide a more complete description of mental health.

Medical Models

Medicine deals with physical (organic) malfunctions that are due to injury, infection, chemical imbalances, or other causes, and that can often be treated surgically or chemically. Medical models view psychological malfunction in the same way as physical malfunction. Accordingly, psychological abnormality is seen as a disease or illness caused by infection or malfunction and is treated in the same way as organic malfunctions. The process of removing parts of the brain in attempts to "cure" mental disorder is compatible with a medical model.

It should be clear that there is no great conflict between statistical and medical models. Since the types of disorders that have been identified and described following the medical models (sometimes called disease models) are relatively rare in a mathematical sense, they can also be identified by using a purely statistical process. The most obvious advantage of medical models is that they encourage the search for specific organic causes of various disorders and suggest means of dealing with them.

Medical models have been extensively criticized by a number of writers. Szasz (1960) believes strongly that medical models present a false, misleading, and immoral view of mental disturbance. If mental disturbances were diseases, he argues, they should be communicable and curable by conventional means. Most are not. In addition, many severe psychological disorders are simply behaviors that are not accepted or tolerated by society. Ironically, in other societies, and at other times, similar behaviors would be acceptable and would not merit the social stigma that is attached to them in contemporary societies. And over-diagnosis of mental illness may have undesirable consequences that over-diagnosis of physical illness may not have. Thus it might often be better to treat a physically well person as ill rather than to make the error of treating the ill as though they were well; the same is less likely to be true in the area of mental health.

Behavioral Models

The principal difference between medical and behavioral models of abnormality lies in their explanations of causes. Whereas medical models attribute abnormality to internal causes, and focus on the interplay of dynamic, genetically ordained forces, behavioral models claim simply that abnormal behavior is learned just as is any other behavior. Most behavioral models are premised on conditioning models, or variations thereof, and concern themselves principally with manifestations of abnormal behavior without paying great attention to supposed causes. Whereas medical models lead to treatments designed to eliminate the causes of malfunctioning, behavioral models concentrate instead on "unlearning" unacceptable behavior, and learning (or relearning) more normal forms of behavior.

Cognitive Models

A relatively new interpretation of psychological disorders revolves around the notion that such disorders involve *cognitive problems* (Beck, 1976) which are frequently expressed in distortions of reality. Patients view themselves as worthless, unhealthy, and unhappy, have unrealistic appraisals of their futures, and react inappropriately. Distorted views of reality are, in fact, one of the principal characteristics of the more serious mental disorders. Whereas medical and behavioral models concentrate on the organic or behavioral causes and manifestations of these distortions, the cognitively oriented psychologist seeks to understand psychological malfunction by examining the patient's cognitions. Accordingly, therapies are directed toward altering subjects' perceptions of the world and of themselves—in other words, toward changing cognitions.

Cognitive and behavioral models of psychological disorders have a great deal in common in spite of the controversies that have historically existed between the two orientations. If inappropriate cognitions are at the root of many mental disorders, altering these cognitions assumes paramount importance. Techniques for so doing can most easily be derived from conventional learning theories including behavioristic models. An increasing number of clinical psychologists are moving toward a synthesis of cognitive and behavioristic approaches. Mahoney (1977) suggests that this new approach, one that he labels a *cognitive-learning perspective,* "may well mark the development of a new and challenging era in clinical psychology" (p. 12). In his view, cognitive-learning trends in psychotherapy are not narrowly restricted to a single point of view, but recognize the importance of a variety of causes and treatments. More about the cognitive therapies in the next chapter.

Psychodynamic Models

The model which has probably been most influential in providing both descriptions and treatments for mental disorders is based largely on Freud's theorizing. This psychodynamic model, described in some detail in Chapter 13, is premised on Freud's description of human personality as involving three levels: id, ego, and superego. Within this model the id, source of powerful instinctual tendencies which are primarily sexual and aggressive, finds itself in continual conflict with the ego, the reality-based aspect of personality, and more importantly with the superego, which embodies social and cultural beliefs about morality and immorality. It is as though our basic sexual urges (id) are continually being thwarted by our immediate circumstances (ego) as well as by the fact that society does not permit unbridled expression of sexuality. The result of this conflict is anxiety which, if sufficiently severe, may manifest itself in mental disorders of various kinds. In brief, then, one of the principal causes of mental disorder is anxiety stemming in large part from conflict between our urges (many of which are unconscious) and our consciences. And, as noted in Chapter 13, this anxiety may be reduced in a number of ways, including the defense mechanisms described by Freud. Psychodynamic models include, as well, descriptions of normal development through stages (psychosexual stages) as well as abnormal development manifested in fixation at an early stage, or regression to a previous stage. Recall that Freud believed fixation and regression resulted either from too much or too little sexual gratification at a particular stage or from some particularly horrendous experience (commonly labeled *trauma*).

Therapies based on this psychodynamic model have variously been described as *psychoanalytic* or *insight therapies*. They are most commonly associated with our traditional views of therapy. They include, at their stereotypic best, psychoanalyst and couch, dream analysis and free association, complexes, fixations, regressions, and so on. Psychodynamic therapy is described in the next chapter.

Which Model?

It is not possible to say that one of these models is correct and the others not. Nor is it possible to state categorically that one is more useful than any other. Each leads to a different view of mental disorders; and each leads to different forms of intervention or treatment. The statistical model is useful in providing a relatively objective means of identifying bizarre, unconventional behavior, although its value in increasing our understanding of abnormal behavior or our ability to deal with it is clearly very limited. Medical models are valuable in providing methods for identifying and describing malfunctions, and sometimes in providing specific treatments for them. There is little doubt, however, that they have been abused through misapplication and overapplication, and that treatments premised on them are not always very effective. The principal contribution of the behavioral models has been related to the development of systematic learning therapies that have been highly effective in some situations. Again, however, they are not appropriate or effective in all circumstances. Cognitive models, although promising, would be highly limited as well if they did not take organic and metabolic factors into account. Psychodynamic approaches, despite their historical influence, tend to be imprecise and speculative. The various models of mental disorder are summarized in Table 15.1.

The consequences of adopting a single model of mental disorder should be clear. Not only is classification, description, and explanation of disorders determined by the model adopted, but so is choice of treatment (Fisher & Farina, 1979). Although all models have their usefulness, all have their limitations as well.

A Definition

Most of the difficult concepts in psychology cannot easily be defined in a single sentence or paragraph. This text requires no less than 250,000 words to define *psychology;* it requires most of a chapter to define *abnormality*. One global definition is provided by Farina (1976), who says the term *mental illness* refers to *"a pattern of behavior that is not reasonable or easily understood, that is deviant and unusual, and that is unacceptable to society"* (p. 18). Although the definition does have some intuitive validity, it fails to specify either what it is like to be "mentally ill" or the sorts of behaviors that might be expected of individuals so identified. In addition, it is so general that it includes a variety of behaviors that are also "deviant," "unusual," and "unacceptable," but that we do not ordinarily consider symptomatic of mental disorders (stealing, for example).

Spitzer et al. (1976) provide a more precise definition in their description of the criteria that have been employed by the American Psychiatric Association in efforts to diagnose and classify mental disorders. According to these authors, mental disorders share the following common features: "In their extreme or fully developed form, they are directly associated with either distress, disability, or in the absence of either of these, disadvantage in coping with unavoidable aspects of the environment" (p. 3). A fuller explanation of this definition follows.

Table 15.1 Models of Mental Disorders

Model	Definition of Abnormality	What Therapist Looks For	Therapeutic Approach
Statistical	A rare behavior	Uncommon behavior in a statistical sense	None
Medical	System malfunction	Medical basis	Chemotherapy, surgery
Behavioral	Learned behavior	Symptoms, not causes	Learning therapies (such as behavior modification)
Cognitive	Inappropriate cognitions (beliefs, thoughts, perceptions)	Irrational or inappropriate beliefs about self or others	Attempts to change cognitions, sometimes through learning therapies
Psychodynamic	Psychic conflicts, anxiety	History, relationships	Psychoanalysis

DSM III Classifications of Mental Disorders

The American Psychiatric Association (1980) publishes a manual that classifies mental disorders in major and minor categories, and that thereby says much more about abnormality than a single definition can. Called **DSM III** (Diagnostic and Statistical Manual, 3rd ed.), it is used extensively in psychiatric diagnosis.

DSM III presents seventeen separate major categories of mental disorders, together with some well-defined operational criteria for classifying individuals (Table 15.2). These are based largely on explicit diagnostic criteria developed by Feighner et al. (1972). To make a diagnosis, the clinician need not rely on individual interpretation, but need only ascertain whether certain symptoms are present and apply relatively definite rules for making the diagnosis. For example, in addition to being given information that highlights the differences among schizophrenia, transsexualism, and transvestism, the clinician is presented with the following five operational criteria for transsexualism:

a. *Sense of discomfort and inappropriateness in one's anatomic sex*
b. *Wish to be rid of one's own genitals and to live as a member of the other sex*
c. *The disturbance has been continuous (not limited to periods of stress) for at least two years*
d. *Absence of physical intersex or genetic abnormality*
e. *Not due to another mental disorder, such as schizophrenia (DSM III, 1980, 263–264)*

Not only does DSM III present criteria for mental disorders, but it also provides for *multiaxial* classification. That is, the clinician diagnoses and evaluates the patient on more than one dimension. DSM III specifies five separate dimensions, or axes, and provides specific rules for assigning number or letter codes for each subject on all five dimensions. The nature of the five axes is of particular importance. The first two refer specifically to the diagnostic classification provided by DSM III, and include all of these classifications. Axis I refers to all mental disorders except personality disorders; personality disorders are coded on Axis II. Mental disorders are separated in this fashion to enable the clinician to take into account the possibility that a patient may be suffering from more than one disorder. Frequently, a subject who might be classified as schizophrenic on the basis of present symptoms also has a history

DSM III (Diagnostic and Statistical Manual, 3rd ed.) A comprehensive classification of mental disorders published by the American Psychiatric Association for use as a diagnostic tool. Using DSM III, clinicians code patients as belonging to any of seventeen different major categories, and along five axes.

Table 15.2 Major Categories of Mental Disorders According to the Third Edition of the Diagnostic and Statistical Manual (DSM III) of the American Psychiatric Association (1980)

Mental Disorder	Example
Disorders usually first evident in infancy, childhood, or adolescence	Mental retardation
Organic mental disorders	Delirium
Substance-use disorders	Alcoholism
Schizophrenic disorders*	Affective states such as mania
Paranoid disorders	Paranoia
Psychotic disorders not elsewhere classified	Atypical psychoses
Affective disorders*	Depression
Anxiety disorders*	Phobias
Somatoform disorders	Hypochondriasis
Dissociative disorders*	Amnesia
Psychosexual disorders*	Transvestism
Factitious disorders	Deliberate production of symptoms of disorders
Disorders of impulse control not elsewhere classified	Kleptomania
Adjustment disorder	Inability to cope with work
Psychological factors affecting physical condition	Obesity; tension headache
Personality disorders*	Narcissism
V Codes	Marital problems; malingering†

*Discussed in this chapter.

†Note that many of these examples are *not* mental disorders unless they are accompanied by significant personal distress and/or impairment of ability to function in one or more important areas. In particular, disorders classified under V Codes include behaviors not attributable to other known mental disorders, but nevertheless serious enough for the individual to seek psychiatric help.

of mental disorder that might be classified as an antisocial personality disorder on Axis II.

Axis III is provided for coding nonmental medical problems that might be important in understanding and treating relevant mental disorders. Thus, a patient's diagnostic chart includes classification in accordance with the diagnostic categories of mental disorders, as well as a medical diagnosis wherever appropriate. Axis IV is of particular importance for research, as well as for treatment. It concerns the presence and severity of stress in the patient's recent history, and provides seven codes and descriptive terms for "psychosocial stressors," ranging from "none" and "minimal" to "extreme" and "catastrophic." Catastrophic stressors would include such events as multiple family deaths, concentration-camp experience, or a devastating natural disaster. An extreme stressor might be the death of a close relative; moderate stress might be involved in pregnancy, having a child leave home, and so on. Given the apparently close relationship between stress and mental disorders, this axis may prove to be of tremendous value for research.

Axis V attempts to describe the patient's highest level of functioning during the previous year. Clinical experience and research have shown that prognosis for recovery is frequently closely related to how well-adjusted the patient was before diagnosis. Therefore, Axis V is designed to reveal the optimal level of functioning in day-to-day activities. Patients may be described in terms ranging from superior (unusually effective functioning in a wide range of activities and relationships) to grossly impaired (unable to function in most areas). The DSM III classification scheme is illustrated in Figure 15.3.

DSM III classifications are a recent replacement of the older DSM II classifications, and have not been universally accepted by the psychiatric community. Some

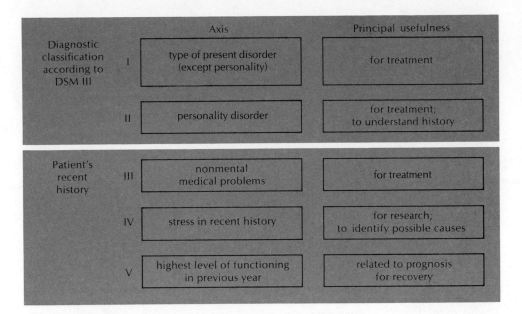

	Axis	Principal usefulness
Diagnostic classification according to DSM III	I — type of present disorder (except personality)	for treatment
	II — personality disorder	for treatment; to understand history
Patient's recent history	III — nonmental medical problems	for treatment
	IV — stress in recent history	for research; to identify possible causes
	V — highest level of functioning in previous year	related to prognosis for recovery

Figure 15.3 The DSM III scheme for classifying mental disorders on five axes. The first two axes permit classification according to the seventeen categories listed in Table 15.2; the division between I and II allows a double classification for individuals who are diagnosed as having both a personality disorder and another mental disorder. Axes III and IV evaluate nonmental or external factors that may have affected functioning; and Axis V evaluates the individual's level of functioning in order to make a prognosis for recovery.

have objected to its elimination of traditional categories such as neuroses; others are apprehensive about the length and detail of DSM III, and about its inclusion of behaviors that were not previously considered to be symptomatic of mental disorders (for example, tobacco-use disorder, which is a disorder only if it is accompanied by distress at the need to use tobacco, or by medical problems associated with the behavior). It is likely that a number of practitioners will continue to use classifications and diagnoses with which they are most familiar and comfortable. Here, as elsewhere, practice often lags some distance behind theory.

In this chapter we have neither the space nor the need to consider in detail all the classifications of mental disorders described in DSM III. Accordingly, this chapter focuses on the most common mental disorders, with emphasis on the behavioral symptoms of individuals who might be classified as suffering from them. It is important to note at the outset that individuals do not always bring with them a simple and clearly identifiable set of symptoms when they seek help for various disorders. And although classification schemes are highly useful for the therapist, they are often somewhat misleading. A person diagnosed as schizophrenic, for example, does not always and necessarily behave as textbook descriptions of that individual would predict. Nor are the conceptual distinctions that can be made among various types of mental disorders always evident in practice. There is sometimes a fuzzy distinction between behaviors that might be seen as schizophrenic and others that might be more neurotic. So too, there is sometimes a vague distinction between what is generally considered to be normal and what might be considered abnormal. A large majority of people with serious emotional problems appear, in most situations, to be well adjusted and reasonably happy. Mental disorders do not always announce themselves like chicken pox or a cold (see Box 15.1).

Six of the seventeen DSM III classifications of mental disorders are discussed in the following pages. The first two, anxiety and dissociative disorders, have historically been called *neuroses*. They seldom require hospitalization and are among the less severe mental disorders. The next two disorders, schizophrenia and affective disorders, are forms of what has traditionally been labeled **psychoses**. These are severe, often debilitating, mental disorders for which hospitalization is common. Distortions of thought, speech, and perception are some of their symptoms.

The *personality disorders* (sometimes called *character disorders*) are evident primarily in behaviors that are socially inappropriate, unacceptable, or dangerous. Most of these behaviors typically become apparent during childhood or adolescence

Psychosis (plural psychoses) Any of a number of severe, often debilitating mental disorders, characterized sometimes by distortions of thought, speech, and perception. Hospitalization is common for victims of psychosis.

and are manifested as relatively stable, although sometimes highly maladjustive, personality characteristics. The *psychosexual disorders* include the range of sexual-identity or sexual-role problems that cause distress either to the patient or to others. Transsexualism and transvestism are two manifestations of psychosexual disorders. We now move to a consideration of each of these six major classes of disorders.

Anxiety Disorders

Anxiety is among the most devastating and the most baffling of human emotions. It can take many forms, ranging from acute panic to mild trepidation, and can occur

---

BOX 15.1

Labels and Insanity

Eight "normal" individuals, five women and three men, presented themselves to the admitting wards of twelve psychiatric hospitals (Rosenhan, 1973). Each complained of identical symptoms: an unidentified, same-sexed voice saying "empty," "hollow," and "thud." In subsequent interviews, they presented their life histories accurately and honestly (although they did not use their own names), and each behaved as normally as you or I. All subjects were admitted immediately as patients. Their behavior as inmates was "normal": they reported no more auditory hallucinations or any other psychiatric symptom, each was cooperative and helpful, and almost all wanted to leave immediately. Each, save one, was diagnosed as schizophrenic, and each was later released with a diagnosis of "schizophrenia in remission." Length of hospitalization ranged from three to fifty-two days and averaged nineteen days.

On the basis of this experiment, Rosenhan concludes that "the normal are not detectably sane" and that there is a tendency among psychiatric personnel to err on the side of diagnosing the sane as insane. A second experiment, designed to see whether this tendency could be reversed, involved informing the staff of one hospital that a number of "pseudopatients" of the kind described above would present themselves for admission during the next three months. Staff were asked to indicate the likelihood that each patient they saw during this period might be a pseudopatient. Despite the fact that no pseudopatients actually presented themselves, at least one member of the staff expressed high confidence that a patient was "not real" with respect to 41 of 193 patients. Rosenhan concludes that "any diagnostic process that lends itself so readily to massive errors of this sort cannot be a very reliable one" (p. 257).

Rosenhan's study seemed to show that psychiatrists could easily be duped into making false diagnoses, and that these diagnoses were not likely to be corrected in the face of contradictory evidence. Are these conclusions valid?

Numerous critics of the studies suggest not. The evidence is alleged to be inconclusive and misleading. "Most physicians do not assume that patients who seek help are liars; they can therefore, of course, be duped" (Fleischman, 1973, p. 356). Furthermore, as Fleischman points out, psychiatrists never diagnose individuals as being sane or insane; insanity is a legal term. Hence the question being examined is not whether psychiatrists impose mental-disorder labels on people who present themselves with appropriate symptoms. That they do so is hardly surprising, since people who present themselves to admitting wards of psychiatric institutions are generally in need of help.

Thaler (1973) criticizes the Rosenhan study and its conclusion on other grounds. First, the twelve hospitals chosen were not a random sample of psychiatric hospitals; hence generalizations might not apply to other hospitals. More damaging, only eight subjects were used, a number far too small to permit reliable conclusions. Thaler also voices the opinion that subjects presenting themselves with no more symptoms than those described in the study would *not* ordinarily be admitted as inpatients, particularly in view of the fact that they reported no history of maladjustment. It is perhaps more likely that they would be treated as outpatients. Furthermore, the isolated symptoms they presented were suggestive of drug experiences, brain damage, tumors, and so on. Ordinary procedure might well have involved urine analysis, skull X-rays, electroencephalograms, radioisotope brain scans, lumbar puncture, and other forms of neurological and physiological examination. Several critics have expressed surprise not only at the fact that these "pseudopatients" were admitted, but that no follow-up examinations were undertaken.

Lieberman (1973) contends that the only reasonable conclusion to be drawn from this study is that psychiatrists cannot distinguish between the insane and the "sane-feigning-insanity" when there is no reason to suspect malingering (feigning).

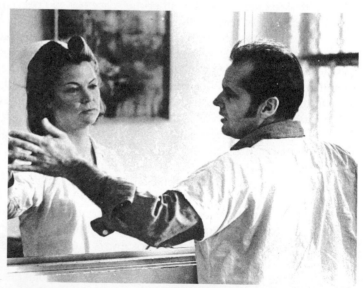

The novel, play, and film *One Flew over the Cuckoo's Nest* (Kesey, 1962) deals with the erroneous commitment of a normal person to an institution. It traces the tragic results of chemotherapy and lobotomy and ends with the patient's death. Although the movie portrays an extreme fictional situation, it dramatizes concern about the arbitrariness of decisions drawing the fine line between "normal" and "abnormal." Despite subsequent criticisms, Rosenhan's 1973 study adds fuel to the fire.

---

in response to a wide variety of situations. In many cases it is both natural and normal; in a number of instances, however, it is maladaptive and irrational, and is the basis of a number of disorders. DSM III classifies several specific anxiety disorders.

Phobic Disorders **Phobias** are intense, irrational fears, recognized by the patient as unreasonable, and often leading to avoidance of certain situations. These disorders are typically chronic and can be distinguished in terms of the objects or situations that bring them about.

Agoraphobia, fear of open spaces, often takes the form of fear of leaving home. Subjects experience anxiety at the thought of leaving, as well as when traveling alone, being apart from friends, or being in strange places. The effects of agoraphobia are not limited to serious personal distress but include the sometimes crippling effects of actively avoiding unfamiliar places and situations. In extreme cases, subjects may become completely "housebound" for prolonged periods. This manifestation of the phobias is among the most common, accounting for some 60 percent of all phobic cases seen in clinical settings (Davison & Neale, 1974). The disorder is seen more frequently in women than in men and most often begins in adolescence or early adulthood, although it may occur considerably later. Box 15.2 is a case report of agoraphobia.

Social phobia involves fear of social situations—that is, fear of situations in which the individual is exposed to judgment of others. Its most common manifestations include the avoidance of social situations and of such public behaviors as speaking formally to a group. Fear of using public washrooms, eating in public, appearing at certain social gatherings, or performing in public are other manifestations of social phobia. Because social phobias frequently lead the individual to adopt a life-style and occupational role that do not demand a great deal of social contact, thus permitting adequate adjustment and functioning, relatively few people seek clinical help for this disorder.

Simple phobias include the variety of other specific fears that are not agoraphobic or social. Some of these are listed in Table 15.3, together with their erudite Greek labels. The list is by no means exhaustive, since it is possible to develop a phobia about virtually any object or situation. The criterion for a phobia is simply that the fear be irrational, completely out of proportion to the potential danger of the feared object or situation, and not shared by a significant number of other people. It is interesting to note, however, that human phobias tend to be limited to a number of common

Phobia An intense, irrational fear, triggered by any one of a number of objects or situations. Generally classified as an anxiety disorder.

Table 15.3 Some Common and Uncommon Phobias

Phobia	Feared Object or Situation
Acrophobia	Heights
Algophobia	Pain
Mysophobia	Germs
Hydrophobia	Water
Claustrophobia	Being enclosed
Agoraphobia	Open places, leaving familiar places
Anthropophobia	People
Thanatophobia	Death
Ochlophobia	Crowds
Monophobia	Being alone
Zoophobia	Animals
Nyctophobia	Dark, night
Syphilophobia	Syphilis

BOX 15.2

Jane

Jane was born and raised in a rural agricultural area.* She attended school in the closest town, some six miles from her farm home, getting to and from school in a bus with about thirty other children. In time she graduated from high school. That summer, she married her school boyfriend, whose parents operated a farm approximately ten miles from her home. Her new husband's parents, finally liberated, turned the farm over to their son and disappeared into retirement.

Happy with her new responsibilities, Jane quickly adjusted to being a farm wife. There is little doubt that she was every bit as excited as her husband when the first crop came in, rich and profitable. Shortly before Christmas, they celebrated their success with a holiday. Jane made all the travel arrangements for a three-week trip, and they left.

Two days later, they were back—Jane confused, frightened, and somewhat depressed; her husband puzzled and angry. They had no sooner left than Jane began to complain of chest pains and dizziness. Medical examination had been unable to find any physical cause for these symptoms. Yet they persisted. In addition, Jane was overwhelmed with a desire to return, convinced that she would feel better once she was at home. And she did.

During the ensuing months, Jane spent progressively more time at home, venturing to town only when in desperate need of groceries. Her habit was to buy huge quantities of goods, a feat that she accomplished in an impressively short time. She would then rush frantically home, never stopping to visit any of the friends with whom she had previously spent so much time. By Easter, even her trips to the grocery store became a thing of the past. She always became ill on days when she had planned to buy groceries or she found some other reason for her husband to go instead.

By the time summer came, Jane was a virtual prisoner in her home, no longer even daring to go to the chicken coop. Her husband was finally able to convince her to seek help.

Diagnosis: agoraphobia with panic.

*From the files of Dr. Sam Bellott. Used by permission.

situations. Thus, although very few people have furniture phobias, a much larger number are afraid of open spaces, heights, closed spaces, and darkness.

Obsession A recurring thought or impulse that seems irrational to the person having it.

Compulsion An urge to engage in a certain behavior which when resisted causes anxiety.

Obsessive-Compulsive Disorders *Obsessive-compulsive disorders* are defined by the presence of recurring thoughts or impulses that appear irrational to the person having them (**obsessions**) but that give rise to intense urges to engage in certain behaviors, and that result in anxiety when they are resisted (**compulsions**). Thus, a compulsion is characterized by both a strongly felt desire to do something and a competing desire to resist. Both obsessions and compulsions are perceived as incompatible with the individual's nature, but neither can easily be resisted. Obsessions most often take the form of repetitive thoughts of violence, accompanied by considerable fear that the individual will engage in some highly undesirable behavior. Alternatively, obsessions can take the form of perpetual indecision and doubting which can be sufficiently severe as to prevent reaching any decision. Compulsions typically involve a strong impulse to repeat some senseless and meaningless act over and over again, as when Lady Macbeth repeatedly washed her hands after Duncan's murder ("Out, damned spot!"). Compulsions often center around washing and cleansing rituals (see Box 15.3).

Generalized Anxiety Disorders Generalized anxiety disorders include general rather than episodic subjective sensations of anxiety in the absence of specific symptoms such as characterize the phobic reactions, and in the absence of specific situations or objects that might be associated with phobic reactions. Individuals suffering from *generalized anxiety,* sometimes termed *free-floating anxiety,* recognize themselves as being predominantly tense, nervous, and fearful, and cannot associate their anxiety with anything specific.

Dissociative Disorders

Dissociative disorders A classification of disorders that apparently involve the splitting of various aspects of personality and functioning. Includes amnesia and multiple personality.

Dissociative disorders are so-called because they apparently involve the splitting or dissociating of aspects of personality and functioning. They include several distinct manifestations.

Amnesia Amnesia is defined by a sudden and temporary loss of memory in the absence of any organic cause of memory loss. It may take one of four different forms, distinguishable in terms of the type of material that cannot be remembered and the time period covered by the amnesia. In *localized* (or *circumscribed*) *amnesia,* the individual is unable to recall anything for a period of time following some event. In *systematized amnesia,* some events may be recalled during the circumscribed period, but many others will have been completely forgotten. *Generalized amnesia,* highly

---

BOX 15.3

Miranda

When Miranda presented herself to the therapist, she seemed pleasant, relaxed, and confident. "I have no real problems," she assured Sam.* Her husband thought otherwise. He described a typical day in Miranda's life as follows:

Upon awakening in the morning, she would strip the bed and throw all the sheets and pillow cases into the washing machine. She would then immediately vacuum the mattress and pillows. After breakfast, when all the dishes had been washed, polished, and put into their labeled places, she would begin to wash—floors and counters, cupboards and walls, closets and windows—scrubbing and waxing, washing and polishing until her husband returned home. But never through the front door. Always through the back

where, in a small porch, he would remove *all* of his clothing. As he entered, she would hand him a clean towel, and he would tiptoe into the bathroom, leaving as few footprints as possible for fear that Miranda would have to wash the floor again. Meanwhile she would wash his clothes before they could sit down to supper. And if the evening went well, she would get up only four or five times to dust the television or to wipe fingerprints that her husband might inadvertently have left around.

In the end, Miranda confessed to the therapist that she did have problems—that she was beset by an overwhelming urge to make sure that everything was always clean; that she knew that germs bred in dirt and that she could not tolerate any germs in her house. And once during therapy, she left quickly because Sam had sneezed.

Diagnosis (tentative): obsession-compulsion with mysophobia (fear of germs).

---

*From the files of Dr. Sam Bellott. Used by permission.

a   b   c

Figure 15.4 William (Billy) Milligan, recently acquitted of four counts of rape by reason of insanity, suffers from a multiple personality disorder (**a**). Among his ten or more highly distinct personalities are several with artistic talent. The doll (**b**) was drawn by "Ragan," a Slavic male who considers himself the protector of the other personalities. Billy's own artistic talents are illustrated in **c**.

unusual in practice although common as a literary and motion picture subject, involves the sudden inability to recall any detail of one's previous life. Interestingly, ability to speak, intellectual skills, and motor skills are not forgotten. *Continuous amnesia,* also very rare, involves loss of memory from a specific time onward (up to and including the present). Continuous amnesia differs from generalized amnesia in that the individual retains memory of events prior to the onset of amnesia but cannot remember events that have just occurred.

Fugue   Like amnesia, *fugue* involves a loss of memory. In addition, however, it involves wandering, and sometimes the assumption of a new identity. People suffering from a fugue state undergo an episode during which they have forgotten who they are, but are unaware of having been anyone else. During this time, they may wander, leaving their homes, and sometimes establishing very different lives somewhere else. Both onset and recovery are usually rapid, but the individual may then be left with a feeling of disorientation and confusion.

Multiple Personality   The dissociative aspects of amnesia and fugue states are obvious. In both cases, it is as though parts of the individual's personality and memory become separated from one another, some parts remaining temporarily inaccessible to the individual. **Multiple-personality** disorders involve a more complex type of dissociation, where individuals are from time to time dominated by distinctly different, complex, highly integrated personalities. Typically, domination by one personality is complete and does not involve any memory of other personalities, although it sometimes does. Shifts from one personality to another may be sudden and dramatic. (See Figure 15.4.)

> **Multiple personality** The dwelling in one person of two or more distinct and highly integrated personalities. Not to be confused with schizophrenia, which often involves distorted perceptions and is a psychosis.

The Three Faces of Eve (Thigpen & Cleckley, 1954) presents a classic illustration of multiple personality. "Eve White," who had been in psychotherapy for a period of time following complaints of severe headaches and blackouts, was a quiet, demure, soft-spoken woman. The therapist had no reason to suspect a multiple personality until one day:

> *As if seized by sudden pain, she put both hands to her head. After a tense moment of silence, both hands dropped. There was a quick, reckless smile,*

and, in a bright voice that sparkled, she said, "Hi, there, Doc!" The demure and constrained posture of Eve White had melted into buoyant repose.
(p. 137)

The "new" woman had no doubt that she was "Eve Black." Later, "Jane" emerged as a third personality.

Multiple personalities and fugue states can be distinguished principally in terms of the repeated shifts of personality that occur in a multiple personality, but do not occur in the fugue state. In addition, the two or more personalities that alternately dominate the individual diagnosed as having a multiple-personality disorder are complete personalities with well-integrated identities.

There is sometimes confusion between schizophrenia and "split" or multiple personalities, but the two are quite different. None of the schizophrenias involve dual (or triple) personalities in the sense of well-integrated, apparently normal, but separate manifestations of identity. In addition, the schizophrenias typically involve serious problems of perceptual or cognitive distortion. In effect, they are psychoses rather than neuroses.

Psychoses are defined as severe, debilitating conditions characterized by "mental functioning . . . sufficiently impaired to interfere grossly with . . . capacity to meet the ordinary demands of life. . . . Deficits in perception, language, and memory may be so severe that the patient's capacity for mental grasp of the situation is effectively lost" (American Psychiatric Association, 1968, p. 23). The two disorders that we turn to next, schizophrenia and affective disorders, are examples of psychoses.

Schizophrenia

Among the most severe and the most common of the psychotic disorders, **schizophrenia** is characterized by emotional, cognitive, and perceptual confusion and a consequent breakdown of effective contact with others and with reality. Although there are general characteristics of schizophrenia, the most notable of which involves distorted perceptions of reality, the term actually includes a number of distinct disorders, each distinguishable by its specific symptoms.

Disorganized schizophrenia involves severe disintegration of behavior and thought. Delusions, hallucinations (primarily auditory, rarely visual), and extremely bizarre behaviors are typical. Patients may laugh hysterically and inappropriately one minute, become seriously convinced that they are some historical personage the next, and subsequently become involved in a long, incoherent conversation with some imaginary individual. Disorganized schizophrenics live in their dreams and hallucinations, contacting reality only rarely and inappropriately. The hallmark of disorganized schizophrenia is an almost total unpredictability of behavior.

Catatonic schizophrenia is so named because of the rigid, immobile (catatonic) postures frequently adopted, sometimes for hours, by patients (Figure 15.5). Typically, immobility is absolute during a catatonic stupor: patients sometimes have no bowel or bladder control and have to be fed intravenously. Indeed, the rigidity may be so complete that saliva runs unchecked down their chins, since patients do not even swallow. Two different types of immobility are identified. The one just described is labeled *catalepsy* and is characterized by complete rigidity of posture. The second, termed *waxy flexibility,* permits the patient to be placed in almost any position, which will then be retained, sometimes for hours, no matter how difficult or impossible the position might seem.

Catatonic patients generally alternate between periods of immobility (catatonia) and periods of intense physical activity accompanied by a great deal of excitement. Changes from one to the other are sometimes violent and dramatic. Periods of intense activity are sometimes accompanied by overtly aggressive and manifestly dangerous behavior. Not surprisingly, if precautions are not taken, catatonic patients frequently hurt themselves as a result of prolonged immobilization and hampered blood circulation as well as muscular strain, or as a result of doing themselves violence and injury while in a frenzy of catatonic excitement.

Schizophrenia A severe and relatively common mental disorder, the most general characteristic of which is distorted perceptions of reality. There are a number of distinct forms of schizophrenia, among them disorganized schizophrenia, catatonic schizophrenia, and paranoid schizophrenia.

Paranoid schizophrenia is probably the most common of the schizophrenias. Its symptoms are not always as obvious as those of disorganized schizophrenia or catatonia and may remain undetected for a time. Chief among these are delusions of grandeur and feelings of persecution, which go hand in hand. That is, paranoid schizophrenics typically suffer from delusions that they are someone of extreme importance, believing, for example, that they are some historical figure such as Napoleon or Jesus Christ (see Box 15.4). At the same time, they are overwhelmed by a conviction that someone or something is after them—that they are being persecuted because they are important, because they know something that someone else wants, or simply because the historical figure they know themselves to be was persecuted. Such individuals may spend a lifetime running from these imaginary persecutors, gathering evidence that they are being persecuted, sometimes hearing voices belonging to their enemies and hallucinating their presence. In severe cases, subjects may seek retaliation or defense, and can become extremely dangerous. Sirhan B. Sirhan, assassin of Robert F. Kennedy, has been diagnosed as a paranoid schizophrenic who believed himself to be the savior of his people.

This classification of schizophrenias is not nearly so clear in practice as it might appear in theory. Numerous apparently schizophrenic patients cannot easily be classified within a single division, since symptoms often overlap or change over time. An alternative classification has also been proposed and is employed extensively, sometimes in place of this traditional classification and sometimes in addition to it. It involves two broad groupings of schizophrenia, not in terms of symptoms so much as in terms of victims' histories (Kantor et al., 1953). Thus, *process schizophrenia* is marked by a long history of maladjustment, childhood traumas, and instability prior to the onset of schizophrenia. A second type, *reactive schizophrenia,* is preceded by an apparently normal history, and can sometimes be identified as having been caused by a specific, highly stressful event. Not surprisingly, the prognosis is considerably better for reactive schizophrenias than it is for process schizophrenias.

Affective Disorders

Affective disorders A classification of disorders marked by severe distortions or disturbances of affect (emotion).

There are a number of severe **affective** (emotional) **disorders**, the best-known of which are bipolar disorder and major depression. The principal differences between these affective reactions and the schizophrenias include the greater cognitive and perceptual disintegration of the schizophrenias, and the marked emotional component of the affective disorders.

Bipolar disorder A major affective disorder characterized by attacks of mania (euphoria, intense activity, or excitement) and depression.

Bipolar disorder is characterized by periodic attacks of mania and depression. Sometimes the attacks are cyclical. That is, mania is followed by depression which may then be followed by another period of mania, and so on. More frequently, subjects experience a single episode of mania and one of depression, not necessarily in that order, and may then be free of both for long periods—sometimes even decades.

Mania is characterized by periods of extreme and intense activity, irrepressible good humor, grandiose plans and involvements, and overwhelming displays of energy and joie-de-vivre. In sharp contrast, depression is marked by periods of extreme apathy, listlessness, feelings of worthlessness, hypochondriacal fears (concerns over health and bodily functions), and preoccupation with suicide (see Box 15.5). Cognitively oriented psychologists generally agree that feelings of helplessness and hopelessness are central in the development of depression (R. J. Friedman & Katz, 1974), as do a number of behaviorists (Seligman, 1975).

Major depression An affective disorder characterized by extreme depression, sometimes leading to suicide.

Whereas bipolar disorder is always characterized by at least one period of mania, **major depression** is characterized only by extreme apathy and listlessness, and frequently by loss of contact with portions of reality. Sometimes the depression appears to originate with a specific event such as menopause or the climacteric—the change of life, where the sexual organs are no longer capable of procreating. This type of depression was once termed *involutional melancholia,* a label that is no longer employed in DSM III. Less severe forms of depression are far more common than major depression, and are sometimes called neurotic depression or dysthymic disorder. Dysthymic disorders often result from a specific tragic event such as the death of a friend or relative, loss of employment, or some significant failure.

Personality Disorders

A large group of mental disorders involve long-term, relatively fixed and stable, maladaptive patterns of social behavior and emotional responsiveness. Most of these become manifest during childhood or adolescence, are identifiable as character traits, lead to poor social adjustment, and sometimes result in considerable personal distress.

BOX 15.4

George

George, an intelligent, twenty-one-year-old Catholic, presented himself for treatment at the insistence of a priest (Angers, 1975). He personally felt that he had no problems. His work history was varied and menial; he had held more than twenty short-term, unskilled jobs. He had also been evicted from a large number of boarding houses.

George walked into the therapist's office wearing his usual twelve sweaters—his twelve apostles, he insisted. There, he described his

purpose. God had appointed him the savior of mankind, and especially of Russia, where corruption and sin were rampant. Striking a Christ-like pose, his beard jutting out dramatically, he attempted to orate on evil, and he spoke of his delusion of appearing before the pope and convincing him of the measures that must be taken to save the world. But his speech was disorganized and confused, he slurred his words and giggled inappropriately, and when interrupted with a question, he stared vacantly and uncomprehendingly.

An Adlerian interpretation of George's difficulties was that in order to overcome tremendous feelings of inferiority, he had overcompensated by becoming Christ.

Diagnosis: Schizophrenia—paranoid type with emphasis on delusions.

(A treatment for George is described in Chapter 16.)

A number of individuals suffer from more than one **personality disorder**. Unlike most schizophrenics, however, persons suffering from personality disorders usually continue to function in society. Typically, too, such individuals suffer little anxiety over their behaviors since they are ordinarily unaware of their maladaptive nature. Unlike those suffering from anxiety disorders, schizophrenia, or affective disorders, they are not likely to seek help on their own. A relatively high number of individuals who suffer from one of the other mental disorders are also characterized by a long-standing history of personality disorder.

DSM III lists twelve different types of personality disorder, only one of which is considered in detail here (antisocial personality disorder). A number of others are described briefly in Box 15.6. A word of caution is appropriate at the outset, however. The behaviors characteristic of each of these disorders are displayed by each of us at one time or another. These behaviors do not constitute a mental disorder unless they are long lasting, and unless they "become inflexible and maladaptive, causing significant impairment in social or occupational functioning, or subjective distress" (Spitzer et al., 1979, p. 161).

Personality disorder One of a number of maladaptive patterns of functioning and response. Personality disorders are usually not incapacitating but can result in considerable personal distress.

BOX 15.5

Depression, the Moon, and Suicide

Depressive disorders are the most common of all affective disorders (Winokur, 1973). They are characterized by a conglomerate of symptoms, including apathy, listlessness, despair, loss of appetite, sleep disturbances, unwavering pessimism, and a preoccupation with physical complaints as well as with suicide (although not all of these symptoms need be present in any single case). Indeed, some 15 percent of all depressives reportedly attempt suicide (Arieti, 1959); 15 percent of these succeed.

Although there appears to be a clear relationship between suicide and depression, it is by no means a simple relationship. Under most conditions, depression is positively related to suicide (Fawcett, 1972), but under certain conditions, the opposite seems to be true. Durkheim (1897/1951), who conducted the first large-scale studies of suicide, suggested that when events that would ordinarily be closely associated with depression and that might therefore lead to an increase in suicide rates also served to focus the attention of a large group of individuals, the suicide rate would not increase in this group. Biller (1977) investigated this hypothesis by looking at suicide rates in twenty-nine U.S. cities over a seventeen-year period (1956–1972), but only during the same nine-day period for each of those years. The nine days selected spanned November 22 to November 30. John F. Kennedy was killed on November 22, 1963. The hypothesis that depression would increase in the United States during that period following widespread media coverage of the assassination seems reasonable.

There were seventy-five reported suicides (forty-eight male, twenty-six female) in these twenty-nine cities during the relevant days over the seventeen years; not a single one of these occurred in 1963. This finding far exceeds chance expectations. Biller suggests that a national or widespread catastrophe or emergency might focus people's attention on events outside themselves, thereby relieving depressed people's preoccupations with their own situations. This has the indirect effect of lowering the suicide rate. In fact, it is not unlikely that it might reduce depression as a psychiatric disorder.

The role of the moon, too, has been systematically investigated. Does the moon, which affects tides, also affect humans? Was folklore correct when it claimed that the moon had much to do with strange behavior? Is it significant that the term *lunacy* relates directly to the Latin word for moon *(luna)*?

There are a handful of studies that have apparently found an ill-explained relationship between phases of the moon and such behaviors as suicide or homicide, but for every one of these studies there are a larger number that have failed to replicate original findings (Kelly, 1981). There appears to be no convincing scientific evidence to link the moon with police activity, human births, drug overdoses, homicide, suicide, epileptic seizures, birthrate, or bleeding during surgery (Campbell & Beets, 1978).

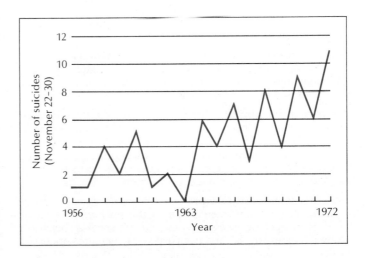

In general, depression is positively related to suicide. But research by Biller indicates that some types of depression reduce incidence of suicide. Tragic events which focus public attention are likely to lower suicide rates: they take people's minds off their own troubles. The graph shows the number of suicides in twenty-nine cities during a nine-day period (November 22–30) from 1956 to 1972. On November 22, 1963, John F. Kennedy was killed.

Sociopath An individual suffering from antisocial personality disorder, characterized by violation of laws, rules, and rights of others with no apparent remorse.

Individuals suffering from *antisocial personality disorder,* often labeled **sociopaths,** frequently present significant problems for society, and particularly for people near them. Such individuals are indifferent to the feelings of others, are selfish and manipulative in the extreme, experience no guilt whatsoever at any of their wrongdoings, seem to be incapable of emotional attachments, and frequently find themselves in trouble with the law. The antisocial personality is not antisocial in the sense of not being sociable. Quite the contrary. Such people are frequently pleasant, charming, "the life of the party." Their behaviors are antisocial in that they violate established customs, laws, and rules *with no apparent remorse.*

Manifestations of an antisocial personality disorder are far more common among males than females, and usually begin before the age of fifteen. Delinquency is one common early manifestation, as are underachievement in school, aggressive or exceptionally early sexual behavior, and repeated violation of rules. After the age of eighteen,

---

Personality Disorders

Personality disorders are characterized by specific, enduring patterns of maladaptive behavior. Unlike schizophrenia, they do not involve significant distortions of reality; and unlike the affective and anxiety disorders, they are not usually associated with profound guilt, anxiety, and/or depression. Although they are sometimes distressing for the victim and for the people around the victim, quite often the person is totally unaware of the disorder, and would remain quite incredulous if someone were to suggest that there is a problem. Among specific personality disorders are the following:

Paranoid Personality Disorder The *paranoid personality* is suspicious, mistrustful, and reluctant to assume blame for anything. Unlike the more serious schizophrenic or paranoid disorders, however, a paranoid personality disorder does not involve hallucinations or delusions.

Asocial Personality Disorder The *asocial personality disorder* is evident in an inability to form lasting and meaningful social relationships with others, and is frequently manifested in the individual's withdrawal from social contact.

Schizotypal Personality Disorders *Schizotypal personality disorders,* also described as borderline schizophrenia, are manifested in marked peculiarities of behavior, thinking, or emotional reaction. Belief in supernatural or extrasensory powers is common, as are disordered speech processes (vague, tangential), suspiciousness, social isolation, and emotional aloofness.

Histrionic Personality Disorder A relatively common disorder, more frequent in women than men, the *histrionic personality disorder* is marked by excessive, overt, attention-seeking behavior, and by overly expressed and not particularly genuine emotional reaction.

Narcissistic Personality Disorder Narcissus of the Greek legend loved himself above all else. Self-love, extreme arrogance, disregard for social convention and the rights of others, supreme confidence, and selfish exploitation of others are the principal characteristics of the *narcissistic personality.* Not surprisingly, such individuals appear only rarely in clinics. According to Kernberg (1978), narcissists love themselves but cannot love others.

Unstable Personality Disorder The primary features of *unstable personality disorder* are inconstancy in mood, in interpersonal relationships, and in feelings of identity. These are often apparent in the individual's inability to *maintain* relationships, despite a tendency to enter into many intimate and highly intense relationships. They are also apparent in rapid and seemingly uncontrollable shifts of mood, with sudden bursts of anger being prevalent. In addition, individuals described as having unstable personalities tend to be impulsive and unpredictable, and frequently embark on excesses of spending, drinking, sexual behavior, gambling, and so on. There is evidence, as well, of considerable personal distress accompanying unstable personality disorders. Being alone is not easily tolerated and frequently leads to depression. Loss of friends, jobs, and so on, a frequent consequence of the unstable person's impulsivity and emotional instability, may also lead to feelings of self-deprecation and depression.

Avoidant Personality Disorder *Avoidant personality disorder* is superficially similar to social phobia. In both cases, individuals exhibit excessive apprehension about social situations and tend to be withdrawn. Social phobias, however, are characterized by intense fear and anxiety. Avoidant personality disorders do not share these characteristics. In addition, individuals diagnosed as having avoidant personality disorders are typically highly desirous of intense and warm social relationships despite the fact that they are hypersensitive to social criticism. Given their fear of humiliation and rejection, they tend not to enter into many close relationships unless they can be well assured of uncritical acceptance.

Dependent Personality Disorder As the label implies, the *dependent personality* is marked by an overwhelming need to be closely associated with other people, to be surrounded by supportive people. Such individuals are self-effacing, highly tolerant, nonassertive, noncompetitive, and passionately committed to not being alone.

Compulsive Personality Disorder The *compulsive personality* is characterized by meticulousness, perfectionism, and a rigid adherence to convention. Such individuals are preoccupied with details, find it very difficult to relax, and tend to be excessively reserved in social situations. They are the individuals who do not easily "let go," whose concern with order and organization pervades their existence and makes it very difficult for them to make final decisions or to complete projects. Many tend to be indecisive and to procrastinate.

---

symptoms include inability to keep jobs, heavy drinking, marital difficulties, and legal difficulties.

Dan, a fourteen-year-old boy whom I recently interviewed in a detention center, presents a typical profile of an antisocial personality disorder (Lefrancois, 1981). Dan is an only child who lives with his mother occasionally, but who readily admits that he does not really like her, and doesn't remember ever doing so. He has a long history of minor trouble with law enforcement officers, and is presently serving an eighteen-month sentence following conviction on a theft charge. He seems proud of the fact that he has appeared in court on nine separate occasions, claims to have tried every drug on the street, and looks forward to getting out so that he can get involved once more with girls, drugs, fighting, and motorcycles. His supervisors describe Dan as having a nice personality, and as being very good at "conning" people. He lies and schemes to obtain favors, and has been successful in running away from the center on three occasions. On each of those occasions, he had been able to convince detention center staff that he was sufficiently ill to be taken to a nearby hospital; he had then succeeded in running away from the hospital. Local police always picked him up within a few days, either as a result of a fight or following some impulsive crime.

When he approaches the detention center counsellor, ostensibly for help, it is usually because Dan wants to try to manipulate her into doing him a favor. Like most individuals suffering from an antisocial personality disorder, he sees little wrong with his behavior and is, accordingly, highly resistant to treatment.

Psychosexual Disorders

DSM III recognizes three major subgroups of psychosexual disorders: those having to do with gender and associated role and identity problems; those relating to unusual objects of sexual gratification and unusual modes of sexual expression (the paraphilias); and those relating to sexual dysfunction (psychosexual dysfunctions).

Gender Identity Disorders   These disorders manifest themselves in conflict between anatomical sex (male or female, genetically) and gender role or gender identity. **Gender identity** refers to the subjective feelings individuals have concerning their sexuality. In the absence of gender identity problems, anatomical males *feel* that they are male. *Gender role* is actual behavior related to sexual identity. Thus, the gender identity of a normal female is a feeling of being female; gender role of a normal female is manifested in behaviors that are typically female and are congruent with gender identity.

Transsexualism, a rare disorder more common in males than in females, involves a feeling of discomfort with one's anatomical sex. In other words, transsexualism is a conflict between genetic sex and gender identity. Manifestations of transsexualism frequently take the form of reversed sex-role behavior. Transsexual males, who often dress and behave like females, sense themselves as female rather than male—hence their gender-identity problem.

Transvestism is a male disorder defined by repeatedly dressing as a female. Unlike the transsexual male, the transvestite sees himself as a male and has little wish to become female. Sexual arousal frequently accompanies "cross-dressing" but is not a necessary part of the disorder. Nor is the transvestite homosexual, although he may sometimes engage in homosexual acts.

Paraphilias   The **paraphilias** are a variety of sexual deviations (*para:* deviation; *philia:* attraction or love). Among these are the *fetishes,* involving sexual attraction to nonliving objects, like women's undergarments, shoes, hats, and other accessories. Fetishism occurs primarily in males. *Zoophilia* denotes sexual attraction to animals and the exclusive or preferred use of animals for sexual arousal or release. The condition is apparently rare. Given the highly secretive nature of many sexual deviations, however, all estimates must be considered tentative. *Pedophilia* describes a condition where prepubertal children are employed as sexual partners or objects. Pedophilia predominantly involves heterosexual rather than homosexual behavior and

Gender identity   One's subjective feelings of sexuality. If one's gender identity conflicts with one's anatomical sex, gender identity disorders may result.

Paraphilia   Attachment to unusual objects of sexual gratification and unusual modes of sexual expression. Paraphilia is classified as a psychosexual disorder.

is, according to news reports, becoming increasingly common. In particular, the use of children in pornographic books and films has increased dramatically.

Ego-dystonic homosexuality involves significant personal distress and conflict as a result of engaging in homosexual activities, or as a result of being aroused by fantasizing such activities. Note that homosexuality is not considered a disorder, but that the individual's reactions to homosexuality, where there is a serious conflict between conscience (self-ideal) and fantasy or behavior, may present a significant problem. *Exhibitionism* describes a condition where sexual arousal is obtained by exposing the genitals to an unsuspecting stranger. Thus a nude or "exotic" dancer cannot be classified as an exhibitionist. In fact, exhibitionists are almost invariably male. *Voyeurism* (peeping-tommery) involves achieving sexual arousal and frequently orgasm by observing others naked when they are unaware of being watched, and sometimes when they are engaged in sexual acts. The condition is probably exclusively male. The person who frequents "adult" and "stag" movie houses cannot, as a result of that behavior alone, be classified as a voyeur.

Sexual masochism denotes the achievement of sexual arousal as a result of personal suffering. It requires that the individual deliberately engage in behavior that brings about physical harm for the purpose of achieving sexual arousal. The condition is apparently rare, and is more common in men than in women. *Sadism,* in one sense the opposite of masochism, involves the persistent use of pain and injury inflicted on another person as a source of sexual excitement, or involves persistent fantasies related to inflicting injury in order to bring about sexual excitement. In some cases, injury is psychological rather than physical, and various forms of "bondage" and "slave-master" relationships may be employed in that way. In its most extreme forms, sadism may be directly associated with rape and murder of sexual victims. Sadism is not a necessary condition for rape, however (see Chapter 17). The condition is far more common in men than in women.

Psychosexual Dysfunctions The *psychosexual dysfunctions* include impediments to the enjoyment of normal sexual activity. Their principal psychological consequence is one of distress that may vary in severity depending on the individual concerned. Among sexual dysfunctions included in the DSM III classification are inhibited sexual desire, inhibited sexual excitement (frigidity or impotence), inhibited female orgasm, inhibited male orgasm, premature ejaculation, dyspareunio (pain during coitus), and vaginismus (spasms of the vagina making coitus painful).

For all of the disorders we have discussed, there are a number of possible therapies. Some are occasionally highly effective; others, less so. We look at therapy in the next chapter.

Causes of Mental Disorders

The area of psychological abnormality is certainly no less complex than that of normality. Recall the tremendous difficulties experienced by personality theorists in their attempts to account for the development of personality characteristics. Similar difficulties arise in the area of abnormality. In fact, the explanations and theoretical speculation presented in Chapter 13 are as pertinent to an understanding of abnormal psychology as they are to an understanding of the normal. Thus we can say without hesitation that genetic, biological, social, and psychological factors are intimately involved in mental disorders. The nature of their involvement is neither simple nor clear.

As noted earlier in this chapter, a variety of explanations for mental disorders are implicit in the models the psychologist adopts. Thus, the medical model looks for causes in physiological systems; the psychodynamic model looks for causes in psychodynamic conflicts; and behavioral models look at environmental influences on the assumption that maladaptive behavior is learned and can be unlearned. Preceding descriptions of various classifications of mental disorders should make it clear that each of these models, although useful, is insufficient by itself.

It would be both impossible and presumptuous to attempt here to detail the role of the many specific factors that might be implicated in the development of mental disorders. Not only would such a discussion necessarily repeat a great deal that has already been said concerning environmental factors, learning, and development, but it would also consume a great deal more space than is available. Accordingly, we limit our discussion of causes to three important sources of influence on mental functioning: genetic and organic factors; stress; and learning, specifically as it is reflected in feelings of helplessness.

Genetic and Organic Factors

Evidence of the importance of genetic factors in mental disorders is manifold. There is little doubt that many forms of mental retardation and schizophrenia are genetically influenced (Gottesman & Shields, 1972). In addition, there are numerous reports of higher incidence of related mental disorders among relatives than among unrelated individuals.

The most convincing evidence of the role of heredity in mental disorders is derived from studies of twins. Based on such studies, many researchers have concluded that a genetic predisposition is a necessary condition for the development of schizophrenia (Suinn, 1975). Gottesman and Shields (1966), for example, found that in twenty-eight pairs of identical twins, there was 42 percent concordance with respect to schizophrenia. That is, they identified members of a schizophrenic population who had identical twins and then determined how many of these twins were also schizophrenic; 42 percent were. Concordance for nonidentical twin pairs identified in the same fashion was only 9 percent. Further evidence of a genetic factor in schizophrenia has been provided by studies of schizophrenic mothers and their children. In one such study, Heston (1966) compared a group of infants born to institutionalized schizophrenic mothers and placed immediately in adoptive homes with a comparable group of adopted children born to normal mothers. Of the forty-seven children whose mothers were schizophrenic, five were themselves later diagnosed as schizophrenic, and a large number of the remaining forty-two were found to be suffering from psychosocial problems. None of the control group were found to be schizophrenic, and only a few suffered from psychosocial problems. Table 15.4 summarizes the results of a number of studies of schizophrenia in twins.

Table 15.4 Studies of Schizophrenia in Twins

		Percentage of Concordance*	
Investigator	Country	Identical Twins	Fraternal Twins (same sex)
Early studies			
Luxenburger (1928)	Germany	58	0
Rosanoff and others (1934)	USA	61	13
Essen-Moller (1941)	Sweden	64	15
Kallmann (1946)	USA	69	11
Slater (1953)	UK	65	14
Inouye (1961)	Japan	60	18
Later studies†			
Kringlen (1967)	Norway	45	15
Fischer and others (1969)	Denmark	56	26
Tienari (1971)	Finland	35	13
Allen and others (1972)	USA	43	9
Gottesman and Shields (1972)	UK	58	12

Source: Gottesman and Shields (1973).

*Concordant pairs are those in which both members are schizophrenic.

†The later studies used a more carefully controlled method for diagnosing schizophrenia, which probably accounts for their slightly lower concordance rates for identical twins.

The relationship of heredity to other disorders (personality disorders, for example) is not yet clear (see Schulsinger, 1980). It should also be noted that even where heredity appears to be related to the later manifestation of mental disorders, genetic make-up cannot be said to *cause* the disorder. The most logical affirmation that can be made on the basis of the data we have thus far is that heredity probably predisposes the individual to certain disorders, but that here, as elsewhere, manifestation of the disorder will also be a function of social and environmental factors.

A number of mental disorders can be attributed directly to nongenetic organic factors. Thus, infections such as syphilis and rubella (German measles), intoxicants such as carbon monoxide, vitamin deficiencies, metabolic malfunctions, brain injury or strokes, tumors, nutritional disorders, various drugs, endocrine gland disorders, circulatory diseases, and various degenerative diseases of the central nervous system may be implicated in **organic mental disorders**. Although nonorganic mental disorders are, by definition, not related directly to organic malfunction, our knowledge of medicine and psychiatry seldom allows us to rule out organic factors with complete assurance. And it is frequently difficult to determine whether other contributing factors are organic or not. Stress is a case in point since it appears to have physical as well as psychological effects (Chapter 10).

Organic mental disorders Mental disorders stemming demonstrably from some malfunction in the biological systems of the body. Organic factors may also be implicated, although they cannot be identified, in nonorganic disorders.

Stress

As was noted earlier in this chapter, the immediate onset of many mental disorders can be traced to specific traumatic experiences (Wills & Langner, 1980). This is most notably true of depressive reactions frequently triggered by a tangible loss or by a sense of hopelessness accompanying an anticipated loss. Losses, particularly serious and unusual ones, are, in fact, a considerable source of stress. Similarly, several of the amnesias can often be traced to a single overwhelming event, again presumably a source of intense stress.

War, natural catastrophe, economic depressions, and similar events are sources of stress for a great number of individuals. They provide a natural, though regrettable, opportunity for studying the more general effects of stress. Of these, wars have been studied most extensively. Such studies have, in fact, provided convincing evidence that many mental disorders may be precipitated by stressors of this nature. However, it has not usually been possible to determine the extent to which stress interacts with predispositions in bringing about a disorder. Not all individuals exposed to stressful situations react the same way; a great many have no clinically significant adverse reactions (Minter & Kimball, 1980). Nevertheless, the incidence of mental disorder in wartime has been common enough to bring into vogue a number of distinct descriptive terms. Psychologists, like other scientists, like to order their observations; classifications provide simple order. Thus, veterans have variously been described as suffering from shell shock, traumatic war neuroses, combat exhaustion, operational fatigue, and more recently, posttraumatic stress disorder.

Grinker and Spiegel (1963) have provided extensive studies of men in combat. Their conclusion is that all who are exposed to combat experiences are, to some degree, adversely affected. They present numerous case histories of Air Force personnel who, following traumatic experiences, displayed mental disorders ranging from mild disturbance to psychosis, and including the entire range of personality and affective disorders. Although a number of these individuals might have been diagnosed as having suffered disorders previously, particularly in childhood, the majority would have been classed as normal. All had been accepted for flight training.

Shaffer (1947), in a study of Air Force personnel, reports that virtually all airmen in combat were afraid (see Figure 15.6). Perhaps more important, the after-effects of this fear included fatigue, restlessness, depression, loss of appetite, obsessive thoughts, tremors, and tics—all of which are symptoms of possible anxiety disorders. These, and related findings, suggest strongly that stress may be an important factor in mental disorders.

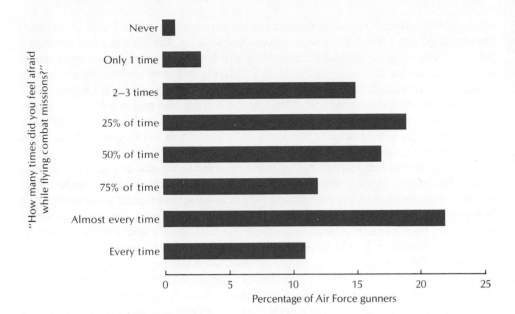

"How many times did you feel afraid while flying combat missions?"

Never
Only 1 time
2–3 times
25% of time
50% of time
75% of time
Almost every time
Every time

0   5   10   15   20   25
Percentage of Air Force gunners

Figure 15.6 Behavioral and emotional disorders are not uncommon following wartime experiences, as is evidenced by such psychiatric labels as shell shock, battle fatigue, war neuroses, and posttraumatic stress disorder. Stress, often manifested in fear and anxiety, is believed to be centrally implicated in such disorders. The chart at left depicts graphically how common stress is among one group of Air Force personnel.

Learned Helplessness

A recent explanation for anxiety, depression, and some otherwise unexplained deaths derives from parallels between the laboratory phenomenon of **learned helplessness** and human behavior in nonlaboratory situations. Recall from Chapter 6 that dogs who learn that their behaviors do not control the presentation of an aversive stimulus (who learn helplessness, in other words) subsequently "give up" when placed in situations where they would otherwise have learned a simple behavior that would have given them control (M. E. P. Seligman, 1975). In the original experiments, dogs were shocked while being restrained and were later released in a two-compartment shuttle box where escaping from a shock required only that they learn to jump over a low barrier. Animals who had learned helplessness frequently lay down, whining, passively accepting electric shocks.

Seligman (1974, 1975) advances the hypothesis that depression in humans may result from an analogous phenomenon. When we become convinced, for whatever reason, that our behaviors are inconsequential—that we are powerless and helpless—we abandon ourselves to feelings of depression and sometimes to death. It follows that as long as we retain some feeling of power, of helpfulness, we are more likely to escape from the consequences of depression.

In support of this theory, Seligman (1975) points to several parallels between depression in humans and learned helplessness in animals. Animals who have learned helplessness initiate fewer voluntary responses, have difficulty learning that behavior can affect outcomes, are less aggressive and competitive, display reduced appetites, and sometimes manifest chemical changes in neurotransmitters (particularly norepinephrine depletion). In much the same way, individuals diagnosed as depressed initiate fewer activities, are less likely to consider themselves in control, are typically nonaggressive and noncompetitive, often lose weight, become less active sexually, and often manifest changes in neurotransmitter substances.

Additional evidence of the importance of control (or "felt powerfulness") has been found in studies of aging. In one experiment, Langer and Rodin (1976) gave a group of institutionalized elderly people control over a large number of decisions that would affect their lives directly. In addition, they were each given a plant for which they were to be completely responsible. A second group were also given plants, but were told that nurses would water and care for them. In addition, emphasis was placed on the staff's eagerness to take care of the residents, so that they, in effect, would not

Learned helplessness A phenomenon, described by Seligman, characterized by feelings of powerlessness that appear to result from negative experiences over which we have no control, and that might account for depression and perhaps even for death.

be required to make any important decisions for themselves. Differences between these two groups a mere three weeks later were striking. The "greater responsibility" group scored significantly higher than the comparison group on measures of happiness, participation, alertness, and general well-being. A follow-up comparison undertaken a year and a half later was perhaps even more striking (Rodin & Langer, 1977). To begin with, twice as many individuals in the comparison group had died, relative to the control group (thirteen out of forty-four compared with seven out of forty-seven). In addition, measures of physical well-being as well as of psychological health all favored the experimental group.

To the extent that learned helplessness explains some manifestations of depression, it has some obvious, although still speculative, implications for treatment and, perhaps most important, for prevention. Whereas treatment would involve efforts to bring about feelings of control (that is, to reduce helplessness), prevention might involve the presentation of situations where the individual learns that outcomes are affected by behavior. In this connection, Seligman speaks of "immunizing" against depression. When dogs are first taught an avoidance behavior by being placed in a situation where they can remove themselves from an aversive situation, subsequent attempts to induce "learned helplessness" are frequently unsuccessful. Perhaps the same is true of humans who have been exposed to enough success experiences. A series of situations which demonstrate their helplessness might not be nearly so devastating for these individuals as for others who have repeatedly failed, and who have learned to perceive themselves as relatively helpless.

Mental Disorders in Perspective

Mental disorders, unlike the more common organic disorders, lend themselves reluctantly to classification. "Disordered" individuals bring with them a sometimes bewildering and unpredictable assortment of symptoms and feelings, and the task of sorting these into established categories frequently requires stretching the category or the symptoms. Indeed, one of the principal criticisms of diagnostic schemes such as those of the American Psychiatric Association is that distinctions among categories are often unclear, and manifested disorders of many patients cover aspects of many different categories. A second objection to systematic classification concerns the application of labels to individuals. A ruptured appendix is seldom unique: it is tangible, and has easily identified symptoms and predictable effects. Labeling the condition presents no problems. A disturbed psyche *is* unique: its symptoms are intangible and sometimes very difficult to identify; and its effects are all too often quite unpredictable. Labeling it is difficult and may, in the end, be unfair to the individual concerned.

In spite of these difficulties, progress in treating mental disorders has been dramatic in the past several decades. And that progress has, in large part, been due to the therapist's ability to identify and label separate manifestations of mental disorders, and to apply treatments that appear to be warranted by the nature of the disorder and its symptoms.

Madness Elsewhere

As noted earlier, a number of writers have argued that there are no "mental illnesses," only "problems in living" (Laing, 1964; Szasz, 1960); that, in fact, mental disorders are socially defined and take the form of socially unacceptable behaviors. Such writers sometimes argue that if society accepted the behaviors we view as "disordered," the number of individuals identified as disturbed would be drastically reduced.

Although these observations might be true for some of the milder disorders, particularly for those described as personality disorders, they are misleading with respect to the more serious disorders of thinking and perception that are manifested in the schizophrenias, for example, or in some of the organic brain disorders. Persistent delusions, hallucinations, other perceptual distortions, and inability to function in day-to-day living present real and significant problems, no matter how they are labeled or explained. And arguments concerning the "reality" of mental illness and the advisability of labeling do little to ameliorate the lives of those who find themselves beset with problems, or the lives of those who are affected by the sociopaths of society.

Interestingly, however, societies do appear to have their own special forms of madness. For reasons that are still unclear, eighteenth-century Europe, in addition to its dwindling numbers of witches, was swept by a wave of hysterical disorders. These disorders were marked by a variety of "conversion" symptoms, the most common of which were paralysis, deafness, blindness, and other physical incapacities that could not be accounted for by organic factors. Hysteria is no longer a popular form of disorder.

Farina (1976) describes a number of other disorders that appear to be highly specific to certain societies. One example is a condition labeled *amok* (whence our expression "to run amok"), prevalent in Malaysia. Victims are suddenly possessed by overwhelming aggressive and violent urges, and run about destroying property and attempting to kill anyone in sight. The condition sometimes lasts until the victims manage to kill themselves, knock themselves senseless, or drop into a coma. After recovery from the coma, amnesia covering the period of being "amok" is common.

Pibloktog is a peculiar form of madness observed by Admiral Peary among Eskimo women. Its primary symptoms include a short period of intense mania where victims run about in extreme excitement, singing, shouting, and tearing off their clothes—a behavior that is not entirely sensible in Arctic regions. Subsequently, victims may weep, lose consciousness, or fall asleep and later awaken apparently normal.

Certain natives of northern Siberia reportedly suffer from a strange disorder called *Arctic hysteria,* which affects both men and women, and which is evident in extreme suggestibility highly reminiscent of a hypnotic trance.

One additional example of culture-specific disorder is presented by Farina (1976). Members of the Canadian Ojibway and Chippewa tribes are sometimes "bewitched" and turned into cannibals. This condition, termed *witigo, wihtigo,* or *windigo* after the "spirit" which causes the disorder, presents itself with warning signals such as nausea, vomiting, and increased anxiety. Many suffering from these initial symptoms become afraid that they will kill and eat a friend, and may even ask to be killed themselves before they become completely "mad."

Consequences of Mental Disorders

I promised to provide a chapter-length definition of abnormality. This promise has been delivered and may be summarized as follows: Mental disorders are those conditions of human thought, affect, and behavior leading to personal distress, functional disability, or, at the very least, some disadvantage in coping with unavoidable aspects of the environment (Spitzer et al., 1976). The consequences of being the victim of a mental disorder are implicit in this definition. They range from mild to serious personal distress and include the possibility of mild to severe impairment of ability to function normally.

When distress results, the individual affected is usually aware of the disorder. It should be clear from preceding discussions, however, that with many forms of mental disorder, including personality disorders and sometimes the schizophrenias, individuals remain unaware that they are disordered and do not seek help. In such cases, they may be compelled to submit to treatment either as a result of their maladaptive and sometimes dangerous behaviors, or as a result of social pressure.

Not all individuals who might be diagnosed as suffering from a mental disorder are so diagnosed and treated; nor do all suffer noticeably from personal distress. Many continue to function quite well in society in spite of varying degrees of unhappiness and strife. Some, overwhelmed by melancholia, commit suicide; others manifest their disorders in abnormal but sometimes undetected behaviors. The pyromaniacs, kleptomaniacs, sadists, and masochists might be sitting right next to you. And if that concerns you overly, you might need to look no further than a mirror to observe a paranoiac!

A word of caution might be in order at this point. It is not uncommon for medical students to suffer from a succession of exotic diseases as they progress through medical school, or at least to imagine that they suffer from these diseases as they recognize symptoms in themselves. Similarly, as you were reading these pages, you may have occasionally recognized in yourself the symptoms of a narcissistic personality disorder or schizophrenia. Relax. Not only is the stress and worry not particularly good for you, but it most likely has no basis in fact. You are probably not constitutionally suited to be schizophrenic; the personality disorders typically require a history of adjustment problems; and if you have survived happily till now, you will probably continue to do so.

Main Points

1 Mental disorders have historically been attributed to demons, witchcraft, masturbation, and a variety of other factors. Accordingly, historical methods of treatment have included exorcism, torture, blood-letting, and making holes in the head (trephining).

2 Insanity is a legal term, defined by courts of law, and not ordinarily employed in psychology.

3 Abnormality may be defined statistically as including those behaviors or personality traits that are extremely rare.

4 Medical models of abnormality are based on the idea that mental disorders are diseases or malfunctions in the same way as physical disorders represent disease or malfunction.

5 Behavioral models of abnormality maintain that abnormal behavior is learned just as is any other behavior, and that it can be modified in the same way.

6 Cognitive models of abnormality argue that psychological disorders generally result from distortions of reality—these distortions being essentially cognitive problems.

7 Psychodynamic models are premised on the assumption that disorders result from the interplay of powerful and often unconscious psychic forces.

8 Mental disorders may be defined as psychological or emotional states which are associated with distress, disability, or, at the very least, some disadvantage in coping with the environment.

9 The Diagnostic and Statistical Manual of the American Psychiatric Association (DSM III) describes seventeen major classes of mental disorders, and provides specific criteria which clinical psychologists can use in arriving at a diagnosis.

10 DSM III provides for classification of disorders on five axes: all disorders except for personality disorders; personality disorders; medical problems not directly associated with the mental disorder; presence and severity of stress in the patient's life; and an indication of the patient's recent level of functioning.

11 Anxiety disorders include phobias (intense, irrational fears, of which agoraphobia—fear of leaving home or of being in strange places—is relatively common); obsessive-compulsive disorders, which are marked by the recurrence of impulses and thoughts that the individual finds disturbing; and generalized anxiety disorders, which involve pervasive feelings of anxiety in the absence of any specific cause.

12 Dissociative disorders involve the splitting of aspects of personality and behavior and include amnesia (loss of memory, sometimes of personal history); fugue states (wandering and loss of memory); and multiple personality, often confused with schizophrenia in popular literature.

13 Schizophrenia, one of the more severe forms of what have often been labeled *psychoses* (as opposed to what were once termed *neuroses*), includes disorganized schizophrenia (marked by delusions, hallucinations, and severe disintegration of behavior and thought); catatonic schizophrenia (where patients might remain immobile for prolonged periods); and paranoid schizophrenia (probably the most common form of schizophrenia, marked by delusions of grandeur and feelings of persecution).

14 Major affective disorders include bipolar disorders (sometimes called manic-depression) and major depression. Less severe forms of depression are extremely common, and are sometimes called neurotic depression or dysthymic disorder.

15 Personality disorders include a large group of disorders that generally begin in childhood or adolescence, and that are characterized by maladaptive patterns of behavior or of emotional responsiveness. Antisocial personality disorders (sometimes labeled *sociopathy*) are marked by repeated transgression of rules and laws with no apparent feelings of remorse. Truancy, delinquency, and eventual criminality are not uncommon among such individuals.

16 Psychosexual disorders include gender identity disorders (transsexualism and transvestism), paraphilias, and psychosexual dysfunctions (inhibited sexual desire, inhibited sexual excitement, inhibited orgasm, premature ejaculation, and pain during coitus).

17 A number of mental disorders appear to have a genetic basis. Important nongenetic organic factors in mental disorders include infections as well as various drugs, vitamin deficiencies, metabolic malfunctions, brain injury or disease, nutritional disorders, and various nervous system diseases.

18 Stress is closely associated with a variety of physical and mental disorders. Its effects have been particularly evident in times of war, and are sometimes manifested in what is labeled *posttraumatic stress disorder*.

19 Some anxiety and depression may result from feelings of powerlessness and helplessness. These feelings may be learned as a result of negative experiences over which we have no control.

20 Some forms of madness appear to be peculiar to specific ages (hysteria in eighteenth-century Europe) and to specific cultures (*windigo* among Ojibway or Chippewa Indians; *pibloktog* among Eskimo women).

Further Readings

Numerous textbooks are devoted to an examination of psychopathology. Among them, the following present clear and comprehensive surveys:

Coleman, J. *Abnormal psychology and modern life* (6th ed.). Chicago: Scott, Foresman, 1980.

Davison, G. C., and Neale, J. M. *Abnormal psychology: An experimental clinical approach* (2nd ed.). New York: John Wiley, 1978.

Goldenberg, H. *Abnormal psychology: A social/community approach.* Monterey, Calif.: Brooks/Cole, 1977.

Szasz's books stand in sharp contrast to traditional approaches to mental disorders, claiming that they are, in many ways, mythical:

Szasz, T. S. *The myth of mental illness: Foundations of a theory of personal conduct.* New York: Dell, 1967.

Szasz, T. S. *The manufacture of madness.* New York: Harper & Row, 1970.

An intriguing, sometimes controversial learning-theory approach to mental disorders is presented in:

Seligman, M. E. P. *Helplessness: On depression, development and death.* San Francisco: W. H. Freeman, 1975.

The role of stress in mental disorder and suggestions for avoiding and coping with it are elaborated in the classic book:

Selye, H. *Stress without distress.* Philadelphia: J. B. Lippincott, 1974.

Insights into what mental disorders are like from the patient's point of view are implicit in the personal accounts of madness in:

Kaplan, B. (Ed.). *The inner world of mental illness.* New York: Harper & Row, 1954.

A well-known, fictional description of mental disorder and its treatment is presented in:

Kesey, K. *One flew over the cuckoo's nest.* New York: Viking Press, 1962.

A massive and detailed compendium of articles relating to abnormality is the following:

Eysenck, H. J. (Ed.). *Handbook of abnormal psychology* (2nd ed.). London: Sir Isaac Pitman and Sons, 1973.

Therapy

16

Bezekia has an absolutely fascinating medical and psychotherapeutic history. Twice married and twice divorced, she now lives with her aging mother. Together they discuss symptoms of their countless ailments. The old lady treats hers with herbs, spices, salves, prayers, and overproof rum; Bezekia looks elsewhere for treatment.* Some of the therapies she has tried:

Tranquilizers for her anxiety (chemotherapy). She asked as well for a frontal lobotomy, having read that the procedure might alleviate her occasional fits of violence, and for electroconvulsive therapy, fearing she was badly depressed. But these were denied.

Psychoanalysis for her unresolved Electra complex, intuitively and cleverly diagnosed by Bezekia herself after an introductory psychology course. The analyst reportedly enjoyed her rich and varied dream life.

Adlerian therapy in a futile attempt to identify her nagging feelings of inferiority.

Systematic desensitization following a particularly harrowing experience with a small garter snake in southern Saskatchewan.

Aversive conditioning in a brave attempt not to smoke. Bezekia has never smoked but wished to take no chances in case the urge ever arose.

Positive reinforcement for losing weight. She was not particularly overweight but thought it would be nice to reward herself with a short trip to the Fiji Islands with a rational-emotive therapist she had recently met.

---

*With apologies to those therapists who might take all of this seriously.

Rational-emotive therapy because she wanted to go to the Fiji Islands with the therapist. He was highly sympathetic but had some difficulty identifying specific problems although there were a large number of more general difficulties. His wife was one of them. She thought the idea was irrational.

Gestalt therapy because Esalen is beautiful and the baths warm.

Transactional analysis in a genuine attempt to discover the games she had been playing and the scripts she was living. The analyst informed her she specialized in Life Games with emphasis on "Now I've Got You, You Son of a Bitch" (NIGYYSOB) and "Kick Me" (KM). Subsequently she stopped playing NIGYYSOB with her mother, but still plays KM with me.

Client-centered therapy in an effort to discover herself, to grow, and to become. Something. Anything. Her mother is tired of supporting her.

Primal-scream therapy because my Uncle Robert suggested it at a Halloween party.

Orgone therapy because she had read, and believed, that the measure of mental health is the frequency and intensity of orgasm.

Sex therapy because she believed in orgone therapy.

Countless "growth" groups, there being a great many of them, and Bezekia having a profound interest in the promises of each. And in the activities of some.

And in spite of all this therapy, Bezekia continues to thrive on her self-conscious unhappiness—a fact that says less about therapies and their effectiveness than it does about Bezekia herself.

Treatments for Mental Disorders

The object of this chapter on the various therapies is not to make a therapist of you, but simply to acquaint you with some traditional and current approaches. There are no panaceas in the treatment of mental disorders. Symptoms can sometimes be removed; joy can sometimes be restored to saddened lives; distortions of reality can sometimes be repaired; the ability to relate to other humans can sometimes be improved. There may be some magic in the methods that are employed for these purposes. But you and I are hard-headed scientists who deal neither in mystery nor in magic. We categorize and label; we describe and evaluate according to established procedures and well-defined criteria. And sometimes we find ourselves overwhelmed, because our sciences are not always adequate. Yet.

Consider that there are easily hundreds of different therapies for mental disorders, each with their passionate advocates, their handfuls of documents, their case histories of cures, walking proof of their effectiveness and superiority. In addition to these therapies, there are the surgical, chemical, and nutritional treatments. And in addition to all these, there is the magic of the witch doctor. These many treatments and approaches have been described and labeled in a variety of ways. This chapter presents descriptive information about the major classes of treatment: medical approaches, insight therapies, behavior therapies, and other approaches. A critical evaluation of these therapies follows their presentation.

Medical Approaches

At first glance, it might seem that medical therapies would be appropriate only in the case of organically based disorders. In other words, if an organic basis can be found for a specific disorder, then it might seem reasonable to suppose that physiological intervention might, in some cases, help "cure" it. That is the case on occasion, particularly with respect to certain metabolic conditions or infections known to have psychological and neurological effects. Treatment in many such cases consists of arresting the disease or rectifying the condition before its more extreme results appear. Syphilis, for example, can, if unchecked, lead to neurological impairment and the manifestation of various mental disorders. Simple and highly effective treatment with penicillin or related drugs in its early stages prevents their appearance. Similarly, thyroid problems, insulin problems, and a variety of metabolic and glandular problems can be controlled chemically.

Medical therapies are not limited to the treatment of disorders that clearly have organic origins, however, but are applied to a large number of other disorders. Such therapies may be chemical (drug therapy or chemotherapy) or surgical, or may involve the use of electric shocks (electroconvulsive therapy).

Chemotherapy

Mild tranquilizers (Miltown, Valium, Librium) reduce anxiety and are useful for treating phobias, somatoform disorders, some sleep disorders, and so on; drugs known as *psychic energizers* or antidepressants (Tofranil, Elavil) are widely used in the treatment of depression; major tranquilizers (chlorpromazine, Mellaril), called *antipsychotic drugs,* are used extensively with schizophrenic patients. There is considerable controversy over the effectiveness of these chemical substances. Their use frequently accompanies other forms of therapy, where they might be employed simply to control anxiety or depression sufficiently that the therapist can more effectively employ other treatments. In addition, many of these drugs have unpleasant side effects.

Other drugs sometimes used in the treatment of mental disorders include lithium carbonate for manic-depressive disorders, disulfiram (Antabuse) for alcoholism, and methadone for heroin addiction. It should be noted, however, that despite their widespread use, drugs have not been clearly established as the best of all possible forms of therapy. Their primary effects and many of their side effects vary from one person to another, are frequently unpredictable, and are sometimes highly undesirable. The mildest of these include lethargy, mood fluctuations, and insomnia. Prolonged use of heavy doses of antipsychotic drugs has been associated with symptoms typical of Parkinson's disease (stiffness, drooling, tremors), with stupor and "zombie-like" behaviors, with brain damage, and with *tardive dyskinesia,* a condition characterized by grotesque, involuntary facial movements (MacDonald, Lidsky, & Kern, 1979; Widroe & Heisler, 1976). Considerable research still needs to be undertaken with psychotherapeutic drugs. In spite of this, however, the relative decline in inpatient populations of psychiatric institutions since the 1950s is due largely to the discovery and widespread use of these drugs.

Psychosurgery

A second, highly controversial medical therapy involves surgical intervention. Among the most highly publicized of the surgical treatments is that of excising (removing) or making lesions (cuts) in the frontal lobes of the brain (prefrontal lobotomy), a procedure that is sometimes successful in reducing anxiety and alleviating depression. Among its frequent side effects, however, are a general dulling of emotional reaction, occasional epileptic seizures, listlessness, and sometimes stupor (Barahal, 1958). Given the irreversibility of this operation, it is not surprising that chemotherapy has largely replaced it. Recent findings that it is possible to control a number of emotions through the simpler procedure of producing lesions in appropriate parts of the brain, as well as fears of the political use of psychosurgery for controlling criminals or the dangerously insane (and perhaps other "undesirables"), have led to a strong public reaction against psychosurgery.

It should be noted, however, that recent advances in neurological techniques have made it possible to determine in advance what the effects of brain lesions will be (Sem-Jacobsen & Styri, 1975). The general procedure is to stimulate specific portions of the brain with microelectrodes before surgery to determine precisely where lesions should be made. The therapeutic value of surgery has accordingly increased, and the risk of undesirable side effects has decreased dramatically. It should also be noted that surgical techniques are used very rarely and only after the patient has been unsuccessfully exposed to other available therapies, including chemotherapies, over a long period of time. Even then, psychosurgery would not be employed unless the condition was sufficiently serious to warrant what is recognized as the most drastic of all therapies.

Electroconvulsive Therapy

Popularly called "shock treatments," *electroconvulsive therapy (ECT)* has sometimes proven effective for severely depressed patients. The procedure is to pass an alternating current of between 110 and 150 volts across the temples for 0.1 second, two or three times a week, for approximately four weeks (eight to twelve treatments). The immediate effect is a convulsion lasting approximately one minute, a recovery period of about thirty minutes, and subsequent amnesia for the period immediately preceding administration of the shock and sometimes for a period of an hour or so following treatment. In some cases amnesia is more profound and covers a longer period of time, causing severe disorientation, with patients unable to remember where they are or why. A second undesirable side effect involves the bruises and fractures that sometimes result from the violence of the convulsions. More recently, ECT has been employed in conjunction with relaxing drugs in order to minimize the risk of physical injury (Kalinowsky, 1975).

Although the reasons why ECT should work remain obscure, research indicates that it is effective with as many as 80 percent of all severely depressed patients (Greenblatt et al., 1964). Since it is a particularly violent form of therapy that does carry a risk of physical injury and sometimes even brain damage, it remains highly controversial (Figure 16.1).

Psychotherapeutic Approaches

Medical treatments present one method of dealing with mental disorders. The psychotherapeutic approaches are a second alternative. Essentially, **psychotherapy** attempts to "cure" or ameliorate mental disorders through interaction between a professional therapist and one or more patients, or sometimes simply through interaction among a number of patients.

Professional therapists, like patients, come in a variety of forms, including but not limited to psychiatrists and clinical psychologists. The principal difference between these two groups is that psychiatrists have undergone extensive medical training in addition to their psychological training. In effect, a psychiatrist is a medical doctor who has also taken postdoctoral training in mental disorders. A psychiatrist whose training and practice are primarily Freudian is often described as a psychoanalyst. A clinical psychologist generally has a Ph.D. in psychology and has been trained in hospital or clinical settings to develop competence in the diagnosis and treatment of mental disorders. In addition to psychiatrists and clinical psychologists, there are counseling psychologists and a variety of other "counselors." Counseling psychologists possess graduate degrees in psychology (or from related faculties and departments) and have been trained in the recognition and treatment of a variety of problems, often involving personal adjustment or vocational decision making, and not ordinarily classified as mental disorders (see Table 16.1). Other "counselors" cannot easily be described. Some are self-appointed, well-intentioned, and effective; others, also self-appointed, are less well intentioned. There is money to be made from exploiting the miserable. However, not all that the quacks and charlatans do in the name of self-aggrandizement or money should be dismissed out of hand. Very often, and in spite of themselves, they are extremely effective.

What therapies do psychotherapists employ? The literature presents a vast and bewildering array of therapies, many of which have appeared very recently. A great number of these are intended less for the treatment of more serious mental disorders

Figure 16.1 Here a patient is readied for "shock treatment," or *electroconvulsive therapy*. Although research indicates this can be an effective therapy for severe depression, it remains highly controversial.

Psychotherapy An extremely general term that refers to the use of a great variety of techniques to alleviate mental disorders or emotional problems. Although not limited to traditional psychoanalysis, it is usually restricted to treatments supervised or conducted by trained people such as clinical psychologists or psychiatrists. Nor is psychotherapy limited to the treatment of such serious disorders as schizophrenia or personality disorders; it may be used for a variety of conditions related to personal distress, problems of adjustment, and related difficulties. Indeed, psychotherapy is sometimes appropriate for such behaviors as nail-biting, thumb-sucking, stuttering, smoking, overeating, and chasing rabbits while naked.

Table 16.1 Practitioners of Psychotherapeutic Approaches

Practitioner	Qualifications
Psychiatrist	Medical degree; postdoctoral training in treatment of mental disorders; only practitioner qualified to employ chemotherapy or use radical medical intervention
Psychoanalyst	Psychiatrist whose practice is based on the principles of Freudian therapy
Clinical psychologist	Psychology training, usually including a Ph.D. in psychology; hospital or clinical training in diagnosis and treatment
Counseling psychologist	Graduate degree in psychology or related field; training in diagnosis and treatment of problems not usually classified as mental disorders
Other counselors	Variety of backgrounds and credentials; some well-meaning and effective, others self-appointed and unqualified

than for the alleviation of relatively minor problems. A significant number are intended to enhance personal growth and development, to promote better social adjustment, and to increase happiness. Accordingly, many therapies have moved out of clinical and hospital settings and are flourishing in resort areas, in suburban homes and downtown offices, in parks and on beaches.

Distinctions among these many therapies are not always obvious; they lend themselves poorly to the type of organization required in a textbook such as this. Nevertheless, it is possible to differentiate among therapies directed primarily toward achieving insight into psychodynamic forces that are presumably at the root of present problems; therapies that emphasize immediate behavior rather than its causes; and a number of other therapies that do not fit easily into these categories. Accordingly, this chapter deals first with the insight therapies, next with behavioral therapies, and finally with an assortment of other therapies. No evaluative comments are made during the initial descriptions of these therapies, but a major section is devoted to evaluation at the end of this chapter.

Insight Therapies

The major *insight therapies* are premised on Freudian theory. Their common feature is the belief that alleviating mental disorders and more minor personality and adjustment problems depends upon achieving insight into the causes of present behavior. Two examples of insight therapies are described here: Freudian psychoanalysis and Adlerian psychotherapy.

Freudian Psychoanalysis

From Freud's psychodynamic theories have grown elaborate therapies, some of which he originated and practiced himself, many of which represent developments and modifications introduced by his followers over the years. These are widespread and immensely popular therapies. Indeed, the lay person's stereotype of the psychiatrist, complete with couch, notebook, and fascinating insight into the symbols of dreams, is based on a psychoanalytic model.

The psychoanalytic model, elaborate and detailed though it is, may be simplified as follows. Recall that Freud considered mental disturbances to result from psychodynamic conflict. More specifically, conflict between basic impulses (id) and conscience (superego) gives rise to anxiety. One of the major roles played by the ego is to find means of reducing this anxiety. This may be accomplished through one of a number of defense mechanisms (repression, reaction formation, and so on). Accordingly, the psychoanalyst's primary task is to uncover basic sources of conflict, many of

Free association A psychoanalytic technique wherein the patient is asked to say whatever comes to mind without evaluating or discarding material.

Mental blocks A Freudian term for what are assumed to be the ego's defenses against revealing sensitive issues.

Transference A psychoanalytic process whereby the patient transfers emotions and feelings originally directed toward other people or objects to the therapist.

which will have a sexual basis. Psychoanalysis provides a number of techniques for doing this. They are generally employed in one-hour sessions, sometimes as often as five times a week, and often lasting many years.

In **free association**, the patient, reclining comfortably on the proverbial psychiatrist's couch, is encouraged to say whatever comes to mind without evaluating or discarding material. The hope is that these *associated ideas* will eventually lead therapist and patient back to a fundamental source of conflict or, failing that, that the therapist will recognize where blocks to association occur. These **mental blocks** are assumed to be the ego's defenses against revealing sensitive issues. Through repeated verbal probing, the analyst may eventually understand these blocks, and perhaps even remove them.

The analysis of dreams is a second, fascinating technique employed in psychoanalysis. Freud believed that ego defenses (including mental blocks and other defense mechanisms) were at their weakest during sleep, and that sources of intense psychodynamic conflict are therefore often revealed during dreams. He distinguished between the apparent or *manifest* meaning of dreams (a baseball bat is a baseball bat, whether in a dream or in a batter's hand) and their true or symbolic meaning (for all that you and I know, a baseball bat might be a symbol of penis envy in a dream, although it presumably continues to be a baseball bat in the batter's hands).

In the course of repeated psychoanalytic sessions, the therapist pays particular attention to the relationship that develops between analyst and patient. According to Freud, this relationship often illustrates **transference**: the therapist becomes somebody of importance in the patient's life, perhaps embodying a source of historical conflict. Thus, patients react to their therapists as they would to a parent or a lover, displaying in their behavior many of the attitudes they might have had toward that important person, perhaps at a time when conflict was being born. In effect, attitudes and feelings that might be the basis of conflict are *transferred* to the analyst. Recognizing this, the analyst may then interpret this transference, along with information derived from dreams and from free association, thereby arriving at some *insight* into the source of the patient's conflict. If the objective of psychoanalysis were to be described in a single word, that word would be *insight*. In short, the purpose of psychoanalysis is to help patients understand the reasons for their present difficulties. The assumption is that if a "cure" is to be achieved, it will be achieved through insight (see Box 16.1).

Adlerian Therapy

Recall that in Adler's description of personality, presented in Chapter 13, one of the fundamental facts of human existence is inferiority. To be human is to feel inferior, and it is this feeling of inferiority, recognized extremely early in life, that provides the principal source of motivation for all our later behaviors. Failure to overcome inferiority may lead to an inferiority complex; overcompensation for feelings of inferiority may lead to a superiority complex.

Among the most important forces in the child's life are early experiences that communicate inferiority or superiority. Accordingly, the Adlerian therapist is highly interested in the individual's first vivid recollections, in parent-child relationships, and in the individual's birth order, which is important in determining parent-child relationships, child-sibling relationships, and life-style—characteristic ways of coping with life's problems, manifested in personality and directed toward the elimination of feelings of inferiority. The first goal of the therapist is to uncover these historical factors through intensive interviews. A second goal is to explain to patients the roots of their behavior. In this sense, *Adlerian therapy* is similar to Freudian psychoanalysis: both strive to achieve and to communicate insight into the reasons for the patient's problems.

A third, highly important goal of the Adlerian therapeutic process is to bring about a feeling of worth in clients, to develop their interests in areas where they can manifest reasonable competence. The desired result is a reduction in the inferiority which lies at the root of the problem or a reduction in the superiority complexes that sometimes manifest themselves in delusions of grandeur (see Box 16.2).

Behavior Therapy

Whereas the insight therapies are centrally concerned with the historical antecedents of present behavior, the behavior therapies deal with immediate manifestations of deviant behavior. Their assumption is that abnormal behavior can be unlearned or at least replaced with more acceptable behavior. Accordingly the principal behavior therapies are based directly on learning theories, particularly of the operant and classical conditioning variety, and make extensive use of learning principles in approaches collectively labeled *behavior modification*.

Although there are a variety of approaches to behavior modification, most are based on the general principle that people are influenced by the consequences of their behavior—that their immediate environmental circumstances are more relevant than most early experiences, psychic conflicts, or personality structure (Stolz et al., 1975). Examples of the major approaches to behavior modification are described and illustrated here.

BOX 16.1

Psychoanalytic Treatment of the Little Prince

At the age of nine, Uri was referred for psychiatric treatment because of enuresis (bed-wetting), but that was only one of his problems (Aleksandrowicz, 1975). His mother provided much of his history. He had been a "strange" baby, unresponsive and rejecting. He slept much of the time and adamantly refused to be cuddled when awake. At the age of eight months he had been brought to visit a relative in a strange place and had spent the entire day screaming. Afterward he manifested a deep fear of strange places and of strangers, and was terrified of moving objects. Between the ages of nine months and five years, he woke up every night, screaming, from nightmares.

Uri was musically talented and had a remarkable memory for numbers and dates. He refused to take music lessons, however, and became highly agitated when his sister played and made mistakes. At nursery school he refused to become involved in activities with other children, but insisted on playing with mechanical toys. Any attempt to involve him resulted in a violent temper tantrum.

At the age of five, Uri was placed in a psychiatric ward for one week because of a "key mania" that he had developed (he had collected hundreds of keys, and spoke of nothing else). Minimal brain damage was diagnosed at that time.

He adjusted somewhat in school but continued to be hypersensitive to sights, sounds, and smells, and developed a number of intense phobias, the most striking of which was his fear of thieves. In addition, he became increasingly accident-prone, suffering numerous cuts, bruises, and bone fractures as a result of daring or foolish activities. He continued to have temper tantrums periodically.

Diagnosis: early infantile autism (symptoms: avoidance of people, fear of physical contact, absorption in mechanical objects, memory for numbers, minimal brain damage); later symptoms manifesting anxiety disorders (particularly phobias), and personality disorders (aggressiveness and tantrums). Treatment undertaken was psychoanalytically oriented.

First a detailed and extensive history of Uri was obtained from his parents. Similarly, both mother and father were examined in terms of their histories and present relationships, particularly as these related to Uri. Uri then came to two sessions per week for a total of two years. Early sessions revealed anger and envy directed largely toward his sister. A recurrent dream involving a black water boiler hanging over his head and about to explode was interpreted as relating to his sister. More pertinent was a second dream in which a thief (about whom he had severe phobias) stood by his sister's bed, but disappeared and became a bone when illuminated by Uri's flashlight, leaving only a shoe behind him. The Freudian interpretation recognizes the "thief" motive as well as some incestuous motives (he wanted to steal his sister's "shoe-vagina"), in addition to a fear of punishment (becoming a skeleton—a bone).

The psychotherapist also inferred an acute Oedipal conflict, poorly resolved because Uri was intensely narcissistic (that is, he loved himself and expressed feelings of grandeur), and because his father was not a perfect model for identification. Over a number of months, therapist and patient struggled with this conflict, the therapist explaining to Uri the source of his "bisexual identity" problems.

Over the ensuing months, they continued to explore Uri's fantasies and fears, his conflicts and defense mechanisms, eventually breaking through to some new personal insights. Concomitant with this therapeutic progress, Uri began to engage in independent activities he had previously feared intensely. He joined a scout group, began to take swimming lessons, and stopped wetting his bed. Sessions with Uri were complemented with long discussions with his parents who, as a result, learned to cope with his behavior without encouraging his symptoms. And, in the end "the little prince finally descended from his lonely star to join the crowded world of ordinary people" (Aleksandrowicz, 1975, p. 425).

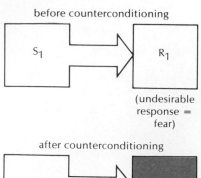

before counterconditioning

(undesirable response = fear)

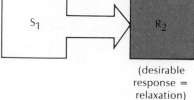

after counterconditioning

(desirable response = relaxation)

Figure 16.2 The theoretical "before" and "after" of counterconditioning, or systematic desensitization. The object is to replace R_1 with R_2 for a given situation (S_1).

Systematic desensitization A behavior modification technique that attempts to replace undesirable responses with more desirable responses through a conditioning procedure.

Aversive conditioning A behavior modification technique that attempts to bring about avoidance behavior with respect to certain situations by attaching negative feelings to the situation.

Systematic Desensitization

Systematic desensitization involves an attempt to replace an undesirable response with another response which is incompatible with the first and which is more desirable. Recall, for example, Watson and Rayner's conditioning experiment where Little Albert was eventually made to fear a white rat through a classical conditioning procedure (see Chapter 6). A procedure that, in principle, is identical to that employed by Watson and Rayner has been described and used extensively by Wolpe (1958, 1976). It is alternatively called *counterconditioning, systematic desensitization,* or *reciprocal inhibition.* The procedure is particularly effective for phobias and is best illustrated in relation to them.

Imagine if you will, a copy editor whose fear of pencils and related objects has driven her to distraction and who, as a result of this well-developed phobia, finds herself in the office of a therapist inclined toward the use of counterconditioning. The therapist begins by training the patient in relaxation. Once she has achieved the ability to relax, she is presented with the first item on a list of fear-inducing situations that she has previously described. The list is hierarchically arranged, proceeding from the least anxiety-laden stimulus to the situation that would bring about the greatest amount of fear. In this case, the first item on the list is a piece of straw; the last item is a large wooden pencil. The patient is then asked to imagine the first item, while being encouraged to relax. The theory is simply that relaxation is incompatible with anxiety, and if stimuli are introduced in such a way that they do not produce anxiety, the patient will eventually learn to respond to them by relaxing (see Figure 16.2). In successive sessions, the patient is encouraged to imagine other situations until she can imagine the great wooden pencil without any anxiety. Research indicates that being able to tolerate anxiety-related situations in imagination is related to a reduction in anxiety when these situations are actually encountered. Following this phase of the treatment, the patient is then encouraged to confront pencils and related objects in real life.

Considerable research, in addition to Wolpe's own clinical evidence, suggests that counterconditioning procedures can be remarkably effective in relieving anxiety related to phobias, as well as in the treatment of certain obsessions, compulsions, and related disorders.

Aversive Conditioning

A related behavioral technique, labeled **aversive conditioning**, attempts to attach negative feelings and to bring about avoidance behavior with respect to certain

---

BOX 16.2

Adlerian Therapy: George

In Box 15.4 (p. 460) we described George, a schizophrenic individual, paranoid type. Complete with twelve sweaters (his apostles), he had deluded himself into believing he was the chosen savior of mankind—a contemporary Christ. The therapist (Angers, 1975) interpreted his delusions and paranoia within an Adlerian framework. Tremendous feelings of inferiority had led to an inferiority complex that had then been surmounted through overcompensation and resultant feelings of vast superiority. Who, in George's mind, would be more powerful and more superior than Christ?

Therapy involved establishing a close, caring relationship with the patient, expressing interest in his abilities and skills (George was something of an expert on Russian customs and language), and attempting in this way to engender feelings of confidence that would eventually replace his schizophrenic delusions of superiority. True to Adlerian theory, the therapist delved back into George's first vivid recollection (Adler believed that sources of inferiority and a consequent life-style were established very early in life); inquired as to his ordinal position in the family (he was a rejected only child, spoiled by nursery attendants); and attempted to determine the principal characteristics of his parents (his father was domineering and cruel; his mother, weak and ineffectual). His parents had separated after a period of bitter arguments. George had interpreted this as being sinful and had incorporated their guilt. Over succeeding sessions, the therapist showed George that he was not guilty for his parents' sins, and that his behavior was incompatible with the teachings of Christ, who simply wanted people to be Christlike without assuming that they were actually Christ. In this latter endeavor he was helped by a cooperative priest. George spoke progressively more clearly, began to go out socially, acquired a position as a language tutor; in short, he accepted himself as a human being. He also removed all but one of his sweaters.

situations. Some sexual disorders may, for example, be effectively treated employing this approach. Raymond (1956) reports the case of a male client who had a fetish for handbags and baby carriages. He had developed the rather crude habits of smearing mucus on ladies' handbags and destroying baby carriages by running into them with his motorcycle. Treatment, employing aversive conditioning, consisted of presenting the patient with photographs of handbags and/or baby carriages, objects of sexual arousal for him, just before the onset of violent sensations of nausea induced through the injection of a drug (apomorphine). Initial treatment occurred every two hours for a week (twenty-four hours a day) and included follow-up sessions eight days later, and then six months later. The fetish was successfully eliminated.

Attempts to eliminate smoking using similar techniques have met with mixed success (Chapman et al., 1971; McFall, 1978). But then, *most* attempts to eliminate smoking have met with mixed success.

Positive Reinforcement

Other behavioral therapies make use of positive reinforcement, social imitation, or the withdrawal of reinforcement. For example, highly withdrawn patients might be placed on a **token economy**, an arrangement where they receive tokens for social interaction, and where these tokens can then be exchanged for more tangible reinforcement. Alternatively, verbal reinforcement may be employed. Alcoholics Anonymous, Weight Watchers, and similar organizations make extensive use of social imitation, presenting members with a variety of models that they are encouraged to imitate. Withdrawal of reinforcement is particularly effective for eliminating behavior which is apparently maintained by reinforcement that is potentially under the therapist's control. Ayllon and Michael (1959), for example, describe the case of a schizophrenic patient whose "psychotic talk" was drastically reduced after her attendants were instructed not to pay any attention to her descriptions of delusions, but to reinforce only her more "social" conversations.

> **Token economy** An arrangement where patients receive positive reinforcement in the form of tokens for desirable behavior. Tokens are typically chips, markers, or other worthless items that can later be exchanged for things of value.

One fairly common use of positive reinforcement in behavior management involves what is termed *behavioral contracting* (or *contingency contracting*). In behavioral contracting, the therapist and client decide *together* what the behavioral goals and reinforcers will be. For example, a person fighting obesity might contract to reduce weight at the rate of one kilogram per week, in return for which he might earn points toward a vacation. Having accumulated a specified number of points, he would then earn his reward. Simple contracts such as this might also contain a *response-cost* clause, whereby failure to reach behavioral objectives in any given week would cost the client a specified number of points already earned. Thus the contract would involve *punishment* as well as positive reinforcement.

Various positive reinforcement therapies have proven quite successful with habit disorders such as smoking, alcoholism, overeating, and drug abuse (Phillips & Bierman, 1981).

Implosive Therapy

Stampfl (1975) advances the notion that neuroses are the result of a learning process whereby we learn, through conditioning, to avoid anxiety-producing stimuli. Many of the stimuli that we now avoid need no longer be anxiety-laden at all. Accordingly, the goal of **implosive therapy** is to have the client *learn* that this is so. The learning is accomplished by challenging patients to confront their anxieties directly. The therapist finds out from the patient as many specific stimuli (situations) as possible that might provoke anxiety. The client is then encouraged to imagine these as vividly as possible. No attempt is made to bring about relaxation, as in a desensitization procedure; instead, the therapist simply overwhelms the patient with anxiety. The hope is that when the client realizes that no dire consequences have resulted, the stimuli will have lost their fear-related properties.

> **Implosive therapy** A behavior modification technique that seeks to reduce the potency of anxiety-provoking stimuli by overwhelming the individual with them in imagination.

Like a number of other therapies, behavior modification may be employed in groups as well as individually. In recent years, for example, use of behavior-modification principles has become common in a number of schools and institutions (see, for example, O'Leary, 1972; O'Leary & Drabman, 1971). It may be employed to correct disruptive behavior or to improve classroom performance in subject areas. It is used to alleviate phobias and anxieties, and to eliminate stuttering, compulsive behavior, impotence and sexual unresponsiveness, exhibitionism, and insomnia. It has proven useful with institutionalized retarded children in a variety of areas including language, school achievement, cooperation, and the control of dangerous or disruptive behavior. In addition, behavioral programs have been successful with toilet-training problems, alcoholism, smoking, and a variety of other problems (Stolz et al., 1975). (See Box 16.3.)

Is it suitable for all problems? Does it always result in permanent "cures"? Is it a panacea delivered to humanity by the behavioral sciences? Perhaps not quite. A later section presents an evaluation of behavior modification.

Other Therapies

Medical therapies are concerned with the organism and its systems, and intervene by means of chemicals, surgery, or induced convulsions; psychoanalysis deals with internal forces and conflicts; behavioral therapies focus on manifested behavior and on mental disorders as examples of behavior that can be "unlearned."

In addition to these three broad classifications of treatments, there are a large number of other approaches sometimes described as humanistic or existential therapies, cognitive therapies, rational therapies, and so on. Further, distinctions are made between individual therapies, where a single patient and therapist interact, and group therapies, which involve a number of patients interacting together and/or with one or

---

BOX 16.3

Behavioral Therapy for Anorexia Nervosa

Among the eating disorders that often appear in childhood or adolescence but that can also appear considerably later is a little-understood condition labeled *anorexia nervosa,* which, literally translated, means loss of appetite as a function of nerves. It is much more common among women than men (over 90 percent of all cases), and is often related to an excessive fear of gaining weight. People suffering from this condition typically have a distorted body image and continue to see themselves as overweight or normal even after they have become extremely emaciated and weak from undernourishment. Another consistent feature of anorexia nervosa is that patients continue to engage in excessive physical activity long after their physical conditions have deteriorated significantly. Several studies have found that as many as 60 percent of all such patients eventually die as a result of not eating (for example, Bruch, 1973; Seidensticker & Tzagournis, 1968).

A twenty-two-year-old serviceman, single and previously healthy, was ordered to seek medical help by his superior officers (Davidson, 1976). The patient, a bright, successful, ambitious, and com-

pulsive individual, came with a five-month history of fatigue, depression, and insomnia. During this time he had dropped from 158 to 114 pounds.

Extensive examination revealed no medical condition that might account for his weight loss, except for a possible reduction of hypothalamic stimulation of the pituitary. He denied eating less than normal, but careful observation revealed that his daily intake was less than 500 calories. During his first fifteen days in the hospital, in spite of a variety of arrangements for selecting nourishing and highly palatable foods, and hospital staff efforts to encourage him to eat, he lost another 15 pounds. He now weighed a mere 99 pounds.

On the sixteenth day he was placed on an operant conditioning program. One of the common features of anorexic patients is their constant engagement in physical activities such as walking. Accordingly, the patient was confined to his room for one week without privileges. After this first week, free-time privileges (being allowed to leave the room to engage in private activities) were made contingent upon his gaining weight daily.

The operant conditioning principles are clear: eating (the measurable effects of which are weight gains) is an operant; being allowed to leave the room is the contingent reinforcement. The object is to achieve control of eating behavior by controlling reinforcement. The results indicate that this behavior modification treatment was highly effective.

During the next thirty-six days, the patient gained 37 pounds. In addition, his depression and self-concern appeared to have been replaced by his previous optimism and concern for others.

---

more therapists. In recent years a number of group therapies have become increasingly popular. Some of these and other representative and popular therapies are described briefly in the remainder of this section. The list is far from exhaustive.

Rational-Emotive Therapy

Rational therapy (or **rational-emotive therapy**) is essentially a cognitive therapy developed by Ellis (1962, 1974, 1975). It is premised on the assumption that our cognitive interpretations of events and situations are the root of emotional turmoil, and that therapy should therefore focus on the individual's immediate interpretation of the meanings of events. More specifically, Ellis lists a number of erroneous assumptions that people make. When these assumptions are violated, the individual experiences anxiety and unhappiness. The goal of the therapist is simply to *direct* the patient's attention to these false assumptions, termed *irrational ideas,* and, through cognitive and verbal means, to supplant them with more rational ones. Among common irrational ideas are the following (Ellis, 1962, pp. 61–85):

Rational-emotive therapy (RET) A cognitive approach to "curing" mental disorder that helps the individual recognize and replace irrational beliefs.

It is necessary to be loved by everyone.

It is necessary to be thoroughly competent in everything if one is to consider oneself worthwhile.

Certain people are basically bad and should be punished accordingly.

Things *should* be the way one would like them to be.

Past history is an all-important determiner of the present.

Ellis (1976) describes these irrational ideas as *beliefs* (B) in his *A-B-C theory of disturbance*. According to this theory, an emotional reaction or consequence (C) is usually ascribed to some specific experience (A, for activating event). In fact, however, the emotional consequence (C) is not a function of the event (A), but of the beliefs (B) the individual has. Since the majority of these beliefs are irrational (if they were rational, the emotional consequences would not ordinarily be disturbing), the goal of therapy is to replace irrational with rational beliefs (Figure 16.3).

As an illustration, consider the case of a twenty-seven-year-old man who felt shy and inhibited with women, who suffered feelings of worthlessness, and who lived in constant fear of failing (Ellis, 1976). He attributed his feelings of worthlessness (C) in part to his rejection by women (A), because of his belief (B) that his inability to perform well in bed (premature ejaculation) would inevitably lead to rejection. During the therapy, Ellis attempted to show the client that his beliefs were, in fact, irrational. Below is a short excerpt from one session:

Therapist: You seem to be terribly afraid that you will fail at making a good initial contact with a woman and also at succeeding sexually.

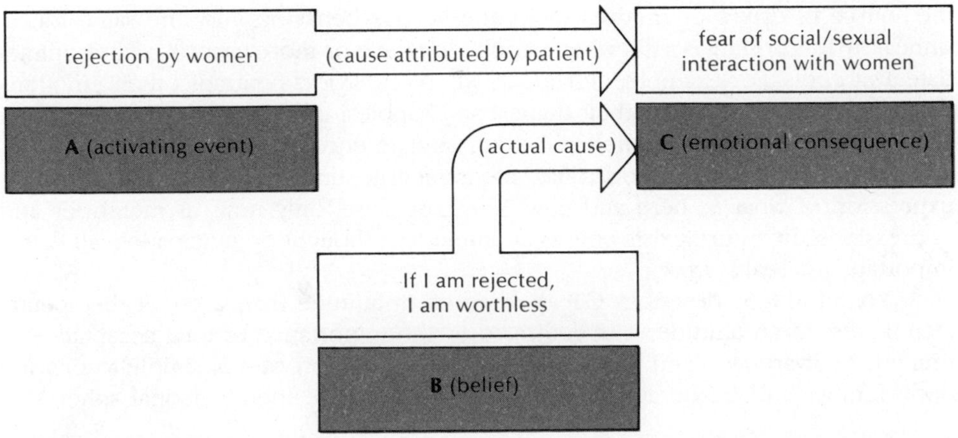

Figure 16.3 Ellis's A-B-C theory of disturbance. An event (A) leads to an emotional consequence (C) only because of the individual's beliefs (B). If you reject me and I am upset, my upset is due not to your rejection, but to my irrational belief that I should never be rejected.

Client: Hell, yes! To say the least, I'm scared shitless in both these areas.

Therapist: Because if you fail in either area, what—?

Client: If I fail, I'll be an utter slob!

Therapist: Prove it!

Client: Isn't it obvious?

Therapist: Not for me! It's fairly obvious that if a woman rejects you, socially or sexually, it'll hardly be a great thing. But how will that prove that *you,* a total person, will be no good? (p. 76)

Note how the therapist identifies the irrational belief ("If I am rejected, it proves that I am worthless") and attempts to convince the client that the belief is irrational. The assumption is that if irrational beliefs are replaced with more rational ones, individuals will better accept themselves as they are. In short, the therapy strives for a "worthwhile philosophic solution to people's fundamental emotional problems" (Ellis, 1976, p. 33).

Ellis's rational-emotive therapy (often abbreviated RET) is similar to the behavioral approaches because of its emphasis on immediate behaviors rather than on historical antecedents. In addition, rational therapists frequently use operant conditioning techniques to change behavior and thoughts. As Ellis describes the process, clients are sometimes successful in replacing irrational beliefs with more rational ones by reinforcing themselves for spending a specific amount of time disputing their irrational beliefs privately after they have been identified by client and therapist.

Gestalt Therapy

The first two of the insight therapies considered in this chapter, Freud's psychoanalysis and Adlerian psychotherapy, are principally concerned with the historical antecedents of present conditions. In these therapies, the burden of interpretation lies with the therapist, who is called upon to uncover the roots of present maladjustment and, having achieved insight, to help the client understand. Their explicit common assumption is that personal insight is fundamental to the alleviation of psychological problems.

Gestalt therapy also had its roots in psychoanalysis, one of its chief early exponents, Fritz Perls, having been a psychoanalyst (Latner, 1973; Perls, 1973; Stephenson, 1975). The major differences between psychoanalysis and Gestalt therapy (abbreviated GT) are two: (1) GT is largely unconcerned with the *history* of present problems, but deals instead with the *now;* (2) the burden of interpretation is not on the therapist but on the individual who, through a variety of activities, is encouraged to explore immediate personal awareness.

The central concept of the Gestalt position is that healthy functioning is a direct result of full immediate awareness, involving cognitive, sensorimotor, emotional, and *energetic* aspects of the individual (the expression *energy* may be interpreted to mean the source of drives or motives that underlie our behaviors). By the same token, unhealthy functioning occurs when people deny one or more aspects of their immediate awareness. For example, individuals whose behaviors contradict their emotions would not be functioning at their highest and happiest level. Accordingly, the goal of GT is to remove blocks to emotional expression, to encourage the immediate acceptance of present cognitions, to facilitate the immediate, unrestrained, completely *aware* expression of what *is,* here and now. The past exists only now, as memories and impressions; the future exists only as an immediate thought or anticipation; all that is important and real is *now.*

Yontef (1976) describes GT as more of an attitude than a set of therapeutic techniques. As an attitude, it is dedicated to the importance of total acceptance of immediate awareness, and the goal of the therapeutic process is simply to provide opportunities and encouragement for clients to explore their personal spheres of

Gestalt therapy (GT) A therapeutic approach that encourages the individual to explore immediate personal awareness. More an attitude than a set of techniques, it often uses games to encourage individuals to deal with "unfinished business."

Figure 16.4 Gestalt therapy employs a number of "games" as techniques for enhancing recognition and acceptance of feelings. Here a couple involved in marriage counseling confront each other by completing (as honestly as possible) sentences such as "What I don't like about you is...," or "I wish you...." On other occasions, partners might approach each other more positively: "What I like most about you is...."

awareness. Accordingly, a wide variety of specific techniques may be borrowed from other therapies as long as they are compatible with the goals of GT.

A number of "games" are often employed in GT (Levitsky & Perls, 1970). These games follow certain "rules" which emphasize immediacy (now), recognition and acceptance of personal feelings (do not say "It doesn't feel good" but rather "*I* feel sad"), and direct confrontation (if you think something about someone, say it directly to that person rather than to someone else).

The "games" themselves are varied. Marriage partners might be asked to "confront" each other and to express honestly how they feel by completing such sentence stems as: "I am jealous of you because ..."; "What annoys me most about you is ..."; "What I really like about you is ..."; "I wish you...." Clients may be encouraged to identify exactly what their feelings are, *right now,* in their stomach, their head, their foot (Figure 16.4).

Many of these games have a dual purpose: one is to increase the client's acceptance and awareness of all feelings and thoughts that are immediate; the other is to encourage the client to deal with "unfinished business." Gestalt therapy maintains that many of our problems and conflicts are related directly to emotional "business" that has never been finished—intense or mild feelings of love or hate, for example, that have been bottled up and have become part of the individual's "character armor." To some extent, much of this business can be finished simply by being accepted and "owned" by the individual.

Transactional Analysis

Eric Berne ascribes the beginning of **transactional analysis** to the fact that, after several decades of psychoanalytic training and practice, he began to listen to his patients rather than his teachers. His teachers had described the hidden psychodynamic forces that move each of us, the conflicts that rage undetected in our psyches, the defenses we establish to quell dark depths of anxiety; his patients told him simply that they were sometimes children, sometimes parents, and sometimes adults. As children, they spoke impulsively and emotionally; they intuited and manipulated; they were demanding. As parents, they were controlling and critical; they reflected the

Transactional analysis (TA) A therapeutic approach that attempts to analyze interactions in terms of the personality levels, or "ego-states," of the individuals involved: Parent, Child, or Adult.

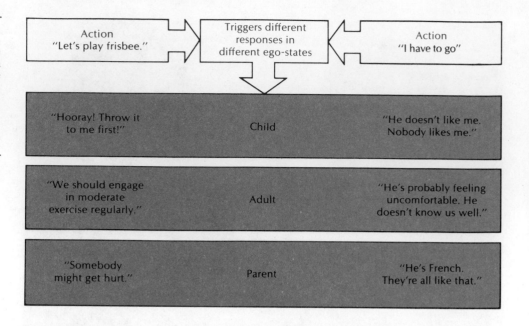

Figure 16.5 Structural analysis. Responses characteristic of the three ego-states, all made to the same situations (the invitation to play or the apparent rejection by a French person). Note that each of the ego-states may be characterized in a number of ways. The *Child* might be dependent, spoiled, petulant, carefree, or happy; the *Adult,* analytical, unemotional, and logical; the *Parent,* prejudiced, authoritarian, nurturing, or protective.

Action "Let's play frisbee."	Triggers different responses in different ego-states	Action "I have to go"
"Hooray! Throw it to me first!"	Child	"He doesn't like me. Nobody likes me."
"We should engage in moderate exercise regularly."	Adult	"He's probably feeling uncomfortable. He doesn't know us well."
"Somebody might get hurt."	Parent	"He's French. They're all like that."

values of *their* parents. And as adults, they were logical, unemotional, informed, and realistic.

Transactional theory maintains that these states exist in each of us, and that they are revealed in our verbal and nonverbal communication (Corey, 1977). *Structural analysis* is the process of identifying these "ego-states." It is a fundamental first step in the actual application of transactional analysis. Clients are typically asked to read one or more transactional books in order to familiarize themselves with the terminology, and are then given practice, usually in group situations, in recognizing these three states in their own behavior. The books recommended generally include one or more of Berne's (1964, 1972) or Harris's (1967). Figure 16.5 illustrates typical Parent, Adult, and Child responses.

One of the fundamental goals of transactional therapy is to assist people in making new decisions about their lives. Harris (1967) cites three reasons why people might be motivated to change: they hurt sufficiently, they are bored, or they have simply realized that change is possible. These are not descriptions of people in serious difficulty; accordingly, TA is not intended specifically for the treatment of the sorts of mental disorders described in the preceding chapter.

The techniques of transactional therapy are sometimes varied in that they often borrow extensively from Gestalt therapy. The general procedure, however, is uniform. Therapy generally occurs in small groups (six to ten individuals) with a single therapist. Clients are familiarized with structural and transactional analysis, and are usually required to read one or more relevant books or articles. The therapist then enters into a *contract* with each client, specifying exactly what the client would like as a result of therapy. General objectives such as "I want to be happier" are not accepted. Typically the contracts are sufficiently precise and objective that it is possible to describe what the patient should be able to do or feel if the contract is successfully completed. If, for example, the client has difficulty relating intimately with people of the opposite sex, the contract might include a specific task or exercise as an intermediate or final goal (for example, speaking intimately with three opposite-sexed members of the group).

It is important to note that the contract is essential to transactional analysis. Both client and therapist must accept the contract, and neither is permitted to stray far from its limits. In particular, the therapist is expected to refrain from delving into the client's past or into unrelated present experiences and feelings.

Once clients are familiar with TA principles and methods and have arrived at their contracts, they may engage in a variety of transactions, some structured as "games," and some spontaneous. One of the important early functions of the therapist is to interpret transactions and analyze them in terms of the ego-states involved, as well as in terms of the "games" being played. In this connection, Eric Berne (1964) described a large number of "games" in which people engage. He defines these as standardized, ritualistic, superficial social exchanges with clearly predictable outcomes. In essence, games are transactions with ulterior motives. Some of their self-explanatory labels are "Poor Me," "Yes, But," "Look What You Made Me Do," and "Wooden Leg."

Other TA procedures might include role-playing; the "empty chair" game, where the client has a transaction with an imaginary but personally important individual sitting in an "empty chair," and where he might occasionally take the part of the person in the chair; procedures where clients are *taught* TA and where principles are demonstrated for them; and other games or exercises directed toward the accomplishment of contractual goals. In summary, transactional analysis provides methods for the rational analysis of interpersonal communication with the ultimate goal of freeing individuals from their games and scripts, and making them aware of their separate ego-states so that they might understand their behavior more clearly. It is a rational and emotional therapy designed for groups and not particularly suitable for individual therapy.

Client-Centered Therapy

Rogers's (1951, 1961) **client-centered therapy** stands in sharp contrast to most of the traditional approaches. It is premised on the belief that all individuals possess both the need and the ability to develop themselves—to actualize—and that this process of growth is incompatible with mental disorders. Accordingly, client-centered therapy is not concerned with interpreting in the psychoanalytic sense, or with diagnosing and classifying mental disorder, but is concerned instead with providing patients with an environment in which they can explore their own feelings and achieve their own methods of growing. The emphasis is on the development of a warm, supportive, uncritically accepting relationship between the therapist and the client. In essence, the therapist *reflects* the patient's feelings, often by repeating the patient's expressions: "You feel sad," the therapist says in response to the patient's expression of sadness, "Tell me about it." In addition, the therapist makes extensive use of noncommittal but supportive monosyllabic utterances: "Yes," "Mmm-hmm." The therapy is nondirective. The therapist does not search for a cure, but simply establishes an environment and a relationship where clients will be moved toward greater openness to experience, growth, self-actualization, and the eventual realization of personal solutions for whatever problems brought them to the therapist.

Client-centered therapy does not present techniques or roles for the therapist, but presents instead an exhortation to be "real" and "genuine"—to encounter the client on a "person-to-person" level. In effect, it encourages the development of attitudes rather than of techniques; and the adoption of a prescribed role would be incompatible with these attitudes.

Rogers (1961) believes that the fundamental question that brings most people to a therapist is an existential one: "Who am I?" Accordingly, the principal goal of the client-centered therapeutic process is to establish the sort of climate that will encourage clients to discover personally who they are; and that goal will have been reached when clients realize and accept that concepts such as *self, growth,* and *awareness* describe a process rather than a product. Growth and positive change are the measure of therapeutic success. The therapist is neither the director nor the interpreter of these processes, but is simply their facilitator.

Sex Therapy

Prior to the Masters and Johnson (1966, 1970) books, therapy for sexual problems was largely psychoanalytic—and often unsuccessful. More than any other researchers in the field, Masters and Johnson objectified the study of human sexual responsiveness and developed highly effective therapeutic procedures for the common dysfunctions:

Client-centered therapy A therapeutic approach that seeks to provide a supportive environment within which individuals may explore feelings and find methods of growth.

premature ejaculation and impotence in males, and orgasmic unresponsiveness in women.

Treatment for the various disorders depends upon the nature of the disorder and the relationship between the partners. Therapists, many of whom are now members of the American Association of Sex Educators and Counselors, work in male-female pairs. Initially, the couple seeking therapy are interviewed *individually* by the same-sexed member of the therapeutic pair. The next day, they are again interviewed individually, but this time by the opposite-sexed therapist. The interviews are intensive and deal primarily with medical and sexual history. In addition, a medical examination is a standard requirement, although sexual dysfunction is only rarely linked directly to a physiological problem.

After the interviews, the therapists attempt to arrive at some picture of how husband and wife relate, and what treatment might be most effective. A "roundtable" discussion follows in which the therapists' observations are discussed and therapeutic procedures are described. The couple now has to agree to abide by the therapists' instructions.

The next step is termed "sensate focus" and involves encouraging the couple to learn *how* and *where* to touch each other. Genital and breast areas are out of bounds, and orgasm is prohibited. Later, couples are allowed to stimulate the genital areas, but are again asked not to engage in intercourse. They are simply to *learn* what feels good, both for themselves and for their partner. After this part of the therapy, procedures are determined by the nature of the problem. Premature ejaculation and impotence often require that the woman be taught specific techniques for preventing ejaculation or for stimulating the penis. If the problem involves nonorgasmic response in the woman, other procedures are described.

The central theme in Masters and Johnson's therapy is not so much the physical knowledge and skills that the couples are taught, but the changes that take place in their communication. Its effectiveness, according to Masters and Johnson, is impressive. Between 60 and 74 percent of impotent men become potent; premature ejaculation is significantly improved in more than 97 percent of all subjects; and 80.7 percent of nonorgasmic women become orgasmic (Masters & Johnson, 1970).

However, most other studies that have looked at the effectiveness of therapeutic procedures similar to those employed by Masters and Johnson report far lower success rates (Hogan, 1978). Zilbergeld and Evans (1980), two of several researchers who have attempted to replicate Masters and Johnson's results and who have not been able to do so, report considerable difficulty in determining exactly what Masters and Johnson did. What were their criteria for success, did they include as "failures" those who must surely have dropped out of therapy before its completion (no such cases are mentioned by Masters and Johnson), and how long did each client spend in therapy? Zilbergeld and Evans have not been able to establish answers to these questions.

There is little doubt that the Masters and Johnson approach works very well for some dysfunctions and for some individuals. But that it is as remarkably effective as Masters and Johnson claim has not yet been established.

Growth Groups

Variously referred to as *T-groups* (T for training), *encounter groups, sensitivity groups,* or **growth groups**, this form of therapy became immensely popular in the 1970s. Most of the approaches represented by encounter and sensitivity groups are not therapies in the sense that the more traditional approaches are therapies. In effect, they deal primarily with relatively normal individuals (Figure 16.6).

Encounter groups are designed primarily to foster an open and honest examination of one's behavior and one's self, and to encourage more authentic interpersonal interaction. Groups typically consist of one or more "leaders" and an indefinite number of participants (usually eight to twenty, but sometimes more or less). Leaders ordinarily adopt a participant role in addition to an imprecisely defined leadership

Growth groups A global term for a variety of group approaches to therapy designed primarily to foster open and honest examinations of behavior and self and to encourage more authentic interpersonal interaction.

Figure 16.6 Growth groups often reduce loneliness and boredom. The scene at right, from an encounter session, contrasts with the impersonal space between the people in the left picture.

role. Groups may have religious, entertainment, or psychotherapeutic orientations. Their most common promise, sometimes explicit but often implicit, is a change in life-style or personality, the removal of "unhealthy" impediments to genuine emotional feeling and expression, a more sensitive knowledge of the self, a deeper understanding of others, the development of compassion, trust, and other celebrated human attitudes and feelings. In short, encounter experiences promise *growth,* a concept that is difficult to define, virtually impossible to measure, and most reluctant to be evaluated.

One of the great attractions of growth groups is that they encourage behaviors not ordinarily accepted in everyday life. The cold, impersonal, crowded, and lonely cities in which we live do not encourage casual intimacy. We touch unwillingly in subways and elevators; we avoid eye contact on sidewalks and in public buildings; we speak only briefly and purposefully; we smile rarely. It is little wonder that so many should flock hungrily to group meetings that allow them complete freedom of emotional expression, that encourage them to touch and to feel.

There are potential dangers in group experiences, however. Psychoanalytically speaking, gullible individuals sometimes reveal too much of themselves. Consequently, they sometimes find themselves emotionally naked and helpless, and poorly trained leaders are not always equipped to deal with individual problems. Serious criticism of growth groups has focused on potential psychological casualties. Follow-up research is rare, but what does exist documents the possibility (although not necessarily the probability) of serious problems among some participants (Maliver, 1973; Yalom & Lieberman, 1971).

Criticisms of growth groups have also been directed at the unethical practices sometimes evident. Some "therapists" advertise for clients, make extravagant claims concerning potential benefits, do not screen applicants, and employ subtle forms of compulsion—sometimes in enrolling group members, but more frequently in the group itself, where social pressure frequently forces individuals to engage in behaviors with which they are highly uncomfortable. Critics argue that leaders should not advertise for clients (psychiatrists do not advertise); applicants should be screened and other professionals should be consulted where appropriate; leaders should be adequately trained and certified; and no compulsion should be employed. With respect to this last point, university courses and business seminars that incorporate "growth experiences" as a *compulsory* component are unethical. The American Psychological Association (1973) has attempted to develop standards and a code of ethics for growth groups, concerned primarily with leader qualifications, absence of compulsion, methods of obtaining clients, screening procedures, and the availability of additional individual help by the leader or other professionals where it is needed.

These criticisms should not be interpreted as a wholesale condemnation of growth groups, but simply as a caution. There is money to be made from loneliness. And psychological endeavors (or quasi-psychological endeavors) have too often been the playground of the charlatan and the unscrupulous opportunist.

Situational Therapy

Most of the therapies described in this chapter require a specific type of interaction between one or more therapists and one or more patients. The nature of the therapy and of the disturbance determine what the precise interaction will be, its frequency, and its duration. In general, most of the therapies do not consume a great deal of the patient's time, even in institutional settings.

Treatment of institutionalized patients is seldom limited to just one of these therapies, however. An increasing number of institutions make use of what is termed situational or milieu therapy. **Situational therapy** is an attempt to make the patient's entire physical and social environment therapeutic. In hospitals geared toward milieu therapy, all members of the staff, from kitchen help to administrators, are encouraged to interact with patients, open ward meetings are held so that inmates can participate in important decisions, and recreational as well as occupational activities are made an integral part of hospital life. Thus the principal method of situational therapy is constant socialization and interaction; and its principal goals are to prevent isolation and withdrawal, to provide a model of normal social functioning, and to increase self-esteem in patients. In a great many cases, situational therapy may be one of the most important factors contributing to the recovery and rehabilitation of persons suffering from mental disorders (Kernberg, 1975).

Table 16.2 summarizes the theoretical bases and therapeutic techniques of the various therapies discussed in this chapter.

Situational therapy A therapeutic approach that seeks to make an institutionalized patient's entire environment supportive of normal functioning and increased self-esteem.

An Evaluation of Therapies

Few evaluative comments have been made and little evaluative research has been cited in the preceding accounts of the various therapies. This is partly because research in this area is difficult and consequently scarce, and partly because it is perhaps more valuable and more meaningful to provide an assessment of these approaches after each has been impartially presented.

Much of the difficulty in systematically evaluating therapies relates to problems of definition. Not only is there considerable disagreement concerning diagnoses, and considerable variation among therapists and psychiatrists in their assessment of individuals, but it is perhaps even more difficult to determine what constitutes a "cure" or, at the very least, an improvement. A great deal of the evidence that has been cited in support of individual approaches consists of isolated case reports where the same therapist defines the problem, describes the treatment, and assesses, often very informally, the improvement. Although this type of "evidence" might provide weak justification for alleging that a therapeutic procedure is effective, it does not address what must surely be a more crucial question for a beginning therapist: Which therapy is most effective, and for which purpose or with which problem?

The usefulness of *any* and *all* therapeutic intervention has sometimes been called into question. Most often cited in this connection are Eysenck's (1960, 1965) reviews of the major studies that have looked at the *outcomes* of therapy. His conclusion: two out of three neurotics who undergo psychotherapy are improved. A second highly relevant finding: two out of three neurotics who do *not* undergo treatment also improve. Similar findings are reported by Truax and Carkhuff (1967) and by E. E. Levitt (1971).

Table 16.2 Summary of Therapies

Therapy	Basic Assumptions	Techniques
Medical therapies	Abnormal behavior can be cured by physiological treatment	
Chemotherapy		Use of drugs to alleviate or remove symptoms
Psychosurgery	Look for chemical or organic malfunctions (disease, tumors, brain damage)	Employing surgical procedures, sometimes to remove brain structures associated with emotion, or to sever connections between brain structures
Electroconvulsive therapy		Running a mild electrical current through the cranium, sometimes effective in cases of severe depression
Insight therapies	Understanding of problem is essential first step to solution	
Freudian psychoanalysis	Disorders are based in psychodynamic conflict (id, ego, superego)	Free association to uncover mental blocks Dream analysis Awareness of transference of patient's feelings to analyst
Adlerian therapy	Disorders are based in developmental factors, early relationships	Reconstruction of childhood Development of feelings of worth to overcome sense of inferiority
Behavior therapies	Abnormal behavior is learned; it can also be unlearned	
Systematic desensitization (counterconditioning, reciprocal inhibition)	Look at present manifestations of unwanted behavior; no attempt to induce insight or otherwise treat historical or developmental factors	Replacement of undesirable response with a desirable response incompatible with unwanted behavior
Aversive conditioning		Pairing of undesirable response with negative experience
Positive reinforcement		Use of reinforcers for desirable behaviors; withdrawal of reinforcers for undesirable behavior Token economies; behavioral contracts
Implosive therapy	Neuroses stem from avoiding anxiety, but not overcoming it	Exposing patient repeatedly to anxiety situations until patient realizes that fear is groundless
Other therapies Rational-emotive therapy (RET)	Disorders are based in present misinterpretations of situations and events	Identification of irrational beliefs, replacement with rational ones Some use of operant techniques
Gestalt therapy (GT)	Dysfunctions result when people deny full expression or awareness of themselves; focus on the present	Increasing self-awareness and expressiveness, often through "games"
Transactional analysis (TA)	Inappropriate "ego-states" (Child or Parent) underlie and hinder Adult interactions with other people	Awareness and analysis of inappropriate ego-states and of "scenarios" Contracts and games within groups to help individuals recognize and overcome specific problems
Client-centered therapy	Disorders result when individuals haven't realized their own ability to develop self	Providing individual with most supportive environment for self-exploration and growth
Sex therapy	Appropriate sexual functioning can be learned, and communication between sexual partners improved	Interviews, open discussion, "sensate focus" experiences, and specific techniques for specific dysfunctions
Growth groups	Disorders are based in failure to understand self or interact honestly with others	Common experiences with one or more leaders and eight to twenty participants
Situational therapy	Disorders have multiple causes, but generally involve problems of social interaction and self-esteem	Constant socialization and interaction; participation in decisions; occupational and recreational therapy

Does this mean that psychotherapy is no more effective than no therapy, and therefore a waste of time and money? A hoax perpetrated on a gullible public by a misguided and misguiding profession?

The answer is no. It appears, to begin with, that Eysenck's research probably exaggerated the ineffectiveness of psychotherapy. Specifically, Eysenck's estimate of the number of neurotics who improved without therapy was based on his interpretation of only six separate studies. Bergin's (1971) review of twenty-three controlled studies indicates that the percentage of neurotics who recover spontaneously is probably closer to 40 than to 75. In addition, a spate of more recent studies have repeatedly found evidence for the effectiveness of psychotherapy (for example, Luborsky et al., 1975; Meltzoff & Kornreich, 1970). Perhaps more pertinent, demonstrating that neurotics are as likely to improve without therapy as with therapy is a poor argument against the effectiveness of therapy in general. In fact, the most valid general conclusion from the widely cited Eysenck (1965) review is that two-thirds of those who undergo therapy are improved *immediately* after therapy, whereas those who do not undergo therapy tend to manifest improvement considerably later.

It should also be pointed out that the general effectiveness of therapy cannot be judged with reference only to those disorders that have traditionally been labeled *neuroses*. There is very clear evidence of the effectiveness of chemotherapy for certain schizophrenic and manic-depressive reactions; and the effectiveness of drugs in dispelling or reducing symptoms of anxiety is beyond question (R. A. Levitt, 1975).

So the conclusion that therapy *in general* is more effective than no therapy appears to be fully warranted by the evidence (Frank, 1973, 1974; Sloane et al., 1975). This does not mean that *any* therapy is effective for *any* disorder. There is at least some evidence, although not always undisputed, that certain therapies are more effective for some purposes than are others. Frank (1973) cites evidence, for example, that chemotherapy alone is as effective for schizophrenia as chemotherapy in combination with insight therapy; and, in general, chemotherapy is *more* effective than insight therapy alone. But even with chemotherapy, there is an obvious need for the type of personal support and encouragement that is provided by other forms of therapy. Similarly, there is evidence that behavior modification is highly effective with specific phobias. Except for these two demonstrations, however, there is no widely accepted evidence that any specific therapy produces better results than any other (Frank, 1974).

Indeed, Smith and Glass (1977), following a detailed analysis of 375 psychotherapy outcome studies, conclude, "despite volumes devoted to the theoretical differences among different schools of psychotherapy, the results of research demonstrate negligible differences in the effects produced by different therapy types" (p. 760). What is highly reassuring about this major analysis, however, is a second conclusion: "On the average, the typical therapy client is better off than 75 percent of untreated individuals" (p. 752). One possible and plausible explanation for the apparent lack of substantial differences in the effectiveness of different therapies is discussed following a brief, critical examination of each of the major therapies.

Medical Therapies

The effectiveness of the medical therapies for some problems is well established. This is particularly true of the chemotherapies, but less true of psychosurgery and electroconvulsive therapy. Psychosurgery, in particular, is generally a last resort, given that its effects are usually irreversible. Electroconvulsive therapy, although it has proven effective in the treatment of severe depression, has engendered negative reaction because of the physical violence of the method.

Some therapists have also been highly concerned at the sometimes unpredictable side effects of the more powerful antipsychotic drugs. In addition, evidence suggests that these drugs are *not* effective for some chronic schizophrenics (Levitt & Lonowski, 1975). It is clear that they can be abused and misused in these and other cases. But most powerful therapies can be misused; if they could not be, they would not be very powerful.

Insight Therapies

Freudian psychoanalysis and Adlerian therapy, like many other therapeutic approaches, deal with inferred entities, hypothetical concepts, and assumed conflicts.

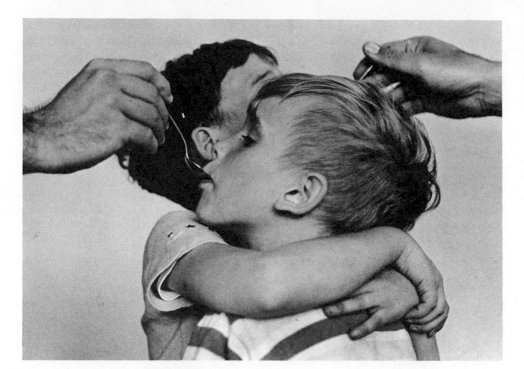

The assumptions most basic to these positions cannot be empirically verified and are thus open to severe criticism from a scientific and empirical point of view (Corey, 1977). The main thrust of these criticisms may not be particularly relevant, however. That is, it is unnecessary to prove the existence of id, ego, and superego and to establish their relationships and their role in the development of mental disorders if it can be shown that the methods based on these beliefs are effective. Unfortunately, however, evidence of effectiveness is not entirely unquestioned, since the bulk of it rests on unsubstantiated case reports. And even if we do accept the evidence at face value, we can never be certain that the outcome of the therapeutic process was a function of specific psychoanalytic techniques. In fact, other therapies employing dramatically different methods can demonstrate a similar degree of effectiveness (Frank, 1974).

One clear limitation of the insight therapies concerns the lengthy and difficult training necessary to become proficient in their use, not to mention the lengthy and expensive commitment required of the client. It is perhaps for these reasons, as much as because of a general discomfort with psychoanalytic terms and concepts, that many of the "modern therapies" have departed dramatically from the insight therapies. Nevertheless, there are very few contemporary therapies that do not owe a great deal to the monumental pioneering efforts of Freud and his followers.

Behavior Therapies

There is considerable evidence for the effectiveness of various behavior modification techniques (Stolz et al., 1975). Since the approach lends itself particularly well to objective evaluation (indeed, it often requires it), a great deal of empirical evidence has accumulated in recent years. Behavior modification has successfully been employed to reduce fears, relieve anxiety, cure enuresis, relieve insomnia, eliminate impotence, and ameliorate stuttering; it has been employed to teach mentally retarded individuals a variety of tasks and skills, to foster cooperative behavior among highly withdrawn children, and to remove many of typical symptoms of childhood schizophrenia (Phillips & Bierman, 1981) (Figure 16.7). In the Paul (1966) study of public-speaking anxiety mentioned in Chapter 14, insight and behavioristic therapies were compared. The behavior therapies were considerably more effective.

Although fervent advocates of behavior therapies sometimes assume that this approach is appropriate for any behavioral or mental disorder, it does not appear to be easily applicable in certain situations. Mental disorders whose origins are clearly organic, schizophrenia, manic-depression, and existential dilemmas such as are reflected in the question "Who am I?" do not always lend themselves well to behavioral therapies. In spite of this, however, there are instances when disorders of biological origin can be improved through behavior modification, sometimes in conjunction with chemotherapy (Birk et al., 1973). Research has not yet determined whether behavior modification is *more* effective than other forms of therapy, except, as mentioned earlier, with respect to specific phobias (Frank, 1974; Paul, 1967). Considerably more systematic research is required before a useful conclusion can be reached.

In addition to the general questions of whether behavior modification is effective and for what purposes, and how effective it is in comparison with other therapies, a number of important and sometimes highly controversial issues are implicit in its use. Stolz et al. (1975) present a highly informed review of these issues.

Perhaps the most widespread concern over the use of behavior modification is based on a misconception of its effectiveness. There are many who fear that those in power (those who control reward and punishment) can, through a deliberate and systematic application of operant conditioning principles, achieve a high degree of control over individual lives. Stolz et al. point out that behavior modification techniques are generally ineffective for those who are unwilling to be "shaped" or "controlled." Those in power do not often have control of rewards or punishments sufficiently powerful that they can change our behaviors in spite of ourselves.

The use of behavior modification techniques with certain institutionalized groups (prisoners and the mentally retarded, for example) and with children in schools presents a different issue. The ethical concerns are not simple. If, for example, the goals of a behavior-modification program are concerned more with social order than with individual good, then perhaps the rights of individuals are being violated. Some have expressed fear that behavior modification might be employed to impose acceptable conduct on political dissidents and agitators who could, in fact, be imprisoned for that purpose (Heldman, 1973). Others have been highly concerned, sometimes justifiably so, at the use of aversive control (electric shocks and other forms of punishment) which can be simply a new label for very old forms of punishment (solitary confinement in prison, for example).

As a result of these concerns, as well as of specific events involving behavior modification, a number of legal rulings have recently emerged (Stolz et al., 1975). One legal decision *(Wyatt* vs. *Stickney)* in which the presiding judge ruled that institutionalized individuals would be compensated at a rate no less than the current minimum wage has implications for token economy programs where inmates are often required to perform real chores in exchange for tokens. According to legal precedent, such programs are probably illegal in certain jurisdictions.

Other concerns and criticisms of behavioral therapies have been directed at their long-term effectiveness. Some therapists argue that, since behavior therapies treat symptoms (actual behavior) rather than causes, the disorders that are apparently "cured" may reappear, sometimes in different form. This is most notably true for substance-use disorders such as alcoholism, and for obesity (Jeffery & Coates, 1978).

Other Therapies

The various therapies presented in this chapter are each subject to criticism. Much of this criticism stems from theoretical beliefs that are at variance; some is based on the supposed ineffectiveness of a given therapy or on the alleged superiority of another therapy. As noted earlier, there is, in fact, no substantial evidence that any of these therapies is better than any other for any given purpose. But there is evidence that each has its degree of effectiveness. Which should a therapist embrace? Or should we pick and choose bits and morsels from each? In fact, many contemporary therapists, contrary to the impression that may have been given, do just that.

A Resolution

Frank (1974) suggests that all therapies have a number of common features which, together with the fact that all clients have something in common as well, accounts for their approximately equal effectiveness. He argues, first, that those who come for help are *demoralized,* no matter what the nature of their symptoms. Thus, the two most common symptoms of mental disorder, anxiety and depression, are both manifestations of demoralization (helplessness, despair, and hopelessness). The function of therapy is, then, to restore morale; and therapy is successful to the extent that it does so.

All therapies share certain common features. First, each (whether it be a group or an individual approach) involves a psychotherapeutic relationship that is geared toward helping patients achieve better concepts of themselves, to adjust, orient, become happier—in short, that is geared toward the restoration of morale. Second, all therapies offer a *believable* rationale: an explanation for the patient's symptoms and a reason for using a certain collection of methods for alleviating these symptoms. The important point is not what these methods are or what the rationale is, but that both the therapist and the patient *believe* in their rightness and appropriateness. Does this mean that, since all therapies are equally effective, and since the rationales and techniques of each are therefore equivalent, there should be but one therapy? Frank

"What a shame! With a little professional help early on, all this could have been avoided."
Drawing by Sempé; © 1981 The New Yorker Magazine, Inc.

(1974) argues against this—that therapists, given their individuality, their personal styles, should select therapies with which they are comfortable. At the same time, each should learn as much as possible from other therapies so that a choice can be made that will also reflect the needs and wishes of individual patients. Not all clients want to be part of a group; nor do all therapists enjoy delving into clouded childhood histories.

In summary, the various therapies should not be discarded out of hand as exercises in small-scale empire-building. Each has its strengths and weaknesses; each claims its passionate adherents, and its passive or vocal dissenters. And, in the end, each might help someone become a little happier—or at least a little less unhappy.

Community Mental Health

The treatment of mental disorders has seen a number of massive reforms through the course of history, as noted in the early pages of Chapter 15. We no longer burn witches, exile the "insane," imprison them, or leave them to the dogs and the children. Throughout most of this century, we have institutionalized them in more or less humane environments. Now we find ourselves in the second decade of another massive reform: the community mental health program.

Community mental health A recent movement that emphasizes promoting mental health rather than offering specific therapies.

Social psychiatry in the form of **community mental health** programs does not adopt a primarily therapeutic role. In effect, such programs are concerted social attempts to improve the level of mental health in communities, thereby enhancing quality of life. Although these programs vary widely, they typically have a number of goals in common. Chief among these are the promotion of mental health through educational programs, the prevention of mental disorders, and the care of those who have suffered mental disorders and received treatment elsewhere. With these goals in mind, community mental health centers may establish crisis-intervention centers (suicide prevention hotlines, unwanted pregnancy counseling, rape hotlines, and so on); centers for the aged, single parents, and others potentially lonely; school visitation programs; therapeutic workshops; newsletters and articles; and a variety of other programs (Figure 16.8).

Figure 16.8 The community mental health movement emphasizes prevention, rehabilitation, and perhaps more important, the restoration of joy to saddened lives. (**a**) A volunteer answers calls at a suicide prevention center; and (**b**) a young woman visits in a senior citizens' home.

a

b

Among the newer programs associated with community mental health, those involving **planned short-term therapy (PSTT)** are of particular interest since they represent a major departure from traditional attitudes toward the treatment of mental disorders. PSTT is defined as a therapeutic program that is *planned* to last for only a short period of time, and that typically has specific, identifiable goals. The actual duration of PSTT may vary from a single session (which is not altogether rare) to perhaps a dozen sessions. Many different approaches, including a variety of behavioral therapies, have been employed in short-term therapy (Grayson, 1979). Bloom suggests that there are three important reasons for the increasing popularity of planned short-term therapy. The first relates to the savings, both in terms of time and cost, associated with short-term as opposed to long-term therapy. Second, the popularization of newer therapies as alternatives to the more time-consuming insight therapies favors the use of shorter-term treatments. Third, and perhaps more important, an impressive number of studies indicate that there is little difference between the eventual outcomes of short-term as opposed to longer-term therapies (Shoulberg, 1976).

One of the major initial goals of the community mental health program was to deinstitutionalize patients and rehabilitate them within their communities. The recent discovery of the psychoactive drugs made the goal seem realistic. Following implementation of the program, a wide variety of community mental health centers were established throughout the United States (507 by mid-1975) (Bassuk & Gerson, 1978), and inpatient population has declined dramatically, from over 500,000 in the late 1950s to under 200,000 at present (Figure 16.9). State mental hospitals, which had previously been a tremendous financial burden, now cost vastly less than they might otherwise have cost. But community mental health has more than taken up the slack.

There is a very real possibility, argue Bassuk and Gerson (1978), that reduction in the number of institutionalized patients does not mean that the community mental health program has been successful. They point out that the dramatic reduction in the number of patients hospitalized at any given time simply reflects a policy of keeping people in hospitals for a shorter period (approximately one-third as long as in the early 1950s). Furthermore, the number of admissions has increased dramatically during this time, as has the number of of readmissions. Half of all patients released from mental institutions are readmitted within a year, and the readmission rate has more than doubled since 1950. This suggests that, although community mental health programs have apparently been successful in relieving some of the pressure of numbers on mental institutions, they have not been successful in their rehabilitative functions. Furthermore, a great many community centers are drastically short of funds and of personnel, a situation that is not likely to be alleviated very soon given the fact that an additional 1,000 centers are needed to provide adequate service to the entire population (Bassuk & Gerson, 1978).

Planned short-term therapy (PSTT) Therapeutic programs that are goal-oriented and planned to last for only a short time. A variety of specific therapies may be used.

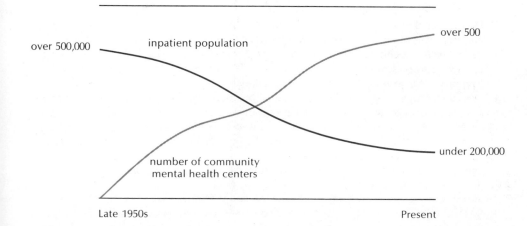

Figure 16.9 Growth of community mental health centers has been related to a sharp decline in the inpatient population of mental hospitals. Figures also reflect changed medical policies since the 1950s, with much shorter average hospital stays for most patients. (Based on data from Bassuk and Gerson, 1978.)

In spite of these problems, community mental health movements represent a major social change in terms of public acceptance of responsibility, not only for the care and treatment of those who identify themselves (or who are identified by others) as having serious mental disorders, but also for the general health and welfare of all.

Main Points

1 Medical therapies are not limited to use with disorders that have clearly organic bases. These therapies include chemotherapy, surgery, and the use of electric shocks (electroconvulsive therapy, ECT).

2 Mild tranquilizers are used extensively in the treatment of anxiety and other disorders. Major tranquilizers, certain drugs termed *antipsychotic*, and a variety of other drugs are also employed. Some of these are very effective, but a number sometimes have unfortunate side effects.

3 Psychosurgery is used relatively rarely to alleviate mental disorders, typically only when the condition is highly serious and all other approaches have proven ineffective.

4 Electroconvulsive therapy is often highly effective, particularly for major depressions, although why it works is still not clear.

5 A wide range of psychotherapies are employed by psychiatrists, psychoanalysts, clinical psychologists, counseling psychologists, and a variety of other counselors.

6 Freudian psychoanalysis makes use of free association and dream analysis in an attempt to get around the ego's defenses against revealing sensitive issues (termed *mental blocks*). An important phenomenon in psychoanalysis is transference—a process whereby the therapist comes to represent someone important in the patient's life, perhaps embodying a source of anxiety-related conflict.

7 Adlerian therapy, similar in some ways to Freudian psychoanalysis, attempts to achieve *insight* into the patient's problems and to bring about feelings of worth in patients, thus overcoming feelings of inferiority. On occasion, the therapy helps patients overcome feelings of superiority that might result from having *overcompensated* for feelings of inferiority.

8 Behavior therapies are concerned less with the historical causes of mental disorders and with attempts to achieve *insight* into these as with the behavioral manifestations of these disorders.

9 In systematic desensitization, an attempt is made to replace an undesirable response with another response incompatible with the first. The most common way of accomplishing this is by *desensitizing* the patient to specific anxiety-related stimuli, sometimes by initially exposing the patient to very mild forms of the stimulus, and progressively increasing the potency of the stimulus.

10 In *aversive conditioning*, an attempt is made to associate negative feelings (and hence to bring about avoidance behavior) with respect to certain undesirable habits (smoking, for example).

11 Positive reinforcement as a behavior therapy is highly common, particularly when the intention is to bring about some socially desirable behavior. Token economies are sometimes employed in these behavior therapies.

12 Ellis's rational-emotive therapy is a cognitive therapy based on the notion that the emotional consequences of various situations result from irrational beliefs concerning the way things should be (for example, we irrationally believe that everyone should like us, and become upset when we discover that someone doesn't). Rational-emotive therapy attempts to replace irrational ideas with others that are more rational.

13 Gestalt therapy is based on the fundamental belief that psychological health is a function of total immediate awareness involving cognitive, sensory, motor, and emotional aspects of living. Gestalt therapy is frequently employed to *enhance* the process of living rather than to alleviate mental disorders. A variety of growth groups are based on Gestalt therapy.

14 Transactional analysis attempts to analyze interactions in terms of the personality levels, or ego states, involved in interpersonal interaction. *Adult, Parent,* and *Child* states characterize the way we react. A variety of games and other approaches are designed to make participants aware of the states involved in their behavior, and to control these.

15 Rogers's client-centered therapy, also called nondirective therapy, is based on the notion that the central role of the therapist should be one of *facilitating*, rather than directing,

improvement in patients. This approach does not present specific techniques so much as advice concerning the humanistic, caring relationship that must exist between therapist and client if growth is to occur. Client-centered therapy is essentially humanistic (in contrast with behavioristic or cognitive approaches).

16 Therapeutic techniques for sexual dysfunctions, pioneered by Masters and Johnson, focus on changes in a couple's communication. Effectiveness of these techniques has not yet been established.

17 *Growth group* is the collective label applied to a wide variety of sometimes-therapeutic programs, exercises, and experiences available not only to those who are unhappy or who have identifiable psychological problems, but also to those who simply want to know more about themselves and perhaps to experience living more fully and more happily.

18 Situational therapy, probably the most extensively employed form of institutional therapy, involves an attempt to make the entire environment therapeutic. Situational therapy thus makes use of social interaction, work, play, and a variety of other activities.

19 Although it appears that a number of patients improve without therapy, evidence suggests strongly that many forms of psychotherapy, chemotherapy, and medical therapy are highly effective. In general, however, there are few substantial differences among the effects produced by different types of therapy, although the behavioral therapies appear to be most effective with specific phobias.

20 The community mental health movement, one of the more recent reforms in the field of mental disorders, is most evident in the various centers established to provide crisis assistance (suicide prevention, rape, and drug abuse hotlines), as well as in drop-in centers for the aged and others who might be lonely. In addition, the community mental health movement includes various forms of therapy, such as planned short-term therapy (PSTT).

Further Readings

The following three books are recommended as informative descriptions of a great variety of therapeutic approaches, including many that are more idiosyncratic and less well known than those covered in this chapter.

Corey, G. *Theory and practice of counseling and psychotherapy.* Monterey, Calif.: Brooks/Cole, 1977.

Garfield, S. L., and Bergin, A. E. (Eds.). *Handbook of psychotherapy and behavior change: An empirical analysis.* New York: John Wiley, 1978.

Belkin, G. S. *Contemporary psychotherapies.* Chicago: Rand McNally, 1980.

Students interested in Freud and in psychoanalysis are strongly urged to read the excellent biography of Freud and exposition of psychoanalysis offered in three volumes by his close friend, Ernest Jones, who was also a psychoanalyst. Jones was instrumental in encouraging and helping Freud to leave Vienna. Clark's more recent biography is less comprehensive.

Jones, E. *The life and work of Sigmund Freud* (3 vols.). New York: Basic Books, 1953–1957.

Clark, R. W. *Freud: The man and the cause.* New York: Random House, 1980.

Behavior therapy, its effectiveness and its abuses, is dealt with in detail in:

O'Leary, K. D., and Wilson, G. T. *Behavior therapy: Application and outcome.* Englewood Cliffs, N.J.: Prentice-Hall, 1975.

An excellent collection of articles dealing with behavioral approaches to problems of lifestyle is:

Davidson, P. O., and Davidson, S. M. *Behavioral medicine: Changing health lifestyles.* New York: Brunner/Mazel, 1980.

We are not alone with our genetic and biological predispositions, our intellectual abilities and skills, our motives and emotions, our personality characteristics. Quite the contrary. We are surrounded by others—others who see and watch even when they aren't there. *They* say that. . . . What will *they* think? Much as we might like to deny it, we are very concerned with what *they* say and think. We want *them* to like us. Most of us, consciously or otherwise, spend a great deal of time and energy conforming to what we think *they* expect of us. Chapter 17 discusses the nature of social influences and some important social behaviors; Chapter 18 looks at interpersonal relationships, particularly as they are reflected in loving and liking.

PART SIX

Relationships and Others

Chapter 17
Social Influence
Chapter 18
Interpersonal Relationships

Social Influence

My friend Rob was once highly susceptible to social influence. True, he had definite opinions, but the few that he did not borrow from friends, he stole from newspapers; he had well-articulated attitudes, but they were invariably the attitudes of his immediate friends; and he had very clear intentions, but he was always open to persuasion.

Until Boris, the cat. For some obscure reason, perhaps related to early social deprivation, Rob had always wanted a cat. And so, just as soon as he met Cathy and she agreed to spend the rest of her life with him beginning sometime soon, he said, very definitely, that they would go out that very afternoon and buy this exquisite Siamese cat for a mere $200. "I know cats," he assured his lady-to-be, "and that Siamese is exactly what I am going to get."

So Cathy and Rob went to the local animal shelter, run by the SPCA, and picked out a scruffy-looking alley specimen with one bad eye, a slightly torn ear, and an absolutely irresistible purr. Rob said, "Let's call him Ralph," and they named him "Boris."

The cat moved in with Cathy, made himself right at home, became hers at once, and Rob said, "I intend to get a cat someday. A Siamese. Probably."

Two days later, the cat got sick and became half Rob's. "We should share in this, like we will in everything else after we get married, so we'll each pay half the veterinary bill," Cathy informed Rob.

Boris was diagnosed as having distemper. Cats don't often survive distemper. But Boris, as a result of exceptional medical attention, a private nurse, and sheer luck, did survive. The total medical bill was $600. Cathy and Rob each paid half, and brought Boris back home with them.

Two days later, Boris strutted out of the house and never returned. And Rob, a little poorer, may also be a little less susceptible to Cathy's social influence. Sometimes.

Social Psychology

A simple definition of sociology is that it is the social science that concerns itself with groups; a simple definition of psychology is that it is the social science that concerns itself with individuals. And a simple definition of **social psychology** is that it is the social science concerned with the intersection of sociology and psychology. Specifically, social psychology looks at relationships between individuals or between individuals and groups. In G. W. Allport's (1968) terms, "social psychologists regard their discipline as an attempt to understand how *thought, feeling,* and *behavior* of individuals are influenced by the *actual, imagined,* or *implied* presence of others" (p. 3). Accordingly, the subject matter of social psychology spans almost all facets of human behavior save those that are clearly individual and are not affected by the presence of others. Most of what we learn, think, feel, and do can be shown to be influenced by others. The nature of that influence presents a fascinating study.

There are very few people whose lives are totally devoid of relationships with others. Indeed, to be completely isolated socially requires absolute geographic isolation, or some form of madness that results in total social withdrawal. The total recluse, interesting though he or she may be, is not of primary concern to the social psychologist. You, on the other hand, are. You who can love and hate, envy and emulate, fear and avoid, dislike and aggress; you whose dress is of this decade, and whose range of interests and behaviors is more like that of your peers than like that of any other group; you whose daily activities are shaped and molded as much by social realities as by anything that might be completely and exclusively you.

Given the vast range of topics that might be included in a comprehensive discussion of social psychology, and the fact that many of these topics have been considered in earlier chapters, this book has had to be at least as selective in this chapter as it has been in others. The following pages deal with behavior toward others ranging from violence and aggression through apathy to helping and altruistic behavior; with attitudes, and with obedience and conformity. Note that each of these topics concerns behaviors, thoughts, and emotions that are meaningful only in relation to other individuals or to groups of individuals; hence these are the proper concerns of social psychology.

Social psychology While psychology is the science that concerns itself with individuals, social psychology is the science that studies relationships between individuals or between individuals and groups.

Aggression and Violence

A popular stereotype of the North American male is that of an assertive, intrusive, domineering individual—in short, of an aggressive person. This view is based on the observation that aggression is basic to organized competitive activities such as football and hockey, is the key to success in the business and academic worlds, is one of the principal subjects of the entertainment media, and is characteristic of much human interaction (see Figure 17.1). In fact, none of these observations is difficult to document, since **aggression**, defined as intrusive, assertive, or domineering behavior, can readily be found and described.

Theories of Aggression

Psychological research provides us with an abundance of theoretical explanations of aggression as well as with a bewildering assortment of definitions. Much of this research has been concerned with the apparent causes of aggression, and with methods of controlling it. Two things should be noted at the outset, however: first, aggression, when defined primarily in terms of assertiveness and competition, is not undesirable in all circumstances; second, the forms of aggression that have been of most interest to social psychologists are more properly described as instances of *violence,* an extreme form of aggression (Figure 17.2). Whereas aggression may be no more than verbal or symbolic, violence denotes "a form of human aggression that involves inflicting physical damage on persons or property" (Moyer, 1976). Much of

Aggression Hostile or forceful action intended to dominate or violate. Violence is the most extreme form of aggression; assertiveness, the least. Social psychology has attempted to understand and explain aggression.

Figure 17.1 Aggression is basic to many sports. Does this mean that violence is also necessary?

this section deals with violence rather than with more general manifestations of aggression.

Frustration-Aggression A number of opposing beliefs have dominated social psychology's attempts to understand and explain aggression. Among them is Berkowitz's (1965) contention that aggression is the logical result of anger. Anger itself may result from a number of causes, most important among which is **frustration.** To be frustrated is to be prevented from reaching a goal. Berkowitz argues that, following frustration, anger is experienced; but anger will result in aggression only if a suitable object or person releases the aggression. This explanation of aggression is highly similar to that presented earlier by Dollard et al. (1939), often referred to as the *frustration-aggression hypothesis.* The principal difference between the two is that Dollard believed that aggression results directly and inevitably from frustration; Berkowitz believes that anger results from frustration, with aggression following in the presence of suitable stimuli (Figure 17.3).

Territoriality Another explanation, attributed to a number of **ethologists**, is based on the assumption that we are by nature aggressive (Ardrey, 1966; Lorenz, 1966). This explanation relies heavily on observations of aggression among lower animals, and makes the assumption that since aggression appears to be common among other animals, it must have an instinctual basis.

According to this theory, certain stimuli in the environment serve as *releasers* for aggression. In some cases, the stimuli are highly specific, and have clear survival or reproductive significance. For example, the male stickleback, a small spiny fish, will protect its nest feverishly against invasion by other males (Tinbergen, 1951). The *releaser* for its aggressive behavior is red on the belly of a rival male. A fish with red on its back, or with no red anywhere, will not be attacked.

In much the same way, wolves and a variety of other **territorial** animals will violently defend their territory against intruders (Ardrey, 1966); and it seems that in many of these territorial fights, the animal fights progressively more fiercely, the closer it is to its home. Home, after all, is where the animal lives and breeds. However, animals do not *invite* attack or aggress randomly against their species or members of

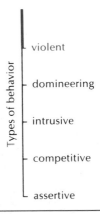

Figure 17.2 A simple aggression continuum. Social psychologists have been most interested in the extreme forms of aggression.

Frustration The prevention of an activity that is directed toward a goal, or interference with that activity; also, the emotional state that results from being prevented from reaching a goal.

Ethologist One who studies behavior of animals in their natural habitats. Ethology looks at the influence of biology on behavior.

Territorial An adjective employed to describe individuals or species whose instinctual behavior patterns include the establishment and protection of an identifiable geographic area. Wolves, bears, and many other predatory animals are territorial.

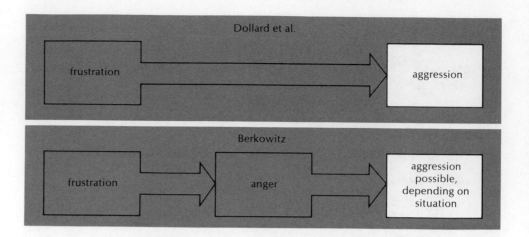

Figure 17.3 Frustration-aggression: two related models.

other species. Many animals mark their territories, sometimes by urinating at selected locations around its perimeter (wolves); sometimes by scratching on trees (certain species of bears; Becker, 1973). One widely accepted explanation for this is that it prevents other animals from inadvertently encroaching on territory that is not theirs. This is of considerable genetic value to the species, since it prevents many encounters where one or both of the aggressors might be killed or injured. It should be noted, however, that many aggressive encounters among animals of the same species do not lead to death or injury (although some do; Wilson, 1973).

Lorenz describes in detail the ritualistic "fights" of many animals, particularly in courtship sequences, but also in some territorial fights. Wolves, for example, commonly expose their jugular as a sign of submission when fighting with other wolves. After one or two mock passes at the exposed throat, the victor allows the vanquished to leave. The entire process is not unlike our traditional military gun salutes, a ritual which originated at a time when firing one's weapon meant, in effect, "The fact that I am unarmed and you could now kill me proves that I am your friend."

The survival value of certain aggressive behaviors in nonhuman animals and their frequent instinctlike specificity (that is, the fact that aggression usually occurs only in response to specific internal and external conditions) provide strong evidence for the belief that aggression in animals is, at least to some degree, genetically based. The situation with respect to humans is not as clear, however. Although there is a possibility that we have (or had) instinctual tendencies toward aggressiveness, perhaps predicted on territoriality as Ardrey (1966) argues, learning and environment affect so much of our behavior that "instinctual" tendencies are difficult to isolate (Barnett, 1973). In addition, there are human societies where aggressive behavior is at an extreme minimum (the Zuni and the Hutterites)—and others where it is at the opposite extreme (the Kwakiutl Indians and the Mundugumor). Although these societies do not provide proof that we have no genetic tendencies toward aggression, they do indicate that environmental factors are probably more important in *manifestations* of aggression than are genetic forces. (See Figure 17.4).

Social Learning A third explanation for aggressive behavior is derived from a behavioristic or social-learning model and has been extensively developed by Bandura (1973). According to this model, aggressive behavior is learned largely as a result of the reinforcing consequences of being aggressive, or simply as a result of social imitation. If violence on television increases aggressive behavior in viewers, social imitation may provide an explanation. We look at this question more thoroughly later in this chapter.

Physiology There are a number of other explanations for aggression as well, many of which do not pretend to be as comprehensive as the three just described. Recent evidence suggests that aggression may be associated with hormones (injections of

Figure 17.4 Human societies such as the Mennonites, where aggressive behavior is at an extreme minimum, give evidence that environmental influences may be more important than genetic influences in manifestations of aggression.

testosterone increase aggressiveness in monkeys), with olfaction (certain strains of mice respond aggressively to other mice who have been smeared with urine from mice that would ordinarily be aggressed upon), with brain damage or dysfunction, or with stimulation of appropriate areas of the thalamus (rage can be produced in cats as a result of electrical stimulation). Clearly, then, aggression has a physiological basis. In fact, however, this is not an adequate explanation, since all aspects of human behavior have physiological bases. Nevertheless, knowledge of the physiological underpinnings of aggression may prove useful in controlling extremes of violence (using psychosurgery and drugs, for example).

Figure 17.5 summarizes the four major theories of aggression.

Common Forms of Aggression

Moyer (1976) describes six forms of aggression that are commonly observed among various animal species. Although not all of these can readily be observed among humans, they are described briefly here since they provide an interesting basis for comparison.

Predatory Aggression   A highly specific form of behavior, predation is usually associated with hunger and is clearly evident among members of the cat and dog families, and a number of birds. Few sex differences exist among these animals with respect to predation. That is, both males and females of predatory species generally engage in killing and eating. Among predatory baboons, however, dominant males do almost all the killing *and the eating* (Harding, 1973).

Predation almost always occurs between species rather than within. Wolves, for example, do not prey on other wolves, but on members of other species. Lorenz (1966) makes an important distinction between interspecies (between species) aggression (predation) and intraspecies (within species) aggression. Predation occurs primarily as a result of hunger motives, involves no anger or self-defense, and is therefore very different from intraspecies aggression. The forms of aggression that are of greatest interest to social psychologists are intraspecies.

Although it might be argued that hunting and cannibalism are examples of predatory aggression in humans, these activities are by no means common to all members of our species. And science's imagination will not stretch so far as to declare that these

frustration-aggression
aggression following impediments to reaching a goal

territoriality
aggression based on instinctual tendencies

social learning
aggression as a learned response

physiology
aggression as caused by hormones, brain damage, and other physiological events or conditions

Figure 17.5 Explanations of aggression. These should not be interpreted as mutually exclusive, since aggressive behavior may well be a function of several underlying factors.

behaviors provide evidence that predatory aggression is instinctual in humans. Pronouncements concerning the possibility of a predatory instinct in our evolutionary history should also be filed under speculation, although the fact that a number of cows, pigs, and chickens have fallen prey to us is beyond speculation. What is important from the social psychologist's viewpoint is that we are seldom angry when we eat a chicken.

Intermale Aggression Among almost all species, including humans, males are more aggressive than females. Furthermore, interspecies aggression typically involves male pairs or groups. Males do not often aggress against females or, typically, against the young of their species.

Among humans, the vast majority of violent crimes are committed by males. Recall that the male sex hormone testosterone may be directly related to aggression. Injections of testosterone in monkeys increase aggressive behavior. By the same token, castration (which involves removal of the glands responsible for producing testosterone) results in a decline in aggressive behavior. Thus, not only does aggressiveness in at least some nonhuman animals have a biological basis, but its basis also provides for clear sex differences. Chapter 11 presented a discussion of sex differences among children. Recall that the one area in which there is consistent agreement among researchers concerning the existence of psychological differences between the sexes is that of aggression (Maccoby & Jacklin, 1974).

Under special circumstances, many nonhuman females also become aggressive. These circumstances relate to ovulation, lactation, and the care of the young. Hence, when females display predictable aggressiveness, it is seldom as general as it is among males, and it relates to reproduction and the rearing of young. Recall, too, that nonhuman males of one species often do not kill one another or even inflict injury. Fights are often highly ritualized mating or territorial displays, or struggles for dominance.

Sex-Related Aggression Sex without violence is the norm in contemporary human societies, in terms of both expectations and observations. In fact, however, it is extremely difficult to estimate the incidence of sex-related violence. Police reports of rape and sexual assault are clearly underestimates, given the reluctance of many victims to report their experiences, and given the legal difficulties involved in obtaining convictions. Psychology's understanding of the rapist is unclear at best. M. L. Cohen et al. (1971) describe a variety of classifications for violent sexual offenders, most of them based on motivation. Thus, there are individuals for whom aggression appears to be the primary or at least the secondary motive, and where victims are typically assaulted and sometimes killed before, during, or after intercourse. Such individuals describe their primary emotion as anger. In some instances intercourse is of little importance as a motivational factor, and the aggressive act may involve such cruel and bizarre behaviors as mutilating the breasts or genitals and other forms of torture.

A second classification of rapists includes offenders for whom sexual intercourse appears to be the primary motive, and where violence is employed only to that end. In such cases, the victim's compliance typically prevents violence beyond the act of rape itself. Furthermore, Cohen et al. report that potential victims who struggle or cry out often frighten their attacker and chase him away.

The third classification described by Cohen et al. includes offenders whose motivation is sexual, but who are unable to achieve sexual arousal or release in the absence of violence. Their behavior presents a clear example of sexual sadism. Many of these rapists firmly believe that women like to be raped, that their struggles and cries are evidence of sexual excitement.

These three classifications describe men who are clearly dangerous, whether their primary motivation is sexual, aggressive, or sadistic. Each is prone to use physical force or threat to obtain satisfaction of his wishes. Nor is the picture as simple as might be implied by this classification. There are a large number of sexual offenders whose motives and behaviors are both less clear and less predictable than can be provided for by any classification system. Nor is rape limited to males attacking females. Occasionally males are raped by other males and even by women. Box 17.1 discusses sex-related violence in nonhuman animals.

Fear-Induced Aggression   Captured or cornered animals who are ordinarily docile sometimes become fiercely aggressive. In such cases the aggression is ordinarily interpreted as an innate self-protective reaction. In most cases of fear-induced aggression, the animal will flee rather than aggress if given a recognizable opportunity to do so. Moyer (1976) points out that aggression is only one of many possible responses to fear. Cornered animals will sometimes simply cower, faint, or enter a cataleptic state. In other cases, fear may result in approach and appeasement behavior, particularly among nonhuman primates, when an inferior animal threatened by a dominant male might present gestures of submission rather than fleeing or fighting.

Although fear-induced aggression has not been carefully studied under controlled circumstances, anecdotal evidence suggests that it may also be characteristic of humans. Children who are goaded into fights may attack out of fear. Can some wars be explained in this way?

Maternal Aggression   This type of aggression is very much in evidence among female nonhuman animals when there is a possibility that their young might be threatened. Human mothers do not appear to react instinctively with aggression when their nests are approached. There is little doubt, however, that in the same way as most of us will aggress in order to protect things that are important to us, so human mothers would surely become highly aggressive if doing so were compatible with preventing harm or injury to their offspring.

Irritable Aggression   Unlike the other classifications of aggression described thus far, irritable aggression is not directed toward specific people, animals, or objects in clearly prescribed circumstances. Instances of irritable aggression are less common among most animals than are other forms of aggression (intermale, predatory, or maternal, for example); they are highly common among humans, however (Figure 17.6).

Psychologists recognize three primary sources of irritable aggression. One is frustration, and is often explained by reference to Dollard et al.'s (1939) frustration-aggression hypothesis or Berkowitz's (1965) frustration-anger hypothesis. The second is deprivation rather than frustration. Recall that frustration is defined as the effect of being prevented from reaching a goal. Deprivation differs from frustration in that it involves the absence of a goal, rather than an obstacle to an otherwise attainable goal. A third source of irritable aggression is pain.

BOX 17.1

Sexual Violence among Animals

Sexual aggression is not uncommon among various animal species. Those of you who have observed cats on hot tin roofs or elsewhere may have been impressed by the violence of their mating. Lax (1976) reports that male orangutans are typically rapists, and that wild horses and zebras kick each other in the chest and bite, often drawing blood, before having intercourse. Monkeys and baboons present numerous examples of sex-related aggression, many of them involving females who become highly aggressive when they are sexually receptive, and who, in some cases, temporarily supplant the dominant male in the tribe. Among rhesus monkeys, males are often highly aggressive during intercourse. Carpenter (1942) observed forty-five separate oestrous periods (periods of female ovulation and receptivity). In twenty-two of these, females suffered serious attacks. Six were severely wounded, and one was permanently crippled as a result of damage to a major motor nerve in her thigh.

None of these observations can be interpreted as evidence that aggressiveness and sexual behavior are "naturally" related in humans. Cohen et al.'s (1971) description of the psychology of rapists suggests strongly that the majority of sexual offenders have not had normal childhoods. Their pathologies can frequently be traced to physical abuse and cruelty at the hands of parents, to frightening sexual experiences at young ages, often with parents, aunts, or acquaintances, or to a variety of other childhood traumas.

Figure 17.6 Most types of irritable aggression, caused primarily by frustration or deprivation, have little parallel in nonhuman animals.

There is considerable experimental evidence relating frustration to aggression (Berkowitz, 1969). Violence among minority groups has sometimes been explained by reference to the observation that such groups are typically oppressed and prevented from reaching many of the goals available to other members of society. Thus racial violence, collective violence (in labor disputes, for example), and violence among nations might all have frustration or deprivation as a cause.

There is evidence as well that a tendency toward aggressiveness—or simple irritability—may be a personality predisposition that varies from individual to individual. Certainly, males appear to be more prone to irritable aggression than females. Similarly, some males and females are less likely than others to respond to frustration, deprivation, or pain in aggressive ways.

The six common forms of aggression are summarized in Table 17.1.

Violence in Society

The most obvious instances of aggression in society are those involving overt acts of violence: rape, homicide, assault, and destruction of property. Interpersonal violence, which includes the first three of these, is committed primarily by males. The extent to which these acts can be attributed to frustration, deprivation, pain, or sex-related factors, and the extent to which character and personality disorders or other factors are involved, is not clear. There is little doubt, however, that each can play a significant role.

Table 17.1 Common Forms of Aggression

Type	Instance
Predatory	Feeding behavior of predatory carnivore
Intermale	Intraspecies aggression (for mates or territory); also interspecies (as in war)
Sex-related	Rape
Fear-induced	Violent reaction of cornered organism
Maternal	A bear sow with cubs
Irritable	Fight at a hockey game

Note. Based in part on Moyer, 1976.

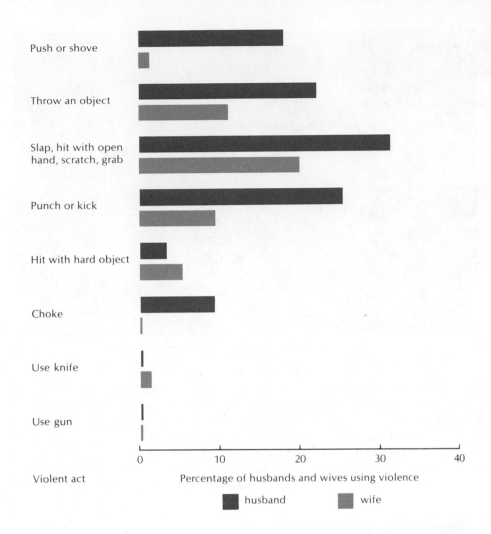

Push or shove

Throw an object

Slap, hit with open
hand, scratch, grab

Punch or kick

Hit with hard object

Choke

Use knife

Use gun

| 0 | 10 | 20 | 30 | 40 |

Violent act

Percentage of husbands and wives using violence

■ husband   ■ wife

Figure 17.7 A graphic presentation of the results of Gelles's study on the percentage of husbands and wives who have ever used physical violence on each other. (This graph has been adapted from *The Violent Home: A Study of Physical Aggression between Husbands and Wives* by R. J. Gelles, Sage Library of Social Research, Vol. 13, © 1972, p. 53, by permission of the Publisher, Sage Publications, Inc., Beverly Hills/London.)

The incidence of violent crimes in Western industrialized societies appears to have risen sharply during the last decades, according to police reports. It is possible, however, that these statistics do not reflect actual increases in violent crimes so much as increases in the effectiveness of detection, apprehension, and conviction machinery. Graham and Gurr (1969) suggest, for example, that crime rates in major U.S. cities are lower now than they were in the early part of this century. Thus, we cannot categorically accept the frequently expressed opinion that crime is rising at an alarming rate; but we can accept as fact that the crime rate is very high.

Violence in society is reflected not only in crime, but in international aggression as well. In this century alone, well over half of all nations have been involved in war. As of this writing, many still are. And while nations fight, so do individuals within families. Violence in the home is not always obvious. Child abuse presents one inexact index; the fact that 25 percent or more of all homicides and assaults involve members of the same family provides a second index (Gelles, 1972).

In an intensive study of violence in the home, Gelles interviewed eighty couples. Forty of these had either been reported to the police for domestic violence or at least one member had gone to a private marital agency with violence as a complaint. The other forty couples were chosen from houses neighboring those of the initial forty couples. It is significant that violence was reported in over 30 percent of these neighboring homes. The nature and incidence of violence between spouses is described in Figure 17.7. Violence toward children was considerably higher (96 percent of all cases) in those homes Gelles studied. Although predominant forms of violence (spanking,

Figure 17.8 Research has not established clearly whether television viewing among children is often implicated in significant aggressive acts.

slapping) are not serious enough to warrant the label of child abuse, their high incidence suggests a general acceptance of physical violence as a child-rearing technique. Research reported by Bandura (1973) indicates that children who are punished aggressively (usually physically) are more likely to be aggressive. In other words, there appears to be a relationship between aggression in the home and subsequent aggression as adults. This observation is further substantiated by the fact that many who engage in sexually aggressive acts had been severely beaten as children (Cohen et al., 1971).

Violence and Television

Is there also a relationship between violence in the mass media and violence in society? The answer is somewhat equivocal—and not for lack of research, as was shown in Chapter 11. What we do know is that most people have television sets (over 99 percent of all homes with small children; J. P. Murray, 1973), and many people watch these sets for long periods of time. We also know with great certainty that television programs abound in violence, and that this is, perhaps sadly, more true of programs designed expressly for children than it is for adult programs. But what we do not know, in spite of the fact that the U.S. government allocated 1 million dollars in 1969 expressly for research on this question, is the effect of television violence on the behavior and attitudes of viewers. The five-volume report that resulted from this research concludes that there is evidence of short-term *causation* of aggressive behavior as a function of exposure to television violence (see Liebert & Schwartzberg, 1977). However, as we saw in Chapter 11, the evidence is not entirely clear, and our conclusions need to be tentative. (See Figure 17.8.)

Three theories are currently resorted to by those who are concerned about the impact of television violence. Felsenthal (1976) identifies these as the catharsis hypothesis, the modeling hypothesis, and the catalytic hypothesis (Figure 17.9). The **catharsis hypothesis** maintains that watching violence may serve as a release (catharsis) for pent-up hostilities and aggressive urges; that, in short, a person who would like to hit a neighbor over the head with a lawnmower handle may be partially satisfied after watching an Indian scalp a white scout, and may be less likely to use the lawnmower handle. In fact, some research has shown a decline in aggression among highly hostile viewers following exposure to television violence.

Catharsis hypothesis Theory about the impact of television violence that proposes that viewing violence may have the beneficial effect of releasing pent-up emotions.

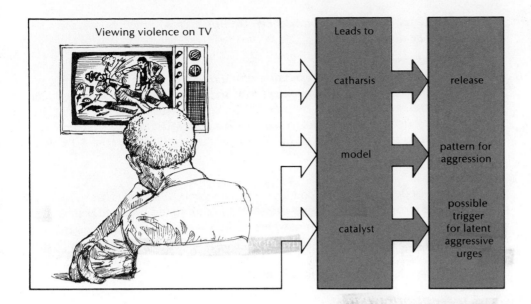

The **modeling hypothesis** maintains that television violence serves as a model for violence in real life; that children become progressively more violent as they are exposed to a variety of aggressive models. This hypothesis, too, has received its share of support from science.

The **catalyst hypothesis** is based on the observation that not all people are affected in the same way by television violence. This hypothesis maintains that for certain individuals, violence on television serves as a catalyst, triggering the release of their own pent-up aggressive urges. Other individuals remain unaffected. Pember (1977) refers to NBC's 1966 telecast of *The Doomsday Flight* as a case in point. The film dealt with an attempt to extort money from a major airline by an individual who placed a bomb aboard a plane and offered to tell authorities where the bomb was in exchange for money. Shortly after the show was aired, several airlines received telephone calls with similar threats. Apparently, the film served as a catalyst for a small number of individuals; it did not affect the majority of viewers in the same way.

In summary, then, all hypotheses are, to some degree, supported by relevant research. Television violence may serve as a catharsis for some individuals and may, for that reason, have a limited but useful purpose; it may serve as a general model for violence; or it may have a catalytic effect on a small number of individuals. It is conceivable, as well, that television may often have very little effect on its viewers; that it may be no more than a cloudy mirror of the actual state of affairs in contemporary society.

Clearly, however, we are not aggressive in all places and at all times. Indeed, there are many who are seldom aggressive under any circumstances. And even among those who are often aggressive, there are some who are sometimes altruistic.

But not all of us are altruistic if we are not aggressive: a great many are simply apathetic. We neither aggress nor help. In some circumstances, however, the end result of apathy—of doing nothing—can be almost as bad as the results of violent aggression. Kitty Genovese's story is a case in point.

Modeling hypothesis Theory about the impact of television violence that proposes that it may serve as a model for aggression in real life.

Catalyst hypothesis A catalyst is a substance that facilitates or makes possible a chemical reaction. In a more general sense, catalysts are individuals, events, or experiences that facilitate, initiate, or make possible certain reactions. The catalyst hypothesis of television violence proposes that viewing violence may trigger latent aggressive urges in some individuals.

Apathy and Altruism

Kitty Genovese is set upon by a maniac as she returns home from work at 3 A.M. Thirty-eight of her neighbors in Kew Gardens come to their windows when she cries out in terror; none come to her assistance even though her stalker takes over half an hour to murder her. No one even so much as calls the police. She dies.

A second case in point:

An 18-year-old switchboard operator, alone in her office in the Bronx, is raped and beaten. Escaping momentarily, she runs naked and bleeding to the street, screaming for help. A crowd of 40 passersby gathers and watches as, in broad daylight, the rapist tries to drag her back upstairs; no one interferes. Finally, two policemen happen by and arrest her assailant. (Latané & Darley, 1970, pp. 1–2)

Bystander effect Label given to the phenomenon where individuals who witness emergency situations do not offer assistance or respond in any way.

These episodes, only two of countless similar events, illustrate what social psychologists have termed the **bystander effect**. Most of us would prefer to believe that if a number of people witness an event where someone desperately needs assistance, the more people witnessing the act, the more likely it is that one of them will give help. In fact, however, it appears that in some circumstances the more witnesses there are, the less likely it is that someone will intervene.

The Bystander Effect

Latané and Darley (1970) conducted experiments investigating the alleged apathy of bystanders and their unwillingness to become involved. In one series of studies, subjects alone in a room overheard an epileptic seizure apparently suffered by another "subject" (in fact, a tape-recorded "seizure"). Experimental conditions were such that subjects either thought they were the only ones listening to the person having a seizure, or they thought that one or more others were also listening in different rooms. The dependent variable was whether or not the subject reported the seizure or otherwise attempted to provide assistance, and how much time elapsed before helping behavior occurred. Table 17.2 presents the results. Note that all subjects who thought they were alone with the victim responded; in contrast, when subjects thought there were four others besides the victim, only 62 percent responded.

In another experiment, subjects were left in a room ostensibly to wait for an interviewer (Latané & Darley, 1968). They were asked to fill out an information questionnaire while waiting. Shortly after the subjects were left alone, artificial smoke was introduced into the room through a wall vent. The smoke continued in irregular gusts, eventually filling the room, irritating the eyes, and making breathing difficult. If subjects had not reported the smoke after six minutes, the experiment was discontinued and subjects were debriefed. In one experimental condition, subjects waited alone; in another, they waited with two other individuals, ostensibly subjects but in fact assistants of the experimenter who had been instructed to remain passive and who continued to fill out their questionnaires, fanning away the smoke, until relieved at the end of six minutes. In a third condition, two naive subjects waited together.

The results of these experiments are as would be predicted in view of the fact that larger groups are less likely to react to emergencies. Subjects alone reported the smoke 75 percent of the time; subjects in pairs reported it only 30 percent of the time and took longer before doing so. Most striking, only one of ten subjects paired with passive assistants reported the smoke.

These and related studies seem to indicate that individuals who have reason to believe themselves the only witnesses and hence the only immediate sources of intervention are more likely to involve themselves, either by reporting a potentially dangerous situation or by offering direct assistance. It seems that when there are a number of apparent witnesses, people are more reluctant to become involved. This does not mean, however, that witnesses remain apathetic. In fact, there is considerable evidence that they do *care*. Subjects who did not report the "epileptic seizure" were often visibly shaken, their hands trembling, their faces pale and drawn.

Table 17.2 Effects of Group Size on Likelihood and Speed of Response to Help "Victim" Feigning an Epileptic Seizure

Group Size	Number of Trials	Percentage Responding by End of Fit	Percentage Ever Responding	Time Taken to Respond (in seconds)
2 (subject and victim)	13	85	100	52
3 (subject, victim, and one other)	26	62	85	93
6 (subject, victim, and 4 others)	13	31	62	166

Note. Adapted from *The Unresponsive Bystander: Why Doesn't He Help?* by Bibb Latané and John M. Darley. Copyright © 1970. Reprinted by permission of Prentice-Hall, Inc., Englewood Cliffs, New Jersey.

Explaining Differences in Bystander Intervention

What causes the greater reluctance of people to become involved when others could also be involved? A number of factors may be responsible. They may not see themselves as the most competent; perhaps they simply assume that someone else has already intervened; perhaps, too, there is a fear of making a wrong judgment and of appearing foolish. J. M. Darley and Latané (1968) attribute the bystander effect to one of three sources (or a combination of these): a process of diffusion of responsibility, where the presence of others reduces the cost of nonintervention; a process of social influence, where the nonintervention of others leads the subject to misinterpret the seriousness of the situation; and a process of audience inhibition, where the presence of others brings about fear of making a wrong decision and acting unwisely. Other studies have arrived at other conclusions. We look at some of them here.

Situation Ambiguity   It is perhaps reassuring that a great many later studies have not found a bystander effect, or have found a considerably less dramatic one than might have been expected. R. D. C. Clark and L. E. Word (1974) suggest that one of the reasons might be that many of the early studies presented ambiguous "emergencies" (for example, smoke from a ventilator, or noise without visual cues). They suggest that the bystander effect, when it does occur, is perhaps due more to the ambiguity of the situation and to the potential dangers of intervention than to social influence, audience effects, or diffusion of responsibility. To test their hypotheses, they arranged for subjects to witness a technician apparently receiving a severe electric shock. In some conditions, the accident occurred in full view, with the victim calling for help before fainting (unambiguous); in others, the victim was hidden behind a counter but called for help (moderately ambiguous); and in others, the victim was hidden, and although sounds of his falling could be heard, he did not cry out for help (highly ambiguous). Other experimental conditions varied the amount of danger involved. In the nonambiguous condition, the victim either fell on wires with his hand still on a control box where the short had apparently occurred (high danger) or he fell some distance away from the wires and the box (low danger).

Results are striking. When the emergency is unambiguous and the danger low, all subjects, whether alone or in pairs, come to the victim's assistance. There is virtually no bystander effect. In the high-danger situation, 91 percent of subjects alone attempt to help; and subjects in pairs always provide help. But the bystander effect *is* manifested when the situation is ambiguous, although it only occurs 50 percent of the time when subjects are in pairs.

Perceived Danger   Related to this study, a number of other investigations have shown that perceived danger is an important factor in determining whether bystanders will help or not (Schwartz & Gottlieb, 1976). Shotland and Straw (1976) had subjects witness a man attacking a woman. The bystander effect was most evident when the fight occurred between married couples, and seldom evident when it occurred between strangers. Subjects apparently reasoned that the wife was less likely to want intervention if the fight occurred between her and her husband, and that the husband would be less likely to run away. By the same token, they assumed that when the fight occurred between strangers, the man would likely run away. A lovers' quarrel or a quarrel between man and wife presents an ambiguous situation, and a potentially dangerous one. Shotland and Straw argue that the assumption that a man and woman who are fighting have a relationship is reasonable in the absence of any evidence to the contrary (such as rape or theft). This might explain the bystander effect in natural situations.

Commitment to Victim   There is research to indicate, as well, that intervention is much more likely when subjects have a commitment to the victim. When subjects were asked to watch the victim's belongings while he or she went away for a short while, they were much more likely to report a theft or even to prevent it than if they simply observed the same theft without having been asked to commit themselves beforehand (Moriarty, 1975).

Location Familiarity   In an experiment conducted at La Guardia Airport and in a New York subway, a young man on crutches fell moaning to the floor, clutching his knee in pain. When the incident occurred at the airport (there were sixty stagings of the incident in each place), 41 percent of the bystanders attempted to help; when it occurred in the subway, a reassuring 83 percent came to the man's assistance (Latané & Darley, 1970). Differences in bystander intervention in these two locations have tentatively been explained on the basis of the familiarity of bystanders with the location (subway users are typically more familiar with subway stations than airport users are with airports). (See Box 17.2.) Subsequent interviews with bystanders indicated that the higher the individual's socioeconomic class, the less likely it was that assistance would be offered. This does not provide an explanation; it is simply an observation.

Situation Seriousness   Willingness to help is also related to the seriousness of the situation. Extreme emergencies are often less likely to elicit immediate assistance than are more common occurrences, where the assistance required is less costly. Emergencies involving violence may present a potential danger to those who would render assistance; in addition, these usually present unfamiliar situations to which a bystander might be uncertain as to how to respond. As Latané and Darley (1970) note, before

---

BOX 17.2

Can You Spare a Dime?

Incidents such as the highly publicized murder of Kitty Genovese can too easily lead to a cynical and inaccurate view of life in contemporary society. It is reassuring to note that examples of altruism are in fact common. When Columbia University students asked strangers in New York for a dime, 34 percent of all those asked did give subjects a dime, even when the request was not accompanied by any form of explanation. That 66 percent did not comply with the request is not nearly as surprising as the fact that the remainder did. And when students explained that they needed the dime because their wallets had been stolen, an amazing 72 percent of those asked provided the money (Latané & Darley, 1970). It is perhaps unfortunate that instances of altruism like this are not dramatic and consequently don't often receive the media coverage accorded more sensational, if more lurid, events such as public rapes, thefts, and murders.

On occasion, however, there are instances of altruism so compelling that even a media that gorges itself callously on violence and aggression, pauses. Such was the case when Flight 90, departing from Washington, D.C. for Miami, crashed into the Potomac River in January 1982. There, in the numbing cold of an ice-covered river, a handful of people were saved through actions that were truly self-sacrificing. One man on shore jumped into the freezing water to save a woman; a helicopter crew hovered dangerously above the river with landing skids often touching the water as they hauled victims to safety; and as millions later saw on television, a lone male crash victim in the water passed the life-saving ring lowered from the helicopter to four or five others, each of whom was pulled immediately to safety. He paid the highest price that altruism can ask. He died.

bystanders intervene, they must notice an event, interpret it as an emergency, make a decision as to their personal responsibility, select a form of assistance, and implement that assistance. When Kitty Genovese was murdered in front of thirty-eight witnesses, it is likely that each of these witnesses interpreted the situation as an emergency. It is unlikely that each would then decide to take personal responsibility for bringing assistance. In fact, many might have thought that someone else *must* have called the police. If all thirty-eight reasoned that way, the incident, shocking though it might be, is not as difficult to understand as it might otherwise be, given our implicit beliefs in the goodness of human nature. Choosing a form of assistance, other than calling on someone else (the police) for assistance, also presents a real problem. The man who was killing Kitty Genovese might not have hesitated to attack anyone else coming to her assistance directly. There might be, in addition, the paranoiac speculation that her murder was connected with organized crime, and that the eventual consequences of intervention might be disastrous. In summary, the Kitty Genovese case presents an extreme where the possibility of intervening and the desirability of doing so are difficult and costly. It is not surprising that the likelihood of intervention is lessened by the presence of others who might also intervene. In fact, only rather stupid people react without taking into account how other people are reacting.

Attitudes and Attitude Change

Understanding social influence is basic to understanding attitudes and opinions, stereotypes and prejudices—topics that have always been of great interest and concern for social psychology. Unfortunately, they are difficult to research, partly because of problems of definition and measurement, and partly because they are elusive and changing characteristics of human thought and behavior.

An **attitude** is typically defined as a prevailing and consistent tendency to react in a given way. In addition, it has important emotional connotations. Thus, attitudes may be described as positive or negative; they therefore have strong motivational consequences, a fact that distinguishes them from **opinions**. Whereas an opinion is also an evaluation, opinions do not lead people to action as do attitudes.

Stereotypes are widely held attitudes and opinions concerning identifiable groups. They usually include value-laden beliefs. In social psychology the term has most often referred to erroneous beliefs based on emotional reaction, illogical reasoning, and faulty generalization (Lippmann, 1922). More recently, psychologists have recognized that generalized beliefs about groups—in other words, stereotypes—are virtually indispensable in daily interaction (Figure 17.10). Research has shown, as well, that there is remarkable agreement between many stereotypes, including those applied to ethnic groups, and more objective evaluations. This does not mean that stereotypes are invariably accurate and useful; bigoted, inappropriate, unjust, and frankly immoral stereotypes are rampant in virtually all social groups. However, their existence should not lead us to overlook the usefulness of relatively accurate stereotypes. Unlike stereotypes, which are widely held beliefs about groups, **prejudices** are personal and individualistic prejudgments. To be prejudiced implies having arrived at an opinion prior to obtaining relevant facts.

To illustrate the distinction among attitudes, opinions, stereotypes, and prejudice, consider these four reactions. A man feels strongly that involvement in war is immoral, and tries to persuade those of draft age to protest. Besides, he agrees with his father that military personnel are highly immoral, although he has had little exposure to them. He also believes that seatbelt legislation is unnecessary and uneconomical, and that the American people are sufficiently resourceful and industrious that they will cope with energy shortages and other national and international problems. His beliefs concerning war are individual, affective, and motivating; they illustrate a

Figure 17.10 Would you be inclined to give a ride to this person? Stereotypes guide many of our social interactions. You probably have some definite feeling about the kind of relationship (if any) you would like with him.

Attitude A prevailing and consistent tendency to react in a given way, describable as being positive or negative and having important motivational consequences.

Opinion A personal evaluation, describable as being good or bad, often manifested as a personal belief, and not having strong motivational consequences.

Stereotype Widely held attitude or opinion concerning identifiable groups.

Prejudice Literally, a prejudgment; thus a prejudice is a preconceived attitude or opinion that is, by definition, arrived at before a person obtains relevant facts and information.

clearly negative *attitude* toward war. His estimate of the morality of the military is clearly a *prejudice*. His beliefs concerning seatbelts represent an *opinion*. And his beliefs with respect to the American people are the result of a *stereotype* he shares with a significant number of other people.

Compliance and Conformity

Conformity A change in attitudes or beliefs as a result of social pressure. Whereas compliance involves agreement in behavior, conformity involves agreement in principle.

One reason why the study of attitudes is so important is that they are powerful motives for behavior. Psychology has established clearly that behavior can sometimes be controlled through the administration of rewards and punishments—that is, through coercion. It can also be controlled to some extent through persuasion. When persuasion is successful in effecting a long-term change in behavior, attitudes have been affected, opinions modified, or stereotypes and prejudices altered; in short it has led to **conformity**. Short-term changes in behavior that do not significantly alter any of these types of beliefs illustrate **compliance**. The distinction is sometimes more subtle in practice than in theory. If I hold a carrot a tantalizing distance in front of a mule, thereby inducing that dumb animal to swim across a small body of water, I have simply succeeded in getting a mule to *comply* with my pointless wishes. Assuming that the mule does not like water and is not in the habit of taking off its shoes and wading for pleasure of a Sunday morning, it cannot be argued that I have developed a conforming mule simply by bullying one into complying. To become a *conforming* mule, the creature would have to change its attitude toward water and deliberately wade with the other wading mules as a result of its attitude, rather than for a meager carrot. If you happened along and saw the mule swimming, however, you could not tell whether it was complying or conforming.

Compliance Acceding to the wishes and desires of others. To comply is to behave according to instruction or expectation.

To bring the illustration closer to home, you may be said to conform to social norms to the extent that you approve of them and therefore act accordingly. Complying with the same social norms does not involve different overt behavior, but it is premised on motives other than your approval of the norms.

For those who attempt to control others, compliance is probably a lot more threatening than conformity. To the extent that compliance is grudging and forced, there is always the possibility of rebellion. Conformity, by contrast, implies approval and is less likely to lead to revolt.

Among the most important studies of compliance and conformity are those that have looked at a phenomenon termed *cognitive dissonance*. Many of these studies have asked individuals to do something that runs counter to their predominant beliefs. In one study, subjects were asked to tell a lie about the interest and usefulness of an exceedingly boring hour-long experimental procedure (Festinger & Carlsmith, 1959). Subjects who told the lie *complied*. Only those who also changed their attitudes actually *conformed*.

Cognitive Dissonance and Attitude Change

Cognitive dissonance A state of conflict between beliefs and behavior or between expectations and behavior.

Cognitive dissonance is what results from a situation where there is conflict between behavior, beliefs, or attitudes (Festinger, 1962). Cognitive dissonance theory maintains that whenever there is conflict between cognitions (items of information, beliefs, values, and so on), people will engage in behaviors designed to eliminate or reduce the conflict. Cognitive dissonance may arise, for example, when people do things contrary to their beliefs; when they violate certain notions they have about themselves; when they compromise principles; when they observe people doing things they don't expect of them; and so on. Cognitive dissonance theory predicts that something will then be done to reduce the conflict. This theory is useful for understanding social behavior.

In the Festinger and Carlsmith (1959) study, college students were asked to place twelve spools on a tray using only one hand, remove these spools, place another twelve on the tray, remove them, replace them, and so on (always using only one hand). After one hour of this, they were asked to spend a second hour turning forty-eight pegs a quarter-turn, again using only one hand. Once all pegs had been turned, they were to be turned another quarter-turn, and again, and again. After this, subjects were asked to judge the usefulness and interest of the experiment. They were then divided into three groups, one of which did nothing further, serving as a control group. The remaining two groups were asked to help the experimenter with the project by talking individually to upcoming subjects. They were told that the experiment would look at the role of attitude in the performance of motor tasks, and that it was therefore important for new subjects to have appropriate attitudes. To this end, they were asked to lie to the new subjects, telling them that the experiment was interesting, exciting, and useful. For their services, subjects would be paid. Members of one group were to receive one dollar; members of the second group would be paid twenty dollars. Neither group knew that the other group was being paid a different amount.

After members of these two groups had each spoken to what were allegedly new subjects (they were, in fact, confederates of the investigators), they were interviewed by a neutral person who attempted to uncover their actual feelings about the experiment. The control group, not surprisingly, still found the experiment boring and useless. The twenty-dollar group also found it boring; they had not changed their minds. Amazingly, the group who had been paid one dollar had changed their minds in a positive direction. Many now agreed that the experiment was useful and quite interesting (Figure 17.11).

The results, surprising at first glance, are easily explained by reference to cognitive dissonance theory. Subjects could be expected to experience dissonance as a result of the lie they told. Presumably, there would be conflict between whatever principles they adhered to that opposed telling lies and their actual behavior. When they were paid a great deal of money for telling a lie, there was little dissonance, since the behavior was amply justified. Accordingly, subjects who were paid twenty dollars did not change their minds about the value of the experiment and its interest. Those who were paid very little money had less justification for lying, and would therefore be expected to experience considerably more dissonance. The most obvious method of reducing this dissonance would be to *believe* that the experiment was not boring. That was, in fact, what happened.

Cognitive dissonance theory leads to a number of interesting observations and applications. It answers a perennially important question concerning grass, for example. Many have long believed that the grass is greener on the other side of the fence, mountain, or what have you. In short, people want what they do not have. Festinger (1957) had young girls rank five phonograph records according to which they would most like to have. He then selected two records for each girl, each of which had been ranked as moderately, and approximately equally, attractive by the girl. The girls were then led to believe that they might receive both records, none, or one, and were asked which of the two they would prefer should they receive only one. After this, some girls received their chosen records, others received both, and some received none. Those who received both records or no records would not be expected to experience any dissonance, since their choices were largely irrelevant. Those who received only one record, however, might be expected to experience some conflict, since they could as easily have chosen the other record. If the grass is indeed greener, these girls should have found the other record more attractive than their own. But the grass is not greener. Subjects, when reevaluating the records, consistently judged their selection as being the more desirable. Cognitive dissonance theory provides an easy explanation. Whatever conflict results from having had to make an uncertain choice is quickly reduced when the subject convinces herself that she has made the best choice. It is not particularly surprising that people who make major decisions to buy houses, cars, and other objects immediately begin to exaggerate the positive aspects of their choices. They are simply reducing dissonance, or guarding against its appearance.

There are several ways of reducing dissonance, depending on the behavior from which dissonance originated (Figure 17.12). Changing attitudes is one common method, illustrated in the experiments just described. A second method involves changing

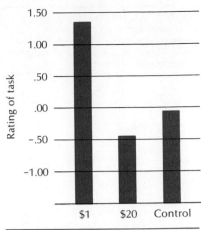

Figure 17.11 Cognitive dissonance and forced compliance. After performing particularly boring tasks, one group of students was paid $1 each to report to "potential subjects" that the tasks were exciting; another group was paid $20 each to do the same thing; and a control group was neither paid nor asked to describe the tasks (Festinger & Carlsmith, 1959). The graph reflects each group's rating of the tasks to a neutral interviewer after the experiment was completed. The $1 group's memories were most positive. Why? Unlike the control group, they had been asked to lie; unlike the $20 group, they had not been paid enough to feel the lie was justified. As a result, they felt more cognitive dissonance than the other groups. One way to reduce that dissonance was to talk themselves into believing their own descriptions. (From "Cognitive Consequences of Forced Compliance" by L. Festinger and J. M. Carlsmith, *Journal of Abnormal and Social Psychology,* 1959, *58,* 203–210. Copyright 1959 by the American Psychological Association. Reprinted by permission.)

Figure 17.12 A model of cognitive dissonance. Everyone experiences conflicts between beliefs or desires and reality. There are many ways of trying to reduce cognitive dissonance.

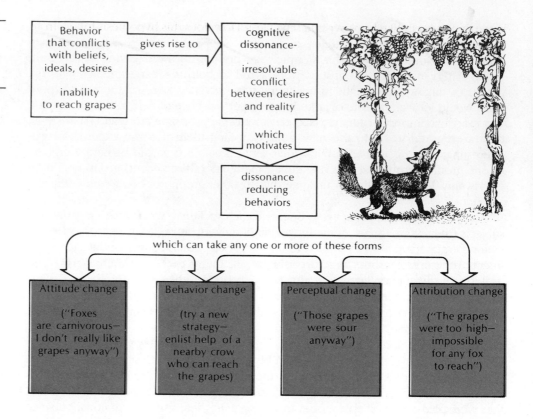

behavior. Those who stop smoking, for example, reduce dissonance created by their smoking by changing their behaviors.

Distorting information or perceptions is another way to reduce dissonance. For example, an individual who is fired from his position might interpret his dismissal as a function of prejudice—even if doing so requires that he distort his perceptions of the individuals responsible for his dismissal. A fourth way of reducing dissonance in situations like these is to attribute failure to external factors over which we have no control. Failure will create dissonance to the extent that internal factors are seen as being responsible for the failure. As Collins and Hoyt (1972) argue, people must feel personal responsibility for their behavior in order to experience dissonance. It follows, then, that those who attribute events to internal factors are more likely to feel dissonance when they fail, and that those who are externally oriented are unlikely to feel much dissonance. Shifting the blame for failure to causes over which we have no control is likely to reduce whatever dissonance we feel as a result of failure.

Overjustification

Attribution theories of attitude change in situations of forced compliance (dissonance-creating situations) maintain that when there is low justification for engaging in dissonant behavior, subjects *infer* that they did so because they wanted to. In contrast, when there is high justification, they attribute their behavior to external circumstances (compulsion or reward, for example).

Lepper et al. (1973), Lepper and Greene (1975, 1978), Nisbett and Valins (1971), and others have recently investigated the effects of justification on *consonant* behavior (behavior that is consistent with one's attitudes and beliefs). These authors have proposed an **overjustification** hypothesis which says, in effect, that large external rewards for behavior that is initially intrinsically motivated may undermine our attitudes relating to the behavior. Put more simply, if I write a book initially because I like writing books (intrinsic motivation: positive attitudes toward book-writing), and later some misguided individual promises me too high a reward for doing another book, I might

Overjustification Providing large external rewards for behavior that is initially internally motivated. The overjustification hypothesis says that this may result in undermining positive attitudes.

in the end come to like book-writing much less. How does this hypothesis follow from attribution theory?

The reasoning is as follows: Initially, I attribute my book-writing to intrinsic factors: I like writing books. But when extrinsic reinforcers become too powerful, I begin to attribute the same behavior to extrinsic reinforcers. In effect, what has now happened is that my behavior (book-writing) is so well-justified by external reinforcers that I slowly begin to change my attitude toward the behavior, attributing it more to external rewards (money) and less to intrinsic reward (satisfaction). I become less positively disposed toward the behavior.

This analysis might seem to contradict common sense. We have long assumed that people like to do things that are highly rewarded, and have perhaps naively assumed that if we increase rewards associated with a behavior, positive attitudes toward that behavior should also increase. But research indicates that these beliefs are wrong at least some of the time, and that the overjustification hypothesis is right, at least part of the time.

In an initial investigation of the overjustification hypothesis, Lepper et al. (1973) had groups of children engage in an activity for which they had high intrinsic motivation, previously determined by observing the amount of time the children engaged in the activity when given a choice among a number of presumably attractive activities. Three experimental conditions were employed. In the "expected reward" condition, subjects were told that they could engage in the activity (drawing) and earn a "good player" award if they did so. The "unexpected award" condition was identical except that players were not told beforehand that there would be an award. In a third condition, "no award," subjects neither expected nor received an award.

The dependent variable in the experiment was the interest shown by subjects in the same activity two weeks later, as manifested in whether they spontaneously engaged in the activity when permitted to do so (reflecting their attitude toward the activity). As predicted, children in the "expected award" condition showed significantly less interest in the activity. Presumably, they had now attributed their earlier engagement in the activity to external conditions (award) rather than to their intrinsic interest. Subjects in the "no award" and in the "unexpected award" conditions showed no change in interest.

Similar studies have replicated these findings a number of times (Lepper et al., 1973). It seems clear that expectation of a significant reward following what might otherwise have been an intrinsically motivated behavior reduces subsequent interest in that activity. In contrast, the same reward has no effect on interest when it is initially unexpected (M. Ross, 1975).

It is important to note that these findings do not contradict the widely accepted results of programs with positive reinforcement (token economies and so on). There are some important differences between situations where positive reinforcement has been found to be highly effective and overjustification studies where reinforcement reduces subsequent interest in the task (Feingold & Mahoney, 1975). First, in the overjustification studies, performance rather than learning is the crucial variable. That is, reward is not employed to bring about new learning (or to "shape" learning), but is contingent upon the performance of a previously learned task. Second, in systematic reinforcement programs, multiple-response procedures are employed. That is, subjects perform a number of responses and frequently receive a number of reinforcements. S. Reiss and Sushinsky (1975) have shown that the overjustification effect is not obtained in multiple-trial procedures and that, in fact, subsequent task engagement may increase after reinforcement is discontinued.

The implications of overjustification research are not yet entirely clear. Tentatively, it appears that attitudes are not likely to be changed positively by promising individuals great rewards for behaviors that reflect these attitudes. In contrast, the same rewards are not likely to undermine attitudes when they are unexpected, and when they follow behavior that was initially intrinsically motivated.

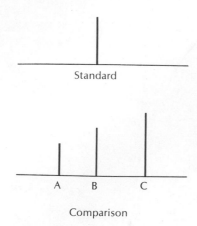

Figure 17.13 Asch (1955) used a simple visual perception test to determine the effects of social pressure. Subjects were asked which comparison line is the same length as the standard line.

Confederates Allies or accomplices. In psychological research, confederates are frequently employed to help the investigator reach the objectives of the experiment. These objectives often require that the real subjects be made to believe that the confederates are also subjects. An alternative term for confederate is *stooge.*

Obedience Like compliance, obedience involves yielding to the desires, suggestions, or wishes of other people. But obedience implies unwillingness or reluctance, and response to specific suggestions or commands. Thus, if I *tell* you to smile, you might *obey* even if you do not particularly feel like smiling at this time. If I suggest that you should be more friendly, you might comply with my suggestion by smiling.

Social Pressure

The classic studies of compliance, frequently described as studies of conformity, are those conducted by Asch (1955). In a typical experiment, "subjects" are placed in a semicircle facing an easel on which the experimenter places two large cards (see Figure 17.13). One of these cards has a single vertical line on it (the standard); the other has three vertical lines of different lengths, one of which is equal in length to the standard. In a "test of perceptual accuracy," subjects are required to determine which of the three lines is equal to the standard. In fact, the test is not of perceptual accuracy, but of social pressure and its effects on compliance, and only one of the "subjects" is actually a subject; the others are **confederates**. The confederates have been instructed to answer correctly for a number of trials, and then to answer incorrectly, but to agree on the incorrect answer. The real subject, who has no reason to suspect that the others are not also subjects, is the last to answer. The results show compliance on a high percentage of responses. Only thirteen of fifty subjects (26 percent) made no errors in the face of contrary social pressure. A control group not exposed to social pressure answered without error 94 percent of the time. Typically, subjects have been confronted with the conflicting opinions of as many as eight confederates. Other studies have shown, however, that a majority of three is equally effective in eliciting compliance with the group (Asch, 1955). In effect, the majority establishes a norm with which the subject then complies. When subjects are questioned later, however, it turns out that they knew all along that their responses and those of the confederates were in error, but for a variety of reasons they went along with the error.

These experiments have often been interpreted as showing the gullibility of individuals and their susceptibility to group pressure, the implication being that these are undesirable qualities. In fact, however, it is precisely because we are susceptible to group pressures that complex social institutions such as governments, schools, and churches work. It is also because we are sensitive to the opinions and attitudes of others that we are able to interact effectively with them. This should not be taken to mean that compliance and conformity are always good; it does mean, however, that they are not always bad, in the same way as stereotypes are not always bad.

Obedience

A special case of compliance involves unquestioning **obedience** to authority. It has been dramatically illustrated by concentration-camp atrocities performed under direct orders from powerful, potentially highly punitive or highly reinforcing superiors. More recently, it has been flagrantly demonstrated in the Watergate affair, where a number of "moral" and well-intentioned individuals succumbed to authority and to group pressure and engaged in acts that they would not privately have condoned.

In a series of controversial experiments (Milgram, 1963, 1965), subjects were duped into believing that they were confederates of an experimenter studying the effects of punishment on learning. An alleged subject (actually a confederate, termed a *stooge* in this experiment) was to be presented with a series of learning tasks while attached to electrodes so that shocks could be administered to him whenever he made an error. The real subjects' task was to depress the toggle switch that would deliver the shock. Subjects were first connected to the electrodes and administered a mild shock so that they would have no reason to think that the shocks would not be real. They were then seated in front of an instrument panel containing a series of toggle switches labeled from 15 to 450 volts, in 15-volt increments. Verbal descriptions above the switches ranged from "Slight shock" to "Danger: severe shock" at 390 volts and "XXX" at 435 volts.

In the first Milgram (1963) experiment, "victims" (stooges who did not actually receive any shocks) were placed in a separate room from the real subject and were instructed to make a predetermined number of errors. The subjects, who controlled the toggle switches, were instructed to administer a shock for every error made by the victim, beginning with the first switch and progressing as high as necessary, in one-step increments. If a subject hesitated or indicated any unwillingness to continue, the experimenter would employ a predetermined "prod"; that prod failing, a second would be employed, then a third, and finally a fourth. In all cases, the prods were given in sequence:

Prod 1. "Please continue," or "please go on."
Prod 2. "The experiment requires that you continue."
Prod 3. "It is absolutely essential that you continue."
Prod 4. "You have no other choice. You must go on." (p. 374)

Several findings of this experiment are noteworthy. Of the forty original subjects, twenty-six obeyed the experimenter's instructions (and exhortations) until the very end ("victims" committed sufficient errors to ensure that subjects would have an opportunity to administer the most severe shock—450 volts). The remaining fourteen all obeyed until at least the 300-volt level (Figure 17.14); none categorically refused to obey from the outset.

In related studies, Milgram (1965) looked at the effect of the distance between subject and victim. Four experimental conditions were employed. In one the subject could see, hear, and touch the victim, since both were in the same room. In a second, the subject could hear and see the stooge, but the latter was far enough away that he could not be touched. In a third condition, the subject could hear the stooge, but not see him, a curtain having been drawn between the two. In a final experimental condition, the subject could neither see nor hear the victim. The experimental procedure was similar to that described for the first Milgram experiment. Results are presented in Figure 17.15. There are two striking findings. One is that, again, most subjects complied with the experimenter's requests; the second is that average intensity of shocks increased in direct proportion with the distance between the subject and the victim, with the greatest average intensity of maximum shocks being administered when the subject could not see or hear the victim.

One finding that is sometimes overlooked when reporting the more sensational results of the Milgram obedience studies is that most subjects, whether or not they obeyed, were disturbed by the procedure. As Milgram (1963) notes:

In a large number of cases the degree of tension reached extremes that are rarely seen in sociopsychological laboratory studies. Subjects were observed to sweat, tremble, stutter, bite their lips, groan, and dig their fingernails into their flesh. These were characteristic rather than exceptional responses to the experiment. . . . On one occasion we observed a seizure so violently convulsive that it was necessary to call a halt to the experiment. (p. 375)

Studies such as these are disturbing for a number of reasons. They reveal aggressive aspects of humanity that many would prefer not to admit; they accentuate the

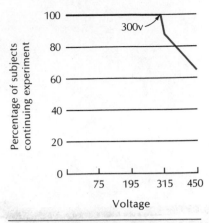

Figure 17.14 The percentage of subjects who "went all the way" and the point at which others refused in the Milgram obedience study. (Based on data from Milgram, 1963.)

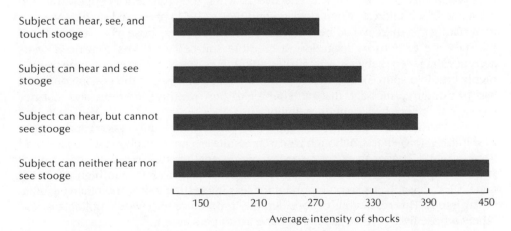

Figure 17.15 The average intensity of shocks increases in direct proportion to the distance between the subject and the stooge. (Adapted from "Some Conditions of Obedience and Disobedience to Authority" by S. Milgram, *Human Relations*, 1965, *18*, 57–76. Reprinted by permission.)

power of authority and conformity in contrast to individual choice and freedom; and they present some serious moral issues with respect to deceiving subjects into engaging in behaviors that potentially are psychologically damaging. In fairness, however, it must be pointed out that care is taken to debrief subjects, to advise them of the true nature of the experiment, and to assure them that no physical harm has actually been inflicted. Unfortunately, this procedure presents no guarantee that all subjects will emerge completely unscathed.

Persuasion

Social influence is a difficult and comprehensive topic. We have seen that people are influenced by norms expressed in the behaviors and attitudes of others, and that they respond to authority. Research and common sense also indicate that there are many subtle forms of social influence to which we are responsive. **Persuasion** is a global term for some of these influences. More specifically, persuasion generally refers to deliberate attempts to alter beliefs or behavior, usually by verbal methods—written, spoken, or both. Television commercials, religious and political propaganda, newspaper and magazine advertising, and so on all represent attempts at persuasion. How effective are they, and under what circumstances? (See Figure 17.16.)

> **Persuasion** Deliberate attempts, more subtle than coercion, to influence attitudes or behavior.

The most powerful forms of persuasion are those that succeed in changing attitudes rather than simply behavior. Attitudes may change as a result of events within the person, a process that is typically slow although it may result from resolutions and rational decisions and occur very rapidly. Attitudes may also change as a result of external events that are accidental rather than deliberately persuasive. Thus, an individual who is rescued from death by a member of a minority group toward which he has held highly negative attitudes may quite suddenly develop positive attitudes toward the group. Finally, attitudes may change as a result of persuasion, a topic that has been extensively researched in social psychology.

The results of this research indicate, to no one's great surprise, that the source of persuasion is of considerable importance in determining its effectiveness. Osgood and Tannenbaum (1955) presented subjects with statements attributed to some labor leaders concerning legalized gambling, and with statements attributed to a relatively prestigious newspaper, the *Chicago Tribune,* concerning abstract art. Subject attitudes toward these topics had been determined by means of questionnaires administered earlier. As expected, attitudes changed most in the direction of conforming with the more respected source. Similarly, in the pioneering studies of Hovland et al. (1953), subjects were exposed to statements attributed either to an eminent nuclear physicist or to the Russian newspaper *Pravda.* As predicted, subjects tended to change their attitudes when confronted with what they would interpret as the more trustworthy source.

Motives that might be attributed to the persuader also play an important role. Research suggests that when persuaders are arguing in their own best interests, the persuasion may not be nearly as effective as when the argument is opposed to the persuader's self-interest. When Hovland and Weiss (1951) presented subjects with an item stating that there would be a decline in movie theaters, those who had attributed the message to *Fortune* magazine (a credible source) were less convinced of its accuracy than were subjects who attributed the message to a gossip columnist (not a highly credible source). The most plausible explanation is that the gossip columnist was presenting a message that ran counter to her own best interests, and that her message therefore had higher credibility.

Persuasion also appears to be subject to primacy (first impression) and recency (last impression) effects, although research results are not entirely clear. Rosnow and Robinson (1967), after an extensive review of relevant literature, conclude that primacy is most important for interesting topics, controversial subjects, and highly familiar issues. Recency appears most important for less interesting topics and relatively unfamiliar issues. This research is of considerable importance for lawyers, politicians, and others whose lives revolve around the fine art of persuasion.

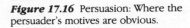
Figure 17.16 Persuasion: Where the persuader's motives are obvious.

In conclusion, it should be noted that in spite of these studies, attitudes are, by definition, pervasive predispositions to respond in given ways. To the extent that they are pervasive, they resist change. Thus, although it may be relatively simple for a skilled social psychologist to persuade individuals to vote for her, she may experience considerably more difficulty in getting them to love members of minority groups against whom they have highly negative prejudices. In fact, research shows that persuasion is not likely to be at all effective in such endeavors, but that prolonged face-to-face contact in a cooperative situation might be. Then again, it might not. When considering the power of social influence, our tendency to conform, comply, and obey, and our susceptibility to persuasion, we tend to overlook the fact that there are marked individual differences in the extent to which we are susceptible to social influence. Put another way, our social motives are not all identical.

Social Motives

Social motives are most easily described as tendencies that we appear to have that influence how we interact with others. Among the most important of these with respect to social influence are our tendencies to compete or cooperate, and to conform to norms. These are discussed here.

Competition and Cooperation

Margaret Mead (1937) presents a varied collection of evidence that **competition** and **cooperation** are acquired social motives. Indeed, all social motives, although they may be influenced to an unknown degree by innate predispositions, are also influenced by experience. In particular, Mead's book includes a description by Irving Goldman of two diametrically contrasting cultures: the Kwakiutl Indians of Vancouver Island, and the Zuni of New Mexico.

Goldman describes the Kwakiutl culture as one that glorifies competitiveness above all else, where aggression and violence are a way of life. Individuals inherit social rank and, with it, sacred obligations to subjugate, malign, and abuse all individuals of lower rank. So powerful are the resulting social motives that lower-class children are sometimes stoned by those of higher classes. In addition, intense rivalries develop among individuals of equivalent social levels and are manifested in orgies of public adornment and consumption. Perhaps best known among their customs is that of the potlatch. On the surface, this appears to be a friendly and cooperative under-

Social motives Tendencies that we appear to have, such as toward competition or cooperation, that influence how we interact with others.

Competition A condition manifested when two or more individuals or groups strive for the same goal, and when success is perceived, at least to some degree, as being dependent on the other group or individual not attaining the goal. Competition implies some degree of personal rivalry and mutual opposition.

Cooperation A condition manifested when two or more individuals or groups strive together to achieve a common goal. Cooperation implies lack of rivalry or mutual opposition. It implies as well that obtaining the goal is at least to some degree dependent on the activities of all members of the groups or individuals involved.

Figure 17.17 Two diametrically
different cultures. The Kwakiutl (**a**),
characterized by orgies of consumption,
competition, violence, and aggression;
and the Zuni (**b**), pacific, nonaggressive,
and cooperative. Cross-cultural evidence
of this kind supports the belief that
personality characteristics are highly
susceptible to environmental influence.

a

b

taking. One Kwakiutl, in public ceremony, gives material goods to another, thereby enhancing the recipient's status. In fact, however, the gesture is not friendly, for the recipient must reciprocate within one month, not with goods of equal value, but with goods worth twice as much. And one month later, the original donor must reciprocate again, this time with goods worth four times the value of the first gift. Not to reciprocate in kind brings ridicule, humiliation, and ostracism to the last recipient and greatly increases the prestige of the last donor. It is a precarious prestige, however, since the humiliated Kwakiutl may openly resort to murder. By so doing, he will inherit all his victim's possessions and titles.

In contrast, consider the Zuni of New Mexico, pacific and cooperative to a degree almost beyond our comprehension (Figure 17.17). Although Zunis own possessions, these bring no status. Indeed, Goldman reports that Zunis who own too much are social misfits. Status derives not from owning goods, or from power, but from friendship. And so the successful and happy Zuni is not one who has planted many fields and hoarded many crops, or one who is faster and stronger than all others, but the one who has the most friends. The Zuni who can appear in public with entirely borrowed clothing is accorded status. Such dress says, in effect, "Look at what good friends I have that they have dressed me in these turkey feathers." Violent crimes—murder, rape, assault—are as uncommon among the Zuni as they are common among the Kwakiutl.

Anthropological evidence would suggest, then, that there is no universal tendency to be competitive or, alternatively, to be cooperative. Nor can we categorically state that most contemporary cultures (such as ours) are predominantly competitive or cooperative. That there are highly competitive individuals within the culture is obvious; that there are highly cooperative individuals is no less obvious. Indeed, that there are individuals who are sometimes, and in certain situations, competitive, while at other times highly cooperative, is equally obvious. In short, competitiveness and cooperation in highly diverse cultures are social motives that manifest themselves in specific situations. Accordingly, much of the research that has been done on these social motives has been concerned with examining factors relating to prosocial and antisocial behavior in children, and with looking at situations where cooperation is most likely to be manifested.

Additional evidence that cooperation is an acquired social motive derives from a study in which two children were placed in separate cubicles, and each had access to a control device which allowed her or him to present the other child with a cookie (Wolfle & Wolfle, 1939). They could not obtain cookies for themselves (see Figure 17.18). Not until children can communicate verbally—"You pull my cookie and I'll pull yours"—do they cooperate.

Studies of altruism among children provide evidence that helping behavior can be fostered through the use of models. Paulson (1974) compared thirty-six children who had watched all programs in the Sesame Street series designed to promote cooperative behavior, with forty-two children who had not been exposed to the series. He found significantly more cooperative behavior among the experimental group (see Figure 17.19). However, this difference was not generalized to testing situations that were different from those depicted in the series. The most logical conclusion is that cooperative behavior can be increased, but that in order for this behavior to be general, models of cooperative behavior have to be provided in a great variety of social situations. Presumably, competitive, aggressive, and apathetic behavior could also be fostered in the same way. Cross-cultural comparisons such as those between the Kwakiutl and the Zuni, or between Israeli children (typically in kibbutzes) and U.S. whites (Shapira & Madsen, 1974), would warrant such a conclusion.

Conformity to Norms

Perhaps the most powerful of all social motives derives from a widespread tendency of individuals to conform to social **norms**. Indeed, conformity may well be the best explanation for other social motives such as competitiveness and cooperation. Cross-cultural studies reveal clearly that where social norms reinforce competitiveness, individuals are competitive; where they reinforce cooperation and sharing, individuals are cooperative.

In essence, social norms either direct or prohibit certain behaviors. Many of these norms are implicit, although they are well understood by society's members; others are explicit, taking the form of civil and religious laws. The fact that many of us are motivated to marry only one person may not be related to any innate tendencies in that direction, but simply to adherence to a powerful social norm, expressed in the laws of our countries. Indeed, to understand a great deal of human behavior, it is often unnecessary to go beyond a careful examination of prevailing social norms. We can be relatively sure that adherence to these norms will be typical rather than atypical. F. H. Allport (1935) describes this phenomenon as the **conformity curve**, depicted in ideal form in Figure 17.20. In essence, the conformity curve maintains that most people exhibit complete conformity to social norms, with fewer and fewer people exhibiting greater and greater deviance. In short, the individual who fails to stop at a stop sign is rare; the bigamist is even rarer.

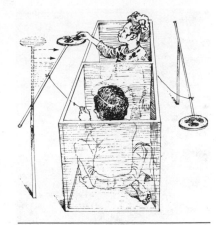

Figure 17.18 The Wolfle and Wolfle (1939) experiment on cooperation. Not until children were old enough to communicate verbally did they cooperate. (From "The Development of Cooperative Behavior in Monkeys and Young Children" by D. L. Wolfle and H. M. Wolfle, *Journal of Genetic Psychology*, 1939, *55*, 137–175. Reprinted by permission.)

Norm Behavior that is usual or expected, acceptable, or socially prescribed. Thus, norms may be explicit, taking the form of rules or laws, or implicit, being implied in the prevailing moral standards of a society.

Conformity curve A phenomenon described by F. H. Allport whereby the majority of individuals within a culture conform to prevailing cultural norms with fewer and fewer individuals manifesting behaviors that deviate from the norm.

Figure 17.19 Helping behavior in children can be fostered by models provided in a variety of social situations.

Sociobiology A relatively new discipline that attempts to apply findings from biology, anthropology, ethology, and other related disciplines to the understanding of social behavior in humans. Essentially, sociobiology looks for biological explanations for social phenomena.

In essence, norms are quasi-compulsory patterns of behavior, attitudes, and opinions that are characteristic of a social group, and that account for the validity of a great many of our stereotypes. We are, in fact, expected to believe and behave in certain ways. Social norms may take a variety of forms. They sometimes encourage (honor thy mother and love thy country); they sometimes discourage (do not lie or steal). They take the form of widely held beliefs and opinions, and are manifested in redundant and predictable forms of dress, speech, and behavior. They are perhaps most obvious in fads and fashions, but are no less important in customs and mores (Box 17.3).

It is not the mere existence of fads, fashions, customs, and mores that is of primary interest to the social psychologist, but the social influence implicit in these manifestations of social norms. It is because we are extremely responsive to mores and customs (less to fads and fashions) that we are identifiable as groups, and that others are identifiable as different groups. Concerned as we are with ourselves and our individualities, we often overlook or minimize the fact that at least part of our public identities reflect the patterns of behavior and beliefs that define the norms of our societies. At the same time, however, we are not infinitely plastic and subject to the whims and logic of fads, fashions, and customs. Our apparent submissiveness to social influences belies our individualities. Not all conform or obey, respond to fads and fashions, or even respect mores when society imposes severe penalties for not doing so. And from an ethical point of view, a strong argument can be mounted in support of the violation of mores that have become immoral and that should be discarded.

One of the great paradoxes of our times is that, although society runs smoothly to the extent that its members adhere to its mores, its hope for the future lies in the possibility of dramatic and fundamental change. How easily can we change? The question may not be entirely frivolous. An emerging and controversial new discipline, sociobiology, suggests that a great many of our social behaviors are genetically based, and thus relatively unchangeable. We conclude this chapter with an examination of sociobiology.

Sociobiology

Sociobiology defines itself as "the systematic study of the biological basis of all social behavior" (Wilson, 1975, p. 4). Its primary focus is on social structures and behavior among nonhuman species, but it extends its concerns from other animal societies to

573

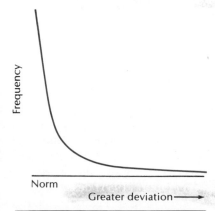

Figure 17.20 F. H. Allport's idealized J-curve of conformity. Most individuals are at, or close to, the norm, with fewer and fewer deviating more and more.

early and even contemporary human societies. Its single most striking and most controversial belief is that human social behavior is genetically based—that it is the result of a lengthy evolutionary process. Chief advocates of this position are Trivers (1971, 1972, 1974), Wilson (1975, 1976), and a growing number of biologists, zoologists, and social scientists (estimated by *Time* magazine at 250 in August 1977). Wilson's (1975) 700-page book, *the* sociobiology text, written over three years of ninety-hour weeks, is a massive compilation of sociobiological research, the bulk of which deals with social groups and mechanisms in nonhuman societies; only one rather tentative chapter deals specifically with humans.

The Theory

There is a fundamental problem in a simplistic interpretation of Darwinian evolutionary theory. Specifically, the conviction that evolutionary forces move the organism toward behaviors that ensure its survival and its consequent reproduction (survival of the fittest) could never explain why some individuals behave in ways that might be termed *altruistic* (that demonstrate affection, kindness, helpfulness, concern, and care for others), when doing so is clearly not to their advantage. Why, for example, does a blackbird noisily signal the approach of a hawk when doing so might mean that it will

---

BOX 17.3

Fads, Fashions, Customs, and Mores

J. Cohen (1970) describes *fads* as "grotesque and bizarre social norms (often termed crazes)" (p. 23). They appear suddenly, last a short while, and disappear. Pet rocks, goldfish-swallowing, phone-booth stuffing, streaking, "knock-knock, who's there?" jokes, marathon dances, and Rubic's Cube are fads. That social fads exert a powerful influence is evident in their rapidly contagious nature. Beards are in, then out; one year, things are cool, the next, neat, the next, far out, and the next, outasight. Rock singing groups come and go; hemlines rise and fall; pants loosen and tighten.

Fads that endure become *fashions*. And one of the most obvious marks of social ineptitude and lack of savoir-faire is to be "old-fashioned" or "out of fashion." Fashions rule in dress, hair styles, music, art, architecture, gardens, and use of leisure time. If the Joneses are doing it, it must be the fashion. The trend setters are to be envied, for they are always in fashion; they have style, and style is good.

Whereas fads and fashions might, when considered in an academic textbook, appear trivial and laughable, *customs* are stable, long-lasting, and highly respected expressions of social norms. It is *customary* to eat with cutlery, to dine after six, to eat soup before dinner and dessert after. It is customary for men to initiate dating behavior (customs do change, although very slowly), for people to present gratuities in expensive restaurants, and for men and women to dress differently. Elsewhere customs are different. Social psychology did not originate the piece of wisdom that one should do as the Romans do when in Rome.

Customs that become fixed, virtually permanent, and morally or legally binding are *mores*. Contemporary mores are expressed in laws and principles that guide behavior, and are enforced by such institutions as governments, churches, schools, and the family. These mores prohibit murder and polygamy, and enforce child support and education; they also lead to the ritual and pomp of group social activities (bands and parades, wedding gowns and funeral robes).

Fads are "grotesque and bizarre social norms (often termed crazes)." Are wheels attached to one's feet grotesque and bizarre?

---

be discovered and eaten (Marler & Hamilton, 1966)? Why do certain species of termites explode themselves as warning signals, thus protecting their colony from predators, but dying in the process (Wilson, 1975)? Why do honeybees sting intruders when doing so means that they will injure themselves fatally (Sakagami & Akahira, 1960)?

Darwin noted a similar problem in his observation that certain social insects such as ants produce a class of sterile insects (workers or drones) who are important to the physical survival of the colony, but who cannot themselves reproduce. In view of this observation, he modified his original thinking and contended that the pressures of natural selection might operate at the level of the family or group rather than at the level of the individual.

Sociobiology has introduced a more general and far-reaching principle to account for the production of nonreproducing but species-important individuals. In essence, this principle maintains that the concept of survival of the fittest is applicable at the molecular level rather than at the level of the individual or the group. It is the DNA molecule, the basis of all life, that is the fundamental unit in evolution. Interpreted in this manner, the struggle for survival may be seen as a cosmic struggle among DNA arrangements to reproduce themselves. Organisms are merely the carriers of DNA: their biological nature is determined by DNA, and their reproduction simply ensures that particular complements of DNA will not become extinct. Thus, it is not the individual who is important in an evolutionary sense, but the group of individuals who carry related genes. It follows, then, that evolutionary pressures would not necessarily favor those behaviors that ensure the survival of the individual, except when survival of the individual is compatible with survival of the group. In Wilson's terms, "the ruling principle [is] the maximum *average* survival and fertility of the group as a whole" (1975, p. 107). The sacrifice of one termite, one bird, or one bee is a small price to pay for the possible survival of an entire colony or flock.

This line of thinking has led to a sociobiological theory of altruism (Hamilton, 1970, 1971, 1972). In this theory, altruism is nothing more complicated than *genetic selfishness*. If an altruistic act increases the probability of reproduction of genes related to those carried by the individual who is altruistic, the interests of the DNA have been served. Thus, if I risk my own life in an attempt to save someone else's, it is because the probability of our both living is greater than that of our both dying, and the net genetic advantage to the species is high. It follows that if my own son were drowning, I would be willing to take a greater risk, since he carries more of my genes than does a stranger. Following this line of reasoning still further leads to the possibility that ethnic pride and racism are genetically rooted: they stem from the greater genetic similarity among individuals of the same ethnic background than among individuals of different races (Figure 17.21).

In similar manner, sociobiological theory suggests genetic explanations for such human social behaviors as aggression, spitefulness, sexual mores, maternal love, and, indeed, virtually the entire range of human social actions.

Some Reactions

A theoretical position that can be interpreted as meaning that social behavior is shaped by genetic rather than by environmental forces will inevitably give rise to strong negative reactions. In particular, many sociologists have reacted negatively (Wade, 1976b). Some interpret sociobiological theory as offering a rationalization for ethnic and racial prejudice, and as an attempt to substantiate the claim that differences among races are genetically determined. In addition, a number of scientists have been dismayed at the speculative theorizing that has stemmed from a handful of unproven and probably untestable assumptions, theorizing that draws its illustrations liberally from zoological and biological research with nonhuman groups, and which then generalizes perhaps too liberally to the human situation.

More specifically, Eckland (1977) argues that Wilson's views are overstated, that he has not succeeded in reducing human social behavior to basic biological urges implicit in DNA structure. But he cautions that the main content of Wilson's book is

Figure 17.21 Can sociobiological theory explain human behaviors like prejudice and altruism?

not concerned with the genetic basis of sexism and racism, topics that have elicited the greatest negative reaction, but is more concerned with altruism.

Mazur (1977) draws attention to the fact that the basic premises of sociobiological theory are really untestable. The theory states, for example, that the concept of *genetic fitness* (maximum average survival) accounts for human social behavior. In other words, if a behavior occurs, it is because that behavior as opposed to another increased the genetic fitness of the individual or of a group of genetically related individuals. How do we know this is so? Because the behavior occurred. Why did the behavior occur? Because it increases genetic fitness. This type of reasoning is not uncommon, but it offers no proof and no means of obtaining proof. As Mazur notes, "If we are to make evolutionary theory testable, then genetic fitness must also be defined in some way that is independent of the behavior it is supposed to explain" (p. 699).

Implications

Wilson (1976) and other sociobiologists have been quick to defend themselves against what have sometimes been emotional attacks premised on the presumed political and racial messages of sociobiology. Although it is true that sociobiology may have underrated the importance of the human brain and of our ability to predict and plan the consequences of our behaviors (*Time,* 1977), Wilson stresses that we are not entirely imprisoned by our genes. We have an inherited range of possibilities, some made more likely than others by pressures of genetic survival. Furthermore, genetic pressures that might have been highly valid in prehistoric times are not nearly so valid in contemporary society. Certainly it would be genetically foolhardy, for example, to reproduce as much as possible, given present environmental constraints.

The long-range implications of sociobiological theory have not yet been clearly interpreted. There are indications that psychology, sociology, anthropology, and other social sciences are drawing increasingly on biology in their varied quests to understand the nature of human behavior and its causes (Campbell, 1975; Dupree, 1975; Platt, 1975; Wade, 1976b). This does not mean that there will be a large-scale acceptance of the notion that social behavior is entirely, or even primarily, explainable in genetic terms. It may mean that the various disciplines that attempt to understand humans will become progressively less reluctant to pool their contributions.

Main Points

1 Social psychology is concerned with human relationships; it examines how groups and individuals influence each other's behavior.

2 Aggression may be defined as intrusive, assertive, or domineering behavior. Instances of mild aggression are common in contemporary societies, and are not only tolerated, but also expected. More severe forms of aggression are less acceptable.

3 Dollard et al.'s model maintains that frustration (being prevented from reaching a goal) inevitably leads to aggression. Berkowitz suggests that frustration leads to anger, which might then be manifested in aggression, depending on the specific situation.

4 An ethological explanation of aggression is that we are by nature aggressive. Instances of unlearned aggressiveness among animals are common; they are less common among humans.

5 Cross-cultural research suggests that aggressive behavior is often learned. Other research indicates that at least some manifestations of aggression are physiologically based. Thus injury or disease affecting certain brain structures, including the amygdala, can sometimes give rise to aggression and even violence.

6 Common forms of aggression include predatory aggression (aggressive behavior directed toward preyed-upon animals, and motivated primarily by hunger); intermale aggression, not uncommon as part of a mating ritual among various animal species; sex-related aggression, sometimes present in nonhuman animals, and evident as well in instances of rape; fear-induced aggression, which is primarily defensive in nature; maternal aggression, directed toward the protection of the young; and irritable aggression, which may well result from frustration, and which is common among humans, but far less common among other animals.

7 Violence in society is reflected in crime, in international aggression, in the home, and on television.

8 There is tentative evidence that viewing violence on television may be associated with aggressive behavior in real life. Three theories are relevant here: the catharsis model suggests that viewing television violence may serve as a release for pent-up aggressive tendencies and thus may serve to lessen manifestations of aggression; the modeling theory suggests that televised violence serves as a model, thus increasing manifestations of aggression; and the catalyst model suggests that television violence serves as an inducement to violence for certain individuals.

9 The bystander effect may be defined as the tendency of individuals, particularly when they are members of groups, not to come to the assistance of those in need. The bystander effect is a manifestation of apathy toward others' misfortunes.

10 The bystander effect may be explained in terms of the individual's failure to recognize the seriousness of the situation; fear of acting foolishly in front of others; or fear of personal danger. In situations where the emergency is clear (unambiguous) and the danger is low, the bystander effect is seldom apparent.

11 An attitude is a prevailing, consistent tendency to react in a given way. It may generally be described as positive or negative, and often serves as a powerful motive for behaving.

12 Stereotypes are widely held opinions concerning identifiable groups—frequently social or racial. Prejudices are more personal judgments (not as widely held).

13 To comply is to accede to the wishes and desires of others; to conform is to change one's attitudes or beliefs as a result of social pressure. It is thus possible to comply with someone's wishes without conforming to their beliefs.

14 Studies of cognitive dissonance (conflict between behavior, beliefs, or attitudes) indicate that we often change our behaviors or our attitudes when faced with dissonance. In situations where individuals are compelled to do or say things contrary to their wishes or beliefs, dissonance may be reduced by changing attitudes; by changing behavior (not complying); through perceptual distortion so that the behavior is no longer recognized as contradicting beliefs; or through attribution change where, for example, an individual might deny responsibility for the behavior in question, arguing that the behavior was compelled.

15 Overjustification research indicates that behaviors that might initially have been undertaken for intrinsic reasons (for example, because we enjoy them) might, if they are rewarded too highly (*overjustified*), subsequently become less attractive. An attribution explanation of overjustification is that such behaviors are initially attributed to intrinsic motives, but that the attribution changes to extrinsic motives (external reward, in other words) if extrinsic rewards are highly apparent.

16 There is little doubt that most individuals are susceptible to group pressure. There are important individual differences in degree of susceptibility, however.

17 In situations where authority is obvious and socially approved, many individuals obey instructions, carrying out acts they would probably not undertake if they were solely responsible for them.

18 Persuasion refers to deliberate attempts to alter people's attitudes or beliefs, and perhaps to change their behaviors as well. Research on the effectiveness of persuasion indicates that the source of persuasion is highly important, as are the persuader's motives. In fact, however, attitudes are highly stable, and cannot always be changed through persuasion.

19 Competition and cooperation appear to be acquired social tendencies that serve as motives for a variety of social behaviors. There are dramatic differences among different cultures with respect to the manifestation of these tendencies.

20 The tendency to conform to norms is an important social motive, which accounts at least in part for the fact that most of us drive on the righthand side of the road. It also accounts for the influence of fads, fashions, customs, and mores.

21 Sociobiological theory is based on the idea that a great deal of social behavior is biologically based and therefore inherited. According to this theory, pressures for survival and procreation of genetic material have led to the selection of individuals with social characteristics that contribute to the welfare of other individuals with related genetic material. Thus sociobiology explains altruism, maternal behaviors, and so on. Sociobiological theory, in its more extreme forms, had met with strong negative reactions.

Further Readings

A general overview of social psychology and a more detailed elaboration of many of the topics covered in this chapter and in the next are found in:

Worchel, S., and Cooper, J. *Understanding social psychology* (2nd ed.). Homewood, Ill.: Dorsey Press, 1979.

Latané and Darley's little book is a classic in the field of bystander apathy, as Lorenz's is in the field of human aggression:

Latané, B., and Darley, J. M. *The unresponsive bystander: Why doesn't he help?* New York: Appleton-Century-Crofts, 1970.

Lorenz, K. *On aggression.* New York: Harcourt Brace Jovanovich, 1966.

A current and detailed analysis of aggression is presented in:

Moyer, K. E. *The psychobiology of aggression.* New York: Harper & Row, 1976.

Milgram presents a collection of his pioneering and controversial studies of extreme obedience in:

Milgram, S. *Obedience to authority.* New York: Harper, 1975.

A very short, highly readable description of social motives is:

Cohen, J. *Secondary motivation: II. Social motives.* Skokie, Ill.: Rand McNally, 1970.

Wilson's massive book on sociobiology is highly interesting. Of particular relevance is the final section, which deals more specifically with human behavior.

Wilson, E. O. *Sociobiology: The new synthesis.* Cambridge, Mass.: Belknap, 1975.

Interpersonal Relationships

Sam has been too occupied to read all of this manuscript, but he has taken the time to read the chapter introductions.

"You have no choice," he said. "No choice whatsoever."

"About what?"

"About the introduction for Chapter 18," he answered. "You have to tell them about the time you fell in love with Celine."

I can't. I choose not to. I do not want to tell you about Celine. It would be meaningless for you and embarrassing for me to describe how I lay awake at night dreaming of that girl, planning our incredibly happy future, and listening to my grandmother snoring. I could not show you our poetry—my poetry. "My soul is sick with sores of misery," I wrote in imperfect iambic pentameter, beginning a heart-rending sonnet expressing my fear that she might not love me, for I had not yet spoken with her. Elsewhere I penned, "Oh sweet, oh love! Oh you, my dove" in a burst of romantic agony. And there were other lines, other poems, too private for me to share. Even with Celine.

I could not bring myself to tell you of the countless clever coincidences I arranged to bring us close enough to each other that I might see her, even if only for a brief instant. It would shame me to admit that I almost failed my French class because she sat in the row two over to the right and three desks forward from where I sat, and I could see her out of the corner of my eye whenever Luke left his seat.

Ah, Celine. She was with me night and day. I could not rid my mind of her. I didn't want to. I was in love. At the age of fifteen and for three whole weeks!

I should have spoken to her.

Attribution in Person Perception

It appears axiomatic that much of our behavior is governed by an apparent need or desire to establish and maintain certain relationships with others. It is equally obvious that we spend a great deal of time and effort trying to decide what other people are like and why they behave as they do. In short, we attribute motives to our behavior and to that of others.

If Paul, whom you might not have met, were ever to take Emily on a date, it is inevitable that she would ask herself why he would want to do so. And an amateur psychologist would not be far wrong in assuming that Emily's judgments would reflect both her impressions of Paul and her impressions of herself. If, for example, she thinks of herself as being highly attractive physically, she might decide that Paul took her out because he is physically attracted to her. If she thinks of herself as being unattractive, she will have to attribute his behavior to some other cause. A wide range of possibilities suggest themselves, a number of them based on what Emily might know of Paul. If she knows he has been having a great deal of difficulty with one of his courses, and she knows as well that he is aware of her competence in that course, she might attribute his behavior to that motive. And if his psychology books lie open on the back seat of the car, her initial judgment might become firmer. Again, our amateur psychologist would not be far wrong in suggesting that the eventual nature of their relationship will to a large extent be determined by the attributions Emily makes concerning Paul's motives. By the same token, Paul will most certainly ask himself why Emily would choose to go out with him. His attribution of motives to Emily will also be based on judgments that he makes of himself and of her.

The Theory

Turning for the moment to a simpler situation, consider the case of Raoul, who, last hunting season, shot his friend Joe in the left buttock with a moderately powered air rifle. Joe sat painfully for some time.

Two distinct attributions of Raoul's behavior immediately suggest themselves: **dispositional** or **situational** (E. E. Jones & Davis, 1965; Shaver, 1975). A dispositional explanation would infer that some internal characteristic (in other words, a disposition) of Raoul's is a correct explanation for his behavior. Thus, we might conclude that Raoul is hostile, envious of Joe, and irresponsible, or that his father's early mistreatment of him warped his good sense and arrested his moral development. A situational explanation would look to some external cause. It might claim, for example, that the air rifle had a defective and unsafe firing mechanism, that the light was bad and Joe was foolishly camouflaged as a small game bird, or that Raoul was jostled by a belligerent and aggressive cow moose as he was innocently turning toward Joe.

How, in fact, do we make attributions of this nature? Jones and Davis (1965), Kelley (1971, 1973), and a number of other social psychologists describe a general model which can be summarized as follows: From an observed action and its subsequent effect, we make inferences about a person's intentions based on assumptions concerning that person's knowledge and ability; and, having inferred intentions, we then infer dispositions. If our assumptions about the actor's knowledge and ability do not allow us to infer intention, then we attribute the actions to situational factors rather than to dispositional factors.

Returning to Raoul and Joe, the action and its effects are the firing of the rifle and Joe's subsequent pain. Assumptions about knowledge or ability would be relevant if we *knew* that Raoul was a crack shot, could not hit the proverbial broad side of a barn, knew that Joe was camouflaged as a small chicken, or did not know that Joe was present. If Raoul had both the knowledge and the ability required for an *intentional* action of the type observed, we would in all likelihood infer intention and attribute his behavior to a disposition that we might label hostile, stupid, aggressive, or what

Dispositional attribution Attributing the cause of someone's action to that person's disposition; assuming the action was internally motivated, and thus intentional.

Situational attribution Attributing the cause of someone's action to elements of the situation; thus, assuming the action was externally motivated, and perhaps unintentional.

have you. If, however, he had neither the ability nor the knowledge to justify an inference of intentionality, we would look to a situational attribution.

Other factors would also be important in determining our attribution. Kelley (1971; 1973; Kelley & Michela, 1980) describes us as being something like naive scientists in our quest to attribute people's actions to internal motives or to the environment. He identifies three factors that might be important in making attributions: distinctiveness, consensus, and consistency.

Distinctiveness refers to whether the behavior observed would be likely to occur in response to all similar situations, or whether it is distinctive to this situation. Would Raoul have fired his rifle at Romulus or Alfred, or is this behavior specific to the presence of Joe? Kelley suggests that if the behavior is highly distinctive (it occurs only for Joe and not for others), our attribution is more likely to be external (situational). That is, we would likely conclude that it is not anything about Raoul, but something in Joe that makes others fire their air rifles at his left buttock, or that it was a simple accident.

Consensus refers to the likelihood that others would behave in the same way in the same situation. If shooting Joe is a high-consensus act (many people have done it or would), we would again be likely to attribute the behavior to external factors (something about Joe and not Raoul).

Consistency refers to the likelihood that the same behavior would occur repeatedly in similar circumstances. Would Raoul shoot Joe at every opportunity? Kelley suggests that high consistency is essential for either an internal or an external attribution. If the behavior occurs only once and would not be likely to occur again, we are then likely to attribute it to accidental sources and make no inferences about either Joe or Raoul.

The hedonic relevance of an action also appears to be a crucial factor in determining the nature of our attributions (E. E. Jones & Davis, 1965). *Hedonic relevance* is the effect of the action on us. A behavior has high hedonic relevance if it is especially pleasing or displeasing. In either of these cases, we are likely to make dispositional attributions. If the behavior can be described as hostile, or alternatively as generous, we are likely to infer that the actor is hostile or generous. Similarly, to the extent that we can infer that the behavior was intended specifically to affect us (is personal— hence Jones and Davis's (1965) term, *personalism*), we are more likely to make dispositional attributions. High hedonic relevance and high personalism both tend to increase the extremity of our dispositional attributions.

Figure 18.1 presents the attribution model schematically.

The Reality

Although our attributions seem to conform to the general model just described, we do not always have sufficient information to arrive at accurate attributions. Knowing simply that Raoul shot Joe, for example, does not tell us very much about Raoul's knowledge or ability; nor does it reveal anything about the distinctiveness of the behavior, whether other people would be likely to engage in the same behavior (consensus), or whether Raoul would do it again if given the opportunity (consistency). And attributing behaviors simply on the basis of their effects on us (personalism and hedonic relevance) may cause us to overlook some important facts. How do we then make an attribution, and will it be correct?

Research suggests that, when observing other people's behavior, we are most likely to make dispositional attributions; when observing our own, in many although not all cases, we are more likely to make situational attributions (J. H. Harvey et al., 1974; E. E. Jones & Nisbet, 1971). This is most often true when the behaviors in question are socially deviant or have undesirable results (Lay et al., 1973) (see Figure 18.2).

Thus, when my cousin stole his father's truck, I attributed my behavior to the fact that I happened to be there and simply went along, compelled by the situation, so to speak. A dispositional attribution—specifically, that I was then really a nefarious

Figure 18.1 A general attribution model of social perception. When we observe a behavior and its effects, we make an attribution based on a variety of factors to the extent that we have information about them. We consider intention, based on our knowledge of the actor; we also consider the distinctiveness of the action, likely consensus, the actor's consistency, the action's relevance to us, and whether it was directed toward us.

A professor discloses an important question (and answer) before a final examination.

Checklist to determine whether cause of action is situational (external) or dispositional (internal)

Situational	Attribution	Dispositional
No. I happened to overhear the professor talking with a colleague.	Actor's knowledge and ability (Could she *intend* to do what she did?)	Yes. She could hardly do it without intention.
Yes. None of my classmates was similarly informed.	Distinctiveness (Does the action occur only in this situation?)	No. She told everyone else she saw.
Yes. People are always eager to help me.	Consensus (Would other people behave in the same way?)	No, not usually.
Not deliberately.	Consistency (Would this actor do the same thing again?)	Probably.
No. I would have passed in any case.	Hedonic relevance (Does it affect me?)	Yes. I passed instead of failing.
No. She was talking to someone else.	Personalism (Was the action directed toward me?)	Yes. There was no one else there.
I gave her flowers just before she told me the answer.	Other knowledge, including prejudices, coercion, stereotypes, and so on.	I bet she's partial to men. I've heard she helps them more.

chicken thief at heart—might have been far more accurate. Indeed, my school chums didn't hesitate in the least to attribute my participation in that small crime to my natural tendencies toward delinquency (to my disposition, in other words). Who is correct? Is the observer (who tends to make more dispositional attributions) more accurate than the actor (who tends to make more situational attributions)? Monson and Snyder (1977) suggest that the actor is generally more accurate in attributing an action to certain causes, principally because no one else has quite as much information about the behavior in question. But, as Kelley and Michela (1980) point out, no experimental research has confirmed this hypothesis. Perhaps I really was a chicken thief.

Value of Attribution Theories

Attribution theories, whether they deal primarily with motivational questions (see Chapter 9), with questions of social perception, or with self-perception, are cognitive explanations for human behavior. They assume that we try to make sense of ourselves, our behavior, and that of others, and that one of the common ways of making sense is to develop strategies for making attributions. Insofar as regularities exist in the ways different people make attributions, research in this area is likely to contribute much to our understanding of ourselves and others.

Attribution theory speaks, as well, to one of the most important aspects of being human: the formation of relationships among individuals. And it is in the study of relationships, particularly those based on attraction, liking, loving, or hating, that a number of other factors important in the attribution process are revealed.

Figure 18.2 This person has had "a few too many." Is the cause situational or dispositional? Our attributions of causality for other people's behaviors tend to be dispositional—for instance, "Jerry always overindulges." For our own actions, though, we are more likely to recognize situational causes: "I've been under too much pressure lately," or "A friend pushed me to have that last drink."

Interpersonal Attraction

Recall our opening discussion of Paul, who is about to go somewhere with Emily. Let us assume that Paul has admired Emily from a distance, thinks he will like her, and wants her to like him. What practical advice can social psychology offer? Actually, quite a lot.

Stereotypes

Each of us responds to others in terms of stereotypes, as we mentioned in Chapter 17, no matter how fair and unprejudiced we might consider ourselves to be. We make very different judgments about people we know to be criminals, psychopaths, television stars, writers, hobos, and cuckoos. In spite of ourselves, we tend to trust lawyers more than their clients; guards more than their prisoners; ministers more than their penitents. In short, we have preconceived notions of the predominant characteristics of individuals in these *groups*. And, not surprisingly, many of our stereotypes are highly valid and extremely useful. Not only do they simplify the decisions and judgments we must make, but they frequently assure that these will be correct. At the same time, however, stereotypes can also be misleading, unfair, and highly inaccurate.

Paul's task with respect to the use of stereotypes is quite simply to present the combination of impressions that Emily is most likely to associate with positive stereotypes. Within limits, and to the extent that Paul understands some of Emily's stereotypes, he can deliberately present himself so as to increase his chances of being liked.

First Impressions

There is considerable folk wisdom concerning the importance of first impressions, much of it summarized succinctly and cleverly in the parental admonition, "Put your best foot forward!" For those with two quite different feet, might it not sometimes be better to save the best foot until later? Science has tried to find out.

Luchins (1957a, 1957b) wrote two separate paragraphs describing daily activities attributed to one Jim. One of these paragraphs described activities that would lead one to suppose Jim to be outgoing and friendly (he spoke with people, walked with friends, talked with a girl he had just met, and so on); the other described similar but less sociable activities (he walked alone, waited with others without speaking, and did not greet a girl he had recently met). In other words, one of the paragraphs described

Jim left the house to get some stationery. He walked out into the sun-filled street with two of his friends, basking in the sun as he walked. Jim entered the stationery store, which was full of people. Jim talked with an acquaintance while he waited to catch the clerk's eye. On his way out, he stopped to chat with a school friend who was just coming into the store. Leaving the store, he walked toward school. On his way he met the girl to whom he had been introduced the night before. They talked for a short while, and then Jim left for school.

After school Jim left the classroom alone. Leaving the school, he started on his long walk home. The street was brilliantly filled with sunshine. Jim walked down the street on the shady side. Coming down the street toward him, he saw the pretty girl whom he had met on the previous evening. Jim crossed the street and entered a candy store. The store was crowded with students, and he noticed a few familiar faces. Jim waited quietly until he caught the counterman's eye and then gave his order. Taking his drink, he sat down at a side table. When he had finished his drink he went home. (Luchins, 1957a, pp. 34–35)

Primacy effect Those impressions that we first form of people may be more important than those we might form later.

Recency effect On occasion information that is obtained last may be judged of more importance than that which is obtained first.

an extrovert (E); the second described an introvert (I). The paragraphs were written so that they could be read consecutively in either order and would still appear to be describing the same person. Thus it was possible to present a description of Jim in the E-I order or in the I-E order, the only difference being that Jim would initially appear to be extroverted or introverted. In this way, science attempted to determine whether first impressions are more important than later impressions. In fact, it appears that first impressions are considerably more important when the paragraphs are read consecutively. This has been termed the **primacy effect**. Paul might be well advised to put his best foot forward.

Further studies with the Luchins paragraphs, however, have also demonstrated the existence of a **recency effect** whereby information presented last can become more important than first impressions (Luchins, 1958). This was done by interrupting subjects after they had read the first paragraph and warning them against being misled by first impressions. It was also accomplished by interrupting subjects and having them engage in some unrelated activity before reading the second paragraph. The implication for Paul would appear to be as follows: If he makes a good impression at the beginning of the evening and a poorer impression later, he may still be perceived in terms of the good impression (primacy effect). If, however, he makes a good impression on a first date and a poor impression on a second date, he is more likely to be perceived in terms of the poor impression (recency effect). It should be noted that more recent studies have not always been able to establish the existence of a recency effect. Early studies that demonstrated this effect have been criticized because of the unreal nature of the experiment: reading a description of someone's activities is different from being with that person. In addition, instructions typically have not asked subjects to form a comprehensive impression of a single individual, taking into consideration both their initial and their final impressions. When subjects are explicitly told that both paragraphs refer to a single person, neither a recency nor a primacy effect is observed. Instead, subjects tend to form a more balanced view of Jim (Leach, 1974) (Figure 18.3). In view of these findings, Paul might be well advised to sit on his not-so-good foot.

Averaging or Adding

Our opinions of others are not determined solely by first or last impressions. In the course of learning about people, we acquire a variety of information, not all of which is compatible with a single, specific description. Yet we manage to form impressions. Social psychologists have been particularly interested in how this is accomplished. In addition to looking at the importance of first and last impressions, they have attempted to explain how a variety of different impressions can become a more or less unitary impression.

Suppose you know one highly positive thing about a person. As a result, you have a very favorable impression of that person. Suppose further that you now discover

Table 18.1 Hypothetical Illustration of Anderson's (1974) "Cognitive Algebra"

Person	Trait/Weighted Value	Value of Impression
A		
1 positive trait	Sociable + 10	+ 10
B		
2 positive traits	Sociable +10	10 + 5 = 15
	Honest +5	15/2 = 7½
C		
1 positive trait	Sociable + 10	10 + (−5) = +5
1 negative trait	Dishonest −5	5/2 = 2½

Note. In arriving at a unitary impression of people, we are more likely to average than to add. The average is, in this case, a *weighted* average. It takes into account the importance of different characteristics, and assigns values to them.

one additional only *slightly* positive thing about that person. Would your impression be more favorable or less? If it was more favorable, we might assume that the effects of these two impressions are *additive;* if, however it was less favorable, we might conclude that the impressions have been *averaged.* Research suggests that the latter is most likely the case (N. H. Anderson, 1974). Our impressions of people are not raised indefinitely by an accumulation of positive information; nor are they lowered additively by negative information (Table 18.1).

It would seem, then, that Emily might retain a more positive impression of Paul if she learns only one or two highly positive things about him rather than a wealth of moderately positive things.

Reputations

Our reputations are not unlike the king's messengers: they go before us and prepare others for our coming. How instrumental are they in determining how others see us? Does what you have heard about somebody affect how you will perceive that person?

Kelley (1950) conducted an experiment in which a large group of students in an economics class were informed at the beginning of a class that their regular lecturer would not be present, but would be replaced by a complete stranger. Students were also told that since the department was interested in how classes react to different instructors, they would be given a short questionnaire to fill out after the class. Following this introduction, a brief biographical sketch of the new instructor was handed out to students. This sketch had ostensibly been written by someone who knew the instructor well. In fact, two different sketches were presented to the students, who had also been told not to talk with each other about the new lecturer. The two biographical sketches differed in only one word. Each contained identical biographical information about the new lecturer, but whereas one described him as "a rather warm person, industrious, critical, practical, and determined," the other described him as "a rather cold person, industrious, critical, practical, and determined." Thus the sketches differed only in the use of the adjective *warm* or *cold.*

The new instructor entered, introduced himself, and after a twenty-minute discussion, left the room. Students then filled out the questionnaire. Their responses revealed clearly that those who had been given the "warm" description considered the instructor more sociable, good-natured, humorous, and considerate than those who had been given the "cold" description. Additional evidence of the positive effect of the "warm" rather than "cold" description is the fact that 56 percent of the group with the "warm" impression actually participated in the twenty-minute discussion, compared with 32 percent of the "cold" group (Figure 18.4). Our grandmothers were not entirely wrong when they insisted that we keep our reputations unsullied. Accordingly, if she wants Paul to like her, Emily might be well advised to have others say nice things to Paul about her or to behave so that this will happen.

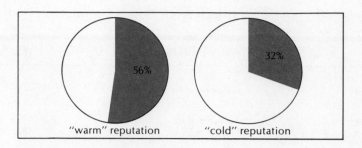

Consistency

Among our most fundamental beliefs about others is that they are *consistent*. Thus, we assume that a generous individual is generous in many situations; that a hostile person is often hostile; that a friendly person is often friendly. In spite of the fact that research on personality (see Chapter 13) has shown human behavior to be variable and unpredictable, it is nevertheless true that people sometimes go to great lengths to project images of themselves that are consistent from one situation to the next. Freedman and Fraser (1966) hired two students to approach suburban home-makers with one of two undemanding and socially positive requests. One involved signing a petition concerning safe driving or keeping California beautiful; the other required that the woman place a small sign in her window relating to the same subject. Several weeks later, a different student approached each woman with a much more demanding request: would she consent to placing a large, unattractive billboard on her lawn? The billboard loudly proclaimed "Drive Safely." Yes, indeed, most who had consented to the rather trivial first request were happy to comply with the second request. In contrast, other homemakers, who had not been asked to comply with a mild, socially desirable request earlier, typically refused to have the billboard erected on their lawns.

Explanation for this behavior, intuitively recognized as valid by any successful door-to-door salesman, is that once the woman had projected an image of herself as being cooperative, helpful, and socially concerned, she had also developed a private image of herself consistent with the public image. Subsequently, her behavior tended to conform with her image of herself (note that this is essentially a cognitive dissonance explanation, as described in Chapter 17).

The tendency to behave consistently, or at least to project a consistent image, has also been observed in a number of studies of racial discrimination. Dutton and Lake (1973) interviewed college students who considered themselves to be racially unprejudiced. In the course of the interview, subjects were connected to a "lie-detector" instrument, and some were led to believe that their responses provided evidence of discrimination. Others were given information consistent with their beliefs that they were unprejudiced. Subsequently, arrangements were made for each subject to be approached by a white or a black panhandler. The experimental prediction is that subjects whose self-images have been contradicted by the "lie-detector test" will go out of their way to show that they are not prejudiced—in short, to maintain a consistent self-image for themselves (rather than for others). This, in fact, was the case, as is shown in Table 18.2.

How might Emily employ this information, assuming that she, like Paul, is interested in being liked? She might, in a subtle way to be sure, *label* Paul, letting him know she thinks he is a warm, caring individual, perhaps on the basis of information that she has allegedly obtained from friends of his. Once this image has been attributed to Paul publicly, the likelihood that he will behave in a warm, caring fashion will presumably increase. Alternatively, should she belong to any group against which the narrow-minded might have baseless prejudices, she might challenge the strength of Paul's broad-minded unprejudiced attitudes. Again, theoretically, it is conceivable that he would then go out of his way to demonstrate that he is in fact unprejudiced.

Table 18.2 Percentage of Subjects Donating and Average Donations to Panhandlers in Each Experimental Condition

Experimental Condition	Self-Image Contradicted		Self-Image Confirmed	
	Percentage Donating	Average Donation (cents)	Percentage Donating	Average Donation (cents)
Black panhandler	85	47.25	45	16.75
White panhandler	50	28.25	65	27.75

Note. Adapted from "Threat of Own Prejudice and Reverse Discrimination in Interracial Situations" by D. G. Dutton and R. A. Lake, *Journal of Personality and Social Psychology*, 1973, *28*, 98.

Ingratiation

Social psychology has conducted extensive studies of the means by which people attempt to obtain approval, friendship, admiration—in other words, to *ingratiate* themselves. E. E. Jones (1964) describes a variety of **ingratiation** tactics. One of them, already discussed, involves the presentation of a favorable image (*self-presentation*). A second tactic, well known and widely practiced, is that of *flattery*. Amazingly, compliments often work even when those receiving them are aware of the flatterer's motives. Although we are sometimes able to attribute dishonest motives to a flatterer, we often appear to be unable to attribute dishonesty to the compliments themselves (she says my eyes are attractive because she wants to seduce me, the witch, but my eyes really are nice). A third tactic, frequently and effectively employed, involves *conformity*. With some obvious exceptions, we are more likely to like those who agree with our opinions and approve of our behaviors, so to be liked we may agree with the opinions of others and let them know we approve of their behaviors. A fourth tactic is rendering *favors*. Unlike bribes, favors do not demand specific reciprocal behaviors (I will pay you to like me). They do, however, increase the probability that the recipient will be positively disposed toward the donor. We tend to like people who do things for us.

Ingratiation Attempts to obtain approval and friendship. A number of ingratiation tactics are widely practiced, including flattery, conformity, and bestowing favors.

Our Public Selves: Real or Role?

If much of this seems to be no more than common sense, do not be alarmed. It's simply that psychology is sometimes capable of being sensible without being surprising.

The advice that has been given to Paul and Emily thus far includes presenting a favorable image by making conscious use of positive stereotypes and by attempting to present a favorable first impression; labeling the partner's attitudes in an effort to evoke behavior consistent with those attitudes; and flattering, agreeing (on important issues, although not necessarily on those more trivial, lest the ploy become too obvious), and rendering favors.

This chapter is now left with an uneasy feeling. There is something distasteful about deliberately manipulating impressions and using ingratiation techniques. There is something about this entire discussion that contravenes our implicit beliefs in our own honesty and openness and in that of our friends. Do we not believe that people like us for what we are, and that we like others, not for what they intentionally do or say to curry our affection, but precisely because they do not intentionally curry favor—because they are real, genuine, warm, sincere people?

Perhaps. But the facts do not always agree with our most profound wishes and beliefs. Although we are not always deliberately insincere, a wealth of research indicates that we often present ourselves insincerely, even if unconsciously. Zanna and Pack (1975) asked female undergraduates to describe themselves to a male partner whom they did not see but about whom they had been given one of two descriptions. In the first case, the partner was described as being physically unattractive, having a close relationship with a woman, and being uninterested in meeting other women. In the second, the partner was described as being tall, physically attractive, unattached, intelligent, and interested in meeting women. When the partner had been described as unattractive and uninterested, subjects described themselves relatively honestly; when he had been described as attractive, they described themselves in much more favorable terms. Furthermore, if the attractive partner was also described as conventional—that is, as believing that women should be emotional, interested in home-making, passive, and so on—subjects tended to describe themselves in traditional terms. When the partner was described as highly liberal—that is, believing that women should be career-oriented, independent, and ambitious—women described themselves as being much more liberated.

Research such as this leaves little doubt that our public presentations of self are significantly affected by the nature of the public to whom we are presenting. And research has not yet been able to separate the genuine from the expedient or the real from the role. We cannot say whether it is good or whether it is bad; like Talleyrand, we can only say that it is.

Characteristics of Likable People

N. H. Anderson (1968) asked one hundred college students to rank 555 different words on a seven-point scale ranging from "least favorable or desirable" to "most favorable or desirable." In this way he arrived at a ranking of 555 specific descriptions of people in terms of the extent to which these descriptions are viewed as being positive or negative (see Table 18.3). Among the highly preferred characteristics are sincerity, honesty, loyalty, and understanding; the least desirable include cruelty, meanness, phoniness, and dishonesty.

Liking people, however, does not appear to be simply a question of determining what a person's characteristics are and then being attracted to those who score highest and repelled by those who score lowest. Who is most likely to be your friend? Folk wisdom is apparently a trifle confused about this important question. We are told that "birds of a feather flock together," the implication clearly being that people who are similar are most likely to associate with one another. But is it not true that "opposites attract," or that "politics makes strange bedfellows"?

Similarly, a related source of wisdom warns young lovers that separation may dampen their affection: "Out of sight, out of mind." Do not fear, young lovers, for is it not true that "absence makes the heart grow fonder"?

"Beauty attracts and ugliness repels," we are told. But "beauty is in the eye of the beholder," is it not?

We will now look at each of these bits of wisdom in an attempt to answer questions relating to the importance of physical attractiveness, similarity, and propinquity (physical proximity).

Attractiveness

Walster et al. (1966) arranged for an elaborate dating experiment at the University of Minnesota. Subjects were 376 men and 376 women who were first in line to purchase tickets for a special "computer dance" held at the beginning of the university term. The dance was described as one where couples would be matched by computer on the basis of interests. Subjects were unaware that the dance had been arranged for experimental purposes, and that the information they provided concerning their expectations of a date, their perceptions of themselves, their popularity, and so on was being employed not for matching but for experimental purposes. After subjects purchased tickets, they were ushered into another room where they filled out questionnaires, and where experimenters surreptitiously assigned them ratings on the basis of their physical attractiveness. Subjects were advised to keep their ticket stubs during the dance, since a drawing for a fifty-dollar prize would be held at intermission. They

Table 18.3 Some Characteristics of Likable and Unlikable People

Likable Characteristics		Unlikable Characteristics	
Rank	Description	Rank	Description
1	Sincere	290	Materialistic
2	Honest	291	Self-satisfied
3	Understanding	292	Rebellious
4	Loyal	293	Eccentric
5	Truthful	294	Opinionated
80	Ethical	551	Dishonest
81	Intellectual	552	Cruel
82	Versatile	553	Mean
83	Capable	554	Phony
84	Courageous	555	Liar

Note. After "Likableness Ratings of 555 Personality-Trait Words" by N. H. Anderson, Journal of Personality and Social Psychology, 1968, 9, 272–279.

Table 18.4 Measures of the Subjects' Desire to Date Their Partners, Arranged According to Physical Attractiveness

	Date's Physical Attractiveness		
	Ugly	Average	Attractive
Percentage of subjects saying they wanted to date partner again			
According to ugly male subjects	.41	.53	.80
According to average male subjects	.30	.50	.78
According to attractive male subjects	.04	.37	.58
According to ugly female subjects	.53	.56	.92
According to average female subjects	.35	.69	.71
According to attractive female subjects	.27	.27	.68

Note. From "Importance of Physical Attractiveness in Dating Behavior" by E. Walster, V. Aronson, O. Abrahams, and L. Rottman, *Journal of Personality and Social Psychology*, 1966, 4, 513. Copyright 1966 by the American Psychological Association. Reprinted by permission.

were also told that they would be provided with an opportunity to evaluate the effectiveness of the computer matching process.

Subjects were divided into three groups on the basis of rated attractiveness: ugly, average, and attractive. They were then matched randomly except that no woman was matched with a partner shorter than she. Of the 376 pairs thus formed, all but 40 actually attended the dance. The majority of those who did not apparently failed to do so for religious reasons. In many of these cases, parents refused to allow their children to date someone of a different religion (most subjects were eighteen years of age).

During the intermission, some two and a half hours after the start of the dance, subjects were asked to fill out an anonymous questionnaire and to turn in their ticket stubs. In fact, ticket stubs identified each subject. The questionnaire dealt with how much they liked their date, how attractive the date was, how comfortable the subject felt, how much the date seemed to like the subject, how similar the subject thought the date was in terms of attitudes and beliefs, how much effort each was putting into making sure that the other had a good time, and whether or not they were likely to date again. Actual frequency of subsequent dating was determined four to six months later by contacting all subjects directly. Some of the results of the study are summarized in Table 18.4. Not particularly surprising, given prevailing cultural values, is the finding that physical attractiveness is of considerable importance in deciding whether continued contact is desired. Note that the more attractive males and females are much less attracted to those classified as "ugly" or "average." Ugly people will, in general, date anybody, although they too would greatly prefer to date those more attractive.

Similarity

Do opposites attract? Some early research suggested that people are attracted to each other on the basis of the dissimilarity of their traits. Thus, perhaps, submissive people are attracted to dominant people. Each can be seen as fulfilling certain needs that the other has. It is not as logical to assume, however, that a highly aggressive individual will be attracted to a highly pacific individual; that an extrovert will naturally gravitate toward an introvert; that liberals and conservatives will love each other; that, to carry the argument to its illogical extreme, the more dissimilar two individuals are, the more they will love each other. Research suggests that the opposite is more often true. Newcomb (1961) provided a house for seventeen male university students so that he could study friendship patterns among them. Not surprisingly, roommates, regardless of similarity of interests and beliefs, tended to be attracted at the beginning. As time passed, however, and students got to know each other better, similarity gradually emerged as the most important factor in determining friendships. A similar study (Griffitt & Veitch, 1974) arranged for thirteen students to live together for ten days under conditions that simulated a fallout shelter. Like Newcomb, they found that the more similar subjects liked each other more with passing time. (See Figure 18.5.)

Figure 18.5 People who are similar in important ways tend to like each other more than those less similar.

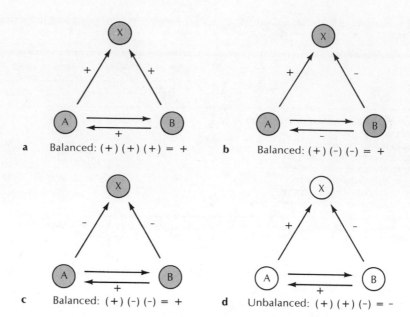

Figure 18.6 The A-B-X model of relationships. The model predicts that there is a tendency to establish relationships that are balanced, or symmetrical. Plus signs indicate attraction (liking); minus signs, the opposite. A relationship is balanced when all signs can be multiplied to yield a positive product. Thus, **a**, where both *A* and *B* like *X* as well as each other, **b**, where *A* likes *X* but not *B*, nor does *B* like *X*, and **c**, where *A* and *B* like each other but neither likes *X*, are all balanced. In **d**, where *A* likes *B* and *X*, and *B* likes *A* but not *X*, the relationship is asymmetrical. According to this theory, asymmetrical relationships would be rare and would not usually last without change.

a   Balanced: (+) (+) (+) = +

b   Balanced: (+) (−) (−) = +

c   Balanced: (+) (−) (−) = +

d   Unbalanced: (+) (+) (−) = −

Numerous other studies of friendship and marriage patterns have established that both friends and spouses tend to be chosen from similar socioeconomic backgrounds and have similar values, interests, and ideals (Byrne, 1971; Hollingshead, 1949).

As a result of these findings, Newcomb (1961) has proposed a *balance* or *symmetry model* of interpersonal attraction, often called the A-B-X model. A simplified version of this model is presented in Figure 18.6. The model looks at attraction from the point of view of individual *A*, who has a relationship with *B*; both also have a relationship with *X*, which might be an object, an event, or a person. The underlying assumption is that individuals tend to establish relationships that are symmetrical or balanced. Symmetry obtains when both individuals (*A* and *B*) share similar feelings about *X* (Figure 18.6a and c), or when *B* has negative feelings about *X* and *A* has negative feelings about *B* (Figure 18.6b). More simply, when the signs that indicate attraction or its opposite (plus or minus) can be multiplied and the result is positive, the system is balanced; when the result is negative, the system is asymmetrical (Figure 18.6d).

The most important finding from this study was that of all the measures employed (intelligence, self-acceptance, extroversion, and a number of other scores in student files based on standardized tests such as the MMPI), physical attractiveness was the only significant variable in determining degree of social attraction. Other research has generally confirmed this finding (for example, Kleck & Rubenstein, 1975). It should be pointed out, however, that studies such as these show only that physical attractiveness is of primary importance at the beginning of a relationship. They do not establish that physical attractiveness will continue to be of primary importance. In fact, as individuals get to know each other at a less superficial level, common sense would suggest that other variables would eventually become more important. Research agrees (Krebs & Adinolfi, 1975).

Several important predictions can be based on this model. If *A* likes *X*, and *B* likes *X*, there will be a tendency for *A* and *B* to like each other (attraction of similars); if *A* likes *X*, and *B* and *A* like each other, there will be a tendency for *B* to like *X*; and if *A* and *B* like each other, and *A* does not like *X*, it is less likely that *B* will like *X*.

In essence, the model postulates that imbalances impose a strain that tends toward balance. If I like you and I also like Sam very much, and you also like me, but you dislike Sam very intensely, the strain may be obvious. Balance theory would predict that you and I will come to like each other less, that you will come to like Sam more, or that I will come to like Sam less. Unfortunately, it cannot predict which of these is most likely to occur.

The research cited earlier with respect to the attraction of opposites is highly compatible with this model. In addition, a long series of studies conducted by Byrne and his associates (for example, Byrne, 1971) has looked at the variables involved in the attraction of similars. The prototypical experiment asks subjects to fill out an attitude inventory, often at the beginning of a university semester, since most of the subjects are college students. Later during the term, subjects are asked to react to people who are described briefly. In this way it is possible to manipulate the amount of similarity between subjects and the people to whom they are reacting. In other words, subjects may be asked to assess their reactions to people who are diametrically opposite them, to people who are very much like them, or to people who are like them in some ways but not in others.

Studies such as these have shown repeatedly that it is not the number of items on which subject and object are similar that is important, but the proportion of items. If a subject is asked to react to an object (person) who is like him or her on six items and different on six, attraction will typically be lower than if the subject and object are alike on three items and dissimilar on none (Byrne & Nelson, 1965).

It has also been found that it is important to be similar on some variables, but that similarity on others is largely irrelevant (Touhey, 1972). It makes little difference whether two people are alike in that they use similar toothpastes and both go to school; that they both believe in reincarnation and sociobiology may be considerably more significant. In general, agreement with respect to opinions, beliefs, and attitudes is important; agreement on more trivial matters is not.

Propinquity

Although attractiveness and similarity are clearly important in determining interpersonal attraction, many apparently lasting relationships cannot easily be explained in these terms. Among other factors that are also important is simple *propinquity,* or physical proximity. In the Newcomb (1961) study, roommates tended to be attracted to each other at the outset of their stay in the house. Similarly, marriage partners tend to come from the same neighborhood, to attend the same colleges, often to have taken the same classes. Note, however, that although these observations have sometimes been interpreted as evidence that simple physical proximity is an important factor in determining friendships, it may well be that proximity results from similar interests and values. It would seem logical to suppose that individuals who live in the same neighborhood, attend the same churches and schools, enroll in the same courses, and go to the same theaters do, in fact, have highly similar interests. And it may be this similarity that attracts them, rather than simple propinquity. Indeed, to say that propinquity is important in determining friendships is perhaps no more revealing than to say that before two people like one another, it is necessary that they meet and know one another. By definition, propinquity is related to the probability that people will meet and discover similar interests.

Criticism, Stupidity, Clumsiness, and Belligerence

So beauty does attract, initially at any rate. Birds of a feather do flock together once they have been given the opportunity to examine one another's plumage. But sadly, absence is not very likely to make the heart grow fonder. Thus it seems folk wisdom is sometimes right, sometimes wrong. As is common sense. It might have seemed common sensical to you that you can attract people by being like them and close to them, and by liking them, being nice to them, and saying nice things about and to them. But winning friends through criticism, stupidity, clumsiness, and belligerence? It doesn't seem possible. Still, science tells us that it happens in certain circumstances.

Science has found, for example, that under certain circumstances, we like those who criticize us better than would-be flatterers. In an ingenious experiment, Aronson

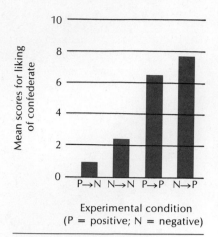

Figure 18.7 Effects of praise and criticism on attraction. We tend to like people who initially criticize and eventually praise us. We do not like those who always criticize and like even less those who praise first and criticize last. (Based on data from Aronson and Linder, 1965.)

and Linder (1965) arranged for subjects to overhear others (confederates) praise or criticize them. Confederates were instructed to make evaluative comments about subjects in accordance with one of four conditions, and over seven experimental sessions. Under the positive-positive condition, the confederate made nothing but flattering statements throughout each of the seven sessions; in the negative-negative condition, the confederate did nothing but criticize the subject; in the other two conditions, the confederate began by criticizing the subject, but flattered the subject in the last half of the sessions (negative-positive), or began by praising the subject during the first three and a half sessions, but criticized the subject during the last three and a half (positive-negative). After these sessions, the experimenter approached the subject and asked what "gut" reactions the subject had to the confederate.

The findings indicated that we like best those people who start out by being critical of us, but who end up apparently liking us; and we like least those people who like us to begin with but who end up critical of us. And although we do like people who like us consistently (positive-positive), we do not like them as well as those who have changed their minds from a negative to a positive position (Figure 18.7).

These findings, perhaps surprising at first glance, have been replicated a number of times (for example, Mettee, 1971). Aronson (1969) suggests that one of the reasons for these results might be that we tend to *believe* people who are initially negative but then become positive. We perceive them as being more critical, more discerning, and therefore value their judgment more highly. Alternatively, it might be that initial negative judgments create tension and dissonance in us, and that subsequent relief of this dissonance when the person becomes positive is highly reinforcing. It may well be that both of these explanations are valid—that our final impressions are a function of the interaction of our "dissonance reduction" and our attribution of greater perceptiveness and sincerity to those who have moved from a critical to a positive position.

But what of stupidity? Cooper (1971) had subjects working in pairs on a number of difficult problems. They were told that they would receive a financial reward only if they *both* did well. In addition, in some experimental conditions, one member of each pair was told that the partner was not expected to do very well, and that they could choose to work with a different partner instead. All subjects agreed to work with the partner initially assigned, even when given this information. And, in a number of cases, the partner did so poorly that, even though the "subject" did very well, they did not earn any reward. In spite of this, subjects liked their partners. In fact, when they had been told that the partner would do poorly, they liked the partner even more when the performance was very poor. Stupidity apparently can earn friendship. Cooper's explanation for this phenomenon is based on cognitive dissonance theory (see Chapter 17). Since subjects had deliberately chosen a partner who was likely to prevent them from obtaining a reward, they might attempt to reduce dissonance by liking the partner very much.

Clumsiness, too, can make people likable, but only if these people seem to be very intelligent, very competent, and not at all the sorts of people from whom you would expect clumsiness. Aronson et al. (1966) had subjects listen to two interviews, one of a highly competent, bright, alert, and intelligent person; the second of a much more mediocre performer. Toward the end of the interview, the interviewee had a clumsy accident. Subjects heard noise, shuffling, and someone saying "I've spilt coffee all over my new suit." Attraction scores for the two interviewees were later obtained. Results indicated that when the superior interviewee spilt his coffee, his attractiveness scores increased dramatically; but when the more ordinary interviewee did the same thing, his attractiveness scores decreased. Thus, clumsiness in a superior person might be endearing; in an ordinary person, it is not. It should also be noted that even without the pratfall, the superior person was seen as being more attractive than the average person, also without a pratfall. In short, clumsiness is endearing only under certain circumstances and only for certain people. Impeccable competence is probably a lot safer if you are interested in "winning friends and influencing people."

Criticism, stupidity, clumsiness, and belligerence. How can belligerence make friends? Again, under very special circumstances. Aronson and Cope (1968) arranged for subjects to overhear someone being highly hostile, obnoxious, and belligerent toward a third person. In situations where the third person had previously been hostile to the subjects themselves, subjects tended to like the belligerent person. As Aronson and Cope put it in the title of their article, "My Enemy's Enemy Is My Friend."

Love

We have now identified some of the variables that are important in determining attraction and, presumably, liking. Many of these same variables are highly important as antecedents of *love*.

Love has long been a subject for poets and novelists, but not for textbooks and science (see Box 18.1). Yet love is a proper subject for social psychology since it is, in effect, a special, severe, and widely prevalent instance of interpersonal attraction,

Table 18.5 Several Items from Rubin's Loving and Liking Scales*

Loving-Scale Items
1. I feel that I can confide in ___ about virtually everything.
2. If I could never be with ___ , I would feel miserable.
3. One of my primary concerns is ___'s welfare.

Liking-Scale Items
1. I think that ___ is unusually well adjusted.
2. I would highly recommend ___ for a responsible job.
3. ___ is the sort of person whom I myself would like to be.

Note. From "Measurement of Romantic Love" by Z. Rubin, *Journal of Personality and Social Psychology,* 1970, *16,* 265–273. Copyright 1970 by the American Psychological Association. Reprinted by permission.

*Each item is answered on a scale from 1 to 9, with 9 indicating highest agreement.

Figure 18.8 Differences between liking and loving are subtle.

not easily defined or measured, and not at all well understood in spite of the fact that many of us spend our lives in love, or alternating between love and the anticipation thereof.

Z. Rubin (1970, 1973) has made serious attempts to measure and investigate romantic love. He has derived two complementary scales: one for liking, and one for loving (Table 18.5). Liking, according to Rubin, is qualitatively different from loving. In other words, loving is not simply more of the same thing as liking; it is something *else*. Liking involves sensing that someone is similar to us, and evaluating that person positively; loving involves affiliation (being close to) and dependence, a more selfless desire to be helpful, and a quality of exclusiveness and absorption. It is perhaps in these last qualities that the differences between loving and liking become most apparent. If you simply like someone, that person does not ordinarily preoccupy your thoughts and dreams; nor are you likely to be concerned about the possibility that others might like the same person. Love, however, brings with it tremendous preoccupation and a sometimes fierce possessiveness—possessiveness in the sense that lovers not only wish for a reciprocation of their feelings, but desire as well that no other person should feel the same way in relation to the object of their love (Figure 18.8).

That Rubin's (1970) liking and loving scales measure different facets of interpersonal attraction is suggested by the fact that those who score high on the love scale are more likely to be contemplating marriage than are those who simply score high on the liking scale. Similarly, love scores are higher for opposite-sexed partners, and lower for same-sexed friends (based on a sample of 158 unmarried couples).

That we can begin to measure love may be a useful first step in a greater understanding of one of the most important of all human emotions and motives.

A Labeling Theory of Love

Rubin (1973) defines love in terms of three components: caring, attachment, and intimacy. These imply, as mentioned earlier, a quality of absorption and selflessness, a desire to be together and to share intimately. But how does one know when it is love? True love? The real thing? Dog love and not puppy love? A romance and not a crush? An *amour* and not an infatuation?

Recall Schachter and Singer's (1962) study, described in Chapter 10, in which subjects reacted emotionally in terms of the *labels* they gave the physiological reactions they experienced. In that study, subjects who were given logical explanations for their emotional reactions (they had been injected with an arousing drug, epinephrine) labeled their arousal appropriately and felt little emotion. Others, who had been misled about their reactions or not told that they would react, tended to label their physiological sensations in terms of appropriate cognitions (labels of euphoria or anger, depending on the experiences they had had).

Walster and Berscheid (1971; Walster, 1971), following Schachter and Singer's labeling theory, have proposed a labeling theory of love. According to this theory, arousal is most likely to be labeled *love* if the circumstances are appropriate. In one intriguing study (Dutton & Aron, 1974), male subjects were interviewed by an attractive female interviewer on a wobbly suspension bridge 230 feet above a canyon. While on the bridge, they were asked to fill out a short questionnaire and to make up a brief story in response to a picture from the thematic apperception test (TAT). A control group crossed the same canyon on a sturdy bridge only ten feet above ground and were interviewed by the same woman. Each subject was given the interviewer's phone number in case they should want further information.

Two findings are striking. Nine of the eighteen subjects on the high suspension bridge later contacted the interviewer; only two of the sixteen on the low bridge did so. Second, subjects in the fear condition (high bridge and high arousal) had significantly more sexual imagery in their TAT stories. The clearest interpretation of these findings is based on a labeling-arousal theory. Although fear associated with being on the bridge should not be directly related to sexual attraction, there is strong evidence that it increased the sexual attraction or, probably more accurately, the sexual arousal of subjects. The same interviewer in nonarousing circumstances apparently did not give rise to the same feelings. Presumably, had there been no female interviewer on the suspension bridge, subjects would have correctly attributed their arousal entirely to the height and precariousness of the bridge and not to sexual inclinations.

The implications of this study are several. First, it points to the importance of labeling in the recognition of emotional states, and, more specifically, in the recognition of love. Given this observation, it is perhaps not surprising that people seem to "fall" in love when they intend to—or at least when they are willing. Without willingness or intention, it is less likely that appropriate labels would be available. A second implication is perhaps more practical. In Romeo's perennial quest for Juliet, or Paul's for Emily, the actors might be well advised to meet in high places. Alternatively, low places might do if they were frightening. Indeed, any place will do if it engenders intense emotional reaction. Perhaps this is one reason why catastrophes bring people together, just as highly stimulating concerts or bingo games might.

Love and Sex

Rubin's love scales do not address themselves specifically to sexual attraction or behavior. A number of recent studies have looked at the relationship between love and sex, however (for example, Hill et al., 1976; Peplau et al., 1977), and have found, among other things, that sexual intercourse and the probability of staying together (for unmarried couples) are largely unrelated. In other words, the probability that a couple will continue to see each other regularly appears to be unaffected by whether or not they have sex together. There are, of course, numerous individual exceptions. A second finding of interest is that sex and love appear to be more closely related for women than for men. That is, among those couples who had engaged in sexual intercourse, more women than men reported increased feelings of love.

As reported in Chapter 9, incidence of premarital sexual intercourse has increased considerably since the beginning of this century. There is strong evidence, as well, that the sexual double standard characteristic of much of our recent history is dissipating. Whereas society once tolerated sexual promiscuity among men (indeed, would not have used the term *promiscuous* with respect to males) and frowned upon similar female activities, it now appears that both men and women can engage in premarital sexual behavior with little disapproval, even if not universal approval, particularly if they are involved in a close personal relationship.

Marriage and Divorce

Attraction to love to marriage: the dream of almost all women and men. Attraction to love to marriage to divorce: a striking reality for a great many.

Divorce rates have risen dramatically during this century (Figure 18.9). R. S. Weiss (1975) reports a 40 percent increase between 1930 and 1960, but that was merely an indication of things to come. During the next ten years, divorce rates climbed another astonishing 70 percent (Glick, 1973). And the trend seems hardly to have slowed, the 1975 Monthly Vital Statistics Report in the United States reporting a 4.5 percent increase from 1973 to 1974. Now somewhere between 40 and 50 percent of all children born since 1970 will spend an average of six years living in a one-parent family (Glick & Norton, 1978). Why?

A wide variety of plausible reasons have been suggested, none of which indicate that people might perhaps like each other less. Indeed, marriage rates would make this seem unlikely. Love is still very much what it was. But laws, religions, social attitudes, and other circumstances are quite different. Laws have made divorces much easier to obtain; religions have softened their traditional hard-line approaches; public attitudes now attach little stigma to divorce; many economic barriers have eroded, particularly with the advent of the economically self-sufficient woman; and new urges

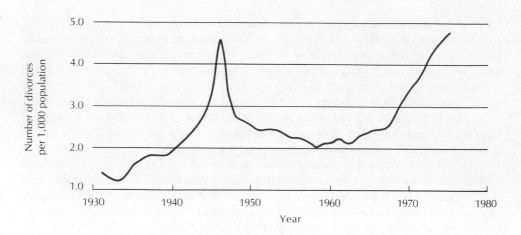

Figure 18.9 Divorce rates (number of divorces per 1,000 population) in the United States from 1930 through 1975. The high rates between 1944 and 1946 reflect family instability in the post-World War II years. Between 1950 and 1966, divorce rates were fairly constant but then began climbing steadily. In 1975, the marriage rate per 1,000 population was 10.0 and the divorce rate was 4.8—almost half the marriages end in divorce. (Based on data from National Center for Health Statistics, Department of Health, Education, and Welfare as cited in *Information Please Almanac Atlas and Yearbook*, 31st ed., Simon and Schuster, 1977.)

toward self-realization, or at least a more open recognition and acceptance of these urges, have impelled more men and women to move out alone in search of themselves (Weiss, 1975). For these reasons, and probably for many other reasons as well, somewhere between 45 and 60 percent of all new marriages eventually terminate in divorce; a large number in addition to these result in separation of indefinite duration.

Accepting that social, religious, and legal changes have made divorce considerably easier does little to provide an understanding of why people want to dissolve their marriages. Weiss (1975) identifies a number of themes that run through divorced people's accounts of their own experiences. In many cases, individuals felt that their marriages were wrong from the very beginning, but having invested considerable time and energy in the relationship, perhaps having produced children, and for many other reasons, continued in unhappy situations sometimes for a relatively long time:

> *It was just a rotten marriage to start with, and it just kept getting worse. But so slowly, over fifteen years, just living in the same house, that you don't realize how yucky it is. I didn't particularly like the way it ended, but I'm glad that it's over. (woman, late thirties; Weiss, 1975, p. 17)*

Differences in values, ambitions, and goals present a second recurring theme:

> *I was trying to find myself, and she wanted to have babies. Well, I did and I didn't. She would have been quite happy with ten children living in a little place. It was a clash of values. (man about thirty; Weiss, 1975, p. 17)*

Other precipitating factors include depression or illness in one of the partners, annoying personality traits usually labeled as defects or at least as annoyers, poor communication between partners, or the discovery of infidelity.

The aftermath of divorce is not easy to predict. It is almost inevitable that the disruption of what was once a highly intimate relationship should lead to considerable social and emotional disruption. But whether individuals will be distressed, relieved and even euphoric, lonely, or satisfied is difficult to predict. Weiss (1975) describes each of these reactions as common, with distress and confusion perhaps most prevalent immediately after separation. The effects of divorce on children have been extensively investigated as well, but here too the results are not clear. Although there is often more evidence of maladjustment and delinquency among children from "broken" homes, deviance in children cannot be attributed solely to the effects of parental separation. In many cases these children have lived in home situations torn by strife, parental arguments, neglect, and sometimes abuse. Indeed, most authorities agree that divorce or separation is better for children than life in a home with warring parents. Whereas divorce counselors (or marriage therapists) were once trained to direct their efforts toward reconciliation, their major emphasis now appears to be geared toward reducing the pain of separation (Framo, 1978).

Attraction, love, marriage, separation, and divorce. Is that the end for the average person who does, in fact, reach that end? The evidence says clearly, no. Nye and Berardo (1973) report that approximately five out of six men who become divorced eventually remarry; the proportion with respect to women is only slightly lower: three out of four divorced women remarry. Nor, of course, are we limited to a single marriage, divorce, and remarriage (Figure 18.10). For an increasing number, the pattern is attraction, love, marriage, separation, divorce, attraction, love, remarriage, separation, divorce, attraction. . . .

Figure 18.10 Despite rising divorce rates, marriage appears to be no less popular than it ever was. The vast majority get married at least once; an increasing number do it more often.

Main Points

1 Much of our behavior is governed by a need to establish and maintain relationships with others. Thus we expend considerable time and effort in attempting to make sense of the behavior of others and of our own. It is important for us to be able to attribute motives and personality characteristics to others.

2 In attributing motives to others, we attempt to determine whether their behavior is intentional or not. Nonintentional behaviors are generally attributed to *situational* factors (to the influence of the immediate situation); behaviors that are intentional are more likely to be attributed to dispositional factors (to personality characteristics, attitudes, and beliefs of the actor).

3 Other factors that are important in making attributions concerning other people's behavior include our knowledge about their ability, how relevant the behavior in question is for us personally, whether its consequences are pleasant or not, and what we know about the behavior of other people in similar circumstances.

4 In general, we are more likely to attribute the behavior of others to dispositions (personal characteristics of the actor); and we are more likely to attribute our own behavior to immediate situations, particularly when the behaviors in question are socially undesirable. There are numerous exceptions to these generalizations, however.

5 Interpersonal attraction is affected by stereotypes (preconceived notions that dispose us toward liking or disliking someone); first impressions, which tend to be more important than later impressions; and our awareness of highly positive or negative qualities in the other person, these being more important than our awareness of a number of qualities that are only moderately positive or negative. In addition, our reputations are important in determining how people will react to us. And even though we tend to behave consistently in different situations (and assume that others do likewise), there are a variety of ingratiation techniques we can use to predispose others toward liking us.

6 The most important factors in determining the establishment of interpersonal relationships include physical attractiveness, which is particularly important in early stages of a relationship; similarity, particularly with respect to areas such as religion, political beliefs, and predominant life-style, and with respect to likes and dislikes (the balance theory); and simple physical proximity.

7 Under special circumstances, if we are first criticized and then praised by someone, we might be more favorably disposed toward them than if they praised us first and criticized us last. Clumsiness, belligerence, and stupidity can also render certain people more endearing under special circumstances.

8 Love is a particularly extreme form of interpersonal attraction which differs from simple liking primarily in terms of absorption, caring, and intimacy.

9 The labeling theory of love is based on the notion that the emotions we feel are labeled according to the context in which we experience them. In other words, we try to provide ourselves with reasonable explanations for our aroused states. In the presence of an attractive person, we might label our emotional reactions "love." In the presence of great danger, we might label a similar emotional response "fear."

10 Sexual intimacy and the probability of staying together do not seem to be highly related for unmarried couples. There is a trend toward permissiveness regarding premarital sex, providing there is affection between the people involved.

11 Divorce rates have risen dramatically in recent decades, due in part to social, religious, and legal changes that have made divorces simpler, easier to obtain, and more socially acceptable.

Further Readings

For this chapter, as for Chapter 17, you are invited to consult Worchel and Cooper's introductory social psychology textbook. It covers the topics of this chapter in some detail:

Worchel, S., and Cooper, J. *Understanding social psychology* (2nd ed.). Homewood, Ill.: Dorsey Press, 1979.

The following two references provide a wealth of interesting information on interpersonal attraction and love. The first is a collection of research papers representative of some of the leading researchers in the area. The second is a stimulating, highly readable paperback concerned specifically with research on attraction and its more practical applications and implications.

Huston, T. L. (Ed.). *Foundations of interpersonal attraction.* New York: Academic Press, 1974.

Rubin, Z. *Liking and loving: An invitation to social psychology.* New York: Holt, Rinehart & Winston, 1973.

Weiss explores the circumstances that lead to marital separation and the possible consequences of separation in:

Weiss, R. S. *Marital separation.* New York: Basic Books, 1975.

Statistics

It is unfortunate that the parts of books that come after the main body are called appendixes, since we have come to associate our own personal appendix with things that not only have no value, but also are sometimes painful. I hasten to assure you that this appendix is both valuable and painless. It describes simple and important statistical concepts in English, illustrates with elementary mathematics, clarifies liberally with examples, and stops some distance short of a complete course in statistics.

What Is It?

Statistics is two things: descriptions, usually numerical; and a body of techniques employed very extensively to make sense of observations. Thus the number 37 might be a *statistic* which describes something specific such as the height of a tall elf, or the average intelligence test scores of a group of five-year-olds. At the same time, the methods by which we arrive at the average intelligence test scores illustrate an important statistical technique. Our primary interest is in statistics as a body of methods for simplifying and making sense of observations.

Statistics, as a collection of techniques, has two clear functions. One is to facilitate description; the other is to make possible intelligent inferences (predictions or logical conclusions). Accordingly, the study of statistics is often divided into two areas: descriptive statistics and inferential statistics. Both are of crucial importance in psychological research.

Descriptive Statistics

I have located a group of children and have a number of measures for each individual: height, weight, intelligence, achievement, motivation, and so on. "How tall are your children?" you ask. And even though it is really none of your concern, I might answer politely: "Winny is 37 inches, Par is 36, Gooh 35, Jes 26. . . ." If I knew the heights of several hundred children, and you had the time and patience to listen to me list each of their heights, you might, in the end, come away with a vague notion of how tall they are. But it would be a vague notion, and my description would be stupidly cumbersome and time-consuming. Statistics suggests a number of obvious ways to simplify my description and to clarify your understanding.

Graphs

Had I been so inclined, I might have drawn a graph of the heights to my ten children and might carry it around with me on a small piece of paper—laminated in plastic, to be sure. It might look like Figure A.1a. If it did, statisticians would call it a

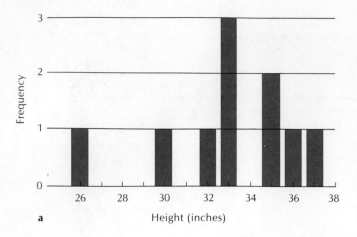

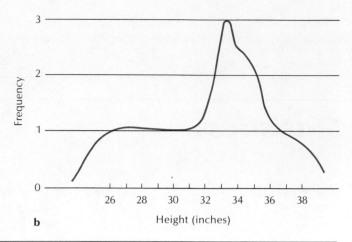

a Height (inches)

b Height (inches)

Figure A.1 (**a**) A histogram. Each bar represents the frequency of individual scores. Thus, one child measured 26 inches, 30, 32, 36, and 37; three measured 33; and two measured 35. (**b**) A frequency polygon representing distribution of height measures in a group of ten children. These distributions are somewhat misleading because they are based on only 10 observations (given in Table A.1). If 200 had been used, the graphs would appear more "normal."

histogram. All I have done is show the frequency of each height score on a graph, where *frequency* is defined as the number of times each score appears. Alternatively, I might join the midpoints of each bar on the histogram and present you with Figure A.1b. Statisticians would refer to this graphic representation as a *frequency polygon.* In essence, it is nothing more than a continuous line that represents within its boundaries the heights of my ten children.

From these graphic portrayals of the physical stature of my subjects, you might arrive at a relatively clear notion of how tall a tall child is, how short a short one is, and what the approximate height of a more ordinary child of this age might be.

Arithmetical Descriptions

I don't have a graph to show you at this time. Nor am I inclined to read you a long list of numbers representing the heights of children. Instead, I would prefer to summarize the information I have. There are a number of simple ways in which I might do this.

Mean First, I might tell you that the *average* height of my children is 33 inches. This arithmetical average is called a *mean.* It is arrived at today in much the same way as it was when you were in elementary school. All relevant scores (numbers, measurements, or what have you) are added, and the total is divided by the number of scores. In the example presented in Figure A.1, the heights of ten children are given. The sum of these heights (330) divided by the number of cases (10) yields the mean (average) of 33 (see Table A.1).

The mean is one of three common measures employed to describe *central tendency* in a group of scores. These measures of central tendency are so called because they are single values that summarize an entire collection of scores by saying something about the *center* points of a distribution. For example, the mean is the point about which the sum of all differences is zero. If you were to subtract the mean from each score and add the differences (some of which would be positive and others negative), the end result would be zero (see Table A.1).

Median A second measure of central tendency, called the *median,* is arrived at by ranking (arranging in order) all scores. It is the point above and below which half the scores fall, respectively. In the example of the heights of ten children, the median

Table A.1 Statistical Description of Heights and IQ Scores

	Height X	X̄	(X-X̄)	(X-X̄)²	Measured IQ Y
Winny	37	33	4	16	130
Par	36	33	3	9	128
Gooh	35	33	2	4	124
Griand	35	33	2	4	124
Elbert	33	33	0	0	124
Prog	33	33	0	0	123
Fret	33	33	0	0	122
Min	32	33	−1	1	122
Ser	30	33	−3	9	120
Jes	26	33	−7	49	102
Sums	330	330	0	92	1,219

$$\text{Mean } (\bar{X}) = \frac{\Sigma \text{(sum) } X}{N \text{ (number of observations)}} = \frac{330}{10} = 33 \qquad \bar{Y} = \frac{1,219}{10} = 121.9$$

Mode $X = 33$ \qquad\qquad Mode $Y = 124$

Median $X = 33$ \qquad\qquad Median $Y = 123.5$

$$\text{SD (standard deviation) } X = \sqrt{\frac{\Sigma(X - \bar{X})^2}{N}} = \sqrt{\frac{92}{10}} = \sqrt{9.2} = 3.03$$

Note: The sum of the differences between the average (mean) and each individual score is zero. One way of defining the mean is in terms of that point in a distribution of scores where the sum of all differences between that point and each individual score is zero.

(midpoint) happens to be identical to the mean: half the scores are above 33 and half are below. In other distributions, however, the mean and median might be quite different. This is the case with respect to the IQ scores of the ten children in question (see Table A.1), where the mean is 121.9 and the median, 123.5 (halfway between 123 and 124).

Mode The third measure of central tendency is nothing more complicated than the most frequently recurring score. Quite often this score will be almost identical to the mean and the median, as it is with respect to the heights of the ten children, where the most frequent score is 33. In other distributions (collections or arrangements of scores) there may be two or more modes (see Figure A.2). There will never be more than a single mean or median for a single distribution.

Mode, Mean, or Median? Each of these measures of central tendency is useful, but sometimes under different circumstances or for different purposes. Each provides a value to describe a collection of scores. Of these the mean is used most often, but it can sometimes mislead. If I tell you, for example, that the average salary in a small factory is $18,800, you might conclude that factory workers are relatively well paid. But if the salary distribution were as depicted in Figure A.3, you would be far more realistically informed if you knew instead that the median salary is only $4,000 (as, incidentally, is the mode). The disadvantage of the mean, dramatically illustrated in this example, is that it is highly sensitive to extreme scores. The supervisor's salary of $150,000 (mom and dad own the factory) inflates the mean. In contrast, both the mode and the median are less affected by extreme scores. In fact, the median often presents a more accurate *description* of a distribution than does the mean, although the mean is more useful for making *inferences*. In some cases, the mode may be most useful. A shoe supplier is not particularly interested in knowing that the average size of shoes sold to men in a one-year period is 8.74 or that the median is 8.50. Knowing that the mode of shoe sizes is 7 or 9 is of far greater importance. In this case, a graph would be even more important.

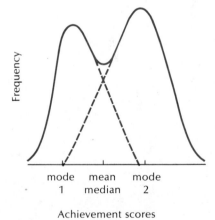

Figure A.2 A bimodal (two-mode) distribution. A class of tenth-grade students was administered a battery (collection) of achievement tests. Because the class consisted in part of students who had been transferred from a school for academically gifted children, but also of more "average" students, achievement scores appear to represent two relatively separate distributions, each with its own mode. Note, however, that there is but one mean and one median.

Figure A.3 The mean, because it is highly sensitive to extreme scores, is not always the best measure of central tendency. In this case, the average salary ($18,800) is far less indicative of the general salary structure than is the mode or median ($4,000). Note that if the single extreme salary is deleted, the average becomes $4,222.22.

Annual salaries (ranked)

$150,000
6,000
5,000
4,000
4,000
4,000
4,000
4,000
3,500
3,500
$188,000 total

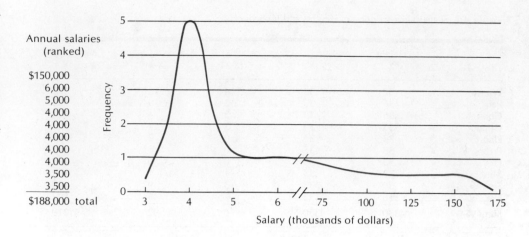

Variation

And so, to be instructive, I tell you that the average height of those children I have measured is exactly 33 inches. Would you like to know more? And can I tell you more (other than the mode and median) without having to list all individual heights? Yes.

I can tell you that the tallest child I measured was 37 inches and the shortest, 26 inches. This would indicate to you that the *range* of height is 11 inches, and you might imagine any of the following:

One 26-inch child, one 37-inch child, and a host of children all very close to 33 inches (Figure A.4a).

A host of 26-inch children, and a flock of 37-inch children (Figure A.4b).

An equal number of children at each height ranging from 26 to 37 inches (Figure A.5a).

A *normal* distribution of children, with the greatest number around 33 inches in height and progressively fewer children in either direction from the mean (Figure A.5b).

A Normal Distribution   Many of the variables with which we are most concerned are distributed in predictable fashion, conforming to a mathematical abstraction known as the *normal curve* (or as a normal distribution). This distribution, when represented graphically, is bell-shaped. In its ideal form, it has certain highly important character-

Figure A.4 (**a**) One 26-inch-child, one 37-inch-child, and a host of 33-inch-children. (**b**) A host of 26-inch-children and a flock of 37-inch-children.

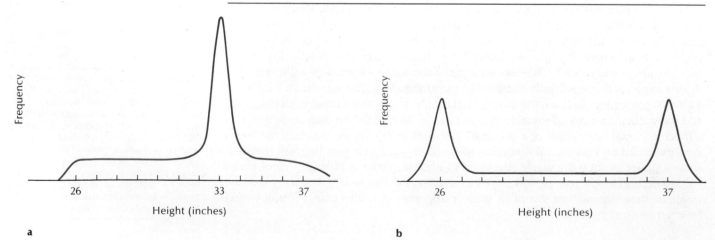

a

b

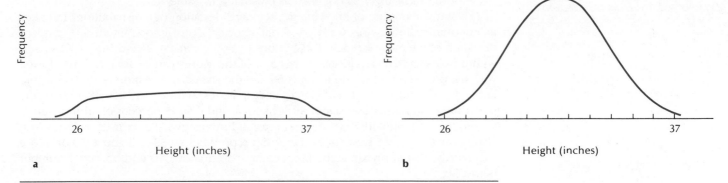

Figure A.5 (**a**) An equal number of children at each height, ranging from 26 to 37 inches. (**b**) A normal distribution of children.

istics (see Figure A.6). For example, in a normal distribution, the mean, mode, and median all fall at the same point. In addition, the majority of the scores are clustered around these measures of central tendency, with progressively fewer scores at either extreme.

Standard Deviation

Only two descriptive statistics are essential for representing a distribution that can be assumed to be normal. The first is the mean, which tells us where the midpoint of the distribution will be. The second is a measure of variation which will indicate how scores are distributed around this mean. The one measure of variation that we have mentioned thus far, the *range*, is the "spread" of scores; it is simply the difference between the highest score and the lowest. Since the range takes into consideration only the lowest and the highest scores, in most instances it says very little about how other scores might be distributed. What is needed, instead, is a measure that takes into account every individual score. This measure is provided by the *standard deviation*.

The standard deviation of a distribution of scores is obtained by taking the difference of every score from the mean of the distribution. This provides an indication of spread (or dispersion). Recall, however, that the sum of these differences is always zero. For this reason, the differences are squared (to eliminate the minus signs), summed, and averaged. The square root of the result is the standard deviation. The process is vastly more simple than it might sound. Mathematically, it is expressed as follows (where Σ is the sum and $\overline{X}$ is the mean of a distribution of scores labeled X; SD is the standard deviation; and N is the total number of observations):

$$SD = \sqrt{\frac{\Sigma(X - \overline{X})^2}{N}}$$

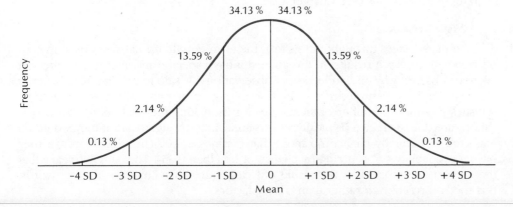

Figure A.6 A normal distribution. Note that approximately two-thirds of all observations fall within one standard deviation from the mean (actually 68.26 percent), and 95 percent fall within two standard deviations (actually 95.44 percent).

More practically, it is obtained as illustrated in Table A.1.

What is the value of knowing the standard deviation of a distribution? In effect, its importance lies in what we know about a normal distribution. Within one standard deviation of the mean in such distributions lie approximately two-thirds of all scores; within two standard deviations, 95 percent of the scores can be found. Thus, if I tell you that on a certain test the mean is 50 and the standard deviation is 10, you would know that two-thirds of all individuals taking the test scored between 40 and 60 (the mean plus and minus one standard deviation), and that 95 percent of all individuals scored between 30 and 70 (the mean plus and minus two standard deviations). You also know that only 5 percent of the group scored below 30 and above 70 or, more specifically, that approximately 2.5 percent scored above 70 and an equal number below 30.

You wanted to know how tall my children were? Had you been as sophisticated then as you are now, I need only have said: "Height among these children appears to be normally distributed with a mean of 33 and a standard deviation of 3.03."

Inferential Statistics

Psychological research does more than gather observations and summarize these so that they might be more easily described. Very often it is called upon to make inferences about groups for whom there are no direct observations, or to answer important questions concerning differences among groups.

Let us assume that you and I are interested in the heights of Saskatchewan elves. More specifically, we want to know the mean and standard deviation for height for the entire *population* of Saskatchewan elves (in much the same way as we might want to know the mean and standard deviation of intelligence test scores of Saskatchewan's fourth-grade population). The term *population* refers to the entire collection of observations in which we are interested. In most cases, however, researchers do not have access to entire populations; even when they do have access to them, obtaining the required measurements for every specific individual is practically and economically impossible. In such cases, a *sample* of relevant observations is selected and inferences about the entire *population* are made on the basis of this sample. As noted in Chapter 1, the validity of these inferences is to a large extent a function of the representativeness of the sample. If our sample of ten elves were chosen entirely from the northern part of the territory, where elves typically do not grow very tall, our sample would be highly biased and any inferences we might make about the entire population would probably be misleading. However, if the sample is representative, we can reasonably infer that the average height of the sample and the nature of the observed distribution will be very close to those which would be obtained employing the entire population. It is for this reason that researchers can sometimes generalize the results of their studies to populations far larger than the samples actually employed in the studies. Indeed, in most cases, research is far more interested in populations than in the samples drawn from these populations (see Chapter 1).

Significance

In many places throughout this text, the term *significant* has been used in connection with research results. In this context it has a specific and special meaning. An event or observation (or a collection of observations) is said to be significant when it can reasonably be assumed not to be due to chance or random factors. Inferential statistics provides a number of techniques for estimating the probability that observations are due to chance. Typically, events are said to be significant if they would be expected to occur by chance no more than 5 times in 100 (in other words, if they have a probability of occurring by chance of less than 0.05). This simply means that these events are most likely the results of factors other than chance—in other words, that they represent *real* rather than chance factors.

Consider, for example, the problem of determining whether an experimental group is different from a control group after treatment as a result of *real* factors in the experimental situation. Assume that the means of both groups are, in fact, mathematically different. Can you conclude immediately that the groups are different because the experimental treatment was effective? Perhaps not. It is conceivable that the observed difference between the means is due to chance factors. If the difference between the means is very small, or if the samples are themselves small, the likelihood of obtaining a difference by chance is considerably greater than if the samples are very large or if the difference is very large. We know intuitively that the mean intelligence test scores of 20 samples consisting of only 5 individuals each, may vary a great deal *by chance*. By the same token, the mean scores of 20 samples consisting of 2,000 individuals each, will be much more similar. A number of statistical techniques widely used in inferential statistics permit researchers to infer the distribution characteristics (mean and standard deviation, for example) of differences between means. Once this has been done, it is a simple matter to determine whether obtained differences would occur more or less than 5 times in 100 *by chance*. Differences that would be expected to occur less than 5 percent of the time by chance would be deemed to be significant—that is, to represent *real* differences between groups.

In much the same way, inferential statistics provides methods for describing expected distributions with respect to measures of relationship (correlation, described in Chapter 1). Expected distributions are those that theoretically would obtain *if* observations were the result of chance factors. Whenever there is a dramatic departure from what would be expected by chance (a less than 5 percent probability of the observation having occurred solely as a result of chance factors), researchers make the inference that other factors are involved. Thus, a relationship between the two sets of observations (intelligence and achievement, for example) is said to be significant if it would be expected only rarely *by chance*.

Testing a Hypothesis by Inference

Loosely defined, the scientific method may be seen as a collection of attitudes and procedures that allow scientists to investigate phenomena in an objective way, and that increase the probability that conclusions based on these investigations will be valid. Statistical inference techniques are an intrinsic part of the scientific method. Also important are *hypotheses:* statements about relationships among variables that can be true or false and whose probability of being true or false can be estimated through statistical methods.

Suppose, by way of illustration, that you have volunteered to participate in research apparently designed to examine the hypothesis that both men and women are more likely to be dishonest when being interviewed by members of the opposite sex. You, and all other subjects, are told that you will be interviewed on six different occasions, and that the interviewers will be randomly selected from a pool of potential interviewers consisting of equal numbers of men and women. Thus, each interviewee would have an equal chance of being interviewed either by a man or by a woman on any given occasion.

Happy to be of service in the cause of science, you appear punctually for each of the six interviews. Being both rational and intelligent, you are not at all surprised when the first interviewer is male or when the second is also male. When the third is again male, you begin to wonder whether the interviewers are indeed being selected randomly; and when the fourth, fifth, and sixth are also male, you might conclude that the experimenters have deliberately chosen to have you interviewed only by men, in spite of their claims to the contrary. At this point you can make use of some simple methods of statistical inference to determine whether you are justified in your suspicions.

Your hypothesis at this point might be worded as follows: "The fact that I was interviewed by six males in a row is due to chance." The alternative hypothesis, one which would be accepted as most likely to be true if the first were rejected, might be

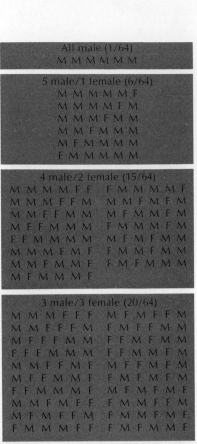

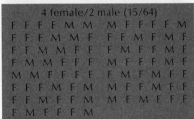

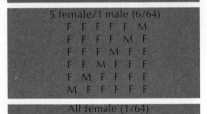

Figure A.7 The 64 possibilities, together with their *chance* probabilities, of being interviewed either by a man or a woman on six different occasions when the probability of being interviewed by either on a given occasion is equal and unaffected by what happens on other occasions. The probability that a coin tossed six times will come up heads or tails each of the six times is theoretically the same as the probability that the interviewers will be either all men or all women. The probability that six coins tossed at the same time will all be heads or tails is also the same.

stated in this way: "The fact that I was interviewed by six males is not due to chance" (that is, it was accomplished deliberately).

The general model of statistical inference now requires that you arrive at an estimate of the *chance* probabilities of each possibility. In this case the estimates can be arrived at quite simply since, if *chance is the determining factor,* the probability of being interviewed by a man or a woman should be equal on each occasion (that is, 1 out of 2). Indeed, the entire procedure should be much like that of flipping a fair coin which, over a large number of flips, will come out heads and tails approximately equally often. With respect to the interviews, therefore, the most likely event is that you will be interviewed by three women and by three men, although it is, as you now know, quite possible that you will be interviewed by five of one and one of the other, or by six of one. Your task is simply to determine the likelihood of this last possibility. This can be done mathematically as follows: on the occasion of each interview, the probability of being interviewed by a male is ½; since each of the interviews is an independent event (the probability of being interviewed by a man or a woman is unaffected by what happened on the previous occasion), the probability of being interviewed by a man six times in a row is $\frac{1}{2} \times \frac{1}{2} \times \frac{1}{2} \times \frac{1}{2} \times \frac{1}{2} \times \frac{1}{2} = 1/64$ or 0.016. Another way of arriving at the same estimate is to compute all possibilities as in Figure A.7. Note that there are sixty-four possible combinations, only one of which is all men (and one of which is all women).

After doing this exercise, you know that being interviewed by six persons of the same sex under these circumstances is rare under the influence of chance alone. Indeed, you might reasonably expect that only one out of every sixty-four people being interviewed (on the average) will have been examined by men only, and one out of sixty-four, by women only. You are now in a position to reject your first hypothesis. Being interviewed by six men in a row is *significantly* different from what might be expected by chance more than 5 percent of the time.

But you might be wrong. Statistical manipulations do not guarantee truth, although they do make it more probable. It is important to keep in mind that research in the social sciences, as elsewhere, is subject to two types of error: that of accepting a hypothesis which is false, and that of rejecting one that is true. Wise use of statistical inference minimizes these errors but does not eliminate them.

Main Points

1 A statistic is a numerical description. Statistics is a body of techniques for simplifying observations and making sense of them.

2 Statistics has two functions: description and inference.

3 Quantified observations may be described in terms of distributions (patterns of observations). These may be graphed, or may be summarized by means of indexes of central tendency or of variability.

4 Common indexes of central tendency are the mean (arithmetical average), the mode (most frequently recurring score), and the median (the point above and below which half the observations fall, respectively).

5 Variability may be indicated in terms of range (the difference between high and low scores), or more often in terms of standard deviation.

6 The standard deviation takes into account the "distance" of each score from the mean of the distribution, and is computed by squaring these differences, summing the squares, averaging them, and taking the square root of the average.

7 For events that conform to the mathematical abstraction known as the normal curve (or the normal distribution), the standard deviation is useful as an indicator of the way in which scores are distributed around the mean. Approximately two-thirds of all scores are within one standard deviation of the mean; 95 percent fall within two standard deviations on either side of the mean.

8 Statistical inference procedures enable researchers to make inferences about populations on the basis of descriptions of samples, and to answer important questions concerning the significance of observed differences and relationships among observations.

9 A sample is a collection of observations derived from a totality of potential observations, and representative of that totality. The totality is referred to as a *population*. Inferences are generally intended for populations rather than for samples.

10 Observations (differences, relationships) are deemed to be significant (not due to chance) when their probability of occurrence *by chance* is less than 0.05 (5 times in 100). On occasion, observations will be accepted as being significant even when they could have occurred by chance more than 5 percent of the time (or less). In either case, there is always the possibility of making an error.

Further Readings

The following are four relatively simple introductions to statistics. Each is directed primarily toward the application of statistics in psychology, and each is far more detailed and comprehensive than this appendix.

Jaccard, J. *Statistics for the behavioral sciences.* Belmont, Calif.: Wadsworth, 1983.

Johnson, R. *Elementary statistics.* North Scituate, Mass.: Duxbury, 1976.

Mendenhall, W., McClave, J. T., and Ramey, M. *Statistics for psychology* (2nd ed.). North Scituate, Mass.: Duxbury, 1977.

Dinham, S. M. *Exploring statistics: An introduction for psychology and education.* Monterey, Calif.: Brooks/Cole, 1976.

Abse, D. W. *Hysteria and related mental disorders.* Baltimore: Williams & Wilkins, 1966.

Adams, R. D. The anatomy of memory mechanisms in the human brain. In B. A. Talland & N. C. Laugh (Eds.), *The pathology of memory.* New York: Academic Press, 1969.

Agnew, N. M., & Pyke, S. W. *The science game: An introduction to research in the behavioral sciences* (3rd ed.).Englewood Cliffs, N.J.: Prentice-Hall, 1982.

Ahlstrom, W. A. & Havighurst, R. J. *400 Losers.* San Francisco: Jossey-Bass, 1971.

Ahsen, A. *Psych eye: Self-analytic consciousness.* New York: Brandon House, 1977. (a)

Ahsen, A. Eidetics: An overview. *Journal of Mental Imagery,* 1977, *1,* 5–38. (b)

Ainsworth, M. D. *Infancy in Uganda.* Baltimore: Johns Hopkins Press, 1967.

Alden, L. Preventive strategies in the treatment of alcohol abuse: A review and a proposal. In Davidson, P. O., & Davidson, S. M. (Eds.), *Behavioral medicine: Changing health lifestyles.* New York: Brunner/Mazel, 1980, 256–278.

Aleksandrowicz, M. K. The little prince: Psychotherapy of a boy with borderline personality structure. *International Journal of Psychoanalytic Psychotherapy,* 1975, *4,* 410–425.

Alexander, G. LSD: Injections early in pregnancy produce abnormalities in offspring of rats. *Science,* 1967, *157,* 459–460.

Allport, F. H. The J-curve hypothesis of conforming behavior. *Journal of Social Psychology,* 1935, *5,* 141–183.

Allport, G. W. Eidetic imagery. *British Journal of Psychology,* 1924, *15,* 99–120.

Allport, G. W. *Personality: A psychological interpretation.* New York: Holt, 1937.

Allport, G. W. The historical background of modern social psychology. In G. Lindzey & E. Aronson (Eds.), *Handbook of social psychology* (Vol. 1) (2nd ed.). Cambridge, Mass.: Addison-Wesley, 1968.

Allport, G. W., & Odbert, H. S. Trait names: A psycholexical study. *Psychological Monographs,* 1936, *47,* 2–11.

Altus, W. D. Birth order and academic primogeniture. *Journal of Personality and Social Psychology,* 1965, *2,* 872–876.

American Psychiatric Association. *Diagnostic and statistical manual of mental disorders* (2nd ed.) (DSM II). Washington, D.C.: American Psychiatric Association, 1968.

American Psychiatric Association. *Diagnostic and statistical manual of mental disorders* (3rd ed.) (DSM III). Washington, D.C.: American Psychiatric Association, 1980.

American Psychological Association. Guidelines for psychologists conducting growth groups. *American Psychologist,* 1973, *28,* 933.

American Psychological Association. *A career in psychology.* Washington, D.C.: PA, 1975.

Ames, R. Physical maturing among boys as related to adult social behavior: A longitudinal study. *California Journal of Educational Research,* 1957, *8,* 69–75.

Amoore, J. E., Johnston, J. W., Jr., & Rubin, M. The stereochemical theory of odor. *Scientific American,* 1964, *210,* 42–49.

Anand, B. K., & Chhina, G. S. Investigations on yogis claiming to stop their heart beats. *Indian Journal of Medical Research,* 1961, *49,* 90–94.

Anand, B. K., Chhina, G. S., & Singh, B. Some aspects of electroencephalographic studies in yogis. *Electroencephalography and Clinical Neurophysiology,* 1961, *13,* 452–456.

Anastasi, A. Heredity environment and the question "how?" *Psychological Review,* 1958, *65,* 197–208.

Anderson, H. H. (Ed.). *Creativity and its cultivation.* New York: Harper, 1959.

Anderson, N. H. Likableness ratings of 555 personality-trait words. *Journal of Personality and Social Psychology,* 1968, *9,* 272–279.

Anderson, N. H. Cognitive algebra: Integration theory applied to social attribution. In L. Berkowitz (Ed.), *Advances in Experimental Social Psychology,* 1974, 7.

Angelino, H., Dollins, J., & Mech, E. V. Trends in the "fears and worries" of school children as related to socio-economic status and age. *Journal of Genetic Psychology,* 1956, *89,* 263–276.

Angers, W. P. Adlerian psychotherapy with schizophrenics. *Journal of Clinical Psychology,* 1975, *31,* 121–126.

Ansbacher, H. L., & Ansbacher, R. R. (Eds.). *The individual psychology of Alfred Adler: A systematic presentation in selections from his writings.* New York: Basic Books, 1973.

Apkom, A., Apkom, K., & Davies, M. Prior sexual behavior of teenagers attending rap sessions for the first time. *Family Planning Perspectives,* 1976, *8,* 203–206.

Ardrey, R. *The territorial imperative.* New York: Atheneum, 1966.

Arieti, S. Manic depressive psychosis. In S. Arieti (Ed.), *American handbook of psychiatry.* New York: Basic Books, 1959.

Aronfreed, J. *Conduct and conscience.* New York: Academic Press, 1968.

Aronson, E. Some antecedents of interpersonal attraction. In W. J. Arnold & D. Levine (Eds.), *Nebraska Symposium on Motivation* (Vol. 17). Lincoln: University of Nebraska Press, 1969.

Aronson, E., & Cope, V. My enemy's enemy is my friend. *Journal of Personality and Social Psychology,* 1968, *8,* 8–12.

Aronson, E., & Linder, D. E. Gain and loss of esteem as determinants of interpersonal attractiveness. *Journal of Experimental Social Psychology,* 1965, *1,* 156–171.

Aronson, E., Willerman, B., & Floyd, J. The effect of a pratfall on increasing interpersonal attractiveness. *Psychonomic Science,* 1966, *4,* 227–228.

Asch, S. E. Forming impressions on personality. *Journal of Abnormal and Social Psychology,* 1946, *41,* 258–290.

Asch, S. E. Opinions and social pressure. *Scientific American,* 1955, 193.

Aserinsky, E., & Kleitman, N. Regularly occurring periods of eye mobility and concomitant phenomena during sleep. *Science,* 1953, *118,* 273–274.

Athanasiou, R. A review of public attitudes on sexual issues. In J. Zubin & J. Money (Eds.), *Contemporary sexual behavior: Critical issues in the 1970's.* Baltimore: Johns Hopkins University Press, 1973.

Atkinson, J. W. *An introduction to motivation.* Princeton, N.J.: Van Nostrand Reinhold, 1964.

Atkinson, R. C., & Shiffrin, R. M. Human memory: A proposed system and its control processes. In K. Spence & J. Spence (Eds.), *The psychology of learning and motivation: Advances in research and theory* (Vol. 2). New York: Academic Press, 1968.

Ausubel, D. P. *The psychology of meaningful verbal learning.* New York: Grune & Stratton, 1963.

Ausubel, D. P., & Robinson, R. G. *School learning: An introduction to educational psychology.* New York: Holt, Rinehart & Winston, 1969.

Ayllon, T., & Michael, J. The psychiatric nurse as a behavioral engineer. *Journal of Experimental Analysis of Behavior,* 1959, *2,* 323–334.

Babrick, H. P., Babrick, P. O., & Wittlinger, R. P. Fifty years of memory for names and faces: A cross-sectional approach. *Journal of Experimental Psychology,* 1975, *104,* 54–75.

Baddeley, A. D. *The psychology of memory.* New York: Basic Books, 1976.

Bagby, J. A cross-cultural study of perceptual predominance in binocular rivalry. *Journal of Abnormal and Social Psychology,* 1957, *54,* 331–338.

Bakan, D. *Slaughter of the innocents.* Toronto, Ont.: CBC Learning Systems, 1971.

Balkhasov, I. Rapid teaching of a foreign language by lessons heard during sleep. In S. Rubin (Ed.), *Current research in hypnopaedia.* New York: American Elsevier, 1968.

Ball, J. C., Ross, A., & Simpson, A. Incidence and estimated prevalence of recorded delinquency in a metropolitan area. *American Sociological Review,* 1964, *29,* 90–93.

Baltes, P. B., Reese, H. W., & Lipsitt, L. P. Life-span developmental psychology. *Annual Review of Psychology,* 1980, *31,* 65–110.

Baltes, P. B., & Schaie, K. W. Aging and IQ: The myth of the twilight years. *Psychology Today,* March 1974, pp. 35–38; 40.

Baltes, P. B., & Schaie, K. W. On the plasticity of intelligence in adulthood and old age: Where Horn and Donaldson fail. *American Psychologist,* 1976, *31,* 720–725.

Bandura, A. *Psychological modeling: Conflicting theories.* Chicago: Aldine, 1971.

Bandura, A. *Aggression: A social learning analysis.* Englewood Cliffs, N.J.: Prentice-Hall, 1973.

Bandura, A., Ross, D., & Ross, S. A. Vicarious reinforcement and imitative learning. *Journal of Abnormal and Social Psychology,* 1963, *67,* 601–607.

Bandura, A., & Walters, R. *Adolescent aggression.* New York: Ronald Press, 1959.

Bandura, A., & Walters, R. *Social learning and personality development.* New York: Holt, Rinehart & Winston, 1963.

Barahal, H. S. 1,000 prefrontal lobotomies: Five to ten year followup study. *Psychiatric Quarterly,* 1958, *32,* 653–678.

Baratz, J. C. A bi-dialectical task for determining language proficiency in economically disadvantaged Negro children. *Child Development,* 1969, *40,* 889–901.

Barber, T. X. *Hypnosis: A scientific approach.* New York: Van Nostrand Reinhold, 1969.

Barber, T. X., & Silver, M. J. Fact, fiction, and the experimenter bias effect. *Psychological Bulletin Monographs Supplement,* 1969–1970, pp. 1–29.

Bard, P., & Mountcastle, V. B. Some forebrain mechanisms involved in the expression of rage, with special reference to suppression of angry behavior. In J. F. Fulton (Ed.), *The Frontal Lobes.* Baltimore: Williams & Wilkins, 1948.

Bardwick, J. N. *Readings on the psychology of women.* New York: Harper & Row, 1972.

Barnett, S. A. *Instinct and intelligence: Behavior of animals and man,* Englewood Cliffs, N.J.: Prentice-Hall, 1967.

Barnett, S. A. On the hazards of analogies. In M. F. A. Montagu (Ed.), *Man and aggression* (2nd ed.). New York: Oxford University Press, 1973.

Barron, F., & Harrington, D. M. Creativity, intelligence, and personality. *Annual Review of Psychology,* 1981, *32,* 439–476.

Bartlett, F. C. *Remembering: A study in experimental and social psychology.* New York: Cambridge University Press, 1932.

Bartley, S. H. *Principles of perception.* (2nd ed.). New York: Harper & Row, 1969.

Bartley, S. H. *Perception in everyday life.* New York: Harper & Row, 1972.

Bartoshuk, L. M., Lee, C. H., & Scarpellino, R. Sweet taste of water induced by artichoke (*Cynara scolymus*). *Science,* 1972, *178,* 988–989.

Basser, L. S. Hemiplegia of early onset and the faculty of speech with special reference to the effects of hemispherectomy. *Brain,* 1962, *85,* 427.

Bassuk, E. L., & Gerson, S. Deinstitutionalization and mental health services. *Scientific American,* 1978, *238,* 46–53.

Bayer, A. E. Birth order and college attendance. *Journal of Marriage and the Family,* 1966, *28,* 480–484.

Beach, F. A. Behavioral endocrinology: An emerging discipline. *American Scientist,* 1975, *63,* 178–187.

Beck, A. T. *Cognitive therapy and the emotional disorders.* New York: International Universities Press, 1976.

Becker, F. D. Study of spatial markers. *Journal of Personality and Social Psychology,* 1973, *26,* 439–445.

Bedichek, R. *A sense of smell.* New York: Doubleday, 1960.

Békésy, G. von. Current status of theories of hearing. *Science,* 1956, *123,* 779–783.

Békésy, G. von. Auditory backward inhibition in concert halls. *Science,* 1971, *171,* 529–536.

Belkin, G. S. *Contemporary psychotherapies.* Chicago: Rand McNally, 1980.

Bell, R. R. *Premarital sex in a changing society.* Englewood Cliffs, N.J.: Prentice-Hall, 1966.

Bem, D. J. Constructing cross-situational consistencies in behavior: Some thoughts on Alker's critique of Mischel. *Journal of Personality,* 1972, *40,* 17–26. (a)

Bem, D. J. Self-perception theory. In L. Berkowitz (Ed.), *Advances in experimental social psychology* (Vol. 6). New York: Academic Press, 1972. (b)

Bem, D. J., & Allen, A. On predicting some of the people some of the time: The search for cross-situational consistencies in behavior. *Psychological Review,* 1974, *82,* 506–520.

Bennett, T. L. *Brain and behavior.* Monterey, Calif.: Brooks/Cole, 1977.

Bennett, W., & Gurin, J. Science that frightens scientists: The great debate over DNA. *Atlantic Monthly,* January 1977, pp. 43–62.

Benson, H. *The relaxation response.* New York: Avon, 1975.

Benson, H. Systemic hypertension and the relaxation response. *New England Journal of Medicine,* 1977, *296,* 1152–1156.

Berg, D. F., & Broeker, L. P. *Illicit use of dangerous drugs in the United States: A compilation of studies, surveys, and polls.* Bureau of Narcotics and Dangerous Drugs, U.S. Department of Justice. Washington, D.C.: U.S. Government Printing Office, 1972.

Berger, R. J. Experimental modification of dream content by meaningful verbal stimuli. *British Journal of Psychiatry,* 1963, *109,* 722–740.

Bergin, A. E. The evaluation of therapeutic outcomes. In A. E. Bergin & S. L. Garfield (Eds.), *Handbook of psychotherapy and behavior change.* New York: John Wiley, 1971.

Berkowitz, L. The concept of aggressive drive: Some additional considerations. In L. Berkowitz (Ed.), *Advances in experimental social psychology* (Vol. 2). New York: Academic Press, 1965.

Berkowitz, L. *Roots of aggression.* New York: Appleton-Century-Crofts, 1969.

Berlyne, D. E. The influence of complexity and novelty in visual figures on orienting responses. *Journal of Experimental Psychology,* 1958, *55,* 289–296.

Berlyne, D. E. *Conflict, arousal, and curiosity.* New York: McGraw-Hill, 1960.

Bernard, L. L. *Instinct: A study in social psychology.* New York: Holt, Rinehart & Winston, 1924.

Berne, E. *Games people play.* New York: Grove Press, 1964.

Berne, E. *What do you say after you say hello?* New York: Grove Press, 1972.

Bernstein, B. Social class and linguistic development: A theory of social learning. *British Journal of Sociology*, 1958, *9*, 159–174.

Bernstein, B. Language and social class. *British Journal of Sociology*, 1961, *11*, 271–276.

Bersoff, D. N. Silk purses into sow's ears: The decline of psychological testing and a suggestion for its redemption. *American Psychologist*, 1973, *28*, 892–899.

Bettelheim, B. *The uses of enchantment: The meaning and importance of fairy tales.* New York: Alfred A. Knopf, 1976.

Biller, O. A. Suicide related to the assassination of President John F. Kennedy. *Suicide and Life-Threatening Behavior*, 1977, *7*, 40–45.

Bindra, D. How adaptive behavior is produced: A perceptual-motivational alternative to response-reinforcement. *The Behavioral and Brain Sciences*, 1978, *1*, 41–52.

Birch, D., Atkinson, J. W., & Bongort, K. Cognitive control of action. In B. Weiner (Ed.), *Cognitive views of human motivation.* New York: Academic Press, 1974.

Birch, H. G. Sources of order in maternal behavior of animals. *American Journal of Orthopsychiatry*, 1956, *26*, 279–284.

Birdwhistell, R. L. The kinesic level in the investigation of emotions. In P. H. Knapp (Ed.), *Expression of emotions in man.* New York: International Universities Press, 1963.

Birk, L. *Behavior therapy in psychiatry.* Washington, D.C.: American Psychiatric Association, 1973.

Bischof, L. J. *Adult psychology.* New York: Harper & Row, 1969.

Blakemore, C. *Mechanics of the mind.* Cambridge: Cambridge University Press, 1977.

Bland, J. The junk-food syndrome. *Psychology Today*, January 1982, *92*.

Bloch, H. A., & Niederhoffer, A. *The gang: A study in adolescent behavior.* New York: Philosophical Library, 1958.

Block, J. *Lives through time.* Berkeley, Calif.: Bancroft Books, 1971.

Bloom, B. L. Social and community interventions. *Annual Review of Psychology*, 1980, *31*, 111–142.

Blum, R. H., & Associates. *Society and drugs.* San Francisco: Jossey-Bass, 1970.

Blumer, D., & Walker, E. Sexual behavior in temporal lobe epilepsy. *Archives of Neurology*, 1967, *16*, 37–43.

Boden, M. A. *Artificial intelligence and natural man.* Hassocks, Sussex, England: The Harvester Press, 1977.

Bolles, R. C. Species-specific defense reactions and avoidance learning. *Psychological Review*, 1970, *77*, 32–48.

Bolles, R. C. Cognition and motivation: Some historical trends. In B. Weiner (Ed.), *Cognitive views of human motivation.* New York: Academic Press, 1974.

Bolles, R. C. *Learning theory* (2nd ed.). New York: Holt, Rinehart & Winston, 1979.

Bolles, R. C., & Fanselow, M. S. Endorphins and behavior. *Annual Review of Psychology*, 1982, *33*, 87–101.

Boring, E. G. Intelligence as the tests test it. *New Republic*, 1923, *35*, 35–37.

Boring, E. G. *A history of experimental psychology* (2nd ed.). New York: Appleton-Century-Crofts, 1950.

Bornstein, M. H., & Marks, L. E. Color revisionism. *Psychology Today*, January 1982, 64–73.

Botwinick, J. Disinclination to venture response versus cautiousness in responding: Age differences. *Journal of Genetic Psychology*, 1969, *119*, 241–249.

Botwinick, J. *Aging and behavior.* New York: Springer, 1973.

Bouchard, T. J., Jr., & McGue, M. Familial studies of intelligence: A review. *Science*, 1981, *212*, 1055–1059.

Bower, G. H. Mental imagery and associative learning. In L. Gregg (Ed.), *Cognition in learning and memory.* New York: John Wiley, 1972.

Bower, G. H. Educational applications of mnemonic devices. In K. O. Doyle, Jr. (Ed.), *Interaction: Readings in human psychology.* Boston: D. C. Heath, 1973.

Bower, G. (Ed.). *Human memory: Basic processes.* New York: Academic Press, 1977.

Bower, G. H. Mood and memory. *American Psychologist*, 1981, *36*, 129–148.

Bowerman, C. E., & Kinch, J. W. Changes in family and peer orientation of children between the fourth and tenth grades. *Social Forces*, 1959, *37*, 206–211.

Bowers, K. S. *Hypnosis for the seriously curious.* Monterey, Calif.: Brooks/Cole, 1976.

Bowes, W. A., Jr., Brackbill, Y., Conway, E., & Steinschneider, A. The effects of obstetrical medication on fetus and infant. *Monographs of the Society for Research in Child Development*, 1970, *35*(4).

Bowlby, J. Some pathological processes set in train by early mother-child separation. *Journal of Mental Science*, 1953, *99*, 265–272.

Bradburn, N. M., & Caplovitz, D. *Reports on happiness: A pilot study of behavior related to mental health.* Chicago: Aldine, 1965.

Brady, J. V. Ulcers in "executive" monkeys. *Scientific American*, 1958, *199*, 95–100.

Brady, J., & Nauta, W. Subcortical mechanisms in emotional behavior: The duration of affective changes following septal and habenular lesions in the albino rat. *Journal of Comparative and Physiological Psychology*, 1955, *48*, 412–420.

Braine, M. D. S. The ontogeny of English phrase structure: The first phrase. *Language*, 1963, *39*, 1–13.

Bransford, J. D., & Franks, J. J. The abstraction of linguistic ideas. *Cognitive Psychology*, 1971, *2*, 331–350.

Brazziel, W. S. A letter from the South. *Harvard Educational Review*, Reprint Series No. 2, 1969, pp. 200–208.

Breland, K., & Breland, M. A field of applied animal psychology. *American Psychologist*, 1951, *6*, 202–204.

Breland, K., & Breland, M. The misbehavior of organisms. *American Psychologist*, 1961, *16*, 681–684.

Broadbent, D. E. Speaking and listening simultaneously. *Journal of Experimental Psychology*, 1952, *43*, 267–273.

Broadbent, D. E. *Perception and communication.* London: Pergamon Press, 1958.

Broadbent, D. E. The magic number seven after fifteen years. In A. Kennedy & A. Wilkes (Eds.), *Studies in long term memory.* New York: John Wiley, 1975.

Brome, V. *Jung: Man and myth.* London: Macmillan, 1978.

Broughton, W. J. Sleep disorders: Disorders of arousal? *Science*, 1968, *159*, 1070–1078.

Brown, B. B. Recognition of aspects of consciousness through association with EEG alpha activity represented by a light signal. *Psychophysiology*, 1970, *6*, 442–452.

Brown, H. *Brain and behavior: A textbook of physiological psychology.* New York: Oxford University Press, 1976.

Brown, J. A. C. *Freud and the post-Freudians.* Middlesex, Eng.: Penguin Books, 1961.

Brown, J. L. States in newborn infants. *Merrill-Palmer Quarterly*, 1964, *10*, 313–327.

Brown, P. L., & Jenkins, H. M. Auto-shaping of the pigeon's key-peck. *Journal of the Experimental Analysis of Behavior*, 1968, *11*, 1–8.

Brown, R. *A first language: The early stages.* Cambridge, Mass.: Harvard University Press, 1973.

Brown, R., & McNeill, D. The "tip of the tongue" phenomenon. *Journal of Verbal Learning and Verbal Behavior*, 1966, *5*, 325–337.

Bruch, H. *Eating disorders.* New York: Basic Books, 1973.

Bruner, J. S. The course of cognitive growth. *American Psychologist*, 1964, *19*, 1–15.

Bruner, J. S. (Ed.). *Beyond the information given: Studies in the psychology of knowing.* New York: W. W. Norton, 1973.

Bruner, J. S., Goodnow, J. J., & Austin, G. A. *A study of thinking.* New York: John Wiley, 1956.

Buffery, A. W. H., & Gray, J. A. Sex differences in the development of spatial and linguistic skills. In C. Ounsted & D. C. Taylor (Eds.), *Gender differences: Their ontogeny and significance.* Edinburgh: Churchill Livingstone, 1972.

Bugelski, B. R. Words and things and images. *American Psychologist*, 1970, *25*, 1002–1012.

Buros, O. K. *Personality, tests and reviews: II.* Highland Park, N.J.: Gryphon Press, 1975.

Buros, O. K. (Ed.). *The eighth mental measurements yearbook, Vol. II.* Highland Park, N.J.: Gryphon Press, 1978.

Burrell, R. J. W. The possible bearing of curse death and other factors in Bantu culture on the etiology of myocardial infarction. In T. N. James & J. W. Keyes (Eds.), *The etiology of myocardial infarction*. Boston: Little, Brown, 1963.

Burt, C. L. Review of Getzels and Jackson, *Creativity and intelligence*, *British Journal of Educational Psychology*, 1962, *32*, 292–298.

Burt, C. The genetic determination of differences in intelligence: A study of monozygotic twins reared together and apart. *British Journal of Psychology*, 1966, *57*, 137–153.

Burtt, H. E. An experimental study of early childhood memory. *Journal of Genetic Psychology*, 1941, *58*, 435–439.

Buxton, C. E. Latent learning and the goal gradient hypothesis. *Contributions to Psychological Theory*, 1940, *2*, 6.

Byrne, D. *The attraction paradigm*. New York: Academic Press, 1971.

Byrne, D., & Nelson, D. Attraction as a linear function of properties of positive reinforcement. *Journal of Personality and Social Psychology*, 1965, *1*, 659–663.

Cahalan, D., Cisin, I. H., & Crossley, H. M. *American drinking practices: A national study of drinking behavior and attitudes*. New Brunswick, N.J.: Rutgers Center of Alcohol Studies, 1969.

Campbell, B. G. *Human evolution*. Chicago: Aldine, 1966.

Campbell, D. E., & Beets, J. L. Lunacy and the moon. *Psychological Bulletin*, 1978, *85*, 1123–1129.

Campbell, D. T. On the conflicts between biological and social evolution and between psychology and moral tradition. *American Psychologist*, 1975, *30*, 1103–1126.

Cannon, W. B. The physiological basis of thirst. *Proceedings of the Royal Society of London*, 1918, *90*, 283–301.

Cannon, W. B. *Bodily changes in pain, hunger, fear, and rage* (2nd ed.). New York: Appleton-Century-Crofts, 1929.

Cannon, W. B. *The wisdom of the body*. New York: Norton, 1939.

Cannon, W. B., & Washburn, A. L. An explanation of hunger. *American Journal of Physiology*, 1912, *29*, 441–454.

Cantor, N., & Mischel, W. Traits as prototypes: Effects on recognition memory. *Journal of Personality and Social Psychology*, 1977, *35*, 38–48.

Capra, F. *The turning point: Science, society, and the rising culture*. New York: Simon & Schuster, 1982.

Carlson, N. R. *Physiology of behavior* (2nd ed.). Boston: Allyn & Bacon, 1980.

Carpenter, C. R. Sexual behavior of free ranging rhesus monkeys *(Macaca mulatta)*. *Journal of Comparative Psychology*, 1942, *33*, 113–142.

Carrington, R. *Elephants*. New York: Basic Books, 1959.

Cartwright, D. S., Howard, K. I., & Reuterman, N. A. Multivariate analysis of gang delinquency: III. Age and physique of gangs and clubs. *Multivariate Behavioral Research*, 1971, *6*, 75–90.

Cartwright, D. S., Thomson, B., & Schwarts, H. *Gang delinquency*. Monterey, Calif.: Brooks/Cole, 1975.

Cartwright, R. D. Sleep fantasy in normal and schizophrenic persons. *Journal of Abnormal Psychology*, 1972, *80*, 275–279.

Cartwright, R. D. Problem solving: Waking and dreaming. *Journal of Abnormal Psychology*, 1974, *83*, 451–455.

Cartwright, R. D. *Night life: Explorations in dreaming*. Englewood Cliffs, N.J.: Prentice-Hall, 1977.

Casler, L. Maternal deprivation: A critical review of the literature. *Monograph of the Society for Research in Child Development*, 1961, *26* (2).

Castañeda, C. *The teachings of Don Juan: A Yaqui way of knowledge*. New York: Simon & Schuster, 1968.

Castañeda, C. *A separate reality*. New York: Simon & Schuster, 1971.

Castañeda, C. *Journey to Ixtlan: The lessons of Don Juan*. New York: Simon & Schuster, 1972.

Castañeda, C. *Tales of power*. New York: Simon & Schuster, 1974.

Castañeda, C. *The second ring of power*. New York: Simon & Schuster, 1978.

Castañeda, C. *The eagle's gift*. New York: Simon & Schuster, 1981.

Cates, J. Psychology's manpower: Report on the 1968 National Register of Scientific and Technical Personnel. *American Psychologist*, 1970, *25*, 254–264.

Cattell, R. B. *Description and measurement of personality*. New York: Harcourt Brace & World, 1946.

Cattell, R. B. *Abilities: Their structure, growth and action*. Boston: Houghton Mifflin, 1971.

Cattell, R. B. Travels in psychological hyperspace. In T. S. Krawiec (Ed.), *The psychologists* (Vol. 2). New York: Oxford University Press, 1974.

Cermak, L. S., & Craik, F. I. (Eds.). *Levels of processing in human memory*. Hillsdale, N.J.: Erlbaum, 1979.

Chambliss, W. J. The state, the law, and the definition of behavior as criminal or delinquent. In D. Glaser (Ed.), *Handbook of Criminology*. Chicago: Rand McNally, 1974.

Chance, P. *Learning and behavior*. Belmont, Calif.: Wadsworth, 1979.

Chapman, R. S., Smith, J. W., & Layton, T. A. Elimination of cigarette smoking by punishment and self-management training. *Behavior Research Therapy*, 1971, *9*, 255–264.

Chase, W. G., & Simon, H. A. The mind's eye in chess. In W. G. Chase (Ed.), *Visual information processing*. New York: Academic Press, 1973.

Cherry, E. C. Some experiments on the recognition of speech with one and two ears. *Journal of the Acoustical Society of America*, 1953, *25*, 975–979.

Cherry, E. C., & Taylor, W. K. Some further experiments on the recognition of speech with one and two ears. *Journal of the Acoustical Society of America*, 1954, *26*, 554–559.

Chertok, L. *L'hypnose: Les problèmes théoriques et pratiques* (2nd ed.). Paris: Masson et Cie, 1961.

Chomsky, N. *Syntactic structures*. The Hague: Mouton, 1957.

Chomsky, N. *Aspects of the theory of syntax*. Cambridge, Mass.: MIT Press, 1965.

Chomsky, N. *Language and mind* (Enl. ed.). New York: Harcourt Brace Jovanovich, 1972.

Clarizio, H. F., & Yelon, S. L. Learning theory approaches to classroom management: Rationale and intervention techniques. In A. R. Brown & C. Avery (Eds.), *Modifying children's behavior: A book of readings*. Springfield, Ill.: Charles C Thomas, 1974.

Clark, H. H. Space, time, semantics, and the child. In T. E. Moore (Ed.), *Cognitive development and the acquisition of language*. New York: Academic Press, 1973.

Clark, H. H., & Clark, E. V. *Psychology and language: An introduction to psycholinguistics*. New York: Harcourt Brace Jovanovich, 1977.

Clark, R. D. C., III, & Word, L. E. Where is the apathetic bystander? Situational characteristics of the emergency. *Journal of Personality and Social Psychology*, 1974, *29*, 279–287.

Clark, R. W. *Freud: The man and the cause*. New York: Random House, 1980.

Clarke, M. R. B. Some ideas for a chess compiler. In A. Elithorn & D. Jones (Eds.), *Artificial and human intelligence*. New York: American Elsevier, 1973.

Clausen, J. A. The social meaning of differential physical and sexual maturation. In S. E. Dragastin & G. H. Elder (Eds.), *Adolescence in the life cycle: Psychological change and social context*. New York: John Wiley & Sons, 1975, 25–46.

Cofer, C. N. *Motivation and emotion*. Chicago: Scott, Foresman, 1972.

Cofer, C. N., & Appley, M. H. *Motivation: Theory and research*. New York: John Wiley, 1964.

Cohen, D. *Psychologists on psychology*. London: Routledge & Kegan Paul, 1977.

Cohen, D. K. Does IQ matter? *Current*, 1972, *141*, 19–30.

Cohen, J. *Secondary motivation: II. Social motives*. Skokie, Ill.: Rand McNalley, 1970.

Cohen, M. L., Garofalo, R., Boucher, R., & Seghorn, T. A psychology of rapists. *Seminars in Psychiatry*, 1971, *3*(3).

Cohen, S. Mr. Robinson answered. In C. C. Brown & C. Savage (Eds.), *The drug abuse controversy*. Baltimore: National Educational Consultants, 1971.

Cohen, S. *The drug dilemma* (2nd ed.). New York: McGraw-Hill, 1976.

Cole, M., Gay, J., Glick, J. A., & Sharp, D. W. (Eds.). *The cultural context of learning and thinking: An exploration in experimental anthropology.* New York: Basic Books, 1971.

Coleman, J. C., Butcher, J. N., & Carson, R. C. *Abnormal psychology and modern life* (6th ed.). Glenview, Ill.: Scott Foresman, 1980.

Collins, B. E., & Hoyt, M. F. Personal responsibility for consequences: An integration and extension of the "forced compliance" literature. *Journal of Experimental and Social Psychology,* 1972, *8,* 558–593.

Collins, J. K. Adolescent dating intimacy: Norms and peer expectations. *Journal of Youth and Adolescence,* 1974, *3,* 317–328.

Coltheart, M., Lea, C. D., & Thompson, K. In defense of iconic memory. *Quarterly Journal of Experimental Psychology,* 1974, *26,* 633–641.

Commission on Obscenity and Pornography. *Report.* Washington, D.C.: U.S. Government Printing Office, 1970.

Commons, W. D., & Fagin, B. *Principles of educational psychology.* New York: Ronald Press, 1954.

Conrad, R., & Hille, B. A. The decay theory of immediate memory and spaced recall. *Canadian Journal of Psychology,* 1958, *12,* 1–6.

Consumer Reports. Sleeping students don't learn English. May 1970, *35,* 313.

Contreras, R. J. Salt taste and disease. *The American Journal of Clinical Nutrition,* 1978, *31,* 1088–1097.

Cooper, J. Personal responsibility and dissonance: The role of foreseen consequences. *Journal of Personality and Social Psychology,* 1971, *18,* 354–363.

Coopersmith, S. *The antecedents of self esteem.* San Francisco: W. H. Freeman, 1967.

Coren, S., Porac, C., & Ward, L. M. *Sensation and perception.* New York: Academic Press, 1979.

Corey, G. *Theory and practice of counseling and psychotherapy.* Monterey, Calif.: Brooks/Cole, 1977.

Cortes, J. B., & Gatti, F. M. Physique and self-description of temperament. *Journal of Consulting Psychology,* 1965, *29,* 432–439.

Coyne, M. L. Some problems and parameters of sleep learning. In S. Rubin (Ed.), *Current research in hypnopaedia.* New York: American Elsevier, 1968.

Craik, F. I., & Lockhart, R. S. Levels of processing: A framework for memory research. *Journal of Verbal Learning and Verbal Behavior,* 1972, *11,* 671–684.

Craik, F. I. M., & Watkins, M. J. The role of rehearsal in short-term memory. *Journal of Verbal Learning and Verbal Behavior,* 1973, *12,* 599–607.

Cropley, A. J. *Originality, intelligence and personality.* Unpublished doctoral dissertation, University of Alberta, Edmonton, 1965.

Crow, J. S. Genetic theories and influences: Comments on the value of diversity. *Harvard Educational Review,* Reprint Series No. 2, 1969, pp. 153–161.

Crowder, N. A. Characteristics of branching programs. In D. T. Scrannell (Ed.), *Conference on programmed learning.* Lawrence: University of Kansas, Studies in Education, 1961.

Curtis, D. *Learn while you sleep.* New York: Libra, 1960.

Dallenbach, K. M. Twitmeyer and the conditioned response. *American Journal of Psychology,* 1959, *72,* 633–638.

Dallos, P. Cochlear physiology. *Annual Review of Psychology,* 1981, *32,* 153–190.

Darian-Smith, I. Touch in primates. *Annual Review of Psychology,* 1982, *33,* 155–194.

Darley, J. M., & Latané, B. Bystander intervention in emergencies: diffusion of responsibility. *Journal of Personality and Social Psychology,* 1968, *8,* 377–383.

Darley, S. A., & Cooper, J. Cognitive consequences of forced noncompliance. *Journal of Personality and Social Psychology,* 1972, *24,* 321–326.

Darwin, C. *The expression of emotions in man and animals.* London: John Murray, 1872. Reprinted Chicago: University of Chicago Press, 1965.

Davidson, D. M. Anorexia nervosa in a serviceman: A case report. *Military Medicine,* 1976, *141,* 617–619.

Davidson, P. O., & Davidson, S. M. (Eds.). *Behavioral medicine: Changing health lifestyles.* New York: Brunner/Mazel, 1980.

Davis, A. *Let's have healthy children* (3rd ed.). New York: Harcourt Brace Jovanovich, 1972.

Davis, D. M. Self selection of diet by newly weaned infants. *American Journal of the Disabled Child,* 1928, *36,* 651–679.

Davis, R. C., Garafalo, L., & Klein, K. Conditions associated with gastrointestinal activity. *Journal of Comparative and Physiological Psychology,* 1959, *52,* 466–475.

Davison, G. C., & Neale, J. M. *Abnormal psychology: An experimental clinical approach* (2nd ed.). New York: John Wiley, 1978.

Davitz, J. R. *The language of emotion.* New York: Academic Press, 1969.

Dawkins, R. *The selfish gene.* London: Oxford University Press, 1976.

Deaux, K. *The behavior of women and men.* Monterey, Calif.: Brooks/Cole, 1976.

De Bono, E. *Lateral thinking: A textbook of creativity.* London: Ward Lock Educational Limited, 1970.

De Bono, E. *Teaching thinking.* London: Temple Smith, 1976.

Deci, E. L. *Intrinsic motivation.* New York: Plenum Press, 1975.

DeFries, J. C., & Plomin, R. Behavioral genetics. *Annual Review of Psychology,* 1978, *29,* 473–515.

Deikman, A. J. Experimental meditation. *Journal of Nervous and Mental Disease,* 1963, *136* (4), 329–343.

Deikman, A. J. Deautomatization and the mystic experience. *Psychiatry,* 1966, *29,* 324–338. (a)

Deikman, A. J. Implications of experimentally induced contemplative meditation. *Journal of Nervous and Mental Disease,* 1966, *142*(2), 101–116. (b)

Delgado, J. M. R. *Physical control of the mind.* New York: Harper & Row, 1969.

De Martino, M. S. A review of the literature on children's dreams. *Psychiatric Quarterly Supplement,* 1955, *29* (Pt. 1), 90–101.

De Martino, M. S. *Dreams and personality dynamics.* Springfield, Ill.: Charles C Thomas, 1959.

DeMause, L. Our forebears made childhood a nightmare. *Psychology Today,* April 1975, pp. 85–88.

Dember, W. N. Response by the rat to environmental change. *Journal of Comparative Physiological Psychology,* 1956, *49,* 93–95.

Dement, W. Dream recall and eye movements during sleep in schizophrenics and normals. *Journal of Nervous and Mental Disease,* 1955, *122,* 263–269.

Dement, W. The effect of dream deprivation. *Science,* 1960, *131,* 1705–1707.

Dement, W. *Some must watch while some must sleep.* San Francisco: Newman, 1974.

Dement, W., & Kleitman, N. The relation of eye movement during sleep to dream activity: An objective method for the study of dreaming. *Journal of Experimental Psychology,* 1957, *53,* 339–346.

de Mille, R. *Castaneda's journey.* Santa Barbara: Capra Press, 1976.

Demuth, P. Wobbly biorhythms. *Human Behavior,* April 1979, 53–55.

Dennis, W. The significance of feral man. *American Journal of Psychology,* 1941, *54,* 425–432.

Dennis, W. A further analysis of reports of wild children. *Child Development,* 1951, *22,* 153–158.

Dethier, V. G. Insects and the concept of motivation. In D. Levine (Ed.), *Nebraska Symposium on Motivation* (Vol. 14). Lincoln: University of Nebraska Press, 1966.

Dethier, V. G. The hungry fly. *Psychology Today,* June 1967, pp. 64–72.

Deutsch, A. *The mentally ill in America.* New York: Doubleday, 1937.

De Valois, R. L., & De Valois, K. K. Spatial vision. *Annual Review of Psychology,* 1980, *31,* 309–341.

Dick, A. O. Relations between the sensory register and short-term storage in tachistoscopic recognition. *Journal of Experimental Psychology,* 1969, *82,* 279–284.

Dinham, S. M. *Exploring statistics: An introduction for psychology and education.* Monterey, Calif.: Brooks/Cole, 1976.

Dobzhansky, T. *Genetics of the evolutionary process.* New York: Columbia University Press, 1970.

Dollard, J., Doob, L. W., Miller, N. E., Mowrer, O. H., & Sears, R. R. *Frustration and aggression.* New Haven: Yale University Press, 1939.

Donnerstein, E., & Barrett, G. Effects of erotic stimuli on male aggression toward females. *Journal of Personality and Social Psychology,* 1978, *36,* 180–188.

Douglas, J. W. B., & Ross, J. N. Age of puberty related to educational ability, attainment, and school leaving age. *Journal of Child Psychology and Psychiatry,* 1964, *5,* 185–196.

Dreyer, P. H. Sex, sex roles, and marriage among youth in the 1970s. In R. J. Havighurst & P. H. Dreyer (Eds.), *Youth: The seventy-fourth yearbook of the National Society for the Study of Education (Part I).* Chicago: University of Chicago Press, 1975, 194–223.

Droscher, V. B. *The magic of the senses.* New YorK: Dutton, 1969.

Duncker, K. The influence of past experience upon perceptual properties. *American Journal of Psychology,* 1939, *52,* 255–265.

Duncker, K. On problem solving. *Psychological Monographs,* 1945, *58* (Whole No. 270).

Dunn, A. J. Neurochemistry of learning and memory: An evaluation of recent data. *Annual Review of Psychology,* 1980, *31,* 343–390.

Dunphy, D. C. The social structure of urban adolescent peer groups. *Sociometry,* 1963, *26,* 230–246.

Dupree, A. H. Biological and social theories—a new opportunity for a union of systems. In N. H. Steneck (Ed.), *Science and society.* Ann Arbor: University of Michigan Press, 1975.

Durkheim, E. *Suicide.* Glencoe, Ill.: Free Press, 1951. (Originally published, 1897.)

Dutton, D. C., & Aron, A. P. Some evidence for heightened sexual attraction under conditions of high anxiety. *Journal of Personality and Social Psychology,* 1974, *30,* 510–517.

Dutton, D. G., & Lake, R. A. Threat of own prejudice and reverse discrimination in interracial situations. *Journal of Personality and Social Psychology,* 1973, *28,* 94–100.

Ebbinghaus, H. *Memory.* (H. A. Ruger & C. E. Busenius, Trans.). New York: Dover, 1964. (Originally published, 1885.)

Ebin, D. (Ed.). *The drug experience: First person accounts of addicts, writers, scientists, and others.* New York: O'Ryan Press, 1961.

Eccles, J. C. *The understanding of the brain.* New York: McGraw-Hill, 1973.

Eckland, B. K. Darwin rides again. *American Journal of Sociology,* 1977, *82,* 693–697.

Edwards, A. L. *Edwards personal preference schedule.* New York: Psychological Corporation, 1954.

Eibl-Eibesfeldt, I. *Love and hate: The natural history of behavior patterns.* New York: Schocken Books, 1974.

Eiseley, L. *The immense journey.* New York: Random House, 1957.

Eisenberg, R. B., Griffin, F. J., Coursin, D. B., & Hunter, M. A. Auditory behavior in the neonate. *Journal of Speech and Hearing Research,* 1963, *7,* 245–269.

Ekman, P. Universal and cultural differences in facial expressions of emotion. In J. K. Cole (Ed.), *Nebraska symposium on motivation, 1971.* Lincoln, Nebraska: University of Nebraska Press, 1972.

Ekman, P. Cross cultural studies of facial expression. In P. Ekman (Ed.), *Darwin and facial expression: A century of research in review.* New York: Academic Press, 1973, 169–220.

Ekman, P., Sorenson, E. R., & Friesen, W. V. Pan-cultural elements in facial displays of emotion. *Science,* 1969, *164,* 86–88.

Eliseo, T. S. The Hypnotic Induction Profile and hypnotic susceptibility. *International Journal of Clinical and Experimental Hypnosis,* 1974, *22,* 320–326.

Elliot, R., & Vesta, R. The modelling of sharing: effects associated with vicarious reinforcement, symbolization, age and generalization. *Journal of Experimental Child Psychology,* 1970, *10,* 8–15.

Ellis, A. *Reason and emotion in psychotherapy.* New York: Lyle Stewart, 1962.

Ellis, A. *Humanistic psychotherapy: The rational-emotive approach.* New York: Julian Press, 1974.

Ellis, A. *How to live with a "neurotic"* (Rev. ed.). New York: Crown, 1975.

Ellis, A. Rational-emotive therapy. In V. Binder, A. Binder, & B. Rimland (Eds.), *Modern therapies.* Englewood Cliffs, N.J.: Prentice-Hall, 1976.

Emmons, W. H., & Simon, C. W. The nonrecall of material presented during sleep. *American Journal of Psychology,* 1956, *69,* 76–81.

Epstein, A. N., & Teitelbaum, P. Regulation of food intake in the absence of taste, smell, and other oropharyngeal sensations. *Journal of Comparative and Physiological Psychology,* 1962, *55,* 753–759.

Epstein, R., Lanza, R. P., & Skinner, B. F. Symbolic communication between two pigeons *(Columba livia domestica).* *Science,* 1980, *207,* 543–545.

Epstein, S. M. Toward a unified theory of anxiety. In B. A. Maher (Ed.), *Progress in experimental personality research (Vol 4).* New York: Academic Press, 1967.

Erikson, E. H. *Childhood and society.* New York: W. W. Norton, 1950.

Erikson, E. H. *Identity: Youth and crisis.* New York: W. W. Norton, 1968.

Erlenmeyer-Kimling, L., & Jarvik, L. S. Genetics and intelligence: A review. *Science,* 1963, *142,* 1477–1478.

Estes, W. K. Is human memory obsolete? *American Scientist,* 1980, *68,* 62–69.

Evans, F. J., & Orne, M. T. The disappearing hypnotist: The use of simulating subjects to evaluate how subjects perceive experimental procedures. *International Journal of Clinical and Experimental Hypnosis,* 1971, *19,* 277–296.

Evans, R. I. *The making of psychology: Discussions with creative contributors.* New York: Alfred A. Knopf, 1976.

Eysenck, H. J. *Dimensions of personality.* London: Routledge & Kegan Paul, 1947.

Eysenck, H. J. What's the truth about psychoanalysis? *Reader's Digest,* 1960, *76,* 38–43.

Eysenck, H. J. The effects of psychotherapy. *International Journal of Psychiatry,* 1965, *1,* 97–142.

Eysenck, H. J. *The biological basis of personality.* Springfield, Ill.: Charles C Thomas, 1967.

Eysenck, H. J. (Ed.). *Handbook of abnormal psychology* (2nd ed.). London: Sir Isaac Pitman and Sons, 1973.

Falek, A. Ethical issues in human behavior genetics: Civil rights, informed consent and ethics of intervention. In K. W. Schaie, V. E. Anderson, G. E. McClearn, & J. Money (Eds.), *Developmental human behavior genetics.* Boston: D. C. Heath, 1975.

Falk, J. L. Control of schedule-induced polydipsia: Type, size, and spacing of meals. *Journal of the Experimental Analysis of Behavior,* 1967, *10,* 199–206.

Falk, J. L. Conditions producing psychogenic polydipsia in animals. *Annals of the New York Academy of Science,* 1969, *157,* 569–593.

Falk, J. L. The nature and determinants of adjunctive behavior. In *Schedule-induced and schedule-dependent phenomena* (Vol. 2). Toronto: Addiction Research Foundation, 1970.

Fancher, R. E. *Pioneers of psychology.* New York: W. W. Norton, 1979.

Fantino, E., & Logan, C. A. *The experimental analysis of behavior: A biological perspective.* San Francisco: W. H. Freeman, 1979.

Fantz, R. L. The origin of form perception. *Scientific American,* 1961, *204,* 66–72.

Fantz, R. L. Pattern vision in newborn infants. *Science,* 1963, *140,* 296–297.

Fantz, R. L. Visual experience in infants: Decreased attention to familiar patterns relative to novel ones. *Science,* 1964, *146,* 668–670.

Fantz, R. L. Visual perception from birth as shown by pattern selectivity. *Annals of the New York Academy of Science,* 1965, *118,* 793–814.

Faraday, A. *Dream power.* New York: Coward, McCann & Geoghegan, 1972.

Farina, A. *Abnormal psychology.* Englewood Cliffs, N.J.: Prentice-Hall, 1976.

Fawcett, J. Suicidal depression and physical illness. *Journal of the American Medical Association,* 1972, *219,* 1303–1306.

Feffer, M. *The structure of Freudian thought: The problem of immutability and discontinuity in developmental theory.* New York: International Universities Press, 1982.

Feighner, J. P., Robbins, E., Guze, S. B., et al. Diagnostic criteria for use in psychiatric research. *Archives of General Psychiatry,* 1972, *26,* 57–63.

Feingold, B. D., & Mahoney, M. J. Reinforcement effects on intrinsic interest: Undermining the overjustification hypothesis. *Behavior Therapy,* 1975, *6,* 367–377.

Feldman, S. E., & Feldman, F. T. Transition of sex differences in cheating. *Psychological Reports,* 1967, *20,* 957–958.

Felsenthal, N. *Orientations to mass communication.* Chicago: Science Research Associates, 1976.

Feshbach, S., & Singer, R. D. *Television and aggression.* San Franciso: Jossey-Bass, 1971.

Festinger, L. *A theory of cognitive dissonance.* Stanford, Calif.: Stanford University Press, 1957.

Festinger, L. Cognitive dissonance. *Scientific American,* 1962, *207,* 93–100.

Festinger, L., & Carlsmith, J. M. Cognitive consequences of forced compliance. *Journal of Abnormal and Social Psychology,* 1959, *58,* 203–210.

Fishbein, W., & Gutwein, B. M. Paradoxical sleep and memory storage processes. *Behavioral Biology,* 1977, *19,* 425–464.

Fisher, C., Kahn, F., Edwards, A., & Davis, D. M. A psychophysiological study of nightmares and night terrors. *Archives of General Psychiatry,* 1973, *28,* 252–259.

Fisher, J. D., & Farina, A. Consequences of beliefs about the nature of mental disorders. *Journal of Abnormal Psychology,* 1979, *88,* 320–327.

Fisher, S., & Greenberg, R. P. *The scientific credibility of Freud's theories and therapy.* New York: Basic Books, 1977.

Fisher, W. A., & Byrne, D. Sex differences in response to erotica? Love versus lust. *Journal of Personality and Social Psychology,* 1978, *36,* 117–126.

Fleischman, P. R. Letter in response to Rosenhan's 1973 article. *Science,* 1973, *180,* 356.

Flexner, L. Disruption of memory in mice with antibiotics. *Proceedings of the American Philosophical Society,* 1967, *111,* 343–346.

Flynn, J. P. The neural basis of aggression in cats. In D. C. Glass (Ed.), *Neurophysiology and emotion.* New York: Rockefeller University Press, 1967.

Fodor, E. N. Delinquency and susceptibility to social influence among adolescents as a function of level of moral development. *Journal of Social Psychology,* 1972, *86,* 257–260.

Fouts, R. S. Acquisition and testing of gestural signs in four young chimpanzees. *Science,* 1973, *180,* 978–980.

Fowler, H. Response to environmental change: A positive replication. *Psychological Review,* 1958, *4,* 506.

Fowler, H. *Curiosity and exploratory behavior.* New York: Macmillan, 1965.

Fowler, R. D., & Miller, M. L. Computer interpretation of the MMPI. *Archives of General Psychiatry,* 1969, *21,* 502–508.

Fowler, W. L. Hypnosis and learning. *International Journal of Clinical and Experimental Hypnosis,* 1961, *9,* 223–233.

Framo, J. L. The friendly divorce. *Psychology Today,* February 1978, 77–79; 100–102.

Frank, J. D. *Persuasion and healing: A comparative study of psychotherapy.* Baltimore: Johns Hopkins University Press, 1973.

Frank, J. D. Psychotherapy: The restoration of morale. *American Journal of Psychiatry,* 1974, *131,* 271–274.

Franklin, K. B. J., & Herberg, L. J. Ventromedial syndrome: The rat's "finickiness" resulting from the obesity, not from the lesions. *Journal of Comparative and Physiological Psychology,* 1974, *87,* 410–414.

Freedman, J. L., & Fraser, S. C. Compliance without pressure: The foot-in-the-door technique. *Journal of Personality and Social Psychology,* 1966, *4,* 195–202.

French, E. G. *Development of a measure of complex motivation.* Lackland Air Force Base, Texas: Research, REP. ASPTRC-TN-56-48, Air Force Personnel and Training Research Center, 1956. (a)

French, E. G. Motivation as a variable in work partner selection. *Journal of Abnormal and Social Psychology,* 1956, *53,* 96–99. (b)

French, J. D. The reticular formation. *Scientific American,* 1957, *196,* 54–73.

Freud, S. *On the history of the psychoanalytic movement.* London: Hogarth Press, 1914.

Frick, W. B. *Humanistic psychology: Interviews with Maslow, Murphy, and Rogers.* Columbus, Ohio: Charles E. Merrill, 1971.

Friedman, A. S. The family and the female delinquent: An overview. In O. Pollak & A. S. Friedman (Eds.), *Family dynamics and female sexual delinquency.* Palo Alto, Calif.: Science and Behavior Books, 1969.

Friedman, M. I., & Stricker, E. M. The physiological psychology of hunger: A physiological perspective. *Psychological Review,* 1976, *83*(6), 409–431.

Friedman, R. J., & Katz, M. M. (Eds.). *The psychology of depression: Contemporary theory and research.* Washington, D.C.: V. H. Winston, 1974.

Frieze, I. H., Parsons, J. E., Johnson, P. B., Ruble, D. N., & Zellman, G. L. *Women and sex roles: A social psychological perspective.* New York: W. W. Norton, 1978.

Frisch, Karl von. *The dancing bees: An account of the life and senses of the honey bee.* New York: Harcourt Brace & World, 1953.

Frodi, A. Sexual arousal, situational restrictiveness, and aggressive behavior. *Journal of Research in Personality,* 1977, *11,* 48–58.

Gagnon, J. H., & Simon, W. They're going to learn in the street anyway. *Psychology Today,* 1969, *3,* 46–47; 71.

Gallagher, J. J. *Analysis of research on the education of gifted children.* Springfield, Ill.: State of Illinois, Office of the Superintendent of Public Instruction, 1960.

Galton, S. *Hereditary genius: An inquiry into its laws and consequences.* London: Macmillan, 1869.

Garcia, J., Ervin, F. E., & Koelling, R. A. Learning with prolonged delay of reinforcement. *Psychonomic Science,* 1966, *5,* 121–122.

Garcia, J., & Koelling, R. A. Relation of cue to consequence in avoidance learning. *Psychonomic Science,* 1966, *4,* 123–124.

Gardiner, W. L. *Psychology: The story of a search* (2nd ed.). Monterey, Calif.: Brooks/Cole, 1974.

Gardner, M. Monkey business. *New York Review of Books,* March 20, 1980, 3–5.

Gardner, R. A., & Gardner, B. T. Teaching sign language to a chimpanzee. *Science,* 1969, *165,* 664–672.

Garfield, S. L., & Bergin, A. E. (Eds.). *Handbook of psychotherapy and behavior change: An empirical analysis.* New York: John Wiley, 1978.

Gazzaniga, M. S. The split brain in man. *Scientific American,* 1967, *217,* 24–29.

Gazzaniga, M. S. *The bisected brain.* New York: Appleton-Century-Crofts, 1970.

Gazzaniga, M. S. One brain—two minds? *American Scientist,* 1972, *60,* 311–317.

Gazzaniga, M. S., & LeDoux, J. E. *The integrated mind.* New York: Plenum, 1978.

Gelles, R. J. *The violent home: A study of physical aggression between husand and wife.* Beverly Hills, Calif.: Sage Publications, 1972.

Gerbner, G. Violence in television drama: Trends and symbolic functions. In G. A. Comstock & E. A. Rubinstein (Eds.), *Television and social behavior* (Vol. 1. *Media content and control*). Washington, D.C.: U.S. Government Printing Office, 1972.

Gershon, S., & Angrist, D. Drug induced psychosis: II. *Hospital Practice,* 1967, *2,* 50–53.

Getzels, J. W., & Jackson, P. W. *Creativity and intelligence.* New York: John Wiley, 1962.

Gewirtz, J. L. The course of infant smiling in four child-rearing environments in Israel. In B. M. Foss (Ed.), *Determinants of infant behavior III.* London: Methuen, 1965.

Gibson, E. J., & Walk, R. D. The "visual cliff." *Scientific American,* 1960, *202,* 64–71.

Gibson, J. J. *The perception of the visual world.* Boston: Houghton Mifflin, 1950.

Gibson, J. J. *The senses considered as perceptual systems.* Boston: Houghton Mifflin, 1966.

Gil, D. G. *Violence against children: Physical child abuse in the United States.* Cambridge, Mass.: Harvard University Press, 1970.

Gill, T. V. Conversations with Lana. In D. M. Rumbaugh (Ed.), *Language learning by a chimpanzee: The Lana Project.* New York: Academic Press, 1977.

Ginsberg, H., & Opper, S. *Piaget's theory of intellectual development* (2nd ed.). Englewood Cliffs, N.J.: Prentice-Hall, 1979.

Glassman, E., Machlus, B., & Wilson, J. E. Phosphorylation of non-histone acid-extractable nuclear proteins (NAEP) from brain. In H. P. Zippel (Ed.), *Memory and transfer of information*. New York: Plenum Press, 1973.

Glick, P. C. Dissolution of marriage by divorce and its demographic consequences. In *International Population Conference* (Vol. 2). Liége, Belgium: International Union for the Scientific Study of Population, 1973.

Glick, P. C., & Norton, A. J. Marrying, divorcing, and living together in the U.S. today. *Population Bulletin*, 1978, *32*, 328–399.

Glueck, S., & Glueck, E. *Unravelling juvenile delinquency*. New York: Commonwealth Fund, 1950.

Goddard, G. V. Functions of the amygdala. *Psychological Bulletin*, 1964, *62*, 89–100.

Goddard, H. H. *Feeble-mindedness: Its causes and consequences*. New York: Macmillan, 1914.

Goffman, E. *The presentation of self in everyday life*. New York: Doubleday, 1959.

Gold, R. M. Hypothalamic obesity: The myth of the ventromedial nucleus. *Science*, 1973, *182*, 488–490.

Golden, R. I. A conditioned reflex technique in lie detection. In S. A. Yegfsky (Ed.), *Law enforcement science and technology*. London: Academic Press, 1967.

Goldenberg, H. *Abnormal psychology: A social/community approach*. Monterey, Calif.: Brooks/Cole, 1977.

Goldstein, E. B. *Sensation and perception*. Belmont, Calif.: Wadsworth, 1980.

Goleman, D. Who's mentally ill? *Psychology Today*, January 1978, pp. 34–41.

Goleman, D., & Davidson, R. J. (Eds.). *Consciousness: Brain, states of awareness, and mysticism*. New York: Harper & Row, 1979.

Goodall, J. Van Lawick. *In the shadow of man*. New York: Dell, 1972.

Goode, E. (Ed.) *Marijuana*. New York: Walter, 1969.

Goodenough, S. *Measurement of intelligence by drawings*. New York: Harcourt Brace & World, 1926.

Gordon, S., Scales, P., & Everly, K. *The sexual adolescent: Communication with teenagers about sex* (2nd ed.). North Scituate, Mass.: Duxbury Press, 1979.

Gordon, W. J. J. *Synectics: The development of creative capacity*. New York: Harper & Row, 1961.

Gorn, G. J., Goldberg, M. E., & Kanungo, R. N. Changing the intergroup attitudes of children. *Child Development*, 1976, *47*, 277–280.

Gottesman, I. I., & Shields, J. Schizophrenia in twins: Sixteen years' consecutive admissions to a psychiatric clinic. *British Journal of Psychology*, 1966, *112*, 809–818.

Gottesman, I. I., & Shields, J. *Schizophrenia and genetics*. New York: Academic Press, 1972.

Gough, H. G. *A preliminary guide for the use and interpretation of the California Psychological Inventory*. Berkeley, Calif.: University of California Institute for Personality Assessment and Research, 1954.

Graham, H. D., & Gurr, T. R. (Eds.). *Violence in America: Historical and comparative perspectives*. New York: New American Library, 1969.

Grambs, J. D., & Waetjen, W. B. *Sex: Does it make a difference?* North Scituate, Mass.: Duxbury Press, 1975.

Gray, P. H. Theory and evidence of imprinting in human infants. *Journal of Psychology*, 1958, *46*, 155–166.

Grayson, H. (Ed.). Short-term approaches to psychotherapy. New York: Human Sciences Press, 1979.

Graziadei, P. P. C., & Dehon, R. S. Neuronal regeneration in frog olfactory system. *Journal of Cell Biology*, 1973, *59*, 525–530.

Greenblatt, M., Grosser, G. H., & Wechsler, H. Differential responses of hospitalized depressed patients to somatic therapy. *American Journal of Psychiatry*, 1964, *120*, 935–943.

Greene, J. *Thinking and language*. London: Methuen, 1975.

Gregory, R. L. *The intelligent eye*. New York: McGraw-Hill, 1970.

Gregory, R. L. *Eye and brain: The psychology of seeing* (2nd ed.). New York: McGraw-Hill, 1973.

Griffin, D. R. *Echoes of bats and men*. New York: Doubleday, 1959.

Griffitt, W., & Veitch, R. Pre-acquaintance attitude similarity and attraction revisited: Ten days in a fall-out shelter. *Sociometry*, 1974, *37*, 163–173.

Grinker, R. R., & Spiegel, J. P. *Men under stress*. New York: McGraw-Hill, 1963.

Grossman, S. P. The biology of motivation. *Annual Review of Psychology*, 1979, *30*, 209–242.

Grossman, S. P. *A textbook of physiological psychology*. New York: John Wiley, 1967.

Grotevant, H. D., Scarr, S., & Weinberg, R. A. Intellectual development in family constellations with adopted and natural children: A test of the Zajonc and Markus model. *Child Development*, 1977, *48*, 1699–1703.

Guilford, J. P. Three faces of intellect. *American Psychologist*, 1959, *14*, 469–479.

Guilford, J. P. *The nature of human intelligence*. New York: McGraw-Hill, 1967.

Gulevich, G., Dement, W. C., & Johnson, L. Psychiatric and EEG observations on a case of prolonged (264 hours) wakefulness. *Archives of General Psychiatry*, 1966, *15*, 29–35.

Gunderson, K. The imitation game. In A. R. Anderson (Ed.), *Mind and machines*. Englewood Cliffs, N.J.: Prentice-Hall, 1964.

Gurdon, J. B. Adult frogs derived from the nuclei of single somatic cells. *Developmental Biology*, 1962, *4*, 256–273.

Gurney, R. *Language, brain and interactive processes*. London: Edward Arnold, 1973.

Haan, N., Smith, N. B., & Block, J. Moral reasoning of young adults: Political-social behavior, family background, and personality correlates. *Journal of Personality and Social Psychology*, 1968, *10*, 183–201.

Haber, R. N., & Haber, R. B. Eidetic imagery I: Frequency. *Perceptual and Motor Skills*, 1964, *19*, 131–138.

Haber, R. N., & Hershenson, M. *The psychology of visual perception*. New York: Holt, Rinehart & Winston, 1973.

Haefele, J. W. *Creativity and innovation*. New York: Reinholt, 1962.

Haith, M. M. The response of the human newborn to visual movement. *Journal of Experimental Child Psychology*, 1966, *3*, 235–243.

Hall, C. What people dream about. *Scientific American*, 1951, *184*, 60–63.

Hall, C. S., & Lindzey, G. *Theories of personality* (3rd ed.). New York: John Wiley, 1978.

Hall, G. S. *Adolescence*. New York: Appleton, 1905.

Hall, J. F. *Classical conditioning and instrumental learning: A contemporary approach*. Philadelphia: J. B. Lippincott, 1976.

Hamerton, J. L., Briggs, S. M., Gianelli, F., & Carter, C. O. Chromosome studies in detection of parents with high risk of second child with Down's syndrome. *Lancet*, 1961, *281*, 788–791.

Hamilton, W. D. Selfish and spiteful behaviour in an evolutionary model. *Nature*, 1970, *228*, 1218–1220.

Hamilton, W. D. Geometry for the selfish herd. *Journal of Theoretical Biology*, 1971, *31*, 295–311.

Hamilton, W. D. Altruism and related phenomena, mainly in social insects. *Annual Review of Ecology and Systematics*, 1972, *3*, 193–232.

Hanlon, J. Uri Geller and science. *New Scientist*, 1974, 170–185.

Hansel, C. E. M. *ESP: A scientific evaluation*. New York: Charles Scribner's, 1966.

Harding, R. S. Tradition by a troupe of olive baboons. *American Journal of Physical Anthropology*, 1973, 587–591.

Hardt, J. V., & Kamiya, J. Some comments on Plotkin's self-regulation of electroencephalographic alpha. *Journal of Experimental Psychology*, 1976, *105*, 100–108.

Harger, R. N. The sojourn of alcohol in the body. In R. G. McCarthy (Ed.), *Alcohol education for classroom and community*. New York: McGraw-Hill, 1964.

Harlow, H. F. Mice, monkeys, men, and motives. *Psychological Review*, 1953, *60*, 23–32.

Harlow, H. F. The nature of love. *American Psychologist*, 1958, *12*, 673–685.

Harlow, H. F. Love in infant monkeys. *Scientific American*, 1959, *200*, 68–74.

Harlow, H. F. *Learning to love*. San Francisco: Albion, 1971.

Harlow, H. F., Blazek, N. C., & McClearn, G. E. Manipulatory motivation in the infant rhesus monkey. *Journal of Comparative Physiological Psychology*, 1956, *49*, 444–448.

Haronian, F., & Saunders, D. R. Some intellectual correlates of physique: A review and a study. *Journal of Psychological Studies*, 1967, *15*, 57–105.

Harris, D. *Children's drawings as measures of intellectual maturity*. New York: Harcourt Brace & World, 1963.

Harris, T. *I'm OK—you're OK*. New York: Avon, 1967.

Hart, J. T. Auto-control of EEG alpha. *Psychophysiology*, 1968, *4*, 506.

Hartshorne, H., & May, M. A. *Studies in deceit*. New York: Macmillan, 1928.

Harvey, J. H., Arkin, R. M., Gleason, J. M., & Johnson, S. Effect of expected and observed outcome of an action on the differential causal attributions of actor and observer. *Journal of Personality*, 1974, *42*, 62–77.

Harvey, O. J. System structure, flexibility, and creativity. In O. J. Harvey (Ed.), *Experience, structure, and adaptability*. New York: Springer, 1966.

Harvey, O. J., Hunt, D. E., & Schroder, H. M. *Conceptual systems and personality organization*. New York: John Wiley, 1961.

Hassett, J. Sex and smell. *Psychology Today*, March 1978, pp. 40–45.

Hassett, J. Teaching yourself to relax. *Psychology Today*, August 1978, 125–126.

Havighurst, R. J., & Taba, H. *Adolescent character and personality*. New York: John Wiley, 1949.

Hawkes, J. (Ed.). *The world of the past*. New York: Alfred A. Knopf, 1963.

Hawkes, J. *The atlas of early man*. New York: St. Martin's Press, 1976.

Hawkins, D. *The science and ethics of equality*. New York: Basic Books, 1977.

Hayes, C. *The ape in our house*. New York: Harper & Row, 1951.

Hayes, H. T. P. The pursuit of reason. *New York Times Magazine*, June 12, 1977, pp. 21–24; 74–79.

Hayes, K. J., & Hayes, C. Intellectual development of a home-raised chimpanzee. *Proceedings of the American Philosophical Society*, 1951, *95*, 105–109.

Hayflick, L. Why grow old? *Stanford Magazine*, September 1975, pp. 36–43.

Haynes, S. G., Feinleib, M., & Kannel, W. B. The relationship of psychosocial factors to coronary heart disease in the Framingham study: III. Eight-year incidence of coronary heart disease. *American Journal of Epidemiology*, 1980, *111*, 37–58.

Haywood, K. M. Skill performance on biorhythm theory's physically critical day. *Perceptual and Motor Skills*, 1979, *48*, 373–374.

Hearse, F., & Jenkins, H. M. Sign-trading: The stimulus-reinforcer relation and directed action. *Psychonomic Society Monographs* (Austin, Tex.), 1975.

Heath, R. G. Pleasure response of human subjects to direct stimulation of the brain: Physiologic and psychodynamic considerations. In R. G. Heath (Ed.), *The role of pleasure in behavior*. New York: Harper & Row, 1964.

Hebb, D. O. On the nature of fear. *Psychological Review*, 1946, *53*, 259–276.

Hebb, D. O. The effects of early experience on problem-solving at maturity. *American Psychologist*, 1947, *2*, 306–307.

Hebb, D. O. *The organization of behavior*. New York: John Wiley, 1949.

Hebb, D. O. *A textbook of psychology* (2nd ed.). Philadelphia: W. B. Saunders, 1966.

Hebron, M. E. *Motivated learning: A developmental study from birth to the senium*. London: Methuen, 1966.

Heider, F. *The psychology of interpersonal relations*. New York: John Wiley, 1958.

Heim, A. Remarks on fatal falls. *Yearbook of the Swiss Alpine Club* 1892, *27*, 327–337. Trans. R. Noyes and R. Kletti in *Omega*, 1972, *3*, 45–52.

Held, R., & Hein, A. Movement produced stimulation in the development of visually guided behavior. *Journal of Comparative and Physiological Psychology*, 1963, *56*, 872–876.

Heldman, A. W. Social psychology versus the first amendment freedoms, due process, liberty, and limited government. *Cumberland-Samford Law Review*, 1973, *4*, 1–40.

Hellyer, S. Supplementary report: Frequency of stimulus presentation and short-term decrement in recall. *Journal of Experimental Psychology*, 1962, *64*, 650.

Henderson, J. "Reading and writing" and hypnotic state—Hypnosis may triple learning. *New York Times*, September 29, 1968, pp. 5; 21.

Hendry, L. S. *Cognitive processes in a moral conflict situation*. Unpublished doctoral dissertation, Yale University, 1960.

Herold, E. S., & Goodwin, M. R. The adoption of oral contraceptives among adolescent females: Reference group influence. In K. Ishwaran (Ed.), *Childhood and adolescence in Canada*. Toronto: McGraw-Hill Ryerson, 1979, 232–248.

Heron, W. The pathology of boredom. *Scientific American*, 1957, *196*, 52–69.

Herrnstein, R. J. *IQ in the meritocracy*. Boston: Little, Brown, 1973.

Herrnstein, R. J. Doing what comes naturally: A reply to Professor Skinner. *American Psychologist*, 1977, *32*, 1013–1016. (a)

Herrnstein, R. J. The evolution of behaviorism. *American Psychologist*, 1977, *32*, 593–605. (b)

Herzog, E., & Sudia, C. *Boys in fatherless homes*. Washington, D.C.: U.S. Department of Health, Education, and Welfare, 1970.

Hess, E. H. Imprinting and the "critical period" concept. In E. L. Bliss (Ed.), *Roots of behavior*. New York: Harper & Row, 1962.

Hess, E. H., & Polt, J. M. Pupil size as related to interest value of visual stimuli. *Science*, 1960, *132*, 349–350.

Hess, W. R., & Akert, K. Experimental data on role of hypothalamus in mechanism of emotional behavior. *Archives of Neurological Psychiatry*, 1955, *73*, 127–129.

Heston, L. L. Psychiatric disorders in foster home children of schizophrenic mothers. *British Journal of Psychiatry*, 1966, *112*, 819–825.

Hetherington, A. N., & Ranson, S. W. Spontaneous activity and food intake of rats with hypothalamic lesions. *American Journal of Physiology*, 1942, *136*, 609–617.

Higbee, K. L. *Your memory: How it works and how to improve it*. Englewood Cliffs, N.J.: Prentice-Hall, 1977.

Hilgard, E. R. *Hypnotic susceptibility*. New York: Harcourt Brace & World, 1965.

Hilgard, E. R. A neo-dissociation theory of pain-reduction in hypnosis. *Psychological Review*, 1973, *80*, 396–411.

Hilgard, E. R. Hypnosis. *Annual Review of Psychology*, 1975, *26*, 19–44.

Hilgard, E. R. *Divided consciousness: Multiple controls in human thought and action*. New York: John Wiley, 1977.

Hill, O. T., Rubin, Z., & Peplau, L. A. Break-ups before marriage: The end of 103 affairs. *Journal of Social Issues*, 1976, *32*, 147–168.

Himmelweit, H. T., Oppenheim, A. N., & Vince, P. *Television and the child*. New York: Oxford University Press, 1958.

Hinde, R. A., & Stevenson-Hinde, R. (Eds.). *Constraints on learning: Limitations and predispositions*. New York: Academic Press, 1973.

Hindley, C. B., Filliozat, A. M., Klackenberg, G., Nicolet-Meister, D., & Sand, E. A. Differences in age of walking in five European longitudinal samples. *Human Biology*, 1966, *38*, 364–379.

Hobson, J. A., & McCarley, R. W. The brain as a dream state generator: An activation-synthesis hypothesis of the dream process. *American Journal of Psychiatry*, 1977, *134* (12).

Hochberg, J. *Perception* (2nd ed.). Englewood Cliffs, N.J.: Prentice-Hall, 1978.

Hoffman, L. W. Early childhood experiences and women's achievement motives. *Journal of Social Issues*, 1972, *28*, 129–155.

Hoffman, M. C. Empathy, role-taking, guilt and development of altruistic motives. In T. Lick (Ed.), *Moral development and behavior*. New York: Holt, Rinehart & Winston, 1976.

Hogan, D. R. The effectiveness of sex therapy: A review of the literature. In J. LoPiccolo & L. LoPiccolo (Eds.), *Handbook of sex therapy*. New York: Plenum, 1978.

Holland, J. L., Magoon, T. M., & Spokane, A. R. Counseling psychology: Career interventions, research, and theory. *Annual Review of Psychology*, 1981, *32*, 279–305.

Hollander, M. J., & McCurdy, E. A. *Alcohol and drug use among Vancouver secondary school students: 1970, 1974, 1978. Summary of findings*. Vancouver, B.C.: Alcohol and Drug Commission of British Columbia, 1978.

Hollingshead, A. B. *Elmtown's youth*. New York: John Wiley, 1949.

Holmes, T. H., & Rahe, R. H. The social readjustment rating scale. *Journal of Psychosomatic Research*, 1967, *11*, 213–218.

Holroyd, S. *Psi and the consciousness explosion*. New York: Taplinger, 1976.

Hood, A. B. A study of the relationship between physique and personality variables measured by the MMPI. *Journal of Personality*, 1963, *31*, 97–107.

Horn, J. L. Psychometric studies of aging and intelligence. In S. Gerscon and A. Raskin (Eds.), *Aging* (Vol. 2. *Genesis and treatment of psychological disorders in the elderly*). New York: Raven, 1975.

Horn, J. L. Human abilities: A review of research and theory in the early 1970's. *Annual Review of Psychology*, 1976, *27*, 437–485.

Horn, J. L., & Donaldson, G. On the myth of intellectual decline in adulthood. *American Psychologist*, 1976, *31*, 701–719.

Horn, J. M., Loehlin, J. C., & Willerman, L. Intellectual resemblance among adoptive and biological relatives: The Texas Adoption Project. *Behavior Genetics*, 1979, *9*, 177–207.

Horner, M. Women's will to fail. *Psychology Today*, 1969, pp. 36–38.

Horvath, F. S., & Reid, J. E. The reliability of polygraph examiner diagnosis. In J. E. Reid & F. E. Inbau, *Truth and deception: The polygraph ("lie-detector") technique* (2nd ed.). Baltimore: Williams & Wilkins, 1977.

Hovland, C. I. Computer simulation of thinking. *American Psychologist*, 1960, *15*, 687–693.

Hovland, C. I., & Hunt, E. B. Computer simulation of concept attainment. *Behavioral Science*, 1960, *5*, 265–267.

Hovland, C., Janis, I., & Kelley, H. H. *Communication and persuasion*. New Haven: Yale University Press, 1953.

Hovland, C. I., & Weiss, W. The influence of source credibility on communication effectiveness. *Public Opinion Quarterly*, 1951, *15*, 635–650.

Howard, M. How to look and outreach for the younger father. *American Journal of Orthopsychiatry*, 1971, *41*, 294–295.

Howe, M. J. A. *Introduction to human memory*. New York: Harper & Row, 1970.

Hubel, D. H., & Wiesel, T. N. Receptive fields and functional architecture of monkey striate cortex. *Journal of Physiology*, 1968, *195*, 215–243.

Hubel, D. H., & Wiesel, T. N. The period of susceptibility to the physiological effects of unilateral eye closure in kittens. *Journal of Physiology*, 1970, *206*, 419–436.

Hubel, D. H., & Wiesel, T. N. Sequence regularity and geometry of orientation columns in the monkey striate cortex. *Journal of Comparative Neurology*, 1974, *158*, 267–294.

Hudson, L. *Frames of mind*. Harmondsworth, Eng.: Penguin, 1968.

Hudson, W. Pictorial depth perception in subcultural groups in Africa. *Journal of Social Psychology*, 1960, *52*, 183–208.

Hudspeth, W. J., McGaugh, J. L., & Thompson, C. W. Aversive and amnesic effects of electroconvulsive shock. *Journal of Comparative and Physiological Psychology*, 1964, *57*, 61–64.

Huesmann, L. R. (Ed.). Special issue: Learned helplessness as a model of depression. *Journal of Abnormal Psychology*, 1978, *87* (1).

Hull, C. L. *Principles of behavior*. New York: Appleton-Century-Crofts, 1943.

Hull, C. L. *A behavior system*. New Haven: Yale University Press, 1952.

Hulse, S. E. Reinforcement contrast effects in rats following experimental definition of a dimension of reinforcement magnitude. *Journal of Comparative and Physiological Psychology*, 1973, *85*, 160–170.

Hulse, S. E., Deese, J., & Egeth, H. *The psychology of learning*. New York: McGraw-Hill, 1975.

Hunt, J. M. *Intelligence and experience*. New York: Ronald Press, 1961.

Hunt, J. M. The psychological basis for preschool enrichment as an antidote for cultural deprivation. *Merrill-Palmer Quarterly*, 1964, *10*, 209–248.

Hunt, J. M. Has compensatory education failed? Has it been attempted? *Harvard Educational Review*, Reprint Series No. 2, 1969, pp. 130–152.

Hunt, M. *Sexual behavior in the 1970's*. Chicago: Playboy Press, 1974.

Husband, R. W. Sex differences in dream contents. *Journal of Abnormal and Social Psychology*, 1936, *30*, 513–521.

Huston, T. L. (Ed.). *Foundations of interpersonal attraction*. New York: Academic Press, 1974.

Hyde, T. S., & Jenkins, J. J. The differential effects of incidental tasks on the organization and recall of a list of highly associated words. *Journal of Experimental Psychology*, 1969, *82*, 472–481.

Hyden, H. Neuronal plasticity, protein conformation and behavior. In H. P. Zippel (Ed.)., *Memory and the transfer of information*. New York: Plenum Press, 1973, 511–520.

Hyden, H., & Lange, P. W. Protein changes in different brain areas as a function of intermittent training. *Proceedings of the National Academy of Sciences*, 1972, *69*, 1980–1984.

Interview with Candace Pert. *Omni*, February 1982, 63–65; 110–112.

Interview with David Levy. *Omni*, April 1979, 65–67; 134–135.

Involvement in developmental psychology today. Del Mar, Calif.: C. R. M. Books, 1971.

Irwin, O. C. Infant speech. *Scientific American*, 1949, *18*, 22–24.

Itakura, K., Hirose, T., Crea, R., Riggs, A. D., Heyneker, H. L., Bolivar, R., & Boyer, H. W. Expression in *Escherichia coli* of a chemically synthesized gene for the hormone somatostatin. *Science*, 1977, *198*, 1056–1063.

Izard, C. E. *Human emotions*. New York: Plenum Press, 1977.

Jackson, D. N., & Paunonen, S. V. Personality structure and assessment. *Annual Review of Psychology*, 1980, *31*, 503–551.

Jacobi, J. *The psychology of C. G. Jung* (7th ed.). New Haven: Yale University Press, 1968.

Jacobson, A., & Kales, A. Somnambulism: All-night EEG and related studies. In S. S. Key, E. V. Evarts, & H. L. Williams (Eds.), *Sleep and altered states of consciousness*. Baltimore: Williams & Wilkins, 1967.

Jaffee, C. L., Millman, F., & Gorman, B. An attempt to condition an eyeblink response to verbal deception. *Psychological Reports*, 1966, *19*, 421–422.

Jahnke, J. C. Serial position effects in immediate serial recall. *Journal of Verbal Learning and Verbal Behavior*, 1963, *2*, 284–287.

Jalkanen, A. W. Drug use and the adolescent. In J. F. Adams (Ed.), *Understanding adolescence: Current developments in adolescent psychology* (2nd ed.). Boston: Allyn & Bacon, 1973.

James, W. What is an emotion? *Mind*, 1884, *9*, 188–205.

James, W. *The principles of psychology*. New York: Holt, Rinehart & Winston, 1890.

Jarvik, L. F., Klodin, V., & Matsuyama, S. S. Human aggression and the extra Y chromosome: Fact or fantasy? *American Psychologist*, 1973, *28*, 674–682.

Jaynes, J. *The origin of consciousness in the breakdown of the bicameral mind*. Boston: Houghton Mifflin, 1976.

Jeffrey, R. W., & Coates, T. J. Why aren't they losing weight? *Behavior Therapy*, 1978, *9*, 856–860.

Jenkins, J. G., & Dallenbach, K. M. Obliviance during sleep walking. *American Journal of Psychology*, 1924, *35*, 605–612.

Jensen, A. R. Social class, race, and genetics: Implications for education. *American Educational Research Journal*, 1968, *5*, 1–42.

Jensen, A. R. How much can we boost IQ and scholastic achievement? *Harvard Educational Review*, 1969, *39*, 1–123.

Jensen, A. R. A review of the Rorschach. In O. K. Buros (Ed.), *Personality tests and reviews.* Highland Park, N.J.: Gryphon Press, 1970.

Jensen, A. R. Kinship correlations reported by Sir Cyril Burt. *Behavior Genetics,* 1974, *4,* 1–28.

Johnson, H. R., Myhre, S. A., Ruvalcaba, R. H. A., Thuline, H. C., & Kelley, V. C. Effects of testosterone on body image and behavior in Klinefelter's syndrome: A pilot study. *Developmental Medicine and Child Neurology,* 1970, *12,* 454–460.

Johnson, M. K., Bransford, J. D., & Solomon, S. Memory for tacit implications of sentences. *Journal of Experimental Psychology,* 1973, *98,* 203–205.

Johnson, N. Through the video-screen darkly. *Christian Science Monitor,* February 1969.

Johnson, R. *Elementary statistics.* North Scituate, Mass.: Duxbury, 1976.

Johnston, L. *Drugs and American youth.* Ann Arbor, Mich.: Institute for Social Research, University of Michigan, 1973.

Jolly, A. *The evolution of primate behavior.* New York: Macmillan, 1972.

Jones, D. E. H. The stability of the bicycle. *Physics Today,* 1970, *4,* 34–40.

Jones, E. *The life and work of Sigmund Freud* (3 vols.). New York: Basic Books, 1953–1957.

Jones, E. E. *Ingratiation.* New York: Appleton-Century-Crofts, 1964.

Jones, E. E., & Davis, K. E. From acts to dispositions: The attribution process in person perception. In L. Berkowitz (Ed.), *Advances in experimental social psychology* (Vol. 2). New York: Academic Press, 1965.

Jones, E. E., & Nisbett, R. E. *The actor and the observer: Divergent perceptions of the causes of behavior.* Morristown, N.J.: General Learning Press, 1971.

Jones, M. C. The later careers of boys who are early or late maturing. *Child Development,* 1957, *28,* 113–128.

Jones, M. C. Psychological correlates of somatic development. *Child Development,* 1965, *36,* 899–911.

Jones, M. C., & Mussen, T. H. Self conceptions, motivations, and interpersonal attitudes of early and late maturing girls. *Child Development,* 1958, *29,* 491–501.

Jones, P. K, & Jones, S. L. Lunar association with suicide. *Suicide and Life Threatening Behavior,* 1977, *7,* 31–39.

Jung, C. G. *Psychological types.* New York: Harcourt Brace & World, 1923.

Kagan, J. S. Inadequate evidence and illogical conclusions. *Harvard Educational Review,* Reprint Series No. 2, 1969, pp. 126–129.

Kagan, J. S., & Madsen, M. C. Experimental analyses of cooperation and competition of Anglo-American and Mexican children. *Developmental Psychology,* 1972, *6,* 49–59.

Kahneman, D. *Attention and effort.* Englewood Cliffs, N.J.: Prentice-Hall, 1973.

Kalat, J. W. *Biological psychology.* Belmont, Calif.: Wadsworth, 1981.

Kalinowski, L. B. The convulsive therapies. In A. M. Freedman, H. I. Kaplan, & B. J. Sadock (Eds.), *Comprehensive textbook of psychiatry—II,* Vol. 2. Baltimore, Md.: Williams & Wilkins, 1975, 1969–1975.

Kamin, L. J. Predictability, surprise, attention, and conditioning. In B. A. Campbell & R. .M. Church (Eds.), *Punishment and aversive behavior.* New York: Appleton, 1969.

Kamin, L. J. *The science and politics of IQ.* Potomac, Md.: Erlbaum, 1974.

Kamiya, J. Conscious control of brain waves. *Psychology Today,* 1968, pp. 57–60.

Kantor, R. E., Wallner, J. M., & Winder, C. L. Process and reactive schizophrenia. *Journal of Consulting Psychology,* 1953, *17,* 157–162.

Kaplan, B. (Ed.). *The inner world of mental illness.* New York: Harper & Row, 1954.

Kapleau, P. Zen meditation. In P. Kapleau (Ed.), *The three pillars of Zen.* New York: John Weatherhill, 1965.

Kasamatsu, A., & Hirai, T. An electroencephalographic study on the Zen meditation (Zazen). *Folia Psychiatrica and Neurologica,* 1966, *20,* 315–336.

Kasl, S. V., & Cobb, S. Blood pressure changes in men undergoing job loss: A preliminary report. *Psychosomatic Medicine,* 1970, *6,* 95–106.

Kastenbaum, R., & Costa, P. T. Psychological perspectives on death. *Annual Review of Psychology,* 1977, *28,* 225–249.

Katona, G. *Organizing and memory.* New York: Hafner, 1940.

Kaufman, L., & Rock, I. The moon illusion, I. *Science,* 1962, *136,* 953–961. (a)

Kaufman, L., & Rock, I. The moon illusion, II. *Science,* 1962, *136,* 1023–1031. (b)

Kazdin, A. E., & Bootzin, R. R. The token economy: An evaluative review. *Journal of Applied Behavior Analysis,* 1972, *5,* 343–372.

Keith-Lucas, T., & Guttman, N. Robust-single-trial delayed backward conditioning. *Journal of Comparative and Physiological Psychology,* 1975, *88,* 468–476.

Keller, F. S. *Learning: Reinforcement theory* (2nd ed.). New York: Random House, 1969.

Kelley, H. H. The warm-cold variable in first impressions of persons. *Journal of Personality,* 1950, *18,* 431–439.

Kelley, H. H. *Attribution in social interaction.* Morristown, N.J.: General Learning Press, 1971.

Kelley, H. H. The processes of causal attribution. *American Psychologist,* 1973, *28,* 107–128.

Kelley, H. H., & Michela, J. L. Attribution theory and research. *Annual Review of Psychology,* 1980, *31,* 457–501.

Kellogg, W. N. Communication and language in the home raised chimpanzee. *Science,* 1968, *162,* 423–427.

Kellogg, W. N., & Kellogg, L. A. *The ape and the child.* New York: McGraw-Hill, 1933.

Kelly, I. The scientific case against astrology. Part II: Cosmobiology and moon madness. *Mercury,* January–February 1981, 13–30.

Kennell, J. H., Trause, M. A., & Klaus, M. H. Evidence for a sensitive period in the human mother. In *Parent-infant interaction, Ciba Foundation symposium* (new series), 1975, *33,* 87–102.

Kermis, M., Monge, R., & Dusek, J. Human sexuality in the hierarchy of adolescent interests. Paper presented at the annual meeting of the Society for Research in Child Development, Denver, 1975.

Kernberg, O. F. Modern hospital milieu treatment of schizophrenia. In S. Arieti & G. Chrzanowski (Eds.), *New dimensions in psychiatry.* New York: John Wiley, 1975.

Kernberg, O. Why some people can't love (interviewed by Linda Wolfe). *Psychology Today,* June 1978, pp. 55–59.

Kesey, K. *One flew over the cuckoo's nest.* New York: Viking Press, 1962.

Kessen, W. *The child.* New York: John Wiley, 1965.

Kiesler, C. A., & Munson, P. A. Attitudes and opinions. *Annual Review of Psychology,* 1975, *26,* 415–456.

Kilhstrom, J. F. Hypnosis and psychopathology: Retrospect and prospect. *Journal of Abnormal Psychology,* 1979, *88,* 459–473.

King, W. L., & Gruber, H. T. Moon illusion and Emmert's law. *Science,* 1962, *135,* 1125–1126.

Kinsbourne, M., & Cook, J. Generalized and lateralized effects of concurrent verbalization on a unimanual skill. *Quarterly Journal of Experimental Psychology,* 1971, *23,* 341–345.

Kinsey, A. C., Pomeroy, W. D., & Martin, C. E. *Sexual behavior in the human male.* Philadelphia: W. B. Saunders, 1948.

Kinsey, A. C., Pomeroy, W. D., Martin, C. E., & Gebhard, T. H. *Sexual behavior in the human female.* Philadelphia: W. B. Saunders, 1953.

Klatzky, R. L. *Human memory: Structures and processes* (2nd ed.). San Francisco: W. H. Freeman, 1980.

Klaus, M., & Kennell, J. *Maternal-infant bonding.* St. Louis: Mosby, 1976.

Kleck, R. F., & Rubenstein, C. Physical attractiveness, perceived attitude similarity, and interpersonal attraction in an opposite-sex encounter. *Journal of Personality and Social Psychology,* 1975, *31,* 107–114.

Klein, G. S. Semantic power of words measured through interference with color naming. *American Journal of Psychology,* 1964, *77,* 576–588.

Klein, K. E., Wegmann, H. M., & Hunt, B. M. Desynchronization of temperature and performance circadian rhythms as a result of outgoing and homegoing transmeridian flights. *Aerospace Medicine,* 1972, *43,* 119–132.

Kleitman, N. *Sleep and wakefulness* (2nd ed.). Chicago: University of Chicago Press, 1963.

Kline, P. *Fact and fantasy in Freudian theory.* London: Methuen, 1972.

Klineberg, O. Emotional expression in Chinese literature. *Journal of Abnormal and Social Psychology,* 1938, *33,* 517–520.

Klineberg, O. *Race and psychology.* Paris: UNESCO, 1951.

Knowlis, D. T., & Kamiya, J. The control of electroencephalographic alpha rhythms through auditory feedback in the associated mental activity. *Psychophysiology,* 1970, *6,* 476–484.

Knox, V. M., Morgan, A. H., & Hilgard, E. R. Pain suffering in ischemia. *Archives of General Psychiatry,* 1974, *30,* 840–847.

Koch, H. L. Some personality correlates of sex, sibling position, and sex of sibling among five and six year old children. *Genetic Psychology Monographs,* 1955, *52,* 3–50.

Koffka, K. *The growth of mind.* New York: Harcourt Brace & World, 1925.

Koffka, K. *Principles of Gestalt psychology.* New York: Harcourt Brace & World, 1935.

Kohlberg, L. Development of moral character and moral ideology. In M. L. Hoffman & L. W. Hoffman (Eds.), *Review of child development research* (Vol. 1). New York: Russell Sage Foundation, 1964.

Kohlberg, L. Stage and sequence: The cognitive-developmental approach to socialization. In D. Gosslin (Ed.), *Handbook of socialization theory and research.* Skokie, Ill.: Rand McNally, 1969.

Kohlberg, L. Implications of developmental psychology for education: Examples from moral development. *Educational Psychologist,* 1973, *10,* 2–14.

Kohlberg, L., & Turiel, E. *Research in moral development: A cognitive developmental approach.* New York: Holt, Rinehart & Winston, 1971.

Kohler, I. Experiments with goggles. *Scientific American,* 1962, *206,* 62–85.

Köhler, W., *The mentality of the apes.* New York: Harcourt Brace & World, 1927.

Köhler, W. Gestalt psychology today. *American Psychologist,* 1959, *14,* 727–737.

Kolodny, R. C., Masters, W. H., Kolodner, R. M., & Toro, G. Depression of plasma testosterone levels after chronic intensive marihuana use. *New England Journal of Medicine,* 1974, *290,* 872–874.

Koriat, A., Melkman, R., Averill, J. R., & Lazarus, R. S. Self control of emotional reactions to a stressful film. *Journal of Personality,* 1972, *40,* 601–619.

Krauss, I. Predictors of competence in the elderly. Paper presented at the annual meeting of the Western Psychological Association, Los Angeles, 1976.

Krebs, D., & Adinolfi, A. A. Physical attractiveness, social relations, and personality style. *Journal of Personality and Social Psychology,* 1975, *31,* 245–253.

Krech, D. The genesis of "hypotheses" in rats. *University of California Publications in Psychology,* 1932, *6,* 45–64.

Krech, D., Rosenzweig, M., & Bennett, E. L. Environmental impoverishment, social isolation, and changes in brain chemistry and anatomy. *Physiology and Behavior,* 1966, *1,* 99–104.

Krikstone, B. J., & Levitt, R. A. Distorting drugs. In R. A. Levitt (Ed.), *Psychopharmacology: A biological approach.* Washington, D.C.: Hemisphere Publishing Corp., 1975.

Kripke, D. F. Circadian rhythms in sleep and wakefulness. In E. D. Weitzman (Ed.), *Advances in sleep research* (Vol. 2). New York: Spectrum, 1975.

Kripke, D. F., & Simons, R. N. Average sleep, insomnia, and sleeping pill use. *Sleep Research,* 1976, *5,* 110.

Krueger, W. C. F. The effects of overlearning on retention. *Journal of Experimental Psychology,* 1929, *12,* 71–78.

Kryter, K. D. *The effects of noise on men.* New York: Academic Press, 1970.

Kübler-Ross, E. *On death and dying.* New York: Macmillan, 1969.

Kübler-Ross, E. *Questions and answers on death and dying.* New York: Macmillan, 1974.

Kuhn, T. S. *The structure of scientific revolutions* (2nd ed., enl.). Chicago: University of Chicago Press, 1970.

Laing, R. D. Is schizophrenia a disease? *International Journal of Social Psychiatry,* 1964, *10,* 184–193.

Laird, D. A., & Muller, C. G. *Sleep.* London: Williams and Norgate, 1930.

Lambert, M. J., DeJulio, S. S., & Stein, D. M. Therapist interpersonal skills: Process, outcome, methodological considerations, and recommendations for future research. *Psychological Bulletin,* 1978, *85,* 467–489.

Lambert, W., Yackley, A., & Hein, R. N. Child training values of English Canadian and French Canadian parents. *Canadian Journal of Behavioral Science,* 1971, *3,* 217–236.

Land, E. H. The retinex theory of color vision. *Scientific American,* 1977, *237,* 108–129.

Land, E. H., & McCann, J. J. Lightness and retinex theory. *Journal of the Optical Society of America,* 1971, *61*(1), 1–11.

Landis, J. T., & Landis, M. G. *Building a successful marriage.* Englewood Cliffs, N.J.: Prentice-Hall, 1963.

Langer, E. J., & Rodin, J. The effects of choice and enhanced personal responsibility for the aged. *Journal of Personality and Social Psychology,* 1976, *34,* 191–198.

Lanyon, R. I., & Goodstein, L. D. *Personality assessment.* New York: John Wiley, 1971.

Lassner, J. L'hypnose en anesthésiologie. *Cahiers d'anesthésiologie,* 1960.

Latané, B., & Darley, J. M. Group inhibition of bystander intervention. *Journal of Personality and Social Psychology,* 1968, *10,* 215–221.

Latané, B., & Darley, J. M. *The unresponsive bystander: Why doesn't he help?* New York: Appleton-Century-Crofts, 1970.

Latner, J. *The Gestalt therapy book.* New York: Julian Press, 1973.

Lax, E. Birds do it, bees do it, but how do they do it? *Esquire,* July 1976, pp. 89–93.

Lay, C. H., Burron, B. F., & Jackson, D. N. Base rates and informational value in impression formation. *Journal of Personality and Social Psychology,* 1973, *28,* 390–395.

Lazarus, R. S. Cognitive and coping processes in emotion. In B. Weiner (Ed.), *Cognitive views of human motivation.* New York: Academic Press, 1974.

Leach, C. The importance of instructions in assessing sequential effects in impression formation. *British Journal of Social and Clinical Psychology,* 1974, *13,* 151–156.

Leaf, A. Getting old. *Scientific American,* September 1973.

Leakey, L. S. *Adam or ape: A sourcebook of discovery about early man.* New York: Schenkman, 1971.

Leander, J. American Indians in 1626. In G. Andrews & S. Vinkenoog (Eds.), *The book of grass: An anthology of Indian hemp.* New York: Grove Press, 1967.

Ledain, G., Committee Chairman. *A report of the Commission of Inquiry into the Non-Medical Use of Drugs.* Ottawa: Canada Crown Copyright, Information Canada, 1972.

Lefkowitz, M., Erom, L., Walder, L., & Heusmann, L. R. Television violence and child aggression: A followup study. In G. A. Comstock & E. A. Rubinstein (Eds.), *Television and social behavior* (Vol. 3. *Television and adolescent aggressiveness*). Washington, D.C.: U.S. Government Printing Office, 1972.

Lefrancois, G. R. *Adolescents* (2nd ed.). Belmont, Calif.: Wadsworth, 1981.

Lefrancois, G. R. *Psychological theories and human learning* (2nd. ed.). Monterey, Calif.: Brooks/Cole, 1982.

Lefrancois, G. R. *Psychology for teaching: A bear sometimes faces the front* (4th ed.). Belmont, Calif.: Wadsworth, 1982.

Lefrancois, G. R. *Of children: An introduction to child development* (4th ed.). Belmont, Calif.: Wadsworth, 1983.

Lehman, H. C. *Age and achievement.* Princeton: Princeton University Press, 1953.

Leight, K. H., & Ellis, H. C. Emotional mood states, strategies, and state dependency in memory. *Journal of Verbal Learning and Verbal Behavior,* 1981, *20,* 251–266.

Lcippe, M. R., Wells, G. L., & Ostrom, T. M. Crime seriousness as a determinant of accuracy in eyewitness identification. *Journal of Applied Psychology,* 1978, *63,* 345–351.

LeMagnen, J. Advances in studies in the physiological control and regulation of food intake. In E. Stellar & J. M. Sprague (Eds.), *Progress in physiological psychology.* New York: Academic Press, 1974.

Lenneberg, E. H. *Biological foundations of language.* New York: John Wiley, 1967.

Lenneberg, E. H. On explaining languge. *Science,* 1969, *164,* 635–643.

Lenneberg, E. H., Nichols, I. A., & Rosenberger, E. S. Primitive stages of language development in mongolism. In *Disorders of Communication* (Vol. 42). Baltimore: Williams & Wilkins, 1964.

Lepper, M. R., & Greene, D. Turning play into work: Effects of adult surveillance and extrinsic rewards on children's intrinsic motivation. *Journal of Personality and Social Psychology,* 1975, *31,* 479–486.

Lepper, M. R., & Greene, D. Overjustification research and beyond: Toward a means-ends analysis of intrinsic and extrinsic motivation. In D. Greene & M. R. Lepper (Eds.), *The hidden costs of reward.* Hillsdale, N.J.: Lawrence Erlbaum Associates, 1978.

Lepper, M. R., Greene, D., & Nisbett, R. E. Undermining children's intrinsic interest with extrinsic rewards: A test of the "overjustification" hypothesis. *Journal of Personality and Social Psychology,* 1973, *28,* 129–137.

Lerner, I. M. *Heredity, evolution, and society.* San Francisco: W. H. Freeman, 1968.

Levenson, R. W. Feedback effects and respiratory involvement in voluntary control of heart rate. *Psychophysiology,* 1976, *13,* 108–114.

LeVere, T. E. Neural stability, sparing, and behavioral recovery following brain damage. *Psychological Review,* 1975, *82*(5), 344–358.

Levinson, D. J. *The seasons of a man's life.* New York: Alfred A. Knopf, 1978.

Levison, P. K., & Flynn, J. P. The objects attacked by cats during stimulation of the hypothalamus. *Animal Behavior,* 1965, *13,* 217–220.

Levitsky, A., & Perls, F. The rules and games of Gestalt therapy. In J. Fagan & I. L. Shepherd (Eds.), *Gestalt therapy now: Theory, techniques, applications.* New York: Harper & Row, 1970.

Levitt, E. E. Research on psychotherapy with children. In A. E. Bergin & S. L. Garfield (Eds.), *Handbook of psychotherapy and behavior change.* New York: John Wiley, 1971.

Levitt, R. A. *Psychopharmacology: A biological approach.* Washington, D.C.: Hemisphere, 1975.

Levitt, R. A., & Lonowski, D. J. Adrenergic drugs. In R. A. Levitt (Ed.), *Psychopharmacology: A biological approach.* Washington, D.C.: Hemisphere, 1975.

Levy, L. H. *Concepts of personality: Theories and research.* New York: Random House, 1970.

Lewin, K. *A dynamic theory of personality* (B. K. Adams & K. E. Zener, Trans.). New York: McGraw-Hill, 1935.

Lewin, R. Starved brains. *Psychology Today,* September 1975, pp. 29–33.

Lewis, M. Parents and children: Sex role development. *School Review,* 1972, *80,* 229–240.

Leyens, J. P., Camino, L., Parke, R. D., & Berkowitz, L. Effects of movie violence on aggression in a field setting as a function of group dominance and cohesion. *Journal of Personality and Social Psychology,* 1975, *32,* 346–360.

Lieberman, L. R. Letter in response to Rosenhan, 1973. *Science,* 1973, *180,* 361.

Liebert, R. M., & Baron, R. A. Short term effects of televised aggression on children's aggressive behavior. In J. P. Murray, E. A. Rubinstein, & G. A. Comstock (Eds.), *Television and social behavior* (Vol. 2. *Television and social learning*). Washington, D.C.: U.S. Government Printing Office, 1972.

Liebert, R. M., & Schwartzberg, N. S. Effects of mass media. *Annual Review of Psychology,* 1977, *28,* 141–173.

Liebert, R. M., & Spiegler, M. E. *Personality: Strategies for the study of man.* Homewood, Ill.: Dorsey Press, 1975.

Lief, H. I., & Fox, R. S. Training for "detached concern" in medical students. In H. I. Lief, V. F. Lief, & N. R. Lief (Eds.), *The psychological basis of medical practice.* New York: Harper & Row, 1963.

Lilly, J. C. *The center of the cyclone: An autobiography of inner space.* New York: Julian Press, 1972.

Linden, E. Talk to the animals. *Omni,* January 1980.

Lindsay, P. H., & Norman, D. A. *Human information processing.* New York: Academic Press, 1972.

Lippmann, W. *Public opinion.* New York: Harcourt Brace, 1922.

Lipsitt, L. P. Babies: They're a lot smarter than they look. *Psychology Today,* December 1971, pp. 70–72, 88–89.

Lipsitt, L. P., Engen, T., & Kaye, H. Developmental changes in the olfactory threshold of the neonate. *Child Development,* 1963, *34,* 371–376.

Loehlin, H. C., Lindzey, G., & Spuhler, J. N. *Race differences in intelligence.* San Francisco: W. H. Freeman, 1975.

Loftus, E. F. *Eyewitness testimony.* Cambridge, Mass.: Harvard University Press, 1979. (a)

Loftus, E. F. The malleability of human memory. *American Scientist,* 1979, *67,* 312–320. (b)

Lorayne, H., & Lucas, J. *The memory book.* New York: Ballantine Books, 1974.

Lorenz, K. *King Solomon's ring.* London: Methuen, 1952.

Lorenz, K. *On aggression.* New York: Harcourt Brace Jovanovich, 1966.

Louis, A. M. Should you buy biorhythms? *Psychology Today,* April 1978, 93–96.

Lovett Doust, J. W. Studies in the physiology of awareness: The incidence and content of dream patterns and their relationship to anoxia. *Journal of Mental Science,* 1951, *97,* 801–811.

Lubin, A. A note on Sheldon's table of correlations between temperamental traits. *British Journal of Psychology,* 1950, *3,* 186–189.

Luborsky, L., Singer, B., & Luborsky, L. Comparative studies of psychotherapies. Is it true that "everyone has won and all must have prizes"? *Archives of General Psychiatry,* 1975, *32,* 995–1008.

Luce, G. G., & Segal, J. *Sleep.* New York: Coward-McCann, 1966.

Luchins, A. S. Experimental attempts to minimize the impact of first impressions. In C. I. Hovland (Ed.), *The order of presentation in persuasion.* New Haven: Yale University Press, 1957. (a)

Luchins, A. S. Primacy-recency in impression formation. In C. I. Hovland (Ed.), *The order of presentation in persuasion.* New Haven: Yale University Press, 1957. (b)

Luchins, A. S. Definitiveness of impression and primacy-recency in communications. *Journal of Social Psychology,* 1958, *48,* 275–290.

Luchins, A. S., & Luchins, E. H. New experimental attempts at preventing mechanization in problem solving. *Journal of General Psychology,* 1950, *42,* 279–297.

Luckey, F. B., & Nass, G. D. The comparison of sexual attitudes and behavior in an international sample. *Journal of Marriage and the Family,* 1969, *31,* 364–378.

Luckiesch, M. *Visual illusions: Their causes, characteristics and applications.* New York: Dover, 1965.

Lumsden, C. J., & Wilson, E. O. *Genes, mind, and culture: The coevolutionary process.* Cambridge: Harvard University Press, 1981.

Lundin, R. W. *Personality: A behavioral analysis* (2nd ed.). New York: Macmillan, 1974.

Luria, A. R. *The mind of a mnemonist.* New York: Avon Books, 1968.

Lynn, D. B. *The father: His role in child development.* Monterey, Calif.: Brooks/Cole, 1974.

Maccoby, E. E., & Jacklin, C. N. *The psychology of sex differences.* Stanford, Calif.: Stanford University Press, 1974.

MacDonald, M. L., Lidsky, T. I., & Kern, J. M. Drug instigated effects. In A. P. Goldstein and F. H. Kanfer (Eds.), *Maximizing treatment gains: Transfer enhancement in psychotherapy.* New York: Academic Press, 1979, 429–445.

Maddi, S., & Costa, P. T. *Humanism in personality.* Chicago: Aldine-Atherton, 1972.

Mahoney, M. J. Reflections on the cognitive learning trend in psychotherapy. *American Psychologist,* 1977, *32,* 5–12.

Maier, N. F. Reasoning in humans. *Journal of Comparative Psychology,* 1931, *12,* 181–194.

Maier, S. F. Failure to escape traumatic shock: Incompatible skeletal motor responses or learned helplessness? *Learning and Motivation,* 1970, *1,* 157–170.

Maier, S. F., Albin, R. W., & Testa, T. J. Failure to learn to escape in rats previously exposed to inescapable shock depends on the nature of the escape response. *Journal of Comparative and Physiological Psychology,* 1973, *85,* 581–592.

Maliver, B. L. *The encounter game.* New York: Stein & Day, 1973.

Mann, J., Berkowitz, L., Sidman, J., Stair, S., & Weso, S. Satiation of the transient stimulating effect of erotic films. *Journal of Personality and Social Psychology,* 1974, *30,* 729–735.

Maranon, G. Contribution à l'étude de l'action émotive de l'adrénaline. *Revue Française Endocrinologique,* 1924, *2,* 301–325.

Margules, D. L., Moisset, B., Lewis, M. J., Shibuya, H., & Pert, C. B. Beta-endorphin is associated with overeating in genetically obese mice (ob/ob) and rats (fa/fa). *Science,* 1978, *202,* 988–991.

Marler, P. R., & Hamilton, W. J., III. *Mechanisms of animal behavior.* New York: John Wiley, 1966.

Marquet, P. B. *Rogers.* Paris: Psychotheque, Editions Universitaires, 1971.

Maslow, A. H. *Motivation and personality* (2nd ed.). New York: Harper & Row, 1970.

Masters, W. H., & Johnson, V. E. *Human sexual response.* Boston: Little, Brown, 1966.

Masters, W. H., & Johnson, V. E. *Human sexual inadequacy.* Boston: Little, Brown, 1970.

Mayer, R. E. *Thinking and problem solving: An introduction to human cognition and learning.* Glenview, Ill.: Scott, Foresman, 1977.

Mazur, A. On Wilson's sociobiology. *American Journal of Sociology,* 1977, *83,* 697–700.

McCain, G., & Segal, E. M. *The game of science* (4th ed.). Monterey, Calif.: Brooks/Cole, 1982.

McCall's Magazine. I have never again been afraid of death. November 1976, pp. 96–100.

McCary, J. L. *Human sexuality.* New York: D. Van Nostrand, 1978.

McClearn, G. E., & DeFries, J. C. *Introduction to behavioral genetics.* San Francisco: W. H. Freeman, 1973.

McClelland, D. C. Risk taking in children with high and low need for achievement. In J. W. Atkinson (Ed.), *Motives in fantasy, action, and society.* New York: Van Nostrand Reinhold, 1958.

McClelland, D. C., Atkinson, J. W., Clark, R. A., & Lowell, E. L. *The achievement motive.* New York: Appleton-Century-Crofts, 1953.

McClothlin, W. H. Drug use and abuse. *Annual Review of Psychology,* 1975, *26,* 45–64.

McConnell, J. V. Memory transfer through cannibalism in planarians. *Journal of Neuropsychiatry,* 1962, *3,* monograph supp. 1.

McConnell, J. V. Worm-breeding with tongue in cheek and the confessions of a scientist hoist by his own petard. *UNESCO Courier,* April 1976, pp. 12–15; 32.

McDaniel, E., Guay, R., Ball, L., & Kolloff, M. A spatial experience questionnaire and some preliminary findings. Unpublished paper presented at the annual meeting of the American Psychological Association, Toronto, Canada, August 1978.

McDougall, W. *An introduction to social psychology.* London: Methuen, 1908.

McFall, R. M. Smoking-cessation research. *Journal of Consulting and Clinical Psychology,* 1978, *46,* 703–712.

McGraw, M. B. *The neuromuscular maturation of the human infant.* New York: Columbia University Press, 1943.

McKee, J. T., & Leader, F. The relationship of socio-economic status and aggression to the competitive behavior of pre-school children. *Child Development,* 1955, *26,* 135–142.

Mcloskey, M., & Santee, J. Are semantic memory and episodic memory distinct systems? *Journal of Experimental Psychology: Human Learning and Memory,* 1981, *7,* 66–71.

McNeill, D. *The acquisition of language: The study of developmental psycholinguistics.* New York: Harper & Row, 1970.

McPhail, P., Ungoed-Thomas, J. R., & Chapman, H. *Moral education in the secondary school.* London: Longmans, 1972.

Mead, G. H. *Mind, self, and society.* Chicago: University of Chicago Press, 1934.

Mead, G. H. *Mind, self, and society* (C. W. Morris, Ed.). Chicago: University of Chicago Press, 1967.

Mead, M. *Sex and temperament in three primitive societies.* New York: New American Library, 1935.

Mead, M. (Ed.). *Cooperation and competition among primitive peoples.* New York: McGraw-Hill, 1937.

Mead, M. *Culture and commitment: The new relationships between the generations in the 1970's* (rev. ed.). New York: Columbia University Press, 1978.

Mednick, S. A. The associative basis of the creative process. *Psychological Review,* 1962, *69,* 220–232.

Meeker, W. B., & Barber, T. X. Toward an explanation of stage hypnosis. *Journal of Abnormal Psychology,* 1971, *77,* 61–70.

Melican, G. J., & Feldt, L. S. An empirical study of the Zajonc-Markus hypothesis for achievement test score declines. *American Educational Research Journal,* 1980, *17,* 5–19.

Meltzoff, J., & Kornreich, J. *Research in psychotherapy.* New York: Atherton, 1970.

Melzack, R. Phantom limbs. *Psychology Today,* October 1970, pp. 63–68.

Melzack, R., & Perry, C. Self-regulation of pain: The use of alpha-feedback and hypnotic training for the control of chronic pain. *Experimental Neurology,* 1975, *46,* 452–469.

Melzack, R., & Wall, P. D. Pain mechanisms: A new theory. *Science,* 1965, *150,* 971–979.

Mendenhall, W., McClave, J. T., and Ramey, M. *Statistics for psychology* (2nd ed.). North Scituate, Mass.: Duxbury, 1977.

Mervis, C. V., & Rosch, E. Categorization of natural objects. *Annual Review of Psychology,* 1981, *32,* 89–115.

Mettee, D. R. Rejection of unexpected success as a function of the negative consequences of accepting success. *Journal of Personality and Social Psychology,* 1971, *17,* 332–341.

Milgram, S. Behavioral study of obedience. *Journal of Abnormal and Social Psychology,* 1963, *67,* 371–378.

Milgram, S. Some conditions of obedience and disobedience to authority. *Human Relations,* 1965, *18,* 67–76.

Milgram, S. *Obedience to authority.* New York: Harper & Row, 1975.

Miller, D. T. Locus of control and ability to tolerate gratification delay: When it is better to be an external. *Journal of Research in Personality,* 1978, *12,* 49–56.

Miller, G. A. The magical number seven, plus or minus two: Some limits on our capacity for processing information. *Psychological Review,* 1956, *63,* 81–97.

Miller, G. A., Galanter, E., & Pribram, K. H. *Plans and the structure of behavior.* New York: Holt, Rinehart & Winston, 1960.

Miller, N. E. Learning of visceral and glandular responses. *Science,* 1969, *163,* 434–445.

Miller, N. E. Biofeedback and visceral learning. *Annual Review of Psychology,* 1978, *29,* 373–404.

Miller, N. E., & Dollard, J. C. *Social learning and imitation.* New Haven: Yale University Press, 1941.

Milner, B. Hemispheric specialization: Scope and limits. In F. O. Schmitt & F. G. Worden (Eds.), *The Neurosciences: Third study program.* Cambridge, Mass.: MIT Press, 1974.

Milstein, R. M. Responsiveness in newborn infants of overweight and normal weight parents. *Appetite,* 1980, *1,* 65–74.

Minter, R. E., & Kimball, C. P. Life events, personality traits and illness. In I. L. Kutach, L. B. Schlesinger, & Associates (Eds.), *Handbook on stress and anxiety.* San Francisco: Jossey Bass, 1980, 189–206.

Mischel, W. *Personality and assessment.* New York: John Wiley, 1968.

Mischel, W. Toward a cognitive, social learning reconceptualization of personality. *Psychological Review,* 1973, *80,* 252–283.

Mischel, W. On the future of personality measurement. *American Psychologist,* 1977, *32,* 246–254.

Mischel, W. On the interface of cognition and personality: Beyond the person-situation debate. *American Psychologist*, 1979, *34*, 740–754.

Mishlove, J. *The roots of consciousness*. New York: Random House, 1975.

Mitchell, E. D. *Psychic exploration: A challenge for science*. New York: G. P. Putnam's Sons, 1974.

Mitchell, G. D., Arling, G. L., & Moller, G. W. Long term effects of maternal punishment on the behavior of monkeys. *Psychonomic Science*, 1967, *32*, 209–210.

Mitler, M. M., Guilleminault, C., Orem, J., Zarcone, V. P., & Dement, W. C. Sleeplessness, sleep attacks, and things that go wrong in the night. *Psychology Today*, December 1975, pp. 45–50.

Moffitt, A. R. Consonant perception by 20–24 week old infants. *Child Development*, 1971, *42*, 717–731.

Mollon, J. D. Color vision. *Annual Review of Psychology*, 1982, *33*, 41–85.

Monahan, L., Kuhn, D., & Shaver, P. Interpsychic versus cultural explanations of the "fear of success" motive. *Journal of Personality and Social Psychology*, 1974, *29*, 60–64.

Money, J. Psychosexual differentiation. In. J. Money (Ed.), *Sex research: New developments*. New York: Holt, Rinehart & Winston, 1965.

Money, J. Counselling in genetics and applied behavior genetics. In K. W. Schaie, V. E. Anderson, G. E. McClearn, J. Money (Eds.), *Developmental human behavior genetics*. Boston: D. C. Heath, 1975.

Money, J., & Erhardt, A. A. Prenatal hormonal exposure: Possible effects on behavior in men. In R. P. Michael (Ed.), *Endocrinology and human behavior*. London: Oxford University Press, 1968.

Money, J., & Erhardt, A. A. *Man and woman, boy and girl: Differentiation and dimorphism of gender identity*. Baltimore: Johns Hopkins Press, 1972.

Monson, T. C., & Snyder, M. Actors, observers, and the attribution process. *Journal of Experimental and Social Psychology*, 1977, *13*, 89–111.

Monthly vital statistics report (births, marriages, divorces and deaths for 1974). Washington, D.C.: Department of Health, Education, and Welfare, 1975.

Moody, R. A. *Life after life*. Covington, Ga.: Mockingbird Books, 1976.

Moray, N. Attention in dichotic listening: Effective cues and the influence of instruction. *Quarterly Journal of Experimental Psychology*, 1959, *11*, 56–60.

Moriarty, R. Crime, commitment, and the responsive bystander: Two field experiments. *Journal of Personality and Social Psychology*, 1975, *31*, 370–376.

Morris, D. *Manwatching: A field guide to human behaviour*. London: Jonathan Cape, 1977.

Mosher, D. L. Psychological reactions to pornographic films. In D. M. Amoroso et al., *An investigation of behavioral, psychological, and physiological reactions to pornographic stimuli*. Technical report of the Commission on Obscenity and Pornography. Washington, D.C.: U.S. Government Printing Office, 1970.

Moyer, K. E. *The psychobiology of aggression*. New York: Harper & Row, 1976.

Moyer, W. W. Effects of loss of freedom on subjects with internal or external locus of control. *Journal of Research on Personality*, 1978, *12*, 253–261.

Murchison, C. (Ed.). *A history of psychology in autobiography* (Vol. 3). Worcester, Mass.: Clark University Press, 1936.

Murphy, G., & Korach, J. *Historical introduction to modern psychology* (3rd ed.). New York: Harcourt Brace Jovanovich, 1972.

Murray, H. A. *Explorations in personality*. New York: Oxford University Press, 1938.

Murray, H. A. *Thematic apperception test*. Cambridge, Mass.: Harvard University Press, 1943.

Murray, J. P. Television and violence: Implications of the Surgeon General's research program. *American Psychologist*, 1973, 472–478.

Murray, J. P., Rubinstein, E. A., & Comstock, G. A. (Eds.). *Television and social behavior* (Vol. 2. *Television and social learning*). Washington, D.C.: U.S. Government Printing Office, 1972.

National Survey on Drug Abuse: 1977. Vol. I: Main Findings. Washington, D.C.: Government Printing Office, 1977.

Neisser, U. *Cognitive psychology*. New York: Appleton-Century-Crofts, 1967.

Neisser, U. *Cognition and reality: Principles and implications of cognitive psychology*. San Francisco: W. H. Freeman, 1976.

Newcomb, T. M. *The acquaintanceship process*. New York: Holt, Rinehart & Winston, 1961.

Newell, A., Shaw, J. C., & Simon, H. A. Empirical explorations with a logic theory machine. *Proceedings of the Joint Western Computer Conference, Institute of Radio Engineers*, 1957, 218–230.

Newell, A., Shaw, J. C., & Simon, H. A. Elements of a theory of human problem solving. *Psychological Review*, 1958, *65*, 151–166.

Newell, A., & Simon, H. A. The logic theory machine: A complex information processing system. *Transactions on Information Theory, Institute of Radio Engineers*, 1956, IT-2, pp. 61–69.

Newell, A., & Simon, H. A. *Human problem solving*. Englewood Cliffs, N.J.: Prentice-Hall, 1972.

Newsweek, December 7, 1942, pp. 43–44.

Newsweek, January 6, 1969, p. 37.

Nisbitt, R. E., & Valins, S. *Perceiving the causes of one's own behavior*. Morristown, N.J.: General Learning Press, 1971.

Nordby, V. J., & Hall, C. S. *A guide to psychologists and their concepts*. San Francisco: W. H. Freeman, 1974.

Noyes, R., Jr., & Kletti, R. Depersonalization in the face of life-threatening danger: A description. *Psychiatry*, 1976, *39*, 19–27.

Nye, F. I., & Berardo, F. M. *The family: Its structure and interaction*. New York: Macmillan, 1973.

Olds, J. Pleasure centers in the brain. *Scientific American*, 1956, *195*.

Olds, J., & Milner, P. Positive reinforcement produced by electrical stimulation of septal area and other regions of rat brain. *Journal of Comparative and Physiological Psychology*, 1954, *47*, 419–427.

O'Leary, K. D. Behavior modification in the classroom: A rejoinder to Winett and Winkler. *Journal of Applied Behavior Analysis*, 1972, *5*, 505–511.

O'Leary, K. D., & Drabman, R. Token reinforcement programs in the classroom: A review. *Psychological Bulletin*, 1971, *75*, 379–398.

O'Leary, K. D., & Wilson, G. T. *Behavior therapy: Application and outcome*. Englewood Cliffs, N.J.: Prentice-Hall, 1975.

Olton, D. S., & Samuelson, R. J. Remembrance of places past: Spatial memory in rats. *Journal of Experimental Psychology: Animal Behavior Processes*, 1976, *2*, 97–116.

Orne, M. T. The mechanisms of hypnotic age regression: An experimental study. *Journal of Abnormal and Social Psychology*, 1951, *46*, 213–225.

Orne, M. T., & Evans, F. J. Social control in psychological experiments: Antisocial behavior and hypnosis. *Journal of Personality and Social Psychology*, 1965, *1*, 189–200.

Orne, M. T., & Evans, F. J. Inadvertent termination of hypnotized and simulating subjects. *International Journal of Clinical and Experimental Hypnosis*, 1966, *14*, 61–78.

Ornstein, R. E. (Ed.). *The nature of human consciousness: A book of readings*. New York: Viking Press, 1973.

Osborn, A. *Applied imagination*. New York: Charles Scribner's, 1957.

Osgood, C. E. A behavioristic analysis of perception and language as cognitive phenomena. In *Contemporary approaches to cognition*. Cambridge, Mass.: Harvard University Press, 1957.

Osgood, C. E., & Tannenbaum, T. H. The principle of congruity in the prediction of attitude change. *Psychological Review*, 1955, *62*, 42–55.

Osmond, H. Psychopharmacology: The manipulation of the mind. In D. Soloman (Ed.), *LSD: The consciousness-expanding drug*. New York: G. P. Putnam's, 1964.

Otis, A. S., & Lennon, R. T. *Otis-Lennon Mental Ability Test.* New York: Harcourt Brace Jovanovich, 1967.

Otis, A. S., & Lennon, R. T. *Otis-Lennon School Ability Test.* New York: Harcourt Brace Jovanovich, 1979.

Ounsted, C., & Taylor, D. C. (Eds.). *Gender differences: Their ontogeny and significance.* Edinburgh: Churchill Livingstone, 1972.

Over, R. Van. *Psychology and extrasensory perception.* New York: New American Library, 1972.

Packard, V. *The sexual wilderness.* New York: Pocket Books, 1968.

Page, E. B., & Grandon, G. M. Family configuration and mental ability: Two theories contrasted with U.S. Data. *American Educational Research Journal,* 1979, *16,* 257–272.

Paivio, A. *Imagery and verbal processes.* New York: Holt, Rinehart & Winston, 1971.

Papalia, D. F. The status of several conservation abilities across the life-span. *Human Development,* 1972, *15,* 229–243.

Parke, R. D. The role of punishment in the socialization process. In R. A Hoppe, G. A. Milton, & E. C. Simmol (Eds.), *Early experiences and the processes of socialization.* New York: Academic Press, 1970.

Parnes, S. J. *Creative behavior workbook.* New York: Charles Scribner's Sons, 1967.

Parnes, S. J., & Harding, H. F. (Eds.) *A source book for creative thinking.* New York: Charles Scribner's, 1962.

Passman, R. H. *The effects of mothers and security blankets upon learning in children (should Linus bring his blanket to school).* Paper presented at the American Psychological Association convention, New Orleans, September 1974.

Passman, R. H., & Weisberg, P. Mothers and blankets as agents for promoting play and exploration by young children in a novel environment: The effects of social and non-social attachment objects. *Developmental Psychology,* 1975, *11,* 170–177.

Patterson, F. Conversations with a gorilla. *National Geographic,* 1978, *154,* 438–465.

Paul, G. L. *Insight vs. desensitization in psychotherapy.* Stanford, Calif.: Stanford University Press, 1966.

Paulson, F. L. Teaching cooperation on television: An evaluation of Sesame Street social goals programs. *AV Communication Review,* 1974, *22,* 229–246.

Pavlov, I. P. *Conditioned reflexes* (G. V. Anrep, Trans.). London: Oxford University Press, 1927.

Pearce, J. C. *The crack in the cosmic egg.* New York: Fawcett Books, 1971.

Peck, R. C. Psychological developments in the second half of life. In B. L. Neugarten (Ed.), *Middle age and aging.* Chicago: University of Chicago Press, 1968.

Pember, D. R. *Mass media in America* (2nd ed.). Chicago: Science Research Associates, 1977.

Penfield, W. Consciousness, memory and man's conditioned reflexes. In K. H. Pribram (Ed.), *On the biology of learning.* New York: Harcourt Brace Jovanovich, 1969.

Penfield, W., & Roberts, L. *Speech and brain mechanisms.* Princeton: Princeton University Press, 1959.

Peplau, L. A., Rubin, Z., & Hill, C. T. Sexual intimacy in dating relationships. *Journal of Social Issues,* 1977, *33,* 86–110.

Perls, F. *The Gestalt approach.* Palo Alto, Calif.: Science and Behavior Books, 1973.

Peskin, H. Pubertal onset and ego functioning. *Journal of Abnormal Psychology,* 1967, *72,* 1–15.

Peskin, H. Influence of the developmental schedule of puberty on learning and ego functioning. *Journal of Youth and Adolescence,* 1973, *2,* 273–290.

Peters, R. *The place of Kohlberg's theory in moral education.* Paper presented at the first International Conference on Moral Development and Moral Education, Leicester, Eng., 1977.

Peterson, L. R., & Peterson, N. J. Short term retention of individual verbal items. *Journal of Experimental Psychology,* 1959, *58,* 193–198.

Petrel-Petrelevicius, E. *New explorations in mind and learning: An introduction to educational suggestology.* Philadelphia: Lawrence, 1975.

Petrie, H. L. *Motivation: Theory and research.* Belmont, Calif.: Wadsworth, 1981.

Pfeiffer, E., Verwordt, A., & Davis, G. C. Sexual behavior in middle life. *American Journal of Psychiatry,* 1972, *128,* 1262–1267.

Phillips, J. L. *The origins of intellect.* San Francisco: W. H. Freeman, 1969.

Phillips, J. S., & Bierman, K. L. Clinical psychology: Individual methods. *Annual Review of Psychology,* 1981, *32,* 405–438.

Piaget, J. *Le langage et la pensée chez l'enfant.* Neuchâtel: Delachaux et Niestle, 1923.

Piaget, J. *The moral judgment of the child.* London: Kegan Paul, 1932.

Piaget, J. Intellectual development from adolescence to adulthood. *Human Development,* 1972, *15,* 1–12.

Piaget, J. *Adaptation vitale et psychologie de l'intelligence: Phonocopie et selection organizée.* Neuchâtel: Delachaux et Niestle, 1974.

Piaget, J. *L'equilibration des structures cognitives.* Neuchâtel: Delachaux et Niestle, 1975.

Piaget, J. *The grasp of consciousness.* Cambridge: Harvard University Press, 1976.

Pincus, J. H., & Tucker, G. J. *Behavioral neurology.* New York: Oxford University Press, 1974.

Platt, G. M. Another wedding of biology and sociology: Can molecular genetics and Parsonian theory of action live together? In N. H. Steneck (Ed.), *Science and society.* Ann Arbor: University of Michigan Press, 1975.

Potter, E. L. Pregnancy. In M. Fishbein & R. J. R. Kennedy (Eds.), *Modern marriage and family living.* New York: Oxford University Press, 1957.

Pratt, J. G., & Blom, J. G. A confirmatory experiment with a "borrowed" outstanding ESP subject. *Journal of Personality and Social Psychology,* 1964, *17,* 381–389.

Pratt, K. C. The neonate. In M. L. Carmichael (Ed.), *Manual of child psychology* (2nd ed.). New York: John Wiley, 1954.

Prechtl, H. F. R., & Beintema, D. J. The neurological examination of the full term newborn infant. *Clinical and Developmental Medicine,* No. 12. London: Heinemann, 1964.

Premack, A. J., & Premack, D. Teaching language to an ape. *Scientific American,* 1972, *227,* 92–99.

Premack, D. Why chimps can read. New York: Harper, 1976.

Pressey, S. L. A third and fourth contribution toward the coming "industrial revolution" in education. *School and Society,* 1932, *36,* 668–672.

Pribram, K. H. The new neurology: Memory, novelty, thought, and choice. In C. N. Glaser (Ed.), *EEG and behavior.* New York: Basic Books, 1963.

Pribram, K. H. *Languages of the brain: Experimental paradoxes and principles in neuropsychology.* Englewood Cliffs, N.J.: Prentice-Hall, 1971.

Prytula, R. E., Sadowski, C. J., Ellisor, J., Corritore, D., Kuhm, R., & Davis, S. F. Studies on the perceived predictive accuracy of biorhythms. *Journal of Applied Psychology,* 1980, *65,* 723–727.

Rachman, S. Behavior therapy. In B. Berenson & R. Carkhuff (Eds.), *Sources of gain in counseling and psychotherapy.* New York: Holt, Rinehart & Winston, 1967.

Radner, D., & Radner, M. *Science and unreason.* Belmont, Calif.: Wadsworth, 1982.

Rahe, R. H. Subjects' recent life changes and their near-future illness susceptibility. In Z. J. Lipowski (Ed.), *Advances in psychosomatic medicine* (Vol. 8. *Psychosocial aspects of physical illness*). Basel, Switzerland: S. Karger, 1972.

Randi, J. R. *The magic of Uri Geller.* New York: Random House, 1975.

Randi, J. R. Geller is a fake. *Science Digest,* April 1976, pp. 63–66.

Randi, J. R. *Flim-flam: The truth about unicorns, parapsychology, and other delusions.* New York: Lippincott and Crowell, 1980.

Raphael, B. *The thinking computer: Mind inside matter.* San Francisco: W. H. Freeman, 1976.

Raymond, M. S. Case of fetishism treated by aversion therapy. *British Medical Journal,* 1956, *2,* 854–856.

Reid, J. E., & Inbau, F. E. *Truth and deception: The polygraph ("lie-detector") technique* (2nd ed.). Baltimore: Williams & Wilkins, 1977.

Reiss, I. L. *The social context of premarital sexual permissiveness.* New York: Holt, Rinehart & Winston, 1966.

Reiss, S., & Sushinsky, L. W. Overjustification, competing responses, and the acquisition of intrinsic interest. *Journal of Personality and Social Psychology,* 1975, *31,* 116–125.

Rescorla, R. A. Probability of shock in the presence and absence of CS in fear conditioning. *Journal of Comparative and Physiological Psychology,* 1968, *66:* 1–5.

Rescorla, R. A., & Holland, P. C. Some behavioral approaches to the study of learning. In Rosenzweig, M. R., & Bennet, E. L. *Neuromechanisms of learning and memory.* Boston: MIT Press, 1976, 165–192.

Rescorla, R. A., & Holland, P. C. Behavioral studies of associative learning in animals. *Annual Review of Psychology,* 1982, *33,* 265–308.

Rescorla, R. A., & Wagner, A. R. A theory of Pavlovian conditioning: Variations in the effectiveness of reinforcement and non-reinforcement. In Black, A. H., and Prokasy, W. F. (Eds.). *Classical conditioning II.* New York: Appleton Century, 1972.

Reykowski, J. Social motivation. *Annual Review of Psychology,* 1982, *33,* 123–154.

Reynolds, G. S. *A primer of operant conditioning* (rev. ed.). Chicago: Scott, Foresman, 1975.

Rice, B. The new truth machines. *Psychology Today,* 1978, *12,* 61–78.

Rice, B. The Hawthorne defect: Persistence of a flawed theory. *Psychology Today,* February 1982, 70–74.

Richter, C. F. Total self regulatory functions in animals and human beings. *Harvey Lectures,* 1942–1943, *38,* 63–103.

Riegel, K. F. Dialectic operations: The final period of cognitive development. *Human Development.* 1973, *16,* 346–370.

Riesen, A. H. The effects of stimulus deprivation on the development and atrophy of the visual sensory system. *American Journal of Orthopsychiatry,* 1960, *30,* 23–36.

Rivers, W. H. R. Primitive color vision. *Popular Science Monthly,* 1901, *59,* 44–58.

Roazen, P. *Freud and his followers.* New York: Alfred A. Knopf, 1975.

Rockstein, M., & Sussman, M. *Biology of aging.* Belmont, Ca.: Wadsworth Publishing, 1979.

Rodin, J. Current status of the internal-external hypothesis for obesity: What went wrong? *American Psychologist,* 1981, *36,* 361–372.

Rodin, J., & Langer, E. J. Long-term effects of a control-relevant intervention with the institutionalized aged. *Journal of Personality and Social Psychology,* 1977, *35,* 897–902.

Roethlisberger, S. J., & Dickson, W. J. *Management and the worker.* Cambridge, Mass.: Harvard University Press, 1939.

Rogers, C. R. *Client-centered therapy: Its current practice, implications and theory.* Boston: Houghton Mifflin, 1951.

Rogers, C. R. *On becoming a person: A therapist's view of psychotherapy.* Boston: Houghton Mifflin, 1961.

Rogers, C. R., & Skinner, B. F. Some issues concerning the control of human behavior: A symposium. *Science,* 1956, *124,* 1057–1066.

Rose, G. A., & Williams, R. T. Metabolic studies of large and small eaters. *British Journal of Nutrition,* 1961, *15,* 1–9.

Rosenberg, M. *Conceiving the self.* New York: Basic Books, 1979.

Rosenblueth, A. *Mind and brain: A philosophy of science.* Cambridge, Mass.: MIT Press, 1970.

Rosenhan, D. L. On being sane in insane places. *Science,* 1973, *179,* 250–258.

Rosenkrantz, P. S., Vogel, S. R., Bee, H., Broverman, I., & Broverman, D. Sex role stereotypes and self concept in college students. *Journal of Consulting and Clinical Psychology,* 1968, *32,* 287–295.

Rosenthal, R., & Fode, K. L. The effect of experimenter bias on the performance of the albino rat. *Behavioral Science,* 1963, *8,* 183–189.

Rosenthal, R., & Jacobsen, L. *Pygmalion in the classroom: Teacher expectations and pupils' intellectual development.* New York: Holt, Rinehart & Winston, 1968.

Rosenzweig, S. Available methods for studying personality. *Journal of Psychology,* 1949, *28,* 345–368.

Rosnow, R., & Robinson, E. (Eds.). *Experiments in persuasion.* New York: Academic Press, 1967.

Ross, A. O., & Pelham, W. E. Child psychopathology. *Annual Review of Psychology,* 1981, *32,* 243–278.

Ross, L. B. *Cue and cognition controlled eating among obese and normal subjects.* Unpublished doctoral dissertation, Columbia University, 1969. (Cited in R. S. Thompson, *Introduction to physiological psychology.* New York: Harper & Row, 1975.)

Ross, M. Salience of reward and intrinsic motivation. *Journal of Personality and Social Psychology,* 1975, *32,* 245–254.

Roszak, B., & Roszak, T. (Eds.). *Masculine-feminine: Readings in sexual mythology and the liberation of women.* New York: Harper & Row, 1969.

Rothstein, E. The scar of Sigmund Freud. *New York Review of Books,* October 9, 1980, 14–20.

Rotter, J. B. *Social learning and clinical psychology.* Englewood Cliffs, N.J.: Prentice-Hall, 1954.

Rotter, J. B. Generalized expectancies for internal versus external control of reinforcement. *Psychological Monographs,* 1966, *80*(1, Whole No. 609).

Rotter, J. B. Some problems and misconceptions related to the construct of internal versus external control of reinforcement. *Journal of Consulting and Clinical Psychology,* 1975, *43,* 36–67.

Rowland, L. W. Will hypnotized persons try to harm themselves or others? *Journal of Abnormal and Social Psychology,* 1939, *34,* 114–117.

Rozin, P., & Kalat, J. W. Specific hungers and poison avoidance as adaptive specializations of learning. *Psychological Review,* 1971, *78,* 459–486.

Rubin, K. H., Attewell, P. W., Tierney, M. C., & Tumolo, P. Development of spatial egocentrism and conservation across the life span. *Developmental Psychology,* 1973, *9,* 432.

Rubin, S. *Current research in hypnopaedia.* New York: American Elsevier, 1968.

Rubin, Z. Measurement of romantic love. *Journal of Personality and Social Psychology,* 1970, *16,* 265–273.

Rubin, Z. *Liking and loving: An invitation to social psychology.* New York: Holt, Rinehart & Winston, 1973.

Rumbaugh, D. M. (Ed.). *Language learning by a chimpanzee: The Lana Project.* New York: Academic Press, 1977.

Rumbaugh, D. M., & Gill, T. M. Lana's acquisition of language skills. In D. M. Rumbaugh (Ed.), *Language learning by a chimpanzee: The Lana Project.* New York: Academic Press, 1977.

Rumbaugh, D. M., Gill, T. V., & Glaserfeld, E. C. von. Reading and sentence completion by a chimpanzee. *Science,* 1973, *182,* 731–733.

Ryle, G. Thinking and language. *Proceedings of the Aristotelian Society,* 1951, *25* (supp.), 65–82.

Sabom, M. B. *Recollections of death.* New York: Harper & Row, 1982. (a)

Sabom, M. B. Recollections of death. *Omni,* February 1982, 58–60; 103–109. (b)

Sakagami, S. F., & Akahira, Y. Studies on the Japanese honeybee, *Apis cerana cerana Fabricius: 8,* two opposing adaptations in the post-stinging behavior of honeybees. *Evolution,* 1960, *14,* 29–40.

Sakitt, B. Iconic memory. *Psychological Review,* 1976, *83,* 257–276.

Sampson, E. E. Birth order, need achievement, and conformity. *Journal of Abnormal and Social Psychology,* 1962, *64,* 155–159.

Sanford, F. H., & Wrightsman, L. S., Jr. *Psychology; a scientific study of man* (3rd ed.). Monterey, Calif.: Brooks/Cole, 1970.

Sapir, E. The unconscious patterning of behavior in society. In E. S. Dummer (Ed.), *The unconscious: A symposium.* New York: Alfred A. Knopf, 1928.

Savage, C., & McCabe, O. L. Psychedelic therapy of drug addiction. In C. C. Brown & C. Savage (Eds.), *The drug abuse controversy.* Baltimore: National Educational Consultants, 1971.

Sawrey, W. L., & Weisz, J. D. An experimental method of producing gastric ulcers: Role of psychological factors in the production of gastric ulcers in the rat. *Journal of Comparative and Physiological Psychology,* 1956, *49,* 457–461.

Scarr, S., & Salapatek, T. Patterns of fear development during infancy. *Merrill-Palmer Quarterly,* 1970, *16,* 59–60.

Scarr, S., & Weinberg, R. A. Intellectual similarities within families of both adopted and biological children. *Intelligence,* 1977, *1,* 170–191.

Scarr, S., & Weinberg, R. A. Attitudes, interests, and IQ. *Human Nature,* April 1978, 29–36.

Schachter, S. Some extraordinary facts about obese humans and rats. *American Psychologist,* 1971, *26,* 129–144.

Schachter, S., Goldman, R., & Gordon, A. Effects of fear, food deprivation and obesity on eating. *Journal of Personality and Social Psychology,* 1968, *10,* 91–97.

Schachter, S., & Singer, J. E. Cognitive, social, and physiological determinants of emotional state. *Psychological Review,* 1962, *69,* 379–399.

Schaefer, C. E. Imaginary companions and creative adolescents. *Developmental Psychology,* 1969, *1,* 747–749.

Schaefer, V. H. Teaching the concept of interaction and sensitizing students to its implications. *Teaching of Psychology,* 1976, *3,* 103–114.

Schaffer, H. R. The onset of fear of strangers and the incongruity hypothesis. *Journal of Child Psychology and Psychiatry,* 1966, *7,* 95–106.

Schaie, K. W. Translations in gerontology— from lab to life: Intellectual functioning. *American Psychologist,* 1974, *29,* 802–807.

Schaie, K. W., & Gribbin, K. Adult development and aging. *Annual Review of Psychology,* 1975, *256,* 65–96.

Schaie, K. W., & Labouvie-Vief, G. Generational versus ontogenetic components of change in adult cognitive behavior: A fourteen year cross-sequential study. *Developmental Psychology,* 1974, *10,* 305–320.

Schlosberg, H. The description of facial expression in terms of two dimensions. *Journal of Experimental Psychology,* 1952, *44,* 229–237.

Schmeidler, G. R. ESP breakthroughs: Paranormal effects in real life. In R. Van Over (Ed.), *Psychology and extra sensory perception.* New York: New American Library, 1972.

Schmidt, G., & Sigusch, V. Women's sexual arousal. In J. Zubin & J. Money (Eds.), *Contemporary sexual behavior: Critical issues in the 1970's.* Baltimore: Johns Hopkins University Press, 1973.

Schmidt, H. Precognition of a quantum process. *Journal of Parapsychology,* 1969, *33,* 99–108.

Schneider, D. J. Implicit personality theory: A review. *Psychological Bulletin,* 1973, *79,* 294–309.

Schneider, W., & Shiffrin, R. M. Controlled and automatic human information processing. I. Detection, search and attention. *Psychological Review,* 1977, *84,* 1–66.

Schramm, W. *The research on programmed instruction: An annotated bibliography.* Washington, D.C.: U.S. Government Printing Office, 1964.

Schramm, W., Lyle, J., & Parker, E. G. *Television in the lives of our children.* Stanford, Calif.: Stanford University Press, 1961.

Schroeder, D. D. *The silent epidemic.* Pasadena, Calif.: Ambassador College, 1977.

Schulsinger, F. Biological psychopathology. *Annual Review of Psychology,* 1980, *31,* 585–606.

Schultz, D. P. *Panic behavior.* New York: Random House, 1964.

Schultz, D. P. *A history of modern psychology.* New York: Academic Press, 1969.

Schultz, D. P. *Theories of personality.* Monterey, Calif.: Brooks/Cole, 1976.

Schwartz, C. J. Toward a medical understanding of marihuana. *Canada Psychiatric Association Journal,* 1969, *14,* 591–600.

Schwartz, S., II, & Gottlieb, A. Bystander reactions to a violent theft: Crime in Jerusalem. *Journal of Personality and Social Psychology,* 1976, *34,* 1188–1199.

Schwitzgebel, R. K., & Kolb, D. A. *Changing human behavior: Principles of planned intervention.* New York: McGraw-Hill, 1974.

Sclafani, A. Appetite and hunger in experimental obesity syndromes. In D. Novin, W. Wyrwicka, & G. A. Bray (Eds.), *Hunger: Basic mechanisms and clinical implications.* New York: Raven Press, 1976.

Sclafani, A., & Springer, D. Dietary obesity in adult rats: Similarities to hypothalamic and human obesity syndromes. *Physiology and Behavior,* 1976, *17,* 461–471.

Seamon, J. G. *Memory and cognition: An introduction.* New York: Oxford, 1980.

Sears, R. R., Maccoby, E. P., & Lewin, G. *Patterns of child rearing.* Evanston, Ill.: Row Peterson, 1957.

Sebeok, T. A., & Umiker-Sebeok, D. J. Performing animals: Secrets of the trade. *Psychology Today,* November 1979, 78–91.

Sebeok, T. A., & Umiker-Sebeok, D. J. (Eds.). *Speaking of apes: A critical anthology of two-way communication with man.* New York: Plenum, 1980.

Seeman, M. Powerlessness and knowledge: A comparative study of alienation and learning. *Sociometry,* 1967, *30,* 359–367.

Segall, M. H., Campbell, D. T., & Herskovips, M. J. *The influence of culture on visual perception.* New York: Bobbs-Merrill, 1966.

Seidensticker, J. F., & Tzagournis, M. Anorexia nervosa—clinical features and long term follow-up. *Journal of Chronic Diseases,* 1968, *21,* 361–367.

Seligman, M. E. P. Submissive death: Giving up on life. *Psychology Today,* May 1974, pp. 80–85.

Seligman, M. E. P. *Helplessness: On depression, development and death.* San Francisco: W. H. Freeman, 1975.

Seligman, M. E. P., & Hager, J. L. *Biological boundaries of learning.* New York: Appleton-Century-Crofts, 1972.

Seligmann, J., & Begley, S. What's in a dream? *Newsweek,* January 16, 1978, p. 50.

Selye, H. *The stress of life.* New York: McGraw-Hill, 1956.

Selye, H. *From dreams to discovery: On being a scientist.* New York: McGraw-Hill, 1964.

Selye, H. *Stress without distress.* Philadelphia: J. B. Lippincott, 1974.

Selye, H. (Ed.). *Selye's guide to stress research,* Vol. 1. New York: D. Van Nostrand, 1980.

Sem-Jacobsen, C. W., & Styri, O. B. Manipulation of emotion: Electrophysiological and surgical methods. In L. Levi (Ed.), *Emotions: Their parameters and measurement.* New York: Raven Press, 1975.

Shaffer, L. F. Fear and courage in aerial combat. *Journal of Consulting Psychology,* 1947, *2,* 137–143.

Shapira, A., & Madsen, M. C. Between and within group cooperation and competition among kibbutz and non-kibbutz children. *Developmental Psychology,* 1974, *10,* 140–145.

Shaver, K. G. *An introduction to attribution processes.* Cambridge, Mass.: Winthrop, 1975.

Shaw, G. B. *The adventures of the Black girl in search of her God.* London: Constable, 1932.

Sheldon, W. H. *The varieties of temperament: A psychology of constitutional differences.* New York: Harper & Row, 1936.

Sheldon, W. H. *Atlas of men: A guide to somatotyping the adult male of all ages.* New York: Harper, 1954.

Shepherd, D. M. Microcircuits in the nervous system. *Scientific American,* 1978, *238,* 92–103.

Sherman, M. *Hollow folk.* New York: Thomas Y. Crowell, 1933.

Sherman, M., & Key, C. B. The intelligence of isolated mountain children. *Child Development,* 1932, *3,* 279–290.

Short, J. F., Jr., & Nye, F. I. Reported behavior as a deviant behavior. *Social Problems,* 1957–1958, *5,* 207–213.

Shotland, R. L., & Straw, M. K. Bystander response to an assault: When a man attacks a woman. *Journal of Personality and Social Psychology,* 1976, *34,* 990–999.

Shoulberg, D. J. Psychoanalytically oriented brief psychotherapy and the community mental health clinician. *Journal of Social Welfare,* 1976, *3,* 65–74.

Siegel, J., & Gordon, T. P. Paradoxical sleep: Deposition in the cat. *Science,* 1965, *148,* 978–980.

Siegel, R. K. The psychology of life after death. *American Psychologist*, 1980, *35*, 911–931.

Singer, J. L. *The child's world of make believe: Experimental studies of imaginative play.* New York: Academic Press, 1973.

Singh, J. A., & Zingg, R. N. *Wolf-children and feral man.* New York: Harper, 1942.

Skeels, H. M. Adult status of children with contrasting early life experiences. *Monograph of the Society for Research in Child Development*, 1966, *31*(3).

Skeels, H. M., & Skodak, M. Techniques for a high yield follow up study in the field. *Public Health Reports*, 1965, *80*, 249–257.

Skinner, B. F. *The behavior of organisms.* New York: Appleton-Century-Crofts, 1938.

Skinner, B. F. "Superstition" in the pigeon. *Journal of Experimental Psychology*, 1948, *38*, 168–172. (a)

Skinner, B. F. *Walden II.* New York: Macmillan, 1948. (b)

Skinner, B. F. How to teach animals. *Scientific American*, 1951, *185*, 26–29.

Skinner, B. F. *Science and human behavior.* New York: Macmillan, 1953.

Skinner, B. F. The science of learning and the art of teaching. *Harvard Educational Review*, 1954, *24*, 86–97.

Skinner, B. F. *Verbal behavior.* New York: Appleton-Century-Crofts, 1957.

Skinner, B. F. *Cumulative record* (rev. ed.). New York: Appleton-Century-Crofts, 1961.

Skinner, B. F. *Beyond freedom and dignity.* New York: Alfred A. Knopf, 1971.

Skinner, B. F. The shaping of phylogenic behavior. *Acta Neurobiologiae Experimentalis*, 1975, *35*, 409–415.

Skinner, B. F. Herrnstein and the evolution of behaviorism. *American Psychologist*, 1977, *32*, 1006–1012.

Sloane, R. B., Staples, F. R., Cristol, A. H., Yorkston, N. J., & Whipple, K. *Psychotherapy versus behavior therapy.* Cambridge, Mass.: Harvard University Press, 1975.

Sluckin, W. *Imprinting and early learning.* Chicago: Aldine, 1965.

Smith, B. E., & Sternfield, J. The hippie communal movement: Effects on childbirth and development. *American Journal of Orthopsychiatry*, 1970, *40*, 527–530.

Smith, M. E. An investigation of the development of the sentence and the extent of vocabulary in young children. *University of Iowa Studies in Child Welfare*, 1926, *3*(5).

Smith, M. L., & Glass, G. V. Meta-analysis of psychotherapy outcome studies. *American Psychologist*, September 1977, 752–760.

Sokolov, A. N. Studies on the problem of speech mechanisms in thinking. *Psychological Science in the USSR*, 1959, *1*, 669–704.

Solomon, R. C. Freud and "unconscious motivation." *Journal for the Theory of Social Behavior*, 1974, *34*, 191–216.

Solomon, R. L. An opponent-process theory of acquired motivation: IV. The affective dynamics of addiction. In J. D. Maser & M. E. P. Seligman (Eds.), *Psychopathology: Experimental models.* San Francisco: Freeman, 1977, 66–103.

Solomon, R. L. The opponent-process theory of acquired motivation: The costs of pleasure and the benefits of pain. *American Psychologist*, 1980, *35*, 691–712.

Solomon, R. L., & Corbit, J. D. An opponent-process theory of motivation. *Psychological Review*, 1974, *81*, 119–145.

Solso, R. L. *Cognitive psychology.* New York: Harcourt Brace Jovanovich, 1979.

Sonderegger, T. B. Intracranial stimulation and maternal behavior. *APA convention proceedings*, 78th meeting, 1970, 245–246.

Sorensen, R. C. *Adolescent sexuality in contemporary America.* New York: World Publishing, 1973.

Spiegel, H. An eye roll test for hypnotizability. *American Journal of Clinical Hypnosis*, 1972, *15*, 25–28.

Spiegel, H. *Manual for the Hypnotic Induction Profile.* New York: Soni Medica, 1974.

Spiegel, H. The Hypnotic Induction Profile (HIP): A review of its development. *Annals of the New York Academy of Sciences*, 1979, *296*, 129–142.

Spelt, D. K. The conditioning of the human fetus in utero. *Journal of Experimental Psychology*, 1948, *38*, 375–376.

Spence, J. T., & Helmreich, R. L. *Masculinity and femininity: Their psychological dimensions, correlates and antecedents.* Austin: University of Texas Press, 1978.

Sperber, M. *Masks of loneliness: Alfred Adler in perspective.* New York: Macmillan, 1974.

Sperling, G. The information available in brief visual presentations. *Psychological Monographs*, 1960, *74* (11, Whole No. 498).

Sperling, G. A model for visual memory tests. *Human Factors*, 1963, *5*, 19–31.

Sperry, R. W. The great cerebral commissure. *Scientific American*, 1964, *210*, 42–62.

Sperry, R. W. Hemisphere deconnection and unity in conscious experience. *American Psychologist*, 1968, *23*, 723–733.

Spitz, R. A. Hospitalism: An inquiry into the genesis of psychiatric conditions in early childhood. Part I. *Psychoanalytic Studies of the Child*, 1945, *1*, 53–74.

Spitz, R. A. Unhappy and fatal outcomes of emotional deprivation and stress in infancy. In I. Galdston (Ed.), *Beyond the germ theory.* Health Education Council, 1954.

Spitzer, R. L., Sheehy, M., & Endicott, J. *DSM-III: Guiding principles.* Paper presented at the fourth C. M. Hincks Memorial Lectures, Symposium on Psychiatric Diagnosis, University of Toronto, 1976.

Spitzer, R. L., Williams, J. B. W., & Skodol, A. E. DSM-III: The major achievements and an overview. *The American Journal of Psychiatry*, 1980, *137*, 151–164.

Springer, S. P., & Deutsch, G. *Left brain, right brain.* San Francisco: W. H. Freeman, 1981.

Staats, A. W. Paradigmatic behaviorism, unified theory, unified theory construction methods, and the zeitgeist of separatism. *American Psychologist*, 1981, *36*, 239–256.

Staddon, J. E. R., & Simmelhag, V. L. The "superstition" experiment: A reexamination of its implications for the principles of adaptive behavior. *Psychological Review*, 1971, *78*, 3–43.

Stagner, R. The gullibility of personnel managers. *Personnel Psychology*, 1958, *11*, 347–352.

Stampfl, T. Implosive therapy: Staring down your nightmares. *Psychology Today*, February 1975, pp. 66–73.

Standing, L. Learning 10,000 pictures. *Quarterly Journal of Experimental Psychology*, 1973, *25*, 207–222.

Stearns, G. Nutritional state of the mother prior to conception. *Journal of the American Medical Association*, 1958, *168*, 1655–1659.

Stein, A., & Friedrich, L. K. Television content and young children's behavior. In J. P. Murray, E. A. Rubinstein, & G. A. Comstock (Eds.), *Television and social behavior* (Vol. 2. *Television and social learning*). Washington, D.C.: U.S. Government Printing Office, 1972.

Stein, L., & Wise, C. D. Possible etiology of schizophrenia: Progressive damage to the noradrenergic reward system by 6-hydroxydopamine. *Science*, 1971, *171*, 1032–1036.

Stephenson, F. D. (Ed.). *GT primer.* Springfield, Ill.: Charles C Thomas, 1975.

Stern, C. Hereditary factors affecting adoption. In *A study of adoption practices* (Vol. 2). New York: Child Welfare League of America, 1956.

Sternberg, S. High speed scanning in human memory. *Science*, 1966, *153*, 652–654.

Sternberg, S. Two operations in character recognition: Some evidence from RT measurements. *Perception and Psychophysics*, 1967, *2*, 45–53.

Sternberg, S. Memory scanning: Mental processes revealed by reaction time experiments. *American Scientist*, 1969, *57*, 421–457.

Stevens, J. The electroencephalogram: Human recordings. In R. F. Thompson & M. Patterson (Eds.), *Bioelectric recording techniques.* New York: Academic Press, 1973.

Stimbert, V. E. A comparison of learning based on social or nonsocial discriminative stimuli. *Psychonomic Science*, 1970, *20*, 185–186.

Stolz, S. B., Wienckowski, L. A., & Brown, B. S. Behavior modification: A perspective on critical issues. *American Psychologist*, 1975, *30*, 1027–1048.

Strand, B. Z. Change of context and retroactive inhibition. *Journal of Verbal Learning and Verbal Behavior*, 1970, *9*, 202–206.

Stromeyer, C. S., III. Eidetikers. *Psychology Today,* November 1970, pp. 46–50.

Stroop, J. R. Studies of interference in serial verbal reactions. *Journal of Experimental Psychology,* 1935, *18,* 643–662.

Stuart, R. B. *Trick or treatment: How and when psychotherapy fails.* Champaign, Ill.: Research Press, 1970.

Stuart, R. B., & Davis, B. *Slim chance in a fat world: Behavioral control of obesity.* Champaign, Ill.: Research Press, 1972.

Stunkard, A. J. *Obesity.* Philadelphia: W. B. Saunders, 1980.

Stunkard, A. J., Van Itallie, T. B., & Reis, B. B. The mechanism of satiety: Effect of glucagon on gastric hunger contractions in man. *Proceedings of the Society for Experimental and Biological Medicine,* 1955, *89,* 258–261.

Suinn, R. M. *Fundamentals of behavior pathology* (2nd ed.). New York: John Wiley, 1975.

Suinn, R. M., & Oskamp, S. *The predictive validity of projective measures: A fifteen year evaluative review of research.* Springfield, Ill.: Charles C Thomas, 1969.

Sullivan, F. V. *A study of Kohlberg's structural theory of moral development: A critique of liberal social science ideology.* Unpublished manuscript, Ontario Institute for Studies in Education, Toronto, 1977.

Sweet, W. H., Ervin, F., & Mark, V. H. The relationship of violent behavior to focal cerebral disease. In S. Garattini and E. Sigg (Eds.), *Aggressive behavior.* New York: Wiley, 1969.

Szasz, T. S. The myth of mental illness. *American Psychologist,* 1960, *15,* 113–118.

Szasz, T. S. *The myth of mental illness: Foundations of a theory of personal conduct.* New York: Dell, 1967.

Szasz, T. S. *The manufacture of madness.* New York: Harper & Row, 1970.

Tallmer, M., Formanek, R., & Tallmer, J. Factors influencing children's concepts of death. *Journal of Clinical Child Psychology,* 1974, *3,* 17–19.

Targ, R., & Puthoff, H. Information transmission under conditions of sensory shielding. *Nature,* 1974, *251,* 602–607.

Targ, R., & Puthoff, H. *Mind reach: Scientists look at psychic ability.* New York: Delacorte, 1977.

Tavris, C. The end of the IQ slump. *Psychology Today,* April 1976, pp. 69–73.

Taylor, C. W., & Holland, J. W. Development and application of tests of creativity. *Review of Educational Research,* 1964, *33,* 91–102.

Taylor, J. *Superminds.* New York: Viking Press, 1975.

Taylor, J. Geller's powers are genuine. *Science Digest,* April 1976, pp. 56–62.

Teahan, J., & Kastenbaum, R. Subjective life expectancy and future time perspective as predictors of job success in the "hard core unemployed." *Omega,* 1970, *1,* 189–200.

Telfer, M. A., Baker, D., Clark, G. R., & Richardson, C. E. Incidence of gross chromosomal errors among tall, criminal American males. *Science,* 1968, *159,* 1249–1250.

Terman, L. M. (Ed.). *Genetic studies of genius,* Vol. V. Stanford, Calif.: Stanford University Press, 1959.

Terman, L. M., & Merrill, M. A. *Stanford-Binet Intelligence Scale.* Boston: Houghton Mifflin, 1960.

Terrace, H. S. How Nim Chimpsky changed my mind. *Psychology Today,* November 1979, 65–76. (a)

Terrace, H. S. Can an ape create a sentence? *Science,* November 23, 1979, *206,* 891–902. (b)

Terrace, H. S. *Nim: A chimpanzee who learned sign language.* New York: Knopf, 1980.

Thaler, O. F. Letter in response to Rosenhan's 1973 article. *Science,* 1973, *180,* 358.

Thigpen, C. H., & Cleckley, H. *The three faces of Eve.* Kingsport, Tenn.: Kingsport Press, 1954.

Thommen, G. *Is this your day?* New York: Crown Publishers, 1973.

Thompson, R. F. *Introduction to physiological psychology* (2nd ed.). New York: Harper & Row, 1975.

Thorndike, E. L. *Animal intelligence.* New York: Macmillan, 1911.

Thorndike, E. L. *Psychology of learning.* New York: Teacher's College, 1913.

Thorndike, R. L., & Hagen, E. *Measurement and evaluation in psychology and education* (4th ed.). New York: John Wiley, 1977.

Thorpe, W. H. *Learning and instinct in animals* (2nd ed.). London: Methuen, 1963.

Thouless, R. H. *From anecdote to experiment in psychical research.* London: Routledge & Kegan Paul, 1972.

Thurstone, L. L. Primary Mental Abilities. *Psychometric Monographs,* No. 1. Chicago: University of Chicago Press, 1938.

Time Magazine. Why you do what you do: Sociobiology: A new theory of behavior. August 1, 1977, pp. 36–41.

Timiras, P. S. *Developmental physiology and aging.* New York: Macmillan, 1972.

Tinbergen, N. *The study of instinct.* Oxford: Clarendon Press, 1951.

Tobias, S. Sexist equations. *Psychology Today,* January 1982, 14–17.

Tolman, E. C. *Purposive behavior in animals and man.* New York: Appleton, 1932.

Tolman, E. C., & Honzik, C. H. Insight in rats. *University of California Publications in Psychology,* 1930, *4,* 215–232.

Touhey, J. C. Comparison of two dimensions of attitude similarity on heterosexual attraction. *Journal of Personality and Social Psychology,* 1972, *23,* 8–10.

Tournier, P. *The meaning of persons* (E. Hudson, Trans.). New York: Harper & Row, 1957.

Treisman, A. M. Verbal cues, language and meaning in selective attention. *American Journal of Psychology,* 1964, *77,* 206–219.

Trivers, R. L. The evolution of reciprocal altruism. *Quarterly Review of Biology,* 1971, *46,* 35–57.

Trivers, R. L. Parental investment and sexual selection. In B. Campbell (Ed.), *Sexual selection and the descent of man, 1871–1971.* Chicago: Aldine, 1972.

Trivers, R. L. Parent-offspring conflict. *American Zoologist,* 1974, *14,* 249–264.

Truax, C. B., & Carkhuff, R. R. *Toward effective counseling and psychotherapy: Training and practice.* Chicago: Aldine, 1967.

Tryon, R. C. Genetic differences in maze learning in rats. *Yearbook of the National Society for Studies in Education,* 1940, *39,* 111–119.

Tulving, E. Retrograde amnesia in free recall. *Science,* 1969, *164,* 88–90.

Tulving, E. Episodic and semantic memory. In E. Tulving & W. Donaldson (Eds.), *Organization of memory.* New York: Academic Press, 1972.

Tulving, E. Cue-dependent forgetting. *American Scientist,* 1974, *62,* 74–82.

Tulving, E., & Madigan, S. A. Memory and verbal learning. *Annual Review of Psychology,* 1970, *21,* 437–484.

Turing, A. M. Computing machinery and intelligence. *Mind,* 1950, *59* (236), 433–460.

Turnbull, C. M. Observations. *American Journal of Psychology,* 1961, *7,* 304–308.

Udry, J. R., & Morris, N. M. Distribution of coitus in the menstrual cycle. *Nature,* 1968, *220,* 593–596.

Vandenbergh, J. G. Endocrine coordination in monkeys: Male sexual responses to the female. *Physiology and Behavior,* 1969, *4,* 261–264.

Van den Daele, L. D. Modification of infant state by treatment in a rocker box. *Journal of Psychology,* 1970, *74,* 161–165.

Van Der Horst, B. Cartographer of consciousness. *Omni,* September 1980, 55–58.

Vaughan, E., & Fisher, A. E. Male sexual behavior induced by intracranial electrical stimulation. *Science,* 1962, *137,* 758–760.

Vaz, E., & Lodhi, A. *Crime and delinquency in Canada.* Scarborough, Ontario: Prentice-Hall, 1979.

Veilleux, S., & Melzack, R. Pain in psychotic patients. *Experimental Neurology,* 1976, *52,* 535–543.

Vernon, P. E. (Ed.). *Creativity.* Harmondsworth, Eng.: Penguin, 1970.

Vernon, P. E. *Intelligence, heredity and environment.* San Francisco: W. H. Freeman, 1979.

Vinacke, W. Z. Illusions experienced by aircraft pilots while flying. *Journal of Aviation Medicine,* 1947, *18,* 308–325.

Vygotsky, L. S. *Thought and language* (E. Hansmann & G. Vaker, Eds. and Trans.). New York: John Wiley, 1962.

Waddington, C. H. *The evolution of an evolutionist.* Edinburgh: Edinburgh University Press, 1975.

Wade, N. IQ and heredity: Suspicion of fraud beclouds classic experiment. *Science,* 1976, *194,* 916–919. (a)

Wade, N. Sociobiology: Troubled birth for a new discipline. *Science,* 1976, *191,* 1151–1155. (b)

Wade, T. C., & Baker, T. B. Opinions and use of psychological tests: A survey of clinical psychologists. *American Psychologist,* 1977, *32,* 874–882.

Wagner, A. R., & Rescorla, R. A. Inhibition in Pavlovian conditioning: Application of a theory. In Boakes, R. A., & Halliday, S. (Eds.). *Inhibition and learning.* New York: Academic Press, 1972.

Wald, G. The receptors of human color vision. *Science,* 1964, *145,* 1007–1017.

Walker, R. N. Body build and behavior in young children: Body build and nursery school teachers' ratings. *Monographs of the Society for Research in Child Development,* 1962, *27,* No. 84.

Wallace, R. K., & Benson, H. The physiology of meditation. *Scientific American,* 1972, *226,* 85–90.

Wallach, M. A., & Kogan, N. *Modes of thinking in young children: A study of the creativity-intelligence distinction.* New York: Holt, Rinehart & Winston, 1965.

Walster, E. Passionate love. In B. Murstein (Ed.), *Theories of attraction and love.* New York: Springer, 1971.

Walster, E., & Berscheid, E. Adrenaline makes the heart grow fonder. *Psychology Today,* June 1971, pp. 46–50.

Walster, E., & Walster, G. W. *A new look at love.* Reading, Mass.: Addison-Wesley, 1978.

Walster, E., Aronsen, V., Abrahams, D., & Rottman, L. Importance of physical attractiveness in dating behavior. *Journal of Personality and Social Psychology,* 1966, *4,* 508–516.

Walters, G. C., & Grusec, J. F. *Punishment.* San Francisco: W. H. Freeman, 1977.

Wardaugh, R. *The contents of language.* Rowley, Mass.: Newbury House, 1976.

Wason, P. C., & Johnson-Laird, P. N. *Psychology of reasoning.* London: Batsford, 1972.

Watson, J. B. *Behaviorism* (2nd ed.). Chicago: University of Chicago Press, 1930.

Watson, J. B., & Rayner, R. Conditioned emotional reactions. *Journal of Experimental Psychology,* 1920, *3,* 1–14.

Watson, J. D., & Crick, F. H. The structure of DNA. *Cold Spring Harbor Symposium on Quantitative Biology,* 1953, *18,* 123–131.

Watson, R. I. *The great psychologists* (3rd ed.). Philadelphia: J. B. Lippincott, 1971.

Webb, W. B., & Agnew, H. W., Jr. *Sleep and dreams.* Dubuque, Iowa: Brown, 1973.

Webb, W. B., & Cartwright, R. D. Sleep and dreams. *Annual Review of Psychology,* 1978, *29,* 223–252.

Wechsler, D. *The measurement and appraisal of adult intelligence* (4th ed.). Baltimore: Williams & Wilkins, 1958.

Weil, A. T., Zinberg, N. E., & Nelson, J. M. Clinical and psychological effects of marijuana in man. *Science,* 1968, *162,* 1234–1242.

Weiner, B. *Theories of motivation: From mechanisms to cognition.* Skokie, Ill.: Rand McNally, 1972.

Weiner, B. Attributional interpretation of expectancy-value theory. In B. Weiner (Ed.), *Cognitive views of human motivation.* New York: Academic Press, 1974. (a)

Weiner, B. (Ed.). *Cognitive views of human motivation.* New York: Academic Press, 1974. (b)

Weiner, B., Frize, I., Kukla, A., Reed, L., Rest, S., & Rosenbaum, R. M. *Perceiving the causes of success and failure.* New York: General Learning Press, 1971.

Weisberg, P., & Russell, J. E. Proximity and interactional behavior of young children to their "security" blanket. *Child Development,* 1971, *42,* 1575–1579.

Weisenberg, M. Pain and pain control. *Psychological Bulletin,* 1977, *84,* 1008–1044.

Weiss, D. J., & Davison, M. L. Test theory and methods. *Annual Review of Psychology,* 1981, *32,* 629–658.

Weiss, J. M. Effects of coping responses on stress. *Journal of Comparative and Physiological Psychology,* 1968, *65,* 251–260.

Weiss, J. M. Effects of coping behavior in different warning signal conditions on stress pathology in rats. *Journal of Comparative and Physiological Psychology,* 1971, *77,* 1–13.

Weiss, R. S. *Marital separation.* New York: Basic Books, 1975.

Weitzenhoffer, A. M., & Hilgard, E. R. *Stanford hypnotic susceptibility scales, forms A and B.* Palo Alto, Calif.: Consulting Psychologists Press, 1959.

Weitzenhoffer, A. M., & Hilgard, E. R. *Stanford hypnotic susceptibility scale, form C.* Palo Alto, Calif.: Consulting Psychologists Press, 1962.

Weitzenhoffer, A. M., & Hilgard, E. R. *Revised Stanford profile scales of hypnotic susceptibility, forms I and II.* Palo Alto, Calif.: Consulting Psychologists Press, 1967.

Weitzman, E. D. (Ed.). *Advances in sleep research* (Vol. 1). New York: Spectrum, 1974.

Weitzman, E. D. (Ed.). *Advances in sleep research* (Vol. 2). New York: Spectrum, 1975.

Wells, G. L., Lindsay, P. C. L., & Ferguson, T. J. Accuracy, confidence, and juror perceptions. *Journal of Applied Psychology,* 1979, *64,* 440–448.

Wertham, F. *Seduction of the innocent.* New York: Rinehart, 1954.

Wertheimer, M. *Productive thinking* (Enl. ed.). New York: Harper & Row, 1959.

Wever, E. G., & Bray, C. W. The nature of the acoustic response: A relation between sound frequency and frequency of impulses in the auditory nerve. *Journal of Experimental Psychology,* 1930, *13,* 373–387.

Whitehead, A. N., & Russell, B. *Principia mathematica* (Vol. 1) (2nd ed.). Cambridge: Cambridge University Press, 1925.

Whorf, B. L. Science and linguistics. *Technology Review,* 1940, *54,* 229–231; 247; 248.

Whorf, B. L. The relation of habitual thought and behavior to language. In L. Spier (Ed.), *Language, culture and personality.* Salt Lake City: University of Utah Press, 1941.

Whorf, B. L. *Language, thought, and reality.* New York: John Wiley, 1956.

Wickelgren, W. A. Human learning and memory. *Annual Review of Psychology,* 1981, *32,* 21–52.

Widroe, H. J., & Heisler, S. Treatment of tardive dyskinesia. *Diseases of the Nervous System,* 1976, *37,* 162–164.

Wiener, N. *Cybernetics.* New York: John Wiley, 1948.

Wilbur, M. P., & Wilbur, J. R. Counselor educator: Nonverbal behavior in the supervision process. Counselor Education and Supervision, December, 1979, 101–108.

Wilcoxon, H. C., Dragoin, W. B., & Kral, P. A. Illness-induced aversions in rat and quail: Relative salience of visual and gustatory cues. *Science,* 1971, *171,* 826–828.

Willerman, L. Effects of families on intellectual development. *American Psychologist,* 1979, *34,* 923–929.

Williams, D. R., & Williams, H. Auto-maintenance in the pigeon: Sustained pecking despite contingent non-reinforcement. *Journal of the Experimental Analysis of Behavior,* 1969, *12,* 511–520.

Wills, T. A., & Langner, T. S. Socioeconomic status and stress. In I. L. Kutash, L. B. Schlesinger, & Associates (Eds.), *Handbook on stress and anxiety.* San Francisco: Jossey Bass, 1980, 159–173.

Wilson, E. O. The natural history of lions. *Science,* 1973, *179,* 466–467.

Wilson, E. O. *Sociobiology: The new synthesis.* Cambridge, Mass.: Belknap, 1975.

Wilson, E. O. Academic vigilantism and the political significance of sociobiology. *BioScience,* 1976, *183,* 187–190.

Winokur, G. The types of affective disorders. *Journal of Nervous and Mental Disorders,* 1973, *156,* 82–96.

Winsten, S. *Days with Bernard Shaw.* New York: Vanguard Press, 1949.

Witkin, H. A. The perception of the upright. *Scientific American,* 1959, *200,* 50–56.

Witkin, H. A., Mednick, S. A., Schulsinger, F., Bakkestrom, E., Christiansen, K. O., Goodenough, D. R., Hirschhorn, K., Lundesteen, C., Owen, D. R., Philip, J., Rubin, D. B., & Stocking, M. Criminality in XYY and XXY men. *Science,* 1976, *193,* 547–555.

Wolcott, J. H., McMeekin, R. R., Burgin, R. E., & Yanowitch, R. E. Biorhythms—Are they a waste of time? *TAC Attack,* 1975, *15,* 4–9.

Wolcott, J. H., McMeekin, R. R., Burgin, R. E., & Yanowitch, R. E. Correlation of general aviation accidents with the biorhythm theory. *Human Factors,* 1977, *19,* 283–293.

Wolff, P. H. Observations on newborn infants. *Psychosomatic Medicine,* 1959, *21,* 110–118.

Wolff, P. H. Observations of the early development of smiling. In B. M. Foss (Ed.), *Determinants of infant behavior II.* London: Methuen, 1963.

Wolff, P. H. The causes, controls, and organization of behavior in the neonate. *Psychological Issues,* 1966, *5,* Monograph 17.

Wolfle, E., & Wolfle, H. M. The development of cooperative behavior in monkeys and young children. *Journal of Genetic Psychology,* 1939, *55,* 137–175.

Wollheim, R. *Sigmund Freud.* New York: Viking Press, 1971.

Wolpe, J. *Psychotherapy by reciprocal inhibition.* Stanford, Calif.: Stanford University Press, 1958.

Wolpe, J. *Theme and variations: A behavior therapy casebook.* New York: Pergamon Press, 1976.

Wood, B. S. *Children and communication: Verbal and non-verbal language development.* Englewood Cliffs, N.J.: Prentice-Hall, 1976.

Wood, L. A., Krider, D. W., & Fezer, K. D. Emergency room data on 700 accidents do not support biorhythm theory. *Journal of Safety Research,* 1980, *11,* 172–175.

Woodrow, H. The effect of type of training upon transference. *Journal of Educational Psychology,* 1927, *18,* 159–172.

Woods, P. J. A taxonomy of instrumental conditioning. *American Psychologist,* August 1974, 584–597.

Woods, S. C., West, D. B., Stein, L. J., McKay, L. D., Lotter, E. C., Porte, S. G., Kenney, N. J., & Porte, D. Jr. Peptides and the control of meal size. *Diabetologia,* 1981, *20,* 305–313.

Woodward, K. L. There is life after death. *McCall's,* August 1976, pp. 97; 134–139.

Woodworth, R. S., & Schlosberg, H. *Experimental psychology* (Rev. ed.). New York: Holt, 1954.

Worchel, S., & Cooper, J. *Understanding social psychology* (2nd ed.). Homewood, Ill.: Dorsey Press, 1979.

Wozny, J. R. *Psychological and sociological correlates of use and non-use of marijuana.* Unpublished master's thesis, University of Alberta, Edmonton, 1971.

Yalom, I. D., & Lieberman, M. A. A study of encounter group casualties. *Archives of General Psychiatry,* 1971, *25,* 16–30.

Yamamoto, K. *Experimental scoring manual for Minnesota tests of creative thinking and writing.* Kent, Ohio: Bureau of Educational Research, Kent State University, 1964.

Yarmey, A. D. *The psychology of eyewitness testimony.* New York: Free Press, 1979.

Yarrow, L. J., & Goodwin, M. S. The immediate impact of separation: Reactions of infants to a change in mother figures. In L. J. Stone, H. T. Smith, & L. B. Murphy (Eds.), *The competent infant: Research and commentary.* New York: Basic Books, 1973.

Yensen, R. On the measurement of happiness and its implications for welfare. In L. Levi (Ed.), *Emotions: Their parameters and measurement.* New York: Raven Press, 1975.

Yontef, G. M. Gestalt therapy: Clinical phenomenology. In V. Binder, A. Binder, & B. Rimland (Eds.), *Modern therapies.* Englewood Cliffs, N.J.: Prentice-Hall, 1976.

Young, P. C. Antisocial uses of hypnosis. In L. M. LeCron (Ed.), *Experimental hypnosis.* New York: Macmillan, 1952.

Young, W. C., Goy, R. W., & Phoenix, C. H. Hormones in sexual behavior. *Science,* 1964, *143,* 212–218.

Zajonc, R. B. Birth order and intelligence: Dumber by the dozen. *Psychology Today,* 1975, pp. 37–43.

Zanna, M. T., & Pack, S. J. On the self fulfilling nature of the apparent sex differences in behavior. *Journal of Experimental Social Psychology,* 1975, *11,* 583–591.

Zeaman, D. Response latency as a function of amount of reinforcement. *Journal of Experimental Psychology,* 1949, *39,* 466–483.

Zelman, A., Kabot, L., Jacobsen, R., & McConnell, J. V. Transfer of training through injection of "conditioned" RNA into untrained worms. *Worm Runners Digest,* 1963, *5,* 14–21.

Zepelin, H., & Rechtschaffen, A. Mammalian sleep, longevity, and energy metabolism. *Brain, Behavior, and Evolution,* 1974, *10,* 425–470.

Zilbergeld, B., & Evans, M. The inadequacy of Masters and Johnson. *Psychology Today,* August 1980, 28–43.

Zilboorg, G., & Henry, G. W. *A history of medical psychology.* New York: W. W. Norton, 1941.

Zubek, J. P. *Sensory deprivation: Fifteen years of research.* New York: Appleton-Century-Crofts, 1969.

Zuckerman, M. *Sensation seeking: Beyond the optimal level of arousal.* Hillsdale, N.J.: Erlbaum, 1979.

Photo Credits

Page xvi, top left, Louvre Museum, Paris (*Mona Lisa* by Leonardo Da Vinci)

Page xvi, bottom left, Baron Hugo van Lawick © National Geographic Society

Page xvi, bottom right, © Leonard Freed/ Magnum Photos

Page 1, center, © Bohdan Hrynewych/Stock, Boston

Page 2, © Peeter Vilms/Jeroboam

Page 6, The Bettmann Archive

Page 7, left, The Bettmann Archive

Page 7, center, National Library of Medicine

Page 7, right, National Library of Medicine

Page 8, left, © Leonard Freed/Magnum Photos

Page 8, right, Louvre Museum, Paris (*Mona Lisa* by Leonardo Da Vinci)

Page 10, Baron Hugo van Lawick © National Geographic Society

Page 23, © Bohdan Hrynewych/Stock, Boston

Page 28, top left, William Vandivert, from *Scientific American,* 1961

Page 28, top center, Goethe Museum, Frankfurt (*The Nightmare* by John Henry Fuseli)

Page 28, top right, Peter M. Witt, North Carolina Department of Mental Health

Page 28, bottom right, © Kent Reno/Jeroboam

Page 29, bottom left, Courtesy Carolina Biological Supply Company

Page 30, © Christopher Springmann

Page 32, © Ira Kirschenbaum/Stock, Boston

Page 37, top, Courtesy Carolina Biological Supply Company

Page 37, bottom, Dr. Edwin Lewis, University of California, Berkeley

Page 41, American Museum of Natural History

Page 54, © Bonnie Freer

Page 56, The Bettmann Archive

Page 59, The Bettmann Archive

Page 60, © Ian Berry/Magnum Photos

Page 62, Wide World Photos

Page 65, © Erich Hartmann/Magnum Photos

Page 68, Goethe Museum, Frankfurt (*The Nightmare* by John Henry Fuseli

Page 71, left, Brown Brothers

Page 71, right, © Mimi Forsyth

Page 78, © Bonnie Freer

Page 79, © Bonnie Freer

Page 86, © Joan Liftin/Archive Pictures

Page 89, Peter M. Witt, North Carolina Department of Mental Health

Page 92, © Charles Gatewood/Magnum Photos

Page 96, © Kent Reno/Jeroboam

Page 102, David Linton, from *Scientific American,* 1959

Page 105, U.S. Navy

Page 113, © Elizabeth Crews

Page 118, © Burk Uzzle/Magnum Photos

Page 130, © Peeter Vilms/Jeroboam

Page 131, © Jonas Grushkin

Page 132, © Peter Simon/Stock, Boston

Page 133, © Kent Reno/Jeroboam

Page 135, top, © Emile Schulthess/Black Star

Page 135, bottom, Library of Congress

Page 141, William Vandivert, from *Scientific American,* 1961

Page 148, bottom, © Fred Kaplan/Black Star

Page 149, center, Collection, The Museum of Modern Art, New York, gift of Nelson A. Rockefeller (*The Dream* by Henri Rousseau)

Page 150, © Audrey Ross

Page 155, National Library of Medicine

Page 156, Culver Pictures

Page 162, Courtesy B. F. Skinner

Page 163, Christopher S. Johnson, courtesy B. F. Skinner

Page 167, left, © Bill Owens/Magnum Photos

Page 167, right, © Bob Adelman/Magnum Photos

Page 170, left, © Allan Grant

Page 170, right, © Cheryl A. Traendly/ Jeroboam

Page 174, Yerkes Regional Primate Research Center, Atlanta

Page 177, © Fred Kaplan/Black Star

Page 182, © Joseph Schuyler/Stock, Boston

Page 188, Collection, The Museum of Modern Art, New York, gift of Nelson A. Rockefeller (*The Dream* by Henri Rousseau)

Page 197, © Robert Eckert/EKM-Nepenthe

Page 214, © Sergio Larrain/Magnum Photos

Page 216, © Robert Eckert/EKM-Nepenthe

Page 219, Wide World Photos

Page 225, © Paul S. Conklin

Page 231, © Elizabeth Hamlin/Stock, Boston

Page 235, © Richard Smolan/Stock, Boston

Page 240, © Paul Fusco/Magnum Photos

Page 241, News and Publications Service, Stanford University

Page 242, Yerkes Regional Primate Research Center, Atlanta

Page 254, © Martin A. Levick/Black Star

Page 258, left, © Peeter Vilms/Jeroboam

Page 258, right, © Kent Reno/Jeroboam

Page 259, © Clay Templin/Jeroboam

Page 260, © Clay Templin/Jeroboam

Page 263, © Jonas Grushkin

Page 264, Grant Heilman

Page 266, Nina Leen © 1965 Time Inc., from Life Nature Library—Animal Behavior

Page 269, © H. S. Chapman/Jeroboam

Page 278, © Peter Menzel

Page 280, Yale University Library

Page 285, © Mark Chester

Page 294, © Peter Menzel/Stock, Boston

Page 296, © Kent Reno/Jeroboam

Page 297, © Owen Franken/Stock, Boston

Page 301, © Michael Hayman/Stock, Boston

Page 303, © Peeter Vilms/Jeroboam

Page 304, © Peeter Vilms/Jeroboam

Page 307, © Chris Maynard/Magnum Photos

Page 311, Department of the Army, Walter Reed Army Institute of Research

Page 312, © Joan Liftin/Archive Pictures

Page 314, © Bonnie Freer

Page 315, University of Wisconsin Primate Laboratory

Page 316, © William Strode/Woodfin Camp & Associates

Page 318, top left, Robert Capa/Magnum

Page 318, top right, © Elizabeth Crews

Page 318, bottom left, © Peter Vandermark/ Stock, Boston

Page 318, bottom right, Courtesy S. Brecher

Page 320, © J. Scott Applewhite

Page 323, Library of Congress

Page 324, © Jean-Claude Lejeune/Stock, Boston

Page 325, © Mimi Forsyth

Page 326, Courtesy S. Brecher

Page 329, © Timothy Eagan/Woodfin Camp & Associates

Page 330, National Foundation, March of Dimes

Page 331, © Cheryl A. Traendly/Jeroboam

Page 333, © Peter Vandermark/Stock, Boston

Page 334, © Arthur Grace/Stock, Boston

Page 337, left, © J. W. Berndt/Stock, Boston

Page 337, right, © Frank Siteman/Stock, Boston

Page 340, Eric Schwab/World Health Organization

Page 341, © Terry Evans/Magnum Photos

Page 346, © Charlotte Brooks/Magnum Photos

Page 347, © Bonnie Freer

Page 350, top left, © Bonnie Freer

Page 350, bottom left, © Bill Owens/Magnum Photos

Name Index

Italic page numbers refer to illustrations.

Carlsmith, J. M., 518, *519*
Carlson, N. R., 37, 52, 61, 66, 293
Carpenter, C. R., 509
Carson, R. C., 86
Cartwright, D. S., 363
Cartwright, R. D., 67, 69, 70, 91
Casler, L., 348
Castaneda, C., 91
Cates, J., 4, 5, *5*
Cattell, James McKeen, 6
Cattell, R. B., 373, 386, 408, *386*
Cermak, L. S., 198, 213
Chambard, 73
Chambliss, W. J., 363
Chance, P., 181
Chapman, R. S., 481
Chase, W. G., 189
Cherry, E. C., 96–97
Chertok, L., 75
Chhina, G. S., 81
Chomsky, Noam, 244, 248, 250–251, *251*
Cisin, I. H., 83
Clarizio, H. F., 168
Clark, E. V., 251
Clark, H. H., 251, 253
Clark, R. D. C., III, 515
Clark, R. W., 398, 411, 499
Clausen, J. A., 359
Cleckley, H., 59, 457
Coates, T. J., 494
Cobb, S., 310
Cofer, C. N., 268, 293
Cohen, D. K., 390, 430
Cohen, J., 529, 533
Cohen, M. L., 508, 509, 512
Cohen, S., 87, 88
Cole, M., 228
Coleman, J. C., 86, 471
Collins, B. E., 520
Collins, J. K., 364
Commons, W. D., 173
Conrad, R., 189
Contreras, R. J., 274
Cook, Eliza, 549
Cook, J., *50*
Cooper, J., 533, 548, 554
Coopersmith, S., 361
Cope, V., 549
Corbit, J. D., 307–308
Coren, S., 111, 116, 127
Corey, G., 486, 493, 499
Cortes, J. B., 390
Costa, P. T., 376, 377, 406, 411
Cotzin, Milton, 105
Coyne, M. L., 62
Craik, F. I., 198, 199, 213
Crick, F. H., 325
Cropley, A. J., 232
Crossley, H. M., 83
Crow, J. S., 435
Crowder, N. A., 178, *178*
Curtis, D., 70

Dallenbach, K. M., 105, 205, *205*
Dallos, P., 109
Darian-Smith, I., 110
Darley, John M., 514, 515, 516, 533, *515*
Darwin, C., 298, 338
Davidson, D. M., 482
Davidson, P. O., 499

Davidson, R. J., 91
Davidson, S. M., 499
Davis, Adelle, 332
Davis, B., 293
Davis, D. M., 272
Davis, K. E., 536, 537
Davis, R. C., 268, *268*
Davison, G. C., 455, 471
Davison, M. L., 425
Davitz, J. R., 297
Dawkins, R., 53
Deaux, K., 293
De Bono, E., 216, 233–234, 255, 256, *234*
Deci, E. L., 280
DeFries, J. C., 354, 436
Dehon, R. S., 115
Deikman, A. J., 78, 79
Delgado, J. M. R., 309
DeMartino, M. S., 67, 68
DeMause, L., 322, 323
Dember, W. N., 98, 281
Dement, William C., 62, 65, 66, 68, 70
de Mille, R., 91
Demuth, P., 63
Descartes, René, 51
Dethier, V. G., 269
Deutsch, A., 446
Deutsch, G., 53
De Valois, K. K., 133
De Valois, R. L., 133
Dickson, W. J., 16
Dinham, S. M., 563
Dollard, J. C., 402, 505, 509, 532
Donne, John, 549
Donnerstein, E., 278
Douglas, J. W. B., 359
Dove, Adrian, 438
Drabman, R., 482
Drayton, Michael, 444
Dreyer, P. H., 364
Droscher, V. B., 113
Dryden, John, 444
Duncker, K., 134, 229
Dunn, A. J., 211
Dunphy, D. C., 360–361, *362*
Dupree, A. H., 532
Durkheim, E., 461
Dusek, J., 363
Dutton, D. C., 542, 550, *543*

Ebbinghaus, H., 188, 201
Ebin, D., 86
Eckland, B. K., 530
Edwards, A. L., 386
Eibl-Eibesfeldt, I., 298
Einstein, Albert, 291, *407*
Eiseley, L., 53
Eisenberg, R. B., 345
Ekman, P., 298–300, *299*
Eliseo, T. S., 74
Elliot, R., 352
Ellis, A., 483–484, 498, *483*
Ellis, H. C., 192
Emmons, W. H., 70
Epstein, A. N., 270, *270*
Epstein, R., 243
Epstein, S. M., 308
Erhardt, A. A., 277, 336
Erikson, Erik Homburger, 339, 361, 368–371, 379, 398, *369, 372, 400,* biography, 370
Erlenmeyer-Kimling, L., 433, *435*
Eron, 311
Ervin, F., 301
Essen-Moller, *465*

Estes, W. K., 197
Evans, F. J., 71, 76
Evans, M., 488
Evans, R. I., 390, 408
Everly, K., 379
Eysenck, Hans J., 388, 391–392, 402, 410, 423, 471, 490, 491, 492, *391, 393,* biography, 390

Fagin, B., 173
Falek, A., 332
Fancher, R. E., 26
Faneslow, M. S., 38, 111
Fantino, E., 50, 181
Fantz, R. L., 140, 345, *141*
Farina, A., 450, 469
Farquhar, George, 549
Fawcett, J., 461
Feffer, M., 411
Feighner, J. P., 451
Feingold, B. D., 521
Feinleib, M., 310
Feldman, F. T., 351, *351*
Feldman, S. E., 351, *351*
Feldt, L. S., 430
Felsenthal, N., 512, *513*
Ferguson, T. J., 194
Feshbach, S., 335
Festinger, L., 518, 519, *519*
Fezer, K. D., 63
Fielding, Henry, 549
Fischer, *465*
Fishbein, W., 62
Fisher, A. E., 276
Fisher, C., 66
Fisher, J. D., 450
Fisher, S., 398, 411
Fisher, W. A., 278, 364
Fleischman, P. R., 454
Flexner, L., 211
Flynn, J. P., 301, 309
Fode, K. L., 16
Fodor, E. N., 351
Fouts, Roger, 239, 241, 244
Fowler, H., 98, 281, 293
Fowler, R. D., *424*
Fowler, W. L., 77
Framo, J. L., 552
Frank, J. D., 492, 493, 494, 495
Franks, J. J., 200
Fraser, S. C., 542
Freidman, J. L., 542
French, J. D., 45, 289
Freud, Anna, 370
Freud, Sigmund, 68–69, 90, 203, 339, 370, 390, 392–399, 400, 401, 402, 410, 411, 449, 450, 477, 478, 484, *395, 396,* biography, 398
Frick, W. B., 406
Friedman, A. S., 363
Friedman, M. I., 271
Friedman, R. J., 460
Friedrich, L. K., 335
Friesen, W. V., 298
Frieze, I. H., 355
Frisch, Karl von, 237, *238*
Frodi, A., 278

Gage, Phineas, 41, 42
Gagnon, J. H., 365
Galanter, E., 221, 222, *224*
Galen, 386
Gallagher, J. J., 232
Galton, S., 333, 432

Italic page numbers refer to illustrations.

Italic page numbers refer to illustrations.

Italic page numbers refer to illustrations.

Italic page numbers refer to illustrations.

Italic page numbers refer to illustrations.

Italic page numbers refer to illustrations.

Subject Index and Glossary

Italic page numbers refer to illustrations.

It disseminates psychological information through a large number of publications and through meetings and conventions. 489
   areas of specialization of members, 4, *5, 6*
   defined, 6
American Sign Language, for nonhuman speech, 239–240, *240*
   review of, 256
Ames room, 130, 134, 135, *130*
Amino acids, as neurotransmitter substances, 37–38
Amnesia Sudden and temporary loss of memory for no apparent organic reason. Amnesia may take a variety of forms and is sometimes associated with mental disorders. In hypnosis, amnesia can be induced in subjects if they are told they will remember nothing of what transpired while in a hypnotic state. 456–457
   review of, 470
   under hypnosis, 74
      review of, 91
Amok, 469
Amphetamines A class of drugs known as stimulants (uppers). Methedrine (speed), Dexedrine, and Benzedrine are trade names of common amphetamines. 88, *85, 89*
Amplitude, auditory One of three characteristics of waves that produce sounds, defined physically as the height of wave peaks. Amplitude corresponds to the violence of the vibratory event that gave rise to the wave, and is related to perception of loudness. 125, *126*
Amplitude, visual, 104, *104*
   relation to brightness, 125, *126*
      review of, 146
   review of, 116
Amygdala, role in anger, aggression, and violence, 300–301, 532
   review of, 316
Anal characters Individuals with a pattern of personality traits associated with fixation at the anal stage of development or regression to that stage. Freud believed that two kinds of sexually related pleasures were associated with the anal period: those related to the expulsion of feces, and those related to their retention. He suggested that pleasures associated with anal expulsion would be associated with ambition, generosity, conceit, and suspicion; those associated with anal retention would lead to compulsiveness, orderliness, and stubbornness. Since an anal character might have resulted from both types of pleasures, all of these characteristics or any combination of them might be descriptive of that person. 395
Anal stage, 394, *395*
   review of, 410
Analytical theory (Jung) Pertaining to *analysis,* a logical thought process that involves separating a problem into its elements and examining its parts. To analyze is, in essence, to break down. In a highly specialized sense, analytical refers to the psychological system advanced by Jung. 401–402, *401*
   collective unconscious, 401
   personality functioning, 401–402
   review of, 411

Italic page numbers refer to illustrations.

Androgens Male sex hormones. The principal androgens are testosterone and androsterone. 275. *See also* Testosterone
Androsterone, role in sexual motivation, 275
Anesthesia Loss of sensitivity to stimulation. Anesthesia is often induced through drugs for surgical reasons and may also be a characteristic of a hypnotic state.
   as cause of hypnotic trance, 75
   under hypnosis, 72–73, *73*
   review of, 90
Angel's dust, 87
Anger stage of dying, 377
   review of, 379
Anima/animus, 401
Animalculists, 99
Animals:
   communication systems of, 237–238, *238*
   imprinting in, 265–266, *265, 266*
   language learned by, 237–244, *238, 240, 241, 242*
   sexual violence among, 509
   and sleep deprivation, 62
   use in research, 14
Anorexia nervosa, therapy for (case study), 482
Anosmatic noses, 115
Antabuse, 475
Anthropophobia, *455*
Antipsychotic drugs, 475
   review of, 498
Antisocial behavior, under hypnosis, 70–72
Antisocial personality disorder, 462–463
   review of, 471
Anvil, 107, *107*
Anxiety An unpleasant emotional reaction whose most identifiable characteristic is fear. Anxiety can vary from mild trepidation, frequently not associated with any specific situation or stimulus, to severe panic. One of the most common characteristics of a great number of mental disorders is anxiety; in fact, psychoanalytic theory suggests that anxiety is at the root of virtually all mental disorders. 298
   relation to stress, 310
Anxiety disorders, 453, 454–456, *452, 455*
   generalized anxiety disorders, 456
   obsessive-compulsive disorders, 456
   phobic disorders, 455–456, *455*
   review of, 470
APA. *See* American Psychological Association
Apathy:
   bystander effect, defined, 514, *515*
   causes, 515–517
   versus altruism, 513–517, *515*
Aphagia The Latin prefix *a* signifies "against" or "opposed to." Aphagia therefore indicates insufficient eating. 271
Aphasia Any of a number of language disorders or impairments that result from brain damage. Difficulties with language which are not related to brain damage (for example, stuttering or stammering) are not examples of aphasia. 42
Apnea, 66
Apomorphine, 481
Apprehend Literally, to take hold of or seize, as in "to apprehend a criminal." As a psychological term, it refers to the simple awareness of an object, or the process of becoming aware. Apprehension goes somewhat beyond perception, but implies something less than comprehension. 94

Aptitude A specific ability or capacity to learn. Aptitude tests measure the extent to which individuals are likely to profit from future experiences. When psychologists speak of *special aptitudes* they mean specific aptitudes (for example, music aptitude), rather than aptitudes that are most outstanding. They speak as well of *general aptitudes:* a capacity for acquiring knowledge or proficiency in a number of areas. *Scholastic aptitude* tests measure the capacity to profit from educational experience and are very similar to intelligence tests. 427
Aqueous humor, 121, *122*
Archetype The first, or original, model. For Jung, a sort of universal thought—a thought present in all our minds, throughout human history, but essentially unconscious. 401
   review of, 411
Arctic hysteria, 469
Arousal Both a physiological and a psychological concept. As a physiological concept, it refers to changes in heart rate, respiration, electrical activity in the cortex, and the skin's electrical conductivity. Psychologically, the term relates to degree of alertness, awareness, vigilance, or wakefulness. 286–289, *287, 289*
   cognitive arousal theory, 289, *289*
   defined, 45
   level of, 286–288, *287*
   panic, 287
   as physiological term, 286
   as psychological term, 286
   review of, 293
   sources of, 288–289
Arousal function of stimulus, 288–289
Arousal theory Arousal theory refers to activity of the sympathetic nervous system, and therefore relates to emotion; it also relates to degree of alertness. Arousal theory maintains that we behave so as to maintain arousal at an optimal level, sometimes seeking stimulation and sometimes trying to reduce it. 286
Artificial intelligence A branch of computer science concerned with the use of machine or computer models either to stimulate human behavior or as metaphors for some aspects of human cognitive processes. 217–219
   review of, 255
ASL. *See* American Sign Language
Asocial personality disorders, 462
Assassin, origin of term, 83
Assimilation The act of incorporating objects or aspects of objects in previously learned activities.
   in Piaget's theory, 339
   review of, 354
Association areas of brain, 43
   review of, 52
Associationistic models of memory Models of memory that concern themselves with the way items of information in our memories are associated with each other. The levels of processing model is associationistic. 197–200
   review of, 212
Associationistic theories of learning. *See* Behavioristic theories
Assumption A judgment or belief that is accepted as true even though it has not been proven and in most instances, cannot be

proven. Assumptions, many of which are not consciously recognized, are fundamental in most sciences, although they are often sources of error. Later investigations may prove assumptions false; or they may verify them, in which case they become principles or laws. 20–21
  review of, 26

Asylum A once common term for institutions in which individuals suffering from mental disorders were held. The term is now actively avoided, as is the equivalent expression *mental hospital*. Instead, such euphemisms as *state hospital, sanitarium, "home,"* or *treatment facility* are employed. 446

Attention A state of the reacting organism which, as it increases, narrows the focus of perception. Attention denotes a state of readiness to perceive and/or respond. In addition, it implies selection and emphasis. It is both a state (wherein an individual is more likely to respond to certain events than to others) and a process (whereby an individual increases the probability of responding to one event and not another).
  relation to perception, 96–99
  cocktail party problem, 96–97, *97*
  defined, 96, 136
  determinants of, 97–99, *99*
  review of, 116
Attention span, 196
  review of, 212

Attitudes and attitude change A prevailing and consistent tendency to react in a given way describable as being positive or negative and having important motivational consequences. 517–525, *517, 519, 520, 522, 523, 525*
  cognitive dissonance, 518–520, *519, 520*
  compliance and confirmity, 518
  defined, 517
  obedience, 522–524, *523*
  overjustification, 520–521
  persuasion, 524–525, *525*
  review of, 532
  social pressure, 522, *522*
Attractiveness, role in interpersonal attraction, 544–545, *545*
  review of, 553
Attributions, affected by personality, 404

Attribution theory Attribution theories in personality, social psychology, motivation, and other topics in psychology look at external circumstances and personality characteristics that influence processes of assessing and assigning responsibility or cause. 281
  of achievement motivation, 285–286, *285*
  review of, 293
  of attitude change, 520
  of emotion, 306–307, *307*
  review of, 316
  of person perception, 536–538, *538, 539*
  review of, 553
  review of, 293
Auditory canal, 107, *107*
  function of, 108

Auditory system A perceptual system whose principal sensory organs are the ears and whose function is to permit detection of

---

sounds, of their direction and distance, and of other characteristics of vibrations that are important in our understanding of the environment. 102–109, *95, 104, 106, 107, 108, 109*
  anatomy of, 107–108, *107*
  function of, 102–103
  physiology of, 108–109, *108, 109*
  review of, 116
  sound waves and our perception of, 103–107, *104, 106*

Authoritarian An adjective descriptive of people who consistently exhibit the need to dominate. Such individuals are frequently aggressive, imperious, intolerant, and demanding. 363

Autokinetic effect A phenomenon whereby stationary objects are perceived as though they were in motion. 134
  review of, 146

Autonomic nervous system That part of the peripheral nervous system not ordinarily under conscious control. It regulates physiological functions such as respiration, heart rate, temperature, and digestion, and includes the sympathetic and parasympathetic systems. 39–41, *39, 40*
  review of, 52
  role in emotion, 300, *301*
    review of, 315
Autonomy versus shame and doubt, 368, *369, 372*

Autoshaping Refers to responses that are learned in experimental situations in spite of the fact that they are not related to reinforcement. In some cases, autoshaped behaviors may be learned even though they actually prevent reinforcement. 172
  review of, 180

Average A mathematical indication of central tendency. An average is obtained by summing the numbers that relate to a particular characteristic among a group of individuals and dividing the sum by the total number of observations involved. Although averages are often good descriptions of characteristics or qualities of groups, they do not describe individual members of groups. 11
  person, child, nonexistence of, 11, 24, 259, 323–324, *324*
  in statistics. *See* Mean
Averaging and adding, in person perception, 540–541, *541*
  review of, 553

Aversive conditioning A behavior modification technique that attempts to bring about avoidance behavior with respect to certain situations by attaching negative feelings to the situation. 480–481, *491*
  review of, 498

Avoidance learning A type of conditioning in which the organism learns responses that prevent the occurrence of unpleasant stimuli. 168
Avoidant personality disorder, 462
Awakening, after hypnosis, 75
Awareness, 57. *See also* Consciousness

Axon The elongated part of a neuron. Axons ordinarily transmit impulses from the cell body to adjoining dendrites. 35, *37*

Babbling, 245
  review of, 256

Backward conditioning, 155–156, *155*
  review of, 180
Balance model of interpersonal attraction, 546, *546*
  review of, 553

Barbiturates Any of a large number of drugs that have a powerful sedating influence on the body, and that are also addictive. Barbiturates are often prescription drugs. 88, *85*
  as cause of hypnotic trance, 75
  effects when mixed with alcohol, 88
  review of, 91
Bargaining stage of dying, 377
  review of, 379
Basic needs, 290, 291
  review of, 293

Basic orienting system The perceptual system whose principal function is to provide the organism with information relating to positions of the body, body movements, and relationship to the gravitational plane. It allows us to remain upright, informs us which way is up and which way is down, and allows us to determine whether we are moving and in what direction. The organ that appears to be most central to the basic orienting system is the vestibular organ. 94, 99–102, *95, 101, 102*
  deceiving the, 101–102, *102*
  defined, 99
  functions, 100
  review of, 116
  vestibular organ, 100–101, *101*
  and visual system, 101–102, *102*
Basilar membrane, 108, *107, 108*
  function of, 108
Bats, echolocation of, 31, 106
The Beaux Stratagem, 549
Bed-wetting, 66
Bees:
  altruism in, 530
  communication among, 237, *238*
Behavioral contracting, 481
Behavioral models of mental disorder, 449, 450, 464, *451*
  review of, 470
Behavioral observation, in assessing personality, 418, *419*
  review of, 439

Behaviorism An approach to psychology that considers only objective evidence of behavior and does not consider consciousness and mind. 153, 171–178, 216, *174, 175, 177, 178*
  applications of, 177–178, *177, 178*
  challenges to, 171–175, *174, 175*
  current directions in, 175–177
  review of, 255
Behavioristic theories:
  of learning, 153
  of motivation, 280
  review of, 292

Behavior modification Changes in the behavior of an individual. Also refers to psychological theory and research concerned with applying psychological principles in attempts to change behavior. Since many of these attempts relate directly to behavior problems or mental disorders, the expression *behavior therapy* is often used as a synonym. 178, 479
  review of, 181
The Behavior of Organisms, 163

Italic page numbers refer to illustrations.

A *Behavior System,* 280
Behavior therapy, 178, 479–482, 493–494, *480, 491, 493*
  aversive conditioning, 480–481
  case study, 482
  implosive therapy, 481–482
  positive reinforcement, 481
  review of, 498
  systematic desensitization, 480, *480*
Beliefs Acceptance of something as accurate or truthful. Beliefs are more personal and less universal than principles, and ideally compose only a small portion of the body of knowledge characterizing a discipline. 3
  defined, 3
  illustrated, 4, 21
Belligerence, as factor in interpersonal attraction, 549
  review of, 553
Benzedrine, 88, *85*
Bernstein's language codes, 253
Beta-endorphins, role in appetite control, 271
  review of, 292
Beta waves, *61*
Beyond Freedom and Dignity, 163
Bias, in experiments, 16–18
Bible, 444
Binocular cues to perception, 132–133
  review of, 146
Biofeedback The information we obtain about our biological functioning. In a more specialized sense, it refers to procedures whereby subjects are given information about physiological functioning that they would not ordinarily have with the object of achieving control over specific aspects of physiological functioning. 80–82, 288, *82*
  medical applications, 82
  review of, 91
Biological approaches to personality theories, 387, 388–392, *388, 389, 391, 393*
  Eysenck's biological theory, 391–392, *391, 393*
  review of, 410
  Sheldon's body types, 389–391, *389*
The Biological Basis of Personality, 393
Biological clocks, 64, *65*
Biological constraints A highly general term referring to the observation that certain behaviors are more easily learned by some organisms than by others and, conversely, that other specific behaviors are not learned at all easily. Biological constraints are essentially genetic predispositions that either *prepare* or *contraprepare* organisms for specific learning. 172
  review of, 181
Biological Foundation of Language, 249
Biological theory (Eysenck), 391–392, *391, 393*
  review of, 410
Biological theory of sleep, 62, 64
  review of, 90
Biology, relation to behavior, 50–51
  review of, 52
Biorhythm theory, 63, *63*
Bipolar disorder A major affective disorder characterized by attacks of mania (euphoria, intense activity, or excitement) and depression. 460
  review of, 470

Italic page numbers refer to illustrations.

Bipolar layer of retina, *123*
Birth order:
  in Adlerian theory and therapy, 400, 478
  influence on development, 333
    review of, 353
  relation to IQ, 430
Birth trauma, 397
Blackbirds, altruism in, 529–530
Blacks, language code of, 253
Blind spot, 122, 138, *122, 123*
Blocked-path study, 174, 175, *175*
Blocking, 160
Block problems, 233–234, *234*
Blood sugar level, relation to hunger, 270, 271
  review of, 292
Blowfly, feeding behavior of, 269
Body-sway test, 74
Body types, theory of, 389–391, *389*
  review of, 410
Body versus mind, philosophical problem of, 51
Booee, 241
Botulism toxin, effects of, 36
Box problem, 174, 229
Brain A complex cluster of nerve cells centrally involved in coordinating activities and events in various parts of an organism. The human brain is reputedly the most complex structure in the universe. 34, 41–49, *41, 44, 45, 46, 47, 49, 50*
  association areas, 43
    review of, 52
  cerebrum, 43, *44*
  compared to other animals, 34–35, *35*
  hemispheres of, 46–49, 50, *47, 49*
    review of, 52
  importance of in evolution, 32, 33, 34
    review of, 51
  mapping functions of, 42–43
  other structures, 44–45, *45*
  role in emotion, 300–303
    review of, 316
  role in hunger sensation, 271–272
    review of, 292
  role in sexual motivation, 276
  role in vision, 129
  split brain, 46–49, *47, 49, 50*
  surgery on, 309, 475–476, 492
    review of, 316, 498
Brain stem, 45
Brainstorming, 233, *234*
  review of, 255
Brain waves:
  control of, 80–82
  graphing of, *61*
  in hypnosis, 70
  in meditation, 80
  in sleep, 60, 65, *61*
  in sleep deprivation, 62
  types of, 60, 65, *61*
Branching program, 178, *178*
Breland effect, 171
Brightness, relation to amplitude, 125, *126*
  review of, 146
Broca's region, 42
Bruno, 241
Bystander effect Label given to the phenomenon where individuals who witness emergency situations do not offer assistance or respond in any way. 514
  causes, 515–517
  defined, 514, *515*
  review of, 532

California Personality Inventory. *See* the CPI
Camera, as analogy for eye, 121, 122
Cannibal experiments, 210–211
Cannon-Bard theory of emotion, 303–304, *305*
  review of, 316
Carbon dioxide elimination, during meditation, 80, *80*
Cartesian position, 51
Case study A method of observation which involves the intensive examination of a single subject or unit. 9–11, *10, 14*
  review of, 25
Castration, effect on sexual motivation, 275
Cat:
  righting reflex in, 100
  vision in, 119
Catalepsy A state in which the body adopts a rigid, immobile position in which it may remain for a considerable period. It is occasionally a symptom of some mental disorders and is also possible in some of the deeper states of hypnosis. 458, *459*
  under hypnosis, 72, *73*
  review of, 90
Catalyst hypothesis of television violence A catalyst is a substance that facilitates or makes possible a chemical reaction. In a more general sense, catalysts are individuals, events, or experiences that facilitate, initiate, or make possible certain reactions. The catalyst hypothesis of television violence proposes that viewing violence may trigger latent aggressive urges in some individuals. 513, *513*
  review of, 532
Catatonic schizophrenia, 458, *459*
  review of, 470
Categorization, as stage of language development, 247, *245*
Categorizing A process described by Bruner which involves placing objects or events into groups (categories) on the basis of their common characteristics. To categorize is to form concepts. 226
  defined, 226
Catharsis hypothesis of television violence Theory about the impact of television violence that proposes that viewing it may have the beneficial effect of releasing pent-up emotions. 512, *513*
  review of, 532
Cathectic flexibility versus cathectic impoverishment, 371, *372*
  review of, 379
Central nervous system The human nervous system that includes the brain and the spinal cord. 38–39, *39*
  review of, 52
CER. *See* Conditioned emotional reaction
Cerebellum One of the major portions of the brain, attached to the rear of the brain stem. Its principal functions appear to be coordinating motor activity and maintaining balance. 45, *45*
Cerebral cortex, 43, *41*
  review of, 52
Cerebral lobes, 43, *44*
Cerebral palsy A syndrome (collection of symptoms) that results from brain injury. The motor areas of the brain are most often affected, which accounts for the motor problems and occasional paralysis that sometimes accompany cerebral palsy. The

condition is usually due to brain damage which occurs during birth. A minority of affected individuals are also mentally deficicient. 309

Cerebrotonic temperament, 389

Cerebrum The most highly developed part of the human brain relative to the brains of lower animals. It is a wrinkled mass of brain tissue, the outer covering of which is labeled the *cerebral cortex.* The cerebrum contains the major association areas of the brain, and its principal functions appear to relate to higher mental processes. Its major divisions include the cerebral lobes. 43, *44*
   review of, 52

C-fibers, 111, *111*

Chance, in inferential statistics, 562
   review of, 563

Change:
   as determiner of attention, 98, *99*
   relation to stress, 310–311, *313*
     review of, 317
   role in curiosity, 281, 282

Character disorders, 453

Chemical nature of memory, 210–211
   review of, 212

Chemical theory of sleep, 62, 64
   review of, 90

Chemotherapy, 475, 492, *491*
   review of, 498

Child development, 321–355
   attitudes toward children, 322–323
   average child, 323–324, *324*
   cognitive, social and emotional
      development, 345–353, *346, 347, 348,*
      350, 351, 352
   environmental forces, 332–337, *333, 334,*
      337
   genetic forces, 324–332, *325, 326, 327,*
      329, 330, 331
   nature-nurture interaction, 337–338
   Piaget's theory of, 339–344, *340, 341, 342,*
      344, 345

Child ego-state, 485–486, *486*
   review of, 498

Childe Harold, 444

Children and Communication: Verbal and Non-Verbal Language Development, 245

Children's Drawings as Measures of Intellectual Maturity, 431

Chimpanzee, language learning in, 238–244, *240, 242*
   evaluation of, 241–244
   review of, 256

Chitling Test, 438

Chloroform, as cause of hypnotic trance, 75

Chlorpromazine, 475

Choleric personality type, 386, *387*

Chorea A neurological disorder characterized by spasmic, jerky, involuntary movements of large groups of muscles. These movements are particularly evident in the face, tongue, hands, and arms, and are often of short duration. 38, *38*
   relation to dopamine, 38, *38*

Chromosomal aberrations Abnormalities, inconsistencies, deformities, or other abnormal characteristics of chromosomes. Those that involve the sex chromosomes are sometimes manifested in inappropriate or arrested development of secondary sexual

characteristics. 275, 329, 331–332, *331*

Chromosomes Microscopic bodies in the nucleus of all animal and plant cells containing the genes—the carriers of heredity. Each mature human sex cell (sperm or ovum) contains twenty-three chromosomes. 325–332, *326, 327, 329, 330, 331*
   aberrations. *See* Chromosomal aberrations
   defined, 325
   determiner of sex, 328
   illustrated, *326*

Chunking, 189–190, 206, *190, 192*

Cigarette smoking. *See* Nicotine; Smoking

Cindy, 241

Circadian rhythm *Circadian* means "around one day"; circadian rhythms are the twenty-four-hour cycles that appear to exercise some influence on the lives of lower animals as well as humans. Also termed *biological clocks,* they are most evident in sleep-waking cycles and in temperature cycles. 64
   review of, 90

Circulatory theory of sleep, 62, 64
   review of, 90

Circumscribed amnesia, 456

Clairvoyance, 143
   review of, 147

Clarity, as monocular cue, 133, *133*

Classical conditioning A process whereby the repeated pairing of two stimuli, one of which is associated with a specific response and one of which is not, eventually leads to the association of the response with the stimulus not ordinarily associated with that response. Classical conditioning is also sometimes referred to as stimulus substitution, since once learning has occurred it is possible to substitute one stimulus for another in order to evoke highly similar responses. 153–160, *154, 155, 157, 158*
   acquisition in, 154–156, *155*
   contiguity explanation for, 159–160
   contingency explanation for, 160
   defined, 153
   discrimination in, 156–157
   extinction in, 157–158, *158*
   of fetus, 346
   generalization in, 156–157, *157*
   as lie detector, 159
   review of, 170–171, 180
   why it works, 158–160

Classification, errors in, 342

Claustrophobia, *455*

Client-centered therapy A therapeutic approach that seeks to provide a supportive environment within which individuals may explore feelings and find methods of growth. 487, *491*
   review of, 498–499

Clinical psychologist and psychology, 4, 476, *5, 6, 477*

Clique, 360–361, *362*

Closure principle of perception, 137, 138, 174, 192, *137*

Clumsiness, as factor in interpersonal attraction, 548
   review of, 553

Cocaine A stimulant drug which, in its pure form, is a white powder that is typically sniffed. 87, *85*
   incidence of use, 84

Cochlea, 108, *107, 108*
   function of, 108, 109, *109*

Cocktail party problem, 96–97, *97*
   review of, 116

Co-consciousnesses, 59

Coconut Grove fire, 1942, 287

Codeine, 87, *85*

Coding system (in concept attainment) A hierarchical arrangement of related categories. Since categories are concepts, coding systems are arrangements of concepts in terms of their generality. In a coding system, the most inclusive concept is at the apex of the system, with progressively more specific concepts falling lower in the hierarchy. 227, *227*

Cognitive Pertaining to intellectual processes. Since to *cognize* is to *know,* cognitive theories are principally concerned with the processes whereby organisms obtain knowledge. approaches:
   to emotion, 304–306
     review of, 311
   to learning, 153
     review of, 179
   to mental disorders, 449, 450, *451*
     review of, 470
   to motivation, 280–281
     review of, 292
   to personality theories, 387, 404–405, *388, 405*
     review of, 411

"Cognitive algebra," *541*

Cognitive arousal theory, 289, *289*
   review of, 293

"Cognitive Consequences of Forced Compliance," *519*

Cognitive development and changes:
   during adolescence, 366–368, *367*
     review of, 379
   during aging, 373–375, *374*
     review of, 379
   Piaget's stages of, 340–344, *340, 341, 342, 344, 345*

Cognitive dissonance A state of conflict between beliefs and behavior or between expectations and behavior. 518–520, *519, 520*
   review of, 533

Cognitive labeling theory of emotion, 304–306
   review of, 316

Cognitive-learning perspective of mental disorder, 449

Cognitive map A mental representation of physical space. That we know how to get from home to school is evidence of the existence of a relevant cognitive map. 174–175, *175*
   review of, 181

Cognitive motives, 267, 281–286, *267, 282, 283, 285*
   achievement motivation, 283–286, *283, 285*
   curiosity, 281–283, *282*

Cognitive psychology, 185

Collective unconscious (also called racial unconscious) A Jungian term for the inherited aspects of our unconscious minds. Jung believed that the elements of the collective unconscious arose from primitive models (archetypes) reflected in concepts that appear to be nearly universal. These concepts appear among peoples who have

---

Italic page numbers refer to illustrations.

never been in contact, and have done so throughout history. They are particularly evident in religious worship and ritual that revolve around such central themes as birth, rebirth, death, God, hero, man, and woman. All of these are, in fact, Jungian archetypes. 401

    review of, 411

Color:

    blindness, 126–127

      review of, 146

    brightness, relation to amplitude, 125, *126*

    constancy, 129

      review of, 146

    purity, relation to complexity, 125–126, *126*

    review of, 146

    and wavelength, 124

Color-stereo effect, 140

Color vision:

    among animals, 120–121

    influence of language on, 139

    opponent process theory, 127

    review of, 146

    trichromatic theory, 127

Combinativity, 343

Comic books, 333–334

Commission on Obscenity and Pornography, 278

Commitment to victim, relation to bystander effect, 516

Common-sense approach to personality theories, 387–388, *388*

    review of, 410

"Communitie," 549

Community mental health programs A recent movement that emphasizes promoting mental health rather than offering specific therapies. 496–498, *496, 497*

    review of, 499

Comparability of subjects, in sampling, 18

Comparative psychology, *5, 6*

Competition A condition manifested when two or more individuals or groups strive for the same goal, and when success is perceived, at least to some degree, as being dependent on the other group or individual not attaining the goal. Competition implies some degree of personal rivalry and mutual opposition. 525

    versus cooperation, 525–527, *526, 527*

    review of, 533

Complexity One of three characteristics of sound waves, physically defined in terms of the mixture of waves that emanate from a vibration source. Complexity of sound waves corresponds to subjective impressions of timbre. 104

    defined, 104, *104*

      review of, 116

    as determiner of attention, 98

    relation to color purity, 125–126, *126*

      review of, 146

    role in curiosity, 281, 282, *282*

    as source of arousal, 289

Complex structures, as phase of language development, 247–248, *245*

Compliance Acceding to the wishes and desires of others. To comply is to behave according to instruction or expectation. 518

    review of, 532

Italic page numbers refer to illustrations.

Componential approach to meaning, 252

Compound eye, 119, *120*

Compulsion An urge to engage in a certain behavior which when resisted causes anxiety. 456

Compulsive personality disorder, 462

Computer:

    analogies, 219–224, *222, 223, 224*

      review of, 255

    intelligence of, 217–219, *219*

"Computer Interpretation of the MMPI," *424*

Concept A meaning, an idea, a categorization, or a property that relates two or more objects or events. 226

Concept attainment, use in problem solving, 226–229, *227, 228*

    review of, 255

    strategies for, 228, *228*

Conceptualization, errors of, effects on research, 19

    review of, 26

Concrete operations stage (Piaget), 343, 366, *340, 344, 345, 367*

    review of, 354

Concurrent validity, 417

    review of, 439

Conditioned emotional reaction, 157

    review of, 180

Conditioned reinforcer, 167

Conditioned response A response that is elicited by a conditioned stimulus. In some obvious ways, a conditioned response resembles its corresponding unconditioned response. The two are not identical, however. 154

    review of, 180

Conditioned stimulus A stimulus that does not elicit any response initially but, as a result of being paired with an unconditioned stimulus and its response, acquires the capability of eliciting that same response. For example, a stimulus that is always present at the time of a fear reaction may become a conditioned stimulus for fear. 154

    defined, 154

    distinctiveness of, importance to acquisition of CR, 154–155

    and extinction, 157–158, *158*

    review of, 180

    timing of, importance to acquisition, 155–156, *155*

Conditioning A process whereby a response becomes dependent upon specific circumstances (stimuli). Conditioning theory is therefore a learning theory—that is, a theory that seeks to explain processes involved in learning. It gives two specific explanations for learning: classical conditioning and operant conditioning. 153 *See also* Aversive conditioning; Classical conditioning

    review of, 180

Cones Light-sensitive cells on the retina; cones respond primarily to color and are extensively involved in daylight vision. 122, *123*

    in color vision, 127

    in low light, 128, *128*

    review of, 146

Confederates Allies or accomplices. In psychological research, confederates are frequently employed to help the investigator reach the objectives of the experiment. These objectives often require that the real subjects

---

be made to believe that the confederates are also subjects. An alternative term for confederate is *stooge*. 522

Conformity A change in attitudes or beliefs as a result of social pressure. Whereas compliance involves agreement in behavior, conformity involves agreement in principle. 518

    as ingratiation tactic, 543

    review of, 532

Conformity curve A phenomenon described by F. H. Allport whereby the majority of individuals within a culture conform to prevailing cultural norms with fewer and fewer individuals manifesting behaviors that deviate from the norm. 527, *528*

Conjunction, in language acquisition, 247

Connectors, 35, *36*

Conscience An internalized set of rules governing an individual's behavior. Conscience may or may not reflect the teaching of religious principles in childhood. 352

Consciousness, 57–59, *59*

    effects of drugs upon, 89–90

    review of, 90

    stream of, 58, *59*

Consensus of behavior, relation to attribution, 537

Conservation, problems of, 341–342, *344*

Conservative focusing, 228

Consistency of behavior:

    expectation of, role in interpersonal attraction, 542, *543*

      review of, 553

    relation to attribution, 537

Consolidation theory of memory In this context, a theory that suggests that the physiological activities that accompany learning and that therefore underlie memory continue for a period of time following the actual activities associated with learning. 194

    review of, 212

Constancies Properties of visual perception that enable us to perceive color, size, and shape of objects as being constant under a great variety of conditions even though the light waves reflected from these objects would be different under different conditions. Although these constancies govern much of our visual perception, there are numerous circumstances under which perception of size, shape, and color are inaccurate. 129–131, *130, 131*

    color, 129

    defined, 129

    review of, 146

    shape, 131, *131*

    size, 129–131, *130, 131*

Construct validity, 417

    review of, 439

Consumer Reports, 70

Content validity, 417

    review of, 439

Contextualists, 408

Contiguity Closeness in time. Two events are said to be contiguous (or in contiguity) when they are simultaneous or nearly simultaneous. Contiguity provides one important explanation for the effects of classical conditioning procedures. Contiguity explanation for classical conditioning, 159–160, 170

Contiguity (continued)
    objection to, 159–160
    review of, 180
Contingency A dependency relationship. An event is said to be contingent upon another when its occurrence is dependent upon the occurrence of the other. The Rescorla-Wagner conditioning model maintains that learning involves the discovery of contingencies. 160
Contingency contracting, 481
Contingency explanation for classical
    conditioning, 160
    review of, 180
Continuity principle of perception, 137, 138,
    174, *137*
    review of, 147
Continuous amnesia, 457
Continuous culture A culture that does not clearly demarcate passage from one period of life to another. 358
    review of, 378
Continuous reinforcement, 164–165, *165*
    effectiveness of, 165–166, *166*
    review of, 180
Contrapreparedness, 172
    review of, 181
Control, as goal of psychology, 22, 23
Control group A group of subjects as comparable to the experimental group as possible—ideally, identical to the experimental group in all respects save that they are not exposed to the treatment (independent variable) under investigation. Subsequent differences between experimental and control groups can then be assumed to be due to the only apparent differences between them—the independent variable. 15, 17, 18, *15*
    review of, 25–26
Conventional role conformity level of
    morality, *352*
    review of, 354
Convergence, 132–133
    review of, 146
Convergent thinking To *converge* is to come together. Hence, convergent thinking is a type of thinking that leads to a single solution or thought. Problems that have a single correct solution generally require convergent thinking. 225
    review of, 255
Conversion symptoms, 469
Cooperation A condition manifested when two or more individuals or groups strive together to achieve a common goal. Cooperation implies lack of rivalry or mutual opposition. It implies as well that obtaining the goal is at least to some degree dependent on the activities of all members of the groups or individuals involved. 525–527, *526, 527*
    review of, 533
Cornea The transparent coating that covers the eyeball in humans. The visible white of the eye seen through the cornea is the sclera. 121, *122*
Corpus callosum The major neural link between the two cerebral hemispheres. In "split-brain" research on animals, the corpus callosum is frequently cut surgically. The human corpus callosum is sometimes

severed to eliminate or alleviate epileptic seizures. 43, 46
Correlation A mathematical expression of relationship between two variables. Correlations may vary from highly positive relationships, where high or low values of one variable are always associated with corresponding high or low values in the second variable; highly negative, where high values in one variable are always associated with low values of the other and vice versa; or at or near zero, where values of one variable cannot be used to make systematic predictions about the second variable. 19, 415–416, *20*
    review of, 26
Correlational fallacy, 19
Cortex, 123
    role in sexual motivation, 276
Counseling psychologist and psychology, 4, 476, *5, 6, 477*
Counterconditioning. *See* Systematic desensitization
the CPI, 423
    cautions in use, 425, 437–439
    described, 423
    use of, 423, 425, 437–439, *425*
CR. *See* Conditioned response
Creative An adjective that may be used to describe people, products, or a process. The term *creativity* generally refers to the capacity of individuals to produce novel or original answers or products. 231
Creativity, 230–234
    changes during aging, 373–375, *374*
    review of, 379
    defined, 230–231
    measuring, 231–232, *232*
    promoting, 232–234, *234*
    review of, 255
Criterion A standard, value, or goal by which something is judged; a necessary condition. 17
Critical period The period during which exposure to appropriate experiences or stimuli will bring about specific learning much more easily than is the case at other times. 265
    review of, 292
Criticism, as factor in interpersonal attraction, 547–548, *548*
    review of, 553
"Cross Cultural Studies of Facial Expression," 299
Cross-sectional study Method of investigation that involves observing and comparing different subjects, usually at different age levels, at one time. 9, 12, 373, *13, 14*
    review of, 25
Crowds, 360–361, *362*
Crystallized intellectual abilities, 373–374
CS. *See* Conditioned stimulus
Cue-dependent forgetting Explanation of forgetting that suggests that much that we cannot remember is not necessarily gone from memory but simply cannot be retrieved because of organization or the individual's inability to make use of cues. 204
    review of, 212
Cue function of stimulus, 288–289
Curiosity A tendency to act that does not have specific, identifiable goals other than whatever might be gained from investigating,

obtaining information, experiencing, or doing. Defined another way, *curiosity* describes behaviors whose primary motive appears to reside in the activities themselves rather than in identifiable objectives. 281
    as cognitive motive, 281–283, *282*
    review of, 292
Customs, 529
Cybernetics Theoretical approach that sees thinking as self-regulating, based on feedback. 220
Cybernetic theories of thinking, 221, *222, 223*
Cyclical nature of sexual behavior, 275, 276–277

Darwin and Facial Expression: A Century of Research in Review, 299
Daydreaming, 350
Death, 376–377, 378, *377*
    review of, 379
Death wish, 392
Decibel A measure of perceived loudness of sounds. Zero decibels is the threshold for human hearing. 106
    defined, 106
    values of ordinary sounds, *106*
Decoding, 250
Deep structure The meaning of a language expression. Meaningfulness is derived from the surface structure of a sentence or of a verbal expression, but often requires as well that the interpreter take context and other cues into consideration. 250–251
Defense mechanisms Relatively irrational, unconscious, and sometimes unhealthy methods people use to compensate for their inability to satisfy their basic drives and to overcome the anxiety accompanying this inability. 395–397, 449–450, 477, *396*
    review of, 410
Deferred evaluation Deliberately refraining from evaluating an idea. This is considered an important aid to creativity. 233
    review of, 255
Deficiency needs, 290–291
    review of, 293
Delayed conditioning, 155, *155*
    review of, 180
Delinquency, 362–363, *364*
    review of, 378
Delta waves, 60, 65, *61*
Demonology, 444–445
Dendrite Hairlike extension emanating from the cell body of the neuron. Dendrites ordinarily receive impulses from adjoining axons. 35, 36, *37*
Denial stage of dying, 377
    review of, 379
Dependent personality disorder, 462
Dependent variable The phenomenon (variable) being observed in an experimental situation where the object is to determine which of one or more specific factors (independent variables) is causally related to the phenomenon. 12, 13, 15, 17, *15*
    review of, 25
Deprivation
    and aggression, 509, *510*
    of dreams, 69
    of sleep, studies of, 61–62, 67, *62*
    review of, 90
Depth, perception of, 131–133, *133*
    binocular cues, 132–133

Italic page numbers refer to illustrations.

Depth, perception of (continued)
   monocular cues, 133, *133*
   review of, 146
Descriptive statistics, 555–560, *556, 557, 558, 559*
   arithmetical descriptions, 556–557, *557*
   graphs, 555–556, *556*
   review of, 562
   standard deviation, 559–560, *557*
   variation, 558–559, *558, 559*
Desensitization, systematic, 480, *480, 491*
   review of, 498
Determinism versus free will assumption, 21, 23
   review of, 26
Deterministic models Models that assume that, given complete, accurate, and adequate information concerning all variables involved in an operation, it is possible to predict the outcome of the operation precisely. 220
Developmental psychology, 4, *5, 6*
"The Development of Cooperative Behavior in Monkeys and Young Children," *527*
Deviation IQ, 427–428
Dexedrine, 88, *85*
Diagnosis Classification on the basis of symptoms. Essentially, diagnosis involves identifying a condition (for example, a disease or abnormality) on the basis of its observable manifestations and origin. 422
Diagnostic and Statistical Manual, 3rd ed. *See* DSM III
Differential reinforcement of successive approximations, method of, 164
Discrimination, in classical conditioning. A process of detecting differences; essentially opposite to that involved in generalization. Whereas to generalize is to respond to similarities in different situations, discrimination involves responding to differences. In discrimination, an organism reacts differently to similar but not identical situations (that is, it discriminates between situations where the response is appropriate and similar situations where the response is not appropriate). 157
   review of, 180
Discriminative stimulus, 163, *164*
Disease models. *See* Medical models of mental disorder
Disharmony, role in curiosity, 282, *282*
Disorganized schizophrenia, 458
   review of, 470
Displacement A Freudian defense mechanism referring to the appearance of previously suppressed behavior in a somewhat more acceptable form. 396
   as defense mechanism, 395, 396, *396*
      review of, 410
   in language, 236
   review of, 256
Dispositional attribution Attributing the cause of someone's action to that person's disposition; thus assuming the action was internally motivated, and thus intentional. 536
   defined, 536, *538*
   factors determining, 537–538, *539*
   review of, 553
Dispositions, defined, 21
Dissociated self, under hypnosis, 77
Dissociative disorders A classification of

_____

Italic page numbers refer to illustrations.

disorders that apparently involve the splitting of various aspects of personality and functioning. Includes amnesia and multiple personality. 453, 456–458, *452, 457*
   amnesia, 456–457
   fugue, 457
   multiple personality, 457–458, *457*
   review of, 470
Distance, perception of, 131–133, *133*
   binocular cues, 132–133
   monocular cues, 133, *133*
   review of, 146
Distinctiveness of behavior, relation to attribution, 537
Distortion theory of forgetting, 203, 204, *202*
   review of, 212
"Distribution of Coitus in the Menstrual Cycle," 277
Disulfiram, 475
Divergent thinking To diverge is to go in different directions, to come apart. Hence, divergent thinking involves the production of a variety of thoughts or solutions. 225
   review of, 255
Divine Creation assumption The belief that present life forms were created by a Supreme Being. 32
Divorce:
   rate of, 551–552, *552*
   reasons for, 552
   review of, 553
D-lysergic acid diethylamide tartrate. *See* LSD-25
DNA:
   as fundamental unit in evolution, 530
   role in molecular genetics, 325
   review of, 353
Dogs:
   in classical conditioning, 153–154, 157, *154*
   hearing in, 105–106
   and learned helplessness, 169
   olfaction in, 113
Dolphins:
   communication system of, 237
   echolocation, 105, 106
Dominance (of brain hemisphere) With respect to the brain, describes (but does not explain) the fact that certain portions may take precedence over others in controlling certain motor or sensory activities. 48
Dominant gene The gene that takes precedence over other related genes in genetically determined traits. Because genes occur in pairs (alleles) on corresponding chromosomes (one from the male and one from the female), the presence of a dominant gene as one member of the pair means that the hereditary characteristics it controls will be present in the individual. 328, *329*
   review of, 353
The Doomsday Flight, 513
Dopamine, 36, 37, *38*
   relation to chorea, 38, *38*
   relation to depression, 38
   relation to mania, 38
   relation to Parkinsonism, 38, *38*
   review of, 52
Dopaminergic neurons, 37
Dorsal horn cells, 111
Double-blind procedure An experimental procedure where neither the subject nor the examiners know who is in the control group and who is in the experimental group. 16, 17
   review of, 26

Dove Counterbalance General Intelligence Test, 438
"Downers," 88, *85*
Down's syndrome, 331, *331*
Dragonfly, vision in, 119, *120*
Draw-a-Man Test, 429, *431*
   review of, 440
Draw-a-Woman Test, 429
Dream A noun with connotations of unreality. Dreams may take one of two forms: daydreams (which typically involve sequences of fantasy); and night dreams (relatively coherent sequences of imagery, primarily visual). Although the reasons for and functions of dreaming remain unclear, we know that it is almost universal. 67–70, *67, 68*
   content of, 67, *67*
   defined, 67
   deprivation of, 69
   purpose of, 68–69
   remembering, 67
   review of, 90
   theories of, 68–69
   usefulness of, 69–70
Drive, 267
   review of, 292
Drive reduction model A motivational theory based on the notion that a need gives rise to tensions which are reduced when the need is satisfied. 279
   objections to, 279
   review of, 292
Drug abuse Refers primarily to the "recreational" use of drugs as opposed to the use of drugs for medical or psychiatric purposes. Drug abuse is classified as a disorder by the American Psychiatric Association because behaviors apparently resulting from drug use impair social or occupational functioning. Defined in this way, drug abuse stops short of drug dependence. 83
   therapy for, 481
Drug addiction, as explained by opponent process model, 308
Drug dependence Also a disorder as defined by the American Psychiatric Association. It results from repeated use of a drug in sufficient dosages that a strong desire to continue taking the drug develops. *Physiological dependence,* frequently referred to as *addiction,* is a type of dependence in which the desire to continue taking a drug is partly or entirely organically based, that is, the body eventually becomes dependent upon the drug. Physiological dependence is characteristic of the "hard drugs," for example, heroin, morphine, and codeine. After the individual has become physiologically dependent, cessation of drug use typically results in "withdrawal" symptoms. *Psychological dependence,* sometimes referred to as *habituation,* is a strong, sometimes overwhelming, desire to continue using a drug, usually attributed to its psychological rather than its physiological effects. Drugs that relieve anxiety or that lead to euphoric (intensely happy) states may lead to psychological dependence even in the absence of physiological dependence. 83
Drugs Chemical or organic substances that have one or more of a wide range of effects on the human body and nervous system.

Italic page numbers refer to illustrations.

involved in sexual maturation and sexual arousal of females. It is also found in males, although in lesser quantities. 275
  review of, 292
Ethologist One who studies behavior of animals in their natural habitats. Ethology looks at the influence of biology on behavior. 505
Evolution A scientific theory that holds that present life forms have developed from preexisting species through a series of modifications governed by laws of natural selection and diversification of species. 32, 338
  of early *Homo sapiens,* 33–34
  of nervous system and brain, 32–35, *33, 35*
  review of, 51
  in sociobiology theory, 529–530
Exhibitionism, 464
Expectancy A belief about likely sources of reinforcement. Cognitive theorists regard this as an important determinant of some aspects of personality. 405
Expectations, as determiner of attention, 99
Experience, influence on visual perception, 138–140
  review of, 147
Experiment A definite, deliberately controlled arrangement of circumstances under which a phenomenon is observed. 12–15, *14, 15*
  animals, use in, 14
  correlation, 19, *20*
  errors in interpreting, 15–20, *17, 20*
  experimental groups, 15, *15*
  experimenter bias, 16, *17*
  ex post facto studies, 13–14, *14*
  review of, 25
  sampling bias, 17–18
  subject bias, 16–17
Experimental group The group of subjects which, in an experiment, is exposed to a treatment (independent variable) that is assumed to have an effect on the phenomenon under observation. 15, 17, 18, *15*
  review of, 25–26
Experimental psychology, *5, 6*
Experimenter bias The observation that experimenters' expectations may influence their observations. Experimenter bias is an unconscious process and is not to be equated with experimenter dishonesty. It is sometimes referred to as the *Rosenthal effect.* 16, *17*
  review of, 26
Explaining, as goal of psychology, 22, 23
Ex post facto study A study in which the experimenter does not assign subjects to experimental conditions or exercise control over these conditions; the experimenter simply selects subjects for study on the basis of differences that already exist among them. 13–14, *14*
  cautions in use, 13–14
  review of, 25
Expression of emotion, 297–300, *299*
  culture-specific versus innate, 298–300, *299*
  review of, 315
External orientation or externality A

personality characteristic identifiable in terms of the extent to which individuals will attribute the causes of their successes and failures to external factors (for example, luck or task difficulty). 285, 404–405, *405*
External stimulation:
  role in sexual motivation, 276–277, *277*
  as source of arousal, 288–289
Extinction A conditioning procedure whereby a learned response is eliminated. Extinction may involve the repeated presentation of a conditioned stimulus without the accompanying unconditioned stimulus, or may involve the withdrawal of reinforcement. Extinction is said to have occurred when a previously conditioned stimulus no longer elicits a conditioned response, or when a previously reinforced behavior is no longer reinforced and ceases to occur. 157–158, *158*
  rate of, effects of reinforcement schedules on, 165–166, *166*
  review of, 180
Extrasensory perception Perception of phenomena without use of the ordinary senses. Instances of ESP are sometimes described as *paranormal* (beyond the normal). The scientific study of ESP is called *parapsychology.* 143–145, *143, 145*
  against, 145
  for, 144
  review of, 147
Extrinsic reinforcement, 167–168, *167*
Extroversion, extroverted An adjective which describes behaviors (or individuals) that are predominantly oriented toward the outside rather than the inside. Principal characteristics include concern with and involvement in social activity and a relative disinterest in subjective states. 386
  Eysenck, 391
    review of, 410
  Jung, 386, 402
    review of, 410, 411
Eye. *See also* Visual system
  anatomy of, 121–122, *122, 123*
  of cat, 119
  changes in, during aging, 372
  interaction with brain, 123, *124*
  review of, 146
Eye-head system of perceiving movement, 134
Eye-rolling ability, relation to suggestibility to hypnosis, 74–75, *74*
Eyewitness testimony, unreliability of, 194

Fad, defined, 529
Fading theory of forgetting, 201, 204, *201, 202*
  review of, 212
Fairy tales, and violence, 334
Fallopian tubes Tubes that link the ovaries and the uterus; where fertilization (conception) ordinarily occurs. 325
Family, influence on development, 333, *333*
  and IQ, 430
  review of, 353
Fascination, hypnosis by, 75
Fashions, defined, 529
Fathers, relation to delinquency, 363
  review of, 378
Favors, giving, as ingratiation tactic, 543
Fear-induced aggression, 509, *510*
  review of, 532

Fear of failure A motive or personality characteristic that acts in opposition to forces that direct the individual toward achievement. 284
  review of, 293
Feedback Information that an organism or a machine receives about its functioning. 220
Feedback analogies of thought, 220–222, *222, 223, 224*
  review of, 255
Felt powerfulness, 467–468
Feminine traits, 336
Feminism, 336
Fetishes, 463
Figure-ground principle of perception, 137–138, *137*
Filing cabinet, memory as, 185–186
  compared to other models of memory, 199–200
  review of, 211
First impressions, role in interpersonal attraction, 539–540, *540*
  review of, 553
Fixation, 395, 450
  review of, 410
Fixed interval reinforcement, 165, *165*
  effectiveness of, 165–166, *166*
  review of, 180
Fixed-object technique, for hypnosis, 75
Fixed ratio reinforcement, 165, *165*
  effectiveness of, 165–166, *166*
  review of, 180
Flattery, as ingratiation tactic, 543
Flower pot technique, 62
Fluid intellectual abilities, 373–374
Focused activity, 346
Focus gambling, 228
Forgetting, 201–204, *202, 203*
  distortion theory, 203, *202*
  fading theory, 201, *201, 202*
  interference theory, 203–204
  repression theory, 203, *202*
  review of, 212
  versus retrieval failure, 204
Formal operations stage (Piaget), 343–344, 366–368, *367*
  criticism of, 367–368
  review of, 354
Forward-order conditioning, 155, *155*
  review of, 180
Fovea, 122, *122*
Fractional relaxation method for hypnosis, 75
Free association A psychoanalytic technique wherein the patient is asked to say whatever comes to mind without evaluating or discarding material. 478
  review of, 498
Free-floating anxiety, 456
Free recall, as way to measure memory, 200, *201*
Free will versus determinism assumption, 21, 23
  review of, 26
Frequency One of three characteristics of waves that give rise to perceptions of sound. Frequency is defined as the number of waves per second, measured in Hertz units. Frequency of sound waves is related to perception of pitch. 103, *104*
  review of, 116
Frequency polygon, 556, *556*
Frequency theory of hearing The frequency theory of hearing suggests that neural impulses correspond in frequency to

Italic page numbers refer to illustrations.

Hashashi, 83

Hashish, origin of term, 83

Hawthorne effect The observation that experimental subjects who are aware that they are members of experimental groups often perform better than subjects who are not aware they are. 17
  review of, 26

Hearing loss, during aging, 372

Hedonic relevance, relation to attribution, 537

Hedonism, as theory of motivation, 266–267
  review of, 292

Hemisphere (brain) Literally, half of a sphere. The cerebral hemispheres are the two halves of the cerebrum. The major neurological and physical link between them is a thick tract of nerve tissue, the corpus callosum. *See also* Split brain
  defined, 46
  functions of, 46–49, *47, 49, 50*
    review of, 52
  and vision, 123, *124*

Heredity-environment debate, 50–51, 432–437, *433, 434, 435, 437*
  in animal intelligence, 432–433, *433*
  as assumption, 21
    review of, 26
  interaction of, 332, 337–338
    review of, 354
  Jensen hypothesis, 434–436
    review of, 440
  rubber band hypothesis, 436, *437*
  in twins, 433–434, *434, 435*

Hering's opponent process theory of color vision, 127
  review of, 146

Heritability coefficient An index that generally indicates the extent to which variation in characteristics is related to genetic factors. A heritability coefficient of 70 does not indicate that 70 percent of a characteristic (for example, intelligence) is determined by heredity; it indicates that 70 percent of the *variation* in intelligence scores appears to be accounted for by genetic factors. In other words, a heritability coefficient is an index of variation rather than of absolute amount. 435

Hermaphrodite, defined, 276

Heroin, 87, *85*
  incidence of use, 84
  treatment for addiction, 475

Herpes, 365

Heterogeneity, role in curiosity, 282, *282*

Heuristics A problem-solving procedure where strategies are employed to maximize the probability of being correct as well as to minimize the time and effort involved in the solution. 220

"Hidden observer," under hypnosis, 76–77, 77
  review of, 91

Hierarchy of needs (Maslow), 290–292, *291*
  review of, 293

Hierarchy of personality (Eysenck), 392, *393*
  review of, 410

Higher-order conditioning, 161

HIP. *See* Hypnotic Induction Profile

Histogram, 556, *556*

Histrionic personality disorder, 462

———————————

Italic page numbers refer to illustrations.

Holophrase A single word or sound which, early in the development of language, may take on a great variety of meanings. If a child uses the word *cat* to mean cats, horses, light bulbs, mothers, and other things, then *cat* is a holophrase for that child. 246, *245, 246*

Homeostasis Tendency to maintain balance, evident at both a physiological and a psychological level. Homeostasis is the basis of the opponent process theory of emotion. 307
  defined, 307
  review of, 316
  role in regulation of emotion, 307–308

Homologous pairs of chromosomes, 326

Homo sapiens:
  classification of, *33*
  evolution of, 32–35, *33, 35*

Honesty, importance of to surveys, 18–19
  review of, 26

Hopkins Beast, 223

Hormone One of a variety of chemical substances produced by endocrine glands and secreted into the bloodstream. Hormones have important effects on growth, maturation, behavior, and emotions. 44
  defined, 44
  role in emotion, 302
  role in sexual motivation, 275–276, *276*
  review of, 292

Humanism A philosophical and psychological orientation that is primarily concerned with *humanity*—the worth of humans as individuals and those processes that augment their human qualities. The humanistic movement in psychology is also referred to as *third-force psychology,* the other two forces being behaviorism and psychoanalytic theory. The principal concerns of humanistic psychology are the self and emotions. 153
  defined, 153
  review of, 179

Humanistic approaches to personality theories, 387, 405–407, *388, 407*
  Maslow's self-actualization, 406–407, *407*
  review of, 411

Humors (body fluids), 386, *387*

Hunger, 268–273, *268, 269, 270, 272, 273*
  junk food, 272, *272*
  metabolic factors, 270–271
  obesity, 273, *273*
  review of, 292
  role of brain, 271
  and stomach contractions, 268, 271, *268*
  taste-smell factors, 269–270, *270*

Huntington's chorea, 330

Hunzukuts, life spans of, 376

Hutterites, 506

Hybrid, defined, 324

Hydrophobia, *455*

Hyperphagia Derived from Latin terms meaning excessive (*hyper*) and eating (*phagia*). 271

Hypersomnia, 66

Hypnagogic state An adjective that relates to drowsiness, or more specifically to the state that precedes sleep. It has not been extensively investigated, but it is generally recognized that hallucinations are not uncommon during this state. 64

Hypnopaedia, 70

Hypnosis A state characterized by heightened suggestibility (willingness of the subject to perform whatever acts are required by the hypnotist; readiness to believe whatever is suggested). *Hypnotism* is the process by which this state may be induced. 70–77, *71, 73, 74, 77*
  antisocial behavior under, 70–72
  behavior under, 72–74
  characteristics of, 70–72
  and learning, 77
  memory under, 201
  review of, 90
  stages of, *73*
  as state of consciousness, 75–77, *77*
  suggestibility, 72, 74–75, *74*
  techniques for inducing, 75

Hypnotic Induction Profile, 74

Hypothalamus A small structure at the base of the brain centrally involved in a variety of bodily functions, as well as in the functioning of most of the body's endocrine glands. 44
  anatomy, 44, *45*
    review of, 52
  pain center in, 302
  pleasure center in, 302, *302*
  role in emotion, 300, 301, 303
    review of, 316
  role in hunger sensation, 271
    review of, 292
  role in sexual motivation, 276
  role in thirst drive, 274, *274*
    review of, 292

Hypothesis A prediction based on theory; an educated guess derived from the explanations and assumptions that make up theories. 9
  defined, 9
  testing, through statistics, 561–562, *562*
  use in problem solving, 225–226, *226*

Hysterical disorders A classification of mental disorders, not usually employed by contemporary psychiatrists, whose primary symptoms include loss of perceptual functioning in one sensory mode. There is no apparent physiological or neurological basis for the disorder. Thus there is hysterical blindness (individuals cannot *see* although the eyes and all related neurological systems are intact); hysterical mutism (individuals cannot speak); hysterical anesthesia (they cannot sense pain); hysterical deafness (they cannot hear); and hysterical paralysis (they cannot use one or more limbs). Waves of hysteria swept through Europe in the eighteenth century, but the disorder has virtually disappeared. 391, 469
  review of, 471

Iconic memory, 186. *See also* Sensory memory

Id In Freudian theory, all the instinctual urges that humans are heir to; the level of personality that contains human motives; in short, eros and thanatos. 393–394, 449, 477, *394, 395*
  review of, 410

Idealism, 51

Identification The process of assuming the goals, ambitions, mannerisms, and other personality characteristics of another person—of *identifying* with that person. 394

Identity:
  as concrete operation, 343
  development of in adolescence, 361–362
  review of, 378

Italic page numbers refer to illustrations.

Interpersonal relationships (continued)
attribution in person perception, 536–538, *538, 539*
interpersonal attraction, 539–544, *540, 541, 542, 543*
likable people, characteristics of, 544–549, *544, 545, 546, 548*
love, 312–315, 549–553, *314, 315, 550, 552, 553*
Interposition, as monocular cue, 133, *133*
review of, 146
Interpretation, errors in, effects on research, 19
Interval reinforcement, 164–165, *165*
effectiveness of, 165–166, *166*
review of, 180
Intimacy and solidarity versus isolation, 370, *369, 372*
review of, 379
Intrinsic reinforcement, 167

Introversion, introverted An adjective descriptive of behaviors (or persons) that turn inward. The most obvious introverted behaviors involve a disinterest in social contact or a preoccupation with internal states. 386
Eysenck, 391
review of, 410
Jung, 386, 401–402
review of, 410, 411
Intuitive thought (Piaget), 341–342, *340, 342*

Inventories and scales An inventory is a list. Personality inventories are, accordingly, lists that may be employed to assess personality. Such lists typically take the form of sentences that describe personality, or simply of questions that are typically answered yes or no. Although inventories are usually not characterized by specific rules governing the assignment of numbers to different responses, they often provide *norms,* based on the typical responses of large numbers of individuals, to facilitate interpretation of results. 421–423, *424*
cautions in use, 425, 437–439
the CPI, 423
the MMPI, 421–423, *424*
review of, 440
use of, 423, 425, 437–439, *425*
"An Investigation of the Development of the Sentence and the Extent of Vocabulary in Young Children," *245*
Involutional melancholia, 460
Involvement in Developmental Psychology Today, 364

IQ A simple way of describing intelligence by assigning it a number: the ratio of mental to chronological age, multiplied by 100. Average IQ is thus 100, and is based on a comparison between an individual and comparable others. 427
defined, 427
heredity versus environment as cause of, 432–437, *433, 434, 435, 437*
myths about, 429–432
normal distribution of, 428, *429*
review of, 440
slump in, 430
tests to measure, 428–429, *431*

Iris A muscle in the eye that creates the pupil. The iris is the colored portion of the eye. 121, *122*
Irregularity, role in curiosity, 282, *282*
Irritable aggression, 509–510, *510*
review of, 532

Jackson Personality Research Form, 423
James-Lange theory of emotion, 303, *305*
review of, 316
Jensen hypothesis, 434–436
review of, 440
Jet lag, 64, *65*
Johns Hopkins Beast, 223
JPRF. *See* Jackson Personality Research Form
Junk food, 272, *272*
Juvenile delinquency. *See* Delinquency

Kidney, role in thirst drive, 274
Kinesthesis A part of the haptic perceptual system, relating specifically to knowledge of the movements of the body or of its limbs. Sometimes considered to include three separate sensory systems: the muscle sense, the tendon sense, and the joint sense. 112
defined, 110
review of, 116
Klinefelter's syndrome, 331–332
Koan, 81
Koko, 241, 243, 244, *241*
Kuder Occupational Interest Survey, 423
Kwakiutl Indians, 506, 525–526, *526*

Labeling theory of love, 550–551
review of, 553
LAD. *See* Language acquisition device
Lalling, 245
Lana, 241, 242, *242*
Language Verbal forms of communication. Language is not necessary for communication, but it is nevertheless a form of communication. Animals communicate but, as far as we know, do not employ language. 235–254
acquisition of, 244–248, *245, 246, 247, 249*
review of, 256
defined, 235
development of, correspondence with motor development, 248, *249*
elements and characteristics of, 235–237, *237*
importance of in evolution, 32, 34
influence on color vision, 139
of nonhumans, 237–244, *238, 240, 241, 242*
psycholinguistics, 250–252, *251*
relation to thought, 252–254, *254*
review of, 256
and speech, left hemisphere control of, 48, 49, *49, 50*
review of, 52
Language acquisition device (LAD) A label employed by Chomsky to describe the neurological *something* that corresponds to grammar and that is assumed to be innate. 248
Language codes, 253
Language Learning by a Chimpanzee: The Lana Project, 242
Late maturation, 359
review of, 378
Latency stage (Freud), 394, *395*
review of, 410

Latent meaning of dreams (Freud), 69
review of, 90
Lateral part of hypothalamus. *See* LH
Lateral thinking, 233–234, *234*
review of, 255
Laws Statements whose accuracy is beyond reasonable doubt. Laws should not be confused with truths, since laws can be refuted by sufficient contrary evidence. Physics has many laws (for example, $e = mc^2$); psychology, however, has very few. 3, 20
"The Lay of the Last Minstrel," 549
L-Dopa, 38
Learned helplessness A phenomenon, described by Seligman, characterized by feelings of powerlessness that appear to result from negative experiences over which we have no control, and that might account for depression and perhaps even for death. 169
as cause of mental disorders, 467–468
review of, 471
Learning An actual or latent change in behavior due to experience.
approaches to, 152–153
behaviorism, 171–178, *174, 175, 177*
changes in ability during aging, 373–375, *374*
classical conditioning, 153–160, *154, 155, 157, 158*
defined, 152, 262
under hypnosis, 77
review of, 91
improving, 204–210, *205, 208, 209*
review of, 212
as latent, 152
review of, 179
in newborn, 346
review of, 354
operant conditioning, 160–170
role in sexual behavior, 277
role in visual perception, 142–143
review of, 147
Learning expectancies, 176
Ledain Commission, 84, 85
Lens In the human eye, a transparent structure capable of changing its shape, thereby focusing light waves emanating from closer or farther objects directly on the retina. 121–122, *122*
changes in during aging, 372
Lesions Structural changes in tissue. Lesions may be caused by injury or disease, or surgically—as is often the case in research. 271
Let's Have Healthy Children, 332
Level of arousal, maintaining optimum, 286–288, *287*
review of, 293
Levels of processing model of memory, 196–199
compared to other models, 199–200
criticism of, 199
review of, 212
LH, role in aphasia, 271
Libido A Freudian term denoting sexual urges. 392
review of, 410
Librium, 475
Life after life, 378
Life After Life, 378
Life-change events, 311, *313*
review of, 317

Italic page numbers refer to illustrations.

Life expectancy The expected duration of human life. 375–376, *375*
    review of, 379

Life span The total length of an individual life, as opposed to statistical predictions of its average length. 375–376, *375*
    review of, 379

Life-style As an Adlerian term, *life-style* refers not only to individuals' characteristic ways of reacting to life, but more specifically to the methods by which people overcome feelings of inferiority. Adler employed the terms *life-style, personality,* and *character* almost synonymously. 400

Light waves, characteristics of, 124–126, *126*
    amplitude of, 125
    color, 124
    complexity, 125–126
    review of, 146

"Likableness Ratings of 555 Personality-Trait Words," *544*

Likable people, characteristics of, 544–549, *544, 545, 546, 548*
    attractiveness, 544–545, *545*
    criticism, stupidity, clumsiness, and belligerence, 547–549, *548*
    propinquity, 547
    similarity, 545–547, *545, 546*

Liking versus loving, 550, *550*
    review of, 553

Limbic system A grouping of brain structures involved in motivation and emotion. The limbic system includes the hypothalamus, part of the thalamus, the amygdala, and other structures. 276
    role in emotion, 300, 302
        review of, 316
    role in sexual motivation, 276

Linear perspective, as monocular cue, 133, *133*

Linear program, 178, *178*

Link system of mnemonics, 207, *208*
    review of, 212

Lithium carbonate, 475

Liver, role in hunger sensation, 271

Localized amnesia, 456

Location familiarity, relation to bystander effect, 516

Loci system of mnemonics, 207–208, *208*
    review of, 212

Locus of control (Rotter), 404–405
    review of, 411

Logic, importance of in intellectual development, 343

Longitudinal study Psychological investigation where the same subjects are examined over time. 9, 11–12, 373, 374, *13, 14*
    review of, 25

Long-term memory A type of memory whereby with continued rehearsal and recoding of sensory input, material may become available for recall for an indefinite period of time. 191–196, *193, 195, 197, 198*
    characteristics, 191–192, *193*
    compared to short-term memory, 196, *198*
    consolidation theory, 194–195
    review of, 211, 212
    two kinds of, 195, *195*
    verbal versus pictorial storage, 192–193

Loudness, 104, 106–107, *104, 106*
    review of, 116

Love, 312–315, 549–553, *314, 315, 550, 552, 553. See also* Interpersonal attraction
    labeling theory of, 550–551
    marriage and divorce, 551–553, *552, 553*
    in poetry, 549
    review of, 553
    and sex, 551
    versus liking, 550, *550*

"Love in Infant Monkeys," *315*

Love in Several Masques, 549

LSD-25 (D-lysergic acid diethylamide tartrate) A particularly powerful hallucinogenic drug that is a relatively inexpensive, easily made, synthetic chemical. 86–87, *85*
    review of, 91
    symptoms of use and abuse, *89*

LTM. *See* Long-term memory

McCall's, 378

Madness. *See* Mental disorders

Macrosmatic noses, 115

Magazine training, 163

Maier string (pendulum) problem, 229–230, *229, 230*

Major Barbara, 315

Major depression An affective disorder characterized by extreme depression, sometimes leading to suicide. 460
    review of, 470

Major gene determination Determination of a characteristic as a result of the presence or absence of dominant and recessive genes in a single pair. 328
    review of, 353

Malaria, relation to sickle-cell anemia, 330

Mandala, 81, 401, *401*

Mands, 248

Manic-depressive disorders, 470. *See also* Major depression
    treatment for, 475

Mantra, 81

Marijuana A mildly hallucinogenic drug derived from the hemp plant *Cannabis sativa* and containing the active ingredient tetrahydrocannabinol (THC). Hash or hashish is derived from the same plant and contains the same active ingredient, but in a higher concentration. 84–86, *85, 86*
    defined, 84
    incidence of use, 84
    physiological effects, 84
    psychological effects, 84–86
    review of, 91
    symptoms of use and abuse, *89*

Marriage, rate of, 553

Masculine and feminine traits Those traits and characteristics ordinarily associated with the male and female, respectively. Their use should not be taken to imply that the traits they subsume are limited to people of one sex and therefore are undesirable in people of the other. 336

Masochism, 464

Master gland, pituitary as, 44

Masturbation, 445
    incidence of, 365
    review of, 379

Materialism, 51

Maternal aggression, 509, *510*
    review of, 532

Maudsley Personality Inventory, 423

MDA, 87

Mean, 556, 557, *557, 558*
    review of, 562

Meaning, theories of, 251–252
    componential approach, 252
    image theory, 252
    quantificational approach, 252
    referential theory, 251

Meaningfulness:
    in language, 236
        review of, 256
    as source of arousal, 289

Measurement, 413–439
    characteristics of instruments used, 414–417, *417*
    of intelligence, 425–437, *427, 428, 429, 431, 433, 434, 435, 437*
    misuses and abuses of, 437–439
    of personality variables, 418–425, *419, 421, 424, 425*

"Measurement of Romantic Love," *550*

Mechanoreceptors, 110

Median, 556–557, *557, 558*
    review of, 562

Medical models of mental disorder, 448–449, *450, 464, 451*
    review of, 470

Medical therapies, 474–476, 492, *476, 491*
    chemotherapy, 475, 492, *491*
    electroconvulsive therapy, 476, 492, *476, 491*
    evaluation, 492
    psychosurgery, 475–476, 492, *491*
    review of, 498

Medicine, role in beginnings of psychology, 5

Meditation A process or state involving serious contemplation or thought, typically with the object of achieving a mystical experience. A wide variety of processes is involved, many of them with little in common. Zen and yoga are traditional meditative techniques. 77–81, *78, 79, 80*
    and mystical experience, 77–79
    physiological functioning during, 79–80, *80*
    review of, 91
    techniques of, 81

Medulla The lowest part of the brain, found at the very top of the spinal cord and containing nerve centers involved in regulating physiological activity such as breathing, digestion, and heart functioning. 45, *45*

Meiosis The division of a single cell into two separate cells, each consisting of 23 chromosomes rather than 23 pairs of chromosomes. 326–328, *327*
    review of, 353

Melancholic personality type, 386, *387*

Mellaril, 475

Memory, 183–213
    distortion of, effect on research, 19
        review of, 26
    as filing cabinet, 185–186
    forgetting, 201–204, *202, 203*
    generative theory, 200
    improving, 204–210, *205, 208, 209*
    levels of processing model, 196–199
    physiology of, 210–211
    role of, 184–185
    three-stage model of, 186–196, *186, 188, 189, 190, 191, 192, 193, 195, 197, 198*
    ways to measure, 200–201

Memory traces, 201

Italic page numbers refer to illustrations.

Menarche, 359
Mendelian genetics, defined, 324. *See also* Genes; Genetics
  review of, 353
Mennonites, *507*
Mental blocks A Freudian term for what are assumed to be the ego's defenses against revealing sensitive issues. 478
  review of, 498
Mental disorders, 443–471
  affective disorders, 453, 460, *452*
  anxiety disorders, 453, 454–455, *452*
  causes of, 464–468, *465, 467*
  consequences of, 469–470
  definitions and models, 446, 448–450, *448, 451*
  dissociative disorders, 453, 456–458, *452, 457*
  DSM III classifications, 451–464, *452, 453, 455, 457, 459*
  errors in diagnosing, 454
  history of treatments, 444–446, *447*
  personality disorders, 453, 461–463, *452*
  psychosexual disorders, 454, 463–464, *452*
  review of, 470
  schizophrenia, 453, 458–460, *452, 459*
  special forms, 469
  treatment for, *See* Therapy
Mental flexibility versus mental rigidity, 371, *372*
  review of, 379
Mental illness. *See* Mental disorders
Mental image, 187
Mental monism, 51
Mescaline A drug originally derived from the peyote cactus that has now been synthesized and can be made in the laboratory as a white powder. 87, *85*
Mesmerism, *71*
Mesomorph One of Sheldon's somatotyping classifications; mesomorphs are believed to love adventure, exercise, and activities that demand boldness and courage. 389–391, *389*
  review of, 410
Metabolic factors in obesity, 273
  review of, 292
Metabolism The biological processes concerned with building up or breaking down living cellular material and tissue. Basic metabolic processes include those involved in digestion, elimination, and the oxygenation of red blood cells. 269
Metaneeds A term coined by Maslow to describe a group of human needs that are superior to the basic physiological needs. Metaneeds include aesthetic needs and the need for self-actualization. 290, 291
  review of, 293
Methadone, 475, *85*
Methedrine, 88, *85*
Method of savings, 201
Microsmatic noses, 115
Middle ear:
  anatomy of, 107, *107*
  function of, 108
Miltown, 475
The Mind of a Mnemonist: A Little Book about a Vast Memory, 10
Mind versus body, philosophical problem of, 51

Minnesota Multiphasic Personality Inventory. *See* the MMPI
Minnesota Tests of Creative Thinking, 231–232, *232*
Mirages, 135, *135*
Misperception, 134–136, *135, 136*
  illusory movement, 134–135
  mirages, 135, *135*
  visual illusions, 135–136, *135, 136*
Mitosis The division of a single cell into two identical cells. Mitosis occurs in body cells rather than in sex cells. 326
the MMPI, 421–423, *424*
  cautions in use, 425, 437–439
  described, 421–423
  review of, 440
  use of, 423, 425, 437–439, *425*
Mnemonic Pertaining to memory.
Mnemonic devices, 206–209, *208*
  link system, 207, *208*
  loci system, 207–208, *208*
  peg system, 208–209
  phonetic system, 209, *209*
  review of, 212
Mode, 557, *557, 558*
  review of, 562
Modeling hypothesis of television violence Theory about the impact of television violence that proposes that it may serve as a model for aggression in real life. 513, *513*
  review of, 532
Models Patterns for behavior that can be copied by someone else, or people who provide the patterns that will be imitated. The term is not restricted to human models, but includes symbolic models such as movies, television programs, verbal and written instructions, and religious, literary, musical, or folk heroes. 403
Modification, as stage of language development, 246, *245, 247*
Molar plan, 221, *224*
Molecular genetics, defined, 324–325
  review of, 353
Molecular plan, 221, *224*
Money Madness, 444
Mongolism, 331, *331*
Monism, 51
Monkeys:
  breeding in, 275
  curiosity in, 281
  insight in, 174, 229, *174*
  love in, 312–314, 316, 348, *315*
  sexual violence in, 509
Monocular cues to perception, 133, *133*
  review of, 146
Monophobia, *455*
Moon illusion, 132, *132*
Morality The ethical aspects of human behavior. Morality is intimately bound to the development of an awareness of accepted and unacceptable behaviors and is therefore linked to what is often called *conscience.* 351
  development of, 351–352, *351, 352*
  review of, 354
  stages of, 351–352, *352*
Mores, defined, 529
Morpheme Combinations of phonemes that make up the meaningful units of a language. 236, *237*
  review of, 255
Morphine, 87, *85*
  role in reducing pain, 111

Mothers:
  interaction with infants, 348, *348*
  surrogate. *See* Surrogate mother studies
Motivation, 261–293
  arousal, 286–289, *287, 289*
  cognitive theories and motives, 280–286, *282, 283, 285*
  defined, 262, 267, *263*
  drive reduction and incentives, 279–280, *279, 280*
  hedonism, 266–267
  hierarchy of needs, 290–292, *291*
  imprinting, 265–266, *265, 266*
  instincts, 262–265, *264*
  panic, 287
  physiological motives, 267–278, *267, 268, 270, 271, 272, 273, 274, 276, 277, 278*
  review of, 292
  social motives, 290
Motor development, correspondence with language development, 248, *249*
Mouth, role in thirst drive, 274
Movement, perception of, 133–134
  review of, 146
MPI. *See* Maudsley Personality Inventory
Müller-Lyer illusion, 136, *136*
Multiple-personality disorder The dwelling in one person of two or more distinct and highly integrated personalities. Not to be confused with schizophrenia, which involves distorted perceptions and is a psychosis. 457–458, *457*
  compared to schizophrenia, 458
  review of, 470
Mundugumor, 506
Muscle, tendon, and joint sense. *See* Kinesthesis
Musical ability, right hemisphere superiority in, 49, *50*
  review of, 52
Mutation, 328
Myelin sheath, 35, *37*
"My Enemy's Enemy Is My Friend," 549
Mysophobia, 456, *455*
Mystical experience:
  as goal of meditation, 77
  qualities of, 77–79
  review of, 91

nAch. *See* Achievement motivation
Names, remembering, 209–210
Nanometer, 124
Narcissistic personality disorder, 462
Narcolepsy, 66
Narcotics, 84, *85. See also* Drugs
  symptoms of use and abuse, *89*
National Survey on Drug Abuse, 83
Naturalistic observation Observation that takes place in naturally occurring circumstances or environments rather than in contrived environments. Observation is said to be naturalistic when the phenomena being observed are not affected by the observer or by the requirements of the observation. Observations that occur in laboratory settings are not naturalistic. 9, *10*
  review of, 25
Nature-nurture controversy, 50–51, 432–437, *433, 434, 435, 437*
  in animal intelligence, 432–433, *433*
  as assumption, 21
  review of, 26

Italic page numbers refer to illustrations.

Nature-nurture controversy (continued)
   interaction of, 332, 337–338
      review of, 354
   Jensen hypothesis, 434–436
   review of, 440
   rubber band hypothesis, 436, *437*
   in twins, 433–434, *434, 435*
Necker, cube, *136*
Needs and drives Terms such as *need, drive,* and *motive* are often used synonymously, although each can be distinguished. *Motive* refers to all forces, internal or external, involved in accounting for the instigation, direction, and termination of behavior. *Needs* are specific deficits or lacks in an organism, the satisfaction of which will increase the organism's welfare. *Drives* are the effects of the deficits or lacks that define needs. More specifically, drives are tendencies or urges to act in specific ways, determined by the nature of the need that gives rise to the drive. 267
   review of, 292
Need for achievement. *See* Achievement
   motivation
Negative feedback, 221
Negative identities, 370
Negative reinforcers Stimuli that have the effect of increasing the probability of occurrence of the desired response when they are removed from the situation. 168, *169*
   compared to punishment, 168
   review of, 180
Neglect (Adler), 399, *400*
   review of, 411
Nerve cell. *See* Neuron
Nervous system Parts of the body composed of nerve cells. Nervous systems are communication systems; they transmit messages. The major components of the human nervous system are the brain, the spinal cord, receptor systems associated with the major senses, and effector systems implicated in the functioning of muscles and glands. 31–53
   brain, 41–46, *41, 44, 45, 46*
   compared to other animals, 34–35, *35*
   defined, 34
   evolution, 32–35, *33, 35*
   the neuron, 35–38, *36, 37, 38*
   organization of, 38–41, *39, 40*
   relation to behavior, 50–51
   review of, 51
   split brain, 46–49, *47, 49, 50*
Neural transmission, 36–38, *38*
   review of, 52
Neurological theory of sleep, 62, 64
   review of, 90
Neuromodulators, 38
Neuron A single nerve cell, the smallest unit of the nervous system, and its basic structural unit. Neurons may have various shapes, but typically consist of a cell body and two types of branches: dendrites, which are typically very short; and axons, which may be as long as three feet. The function of the neuron is to transmit impulses. 35–38, *36, 37, 38*
   chemical transmitters and behaviors, 38, *38*
   defined, 35

   review of, 51
   transmission between, 36–38, *38*
Neurosis, neuroticism Any of a wide range of mild mental disorders characterized by underlying feelings of anxiety. Since anxiety also underlies many disorders not ordinarily classified as neuroses, this general label is not used in DSM III, in favor of more specific labels like *anxiety disorder* and *dissociative disorder*. Although neuroticism may be associated with considerable personal distress (unhappiness), it does not involve bizarre behaviors, loss of contact with reality, or other symptoms of the more serious disorders. 453
   Eysenck, 391
      review of, 410
   review of, 470
Neurotic depression, 460
   review of, 470
Neurotransmitters:
   role in appetite control, 271
      review of, 292
   role in emotions, 302–303
      review of, 316
Newborn. *See* Infants
Newsweek, 287, 333
Nicotine The principal active ingredient in tobacco. Although its psychological effects remain unclear, it is highly habituating. Its physiological effects are more clearly established. 89, *85. See also* Smoking
   incidence of use, 83
   review of, 91
Nightmares, 66, 67, *68*
   review of, 90
Nim Chimpsky, 244
Nine-dot problem, 229, *229, 230*
Node, 199
Nondirective therapy, 498
Non-sex-linked genetic defects, 330, *330*
Nonverbal expression of emotion, 298–300, *299*
   culture-specific versus innate, 298–300, *299*
   review of, 315
Noradrenalin. *See* Norepinephrine
Noradrenergic neurons, 37
No rapid eye movement sleep. *See* NREM sleep
Norepinephrine, 36, 37, *38*
   relation to depression, 38
   relation to mania, 38
Norm Behavior that is usual or expected, acceptable, or socially prescribed. Norms may be explicit, taking the form of rules or laws, or implicit, being implied in the prevailing moral standards of a society. 527
   conformity to, 527–528
   defined, 527
   review of, 533
Normal distribution A mathematical function which can be represented in the form of an inverted U-shaped curve (or a bell-shaped curve right side up). A large number of naturally occurring events, or events determined by chance, are normally distributed. What this means, essentially, is that the vast majority of scores cluster around the middle of the distribution (around the average or median), with progressively fewer scores being further and further away from the average. 428, 558–559, *429, 559*
   review of, 562

Novelty:
   as determiner of attention, 98
   role in curiosity, 281, 282, *282*
   as source of arousal, 289
NREM sleep Stage of sleep that is not characterized by rapid eye movements (hence NREM). 58, 65–67, *66*
   deprivation of, 66–67
   nightmares during, 67, *68*
   review of, 90
   sleepwalking and sleeptalking during, 68
Nurture versus nature. *See* Nature-nurture
   controversy
Nutrition, influence on development, 332–333, *333*
   review of, 353
Nyctophobia, *455*

Obedience Like compliance, obedience involves yielding to the desires, suggestions, or wishes of other people. But obedience implies unwillingness or reluctance in response to specific suggestions or commands. 522–524, *523*
   review of, 533
Obesity, 273, *273*
   review of, 292
   therapy for, 481
"Oblivescence during Sleep and Waking," *205*
Observational learning, 177, 402–403
   review of, 411
Obsession A recurring thought or impulse that seems irrational to the person having it. 456
Obsessive-compulsive disorders, 456
   case study, 456
   review of, 470
Occipital lobes, *44*
Ochlophobia, *455*
"An Ode Upon a Question moved, Whether Love should continue forever," 549
Odors, classification of, 114
Oedipus complex A Freudian concept denoting the developmental stage (around four years) when a boy's increasing awareness of the sexual meaning of his genitals leads him to desire his mother and envy his father. 394, *395*
   review of, 410
"Of Marriage and Single Life," 549
Of Poets and Poesie, 444
Olfaction, 113–115, *114*
   anatomy of, 114–115, *114*
   function of, 113–114
   related to sexual behavior, 115
   review of, 116
Olfactory epithelium (plural, epithelia) The true olfactory organ, the olfactory epithelium is a thin mucous membrane located in each nostril. Odor-sensitive cells are located on the olfactory epithelium. 114, *114*
Ololiuqui, 83
Omni magazine, 217, 218
Onania or a Treatise upon the Disorders Produced by Masturbation, 445
One Flew over the Cuckoo's Nest, 454
Open words, 246, *247*
Operant, and operant behaviors A response not elicited by any known or obvious stimulus. Most significant human behaviors appear to be of the operant variety. Such behaviors as writing a letter and going

Peripheral nervous system The neural networks that fan out from the central nervous system to various parts of the body. 38, 39–41, *39, 40*
  review of, 52
Permutation, 247
Personae (singular persona) The masks we choose to show the world; the different roles we adopt in different situations. 384, *384*
  review of, 410
Personage, defined, 384
Personalism, 537
Personality The set of characteristics that we typically manifest in our interactions with others. Psychologists usually distinguish between the self, the persona, and the personality. The personality is the glimpse others get of the self through the persona. Personality, measuring of variables in, 418–425, *419, 424, 425*
  behavioral observation, 418, *419*
  projective techniques, 418–421, *419, 421*
  scales and inventories, 421–423, *424*
  self-reports and ratings, 418
  use of tests, and cautions, 423, 425, 437–439, *425*
Personality, theories of:
  biological approaches, 387, 388–392, *388, 389, 391, 393*
  cognitive approaches, 387, 404–405, *388, 405*
  common-sense approach, 387–388, *388*
  defined, 384–385
  psychodynamic approaches, 387, 392–402, *388, 394, 395, 396, 400, 401, 402*
  social approaches, 387, 402–404, *388, 403*
  trait approach, 385–386, *386*
  traits and situations, 408–409, *409*
  types approach, 385–386, *387*
Personality disorder One of a number of maladaptive patterns of functioning and response. Personality disorders are usually not incapacitating but can result in considerable personal distress. 453, 461–463, *452*
  review of, 471
Personality psychology, *5, 6*
Personal unconscious (Jung), 401
Person-centered psychology (Rogers), 406–407
  review of, 411
Personnel psychology, *5, 6*
Perspective, as monocular cue, 133, *133*
  review of, 146
Persuasion Deliberate attempts, more subtle than coercion, to influence attitudes or behavior. 524–525, *525*
  review of, 533
Peyote, 83, 87
Phallic characters Among many ancient peoples, the phallus, representing the penis and testes, has been an object of religious worship, often as a symbol of fertility and power. For these people, phallic worship was normal; in a Freudian sense, arrestation of development at the phallic stage or regression to that stage, manifested in the phallic character, is abnormal. According to Freud, largely because of excessive pleasures associated with masturbation during the period of phallic development, phallic

characters later manifest an overwhelming preoccupation with immediate and selfish sexual satisfaction without regard for the objects of their satisfaction. 395
Phallic stage, 394, *395*
  review of, 410
Phantom limb pain, 111
Phenomena Observable events or happenings that can be experienced, reported on, and analyzed. What we observe are phenomena; hence phenomena are the data of psychology. 5
Phenomenology A phenomenon is an event, or occurrence. Thus phenomenology is concerned with the world of appearance; that is, with the world as it appears to the individual. 406
Phenotype The observable characteristics in an individual that are assumed to be genetically determined. 328
  review of, 353
Phenylketonuria, 330
Philosophy The pursuit of wisdom; the study of realities, laws, and principles in an attempt to arrive at an accurate and unified conception of the universe and its nature. Since people are part of the universe, philosophy originally included attempts to understand humans. 4–5
Phi phenomenon (fie) The illusion of motion created by presenting a succession of static pictures. 134
  review of, 146
Phlegmatic personality type, 386, *387*
Phobia, phobic disorders An intense, irrational fear, triggered by any one of a number of objects or situations. Generally classified as an anxiety disorder. 455–456, *455*
  case study, 455
  review of, 470
  treatment for, 475, 480
Phoneme The simplest unit of language, consisting of a single sound. 235–236, *237*
  review of, 255
Phonetic system, 209, *209*
  review of, 212
Photographic memory. *See* Eidetic imagery
Phrase-structure rules, 250
  review of, 256
Physical changes:
  of adolescence, 358–359, *359*
    review of, 378
  during aging, 372
    review of, 379
Physical monism, 51
Physics, role in beginnings of psychology, 5
  review of, 25
Physiological dependence, drug, 83, 84
Physiological motives, 267–278
  defined, 267, *267*
  hunger, 268–273, *268, 269, 270, 272, 273*
  sexual motivation, 274–278, *276, 277, 278*
  thirst, 274, *274*
Physiological psychology, *5, 6*
Physiology of aggression, 506–507, *507*
  review of, 532
"The Physiology of Meditation," *80*
Pibloktog, 469
  review of, 471
Pictorial storage, in long-term memory, 192–193
  review of, 212
Pigeons, communication, 243

Pinna The Latin term for the outer ear; the skin and cartilage that we identify as ears. 102, 107, *107*
  function of, 108
Pitch, 104, 105–106, 124, *104, 126*
  review of, 116
Pituitary, 44
Pivot words, 246, *247*
PK. *See* Psychokinesis
PKU. *See* Phenylketonuria
Placebo A "sham" drug; often a harmless and ineffective saline (salt) injection or a "sugar" pill. Placebos typically have little direct physiological effect, although research indicates that they can often have powerful psychological effects. 304
Placenta A flat, thick membrane attached to the inside of the uterus during pregnancy and to the developing fetus by means of the umbilical cord. 325
Place theory of hearing A theory of hearing that suggests that different waves give rise to different neural impulses because they cause displacement of different parts of the basilar membrane. 109
Planaria, in cannibal experiments, 210–211
Planned short-term therapy (PSTT) Therapeutic programs that are goal-oriented and planned to last for only a short time. A variety of specific therapies may be used. 497
  review of, 499
Play Activities with no goal other than the enjoyment derived from them. 348–351, *350*
  defined, 349
  imaginative, 349–351, *350*
  review of, 354
  sensorimotor, 349, *350*
  social, 349, *350*
"Plea for Less Malice Toward None," 549
Pleasure centers, in brain, 302
Po, 234
Polygenetic determination Determination of a characteristic as a result of the interaction of more than a single pair of genes. Most human characteristics are determined polygenetically. 328
  review of, 353
Polygraph, 159
Ponzo illusion, 136, *136*
Population, 560
  review of, 563
Pornography, 278
  and aggression, 278
  and sexual behavior, 278
Porpoises. *See* Dolphins
Positive feedback, 221
Positive reinforcement, 481, *491*
  review of, 498
Positive reinforcer, 168, *169*
  review of, 180
Posthypnotic suggestion A command given to the subject, not after the hypnotic trance is over, but during the trance. The suggestion is *post*hypnotic in that it relates to activities the subject is being asked to engage in after the trance. When subjects are given a definite time span after which they must perform the commanded activity, the posthypnotic act typically takes place at almost exactly the appointed time, in spite of the fact that subjects do not appear to be conscious beforehand that they will feel impelled to perform the activity. 73–74, 75
  review of, 90–91

Italic page numbers refer to illustrations.

Posttraumatic stress disorder, 471
Potlatch, 525–526
Praegnanz principle of perception, 137, 138, 174, *137*
   review of, 147
Precocious Advanced; more developed than would ordinarily be expected. Early-maturing adolescents may be said to be sexually precocious. Children who are highly advanced in motor or intellectual skills are sometimes described as being precocious in a more general sense. 359
Precognition, 143
   review of, 147
Preconceptual thought (Piaget), 341, *340, 342*
Predation and eye direction, 120
   review of, 146
Predatory aggression, 507–508, *510*
   review of, 532
Prediction, as goal of psychology, 22, 23
Predictive validity, 417
   review of, 439
Prefrontal lobectomy Surgical removal of the prefrontal areas of the frontal lobes. Not to be confused with the lobotomy, a surgical procedure whereby nerve fibers that connect the frontal lobes with the thalamus are cut. 309
Prefrontal lobotomy, 475
Pregnancy in adolescence, incidence of, 366
   review of, 379
Prejudice Literally, a prejudgment; thus a prejudice is a preconceived attitude or opinion that is, by definition, arrived at before a person obtains relevant facts and information. 517
   review of, 532
Premoral level of morality, 352, *352*
   review of, 354
Preoperational thought stage (Piaget), 341–342, *340, 342*
   review of, 354
Preparedness, 172
   review of, 181
Prespeech stage of language development, 245
Primacy effect Those impressions that we first form of people may be more important than those we might form later. 189, 196, 540, *540*
"Primacy-Recency in Impression Formation," *540*
Primary memory, 186. *See also* Short-term memory
Primary mental abilities (Thurstone), 425–426
Primary reinforcers Stimuli that are reinforcing in the absence of any learning. Such stimuli as food and drink are primary reinforcers since, presumably, an organism does not have to learn that they are pleasant. 167, *167*
   review of, 180
Principles Statements usually relating to some uniformity or predictability. Principles do not have the same status as laws, since they are often open to doubt. Psychology is characterized more by principles than by laws although the term *law* is frequently

Italic page numbers refer to illustrations.

used where *principle* would be more accurate. 3, 20
Principles of Psychology, 59
Proactive interference (or inhibition), 203, 204, *203*
Problem An incomplete situation; a situation where certain elements are known but others must be found, discovered, provided, implemented, begged, borrowed, or stolen. 224
Problem solving, 224–230
   Level 3: strategies and hypotheses, 225–226, *226, 227*
   Level 4: concept attainment, 226–229, *227, 228*
   Levels 5 and 6: insight and set, 229–230, *229, 230*
Problem-solving analogies of thought, 220
   review of, 255
Processing, in cybernetic theories, 221
Process schizophrenia, 459–460
Productiveness, in language, 236
   review of, 256
Productivity, changes in during aging, 373–375, *374*
   review of, 379
Programmed instruction An instructional procedure that systematically presents information in small steps (frames), usually in a textbook or some other device. Programs typically require learners to make responses and provide them with immediate knowledge of results. Knowledge of being right is assumed to act as a reinforcer. 177–178, *177, 178*
   review of, 181
Projection A Freudian defense mechanism whereby individuals attribute anxieties that are really their own to someone else. 395, 397, *396*
   review of, 410
Projective techniques for personality assessment, 418–421, *419, 421*
   cautions in use, 425, 437–439
   review of, 439
   Rorschach inkblot test, 419–420, *419*
   the TAT, 420–421, *421*
   use of, 423, 425, 437–439, *425*
Propinquity, as factor in interpersonal attraction, 547
   review of, 553
Proposition, defined, 366
Prosocial behavior, development of, 352–353
   review of, 354
Prosody Modes of expression, intonations, accents, and pauses peculiar to a particular language. 236, *237*
   review of, 255
Proximity principle of perception, 137, 138, *137*
   review of, 147
Psi. *See* Extrasensory perception
Psilocybin, 85
PSTT. *See* Planned short-term therapy
Psychiatrist An individual who, in addition to having medical degrees, has undergone intensive training and study in mental disorders. 22, 476, *477*
Psychic energizers, 475
Psychic phenomena. *See* Extrasensory perception
Psychoanalysis, Freudian The elaborate psychotherapeutic system developed by Freud and based on his theories of

personality. Its principal techniques involve free association, analysis of dreams, and interpretation of manifestations of unconscious impulses as might be revealed, for example, in "Freudian slips." The object of psychoanalysis is to provide patients with insight into the source of their difficulties. The assumption is that insight may cure or at least alleviate the disorder. 399, 450, 477–478, 479, 484, 492–493, *491*
   case study, 479
   evaluation, 492–493
   review of, 498
"Psychoanalysis and Mental Hygiene as Status Quo Social Philosophy," 406
Psychoanalyst, defined, 476, *477*
Psychoanalytic theory (Freud), 392–399, *394, 395, 396*
   defense mechanisms, 395–397, *396*
   evaluated, 397–399
   normal and abnormal personality, 395
   psychosexual stages, 394, *395*
   review of, 410
   structure of personality, 392–394, *394*
Psychodynamic approaches to personality theories, 387, 392–402
   Adler's individual psychology, 399–401, *400*
   Freud's psychoanalytic theory, 392–399, *394, 395, 396*
   Jung's analytical theory, 401–402, *402*
   review of, 410–411
Psychodynamic models of mental disorder, 449–450, 464, *451*
   review of, 470
Psychokinesis, 143
   review of, 147
Psycholinguistics, 250–252, *251*
Psychological dependence (drug), 83, 84
Psychological hedonism, as theory of motivation, 266–267
Psychological studies, 9–12, *10, 13, 14*
   case studies, 9–11, *10, 14*
   cross-sectional studies, 9, 12, *13, 14*
   longitudinal studies, 9, 11–12, *13, 14*
   surveys, 9, 11, *13, 14*
Psychologist A person who has studied psychology under professional guidance. In the strict sense, to be a psychologist requires certification or at least having met the criteria for certification by a psychological association. The APA certifies individuals as psychologists after two years of graduate training and one year of experience that relates directly to being a psychologist, or after three years of graduate training. 22
   areas of specialization, 4, *5, 6*
   defined, 22, *23*
Psychology. *See also* Clinical psychology; Gestalt psychology; Psychoanalysis; Therapy
   areas of specialization, 4, *5, 6*
   defined, 4, 22, 24, *25*
      review of, 26
   goal of, 22, 23
      review of, 26
   history of, 4–7, *7*
      review of, 24–25
   origin of term, 5
      review of, 24
Psychology: A Scientific Study of Man, 268
Psychometrics, *5, 6*
Psychopathology. *See* Mental disorders
Psychosexual disorders, 453, 463–464, *452*

Psychosexual disorders (continued)
  gender identity disorders, 463
  paraphilias, 463–464
  psychosexual dysfunctions, 464
  review of, 471
Psychosexual dysfunctions, 464
  review of, 471
Psychosexual stages (Freud), 394, *395*
  review of, 410
Psychosis (plural psychoses) Any of a number of severe, often debilitating mental disorders, characterized sometimes by distortions of thought, speech, and perception. Hospitalization is common for victims of psychosis. 453
  review of, 470
Psychosurgery, 475–476, 492, *491*
  review of, 498
Psychotherapy An extremely general term that refers to the use of a great variety of techniques to alleviate mental disorders or emotional problems. Although not limited to traditional psychoanalysis, it is usually restricted to treatments supervised or conducted by trained people such as clinical psychologists or psychiatrists. Nor is psychotherapy limited to the treatment of such serious disorders as schizophrenia or personality disorders; it may be used for a variety of conditions related to personal distress, problems of adjustment, and related difficulties. 476 *See also* Therapy
  defined, 476–477
Puberty Sexual maturity following pubescence. 358–359
  review of, 378
Pubescence Changes that occur in late childhood or early adolescence and that result in sexual maturity. 358–359, *359*
  review of, 378
Public Law, 439
Pulfrich Pendulum effect, 128
Punishment The presentation of an unpleasant stimulus or the withdrawal of a pleasant stimulus as a consequence of behavior. Punishment should not be confused with negative reinforcement. 168, *169*
  compared to negative reinforcement, 168
  defined, 168, *169*
  objections to, 168–170
  review of, 180
Pupil, 121, *122*
Purity of color, relation to complexity, 125–126, *126*
  review of, 146

Quail, and taste aversion, 173
Quantificational approach to meaning, 252

Racial unconscious (Jung), 401
Radio waves, 124
Random Due solely to chance. A sample is said to have been chosen randomly when every potential subject for the sample had an equal chance of being selected. 12
Random interval reinforcement, 165, *165*
  effectiveness of, 165–166, *166*
  review of, 180
Random ratio reinforcement, 165, *165*

effectiveness of, 165–166, *166*
  review of, 180
Random sampling, defined, 12, 18
Rapid eye movement sleep. *See* REM sleep
Rapists, classifications of, 508–509
Rational-emotive therapy (RET) A cognitive approach to "curing" mental disorder that helps the individual recognize and replace irrational beliefs. 483–484, *483, 491*
  review of, 498
Rationalization A defense mechanism whereby anxiety-provoking behavior is justified (excused) on "rational" grounds, and thus rendered less anxiety-provoking. 395, 396, *396*
  review of, 410
Rational therapy. *See* Rational-emotive therapy
Ratio reinforcement, 164–165, *165*
  effectiveness of, 165–166, *166*
  review of, 180
Rats:
  curiosity in, 281
  developing cognitive maps, 174–175, *175*
    review of, 181
  feeding of, 270, *270*
  and junk food, 272, *272*
  maze learning in, 432–433, *433*
  problem-solving by, 226, *227*
  taste aversion in, 173
Reaction formation A Freudian defense mechanism whereby individuals behave in a manner opposite from their inclinations. 395, 396–397, *396*
  review of, 410
Reactive schizophrenia, 459–460
Realness, as quality of mystical experience, 78
  review of, 91
Recall The retrieval of material from memory. 200, *201*
  review of, 212
Recency effect On occasion information that is obtained last may be judged of more importance than that which is obtained first. 189, 196, 540, *540*
Recency principle, 194, *195*
Receptor layer of retina, 123
Receptors, 35, *36*
Recessive gene A gene whose characteristics are not manifest in the offspring unless it is paired with another recessive gene. When a recessive gene is paired with a dominant gene, the characteristics controlled by the dominant gene will be manifest. 328, *329*
  review of, 353
Reciprocal inhibition. *See* Systematic desensitization
Recognition Literally, to cognize (understand, know) over again. Recognition is the awareness that objects or items have been experienced previously. 200–201, *201*
  review of, 212
Reducing interference, to improve memory, 205–206
  review of, 212
Redundancy, importance to perception, 94
Referential theory of meaning, 251
Reflex An unlearned connection between a stimulus and a response such that the presentation of the stimulus leads automatically to a simple, predictable, and uncontrollable response. Blinking in

response to a puff of air blown in the eyes is an example of a reflex; an infant's sucking in response to stimulation of the mouth is another. 46, 154, *46*
  review of, 52
Refractory period, in neural impulse, *38*
Regression, 395, 450
  review of, 410
"Regulation of Food Intake in the Absence of Taste, Smell, and Other Oro-pharyngeal Sensations," 272
Rehearsal of material, effect on retention, 199
Reinforcement The effect of a reinforcer; specifically, an increase in the probability of a response reoccurring. 162
Reinforcer A stimulus that increases the probability that a response will reoccur. 162
Reinforcer and reinforcement:
  in operant conditioning, 162–163
    review of, 180
  schedules of, and effects, 164–166, *165, 166*
  types, 166–168, *167*
The Relaxation Response, 81
Relearning A highly sensitive measure of memory in which subjects are asked to relearn material they have previously learned or been exposed to but have since forgotten. Evidence of memory is implicit in the observation that material being relearned is typically learned more easily than original material. 201, *201*
  review of, 212
Releaser The stimulus or situation to which an organism must be exposed during the critical period in order for imprinted behaviors to become manifest. 265
  in imprinting, 265
    review of, 292
  in territoriality aggression, 505
Reliability The extent to which a psychological test measures consistently what it is supposed to measure. A good instrument has both validity and reliability. 414
  defined, 414
  estimating, 415–416
  review of, 439
  of a ruler, 416
Relief, 168, *169*
REM sleep A stage of sleep characterized by rapid eye movements (REM). Also called *paradoxical sleep* because of the presence of EEG patterns similar to those characteristic of the waking state. 58, 65–67, *66*
  deprivation of, 66, 67
  dreams during, 65
  review of, 90
Repetition, as determiner of attention, 98
Representativeness of subjects, in sampling, 17–18
  review of, 26
Repression A defense mechanism whereby anxiety-provoking thoughts and experiences become inaccessible to the waking mind. 395, 396, *396*
  review of, 410
Repression theory of forgetting, 203, 204, *202*
  review of, 212
Reputations, role in interpersonal attraction, 541, *542*
  review of, 553
Rescorla-Wagner model of conditioning, 160, 175–176

Italic page numbers refer to illustrations.

Italic page numbers refer to illustrations.

Skin senses, 110, 112
   mapping of, 110, *112*
   review of, 116
   tricking the, 110, *112*
Sleep An altered state of consciousness characterized by loss of muscle tone, loss of immediate awareness of surroundings, and changes in such physiological functions as heart rate, blood pressure, respiration rate, body temperature, and electrical activity of the brain. Sleep appears to be universal among animals and occurs in regular cyclical fashion. 60–67, *60, 61, 62, 63, 65, 66*
   biological clocks, 63, 64, *65*
   biorhythm theory, 63
   defined, 60
   deprivation studies, 61–62, 67, *62*
   disorders, 475
   disturbances of, 66
   explanations for, 61–62, 64
   review of, 90
   stages of, 58, 64–67, *65, 66*
   talking in, 68
   walking in, 66, 68
Sleep attack, 66
Sleep center theory of sleep, 62, 64
   review of, 90
Smell factors, in hunger sensation, 269–270, 273, *270*
   review of, 292
Smiling, in infant, 348
Smoking, therapy for, 481. *See also* Nicotine
Social approaches to personality theories, 387, 402–404, *388, 403*
   Bandura and Walters's observational learning, 402–403, *403*
   relevance of, 403–404
   review of, 411
Social class, relation to delinquency, 363
   review of, 378
Socialization
   in child, 348–349
   during adolescence, 360–361, *361*
      review of, 378
Socializing versus sexuality, 370–371, *372*
   review of, 379
Social learning, as cause of aggression, 506, *507*
   review of, 532
Social motives Tendencies that we appear to have, such as toward competition or cooperation, that influence how we interact with others. 267, 290, 525, *267*
   review of, 293
Social phobia, 455
Social play Play activity that involves interaction between two or more children and frequently takes the form of games with more or less precisely defined rules. 349, *350*
   review of, 354
Social pressure, and attitude change, 522, *522*
   review of, 533
Social psychology While psychology is the science that concerns itself with individuals, social psychology is the science that studies relationships between individuals or between individuals and groups. 504, *5, 6*
   review of, 532
"The Social Readjustment Rating Scale," *313*

Social sciences Sciences concerned with the relationships of people to other people and to social institutions. The social sciences attempt to understand the organization of societies and the relationships between groups and individuals with respect to these societies. 5
"The Social Structure of Urban Adolescent Peer Groups," *362*
Sociobiology A relatively new discipline that attempts to apply findings from biology, anthropology, ethology, and other related disciplines to the understanding of social behavior in humans. Essentially, sociobiology looks for biological explanations for social phenomena. 50, 528–532, *531*
   criticisms of, 530–531
   explained, 529–530
   implications of, 531–532
   review of, 533
Sociopath An individual suffering from antisocial personality disorder, characterized by violation of laws, rules, and rights of others with no apparent remorse. 462–463
   review of, 471
Sodium pentathol, as cause of hypnotic trance, 75
Soft drugs, 84
Solvents, use as inhalant, 87–88, *85*
Soma, 83
Somatic system Part of the peripheral nervous system concerned with bodily sensations (heat, cold, pain, and pressure) and with muscular movement. 39
   review of, 52
Somatoform disorders, treatment for, 475
Somatotonic temperament, 389
"Some Conditions of Obedience and Disobedience to Authority," *523*
"Some Extraordinary Facts about Obese Humans and Rats," *273*
Sound waves Displacements of air molecules caused by vibratory events, whose subjective effect is the perception of sound. Waves are physical events definable in terms of molecular changes; sound is a subjective interpretation of the effects of these waves. 103
   characteristics of, 103–104, *104*
   our perception of, 104–107, *106, 107*
   review of, 116
   use to detect direction and distance, 102–103
Sources of psychological information, 9–15, *10, 13, 14, 15*
   experiments, 12–15, *14, 15*
   observation, 9, *10*
   psychological studies, 9–12, *10, 13, 14*
Spatial tasks, right hemisphere superiority in, 49, *49, 50*
   review of, 52
Spatial-visual ability Ability to see relationships among objects in space, to identify objects and, in short, to deal with the world of physical space as it is perceived through vision. The ability to maintain orientation in a strange place is sometimes a manifestation of spatial-visual ability. 336
Special abilities theory A theory of intelligence that does not recognize the existence of a single underlying factor but instead proposes that intelligence consists of separate, identifiable abilities. 425–426, *427*
   review of, 440

Speed, 88
Speedball, 87
Sperm, 325
Spinal cord The major link between the brain and the sensory and motor areas of the body. It is involved in reflexes—automatic reactions to physical stimulation such as the knee-jerk reflex. 45
   anatomy, 45–46, *46*
      review of, 52
   role in sexual motivation and behavior, 276
Split brain, 46–49, 59, *47, 49, 50*
   dual functions, 46–47, *47*
   implications, 48–49, *49, 50*
   results of research, 48, *47*
   review of, 52
Split-half reliability, 416
   review of, 439
Spoiling (Adler), 399, *400*
   review of, 411
Spontaneous recovery, 158
SQ3R, 206
   review of, 212
Squid, use to study nerve cells, 14, 36
S-R theories, 152
Stages of sleep, 64–67, *65, 66*
Standard deviation, 559–560, *557*
   review of, 562
Standardization, standardized The procedures by which test makers arrive at scores that describe the expected performance of groups or individuals on tests. Most contemporary intelligence tests are standardized so that the average performance of large groups is 100 and scores are distributed in predictable ways around this average. 11
Stanford-Binet test, 340, 427, 428, 429, *431*
   review of, 440
Stanford Hypnotic Susceptibility Scales, 74
Stanford Profile Scales, 74
Star Wars, 224
States of consciousness, 55–91
   biofeedback, 80–82, *82*
   consciousness, 57–59, *59*
   dreams, 67–70, *67, 68*
   drugs, 83–90, *85, 86, 89*
   hypnosis, 70–77, *71, 73, 74, 77*
   meditation, 77–81, *78, 79, 80*
   sleep, 60–67, *60, 61, 62, 63, 65, 66*
   waking, 59
Statistical model of mental disorder, 446, 448, 450, *448, 451*
   review of, 470
Statistics, 555–563
   defined, 555
   descriptive, 555–560, *556, 557, 558, 559*
   inferential, 560–562, *562*
Stereoscopic vision, 133
   review of, 146
Stereotype Widely held attitude or opinion concerning identifiable groups. 517
   defined, 517, *517*
      review of, 532
   role in interpersonal attraction, 539
      review of, 553
Stick problem, 174, 229, *174*
Stimulants, 84, *85*
   symptoms of use and abuse, 89
Stimulus (plural, stimuli) Something, either internal or external to the organism, which has an effect on an organism. Stimuli are ordinarily associated with sensory processes

---

Italic page numbers refer to illustrations.

(that is, they are usually visual, auditory, tactile, and so on). 152

Stimulus control, in operant conditioning, 166–167

Stimulus-response theories. *See* S-R theories

Stimulus substitution, 153

Stirrup, 107, *107*
  function of, 108, *109*

STM. *See* Short-term memory

Stochastic models Probabilistic models, where the outcome cannot be determined precisely beforehand but can be predicted with increasing accuracy as the number of operations increases. The outcome of flipping coins is stochastic. 220

Stomach contractions, relation to hunger, 268, 271, *268*
  review of, 292

STP, 87, *85*

Stranger anxiety, 347

Strategy A plan of attack; an orderly, sequential, and purposeful approach to the solution of problems or to the execution of behavior. Strategies typically have heuristic value in that they facilitate the solution of problems while at the same time reducing the amount of energy and effort required for solution. 225–226, *226*
  review of, 255

Stream of consciousness A descriptive phrase employed by William James to emphasize that consciousness is continuous rather than a series of discrete states or events. 58, *59*

Stress A physiological and essentially adaptive response to disturbances which may result from emotional experiences, physical injury or disease, or other factors. Since anxiety is one of the principal results of stress, the two terms are often used interchangeably. 309–312, *311, 312, 313*
  defined, 304
  identifying, 310–311, *313*
  measuring, with DSM III, 452, *453*
  physiology of, 310
  relation to mental disorders, 466, *466*
    review of, 471
  review of, 316–317
  theory of, 311–312, *312*

Stressors, defined, 309–310

Striate cortex, 142, 143

Strong Vocational Interest Blank, 423

Structural analysis, 486, *486*

Structure, as stage of language development, 246–247, *245*

Stupidity, as factor in interpersonal attraction, 548
  review of, 553

Subject bias, 16–17
  review of, 26

Subsonic waves, 105

Substantia gelatinosa, 111

Successive approximations, method of, 164

Successive scanning, 228

Suggestibility, in hypnosis, 72, 74–75, *74*
  review of, 91

Suicide, relation to depression, 461

Superego According to Freud, the level of personality that defines the moral or ethical aspects of personality. 393–394, 449, 477, *394, 395*

review of, 410

Superiority complex (Adler), 399, 478, *400*
  review of, 411, 498

Supermale syndrome, and criminality, 332

Supermarket diet, and obesity in rats, 272, *272*

Supersonic waves, 105

Superstitious behavior, in operant conditioning, 166

Superstitious schedule, 166

Surface structure The sounds of a verbal expression. Surface structure is not to be confused with meaning, since it does not go beyond the outward appearnce or sound of a language expression. 250–251

Surprisingness, as source of arousal, 289

Surrogate mother studies, 312–314, 316, 348, *315*

Survey A method of observation that involves large groups of individuals. 9, 11, *13, 14*

Survival of fittest, 34. *See also* Evolution

Swinging-pendulum technique, for hypnosis, 75

Symmetry model of interpersonal attraction, 546, *546*

Sympathetic nervous system Part of the autonomic nervous system that instigates the physiological responses that accompany emotion. 39, *39, 40*
  review of, 52

Synapse, 36, *37*

Synaptic knob, 36, *37*

Syncretic reasoning (Piaget), 341

Syntax The grammar of a language, consisting of the set of implicit or explicit rules that govern the combinations of words comprising a language. 236, *237*
  review of, 256

Syphilis The most dangerous, although not the most common, of the venereal diseases. It is ordinarily transmitted through sexual intercourse, but in later stages it may be communicated through other bodily contact. Its initial symptoms are neither obvious nor painful in the male or the female and may go undetected. Its long-term neurological effects, if left unchecked, include progressive deterioration of both physical and mental abilities characterized by delusions, mental disorder, and eventual paralysis. The technical term for the resulting "disease" is *general paresis.* 275, 446

Syphilophobia, *455*

Systematic desensitization A behavior modification technique that attempts to replace undesirable responses with more desirable responses through a conditioning procedure. 480, *480, 491*
  review of, 498

Systematized amnesia, 456

TA. *See* Transactional analysis

Tacts, 248

Tapetum, 119

Tardive dyskinesia, 475

Taste, 115, *115*
  aversion. *See* Taste aversion
  classification of different, 115
  role in hunger sensation, 269–270, 273, *270*
    review of, 292
  review of, 116

Taste aversion An inclination to avoid

certain tastes. Organisms appear to be biologically predisposed to acquire marked aversions for substances that make them ill. These predispositions illustrate biological constraints. 172–173

Taste buds, 115

the TAT, 420–421, *421*
  cautions in use, 425, 437–439
  described, 420–421, 437–439
  as measure of nAch, 283, 284, *284*
  review of, 439
  use of, 423, 425, *425*

Telepathy, 143
  review of, 147

Television:
  beneficial effects, 335–336
  influence on development, 333–336, *334*
  relation to violence, 333–335, 506, 512–513, *512, 513*
  review of, 353, 532

Temporal lobes, *44*

Teonanacatl, 83

Terminal behavior, 164

Termites, altruism in, 530

Territorial An adjective employed to describe individuals or species whose instinctual behavior patterns include the establishment and protection of an identifiable geographic area. 505

Territoriality:
  as cause of aggression, 505–506
  defined, 505, *507*
  review of, 532

Testes, 44

Testing. *See* Measurement

Testosterone:
  as cause of aggression, 507, 508
  role in sexual motivation, 275–276
    review of, 292

Test-retest reliability, 415–416
  review of, 439

Tetrahydrocannabinol, 84

T-groups. *See* Growth groups

Thalamus A small structure at the base of the brain that serves as a major relay center between incoming sensory stimulation and other parts of the brain. Almost all sensory information is channeled through the thalamus. 44–45, 123, 507, *45, 124*
  review of, 52

Thanatophobia, *455*

Thanatos A Freudian term denoting the death wish or death instinct. 392

THC. *See* Tetrahydrocannabinol

Thelma, 241

Thematic apperception test. *See* the TAT

Theory In its simplest sense, an explanation of facts, where facts are observations. Theories emphasize which facts are important for understanding, and which relationships among facts are most important. 7, 338–339

Therapy, 473–499
  behavior therapies, 479–482, 493–494, *480, 491, 493*
  community mental health programs, 496–498, *496, 497*
  evaluations of, 490–496, *493*
  insight therapies, 477–479, 480, 492–493, *491*
  medical treatments, 474–476, 492, *476, 491*
  other therapies, 482–490, *494 495, 483, 485, 486, 489, 491*

Italic page numbers refer to illustrations.

Verbal storage, in long-term memory, 192–193
  review of, 212
Vestibular organ A part of the inner ear consisting of the semicircular canals, the utricle, and the saccule. It is centrally involved in detecting movement and in maintaining balance, and is the principal organ of the basic orienting system. 100–101, *101*
  review of, 116
Vibrations, of sound waves, 103
  review of, 116
Vibratory event, 103
Vienna Psychoanalytic Society, 370, 400
Viki, 239
Vilcabambans, life spans of, 376
Violence:
  and aggression. *See* Aggression
  in society, incidence of, 510–512, *511*
    review of, 532
  and television, 333–335, 506, 512–513, *512, 513*
    review of, 353
The Violent Home: A Study of Physical Aggression between Husbands and Wives, 511
Viscerotonic temperament, 389
"Visual cliff" studies, 140–142, *141*
Visual illusions, 135–136, *135, 136*
  review of, 147
Visual perception:
  characteristics of, 129–138, *130, 131, 133, 135, 136, 137, 138*
  function of, 121
  review of, 146
Visual system, 119–147, *95*
  anatomy of, 121–122, *122, 123*
  color blindness and color vision, 126–127
  extrasensory perception, 143–145, *143, 145*
  and inborn capacities, 138–143, *141*
  interrelation of eye and brain, 123, *124*
  and learning, 138–143, *141*

lightwaves, 124–126, *126*
perception, 121, 129–138, *130, 131, 133, 135, 136, 137, 138*
vision in low light, 128, *128*
VMH, role in hyperphagia, 271
Volley thoery A theory of hearing which hypothesizes that for sounds that are of such high frequency that neural impulses cannot correspond to them in one-to-one fashion, single neurons fire rhythmically in alternating fashion. 109
Voyeurism, 464
Vygotsky's theory of language and thought, 253
  review of, 256

WAISr. *See* Wechsler Adult Intelligence Scale
Walden II, 163
Waking state, 59
Walking upright, importance of in evolution, 32, 33–34
  review of, 51
Wars, as cause of mental disorders, 466, *467*
  review of, 471
Washoe, 239–240, 243, 244, *240*
Waterfall effect A visual illusion involving perception of movement in a direction opposite to that previously perceived. 134
  review of, 146
Wavelength In vision, a property of light waves measured in nanometers (a nonometer is one-billionth of a meter) and related to the perception of color. The shortest wavelengths visible to the human eye are approximately 400 nanometers and are perceived as violet or dark colors; the longest perceptible wavelengths are between 700 and 800 nonometers and are perceived as red. Between are all the colors of the rainbow. 124
  and color, 124
  defined, 124
  review of, 146
Waxy flexibility, 458

Wechsler Adult Intelligence Scale, 423, 429
Wechsler Intelligence Scale for Chidlren, 429
Wechsler Preschool and Primary Scale of Intelligence, 429
Wechsler scales, 428–429
  review of, 440
Weight changes, during aging, 372
Weight Watchers, 481
Whales, echolocation of, 105
Whorf's hypothesis of language and thought, 252
  review of, 256
WISCr. *See* Wechsler Intelligence Scale for Children
Witchcraft, 445
Witigo, wihtigo, windigo, 469
  review of, 471
Witkin tilting chair and room apparatus, 101, *102*
WPPSI. *See* Wechsler Preschool and Primary Scale of Intelligence
Wyatt vs. Stickney, 494

X rays, 124
XYY syndrome, and criminality, 332

Y-maze, 98, *99*
Young-Helmholtz trichromatic theory of color vision, 127
  review of, 146
Your Memory: How It Works and How to Improve It, 209

Zeigarnik effect The tendency of individuals to remember those problems or tasks that they have not yet finished rather than those they have finished. 192
Zen meditation, 81, *79*
Zoophilia, 463
Zoophobia, *455*
Zuni Indians, 403, 506, 525, 526–527, *526*
Zygote, 325

Italic page numbers refer to illustrations.

To the owner of this book:

I hope that you have enjoyed *Psychology* as much as I enjoyed writing it. I would like to know as much about your experience as you would care to offer. Only through your comments and those of others can I learn how to make this a better text for future readers.

School ——————————————————————— Your Instructor's Name ——————————————

1. What did you like the most about *Psychology?* ————————————————————

——

——

2. What did you like the least about the book? ——————————————————————

——

——

3. Were any chapters assigned in part or not at all? If so, which ones weren't? ————————————

——

4. How useful did you find the marginal glossary for understanding new terms? Do you recommend its expansion? ——

——

——

5. How useful were the graphics (figures, tables, photographs) and how would you compare them to those in other college texts you have used? ——————————————————————————————

——

6. In the space below or in a separate letter, please let me know what other comments about the book you'd like to make. (For example, were any chapters *or* concepts particularly difficult?) I'd be delighted to hear from you!

Optional:

Your Name _____ Date _____

May Wadsworth quote you, either in promotion for *Psychology* or in future publishing ventures?

Yes _____ No _____

Thanks!

FOLD HERE

FOLD HERE